Sociology

*This book is offered to teachers of sociology in the hope that it
will help our students understand their place in today's society
and, more broadly, in tomorrow's world.*

John J. Macionis

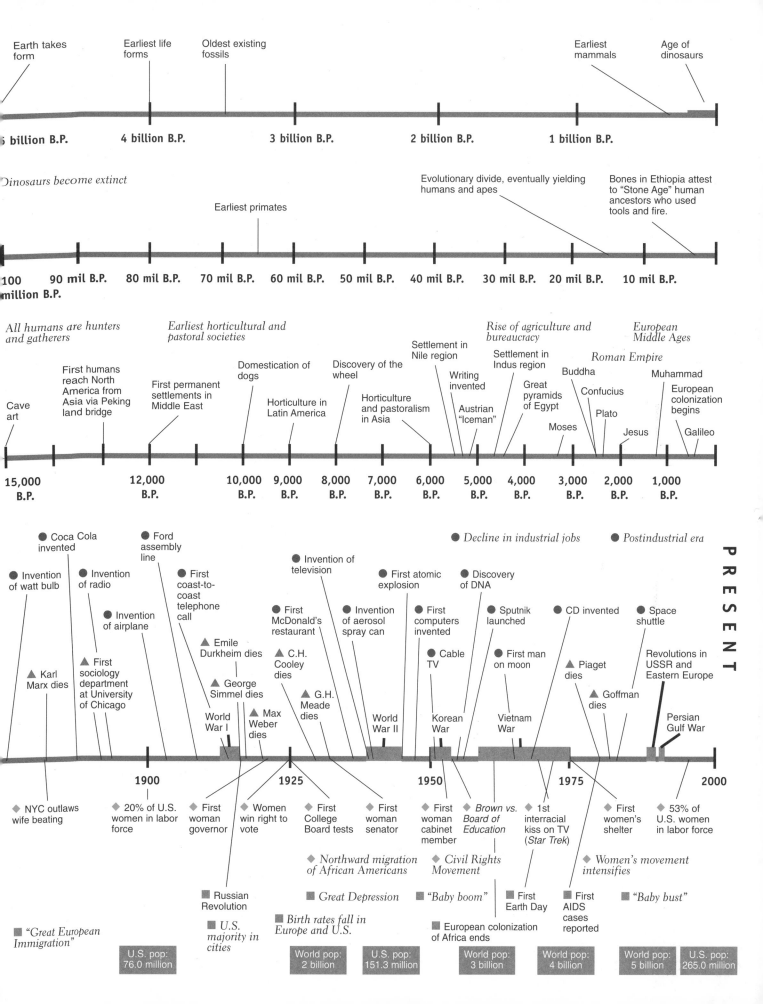

Annotated Instructor's Edition
Sociology
SIXTH EDITION

John J. Macionis
Kenyon College

Prentice Hall, Upper Saddle River, New Jersey 07458

Acquisitions Editor: Nancy Roberts
Editorial Director: Charlyce Jones Owen
Development Editor-in-Chief: Susanna Lesan
Development Editor: Diana Drew
Director of Production and Manufacturing: Barbara Kittle
Production Editor: Barbara Reilly
Copy Editor: Amy Macionis
Proofreader: Rebecca Rolfe
Editorial Assistant: Pat Naturale
Director of Marketing: Gina Sluss
Marketing Manager: Chaunfayta Hightower
Manufacturing Manager: Nick Sklitsis
Prepress and Manufacturing Buyer: Mary Ann Gloriande
Creative Design Director: Leslie Osher
Cover and Interior Design: Circa 86
Line Art Coordinator: Michele Giusti
Photo Editor: Melinda Reo
Photo Researchers: Barbara Salz, Joelle Burrows
Cover Coordinator: Karen Branson
Cover Art: L'Arena di Arles, Vincent van Gogh, Hermitage, St. Petersburg, Russia/Art Resource.

This book was set in 10/11 Elante by Lithokraft II
and was printed and bound by Quebecor Printing.
Color separations and electronic line art illustrations
were done by Lithokraft II. The cover was printed
by Phoenix Color Corp.

 © 1997, 1995, 1993, 1991, 1989, 1987 by Prentice-Hall, Inc.
Simon & Schuster/A Viacom Company
Upper Saddle River, New Jersey 07458

Printed in the United States of America
10 9 8 7 6 5 4 3 2 1

STUDENT ISBN 0-13-237264-9
AIE ISBN 0-13-466301-2

Prentice-Hall International (UK) Limited, London
Prentice-Hall of Australia Pty. Limited, Sydney
Prentice-Hall Canada Inc., Toronto
Prentice-Hall Hispanoamericana, S.A., Mexico
Prentice-Hall of India Private Limited, New Delhi
Prentice-Hall of Japan, Inc., Tokyo
Simon & Schuster Asia Pte. Ltd., Singapore
Editora Prentice-Hall do Brasil, Ltda., Rio de Janeiro

Printed on Recycled Paper

Brief Contents

v

Contents

PART III

Social Inequality

PART IV
Social Institutions

15 The Economy and Work   **403**

16 Politics and Government   **429**

PART V
Social Change

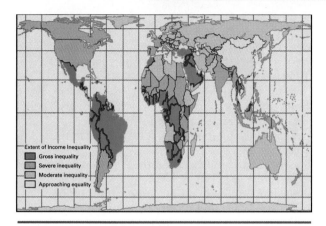
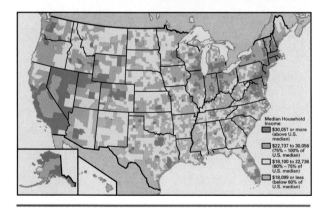

Boxes

Global Sociology

Social Diversity

Critical Thinking

Preface

As we approach the twenty-first century, across the country a wave of anticipation is building. Many people share a sense that change is accelerating and the future is fraught with uncertainty. Our national economy has been transformed over the past generation as work has flowed from industrial factories to a host of new service companies. More and more, earning a living demands working with ideas rather than with things, manipulating symbols rather than, say, bending steel. Is it any wonder, in light of this change, that jobs are less secure? And, just as important, for those lucky enough to be working steadily, income seems to have stalled. Even though women are now a mainstay of the labor force, many two-earner couples are struggling to hold on to their standard of living.

At a broader level, a vast global economy now connects nations the way the burgeoning national economy linked cities a century ago. Changes wrought by this process of globalization are rippling through the world's political systems, setting off waves of migration, especially to the United States, and challenging educators everywhere to rethink their curricula. Even the stunning cultural diversity that has long fascinated and frustrated humankind may now be eroding as communications technology—from satellite transmissions to facsimile machines—draws members of thousands of world societies into a global conversation.

Against this backdrop of ongoing change—indeed, because of it—sociology is gaining in popularity with close to one million students enrolling in courses each year. Never before has sociology been so necessary as we seek to understand the ever-more complex world around us. And, to this end, we are pleased to present the sixth edition of *Sociology*. As in the past, this new edition is authoritative, comprehensive, stimulating, and, as daily electronic mail messages from students around the country testify, plain fun to read.

But much is new to *Sociology*, sixth edition, the product of years of planning, writing, and editorial production. As always, our goal is ambitious—to elevate sociology's most popular text to a still higher standard of excellence, in order to support today's instructors as they teach about both our diverse society and the changing world around us.

ORGANIZATION OF THIS TEXT

Part I introduces the foundations of sociology. Underlying the discipline is the *sociological perspective*, the focus of Chapter 1, which explains how this invigorating point of view brings the world to life in a new and instructive way. Chapter 2 spotlights *sociological investigation*, or the "doing of sociology," and explains how to use the logic of science to study human society. We demonstrate major research strategies in action through well-known examples of sociological work. Learning how sociologists see the world and carry out research, passive readers become active, critical participants in the issues, debates, and controversies that frame our discipline.

Part II targets the foundations of social life. Chapter 3 focuses on the central concept of *culture*, emphasizing the cultural diversity that makes up our society and our world. Chapter 4 links culture to the concept of *society*, presenting four time-honored models of social organization developed by Emile Durkheim, Karl Marx, Max Weber, as well as Gerhard and Jean Lenski. Chapter 5 spotlights *socialization*, explaining how we gain our humanity as we learn to participate in society. Chapter 6 provides a micro-level look at the patterns of *social interaction* that make up our everyday lives. Chapter 7 offers full-chapter coverage of *groups and organizations*, two additional and vital elements of social structure. Chapter 8 completes the unit by investigating how the operation of society generates both *deviance and conformity*.

Part III offers unparalleled discussion of social inequality, beginning with three chapters devoted to *social stratification*. Chapter 9 introduces major concepts and presents theoretical explanations of *social inequality*. This chapter is rich with illustrations of how stratification has changed historically, and how it varies around the world today. Chapter 10 surveys *social inequality in the United States*, exploring our perceptions of inequality and assessing how well they square with research findings. Chapter 11 extends the analysis with a look at *global stratification*, revealing the extent of differences in wealth and power between rich and poor societies. *Race and ethnicity*, additional important dimensions of social inequality both in North America and the rest of the world, are detailed in Chapter 12. The focus of Chapter 13, *sex and gender*, begins with the biological foundation of sex and sexuality, and goes on to explain how societies transform the distinction of sex into systems of gender stratification. *Aging and the elderly*, a topic of increasing concern to "graying" societies such as our own, is addressed in Chapter 14.

Part IV includes a full chapter on each social institution. Chapter 15 leads off investigating *the economy and work*, because most sociologists recognize the economy as having the greatest impact on all other institutions. This chapter highlights the processes of industrialization and postindustrialization, explains the emergence of a global economy, and suggests what such transformations mean for the U.S. labor force. Chapter 16, *politics and government*, investigates the roots of social power both in the United States and around the world. In addition, this chapter includes discussion of the U.S. military, the threat of war, and the search for peace. Chapter 17, *family*, explains the central importance of families to social organization, and underscores the diversity of family life both here and in other societies. Chapter 18, *religion*, addresses the timeless human search for ultimate purpose and meaning, surveys world religions, and explains how religious beliefs are linked to other dimensions of social life. Chapter 19, *education*, traces the expansion of schooling in industrial societies. Here again, educational patterns in the United States are brought to life through contrasts with those of many other societies. Chapter 20, *health and medicine*, shows how health is a social issue just as much as it is a matter of biological processes, and compares U.S. patterns to those found in other countries.

Part V examines important dimensions of global social change. Chapter 21 focuses on the powerful impact of *population growth and urbanization* in the United States and throughout the world. Chapter 22 presents issues of contemporary concern by highlighting the interplay of society and *the natural environment*. Chapter 23 explores how people seek or resist social change through various forms of *collective behavior and social movements*. Chapter 24 concludes the text with an overview of *social change* that highlights *traditional, modern, and postmodern societies*. This chapter rounds out the text by explaining how and why world societies change, and by critically analyzing the benefits and liabilities of traditional, modern, and postmodern ways of life.

CONTINUITY: ESTABLISHED FEATURES OF *SOCIOLOGY*

Although introductory sociology texts have much in common, they are not all the same. The extraordinary success of *Sociology* results from a combination of the following distinctive features.

Unsurpassed writing style. Most important, this text offers a writing style widely praised by students and faculty alike as elegant and inviting. *Sociology* is an enjoyable text that encourages students to read, even beyond their assignments.

A comprehensive text that lets instructors choose. No other text matches *Sociology*'s twenty-four-chapter coverage of the field. We offer such breadth—at no greater cost—not with the expectation that instructors will assign every chapter, but to support the topics instructors choose to teach.

Engaging and instructive chapter openings. One of the most popular features of earlier editions of *Sociology* has been the engaging vignettes that begin each chapter. These openings—for instance, using the Titanic tragedy to illustrate the life-and-death consequences of social inequality, citing the Million Man March to highlight our ability to bring about intentional change, and detailing the Oklahoma City bombing to raise questions about the rules of political life—spark the interest of the reader as they introduce important themes. This revision retains the best chapter-opening vignettes found in earlier editions and offers ten new ones as well.

A celebration of social diversity. *Sociology* invites students from all social backgrounds to discover a fresh and exciting way to see their world and understand themselves. Readers will encounter the diversity of U.S. society—people of African, Asian, European, and Latino ancestry, as well as women and men of various class positions and at all points in the life course. Just as important, without flinching from the problems that marginalized people confront, this text does not treat minorities as social problems but notes their achievements.

Inclusive focus on women and men. Beyond devoting a full chapter to the important concepts of sex and gender, *Sociology* "mainstreams" gender into *every* chapter, showing how the topic at hand affects women and men differently, and explaining how gender operates as a basic dimension of social organization.

Instructive and varied examples. Sociologist George Herbert Mead characterized effective teaching as transforming simple information into real knowledge. Mead's insight applies to books as well as people; on virtually every page of *Sociology*, therefore, rich and illuminating examples give life to concepts and demonstrate to students the value of applying sociology to our everyday world.

A global perspective. *Sociology* has taken a leading role in expanding the horizons of our discipline beyond the United States. Each chapter of this text contains comparative material that explores the social diversity of the entire world. Moreover, this text explains that social trends in the United States—from musical tastes, to the price of wheat, to the growing disparity of income—are influenced by what happens elsewhere. Conversely, students will recognize ways in which social patterns and policies that characterize the United States and other rich countries affect poor nations around the world.

Theoretically clear and balanced presentation. *Sociology*, sixth edition, makes theory easy. The discipline's major theoretical approaches are introduced in Chapter 1 and systematically reappear in later chapters. The text highlights not only the social-conflict, structural-functional, and symbolic-interaction paradigms, but incorporates social-exchange analysis, ethnomethodology, cultural ecology, and sociobiology.

Chapter 4—unique to this text—provides students with an easy-to-understand introduction to important social theorists *before* they encounter their work in later chapters. The ideas of Max Weber, Karl Marx, Emile Durkheim, as well as Gerhard and Jean Lenski appear in distinct sections that instructors may assign together or refer to separately at different points in the course.

Emphasis on critical thinking. Critical-thinking skills include the ability to challenge common assumptions by formulating questions, identifying and weighing appropriate evidence, and reaching reasoned conclusions. This text not only teaches but encourages students to discover on their own.

Recent sociological research. *Sociology*, sixth edition, blends classic sociological statements with the latest research, as reported in the leading publications in the field. Hundreds of new studies inform this revision, and the vast majority of cited research has been published since 1980. Statistical data found throughout the text are the most recent available.

Learning aids. This text has many features to help students learn. In each chapter, **Key Concepts**, identified by boldfaced type, are followed by *a precise, italicized definition*. A listing of key concepts with their definitions appears at the end of each chapter, and a complete **Glossary** is found at the end of the book. Each chapter also contains a numbered **Summary** and four **Critical-Thinking Questions**. Chapters end with lists of **Suggested Readings**, which identify classic texts of enduring value, note topical contemporary research, and point up global studies that allow international comparisons.

Outstanding images: photography and fine art. This text offers the finest and most extensive program of photography and artwork available in any sociology textbook. This edition of *Sociology* displays more than one hundred examples of fine art as well as hundreds more color photographs. Each of these images is carefully selected by the author and appears with an insightful caption. Moreover, both photographs and artwork present people of various social backgrounds and historical periods. For example, alongside art by well-known Europeans such as Vincent van Gogh and U.S. artists including George Tooker, this edition has paintings by celebrated African-American artists Jacob Lawrence and Henry Ossawa Tanner, outstanding Latino artists Frank Romero and Diego Rivera, renowned folk artists including Grandma Moses, and the Australian painter and feminist Sally Swain.

Thought-provoking theme boxes. Although boxed material is common to introductory texts, *Sociology*, sixth edition, provides a wealth of uncommonly good boxes. Each chapter typically contains four boxes, which fall into six types that amplify central themes of the text. **Global Sociology** boxes provoke readers to think about their own way of life by examining the fascinating cultural mix that characterizes our world. **Social Diversity** boxes focus on multicultural issues and amplify the voices of women and people of color. **Critical Thinking** boxes teach students to ask sociological questions about their surroundings, and help them to evaluate important, controversial issues. **Sociology of Everyday Life** boxes show how to apply sociological insights to familiar, everyday experiences. **Profile** boxes introduce many of the men and women who have shaped the discipline of sociology. And **Controversy & Debate** boxes, new to this edition, conclude each chapter by presenting different points of view on an issue of contemporary importance. "Continue the debate" questions, which follow each of these boxes, are sure to stimulate spirited class discussion.

Sociology, sixth edition, contains ninety-four boxes in all, revised and updated as necessary with one-third entirely new to this revision. A complete listing of this text's boxes appears after the table of contents.

An unparalleled program of fifty-three global and national maps. Another popular feature of *Sociology*, sixth edition, is the program of global and national maps. **"Windows on the World"** global maps—twenty-six in all and many updated for this edition—are truly sociological maps offering a comparative look at income disparity, favored languages and religions, the extent of prostitution, permitted marriage forms, the degree of political freedom, the incidence of HIV infection, the extent of the world's rain forests, and a host of other issues. **Windows on the World** use a new, non-Eurocentric projection, devised by cartographer Arno Peters, that accurately portrays the relative size of all the continents. A complete listing of **Windows on the World** maps follows the table of contents.

"Seeing Ourselves" national maps—twenty-seven in all with eleven new to this edition—help to illuminate the social diversity of the United States. While a few national maps provide state-by-state data, most offer a close-up look at all of the 3,014 U.S. counties, highlighting suicide rates, median household income, labor force participation, college attendance, divorce rates, most widespread religious affiliation, availability of doctors, air quality, and, as measures of popular culture, where baseball fans live or where households consume white bread or croissants. Each **Seeing Ourselves** map includes an explanatory caption that poses several questions to stimulate students' thinking about social forces. A complete listing of the **Seeing Ourselves** maps follows the table of contents.

INNOVATION: CHANGES IN THE SIXTH EDITION

Each new edition of *Sociology* has broken new ground, which is one reason that more than one million students have learned from this sociological best-seller. A revision raises high expectations, but, after several years of work guided by the generous suggestions of faculty and students, we are confident that no one will be disappointed. Here is a brief overview of the innovations that define *Sociology*, sixth edition.

Controversy & Debate boxes. Twenty-four Controversy & Debate boxes—all new to the sixth edition—raise issues that are at once timely and provocative. One box is found at the end of each chapter, providing an ideal forum to review key chapter themes by addressing a topic sure to provoke class discussion. Among the many topics : "Is Sociology Nothing More Than Stereotypes?" (Chapter 1); "Can People Lie With Statistics?" (Chapter 2); "What Are the 'Culture Wars'?" (Chapter 3); "The Bell Curve Debate: Are Rich People Really Smarter?" (Chapter 9); "The Welfare Dilemma" (Chapter 10); "Should We Save the Traditional Family?" (Chapter 17); "Is Political Correctness Undermining Education?" (Chapter 19); "Apocalypse Soon? Will People Overwhelm the Earth?" (Chapter 21); and "Personal Freedom and Social Responsibility: Can We Have It Both Ways?" (Chapter 24). A complete listing of all sixth edition boxes appears after the table of contents.

Journal entries. Drawn from the author's travels to some fifty countries around the world, journal entries offer a brief, personal, and comparative insight into a topic found in each chapter. One or two of these journal entries amplify ideas in each chapter.

The time line. Have you ever wished there was a way to locate at a glance important historical periods and key events? Then take a look at the time line inside the front cover. This four-level time line locates every era and important development mentioned in the text, and tracks the emergence of crucial trends.

"Global Snapshots." Twenty-two new and colorful figures—included in almost every chapter—offer a quick and insightful comparison between the United States and other countries. Global Snapshots are especially helpful in showing how the United States differs from other industrial countries in terms of *what we have* (automobile and television ownership, for example), *how we act* (a comparative look at crime rates), and *what we think* (attitudes about inequality, romantic love, contraception, and government funding of health care). Many of the Global Snapshots reflect data from the recent multinational World Values Survey (Inter-university Consortium for Political and Social Research, 1994).

More interactive pedagogy. More than ever, *Sociology* now not only speaks to students but elicits their responses. Critical-Thinking Questions, at the end of each chapter, prompt readers to consider key themes and implications; "Continue the debate" questions that follow each Controversy & Debate box further stimulate students to become actively engaged with the material. In addition, many captions are written as questions that provoke further thinking.

Welcome to the Internet! New information technology is changing the way instructors teach and students learn. *Sociology,* sixth edition, provides a brief, user-friendly introduction to the Internet found directly after the preface. In addition, many chapters of this revision contain new material that highlights the shape of the emerging cyber-society.

Sociology Web sites. Prentice Hall and John Macionis are collaborating to provide the most comprehensive Internet program in sociology. A visit to the Prentice Hall home page (address: **http://www. prenhall.com**) will introduce a wide range of textbooks and available supplementary material. The Macionis home page (address: **http://www.prenhall.com/ macionis**) offers a complete cyber-support system for *Sociology,* sixth edition. Here you will find interactive exercises for every chapter of the text that take students to selected Web sites across the country and around the world. In addition, the Macionis home page provides updates on important statistical information—a sociology resource center that identifies hundreds of Web sites where you can download statistical information, follow late-breaking news stories, and even monitor the job market in sociology.

New topics. The sixth edition of *Sociology* also offers dozens of new or expanded discussions. Here is a partial listing, by chapter: ***Chapter 1:*** A new chapter opening demonstrates the power of the sociological perspective; also find a new discussion of applied sociology; an expanded discussion of who attends college; a new journal entry on visiting Fez, Morocco; a new Global Sociology box describing the "Global Village"; and a new Controversy & Debate box asking how sociological generalizations differ from common stereotypes; ***Chapter 2:*** See a new account of how cyber-technology is changing sociological research, and a new Controversy & Debate box on how to lie with statistics; ***Chapter 3:*** A new chapter opening describes the ancient Chinese practice of *feng shui*; a journal entry notes how cats display the same behavior throughout the world—but people do not; a Global Snapshot highlights automobile ownership; a new National Map asks "Who's Upper Crust?" locating consumers of "high culture" croissants and "low culture" white bread; and a new Controversy & Debate box investigates the "culture wars"; ***Chapter 4:*** A new Global Map spotlights high-tech data transmission; and a new Controversy & Debate box asks whether societies are becoming better or worse; ***Chapter 5:*** A new Social Diversity box explores how the mass media portray minorities; also find expanded coverage of the politics of the culture-

makers in Hollywood; a journal entry on U.S. students missing television while at sea; a new Global Snapshot highlighting television ownership; and a new Controversy & Debate box that assesses the extent of human freedom; ***Chapter 6:*** Here we offer a new Global Snapshot about personal happiness; journal entries on the apparent urban chaos of Saigon, Vietnam, and on trying to make jokes with some residents of Kobe, Japan; and a new Controversy & Debate box suggesting how the "cyber-revolution" is changing our construction of reality; ***Chapter 7:*** A new Global Snapshot highlights organization memberships; a new Sociology of Everyday Life box explores the Internet as the world's largest social network; a new section describes self-managed work-teams; a new National Map shows where people most fear a loss of privacy; and a new Controversy & Debate box investigates how large, high-tech organizations intrude into our lives; ***Chapter 8:*** A new chapter opening features a journal entry on facing off against the police in Morocco; new National Maps show the distribution of police and crime; new Global Snapshots focus on handgun deaths and incarceration rates; a new series of "crime clocks" presents relative frequency of various types of crime; and a new Controversy & Debate box presents Travis Hirschi's provocative crime control strategy; ***Chapter 9:*** Note a new Global Snapshot on economic inequality; a journal entry on the worsening economic crisis in Ukraine; and a new Controversy & Debate box assessing the "Bell Curve" thesis that rich people are smarter than the rest of us; ***Chapter 10:*** Find new data and analysis on the distribution of U.S. income and wealth; a new Global Snapshot on income disparity; a new National Map on child poverty; a new journal entry on the plight of one struggling U.S. service worker; and a new Controversy & Debate box on affirmative action; ***Chapter 11:*** A new opening vignette features a journal entry about visiting the Smokey Mountain dump in Manila, the Philippines; a new Global Snapshot highlights the proportion of births attended by trained health-care workers; and a new Controversy & Debate box asks "Will the World Starve?"; ***Chapter 12:*** A new chapter opening introduces the 1954 Brown decision concerning school desegregation; a new Critical Thinking box explains why race seems linked to intelligence; a new journal entry portrays ethnic hostility in Jerusalem, Israel; expanded discussion of affirmative action includes a new Controversy & Debate box; ***Chapter 13:*** We've expanded discussion of sexual orientation and bisexuality; included data from the new Laumann study of U.S. sexual practices; added a new Global Snapshot on the percentage of married women using contraception; featured a new Global Map on women in the paid labor force, plus a new National Map showing where U.S. women's political clout is greatest; and added a new Controversy & Debate box on the men's rights movement asking "Are Men *Really* So Privileged?"; *Chapter 14:* See the new Global Snapshot on the graying of industrial societies; a new journal entry on how Sri Lankans view the elderly; and the new Controversy & Debate box that asks if we will have to limit medical care for the elderly; *Chapter 15:* The new chapter opener is a journal entry on the recent economic development of Saigon, Vietnam; there is expanded discussion of work in postindustrial societies; a new Global Snapshot on the relative size of the three economic sectors; and a new Controversy & Debate box asking "Does 'The Market' Serve the Public Interest?"; *Chapter 16:* Another new chapter-opening vignette highlights the Oklahoma City bombing; a new National Map displays voter turnout; a new journal entry describes the heavy-handed police in Saigon, Vietnam; there is a new discussion of "information war"; and the new Controversy & Debate box evaluates the promise of "on-line democracy"; *Chapter 17:* Another new chapter-opening vignette features the "family values" debate in Japan; there are new discussions and data on interracial and interethnic marriages; a new journal entry describes arranged marriage in Sri Lanka; two new Global Snapshots highlight romantic love and out-of-wedlock births; and the new Controversy & Debate box asks "Should We Save the Traditional Family?"; *Chapter 18:* See the new Global Snapshot on the strength of religious beliefs; a new journal entry prompted by the official Islam of Morocco; plus a new section contrasting eastern and western religions; and a new Controversy & Debate box assessing the threat of science to religion; *Chapter 19:* New discussion highlights schooling in low-income countries with a focus on India; a new journal entry observes Japanese students; a new Global Snapshot focuses on college graduation; updates point up the school-choice debate; and a new Controversy & Debate box asks "Is Political Correctness Undermining Education?"; *Chapter 20:* A new Global Sociology box focuses on the practice of female genital mutilation; a new journal entry notes the effects of poverty on health in India; a new Global Snapshot shows the extent of government funding for health care; there is an update on U.S. health-care policy; and the new Controversy & Debate box is entitled "The Genetic Crystal Ball: Do We Really Want to Look?"; *Chapter 21:* New Global Snapshots highlight several key demographic variables; a new Critical Thinking box explains

how population growth reflects the social standing of women; new journal entries describe visiting the "City of the Dead" in Cairo, Egypt, and the excitement of Hong Kong at night; and a new Controversy & Debate box assesses the threat that population increase poses to our global future; *Chapter 22:* A new chapter-opening vignette describes Nauru—the most environmentally devastated place on earth; there are new discussions of the role of sociology in environmentalism, environmental racism, and cultural ecology; a new Global Map reveals the planet's water consumption; a new journal entry reports the growing prosperity of Cairo's Zebaleen "Dump People"; a new Global Snapshot focuses on how people rate the local environment; and the new Controversy & Debate box asks "Is the Environmental Movement Radical?"; *Chapter 23:* A new chapter-opening vignette describes the "Million Man March"; a new National Map shows support for the Public Broadcasting System; new data support discussion of the extent of political involvement among U.S. college students; and the new Controversy & Debate box asks "Are You Willing to Take a Stand?"; *Chapter 24:* A new Global Snapshot compares support for science; a new discussion describes global variations of modernity; a new National Map displays geographical mobility; and the new Controversy & Debate box assesses the communitarian movement asking "Can We Have Both Personal Freedom and Social Responsibility?"

The latest statistical data. In an age of government cutbacks and even agency shutdowns, the challenge of providing current statistical data is greater than ever. However, we are happy to assure readers that *Sociology,* sixth edition, is again at the cutting edge with the most current data available. The author, collaborating with Carol A. Singer, a professional government documents librarian employed at the District of Columbia Reference Center of the National Agricultural Library, has incorporated new statistics throughout the text—in many cases, with data for 1994, 1995, and even 1996. Updates of key data for each chapter are also available from the Macionis web site. Finally, this revision is informed by the results of 250 new research findings, and the text makes use of familiar current events that elevate the interest of readers.

A WORD ABOUT LANGUAGE

This text's commitment to representing the social diversity of the United States and the world carries with it the responsibility to use language thoughtfully.

In most cases, we prefer the terms *African American* and *person of color* to the word *black*. We use the terms *Hispanic* and *Latino* to refer to people of Spanish descent. Most tables and figures refer to "Hispanics" because the U.S. Bureau of the Census employs this term in collecting statistical data about our population.

Students should realize, however, that many individuals do not describe themselves using these terms. Although the term "Hispanic" is commonly used in the eastern part of the United States, and "Latino" and the feminine form "Latina" are widely heard in the West, across the United States people of Spanish descent identify with a particular ancestral nation, whether it be Argentina, Mexico, some other Latin American country, or Spain or Portugal in Europe.

The same holds for Asian Americans. Although this term is a useful shorthand in sociological analysis, most people of Asian descent think of themselves in terms of a specific country of origin (say, Japan, the Philippines, Taiwan, or Vietnam).

In this text, the term "Native American" refers to all the inhabitants of the Americas (including the Hawaiian Islands) prior to contact with Europeans. Here again, however, most people in this broad category identify with their historical society (for example, Cherokee, Hopi, or Zuni). The term "American Indian" designates only those Native Americans who live in the continental United States, not including Native peoples living in Alaska or Hawaii.

Learning to think globally also leads us to use other language more carefully. This text avoids the word "American"—which literally designates two continents—to refer to just the United States. Thus, for example, the "American economy" is more correctly termed the "U.S. economy." This convention may seem a small point, but it implies the significant recognition that we in this country represent only one society (albeit a very important one) in the Americas.

SUPPLEMENTS

Sociology, sixth edition, is the heart of an unparalleled learning package that includes a wide range of proven instructional aids as well as several new ones. As the author of the text, I maintain a keen interest in all the supplements to ensure their quality and integration with the text. The supplements for this revision have been thoroughly updated, improved, and expanded.

The Annotated Instructor's Edition. The AIE is a complete student text annotated by the author on every page. Annotations—which have been thoroughly revised for this revision—have won praise from instructors for enriching class presentations. Margin notes include summaries of research findings, statistics from the United States or other nations, insightful quotations, information highlighting patterns of social diversity in the United States, and high-quality survey data from the National Opinion Research Center's (NORC) General Social Survey and World Values Survey data from the Inter-university Consortium for Political and Social Research (ICPSR).

Data File. This is the "instructor's manual" that is of interest even to those who have never used one before. The *Data File* provides far more than detailed chapter outlines and discussion questions; it contains statistical profiles of the United States and other nations, summaries of important developments and significant research, and supplemental lecture material for every chapter of the text. The *Data File* is available in DOS format.

Test Item File. A revised test item file is available in both printed and computerized forms. The file contains 2400 items—100 per chapter—in multiple choice, true-false, and essay formats. Questions are identified as more simple "recall" items or more complex "inferential" issues; the answers to all questions are page-referenced to the text. Prentice Hall Custom Test is a test generator designed to allow the creation of personalized exams. It is available in DOS, Windows, and Macintosh formats. Prentice Hall also provides a test preparation service to users of this text that is as easy as one call to our toll-free 800 number.

Core Test Item File. This general test item file consists of over 350 additional test questions appropriate for introductory sociology courses. All of the questions have been class tested, and an item analysis is available for every question.

Social Survey Software, Third Edition. This is the supplement that is changing the way instructors teach and students learn. *Student CHIP Social Survey Software* is an easy yet powerful program that allows users to investigate U.S. society and other nations of the world by calling on the best source of survey data available, the General Social Survey. John J. Macionis and Jere Bruner (Oberlin College) have transformed 260 GSS items into CHIP data sets and linked them to the chapters of *Sociology*, sixth edition. There is an *Instructor's Manual* as well as an easy-to-understand *Social Survey Software Student Manual* that leads students through multivariate analysis of attitudes and reported behavior by sex, race, occupation, level of income and education, and a host of other variables. *Social Survey Software,* which investigators can now manipulate either by keyboard or mouse, also has a new graphing feature. The *Student CHIP* microcomputer program was developed by James A. Davis (Harvard University) and is available in both IBM and Macintosh formats.

 The New York Times Supplement, Themes of the Times. *The New York Times* and Prentice Hall are sponsoring *Themes of the Times,* a program designed to enhance student access to current information relevant to the classroom. Through this program, the core subject matter provided in the text is supplemented by a collection of timely articles from one of the world's most distinguished newspapers, *The New York Times.* These articles demonstrate the vital, ongoing connection between what is learned in the classroom and what is happening in the world around us.

To enjoy the wealth of information of *The New York Times* daily, a reduced subscription rate is available. For information, call toll-free: 1-800-631-1222.

Prentice Hall and *The New York Times* are proud to co-sponsor *Themes of the Times.* We hope it will make the reading of both textbooks and newspapers a more dynamic, involving process.

Seeing Ourselves: Classic, Contemporary, and Cross-Cultural Readings in Sociology, Third Edition. Create a powerful teaching package by combining this text with the third edition of the best-selling anthology, *Seeing Ourselves,* edited by John J. Macionis and Nijole V. Benokraitis (University of Baltimore). Instructors relish this reader's unique format: Clusters of readings—from classic works to well-rounded looks at contemporary issues and cross-cultural comparisons—correspond to each chapter in *Sociology,* sixth edition.

Media Supplements

Sociology on the Internet. This brief guide introduces students to the origin and innovations behind the Internet and provides clear strategies for navigating the complexity of the Internet and World Wide Web. Exercises within and at the end of the chapters allow students to practice searching for the myriad resources available to the student of sociology. This 48-page supplementary book is free to students when shrinkwrapped to *Sociology,* sixth edition.

Sociology: Interactive Edition. This exciting new electronic version of the text on CD-ROM (for IBM/PC and Macintosh) utilizes the technology of *Power*CD, exclusively developed by Zane Publishing, leaders in the field of multimedia technology. The Interactive Edition features over 120 minutes of self-playing multimedia presentations, photographs, over 600 interactive study questions to strengthen the student's understanding of sociology, additional interactive essay review questions, the complete *Webster's New World College Dictionary,* third edition, and the complete text of *Sociology,* sixth edition.

Web site. In tandem with the text, students and professors can now take full advantage of the World Wide Web to enrich their study of sociology through the Macionis Web site. This resource correlates the text with related material available on the Internet. Features of the Web site will include chapter objectives, study questions, and news updates as well as links to interesting material and information from other sites on the Web that can reinforce and enhance the content of each chapter. **Address:** http://www.prenhall.com/macionis

ABCNEWS ***ABC News/Prentice Hall Video Library for Sociology.*** Video is the most dynamic supplement you can use to enhance a class. But the quality of the video material and how well it relates to your course still make all the difference. Prentice Hall and ABC News are now working together to bring you the best and most comprehensive video ancillaries available in the college market.

Through its wide variety of award-winning programs—*Nightline, Business World, On Business, This Week with David Brinkley, World News Tonight,* and *The Health Show*—ABC offers a resource for feature and documentary-style videos related to the chapters in *Sociology,* sixth edition. The programs have high production quality, present substantial content, and are hosted by well-versed, well-known anchors.

The authors and editors of Prentice Hall have carefully selected videos on topics that complement *Sociology,* sixth edition, and included notes on how to use them in the classroom. An excellent video guide in the *Data File* carefully and completely integrates the videos into your lecture. The guide has a synopsis of each video showing its relation to the chapter and discussion questions to help students focus on how concepts and theories apply to real-life situations.

ABC News/Prentice Hall Video Library, Sociology:
Volume I—Social Stratification (013-466228-8)
Volume II—Marriages and Families (013-209537-8)
Volume III—Race and Ethnic Relations (013-458506-2)
Volume IV—Criminology (013-375163-5)
Volume V—Social Problems (013-437823-7)

Prentice Hall Images in Sociology: Laser Videodisc Series II. Using the latest technology, *Images in Sociology* presents illustrations both from within the text and from outside sources in an integrated framework appropriate for classroom use. These images include maps, graphs, diagrams, and other illustrations, as well as video segments taken from the *ABC News/Prentice Hall Video Library for Sociology.* See your local Prentice Hall representative for details on how to preview this videodisc.

Other supplements to aid in classroom teaching are:

Prentice Hall Color Transparencies: Sociology Series IV
Instructor's Guide to Prentice Hall Color Transparencies: Sociology Series IV
Film/Video Guide: Prentice Hall Introductory Sociology, Fifth Edition
Study Guide
Critical Thinking Audiocassette Tape

IN APPRECIATION

The conventional practice of designating a single author obscures the efforts of dozens of women and men that have resulted in *Sociology*, sixth edition. Nancy Roberts, editor-in-chief at Prentice Hall and valued friend, has contributed enthusiasm, support, and sound advice throughout the revision process. Susanna Lesan, development editor-in-chief at Prentice Hall, has played a vital role in the development of this text since its first edition ten years ago, shouldering responsibility for coordinating and supervising the editorial process. Two additional people deserve thanks and praise for their ongoing efforts to maintain the high quality of this text. Barbara Reilly, production editor at Prentice Hall, and Amy Marsh Macionis, freelance "in house" editor, have each worked closely with the author to ensure that each page is designed correctly, countless statistics are correct and consistent throughout the book, and virtually all of the errors of one kind or another that crop up throughout the writing and production process are identified and corrected.

I also have a large debt to the members of the Prentice Hall sales staff, the men and women who have given this text such remarkable support over the years. Thanks, especially, to Gina Sluss and Chaun Hightower, who have directed our marketing campaign. I also offer heartfelt thanks to Pat Naturale, Sharon Chambliss, Charlyce Jones Owen, and Phil Miller for their continuing support of this text.

Thanks, too, to Circa 86 for providing the interior design of the book. Copy editing of the manuscript was provided by Diana Drew and Amy Marsh Macionis. Barbara Salz did a wonderful job of researching photographs, as Joelle Burrows provided much of the fine art, both working under the supervision of Lorinda Morris-Nantz, head of Prentice Hall Photo Archives.

It goes without saying that every colleague knows more about some topics covered in this book than the author does. For that reason, I am grateful to the hundreds of faculty and students who have written to me to offer comments and suggestions. More formally, I am grateful to the following people who have reviewed some or all of this manuscript:

Peter K. Angstadt, Wesley College
Grace Auyang, University of Cincinnati, RWC
Paula Barfield, Southwest Texas State University
Valerie Brown, Cuyahoga Community College
Joseph Carroll, Colby-Sawyer College
Lynn Chamberlain, Scott Community College
Robert E. Clark, Midwestern State University
Nanette J. Davis, Chapman University
Michael Donnelly, University of New Hampshire
Michael Goslin, Tallahassee Community College
Gary Hodge, Collin County Community College
Alicia Hughes-Jones, Tabor College
Bonnie Korn Ach, Chapman University
Mary Ann Maguire, Tulane University
Patrick McGuire, University of Toledo
Antonio V. Menéndez-Alarcón, Butler University
George Miller, University of Utah
Michael V. Miller, University of Texas at San Antonio
Anne Schulte, Des Moines Area Community College
Wen-hui Tsai, Indiana University-Purdue University at Fort Wayne
Ronny E. Turner, Colorado State University
Glenna Van Metre, Wichita State University
Faith Willis, Brunswick College

I also wish to thank the following colleagues for sharing their wisdom in ways that have improved this book: Doug Adams (The Ohio State University), Kip Armstrong (Bloomsburg University), Rose Arnault (Fort Hays State University), Scott Beck (East Tennessee State University), Lois Benjamin (Hampton

University), Philip Berg (University of Wisconsin, La Crosse), Charlotte Brauchle (Southwest Texas Junior College), Bill Brindle (Monroe Community College), John R. Brouillette (Colorado State University), Cathryn Brubaker (DeKalb College), Brent Bruton (Iowa State University), Richard Bucher (Baltimore City Community College), Karen Campbell (Vanderbilt University), Harold Conway (Blinn College), Gerry Cox (Fort Hays State University), Lovberta Cross (Shelby State Community College), Robert Daniels (Mount Vernon Nazarene College), James A. Davis (Harvard University), Sumati Devadutt (Monroe Community College), Keith Doubt (Northeast Missouri State University), Denny Dubbs (Harrisburg Area Community College), Travis Eaton (Northeast Louisiana State University), Helen Rose Fuchs Ebaugh (University of Houston), Heather Fitz Gibbon (The College of Wooster), Kevin Fitzpatrick (University of Alabama-Birmingham), Dona C. Fletcher (Sinclair Community College), Charles Frazier (University of Florida), Karen Lynch Frederick (St. Anselm College), Jarvis Gamble (Owen's Technical College), Steven Goldberg (City College, City University of New York), Charlotte Gotwald (York College of Pennsylvania), Jeffrey Hahn (Mount Union College), Harry Hale (Northeast Louisiana State University), Dean Haledjian (Northern Virginia Community College), Dick Haltin (Jefferson Community College), Marvin Hannah (Milwaukee Area Technical College), Charles Harper (Creighton University), Elizabeth A. Hoisington (Heartland Community College), Peter Hruschka (Ohio Northern University), Glenna Huls (Camden County College), Jeanne Humble (Lexington Community College), Harry Humphries (Pittsburg State University), Cynthia Imanaka (Seattle Central Community College), Patricia Johnson (Houston Community College), Ed Kain (Southwestern University), Paul Kamolnick (East Tennessee State University), Irwin Kantor (Middlesex County College), Thomas Korllos (Kent State University), Rita Krasnow (Virginia Western Community College), Donald Kraybill (Elizabethtown College), Michael Lacy (Colorado State University), Michael Levine (Kenyon College), George Lowe (Texas Tech University), Don Luidens (Hope College), Larry Lyon (Baylor University), Li-Chen Ma (Lamar University), Meredith McGuire (Trinity College), Setma Maddox (Texas Wesleyan University), Errol Magidson (Richard J. Daley College), Alan Mazur (Syracuse University), Jack Melhorn (Emporia State University), Ken Miller (Drake University), Richard Miller (Navarro College), Joe Morolla (Virginia Commonwealth University), Craig Nauman (Madison Area Technical College), Toby Parcel (The Ohio State University), Anne Peterson (Columbus State Community College), Lauren Pivnik (Monroe Community College), Daniel Quinn (Adrian College), Nevel Razak (Fort Hays State College), Jim Rebstock (Broward Community College), George Reim (Cheltenham High School), Virginia Reynolds (Indiana University of Pennsylvania), Laurel Richardson (The Ohio State University), Keith Roberts (Hanover College), Ellen Rosengarten (Sinclair Community College), Howard Schneiderman (Lafayette College), Ray Scupin (Linderwood College), Steve Severin (Kellogg Community College), Harry Sherer (Irvine Valley College), Walt Shirley (Sinclair Community College), Ree Simpkins (Missouri Southern State University), Glen Sims (Glendale Community College), Verta Taylor (The Ohio State University), Vickie H. Taylor (Danville Community College), Mark J. Thomas (Madison Area Technical College), Len Tompos (Lorain County Community College), Christopher Vanderpool (Michigan State University), Phyllis Watts (Tiffin University), Murray Webster (University of North Carolina, Charlotte), Marilyn Wilmeth (Iowa University), Stuart Wright (Lamar University), William Yoels (University of Alabama, Birmingham), Dan Yutze (Taylor University), Wayne Zapatek (Tarrant County Community College), and Frank Zulke (Harold Washington College).

Finally, I would like to dedicate this book to my father, John Joseph Macionis, who reached the milestone of his eightieth birthday in May of 1996. He has always taken a great deal of pride in the accomplishments of "My son, the professor" (even though, I suspect, he still sometimes wonders what sociology is all about). For all the times I never expressed my appreciation clearly enough, I want to say now, "Thanks, Dad, for everything you've done over my whole lifetime." Without the many lessons you taught me, this book would never have been written at all.

ANTONIO RUIZ,
THE BICYCLE RACE, 1938

Philadelphia Museum of Art; purchased by
Nebinger Fund.

The Sociological Perspective

Imagine if someone you had never met walked into your classroom and began telling you and your classmates all about yourselves. Sociologists are not mind-readers or fortune-tellers, but they can confi- dently describe the lives of strangers and even make predictions about the future. Here are a few safe bets.

First, if you are attending a private liberal arts college, your class- mates (on average) come from well-to-do families with about twice the national level of income. At a state university? Your classmates are not quite as privileged, although their families' earnings are still above average. At a community college? In that case, your classmates are from families of more modest means; at some schools, a majority of students are from lower-income families.

Second, regardless of what college or university you attend, more than nine out of ten members of your class have married or will tie the knot sometime in their lives. Later on, half of them will go through at least one divorce. Those who divorce will do so, on average, after seven years of marriage.

Third, students who complete a two-year associate's degree will earn about $1.5 million (in 1996 dol- lars) during their lifetimes; receiving a bachelor's degree raises the figure to $2.0 million; a Ph.D. pushes life- time income up further to about $2.8 million; people who gain a professional degree (say, as a lawyer or physician) can expect lifetime earnings to top $3.5 million. But gender also comes into play: Women will trail men in lifetime earnings by about 25 percent.

Fourth, the members of your class will have one or two children. After that, most of you (or your part- ners) will choose to be surgically sterilized to prevent further childbirth.

Fifth, on average, members of your class will live to their mid-seventies. But here the women have an edge: They will outlive the men by six years, with most women celebrating their eightieth birthday. And, the odds are that your life will come to an end in a hospital as a result of heart disease, cancer, or stroke.

Human lives do not unfold according to sheer chance; nor do people live isolated lives relying solely on what philosophers call "free will" in choosing every thought and action. On the contrary, while individuals make many important decisions every day, we do so within a larger arena called "society"—a family, a campus, a nation, an entire world. The essential wisdom of sociology is that the social world guides our actions and life choices just as the seasons influence our choices of activities and clothing. And, because sociologists know a great deal about how society works, they can analyze and predict with a good measure of accuracy how we all behave.

We can easily grasp the power of society over the individual by imagining how different our world would be had we been born in place of any of these children from, respectively, Bolivia, Sri Lanka, South Africa, Botswana, the People's Republic of China, and Brazil.

THE SOCIOLOGICAL PERSPECTIVE

Formally, the discipline of **sociology** is *the systematic study of human society*. At the heart of sociology is a distinctive point of view.

Seeing the General in the Particular

Peter Berger (1963) characterized the sociological perspective as *seeing the general in the particular*. He meant that sociologists identify general patterns in the behavior of particular individuals. While acknowledging that each individual is unique, in other words, sociologists recognize that society acts differently on various *categories* of people (say, children compared to adults, women versus men, the rich as opposed to the poor). We begin to think sociologically as we start to realize how the general categories

into which we happen to fall shape our particular life experiences.

Each chapter of this text illustrates the general impact of society on the actions, thoughts, and feelings of particular people. For instance, the differences that distinguish children from adults reflect not just biological maturity: By attaching meaning to age, society creates what we experience as distinct stages of life. Following these age-scripts, we expect children to be "dependent" and adults to behave "responsibly." And, further along the life course, our society defines old age as a time of diminishing standing and withdrawal from earlier routines.

How do we know that society (and not simply biology) is at work here? Looking back in time or around the world today, we see that societies define the stages of life quite differently. Later chapters note that the Native-American Hopi confer on children surprising

THE MAP: Comments about the Windows on the World global maps and the Seeing Ourselves national maps.
RESOURCE: An article or book useful for further reading or for enhancing a class discussion.
Q: A noteworthy quotation by a sociologist, a historical figure, or a contemporary newsmaker.
SOCIAL SURVEY: Data from the National Opinion Research

Center's *General Social Survey.* As noted in the annotation, entries are taken from the *Social Survey Software* package available with this text or from the *GSS Codebook*.
NOTE: A theoretical or methodological comment, information on the text's artwork or photography, or the etymology of an important term.
DISCUSS: Topical information or a suggestion for class discussion.

Whenever we come upon people whose habits differ from our own, we become more aware of social patterns. This is why travel is an excellent way to stimulate the sociological perspective. But even within the United States there is striking cultural diversity, which prompts us to become conscious of our social surroundings.

independence while, in Abkhasia (part of the Russian Federation), elderly people enjoy the lion's share of social clout and esteem.

A sociological look around us reveals the power of class position as well. Chapter 9 ("Social Stratification") and Chapter 10 ("Social Class in the United States") provide ample evidence that how we live—and, sometimes, whether we live at all—have a great deal to do with our ranking in the societal hierarchy.

Seeing the world sociologically also makes us aware of the importance of gender. As Chapter 13 ("Sex and Gender") points out, every society attaches meaning to being one sex or the other, according women and men different kinds of work and family responsibilities. Individuals experience the workings of society as they encounter advantages and opportunities characteristic of each sex.

Seeing the Strange in the Familiar

Especially at the beginning, using the sociological perspective amounts to *seeing the strange in the familiar.* This does not mean that sociologists focus on the bizarre elements of society. Rather, observing sociologically requires giving up the familiar idea that human behavior is simply a matter of what people *decide* to do in favor of the initially strange notion that society guides our thoughts and deeds.

For individualistic North Americans, learning to "see" how society affects us may take a bit of practice. Asked why you "chose" to enroll at your particular

college, you might offer any of the following personal reasons:

I wanted to stay close to home.
This college has the best women's basketball team.
A journalism degree from this university ensures a good job.
My girlfriend goes to school here.
I wasn't accepted by the school I really wanted to attend.

Such responses are certainly grounded in reality for the people expressing them. But do they tell the whole story? The sociological perspective provides additional insights that may not be readily apparent.

Thinking sociologically about college attendance, we might first realize that, for young people throughout most of the world, college is all but out of reach. Moreover, had we lived a century or two ago, the "choice" to go to college probably never would have been an option. But even in the here and now, a look around the classroom suggests that social forces still have much to do with whether or not one pursues higher education. Typically, college students are relatively young—generally between eighteen and twenty-four years of age. Why? Because in our society college attendance is associated with this period of life. But more than age is involved, since only about one-third of all college-age men and women actually end up on campus.

SOCIAL SURVEY: "Does everybody have the opportunity to obtain an education corresponding to their abilities and talents?" (GSS 1983–87, N = 1,473; *Codebook*, 1994:97)

"Yes" 69.8%   "No" 27.9%   DK/NR 2.3%

DIVERSITY: Regarding Fig. 1–1, the higher a family's income, the more likely a daughter or son is to attend a private rather than a state college or university. Average tuition, room, and board at private schools topped $15,000 in 1995 versus about $3,000 for public institutions.

NOTE: Of course, it is also true that human action takes place within the context of our biological existence, so that we consciously (and unconsciously) take account of the various demands and limitations of our bodies.

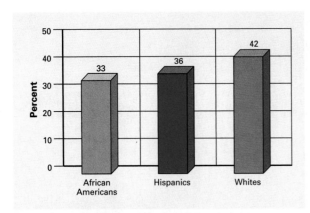

FIGURE 1–1 Share of 1993 High School Graduates Entering College the Following Fall

Source: American Council on Education (1995).

Another factor, alluded to in the opening of this chapter, is that higher education is costly so that college students tend to come from families with above-average incomes. As Chapter 19 ("Education") explains, young people lucky enough to belong to families earning more than $75,000 are three times as likely to go to college as their counterparts in families with annual earnings below $20,000. And, as Figure 1–1 shows, because our society links both race and ethnicity to income, a greater share of white people (42 percent) "choose" to go to college than do African Americans (33 percent) and Hispanics[1] (36 percent) (U.S. Bureau of the Census, 1994).

So it is easy to show that society affects what we do. But society even affects who we are, as a look at the names chosen by celebrities suggests. The box offers examples.

Individuality in Social Context

The sociological perspective often challenges common sense by revealing that human behavior is not as individualistic as we may think. For most of us, daily living carries a heavy load of personal responsibility, so that we pat ourselves on the back when we enjoy success and kick ourselves when things go wrong. Proud of our individuality, even in painful times, we resist the idea that we act in socially patterned ways.

Perhaps the most compelling demonstration of how social forces affect human behavior is the study of suicide. Why? Because nothing is a more personal "choice" than the decision to take one's own life. This is why Emile Durkheim (1858–1917), a pioneer of sociology writing a century ago, chose suicide as a topic of research. He was able to demonstrate that social forces figure in the apparently isolated act of self-destruction.

Durkheim began by examining suicide records in and around his native France. The statistics clearly showed that some categories of people were more likely than others to choose to take their own lives. Specifically, Durkheim found, men, Protestants, wealthy people, and the unmarried each had significantly higher suicide rates compared to women, Catholics and Jews, the poor, and married people. Durkheim deduced that these differences corresponded to people's degree of *social integration*. Low suicide rates characterized categories of people with strong social ties; high suicide rates were found among those who were more socially isolated and individualistic.

In the male-dominated societies studied by Durkheim, men certainly had more autonomy than women. Whatever freedom's advantages for men, concluded Durkheim, autonomy means lower social integration that contributes to a higher male suicide rate.

FIGURE 1–2 Rate of Death by Suicide, by Race and Sex, for the United States

Rates indicate the number of deaths by suicide for every 100,000 people in each category for 1992.
Source: U.S. Bureau of the Census (1995).

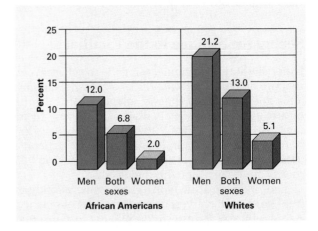

---

[1]Hispanics or Latinos may be of any race; about 85 percent state their race as white. (See "A Word About Language" in the Preface.)

SUPPLEMENTS: The *Data File* contains a chapter outline, discussion topics, and additional lecture material for this chapter.
DIVERSITY: Suicide rates rise with advancing age: 15–24-year-olds, 13.0 (1990); 85 and older, 21.9. (U.S. Bureau of the Census, 1995)
THEN AND NOW: U.S. suicide rate, *1950:* 11.4 per 100,000 people; *1960:* 10.6; *1970:* 11.6; *1980:* 11.9; *1994:* 12.4.

GLOBAL: The meaning of global suicide rates is open to interpretation, but analysis seems to lend support to Durkheim's conclusions. High suicide rates: Hungary (37.0 per 100,000), Finland (27.8), Austria (20.6), Denmark (20.4); moderate rates: Czech Republic (18.8), Bulgaria (16.6), Sweden (15.9), Germany (15.5), United States (12.3); low rates: Netherlands (10.0), Portugal (8.2), Spain (7.1), Italy (6.8). (U. S. Bureau of the Census)

SOCIAL DIVERSITY

What's in a Name? How Social Forces Affect Personal Choices

On July 4th, 1918, twins were born to Abe and Becky Friedman in Sioux City, Iowa. The first to arrive they called Esther Pauline Friedman; the proud parents named her sister Pauline Esther Friedman. Today, these women are known to almost everyone in the United States, but by the new names they later adopted: Ann Landers and Abigail ("Dear Abby") Van Buren.

These two women are among tens of thousands of people in our society who changed their names to advance their careers. At first glance, changing one's name may seem to be little more than a matter of personal preferences. But take a closer look, from a sociological point of view, at the following list:

1. Thomas Mapother
2. Cherilyn Sarkisian
3. Cheryl Stoppelmoor
4. Robert Allen Zimmerman
5. Larry Zeigler
6. Nathan Birnbaum
7. Paul Rubenfeld
8. George Kyriakou Panayiotou
9. Annie Mae Bullock
10. Patricia Andrejewski
11. Malden Sekulovich
12. Jerome Silberman
13. Milton Supman
14. Karen Ziegler
15. Ramon Estevez
16. Henry John Deutschendorf, Jr.
17. Allen Stewart Konigsberg
18. Patsy McClenny
19. Jacob Cohen
20. William Claude Dukenfield
21. Lee Yuen Kam
22. Raquel Tejada
23. Frederick Austerlitz
24. Sophia Scicoloni

Can you see the pattern in these changes? Historically, women and men of various national backgrounds have adopted *English-sounding* names. Why? Because our society has long accorded high social prestige to those of Anglo-Saxon background. Once again, in other words, we see personal choices guided by social forces.

1. Tom Cruise, 2. Cher, 3. Cheryl Ladd, 4. Bob Dylan, 5. Larry King, 6. George Burns, 7. Pee Wee Herman, 8. George Michael, 9. Tina Turner, 10. Pat Benatar, 11. Karl Malden, 12. Gene Wilder, 13. Soupy Sales, 14. Karen Black, 15. Martin Sheen, 16. John Denver, 17. Woody Allen, 18. Morgan Fairchild, 19. Rodney Dangerfield, 20. W. C. Fields, 21. Bruce Lee, 22. Raquel Welch, 23. Fred Astaire, 24. Sophia Loren

---

Likewise, individualistic Protestants were more prone to suicide than Catholics and Jews, whose rituals foster stronger social ties. The wealthy clearly have much more freedom of action than the poor but, once again, at the cost of a higher suicide rate. Finally, single people, with weaker social ties than married people, are also at greater risk of suicide.

A century later, statistical evidence still supports Durkheim's analysis. Figure 1–2 shows suicide rates for four categories of the U.S. population. In 1992, there were 13.0 recorded suicides for every 100,000 white people, almost twice the rate for African Americans (6.8). Also, for both races, suicide is more common among men than among women. White men (21.2) are four times more likely than white women (5.1) to take their own lives. Among African Americans, the rate for men (12.0) is six times that for women (2.0). Following Durkheim's logic, the higher suicide rate among white people and men reflects their greater affluence and autonomy. By contrast, the

lower rate among women and people of color corresponds to their limited social choices. Overall, then, suicide rates reveal general social patterns in the most personal actions of particular individuals.

THE IMPORTANCE OF GLOBAL PERSPECTIVE

December 10, 1994, Fez, Morocco. This medieval city—its labyrinth of narrow streets and alleyways alive with the sounds and movements of playing children, veiled women, and men conducting business over donkeys laden with goods—has changed little over the centuries. We stand in northwest Africa, only a few hundred miles from the more familiar rhythms of Europe; yet this place seems

GLOBAL SOCIOLOGY

The Global Village: A Sociological Snapshot of Our World

The planet Earth is home to some 5.7 billion people who reside in cities and across the countryside of 191 nations. To grasp the social "shape" of the world, imagine for a moment the planet's population reduced to a single settlement of 1,000 people. A visit to this "global village" would reveal that more than half (575) of the inhabitants are Asians, including 200 citizens of the People's Republic of China. Next, in terms of numbers, we would find 130 Africans, 125 Europeans, and about 100 Latin Americans. North Americans—including people from the United States, Canada, and Mexico—would account for a scant 65 village residents.

A study of the settlement's ways of life would yield some startling conclusions: The village is a rich place, with a seemingly endless array of goods and services for sale. Yet most of the inhabitants can do no more than dream longingly of such treasures, since half of the village's total income is earned by just 150 individuals.

Food is the greatest source of concern for the majority of the population. Every year, workers produce more than enough food to feed everyone; even so, half the village's people—including most of the children—are poorly nourished and many fall asleep hungry. The worst-off 200 residents, who lack food, safe drinking water, and secure shelter, do not have the strength to work and are vulnerable to life-threatening diseases.

Villagers boast of their community's many schools, including colleges and universities. About 75 inhabitants have completed a college degree and a few even have doctorates, but half of the village's people can neither read nor write.

We in the United States stand among the most prosperous people of the "global village." The sociological perspective reminds us that many of the achievements we attribute to our personal abilities are also products of the privileged position we occupy in the worldwide social system.

Source: United Nations data and calculations by the author.

a thousand years away. Never have we had such an adventure! Never have we thought so much about home!

In recent years, as even the farthest reaches of the earth have become more easily accessible through advances in technology, many academic disciplines have incorporated a **global perspective,** *the study of the larger world and our society's place in it.* How does a global perspective enhance sociology?

First, global awareness is a logical extension of the sociological perspective. Sociology's basic insight is that where we are placed in our society profoundly affects our individual experiences. It stands to reason, then, that the position of our society in the larger world system also affects everyone in the United States. The box provides a brief sketch of our "global village," indicating that people the world over are far from equal in their quality of life.

Global Map 1–1 provides a visual guide to the relative economic development of the world's countries. The world's **high-income countries** are *industrialized*

nations in which most people enjoy material abundance[2]. High-income countries include the United States and Canada, most of Western Europe, Israel, Japan, and Australia. Taken together, these forty societies generate most of the world's goods and services and control most of the planet's wealth. On average, individuals in these countries live well, not because they are particularly bright or exceptionally hardworking, but because they had the good fortune to be born in an affluent region of the world.

A second category of societies comprises the world's **middle-income countries,** which are *nations characterized by limited industrialization and moderate personal income.* Individuals living in any of the roughly ninety nations at this level of economic development—which include the countries of Eastern Europe and most of Latin America—are more likely to live in rural

[2]The text uses this terminology as opposed to the traditional, but outdated, terms "First World," "Second World," and "Third World." Chapter 11 ("Global Stratification") delves into the reasons for this shift.

THE MAP: About 15% of the world's people live in high-income countries, one-third live in middle-income nations, and just over half live in low-income countries. Per capita GNP for the world as a whole stands at roughly $4,500.

GLOBAL: For details of global income distribution, look ahead to Figure 11–1.

NOTE: Some students may not know that the world is divided into twenty-four time zones. While the U.S. has four, the highly centralized People's Republic of China, although just as "wide," holds to one (everyone uses Beijing time)

THEN AND NOW: Percent of Japanese households with *cars*—1961, 2.8%; 1994, 79.7%. (Japanese Economic Planning Agency)

Window on the World

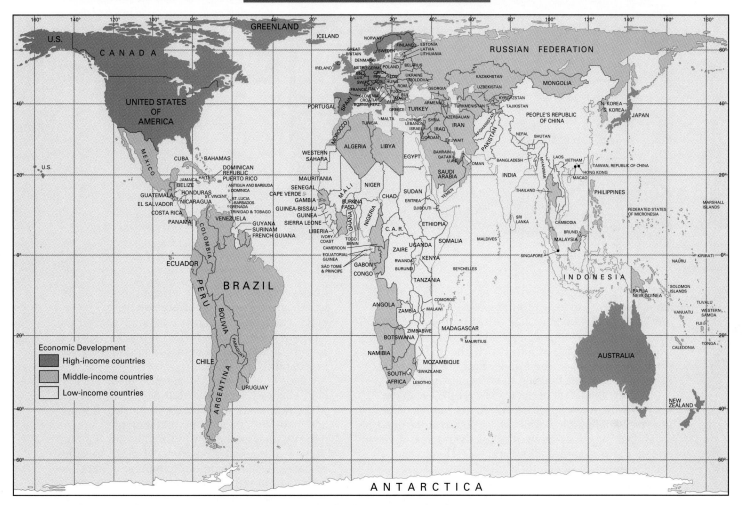

GLOBAL MAP 1–1 Economic Development in Global Perspective*

In high-income countries—the United States, Canada, most of the nations of Western Europe, Israel, Australia, and Japan—industrial technology provides people, on average, with material plenty. Middle-income countries—found throughout Latin America and including the nations of Eastern Europe—have limited industrial capacity and offer their people a standard of living that, while about average for the world as a whole, is far below that familiar to most people in the United States. The populations of these nations also encompass a significant share of poor people who barely scrape by with meager housing and diet. In the low-income countries of the world, poverty is severe and extensive. Although small numbers of elites live very well in these poorest nations, the majority of people struggle to survive on a small fraction of the income common in the United States.

*Note: Data for this map are provided by the World Bank and the United Nations. High-income countries have per capita gross domestic product (GDP) of at least $10,000. Many are far richer than this, however; the figure for the United States exceeds $25,000. Middle-income countries have a per capita GDP ranging from $2,500 to $10,000. Low-income countries have a per capita GDP below $2,500. Figures used here reflect the new United Nations "purchasing power parities" system. Rather than directly converting income figures to U.S. dollars, this calculation estimates the local purchasing power of each domestic currency.

Prepared by the author using data from The World Bank (1995). Map projection from *Peters Atlas of the World* (1990).

GLOBAL: Evidence of ties linking the United States and the rest of the world: Many rock stars sell more records abroad than in the United States; conversely, salsa has replaced ketchup as this nation's favorite condiment.

Q: "One can be an excellent physicist without ever stepping outside of one's society; I know this is not so for a sociologist." Peter Berger (1992)

NOTE: Leonardo Di Vinci sketched a flying machine in the fifteenth century; however, despite his great genius (both as a painter and a scientist), the technology of his times was not sufficiently advanced to make this device a reality.

THEN AND NOW: The number of telephone calls made from the United States to some other country: *1970*, 23 million; *1980*, 200 million; *1993*, 3.1 billion. (FCC data)

One important reason to gain a global understanding is that, living in a high-income society, we scarcely can appreciate the suffering that goes on in much of the world. The life of this Rwandan boy has been shredded by civil war. But even in more peaceful nations of Africa, children have less than a fifty-fifty chance to grow to adulthood.

areas than in cities, to walk or ride bicycles, scooters, or animals rather than to drive automobiles, and to receive only a few years of schooling. Most middle-income countries also have marked social inequality so that while some people are extremely rich (the sheiks of oil-producing nations in the Middle East, for example), many more lack safe housing and adequate nutrition.

Finally, about half of the world's people live in the sixty **low-income countries,** which are *nations with little industrialization in which severe poverty is the rule.* As Global Map 1–1 shows, most of the poorest societies in the world are in Africa and Asia. Here, again, a small number of people in each of these nations is rich; but the majority barely get by with poor housing, unsafe water, too little food, little or no sanitation, and, perhaps most seriously of all, little chance to improve their lives.

Chapter 11 ("Global Stratification") explores the causes and consequences of global wealth and poverty in detail. But every chapter of this text highlights life in the world beyond our own borders. Why? Here are three reasons that global thinking figures prominently in the sociological perspective.

1. **Societies the world over are increasingly interconnected.** People in the United States have long been rather indifferent to the world around us. Separated from Europe and Asia by vast oceans, we have taken only passing note of our neighbors to the north (Canada) and south (Mexico and other Latin American nations). In recent decades,

however, the United States and the rest of the world have become linked as never before. Jet aircraft whisk people across continents in hours, while new electronic devices transmit pictures, sounds, and written documents around the globe in seconds.

One consequence of this new technology, as later chapters explain, is that people all over the world now share many tastes in music, clothing, and food. With their economic clout, high-income nations such as the United States cast a global shadow, influencing members of other societies who eagerly gobble up our hamburgers, dance to rock-and-roll music, and, more and more, speak the English language.

But as we project our way of life onto much of the world, the larger world, too, has an impact on us. More than 1 million documented immigrants entered the United States annually during the 1990s, and we are quick to adopt many of their favorite sights, sounds, and tastes as our own. All this, of course, has greatly enhanced the racial and cultural diversity of this country.

Commerce across national borders has also propelled a global economy. Large corporations manufacture and market goods worldwide, just as global financial markets linked by satellite communications now operate around the clock. Today, no stock trader in New York dares to ignore what happens in the financial markets in Tokyo and Hong Kong, just as no wheat farmer in Kansas can

Q: "For the most part we do not first see then define; we define and then see." U.S. social critic Walter Lippman

Q: "O, when degree is shak'd,
Which is the ladder of all high designs,
The enterprise is sick! . . .
Take but degree away, untune that string,
And hark what discord follows!"

Shakespeare (*Troilus and Cressida*) reflecting on the erosion of the traditional feudal hierarchy, which would only accelerate with the coming of the Industrial Revolution.

Q: "The world is a book and those who study just their own society read only a single page." Old saying

afford to overlook the price of grain in the former Soviet republic of Georgia. Because eight out of ten new U.S. jobs involve international trade, gaining greater global understanding has never been more critical (Council on International Educational Exchange, 1988).

2. **A global perspective enables us to see that many human problems we face in the United States are far more serious elsewhere.** Poverty is certainly a serious problem in the United States. But, as Chapter 11 ("Global Stratification") explains, poverty is both more widespread and more severe throughout Latin America, Africa, and Asia. Similarly, the social standing of women (which is below that of men in the United States) is especially low in poor countries of the world.

   Then, too, many of the toughest problems we grapple with at home are global in scope. Environmental pollution is one example: As Chapter 22 ("Environment and Society") demonstrates, the world is a single ecosystem in which the action (or inaction) of one nation has implications for all others.

3. **Thinking globally is an excellent way to learn more about ourselves.** We cannot walk the streets of a distant city without becoming keenly aware of what it means to live in the United States. Making global comparisons also leads to unexpected lessons. For instance, Chapter 11 ("Global Stratification") transports us to a squatter settlement in Madras, India. There, despite a desperate lack of basic material comforts, we are surprised to find people thriving in the love and support of family members. Such discoveries prompt us to think about why poverty in the United States so often involves isolation and anger, and whether material things—so crucial to our definition of a "rich" life—are the best way to gauge human well-being.

In sum, in an increasingly interconnected world, we can understand ourselves only to the extent that we comprehend others (Macionis, 1993).

THE SOCIOLOGICAL PERSPECTIVE IN EVERYDAY LIFE

Encountering people who differ from ourselves—whether around the world or in our own hometowns—inevitably reminds us of the power of social forces to shape our lives. But two other kinds of situations stimulate a sociological outlook, even before we take a first course in sociology.

Sociology and Social Marginality

Sociological thinking is especially common among social "outsiders." Social marginality is something we all experience from time to time. For some categories of people, however, being an outsider is part of daily living. The more acute people's social marginality, the more likely they are to be keenly aware of their surroundings and to embrace the sociological perspective.

No African American, for example, lives for long in the United States without learning how much race affects personal experience. But because white people are the dominant majority, they think about race only occasionally and often take the attitude that race affects only people of color rather than themselves as well.

Much the same is true of women, gay people, people with disabilities, and the very old. All those relegated to the outskirts of social life typically become aware of social patterns others take for granted. Turning the argument around, for any of us to develop a sociological perspective we must step back a bit from our familiar routines to look on our lives with a new awareness and curiosity.

Sociology and Social Crisis

Periods of massive social change or social crisis throw everyone a little off balance, and this, too, stimulates sociological vision. C. Wright Mills (1959), a noted U.S. sociologist, illustrated this principle by recalling the Great Depression of the 1930s. As the nation's unemployment rate soared to 25 percent, people out of work could not help but see general social forces at work in their particular lives. Rather than personalizing their plight by claiming, "Something is wrong with me; I can't find a job," they took a more sociological approach, observing: "The economy has collapsed; there are no jobs to be found!"

Conversely, sociological thinking often fosters social change. The more we learn about the operation of "the system," the more we may wish to change it in some way. As women and men have confronted the power of gender, for example, many have actively tried to reduce the traditional differences that distinguish men and women.

In short, an introduction to sociology is an invitation to learn a new way of looking at familiar patterns

RESOURCE: Compare the classic essays by C. Wright Mills and Peter Berger in the Macionis and Benokraitis reader, *Seeing Ourselves: Classic, Contemporary, and Cross-Cultural Readings in Sociology*, 3d ed., Prentice Hall, 1995. For Mills, sociology transforms the personal into the political; for Berger, embracing sociology constitutes a step toward personal enrichment.

Q: Recognizing the power of society to confer or withhold greatness, Theodore Roosevelt commented, "A man has to take advantage of his opportunities, but the opportunities have to come. If there is not the war, you don't get the great general. If there is not the great occasion, you do not get the great statesman. If Lincoln had lived in times of peace, no one would know his name now."

of social life. At this point, we might well consider whether this invitation is worth accepting. In other words, what are the benefits of learning to use the sociological perspective?

Benefits of the Sociological Perspective

As we learn to use the sociological perspective, we can readily apply it to our daily lives. Doing so provides four general benefits.

1. **The sociological perspective challenges familiar understandings of ourselves and of others, so that we can critically assess the truth of commonly held assumptions.** Thinking sociologically, in other words, we may realize that ideas we have taken for granted are not always true. As we have already seen, a good example of a widespread but misleading "truth" is that the United States is populated with "autonomous individuals" who are personally responsible for their lives. Thinking this way, we are sometimes too quick to praise particularly successful people as superior to others whose more modest achievements mark them as personally deficient. A sociological approach prompts us to ask whether these beliefs are actually true and, to the extent that they are not, why they are so widely held.

2. **The sociological perspective enables us to assess both the opportunities and the constraints that characterize our lives.** Sociological thinking leads us to see that, for better or worse, our society operates in a particular way. Moreover, in the game of life, we may decide how to play our cards, but it is society that deals us the hand. The more we understand the game, then, the more effective players we will be. Sociology helps us to understand what we are likely and unlikely to accomplish for ourselves and how we can pursue our goals most effectively.

3. **The sociological perspective empowers us to be active participants in our society.** Without an awareness of how society operates, we are likely to accept the status quo. The greater our understanding of the operation of society, however, the more we can take an active part in shaping social life. For some, this may mean embracing society as it is; others, however, may attempt nothing less than changing the entire world in some way. The discipline of sociology advocates no one particular political orientation, and sociologists themselves weigh in at many points across the political

spectrum. But evaluating any aspect of social life—whatever one's eventual goal—depends on the ability to identify social forces and to assess their consequences.

Some thirty years ago, C. Wright Mills claimed that developing what he called the "sociological imagination" would help people to become more active citizens. This major sociological thinker is highlighted in the Profile box. Other notable sociologists are featured in Profile boxes throughout this book.

4. **The sociological perspective helps us to recognize human diversity and to confront the challenges of living in a diverse world.** Sociological thinking highlights our world's remarkable social variety. North Americans represent a scant 5 percent of the world's population, and, as the remaining chapters of this book explain, many of our fellow human beings live in societies dramatically different from our own. Like people everywhere, we tend to define our own way of life as proper and "natural," and dismiss the lifestyles of those who differ from ourselves. But the sociological perspective encourages us to think critically about the relative strengths and weaknesses of all ways of life—including our own.

Applied Sociology

The benefits of sociology go well beyond intellectual growth. Indeed, the American Sociological Association notes that sociology is sound training for literally hundreds of jobs in various fields, including advertising, banking, criminal justice, education, government, health care, public relations, and research (Billson & Huber, 1993).

Currently, most men and women who continue beyond a bachelor's degree to pursue advanced training in sociology go on to careers in teaching and research. But an increasing proportion of professional sociologists work in all sorts of applied fields. One option is clinical sociology, in which practitioners serve the needs of troubled clients much as clinical psychologists do. But the two fields have a basic difference in orientation: While psychologists focus on the individual, sociologists locate difficulties in a person's web of social relationships. Evaluation research constitutes another type of applied sociology. In today's cost-conscious political climate, government and corporate administrators must evaluate the effectiveness of virtually every kind of program and policy. Sociologists—

PROFILE

C. Wright Mills: The Sociological Imagination

Charles Wright Mills (1916–1962) managed to cause a stir with most everything he did. Even arriving for a class at New York's Columbia University—clad in a sweat- shirt, jeans, and boots astride his motorcycle—he usually turned some heads. During the conservative 1950s, Mills not only dressed a bit out of the mainstream; he also produced a number of books that challenged most of the beliefs the majority of us take for granted. In the process, he acquired both adherents and adversaries.

Mills's approach to the discipline can be summed up in one sentence: A sociological imagination can transform

individual lives as it changes society. As Mills saw it, sociology is not some dry enterprise detached from life. Rather, he held up sociology as an escape from the "traps" of our lives because it can show us that society— not our own foibles or failings—is responsible for many of our problems. In this way, Mills maintained, sociology transforms personal *problems* into political *issues*.

In the following excerpt* Mills describes the power of society to shape our individual lives:

> When a society becomes indus- trialized, a peasant becomes a worker; a feudal lord is liquidated or becomes a businessman. When classes rise or fall, a man is employed or unemployed; when the rate of investment goes up or down, a man takes new heart or goes broke. When wars happen, an insurance salesman becomes a rocket launcher; a store clerk, a radar man; a wife lives alone; a child grows up without a father. Neither the life of an individual

*In this excerpt, Mills uses male pronouns to apply to all people. It is interesting—even ironic—that an outspoken critic of society like Mills reflected the conventional writing practices of his time as far as gender was concerned.

nor the history of a society can be understood without under- standing both.

> Yet men do not usually define the troubles they endure in terms of historical change. . . . The well- being they enjoy, they do not usually impute to the big ups and downs of the society in which they live. Seldom aware of the intricate connection between the patterns of their own lives and the course of world history, ordinary men do not usually know what this con- nection means for the kind of men they are becoming and for the kinds of history-making in which they might take part. They do not possess the quality of mind essen- tial to grasp the interplay of men and society, of biography and his- tory, of self and world. . . .

> What they need . . . is a quality of mind that will help them to [see] . . . what is going on in the world and . . . what may be hap- pening within themselves. It is this quality . . . that . . . may be called the sociological imagination.

Source: Mills (1959).

especially those with advanced research skills—are in high demand for this kind of work.

THE ORIGINS OF SOCIOLOGY

Like the "choices" made by individuals, major historical events rarely just happen. They are typically products of powerful social forces that are always complex and only partly predictable. So it was with the emergence of

sociology itself. Having described the discipline's dis- tinctive perspective and surveyed some of its benefits, we can now consider how and why sociology emerged in the first place.

Although human beings have mused about soci- ety since the beginning of our history, sociology is of relatively recent origin. It is among the youngest aca- demic disciplines—far newer than history, physics, or economics, for example. Only in 1838 did the French social thinker Auguste Comte, introduced in the box,

---

PROFILE

Auguste Comte: Weathering a Storm of Change

W hat sort of person would invent *sociology*? Certainly someone living in times of momentous change. Comte (1798–1857) grew up in the wake of the French Revolution, which brought a sweeping transformation to his country. And if that wasn't sufficient, another revolution was under way as factories were sprouting up across continental Europe, recasting the lives of the entire population. Just as people enduring a storm cannot help but think of the weather, so those living during Comte's turbulent era became keenly aware of the state of society.

Drawn from his small hometown by the bustle of Paris, Comte was soon deeply involved in the exciting events of his time. More than anything else, he wanted to understand the human drama that was unfolding all around him. Once equipped with knowledge about how society operates, Comte believed, people would be able to build for themselves a better future. He divided his new discipline into two parts: how society is held together (which he called *social statics*), and how society changes (*social dynamics*). From the Greek and Latin words meaning "the study of society," Comte came to describe his work as *sociology.*

---

coin the term *sociology* to describe a new way of looking at the world.

Science and Sociology

The nature of society was a major topic of inquiry for virtually all the brilliant thinkers of the ancient world, including the Chinese philosopher K'ung Fu-tzu, also known as Confucius (551–479 B.C.E.), and the Greek philosophers Plato (c. 427–347 B.C.E.) and Aristotle (384–322 B.C.E.).[3] Similarly, the Roman emperor Marcus Aurelius (121–180), the medieval thinkers St. Thomas Aquinas (c. 1225–1274) and Christine de Pizan (c. 1363–1431), and the English playwright William Shakespeare (1564–1616) all examined the state of human society. Yet, as Emile Durkheim noted almost a century ago, none of these social thinkers approached society from a sociological point of view.

[3]Throughout this text, the abbreviation B.C.E. designates "before the common era." We use this terminology in place of the traditional B.C. ("before Christ") in recognition of the religious plurality of our society. Similarly, in place of the traditional A.D. (*anno Domini*, or "in the year of our Lord"), we employ the abbreviation C.E. ("common era").

Looking back in history . . . we find that no philosophers ever viewed matters [with a sociological perspective] until quite recently. . . . It seemed to them sufficient to ascertain what the human will should strive for and what it should avoid in established societies. . . . Their aim was not to offer us as valid a description of nature as possible, but to present us with the idea of a perfect society, a model to be imitated. (1972:57; orig. 1918)

What sets sociology apart from earlier social thought? Prior to the birth of sociology, philosophers and theologians mostly focused on imagining the ideal society. None attempted to analyze society as it really was. Pioneers of the discipline such as Auguste Comte and Emile Durkheim reversed these priorities. Although they were certainly concerned with how human society could be improved, their major goal was to understand how society actually operates.

The key to achieving this objective, according to Comte, was developing a scientific approach to society. Looking back in time, Comte sorted human efforts to comprehend the world into three distinct stages (1975; orig. 1851–54). The earliest era, extending through the medieval period in Europe, he termed the *theological stage.* At this point, thoughts about the world were guided by religion, so people regarded society as an expression of God's will—at least insofar as humans were capable of fulfilling a divine plan.

NOTE: Comte considered sociology to be the "Queen of the Sciences," an assertion that inspired some of his followers to acts of arrogance. A century ago, for example, sociologists at Brown University suggested that the entire college be reorganized under the sociology department.

NOTE: The first U. S. courses in sociology were taught during the early Industrial Revolution. Williams College offered a course in social ethics in 1865; Johns Hopkins taught social science in its opening year, 1876, the same year William Graham Sumner taught his first sociology course at Yale; Cornell introduced a social science course in 1884; the University of Chicago founded the first formal sociology department in 1892.

This medieval drawing conveys the mix of apprehension and excitement with which early scientists began to question traditional understandings of the universe. Pioneering sociologists, too, challenged many ideas that people had long taken for granted, explaining that society is neither fixed by God's will nor by human nature. On the contrary, Comte and other sociological pioneers claimed, society is a system that we can study scientifically and, based on what we learn, act deliberately to improve.

With the Renaissance, the theological approach to society gradually gave way to what Comte called the *metaphysical stage*. During this period, people came to understand society as a natural, rather than a supernatural, phenomenon. Human nature figured heavily in metaphysical visions of society: The English philosopher Thomas Hobbes (1588–1679), for example, posited that society reflected not the perfection of God as much as the failings of a rather selfish human nature.

What Comte heralded as the final, *scientific stage* in the long quest to understand society was propelled by scientists such as the Polish astronomer Copernicus (1473–1543), the Italian astronomer and physicist Galileo[4] (1564–1642), and the English physicist and mathematician Isaac Newton (1642–1727). Comte's contribution came in applying this scientific approach—first used to study the physical world—to the study of society.

Comte was thus a proponent of **positivism,** defined as *a means to understand the world based on science.* As a positivist, Comte believed that society conforms to invariable laws, much as the physical

world operates according to gravity and other laws of nature.

Sociology emerged as an academic discipline in the United States at the beginning of this century, with early sociologists such as Lester Ward (1841–1913) pursuing Comte's vision of a scientific sociology. Even today, most sociologists agree that science plays a crucial role in sociology. But, as Chapter 2 ("Sociological Investigation") explains, we now realize that human behavior is often far more complex than natural phenomena. Human beings are creatures with considerable imagination and spontaneity, so that our behavior can never be fully explained by any rigid "laws of society."

Social Change and Sociology

Striking transformations in eighteenth- and nineteenth-century Europe drove the development of sociology. As the social ground trembled under their feet, people understandably focused their attention on society.

First came scientific discoveries and technological advances that produced a factory-based industrial economy. Second, factories drew millions of people from the countryside, causing an explosive growth of cities. Third, people in these burgeoning industrial cities soon entertained new ideas about democracy and political rights. We shall briefly describe each of these three changes.

[4]Illustrating Comte's stages, the ancient Greeks and Romans viewed the planets as gods; Renaissance metaphysical thinkers saw them as astral influences (giving rise to astrology); by the time of Galileo, scientists understood planets as natural objects behaving in orderly ways.

The birth of sociology was prompted by rapid social change. The discipline developed in those regions of Europe where the Industrial Revolution most disrupted traditional ways of life, drawing people from isolated villages to rapidly growing industrial cities.

A New Industrial Economy

During the European Middle Ages, most people tilled fields near their homes or engaged in small-scale *manufacturing* (a word derived from Latin words meaning "to make by hand"). But by the end of the eighteenth century, inventors had applied new sources of energy—first water power and then steam power—to the operation of large machines, which gave birth to factories. Now, instead of laboring at home, workers became part of a large and anonymous industrial work force, toiling for strangers who owned the factories. This drastic change in the system of production weakened families and eroded traditions that had guided members of small communities for centuries.

The Growth of Cities

Factories sprouting across much of Europe became magnets attracting people in need of work. This "pull" of work in the new industrialized labor force was accentuated by an additional "push" as landowners fenced off more and more ground, turning farms into grazing land for sheep—the source of wool for the thriving textile mills. This so-called "enclosure movement" forced countless tenant farmers from

the countryside toward cities in search of work in the new factories.

Many villages were soon abandoned; at the same time, however, factory towns swelled rapidly into large cities. Such urban growth dramatically changed people's lives. Cities churned with strangers, in numbers that overwhelmed available housing. Widespread social problems—including poverty, disease, pollution, crime, and homelessness—were the order of the day. Such social crises further stimulated development of the sociological perspective.

Political Change

During the Middle Ages, as Comte noted, most people thought of society as the expression of God's will. Royalty claimed to rule by "divine right," and each person up and down the social hierarchy had some other part in the holy plan. This theological view of society is captured in lines from the old Anglican hymn "All Things Bright and Beautiful":

The rich man in his castle,
The poor man at his gate,
God made them high and lowly
And ordered their estate.

NOTE: Harriet Martineau's lifelong activism was guided by a Comtean view of the world as comprehensible and changeable. Her achievements are all the more impressive in light of her almost total deafness from the age of about twelve.

NOTE: The word "theory" is derived from the Greek *theoria*, meaning "a viewing." The Latin root of the word "structure" (*struct*) means "a piling up of."

Q: "Theories should be as simple as possible, but not more so." Albert Einstein

Q: "The Catholic accepts his faith ready made. . . . The proclivity of Protestantism for suicide must relate to the spirit of free inquiry that animates this religion. . . . Judaism . . . consists of a body of practices minutely governing all the details of life and leaving little free room to individual judgment." Emile Durkheim, *Suicide*

Many women contributed to the emergence of sociology, although their achievements have long been unrecognized. Harriet Martineau (1802–1876) (left), born to a rich English family, translated the writings of Auguste Comte from French in 1853. Soon afterward, she established her own reputation as a sociologist with studies of slavery, factory laws, and women's rights. In the United States, Jane Addams (1860–1935) (right) was a social worker known for her public activism on behalf of poor immigrants to this country. In 1889, Addams founded Hull House, a Chicago settlement house, in a poor, inner-city neighborhood. There, she engaged with intellectuals and immigrants alike in discussions of the pressing problems of her day. Her contribution to the welfare of others earned Addams a Nobel Peace Prize in 1931.

With economic development and the rapid growth of cities, changes in political thought were inevitable. Starting in the seventeenth century, every kind of tradition came under spirited attack. In the writings of Thomas Hobbes, John Locke (1632–1704), and Adam Smith (1723–1790), we see a distinct shift in focus from people's moral obligations to remain loyal to their rulers to the idea that society is the product of individual self-interest. The key phrases in the new political climate, therefore, were *individual liberty* and *individual rights*. Echoing the thoughts of Locke, our own Declaration of Independence asserts that each individual has "certain unalienable rights," including "life, liberty, and the pursuit of happiness."

The political revolution in France that began soon afterward, in 1789, constituted an even more dramatic break with political and social traditions. As the French social analyst Alexis de Tocqueville (1805–1859) surveyed his society after the French Revolution, he exaggerated only slightly when he asserted that the changes we have described amounted to "nothing short of the regeneration of the whole human race" (1955:13; orig. 1856). In this context, it is easy to see why Auguste Comte and other pioneers of sociology soon developed their new discipline. Sociology flowered in precisely those societies—France, Germany, and England—where change was greatest.

Sociologists reacted differently to the new social order then, just as they respond differently to society today. Some, including Auguste Comte, feared that people would be uprooted from long-established local communities and overpowered by change. So, in a conservative approach, Comte sought to shore up the family and traditional morality.

Taking a different view of these massive changes, the German social critic Karl Marx (1818–1883) worried little about the loss of tradition, which he detested. But he could not condone the way industrial technology concentrated its great wealth in the hands of a small elite, while so many others faced hunger and misery. We examine his ideas at length in Chapter 4 ("Society").

Clearly, Comte and Marx advanced radically different prescriptions for the problems of modernity. Yet they had in common the conviction that society rests on much more than individual choice. The sociological perspective animates the work of each, revealing that people's individual lives are framed by the broader society in which they live. This lesson, of course, remains as true today as it was a century ago.

In subsequent chapters of this book, we delve into the major issues that concern sociologists. These pivotal social forces include culture, social class, race, ethnicity, gender, the economy, and the family. They all involve ways in which individuals are guided, united, and divided in the larger arena of society.

SOCIOLOGICAL THEORY

The task of weaving isolated observations into understanding brings us to another dimension of sociology: theory. A **theory** is *a statement of how and why specific facts are related.* Recall that Emile Durkheim observed that certain categories of people (men, Protestants, the wealthy, and the unmarried) have higher suicide rates than others (women, Catholics and Jews, the poor, and the married). He explained these observations by

THE MAP: The highest suicide rate for any state is Nevada (24.6 per 100,000 people), with New Mexico in second place (19.2). The District of Columbia is lowest (5.8). Interestingly, this pattern is almost precisely the opposite in the case of state by state homicide rates.

NOTE: Herbert Spencer was influenced by Thomas Robert Malthus (whose thesis on population is covered in Chapter 21).

Spencer, a friend of industrialist Andrew Carnegie, wrote the first textbook on sociology, *Principles of Sociology*, in 1879 as part of a larger philosophical treatise.

Q: "I imagine that nearly all of us that took up sociology between 1870, say, and 1890 did so at the instigation of Spencer." Charles Horton Cooley (1920) (Spencer's books sold 400,000 copies in the U.S. during those decades.)

Seeing Ourselves

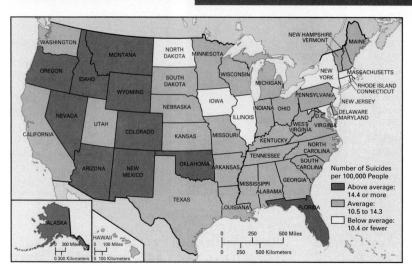

NATIONAL MAP 1–1

Suicide Rates Across the United States

This map identifies states in which suicide rates are particularly high, average, or unusually low. Look for patterns in the map. By and large, high suicide rates are common to states in which people typically live far apart from one another. Low suicide rates, by contrast, characterize states that are more densely populated. Do these data support or contradict Durkheim's theory of suicide? Why?

Prepared by the author using 1992 U. S. Bureau of the Census data.

creating a theory: A high risk of suicide stems from a low level of social integration.

Of course, as Durkheim pondered the issue of suicide, he considered any number of possible theories. But merely linking facts together is no guarantee that a theory is correct. To evaluate a theory, as the next chapter explains, sociologists use scientific research methods to gather evidence. Facts allow sociologists to confirm some theories while rejecting or modifying others. As a scientist, Durkheim was not content merely to identify a plausible cause of suicide; he set about collecting data to see precisely which categories of people committed suicide with the highest frequency. Poring over his data, Durkheim settled on a theory that best squared with all available evidence. National Map 1–1, which displays the recent suicide rate for each of the fifty states, gives you a chance to do some theorizing of your own.

In attempting to develop theories about human society, sociologists face a wide range of choices. What issues should we study? How should we link facts together to form theories? In making sense of society, sociologists are guided by one or more theoretical "road maps" or paradigms (Kuhn, 1970). For them, a **theoretical paradigm** is *a basic image of society that guides thinking and research.*

We noted earlier that two of sociology's founders— Auguste Comte and Karl Marx—made sense of the emerging modern society in strikingly different ways.

Such differences persist today as some sociologists highlight how societies stay the same, while others focus on patterns of change. Similarly, some sociological theorists focus on what joins people together, while others investigate how society divides people according to gender, race, ethnicity, or social class. Some sociologists seek to understand the operation of society as it is, while others actively promote what they view as desirable social change.

In short, sociologists often disagree about what the most interesting questions are; even when they agree on the questions, they may still differ over the answers. Nonetheless, the discipline of sociology is far from chaotic, because sociologists utilize three major theoretical paradigms that allow them to analyze effectively virtually any dimension of society.

The Structural-Functional Paradigm

The **structural-functional paradigm** is *a framework for building theory that envisions society as a complex system whose parts work together to promote solidarity and stability.* As its name suggests, this paradigm begins by recognizing that our lives are guided by **social structure,** meaning *relatively stable patterns of social behavior.* Social structure is what gives shape to the family, directs people to exchange greetings on the street, or steers events in a college classroom. Second, this paradigm leads us to understand social structure

PROFILE

Herbert Spencer: The Survival of the Fittest

The most memorable idea of the English philosopher Herbert Spencer (1820–1903) was his assertion that the passing of time witnesses "the survival of the fittest." Many people associate this immortal phrase with the theory of species evolution developed by the natural scientist Charles Darwin (1809–1882). The expression was actually Spencer's, however, and he used it to refer to society, not to living creatures. In it,

we find not only an example of early structural-functional analysis, but a controversial theory that reflects the popular view in Spencer's day that society mirrored biology.

Spencer's ideas, which came to be known as *social Darwinism,* rested on the assertion that, if left to compete among themselves, the most intelligent, ambitious, and productive people will inevitably win out. Spencer endorsed a world of fierce competition, thinking that as the "fittest" survived, society would undergo steady improvements.

Society rewards its best members, Spencer continued, by allowing a free-market economy to function without government interference. Welfare, or other programs aimed at redistributing money to benefit the poor, Spencer maintained, do just the opposite: They drag society down by elevating its weakest and least worthy members. For such opinions, nineteenth-century industrialists loudly applauded Spencer, and the rich saw in Spencer's analysis a scientific justification for big

business to remain free of government regulation or social conscience. Indeed, John D. Rockefeller, who built a vast financial empire that included most of the U.S. oil industry, often recited Spencer's "social gospel" to young children in Sunday school, casting the growth of giant corporations as merely the naturally ordained "survival of the fittest."

But others objected to the idea that society amounted to little more than a jungle where self-interest reigned supreme. Gradually, social Darwinism fell out of favor among social scientists, although it still surfaces today as an influential element of conservative political thought. From a sociological point of view, Spencer's thinking is flawed because we now realize that ability only partly accounts for personal success, and favoring the rich and powerful does not necessarily benefit society as a whole. In addition, the heartlessness of Spencer's ideas strikes many people as cruel, with little room for human compassion.

---

in terms of its **social functions,** or *consequences for the operation of society.* All social structure—from family life to a simple handshake—contributes to the operation of society, at least in its present form.

The structural-functional paradigm owes much to the ideas of Auguste Comte who, as we have already explained, sought to promote social integration during a time of tumultuous change. A second architect of this theoretical approach, the influential English sociologist Herbert Spencer (1820–1903), is introduced in the box. Spencer was a student of both the human body and society, and he came to see that the two have much in common. The structural parts of the human body include the skeleton, muscles, and various internal organs. These elements are interdependent, with

each contributing to the survival of the entire organism. In the same way, reasoned Spencer, various social structures are interdependent, working in concert to preserve society. The structural-functional paradigm, then, organizes sociological observations by identifying various structures of society and investigating the function of each one.

In France, several decades after Comte's death, Emile Durkheim continued the development of sociology. Durkheim did not share the social Darwinist thinking of his English colleague Spencer; rather, his work is primarily concerned with the issue of *social solidarity,* how societies "hang together." Because of the extent of Durkheim's influence on sociology, his work is detailed in Chapter 4 ("Society").

Q: "The most valid procedure with a historical thinker of this kind is not to try to have sport with his marginal failings but to rescue whatever is viable by cutting out what has proved wrong, tempering what is overstated, tightening what is loosely put, and setting the whole in its proper place among usable perspectives." Richard Hofstadter (referring to Herbert Spencer, but the comment could be applied to Marx or many other thinkers)

NOTE: Some "great inventions" developed as unintended consequences of more modest ambitions. Lee De Forest, inventor of the vacuum tube, envisioned radio as a means of educating millions of people at home; he underestimated the commercial success of radio and, subsequently, television.

NOTE: A positive function is a *eufunction* (*eu* is the Greek prefix "good"), which contrasts with *dysfunction* (*dys* means "ill" or "bad").

The spirit of the structural-functional paradigm is conveyed by the painting I and the Village, *completed in 1911 by Russian-American artist Marc Chagall (1881–1985). Here, recalling the tightly integrated Russian villages of his youth, Chagall conveys the essential unity of human beings who share a social setting; he also suggests that human society is bound up with the natural world.*

Marc Chagall, *I and the Village,* 1911. Oil on canvas, 63 5/8 x 59 5/8 inches. The Museum of Modern Art, New York, Mrs. Simon Guggenheim Fund.

As sociology developed in the United States, many of the ideas of Herbert Spencer and Emile Durkheim were carried forward by Talcott Parsons (1902–1979). The major U.S. proponent of the structural-functional paradigm, Parsons treated society as a system, identifying the basic tasks all societies must perform to survive and the ways they accomplish these tasks.

Contemporary U.S. sociologist Robert K. Merton has expanded our understanding of the concept of social function in novel ways. Merton (1968) explains, first, that the consequences of any social pattern are likely to differ for various members of a society. For example, conventional families may provide crucial support for the development of children, but they also confer privileges on men while limiting the opportunities of women.

Second, Merton notes, people rarely perceive all the functions of a particular social structure. He described as **manifest functions** *the recognized and intended consequences of any social pattern.* By contrast, **latent functions** are *consequences that are largely unrecognized and unintended.* To illustrate, the obvious functions of our nation's system of higher education include providing young people with the information and skills they need to perform jobs effectively. Perhaps just as important, although rarely acknowledged, is college's function as a "marriage broker," bringing together people of similar social backgrounds in a social scene that operates as an ongoing setting for courtship. Another latent function of higher education is keeping millions of young people out of the labor market where, presumably, many of them would not find jobs.

Merton makes a third point: Not *all* the effects of any social structure turn out to be useful. Thus we designate as **social dysfunctions** *any social pattern's undesirable consequences for the operation of society.* And, to make matters still more complex, people may well disagree about what is useful or harmful. In recent years, political conservatives have roundly criticized U.S. college campuses for promoting left-wing thinking that threatens traditional values. Political liberals might dismiss such charges as trivial or simply wrong; yet, from their point of view, higher education is dysfunctional for conferring further privileges on the wealthy (who disproportionately attend college) while college remains out of the financial reach of most lower-income families.

Critical evaluation. The most salient characteristic of the structural-functional paradigm is its vision of society as comprehensible, orderly, and stable. Sociologists typically couple this approach with scientific methods of research aimed at learning "what makes society tick."

At mid-century, the structural-functional paradigm dominated sociology. In recent decades, however, its influence has waned. How can we assume that society has a "natural" order, critics ask, when social patterns vary from place to place and change over time? Further, by emphasizing social integration, structural-functionalism tends to gloss over inequality based on social class, race, ethnicity, and gender—divisions that may generate considerable tension and conflict. This focus on stability at the expense of conflict and change gives the structural-functional paradigm a conservative character. As a critical response to this

Paul Marcus's painting The Greatest Show on Earth *expresses the essential wisdom of social-conflict theory: Some categories of people systematically dominate others. What forms of manipulation and exploitation do you see in the painting? Do you recognize any of the men standing to the rear?*

Marcus, Paul (1953–). *The Greatest Show on Earth.* Oil on etched wood. H. 76 in. W. 96 in. (183.9 x 243.8cm) The Metropolitan Museum of Art, George A. Hearn Fund, 1988. (1988.53a–c)

approach, sociologists have developed another theoretical orientation: the social-conflict paradigm.

The Social-Conflict Paradigm

The **social-conflict paradigm** is *a framework for building theory that envisions society as an arena of inequality that generates conflict and change.* This approach complements the structural-functional paradigm by highlighting not solidarity but division based on inequality. Guided by this paradigm, sociologists investigate how factors such as social class, race, ethnicity, sex, and age are linked to unequal distribution of money, power, education, and social prestige. A conflict analysis points out that, rather than promoting the operation of society as a whole, social structure typically benefits some people while depriving others. The box on page 20 introduces a pioneering U.S. sociologist, whose work was framed by a concern for racial conflict.

Working within the social-conflict paradigm, sociologists spotlight ongoing conflict between dominant and disadvantaged categories of people—the rich in relation to the poor, white people as opposed to people of color, men versus women. Typically, those on top strive to protect their privileges; the disadvantaged counter by attempting to gain more resources for themselves.

To illustrate, a conflict analysis of our educational system might highlight how schooling perpetuates inequality by helping to reproduce the class structure in every new generation. The process begins as secondary schools assign some students to college-preparatory programs while they provide vocational training for others. From a functional point of view, such "tracking" may benefit all of society because, ideally, students receive the training appropriate to their academic abilities. But conflict analysis counters that "tracking" often has less to do with talent than with a student's social background, as well-to-do students are placed in higher tracks and poor students end up in the lower tracks.

In this way, privileged families gain favored treatment for their children from schools. And, with the best schooling behind them, these young people leave college to pursue occupations that confer both prestige and high income. By contrast, the children of poor families are less prepared for college. So, like their parents before them, these young people typically move right from high school into low-paying jobs. In both cases, the social standing of one generation is passed on to another, with schools justifying the practice not in terms of privilege but individual merit (Bowles & Gintis, 1976; Oakes, 1982, 1985).

Social conflict in the United States extends well beyond schools. Later chapters of this book highlight efforts by working people, women, and various racial and ethnic minorities to improve their lives. In each of these cases, the social-conflict paradigm helps us to see

PROFILE

W. E. B. Du Bois: Race and Conflict

One of sociology's pioneers, who has not received the attention he deserves, is William Edward Burghardt Du Bois (1868–1963). Born to a poor Massachusetts family, Du Bois showed extraordinary aptitude as a student. After graduating from high school, he went to college, one of only a handful of the young people in his small town (and the only person of African descent) to do so. After graduating from Fisk University in Nashville, Tennessee, Du Bois realized a childhood ambition and enrolled at Harvard, repeating his junior and senior years and then beginning graduate study. He earned the first doctorate awarded by Harvard to a person of color.

Du Bois believed sociologists should direct their efforts to contemporary problems, and for him the vexing issue of race was the paramount social concern. Although he was accepted in the intellectual circles of his day, Du Bois believed that U.S. society consigned African Americans as a whole to an existence separate and apart. Unlike white people, who can make their way in the world simply as "Americans," Du Bois pointed out, African Americans have a "double consciousness," reflecting their status as Americans who are never able to escape identification based on color.

Politically speaking, his opposition to racial separation led Du Bois to serve as a founding member of the National Association for the Advancement of Colored People (NAACP). Du Bois maintained that his research, too, should attempt to address pressing racial problems. Later in his life, Du Bois reflected (1940:51):

> I was determined to put science into sociology through a study of the condition of my own group. I was going to study the facts, any and all facts, concerning the American Negro and his plight.

After taking a position at the University of Pennsylvania in Philadelphia, Du Bois set out to conduct the research that produced a sociological classic, *The Philadelphia Negro: A Social Study* (1899). In this systematic investigation of Philadelphia's African-American community at the turn of the century, Du Bois chronicled both the strengths and weaknesses of people wrestling with overwhelming social problems. Running against the intellectual current of the times (especially Spencer's social Darwinism), Du Bois rejected the widespread notion of black inferiority, attributing the problems of African Americans to white prejudice. But his criticism extended also to successful people of color, whom he scolded for being so eager to win white acceptance that they abandoned all ties with those still in need. "The first impulse of the best, the wisest and the richest," he lamented, "is to segregate themselves from the mass" (1899:317).

At the time *The Philadelphia Negro* was published, Du Bois was optimistic about overcoming racial divisions. By the end of his life, however, he had grown bitter, believing that little had changed. At the age of ninety-three, Du Bois left the United States for Ghana, where he died two years later.

Sources: Based, in part, on Baltzell (1967) and Du Bois (1967; orig. 1899).

---

how inequality and the conflict it generates are rooted in the organization of society itself.

Finally, many sociologists who embrace the social-conflict paradigm attempt not just to understand society but to reduce social inequality. This was the goal of W. E. B. Du Bois, and also of Karl Marx, the social thinker whose ideas underlie the social-conflict paradigm. Marx had little patience with those who sought merely to understand how society works. In a well-known declaration (inscribed on his monument in London's Highgate Cemetery), Marx asserted: "The philosophers have only interpreted

This painting, Les Réfugiés *by Fateh Al-Moudarres, captures a key insight of the symbolic-interaction paradigm. Society is never at rest; rather, social life is an ongoing process of interaction by which people collectively define and redefine reality.*

Fateh Al-Moudarres (Syrian), *Les Réfugiés.* Institue du Monde Arabe, Paris. Photo (C) Philippe Maillard.

the world, in various ways; the point, however, is to change it."

Critical evaluation. The social-conflict paradigm has developed rapidly in recent decades. Yet, like other approaches, it has come in for its share of criticism. Because this paradigm highlights inequality and division, it glosses over how shared values or interdependence generate unity among members of a society. In addition, say critics, to the extent that the social-conflict approach explicitly pursues political goals, it relinquishes any claim to scientific objectivity. As Chapter 2 ("Sociological Investigation") explains in detail, conflict theorists are uneasy with the notion that science can be "objective." They contend, on the contrary, that the social-conflict paradigm as well as *all* theoretical approaches have political consequences, albeit different ones.

One additional criticism, which applies equally to both the structural-functional and social-conflict paradigms: They envision society in very broad terms, describing our lives as a composite of "family," "social class," and so on. A third theoretical paradigm depicts society less in terms of abstract generalizations and more in terms of people's everyday, situational experiences.

The Symbolic-Interaction Paradigm

Both the structural-functional and social-conflict paradigms share a **macro-level orientation**, meaning *a focus on broad social structures that characterize society as a whole.* Macro-level sociology takes in the big picture, rather like observing a city from high above in a helicopter, noting how highways carry traffic from place to place and the striking contrasts between rich and poor neighborhoods. The symbolic-interaction paradigm takes another tack by providing a **micro-level orientation,** meaning *a focus on social interaction in specific situations.* Exploring urban life in this way occurs at street level, observing how friends interact in public parks or how pedestrians respond to homeless people. The **symbolic-interaction paradigm,** then, is *a theoretical framework that envisions society as the product of the everyday interactions of individuals.*

How does "society" result from the ongoing experiences of tens of millions of people? One answer, detailed in Chapter 6 ("Social Interaction in Everyday Life"), is that society arises as a shared reality that its members construct as they interact with one another. Through the human process of finding meaning in our surroundings, we define our identities, rights, and obligations toward others.

Of course, this process of definition varies a great deal from person to person. On a city street, for example, one person may define a homeless man as "just a bum looking for a handout" and ignore him. Another, however, might define him as a "fellow human being in need" and offer assistance. In the same way, one pedestrian may feel a sense of security passing by a police officer walking the beat, while another may be

Q: "Serious differences among social scientists occur not between those who would observe without thinking and those who would think without observing; the differences have rather to do with what kinds of thinking, what kinds of observing, and what kinds of links, if any, there are between the two." C. Wright Mills

NOTE: Herbert Blumer first used the term "symbolic interactionism" in 1937.

NOTE: One of the earliest "interactionist" thinkers was Renaissance humanist Pico della Mirandola. In "On the Dignity of Man," Pico spells out God's charge to humanity: "We have given to thee, Adam, no fixed seat, no form of thy very own . . . possess as thine own the seat, the form, the gifts that thou thyself shalt desire. A limited nature in other creatures [contrasts with] thy free judgments . . . thou wilt fix limits of nature for thyself." (c. 1480)

TABLE 1–1 The Three Major Theoretical Paradigms: A Summary

Theoretical Paradigm	Orientation	Image of Society	Core Questions
Structural-functional	Macro-level	A system of interrelated parts that is relatively stable based on widespread consensus as to what is morally desirable; each part has functional consequences for the operation of society as a whole	How is society integrated? What are the major parts of society? How are these parts interrelated? What are the consequences of each one for the operation of society?
Social-conflict	Macro-level	A system characterized by social inequality; each part of society benefits some categories of people more than others; conflict-based social inequality promotes social change	How is society divided? What are the major patterns of social inequality? How do some categories of people attempt to protect their privileges? How do other categories of people challenge the status quo?
Symbolic-interaction	Micro-level	An ongoing process of social interaction in specific settings based on symbolic communications; individual perceptions of reality are variable and changing	How is society experienced? How do human beings interact to create, sustain, and change social patterns? How do individuals attempt to shape the reality perceived by others? How does individual behavior change from one situation to another?

seized by nervous anxiety. Sociologists guided by the symbolic-interaction approach, therefore, view society as a mosaic of subjective meanings and variable responses.

The symbolic-interaction paradigm rests, in part, on the thinking of Max Weber (1864–1920), a German sociologist who emphasized the need to understand a setting from the point of view of the people in it. Weber's approach is presented at length in Chapter 4 ("Society").

On this foundation, others have devised their own micro-level approaches to understanding social life. Chapter 5 ("Socialization") examines the ideas of U.S. sociologist George Herbert Mead (1863–1931), who looked at how we build our personalities over time based on social experience. Chapter 6 ("Social Interaction in Everyday Life") presents the work of Erving Goffman (1922–1982), whose *dramaturgical analysis* emphasizes how we resemble actors on a stage as we play out our various roles before others. Other contemporary sociologists, including George Homans and Peter Blau, have developed *social-exchange analysis*. In their view, social interaction amounts to a negotiation in which individuals are guided by what they stand to gain and lose from others. In the ritual of courtship, for example, people typically seek mates who offer at least as much—in terms of physical attractiveness,

intelligence, and social background—as they provide in return.

Critical evaluation.   The social-interaction paradigm helps to correct a bias inherent in all macro-level approaches to understanding society. Without denying the usefulness of abstract social structures such as "the family" and "social class," we must bear in mind that society basically amounts to *people interacting*. Put another way, this micro-level approach helps convey more of how individuals actually experience society.

However, by focusing on day-to-day interactions, the symbolic-interaction paradigm can obscure larger social structures. Highlighting what is unique in each social scene risks overlooking the widespread effects of our culture, as well as factors such as class, gender, and race.

Table 1–1 summarizes the important characteristics of the structural-functional paradigm, the social-conflict paradigm, and the symbolic-interaction paradigm. As we have explained, each paradigm is especially helpful in answering particular kinds of questions. By and large, however, the fullest understanding of society comes from linking the sociological perspective to all three, as we shall now illustrate with an analysis of sports in the United States.

Q: "Situations that are defined as real are real in their consequences." W. I. Thomas

NOTE: Theoretical paradigms sometimes overlap. See, for example, Lewis Coser's (1956) analysis of the functions of social conflict.

NOTE: The assertion that sports function to "build character" was widely expressed at the founding of the Young Men's Christian Association (YMCA) in 1844.

THEN AND NOW: African Americans in the NBA: *1954, 5%; 1993, 77%;* Major League Baseball: *1954, 7%; 1993, 17%;* NFL: *1954, 12%; 1993, 68%.*

DIVERSITY: The National Collegiate Athletic Association (NCAA) reports that African Americans—5% of all college students—comprise 64% of collegiate basketball players and 46% of collegiate football players.

Sports: Three Theoretical Paradigms in Action

To people in the United States, sports seem indispensable. Almost everyone has engaged in some type of sport, and athletics in the United States has evolved into a multibillion-dollar industry. What sociological insights about this familiar element of life can we derive from the three theoretical paradigms?

The Functions of Sports

A structural-functional approach directs attention to the ways sports help society to operate. The manifest functions include providing recreation, physical conditioning, and a relatively harmless way to "let off steam." Sports have important latent functions as well, from fostering social relationships, to generating tens of thousands of jobs. Perhaps most important, sports encourage competition and the pursuit of success, both of which are central to our way of life.

Sports also have dysfunctional consequences, of course. For example, colleges and universities intent on fielding winning teams sometimes recruit students for their athletic ability rather than their academic aptitude. Doing so can pull down the academic standards of a school and may shortchange the athletes themselves, as coaches denigrate academic endeavors so the student-athletes concentrate all their energies on their sport.

Sports and Conflict

A social-conflict analysis begins by pointing out that sports are closely linked to social inequality. Some sports—including tennis, swimming, golf, and skiing—are expensive, so participation is largely limited to the well-to-do. By contrast, football, baseball, and basketball are accessible to people of all income levels. In short, the games people play are not simply a matter of choice but also reflect social standing.

In the United States, sports are oriented primarily toward males. The first modern Olympic Games held in 1896, for example, excluded women from competition; until recently, moreover, even Little League teams in most parts of the country barred girls from the playing field. Such male-only practices have been defended by unfounded notions that girls and women lack the ability to engage in sports or risk losing their femininity if they do. Thus our society encourages men to be athletes while expecting women to be attentive observers and cheerleaders. More women now play professional sports than ever before, yet they continue to take a

African-American artist Jacob Lawrence recognized that sports are more than mere diversion and entertainment. On the contrary, through sports we acknowledge the importance of individualism and competition to our way of life.

Lawrence, Jacob. American, b. 1917 *Munich Olympic Games,* Poster, 1972. Courtesy of the artist and Francine Seders Gallery, Seattle. Photo: Spike Mafford.

back seat to men, particularly in sports that yield the greatest earnings and social prestige.

Although our society long excluded people of color from "big league" sports, the opportunity to earn high incomes in professional sports has expanded in recent decades. Major League Baseball first admitted African-American players when Jackie Robinson broke the "color line" in 1947. By 1993, African Americans—12 percent of the U.S. population)—accounted for 17 percent of Major League

DIVERSITY: In 1993, 191 of 195 owners in the three major sports were white people.
DIVERSITY: The summer Olympics features sports (track and field) that are accessible to people of all social backgrounds; thus, a diverse group of athletes. The winter Olympics focus on expensive sports (skiing, skating, luge) that are socially exclusive; thus, the greater share of white and well-to-do athletes.

NOTE: Each orientation's key thinkers: *functional*, Comte, Durkheim, and Spencer; *conflict*, Marx and Weber; *interactional*, Weber, G. H. Mead, Blumer, Garfinkel. Note that all sociological approaches challenge the utilitarian approach evident in the 18th-century thought of Thomas Hobbes and others (and which is now staging something of a comeback in the form of "rational-choice theory").

Controversy & Debate

Is Sociology Nothing More Than Stereotypes?

"Protestants are the ones who kill themselves!"

"People in the United States? They're rich, they love to marry, and they love to divorce!"

"Everybody knows that you have to be black to play professional basketball!"

Sociologists certainly make generalizations about categories of people. Recognizing this fact, some students who begin the study of sociology may wonder whether statements like those above are *sociological insights* or simply *stereotypes*.

So what, exactly, is the difference between the two? All three statements at the top of this page illustrate the **stereotype**, *an exaggerated description that one applies to all people in some category*. First, rather than describing averages, each statement paints every individual in a category with the same brush; second, each ignores facts and distorts reality (even though each does contain some element of truth); third, each sounds more like a "put down" than a fair-minded assertion.

Good sociology, by contrast, involves making generalizations, but with three important conditions. *First,*

we do not indiscriminately apply these generalizations to individuals; second, we ensure that a generalization squares with available facts; third, we offer it fair-mindedly, with an interest in getting at the truth.

Recall, first, that the sociological perspective reveals "the general in the particular"; therefore, a sociological insight is a generalization about some category of people. An example is the assertion, made earlier in this chapter, that the suicide rate among Protestants is higher than that of Catholics or Jews. However, the statement above—"Protestants are the ones who kill themselves"—is unreasonable since the vast majority of Protestants do no such thing. Moreover, it would be just as wrong-headed to assume a particular friend, because he is a Protestant male, is on the verge of self-destruction. (Imagine refusing to lend money to a roommate who happens to be a Baptist, explaining, "Well, given your risk of suicide, I might never get paid back!")

Second, sociologists base their generalizations on available facts. A more factual version of the second statement above would note that, on average and by world standards, the U.S. population has a very high standard

of living, that our marriage rate is one of the highest in the world, and so is our divorce rate (although few people take great pleasure in divorcing).

Third, sociologists strive to be fair-minded; that is, they are motivated by a passion for learning and for truth. The third statement above about African Americans and basketball fails as good sociology not only because it is simply not true but because it seems motivated by bias rather than truth-seeking.

Good sociology stands apart from stereotyping, then. But a sociology course is an excellent setting for talking over common stereotypes because the classroom encourages discussion and the pursuit of truth, and offers the factual information needed to assess the accuracy of popular wisdom.

Continue the debate . . .

1. Are there stereotypes of sociologists? What are they? Are they valid?

2. Do you think taking a sociology course erodes people's stereotypes? Does it generate new ones?

3. Can you cite a stereotype of your own that sociology challenges?

Baseball players, 68 percent of National Football League (NFL) players, and 77 percent of National Basketball Association (NBA) players (Center for the Study of Sport in Society, 1993).

One reason for the increasing proportion of people of African descent in professional sports is that precisely measured athletic performances cannot be diminished by white prejudice. In addition, some people of color make a particular effort to excel in athletics where they perceive greater opportunity than in other careers (Steele, 1990). In recent years, in fact, African-American

athletes have earned higher salaries, on average, than white players. But racial discrimination still taints professional sports in the United States because almost all managers, head coaches, and owners of sports teams are white.

Taking a wider view, who gains the greatest benefits from professional sports? Although millions of fans follow their teams, the vast sums teams take in are controlled by the small number of people (predominantly white men) for whom teams are income-generating property. In sum, sports in the United States are bound up with inequalities based on gender, race, and economic power.

Sports as Interaction

At a microlevel, a sporting event is a complex drama of face-to-face interaction. In part, play is guided by the players' assigned positions and, of course, everyone takes account of the rules of the game. But players are also spontaneous and unpredictable. Informed by the symbolic-interaction paradigm, then, we see sports less as a system than as an ongoing process.

From this point of view, too, we expect each player to understand the game a little differently. Some thrive in a setting of stiff competition while, for others, love[5] of the game may hold greater rewards than the thrill of victory.

Beyond different attitudes toward competition, team members will also shape their particular realities

according to the various prejudices, jealousies, and ambitions they bring to the field. Then, too, the behavior of any single player also changes over time. A rookie in professional baseball, for example, may feel quite self-conscious during his first few games in the big leagues. In time, however, a comfortable sense of fitting in with the team usually emerges. Coming to feel at home on the field was slow and painful for Jackie Robinson, who was initially all too aware that many white players, and millions of white fans, resented his presence in Major League Baseball (Tygiel, 1983). In time, however, his outstanding ability and his confident and cooperative manner won him the respect of the entire nation.

The three theoretical paradigms certainly offer different insights, but none is more correct than the others. Applied to any issue, each paradigm generates its own interpretations so that, to fully appreciate the power of the sociological perspective, you should become familiar with all three. Together, they stimulate fascinating debates and controversies, many of which are presented in the chapters that follow. The final box reviews many of the ideas presented in this chapter, asking how sociological generalizations differ from common stereotypes.

---

[5]The ancient Romans recognized this fact, evident in our word "amateur," literally, "lover," which designates someone who engages in some activity for the sheer love of it.

SUMMARY

1. The sociological perspective reveals "the general in the particular" or the power of society to shape our lives.

2. Because people in the United States tend to think in terms of individual choice, recognizing the impact of society on our lives initially seems like "seeing the strange in the familiar."

3. Emile Durkheim's research demonstrating that suicide rates are significantly higher among some categories of people than they are among others shows that society affects even the most personal of our actions.

4. Global awareness enhances the sociological perspective because, first, societies of the world are becoming more and more interconnected; second, many social problems are most serious beyond the borders of the United States; and, third, recognizing how others live helps us better understand ourselves.

5. Socially marginal people are more likely than others to perceive the effects of society. For everyone, periods of social crisis foster sociological thinking.

6. There are four general benefits to using the sociological perspective. First, it challenges our familiar understandings of the world, helping us separate fact from fiction; second, it helps us appreciate the opportunities and constraints that frame our lives; third, it encourages more active participation in society; fourth, it increases our awareness of social diversity in the United States and in the world as a whole.

7. Auguste Comte gave sociology its name in 1838. Whereas previous social thought had focused on what society ought to be, Comte's new discipline of sociology used scientific methods to understand society as it is.

8. Sociology emerged as a reaction to the rapid transformation of Europe during the eighteenth and

nineteenth centuries. Three dimensions of change—the rise of an industrial economy, the explosive growth of cities, and the emergence of new political ideas—each focused people's attention on the operation of society.

9. Building theory involves linking insights to gain understanding. Various theoretical paradigms guide sociologists as they construct theories.

10. The structural-functional paradigm is a framework for exploring how social structures promote the stability and integration of society. This approach minimizes the importance of social inequality, conflict, and change.

11. The social-conflict paradigm highlights social inequality, conflict, and change. At the same time, this approach downplays the extent of society's integration and stability.

12. In contrast to these broad, macro-level approaches, the symbolic-interaction paradigm is a micro-level theoretical framework that focuses on face-to-face interaction in specific settings.

13. Because each paradigm spotlights different dimensions of any social issue, the richest sociological understanding is derived from applying all three.

14. Sociological thinking involves generalizations. But, unlike a stereotype, a sociological statement (1) is not applied indiscriminately to individuals, (2) is supported by facts, and (3) is put forward in the fair-minded pursuit of truth.

KEY CONCEPTS

global perspective the study of the larger world and our society's place in it

high-income countries industrial nations in which most people enjoy material abundance

latent functions consequences of any social pattern that are unrecognized and unintended

low-income countries nations with little industrialization in which severe poverty is the rule

macro-level orientation a focus on broad social structures that characterize society as a whole

manifest functions the recognized and intended consequences of any social pattern

micro-level orientation a focus on patterns of social interaction in specific situations

middle-income countries nations characterized by limited industrialization and moderate personal income

positivism a means to understand the world based on science

social-conflict paradigm a framework for building theory that envisions society as an arena of inequality that generates conflict and change

social dysfunction the undesirable consequences of any social pattern for the operation of society

social function the consequences of any social pattern for the operation of society

social structure relatively stable patterns of social behavior

sociology the systematic study of human society

stereotype an exaggerated description applied to every person in some category

structural-functional paradigm a framework for building theory that envisions society as a complex system whose parts work together to promote solidarity and stability

symbolic-interaction paradigm a framework for building theory that envisions society as the product of the everyday interactions of individuals

theoretical paradigm a basic image of society that guides sociological thinking and research

theory a statement of how and why specific facts are related

CRITICAL-THINKING QUESTIONS

1. In what ways does using the sociological perspective make us seem less in control of our lives? In what ways does it give us greater power over our surroundings?

2. Consider this statement: Sociology would not have arisen if human behavior were biologically programmed (like that of, say, ants); nor could sociology exist if our behavior were utterly chaotic. Sociology thrives because human social life falls in a middle ground—as thinking people, we create social patterns but they are variable and changeable.

3. Give a sociological explanation of why sociology developed where and when it did.

4. Guided by the discipline's three major theoretical paradigms, what kinds of questions might a sociologist ask about (a) television, (b) war, (c) humor, and (d) colleges and universities?

SUGGESTED READINGS

Classic Sources

C. Wright Mills. *The Sociological Imagination.* New York: Oxford University Press, 1959.

This classic elaborates on the benefits of learning to think sociologically and links this perspective to the possibilities for social activism.

Peter Berger. *An Invitation to Sociology.* Garden City, N.Y.: Anchor Books, 1963.

Berger's readable classic account of the sociological perspective highlights its value for enhancing human freedom.

Contemporary Sources

John J. Macionis and Nijole V. Benokraitis, eds. *Seeing Ourselves: Classic, Contemporary, and Cross-Cultural Readings in Sociology.* 3d ed. Englewood Cliffs, N.J.: Prentice Hall, 1995.

The new edition of the companion reader to this text is enlarged, offering seventy-five edited readings that follow the chapter flow of this book. For each topic, you'll find classic essays by sociology's "greats," articles on contemporary issues and research, and cross-cultural perspectives.

Janet Mancini Billson and Bettina J. Huber. *Embarking Upon a Career with an Undergraduate Degree in Sociology.* 2d ed. Washington, D.C.: American Sociological Association, 1993.

This publication describing career possibilities in sociology is available for $8.50 from the American Sociological Association, 1722 N Street NW, Washington, D.C. 20036; (202) 833-3410.

Global Sources

Mike Featherstone. *Global Culture: Nationalism, Globalization and Modernity.* Newbury Park, Calif.: Sage, 1991.

Roland Robertson. *Globalization: Social Theory and Global Culture.* Newbury Park, Calif.: Sage, 1992.

These two books provide a sophisticated overview of the process of globalization. The first, a collection of two dozen essays, explains the importance of global thinking to members of our society. The second offers one analyst's reflections on the meanings of globalization for our society as well as for sociology.

JONATHAN GREEN,
LITERARY CIRCLE, 1992

Sociological
Investigation

While on a visit to Atlanta during the holiday season at the close of 1984, sociologist Lois Benjamin (1991) paid a call on the mother of an old friend from college. Benjamin was anxious to learn what had become of her friend, Sheba, who had shared her own dream of earning a graduate degree, finding a teaching position, and writing books. Benjamin was proud that she had fulfilled her dream. But as she soon found out, Sheba had fallen disastrously short of her goal.

There had been early signs of trouble, Benjamin recalled, after they had finished college. Enrolling in a graduate program in Canada, Sheba became increasingly critical of the world around her and cut off from others. In letters to Benjamin, Sheba attributed her bitterness to racism; as an African-American woman, she claimed, she was the target of racial hostility. Before long, her resentment overwhelmed her and she flunked out of graduate school, blaming her white professors for her failure. At this point, she left North America, finally earning a Ph.D. in England and then settling in Nigeria. Since then, Benjamin had not heard a word from her long-time friend.

Entering the house, Benjamin's initial delight at finding that Sheba had returned to Atlanta dissolved into shock when she confronted her comrade. Sheba had suffered a mental breakdown and was barely responsive to anyone.

Many months later, Sheba's emotional collapse still troubled Benjamin. She knew that many factors combine to cause such a personal tragedy. But, having experienced the sting of racism in her own career, Benjamin was convinced that this form of hatred played a major role in Sheba's story. Partly as a tribute to her old friend, Benjamin set out to explore the effects of race in the lives of bright and well-educated people of color in the United States.

Doing so, Benjamin was aware, challenged conventional wisdom that race poses less of a barrier to talented African Americans today than in previous generations (Wilson, 1978). Benjamin knew, too, that some of her colleagues in sociology think of racism as a problem for poor black people far more than for those with prestigious jobs and high incomes. But her own experiences, and those of her friend Sheba, contradicted such thinking.

To test her contention, Benjamin spent the next two years asking one hundred successful African Americans around the country how race affected their lives and shaped their work. In the words of these

GLOBAL: People in other times and places recognize different "truths." In the case of childhood sexuality, the Melanesians of New Guinea typically shrug off as harmless sexual intercourse among children too young to reproduce.

Q: "Philosophers know very little about what is very important; scientists know a great deal about what is far less worth knowing." E. Digby Baltzell

SUPPLEMENTS: The *Data File* contains an annotated outline of Chapter 2, supplemental lecture material, and suggestions for class discussion.

NOTE: Science and religion do not conflict but complement one another. Scientific truths involve proximate causes of events; religious truths deal with ultimate causes. See Chapter 18 ("Religion"), especially the Controversy and Debate box.

"Talented One Hundred"[1] men and women, she found evidence that, even among privileged African Americans, racism remains a heavy burden.

Later in this chapter, we will take a closer look at Lois Benjamin's research. For the moment, notice how the sociological perspective helped this woman to spot broad social patterns operating in the lives of individuals. Just as important, Benjamin's work demonstrates the *doing* of sociology, the process of *sociological investigation*.

Many people think that scientists work only in laboratories, carefully taking measurements using complex equipment. But, as this chapter explains, sociologists also conduct scientific research in the familiar terrain of neighborhood streets, in homes, at workplaces, even in prisons, as well as in unfamiliar locales throughout the world—in short, wherever people can be found.

This chapter highlights the methods that sociologists use to conduct research. Along the way, we shall see that sociological research involves not just procedures for gathering information but controversies about whether that research should strive to be objective or to offer a bold prescription for change. Certainly, for example, Lois Benjamin did not undertake her exploration of racism simply to document its existence; she sought to bring racism out into the open as a way to eradicate it. We shall tackle questions of values after addressing the basics of sociological investigation.

THE BASICS OF SOCIOLOGICAL INVESTIGATION

Sociological investigation begins with two simple requirements. The first was the focus of Chapter 1: *Look at the world using the sociological perspective.* Suddenly, from this point of view, we see all around us curious patterns of behavior that call out for further study.

Lois Benjamin's sociological imagination prompted her to wonder how race affects the lives of

talented African Americans. This brings us to the second requirement for sociological investigation: *Be curious and ask questions.* Benjamin wanted to find out how racial identity figured in the lives of people with significant personal achievements. She asked questions: What effect does being part of a racial minority have on self-identity? Do black people and white people understand racial dynamics in the same way? Are racial tensions easing or becoming more pronounced?

These two requirements—seeing the world sociologically and asking questions—are fundamental to sociological investigation. Yet they are only the beginning. They draw us into the social world, stimulating our curiosity. But then we face the challenging task of finding answers to our questions. To understand the kind of insights sociology offers, we need to realize that there are various kinds of "truth."

Science As One Form of "Truth"

When we say we "know" something, we can mean any number of things. Most members of our society, for instance, claim to believe in the existence of God. Few would assert that they have direct contact with God, but they are believers all the same. We call this kind of knowing "belief" or "faith." A second kind of truth rests on the pronouncement of some recognized expert. Parents with questions about raising their children, for example, often consult child psychologists or other experts about which practices are "right." A third type of truth is based on simple agreement among ordinary people. We come to "know" that, say, sexual intercourse among young children is wrong because virtually everyone in our society says it is.

People's "truths" differ the world over, and we often encounter "facts" at odds with our own. Imagine being a Peace Corps volunteer just arriving in a small, traditional village in Latin America. With the job of helping the local people to grow more food, you take to the fields, observing a curious practice: farmers carefully planting seeds and then placing a dead fish directly on top of each one. In response to your question, they reply that the fish is a gift to the god of the harvest. A local elder adds sternly that the harvest was poor one year when no fish were offered as gifts.

From that society's point of view, using fish as gifts to the harvest god makes sense. The people believe in it, their experts endorse it, and everyone seems to agree that the system works. But, with scientific training in agriculture, you have to shake your head and wonder. The scientific "truth" in this situation is something

---

[1]Benjamin derived her concept from the term "Talented Tenth" used by W. E. B. Du Bois (1899) to describe African-American leaders in his day.

NOTE: Facts, standing alone, do not constitute compelling truth. Myth (from the Greek *mythos*, meaning "story" or "word") is a means of conveying broad cultural truths without relying on factual details. The success of the film *E.T.* was partly due to its mythic elements: (a) a main character who was born elsewhere, (b) who came to earth, (c) underwent a great testing, and (d) finally returned to his origins. The same four elements underlie the lives of Moses, Jesus, and Superman.

NOTE: *Empiricism* (the Greek root means "experience") refers to the philosophical doctrine that only the senses support claims of truth. The closely linked concept of *positivism* defines truth as "positive" facts based on sensory experience, while dismissing as speculation metaphysical or theological claims about ultimate causes of events.

People everywhere try to make sense of their surroundings. In his painting, Whence Do We Come?, *French artist Paul Gauguin (1848–1903) offers a mythic account of human origins. A myth (from Greek meaning "story") may or may not be factual in the literal sense, but it conveys some basic truth about the meaning and purpose of life. It is science, rather than art, that is powerless to address such questions of meaning.*

entirely different: The decomposing fish fertilize the ground, producing a better crop.

Science, then, represents a fourth way of knowing. **Science** is *a logical system that bases knowledge on direct, systematic observation.* Standing apart from faith, the wisdom of "experts," and general agreement, scientific knowledge rests on **empirical evidence**, meaning *information we can verify with our senses.*

Our Peace Corps example does not mean, of course, that people in traditional villages ignore what their senses tell them, or that members of technologically advanced societies reject nonscientific ways of knowing. A medical researcher using science to seek an effective treatment for cancer, for example, may still practice her religion as a matter of faith; she may turn to experts when making financial decisions; and she may derive political opinions from family and friends. In short, we all embrace various kinds of truths at the same time.

Common Sense Versus Scientific Evidence

Scientific evidence sometimes challenges our common sense. Here are six statements that many North Americans assume are "true," even though each is at least partly contradicted by scientific research.

1. **Poor people are far more likely than rich people to break the law.** Watching a television show like "Cops," one might well conclude that police arrest only people from "bad" neighborhoods. And, as Chapter 8 ("Deviance") explains, poor people are arrested in disproportionate numbers. But research also reveals that police and prosecutors are more likely to treat apparent wrongdoing by well-to-do people more leniently. Further, some researchers argue that our society drafts laws in such a way as to reduce the risk that affluent people will be criminalized.

2. **The United States is a middle-class society in which most people are more or less equal.** Data presented in Chapter 10 ("Social Class in the United States") show that the richest 5 percent of U.S. residents control half the nation's total wealth. If people in this country are equal, then, some are much "more equal" than others.

3. **Most poor people ignore opportunities to work.** Research cited in Chapter 10 indicates that this statement is true of some but not most poor people. In fact, about half of poor individuals in the United States are children and elderly people whom no one would expect to work.

4. **Differences in the behavior of females and males reflect "human nature."** Much of what we call "human nature" is created by the society in which we are raised, as Chapter 3 ("Culture") details. Further, as Chapter 13 ("Sex and Gender") argues, some societies define

Common sense suggests that, in a world of possibilities, people fall in love with that "special someone." Sociological research reveals that the vast majority of people select partners who are very similar in social background to themselves.

"feminine" and "masculine" very differently from the way we do.

5. **People change as they grow old, losing many former interests while becoming focused on their health.** Chapter 14 ("Aging and the Elderly") reports that aging actually changes our personalities very little. Problems of health increase in old age but, by and large, elderly people retain their distinctive personalities.

6. **Most people marry because they are in love.** To members of our society, few statements are so self-evident. But as surprising as it may seem, research shows that, in most societies, marriage has little to do with love. Chapter 17 ("Family") explains why.

These examples confirm the old saying that "It's not what we don't know that gets us into trouble as much as the things we *do* know that just aren't so." We have all been brought up believing conventional truths, bombarded by expert advice, and pressured to accept the opinions of people around us. As adults, we must learn to evaluate critically what we see, read, and hear, and sociology can help us to do that. Like any way of knowing, sociology has limitations, as we shall see. But scientific sociology gives us the tools to assess many kinds of information.

THE ELEMENTS OF SCIENCE

Sociologists apply science to the study of society in much the same way that natural scientists investigate the physical world. Whether they end up confirming a widely held opinion or revealing that it is way off base, sociologists use scientific techniques to gather empirical evidence. The following sections of this chapter introduce the major elements of scientific investigation.

Concepts, Variables, and Measurement

A crucial element of science is the **concept**, *a mental construct that represents some part of the world, inevitably in a simplified form.* "Society" is itself a concept, as are the structural parts of societies, including "the family" and "the economy." Sociologists also use concepts to describe individuals, by noting, for example, their "sex," "race," or "social class."

A **variable** is *a concept whose value changes from case to case.* The familiar variable "price," for example, changes from item to item in a supermarket. Similarly, people use the concept "social class" to evaluate people as "upper class," "middle class," "working class," or "lower class."

The use of variables depends on **measurement**, *the process of determining the value of a variable in a specific case.* Some variables are easy to measure, such as adding up our income at tax time. But measuring many sociological variables can be far more difficult. For example, how would you measure a person's "social class"? You might be tempted to look at clothing, listen to patterns of speech, or note a home address. Or, trying to be more precise, you might ask about someone's income, occupation, and education.

Researchers know that almost any variable can be measured in more than one way. Having a very high income might qualify a person as "upper class." But what if the income is derived from selling automobiles, an occupation most people think of as "middle class"? And, would having only an eighth-grade education

SOCIOLOGY OF EVERYDAY LIFE

Three Useful (and Simple) Statistical Measures

We all talk about "averages": the average price of a gallon of gasoline, the average salary for new college graduates, or Barry Bonds's batting average. Sociologists, too, are interested in averages, and they use three different statistical measures to describe what is typical.

Assume that we wish to describe the salaries paid to seven members of a college's sociology department:

$35,000	$43,000	$41,700	$42,000
$35,000	$78,295	$35,000	

The simplest statistical measure is the **mode,** defined as *the value that occurs most often in a series of numbers*. In this example, the mode is $35,000, because that value occurs three times, while each of the others occurs only once. If all the values were to occur only once, there would be no mode; if two values occurred three times (or twice), there would be two modes. Although easy to identify, sociologists rarely make use of the mode because this statistic provides only a crude measure of the "average."

A more common statistical measure, the **mean,** refers to *the arithmetic average of a series of numbers,* and is calculated by adding all the values together and dividing by the number of cases. The sum of the seven incomes is $309,995; dividing by seven yields a mean income of $44,285. But notice that the mean is actually higher than the income of six of the seven sociologists. Because the mean is "pulled" up or down by an especially high or low value (in this case, the $78,295 paid to one sociologist who also serves as a dean), it has the drawback of giving a distorted picture of any distribution with extreme scores.

The **median** is *the value that occurs midway in a series of numbers arranged in order of magnitude or, simply, the middle case*. Here the median income for the seven people is $41,700, since three incomes are higher and three are lower. (With an even number of cases, the median is halfway between the two middle cases.) Since a median is unaffected by an extreme score, it usually gives a more accurate picture of what is "average" than the mean does.

---

make the person "lower class"? To resolve such a dilemma, sociologists sensibly (if somewhat arbitrarily) combine these three measures—income, occupation, and education—into a single composite assessment of social class, called socioeconomic status, which is described in Chapter 9 ("Social Stratification") and Chapter 10 ("Social Class in the United States").

Sociologists also face the challenge of describing thousands or even millions of people according to some variable of interest such as income. Reporting an interminable stream of numbers would carry little meaning and tell us nothing about the people as a whole. Thus sociologists use *statistical measures* to describe people efficiently and collectively. The box explains how.

Measurement is always a bit arbitrary since the value of any variable depends, in part, on how one defines it. **Operationalizing a variable** means *specifying exactly what one is to measure in assigning a value to a variable*. If we were measuring people's social class, for example, we would have to decide if we were going to measure income, occupational prestige, education, or something else and, if we measure more than one of these, how we will combine the scores. When

reporting their results, researchers should specify how they operationalized each variable, so that readers can evaluate the research and fully understand the conclusions.

Reliability and Validity of Measurement

Useful measurement involves two further considerations. **Reliability** is *the quality of consistent measurement*. For a measure to be reliable, in other words, repeating the process should yield the same result. But consistency is no guarantee of **validity**, which is *the quality of measuring precisely what one intends to measure*. Valid measurement, in other words, means more than getting the *same* result time and again—it means obtaining a *correct* measurement.

To illustrate the difficulty of valid measurement, say you want to investigate how religious people are. A reasonable strategy would be to ask how often they attend religious services. But, in trying to gauge *religiosity* in this way, what you are actually measuring is *attendance at services*, which may or may not amount to the same thing. Generally, religious people do attend services more frequently, but people also

NOTE: Earl Babbie envisions the concept of reliability without validity as bullet holes clustered together on a target but not necessarily in the bull's eye; reliability plus validity would be on the bull's eye; neither one would yield holes scattered all over the target.

NOTE: Note that validity implies reliability, but not vice versa.

NOTE: An independent variable in one situation may be a dependent variable in another; the designation is arbitrary and determined by the specific experiment in question.

SUPPLEMENTS: Use the *Student Social Survey*, available with this text, to demonstrate control. This instructional package also lets students discover the relative strength of various factors working together; rarely does one independent variable generate more than a 20% change in the attitude or behavior under study.

Young people who live in the crowded inner city are more likely than those who live in the spacious suburbs to have trouble with the police. But does this mean that crowding causes delinquency? Researchers know that crowding and arrest rates do vary together, but they have demonstrated that the connection is spurious: Both factors rise in relation to a third factor— declining income.

participate in religious rituals out of habit or because of a sense of duty to someone else. Moreover, some devout believers shun organized religion altogether. Thus, even when a measurement yields consistent results (making it reliable), it can still miss the real, intended target (and lack validity). In sum, sociological research is no better than the quality of its measurement.

Relationships Among Variables

Once they achieve valid measurement, investigators can pursue the real payoff, which is determining how variables are related. The scientific ideal is **cause and effect**, *a relationship in which we know that change in one variable causes change in another.* A familiar cause-and-effect relationship occurs when a girl teases her brother until he becomes angry. *The variable that causes the change* (in this case, the teasing) is called the **independent variable**. *The variable that changes* (the behavior of the brother) is known as the **dependent variable**. The value of one variable, in other words, is dependent on the value of another. Why is linking variables in terms of cause and effect important? Because doing so is the basis of *prediction,* that is, researchers using what they do know to predict what they don't know.

Because science puts a premium on prediction, people may be tempted to think that a cause-and-effect relationship is present any time variables change together. Consider, for instance, that the marriage rate in the United States falls to its lowest point in January,

exactly the same month our national death rate peaks. This hardly means that people die because they fail to marry (or that they don't marry because they die). In fact, it is the dreary weather in much of the nation during January (and perhaps also the post-holiday blahs) that causes both a low marriage rate and a high death rate. The flip-side holds as well: The warmer and sunnier summer months have the highest marriage rate as well as the lowest death rate. Thus researchers often have to untangle cause-and-effect relationships that are not readily apparent.

To take a second case, sociologists have long recognized that juvenile delinquency is more common among young people who live in crowded housing. Say we operationalize the variable "juvenile delinquency" as the number of times (if any) a person under the age of eighteen has been arrested, and assess "crowded housing" by looking at the total square feet of living space per person in a home. We would find the variables related; that is, delinquency rates are, indeed, high in densely populated neighborhoods. But should we conclude that crowding in the home (the independent variable) is what causes delinquency (the dependent variable)?

Not necessarily. **Correlation** is *a relationship by which two (or more) variables change together.* We know that density and delinquency are correlated because they change together, as shown in Part (a) of Figure 2–1. This relationship *may* mean that crowding causes misconduct, but often some third factor is at work causing change in both the variables under observation. To see how, think what kind of people live in

GLOBAL: Illustrating spurious correlation, Sweden's National Bureau of Economic Research found that couples who cohabit before marriage are more likely to divorce than those who do not cohabit. Does cohabiting contribute to divorce? Researcher Neil Bennett describes the link as spurious: Cohabiters, he claims, are less religious and less committed to marriage to begin with; this "weak ties" pattern persists among cohabiters who marry.

DISCUSS: As another example of spuriousness, state-by-state tallies of the number of Ph.D.s and the number of mules show a negative correlation. Does a dying mule create a Ph.D.? (Warren Street, Central Washington University)

Q: "We cannot work without hoping that others will advance further than we have." Max Weber

crowded housing: people with less money, power, and choice—the poor. Poor children are also more likely to end up with police records. Thus, crowded housing and juvenile delinquency are found together because *both* are caused by a third factor—poverty—as shown in Part (b) of Figure 2–1. In other words, the apparent connection between crowding and delinquency is "explained away" by a third variable—low income—that causes them both to change. So our original connection turns out to be a **spurious correlation**, *an apparent, although false, association between two (or more) variables caused by some other variable.*

Unmasking a correlation as spurious requires a bit of detective work, assisted by a technique called **control**, *holding constant all relevant variables except one in order to clearly see its effect.* In the example above, we suspect that income level may be behind a spurious connection between housing density and delinquency. To check, we control for income (that is, we hold it constant) by using as research subjects only young people of the same income level and looking again for a correlation between density and delinquency. If, by doing this, a correlation between density and delinquency remains (that is, if young people living in more crowded housing show higher rates of delinquency than young people with the same family income in less crowded housing), we gain confidence that crowding does, in fact, cause delinquency. But if the relationship disappears when we control for income, as shown in Part (c) of the figure, we confirm that we have been dealing with a spurious correlation. Research has, in fact, shown that virtually all correlation between crowding and delinquency disappears if income is controlled (Fischer, 1984). So we have now sorted out the relationship among the three variables, as illustrated in Part (d) of the figure. Housing density and juvenile delinquency have a spurious correlation; evidence shows that both variables rise or fall according to people's income.

To sum up, correlation means only that two (or more) variables change together. Cause and effect rests on three conditions: (1) a demonstrated correlation, but also (2) that the independent (or causal) variable precedes the dependent variable in time, and (3) that no evidence suggests a third variable is responsible for a spurious correlation between the two.

Natural scientists identify cause-and-effect relationships more easily than social scientists because the laboratories used for study of the physical world allow control of many variables at one time. The sociologist, carrying out research in a workplace or on the streets,

FIGURE 2–1 Correlation and Cause: An Example

(a)

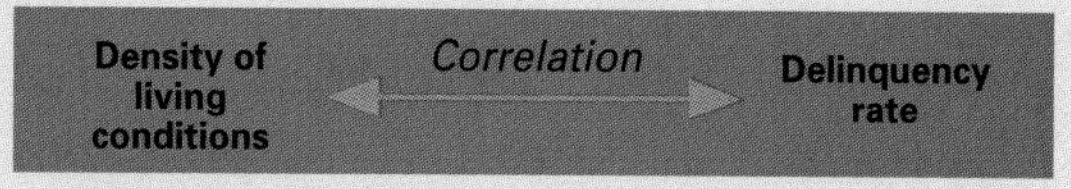

If two variables vary together, they are said to be correlated. In this example, density of living conditions and juvenile delinquency increase and decrease together.

(b)

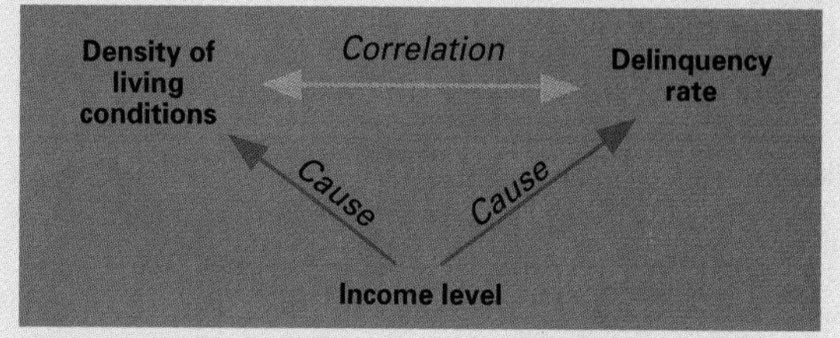

Here we consider the effect of a third variable: income level. Low income level may cause *both* high-density living conditions *and* a high delinquency rate. In other words, as income level decreases, both density of living conditions and the delinquency rate increase.

(c)

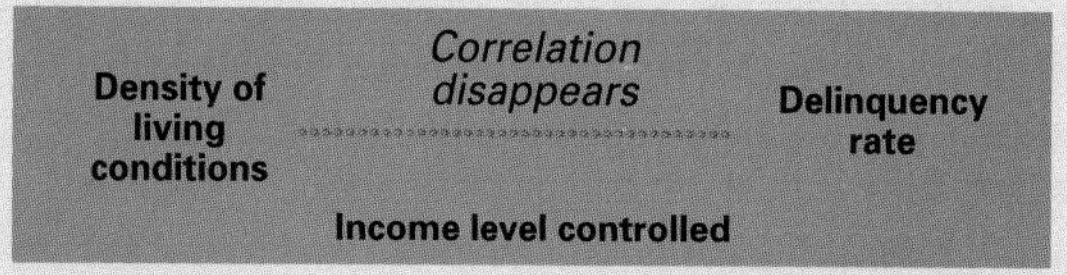

If we control income level — that is, examine only cases with the same income level — do those with higher-density living conditions still have a higher delinquency rate? The answer is *no.* There is no longer a correlation between these two variables.

(d)

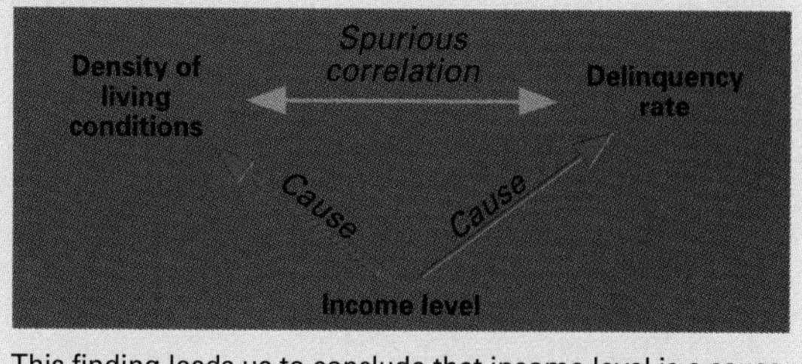

This finding leads us to conclude that income level is a cause of both density of living conditions and the delinquency rate. The original two variables (density of living conditions and delinquency rate) are thus correlated, but neither one causes the other. Their correlation is therefore *spurious.*

Chapter 2 Sociological Investigation **35**

NOTE: David Hume (1711–1776) argued that science can empirically determine (1) correlation and (2) temporal ordering of variables, but not (3) an actual causal connection, which defies observation. Perhaps with Hume's thought in mind, the National Cancer Institute acknowledged higher cancer rates among people living near nuclear power plants but argued that research "can neither confirm nor deny a link . . . because statistical studies, by their very nature, cannot prove cause and effect."

RESOURCE: Max Weber's statement on value-free research is among the classics in the Macionis and Benokraitis reader *Seeing Ourselves: Classic, Contemporary, and Cross-Cultural Readings in Sociology*, 3d ed.

NOTE: Only a small proportion of social science research is actually subjected to replication (far less than in the natural sciences).

faces a considerably more difficult task. Often sociologists must be satisfied with demonstrating only correlation. In every case, moreover, human behavior is highly complex, involving dozens of causal variables at any one time.

The Ideal of Objectivity

Assume that ten writers who work for a magazine in McLean, Virginia, are collaborating on a story about that city's best restaurants. With their editor picking up the tab, they head out on the town for a week of fine dining. Later, they get together to compare notes. Do you think one restaurant would be everyone's clear favorite? That hardly seems likely.

In scientific terms, each of the ten reporters probably operationalizes the concept "best restaurant" differently. For one, it might be a place that serves delicious steaks at reasonable prices; for another, the choice might turn on a rooftop view of Washington, D.C.; for yet another, stunning decor and attentive service might be the deciding factor. Like so many other things in life, the best restaurant turns out to be mostly a matter of individual taste.

Personal values are fine when it comes to restaurants, but they pose a challenge to scientific research. On the one hand, every scientist has personal opinions about the world. On the other, science endorses the goal of **objectivity**, *a state of personal neutrality in conducting research*. Objectivity in research depends on carefully adhering to scientific procedures in order not to bias the results. Scientific objectivity is an ideal rather than a reality, of course, since complete impartiality is virtually impossible for any researcher to achieve. Even the subject a researcher selects to study and the framing of the questions are likely to grow out of personal interest, as the research on race by Lois Benjamin attests. But scientists cultivate detachment and follow specific methods to lessen the chance that conscious or unconscious biases will distort their work. As an additional safeguard, researchers should try to identify and report their personal leanings to help readers evaluate their conclusions in the proper context.

The influential German sociologist Max Weber expected personal beliefs to play a part in a sociologist's selection of research topic. Why, after all, would one person study world hunger, another investigate the effects of racism, and still another examine one-parent families? But Weber (1958; orig. 1918) admonished researchers that even though they select topics that are *value-relevant*, they should conduct research that is *value-free* in their pursuit of conclusions. Only by being dispassionate in their work (as we expect any professional to be), can researchers study the world *as it is* rather than telling others how they think *it should be*. In Weber's view, this detachment was a crucial element of science that sets it apart from politics. Politicians, in other words, are committed to a particular outcome; scientists try to maintain an open-minded readiness to accept the results of their investigations, whatever they may be.

By and large, sociologists accept Weber's argument, although most concede that we can never be completely value-free or even aware of all our biases. Moreover, sociologists are not "average" people: Most are white people who are highly educated and more politically liberal than the population as a whole (Wilson, 1979). Sociologists need to remember that they, too, are affected by their own social backgrounds.

One strategy for limiting distortion caused by personal values is **replication**, *repetition of research by other investigators*. If other researchers repeat a study using the same procedures and obtain the same results, they gain confidence that the original research (as well as their own) was conducted objectively. The need for replication in scientific investigation is probably the reason that the search for knowledge is called *re*search in the first place.

In any case, keep in mind that the logic and methodology of science hold out no guarantee that we will grasp objective, absolute truth. What science offers is an approach to knowledge that is *self-correcting* so that, in the long run, researchers stand the best chance to overcome their own biases and achieve greater understanding. Objectivity and truth, then, lie not in any particular research method, but in the scientific process itself.

Some Limitations of Scientific Sociology

The first scientists probed the operation of the natural world. Contemporary sociologists use science to study the social world; however, the scientific study of people has several important limitations.

1. **Human behavior is too complex to allow sociologists to predict precisely any individual's actions.** Astronomers calculate the movement of planets with remarkable precision, announcing years in advance when a comet will next pass near the earth. But planets and comets are unthinking objects; humans, by contrast, have

NOTE: Consider Plato's idea that "truth" exists as a "form" only approximated by worldly assertions.

Q: "We may remind ourselves that disinterestedness is not disinterest. The passionate commitment to scholarly detachment and free inquiry . . . needs all the self-restraint we can muster to support it precisely because self-restraint goes against our natural preference for our own, including our own views." Pamela Jensen

Q: "As in all sciences, in sociology interpretation is all. A science may be loaded down with too many facts, its vision blurred by peering too intently at the machinery for collecting them. The collected facts can be brought to life, as the statisticians themselves agree, only by a compelling vision of their meaning. Untouched by the magic of a sufficiently powerful and trained imagination, data play dead." Philip Rieff

A basic lesson of social research is that being observed affects how people behave. Researchers can never be certain precisely how this will occur; while some people resent public attention, others become highly animated when they think they have an audience.

minds of their own. Because no two people react to any event in exactly the same way, the best sociologists can do is to show that categories of people typically act in one way or another. This is no failing of sociology; it is simply consistent with the nature of our mission: studying creative, spontaneous people.

2. **Because humans respond to their surroundings, the mere presence of a researcher may affect the behavior being studied.** An astronomer gazing at the moon has no effect whatever on that celestial body. But people usually react to being observed. Some may become anxious, angry, or defensive; others may try to "help" by providing the answers or actions they think researchers expect of them.

3. **Social patterns change constantly; what is true in one time or place may not hold true in another.** The laws of physics apply tomorrow as well as today; they hold true all around the world. But human behavior is too variable for us to set down immutable sociological laws. In fact, some of the most interesting sociological research focuses on social diversity and social change.

4. **Because sociologists are part of the social world they study, being value-free when conducting social research can be difficult.** Barring a laboratory mishap, chemists are rarely personally affected by what goes on in test tubes. But sociologists live in their "test tube"—the society they study. Therefore, social scientists face a greater challenge in controlling—or even recognizing—personal values that may distort their work.

The Importance of Subjective Interpretation

As we have explained, scientists tend to think of "subjectivity" as "bias"—a source of error to be avoided as much as possible. But there is also a good side to subjectivity, since creative thinking is vital to sociological investigation in three key ways.

First, science is basically a series of rules that guide research, rather like a recipe for cooking. But just as more than a recipe is required to make a great chef, so scientific procedure does not, by itself, produce a great sociologist. Also needed is an inspired human imagination. After all, insight comes not from science itself but from the lively thinking of creative human beings (Nisbet, 1970). The genius of physicist Albert Einstein or sociologist Max Weber lay not only in their use of the scientific method but also in their curiosity and ingenuity.

Second, science cannot account for the vast and complex range of human motivations and feelings, including greed, love, pride, and despair. Science certainly helps us gather facts about how people act, but it can never fully explain the complex meanings people attach to their behavior (Berger & Kellner, 1981).

Third, we also do well to remember that scientific data never speak for themselves. After sociologists and other scientists "collect the numbers," they face the ultimate task of *interpretation*—creating meaning from their observations. For this reason, good sociological investigation is as much art as science.

Politics and Research

As Max Weber observed long ago, a fine line separates politics from science. Most sociologists endorse Weber's goal of value-free research. But a growing number of researchers are challenging the notion that politics and science can—or should—be distinct.

Alvin Gouldner (1970a, 1970b) was among the first to claim that the ideal of "value-free" research paints a "storybook picture" of sociology. Every element of social life is political, he argues, in that it benefits some people more than others. If so, Gouldner reasoned, the topics sociologists choose to study and the conclusions they reach also have political consequences.

If sociologists have no choice about their work being political, Gouldner continues, they do have a choice about *which* positions are worthy of support. Moreover, as he sees it, sociologists are obligated to endorse political objectives that will improve society. Although this viewpoint is not limited to sociologists of any one political orientation, it prevails among those with left-leaning politics, especially those guided by the ideas of Karl Marx. Recall Marx's (1972:109; orig. 1845) ringing assertion that the point is not simply to understand the world but to change it.

Such thinking, colliding with the value-free approach, has carried many colleges and universities into a spirited debate over "political correctness." In simple terms, this controversy pits advocates of Weberian value-free teaching and research against proponents of Marx's view that, since all knowledge is political, sociologists should strive to promote positive societal change.

Gender and Research

One political dimension of research involves **gender**, *the significance members of a society attach to being female or male.* Sociologists have come to realize that gender often plays a significant part in their work.

Margrit Eichler (1988) identifies five threats to sound research that relate to gender.

1. **Androcentricity**. Androcentricity (*andro* is the Greek word for "male"; *centricity* means "being centered on") refers to approaching an issue from a male perspective. Sometimes researchers enter a setting as if only the activities of men are important while ignoring what women do. For years, for example, researchers studying occupations focused on the paid work of men while overlooking the housework and child care traditionally performed by women (Counts, 1925; Hodge, Treiman, & Rossi, 1966). Clearly, research that seeks to understand human behavior cannot ignore half of humanity.

   Eichler notes that the parallel situation of *gynocentricity*—seeing the world from a female perspective—is equally limiting to sociological investigation. However, in our male-dominated society, this narrowness of vision arises less frequently.

2. **Overgeneralizing**. This problem occurs when researchers use data drawn from only people of one sex to support conclusions about both sexes. Historically, sociologists have studied men and then made sweeping claims about "humanity" or "society." Gathering information about a community from a handful of public officials (typically, men) and then drawing conclusions about the entire community illustrates the problem of overgeneralizing.

   Here, again, the bias can occur in reverse. For example, in an investigation of child-rearing practices, collecting data only from women would allow researchers to draw conclusions about "motherhood" but not about the more general issue of "parenthood."

3. **Gender blindness**. This refers to the failure of a researcher to consider the variable of gender at all. As we note throughout this book, the lives of men and women typically differ in virtually every setting. A study of growing old in the United States that overlooked the fact that most elderly men live with spouses while elderly women generally live alone would be weakened by its gender blindness.

4. **Double standards**. Researchers must be careful not to distort what they study by applying different standards to men and women. For example, a family researcher who labels a couple as "man and wife" may define the man as the "head of

NOTE: Eichler's gender issues noted here are both threats to sound research and also barriers to gender equality.
RESOURCE: An excerpt from Shulamit Reinharz's article "Feminist Research Methods" is included in the Macionis and Benokraitis reader.
Q: "Advocacy research often justifies playing fast and loose with the facts in service to a noble cause." Neil Gilbert

Q: "Researchers must examine their assumptions about gender . . . Of all the beliefs that anthropologists bring to the field, [these] may be the most difficult to put aside, [operating] on an unconscious level." Maureen Giovannini (1992)
NOTE: Subtle gender biases are evident even in our tendency to speak of "males and females," despite the alphabetical convention that would reverse them.

household" and treat him accordingly, while assuming that the woman simply engages in family "support work."

5. **Interference**. In this case, gender distorts a study because a subject reacts to the sex of the researcher in ways that interfere with the research operation. While studying a small community in Sicily, for instance, Maureen Giovannini (1992) found that many men responded to her as a woman rather than as a researcher, compromising her research efforts. Gender dynamics precluded her from certain activities, such as private conversations with men, that were deemed inappropriate for single women. In addition, local residents denied Giovannini access to places considered off-limits to members of her sex.

Of course, there is nothing wrong with focusing research on one sex or the other. But all sociologists, as well as people who read their work, should stay mindful about how gender can affect the process of sociological investigation.

Feminist Research

Sociology's pervasive attention to men in the past has prompted some contemporary researchers to make special efforts to investigate the lives of women. Advocates of feminist research embrace two key tenets: (1) that their research should focus on the condition of women in society, and (2) that the research must be grounded in the assumption that women generally experience subordination. Thus feminist research rejects Weber's value-free orientation in favor of being overtly political—doing research in pursuit of gender equality.

Some proponents of feminist research advocate the use of conventional scientific techniques, including all those described in this chapter. Others maintain that feminist research must transform the essence of science, which they see as a masculine form of knowledge. Whereas scientific investigation traditionally has demanded detachment, feminists deliberately foster a sympathetic understanding between investigator and subject. Moreover, conventional scientists take charge of the research agenda by deciding in advance what issues to raise and how to study them. Feminist researchers, by contrast, favor a less structured approach to gathering information so that participants in research can offer their own ideas on their own terms (Stanley & Wise, 1983; Nielsen, 1990; Stanley, 1990; Reinharz, 1992).

Feminist research is not concerned simply with studying the social standing of women. It also transforms scientific research so that an investigator assumes a posture of social parity with others, working cooperatively toward solving their common problems.

Such alterations in research premises and methods have led more conventional sociologists to charge that feminist research is less science than simple political activism. Feminists respond that research and politics should not—indeed cannot—ever be distinct. Therefore, traditional notions that placed politics and science in separate spheres have now given way to some new thinking that merges these two dimensions.

Research Ethics

Like all investigators, sociologists must be mindful that research can be harmful as well as helpful to subjects or communities. For this reason, the American Sociological Association—the major professional association of sociologists in North America—has established formal guidelines for the conduct of research (1984).

The prime directive is that sociologists strive to be both technically competent and fair-minded in conducting their research. Sociologists must disclose all their findings, without omitting significant data. Further, they must point out various interpretations of data, and they are ethically bound to make their results available to other sociologists, some of whom may wish to replicate the study.

Whether social scientists need to inform people that they are the objects of study is a matter of continuing debate among sociologists. No one objects to

SOCIAL DIVERSITY

Conducting Research With Hispanics

In a society as racially, ethnically, and religiously diverse as our own, sociological investigators will inevitably confront people who differ from themselves in the course of their work. Learning—in advance—some of the distinctive traits of any category of people being studied can both facilitate the research process and ensure that no hard feelings are left when the work is completed.

Gerardo Marín and Barbara VanOss Marín have identified five key areas of concern for social investigators who plan to conduct research with Hispanics.

1. **Terminology.** The Maríns point out that the term "Hispanic" is a label of convenience used by the

Researchers must always remain respectful of subjects and mindful of their well-being. In part, this means investigators must become familiar— well ahead of time—with the cultural patterns of those they wish to study.

Census Bureau. Few people of Spanish descent think of themselves as "Hispanic" or "Latino"; most identify with a particular country (generally, with a specific nation of Latin America such as Cuba or Argentina, or with Spain).

2. **Cultural values.** By and large, the United States is a nation of individualistic, competitive people. Many Hispanics, by contrast, have a more collective orientation. An outsider may judge the behavior of a Hispanic subject as conformist or overly trusting when, in fact, the person is simply acting in a normative way. Moreover, because Hispanics tend to favor

studying public behavior (say, observing how people interact in a gambling casino or a park) without announcing one's presence. But most sociologists agree that a researcher must not target specific individuals for study without their permission. Taking this debate one step further, should researchers employ deception in their work? Obviously, if researchers tell people exactly what they are looking for, they will not observe natural behavior. On the other hand, misleading subjects may generate understandable resentment. Sociologists disagree about such ethical quandaries, but there is a trend toward greater sensitivity for the well-being of subjects in research.

Virtually everyone agrees, however, that researchers must strive to protect the safety of people involved in a research project. Sociologists are obligated to terminate research, however promising it may seem, if they become aware of any danger to participants. If research is likely to cause subjects substantial discomfort or inconvenience, furthermore, sociologists must ensure in advance that all participants understand and accept any risks.

In addition, sociologists must include in their published results the sources of any and all financial support. They must never accept funding from any organization that seeks to influence the research process for its own purposes.

Finally, there are also global dimensions to research ethics. Before beginning research in other countries, investigators must become familiar enough with the society to be studied to understand what people *there* are likely to perceive as a violation of privacy or a source of personal danger. In a multicultural society like ours, of course, the same rule applies to studying people whose cultural background differs from one's own. The box offers some tips about how outsiders can effectively and sensitively study Hispanic communities.

THE METHODS OF SOCIOLOGICAL RESEARCH

A **research method** is *a systematic plan for conducting research.* The remainder of this chapter introduces four commonly used methods of sociological investigation.

NOTE: The word "experiment" contains the Latin root *per*, "to try out." This is also the root of the word "peril"—a link demonstrated by the Zimbardo research.

Q: "It's not the things we don't know that get us into trouble. It's the things we know that just ain't so." Artemus Ward

Q: "Sciences seek constantly to go beyond their founders, but ideologies do not." Robert Nisbet

Q: "Science is meaningless because it gives no answer to the question, the only question of importance for us: 'What shall we do and how shall we live?'" Leo Tolstoy

Q: "In science as in love, a concentration on technique is likely to lead to impotence." Peter Berger (1963)

Q: "To know is nothing at all. To imagine is everything." Anatole France

harmonious relations, subjects may agree with a researcher's statement out of politeness more than conviction.

3. **Family dynamics.** Generally speaking, Hispanic cultures have strong family loyalties. Asking subjects to reveal information about another family member may make them uncomfortable, and they may even refuse to do so. The Maríns add that, in the home, a researcher's request to speak privately with a Hispanic woman may provoke suspicion or outright disapproval from her husband or father.

4. **Time and efficiency.** Spanish cultures, the Maríns explain, tend to be more concerned with the quality of relationships than with simply getting a job done. Therefore, a non-Hispanic researcher who tries to rush through an interview with a Hispanic family, perhaps out of concern not to delay the family's dinner, may be perceived as rude by those who would prefer to proceed at a more sociable and leisurely pace.

5. **Personal space.** Finally, as the Maríns point out, people of Spanish descent typically maintain closer physical contact with others than many non-Hispanics do. For this reason, researchers who seat themselves across the room from their subjects may come across as "stand-offish." Conversely, researchers may inaccurately label Hispanics as "pushy" when they move closer than the non-Hispanic researcher may find comfortable.

Of course, Hispanics differ among themselves just as people in every other category do, and these generalizations apply to some more than to others. But investigators should be aware of cultural dynamics when carrying out research, especially in the United States, where hundreds of distinctive categories of people make up a multicultural society.

Source: Marín and Marín (1991).

None is inherently better or worse than any other. Rather, in the same way that a carpenter selects a particular tool for a specific task, researchers choose a method according to whom they choose to study and what they wish to learn.

Testing a Hypothesis: The Experiment

The logic of science is most clearly expressed in the **experiment,** *a research method for investigating cause and effect under highly controlled conditions.* Experimental research is *explanatory*, meaning that it asks not just what happens but why. Typically, researchers turn to an experiment to test a specific **hypothesis,** *an unverified statement of a relationship between variables.*

Ideally, we evaluate a hypothesis in three steps. First, the experimenter measures the dependent variable (the "effect"); second, the investigator exposes the dependent variable to the independent variable (the "cause" or "treatment"); and third, the researcher again measures the dependent variable to see if the predicted change took place. If the expected change did occur, the experiment lends support to the hypothesis; if not, the hypothesis is discounted.

But a change in the dependent variable may be due to something other than the assumed cause. To prevent this, researchers must carefully control any and all extraneous factors that might intrude into the experiment and affect what is being measured. Such control is most easily accomplished in a laboratory, an artificial setting specially constructed for research purposes. Another strategy for neutralizing outside influences is dividing subjects into an *experimental group* and a *control group*. At the outset, the researcher measures the dependent variable for subjects in both groups but exposes only the experimental group to the independent variable or treatment (the control group typically gets a "placebo," an apparently comparable treatment known to have no experimental effect). Then the investigator measures the subjects in both groups again. Any factor (such as some news event) occurring during the course of the research that influences people in the experimental group would do the same to the control-group subjects, thus neutralizing the factor. In short, the use of a control group "washes

SUPPLEMENTS: The *Data File* includes an account of how recently celebrated research by the late James Coleman was initially condemned as "politically incorrect."
Q: "People kill each other for prophetic certainties, hardly for falsifiable hypotheses." Peter Berger
Q: "Let us lay the facts aside, for they do not affect the question . . ." Jean Jacques Rousseau

Q: "We can no longer view the world as Descartes and Laplace would have us do, as 'rational onlookers,' from outside. Our place is within the same world that we are studying, and whatever scientific understanding we achieve must be a kind of understanding that is available to participants within the process of nature, i.e., from inside." Stephen Toulmin

An Illustration: The Stanford County Prison

Prisons are often violent institutions, but does the prison setting itself play a part in generating violence and disorder? This question prompted Philip Zimbardo to devise a fascinating experiment to investigate the causes of prison violence (Zimbardo, 1972; Haney, Banks, & Zimbardo, 1973).

Zimbardo's hypothesis was simple: Prison violence is caused not so much by antisocial prisoners or guards as by the nature of prison itself. In other words, Zimbardo suspected, once inside a prison, even emotionally healthy people become prone to violence. Thus Zimbardo treated the *prison setting* as the independent variable capable of causing *violence*, the dependent variable.

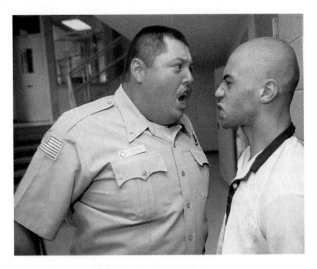

Philip Zimbardo's research helps to explain why violence is a common element in our society's prisons. At the same time, his work demonstrates the dangers that sociological investigation poses for subjects and the need for investigators to observe ethical standards that protect the welfare of people who participate in research.

To test this hypothesis, Zimbardo's research team first constructed a realistic, artificial prison in the basement of the psychology building on the campus of Stanford University. Then they placed an ad in a Palo Alto newspaper, offering to pay young men to help with a two-week research project. To each of the seventy who responded they administered a series of physical and psychological tests, selecting the healthiest twenty-four for their experiment.

The next step was randomly designating half the men as "prisoners" and half as "guards." The plan called for the guards and prisoners to spend the next two weeks in the "Stanford County Prison." The "prisoners" began their part of the experiment soon afterward when the Palo Alto police "arrested" them at their homes. After searching and handcuffing the men, the police took them to the local police station to be fingerprinted. Then they transported their captives to the Stanford "prison" where Zimbardo had the "guards" ready to secure them behind bars. Zimbardo then sat back with a video camera to see what would happen next.

The experiment quickly degenerated into more than anyone had bargained for. Both guards and prisoners soon became embittered and hostile toward one another. Guards humiliated the prisoners by assigning them tasks such as cleaning out toilets with their bare hands. The prisoners, for their part, resisted and insulted the guards. Within four days, the researchers removed five prisoners who displayed "extreme emotional depression, crying, rage and acute anxiety" (1973:81). Before the end of the first week, the situation had deteriorated so much that the researchers called off the experiment entirely. Zimbardo explains (1972:4): "The ugliest, most base, pathological side of human nature surfaced. We were horrified because we saw some boys (guards) treat others as if they were

out" many extraneous factors; comparing before and after measurements of the two groups, a researcher is able to assess how much of the observed change is due only to the independent variable.

Yet subjects may alter their behavior simply in response to a researcher's attention, as one classic experiment revealed. In the late 1930s, the Western Electric Company hired researchers to investigate worker productivity in its Hawthorne factory near Chicago (Roethlisberger & Dickson, 1939). One experiment examined whether increasing the available lighting would raise worker output. To test this idea, researchers measured initial productivity (the dependent variable); then they increased the lighting (the independent variable); finally, they measured productivity a second time. Productivity increased, supporting the hypothesis. But when the research team subsequently *reduced* the lighting, productivity again increased, contradicting the initial hypothesis. In time, the researchers realized that the employees were working harder (even if they could not see as well) simply because people were paying attention to them. From this research, social scientists coined the term **Hawthorne effect** to refer to *a change in a subject's behavior caused simply by the awareness of being studied.*

SOCIAL SURVEY: *Student Social Survey Software*, using the new Student Chip program, is available with this text. It provides 1972 through 1993 NORC General Social Survey data, and now has graphing capability. Each GSS involves about 1,500 subjects, selected from a multistage survey in which researchers first randomly select geographical areas and then randomly select adults over age eighteen from each area. Excluded are individuals who are in any way "institutionalized" (including college students).

NOTE: Sometimes samples produce better results than populations do considering that the tedious work of contacting a whole population can lead to all sorts of nonsampling errors.

NOTE: "Pop" research is often flawed because of poor surveys. For example, the last "Hite survey" of male-female relationships was based on a survey return rate of only 4.5 percent.

despicable animals, taking pleasure in cruelty, while other boys (prisoners) became servile, dehumanized robots who thought only of escape, of their own individual survival and of their mounting hatred for the guards."

The unfolding events in the "Stanford County Prison" supported Zimbardo's hypothesis that prison violence is rooted in the social character of jails themselves, rather than the personalities of guards and prisoners. This finding also raises questions about how and why our society operates prisons, pointing toward the need for basic reform. But also note how this experiment reveals the potential of research to threaten the physical and mental well-being of subjects. Such dangers are not always as obvious as they were in this case. Therefore researchers must carefully consider the potential harm to subjects at all stages of their work and end any study, as Zimbardo responsibly did, if subjects may suffer harm of any kind.

Asking Questions: Survey Research

A **survey** is *a research method in which subjects respond to a series of items in a questionnaire or an interview.* The most widely used of all research methods, surveys are particularly well suited to studying attitudes that investigators cannot observe directly, including political and religious beliefs or the subjective effects of racism. Although surveys can shed light on cause and effect, most often they yield *descriptive* findings, as researchers seek to paint a picture of subjects' views on some issue.

Population and Sample

The researcher begins a survey by designating a **population**, *the people who are the focus of research.* Lois Benjamin, whose research we introduced at the beginning of this chapter, focused on the population of talented African Americans as she explored the effects of racism. As another example, political pollsters try to predict election returns using surveys that treat every adult in the country as the population.

Obviously, however, contacting millions of people would overwhelm even the most well-funded and patient researcher. Fortunately, there is a far easier alternative that produces accurate results: Researchers collect data from a **sample**, *a part of a population that represents the whole.* The box on page 44 describes the evolution of familiar national political surveys, which now utilize a sample of some fifteen hundred people to gauge the political mood of the entire country.

Although the term may be new to you, you use the logic of sampling all the time. If you look around the classroom and notice five or six heads nodding off, you might conclude that the class finds the day's lecture dull. Such a conclusion involves making an inference about *all* the people (the "population") from observing *some* of the people (the "sample"). But how do we know if a sample actually represents the entire population?

One way to do this is through *random sampling*, in which researchers draw a sample from the population in such a way that every element in the population has the same chance of ending up in the sample. If this is the case, the mathematical laws of probability dictate that the sample they select will, in the vast majority of cases, represent the population with a minimal amount of error. Seasoned researchers use special computer programs to generate random samples. Novice researchers, however, sometimes make the mistake of assuming that "randomly" walking up to people on the street produces a sample representative of an entire city. But such a strategy does not give every person an equal chance to be included in the sample. For one thing, any street—whether in a rich neighborhood or a "college town"—contains more of some kinds of people than others. For another, any researcher is apt to find some people more approachable than others, again introducing a bias.

Although good sampling is no simple task, it offers a considerable savings in time and expense. We are spared the tedious work of contacting everyone in a population, while obtaining essentially the same results.

Questionnaires and Interviews

Selecting subjects is only the first step in carrying out a survey. Also needed is a plan for asking questions and recording answers. Surveys fall into two general categories: questionnaires and interviews.

A **questionnaire** is *a series of written questions a researcher supplies to subjects requesting their responses.* One type of questionnaire provides not only the questions but a series of fixed responses (similar to a multiple-choice examination). This *closed-ended format* makes the task of analyzing the results relatively easy, yet narrows the range of responses in a way that might distort the findings. By contrast, a second type of questionnaire, using an *open-ended format,* allows subjects to respond freely, expressing various shades of opinion. The drawback of this approach is

SOCIOLOGY OF EVERYDAY LIFE

National Political Surveys

One hundred million men and women voted in the Congressional elections in 1994. The extent of the Republican victory was a surprise to many people, but the trend favoring Republicans had been correctly predicted by pollsters long before the first vote was cast.

Political surveys, or *polls*, are a familiar part of national life. But how can researchers use information drawn from several hundred subjects to predict what 100 million people will do? The key to accurate prediction lies in selecting a sample *representative* of the entire population.

Gaining the knowledge and skills to do this took a long time. In 1936, the *Literary Digest* surveyed U.S. voters and predicted that Republican Alfred E. Landon would handily defeat Democrat Franklin Delano Roosevelt. The publication could hardly have been more wrong, as Roosevelt buried

Landon in a historic landslide. Why was that poll so wrong? Simply put, the magazine's sample did not represent the voting population. The *Digest* mailed survey ballots to 20 million people (far more than would be included in a poll today) selected from

telephone listings and automobile registrations. But, back then, most people who owned a telephone or car were affluent and, therefore, likely to be Republicans.

This embarrassing prediction did nothing for the prestige of the *Literary Digest*, which soon closed up shop. But that same year a young researcher named George Gallup (1902–1984) not only correctly called the election but warned that the *Literary Digest* would be way off the mark. Gallup went on to become the best-known survey researcher in the United States. Today, the organization he founded carries out surveys around the world, routinely providing accurate predictions about election returns as well as offering information on a host of other issues.

Source: Adapted, in part, from Babbie (1995).

that the researcher later has to make sense out of what can be a bewildering array of answers.

How to present questions to subjects forms another part of the research strategy. Most often, researchers employ a *self-administered survey*, in which they mail questionnaires to respondents with a request to complete the form and mail it back. Since no researcher is present when subjects read the questionnaire, it must be both inviting and clearly written. *Pretesting* a self-administered questionnaire with a small number of people before sending it to the entire sample can preclude the costly problem of finding out—too late—that instructions or questions were confusing.

Using the mail (or, more recently, electronic mail) has the advantage of allowing a researcher to contact a large number of people over a wide geographical area at minimal expense. But many people treat such questionnaires as "junk mail"; typically, no more than half

are completed and returned. Researchers often send out follow-up mailings to coax reluctant subjects to fill out the questionaire.

Finally, keep in mind that many people are not capable of completing a questionnaire on their own. Young children obviously cannot, nor can many hospital patients, as well as a surprising number of adults who simply lack the reading and writing skills needed to wade through a comprehensive questionnaire.

An **interview** is *a series of questions a researcher administers personally to respondents*. In a closed-ended format design, researchers would read a question or statement and then ask the subject to select a response from several alternatives. Generally, however, interviews are open-ended so that subjects can respond in whatever way they choose and researchers can probe with follow-up questions. In the ensuing conversation, however, the researcher must guard

DIVERSITY: The 1990 census showed an unexpected rise from 49 million to 58 million in the number of people of German ancestry. The reason turned out to be that "German" was listed first on the 1990 survey and fourth back in 1980. Similarly, the 1990 form used "French Canadian" as an example in the ancestry section, apparently causing the number of people claiming such ancestry to triple from 780,000 in 1980 to 2.2 million in 1990.

Q: "Information is difference that makes a difference." Gregory Bateson
DISCUSS: Another example of wording affecting survey responses is found in a *Time*/CNN poll (May 18–19, 1994) in which 23% of respondents claimed "government is spending too much on assistance to the poor," yet 53% agreed that government is "spending too much on welfare." (*Time*, June 27, 1994:26)

against influencing a subject, a problem that can creep in through subtle gestures such as the raising of an eyebrow when a person begins to answer.

Comparing the interview with the questionnaire, experienced investigators know that a subject is more likely to complete a survey if contacted personally by the researcher. Yet interviews have some disadvantages: Tracking people down and personally interrogating them is costly and time consuming, especially if all subjects do not live in the same area. And while telephone interviews clearly allow far greater "reach," the impersonality of "cold calls" by telephone may result in a low completion rate.

In both questionnaires and interviews, the wording of questions has a significant effect on answers. When asked if they object to homosexuals serving in the military, for example, most adults in the United States say "yes." Yet, asked if the government should exempt homosexuals from military service, most say "no" (NORC, 1991). Moreover, emotionally loaded language can easily sway subjects. For instance, the term "welfare mothers," as opposed to "women who receive public assistance," injects an emotional element into a survey and encourages respondents to answer more negatively. In still other cases, the wording of questions may hint at what other people think, thereby steering subjects. For example, people are more likely to respond positively to the question "Do you *agree* that the police force is doing a good job?" than to a similar question "Do you *think* that the police force is doing a good job?" Similarly, respondents are more likely to endorse a statement to "*not allow*" something (say, public speeches against the government) than a statement to "*forbid*" the same activity (Rademacher, 1992).

Finally, researchers may inadvertently confuse respondents by asking double questions like "Do you think that the government should cut spending and raise taxes to reduce the deficit?" The problem here is that a subject could very well agree with one part of the question but reject the other, so that saying *yes* or *no* to the two-part question distorts the person's true opinion.

An Illustration: Studying the African-American Elite

We opened this chapter with a brief account of Lois Benjamin's investigation of the effects of racism on talented African-American men and women. Contrary to some published research, she was convinced that personal achievement did not lift minorities above the ordeal of hostility based on color. Her own

Living the good life? Yes and no, according to researcher Lois Benjamin. Based on interviews with one hundred highly successful African-American men and women, Benjamin concluded that "making it" does not eliminate the sting of racial prejudice. On the contrary, she found, even the highest achievers still had to contend with barriers based on skin color.

experiences as the only black professor in the history department of the University of Tampa confirmed this view. But was she the exception or the rule? To answer this question, Benjamin set out to discover whether—and how—racism had tainted the achievements of others like herself.

Opting to conduct a survey, Benjamin chose to do interviews rather than distributing a questionnaire because, first, she wanted to enter into a conversation with her subjects, to ask follow-up questions, and to be able to pursue topics that she could not have anticipated in advance. A second reason she favored interviews over questionnaires is that racism is a sensitive topic. Subjects tend to shy away from painful questions in the absence of a supportive relationship with the investigator.

The choice to conduct interviews carried with it the requirement to limit the number of people in the study. Benjamin settled for one hundred men and women. Given the time needed to complete interviews, even this small number kept Benjamin busy for more than two years scheduling, traveling, and meeting with informants. Another two years was needed to

NOTE: Conducting interviews, as Lois Benjamin did, is something like traveling abroad. We have some idea of our direction and destination, but the unexpected always arises along the way. Imaginative improvisation is needed to make the most of an interview opportunity and sometimes even to "save a situation."

Q: "All human errors are impatience, a premature breaking off of methodological procedure, an apparent fencing in of what is apparently at issue." Franz Kafka

NOTE: Although widely used in survey research, "snowball sampling" is really a crude approach unlikely to represent a population accurately.

NOTE: Lois Benjamin did not clearly operationalize "talented African Americans," so that the population her sample represents remains only vaguely defined.

TABLE 2–1 The Talented One Hundred: Lois Benjamin's African-American Elite

Sex	Age	Childhood Racial Setting	Childhood Region	Highest Educational Degree	Occupational Sector	Income	Political Orientation
Male 63%	35 or younger 6%	Mostly Black 71%	West 6%	Doctorate 32%	College/ University 35%	More than $50,000 64%	Radical 13%
Female 37%	36 to 54 68%	Mostly White 15%	North/ Central 32%	Medical/ Law 17%	Private, Profit 17%	$35,000 to $50,000 18%	Liberal 38%
	55 or older 26%	Racially Mixed 14%	South 38%	Master's 27%	Private, Nonprofit 9%	$20,000 to $34,999 12%	Moderate 28%
			Northeast 12%	Bachelor's 13%	Government 22%	Less than $20,000 6%	Conservative 5%
			Other 12%	Less 11%	Self-Employed 14%		Depends on Issue 14%
					Retired 3%		Unknown 2%
100%	100%	100%	100%	100%	100%	100%	100%

Source: Adapted from Lois Benjamin, *The Black Elite: Facing the Color Line in the Twilight of the Twentieth Century* (Chicago: Nelson-Hall, 1991), p. 276.

transcribe the tapes of her interviews, to sort out what the hours and hours of heartfelt conversation told her about the issue of race, and to write up her results.

Once a researcher selects a survey technique, the next order of business is selecting a sample. At first, Benjamin considered using all the people listed in *Who's Who in Black America* as her population of talented African Americans; from this list, she easily could have drawn a random sample of people to contact. But she rejected this idea in favor of starting out with people she knew and asking respondents to suggest others to include in the sample. This strategy is called *snowball sampling* because the number of individuals included in the sample grows rapidly over time.

Snowball sampling offers an easy and pleasant way to do research—we begin with familiar people who provide easy introductions to their friends and colleagues. However, snowball sampling rarely produces a sample that is representative of the larger population. In this case, the social networks into which Benjamin entered probably contain many like-minded individuals and it was certainly biased toward people willing to talk openly about race. Benjamin understood these problems, and did try to make her sample as varied as she could in terms of sex, age, and region of the country. Table 2–1 provides a statistical profile of the people who participated in her investigation.

Benjamin based all her interviews on a series of questions, but adopted an open-ended format so her subjects could pursue whatever issues they wished. Like many interviewers, Benjamin conducted her interviews in a wide range of settings. She met subjects in offices (hers or theirs), in hotel rooms, and in cars. In each case, Benjamin tape-recorded the conversation—which lasted from two-and-one-half to three hours—so that the task of taking notes would not distract her. After completing all the interviewing, however, she faced the arduous task of transcribing some three hundred hours of tape-recorded conversations.

As research ethics demand, Benjamin offered full anonymity to any individual who wanted it. Even so, many of her respondents—including such notables as Vernon E. Jordan, Jr. (former president of the National Urban League) and Yvonne Walker-Taylor (first woman president of Wilberforce University)—were accustomed to being in the public eye and permitted Benjamin to use their names.

SOCIAL SURVEY: "In general, do you feel that surveys usually serve a good purpose or do you feel that they are usually a waste of time and money?" (GSS 1982, N = 1,506; *Codebook*, 1994:252)

"Good purpose" 70.6%   "Waste of time/money" 14.2%
"Depends" 8.4%   DK/NR 6.8%

NOTE: Among the first systematic participant observers of U.S.

society was Alexis de Tocqueville who, along with his companion Gustave Beaumont, traveled some seven thousand miles across the United States and Canada between May 11, 1831, and February 20, 1832, before writing *Democracy in America*.

Q: "The redeeming power of reflection cannot be supplanted by the extension of technically exploitable knowledge." Jürgen Habermas (1970:61)

CRITICAL THINKING

Table Reading: An Important Skill

A table provides a great deal of information in a small amount of space, so learning to read tables can increase your reading efficiency. When you spot a table, look first at the title to see what information it contains. In Table 2–1, the title tells us that the table provides a profile of the one hundred subjects participating in Lois Benjamin's research. Across the top of the table, you will see eight variables that define these men and women. Reading down under each one, note the various categories, each with a percentage; the percentages in each column add up to one hundred.

Starting at the top left, we see that Benjamin's sample was mostly men (63 percent versus 37 percent women). In terms of age, most of the respondents (68 percent) were in the middle stage of life, and we see, too, that most grew up in a predominantly black community either in the South or in the North-Central region of the United States.

These individuals do, indeed, constitute a professional elite. Notice that half have earned either a doctorate (32 percent) or a medical or law degree (17 percent). Given their extensive education (and Benjamin's own position as a professor), we should not be surprised that the largest share (35 percent) work in academic institutions. In terms of income, these are affluent individuals, with most (64 percent) earning more than $50,000 annually (a salary commanded by only 14 percent of all workers in the United States).

Finally, we see that these one hundred individuals generally claim to be left-of-center in their political orientations. In part, this reflects their extensive schooling (which encourages progressive thinking) and the tendency of academics to lean toward the liberal side of the political spectrum.

What surprised Benjamin the most, however, was how eagerly many informants responded to her request for an interview. These normally busy men and women appeared to go out of their way to contribute to this project. Furthermore, once the interviews were under way, many displayed a high degree of emotion. Benjamin reports that, at some point in the conversation, about forty of her one hundred subjects shed tears. For many, apparently, the interviews provided an opportunity to release feelings and share experiences never revealed before. How did Benjamin, herself, respond to such sentiments? She reports that she laughed, reflected, or cried along with her respondents. In light of this close rapport, we might reasonably wonder whether a more formal and aloof researcher could have completed this research, and whether or not a white investigator could have done so.

As we noted at the beginning of this chapter, other researchers have documented important gains in social standing among African Americans in recent decades. But Benjamin's interviews caution us that race continues to shape the daily lives of talented people of color. Many reported anxiety that their racial identity would at some point undermine their success. Others feared that a race-based "glass ceiling" stands between them and the highest positions in our society. Summing up her respondents' thoughts and feelings, Benjamin states that, despite the improving social standing of African Americans, black people in the United States continue to feel the sting of racial hostility. Just as important, we see that a position in this nation's professional elite is no shield from racism.

Finding a persistent "color line" in U.S. society, Benjamin ends her study by expressing her commitment to change. Following the lead of W. E. B. Du Bois, she asserts that research is not merely a source of knowledge but a strategy for assisting those we study (and, perhaps, ourselves).

In the Field: Participant Observation

Lois Benjamin's research demonstrates that sociological investigation takes place not only in laboratories but "in the field," that is, where people carry on their everyday lives. The most widely used strategy for field study is **participant observation**, *a method by which researchers systematically observe people while joining in their routine activities.*

John Sloan's urban scene, The Lafayette, *piques our imagination. Like Sloan, we have all seen people enter and leave particular places that we know nothing about. Provided, of course, that they can gain access, investigators employ participant observation to gain an insider's understanding of such settings.*

John Sloan (1871–1951). Oil on canvas. 30 1/2 x 36 1/8 inches. Signed (lower left): John Sloan. Painted in 1928. The Metropolitan Museum of Art, Gift of Friends of John Sloan, 1928. (28.18)

Researchers choose participant observation in order to gain an inside look at social life in settings ranging from night clubs to religious seminaries. Cultural anthropologists commonly employ participant observation (which they call *fieldwork*) to study communities in other societies. They term their descriptions of unfamiliar cultures *ethnographies*; sociologists prefer to describe their accounts of people in particular settings as *case studies*.

At the outset of a field study, social scientists typically have just a vague idea of what they will encounter. Thus, most field research is *exploratory* and *descriptive*. Researchers might have hypotheses in mind, but just as likely they may not yet realize what the important questions will turn out to be.

As its name suggests, participant observation has two facets. On the one hand, gaining an "insider's" look depends on becoming a participant in the setting—"hanging out" with others, attempting to act, think, and even feel the way they do. Compared to experiments and survey research, then, participant observation has fewer hard-and-fast rules. But it is precisely this flexibility that allows investigators to explore the unfamiliar and to adapt to the unexpected.

Unlike other research methods, participant observation requires a researcher to become immersed in the

setting, not for a week or two, but for months or even years. For the duration of the study, however, the researcher must maintain some distance as an "observer," mentally stepping back to record field notes and, eventually, to make sense of the action. The tension inherent in this method comes through in the name: "Playing the *participant*" gains for the researcher acceptance and access to people's lives; yet, "playing the *observer*" affords the distance and perspective needed for thoughtful analysis. The twin roles of "insider" participant and "outsider" observer, then, often come down to a series of careful compromises.

Most sociologists carry out participant observation alone, so they must remain mindful that results depend on the interpretations of a single individual. Participant observation is typically **qualitative research**, meaning *investigation by which a researcher gathers impressionistic, not numerical, data.* Unlike experiments or surveys, participant observation usually involves little **quantitative research**, *investigation by which a researcher collects numerical data.* Some scientists disparage a "soft" method like participant observation as lacking in scientific rigor. Yet its personal approach—relying so heavily on personal impressions—is also a strength; while a highly visible team of sociologists attempting to administer formal surveys

NOTE: Other well-known examples of participant-observation studies include Robert and Helen Lynd's *Middletown* and *Middletown in Transition* (Muncie, Ind.), W. Lloyd Warner's Yankee City series (Newburyport, Mass.), Herbert Gans's *The Levittowners* (Willingboro, N.J.), and Elliot Liebow's *Tally's Corner* (Washington, D.C.).
NOTE: The two Lynd studies of Muncie display significant changes in orientation: The first is basically a nontheoretical description, while the second is guided by a vaguely Marxist class analysis. The change was more in the author than in the city. After publishing the first study, Columbia University gave Robert Lynd a Ph.D. and a faculty position; only then did he learn much about theory. Perhaps the second study might better have been titled "Lynd in Transition."

would disrupt many social settings, a sensitive participant-observer can often gain considerable insight into people's natural, day-to-day behavior.

An Illustration: Street Corner Society

In the late 1930s, a young graduate student at Harvard University named William Foote Whyte became fascinated by the lively street life of a nearby, rather rundown section of Boston. His curiosity ultimately led Whyte to carry out four years of participant observation in this neighborhood, which he called "Cornerville," producing a sociological classic in the process.

At the time, Cornerville was home to first- and second-generation Italian immigrants. Many were poor and lived economically precarious lives, quite unlike the more affluent Bostonians familiar to Whyte. Popular wisdom in Boston held that Cornerville was a place to avoid: a poor, chaotic slum inhabited by racketeers. Unwilling to accept easy stereotypes, Whyte set out to discover for himself exactly what kind of life went on inside this community. His celebrated book, *Street Corner Society* (1981; orig. 1943), describes Cornerville as a highly organized community with a distinctive code of values, complex social patterns, and particular social conflicts.

Beginning his investigation, Whyte considered a range of research methods. Of course, he might have taken a pile of questionnaires to one of Cornerville's community centers and asked local people to fill them out. Or he could have asked members of the community to come to his Harvard office for interviews. But it is easy to see that such formal strategies would have prompted little cooperation from the local people and yielded few insights. Whyte decided, therefore, to ease into Cornerville life and patiently seek out the keys to understanding this rather mysterious place.

Soon enough, Whyte discovered the challenges of just getting started in field research. After all, an upper-middle-class Anglo-Saxon graduate student from Harvard did not exactly "fit in" to Cornerville life. And, as Whyte quickly found out, even what he intended as a friendly overture could seem pushy and rude to others. Early on, Whyte dropped in at a local bar, hoping to buy a woman a drink and encourage her to talk about Cornerville. He looked around the room, but could find no woman alone. Presently, he thought he might have an opportunity when a fellow sat down with two women. He gamely remarked, "Pardon me. Would you mind if I joined you?" Instantly, he realized his miscalculation:

> There was a moment of silence while the man stared at me. Then he offered to throw me down the stairs. I assured him that this would not be necessary, and demonstrated as much by walking right out of there without any assistance. (1981:289)

As this incident suggests, gaining entree to a community—that is, becoming a participant—is the crucial (and sometimes hazardous) first step in this type of research. "Breaking in" typically depends on patience, ingenuity, and a little luck. For Whyte, a big break came in the form of a young man named "Doc," whom he met in a local social-service agency. Listening to Whyte's account of his bungled efforts to make friends in Cornerville, Doc sympathetically decided to take Whyte under his wing and introduce him to others in the community. With Doc's help, Whyte soon became a "regular" in the neighborhood.

Whyte's friendship with Doc illustrates the importance of a *key informant* in field research. Such people not only introduce a researcher to a community but often continue to be sources of help and information on a host of issues. But using a key informant also has its risks. Because any person has a particular circle of friends, a key informant's guidance is certain to introduce bias into the study. Moreover, in the eyes of others the reputation of the key informant—for better or worse—usually rubs off on the investigator. In sum, while relying on a key informant at the outset, a participant-observer soon must seek a broader range of contacts.

Now that he had entered the Cornerville world, Whyte began his work in earnest. But he soon realized that the careful field researcher needs to know when to speak up and when to simply listen, look, and learn. One evening, he joined a group of Cornerville people engaged in a discussion of neighborhood gambling. Wanting to get the facts straight, Whyte asked naively, "I suppose the cops were all paid off?" In a heartbeat,

> The gambler's jaw dropped. He glared at me. Then he denied vehemently that any policeman had been paid off and immediately switched the conversation to another subject. For the rest of that evening I felt very uncomfortable.

The next day, Doc offered some sound advice:

> "Go easy on that 'who,' 'what,' 'why,' 'when,' 'where' stuff, Bill. You ask those questions and people will clam up on you. If people accept you, you can just hang around, and you'll learn the answers in the long run without even having to ask the questions." (1981:303)

RESOURCE: In the methodological appendix to *Street Corner Society* (1981; orig. 1943), William Foote Whyte candidly assesses how his own values influenced his work.

RESOURCE: The *Statistical Abstract* is the single best source of statistical data about the population of the United States (order by telephone: 301-763-4100). For global data, see the World Bank's *World Development Report* (202-473-1155), and the United Nations's *Human Development Report* (212-963-8302).

NOTE: In conducting historical research, sociologists can discern the contours and impacts of most significant social developments (such as industrialization or deindustrialization), which come to light only over long periods.

In the months and years that followed, Whyte became familiar with life in Cornerville, and even married a local woman. In the process, he learned that this neighborhood was hardly the stereotypical slum. On the contrary, most immigrants were working hard, many had earned considerable success, and some could even could boast of having sent children to college. In short, his book makes for fascinating reading about the dreams, deeds, and disappointments of one ethnic community, and it contains a richness of detail that only long-term participant observation can provide.

In Whyte's work, we also see that participant observation is a method rife with tensions and contrasts. Its flexibility helps a researcher respond to an unfamiliar setting but makes replication difficult for others. Insight depends on getting close to others, while scientific observation demands detachment. Participant observation calls for little expense, since no elaborate equipment or laboratory is needed, but a comprehensive community study does take time—typically a year or more. Perhaps this long-term commitment explains why participant observation is used less often than other methods described in this chapter. Yet the depth of understanding gained through research of this kind has greatly enriched our knowledge of many types of human communities.

Using Available Data: Secondary and Historical Analysis

Not all research requires investigators to collect their own data personally. In many cases, sociologists engage in **secondary analysis**, *a research method in which a researcher utilizes data collected by others.*

The most widely used statistics in social science are gathered by government agencies. The Bureau of the Census continuously updates information about the U.S. population, and offers much of interest to sociologists. Comparable data on Canada is available from Statistics Canada, a branch of that nation's government. Global investigations benefit from various publications of the United Nations and the World Bank. In short, a wide range of data about the whole world is as close as the college library.

Clearly, using available data—whether government statistics or the findings of individuals—saves researchers time and money. Therefore, this approach holds special appeal to sociologists with low budgets. Just as important, the quality of government data is generally better than what even well-funded researchers could hope to obtain on their own.

Still, secondary analysis has inherent problems. For one thing, available data may not exist in precisely the form one might wish; further, there are always questions about the meaning and accuracy of work done by others. For example, in his classic study of suicide, Emile Durkheim realized that he could not be sure that a death classified as an "accident" was not, in reality, a "suicide" and vice versa. And he also knew that various agencies use differing procedures and categories in collecting data, making comparisons difficult. In the end, then, using secondhand data is a little like shopping for a used car: Bargains are plentiful, but you have to shop carefully to avoid being stuck with a "lemon."

To illustrate, let's assume that reading about Lois Benjamin's account of African-American elites sparks our interest in this country's affluent minorities. How many such people are there? Where do they live? National Map 2–1 graphically displays Census Bureau data that address these questions. These statistics are the best available on the topic, and they are readily available at no cost. Yet to use them means accepting the Census Bureau's racial and ethnic categories as well as the accuracy of people's self-reported income on government questionnaires. Further, if you were to use this map for your own purposes, not only would these problems remain, but you would have to accept our definitions of "affluent" and "above average."

An Illustration: A Tale of Two Cities

Since we are all trapped in the present, secondary analysis provides a key to unlocking the secrets of the past. The award-winning study *Puritan Boston and Quaker Philadelphia*, carried out by E. Digby Baltzell (1979), exemplifies a researcher's power to analyze the past using data from historical sources.

It was a chance visit to Bowdoin College in Maine that prompted Baltzell to launch his investigation. Entering the college library, he was startled to see portraits of celebrated author Nathaniel Hawthorne, the eminent poet Henry Wadsworth Longfellow, and Franklin Pierce, our nation's fourteenth president. All three great men represented a single graduating class at Bowdoin (1825). How could it be, Baltzell mused, that this small college had graduated more famous individuals in a single year than his own, much bigger University of Pennsylvania had done in its entire history? To answer this question, Baltzell was soon poring over historical documents to see if New England had indeed produced more notable individuals than had Pennsylvania.

THE MAP: Generally speaking, African Americans, Asian Americans, and Latinos are concentrated in different regions of the country (look ahead to National Map 12–2). The largest urban regions (surrounding New York and Los Angeles) are home to affluent minorities of all kinds (although they often live in distinctive neighborhoods). In most cases, however, a single county contains a disproportionate share of affluent people of only one minority category. In general, at all income levels, people of various racial and ethnic categories live in different regions of the country as well as in different communities.

NOTE: According to 1990 census data, the most representative places in the United States are Tulsa, Oklahoma and Charleston, West Virginia.

Seeing Ourselves

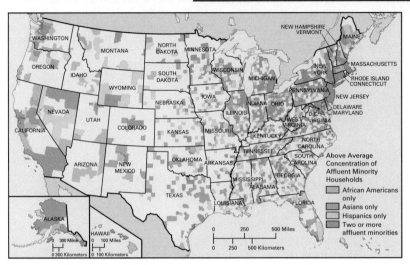

NATIONAL MAP 2–1

Affluent Minorities Across the United States

Based on 1990 census data, this map identifies the counties of the United States that contain an above-average share of affluent minority households—those earning at least $50,000 annually. (For the entire country, 13.2 percent of African Americans, 16.1 percent of Hispanics, and 35.0 percent of Asians fall into this favored category.) Where in the United States do affluent members of each minority category live? Do members of one category tend to live where members of another category predominate? Can you explain this pattern?

Adapted from *American Demographics* magazine, Dec. 1992, pp. 34–35. Reprinted with permission. © 1992, *American Demographics* magazine, Ithaca, New York. Data from the 1990 decennial census.

As his major source of data, Baltzell turned to the *Dictionary of American Biography*, twenty volumes profiling more than thirteen thousand men and women with records of greatness in fields ranging from politics to law and the arts. Baltzell understood that by relying on this source he could consider only those people deemed worthy by the *Dictionary's* editors. Knowing that some bias was inevitable, he proceeded with this line of research simply because there exists no better source of this kind.

The *Dictionary* told Baltzell *who* was great; but he also wanted some way to measure *how* great people were. He decided to base his ranking on the stated policy of the *Dictionary*: The editors claimed that, the more impressive the person's achievements, the longer the biography. So counting the number of lines in a biography yielded a crude "index of greatness." Such a strategy is certainly open to argument, of course, but could Baltzell have done better entirely on his own?

By the time Baltzell had identified the seventy-five individuals with the longest biographies, a striking pattern had emerged. Massachusetts had the most, with twenty-one of the seventy-five top achievers. The New England states, combined, claimed thirty-one of the entries. By contrast, Pennsylvania could boast of only two, and the entire Middle Atlantic region produced just twelve. Looking more closely, Baltzell discovered that most of New England's great achievers had grown up in and around the city of Boston. Again, in stark contrast, almost no people of comparable standing stood out in the history of his native Philadelphia (a city with many more people than Boston).

What could explain this remarkable disparity? Baltzell drew inspiration from the German sociologist Max Weber (1958; orig. 1904–5), who asserted that a region's record of achievement was largely a result of its predominant religious beliefs (see Chapter 4, "Society"). In the religious differences that set Boston apart from Philadelphia, Baltzell found the answer to his puzzle. Boston was a Puritan settlement, founded by people dedicated to the pursuit of public achievement; Philadelphia, by contrast, was settled by Quakers, who were equally determined to shun any sort of elitism or public display of achievement.

Both cities gave refuge to English people fleeing religious persecution. But, convinced of humanity's innate sinfulness, Boston Puritans built a rigid society in which family, church, and school regulated people's behavior. They celebrated hard work as a means to glorify God, and looked upon public prominence as a reassuring sign that one had received God's blessing.

Chapter 2 Sociological Investigation **51**

NOTE: Baltzell describes Boston and Philadelphia as two "social test tubes" into which immigration introduced two distinctive cultural orientations. The study is roughly modeled on Max Weber's analysis of Protestantism and capitalism (see Chapter 4).

NOTE: Interesting, although anecdotal, ways to describe the difference between the two cities: Puritan Boston named streets after great families, Quaker Philadelphia named streets after trees; a

Boston accent often leads people to overestimate someone, a Philadelphia accent lends little prestige to the speaker. Boston's leading university (Harvard) was founded within a decade of the city's settlement and is at the top of the Ivy League; the founders of Philadelphia did not establish their university (University of Pennsylvania) for 60 years, and it remains the least well-known Ivy.

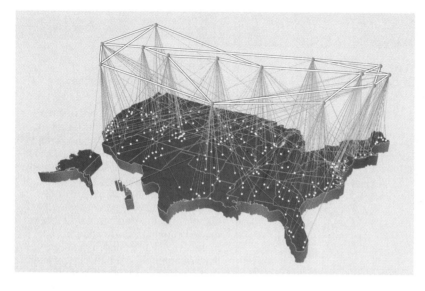

The Internet, an electronic superhighway that connects rapidly increasing numbers of people in the United States as well as around the world, will benefit researchers by improving our ability to communicate with one another and our access to sources of data.

In short, Puritanism fostered a hierarchical and disciplined life in which people vigorously sought and respected achievement.

Philadelphia's Quakers, by contrast, built their way of life on the notion that all human beings are inherently good. They saw little need for strong social institutions to "save" individuals from sinfulness. Although many Quakers became quite rich, their egalitarian way of life demanded that everyone look upon everyone else as a social equal. Even their most affluent members carefully maintained a modest appearance and discouraged one other from standing out by seeking fame or pursuing public office.

In Baltzell's sociological imagination, Boston and Philadelphia took the form of two social "test tubes": Puritanism was poured into one, Quakerism into the other. From our vantage point centuries later, we can see that different "chemical reactions" occurred in each case. Without claiming that one religion is in any sense "better" than the other, Baltzell convincingly argues that the two belief systems certainly set in motion different orientations toward personal achievement, which shaped the history of each region and may mold the accomplishments of people who live there even today. For example, the Kennedy family (despite being Catholic) still exemplifies the Puritan pursuit of fame and leadership. There has never been a family with such public stature in the entire history of Philadelphia.

As in all research, Baltzell's historical data do not *prove* his conclusions in any absolute sense. We can say, however, that the data he collected are consistent with his theory, that his analysis squares with the work of major thinkers like Max Weber, and that his conclusions make basic sense. But keep in mind that, especially when dealing with events far removed from the present, researchers make considerable use of their interpretive talents. Baltzell's research reminds us that, in the end, sociological investigation encompasses a complex weave of scientific skills, personal values, and a lively and practiced imagination.

Table 2–2 summarizes the four major methods of sociological investigation. We now turn to some final considerations: the impact of technology on research, and how to relate specific facts, culled through sociological investigation, to theory.

Technology and Research

In recent decades, new information technology has changed our lives considerably, and this applies to the practice of research as well. Personal computers—which came on the scene only about fifteen years ago—now give individual sociologists remarkable technical ability to randomly select samples, perform complex statistical analysis, and prepare written reports efficiently. Today's average office computer is far more powerful than even the massive mainframe devices that filled entire rooms on the campus a generation ago.

The development of the Internet (the so-called "electronic superhighway") is certain to further enhance our research capabilities in the years to come. First, the Internet now links some 50 million computers in

NOTE: We can perceive the historical influence of Puritanism in U.S. history by noting the expanding meaning of the word "Yankee." Referring to a *Bostonian* at the time of the Revolutionary War, the term designated a *Northerner* by the Civil War, and *any American* by the outbreak of World War I.

Q: "The world belongs to me because I understand it." Honoré de Balzac

DISCUSS: Inductive logical thought amounts to saying "If this is what happens, then what is true?" Deductive logical thought runs the other way: "If this is true, then this is what ought to happen."

GLOBAL: "The world is a book and those who study just their own society read only a page." Old saying

Q: "The most incomprehensible thing about the world is the fact that it is comprehensible." Albert Einstein

175 countries of the world, allowing for an unprecedented level of communication. Contemporary sociologists are capable of building networks across the country and around the globe, which will facilitate collaboration and prompt comparative research. Second, both faculty and students can readily access a rapidly increasing amount of statistical information on the Internet. The U.S. Census Bureau opened a series of Internet addresses in 1994, offering access to Census data and responding to individuals' research queries. Such developments—and other as-yet-unimagined forms of technological change—promise to transform sociological investigation as we enter the next century (Morton, 1995).

The Interplay of Theory and Method

There are, of course, some research tasks that remain unaffected by technological change. No matter how we gather data, sociologists must ultimately transform facts into meaning by building theory.

Actually, sociological investigators move back and forth between facts and theory. **Inductive logical thought** is *reasoning that transforms specific observations into general theory*. In this mode, a researcher's thinking runs from the specific to the general something

like this: "I have some interesting data here; what are the data saying about human behavior?"

E. Digby Baltzell's research illustrates the inductive logical model. His data showed that one region of the country (the Boston area) had produced many more high achievers than another (the Philadelphia region). He worked "upward" from these observations to make the assertion that religious values figured prominently in people's attitude toward achievement.

A second type of logical thought works "downward" in the opposite direction. **Deductive logical thought** is *reasoning that transforms general theory into specific hypotheses suitable for scientific testing*. This time, the researcher's thinking goes from the general to the specific: "I have this hunch about human behavior; let's put it in a form we can test, collect some data, and see if it is correct." Working deductively, the researcher first states the theory in the form of a hypothesis and then selects a method by which to test it. To the extent that the data support the hypothesis, we conclude that the theory is correct; data that refute the hypothesis alert the researcher that the theory should be revised or perhaps rejected entirely.

Philip Zimbardo's Stanford County Prison experiment illustrates how this model operates. Zimbardo

TABLE 2–2 Four Research Methods: A Summary

Method	Application	Advantages	Limitations
Experiment	For explanatory research that specifies relationships among variables; generates quantitative data	Provides greatest ability to specify cause-and-effect relationships; replication of research is relatively easy	Laboratory settings have artificial quality; unless research environment is carefully controlled, results may be biased
Survey	For gathering information about issues that cannot be directly observed, such as attitudes and values; useful for descriptive and explanatory research; generates quantitative or qualitative data	Sampling allows surveys of large populations using questionnaires; interviews provide in-depth responses	Questionnaires must be carefully prepared and may produce a low return rate; interviews are expensive and time consuming
Participant observation	For exploratory and descriptive study of people in a "natural" setting; generates qualitative data	Allows study of "natural" behavior; usually inexpensive	Time consuming; replication of research is difficult; researcher must balance roles of participant and observer
Secondary analysis	For exploratory, descriptive, or explanatory research whenever suitable data are available	Saves time and expense of data collection; makes historical research possible	Researcher has no control over possible bias in data; data may not be suitable for current research needs

NOTE: Sherlock Holmes, celebrated for his great powers of deduction, actually engaged in *inductive reasoning*. While investigating a particular crime scene, for example, Holmes spoke with the woman of the house when he suddenly noticed the housekeeper searching for the cord to close the drapes. "Why did you dismiss your previous servant?" he asked. "How did you know!?" came her startled reply.

"Elementary," he explained, "your present servant is obviously new to her duties."

Q: "Truth must have one face, the same and universal." Michel de Montaigne

Q: "The truth is rarely pure and never simple." Oscar Wilde

Q: "Round numbers are always false." Samuel Johnson

Controversy & Debate   *Can People Lie With Statistics?*

Is scientific research always as objective and "factual" as we think? Not according to the great English politician Benjamin Disraeli, who once noted wryly, "There are three kinds of lies: lies, damned lies, and statistics!" In a world that bombards us with numbers—often in the form of "scientific facts" and "official figures"—it is well worth pausing to consider that "statistical evidence" is not synonymous with truth. For one thing, as this chapter has explained, every method of data collection is prone to error; for another, because data do not speak for themselves, someone has to interpret them to figure out what they mean. And, sometimes, people (even social scientists) "dress up" their data almost the way politicians whip up a campaign speech—with an eye more to winning you over than getting at the truth.

The best way to ferret out statistical manipulation is to understand how these tricks are performed. Here are three ways people can lie with statistics.

1. **People choose their data.** Many times, the data we confront are not wrong, they just do not tell the whole story. Let's say

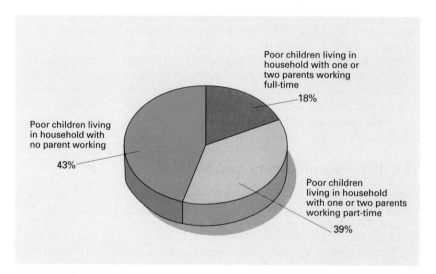

Poor children living in household with one or two parents working full-time — 18%

Poor children living in household with no parent working — 43%

Poor children living in household with one or two parents working part-time — 39%

someone claims that television is ruining our way of life and, as evidence, offers statistics indicating that we watch more TV today than a generation ago and that College Board scores have fallen during that time. Such data are actually correct; however, they are *selectively chosen*. Another person could just as correctly counter that U.S. residents spend much more on books today than we did a generation ago, suggesting that there is no cultural crisis at all. In short, plenty of statistics

are available for people on all sides of a political debate to use as ammunition to bolster their arguments.

2. **People interpret their data.** Another way people manipulate statistics is to "package" them inside a ready-made interpretation, as if to say "Here are the numbers, and this is what they mean." One recent publication, for example, presented the results of a study of U.S. children living in poverty in 1992 (National Center for Children in Poverty, cited in

began with the general idea that prisons alter human behavior. He then fashioned a specific, testable hypothesis: Placed in a prison setting, even emotionally well-balanced young men would exhibit violent behavior. Violence erupted soon after his experiment began, supporting this hypothesis. Had his experiment produced amicable behavior between "prisoners" and "guards," his original theory would clearly have required reformulation.

Just as researchers commonly employ several methods over the course of one study, they

typically make use of *both* types of logical thought. Figure 2–2 on page 56 illustrates the two phases of scientific thinking: inductively building theory from observations and deductively making observations to test our theory.

Finally, it is worth noting that statistics, too, play a key part in the process of turning facts into meaning. Commonly, sociological researchers provide quantitative data as part of their research results. And precisely how they present their numbers affects the conclusions their readers draw. In other words, data

Q: "At least in science, we show the greatest respect for an author by leaving him behind." Peter Berger

NOTE: The motivational paradox of research fraud is that the gains of dishonesty are significant only in situations in which the odds of detection are high.

Q: "As soon as those who are considered promoters of science become persuaded of their infallibility, they naturally proclaim as indubitable things that are not only unnecessary but often absurd, and having proclaimed them they cannot repudiate them." Leo Tolstoy

Population Today, 1995). As the figure shows, the researchers reported that 43 percent of these children lived in a household with no working parent, 39 percent lived in a household with one or two parents employed part-time, and 18 percent lived in a household with one or two parents working full-time. The researchers labeled this figure "Majority of Children in Poverty Live with Parents Who Work." Does this title accurately portray the data or mislead the reader?

3. **People use graphs to "spin" the "truth."** Especially in newspapers and other popular media, we often encounter graphic representations of statistical data. While graphs make comprehending data easy (showing, for example, an upward or downward trend), they also provide the designer with the opportunity to "spin" data in various ways. Where trends are concerned, one common technique for casting data in a particular light involves compressing or expanding the graph's time frame. A graph of the crime rate over only the last several years, for example, would reveal a downward trend; shifting the time frame to include the last few decades, however, would show a sharp increase.

A second manipulation technique occurs when the designer chooses a graph's scale specifically to "inflate" or "deflate" a trend. An illustration of this is shown below. Both graphs present identical data for College Board SAT scores between 1967 and 1993. But the left-hand graph stretches the scale to make a downward trend more pronounced; the right-hand graph compresses the scale to minimize any change over time. So, understanding what statistics *really* mean depends on being a careful reader!

Continue the debate . . .

1. *Why do you think people are so quick to accept "statistics" as true?*

2. *Would Max Weber's "value-free" approach to research forbid "dressing up" one's data? What about a Marxist approach?*

3. *Can you cite a piece of research that you think presented biased data or conclusions? Specify the biases.*

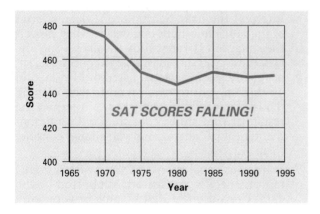

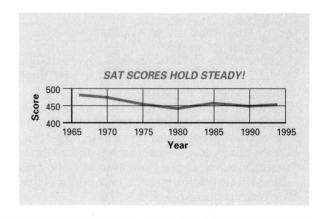

presentation always provides the opportunity to "spin" reality in one way or another.

Often, we conclude that an argument must be true simply because there are statistics to back it up. However, readers must use a cautious eye when encountering statistical data. After all, researchers choose what data to present, they offer interpretations of the statistics, and they may use tables or graphs to encourage others to reach particular conclusions. The final box, above, takes a closer look at these important issues.

PUTTING IT ALL TOGETHER: TEN STEPS IN SOCIOLOGICAL INVESTIGATION

Drawing together the elements of sociological investigation presented in this chapter, a typical project in sociology will include each of the following ten steps.

1. **Define the topic of investigation.** Being curious and looking at the world sociologically can

Q: James D. Wright (1989) asserts that good science makes for bad politics, and vice versa.

Q: "Theories and concepts emerge in sociology like popcorn, puffed up by their own steam." Joseph Gusfield, explaining why no "social scientific Newton" is likely to emerge from sociology

Q: "The direction of our scientific exertions . . . is conditioned by the society in which we live, and most directly by the political climate. . . . [S]tudents turn to research on issues that have obtained political importance." Gunnar Myrdal

Q: "Truth is what serves the German people." Joseph Goebbels, (who had a Ph.D.)

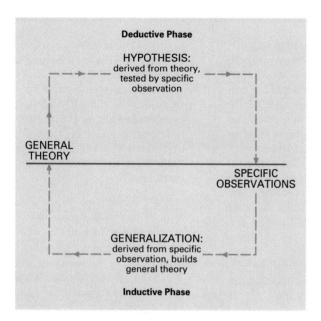

FIGURE 2–2 Deductive and Inductive Logical Thought

generate ideas for social research anywhere. The issue you choose to study is likely to have some personal significance.

2. **Find out what others have learned about the topic.** You are probably not the first person to develop an interest in a particular issue. Spend time in the library to see what theories and methods researchers have applied to your topic in the past. In reviewing existing research, note problems that may have come up before.

3. **Assess the requirements for carrying out the research.** How much time and money will the research require? What special equipment or skills are necessary? Can you do the work yourself? What sources of funding are available to support the research? You should answer all these questions before beginning to design the research project.

4. **Specify the research questions.** Are you seeking to explore an unfamiliar social setting? To describe some category of people? Or to investigate cause and effect among variables? If your study is exploratory, identify general questions that will guide the work. If it is descriptive, specify the population and the variables of interest. If it is explanatory, state the hypothesis to be tested and carefully operationalize each variable.

5. **Consider ethical issues.** Not all research raises serious ethical issues, but you should be sensitive to this matter throughout your investigation. Could the research harm anyone? How might you design the study to minimize the chances for injury? Do you plan to promise anonymity to the subjects? If so, how will you ensure that anonymity will be maintained?

6. **Devise a research strategy.** Consider all major research strategies—as well as innovative combinations of approaches. Keep in mind that the appropriate method depends on the kind of questions you are asking as well as the resources available to support your research.

7. **Gather the data.** The way you collect data depends on the research method you choose. Be sure to record accurately all information in a way that will make sense later (it may be some time before you actually write up the results of your work). Remain vigilant for any bias that may creep into the research.

8. **Interpret the data.** Scrutinize the data in terms of the initial questions and decide what answers they suggest. If your study involves a specific hypothesis, you should be able to confirm, reject, or modify the hypothesis based on the data. In writing up your research report, keep in mind that there may be several ways to interpret the results of your study, consistent with different theoretical paradigms, and you should consider them all.

9. **State your conclusions.** As you write your final report, specify conclusions supported by the data. Consider the significance of your work both to sociological theory and to improving research methods. Of what value is your research to people outside of sociology? Finally, evaluate your own work, noting problems that arose and questions left unanswered. Note ways in which your own biases may have colored your conclusions.

10. **Share your results.** Consider submitting your research paper to a campus newspaper or magazine or making a presentation to a class, campus gathering, or perhaps a meeting of professional sociologists. The important point is to share what you have learned with others and to let others respond to your work.

NOTE: The Utilitarians embraced scientific truth to the exclusion of virtually any other form of knowing; recall Dickens's spoof of this with "Just the facts!" in his novel *Hard Times*.

Q: "Social science is *part* of the social world as well as a *conception* of it. . . . Utilitarian culture . . . fostered acute sentiments of detachment. Positivism transformed this detachment into an ideology and morality." Alvin Gouldner

Q: "Instructors who feel called upon to intervene in the struggles of world views and party opinions . . . may do so outside, in the market place, in the press, in meetings . . . But after all it is somewhat too convenient to demonstrate one's courage in taking a stand where the audience and possible opponents are condemned to silence." Max Weber, "Science as a Vocation"

SUMMARY

1. Science provides the logical foundation of sociological research and, more broadly, helps us to evaluate critically information we encounter every day.

2. Two basic requirements for sociological investigation are (1) viewing the world from a sociological perspective and (2) being curious and asking questions about society.

3. Measurement is the process of determining the value of a variable in any specific case. Sound measurement is both reliable and valid.

4. A goal of science is discovering how variables are related. Correlation means that two or more variables change value together. Knowledge about cause-and-effect relationships is more powerful, however, because a researcher can use an independent variable to predict change in a dependent variable.

5. Although investigators select topics according to their personal interests, the scientific ideal of objectivity demands that they try to suspend personal values and biases as they conduct research.

6. Human curiosity and imagination must infuse the scientific method; moreover, researchers must always bring their data to life through interpretation.

7. Investigators should avoid examining issues from the point of view of only one sex or basing generalizations about humanity on data collected from only men or women.

8. Rejecting conventional ideas about scientific objectivity, some sociologists argue that research inevitably involves political values; with this in mind, research should be directed toward promoting desirable social change.

9. Because sociological research has the potential to cause discomfort and harm to subjects, sociological investigators are bound by ethical guidelines.

10. Experiments, which are performed under controlled conditions, attempt to specify causal relationships between two (or more) variables.

11. Surveys, which gather people's responses to statements or questions, may employ questionnaires or interviews.

12. Through participant observation, a form of field research, sociologists directly observe a social setting while participating in it for an extended period of time.

13. Secondary analysis, or making use of available data, is often preferable to collecting one's own data; it is also essential in the study of historical questions.

14. Theory and research are linked through two kinds of thinking. Deductive thought transforms general ideas into specific hypotheses suitable for testing. Inductive thought organizes specific observations into general ideas.

KEY CONCEPTS

cause and effect a relationship in which change in one variable (the independent variable) causes change in another (the dependent variable)

concept a mental construct that represents some part of the world, inevitably in a simplified form

control holding constant all relevant variables except one in order to observe its effect

correlation a relationship by which two (or more) variables change together

deductive logical thought reasoning that transforms general ideas into specific hypotheses suitable for scientific testing

dependent variable a variable that is changed by another (independent) variable

empirical evidence information we can verify with our senses

experiment a research method for investigating cause and effect under highly controlled conditions

gender the significance members of a society attach to being female or male

Hawthorne effect a change in a subject's behavior caused simply by the awareness of being studied

hypothesis an unverified statement of a relationship between variables

independent variable a variable that causes change in another (dependent) variable

inductive logical thought reasoning that transforms specific observations into general theory

interview a series of questions a researcher administers personally to respondents

mean the arithmetic average of a series of numbers

measurement the process of determining the value of a variable in a specific case

median the value that occurs midway in a series of numbers arranged in order of magnitude or, simply, the middle case

mode the value that occurs most often in a series of numbers

objectivity a state of personal neutrality in conducting research

operationalizing a variable specifying exactly what one intends to measure in assigning a value to a variable

participant observation a research method in which researchers systematically observe people while joining in their routine activities

population the people who are the focus of research

qualitative research investigation by which a researcher gathers impressionistic, not numerical, data

quantitative research investigation by which a researcher collects numerical data

questionnaire a series of written questions a researcher supplies to subjects requesting their responses

reliability the quality of consistent measurement

replication repetition of research by others

research method a systematic plan for conducting research

sample a part of a population researchers select to represent the whole

science a logical system that bases knowledge on direct, systematic observation

secondary analysis a research method in which a researcher utilizes data collected by others

spurious correlation an apparent, although false, relationship between two (or more) variables caused by some other variable

survey a research method in which subjects respond to a series of items in a questionnaire or an interview

validity the quality of measuring precisely what one intends to measure

variable a concept whose value changes from case to case

CRITICAL-THINKING QUESTIONS

1. What does it mean to state that there are various kinds of truth? What is the basic rationale for relying on science as a way of knowing?

2. What sorts of measures do scientists adopt as they strive for objectivity? Why do some sociologists consider objectivity an undesirable goal?

3. Identify several ways in which sociological research is similar to—and different from—research in the natural sciences.

4. What considerations lead a sociologist to select one method of research over another?

SUGGESTED READINGS

Classic Sources

Alvin Gouldner. *The Coming Crisis in Western Sociology*. New York: Avon Books, 1970.

In this volume, Alvin Gouldner provided one of the earliest and best efforts to evaluate the place of values and politics in sociological research.

W. E. B. Du Bois. *The Philadelphia Negro: A Social Study*. New York: Schocken, 1967 (orig. 1899).

Among the very first sociological studies of race in the United States, this milestone work also offers rich insights into the research process.

Contemporary Sources

David J. Miller and Michael Hersen, eds. *Research Fraud in Behavioral and Biomedical Sciences*. New York: Wiley, 1992.

The essays in this collection examine a number of noted cases of research fraud in various disciplines.

Dorothy Ross. *The Origins of American Social Science*. New York: Cambridge University Press, 1991.

This book reviews the development of sociology, political science, economics, and history in the United States, highlighting how they differ from the natural sciences.

Harriet Zuckerman, Jonathan R. Cole, and John T. Bruer, eds. *The Outer Circle: Women in the Scientific Community*. New York: Norton, 1991.

Despite the widespread notion that sex discrimination in the scientific community has all but disappeared, the articles in this edited volume tell a different story.

Global Sources

Gerardo Marín and Barbara VanOss Marín. *Research with Hispanic Populations*. Newbury Park, Calif.: Sage, 1991.

This book explores the meaning of Hispanic ethnicity and its implications for sociological research.

Melvin L. Kohn. *Cross-National Research in Sociology*. Newbury Park, Calif.: Sage, 1989.

Global research offers valuable insights into other societies as well as our own way of life. This provocative paperback includes seventeen essays on global research.

BETTY LADUKE,
MEMORIES OF THE BITTER PAST, 1997

Culture

"I thought they were joking," Barry Lewen, shaking his head in disbelief. Lewen was recalling an unexpected event that capped six months of tough negotiations with a group of Taiwanese investors. On the verge of signing what any broker would regard as a dream deal—the sale of a $14 million building on New York's Madison Avenue—suddenly all bets were off. Although the investors were satisfied with the financial terms of the sale, they soberly informed Lewen of "one final concern." Before any sale would go through, they explained, they would have to enlist the services of a master of *feng shui* (pronounced "fung shway," Chinese words that mean "wind and water"). After flying to New York from Taiwan, this practitioner of the ancient Chinese art would inspect the building; only if he declared the structure to be acceptable would the sale be completed.

Several days later, a jet carrying the *feng shui* master landed at a New York airport and a car whisked him directly to the Madison Avenue building. A small crowd of anxious onlookers had assembled and they watched intently as he surveyed the setting, took account of the surrounding buildings, and, for thirty tense minutes, walked through the structure noting the shape and length of hallways, the location of doorways and elevators, and the presence of mirrors, fountains, and even air conditioners. "I can tell you there were a lot of sweaty palms," recounts Barry Lewen. In the end, the master turned to the apprehensive audience, smiled, and formally approved the building. A wave of relief broke over the group. ·

To our way of thinking, the merit of a building is a matter of its location, size, and the state of its plumbing and other systems. Such concerns are also of great importance to the Chinese. But, historically, members of eastern Asian societies have also considered how physical space affects human feelings and emotions. From this point of view, a "life force" or *qi* (pronounced "chee") flows through all of nature—including buildings—so that the physical design of a home or office building will either help or hinder this flow. A "good" building, that is, one that stands in harmony with nature, will enhance the luck, health, and prosperity of the people living or working inside (Dunn, 1994).

The 5.7 billion people on the earth today are members of a single biological species: *Homo sapiens.* Even so, the differences among people the world over can delight, puzzle, disturb, and sometimes even overwhelm us. Some differences in lifestyles are simply arbitrary matters of convention—the Chinese, for example, wear white at funerals while people in the United States prefer black. Similarly, Chinese people associate the number four with bad luck, in much the same way that people in the United States think of the number thirteen. Or, take the practice of kissing: Most people in the United States kiss in public, most Chinese kiss only in private; the French kiss publicly twice (once on each cheek), while Belgians kiss three times (starting on either cheek); for their part, most Nigerians don't kiss at all. At weddings, moreover, U.S. couples kiss, Koreans bow, and a Cambodian groom touches his nose to the bride's cheek.

Like so many elements of our lives, notions about kissing vary from place to place. People in the United States kiss in public; the Chinese do so only in private; moreover, while we touch lips, the French kiss on each cheek, and New Zealand's Maoris, shown above, rub noses.

Other cultural differences, however, are more profound. The world over, people wear much or little clothing, have many or few children, venerate or shunt aside the elderly, are peaceful or warlike, embrace different religious beliefs, and enjoy different kinds of art and music. In short, although we are all the same creatures biologically, the human beings on this planet have developed strikingly different ideas about what is pleasant and repulsive, polite and rude, beautiful and ugly, right and wrong. This capacity for startling difference is a wonder of our species: the expression of human culture.

WHAT IS CULTURE?

Sociologists define **culture** as *the values, beliefs, behavior, and material objects that constitute a people's way of life.* Culture includes what we think, how we act, and what we own. But as our social heritage, culture is also a bridge to the past as well as a guide to the future (Soyinka, 1991).

To begin to understand all that culture entails, it is helpful to distinguish between thoughts and things. What sociologists call **nonmaterial culture** is *the intangible world of ideas created by members of a society* that span a wide range from altruism to zen. **Material culture**, on the other hand, constitutes *the tangible things*

created by members of a society; here, again, the range is vast, running from armaments to zippers.

Not only does culture shape what we do, it also helps form our personalities—what we commonly (yet inaccurately) describe as "human nature." The warlike Yąnomamö of the Brazilian rain forest look on aggression as natural in their children, just as, halfway around the world, the Semai of Malaysia expect their young to be peaceful and cooperative. The cultures of the United States and China both stress achievement and hard work; but members of our society value individualism more than do the Chinese, who place a stronger emphasis on tradition and group living.

Given the extent of cultural differences in the world and the tendency of all of us to view our own way of life as "natural," it is no wonder that travelers commonly experience **culture shock**, *personal disorientation that comes from encountering an unfamiliar way of life.* The box on page 64 presents one researcher's personal experience of cultural shock.

December 1, 1994, Istanbul, Turkey. Harbors everywhere, it seems, have two things in common: ships and cats. Istanbul, the tenth port of our voyage, is awash with felines, prowling about in search of the easy meal. People certainly change from place to place; cats, by contrast, do not.

No cultural trait is inherently "natural" to humanity, even though most people around the world view their own way of life that way. What is natural to our species is the capacity to create culture in our collective lives. Every other form of life—from ants to zebras—behaves in uniform, species-specific ways. To a world traveler, the enormous diversity of human life stands out in contrast to the behavior of cats and other creatures, which is the same everywhere. Most living creatures are guided by *instincts*, biological programming over which animals have no control. A few animals—notably chimpanzees and related primates—have the capacity for limited culture, as researchers have noted by observing them use tools and teach simple skills to their offspring. But the creative power of humans far exceeds that of any other form of life; in short, *only humans rely on culture rather than instinct to ensure the survival of their kind* (Harris, 1987).

To understand how this came to be, we must briefly review the history of our species on earth.

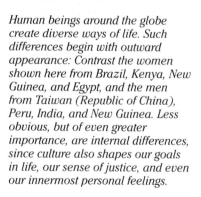

Human beings around the globe create diverse ways of life. Such differences begin with outward appearance: Contrast the women shown here from Brazil, Kenya, New Guinea, and Egypt, and the men from Taiwan (Republic of China), Peru, India, and New Guinea. Less obvious, but of even greater importance, are internal differences, since culture also shapes our goals in life, our sense of justice, and even our innermost personal feelings.

GLOBAL SOCIOLOGY

Culture Shock: Confronting the Yąnomamö

A small aluminum motorboat chugged steadily along the muddy Orinoco River, deep within South America's vast tropical rain forest. Anthropologist Napoleon Chagnon was nearing the end of a three-day journey to the home territory of the Yąnomamö, one of the most technologically primitive societies on earth.

Some twelve thousand Yąnomamö live in villages scattered along the border of Venezuela and Brazil. Their way of life could hardly be more different from our own. The Yąnomamö wear little clothing and live without electricity, automobiles, or other conveniences most people in the United States take for granted. Their traditional weapons, used for hunting and warfare, are the bow and arrow. The Yąnomamö have had few encounters with the outside world. Thus Chagnon would be as strange to them as they would be to him.

By 2:00 in the afternoon, Chagnon had almost reached his destination. The hot sun made the humid air almost unbearable. The anthropologist's clothes were soaked with perspiration, and his face and hands swelled from the bites of innumerable gnats swarming around him. But he scarcely noticed, because of his

anticipation that in just a few moments he would be face to face with people unlike any he had ever known.

Chagnon's heart pounded as the boat slid onto the riverbank near a Yąnomamö village. Sounds of activity came from nearby. Chagnon and his guide climbed from the boat and walked toward the village, stooping as they pushed their way through the dense undergrowth. Chagnon describes what happened next.

I looked up and gasped when I saw a dozen burly, naked, sweaty, hideous men staring at us down the shafts of their drawn arrows! Immense wads of green tobacco were stuck between their lower teeth and lips making them look even more hideous, and strands of

dark green slime dripped or hung from their nostrils—strands so long that they clung to their [chests] or drizzled down their chins.

My next discovery was that there were a dozen or so vicious, underfed dogs snapping at my legs, circling me as if I were to be their next meal. I just stood there holding my notebook, helpless and pathetic. Then the stench of the decaying vegetation and filth hit me and I almost got sick. I was horrified. What kind of welcome was this for the person who came here to live with you and learn your way of life, to become friends with you? (1992:11–12)

Fortunately for Chagnon, the Yąnomamö villagers recognized his guide and lowered their weapons. Reassured that he would survive at least the afternoon, Chagnon was still shaken by his inability to make any sense of the people surrounding him. And this was to be his home for a year and a half! He wondered why he had forsaken physics to study human culture in the first place.

Source: Chagnon (1992).

Culture and Human Intelligence

In a universe some 15 billion years old, our planet is a much younger 4.5 billion years of age (see the time lines inside the front cover of the text). Not for a billion years after the earth was formed did any life at all appear on our planet. Several billion more years went by before dinosaurs ruled the earth and then disappeared. And

then, some 65 million years ago, our history took a crucial turn with the appearance of the creatures we call primates.

What sets primates apart is their intelligence, based on the largest brains (relative to body size) of all living creatures. As primates evolved, the human line diverged from that of our closest relatives, the great apes, about 12 million years ago. But our common lineage shows

NOTE: The early human ancestor Lucy, who lived about 3 million years ago, stood about 3 feet 6 inches tall and weighed 65 pounds; at that time, men might have reached 5 feet and 100 pounds. Sex differences have grown smaller with time: Today's global averages are 5 feet 6 inches tall for men, 5 feet 2 inches for women, 150 pounds for men, 125 for women.

Q: "Man has no nature; what he has is history . . ." José Ortega y Gasset

Q: "There can obviously be no culture without a society [and] no cultureless human society is known; it would even be hard to imagine. But it does not hold on the subhuman level . . . ants and bees do have genuine societies without culture . . ." A. L. Kroeber

Of all forms of life, only human beings inhabit a world of symbols. Every nation on earth represents itself with a flag—and expects people to show proper respect for it. In his painting Three Flags, *contemporary U.S. artist Jasper Johns conveys the power of symbols.*

Jasper Johns b. 1930. *Three Flags* 1958, Encaustic on canvas, 30-7/8 x 45-1/2 x 5" (78.4 x 115.6 x 12.7cm.) 50th Anniv. Gift Gilman Fnd, Inc., The Lauder Fnd, A. Alfred Taubman, anym. donor, pur. Col. of Whitney Museum of American Art NY. Lic by VAGA. Photo: Geoffrey Clements, NY.

through in the traits humans share with today's chimpanzees, gorillas, and orangutans: great sociability, affectionate and long-lasting bonds for child rearing and mutual protection, the ability to walk upright (normal in humans, less common among other primates), and hands that manipulate objects with great precision.

Studying fossil records, scientists conclude that, about 2 million years ago, our distant ancestors grasped cultural fundamentals such as the use of fire, tools, and weapons, created simple shelters, and fashioned basic clothing. Although these Stone Age achievements may seem modest, they mark the point at which our ancestors embarked on a distinct evolutionary course, making culture the primary strategy for human survival.

To comprehend that human beings are wide-eyed infants in the larger scheme of things, Carl Sagan (1977) came up with the idea of superimposing the 15-billion-year history of our universe on a single calendar year. The life-giving atmosphere of the earth did not develop until the autumn, and the earliest beings who resembled humans did not appear until December 31—the last day of the year—at 10:30 at night! Yet not until 250,000 years ago, which is mere minutes before the end of Sagan's "year," did our own species finally emerge. These *Homo sapiens* (derived from Latin meaning "thinking person") have continued to evolve so that, about 40,000 years ago, humans who looked more or less like we do roamed the earth. With larger brains, these "modern" *Homo sapiens* produced culture at a rapid pace, as the wide range of tools and cave art from this period suggests.

Still, what we call "civilization," based on permanent settlements and specialized occupations, began in the Middle East (in what is today Iraq and Egypt) only about 12,000 years ago (Hamblin, 1973; Wenke, 1980). In terms of Sagan's "year," this cultural flowering occurred during the final *seconds* before midnight on New Year's Eve. And what of our modern, industrial way of life? Begun only 300 years ago, it amounts to a mere millisecond flash in Sagan's scheme.

Human culture, then, is very recent and was a long time in the making. As culture became a strategy for survival, our ancestors descended from the trees into the tall grasses of central Africa. There, walking upright, they discovered the advantages of hunting in groups. From this point on, the human brain grew larger allowing for greater human capacity to create a way of life—as opposed to simply acting out biological imperatives. Gradually, culture pushed aside the biological forces we call instincts so that humans gained the mental power *to fashion the natural environment for ourselves.* Ever since, people have made and remade their worlds in countless ways, which explains today's extraordinary cultural diversity.

Culture, Nation, and Society

At this point, we might well pause to clarify several similar terms—"culture," "nation," and "society." *Culture* refers to a shared way of life. A *nation* is a political entity, that is, a territory within designated borders such as the United States, Canada, Argentina,

GLOBAL SOCIOLOGY

Travelers Beware! The Meaning of Gestures in Other Societies

A young man from Wisconsin is enjoying a summer trip in the African nation of Nigeria. He stands by the side of a country road, trying to "thumb a ride" to the next town. A dusty cloud on the horizon soon turns into a truck carrying half a dozen local people. They look him over and come to a screeching halt. But they are not about to offer a ride to our hapless visitor; instead, they pile out of the truck, angrily denounce him, rough him up, and leave him sitting dazed and confused on the ground.

What has happened here? Are Nigerians hostile to foreigners? Not at all. But like people everywhere, they don't take kindly to insults. What the young man from the United States meant as a request for a ride, Nigerians see as a crude and offensive gesture.

Since much human communication involves not words but gestures and body language—especially when we encounter people whose language differs from our own—we need to be mindful that the innocent use of even a simple hand movement may provoke an angry response. Here are six bodily gestures that seem innocent enough to members of our society but that may evoke a stern response from people elsewhere.

Figures (a) and (b) each would offend members of Islamic societies.

(a)

(b)

(c)

or Zimbabwe. *Society*, the topic of the next chapter, is the organized interaction of people in a nation or within some other boundary.

We correctly describe the United States, then, as both a nation and as a society. But many societies—including the United States—are *multicultural*, meaning that they encompass various ways of life that blend (and sometimes clash) in our everyday lives.

In the world as a whole, how many cultures are there? The number of cultures comprising the human record is a matter of speculation. Experts have documented the existence of five to six thousand human languages, suggesting that at least this many cultures

have existed on the earth (Durning, 1993). High-technology communication, rising international migration, and the expanding global economy have combined to lessen the cultural diversity of the contemporary world. Even so, at least one thousand distinct cultures continue to flourish, and hundreds of them thrive in the United States.

The tally of world nations has risen and fallen throughout history as a result of political events. The dissolution of the former Soviet Union and the former Yugoslavia, for example, added nineteen nations to the count. In 1995, there were 191 politically independent nations in the world.

RESOURCE: Leslie White's article "Symbol: The Basic Element of Culture" and Robert Merton's "Manifest and Latent Functions" are two classics on culture found in the Macionis and Benokraitis reader, *Seeing Ourselves*.
GLOBAL: For a deeper look at comparative research on human expressiveness, check out the box "Emotions in Global Perspective" in Chapter 6 ("Social Interaction in Everyday Life").

GLOBAL: Other examples of potential cultural conflict: Because Muslims consider the bottom of the foot to be unclean, they require people to remove shoes before entering a mosque. In Japan, counting change is an insult because it implies distrust.
GLOBAL: Travel implies a commitment to learn; its root is the same as "travail" or work. Touring implies a passive observation of the unfamiliar; literally, this word means simply going in a circle.

Since Muslims typically perform bathroom hygiene with the left hand, they recoil at the sight of a person eating with that hand, illustrated in Figure (a). Islam also holds that the sole of a shoe is unclean; therefore, any display of the bottom of the foot, as in Figure (b), conveys insult. Figure (c) displays the common "A-OK" gesture by which people in North America express approval and pleasure. In France, however, this symbol imparts the snub "You're worth zero," while Germans take this gesture as a crude word for "rectum." Figure (d) shows the simple curling of a finger, meaning "come here." Malaysians attach the same meaning to this gesture as we do, but they use it exclusively for calling animals; thus, they take no pleasure in being beckoned in this way. Figure (e) shows the familiar "thumbs up" gesture widely employed in North America to mean "Good job!" or "All right!" In Nigeria (as the hapless hitchhiker learned), and also in Australia, flashing this gesture (especially with a slight upward motion) transmits the insulting message "Up yours!" Finally, Figure (f) shows a gesture that members of our society read as "Stop!" or "No, thanks." But display this gesture to a motorist or street vendor anywhere in western Africa and you will probably have a fight on your hands. There it means "You have five fathers" or, more simply, "You bastard!"

Sources: Examples are drawn from Ekman et al. (1984) and Axtell (1991).

(d)

(e)

(f)

THE COMPONENTS OF CULTURE

Although the cultures found in all the world's nations differ in many ways, they all are built on five major components: symbols, language, values, norms, and material objects. We shall consider each in turn.

Symbols

Human beings not only sense the surrounding world as other creatures do, we build a reality of *meaning*. In doing so, humans transform elements of the world into **symbols**, *anything that carries a particular meaning recognized by people who share culture*. A whistle, a wall of graffiti, a flashing red light, and a fist raised in the air all serve as symbols. We can see the human capacity to create and manipulate symbols reflected in the very different meanings associated with the simple act of winking the eye. In some settings this action conveys interest; in others, understanding; in still others, insult.

We are so dependent on our culture's symbols that we take them for granted. Occasionally, however, we become keenly aware of a symbol when someone uses it in an unconventional way, as when a person in a political demonstration burns a U.S. flag. Entering an unfamiliar society also reminds us of the power of symbols; culture shock is nothing more than the inability

DISCUSS: The concept of "collective memory" can be introduced here. It refers to significant events that become part of a people's cultural heritage. Paul Revere's ride, Washington crossing the Delaware, M. L. King's "I have a dream" speech, and, more recently, the Rodney King beating and the O. J. Simpson trial have all become part of our "collective memory."

GLOBAL: Sometimes students take linguistic pluralism as a mark of underdevelopment. That is, we assume that industrial societies of the world have one or two dominant languages, while less-developed regions have many "tribal" tongues. This notion does not hold up well to scrutiny, however. Compare Europe and South Asia: Each is about 3 million square miles and contains just over 30 nations, and in each region the population speaks almost 30 different languages.

to "read" meaning in one's surroundings. We feel lost and isolated, unsure of how to act, and sometimes frightened—a consequence of being outside the symbolic web of culture that joins individuals in meaningful social life.

Culture shock is a two-way process. On the one hand it is something the traveler *experiences* when encountering people whose way of life is unfamiliar. On the other hand, it is also what the traveler *inflicts* on others by acting in ways that may well offend them. For example, because North Americans consider dogs to be beloved household pets, travelers to northern regions of the People's Republic of China might well be appalled to find people roasting dogs as a wintertime meal. On the other hand, a North American who orders a hamburger in an Indian restaurant causes offense to Hindus who hold cows to be sacred and thus unfit for human consumption.

Indeed, global travel provides almost endless opportunities for misunderstanding. When in an unfamiliar setting, we need to remember that even behavior that seems innocent and quite normal to us may spark offense among others, whose symbolic system differs from our own. The box on pages 66–67 takes a closer look at this phenomenon.

Then, too, symbolic meanings vary even within a single society. A fur coat, prized by one person as a luxurious symbol of success, may represent to another the inhumane treatment of animals. Similarly, a Confederate flag, which to one individual embodies regional pride, may symbolize racial oppression to someone else.

Cultural symbols also change over time. Blue jeans were created more than a century ago as sturdy and inexpensive clothing for people engaged in physical labor. In the liberal political climate of the 1960s, this working-class aura made jeans popular among affluent students—many of whom wore them simply to look "different" or perhaps to identify with working people. A decade later, "designer jeans" emerged as high-priced "status symbols" that conveyed quite a different message. In recent years, everyday jeans remain as popular as ever; most people choose them simply as comfortable apparel.

In sum, symbols allow people to make sense of their lives, and without them human existence would be meaningless. Manipulating symbols correctly allows us to engage others readily within our own cultural system. In a world of cultural diversity, however, the misuse of symbols may give rise to embarrassment, and loyally supporting one cultural symbol while opposing another can even generate conflict.

Language

Helen Keller (1880–1968) became a national celebrity because she overcame the daunting disability of being blind and deaf from infancy. The loss of two key senses cut off this young girl from the symbolic world, greatly limiting her social development. Only when her teacher, Anne Mansfield Sullivan, broke through Keller's isolation by teaching her sign language did Helen Keller begin to realize her human potential. This remarkable woman, who later became a renowned educator herself, recalls the moment she grasped the concept of language.

> We walked down the path to the well-house, attracted by the smell of honeysuckle with which it was covered. Someone was drawing water, and my teacher placed my hand under the spout. As the cool stream gushed over one hand, she spelled into the other the word *water*, first slowly, then rapidly. I stood still, my whole attention fixed upon the motions of her fingers. Suddenly I felt a misty consciousness as of something forgotten—a thrill of returning thought; and somehow the mystery of language was revealed to me. I knew then that "w-a-t-e-r" meant the wonderful cool something that was flowing over my hand. That living word awakened my soul; gave it light, hope, joy, set it free! (1903:21–24)

Language, the key to the world of culture, is *a system of symbols that allows members of a society to communicate with one another.* These symbols take the form of spoken and written words, which are culturally variable and composed of the various alphabets used around the world. Even conventions for writing differ: In general, people in Western societies write from left to right, people in northern Africa and western Asia write from right to left, and people in eastern Asia write from top to bottom.

Global Map 3–1 shows where in the world one finds the three most widely spoken languages. Chinese is the official language of 20 percent of humanity (about 1.2 billion people). English is the mother tongue of about 10 percent (600 million) of the world's people, with Spanish the official language of 6 percent (350 million). Notice, too, that one can travel virtually anywhere in the world other than much of western Africa and "get by" speaking English. Due to the worldwide economic and political clout of Great Britain and, more recently, the United States, English is now becoming a global tongue that is a favored second language in most of the world's nations.

For people everywhere, language is the major means of **cultural transmission,** *the process by which*

GLOBAL: Sanskrit is the oldest living language.

GLOBAL: Key reasons for the global reach of English are British colonialism, the worldwide U.S. presence in World War II, and the economic power of the U.S. since then. Younger Japanese people speak at least some English, although most older people do not. The strength of the Japanese economy as well as that nation's historic monoculturalism account for this pattern.

GLOBAL: An illustration of global English: International regulations require all Boeing 747 pilots to be fluent in English.

GLOBAL: Another example of the diffusion of the English language and U.S. culture: The rising percentage of box office receipts abroad from U.S. films—France, 59%; Great Britain, 89%; Italy, 85%. English has become the universal language of entertainment, dominating television and pop music as well as film.

Window on the World

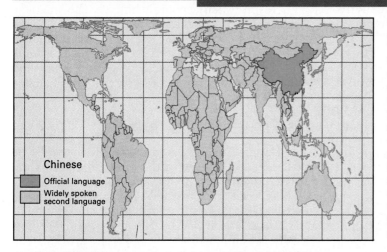

GLOBAL MAP 3–1

Language in Global Perspective

Chinese (including Mandarin, Cantonese, and dozens of other dialects) is the native tongue of one-fifth of the world's people, almost all of whom live in Asia. Although all Chinese people read and write with the same characters, they employ any of several dozen dialects. The "official" dialect, taught in schools throughout the People's Republic of China and the Republic of Taiwan, is Mandarin (the dialect of Beijing, China's historic capital city). Cantonese (the language of Canton, which differs in sound from Mandarin roughly the way French does from Spanish) is the second most common Chinese dialect.

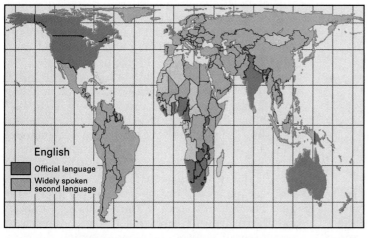

English is the native tongue or official language in several world regions and has become the preferred second language in most of the world.

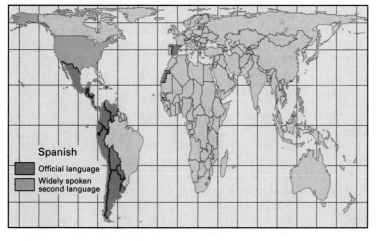

The largest concentration of Spanish speakers is in Latin America and, of course, in Spain. Spanish is also the preferred second language of the United States.

Source: *Peters Atlas of the World* (1990).

NOTE: For decades, a "nurture versus nature" debate has surrounded language. Nurture advocates argue that language systems are distinctive and language is learned along with other cultural elements. Nature advocates counter that all linguistic systems have similar internal structures, suggesting that language construction is "wired" into the human brain. Noam Chomsky, probably the best-known researcher in this area, subscribes to the latter view.

DISCUSS: The argument here contradicts the old adage "Sticks and stones can break my bones, but names can never hurt me." In what sense are symbols real?
NOTE: Although humans have been able to teach chimps to use symbols, little evidence supports the position that chimps are capable of teaching other chimps to do so.

one generation passes culture to the next. Just as our bodies contain the genes of our ancestors, so our symbols carry our cultural heritage. Language gives us the power to gain access to centuries of accumulated wisdom.

Throughout human history, people have transmitted culture through speech, a process sociologists call the *oral cultural tradition.* Only as recently as five thousand years ago did humans invent writing, and, even then, just a favored few ever learned to read and write. It was not until this century that nations (generally the industrial, high-income countries) have boasted of nearly universal literacy. Still, 10 to 15 percent of U.S. adults (20 to 25 million people) cannot read and write—an almost insurmountable barrier to opportunity in a society that increasingly demands symbolic skills. In low-income countries of the world, illiteracy rates range from 30 percent (People's Republic of China) to as high as 80 percent (Sierra Leone in Africa).

Language skills not only link us with others and with the past, they also set free the human imagination. Connecting symbols in new ways, we can conceive of an almost limitless range of future possibilities. Language—both spoken and written—distinguishes human beings as the only creatures who are self-conscious, mindful of our limitations and aware of our ultimate mortality. Yet our symbolic power also enables us to dream, to envision a better world, and to work to bring that world into being.

Is Language Uniquely Human?

Creatures great and small direct sounds, smells, and gestures toward one another. In most cases, these signals are instinctive. But research shows that some animals have at least a rudimentary ability to use symbols to communicate with one another and with humans.

Consider the remarkable achievement of a twelve-year-old pygmy chimp named Kanzi. Chimpanzees lack the physical ability to mimic human speech. But researcher E. Sue Savage-Rumbaugh discovered that Kanzi was able to learn language by listening and observing people. Under Savage-Rumbaugh's supervision, Kanzi has amassed a vocabulary of several hundred words, and he has learned to "speak" by pointing to pictures on a special keyboard. Kanzi has correctly responded to requests like "Will you get a diaper for your sister?" or "Put the melon in the potty." More intriguing, Kanzi's abilities surpass mere rote learning because he can respond to requests he has not heard before. In short, this

remarkable animal has the language ability of a two-and-one-half-year-old human child (Linden, 1993).

Despite such accomplishments, the language skills of chimps, dolphins, and a few other animals are limited. And even specially trained animals cannot, on their own, teach language skills to others of their kind. But the demonstrated language skills of Kanzi and others caution us against assuming that humans alone can lay claim to culture.

Does Language Shape Reality?

Do the Chinese, who think using one set of symbols, actually experience the world differently from North Americans who think in English or Spanish? The answer is yes, since each language has its own, distinct symbols that serve as the building blocks of reality.

Edward Sapir (1929, 1949) and Benjamin Whorf (1956), two anthropologists who specialized in linguistic studies, noted that each language has words or expressions with no precise counterparts in other tongues. In addition, all languages fuse symbols with distinctive emotions. Thus, as multilingual people can attest, a single idea often "feels" different if spoken in, say, Spanish rather than in English or Chinese (Falk, 1987).

Formally, then, what we now call the **Sapir-Whorf hypothesis** states that *people perceive the world through the cultural lens of language.* Using different symbolic systems, a Filipino, a Turk, and a Brazilian actually experience "distinct worlds, not merely the same world with different labels attached" (Sapir, 1949:162).

Of course, the capacity to create and manipulate language also gives humans everywhere the power to alter how they experience the world. For example, many African Americans hailed it as a step toward social equality with white people when the word "Negro" was replaced by the term "black" and, more recently, by "African American" or "person of color." In short, a system of language guides how we understand the world but does not limit how we do so.

Values and Beliefs

What accounts for the popularity of film characters like James Bond, Dirty Harry, Rambo, and Thelma and Louise? Each is ruggedly individualistic, suspicious of "the system," and relies on personal skill and savvy. In applauding such people, we celebrate a sturdy strain of individualism, traditionally for men but increasingly for women, too.

Sociologists call these judgments **values,** *culturally defined standards by which people assess desirability, goodness, and beauty, and which serve as broad*

GLOBAL: Regarding Williams' ten points for traditional societies— *Pts. 1 and 2:* Traditional societies generally embrace fate as a key value; *Pt. 3:* Spiritual comfort and well-being; *Pt. 4:* Greater reflectiveness (especially eastern cultures); *Pt. 5:* Implies a rational world view; this value also suggests why we devalue academics as "eggheads"; *Pt. 6:* Members of most traditional societies are not optimistic (even the Japanese are less so); *Pt. 7:* Religion plays much more of a role than science; *Pt. 8:* Collective sentiment is higher, as is compliance to official authority; for example, Moroccans accept high-handed police direction with little evident complaint; *Pt. 9:* Most of the world is less individualistic than we are; *Pt. 10:* Most of the traditional world is much more group-oriented than we are.

Q: "Social sciences show that values do not fly on their own wings; they must be embodied in our rituals." Amitai Etzioni

guidelines for social living. From the standpoint of a culture, values are statements about what ought to be.

Values are broad principles that underlie **beliefs,** *specific statements that people hold to be true.* While values are abstract standards of goodness, in other words, beliefs are particular matters that individuals consider to be true or false.

Cultural values and beliefs not only color how we perceive our surroundings, they also form the core of our personalities. We learn from families, schools, and religious organizations to think and act according to approved principles, to pursue worthy goals, and to believe a host of cultural truths while rejecting alternatives as false.

In a nation as large and diverse as the United States, of course, few cultural values and beliefs are shared by everyone. In fact, with a long history of immigration from the rest of the world, the United States has become a cultural mosaic. In this regard, we stand apart from China or Japan, which have more homogeneous cultural systems. Even so, there is a broad shape to our national life that may be described as "key values."

Key Values of U.S. Culture

Sociologist Robin Williams (1970) identified the following ten values as central to our way of life:

1. **Equal opportunity.** People in the United States endorse not equality of *condition* but equality of *opportunity.* This means that society should provide everyone with the opportunity to get ahead; at the same time, though, people's varying talents and efforts should end up making some people more successful than others.

2. **Achievement and success.** Our way of life encourages competition so that each person's rewards should reflect personal merit. Moreover, greater success confers worthiness on a person— the mantle of being a "winner."

3. **Material comfort.** Success, in the United States, generally means making money and enjoying what it will buy. People in the United States may quip that "money won't buy happiness," but most diligently pursue wealth all the same.

4. **Activity and work.** U.S. heroes, from Olympic figure skating star Kristi Yamaguchi to film's famed archaeologist Indiana Jones, are "action figures," people who get the job done. Members of our society prefer *action* to *reflection;* through hard work, we try to control events rather than

Australian feminist artist Sally Swain alters a famous artist's painting to make fun of our culture's tendency to ignore the everyday lives of women. This spoof is entitled **Mrs. Toulouse-Lautrec Cleans the Toilet.**

passively accepting our fate. For this reason, many of us take a dim view of cultures that appear more easygoing or philosophical.

5. **Practicality and efficiency.** People in the United States value the practical over the theoretical; "doers" over "dreamers." Activity has value to the extent that it earns money. Moreover, we praise the ability to solve problems with minimal effort. "Building a better mousetrap" is a cultural goal, especially when it is done in the most cost-effective way.

6. **Progress.** We are an optimistic people who, despite periodic waves of nostalgia, believe that the present is better than the past. This embrace

NOTE: Instant gratification is a value on the rise. Seventy percent of U.S. teen respondents agreed with this survey item: "I always try to have as much fun as I possibly can—I don't know what the future holds and I don't care what others think." (Teenage Research Unlimited)

SOCIAL SURVEY: "There is a lot of discussion today about whether Americans are divided or united. Some say that Americans are united and in agreement about the most important values. Others think that Americans are greatly divided when it comes to the most important values. What is your view about this?" (GSS 1994, N = 1,474; *Codebook*, 1994:405)

"Americans are united and in agreement . . ." 39.4%
"Americans are greatly divided . . ." 55.0%
DK/NR 5.6%

SOCIOLOGY OF EVERYDAY LIFE

Don't Blame Me! The New "Culture of Victimization"

A New York man recently leaped in front of a moving subway train; lucky enough to survive, he sued the city, claiming the train failed to stop in time to prevent his serious injuries. (A court awarded him $650,000.) In Washington, D.C., after realizing that he had been videotaped smoking crack cocaine in a hotel room, the city's mayor blamed his woman companion for "setting him up" and charged that the police were racially motivated in arresting him. After more than a dozen women accused former Oregon Senator Bob Packwood of sexual harassment, he tried to defuse the scandal by checking into an alcohol treatment center. In the most celebrated case of its kind, Dan White, who gunned down the mayor of San Francisco and a city council member, blamed this violent episode on insanity caused by his having eaten too much junk food (the so-called "Twinkie defense"). In each of these cases, someone denies personal

Reinforcing "victimization" as an emerging culture, many popular "tell all" television programs feature people who deny personal responsibility for various calamities that have befallen them.

responsibility for an action, claiming instead to be a victim. Rather than taking the blame for our mishaps and misdeeds, in other words, more and more members of our society are pointing the finger elsewhere. Such behavior has prompted sociologist Irving Horowitz to announce a developing "culture of victimization" in which "everyone is a victim" and "no one accepts responsibility for anything."

One indication of this cultural trend is the proliferation of "addictions," a term that people once associated only with uncontrollable drug use. We now hear about gambling addicts, compulsive overeaters, sex addicts, and even people who excuse mounting credit-card debts as a shopping addiction. Bookstores overflow with manuals to help people come to terms with numerous new medical or

---

of progress comes through in marketing that equates the "very latest" with the "very best."

7. **Science.** We often turn to scientists to solve problems, convinced that the work of scientific experts will improve our lives. We believe we are rational people, which accounts for our cultural tendency (especially among men) to devalue emotions and intuition as sources of knowledge.

8. **Democracy and free enterprise.** Members of our society recognize numerous individual rights that cannot be overridden by government. Our political system has come to be based on the ideal of free elections in which all adults select their own leaders. In the same way, we believe that the U.S. economy responds to the needs and choices of individual consumers.

9. **Freedom.** Our cultural value of freedom means that we favor individual initiative over collective conformity. Although we acknowledge that everyone has responsibilities to others, we believe that individuals should be free to pursue personal goals with minimal interference from anyone else.

10. **Racism and group superiority.** Despite prevailing ideas about individualism and freedom, most people in the United States still evaluate individuals according to their sex, race, ethnicity, and social class. Our society values males above females, whites above people of color, people with northwestern European backgrounds above those whose ancestors came from other lands, and more privileged people above those who are disadvantaged. Although we like to describe ourselves as a nation of equals, there is little doubt that some of us rank as "more equal than others."

Values: Inconsistency and Conflict

As the listing above illustrates, cultural values can be inconsistent and even outright contradictory (Lynd,

SOCIAL SURVEY: "People have to realize that they can only count on their own skills and abilities if they are going to win in this world." Percent agreeing: *1989, 75%; 1994, 86%.* (Yankelovich Monitor Perspective surveys)

NOTE: Of course, the notion of victims implies the existence of victimizers, which explains the link between the developing culture of victimization and rising political conflict.

DIVERSITY: Ann M. Beutel and Margaret Mooney Marini (1995) report that men's values are more oriented toward competition and materialism, while women's values emphasize compassion for others and finding meaning in life.

DISCUSS: Does this country's cultural emphasis on independence help explain why three-fourths of workers drive to work alone?

psychological conditions ranging from "The Cinderella Complex" to "The Casanova Complex" and even "Soap Opera Syndrome." And the U.S. courts are ever more clogged by lawsuits driven by the need to blame someone—and often to collect big money—for the kind of misfortune that we used to accept as part of life.

What's going on here? Is U.S. culture changing? Historically, our way of life has been based on a cultural ideal of "rugged individualism," the notion that people are responsible for whatever triumph or tragedy befalls them. But this value has been eroded by a number of factors. First, everyone is more aware (partly through the work of sociologists) of how society shapes our lives. This knowledge has expanded the categories of people claiming to be victims well beyond those who have suffered historical disadvantages (such as African Americans and

women) to include even well-off people. On college campuses, moreover, a sense that "everybody gets special treatment but us" is prompting white males to view themselves as the latest "victims."

Second, since they began advertising their services in 1977, lawyers have encouraged a sense of injustice among clients they hope to shepherd into court. The number of million-dollar lawsuit awards has risen more than twenty-five-fold in the last twenty-five years.

Third, there has been a proliferation of "rights groups" that promote what Amitai Etzioni calls "rights inflation." Beyond the traditional constitutional liberties are many newly claimed rights, including those of hunters (as well as those of animals), the rights of smokers (and nonsmokers), the right of women to control their bodies (and the rights of the unborn), the right to own a gun (and

the right to be safe from violence). Expanding and competing claims for unmet rights, then, generate victims (and victimizers) on all sides.

Does this shift signal a fundamental realignment in our culture? Perhaps, but the new popularity of being a victim also springs from some well-established cultural forces. For example, the claim to victimization depends on a long-standing belief that everyone has the right to life, liberty, and the pursuit of happiness. Yet this new explosion of "rights" does more than alert us to clear cases of injustice; it threatens to erode our sense of responsibility as members of a larger society.

Sources: Based on Etzioni (1991), Taylor (1991), and Hollander (1995).

1967; Bellah et al., 1985). Living in the United States, we sometimes find ourselves torn between the "me first" attitude of an individualistic, success-at-all-costs way of life and the opposing need to belong and contribute to some larger community. Similarly, we affirm our belief in equality of opportunity only to turn around and promote or degrade others because of their race or sex.

Value inconsistency reflects the cultural diversity of U.S. society and the process of cultural change by which new trends supplant older traditions. Recently, for example, what some observers have tagged a new "culture of victimization" has arisen to challenge our society's long-time belief in individual responsibility. The box takes a closer look at this shift.

Whether based on the ethnic mix of U.S. society or changes in our way of life, today's value inconsistency leads to strained and awkward balancing acts in how we view the world. Sometimes we pursue

one value at the expense of another, supporting the principle of equal opportunity, say, yet opposing the acceptance of gays by the U.S. military. At other times, we try to ignore such contradictions. According to one recent national survey, the U.S. population may be losing a sense that the nation shares any core values at all. Asked whether "Americans are united or greatly divided when it comes to the most important values," 39 percent chose the former response while 55 percent endorsed the latter view (NORC, 1994:405).

Values in Action: The Games People Play

Cultural values affect every aspect of our lives. Children's games, for example, may seem like lighthearted fun, but through them we teach young people what our culture deems important.

Using the sociological perspective, James Spates (1976a) sees in the familiar game King of the

DISCUSS: What about "Tag"? Spates observes that the loser in Tag, designated as "It," is singled out as unworthy of joining the group. This experience of being excluded can be so difficult to bear that other players may allow themselves to be tagged just to end "It's" ordeal.

NOTE: "Norm" is derived from Latin *norm(a)*, meaning "a carpenter square, a rule, or a pattern." The root of "moral" is *mor* or *mos*, meaning "custom." The rarely used singular form of mores is *mos*.
NOTE: Not all norms are neatly characterized as mores or folkways; these concepts are most effectively used as endpoints of a continuum.

psychologically, for long. Additionally, the sole victor is likely to feel a certain alienation from others: Whom can one trust? Truly, "it is lonely at the top." (1976a:286)

Just as King of the Mountain conveys our cultural emphasis on winning, Tag, Keep Away, and Monkey in the Middle exemplify the dangers of being a "loser." Drawing on these sociological observations, we can better appreciate the prominence of competitive team sports in U.S. culture and why star athletes are often celebrated as cultural heroes.

Norms

In China, people curious about how much money colleagues are paid readily ask about their salaries. In the United States, people consider such a question rude. Such patterns illustrate the operation of **norms,** *rules and expectations by which a society guides the behavior of its members.* Some norms are *proscriptive,* mandating what we should not do, as when Chinese parents scold young lovers for holding hands in public. *Prescriptive* norms, on the other hand, spell out what we *should* do, as when U.S. schools teach practices of "safe sex."

Most important norms apply virtually anywhere and at any time. For example, parents expect obedience from children regardless of the setting. Many normative conventions, by contrast, are situation-specific. In the United States, we expect audience applause at the end of a musical performance; we accept it (although we do not expect it) when a classroom lecture is over; we discourage applause when a priest or a rabbi finishes a sermon.

Standards of beauty—including the color and design of everyday surroundings—vary significantly from one culture to another. Members of the Ndebele in South Africa lavishly paint their homes. Members of North American and European societies, by contrast, make far less use of bright colors and intricate detail so that their neighborhoods appear much more subdued.

Reprinted by permission of Margaret Courtney-Clarke, © 1990.

Mountain our cultural emphasis on achievement and success.[1]

> In this game, the King (winner) is the one who scrambles to the top of some designated area and holds it against all challengers (losers). This is a very gratifying game from the winner's point of view, for one learns what it is like (however brief is the tenure at the top before being thrown off) to be an unequivocal success, to be unquestionably better than the entire competition. (1976a:286)

Each player endeavors to become number one at the expense of all other players. But success has its price, and King of the Mountain teaches that as well.

> The King can never relax in such a pressurized position and constant vigilance is very difficult to endure,

Mores and Folkways

William Graham Sumner (1959; orig. 1906), an early U.S. sociologist, recognized that some norms are more crucial to our lives than others. Sumner used the term **mores** (pronounced MORE-ays) to refer to *a society's standards of proper moral conduct.* Sumner counted among the mores all norms essential to maintaining a way of life; because of their importance, he contended that people develop an emotional attachment to mores and defend them publicly. In addition, mores apply to everyone, everywhere, all the time. Violation of mores—such as our society's prohibition against sexual relations between adults and children—typically brings a swift and strong reaction from others.

Sumner used the term **folkways** to designate *a society's customs for routine, casual interaction.*

---

[1]The excerpt presented here has been slightly modified, on the basis of unpublished versions of the study, with the permission of the author.

DISCUSS: Ideal culture often is revealed in legends; "legend" is derived from Latin meaning "things to be read." Thus the Greeks celebrated Homer; the Romans, Virgil; the Christians, saints and Joan of Arc; medieval nobles, King Arthur; and moderns, a list of rugged individualists, from Davy Crockett to James Bond, Rambo, and Thelma and Louise. Ask the class to characterize these figures.

Q: "The growth of democracy endowed mass culture with political legitimacy." Paul Jerome Croce

Q: "Myths and taboos are not meant only to reflect reality, but to create it." Richard Farson

NOTE: A detailed discussion of how technology has historically shaped human society is found in the first section of Chapter 4 ("Society").

Folkways, which have lesser moral significance than mores, include notions about proper dress, appropriate greetings, and common courtesy. In short, while mores distinguish between right and wrong, folkways draw a line between right and *rude*. Because they are less important than mores, societies afford individuals a measure of personal discretion in matters involving folkways and punish infractions leniently. For example, a man who does not wear a tie to a formal dinner party is, at worst, guilty of a breach of etiquette. If, however, the man were to arrive at the dinner party wearing *only* a tie, he would be challenging the social mores and inviting more serious sanctions.

Social Control

As participants in cultural systems, we learn to accept mores and many folkways as the basic rules of everyday life, typically responding to the behavior of others with *sanctions*, which take the form of either reward or punishment. Conforming to norms provokes praise and approval from others, just as norm violations prompt avoidance, contempt, or even a formal response from the criminal justice system. Taken together, all kinds of sanctions form the heart of a culture's system of **social control**, *various means by which members of society encourage conformity to norms*.

As we internalize cultural norms, we develop the capacity to respond critically to our own behavior. Doing wrong (say, stealing from someone) can provoke not only *shame*—the painful sense that others disapprove of our actions—but also *guilt*, a negative judgment we make of ourselves. Only cultural creatures can experience shame and guilt: This is probably what Mark Twain had in mind when he quipped that human beings "are the only animals that blush . . . or need to."

"Ideal" and "Real" Culture

Societies devise values and norms as moral guidelines for their members. As such, these cultural elements do not describe actual behavior as much as they tell us how we *should* behave. We must remember, then, that **ideal culture**, *social patterns mandated by cultural values and norms*, is not the same as **real culture**, *actual social patterns that only approximate cultural expectations*.

To illustrate, most women and men acknowledge the importance of sexual fidelity in marriage. Even so, in a recent study, about 25 percent of married men and 10 percent of married women reported being sexually

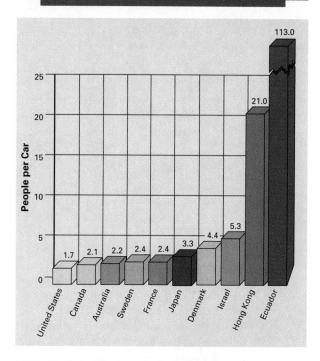

Global Snapshot

FIGURE 3–1 The Number of People Who Share Every Car
Source: U.S. Bureau of the Census (1995).

unfaithful to their spouses at some point in the marriage (Laumann et al., 1994). Such discrepancies are common to all societies, since no one lives up to ideal standards all the time. But a culture's moral prodding is crucial to shaping the lives of individuals all the same, calling to mind the old saying "Do as I say, not as I do."

Material Culture and Technology

In addition to intangible elements such as values and norms, every culture encompasses a wide range of tangible (from Latin meaning "touchable") human creations that sociologists term *artifacts*. The Chinese eat with chopsticks rather than knives and forks, the Japanese place mats rather than rugs on the floor, and many men and women in India prefer flowing robes to the tighter clothing common in the United States. An unfamiliar people's material culture may seem as strange to us as their language, values, and norms.

NOTE: As Donald Kraybill and Marc Olshan (1994) point out, the tension between the Amish and the surrounding society has only increased with the escalation of modern technology.

NOTE: More complex technology empowers humanity to manipulate the natural world; members of industrial societies, therefore, risk losing sensitivity to the natural environment and the requirements of living in an ecological system. Look ahead to Chapter 22 ("Environment and Society").

Q: "Who is the Tolstoy of the Zulus? The Proust of the Papauns? I'd be glad to read him." Saul Bellow

NOTE: Anthropologists have long conceptualized cultural diversity in terms of "big tradition" (dominant cultural patterns) and "little tradition" (folklife).

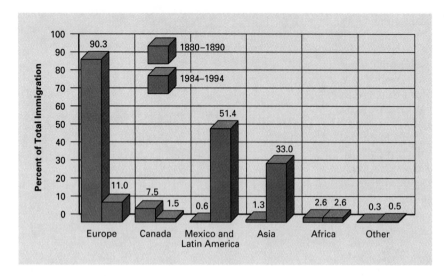

FIGURE 3–2

Recorded Immigration to the United States, by Region of Birth, 1880–1890 and 1984–1994

Source: U.S. Immigration and Naturalization Service (1995).

The artifacts common to a society typically reflect cultural values. The fact that poison-tipped arrows are a prized possession of Yanomamö males in the Amazon rain forest, for example, surely reflects the importance that society places on warfare and militaristic skills. Similarly, our own high regard for the automobile is rooted in cherished values of individuality and independence. Some 4 million miles of freeways already crisscross the United States, and our nation's people own 150 million cars, which represents one car for every licensed driver! Figure 3–1 on page 75 shows that, even compared to other industrial societies, the United States stands out as a car-loving nation.

In addition to reflecting values, material culture also reveals a society's **technology**, *knowledge that a society applies to the task of living in a physical environment*. In short, technology ties the world of nature to the world of culture. Among the most technologically simple people on earth, the Yanomamö interfere little with the natural environment. They remain keenly aware of the cycles of rainfall and the movement of animals they hunt for food. By contrast, technologically complex societies (such as those of North America) have an enormous impact on the natural world, reshaping the environment (for better or ill) according to their own interests and priorities.

Because we accord science such great importance and praise the sophisticated technology it has produced, members of our society tend to judge cultures with simpler technology as less advanced. Some facts would support such an assessment. For example, life expectancy for children born in the United States now exceeds seventy-five years; the lifespan of the Yanomamö stands at only about forty years.

However, we must be careful not to make self-serving judgments about cultures that differ from our own. Although many Yanomamö are eager to gain modern technology (such as steel tools and shotguns), they are generally well fed by world standards and most are quite satisfied with their lives (Chagnon, 1992). Remember, too, that while our powerful and complex technology has produced work-reducing devices and seemingly miraculous forms of medical treatment, it has also contributed to unhealthy levels of stress, eroded the quality of the natural environment, and created weapons capable of destroying in a blinding flash everything that humankind has managed to achieve throughout history.

Finally, technology is another cultural element that varies substantially within the United States. Although many of us cannot imagine life without CD players, televisions, and microwave ovens, some members of our society cannot afford such items, and others reject them on principle. The Amish, for example, live in small farming communities across Pennsylvania, Ohio, and Indiana. These "Plain People" shun most modern conveniences as a matter of religious conviction. With their traditional black garb and horse-drawn buggies, the Amish may seem like a curious relic of the past. Yet their communities flourish, grounded in vibrant families and individuals with a strong sense of identity and purpose. And many of the thousands of outsiders who observe them each year

NOTE: In *Highbrow, Lowbrow: The Emergence of Cultural Hierarchy in America*, Lawrence Levine claims that until the time of the Civil War, all classes were familiar with poetry and quoted Shakespeare. Then as class hierarchy grew, so did cultural hierarchy.

Q: "If *Hamlet* is broadcast on network television, does it represent popular culture (since millions presumably see it) or elite culture, since it is a classic work of art?" Arthur Asa Berger

GLOBAL: Why do people of European background tend to think of people from the Southern Hemisphere as "having rhythm"? The reason is that Western European music emphasizes not rhythm but harmonics. Similarly, European (and U.S.) music has strong bass lines, a trait not found in the music of Native Americans, in India, Peru, or in most of the world.

Cultural patterns are not equally accessible to all members of a society. Formal training in technique, color, and composition, for example, is usually necessary in order to gain standing in the "high culture" pursuit of fine art. We reserve the term "folk art" for the work of people—generally of lower social position—who are drawn by their love of art to paint, even though they have no formal training at all. Anna Mary Robertson (Grandma) Moses, the most popular folk artist of this century, began painting while in her seventies. During the next two decades she produced numerous paintings, yarn pictures, and decorative tiles. Her idyllic landscapes, including Joy Ride, *celebrate U.S. rural traditions and country life.*

Grandma Moses: *Joy Ride,* 1953. Copyright © 1991, Grandma Moses Properties Co., New York.

come away with the suspicion that "local, enduring, and stable" Amish communities may well be "islands of sanity in a culture gripped by commercialism and technology run wild" (Hostetler, 1980:4; Kraybill, 1994:28).

CULTURAL DIVERSITY: MANY WAYS OF LIFE IN ONE WORLD

When contractors and real estate brokers in the United States take account of the Chinese art of *feng shui*, as noted in the opening to this chapter, we can see that our nation is one of striking cultural diversity. In fact, between 1980 and 1990, the number of people in the United States with Chinese or other Asian ancestry more than doubled. Historic isolation makes Japan the most *monocultural* of all industrial nations; heavy immigration over centuries, by contrast, makes the United States the most *multicultural* of all industrial nations.

Between 1820 (when the government began keeping track of immigration) and 1990, more than 55 million people came to these shores from other countries. A century ago, as shown in Figure 3–2, most immigrants hailed from Europe. By the 1980s, however, a large majority of newcomers were arriving from Latin America and Asia.

Cultural variety has always characterized the United States, as we can hear in the distinctive accents of, say, New Englanders or southerners. Ours has also been a nation of religious pluralism, a land of many ethnic traditions, and a home to countless individualists who try to be like no one else.

Given this diversity, sociologists sometimes call our "cloth of culture" a "patchwork quilt." To understand the reality of life in the United States, then, we must move beyond overarching cultural patterns, such as the key values identified by Robin Williams (1970), to consider cultural diversity.

High Culture and Popular Culture

Much cultural diversity has roots in social class. In fact, in everyday conversation, we usually reserve the term "culture" for sophisticated art forms such as classical literature, music, dance, and painting. We praise college professors, film directors, or dance choreographers as "cultured," because they presumably appreciate the "finer things in life." The term "culture" itself has the same Latin root as the word "cultivate," suggesting that the "cultured" individual has cultivated or refined tastes.

By contrast, we speak less generously of ordinary people, assuming that everyday cultural patterns are somehow less worthy. In more concrete terms, we are tempted to judge the music of Mozart as "more

THE MAP: Consumers of croissants (15% of the U.S. population) are higher income, more educated people who live in urban areas. White bread households (44%) are largely in rural, lower-income regions.

DIVERSITY: Subcultural communities such as the Amish are often seen by outsiders as internally homogeneous. John A. Hostetler (1980; see especially Chapter 13) makes clear that the Amish are in many respects internally diverse.

Q: "[The Amish have] polarized over the shape or color of a garment, the style of a house, carriage, or harness, the use of labor-saving farm machinery or the pace of singing. The list is mind-boggling." John A. Hostetler

DIVERSITY: See "The Coming Minority-Majority?" box in Chapter 12 on page 323.

Seeing Ourselves

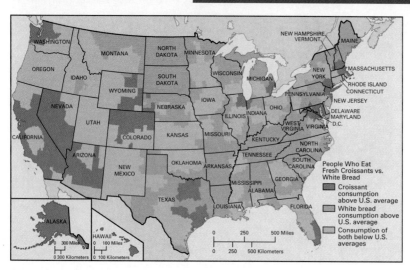

NATIONAL MAP 3–1

Who's "Upper Crust"? High Culture and Popular Culture Across the United States

Patterns of consumption are key indicators of being "highbrow" or "lowbrow." Enjoying croissants—the flaky, delicious pastries served fresh-baked at pricey coffee shops—is one indicator of highbrow standing. These generally well-to-do people drink water from bottles rather than the tap, prefer Grey Poupon to Gulden's mustard, and favor Häagen-Dazs over the local Tastee-Freeze. Being a regular consumer of white bread, by contrast, marks one as "lowbrow." Such a person has modest to low income, consumes above-average quantities of doughnuts, and frequents fast-food restaurants. Looking at the map, do the "highbrows" and "lowbrows" live in the same places? Where, then are the centers of "high culture" and of "popular culture"?

Source: Michael J. Weiss, *Latitudes & Attitudes: An Atlas of American Tastes, Trends, Politics and Passions.* Boston: Little, Brown, and Company 1994.

cultured" than Motown, fine cuisine as better than fish sticks, and polo as more polished than ping pong.

Such judgments imply that many cultural patterns are readily accessible to some but not all members of a society (Hall & Neitz, 1993). Sociologists use the shorthand term **high culture**[2] to refer to *cultural patterns that distinguish a society's elite;* **popular culture**, then, designates *cultural patterns that are widespread among a society's population.*

Common sense may suggest that high culture is superior to popular culture. After all, history chronicles the lives of elites much more than those of ordinary women and men. But sociologists are uneasy with such a sweeping evaluation and generally use the term "culture" to refer to *all* elements of a society's way of life, even as they recognize that cultural patterns vary throughout a population (Gans, 1974).

We should resist quick judgments about the merits of high culture as opposed to popular culture for two key reasons. First, neither elites nor ordinary people have uniform tastes and interests; people in both categories differ in numerous ways. Second, do we praise high culture because it is inherently better than popular culture, or simply because its supporters have more money, power, and prestige to begin with? For example, there is no difference between a violin and a fiddle; however, we refer to the instrument one way when it is used to produce music typically enjoyed by people of higher social position, and the other way when the musician is playing works appreciated by individuals with lower social standing.

National Map 3–1 uses the popularity of two different forms of bread to show where in the United States the "cultural upper crust" resides.

Subculture

The term **subculture** refers to *cultural patterns that set apart some segment of a society's population.* Inner-city teens, elderly Polish Americans, frequent-flyer

[2]The term "high culture" is derived from the more popular term "highbrow." Influenced by phrenology, the bogus nineteenth-century theory that personality was determined by the shape of the human skull, people a century ago contrasted the praiseworthy tastes of those they termed "highbrows" with the contemptible appetites of others they derided as "lowbrows."

NOTE: Most texts offer a common, although technically incorrect, definition of subculture and counterculture as *groups of people* who embrace distinctive cultural patterns. Both terms refer to culture, not people. This text preserves the traditional definitions.

DIVERSITY: Recall the "What's in a Name?" box in Chapter 1 ("The Sociological Perspective"); the so-called "melting pot" in the United States actually involved Anglicizing the cultural patterns of other ethnic categories.

Q: "It is poor strategy, poor history and poor logic . . . to bemoan . . . 'Anglo' culture . . . After all, does anyone expect that there is more tolerance for multiculturalism in Tokyo, Caracas, Istanbul, Copenhagen, Mexico City, or Beijing than there is in New York or Los Angeles?" Kenneth T. Jackson

executives, "Yankee" New Englanders, Colorado cowboys, the southern California "beach crowd," jazz musicians, campus poets, and offshore powerboat racers all display subcultural patterns.

It is easy—but often inaccurate—to place people into subcultural categories. Almost everyone participates simultaneously in numerous subcultures, and we often have little commitment to many of them.

In some cases, however, important cultural traits such as ethnicity or religion do set off people from one another—sometimes with tragic results. Consider the former nation of Yugoslavia in southeastern Europe. The ongoing turmoil there has been fueled by astounding cultural diversity. This *one* small country (which, before its breakup, was about the size of Wyoming with a population of 25 million) made use of *two* alphabets, professed *three* religions, spoke *four* languages, was home to *five* major nationalities, was divided into *six* political republics, and absorbed the cultural influences of *seven* surrounding countries. The cultural conflict that plunged this nation into civil war reveals that subcultures are a source not only of pleasing variety but also of tensions and outright violence (cf. Sekulic et al., 1994).

Historically, we have taught our children to view the United States as a "melting pot" in which many nationalities blend into a single "American" culture. But, considering the extent of our cultural diversity, how accurate is the "melting pot" description? One factor complicating this idealistic notion: Cultural diversity involves not just *variety* but also *hierarchy*. Too often, what we view as "dominant" or "highbrow" cultural patterns are those favored by powerful segments of the population, while we relegate the lives of the disadvantaged to the realm of "subculture." This dilemma has led some researchers to highlight the experiences of less powerful members of our society in a new approach called multiculturalism.

Multiculturalism

In recent years, the United States has been debating the policy of **multiculturalism,** *an educational program recognizing past and present cultural diversity in U.S. society and promoting the equality of all cultural traditions.* This movement represents a sharp turn from the past, when our society downplayed cultural diversity and defined itself primarily in terms of its European (and especially English) immigrants. At this point, scholars and public officials clash over whether we should stress the common elements in our national experience or play up cultural differences (Schlesinger, Jr., 1991; Meyrowitz & Maguire, 1993).

E Pluribus Unum, the familiar Latin phrase that appears on each U.S. coin, means "out of many, one." This motto not only symbolizes our national political confederation, but it also describes the conventional idea that our society forges a new and distinctive way of life from the varied experiences of immigrants who came here from around the world. Even George Washington, the first U.S. president, subscribed to the "melting pot" theory when he confidently predicted that, as future immigrants learned the nation's ways, they would become "one people" (Gray, 1991).

But, from the outset, the many cultures did not melt together as much as harden into a hierarchy. The early English majority established the dominant social institutions (transferring from England the familiar language, economy, legal system, and religions). For their part, members of the non-English minority had little choice but to stay on the sidelines or model themselves after "their betters." This meant that "melting" turned out to be a process of Anglicization—adopting English ways. As multiculturalists see it, early in our history, this society set up the English way of life as an ideal to which all should aspire and by which all should be judged.

For more than two centuries, historians in the United States have highlighted people of English and other European ancestry and chronicled events from their point of view. In the process, little attention has been paid to the perspectives and accomplishments of Native Americans, people of African descent, and immigrants from Asia. Multiculturalists condemn this pattern as **Eurocentrism,** *the dominance of European (particularly English) cultural patterns.* Molefi Kete Asante, a leading advocate of multiculturalism, draws a historical analogy: Like the fifteenth-century Europeans who could not let go of the idea that the earth was the center of the universe, many today find it difficult not to view European culture as the center of the social universe (1988:7).

Few deny that our culture has wide-ranging roots. But multiculturalism is controversial because it demands that we rethink the norms and values at the core of our society. Not surprisingly, battles are now raging over how to describe our nation's culture.

One issue centers on language. By 1996, legislatures in twenty-two states had enacted laws declaring English as an official language, and Congress continues to debate such a law for the entire country. To some, "official English" may seem unnecessary, since a large majority of people in this country are English-speakers. Even so, some 30 million men and women—roughly one in six—communicate in a language other

THE MAP: The most culturally diverse regions of the United States are those with the greatest number of immigrants.

Q: "As long as black people are viewed as 'them,' the burden falls on blacks to do all the cultural and moral work necessary for healthy race relations. The implication is that only certain Americans can define what it means to be an American—and the rest must simply 'fit in.'" Cornel West

GLOBAL: Problems of multiculturalism arise in other societies as well. Consider Sri Lanka, where Sinhalese and Tamil (different languages using different alphabets) replaced English in an effort to end colonial influences. Within two decades, civil war broke out between the two populations. (But remember that in Germany, both the Jews and the Germans spoke German and that didn't prevent the Holocaust.)

Seeing Ourselves

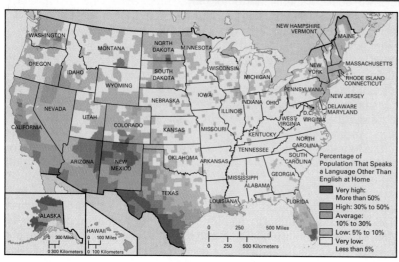

NATIONAL MAP 3–2
Language Diversity
Across the United States

Of 230 million people over the age of five in the United States, the 1990 Census reports, 32 million (14 percent) typically speak a language other than English at home. Of these people, 54 percent speak Spanish, 14 percent use an Asian language, and the remaining 32 percent employ some other tongue (the Census Bureau lists twenty-five languages, each of which is favored by more than 100,000 people). The map shows that these people are concentrated in certain regions of the United States. Which ones? What do you think accounts for this pattern?

Percentage of Population That Speaks a Language Other Than English at Home

Very high: More than 50%
High: 30% to 50%
Average: 10% to 30%
Low: 5% to 10%
Very low: Less than 5%

Source: *Time*, January 30, 1995. Copyright © 1995 *Time*, Inc. Reprinted by permission.

than English at home. Spanish is the second most commonly spoken language here, and several hundred other tongues are heard across the nation, including Italian, German, French, Filipino, Japanese, Korean, Vietnamese and a host of Native-American languages. National Map 3–2 takes a look at where in the United States large numbers of people speak a language other than English at home.

A second controversy involves how our nation's schools—from the early grades through college—should teach about culture. Proponents defend multiculturalism as a strategy to present a more accurate picture of our country's *past*. Multiculturalism, for example, challenges the one-sided praise directed at Christopher Columbus and other European explorers, pointing out that indigenous peoples inhabited the so-called "New World" for tens of thousands of years before Europeans arrived here. Moreover, the European conquest was catastrophic for many of the native peoples of this hemisphere, unleashing centuries of domination and death from war and disease. In short, advocates claim multiculturalism would recover the history and achievements of non-European women and men while offering a fairer and more balanced view of how our nation evolved.

Proponents also paint multiculturalism as a means to come to terms with our country's even more diverse *present*. With the Asian and Hispanic populations of this country increasing rapidly, some analysts predict that children born in the 1990s will live to see people of African, Asian, and Hispanic ancestry become a *majority* of this country's population.

Additionally, some proponents advance multiculturalism as a way to strengthen the academic achievement of African-American children. To counter pervasive Eurocentrism, some multiculturalists are calling for **Afrocentrism**, *the dominance of African cultural patterns*, which they see as a corrective for centuries of minimizing or altogether ignoring the cultural achievements of African societies, and African Americans.

Although multiculturalism has found widespread favor in the last several years, it has provoked its share of criticism as well. Most troubling to opponents of multiculturalism is its tendency to encourage divisiveness rather than unity by urging individuals to identify with their own category rather than with the nation as a whole. Similarly, rather than recognizing any common standards of truth, say critics, multiculturalism maintains that we should evaluate ideas according to the race (and sex) of those who present them. Common humanity thus dissolves into an "African experience," an "Asian experience," and so on.

The bottom line, say the critics, is that multiculturalism may not end up helping minorities, as proponents contend. Critics argue that multiculturalist initiatives (from African-American studies to all-black dorms) seem to demand precisely the kind of racial segregation that our nation has struggled for decades to end. Then, too, an Afrocentric curriculum may well deny children a wide range of crucial knowledge and skills by forcing them to study only certain topics from a single point of view. Historian Arthur Schlesinger, Jr. (1991:21) puts the matter bluntly: "If a Kleagle of the Ku Klux Klan wanted to use the schools to handicap black Americans, he could hardly come up with anything more effective than the 'Afrocentric' curriculum."

Is there any common ground in this debate? Absolutely. Virtually everyone agrees that all people in the United States need to gain greater appreciation of the extent of our cultural diversity. Further, because people of color may well constitute a majority of the population a century from now, we must shift our efforts in this direction right away. But precisely where the balance is to be struck—between the *pluribus* and the *unum*—is likely to remain a divisive issue for some time to come.

Counterculture

Cultural diversity also includes outright rejection of conventional ideas or behavior. **Counterculture** refers to *cultural patterns that strongly oppose those widely accepted within a society.*

In many societies, countercultures spring from adolescence (Spates, 1976b, 1983; Spates & Perkins, 1982). Most of us are familiar with the youth-oriented counterculture of the 1960s that rejected the cultural mainstream as overly competitive, self-centered, and materialistic. Instead, hippies and other counterculturalists favored a cooperative lifestyle in which "being" took precedence over "doing" and the capacity for personal growth—or "expanded consciousness"—was prized over material possessions like homes and cars. Such differences led some people at that time to "drop out" of the larger society.

Counterculture may involve not only distinctive values, but unconventional behavior (including dress and forms of greeting) as well as music. Many members of the 1960s counterculture, for instance, drew personal identity from long hair, headbands, and blue jeans; from displaying a peace sign rather than offering

TABLE 3–1 Attitudes Among Students Entering U.S. Colleges, 1968 and 1995

		1968*	1995	Change
Life Objectives (Essential or Very Important)				
Develop a philosophy of life	Men	79	41	–38
	Women	87	42	–45
Keep up with political affairs	Men	52	32	–20
	Women	52	26	–26
Help others in difficulty	Men	50	51	+ 1
	Women	71	69	– 2
Raise a family	Men	64	70	+ 6
	Women	72	72	0
Be successful in my own business	Men	55	47	– 8
	Women	32	36	+ 4
Be well off financially	Men	51	76	+25
	Women	27	73	+46

*To allow comparisons, data from the early 1970s rather than 1968 are used for some items.

Sources: Richard G. Braungart and Margaret M. Braungart, "From Yippies to Yuppies: Twenty Years of Freshmen Attitudes," *Public Opinion*, vol. 11, no. 3 (September–October 1988): 53–56; Linda J. Sax, Alexander W. Astin, William S. Korn, and Kathryn M. Mahoney, *The American Freshman: National Norms for Fall 1995* (Los Angeles: UCLA Higher Education Research Institute, 1995).

a handshake; and from drug use and the energy of ever-present rock-and-roll music.

Countercultures are still flourishing. In the 1990s the most significant counterculture involves militaristic bands of men and women, deeply suspicious of the federal government, many of whom have dropped out of the political system. Several extremists within this militia counterculture carried out the bombing of the Oklahoma City federal building in 1995, killing 168 people.

Cultural Change

Perhaps the most basic human truth is that "All things shall pass." Even the dinosaurs, who thrived on this planet for some 160 million years (see the time line), exist today only as fossils. Will humanity survive for millions of years to come? No one knows. All we can say with certainty is that, given our reliance on culture, for as long as we survive the human record will be one of continuous change.

Table 3–1 shows changes in student attitudes between 1968 (the height of the 1960s counterculture)

Most people in the affluent United States take for granted that childhood should be a carefree time of life devoted to learning and play. In low-income societies of the world, however, poor families depend on the income earned by children, some of whom perform long days of heavy physical labor. We may not want to accept all cultural practices as "natural" just because they exist. But what universal standards can be used to judge social patterns as either right or wrong?

and 1995. Some things have changed only slightly: Today, as was the case a generation ago, most women and men look forward to raising a family. But a clear trend among contemporary students is the pursuit of affluence, with less interest in developing a philosophy of life.

Change in one dimension of a culture usually accompanies other transformations as well. For example, women's rising participation in the labor force has paralleled changing family patterns, including later age at first marriage, a rising divorce rate, and a growing share of children being raised in households without fathers. Such connections illustrate the principle of **cultural integration**, *the close relationship among various elements of a cultural system.*

But all elements of a cultural system do not change at the same speed. William Ogburn (1964) observed that technology moves quickly, generating new elements of material culture (like "test-tube babies") faster than non-material culture (such as ideas about parenthood) can keep up with them. Ogburn called this inconsistency **cultural lag**, *the fact that cultural elements change at different rates, which may disrupt a cultural system.* In a culture with the technical ability to allow one woman to give birth to a child by using another woman's egg, which has been fertilized in a laboratory with the sperm of a total stranger, how are we to apply the traditional notions of motherhood and fatherhood?

Cultural changes are set in motion in three ways. The first is *invention*, the process of creating new cultural elements. Invention has given us the telephone (1876), the airplane (1903), and the aerosol spray can (1941), all of which have had a tremendous impact on our way of life. The process of invention goes on constantly, as indicated by the thousands of applications submitted annually to the United States Patent Office.

Discovery, a second cause of cultural change, involves recognizing and understanding something not fully understood before—from a distant star, to the foods of another culture, to the athletic prowess of U.S. women. Many discoveries result from scientific research. Yet discovery can also happen quite by accident, as when Marie Curie left a rock on a piece of photographic paper in 1898 and serendipitously discovered radium.

The third cause of cultural change is *diffusion*, the spread of cultural traits from one society to another. The technological ability to send information around the globe in seconds—by means of radio, television, facsimile (fax), and computer—means that the level of cultural diffusion has never been greater than it is today.

Certainly our own society has contributed many significant cultural elements to the world, ranging from computers to jazz music. But diffusion works the other way as well, so that much of what we assume is inherently "American" actually comes from other cultures. Ralph Linton (1937) explained that many commonplace elements of our way of life—most clothing and furniture, clocks, newspapers, money, and even the English language—are all derived from other cultures.

RESOURCE: Another jumping-off point for a discussion of ethnocentrism and cultural relativity is Horace Miner's "Body Ritual Among the Nacirema" (*American Anthropologist* 58, 3 (1956): 503–7), included in the Macionis and Benokraitis reader, *Seeing Ourselves.*
Q: "What the U.S. does best is understand itself. What it does worst is understand others." Carlos Fuentes, Mexican writer

NOTE: Dietary differences offer other illustrations of ethnocentrism. We find the drinking of goat's blood by the Masai of eastern Africa to be revolting; however, few Chinese drink milk, which we consider among the most healthful drinks.
DISCUSS: Why would the Amish demand that children not attend school for more than eight years? Why would they refuse to participate in the Social Security system?

During this century, the culture of Japan has been strongly influenced by Western ways of life. Perhaps this explains the widespread use of Western-looking models in Japanese advertising for various products.

Ethnocentrism and Cultural Relativity

North American travelers are among the world's greatest shoppers. They delight in surveying hand-woven carpets in China or India, inspecting finely crafted metals in Turkey, or collecting beautifully colored porcelain tiles in Morocco. And, of course, all these items are wonderful bargains. But one major reason for the low cost is unsettling: Many products from low- and middle-income countries of the world are produced by children, many as young as five or six, who work long days for extremely low wages.

We think of childhood as a time of innocence and freedom from adult burdens like regular work. In poor countries throughout the world, however, families depend on income earned by children. So what people in one society think of as right and natural, people elsewhere find puzzling and even immoral. Perhaps the Chinese philosopher Confucius had it right when he noted that "All people are the same; it's only their habits that are different."

Just about every imaginable social habit is subject to at least some variation around the world, and such differences cause travelers excitement and distress in about equal measure. The tradition in Japan is to name intersections rather than streets, a practice that regularly confuses North Americans who do the opposite; Egyptians move very close to others in conversation, irritating North Americans used to maintaining several feet of "personal space"; bathrooms lack toilet paper throughout much of Morocco, causing great agitation among Westerners unaccustomed to using one's left hand for bathroom hygiene!

Because a particular culture is the basis for everyone's reality, it is no wonder that people everywhere exhibit **ethnocentrism,** *the practice of judging another culture by the standards of one's own culture.* On one level, some ethnocentrism is inevitable if people are to be emotionally attached to a cultural system. One another level, however, ethnocentrism generates misunderstanding and sometimes conflict.

For example, take the seemingly trivial matter of people in North America referring to China as the "Far East." Such a term, which has little meaning to the Chinese, is an ethnocentric expression for a region that is far east *of Europe.* For their part, the Chinese refer to their country with a word translated as "Middle Kingdom," suggesting that, like us, they see their society as the center of the world.

Maps, too, reveal ethnocentrism. Why does the map, on page 84, appear so odd? Not because it is wrong in any geographical sense; the problem is simply that we are accustomed to seeing the United States "above" the rest of the Americas.

Is there an alternative to ethnocentrism? The logical alternative is to imagine unfamiliar cultural traits from the point of view of *them* rather than *us.* The

Q: "No man ever looks at the world with pristine eyes. He sees it edited by a definite set of customs and institutions and ways of thinking." Ruth Benedict

Q: "Father, mother, and me,
   Sister and Auntie say
   All the people are like We,
   And everyone else is They.

And They live over the sea
While We live over the way,
But—would you believe it?—they look upon We
As only a sort of They!?"
Rudyard Kipling, "We and They"

NOTE: This is a good time to review the differences between Mercator and Peters map projections; see the text's Preface for details.

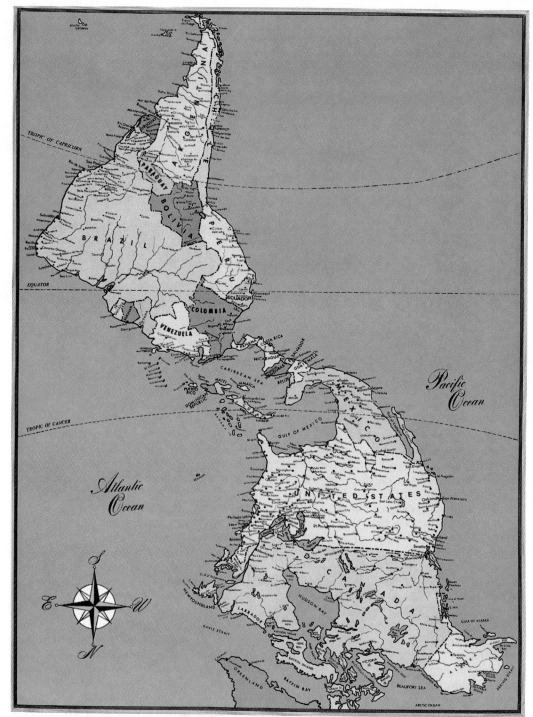

The View from "Down Under"

North America should be "up" and South America "down," or so we think. But, because we live on a globe, such notions are conventions rather than absolutes. The reason that this map of the Western Hemisphere looks wrong to us is not that it is geographically inaccurate; it simply violates our ethnocentric assumption that the United States should be "above" the rest of the Americas.

84 Jesse Levine, Laguna Sales, Palo Alto.

DISCUSS: For a discussion of child labor, look ahead to Global Map 5–1 on page 140.
GLOBAL: Kenneth Jackson points out that there are almost no 24-hour restaurants or grocery stores in Paris. France historically imposed its way of life on colonies and today even has a common vacation period for its people. Compared to France, the United States is more culturally diverse.

Q: "I was a student in the department of anthropology. They taught me that nobody was ridiculous or bad or disgusting." Kurt Vonnegut
Q: ". . . we have failed to understand the relativity of cultural habits, and we remain debarred from much profit and enjoyment in our human relations with people of different cultural standards, and untrustworthy in our dealings with them." Ruth Benedict

casual observer of an Amish farmer tilling hundreds of acres with a team of horses rather than a tractor might initially dismiss this practice as hopelessly backward and inefficient. But, from the Amish point of view, hard work is a foundation of religious discipline. The Amish are well aware of tractors; they simply believe that using such machinery would be their undoing.

This alternative approach, called **cultural relativism**, is *the practice of judging a culture by its own standards*. Cultural relativism is a difficult attitude to adopt because it requires not only understanding the values and norms of another society but also suspending cultural standards we have known all our lives. But, as people of the world come into increasing contact with one another, we are confronting the need to more fully understand other cultures.

U.S. business is learning that success in the ever-expanding global economy depends on cultural sophistication. Consider the troubles several corporations had when they carelessly translated their advertising slogans into Spanish. General Motors soon learned that sales of its Nova were hampered by a product whose name in Spanish means "No Go." Coors' phrase "Turn It Loose" startled customers who read that the beer would make you "Suffer from Diarrhea." Braniff airlines turned "Fly in Leather" into clumsy Spanish reading "Fly Naked." Eastern Airlines transformed its slogan "We Earn Our Wings Daily" into words customers read as "We Fly Daily to Heaven." And even Frank Perdue fell victim to poor marketing when his pitch "It Takes a Tough Man to Make a Tender Chicken" ended up meaning in Spanish "It Takes a Sexually Excited Man to Make a Chicken Affectionate" (Helin, 1992).

The world may need greater cultural understanding, but cultural relativity introduces problems of its own. Virtually any kind of behavior is practiced somewhere in the world; does that mean that everything is equally right? Just because Indian and Moroccan families benefit from having their children work long hours, does that justify such child labor?

Since we all are members of a single species, surely there must be some universal standards of proper conduct. But what are they? And, in trying to develop them, how can we avoid imposing our own standards of fair play on others? There are no simple answers. But here are some general guidelines to keep in mind when dealing with other cultures.

First, while cultural differences fascinate us, they can also be deeply disturbing. Be prepared to experience an emotional reaction when encountering the unfamiliar. Second, resist making a snap judgment so that you can observe unfamiliar cultural surroundings with an open mind. Third, try to imagine the issue from *their* point of view rather than *yours*. Fourth, after careful thought, try to evaluate an unfamiliar custom. After all, there is no virtue in passively accepting every cultural practice. But, in reaching a judgment, bear in mind that—despite your efforts—you can never really experience the world as others do. Fifth, and finally, turn the argument around and think about your own way of life as others might see it. After all, what we gain most from studying others is insight into ourselves.

A Global Culture?

Today, more than ever before, we can observe many of the same cultural patterns the world over. Walking the streets of Seoul (South Korea), Kuala Lumpur (Malaysia), Madras (India), Cairo (Egypt), and Casablanca (Morocco), we find familiar forms of dress, hear well-known pop music, and see advertising for many of the same products we use at home. Just as important, as illustrated by Global Map 3–1, English is rapidly emerging as the preferred second language of most of the world. So are we witnessing the birth of a global culture?

The world is still divided into 191 nation-states and thousands of different cultural systems. Further, as recent violence in the former Soviet Union, the former Yugoslavia, the Middle East, Sri Lanka, and elsewhere attests, many people are intolerant of others whose cultures differ from their own. Yet, looking back through history, we see that societies around the world now have more contact with one another, and enjoy more cooperation, than ever before. These global connections involve the flow of goods, information, and people.

1. **The global economy: the flow of goods.** The extent of international trade has never been greater. The global economy has introduced many of the same consumer goods (from cars to TV shows to T-shirts) the world over.

2. **Global communications: the flow of information.** A century ago, communication around the world depended on written messages delivered by boat, train, horse and wagon, or, occasionally, by telegraph wire. Today's satellite-based communication system enables people to experience sights and sounds of events taking place thousands of miles away—often as they happen.

The flow of immigrants around the world is generally from poor societies to rich nations. Despite vigorous efforts by U.S. authorities to control the border between Mexico and the United States, hundreds of people make their way into this country every day. Here a group of people aspiring to a better life look toward the border, waiting for dark before continuing their journey northward.

3. **Global migration: the flow of people.** Knowledge about the rest of the world motivates people to move where they imagine life will be better. Moreover, today's transportation technology—especially air travel—makes relocating easier than ever before. As a result, most countries contain significant numbers of people born elsewhere (20 million people—about 8 percent of the U.S. population—were born abroad).

These global links have made the cultures of the world more similar at least in superficial respects. But there are three important limitations to the global culture thesis. First, the flow of goods, information, and people has been uneven throughout the world. Generally speaking, urban areas (centers of commerce, communication, and people) have stronger ties to one another, while rural villages remain more isolated. Then, too, the greater economic and military power of North America and Western Europe means that these regions influence the rest of the world more than the other way around.

Second, the global culture thesis assumes that people everywhere are able to *afford* various new goods and services. As Chapter 11 ("Global Stratification") explains, the grinding poverty in much of the world deprives millions of even the basic necessities of a safe and secure life.

Third, although many cultural traits are now found throughout the world, we should not conclude that people everywhere attach the same meanings to them. Do teenagers in Tokyo understand rap music the way their counterparts in New York or Los Angeles do? Similarly, we mimic fashions from around the world with little knowledge of the lives of people who first came up with them. In short, people everywhere look at the world through their own cultural "lenses" (Featherstone, 1990; Hall & Neitz, 1993).

THEORETICAL ANALYSIS OF CULTURE

Through culture, we make sense of ourselves and the surrounding world. Sociologists and anthropologists, however, have the special task of comprehending culture. They do so by using various theoretical paradigms.

Structural-Functional Analysis

Recall from Chapter 1 ("The Sociological Perspective") that structural-functional analysis presents society as a relatively stable system of integrated parts designed to meet human needs. From this point of view, then, the significance of various cultural traits lies in how they function to maintain the overall operation of society.

The reason for the stability of a cultural system, as functionalists see it, is that core values, like the U.S. values noted earlier, anchor its way of life (Parsons, 1964; Williams, 1970). The assertion that ideas (rather than, say, the system of material production) are the basis of human reality aligns structural-functionalism with the philosophical doctrine of *idealism*. Core values give shape to most everyday activities, in the process binding together members of a society. New arrivals, of course, will not necessarily share a society's core orientations. But, according to the functionalist melting-pot scheme, immigrants learn to embrace such values over time.

Thinking functionally is also helpful in making sense of an unfamiliar way of life. Recall, for example, the Amish farmer plowing hundreds of acres with a team of horses. This practice may violate the more widespread cultural value of efficiency; however, from the Amish point of view, hard work functions to generate discipline, which is crucial to Amish religious life. Long days of teamwork, along with family meals and recreation at home, not only make the Amish self-sufficient but unify families and local communities.

Of course, Amish practices have dysfunctions as well. Farm living is hard work, and some people find strict religious discipline too confining, ultimately choosing to leave the community. Then, too, different interpretations of religious principles have generated tensions and sometimes lasting divisions within the Amish world (Hostetler, 1980; Kraybill, 1989; Kraybill & Olshan, 1994).

Because cultures are strategies to meet human needs, we would expect that societies the world over would have some elements in common. The term **cultural universals** refers to *traits that are part of every known culture.* Comparing hundreds of cultures, George Murdock (1945) found dozens of traits common to them all. One cultural universal is the family, which functions everywhere to control sexual reproduction and to organize the care and upbringing of children. Funeral rites, too, are found everywhere, because all human communities cope with the reality of death. Jokes are also a cultural universal, acting as a relatively safe means of releasing social tensions.

Critical evaluation. The structural-functional paradigm shows how culture operates as an integrated system for meeting human needs, yet by emphasizing cultural stability, this approach downplays the extent to which societies change. Similarly, functionalism's assertion that cultural values are embraced by every member of a society overlooks the range of cultural diversity. Finally, the cultural patterns favored by powerful people often dominate a society, while other ways of life are pushed to the margins. Thus, cultures typically generate more conflict than structural-functional analysis leads us to believe.

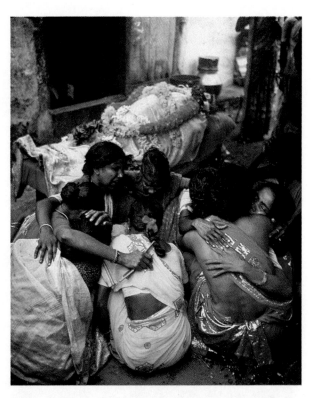

We tend to think of funerals as an expression of respect for the deceased. The social function of funerals, however, has much more to do with the living. For survivors, funerals reaffirm their sense of unity and continuity in the face of separation and disruption.

Social-Conflict Analysis

According to the social-conflict paradigm, a society is a dynamic arena of cultural controversy. Conflict analysis draws attention to links between culture and inequality and highlights the ways in which any cultural trait benefits some members of society at the expense of others.

Conflict theory asks basic questions about why certain values dominate a society in the first place. Sociologists using this paradigm, especially those influenced by Karl Marx, argue that values reflect a society's system of economic production. "It is not the consciousness of men that determines their existence," Marx proclaimed. "It is their social existence that determines their consciousness" (1977:4; orig. 1859). Social-conflict theory, then, is rooted in the philosophical doctrine of *materialism*, the assertion that how people meet their material needs (in the United States, through a capitalist economy) has a powerful effect on

Q: "Between God and ourselves stands nature." Pope Pius XII
NOTE: From the point of view of sociobiology, genes use bodies (and societies) to create more genes. Thus, the chicken and egg dilemma is solved in the following way: eggs come first; eggs use chickens to create more eggs.

RESOURCE: David Barash's *The Whisperings Within* (Harper & Row, 1981) clearly probes the politics of sociobiology (see Chapter 8).
Q: "Although the genes have given away most of their sovereignty, they maintain a certain amount of influence in at least the behavioral qualities that underlie the variations between cultures." Edward O. Wilson

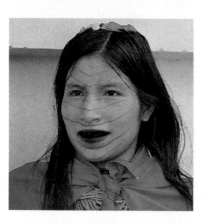

We claim that beauty is in the eye of the beholder, which suggests the importance of culture in setting standards of attractiveness. All of the people pictured here—from Turkey, South Africa, Nigeria, Ecuador, Japan, and Myanmar (Burma)—are beautiful to members of their own society. At the same time, sociobiologists point out that, in every society on earth, people are attracted to youthfulness. The reason is that, as sociobiologists see it, attractiveness underlies our choices about reproduction, which is most readily accomplished in early adulthood.

other dimensions of their culture. Such a materialist approach contrasts with the idealist leanings of structural-functionalism.

Social-conflict analysis ties the competitive values of U.S. society to our capitalist economy, which serves the interests of people who own factories and other businesses. The individualistic culture of capitalism further teaches us to regard rich and powerful people as more energetic and talented than others and therefore deserving of their wealth and privileges. Viewing capitalism as somehow "natural," then, leads people to distrust efforts to decrease the economic disparity found in the United States.

Eventually, however, the strains created by social inequality erupt into drives for social change. The civil rights movement and the women's movement exemplify wide-ranging campaigns for change propelled by disadvantaged segments of the U.S. population. Both, too, have encountered opposition from defenders of the status quo.

Critical evaluation. The social-conflict paradigm reveals that cultural systems address human needs unequally and that a key function of cultural elements is to maintain the dominance of some people over others. This inequity, in turn, generates pressure toward change. Yet by stressing the divisiveness of culture, this paradigm understates the ways in which cultural patterns integrate members of society. Thus we should consider both social-conflict and

NOTE: Scientists discovered fifty years ago that DNA (deoxyribonucleic acid) is analogous to a 3-billion-bit-long computer program, shaped like a double helix, that generates protein and transmits human heredity. Scientists expect to complete the "mapping" of human DNA early in the next century. As this work proceeds, we will learn much more about how genetics affects human culture.

structural-functional insights to gain a fuller understanding of culture.

Sociobiology

We know culture is a human creation; but does our biological humanity influence the development of culture? A third theoretical paradigm, standing with one leg in biology and one in sociology, attempts to answer this question. **Sociobiology**, then, is *a theoretical paradigm that explores ways in which our biology affects how humans create culture.*

A multidisciplinary theoretical scheme, sociobiology rests on the logic of evolution. In *On the Origin of Species*, Charles Darwin (1859) asserted that living organisms change over long periods of time as a result of *natural selection*, a matter of four simple principles. First, all living things live to reproduce themselves. Second, the blueprint for reproduction lies in the genes, the basic units of life that carry traits of one generation into the next. Genes vary randomly in each species; in effect, this genetic variation allows a species to "try out" new life patterns in a particular environment. Third, due to genetic variation, some organisms are more likely than others to survive and to pass on their advantageous genes to their offspring. Fourth and finally, over thousands of generations, specific genetic patterns that promote reproduction survive and become dominant. In this way, as biologists say, a species *adapts* to its environment, and dominant traits emerge as the "nature" of the organism.

In the case of humans, culture itself emerged as human nature. That is, rather than being biologically "wired" for specific behavior, humans developed the intelligence and sociability to devise many ways of life. Such flexibility has allowed our species to flourish all over the planet. Even so, sociobiologists point out, we are all one species—a fact evident in the large number of cultural universals.

Consider, for example, sex researcher Alfred Kinsey's observation: "Among all people everywhere in the world, the male is more likely than the female to desire sex with a variety of partners" (quoted in Barash, 1981:49). What insights does sociobiology offer into the so-called "double standard"?

To begin, we all know that children result from joining a woman's egg with a man's sperm. But the biological significance of a single sperm and a single egg differ dramatically. For healthy men, sperm represent a "renewable resource" produced by the testes throughout most of the life course. A man releases hundreds of millions of sperm in a single ejaculation—technically, enough to fertilize every woman in North America (Barash, 1981:47). A newborn female's ovaries, however, contain her entire lifetime allotment of follicles or immature eggs. A woman commonly releases a single mature egg cell from her ovaries each month. So, while a man is biologically capable of fathering thousands of offspring, a woman is able to bear only a relatively small number of children.

Given this biologically based difference, each sex is well served by a distinctive reproductive strategy. From a strictly biological perspective, a man reproduces his genes most efficiently by being promiscuous, that is, readily engaging in sex. This scheme, however, opposes the reproductive interests of a woman, whose relatively few pregnancies demand that she carry the child for nine months, give birth, and care for the infant for some time afterward. Thus, efficient reproduction on the part of the woman depends on carefully selecting a mate whose qualities (beginning with the likelihood that he will simply stay around) will contribute to their child's survival and successful reproduction (Remoff, 1984).

The "double standard" certainly involves more than biology and is tangled up with the historical domination of women by men (Barry, 1983). But sociobiology suggests that this cultural pattern, like many others, has an underlying bio-logic. Simply put, it has developed around the world because women and men everywhere tend toward distinctive reproductive strategies.

Critical evaluation. Sociobiology has generated intriguing theories about the biological roots of some cultural patterns, especially those that are universal. But sociobiology remains controversial for several reasons.

First, some critics fear that sociobiology may revive biological arguments, common a century ago, touting the superiority of one race or sex. But defenders counter that sociobiology rejects the past pseudo-science of racial superiority. On the contrary, they contend, sociobiology actually unites all of humanity by asserting that all people share a single evolutionary history. With regard to sex, sociobiology does rest on the assumption that men and women differ biologically in some ways that culture cannot overcome—if, in fact, any society sought to. But, far from asserting that males are somehow more important than females, sociobiology emphasizes how both sexes are vital to human reproduction.

Second, say the critics, sociobiologists have as yet amassed little evidence to support their theories. A generation ago, Edward O. Wilson (1975, 1978), generally

NOTE: In his book, *Culture Wars*, Hunter explains that today's political battles have much the same character as religious conflict between Catholics and Protestants during the last century: The issues are set in moral terms, raise powerful passions, and are differences resistant to compromise.

Q: "I define culture conflict very simply as political and social hostility rooted in different systems of moral understanding." James Davison Hunter

DISCUSS: Hunter concludes that the liberals currently have the upper hand in the cultural wars, since they control the symbolic industries, including universities, the press, and Hollywood. Does the class agree? Why or why not?

Controversy & Debate

What Are the "Culture Wars"?

"*Hi, there, this is WOSU's 'Open Line' talk show. This afternoon, we are debating the question 'Should there be a Constitutional amendment outlawing burning of the U.S. flag?' I have Rhonda from the East Side on the line; Rhonda, what do you think . . . ?*"

The easy rhythm of radio talk shows is familiar to just about everyone all across the country. But there is nothing simple about the questions being asked and, more often than not, little agreement on the answers. Indeed, on a host of issues—including flag burning, gender equality, gay rights, welfare, abortion, single parenting, prayer in schools, multiculturalism, and government funding for the arts—there now seems to be a wide and angry gulf in U.S. society. And, on both sides, people are thoughtful, committed to their principles, and concerned about the future of their country. They are fighting the "culture wars."

The "culture wars" represent our nation's latest round of **cultural conflict**, *political opposition, often accompanied by social hostility, rooted in different cultural values.* There is nothing novel about cultural conflict; throughout much of the nineteenth century, for example, Protestants and Catholics clashed over the direction of U.S. society. Many issues at the core of today's "culture wars" are new, of course, but as sociologist James Davison Hunter explains, this conflict remains a "struggle to define America."

Hunter offers several insights into the current cultural conflict. He begins by noting that the diverse touchstones of contemporary culture clashes are related. That is, one's position on any particular issue is likely to predict one's view on another. Why? Because most individuals fall into one of two major camps—"traditionalists" or "progressives"—each of which has distinctive cultural orientations.

Traditionalists, explains Hunter, see the world as a moral system; that is, they recognize "an external, definable, and transcendent authority" that clearly defines right and wrong and to whom everyone is responsible. For many—whether they are Christians, Jews, or Muslims—God is this authority. For others, this authority is the cultural heritage of self-reliance and strong families that has guided this country for centuries. Traditionalists, then, are conservatives who tend to be patriotic, religious, and believe in "old-fashioned family values." Thus traditionalists condemn flag burning as anti-American, oppose abortion as morally wrong, and think that today's public schools have abandoned moral teaching in favor of promulgating a "secular humanism" of tolerance for virtually every imaginable "lifestyle." From this point of view, social problems like the growing tide of violence, divorce, and "illegitimate" births stem from too little moral responsibility and too much personal freedom.

To progressives, on the other hand, a just world is composed of thoughtful people free to act according to their own principles. Progressives recognize no simple distinction between right and wrong. Indeed, they note that, centuries ago, our country deliberately removed religion from public life, making spiritual beliefs a matter of individual conscience. Certainly, some progressives are religious, but they tend to see the Bible or other religious texts as sources of historical wisdom that people must interpret for themselves in light of today's circumstances. Thus, progressives support people's right to protest (even by flag burning), a woman's right to abortion, and current law that bans religious observance from public schools. From this perspective, social problems like poverty and racial discrimination are best remedied not by greater moral discipline, but by more freedom for disadvantaged people so together we can forge a more equal and just society.

One reason that the "culture wars" generate so much heat in the United States, claims Hunter, is that public discussion of issues usually centers around media coverage of groups with extreme positions on one side or the other. But looking beyond how media coverage inflames the "culture wars," we see a solid core of disagreement. Traditionalists and progressives hold diametrically opposing views: What one side sees as the "solution" the other considers to be the "problem."

Continue the debate . . .

1. *Why do you think people find it hard to compromise on so many "culture wars" issues (such as access to abortion or gay rights)?*

2. *Are the "culture wars" evident on your campus? If so, cite examples.*

3. *Which side of the "culture wars" has the upper hand? Why?*

Source: Adapted, in part, from Hunter (1991).

DISCUSS: To what extent do the media—often seeking out the extremists in order to generate a good story—serve to polarize culture conflict?
Q: "Absolute truth can belong to only one class of humans . . . the class of absolute fools." Ashley Montagu

NOTE: The final section of Chapter 5 ("Socialization") explores the "constraint versus freedom" controversy.
Q: "Society is indeed a contract between those who are living, those who are dead, and those who are yet to be born." Edmund Burke
Q: "Don't be so open minded that your brains fall out." Richard Rorty

credited as the founder of this field, optimistically claimed that sociobiology would reveal the biological roots of human culture. But research to date concludes that biological forces do not determine human behavior in any rigid sense. Rather, abundant evidence supports the conclusion that human behavior is *learned* within a cultural system. The contribution of sociobiology, then, lies in its explanation of why some cultural patterns seem "easier to learn" than others (Barash, 1981).

CULTURE AND HUMAN FREEDOM

Throughout this chapter, we have touched on the extent to which cultural creatures are free. Does culture bind us to each other and to the past? Or does culture enhance our capacity for individual thought and independent choices?

Culture as Constraint

Over the long course of human evolution, culture became the human strategy for survival. Truly, we cannot live without culture. But the capacity for culture does have some drawbacks. We may be the only animals who name ourselves; yet, as symbolic beings, we are also the only creatures who experience alienation. Moreover, culture is largely a matter of habit, limiting our choices and driving us to repeat troubling patterns, such as racial prejudice, in each new generation. And, in an electronic age, we may wonder at the extent to which the news media and businesses

manipulate people into believing they must see the latest films or wear the latest styles of clothing.

Moreover, while our society's insistence on competitive achievement urges us toward excellence, this same pattern also isolates us from one another. Material comforts improve our lives in many ways, yet our preoccupation with acquiring things distracts us from seeking the security and satisfaction of close relationships or cultivating spiritual strength. Our emphasis on personal freedom affords us privacy and autonomy, yet our culture often denies us the support of a human community in which to share life's problems (Slater, 1976; Bellah et al., 1985).

Culture as Freedom

Human beings may seem to be prisoners of culture, just as other animals are prisoners of biology. But careful thought about the ideas presented in this chapter reveals a crucial difference. Biological instinct operates in a ready-made world; culture, by contrast, gives us the responsibility to make and remake a world for ourselves.

Therefore, although culture seems at times to circumscribe our lives, it always embodies the human capacity for hope, creativity, and choice. There is no better evidence of this than the fascinating cultural diversity of our own society and the far greater human variety of the larger world. Furthermore, far from being static, culture is ever-changing; it allows our imagination and inventiveness to come to the fore. The more we discover about the operation of our culture, the greater our capacity to use the freedom it offers us.

SUMMARY

1. Culture refers to a way of life shared by members of a society. Several species display a limited capacity for culture, but only human beings rely on culture for survival.

2. As the human brain evolved, the first elements of culture appeared some 2 million years ago; the development of culture reached the point we call "the birth of civilization" approximately 12,000 years ago.

3. Humans build culture on symbols by attaching meaning to objects and action. Language is the symbolic system by which one generation transmits culture to the next.

4. Values represent general orientations to the world around us; beliefs are statements people who share a culture hold to be true.

5. Cultural norms guide human behavior. Mores consist of norms of great moral significance; folkways guide everyday life and afford greater individual discretion.

6. High culture refers to patterns that distinguish a society's elites; popular culture includes patterns widespread in a society.

7. The United States stands among the most culturally diverse societies in the world. Subculture refers to distinctive cultural patterns adopted by a segment of a population; counterculture means

patterns strongly at odds with a conventional way of life. Multiculturalism represents educational efforts to enhance awareness and appreciation of cultural diversity.

8. Invention, discovery, and diffusion all generate cultural change. When parts of a cultural system change at different rates, this is called cultural lag.

9. Because we learn the standards of one culture, we evaluate other cultures ethnocentrically. An alternative to ethnocentrism, cultural relativism, means judging another culture according to its own standards.

10. The structural-functional paradigm views culture as a relatively stable system built on core values. Cultural traits function to maintain the overall system.

11. The social-conflict paradigm envisions culture as a dynamic arena of inequality and conflict. Cultural patterns typically benefit some categories of people more than others.

12. Sociobiology investigates the influence of humanity's evolutionary past on present-day cultural patterns.

13. Culture can constrain human needs and ambitions; yet, as cultural creatures, we have the capacity to shape and reshape the world to meet our needs and pursue our dreams.

14. The concept of cultural conflict refers to political debate ("culture wars") concerning a host of social problems and the general character of our way of life.

KEY CONCEPTS

Afrocentrism the dominance of African cultural patterns

beliefs specific statements that people hold to be true

counterculture cultural patterns that strongly oppose those widely accepted within a society

cultural conflict political opposition, often accompanied by social hostility, rooted in different cultural values

cultural integration the close relationship among various elements of a cultural system

cultural lag the fact that cultural elements change at different rates, which may disrupt a cultural system

cultural relativism the practice of judging a culture by its own standards

cultural transmission the process by which one generation passes culture to the next

cultural universals traits that are part of every known culture

culture the beliefs, values, behavior, and material objects that constitute a people's way of life

culture shock personal disorientation that comes from encountering an unfamiliar way of life

ethnocentrism the practice of judging another culture by the standards of one's own culture

Eurocentrism the dominance of European (especially English) cultural patterns

folkways a society's customs for routine, casual interaction

high culture cultural patterns that distinguish a society's elite

ideal culture (as opposed to real culture) social patterns mandated by cultural values and norms

language a system of symbols that allows members of a society to communicate with one another

material culture the tangible things created by members of a society

mores a society's standards of proper moral conduct

multiculturalism an educational program recognizing past and present cultural diversity in U.S. society and promoting the equality of all cultural traditions

nonmaterial culture the intangible world of ideas created by members of a society

norms rules and expectations by which a society guides the behavior of its members

popular culture cultural patterns that are widespread among a society's population

real culture (as opposed to ideal culture) actual social patterns that only approximate cultural expectations

Sapir-Whorf hypothesis the hypothesis that people perceive the world through the cultural lens of language

social control various means by which members of a society encourage conformity to norms

sociobiology a theoretical paradigm that explores ways in which our biology affects how humans create culture

subculture cultural patterns that set apart some segment of a society's population

symbol anything that carries a particular meaning recognized by people who share culture

technology knowledge that a society applies to the task of living in a physical environment

values culturally defined standards by which people assess desirability, goodness, and beauty, and which serve as broad guidelines for social living

CRITICAL-THINKING QUESTIONS

1. What is the cultural significance of a carefully manicured lawn in a highly mobile and largely anonymous society? What does a well-tended (or untended) front yard say about a person?
2. How does a schoolroom activity such as a "spelling bee" embody U.S. cultural values? What cultural values are expressed by children's stories such as "The Little Engine That Could" and popular board games like "Chutes and Ladders," "Monopoly," and "Risk"?
3. Do you think U.S. cultural values are changing? If so, how and why?
4. Have there been skirmishes in the "culture wars" on your campus? Which side is prevailing? What makes you think so?

SUGGESTED READINGS

Classic Sources

Napoleon A. Chagnon. *Yąnomamö: The Fierce People.* 4th ed. New York: Holt, Rinehart and Winston, 1992.
     Napoleon Chagnon's updated account of the Yąnomamö offers fascinating insights into a culture very different from our own. It is also a compelling tale of carrying out fieldwork in an unfamiliar world.

Margaret Mead. *Coming of Age in Samoa: A Psychological Study of Primitive Youth for Western Civilization.* New York: Wm. Morrow, 1928.
     Margaret Mead, perhaps the best-known student of culture, carried out this study of the Samoan Islands, which demonstrates the variability of cultural systems.

Contemporary Sources

William W. Zellner. *Counter Cultures: A Sociological Analysis.* New York: St. Martin's Press, 1994.
     This recent book investigates a host of groups at the margins of U.S. society, including skinheads, the Ku Klux Klan, satanists, survivalists, and followers of Scientology and the Unification Church.

James Davison Hunter. *Before the Shooting Begins: Searching for Democracy in America's Culture Wars.* New York: The Free Press, 1994.
     This book explains how public discussion of many controversial issues is distorted by the media and various activist organizations.

Global Sources

Mike Featherstone, ed. *Global Culture: Nationalism, Globalization, and Modernity.* London: Sage, 1990.
     These two dozen essays explore various ways in which a global culture is emerging.

Joana McIntyre Varawa. *Changes in Latitude: An Uncommon Anthropology.* New York: Harper & Row, 1990.
     This fascinating book describes how a woman from Hawaii past midlife traveled to Fiji on vacation only to find a new home, a new husband, and a host of new challenges.

Craig Storti. *The Art of Crossing Cultures.* Yarmouth, Minn.: Intercultural Press, 1990.
     This brief book explores the excitement as well as the difficulties of cross-cultural experience.

AMY JONES,
ST. REGIS INDIAN RESERVATION,
1937

Courtesy Janet Marqusee Fine Arts, New York.

Society

"I thought at first it was a doll's head," said Helmut Simon, a German tourist who, in 1991, made one of the scientific finds of the century. Simon was hiking across a huge glacier in southwest Austria near the Italian border when he stumbled upon a familiar shape protruding from the melting ice. He soon realized that it was not a doll but a human body: the so-called Iceman, who died some 5,300 years ago (before the construction of the Great Pyramids of Egypt), making him the oldest member of our species to be discovered essentially intact (see the time lines on the inside front cover).

Experts from around the world soon were buzzing with excitement. At the time of his death, they estimate the Iceman was about thirty years of age, with a height of five feet two inches, and weighing about 110 pounds. He was a shepherd, tending his flock high in the Alps in early fall, scientists speculate, when he was overtaken by a cold storm that forced him to take refuge in a narrow ridge in the mountain. Tired from his ordeal, he lay down and fell asleep, and, as the temperature continued to drop, he painlessly froze to death. Deep snows and a wall of ice soon entombed his body in a massive glacier. There, at a flesh-preserving temperature of twenty-one degrees Fahrenheit, he remained for fifty-three centuries. Only an unusual melt of the glacier—and the luck of a hiker with a sharp eye—led to the Iceman's discovery.

Examining the Iceman's garments, scientists were astonished at how advanced this "cave man's" society was. The Iceman's hair was neatly trimmed, and his body displayed numerous tattoos that probably symbolized his standing in his home community. He wore a skillfully stitched leather coat over which a woven grass cape provided greater protection from the elements. His shoes, also made of leather, were stuffed with grass for comfort and warmth. He carried with him an ax, a wood-handled knife, and a bow that shot feathered arrows with flint points. A primitive backpack held additional tools and personal items, including natural medicines made from plants (Rademaekers & Schoenthal, 1992).

This chapter takes a look back at the historical development of human societies, offers insights about their present state, and points to some future trends. The central concept of **society** refers to *people who interact in a defined territory and share culture.* We shall examine this deceptively simple term from four different angles. **Gerhard Lenski** and **Jean Lenski** describe the changing character of human society over the last ten thousand years. Focusing on how *technology* shapes social life, their analysis shows that a technological breakthrough often has revolutionary consequences for society as a whole. The remainder of the chapter presents classic visions of society developed by three of sociology's founders. Like the Lenskis, **Karl Marx** also understood human history as a long and complex process of social change. For Marx, however, the story of society spins around *social conflict,* which stems from inequality rooted in how people produce material goods. **Max Weber** recognized the importance of productive forces as well, but he sought to demonstrate the power of *human ideas* to animate society. Weber believed that rational thinking underlies modern society and promotes change. Finally, **Emile Durkheim** investigated patterns of *social solidarity,* noting that the bonds uniting traditional societies and their modern counterparts are strikingly different.

NOTE: Instructors may use this chapter in a variety of ways. Assign all of it to give students a detailed introduction to important historical material and key theorists whose ideas inform later chapters. Alternatively, assign sections separately along with later chapters— adding the Weber section to the discussion of bureaucracy in Chapter 7; Durkheim to structural-functional analysis of deviance

in Chapter 8; Marx to the examination of social inequality in Chapter 9. Instructors may also omit the chapter entirely without breaking the flow of the text.

Q: "Technology does not determine all a society's characteristics, of course. It does, however, determine two fundamental things. First it determines the *range of what is possible* . . . Second, its technology determines *the relative costs of its options.*" Gerhard and Jean Lenski

Gerhard Lenski and Jean Lenski: The Evolution of Technology

Gerhard Lenski is a contemporary U.S. sociologist who is well known for his research on

religion, social inequality, and history. Jean Lenski, a writer and poet who passed away in 1994, frequently collaborated with her husband in sociological research. Together, they brought to the attention of their sociological colleagues a wide range of research on the role of technology in human societies.

To the Lenskis, technology underlies all other facets of social life by determining how that society processes material resources from its natural surroundings. With little ability to manipulate nature, technologically simple societies are at the mercy of their surroundings (a situation we sometimes wistfully call living "in

tune" with nature). Technologically simple societies tend to resemble one another; the variations among them basically correspond to their distinctive natural environments. By contrast, technologically sophisticated societies like our own wield enormous power to reshape the physical world according to human designs, and develop the striking cultural diversity described in Chapter 3 ("Culture"). Yet human technology is homogenizing much of the cultural variation in the world today. In light of this increasing global connectedness, it is interesting to wonder whether human cultures are making a shift toward greater similarity once again.

All four visions of society answer key questions: How do societies of the past and present differ from one another? How and why do societies change? What forces divide a society? What forces hold it together? Are societies getting better or worse? The theorists profiled in this chapter all probed these questions, but they disagree on the answers. We shall highlight the similarities and differences in their views as we go along.

GERHARD LENSKI AND JEAN LENSKI: SOCIETY AND TECHNOLOGY

The Iceman, introduced at the opening of this chapter, was a member of a very early human society. He had already died before a great empire flourished in Egypt, before the flowering of culture in ancient Greece, and before any society in Europe could boast of a single city.

As people who take for granted rapid transportation and instant global communication, we look on this ancestor from our distant past with keen curiosity. But sociologists who study the past (working with archaeologists and anthropologists) have learned quite a bit about our human heritage. Gerhard Lenski and

Jean Lenski, introduced in the box, have chronicled the great differences among societies that have flourished and declined throughout human history. Just as important, the work of these researchers helps us better understand how we live today.

The Lenskis call the focus of their research **sociocultural evolution,** *the process of change that results from a society's gaining new information, particularly technology* (Lenski, Nolan, & Lenski, 1995:75). Rather like a biologist examining how a living species evolves over millennia, a sociologist employing this approach observes how societies change over centuries as they gain greater ability to manipulate their physical environments. Societies with rudimentary technology can support only a small number of people who enjoy few choices about how to live. Technologically complex societies—while not necessarily "better" in any absolute sense—develop large populations characterized by diverse, highly specialized lives.

The Lenskis also explain that the greater the amount of technological information a society has in its grasp, the faster the rate at which it changes. Technologically simple societies, then, change very slowly; in fact, some of the clothing worn by the Austrian Iceman differs only slightly from garments used by

DISCUSS: Hunting and gathering people mused over the stars, and we still know the constellations in terms that were relevant to them—mostly animals and hunters. If we were to begin the process from scratch, what meaning would we impose on the stars today?
NOTE: Simple societies have yielded information about the medicinal properties of plants, and also a general model for living in balance with nature. (See Chapter 22, "Environment and Society.")

NOTE: Most likely, shamans practice the "oldest profession," not prostitutes, as the old saying suggests.
NOTE: Hunters and gatherers are animists (from a Latin root meaning "full of life").
NOTE: We can envision the transition from hunting and gathering to pastoralism and horticulture as a shift from *seeking food* to *growing one's own.*

shepherds in the same area early in this century. By contrast, industrial, high-technology societies change so quickly that people witness dramatic transformations in the span of their lifetimes. Consider some familiar elements of North American culture that would probably puzzle, delight, or even alarm people who lived just a few generations ago: beepers, phone sex, artificial hearts, laser surgery, test-tube babies, genetic engineering, computer-based virtual reality, fiber optics, smart bombs, the threat of nuclear holocaust, space shuttles, transsexualism, and "tell-all" talk shows.

As a society extends its technological reach, the effects ripple through the cultural system, generating countless repercussions. When our ancestors first harnessed the power of the wind by using a sail, they set the stage for discovering kites, sailing ships, windmills, and, eventually, airplanes. Consider, as more recent examples, the many ways modern life has been changed by atomic energy or the computer.

Drawing on the Lenskis' work, we will describe five general types of societies distinguished by their technology: hunting and gathering societies, horticultural and pastoral societies, agrarian societies, industrial societies, and postindustrial societies.

Hunting and Gathering Societies

Hunting and gathering refers to *simple technology for hunting animals and gathering vegetation.* From the emergence of our species until about twelve thousand years ago, all humans were hunters and gatherers. Although hunting and gathering societies remained common several centuries ago, only a few persist today, including the Aka and Pygmies of central Africa, the Bushmen of southwestern Africa, the Aborigines of Australia, the Kaska Indians of northwest Canada, and the Batek and Semai of Malaysia (Endicott, 1992; Hewlett, 1992).

With scarcely any technology to make food production efficient, most members of these societies must search continually for game and edible plants. Only in lush areas where food is plentiful would hunters and gatherers have any leisure time. Moreover, foraging for food demands a large amount of land, so hunting and gathering societies comprise small bands of a few dozen people living at some distance from one another. These groups are also nomadic, moving on as they deplete vegetation in one area or in pursuit of migratory animals. Although periodically returning to favored sites, they rarely form permanent settlements.

In technologically simple societies, successful hunting wins men great praise. However, the gathering of vegetation by women is a more dependable and easily available source of nutrition.

Hunting and gathering societies are based on kinship. The family obtains and distributes food, protects its members, and teaches necessary skills to children. Most activities are common to everyone and center on seeking their next meal; some specialization, however, corresponds to age and sex. The very young and the very old contribute only what they can, while healthy adults secure most of the food. The gathering of vegetation—the more reliable food source—is typically the work of women, while men take on the less certain job of hunting. Although the two sexes have somewhat different responsibilities, then, most hunters and gatherers probably accorded men and women comparable social importance (Leacock, 1978).

Hunting and gathering societies have few formal leaders. Most recognize a *shaman,* or spiritual leader, who enjoys high prestige but receives no greater material rewards than other members of the society and must help procure food like everyone else. Other individuals who are especially skillful at obtaining food also bask in high prestige; overall, however, the social organization of hunters and gatherers is relatively simple and egalitarian.

Hunting and gathering societies rarely use their simple weapons—the spear, the bow and arrow, and stone knife—to wage war. Nonetheless they are often ravaged by the forces of nature. Storms and droughts can easily destroy their food supply, and they stand vulnerable to accident and disease. Such risks encourage

Chapter 4 Society **97**

NOTE: The Lenskis explain that hunters and gatherers limited property rights to personal tools and weapons. Natural resources, including fields and forests, were defined as collective property, but ownership was claimed by the group. Thus, members of such societies generally expected outsiders to seek permission before entering an area. Horticulturalists, by contrast, typically (but not always) define land as private property.

DISCUSS: Ask why Christians speak of their "pastor" and refer to the congregation as a "flock."

NOTE: *Hort* is a Latin root meaning "garden." Latin *horti cultura* thus means "cultivation of a garden"; *agri cultura* means "cultivation of a field." "Pastoral" is derived from Latin meaning "shepherd" or, literally, "feeder."

Pastoralism historically has flourished in regions of the world where arid soil does not support crops. Pastoral people still thrive in northern Africa, living today much as they did a thousand years ago.

cooperation and sharing, a strategy that increases everyone's odds of survival. Nonetheless, many die in childhood, and perhaps half perish before the age of twenty (Lenski, Nolan, & Lenski, 1995:104).

During this century, technologically complex societies have slowly closed in on the few remaining hunters and gatherers, reducing their landholdings and depleting game and vegetation. The Lenskis predict that the 1990s may well witness the end of hunting and gathering societies on earth. Fortunately, study of this way of life has already produced valuable information about human history and our fundamental ties to the natural world.

Horticultural and Pastoral Societies

Ten to twelve thousand years ago, a new technology began to change many hunting and gathering societies (see the time line on the inside front cover). **Horticulture** is *technology based on using hand tools to cultivate plants.* The most important tools of horticulturalists are the hoe to work the soil and the digging stick to punch holes in the ground for seeds. Humans first used these tools in fertile regions of the Middle East and, later, in Latin America and Asia. Cultural diffusion spread knowledge of horticulture throughout most of the world by about six thousand years ago.

Not all societies were quick to abandon hunting and gathering in favor of horticulture. Hunters and gatherers living amid plentiful vegetation and game probably saw little reason to embrace the new technology (Fisher, 1979). The Yąnomamö of the Brazilian rain forest (described in Chapter 3, "Culture"), illustrate the common practice of combining horticulture

with more traditional hunting and gathering (Chagnon, 1992).

Then, too, people in particularly arid regions (such as the Middle East) or mountainous areas (such as in the Alps where the Iceman lived) found horticulture to be of little value. Such people turned to a different strategy for survival, **pastoralism,** which is *technology based on the domestication of animals.* Still others combined horticulture and pastoralism to produce a variety of foods. Today, many horticultural-pastoral societies thrive in South America, Africa, and Asia.

The domestication of plants and animals greatly increased food production, enabling societies to support not dozens but hundreds of people. Pastoralists remained nomadic, leading their herds to fresh grazing lands. Horticulturalists, by contrast, formed settlements, moving on only when they depleted the soil. These settlements, joined by trade, comprised multicentered societies with overall populations often in the thousands.

Domesticating plants and animals generates a *material surplus,* more resources than necessary to sustain day-to-day living. A surplus frees some people from the job of securing food, allowing them to create crafts, engage in trade, cut hair, apply tattoos, or serve as priests. In comparison to hunting and gathering societies, then, horticultural and pastoral societies display more specialized and complex social arrangements.

Hunters and gatherers recognize numerous spirits inhabiting the world. Horticulturalists, however, practice ancestor worship and conceive of God as Creator. Pastoral societies carry this belief further, viewing God as directly involved in the well-being of the entire world. This view of God ("The Lord is my shepherd . . . ," Psalm 23) is widespread among members of our own

NOTE: Horticulturalists practice *slash and burn* or *swidden* horticulture. This practice involves regular clearing of new land as land in use suffers depleted nutrients. Trees and other growth are felled and, when dry, burned.

NOTE: Warfare is common among horticulturalists while rare among hunting and gathering people. Why? The increasing population density of horticultural societies limits both available land and game, making competition for these resources stiffer.

Q: "You can lead a horticulture, but you can't make her think." Dorothy Parker

NOTE: At its height, the Roman Empire surrounded most of the Mediterranean Sea (including Europe, the Middle East, and northern Africa).

society because Christianity, Islam, and Judaism originated as Middle Eastern, pastoral religions.

Expanding productive technology also intensifies social inequality. As some families produce more food than others, they assume positions of relative power and privilege. Forging alliances with other elite families ensures that social advantages endure over generations and a formal system of social inequality emerges. Along with social hierarchy, rudimentary government—backed by military force—is formed to shore up the power of elites. However, without the ability to communicate or to travel quickly, a ruler can control only a limited number of people, so empire-building proceeds on a small scale.

The domestication of plants and animals surely made simpler societies more productive. But advancing technology is never entirely beneficial. The Lenskis point out that, compared to hunters and gatherers, horticulturalists and pastoralists display more social inequality and, in many cases, engage in slavery, protracted warfare, and even cannibalism.

Agrarian Societies

About five thousand years ago—around the time the Iceman roamed the earth—another technological revolution was under way in the Middle East that would eventually transform most of the world. This was the discovery of **agriculture,** *the technology of large-scale farming using plows harnessed to animals or more powerful sources of energy.* The Lenskis state that the social significance of the animal-drawn plow, along with other technological innovations of the period—including irrigation, the wheel, writing, numbers, and the expanding use of metals—clearly qualifies this era as "the dawn of civilization" (1995:177).

Farmers with animal-drawn plows cultivated fields vastly larger than the garden-sized plots worked by horticulturalists. Plows have the additional advantage of turning, and thereby aerating, the soil to increase fertility. Such technology encouraged agrarian societies to farm the same land for decades, which, in turn, led to humanity's first permanent settlements. Large food surpluses, transported on animal-powered wagons, allowed agrarian societies to expand to unprecedented land area and population. As an extreme case, the Roman Empire at its height (about 100 C.E.) boasted a population of 70 million spread over some 2 million square miles (Stavrianos, 1983; Lenski, Nolan, & Lenski, 1995).

As always, increasing production meant greater specialization. Tasks once performed by everyone, such as clearing land and securing food, became

Of Egypt's 130 pyramids, the Great Pyramids at Giza are the largest. Each of the three major structures stands more than forty stories high and is composed of 3 million massive stone blocks. Some 4,500 years ago, tens of thousands of people labored to construct these pyramids so that one man, the pharaoh, might have a god-like monument for his tomb. Clearly social inequality in this agrarian society was striking.

distinct occupations. Specialization made the early barter system obsolete and prompted the invention of money as a common standard of exchange. The appearance of money facilitated trade, sparking the growth of cities as economic centers with populations soaring into the millions.

Agrarian societies exhibit dramatic social inequality. In many cases—including the United States early in its history—peasants or slaves constitute a significant share of the population and labor for elites. Freed from manual work, elites can then devote their time to the study of philosophy, art, and literature. This

GLOBAL: For most of our history, our species has lived in hunting and gathering societies; during the last 2,000 years, however, agrarian societies have predominated, and about 70 percent of the world's people still live in agrarian settings.

NOTE: Peter Berger (1986:99) points out that today's average people live better in many respects than the elites of agrarian societies. For example, as late as World War I, Schoenbrunn, the fabulous summer palace of the Habsburgs (monarchs of Austria), had not a single indoor toilet.

NOTE: Worth repeating is the link between agrarian "cultivation" and the flowering of human "culture"—the words share a single root.

RESOURCE: The companion reader *Seeing Ourselves* includes Marvin Harris's article "India's Sacred Cow," which explains the Hindu veneration of the cow in terms of India's ecology and technology.

SOCIAL DIVERSITY

Technology and the Changing Status of Women

In technologically simple societies of the past, women produced more food than men did. Hunters and gatherers valued meat highly, but men's hunting was not a dependable source of nourishment. Thus vegetation gathered by women was the primary means of ensuring survival. Similarly, tools and seeds used in horticulture developed under the control of women, who already had primary responsibility for providing and preparing food. For their part, men engaged in trade and tended herds of animals. Only at harvest time did both sexes work together.

About five thousand years ago, humans discovered how to mold metals. This technology spread by cultural diffusion, primarily along trade networks forged by men. Thus it was men who devised the metal plow and, since they already managed animals, soon thought to hitch the implement to a cow.

This great innovation propelled the transition from horticulture to agriculture and, for the first time, thrust men into a dominant position in the production of food. Elise Boulding explains how this technological breakthrough undermined the social standing of women:

The shift of the status of the woman farmer may have happened quite rapidly, once there were two male specializations relating to agriculture: plowing and the care of cattle. This situation left women with all the many subsidiary tasks, including weeding and carrying water to the fields. The new fields were larger, so women had to work just as many hours as they did before, but now they worked at more secondary tasks. . . . This would contribute further to the erosion of the status of women.

Sources: Based on Boulding (1976) and Fisher (1979).

explains the historical link between "high culture," as noted in Chapter 3 ("Culture"), and social privilege.

Among hunters and gatherers and also among horticulturalists, women are the primary providers of food. The development of agriculture, however, appears to have propelled men into a position of social dominance (Boulding, 1976; Fisher, 1979). The box looks more closely at the declining position of women at this point in the course of sociocultural evolution.

Religion reinforces the power of agricultural elites. Religious doctrine typically propounds the idea that people are morally obligated to perform whatever tasks correspond to their place in the social order. Many of the "Wonders of the Ancient World," such as the Great Wall of China and the Great Pyramids of Egypt, were possible only because emperors and pharaohs wielded virtually absolute power to mobilize their people to endure a lifetime of labor without pay.

In agrarian societies, then, elites gain unparalleled power. To maintain control of large empires, leaders require the services of a wide range of administrators. Consequently, along with the growing economy, the political system becomes established as a distinct sphere of life.

In relation to the societies described so far, the Lenskis conclude, agrarian societies have greater specialization and more social inequality. And, compared to horticultural and pastoral societies, agrarian societies differ more from one another because advancing technology increases human control over the natural world.

Industrial Societies

Industrialism, as found in the United States, Canada, and much of the Northern Hemisphere, is *technology that powers sophisticated machinery with advanced sources of energy.* Until the industrial era, the major source of energy was the muscles of humans and other animals. At the dawning of the *Industrial Revolution,* about 1750, mills and factories relied on flowing water and then steam to power ever-larger and more efficient machinery.

Once this technology was at hand, societies began to change faster, as shown in Figure 4–1. Industrial societies transformed themselves more in a century than they had in thousands of years before. As explained in Chapter 1 ("The Sociological Perspective"), this stunning change stimulated the birth of sociology itself. During the nineteenth century, railroads

NOTE: Until about 150 years ago, the fastest a person traveled (short of falling out of a tall tree) was about 35 mph, the speed of a swift horse.

NOTE: Chapter 15 ("The Economy and Work") details the distinctive elements of the Industrial Revolution: (1) new forms of energy, (2) factories, (3) mass production, (4) productive specialization, and (5) wage labor.

NOTE: The Lenskis point out that the term "Industrial Revolution" did not enter common usage until the final decades of the 19th century; at that point, it already described events that had begun almost two centuries before.

NOTE: Chapter 9 ("Social Stratification") examines the relative degree of social inequality in the types of societies described by the Lenskis. See, especially, Figure 9–2, the Kuznets Curve.

and steamships revolutionized transportation, and steel-framed skyscrapers recast the urban landscape, dwarfing the cathedrals that symbolized an earlier age.

As the twentieth century opened, automobiles further reshaped Western societies, and electricity was fast becoming the basis for countless "modern conveniences." Electronic communication, including the telephone, radio, and television, were mass-producing cultural patterns and gradually making a large world seem smaller and smaller. More recently, transportation technology has given humanity the capacity to fly faster than sound and even to break the bonds of earth. Nuclear power has also forever changed the world. And during the last generation, computers have ushered in the *Information Revolution*, dramatically increasing humanity's capacity to process words and numbers.

Work, too, has changed. In agrarian societies, most men and women work in the home. Industrialization, however, creates factories near centralized machinery and energy sources. Lost in the process are close working relationships and strong kinship ties, as well as many of the traditional values, beliefs, and customs that guide agrarian life.

Industrialism engenders societies of unparalleled prosperity. Although health in industrial cities of Europe and North America was initially poor, a rising standard of living and advancing health-related technology gradually brought infectious diseases under control. Consequently, life expectancy increased, fueling rapid population growth. Industrialization also draws people from the countryside to the cities where the factories are built. So while roughly one in ten members of agrarian societies lives in cities, three out of four people in industrial societies are urbanites.

Occupational specialization, which expanded over the long course of sociocultural evolution, has become more pronounced than ever. Industrial people often size up one another in terms of their jobs rather than according to their kinship ties (as agrarian people do). Rapid change and movement from place to place also generate anonymity and cultural diversity, sparking the formation of numerous subcultures and countercultures, as described in Chapter 3 ("Culture").

Industrial technology recasts the family, too, diminishing its traditional significance as the center of social life. No longer does the family serve as the primary setting for economic production, learning, and religious worship. And, as Chapter 17 ("Family") explains in detail, technological change also underlies the trend away from so-called traditional families to greater numbers of single people, divorced people, single-parent families, and stepfamilies.

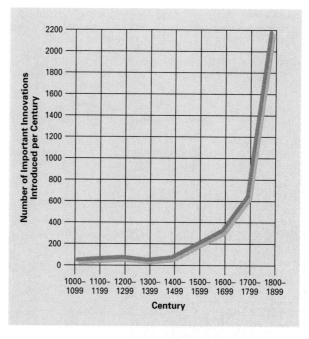

FIGURE 4–1 The Increasing Number of Technological Innovations

This figure illustrates the number of technological innovations in Western Europe after the beginning of the Industrial Revolution in the mid-eighteenth century. Technological innovation occurs at an accelerating rate because each innovation spins off existing cultural elements to produce many further innovations.

Source: Lenski, Nolan, & Lenski (1995).

The Lenskis explain that early industrialization concentrated the benefits of advancing technology on a small segment of the population, with the majority living in poverty. In time, however, the material benefits of industrial productivity spread more widely. Poverty remains a serious problem in industrial societies, but compared to the situation a century ago, the standard of living has risen fivefold, and economic, social, and political inequality has declined. Some social leveling, detailed in Chapter 9 ("Social Stratification"), occurs because industrial societies demand a literate and skilled labor force. While most people in agrarian societies are illiterate, industrial societies provide state-funded schooling and confer numerous political rights on virtually everyone. Industrialization, in fact, intensifies demands for political participation, as seen recently in South Korea, Taiwan, the People's Republic of China, the former Soviet Union, and the societies of Eastern Europe.

GLOBAL: The Lenskis report the following typical densities in persons per square mile: hunting and gathering societies, less than one; horticultural societies, in the range of 10 to 40; agrarian societies, over 100. Industrial societies have densities that range from about 70 (U.S.) to many hundreds (most European nations), nearing 1,000 in a few cases (such as Japan and the Netherlands).

Q: "Society is no comfort to one not sociable." William Shakespeare

GLOBAL: The ratio of inanimate to animate sources of energy is a good index of modernization, according to Marion Levy.

GLOBAL: Marvin Harris (1983) describes the power of expanding technology by estimating that hunters and gatherers had to expend 1 calorie of human energy to produce 3 calories of food value. For horticultural societies, the ratio is 1:15; for agrarian societies, 1:50; and for industrial societies, 1:5,000.

TABLE 4–1 Sociocultural Evolution: A Summary

Type of Society	Historical Period	Productive Technology	Population Size
Hunting and Gathering Societies	Only type of society until about 12,000 years ago; still common several centuries ago; the few examples remaining today are threatened with extinction	Primitive weapons	25–40 people
Horticultural and Pastoral Societies	From about 12,000 years ago, with decreasing numbers after about 3000 B.C.E.	Horticultural societies use hand tools for cultivating plants; pastoral societies are based on the domestication of animals	Settlements of several hundred people, interconnected through trading ties to form societies of several thousand people
Agrarian Societies	From about 5,000 years ago, with large but decreasing numbers today	Animal-drawn plow	Millions of people
Industrial Societies	From about 1750 to the present	Advanced sources of energy; mechanized production	Millions of people
Postindustrial Societies	Emerging in recent decades	Computers that support an information-based economy	Millions of people

Postindustrial Societies

Many industrial societies, including the United States, now appear to be entering yet another phase of technological development, and we can briefly extend the Lenskis' analysis to take account of recent trends. A generation ago sociologist Daniel Bell (1973) coined the term **postindustrialism** to refer to *technology that supports an information-based economy*. While production in industrial societies focuses on factories and machinery generating material goods, postindustrial production focuses on computers and other electronic devices that create, process, store, and apply information. At the individual level, members of industrial societies concentrate on learning mechanical skills; people in postindustrial societies, however, work on honing information-based skills for work involving computers, facsimile machines, satellites, and other forms of communication technology.

As this shift in key skills indicates, the emergence of postindustrialism dramatically changes a society's occupational structure. Chapter 15 ("The Economy and Work") examines this process in detail, explaining that a postindustrial society utilizes less and less of its labor force for industrial production. At the same time, the ranks of clerical workers, managers, and other people who process information (in fields ranging from academia and advertising to marketing and public relations) swell rapidly.

The Information Revolution is, of course, most pronounced in industrial, high-income societies, yet the reach of this new technology is so great that it is affecting the entire world. As explained in Chapter 3 ("Culture"), the unprecedented, worldwide flow of information originating in rich nations like our own has the predictable effect of tying far-flung societies together and fostering common patterns of global culture.

TABLE 4–1 (continued)

Type of Society	Settlement Pattern	Social Organization	Examples
Hunting and Gathering Societies	Nomadic	Family centered; specialization limited to age and sex; little social inequality	Pygmies of central Africa Bushmen of southwestern Africa Aborigines of Australia Semai of Malaysia Kaska Indians of Canada
Horticultural and Pastoral Societies	Horticulturalists form relatively small permanent settlements; pastoralists are nomadic	Family centered; religious system begins to develop; moderate specialization; increased social inequality	Middle Eastern societies about 5000 B.C.E. Various societies today in New Guinea and other Pacific islands Yanomamö today in South America
Agrarian Societies	Cities become common, though they generally contain only a small proportion of the population	Family loses significance as distinctive religious, political, and economic systems emerge; extensive specialization; increased social inequality	Egypt during construction of the Great Pyramids Medieval Europe Numerous nonindustrial societies of the world today
Industrial Societies	Cities contain most of the population	Distinct religious, political, economic, educational, and family systems; highly specialized; marked social inequality persists, diminishing somewhat over time	Most societies today in Europe and North America, Australia, and Japan generate most of the world's industrial production
Postindustrial Societies	Population remains concentrated in cities	Similar to industrial societies with information processing and other service work gradually replacing industrial production	Industrial societies noted above are now entering postindustrial stage

Another pivotal idea from Chapter 3—the concept of cultural lag—has an important application to postindustrial societies. Recall that cultural lag refers to the process by which some cultural elements (especially technology) change faster than others (such as values and norms). Even though information is fast replacing objects as the center of our economy, our legal notions about property are still based on tangible things.

Consider, for example, the national practice by which U.S. government officials monitor the flow of property in and out of this country. Customs officers require travelers to declare all the property that they wish to carry with them when they arrive, and baggage is subject to physical search. Curiously, while people are lining up to discuss purchases of liquor, antiques, or oriental rugs, an individual in possession of valuable ideas or computer programs on a computer disk can easily and legally walk past customs officials announcing "Nothing to declare!" since

our legal system has yet to fully recognize the value of nontangible property. In short, despite rapid technological change in recent decades, many of our ways of thinking remain rooted in an earlier era.

Table 4–1 summarizes how technology shapes societies at different stages of sociocultural evolution.

The Limits of Technology

While technology remedies many human problems, by raising productivity, eliminating disease, and sometimes simply relieving boredom, it provides no "quick fix" for deeply rooted social problems. Poverty remains the plight of millions of women and men in this country (detailed in Chapter 10, "Social Class in the United States") and of 1 billion people worldwide (see Chapter 11, "Global Stratification"). Moreover, with the capacity to reshape the world, technology has created new problems that our ancestors hardly

GLOBAL: James Williams Gibson (*The Perfect War: Technowar in Vietnam*, Boston: Atlantic Monthly, 1986) argues that the American defeat in Vietnam was caused by an ethnocentric view that military power hinges on technology alone.

NOTE: Nuclear power was used for destruction (1945) ten years before it first generated electricity.

Q: "We have too many men of science, too few of God. We have grasped the mystery of the atom and rejected the Sermon on the Mount. . . . Ours is a world of nuclear giants and ethical infants. We know more about war than we do about peace, more about killing than about living." General Omar N. Bradley (1948)

Q: "The truth is that we are all caught in a great economic system which is heartless." Woodrow Wilson

A century ago, the Industrial Revolution drew the labor force together into factories where large machinery and needed energy sources were situated. Today, a countertrend is underway as the Information Revolution now permits people to develop ideas and to process information virtually anywhere.

could have imagined. Industrial societies provide more personal freedom, often at the cost of the sense of community that characterized agrarian life. Further, although the most powerful societies of today's world infrequently engage in all-out warfare, international conflict now poses unimaginable horrors. Should nations ever unleash even a fraction of their present stockpiles of nuclear weapons, human society would almost certainly regress to a technologically primitive state if, indeed, we survived at all.

Another stubborn social problem involves humanity's relation to the physical environment. Each stage in sociocultural evolution has introduced more powerful sources of energy and accelerated our appetite for the earth's resources at a rate even faster than population is growing. We now face an issue of vital concern—one that is the focus of Chapter 22 ("Environment and Society"): Can humanity continue to pursue material prosperity without subjecting the planet to damage and strains from which it will never recover?

In some respects, then, technological advances have improved life and brought the world's people closer together within a "global village." Yet in technology's wake are daunting problems of establishing peace, ensuring justice, and sustaining a safe environment—problems that technology alone can never solve.

KARL MARX: SOCIETY AND CONFLICT

The first of our classic visions of society comes from Karl Marx (1818–1883), who is introduced in the box. Few observed the industrial transformation of Europe as keenly as he did. Marx spent most of his adult life in London, then the capital of the vast British Empire. He was awed by the productive power of the new factories; not only were European societies producing more goods than ever before, but a global system of commerce was funneling resources from around the world through British factories at a dizzying rate.

But what astounded Marx even more was the concentration of industry's riches in the hands of a few. A walk almost anywhere in London revealed dramatic extremes of splendid affluence and wretched squalor. A handful of aristocrats and industrialists lived in fabulous mansions, well staffed by servants, where they enjoyed luxury and privileges barely imaginable by the majority of their fellow Londoners. Most people labored long hours for low wages, living in slums or even sleeping in the streets, where many eventually succumbed to poor nutrition and infectious disease.

Throughout his life, Marx wrestled with a basic contradiction: In a society so rich, how could so many be so poor? Just as important, Marx asked, how can this situation be changed? Many people, no doubt, think of Karl Marx as a man determined to tear societies apart. But he was motivated by compassion for humanity and sought to help a society already badly divided forge what he hoped would be a new and just social order.

The key to Marx's thinking is the idea of **social conflict,** *struggle between segments of society over valued resources.* Social conflict can, of course, take many forms: Individuals may quarrel, some colleges have long-standing rivalries, and nations sometimes go to war. For Marx, however, the most significant form of social conflict involved clashes between social classes that arise from the way a society produces material goods.

Society and Production

Living in the nineteenth century, Marx observed the early stage of industrial capitalism in Europe. This economic system, Marx noted, transformed a small part of the population into **capitalists,** *people who own factories and other productive enterprises.* A capitalist's goal is profit, which results from selling a product for more than it costs to produce. Capitalism

PROFILE

Karl Marx: An Agenda for Change

Few names evoke as strong a response as Karl Marx. Some consider him a genius and a prophet, while others see only evil in his ideas. Everyone agrees that Marx stands among the social thinkers with the greatest impact on the world's people. Today, more than one-fifth of all humanity live in societies that consider themselves Marxist.

Nor was Marx a stranger to controversy during his lifetime. Born in the German city of Trier, he earned a doctorate in 1841 and began working as a newspaper editor. But his relentless social criticism sparked clashes with government authorities, who managed to drive Marx from Germany to Paris. Soon controversy forced him to flee from France as well, and Marx spent the rest of his life in London.

Along with Max Weber and Emile Durkheim, Marx was a major figure in the development of sociology, as we saw in Chapter 1 ("The Sociological Perspective"). However, sociologists in the United States paid relatively little attention to his ideas until the 1960s. Why? The answer lies in Marx's explicit criticism of industrial-capitalist society. Early U.S. sociologists dismissed his ideas as mere "politics" rather than serious scholarship. For Marx, scholarship *was* politics. While most sociologists heeded Max Weber's call for value-free research by attempting to minimize or conceal their own values (see Chapter 2, "Sociological Investigation"), Marx placed values at the center of his thinking. Marx did not merely observe society; he offered a rousing prescription for profound social change. As we have come to recognize the extent to which values shape all ideas, Marx's social analysis has finally received the attention it deserves as a pivotal approach to sociology.

Source: Based, in part, on Ritzer (1983).

transforms most of the population into industrial workers, whom Marx called the **proletariat**, *people who provide labor necessary to operate factories and other productive enterprises.* Workers sell their labor for the wages they need to live. To Marx, an inevitable conflict between capitalists and workers has its roots in the productive process itself. To maximize profits, capitalists must minimize wages, generally their single greatest expense. Workers, however, want wages to be as high as possible. Since profits and wages come from the same pool of funds, ongoing conflict occurs. Marx argued that this conflict would end only when people abandoned the capitalist system.

All societies are composed of **social institutions,** defined as *the major spheres of social life, or society's subsystems, organized to meet basic human needs.* In his analysis of society, Marx contended that one specific institution—the economy—dominates all others when it comes to steering the direction of a society.

Drawing on the philosophical doctrine of *materialism,* which asserts that how humans produce material goods shapes the rest of society, Marx claimed that all the other major social institutions—the political system, family, religion, and education—operated more or less to shore up a society's economy. Just as the Lenskis argue that technology molds the contours of a society, in other words, so Marx argued that the economy is "the real foundation . . . The mode of production in material life determines the general character of the social, political, and spiritual processes of life" (1959:43; orig. 1859).

Marx therefore viewed the economic system as the social *infrastructure (infra* is Latin meaning "below"). Other social institutions, including the family, the political system, and religion, which are built on this foundation, form society's *superstructure.* These institutions extend economic principles into other areas of life, as illustrated in Figure 4–2 on page 106. In practical

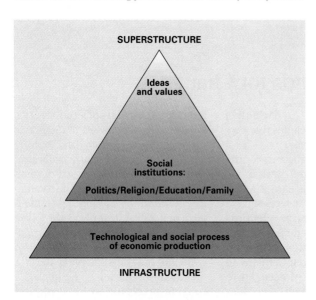

FIGURE 4–2 Karl Marx's Model of Society

This diagram illustrates Marx's materialist view that the process of economic production underlies and shapes the entire society. Economic production involves both technology (industry, in the case of capitalism) and social relationships (for capitalism, the relationship between the capitalists, who control the process of economic production, and the workers, who are simply a source of labor). Upon this infrastructure, or foundation, are built the major social institutions as well as core cultural values and ideas. Taken together, these additional social elements represent the society's superstructure. Marx maintained that every part of a society operates in concert with the economic system.

terms, social institutions reinforce the domination of the capitalists, by legally protecting their wealth, for example, and transferring property from one generation to the next through the family.

Generally speaking, members of industrial-capitalist societies do not view their legal or family systems as hotbeds of social conflict. On the contrary, individuals come to see their rights to private property as "natural." People in the United States find it easy to think that affluent people have earned their wealth, while those who are poor or out of work lack skills or motivation. Marx rejected this kind of reasoning as rooted in a capitalist preoccupation with the "bottom line" that treats human well-being as a market commodity. Poverty and unemployment are not inevitable; as Marx saw it, grand wealth clashing with grinding poverty represents merely one set of human possibilities generated by capitalism (Cuff & Payne, 1979).

Marx rejected capitalist common sense, therefore, as **false consciousness,** *explanations of social problems grounded in the shortcomings of individuals rather than the flaws of society.* Marx was saying, in effect, that industrial capitalism itself is responsible for many of the social problems he saw all around him. False consciousness, he maintained, victimizes people by obscuring the real cause of their problems.

Conflict in History

Marx studied how societies have changed throughout history, noting that they often evolve gradually, although they sometimes change in rapid, revolutionary fashion. Marx observed (as do the Lenskis) that change is partly prompted by technological advance. But he steadfastly held that conflict between economic classes is the major engine of change.

To recast the Lenskis' analysis in Marxist terms, early hunters and gatherers formed primitive communist societies. The word *communism* refers to a social system in which the production of food and other material goods is a common effort shared more or less equally by all members of society. Because the resources of nature were available to all hunters and gatherers (rather than privately owned), and because everyone performed similar work (rather than dividing work into highly specialized tasks), there was little possibility for social conflict.

Horticulture, Marx noted, introduced significant social inequality. Among horticultural, pastoral, and early agrarian societies—which Marx lumped together as the "ancient world"—the victors in frequent warfare forced their captives into servitude. A small elite (the "masters") and their slaves were thus locked in an irreconcilable pattern of social conflict (Zeitlin, 1981).

Agriculture brought still more wealth to members of the elite, fueling further social conflict. Agrarian serfs, occupying the lowest reaches of European feudalism from about the twelfth to the eighteenth centuries, were only slightly better off than slaves. In Marx's view, the power of both the church and the state defended feudal inequality by defining the existing social order as God's will. Thus, to Marx, feudalism amounted to little more than "exploitation, veiled by religious and political illusions" (Marx & Engels, 1972:337; orig. 1848).

Gradually, new productive forces undermined the feudal order. Commerce grew steadily throughout the Middle Ages as trade networks expanded and the power of guilds increased. Merchants and skilled

Q: "The bourgeoisie, wherever it has got the upper hand, has put an end to all feudal, patriarchal, idyllic relations. It has pitilessly torn asunder the motley feudal ties that bound man to his 'natural superiors' and left no other nexus between man and man than naked self-interest, than callous 'cash payment.'" Marx and Engels

NOTE: "Capitalism" is derived from the Latin word *caput*, meaning "head." The term was first used in 12th-century Europe at a time of expanding commerce. "Conflict" is derived from the Latin meaning "a striking together."

NOTE: Political themes have been explicit and broadly evident in the arts in socialist societies, illustrated by the North Korean poster below. As Figure 4–2 (p. 106) indicates, Marx reasoned that a change in the economic foundation ripples through society, politicizing all other social institutions.

All societies use art to convey political ideas. The political use of art is widely evident in countries that seek to engender socialist virtues in their people. In North Korea, one key virtue is loyalty to that nation's leader.

craftsworkers in the cities formed a new social category, the *bourgeoisie* (a French word meaning "of the town"). Profits earned through expanding trade brought the bourgeoisie increasing wealth. After the mid-eighteenth century, with factories at their command, the bourgeoisie became true capitalists with power that soon rivaled that of the ancient, landed nobility. While the nobility regarded this upstart "commercial" class with disdain, their increasing wealth gradually shifted to the capitalists control of European societies. To Marx's way of thinking, then, new technology was only part of the Industrial Revolution; it was also a class revolution by which capitalists overthrew the agrarian elite to preside over the new industrial economy.

Industrialization also fostered the development of the proletariat. English landowners converted fields once tilled by serfs into grazing land for sheep to secure wool for the prospering textile mills. Forced from the land, serfs migrated to cities to work in factories, where they joined the burgeoning industrial proletariat. Marx envisioned these workers one day joining hands across national boundaries to form a unified class, setting the stage for historic confrontation, this time between capitalists and the exploited workers.

Capitalism and Class Conflict

Much of Marx's analysis centers on destructive aspects of industrial capitalism—especially ways it promotes class conflict and alienation. In examining his views on these topics, we will come to see why he advocated the overthrow of capitalist societies.

"The history of all hitherto existing society is the history of class struggles." With this declaration, Marx and his collaborator Friedrich Engels began their best-known statement, the *Manifesto of the Communist Party* (1972:335; orig. 1848). The idea of social class is at the heart of Marx's critique of capitalist society. Industrial capitalism, like earlier types of society, contains two major social classes—the dominant people and the oppressed—reflecting the two basic positions in the productive system. Capitalists and proletarians are the historical descendants of masters and slaves in the ancient world and nobles and serfs in feudal systems. In each case, one class controls the other as productive property. Marx used the term **class conflict** (and sometimes *class struggle*) to refer to *antagonism between entire classes over the distribution of wealth and power in society*.

Class conflict, then, dates back to civilizations long gone. What distinguishes the conflict in capitalist society, Marx pointed out, is how out in the open it has become. Agrarian nobles and serfs, for all their differences, were bound together by long-standing traditions and a host of mutual obligations. Industrial capitalism dissolved those ties so that pride and honor were replaced by "naked self-interest" and the pursuit of profit in a blatant exercise of oppression. With no personal ties to their oppressors, Marx believed that the proletariat had little reason to stand for their subjugation.

But though industrial capitalism brought class conflict out in the open, Marx realized that fundamental social change would not come easily. First, he claimed, workers must *become aware* of their shared oppression and see capitalism as its true cause. Second, they must *organize and act* to address their problems. This means workers must replace false consciousness with **class consciousness,** *the recognition by workers of their unity as a class in opposition to capitalists and, ultimately, to*

Sir Luke Fildes's painting Awaiting Admission to the Casual Ward *shows the numbing poverty common among immigrants drawn to cities as the Industrial Revolution began. Marx saw in such suffering a fundamental contradiction of modern society: Industrial technology promised material plenty for all, yet capitalism concentrated wealth in the hands of a few.*

capitalism itself. Because the inhumanity of early capitalism was plain for him to see, Marx concluded that industrial workers would inevitably rise up en masse to destroy industrial capitalism.

And what of the workers' adversaries, the capitalists? The capitalists' formidable wealth and power, protected by the institutions of society, might seem invulnerable. But Marx saw a weakness in the capitalist armor. Motivated by a desire for personal gain, capitalists fear the competition of other capitalists. Thus Marx thought that capitalists would be reluctant to band together, even though they, too, share common interests. Furthermore, he reasoned, capitalists keep employees' wages low in their drive to maximize profits. This strategy, in turn, bolsters the resolve of workers to forge an alliance against them. In the long run, Marx surmised, capitalists would only contribute to their own undoing.

Capitalism and Alienation

Marx also condemned capitalism for producing **alienation,** *the experience of isolation resulting from powerlessness.* Dominated by capitalists and dehumanized by their jobs (especially monotonous and repetitive factory work), proletarians find little satisfaction in and feel individually powerless to improve their situation. Herein lies another contradiction of capitalist society: As human beings devise technology to gain power over the world, the productive process increasingly assumes power over human beings.

Workers view themselves as merely a commodity, a source of labor, bought by capitalists and discarded when no longer needed. Marx cited four ways in which capitalism alienates workers.

1. **Alienation from the act of working.** Ideally, people work both to meet immediate needs and to develop their long-range personal potential. Capitalism, however, denies workers a say in what they produce or how they produce it. Furthermore, much work is tedious, involving countless repetitions of routine tasks. The modern-day replacement of human labor by machines would hardly have surprised Marx; as far as he was concerned, capitalism had turned human beings into machines long ago.

2. **Alienation from the products of work.** The product of work belongs not to workers but to capitalists, who dispose of it for profit. Thus, Marx reasoned, the more workers invest of themselves into their work, the more they lose.

3. **Alienation from other workers.** Marx saw work itself as the productive affirmation of human community. Industrial capitalism, however, transforms work from a cooperative venture into a competitive one. As the box illustrates, factory work often provides little chance for human companionship.

4. **Alienation from human potential.** Industrial capitalism alienates workers from their human potential. Marx argued that a worker "does not fulfill himself in his work but denies himself, has a feeling of misery rather than well-being, does not freely develop his physical and mental energies, but is physically exhausted and mentally

SOCIAL SURVEY: "Inequality continues to exist because it benefits the rich and powerful." (GSS 1987, N = 1,285; *Codebook*, 1994:559)

"Strongly agree"	12.8%	"Disagree"	17.7%
"Agree"	32.8%	"Strongly disagree"	4.0%
"Neither agree nor disagree"	25.0%	DK/NR	7.8%

SOCIAL SURVEY: "On the whole, how satisfied are you with the work you do—would you say you are very satisfied, moderately satisfied, a little dissatisfied, or very dissatisfied?" (GSS 1994, N = 2,441; *Codebook*, 1994:188). In GSS survey items, workers do not express strong dissatisfaction with their work.

"Very satisfied"	44.2%	"Very dissatisfied"	3.3%
"Moderately satisfied"	38.2%	DK/NR	4.2%
"A little dissatisfied"	10.1%		

SOCIOLOGY OF EVERYDAY LIFE

Alienation and Industrial Capitalism

These excerpts from the book *Working* by Studs Terkel illustrate how dull, repetitive jobs can generate alienation for men and women.

Phil Stallings is a twenty-seven-year-old auto worker in a Ford assembly plant in Chicago.

I start the automobile, the first welds. From there it goes to another line, where the floor's put on, the roof, the trunk, the hood, the doors. Then it's put on a frame. There is hundreds of lines. . . . I stand in one spot, about two- or three-feet area, all night. The only time a person stops is when the line stops. We do about thirty-two jobs per car, per unit. Forty-eight units an hour, eight hours a day. Thirty-two times forty-eight times eight. Figure it out. That's how many times I push that button.

The noise, oh it's tremendous. You open your mouth and you're liable to get a mouthful of sparks. [Shows his arms.] That's a burn, these are burns. You don't compete against the noise. You go to yell and at the same time you're straining to maneuver the gun to where you have to weld.

You got some guys that are uptight, and they're not sociable. It's too rough. You pretty much stay to yourself. You get involved with yourself. You dream, you think of things you've done. I drift back continuously to when I was a kid and what me and my brothers did. The things you love most are what you drift back into.

It don't stop. It just goes and goes and goes. I bet there's men who have lived and died out there, never seen the end of the line. And they never will—because it's endless. It's like a serpent. It's just all body, no tail. It can do things to you. . . .

Twenty-four-year-old Sharon Atkins is a college graduate working as a telephone receptionist for a large midwestern business.

I don't have much contact with people. You can't see them. You don't know if they're laughing, if they're being satirical or being kind. So your conversations become very abrupt. I notice that in talking to people. My conversation would be very short and clipped, in short sentences, the way I talk to people all day on the telephone. . . .

You try to fill up your time with trying to think about other things: what you're going to do on the weekend or about your family. You have to use your imagination. If you don't have a very good one and you bore easily, you're in trouble. Just to fill in time, I write real bad poetry or letters to myself and to other people and never mail them. The letters are fantasies, sort of rambling, how I feel, how depressed I am.

. . . I never answer the phone at home.

Source: Terkel (1974).

---

debased. The worker, therefore, feels himself to be at home only during his leisure time, whereas at work he feels homeless" (1964a:124–25; orig. 1844). In short, industrial capitalism distorts an activity that should express the best qualities in human beings into a dull and dehumanizing experience.

Marx viewed alienation, in its various forms, as a barrier to social change. But he hoped that industrial workers eventually would overcome their alienation by uniting into a true social class, aware of the cause of their problems and galvanized to transform society.

Revolution

The only way out of the trap of capitalism, contended Marx, was deliberately to refashion society. He envisioned a more humane and egalitarian productive system, one that would enhance rather than undermine social ties. He called this system *socialism*. Marx knew well the obstacles to a socialist revolution; even so, he was disappointed that he never lived to see workers in England overthrow industrial capitalism. Still, convinced of the basic immorality of capitalist society, he was sure that, in time, the working majority would realize that they held the key to a better future in their own hands. This transformation would

SUPPLEMENTS: The *Data File* highlights the distinction between Marx's concept of alienation and Durkheim's notion of anomie.
SOCIAL SURVEY: "Owners and workers are still divided. Social standing depends on being upper or lower class." (*CHIP1 Social Survey Software*, USCLAS11; GSS 1984, N = 1,303). Several GSS items provide strong support for Marxist analysis.

RACE/ETH	"Agree"	"Disagree"
Afri Amer	73.2%	26.8%
Hispanics	61.2%	38.8%
Whites	70.6%	29.4%
SES	"Agree"	"Disagree"
High	67.8%	32.2%
Middle	69.6%	30.4%
Low	75.9%	24.1%

"The proletarians have nothing to lose but their chains. They have a world to win."

MAX WEBER: THE RATIONALIZATION OF SOCIETY

With a broad understanding of law, economics, religion, and history, Max Weber (1864–1920) produced what many regard as the greatest individual contribution to sociology. This scholar, introduced in the box, generated ideas so wide ranging that we must limit ourselves to his vision of how modern society differs from earlier types of social organization.

Weber's sociology reflects the philosophical approach known as *idealism,* which emphasizes how human ideas shape society. Weber understood the power of technology, and he shared many of Marx's ideas about social conflict. But he departed from Marx's materialist analysis, arguing that societies differ primarily in terms of the ways in which their members think about the world. For Weber, ideas—especially beliefs and values—have transforming power. Thus he saw modern society as the product, not just of new technology and capitalism, but of a new way of thinking. This emphasis on ideas contrasts with Marx's focus on material production, leading scholars to describe Weber's work as "a debate with the ghost of Karl Marx" (Cuff & Payne, 1979:73–74).

In all his work, Weber contrasted social patterns in different times and places. To sharpen comparisons, he relied on the **ideal type,** *an abstract statement of the essential characteristics of any social phenomenon.* He explored religion by contrasting the ideal "Protestant" with the ideal "Jew," "Hindu," and "Buddhist," knowing that these models precisely described no actual individuals. Note that Weber's use of the word *ideal* does not mean that something is "good" or "the best"; we could analyze "criminals" as well as "priests" as ideal types. We have already compared "hunting and gathering societies" and "industrial societies" as well as "capitalism" and "socialism."

Tradition and Rationality

Rather than categorizing societies in terms of technology or productive systems, Max Weber highlighted differences in the ways people view the world. In simple terms, Weber concluded that members of preindustrial societies hew to *tradition,* while people in industrial-capitalist societies endorse *rationality.*

Marxism, one of the world's most influential social movements, has shaped the economic and political life of one-fifth of the world's people. For years, the conventional wisdom in the United States was that, once established, socialism stifled its opposition, rendering government immune to overthrow. But that notion collapsed along with the socialist regimes of Eastern Europe and the former Soviet Union. The political transformation of this world region is symbolized by the removal of statues of Vladimir Lenin (1870–1924), architect of Soviet Marxism, in city after city during the last few years.

certainly be revolutionary, perhaps even violent. What emerged from the workers' revolution, however, would be a cooperative socialist society intended to meet the needs of all.

The discussion of social stratification in Chapter 9 reveals more about changes in industrial-capitalist societies since Marx's time and why the revolution he championed has not taken place. Later chapters also delve into why people in the societies of Eastern Europe recently revolted against established socialist governments. But, in his own time, Marx looked toward the future with hope (1972:362; orig. 1848):

PROFILE

Max Weber: Expanding the Boundaries of Sociology

To be called merely a "sociologist" probably would have offended Max Weber. Not that he disliked the study of society; in fact, he spent most of his life doing just that. But Weber's contribution to understanding humanity is so broad and rich that no single discipline can claim him.

Born to a prosperous German family, Weber completed law school and set off on a legal career. But he soon felt confined by the work of a lawyer. Continuing his studies, he became a college professor. With his curiosity racing across the entire human condition, he compiled an amazing legacy of scholarship.

The influence of Weber's parents stands out in his work. His mother's devout Calvinism probably encouraged Weber's study of world religions and his classic study of Calvinism and its impact on industrial capitalism, which we take up shortly. From his father, a notable politician, Weber clearly gained insights into the workings of political life and bureaucracy.

Weber flirted with politics, and his wife Marianne was a leading feminist of her time. But Weber found politics to be incompatible with scholarly work. The former, he claimed, demands action and personal conviction, while the latter requires impartiality and patient reflection. Weber tried to resolve this personal dilemma by urging his colleagues to become involved in politics outside the classroom while striving for scientific neutrality in their professional work.

For many reasons, Weber's life was far from happy. He did not get on well with his father, and soon after his father's death Weber began to suffer from psychological problems. Illness sharply limited his ability to work during the remainder of his life. Even so, the exceptional number of major studies he conducted has led many to regard him as the most brilliant sociologist in history.

By **tradition,** Weber meant *sentiments and beliefs passed from generation to generation.* Thus traditional societies are guided by the past. Their members evaluate particular actions as right and proper precisely because they have been accepted for so long.

People in modern societies take a different view of the world, argued Weber, embracing **rationality,** *deliberate, matter-of-fact calculation of the most efficient means to accomplish a particular goal.* Sentiment has no place in a rational world view, which treats tradition simply as one kind of information. Typically, modern people choose to think and act on the basis of present and future consequences, evaluating jobs, schooling, and even relationships in terms of what we put into them and what we expect to receive in return.

Weber viewed both the Industrial Revolution and capitalism as evidence of a historical surge of rationality. He used the phrase **rationalization of society** to denote *the historical change from tradition to rationality as the dominant mode of human thought.* Modern society, he concluded, has been "disenchanted," as scientific thinking and technology have swept away sentimental ties to the past.

The willingness to adopt the latest technology, then, is one good indicator of how rationalized a society is. Indicating the global pattern of rationalization, Global Map 4-1, on page 112, shows where in the world facsimile (fax) machines are found. In general, the high-income countries of North America and Europe utilize these devices to the greatest degree while, in low-income nations, they are quite rare.

Drawing on Weber's comparative perspective—and the data found in the map—we deduce that various societies place different values on technological advancement. What one society might herald as a breakthrough, another might deem unimportant, and a third might strongly oppose as a threat to tradition.

THE MAP: Another indicator of the uneven character of world rationalization is that six nations—the United States, United Kingdom, Japan, the former Soviet Union, France, and Germany—generate half of the world's scientific output.

NOTE: Roughly 10 percent of all people who have ever lived are alive now. However, about 90 percent of all *scientists* who have ever lived are living today.

NOTE: The Protestant ethic and the spirit of capitalism are not synonymous. The former is transformed into the latter only when it is *disenchanted*. The disenchanted spirit of Calvinism can be seen in three impersonal modern "types," all of which are highly disciplined but devoid of piety: (1) the *capitalist* (devotion to profits), (2) the *scientist* (devotion to knowledge), and (3) the *bureaucrat* (devotion to duty). See the drawings of these three types in Chapter 24.

Window on the World

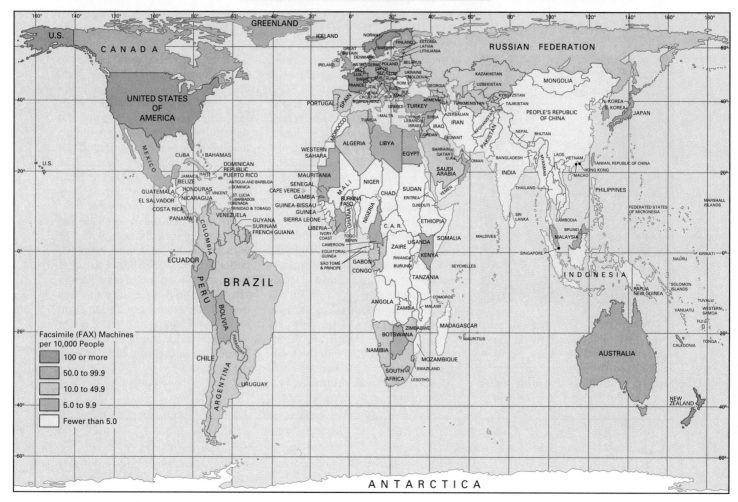

GLOBAL MAP 4–1 High Technology in Global Perspective

Countries with traditional cultures ignore or even resist technological innovation; nations with highly rationalized ways of life eagerly embrace such changes. Facsimile (fax) machines, one common form of high technology, are numerous in high-income countries such as the United States, where 5 million faxes fly along the "information superhighway" every hour. In low-income nations, by contrast, fax machines are unknown to most people. Notice that, in Asia, fax machines are widely available only in Japan, South Korea, Taiwan, and the business centers of Hong Kong and Singapore.

Source: *Peters Atlas of the World* (1990).

Inventors in ancient Greece, for instance, devised many surprisingly elaborate mechanical devices to perform household tasks. But since elites were well served by slaves, they viewed such inventions as mere entertainment. In the United States today, the Amish are guided by their traditions to staunchly oppose modern technology.

In Weber's view, then, technological innovation is promoted or hindered by the way people understand their world. He concluded that people in many

NOTE: The German word *weltanschauung* (*Welt* = world, *Anschauung* = perception), designating the distinctive ideas with which people embrace the world, has no English equivalent. For Weber, early Protestantism was more than a religion, as capitalism was more than an economic system: Both represented a distinctive *Weltanschauung*.

NOTE: To Weber, rationalization represents the eclipse of tradition and sentiment; this loss of deep human passions is one of the costs of modern living in Weber's view. Knowing that many people would struggle to find ultimate meaning in life, Weber concluded his analysis of rationalization by pointing out that "the arms of the old churches are open widely and compassionately . . ."

GLOBAL: Our rational culture encourages us to regard more traditional people as "lazy" and unconcerned with precise time.

societies discovered keys to technological change; however, only in the rational cultural climate of Western Europe did people exploit these discoveries to spark the Industrial Revolution (1958; orig. 1904–5).

Rationality, Calvinism, and Industrial Capitalism

Is industrial capitalism a rational economic system? Here, again, Weber and Marx came down on opposite sides of the issue. Weber considered industrial capitalism as the essence of rationality, since capitalists pursue profit in eminently rational ways. Marx, however, dismissed capitalism as the antithesis of rationality, claiming that it failed to meet the basic needs of most of the people (Gerth & Mills, 1946:49).

But, to look more closely at Weber's analysis, how did industrial capitalism emerge in the first place? Weber contended that industrial capitalism was the legacy of Calvinism—a Christian religious movement spawned by the Protestant Reformation. Calvinists, Weber explained, approached life in a highly disciplined and rational way. Moreover, central to the religious doctrine of John Calvin (1509–1564) was *predestination*, the idea that an all-knowing and all-powerful God has preordained some people for salvation and others for damnation. With everyone's fate set before birth, Calvinists believed that people could do nothing to alter their destiny. Nor could they even know what their future would be. Thus the lives of Calvinists were framed by hopeful visions of eternal salvation and anxious fears of unending damnation.

For such people, not knowing one's fate was intolerable. Calvinists gradually came to a resolution of sorts. Why shouldn't those chosen for glory in the next world, they reasoned, see signs of divine favor in *this* world? Such a conclusion prompted Calvinists to interpret worldly prosperity as a sign of God's grace. Anxious to acquire this reassurance, Calvinists threw themselves into a quest for success, applying rationality, discipline, and hard work to their tasks. This pursuit of riches was not for its own sake, of course, since self-indulgently spending money was clearly sinful. Calvinists also were little moved to share their wealth with the poor, because they saw poverty as a sign of God's rejection. Their ever-present duty was to carry forward what they held to be their personal *calling* from God.

As they reinvested their profits for greater success, Calvinists built the foundation of capitalism. They piously used wealth to generate more wealth, practiced personal thrift, and eagerly embraced whatever technological advances would bolster their efforts.

These traits, Weber explained, distinguished Calvinism from other world religions. Catholicism, the traditional religion in most of Europe, gave rise to a passive, "otherworldly" view of life with hope of greater reward in the life to come. For Catholics, material wealth had none of the spiritual significance that so motivated Calvinists. And so it was, Weber concluded, that industrial capitalism became established primarily in areas of Europe where Calvinism had a strong hold.

Weber's study of Calvinism provides striking evidence of the power of ideas to shape society (versus Marx's contention that ideas merely reflect the process of economic production). But always skeptical of simple explanations, Weber knew that industrial capitalism had many roots. In fact, one purpose of this research was to counter Marx's narrow explanation of modern society in strictly economic terms.

As religious fervor weakened among later generations of Calvinists, Weber concluded, success-seeking personal discipline remained strong. A *religious* ethic became simply a "*work*" ethic. From this point of view, industrial capitalism emerged as "disenchanted" religion, with wealth now valued for its own sake. It is revealing that "accounting," which to early Calvinists meant keeping a daily record of moral deeds, now refers simply to keeping track of money.

Rational Social Organization

Weber contended that, by unleashing the Industrial Revolution and sparking the development of capitalism, rationality had defined the character of modern society. Rational social organization confers the following seven traits on today's social life.

1. **Distinctive social institutions.** Among hunters and gatherers, the family was the center of virtually all activities. Gradually, however, other social institutions, including religious, political, and economic systems, broke away from family life. In modern societies, institutions of education and health care have also appeared. The separation of social institutions—each detailed in a later chapter—is a rational strategy to address human needs more efficiently.

2. **Large-scale organizations.** Modern rationality is exemplified by a proliferation of large-scale organizations. As early as the horticultural era, political officials oversaw religious observances, public works, and warfare. In medieval Europe, the Catholic Church grew larger still with thousands

Max Weber agreed with Karl Marx that modern society is alienating to the individual, but the two thinkers identified different causes of this estrangement. For Marx, economic inequality is the culprit; for Weber, the issue is pervasive and dehumanizing bureaucracy. George Tooker's painting Landscape With Figures *echoes Weber's sentiments.*

George Tooker, *Landscape With Figures*, 1963, egg tempera on gesso panel, 26 x 30 in. Private collection.

of officials. In modern, rational societies, the employees of the federal government number in the millions and most people work for a large organization.

3. **Specialized tasks.** Unlike members of traditional societies, individuals in modern societies pursue a wide range of specialized activities. The enormous breadth of occupations can be seen in any city's "Yellow Pages," which typically runs more than one thousand pages.

4. **Personal discipline.** Modern society puts a premium on self-directed discipline. For early Calvinists, of course, such an approach to life was rooted in religious belief. Although now distanced from its religious origins, discipline is still encouraged by cultural values such as achievement, success, and efficiency.

5. **Awareness of time.** In traditional societies, people measure time according to the rhythm of sun and seasons. Modern people, by contrast, schedule events precisely by the hour and minute. Interestingly, clocks began appearing in European cities some five hundred years ago just as commerce

was starting to expand; soon, people began to think (to borrow Benjamin Franklin's phrase) that "time is money."

6. **Technical competence.** Members of traditional societies evaluate one another largely on the basis of *who* they are—how they are joined to others in the web of kinship. Modern rationality, by contrast, prompts us to judge people according to *what* they are—that is, with an eye toward their skills and abilities.

7. **Impersonality.** Finally, in a rational society technical competence takes priority over close relationships, rendering the world impersonal. Modern social life can be viewed as the interplay of specialists concerned with particular tasks, rather than people broadly concerned with one another. Weber explained that we tend to devalue personal feelings and emotions as "irrational" because they often are difficult to control.

Rationality and Bureaucracy

Although the medieval church grew large, Weber argued that it was never entirely rational because its goal was to preserve tradition. Truly rational organizations, with the principal focus on efficiency, appeared only in the last few centuries. The organizational type Weber called *bureaucracy* became pronounced along with capitalism as an expression of rationality.

Chapter 7 ("Groups and Organizations") explains that bureaucracy is the model for modern businesses, government agencies, labor unions, and universities. For now, note that Weber considered this organizational form to be the clearest expression of a rational world view because its chief elements—offices, duties, and policies—are intended to achieve specific goals as efficiently as possible. By contrast, the inefficiency of traditional organization is reflected in its hostility to change. In short, Weber asserted that bureaucracy transformed all of society in the same way that industrialization transformed the economy.

Still, Weber emphasized that rational bureaucracy has a special affinity to capitalism. He wrote:

Today, it is primarily the capitalist market economy which demands that the official business of public administration be discharged precisely, unambiguously, continuously, and with as much speed as possible. Normally, the very large capitalist enterprises are themselves unequalled models of strict bureaucratic organization. (1978:974; orig. 1921)

PROFILE

Emile Durkheim: Unmasking the Power of Society

Why would being a professor of sociology be controversial? Because there *weren't* any, at least not in France, until Emile Durkheim became the first one in 1887. Up to that time, the study of human behavior was left up to biologists and psychologists. But Durkheim made the assertion—widely disputed at the time—that one can understand people, not by looking at individuals, but only by examining their society.

Durkheim's investigation of suicide, detailed in Chapter 1 ("The Sociological Perspective"), offers persuasive evidence of society's power to shape human behavior. In this classic study, Durkheim showed that people's place within the social system—as women or men, rich or poor, Catholic, Jew, or Protestant—affects even this most personal act.

Durkheim's work, like that of Marx and Weber, is discussed in many later chapters. His contributions to the understanding of crime figure prominently in Chapter 8 ("Deviance"). Durkheim also spent much of his life investigating religion, which he held to be a key foundation of social integration (see Chapter 18, "Religion"). Just as important, Durkheim is also one of the major architects of the structural-functional paradigm, which we refer to in almost every chapter that follows.

Rationality and Alienation

Max Weber joined with Karl Marx in recognizing the unparalleled efficiency of industrial capitalism. Weber also shared Marx's conclusion that modern society generates widespread alienation, although for different reasons. For Weber, the primary problem is not the economic inequality that so troubled Marx, but the stifling regulation and dehumanization that comes with expanding bureaucracy.

Bureaucracies, Weber warned, treat people as a series of cases rather than as unique individuals. In addition, working for large organizations demands highly specialized and often tedious routines. In the end, Weber envisioned modern society as a vast and growing system of rules seeking to regulate everything and threatening to crush the human spirit.

An irony found in the work of Marx reappears in Weber's thinking: Rather than serving humanity, modern society turns on its creators and enslaves them. In language reminiscent of Marx's description of the human toll of industrial capitalism, Weber portrayed the modern individual as "only a small cog in a ceaselessly moving mechanism that prescribes to him an endlessly fixed routine of march" (1978:988; orig. 1921). Thus, knowing well the advantages of modern society, Weber ended his life deeply pessimistic. He feared that the rationalization of society would end up reducing people to robots.

EMILE DURKHEIM: SOCIETY AND FUNCTION

"To love society is to love something beyond us and something in ourselves." These are the words of Emile Durkheim (1858–1917), another architect of sociology, introduced in the box. This curious phrase (1974:55; orig. 1924) distills one more influential vision of human society.

Structure: Society Beyond Ourselves

First and foremost, Emile Durkheim recognized that society exists beyond ourselves. Society is more than the individuals who compose it; society has a life of its own that stretches beyond our personal experiences. It was here long before we were born, it makes claims on us while we are alive, and it will remain long after we are gone. Patterns of human behavior,

Durkheim explained, form established *structures*; they are *social facts* that have an objective reality beyond the lives and perceptions of particular individuals. Cultural norms, values, religious beliefs—all endure as social facts.

And because society looms larger than individual lives, it has the *power* to shape our thoughts and actions, Durkheim noted. So studying individuals alone (as psychologists or biologists do) can never capture the essence of human experience. Society is more than the sum of its parts; it exists as a complex organism rooted in our collective life. A classroom of first graders, a family sharing a meal, people milling about a country auction—all are examples of the countless situations that have an organization apart from any particular individual who has ever participated in them.

Once created by people, then, society takes on a momentum of its own, confronting its creators and demanding a measure of obedience. For our part, we experience society's influence as we come to see the order in our lives or as we face temptation and feel the tug of morality.

Function: Society in Action

Having established that society has structure, Durkheim turned to the concept of *function*. The significance of any social fact, he explained, extends beyond individuals to the operation of society itself.

To illustrate, consider crime. Most people think of lawbreaking as harmful acts that some individuals inflict on others. But, looking beyond individuals, Durkheim saw that crime has a vital function for the ongoing life of society itself. As Chapter 8 ("Deviance") explains, only by recognizing and responding to acts as criminal do people construct and defend morality, which gives necessary shape to our collective life. For this reason, Durkheim rejected the common view of crime as "pathological." On the contrary, he concluded, crime is quite "normal" for the most basic of reasons: A society could not exist without it (1964a, orig. 1895; 1964b, orig. 1893).

Personality: Society in Ourselves

Durkheim contended that society is not only "beyond ourselves," it is also "in ourselves." Each of us, in short, builds a personality by internalizing social facts. How we act, think, and feel—our essential humanity—is drawn from the society that nurtures us. Moreover, Durkheim explained, society regulates human beings through moral discipline. Durkheim held that human beings are naturally insatiable and in constant danger of being overpowered by our own desires: "The more one has, the more one wants, since satisfactions received only stimulate instead of filling needs" (1966:248; orig. 1897). Having given us life, then, society must also instill restraints in us.

Nowhere is the need for societal regulation better illustrated than in Durkheim's study of suicide (1966; orig. 1897), detailed in Chapter 1 ("The Sociological Perspective"). Why is it that, over the years, rock stars have been so vulnerable to self-destruction? Durkheim had the answer long before anyone made electric music: It is the *least* regulated categories of people that suffer the *highest* rates of suicide. The greater license afforded to those who are young, rich, and famous exacts a high price in terms of the risk of suicide.

Modernity and Anomie

Compared to traditional societies, modern societies impose fewer restrictions on everyone. Durkheim acknowledges the advantages of modern freedom, but he warned of a rise in **anomie,** *a condition in which society provides little moral guidance to individuals.* What so many celebrities describe as "almost being destroyed by their fame" is one extreme example of the corrosive effects of anomie. Sudden fame tears people away from their families and familiar routines, disrupting society's support and regulation of an individual, sometimes with fatal results. Durkheim instructs us, therefore, that the desires of the individual must be balanced by the claims and guidance of society—a balance that has become precarious in the modern world.

Evolving Societies: The Division of Labor

Like Marx and Weber, Durkheim witnessed firsthand the rapid social transformation of Europe during the nineteenth century. Analyzing this change, Durkheim saw a sweeping evolution in the forms of social organization.

In preindustrial societies, explained Durkheim, strong tradition operates as the social cement that binds people together. In fact, what he termed the *collective conscience* is so strong that the community moves quickly to punish anyone who dares to challenge conventional ways of life. Durkheim called this system **mechanical solidarity,** meaning *social bonds, based on shared morality, that unite members of preindustrial*

Q: "In a word, we must discover the rational substitutes for those religious notions that for a long time have served as the vehicle for the most essential moral ideas." Emile Durkheim, *Moral Education* (1961:9). (This idea underlies the concept of "civil religion"; see Chapter 18, "Religion.")

Q: "For Durkheim, the sacredness of the person could become one of the few cultural ideals capable of providing a crucial point of unification for an increasingly differentiated, yet interdependent, world." Mike Featherstone (1990:4)

NOTE: By arguing that society has an objective existence, Durkheim (following Comte) may well have been attempting to establish a natural social order as a moral authority to replace declining tradition.

Durkheim's observation that people with weak social bonds are prone to self-destructive behavior stands as stark evidence of the power of society to shape individual lives. When rock-and-roll singers become famous they are wrenched out of familiar life patterns and existing relationships, sometimes with tragic results. The history of rock and roll contains many tragic stories of this kind, including Janis Joplin's death by drug overdose (1970) and Kurt Cobain's suicide (1994).

societies. In practice, then, mechanical solidarity springs from *likeness*. Durkheim described these bonds as "mechanical" because people feel a more or less automatic sense of belonging together.

Durkheim considered the decline of mechanical solidarity to be a defining trait of modern society. But this does not mean that society dissolves; rather, modernity generates a new type of solidarity that rushes into the void left by discarded traditions. Durkheim called this new social integration **organic solidarity,** defined as *social bonds, based on specialization, that unite members of industrial societies.* Where solidarity was once rooted in likeness, in short, it now flows from *differences* among people whose specialized pursuits make them rely on one another.

For Durkheim, then, the key dimension of change is a society's expanding **division of labor,** or *specialized economic activity.* As Max Weber explained, modern societies specialize in order to promote efficiency. Durkheim fills in the picture by showing us that members of modern societies count on the efforts of tens of thousands of others—most complete strangers—to secure the goods and services they need every day.

So modernity rests far less on *moral consensus* (the foundation of traditional societies) and far more on *functional interdependence.* That is, as members of modern societies, we depend more and more on people we trust less and less. Why, then, should we put our faith in people we hardly know and whose beliefs may differ radically from our own? Durkheim's answer: "Because we can't live without them." In a world in which morality sometimes seems like so much shifting sand, then, we confront what might be called "Durkheim's dilemma": The technological power and expansive personal freedom of modern society come only at the cost of receding morality and the ever-present danger of anomie.

Like Marx and Weber, Durkheim had misgivings about the direction society was taking. But, of the three, Durkheim was the most optimistic. Confidence in the future sprang from his hope that we could enjoy greater freedom and privacy while creating for ourselves the social regulation that had once been forced on us by tradition.

CRITICAL EVALUATION: FOUR VISIONS OF SOCIETY

This chapter opened with several important queries about human societies. We will conclude by summarizing how each of the four visions of society answers these questions.

How Have Societies Changed?

According to the Lenskis' model of sociocultural evolution, societies differ primarily in terms of changing technology. Modern society stands out in this regard because of its enormous productive power. Karl

GLOBAL: As Edward A. Tiryakian (1994) points out, neither Durkheim nor other social theorists predicted the reemergence of mechanical solidarity in the form of religious, ethnic, racial, and gender conflict around the world and on U.S. college campuses.

NOTE: Various assessments of social change—corresponding to the ideas of Marx, Weber, and Durkheim—are found in Chapter 24 ("Social Change: Tradition, Modernity, and Postmodernity").

Q: "The nail that stands up gets hit down." Japanese proverb that might describe social control in a traditional society

NOTE: Durkheim linked mechanical solidarity to the extent of repressive (criminal) law and organic solidarity to the extent of restitutive (civil) law.

DISCUSS: Ask how many students are confident that their lives will be better than those of their parents.

Historically, most members of human societies engaged in a narrow range of activities: searching out food and building shelters. Modern societies, explained Durkheim, display a rapidly expanding division of labor. Increasing specialization is evident on the streets of societies beginning to industrialize: Providing people with their weight is the livelihood of this man in Istanbul, Turkey; on a Bombay street in India, another earns a small fee for cleaning ears.

Marx also stressed historical differences in productive systems, yet pointed to the persistence of social conflict throughout human history (except perhaps among simple hunters and gatherers). For Marx, modern society is distinctive only because it brings that conflict out in the open. Max Weber looked at this question from another perspective, tracing evolving modes of thought. Preindustrial societies, he claimed, are guided by tradition, while modern societies espouse a rational world view. Finally, for Emile Durkheim, traditional societies are characterized by mechanical solidarity based on moral consensus. In industrial societies, mechanical solidarity gives way to organic solidarity based on productive specialization.

Why Do Societies Change?

As the Lenskis see it, social change is primarily a matter of technological innovation that, over time, may transform an entire society. Marx's materialist approach pointed to the struggle between social classes as the "engine of history," pushing societies toward revolutionary reorganization. Weber's idealist view argues that modes of thought also contribute to social change. He demonstrated how rational Calvinism bolstered the Industrial Revolution, which, in turn, reshaped much of modern society. Finally, Durkheim pointed to an expanding division of labor as the key dimension of social change.

What Holds Societies Together?

The Lenskis claim that societies are united by shared culture, and that cultural patterns vary according to a society's level of technological development. But they note that inequality divides a society as technology becomes more complex; social stratification diminishes to some extent with the onset of industrialization. Marx spotlighted social division, not unity, treating class conflict as the hallmark of human societies throughout history. From his point of view, elites may force an uneasy peace between the classes, but true social unity would emerge only if production were to become a truly cooperative endeavor. To Weber, members of a society share a distinctive world view. Just as traditional beliefs joined people together in the past, so modern societies have created rational, large-scale organizations with their own organizational cultures that fuse and guide people's lives. Finally, Durkheim made solidarity the focus of his work,

SOCIAL SURVEY: "Do you think that most people would try to take advantage of you if they got a chance, or would they try to be fair?" (GSS 1994, N = 2,011; *Codebook*, 1994:160). This item is one possible index of anomie.

"Would take advantage of you" 39.1%   "Depends" 6.7%
"Would try to be fair"   53.0%   DK/NR   1.2%

THEN AND NOW: Number of people receiving public assistance in New York City, *1943*: 73,000; *1993*: 1 million. Number of gun-shot homicides, *1943*: 44; *1993*: 1,499. (NY's population was 150,000 larger in 1943 than 1993.) Daniel Moynihan (1993)

Q: "Man will never fly. Not in a thousand years." Wilbur Wright

Q: "The optimist proclaims that we live in the best of all possible worlds, and the pessimist fears that this is true." James Cabell

Controversy & Debate

Is Our Society Getting Better or Worse?

Optimism has been a defining trait of U.S. society; as time goes on, we have always thought, life gets better. But these days, our historic optimism seems to be waning. Consider that, in a recent national survey, 67 percent of respondents agreed that life for the average person was getting worse, not better (30 percent disagreed, and 3 percent offered no opinion; NORC, 1994:186).

What's going on here? To begin, we can point to some good reasons for our society's long-time belief in progress. Since the beginning of this century, for example, the scope of education has expanded to an unprecedented level, including a tenfold increase in the share of college graduates among U.S. adults. Moreover, even taking account of inflation, the average U.S. income has quadrupled. In addition, back in 1900, it was the rare home that had a telephone and, outside of large cities, none had access to electricity. No one had even heard of television, and cars were still on the drawing boards. Today, almost every home is served by a telephone, a host of electric appliances, one or more television sets, and a video cassette recorder (VCR); many also are equipped with cable TV and air conditioning. Most important of all, people born in 1900 lived an average of just forty-seven years; children

born today can look forward to thirty additional years of life.

But some trends, especially during the last twenty-five years, have been troubling. Members of our society have been losing confidence that hard work pays off: Despite an increasing share of two-income couples, family earnings have remained almost flat. At the same time, the divorce rate has soared, and rising crime rates have undermined people's sense of personal safety even in their own homes. Our relative affluence coupled with our capacity to move farther and faster than ever before seems to have eroded our sense of responsibility for others, unleashing a wave of individualism that often comes across as unbridled selfishness. As a result, not only is pessimism on the rise, but a majority of U.S. adults report thinking that "they can't be too careful in dealing with people" (NORC, 1994:160).

So, which is it? Is U.S. society getting better or worse?

The theorists whose ideas we have examined in this chapter shed some light on this question. It is easy to equate "high tech" with "progress." But we should make such assumptions cautiously, the Lenskis maintain, because history shows us that, while advancing technology does offer real advantages, it is no guarantee of a "better" life. Marx, Weber, and Durkheim also acknowledged the

growing affluence of societies over time; yet each offered a pointed criticism of modern society because of a dangerous tendency toward individualism. For Marx, capitalism is the culprit, elevating money to godlike status and fostering a culture of selfishness. Weber's analysis claims that the modern spirit of rationality wears away traditional ties of kinship and neighborhood while expanding bureaucracy, which, he warned, both manipulates and isolates people. In Durkheim's view, functional interdependence joins members of modern societies, who are less and less able to establish a common moral framework within which to judge right and wrong.

In the end, what human societies gain through technological advances may be offset, to some extent, by the loss of human community.

Continue the debate . . .

1. *Do you think life in the United States is getting better or worse? Why?*

2. *Is our society's increasing level of affluence entirely good? What might Marx, Weber, and Durkheim say?*

3. *Do you think people in low-income countries generally look up to the United States or not? Why?*

---

contrasting the morality-based mechanical solidarity of preindustrial societies with modern society's more practical organic solidarity.

Like a kaleidoscope that shows us different patterns as we turn it, these four approaches reveal an

array of insights into society. Yet no one approach is, in an absolute sense, right or wrong. Society is exceedingly complex, and we gain the richest understanding from using all of these visions, as we do in the concluding "Controversy and Debate" box.

SUMMARY

Gerhard and Jean Lenski

1. Sociocultural evolution explores the societal consequences of technological advancements.
2. The earliest hunting and gathering societies were composed of a small number of family-centered nomads. Such societies have all but vanished.
3. Horticulture began some twelve thousand years ago as people devised hand tools for the cultivation of crops. Pastoral societies domesticate animals and engage in extensive trade.
4. Agriculture, about five thousand years old, is large-scale cultivation using animal-drawn plows. This technology allows societies to grow into vast empires, more productive, more specialized, and unequal.
5. Industrialization began 250 years ago in Europe, as people harnessed advanced energy sources to power sophisticated machinery.
6. In postindustrial societies, enterprise shifts from the production of material things to the creation and dissemination of information; computers and other information-based technology replace the heavy machinery of the industrial era.

Karl Marx

7. Marx's materialist analysis pointed up historical and contemporary conflict between social classes.
8. Conflict in "ancient" societies involved masters and slaves; in agrarian societies, it places nobles and serfs in opposition; in industrial-capitalist societies, capitalists confront the proletariat.
9. Industrial capitalism alienates workers: from the act of working, from the products of work, from fellow workers, and from human potential.
10. Once workers had overcome their own false consciousness, Marx believed they would overthrow capitalists and the industrial-capitalist system.

Max Weber

11. Weber's idealist approach reveals that modes of thought have a powerful effect on society.
12. Weber drew a sharp contrast between the tradition of preindustrial societies and the rationality of modern, industrial societies.
13. Weber feared that rationality, embodied in efficiency-conscious bureaucratic organizations, would stifle human creativity.

Emile Durkheim

14. Durkheim explained that society has an objective existence apart from individuals.
15. His approach relates social elements to the larger society through their functions.
16. Traditional societies are fused by mechanical solidarity based on moral consensus; modern societies depend on organic solidarity based on the division of labor or productive specialization.

KEY CONCEPTS

agriculture the technology of large-scale farming using plows harnessed to animals or more powerful sources of energy

alienation the experience of isolation resulting from powerlessness

anomie Durkheim's designation of a condition in which society provides little moral guidance to individuals

capitalists people who own factories and other productive enterprises

class conflict antagonism between entire classes over the distribution of wealth and power in society

class consciousness Marx's term for the recognition by workers of their unity as a social class in opposition to capitalists and to capitalism itself

division of labor specialized economic activity

false consciousness Marx's term for explanations of social problems grounded in the shortcomings of individuals rather than the flaws of society

horticulture technology based on using hand tools to cultivate plants

hunting and gathering simple technology for hunting animals and gathering vegetation

ideal type Weber's term for an abstract statement of the essential characteristics of any social phenomenon

industrialism technology that powers sophisticated machinery with advanced sources of energy

mechanical solidarity Durkheim's designation of social bonds, based on shared morality, that unite members of preindustrial societies

organic solidarity Durkheim's designation of social bonds, based on specialization, that unite members of industrial societies

pastoralism technology based on the domestication of animals

postindustrialism technology that supports an information-based economy

proletariat people who provide labor necessary to operate factories and other productive enterprises

rationality deliberate, matter-of-fact calculation of the most efficient means to accomplish a particular goal

rationalization of society Weber's term for the historical change from tradition to rationality as the dominant mode of human thought

social conflict struggle between segments of society over valued resources

social institution a major sphere of social life, or societal subsystem, organized to meet a basic human need

society people who interact in a defined territory and share culture

sociocultural evolution the Lenskis' term for the process of change that results from a society's gaining new information, particularly technology

tradition sentiments and beliefs passed from generation to generation

CRITICAL-THINKING QUESTIONS

1. In terms of sociocultural evolution, assess the notion that technological advance amounts to "progress."
2. As general approaches to understanding society, contrast Marx's concept of materialism with Weber's idealism.
3. How does Marx's concept of alienation differ from Durkheim's concept of anomie?
4. How do these visions of society explain the changing standing of women? What issues might be raised by a feminist critique of each of these theories?

SUGGESTED READINGS

Classic Sources

Robert C. Tucker, ed. *The Marx-Engels Reader.* 2d ed. New York: W. W. Norton, 1978.
This is an excellent source of essays by Karl Marx and Friedrich Engels.

Max Weber. *The Protestant Ethic and the Spirit of Capitalism.* Los Angeles: Roxbury Press, 1995 (orig. 1904–5).
Perhaps Max Weber's best-known study is his analysis of Protestantism and capitalism.

Emile Durkheim. *The Division of Labor in Society.* New York: The Free Press, 1964; orig. 1893.
This is Durkheim's major contribution to our understanding of modern societies.

Contemporary Sources

Gerhard Lenski, Patrick Nolan, and Jean Lenski. *Human Society: An Introduction to Macrosociology.* 7th

ed. New York: McGraw-Hill, 1995.
A comprehensive account of Gerhard and Jean Lenski's analysis of human societies is found in this textbook.

Irving Louis Horowitz. *The Decomposition of Sociology.* New York: Oxford University Press, 1993.
A well-known sociologist argues that the discipline, fraught with political, theoretical, and methodological divisions, is on the decline.

Global Source

Uta Gerhardt, ed. *Talcott Parsons on National Socialism.* Hawthorne, N.Y.: Aldine de Gruyter, 1993.
This book explains how an outstanding theorist applied his research to the Allied effort in World War II and the structuring of a democratic postwar Germany.

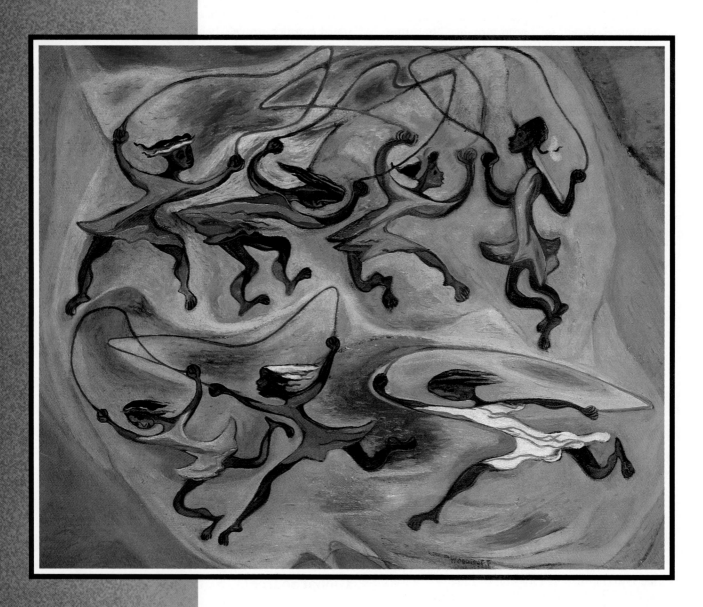

Socialization

On a cold winter day in 1938, a social worker walked anxiously to the door of a rural Pennsylvania farmhouse. Investigating a case of possible child abuse, the social worker soon discovered a five-year-old girl hidden in a second-floor storage room. The child, whose name was Anna, was wedged into an old chair with her arms tied above her head so that she could not move. She was dressed in filthy garments, and her arms and legs—looking like matchsticks—were so frail that she could not use them.

Anna's situation can only be described as tragic. She was born in 1932 to an unmarried and mentally impaired woman of twenty-six who lived with her father. Enraged by his daughter's "illegitimate" motherhood, the grandfather did not even want the child in his house. Anna therefore spent her first six months in various institutions. But her mother was unable to pay for such care, so Anna returned to the hostile home of her grandfather.

At this point, her ordeal intensified. To lessen the grandfather's anger, Anna's mother moved the child to the attic room, where she received little attention and just enough milk to keep her alive. There she stayed—day after day, month after month, with essentially no human contact—for five long years.

Upon learning of the discovery of Anna, sociologist Kingsley Davis (1940) traveled immediately to see the child. He found her at a county home, where local authorities had taken her. Davis was appalled by Anna's condition. She was emaciated and feeble. Unable to laugh, smile, speak, or even show anger, she was completely unresponsive, as if alone in an empty world.

THE IMPORTANCE OF SOCIAL EXPERIENCE

Here is a deplorable but instructive case of a human being deprived of virtually all social contact. Although physically alive, Anna hardly seemed human. Her plight reveals that, isolated in this way, an individual develops scarcely any capacity for thought, emotion, and meaningful behavior. In short, without social experience, an individual is more an *object* than a *person*.

This chapter explores what Anna was deprived of— the means by which we become fully human. This process is **socialization,** *the lifelong social experience by which individuals develop their human potential and learn patterns of their culture.* Unlike other living species whose behavior is biologically set, human beings rely on social experience to learn the nuances of their culture in order to survive.

Social experience is also the foundation of **personality,** *a person's fairly consistent patterns of thinking, feeling,* *and acting.* We build a personality by internalizing our social surroundings. As personality develops, we participate in a culture while remaining, in some respects, distinct individuals. But in the absence of social experience, as the case of Anna shows, personality does not emerge at all.

Social experience is vital for society just as it is for individuals. Societies exist beyond the life span of any person, and thus each generation must teach something of its way of life to the next. Broadly speaking, then, socialization amounts to the ongoing process of cultural transmission.

Human Development: Nature and Nurture

Virtually helpless at birth, the human infant depends on others for care and nourishment as well as learning. Although Anna's short life makes these facts very clear, a century ago most people mistakenly believed that human behavior was the product of biological imperatives.

NOTE: "Nature" has the Latin root *nat(us)*, meaning "born"; "nurture" has the Latin root *nutrit(us)*, meaning "nourished."

GLOBAL: The diversity of economic systems through the years and throughout the world renders claims of "innate competitiveness" suspect.

DISCUSS: Base a discussion on John B. Watson's ideas as evident in the Eddie Murphy and Dan Ackroyd film *Trading Places*.

RESOURCE: Elijah Anderson's *Growing Up on the Streets*, included in the companion reader, *Seeing Ourselves*, demonstrates the effect of environment (especially class and race) on the process of socialization.

Q: "Asking how people grew up may make all men equal yet." Clarence Darrow

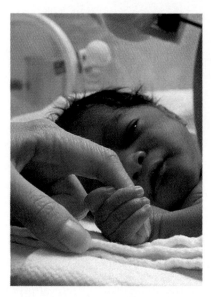
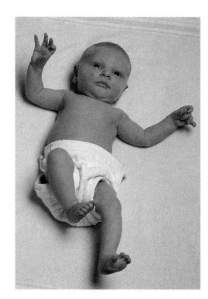

Human infants display various reflexes—biologically based behavior patterns that enhance survival. The sucking reflex, which actually begins before birth, enables the infant to obtain nourishment. The grasping reflex, triggered by placing a finger on the infant's palm causing the hand to close, helps the infant to maintain contact with a parent and, later on, to grasp objects. The Moro reflex, activated by startling the infant, has the infant swinging both arms outward and then bringing them together across the chest. This action, which disappears after several months of life, probably developed among our evolutionary ancestors so that a falling infant could grasp the body hair of a parent.

Charles Darwin, whose groundbreaking ideas are summarized in Chapter 3 ("Culture"), held that each species evolves over thousands of generations as genetic variations enhance survival and reproduction. Biologically rooted traits that enhance survival emerge as a species' "nature." As Darwin's fame grew, people assumed that humans, like other forms of life, had a fixed, instinctive "nature" as well.

Such notions are still with us. People sometimes claim, for example, that our economic system is a reflection of "instinctive human competitiveness," that some people are "born criminals," or that women are more "naturally" emotional while men are "inherently" more rational (Witkin-Lanoil, 1984). We often describe familiar personality traits as *human nature* as if people were born with them, just as we are born with five senses. More accurately, however, our human nature leads us to create and learn cultural traits, as we shall see.

People trying to understand cultural diversity also misconstrued Darwin's thinking. Centuries of world exploration and empire building taught Western Europeans that people around the world behaved quite differently than they did. They attributed such contrasts to biology rather than culture. It was a simple—although terribly damaging—step to conclude that members of technologically simple societies were biologically less evolved and, therefore, less human. Such a self-serving and ethnocentric view helped justify colonial practices, including land seizures and slavery, since it is easier to exploit others if you are convinced that they are not truly human in the same sense that you are.

In the twentieth century, social scientists launched a broad attack on naturalistic explanations of human behavior. Psychologist John B. Watson (1878–1958) devised a theory called *behaviorism*, which held that specific behavior patterns are not instinctive but learned. Thus people the world over have the same claim to humanity, Watson insisted; humans differ only in their cultural environment. For Watson, "human nature" was infinitely malleable:

> Give me a dozen healthy infants . . . and my own specified world to bring them up in, and I will guarantee to take any one at random and train him [or her] to become any type of specialist that I might select—doctor, lawyer, artist, merchant, chief, and yes, even beggar-man and thief—regardless of his [or her] talents, penchants, tendencies, abilities, vocations, and race of his [or her] ancestors. (1930:104)

SUPPLEMENTS: An outline of Chapter 5, along with supplementary lecture material and discussion questions, are found in the *Data File*.

NOTE: We sometimes take highly correlated IQ scores among family members (who share genes) as evidence that intelligence has a genetic component. No doubt, this is so, but the correlation of IQ scores for unrelated individuals reared together is twice as high as that of identical twins reared apart. Thus, "nurture" appears to be the more important in determining "intelligence." (Cf. Thomas J. Bouchard, Jr., and Matthew McGue, "Familial Studies of Intelligence: A Review," *Science* 212, 1981:1055–59.)

Anthropologists weighed in on this debate as well, showing how variable the world's cultures are. An outspoken proponent of the "nurture" view, anthropologist Margaret Mead summed up the evidence: "The differences between individuals who are members of different cultures, like the differences between individuals within a culture, are almost entirely to be laid to differences in conditioning, especially during early childhood, and this conditioning is culturally determined" (1963:280; orig. 1935).

Today, social scientists are cautious about describing any type of behavior as instinctive. Even sociobiology, examined in Chapter 3 ("Culture"), holds that human behavior is primarily guided by the surrounding culture. Of course, this does not mean that biology plays *no* part in human behavior. Human life, after all, depends on the functioning of the body. We also know that children share many biological traits with their parents, especially physical characteristics such as height, weight, hair and eye color, and facial features. Intelligence and various personality characteristics (for example, how one reacts to stimulation or frustration) have some genetic component, as does the potential to excel in such activities as art and music. But whether a person develops an inherited potential depends on the opportunities associated with social position (Herrnstein, 1973; Plomin & Foch, 1980; Goldsmith, 1983).

In sum, the evidence shows that nurture is far more important than nature in determining human behavior. We should not think of nature as opposing nurture, though, since we express our human nature as we build culture. For humans, then, nature and nurture are inseparable.

Social Isolation

For obvious ethical reasons, researchers cannot subject human beings to experimental isolation. Consequently, much of what we know about this issue comes from rare cases of abused children like Anna. Researchers have, however, studied the impact of social isolation on animals.

Effects of Social Isolation on Nonhuman Primates

Psychologists Harry Harlow and Margaret Harlow (1962) conducted a classic investigation of the effects of social isolation on nonhuman primates. They observed the consequences of various conditions of isolation on rhesus monkeys, whose behavior is in some ways remarkably similar to that of humans.

The personalities we develop depend largely on the environment in which we live. When a child's world is shredded by violence, the damage can be profound and lasting. This drawing was made by a child born into the midst of civil war in Yugoslavia. What are the likely effects of such an environment on a young person's self-confidence and capacity to form trusting ties to others?

© 1994 UNICEF. Reprinted by permission of HarperCollins Publishers, Inc.

The Harlows found that complete social isolation for even six months (with adequate nutrition) seriously disturbed the monkeys' development. When these monkeys subsequently returned to their group, they were anxious, passive, and fearful.

The Harlows then isolated infant rhesus monkeys, but provided an artificial "mother" made of wire mesh with a wooden head and the nipple of a feeding tube where the breast would be. These monkeys survived but they, too, subsequently displayed emotional damage.

But when the researchers covered the artificial "mother" with soft terry cloth, the infant monkeys would cling to it, apparently deriving emotional benefit from the closeness. Subsequently, these monkeys revealed less emotional distress. The Harlows thus concluded that normal emotional development requires affectionate cradling as part of parent-infant interaction.

The Harlows made two other discoveries. First, as long as they were surrounded by other infants, monkeys were not adversely affected by the absence of a mother. This finding suggests that deprivation of social experience, rather than the absence of a specific parent, has devastating effects. Second, the Harlows found that lesser periods of social isolation—up to about three months—caused emotional distress, but only temporarily. The damage of short-term isolation,

DISCUSS: Is it simply a coincidence that all the isolated children of record are females?
DIVERSITY: Children of deaf parents sometimes learn sign language first and attempt spoken/written language only later when they enter school. Such children often have difficulty because, as researchers now recognize, the brain loses capacity for language if these skills are not learned within the first few years of life.

NOTE: Susan Curtiss explains that the violence in Genie's family stemmed from a father who wanted no children. The first child in the family died from exposure at 2½ months; the second child died at 2 years; the third child survived, but only after the paternal grandmother took him into her own home; Genie was the family's fourth child.

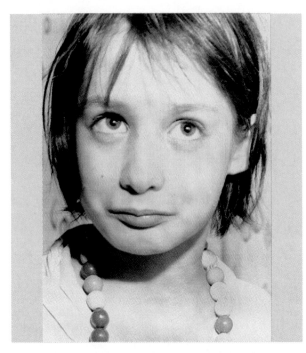

Like other children subjected to prolonged isolation, Genie never did develop a normal facility with language. Many researchers conclude that, unless a child learns language at an early age, this ability is permanently hindered. But others counter that children may well be mentally retarded by such abuse. Thus, cases such as Genie do not settle "nature-nurture" debates about human development.

then, can be overcome; longer-term isolation, however, appears to inflict on monkeys irreversible emotional and behavioral damage.

Effects of Social Isolation on Children

The case of Anna, described earlier, is the best-known instance of the extended social isolation of a human infant. After her discovery, Anna benefited from intense social contact and soon showed improvement. Visiting her in the county home after ten days, Kingsley Davis (1940) noted that she was more alert and even smiled with obvious pleasure. During the next year, Anna made slow but steady progress, showing greater interest in other people and gradually learning to walk. After a year and a half, she could feed herself and play with toys.

Consistent with the observations of the Harlows, however, it was becoming apparent that Anna's five years of social isolation had left her permanently damaged. At the age of eight her mental and social

development was still less than that of a two-year-old. Not until she was almost ten did she begin to grasp language. Of course, since Anna's mother was mentally retarded, perhaps Anna was similarly disadvantaged. The riddle was never solved, because Anna died at age ten from a blood disorder, possibly related to her years of abuse (Davis, 1940, 1947).

A second, quite similar case involves another girl, found at about the same time as Anna and under strikingly similar circumstances. After more than six years of virtual isolation, this girl—known as Isabelle—displayed the same lack of human responsiveness as Anna. Unlike Anna, though, Isabelle benefited from a special learning program directed by psychologists. Within a week, Isabelle was attempting to speak, and a year and a half later, her vocabulary included nearly two thousand words. The psychologists concluded that intensive effort had propelled Isabelle through six years of normal development in only two years. By the time she was fourteen, Isabelle was attending sixth-grade classes, apparently on her way to at least an approximately normal life (Davis, 1947).

A final case of childhood isolation involves a thirteen-year-old California girl victimized in a host of ways by her parents from the age of two (Curtiss, 1977; Pines, 1981; Rymer, 1994). Genie's ordeal included extended periods of being locked alone in a garage. Upon discovery, her condition mirrored that of Anna and Isabelle. Genie was emaciated (weighing only fifty-nine pounds) and had the mental development of a one-year-old. She received intensive treatment by specialists and thrived physically. Yet even after years of care, her ability to use language remains that of a young child, and she lives today in a home for developmentally disabled adults.

All the evidence points to the crucial role of social experience in personality development. Human beings are resilient creatures, sometimes able to recover from even the crushing experience of abuse and isolation. But there is a point—precisely when is unclear from the limited number of cases—at which social isolation in infancy results in irreparable developmental damage.

UNDERSTANDING THE SOCIALIZATION PROCESS

Socialization is a complex, lifelong process. The following sections highlight the work of five men and women who have made lasting contributions to our understanding of human development.

NOTE: Champions of psychoanalysis included Franz Boas, Margaret Mead, and Ruth Benedict, all of whom interpreted this approach as favoring nurture over nature.

RESOURCE: The most sociological of Freud's twenty-four books is *Civilization and Its Discontents*. The sociological implications of Freud's work are explored in Philip Rieff's *Freud: The Mind of the Moralist* (Doubleday, 1961).

RESOURCE: William Golding's *Lord of the Flies* is built on a Freudian model of personality. Jack (and his hunters) represent the power of the id; Piggy consistently opposes them as the superego; Ralph stands between the two as the ego, the voice of reason. Golding wrote the book after participating in the carnage of the D-Day landing in France; he traces the human proclivity for violence (as well as our capacity for learned restraint) to our basic nature.

Sigmund Freud: The Elements of Personality

Sigmund Freud (1856–1939) lived in Vienna at a time when most Europeans considered human behavior to be biologically fixed. Trained as a physician, Freud gradually turned to the study of personality and eventually developed the celebrated theory of psychoanalysis. Many aspects of this work bear directly on our understanding of socialization.

Basic Human Needs

Freud contended that biology plays an important part in social development, although not in terms of the simple instincts that guide other species. Humans, Freud theorized, respond to two general needs or drives. First, humans have a basic need for bonding, which Freud called the life instinct, or *eros* (from the Greek god of love). Second, opposing this need, is an aggressive drive, which Freud termed the death instinct, or *thanatos* (from the Greek meaning "death"). Freud postulated that these opposing forces, operating primarily at the level of the unconscious mind, generate deeply rooted inner tensions.

Freud's Model of Personality

Freud incorporated basic drives and the influence of society into a model of personality with three parts: id, ego, and superego. The **id** represents *the human being's basic drives*, which are unconscious and demand immediate satisfaction. (The word *id* is Latin for "it," suggesting the tentative way in which Freud explored the unconscious mind.) Rooted in our biology, the id is present at birth, making a newborn a bundle of needs demanding attention, touching, and food. But society does not tolerate such a self-centered orientation, so the id's desires inevitably encounter resistance. Because of this cultural opposition, one of the first words a child comprehends is "no."

To avoid frustration, the child learns to approach the world realistically. This accomplishment forms the second component of the personality, the **ego** (Latin for "I"), which is *a person's conscious efforts to balance innate, pleasure-seeking drives with the demands of society*. The ego arises as we gain awareness of our distinct existence; it reaches fruition as we come to understand that we cannot have everything we want.

Finally, the human personality develops the **superego** (Latin meaning "above" or "beyond" the ego), which is *the operation of culture within the individual*.

With the emergence of the superego, we can see *why* we cannot have everything we want. The superego consists of cultural values and norms—internalized in the form of conscience—that define moral limits. The superego begins to emerge as children recognize parental control; it matures as they learn that their own behavior and that of their parents—in fact, everyone's behavior—reflects a broader system of cultural demands.

Personality Development

The id-centered child first encounters the world as a bewildering array of physical sensations and need satisfactions. With gradual development of the superego, however, the child's comprehension extends beyond pleasure and pain to include the moral concepts of right and wrong. Initially, in other words, children can feel good only in the physical sense; but, after three or four years, they feel good or bad as they evaluate their own behavior according to cultural standards.

Conflict between id and superego is ongoing; but, in a well-adjusted person, these opposing forces are managed by the ego. Unresolved conflicts, especially during childhood, typically result in personality disorders later on.

As the source of superego, culture operates to control human drives, a process Freud termed *repression*. Some repression is inevitable, since any society must coerce people to look beyond themselves. Often the competing demands of self and society are resolved through compromise. This process, which Freud called *sublimation*, transforms fundamentally selfish drives into socially acceptable activities. Sexual urges, for example, may lead to marriage, just as aggression gives rise to competitive sports.

Critical evaluation. Freud's work sparked controversy in his own lifetime, and some of that controversy still smolders today. The world he knew vigorously repressed human sexuality, so that few of his contemporaries were prepared to concede that sex is a basic human need. More recently, Freud has come under fire for his depictions of humanity in allegedly male terms, thereby devaluing the lives of women (Donovan & Littenberg, 1982). But Freud provided a foundation that influenced virtually everyone who later studied the human personality. Of special importance to sociology is his notion that we internalize social norms and that childhood experiences have a lasting impact on socialization.

NOTE: Another way to present the theorists is to pose the question "How do we learn?" Freud emphasizes *internalization* of culture; Piaget underscores internal *cognitive development*; behaviorists Watson and Skinner highlight *environmental stimulation*; Mead advances a *social behaviorist* approach based on gaining the capacity for symbolic interaction.

NOTE: Stress that Piaget's stages of development are *maturational*; in this, he stands apart from George Herbert Mead, for whom biology played virtually no role in social development. (Piaget was trained as a biologist.)

NOTE: An example of preoperational thinking: Young children prefer nickels to dimes because they are bigger.

In a well-known experiment, Jean Piaget demonstrated that children over the age of seven had entered the concrete operational stage of development because they could recognize that the quantity of liquid remained the same when poured from a wide beaker into a tall one.

Jean Piaget: Cognitive Development

Jean Piaget (1896–1980) is also among the foremost psychologists of the century. Much of his work centered on human *cognition*—how people think and understand. Early in his career, Piaget was fascinated by the behavior of his three children, wondering not only what they knew but *how* they comprehended the world. His observations led him to conclude that children's thinking undergoes dramatic and patterned changes as children mature biologically and gain social experience. Piaget identified four stages of cognitive development.

The Sensorimotor Stage

In Piaget's scheme, first comes the **sensorimotor stage,** *the level of human development at which individuals experience the world only through sensory contact.* At this stage, roughly the first two years of life, the infant explores the world with the five senses: touching, tasting, smelling, looking, and listening.

Children's social skills at this early point are limited to imitating others; infants cannot yet comprehend symbols. So "knowing" to very young children amounts to direct, sensory experience.

The Preoperational Stage

The second plateau in Piaget's account of development is the **preoperational stage,** *the level of human development at which individuals first use language and other symbols.* At about age two, children begin to engage the world mentally; their capacity to *think* moves reality beyond the senses. The ability to use symbols also gives flight to children's imagination; they learn to distinguish between dreams and reality and they can enjoy the element of fantasy in fairy tales (Kohlberg & Gilligan, 1971; Skolnick, 1986). Unlike adults, however, they attach names and meanings only to specific things. A child at this stage—roughly from age two to six—can describe a favorite toy, for example, but is still unable to describe the qualities of toys in general.

Without abstract concepts, a child also cannot judge size, weight, or volume. In one of his best-known experiments, Piaget placed two identical glasses containing equal amounts of water on a table. He asked several children aged five and six if the amount in each glass was the same. They nodded that it was. The children then watched Piaget take one of the glasses and pour its contents into a taller, narrower glass, raising the level of the water. He asked again if each glass held the same amount. The typical five- and six-year-old now insisted that the taller glass held more water. But children of seven or eight, who are able to think abstractly, could comprehend that the amount of water remained the same.

We have all seen young children place their hands in front of their faces and exclaim, "You can't see me!" They assume that if they cannot see you, then you are unable to see them. This behavior reveals that preoperational children maintain an egocentric view of the world; they cannot yet perceive that any situation may appear different to another person.

The Concrete Operational Stage

Next comes the **concrete operational stage,** *the level of development at which individuals first perceive causal connections in their surroundings.* At this level of development, typically between ages seven and eleven, children begin to grasp how and why things happen, gaining a far greater ability to manipulate their environment.

In addition, girls and boys now can attach more than one symbol to a particular event or object. For instance, if you say to a girl of five, "Today is Wednesday," she might respond, "No, it's my birthday!" indicating the ability to use just one symbol at a time. Within a few years, however, she would be able to respond, "Yes, this Wednesday is my birthday!"

Also during the concrete operational stage, children transcend earlier egocentrism so that they can

Q: "If we examine the intellectual development of the individual . . . we shall find that the human spirit goes through a certain number of stages, each different from the other . . ." Jean Piaget
NOTE: Because of their egocentric world view, young children may see themselves as responsible for family conflict and divorce.

GLOBAL: Kohlberg claims, in essence, that morality spans a continuum from selfishness at one end to selflessness at the other. This is a virtually universal theme of world religions.

now imagine themselves from the point of view of another person. As we shall explain shortly, the ability to "stand in another's shoes" is the key to participating in complex social activities, such as games.

The Formal Operational Stage

The final level in Piaget's model is the **formal operational stage**, *the level of human development at which individuals think abstractly and critically.* By about the age of twelve, children begin to reason in abstract terms rather than thinking only of concrete situations. If, for example, you were to ask a child of seven or eight, "What would you like to be when you grow up?" you might prompt a concrete response such as, "A teacher." But a teenager might well respond abstractly, saying "I would like a job that is exciting." At this point, young people's surging energy is matched by their creativity and imagination, sometimes evident in a passion for science fiction or poetry.

Also at this stage, children can comprehend metaphors. Hearing the phrase "A penny for your thoughts" might lead a young child to ask for a coin, but the adolescent will recognize a gentle invitation to intimacy. Then, too, adolescents begin to favor or reject thoughts or actions "in principle," a trait especially pronounced among teenagers.

Critical evaluation. While Freud envisioned personality as an ongoing battle between opposing forces of biology and society, Piaget viewed the human mind as active and creative. Piaget's contribution to understanding socialization lies in showing that the capacity to engage the world unfolds predictably as the result of biological maturation and increasing social experience.

Some challenge Piaget's scheme by questioning whether people in every society progress through all four of the stages he identified. For instance, living in a traditional society that changes very slowly is likely to inhibit the capacity for abstract and critical thought. Finally, even in our own society, as many as 30 percent of thirty-year-olds may never reach the formal operational stage at all (Kohlberg & Gilligan, 1971:1065). Thus people exposed to little creative and imaginative thinking do not generally develop this capacity on their own.

Lawrence Kohlberg: Moral Development

More recently, Lawrence Kohlberg (1981) used Piaget's theory as a springboard for a study of moral reasoning—the ways in which individuals come to judge situations as right or wrong. Following Piaget's lead, Kohlberg argues that moral development proceeds in stages.

Young children who experience the world in terms of pain and pleasure (Piaget's sensorimotor stage) are at the *preconventional* level of moral development. At this early stage, in other words, "rightness" amounts to "what serves my needs" or "what feels good to me."

The *conventional* level of moral development, Kohlberg's second stage, begins to appear among teenagers (corresponding to Piaget's last, formal operational stage). At this point, young people shed some of their selfishness and begin to define right and wrong in terms of what pleases parents and what is consistent with broader cultural norms. In reaching moral judgments, individuals at this stage try to assess intention in addition to simply observing what others do.

A final stage of moral development, the *postconventional* level, moves individuals beyond the specific norms of their society to ponder more abstract ethical principles. At this level, people philosophically reflect on the meaning of liberty, freedom, or justice. Individuals are now capable of actively criticizing their own society and of arguing, for instance, that what is traditional or legal still may not be right.

Critical evaluation. Like the work of Piaget, Kohlberg's model explains that moral development occurs in more or less definable stages. Thus, some of the criticisms of Piaget's ideas also apply to Kohlberg's work. Whether this model applies to people in all societies, for example, remains unconfirmed. Then, too, many people in the United States apparently do not reach the postconventional level of moral reasoning, although exactly why is also, at present, an open question.

Another problem with Kohlberg's research is that his subjects were all boys. Kohlberg commits the research error, described in Chapter 2 ("Sociological Investigation"), of generalizing the results of male subjects to all of humanity. This problem prompted his colleague Carol Gilligan to investigate how gender affects moral reasoning.

Carol Gilligan: Bringing in Gender

Carol Gilligan, who is introduced in the box on page 130, was disturbed that Kohlberg's research had overlooked girls. This narrow focus, as she sees it, is typical of much social science, which uses the behavior of males as the norm for how everyone should act.

PROFILE

Carol Gilligan: Socialization and Girls' Self-Esteem

Carol Gilligan, an educational psychologist at Harvard University, studies the personality development of young girls. Initially, she attempted to correct a research bias by which others had investigated only boys. As her work progressed, Gilligan discovered that boys and girls employ distinctive standards in making moral decisions.

Gilligan's more recent work targets the issue of self-esteem. Her research team interviewed more than two thousand girls, ranging from six to eighteen years of age, over a five-year period. Their responses point up a clear pattern: Young girls start out with considerable confidence and self-esteem, only to find these vital resources slipping away as they pass through adolescence.

Why? Gilligan claims that the answer lies in culture. Our way of life, she argues, still defines the ideal woman as calm, controlled, and eager to please. Then, too, as girls move from the elementary grades to secondary school, they encounter fewer women teachers and find that most authority figures are men. So by their late teens, women are struggling to regain much of the personal strength they had a decade before.

Illustrating this trend, Gilligan and her colleagues returned to a girls' school—one site of their research—to present their findings. Most younger girls who had been interviewed were eager to have their names appear in the forthcoming book; the older girls, by contrast, were hesitant: Many were fearful that they would be talked about.

Sources: Gilligan (1990) and Winkler (1990).

Therefore Gilligan (1982, 1990) set out systematically to compare the moral development of females and males. Simply put, her conclusion is that the two sexes make moral judgments in different ways. Males, she contends, have a *justice perspective*, relying on formal rules and abstract principles to define right and wrong. Girls, on the other hand, have a *care and responsibility perspective*, judging a situation with an eye toward personal relationships and loyalties. Stealing, as boys see it, is wrong because it breaks the law and violates common moral sentiments. Girls, however, are more likely to wonder why someone would steal, looking less severely upon an individual who did so with the intention of helping another person.

Kohlberg treats the abstract male perspective as superior to the person-based female approach. Yet Gilligan, who takes a more subtly shaded view, points out that the impersonal application of rules has long dominated men's lives in the workplace. Concern for attachments, by contrast, has been more relevant to women's lives as wives, mothers, and caregivers. But, Gilligan asks, should we set up male standards as the norms by which we evaluate everyone?

Critical evaluation. Gilligan's work both sharpens our understanding of human development and highlights the problems related to gender in conducting and evaluating research. Yet what accounts for the differences she documents between females and males? Is it nature or nurture? Although it is impossible to rule out inherent differences between the sexes, Gilligan believes that these patterns reflect cultural conditioning. Thus, we might predict that, as more women organize their lives around the workplace, the moral reasoning of women and men will show greater similarity.

George Herbert Mead: The Social Self

Our understanding of socialization stems in large part from the life work of George Herbert Mead (1863–1931), who is introduced in the box on page 132. Mead (1962; orig. 1934) described his approach as *social behaviorism*, calling to mind the behaviorism of psychologist John B. Watson, described earlier. Both recognized the power of the environment to shape human behavior. But Watson focused on outward

RESOURCE: Mead's statement "The Self" is among the classics included in the *Seeing Ourselves* reader.

Q: "Each to each a looking glass,
      Reflects the other that doth pass."
      Charles Horton Cooley (1964:184; orig. 1902)

RESOURCE: George Herbert Mead also wrote about teaching; see "The Psychology of Social Consciousness Implied in Instruction"

(*Science* XXXI, 1910:688–93) and "The Teaching of Science in College" (*Science* XXIV, 1906:390–97).

Q: "O wad some Power the giftie gie us
      To see oursels as ithers see us!
      It wad frae monie a blunder free us,
      An' foolish notion."
      Scottish poet Robert Burns

behavior, while Mead highlighted inward *thinking*, which he contended was humanity's defining trait.

The Self

Mead's central concept is the **self**, *a dimension of personality composed of an individual's self-awareness and self-image.* Mead's genius lay in seeing that the self is inseparable from society, a connection explained in a series of steps.

First, Mead asserted, *the self emerges from social experience.* The self is not part of the body, and it does not exist at birth. Mead rejected the position that personality is guided by biological drives (as asserted by Freud) or biological maturation (as Piaget claimed). For Mead, the self develops *only* through social experience. In the absence of social interaction, as we see from the cases of isolated children, the body may grow but no self will emerge.

Second, Mead explained, *social experience is the exchange of symbols.* Using words, a wave of the hand, or a smile, people create meaning, which is a distinctively human experience. We can use reward and punishment to train a dog, after all; but the dog attaches no meaning to these actions. Human beings, by contrast, make sense of actions by inferring people's underlying intentions. In short, a dog responds to *what you do*; a human responds to *what you have in mind* as you do it.

Return to our friendly dog for a moment. You can train a dog to walk to the porch and return with an umbrella. But the dog grasps no meaning in the act, no intention behind the command. Thus, if the dog cannot find the umbrella, it is incapable of the *human* response: to look for a raincoat instead.

Third, says Mead, *to understand intention, you must imagine the situation from another person's point of view.* Using symbols, we can imaginatively place ourselves in another person's shoes and thus see ourselves as that person does. This capacity allows us to anticipate how others will respond to us even before we act. A simple toss of a ball requires stepping outside ourselves to imagine how another will respond to our throw. Social interaction, then, involves seeing ourselves as others see us—a process that Mead called *taking the role of the other.*

The Looking-Glass Self

In social life, other people represent the mirror or looking glass in which we perceive ourselves. Charles Horton Cooley (1864–1929), one of Mead's colleagues, used the phrase **looking-glass self** to designate *the image people have of themselves based on how they*

George Herbert Mead wrote: *"No hard-and-fast line can be drawn between our own selves and the selves of others."* The painting Manyness *by Rimma Gerlovina and Valeriy Gerlovin conveys this important truth. Although we tend to think of ourselves as unique individuals, each person's characteristics develop in an ongoing process of interaction with others.*

Rimma Gerlovina & Valeriy Gerlovin, *Manyness*, 1990. Courtesy Steinbaum Krauss Gallery, NY.

believe others perceive them (1964; orig. 1902). Whether we think of ourselves as clever or clumsy, worthy or worthless, depends in large measure on what we think others think of us. This insight goes a long way toward explaining Carol Gilligan's finding that young women lose self-confidence as they come of age in a society that discourages women from being too assertive.

The I and the Me

Our capacity to see ourselves through others implies that the self has two components. First, *the self is subject* as we initiate social action. Humans are innately active and spontaneous, Mead claimed, dubbing this subjective element of the self the *I* (the subjective form of the personal pronoun).

Second, *the self is object* because, taking the role of another, we form impressions of ourselves. Mead called this objective element of the self the *me* (the objective form of the personal pronoun). All social experience begins with someone initiating action

NOTE: Sometimes young children are hurt by adults who seem not to appreciate primitive "homemade" gifts such as artwork from school. This feeling reflects children's limited capacity to "take the role of the other." They cannot comprehend that the adult does not see the same value in the gift as they do.

DISCUSS: We know that children vary with regard to innate talents and temperaments; moreover, biological maturation does affect behavior more than Mead allowed. Would it be more accurate to say that social experience is *necessary but not sufficient* to explain the development of personality?

NOTE: Playing "peek-a-boo" reveals the inability of young children to take the role of the other. *Since they cannot see you*, tots assume, *you cannot see them.*

PROFILE

George Herbert Mead: The Self Is Born of Society

Few people were surprised that George Herbert Mead became a college professor. He was born to a Massachusetts family with a strong intellectual tradition, and both his parents were academics. His father was both a preacher and a teacher at a number of colleges, and his mother served for a decade as president of Mount Holyoke College.

But Mead also had a hand in shaping his own life, rebelling against the strongly religious atmosphere of his home and community. After completing college, he restlessly traveled throughout the Pacific Northwest, surveying for the railroad and reading voraciously. He gradually settled on the idea of studying philosophy, an academic endeavor he pursued at Harvard and in Europe.

Mead took a teaching position at the new University of Chicago. But his outlook still veered from the conventional. For one thing, he rarely published, going against a long-standing tradition among academics. Mead's reputation and stature grew only after his death, when colleagues and former students collected and published his lecture notes. For another, Mead drew together a wide range of ideas to help launch the new field of social psychology.

Finally, never content with life as it was, Mead was an active social reformer. To him, the course of an entire society was as ongoing and changeable as the life of any individual. This insight follows from his basic contention: Society may have the power to shape individuals, but people also have the capacity to mold their society.

Sources: Based, in part, on Coser (1977) and Schellenberg (1978).

(the I-phase of self) and then guiding the action (the me-phase of self) by taking the role of the other. Social experience is thus the interplay of the I and the me: Our actions are spontaneous yet guided by how others respond to us.

Mead stressed that thinking itself constitutes a social experience. Our thoughts are partly creative (representing the I), but in thought we also become objects to ourselves (representing the me) as we imagine how others will respond to our ideas.

Development of the Self

According to Mead, gaining a self amounts to learning to take the role of the other. Like Freud and Piaget, Mead regarded early childhood as the crucial time for this task, but he did not link the development of the self to biological maturation. Mead maintained that the self emerges over time with increasing social experience.

Infants respond to others only in terms of *imitation*. They mimic behavior without understanding underlying intentions. Unable to use symbols, Mead concluded, infants have no self.

Children first learn to use language and other symbols in the form of *play*, especially role playing. Initially, they model themselves on key people in their lives—such as parents—whom we call *significant others*. Playing "mommy and daddy," for example, helps children imagine the world from their parents' point of view.

Gradually, children learn to take the roles of several others at once. This skill is the key to moving from simple play (say, playing catch) involving one other to complex *games* (like baseball) involving many others. Only by the age of seven or eight have most children acquired sufficient social experience to engage in team sports that demand taking the role of numerous others simultaneously.

Figure 5–1 shows the logical progression from imitation to play to games. But a final stage in the development of the self remains. A game involves taking the role of others in just one situation. But

RESOURCE: Besides believing in the plasticity of human personality, George Herbert Mead also believed in people's ability to reform society. For a discussion of his views on social reform, see Dmitri N. Shalin, *American Journal of Sociology* 93, 4 (January 1988):913–51.

RESOURCE: Italian playwright Luigi Pirandello (1867–1936) made use of the sociological perspective in his work. Many of his plays reveal a striking similarity to the ideas of George Herbert Mead (and also Erving Goffman). See, especially, *The Pleasure of Honesty.*

NOTE: An illustration of the significance of the family: Four of the five most powerful "social readjustment" experiences involve family members: death of spouse (100), divorce (73), marital separation (65), death of close family member (63), and jail term (63). (Holmes & Rahe, 1967)

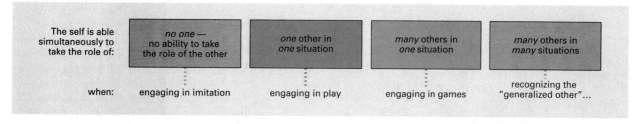

FIGURE 5–1 Building on Social Experience
George Herbert Mead described the development of the self as the process of gaining social experience. This is largely a matter of taking the role of the other with increasing sophistication.

members of a society also need to see themselves as others in general might. In other words, we recognize that people in any situation in society share cultural norms and values, and we begin to incorporate these general patterns into the self. Mead used the term **generalized other** to refer to *widespread cultural norms and values we use as references in evaluating ourselves.*

Of course, the emergence of the self is not the end of socialization. Quite the contrary: Mead claimed that socialization continues as long as we have social experience, so that changing circumstances can reshape who we are. The self may change, for example, with divorce, disability, or unexpected wealth. And we retain some control over this process as we respond to events and circumstances and thereby play a part in our own socialization.

Critical evaluation. The strength of Mead's work lies in exploring the nature of social experience itself. He succeeded in explaining how symbolic interaction is the foundation of both the self and society.

Some critics disparage Mead's view as radically social because it acknowledges no biological element in the emergence of the self. In this position, he stands apart from Freud (who identified general drives within the organism) and Piaget (whose stages of development are tied to biological maturation).

Mead's concepts of the I and the me are often confused with Freud's concepts of the id and the superego. But Freud rooted the id in the biological organism, while Mead rejected any link between the self and biology (although he never specified the origin of the I). Freud's concept of the superego and Mead's concept of the me both reflect the power of society to shape personality. But for Freud, superego and id are locked in continual combat. Mead, however, held that the I and the me work closely and cooperatively together (Meltzer, 1978).

AGENTS OF SOCIALIZATION

Every social experience we have affects us in at least some small way. In modern industrial and postindustrial societies, however, several familiar settings have special significance in the socialization process.

The Family

The family is the most important agent of socialization because it represents the center of children's lives. As we have seen, infants are almost totally dependent on others, and the responsibility to meet their needs almost always falls on parents and other family members. At least until the onset of schooling, the family also shoulders the task of teaching children cultural values, attitudes, and prejudices about themselves and others.

Family-based socialization is not all intentional. Children learn continuously from the kind of environment that adults create. Whether children learn to think of themselves as strong or weak, smart or stupid, loved or simply tolerated, and whether they believe the world to be trustworthy or dangerous largely stem from this early environment.

Parenting styles aside, research points to the importance of parental *attention* in the social development of children. Physical contact, verbal stimulation, and responsiveness from parents and others all foster intellectual growth (Belsky, Lerner, & Spanier, 1984).

The family also confers on children a social position; that is, parents not only bring children into the physical world, they also place them in society in terms of race, ethnicity, religion, and class. In time, all these elements become part of a child's self-concept. Of course, some aspects of social position may change later on, but social standing at birth affects us throughout our lives.

Q: "For most [children of divorce], divorce was the most important cause of enduring pain and anomie in their lives." Judith S. Wallerstein and Sandra Blakeslee (1989)

SUPPLEMENTS: The *Student CHIP Social Survey Software* allows students to analyze the effects of a family's class position on the socialization of children.

SOCIAL SURVEY: "How important is it that a child obey parents well?" (*CHIP1 Social Survey Software*, OBEYS1; GSS 1973–83, N = 7,253)

SES	"Very important"	Other
High	17.1%	82.9%
Middle	30.6%	69.4%
Low	41.1%	58.9%

Sociological research indicates that affluent parents tend to encourage creativity in their children while poor parents tend to foster conformity. While this general difference may be valid, parents at all class levels can and do provide loving support and guidance by simply involving themselves in their children's lives. Henry Ossawa Tanner's painting The Banjo Lesson *stands as a lasting testament to this process.*

Henry Ossawa Tanner, *The Banjo Lesson,* 1893. Oil on canvas. Hampton University Museum, Hampton, Virginia.

National data from the General Social Survey reveal how class position shapes parents' aspirations for children. Asked to pick from a list the three qualities most desirable in a child, lower-class people typically include traits like obedience and conformity. Well-to-do people, by contrast, tend to highlight having good judgment and being creative (*Student CHIP Social Survey Software*, 1992). Why? Melvin Kohn (1977), who discovered the same pattern in his own research, explains the difference in terms of the education and occupations common to parents at each level. People of lower social standing usually have limited education and often perform routine jobs under close supervision. Imagining that their children eventually will hold similar positions, they cultivate obedience and conformity in their offspring. By contrast, with more schooling, well-off parents typically have jobs that provide more autonomy and encourage the use of imagination. These parents, therefore, try to inspire the same qualities in their children.

We know children are born both to rich and poor parents. What is less evident—and probably just as important—is that parents at varying class positions provide children with "cultural capital" in the form of differing aspirations. In many ways, then, parents teach their children to follow in their footsteps.

Schooling

Schooling enlarges children's social world to include people with social backgrounds that differ from their own. As children confront social diversity, they learn the significance society attaches to people's race and sex and often act accordingly: Studies document the tendency of children to cluster together in play groups composed of one race and gender (Lever, 1978; Finkelstein & Haskins, 1983).

Formally, schooling teaches children a wide range of knowledge and skills. But schools convey a host of other lessons informally through what sociologists call the *hidden curriculum.* Activities such as spelling bees and sports teach children key cultural values such as competitive achievement and success. Children also receive countless formal and informal messages promoting their society's way of life as morally good.

Moving beyond the personal web of family life, children entering school soon discover that evaluations of skills like reading and arithmetic are based on impersonal, standardized tests. Here, the emphasis shifts from *who* they are to *how* they perform. Of course, the confidence or anxiety that children develop at home can have a significant effect on how well they perform in school (Belsky, Lerner, & Spanier, 1984).

School is also most children's first experience with rigid formality. The school day runs on a strict time schedule, subjecting children to impersonal regimentation and fostering punctuality. Not surprisingly, these are the same traits expected by most of the large organizations that will employ them later in life.

Finally, schools socialize children with regard to gender. Raphaela Best (1983) points out that, in primary school, boys engage in more physical activities and spend more time outdoors, while girls tend to be more sedentary, sometimes even helping the teacher with

Q: "I am always ready to learn, although I do not always like being taught." Winston Churchill

NOTE: Schooling emerged only with the declining economic value of children. "School" is derived from the Greek word *schole*, meaning "leisure employed in learning."

NOTE: The word "peer" is derived from the Latin *par*, meaning "equal."

GLOBAL: Some 250,000 television sets are built each day; roughly equal to the number of people added to the earth's population. In global perspective, the mass media (especially television) are most widespread in industrial societies that change quickly; however, the media are a powerful force for change when introduced to traditional societies—see the opening dealing with Brazil's Kaiapo Indians in Chapter 24 ("Social Change").

various housekeeping chores. Gender distinctions continue in the higher grades and persist right through college. College women, for example, encounter pressure to select majors in the arts or humanities, while men are steered toward the physical sciences.

The Peer Group

By the time they enter school, children have also discovered the **peer group**, *a social group whose members have interests, social position, and age in common.* A young child's peer group generally consists of neighborhood playmates; later, peer groups are composed of friends from school or elsewhere.

Unlike the family and the school, the peer group allows young people to escape from the direct supervision of adults. With this newfound independence, members of peer groups gain valuable experience in forging social relationships on their own and developing a sense of themselves apart from their families. Peer groups also give young people the opportunity to discuss interests that may not be shared by adults (such as styles of dress and popular music) or looked on favorably by parents (such as drugs and sex).

For the young, the appeal of the peer group lies in the ever-present possibility of activity not condoned by adults; for the same reason, parents express concern about who their children's friends are. In a rapidly changing society, peer groups often rival parents in influence, as the attitudes of parents and children diverge along the lines of a "generation gap." The primacy of peer groups typically peaks during adolescence, as young people begin to break away from their families and think of themselves as responsible adults. At this stage of life, young people often display anxious conformity to peers because this new identity and sense of belonging eases some of the apprehension brought on by breaking away from the family.

The conflict between parents and peers may be more apparent than real, however, for even during adolescence children remain strongly influenced by their families. Peers may guide short-term concerns such as style of dress and musical taste, but parents retain greater sway over the long-term goals of their children. One study, for example, found that parents had more influence than even best friends on young people's educational aspirations (Davies & Kandel, 1981).

Finally, any neighborhood or school operates as a social mosaic composed of numerous peer groups. As we will see in Chapter 7 ("Groups and Organizations"), members tend to perceive their own peer group in positive terms while discrediting others. Moreover,

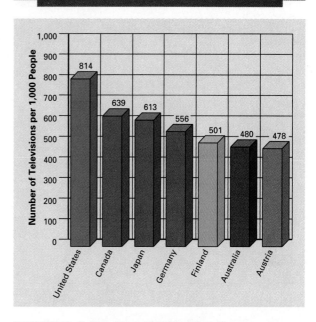

Global Snapshot

FIGURE 5–2 Number of Television Sets per 1,000 People
Source: U.S. Bureau of the Census (1995).

individuals are also influenced by peer groups they would like to join, a process sociologists call **anticipatory socialization**, *social learning directed toward gaining a desired position.* In school, for example, young people may mimic the styles and banter of the group they hope to join. Or, at a later point in life, a young lawyer who hopes to become a partner in her law firm may conform to the attitudes and behavior of the firm's partners to ease her way into this rarefied group.

The Mass Media

September 29, 1994, the Pacific Ocean nearing Japan. We have been out of sight of land for two weeks now, which renders this ship our entire social world. But more than land, many of the students miss television! Tapes of "Beverly Hills 90210" are a hot item . . . .

Seeing Ourselves

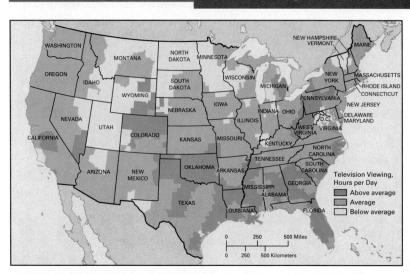

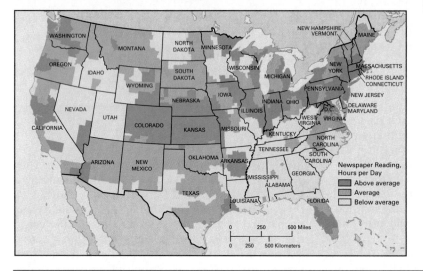

NATIONAL MAP 5–1

Television Viewing and Newspaper Reading Across the United States

The map on the left identifies U.S. counties in which television watching is above average, average, and below average. The map below provides comparable information for time devoted to reading newspapers. What do you think accounts for the high level of television viewing across much of the South and in rural West Virginia? Does your theory also account for patterns of newspaper reading?

Source: *American Demographics* magazine, August 1993, p. 64. Reprinted with permission. © 1993, *American Demographics* magazine, Ithaca, New York. Data from Young and Rubicam, San Francisco.

The **mass media** are *impersonal communications directed to a vast audience*. The term "media" comes from Latin meaning "middle," suggesting that the media function to connect people. The development of *mass* media occurs as communications technologies (first newspapers and, more recently, radio and television) disseminate information on a mass scale.

In the United States today, the mass media have an enormous effect on our attitudes and behavior. For this reason, they are an important component of the socialization process. Television, introduced in 1939, has rapidly become the dominant medium in the United States. In 1950, according to the Census Bureau, only 9 percent of U.S. households could boast one or more television sets. By 1995, this proportion had soared to 98 percent (while only 94 percent had telephones). Videocassette recorders (VCRs) have recently become the fastest growing appliance in history and are found in three-fourths of homes (up from 1 percent in 1980). Two out of three households also have cable television. In fact, as Figure 5–2 on page 135 indicates, the United States has a higher

SOCIAL DIVERSITY

How Do the Media Portray Minorities?

On an old "Saturday Night Live" sketch, Ron Howard tells comedian Eddie Murphy about a new film, *Night Shift*, in which two mortuary workers decide to open their own sideline business—a prostitution ring. Murphy asks whether any black actors are in the film; Howard shakes his head "no." Murphy then thunders, "A story about two pimps and there wasn't no brothers in it? I don't know whether to thank you or punch you in the mouth, man!"

Murphy's ambivalence points up twin criticisms of the U.S. mass media: Films and television portray minorities in stereotypical fashion or exclude them altogether (Press, 1993:219). Certainly, at the beginning of the television age in the 1950s, minorities were almost nowhere to be found on television and in films. Even the wildly successful 1950s comedy "I Love Lucy" originally was turned down by every major television studio because it featured Desi Arnaz—a Cuban—in a starring role. Since then, however, the media have steadily included more minorities, so that the issue of visibility has declined in importance.

But the second issue is just as important: *how* the media portray minorities. The few African Americans who managed to break into television in the 1950s

(for example, the infamous "Amos 'n Andy" or Jack Benny's butler "Rochester") were strictly confined to stereotypical roles portraying uneducated, low-status people. Today, although many television shows feature African-American stars, most are situation comedies ("sitcoms") replete with crude humor and bumbling characters.

Perhaps the most significant exception to this pattern is "The Cosby Show," among the most popular television programs during the past decade. Although Cliff and Claire Huxtable were originally to hold blue-collar occupations (chauffeur and

Should we applaud "The Cosby Show" for demonstrating the ability of African Americans to succeed? Or should we condemn the program for presenting an unrealistic portrait of black people in this white-dominated society?

plumber were one combination), the final decision by TV producers raised them into the white-collar realm of physician and lawyer. Many people praised the show for shattering the stereotype and placing minorities squarely within the middle class. On the other hand, critics charged that the show unrealistically portrayed African Americans, sending a false message to whites that anyone—whatever one's race—can "make it." This, the critics maintain, is doubtful given the barriers of race and class in the United States.

Looking behind the camera, we come to another issue: While a number of minority producers and directors have emerged in recent decades, African Americans and other minorities are largely unrepresented in the executive positions that control the mass media.

Certainly, the mass media can boast of improvement in the portrayal of minorities. But vexing questions remain (cf. MacDonald, 1992). Should the mass media strive to portray minorities *as they are* and risk perpetuating stereotypes? Or—and this has been more the rule—do they portray minorities *as they should be* and risk showing these minorities in unrealistic situations, glossing over racial and ethnic inequality?

rate of television ownership than any other industrial country.

Just how "glued to the television" are we? The latest statistics show that the average household keeps a television on for seven hours each day (U.S. Bureau of the Census, 1995). Years before children learn to

read, watching television has become a regular routine and, as they grow up, young girls and boys spend as many hours in front of a television as they do in school. Indeed, television consumes as much of children's time as interacting with parents (Singer & Singer, 1983; APA, 1993).

SOCIAL SURVEY: "How many hours a day do you watch TV?" (*Student CHIP Social Survey Software*, TVHRS1; GSS 1975–91, N = 14,034)

SES	0–1	2–3	4+
High	36.4%	49.5%	14.1%
Middle	22.7%	47.2%	30.0%
Low	15.9%	41.9%	42.2%
All	24.5%	46.6%	29.0%

High SES only, N = 3,295

NOTE: Rothman and Lichter (1994) report that two-thirds of the people they count as "Hollywood elites" characterize their films or other works as efforts at social reform.

THEN AND NOW: Household television viewing: *1960*, 5 hours daily; *1970*, 6 hours; *1990*, 7 hours.

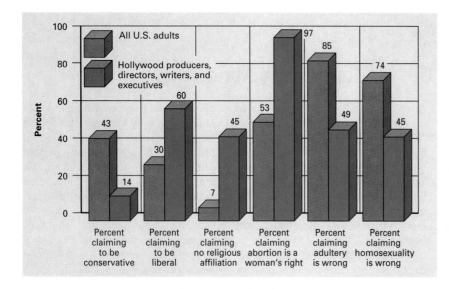

FIGURE 5–3

The Politics of the Hollywood Elite

Recent surveys of leading Hollywood opinion makers, including prominent executives, writers, producers, and directors in television and film, show that the Hollywood elite is far more liberal than U.S. adults as a whole. This discrepancy accounts for critics' charge that Hollywood does not support what conservatives call "American family values."

Sources: The Center for Media and Public Affairs (1991), National Opinion Research Center (1992), and Prindle & Endersby (1993).

Virtually everyone in the United States watches television, but not to an equal degree: National Map 5–1 on page 136 identifies the regions of the country in which television viewing is greatest and compares this with regions where people spend the most time reading newspapers.

Comedian Fred Allen once quipped that we call television a "medium" because it is rarely well done. For a variety of reasons, television (as well as all mass media) has provoked plenty of criticism. Some cite biases in television programming: Liberal critics maintain that television shows mirror our society's patterns of inequality and rarely challenge the status quo. That is, TV shows have traditionally portrayed men and women according to cultural stereotypes, placing men in positions of power and relegating women to roles as mothers or subordinates. Moreover, entertainment programming on television has long portrayed well-to-do people favorably, while depicting less affluent individuals (Archie Bunker is the classic example) as ignorant and wrongheaded. And, although racial and ethnic minorities tend to watch more television than white people, until recent decades minorities have been all but absent from TV programming (Gans, 1980; Cantor & Pingree, 1983; Ang, 1985; Parenti, 1986; Brown, 1990). The box on page 137 offers an overview of how the U.S. entertainment industry has characterized minorities.

On the other side of the fence, conservative critics charge that the television and film industries are dominated by a "cultural elite" who are far more liberal than the population as a whole. Especially in recent years, they maintain, the media have become increasingly "politically correct," advancing various socially liberal causes including feminism and gay rights (Lichter, Rothman, & Rothman, 1986; Woodward, 1992; Prindle, 1993; Prindle & Endersby, 1993; Rothman, Powers, & Rothman, 1993). Figure 5–3, showing the results of several surveys of top "opinion leaders" in Hollywood, reveals that the elite of the entertainment world are, in fact, significantly more liberal than the U.S. population as a whole.

In sum, television and the other mass media have enriched our lives, generating a wide range of entertaining and educational programming. Moreover, the media increase our understanding of diverse cultures and provoke discussion of current issues. At the same time, the power of the media—especially television—to shape how we think continues to fuel controversy on many fronts.

Finally, other spheres of life beyond those just described also play a part in social learning. For most people in the United States, these include religious organizations, the workplace, the military, and social clubs. As a result, socialization inevitably proceeds inconsistently as we absorb different information from disparate sources. In the end, socialization is not a simple learning process; it is a complex balancing act in which we encounter a wide range of ideas as we try to form our own distinctive personalities and world views.

SOCIAL SURVEY: "How many hours a day do you watch TV?" (*Student CHIP Social Survey Software*, TVHRS2; GSS 1975–91, N = 14,073)

EDUC YRS	0–1	2–3	4+
13–20	34.2%	47.9%	18.0%
12	19.5%	47.7%	32.8%
0–11	17.2%	43.3%	39.4%

NOTE: Ariès is an art historian; his interest in the changing conceptions of childhood began when he noted that medieval artists portrayed children as miniature adults. This did not reflect a lack of technical sophistication, he concluded, but rather a different view of childhood.
Q: "One cannot love lumps of flesh, and little infants are nothing more." Samuel Johnson

SOCIALIZATION AND THE LIFE COURSE

Although childhood is critical to the socialization process, learning continues throughout our lives. The following overview of the life course reveals that our society organizes human experience according to age, resulting in distinctive stages of life: childhood, adolescence, adulthood, and, finally, old age.

Childhood

Charles Dickens's classic novel *Oliver Twist* is set in London early in the nineteenth century, when the Industrial Revolution was rapidly transforming English society. Oliver's mother died in childbirth, and, barely surviving himself, he began life as an indigent orphan, "buffeted through the world, despised by all, and pitied by none" (Dickens, 1886:36; orig. 1837–39). As was typical for a poor child of his time, Oliver Twist was soon facing the toil and drudgery of a workhouse, laboring long hours to pay for filthy shelter and meager food.

Today, we think of *childhood*—roughly the first twelve years of life—as a time of freedom from the burdens of the adult world. But until about a century ago, as *Oliver Twist* testifies, children in Europe and North America shouldered most of the burdens of adults. According to historian Philippe Ariès (1965), once they were able to survive without constant care, medieval Europeans expected children to take their place in the world as working adults. Although "child labor" is now scorned in the United States, this historical pattern persists in poor societies today, especially in Africa and Asia. Global Map 5–1 on page 140 shows that work is commonplace for children in low-income nations of the world.

We are shocked by the notion of young children working long hours because common sense tells us that youngsters are very different from adults—physically immature and inexperienced in the ways of the world. But, although this difference is certainly biological, it is also rooted in culture. High-income societies are rich enough that many people—including children—do not need to work. In addition, societies with sophisticated technology extend childhood so young people have time to learn the many complex skills required for adult activities. Thus, we construct the life course so that "irresponsible" children are looked after by "responsible" adults (Benedict, 1938).

Recently, some social scientists have declared that our conception of childhood is changing yet again. In an age of high divorce rates, mothers and fathers in the work force, and an increasing level of "adult" programming on television, they point out, children are no longer "protected" from grown-up concerns as in the past. Rather, we are seeing the development of a "hurried child" syndrome, meaning that children have to grapple with sex, drugs, and violence as well as fend more and more for themselves (Elkind, 1981; Winn, 1983). Critics of this view, however, counter that there is no convincing evidence of any dramatic shift in our society's conception of childhood. Further, they note, the "hurried child" thesis overlooks the fact that children in the lower class have always assumed adult responsibilities sooner than their middle- and upper-class counterparts (Lynott & Logue, 1993).

Adolescence

As industrialization gradually framed childhood as a distinct stage of life, adolescence emerged as a buffer between childhood and adulthood. Corresponding roughly to the teenage years, this is the stage of life when young people establish some independence and learn specialized skills required for adult life.

We generally associate adolescence with emotional and social turmoil; young people experience conflict with their parents and struggle to develop their own, separate identities. Since adolescence commonly occurs at the onset of puberty, we may be tempted to attribute teenage turbulence to physiological changes. However, comparative research indicates that, like childhood, adolescence is a variable product of culture. Studying the Samoan Islanders in the 1920s, Margaret Mead (1961; orig. 1928) found little evidence of stress among teenagers; there, children appeared to move easily to adult standing. Our society, however, defines childhood and adulthood more in opposing terms, making the transition from one to the other more difficult.

Consider the ambivalence our society displays toward young people on the brink of adulthood: Eighteen-year-olds can vote and they may face the adult responsibility of going to war, yet we deny them the privilege of drinking alcohol. Similarly, our way of life also presents mixed messages when it comes to adolescent sexuality. The mass media often encourage sexual activity, while parents urge restraint; for their part, schools try to discourage casual sex even as they hand out condoms to students (Gibbs, 1993).

As is true of all stages of life, the experience of adolescence varies according to social background. Most young people from working-class families move

GLOBAL: The same global variety applies to sexuality. Ruth Benedict found that childhood sexuality, which so disturbs our society, posed little problem for the Melanesian cultures of southwest New Guinea.

Q: "Youth is wholly experimental." Robert Louis Stevenson

Q: "Only a moment, a moment of strength, of romance, of glamour . . . a flick of sunshine upon a strange shore." Joseph Conrad

Q: "Youth, to some extent, lacks experience." Spiro T. Agnew

DISCUSS: Is adolescence expanding? Primarily because of economic uncertainty, 60 percent of 20- to 24-year-olds now live at home with their parents. Ask the class (especially 18- to 22-year-olds) whether or not they consider themselves adults. Why?

Q: "Let me be myself and then I am satisfied. I know that I am a woman with inward strength and plenty of courage." Anne Frank

Window on the World

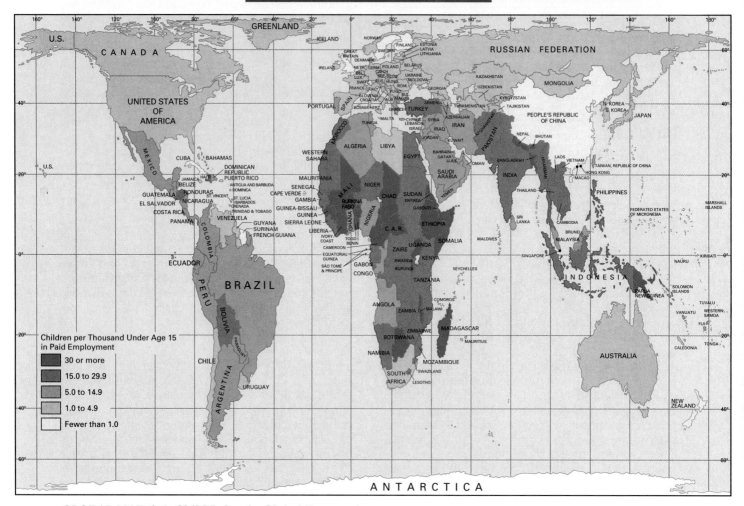

GLOBAL MAP 5–1 Child Labor in Global Perspective

Industrialization prolongs childhood and discourages children from engaging in work and other activities deemed suitable only for adults. Thus child labor is relatively uncommon in the United States and other industrial societies. In less industrialized nations of the world, however, children serve as a vital economic asset, and they typically begin working as soon as they are able.

Source: *Peters Atlas of the World* (1990).

directly from high school into the adult world of work and parenting. Wealthier teens, however, have the resources to attend college and perhaps graduate school, which may extend adolescence into the late twenties and even the thirties. For different reasons, of course, poverty also may extend adolescence. Especially in the inner cities, many young minorities

cannot attain full adult standing because jobs are not available.

Adulthood

At the age of thirty-five, Eleanor Roosevelt, one of the most widely admired women in the United States,

Q: "When I was fourteen my father was so ignorant I could hardly stand to have the old man around. But when I got to be twenty-one, I was astonished at how much he had learned in seven years." Mark Twain

NOTE: "Adult" is derived from the Latin word *adultus*, meaning "grown."

Q: "From birth to age 18, a girl needs good parents; from 18 to 35, she needs good looks; from 35 to 55, she needs a good personality; from 55 on she needs cash." Sophie Tucker

SOCIAL SURVEY: Income peaks among 45- to 54-year-olds. Median income for full-time workers (1992): 25–34, $26,533; 35–44, $34,945; 45–54, $38,219; 55–64, $35,351; 65 and older, $35,256. (U.S. Census Bureau)

wrote in her diary: "I do not think I have ever felt so strangely as in the past year . . . all my self-confidence is gone and I am on the edge, though I never was better physically I feel sure" (quoted in Sheehy, 1976:260). Eleanor Roosevelt may have been troubled by the attention her husband was paying to another, younger woman, or, looking into the future, she may have been trying to imagine what challenges or accomplishments might bring further satisfaction to her life.

But as Eleanor Roosevelt struggled with what today we might call a "midlife crisis," there was much that she could not foresee. Her husband, Franklin Delano Roosevelt, was shortly to become disabled by poliomyelitis, although his rising political career ultimately would lead to the White House. And Eleanor herself was to become one of the most active and influential of all First Ladies. After her husband's death, she would remain in public life, serving as a delegate to the United Nations.

Eleanor Roosevelt's life illustrates two major characteristics of *adulthood*, which our culture defines as beginning during the twenties. First, adulthood is the period during which most of life's accomplishments typically occur, including pursuing careers and raising families. Second, especially in later adulthood, people reflect upon what they have been able to accomplish, perhaps with great satisfaction or with the sobering realization that many of the idealistic dreams of their youth will never come true.

Early Adulthood

By the onset of adulthood, personalities are largely formed. Even so, a marked shift in an individual's life situation—brought on by unemployment, divorce, or serious illness—can significantly change the self (Dannefer, 1984).

Early adulthood—from twenty to about age forty—is generally a time of working toward many goals set earlier in life. Young adults break free of parents and learn to manage for themselves a host of day-to-day responsibilities. With the birth of children, parents draw on experiences from their own upbringing, although, as children, they may have only vaguely perceived what adult life entailed. In addition, young adults typically try to master patterns of intimate living with another person who may have just as much to learn.

Early adulthood is also a period of juggling conflicting priorities: parents, partner, children, schooling, and work (Levinson et al., 1978). Women, especially,

confront the difficulty of "doing it all," since our culture still confers on them primary responsibility for child rearing and household chores, even if they have demanding occupations outside the home (Hochschild, 1989).

Middle Adulthood

Young adults usually cope optimistically with such tensions. But in middle adulthood—roughly age forty to sixty—people begin to sense that marked improvements in life circumstances are less likely. The distinctive character of middle adulthood takes shape as people assess actual achievements in light of earlier expectations. At midlife, people also become more aware of the fragility of health, which the young typically take for granted.

Some women who have already spent many years raising a family find middle adulthood especially trying. Children grow up and require less attention, husbands become absorbed in their careers, leaving these women with spaces in their lives that they find difficult to fill. Women who divorce during middle adulthood may experience serious financial problems (Weitzman, 1985). For all these reasons, an increasing number of women mark middle adulthood by undertaking the challenge of returning to school and then launching careers (U.S. Bureau of the Census, 1993).

Growing older means that both men and women face the reality of physical decline, but our society's traditional socialization has made this prospect more painful for women. Because good looks are defined as more important for women, wrinkles, weight gain, and loss of hair are more traumatic for them. Men, of course, have their own particular difficulties. Some confront limited professional achievement, knowing that their careers are unlikely to change for the better. Others, now realizing that the price of career success has been neglect of family or personal health, harbor uncertainties about their self-worth even as they bask in the praise of others (Farrell & Rosenberg, 1981). Women, too, who devote themselves single-mindedly to careers in early adulthood, may experience regrets about what they have given up in pursuit of occupational success.

Eleanor Roosevelt's midlife crisis may well have involved some of the personal transitions we have described. But her story also illustrates that most people passing midlife have yet to experience their greatest productivity and personal satisfaction. Socialization in our youth-oriented culture has convinced many people (especially the young) that life ends at

GLOBAL: The social standing of the elderly in industrial societies is lower than in agrarian societies, a pattern explained by more rapid change. Hoyt Alverson reports that, for the Tswana in southern Africa, the word "aging" means "seeing with one's own eyes." Similarly, "knowledge" is defined as "remembering things past," so that elders are the wisest of all the Tswana.
NOTE: Figure 14–1 provides data about the rapidly increasing proportion of people in the United States over the age of sixty-five.
DISCUSS: Consider the differing connotations of "elder" and "elderly."
RESOURCE: Cultural variation with regard to death is addressed in E. Bendann's *Death Customs: An Analysis of Burial Rites* (New York: Knopf, 1930).

forty. But as life expectancy in the United States has increased, such limiting notions have begun to dissolve. Major transformations may become less likely, but the potential for learning and new beginnings still infuses this stage of life with promise.

Old Age

Old age comprises the later years of adulthood and the final stage of life itself, beginning about the mid-sixties. Here again, societies attach different meanings to a time of life. Preindustrial people typically grant elders great influence and prestige. As explained in Chapter 14 ("Aging and the Elderly"), traditional societies confer on older people control of most of the land and other wealth; moreover, since their societies change slowly, older people amass a lifetime of wisdom, which earns them great respect (Sheehan, 1976; Hareven, 1982).

In industrial societies, however, most younger people work apart from the family, becoming more independent of their elders. Rapid change and our society's youth orientation combine to define what is older as unimportant or even obsolete. To younger people, then, the elderly are dismissed as unaware of new trends and fashions, and their knowledge and experience are often deemed irrelevant.

No doubt, however, this anti-elderly bias will diminish as the proportion of older people steadily increases. The share of our population over sixty-five has almost tripled since the beginning of this century, so that today more men and women are elderly than in their teens. Moreover, life expectancy is still increasing, so that most men and women in their mid-sixties (the "young elderly") can look forward to decades more of life. Looking to the next century, the Census Bureau (1995) predicts that the fastest-growing segment of our population will be those over eighty-five, whose numbers will soar sixfold.

At present, this final phase of the life course differs in an important way from earlier stages. Growing up typically means entering new roles and assuming new responsibilities; growing old, by contrast, entails the opposite experience of leaving roles that provided both satisfaction and social identity. Retirement, for example, may indeed fit the common image as a period of restful activity. But it may also mean the loss of valued activity and, for some people, outright boredom. Like any life transition, retirement demands learning new and different patterns while simultaneously *un*learning familiar routines. A nearly equal transition is required of the nonworking wife or husband who must now accommodate a partner spending more time at home.

Dying

Through most of human history, death caused by disease or accident came at any stage of life because of low living standards and primitive medical technology. Today, however, almost 85 percent of people in the United States die after the age of fifty-five (U.S. Bureau of the Census, 1995). Therefore, although most senior citizens can look forward to decades of life, growing old cannot be separated from eventual physical decline and ultimate death.

After observing many dying people, Elisabeth Kübler-Ross (1969) described death as an orderly transition involving five distinct responses. A person's first reaction to the prospect of dying is usually *denial*, since our culture tends to ignore the reality of death. The second phase is *anger* by which a person begins to accept the idea of dying but views it as a gross injustice. Third, anger gives way to *negotiation*, the attitude that death may not be inevitable and that one might strike a bargain with God so life can continue. The fourth response, *resignation*, is often accompanied by psychological depression. Finally, adjustment to death is completed in the fifth stage, *acceptance*. At this point, rather than being paralyzed by fear and anxiety, the person whose life is ending sets out to make the most of whatever time remains.

As the proportion of women and men in old age increases, we can expect our culture to become more comfortable with the idea of death. In recent years, for example, people in the United States and elsewhere have been discussing death openly more than in decades past, and the trend is to see dying as preferable to painful or prolonged suffering in hospitals or at home. Moreover, more married couples now anticipate their own deaths with legal and financial planning. This openness may ease the disorientation that generally accompanies the death of a spouse—a greater problem for women, who usually outlive their husbands.

The Life Course: An Overview

This brief examination of the life course points to two sweeping conclusions. First and more important, although each stage of life is linked to the biological process of aging, the life course is largely a social construction. For this reason, people in other societies may experience a stage of life quite differently, or not at all. Second, each stage of any society's life course

Q: "Death means nothing to us; when we are, death has not come yet, and when death has come, we no longer are." Epicurus

GLOBAL: Death practices display remarkable cultural variety. Societies burn, bury, leave out in the weather, embalm, smoke, and even pickle their dead members. Similarly funerals are times for laughter, tears, revelry, solemnity, fighting, or even sex—depending on the culture.

Q: "Just as I choose a ship to sail in or a house to live in, so I choose a death for my passage from life." Seneca, Roman philosopher

Q: "Beware ye as ye pass by,
    As ye be now so once was I.
    As I be now, so must ye be.
    Prepare for death and follow me."
Eighteenth-century New England epitaph

The world's cultures display strikingly different attitudes toward death. Chinese families in Manila, capital city of the Philippines, build tombs big enough to allow the living to gather for meals in the presence of the dead.

presents characteristic problems and transitions that involve learning something new and unlearning familiar routines.

Note, too, that just because societies organize human experience according to age in no way negates the effects of other forces, such as class, race, ethnicity, and gender. Thus, the general patterns we have described are all subject to further modification as they apply to various categories of people.

Finally, people's life experiences also vary depending on when, in the history of the society, they were born. A **cohort** is *a category of people with a common characteristic, usually their age.* Age-cohorts are likely to have been influenced by the same economic and cultural trends so that members typically display similar attitudes and values (Riley, Foner, & Waring, 1988). The lives of women and men born early in this century, for example, were framed by an economic depression and two world wars—events unknown to their children or grandchildren. For their part, younger people today are entering adulthood during a period of economic uncertainty that has dampened the optimism that characterized the generation that came of age during the 1960s.

RESOCIALIZATION: TOTAL INSTITUTIONS

A final type of socialization, experienced by more than 1 million people in the United States at any one time, involves being confined—often against their will—in prisons or mental hospitals. This is the special world of the **total institution**, *a setting in which people are isolated from the rest of society and manipulated by an administrative staff.*

According to Erving Goffman (1961), total institutions have three distinctive characteristics. First, staff members supervise all spheres of daily life, including where residents (often called "inmates") eat, sleep, and work. Second, a rigid system provides inmates with standardized food, sleeping quarters, and activities. Third, formal rules and daily schedules dictate when, where, and how inmates perform virtually every part of their daily routines.

Total institutions impose such regimentation with the goal of **resocialization**, *radically altering an inmate's personality through deliberate manipulation of the environment.* The power of a total institution to resocialize is also enhanced by its forcible segregation of inmates from the "outside" by means of physical barriers such as walls and fences topped with barbed wire and guard towers, barred windows, and locked doors. Cut off in this way, the inmate's entire world can be manipulated by the administrative staff to produce lasting change—or at least immediate compliance—in the inmate.

Resocialization is a two-part process. First, the staff tries to erode the new inmate's autonomy and identity through what Goffman describes as "abasements, degradations, humiliations, and profanations of self" (1961:14). For example, inmates must surrender personal possessions, including clothing and grooming

Q: "Are you going to let the system eat you up and relieve you of your humanity? Or are you going to use the system to human purposes?" Joseph Campbell

Q: "A basic social arrangement in modern society is that the individual tends to sleep, play, and work in different places, with different co-participants, under different authorities, and without an overall rational plan. The central feature of total institutions can be described as the breakdown of the barriers ordinarily separating these three spheres of life." Erving Goffman (1961:6)

The demand by guards that new prisoners publicly disrobe is more than a matter of issuing new clothing; such a degrading ritual is also the first stage in the process by which the staff in a total institution attempts to break down an individual's established social identity.

articles used to maintain their distinctive appearances. In their place, the staff provides standard-issue items that make everyone look alike. In addition, inmates all receive standard haircuts, so that, once again, what was personalized becomes uniform. The staff also subjects new inmates to "mortifications of self," including

searches, medical examinations, and fingerprinting, and then assigns them a serial number. Once inside the walls, individuals surrender the right to privacy; guards may demand that inmates undress publicly as part of the admission procedure and routinely monitor their living quarters.

The second part of the resocialization process includes efforts to systematically build a different self. The staff manipulates inmate behavior through a system of rewards and punishments. The privilege of keeping a book, watching television, or making a telephone call may seem trivial to outsiders, but, in the rigid environment of the total institution, this can form a powerful motivation to conform. Bucking the system, on the other hand, means that privileges will be withdrawn or, in more serious cases, that the inmate will suffer further isolation or additional punishment. The duration of confinement in a prison or mental hospital also depends on how well an inmate cooperates with official rules and regulations. Goffman emphasizes that the staff also seeks to win the hearts and minds of inmates, punishing even those who toe the line but have "an attitude problem."

In principle, total institutions can bring about considerable change in inmates. Yet the resocialization process is extremely complex, and no two people respond to such programs in precisely the same way. Moreover, while some inmates are deemed "rehabilitated" or "recovered," others display little change at all, and still others only become confused, hostile, or bitter. Furthermore, over a long period of time, a rigidly controlled environment may destroy a person's capacity for independent living; such *institutionalized* personalities lose the capacity to deal with the demands of the outside world.

SUMMARY

1. For individuals, socialization is the process of building our humanity and particular identity through social experience. For society as a whole, socialization is the means by which one generation transmits culture to the next.

2. A century ago, people thought most human behavior was guided by biological instinct. Today, the nature-nurture debate has tipped the other way as we understand human behavior to be primarily a product of a social environment. So-called human nature is actually the capacity to create variable cultural patterns.

3. The permanently damaging effects of social isolation reveal the importance of social experience to human development.

4. Sigmund Freud envisioned the human personality as composed of three parts. The id represents general human drives (the life and death instincts), which Freud claimed were innate. The superego embodies cultural values and norms internalized by individuals. Competition between the needs of the id and the restraints of the superego are mediated by the ego.

Q: "Life is like a B-movie: You don't want to leave in the middle, but you also don't want to see it again." Ted Turner

Q: "Idealism is what precedes experience; cynicism is what follows." David Wolf

Q: "After all is said and done, more is said than done." Anonymous

Q: "He was a bold man that first ate an oyster." Jonathan Swift

Q: "It was my fate to be a scholar for awhile." Nietzsche

Q: "For of all sad words, Of tongue or pen;
   The saddest are these: 'It might have been'!"
   John Greenleaf Whittier

Q: "Kites fly highest against the wind." Winston Churchill

Q: "Humility is the final achievement." Anonymous

Controversy & Debate

Are We Free Within Society?

Throughout this chapter we have returned to one key theme: Society shapes how we think, feel, and act. But, if this is so, in what sense are we free? To answer this important question, consider the delightful escapades of the Muppets, puppet stars of television and film. Observing the expressive antics of Kermit the Frog, Miss Piggy, and the rest of the troupe, one almost believes that these puppets are real rather than mere objects animated by movement that originates backstage. The sociological perspective points out that human beings are like puppets in that we, too, respond to backstage forces. Society, after all, imbues us with a culture, places us in a class position, and takes account of our race and sex. In the face of such social constraints, can we really claim to be free?

Sociologists speak with many voices when addressing this question. One response, with politically liberal overtones, is that individuals are *not* free of society—in fact, as social creatures, we never could be. But if we are condemned to live in a society with power over us, it is important to do

what we can to make our home as just as possible, that is, to lessen class differences and eliminate barriers to opportunity based on sex and race. Another approach, this one with conservative overtones, is that we *are* free because society can never control the aspirations or break the will of people committed to their dreams, whatever they may be. Our history as a nation—right from the revolutionary act that led to its founding—is the story of one individual after another who persisted in pursuit of personal goals, often overcoming great odds in the process.

We find both of these orientations in the work of George Herbert Mead, who made a crucial contribution to our understanding of socialization. Mead recognized the power of society to make demands on us, sometimes setting itself before us as a barrier. But he also reminded us that human beings are spontaneous and creative, capable of continually acting back—individually or collectively—on society. Thus Mead acknowledged the power of society while still affirming the human capacity to evaluate, criticize, and, ultimately, to choose and to change.

In the end, then, we may resemble puppets, but only superficially. A crucial difference—one that allows us to claim a significant measure of freedom—is that we have the power to stop, and peer upward at the "strings" that animate much of our action, and perhaps even to jerk down on them defiantly (Berger, 1963:176). If our pull is persistent and powerful enough, we may accomplish more than we might imagine. As Margaret Mead once mused, "Do not make the mistake of thinking that concerned people cannot change the world; it's the only thing that ever has."

Continue the debate . . .

1. *Do you think our society affords more freedom to males than to females? Why, or why not?*

2. *What about modern, industrial countries compared to traditional, agrarian nations: Are some of the world's people more free than others?*

3. *How does an understanding of sociology enhance personal freedom?*

---

5. Jean Piaget believed that human development reflects both biological maturation and increasing social experience. In his view, socialization proceeds through four major stages of development: sensorimotor, preoperational, concrete operational, and formal operational.

6. Lawrence Kohlberg applies Piaget's approach to the issue of moral development. Individuals, he claims, first judge rightness in preconventional terms, according to their individual needs. Next, conventional moral reasoning takes account of the attitudes of parents and the norms of the larger society. Finally, postconventional moral reasoning allows for a philosophical critique of society itself.

7. Beginning with a critique of Kohlberg's reliance on male subjects, Carol Gilligan discovered that gender affects moral reasoning. Females, she asserts, look to the effect of decisions on relationships, while males rely more on abstract standards of rightness.

8. To George Herbert Mead, socialization is based on the emergence of the self, which he viewed as partly autonomous (the I) and partly guided by society (the me). Mead contended that, beginning with imitative behavior, the self develops through play and games and eventually recognizes the "generalized other."

9. Charles Horton Cooley used the term "looking-glass self" to underscore that the self is influenced by how we think others respond to us.

10. Commonly the first setting of socialization, the family has the greatest influence on a child's attitudes and behavior.

11. School exposes children to greater social diversity and introduces the experience of impersonal evaluation. In addition to formal lessons, schools informally teach a wide range of cultural ideas, including attitudes about competitiveness and achievement.

12. Members of youthful peer groups are subject to adult supervision less than in the family or in school. Peer groups take on great significance among adolescents.

13. The mass media, especially television, have a considerable impact on the socialization process. The average U.S. child now spends as much time watching television as attending school.

14. As with each phase of the life course, the characteristics of childhood are socially constructed. Medieval Europeans scarcely recognized childhood as a stage of life. In high-income societies like the United States, people define childhood as much different from adulthood.

15. Adolescence, the transition between childhood and adulthood, is considered a difficult period in our society. This is not the case in all societies, however.

16. During early adulthood, socialization involves settling into careers and raising families. Later adulthood is marked by considerable reflection about initial goals in light of actual achievements.

17. In old age, people make many transitions, including retirement. While the elderly typically enjoy high prestige in preindustrial societies, industrial and postindustrial societies are more youth oriented, relegating older people to the sidelines of life.

18. Members of industrial and postindustrial societies typically fend off death until old age. Adjustment to the death of a spouse (an experience more common to women) and acceptance of one's own death are part of socialization for the elderly.

19. Total institutions such as prisons and mental hospitals strive for resocialization—radically changing the inmate's personality.

20. Socialization demonstrates the power of society to shape our thoughts, feelings, and actions. Yet, as free humans, we also have the capacity to act back on society and, in so doing, shape our lives and our world.

KEY CONCEPTS

anticipatory socialization social learning directed toward gaining a desired position

cohort a category of people with a common characteristic, usually their age

concrete operational stage Piaget's term for the level of human development at which individuals first perceive causal connections in their surroundings

ego Freud's designation of a person's conscious efforts to balance innate, pleasure-seeking drives and the demands of society

formal operational stage Piaget's term for the level of human development at which individuals think abstractly and critically

generalized other George Herbert Mead's label for widespread cultural norms and values that we use as references in evaluating ourselves

id Freud's designation of the human being's basic drives

looking-glass self Cooley's term for the image people have of themselves based on how they believe others perceive them

mass media impersonal communications directed toward a vast audience

peer group a social group whose members have interests, social position, and age in common

personality a person's fairly consistent patterns of thinking, feeling, and acting

preoperational stage Piaget's term for the level of human development at which individuals first use language and other symbols

resocialization radically altering an inmate's personality through deliberate manipulation of the environment

self George Herbert Mead's term for a dimension of personality composed of an individual's self-awareness and self-image

sensorimotor stage Piaget's designation for the level of human development at which individuals experience the world only through sensory contact

socialization the lifelong social experience by which individuals develop their human potential and learn patterns of their culture

superego Freud's designation of the operation of culture within the individual in the form of internalized values and norms

total institution a setting in which people are isolated from the rest of society and manipulated by an administrative staff

CRITICAL-THINKING QUESTIONS

1. What do cases of social isolation teach us about the importance of social experience to human development?

2. Describe the two sides of the nature-nurture debate. In what sense are human nature and nurture not opposed to one another?

3. In what ways does a comparison of the theories of Freud, Piaget, Kohlberg, Gilligan, and Mead suggest that research findings build on one another? In what ways do they seem incompatible?

4. Proportionately speaking, television features far more physically attractive people than there are in the population as a whole. Develop arguments for and against this practice. How does this practice affect the way we think about others—and ourselves?

SUGGESTED READINGS

Classic Sources

George Herbert Mead. *Mind, Self, and Society From the Standpoint of a Social Behaviorist.* Charles W. Morris, ed. Chicago: University of Chicago Press, 1962; orig. 1934.
    Compiled after Mead's death by his students, this paperback presents Mead's analysis of the development of self.

Margaret Mead. *Coming of Age in Samoa.* New York: Dell, 1961; orig. 1928.
    While still in her early twenties, Margaret Mead completed what is probably the best-known book in anthropology, in which she argues that the problems of adolescence are socially created rather than rooted in biology.

Contemporary Sources

Grace Craig. *Human Development.* 7th ed. Englewood Cliffs, N.J.: Prentice Hall, 1995.
    This book is a good general reference for understanding socialization across the life course.

George H. Hill, Lorraine Raglin, and Charles Floyd Johnson. *Black Women and Television.* New York: Garland, 1990.

Mary Ellen Brown, ed. *Television and Women's Culture: The Politics of the Popular.* Newbury Park, Calif.: Sage Publications, 1990.
    The first of these two books about television highlights African-American women and cites interesting "firsts." The second, a collection of thirteen essays, delves into the subject of television and women, as actors and as audience.

Global Sources

Alba N. Ambert and Marie D. Alvarez, eds. *Puerto Rican Children on the Mainland: Interdisciplinary Perspectives.* New York: Garland, 1992.
    This collection of essays sketches a statistical portrait of Puerto Ricans on the mainland and investigates distinctive dimensions of socialization among young people.

M. E. J. Wadsworth. *The Imprint of Time: Childhood, History, and Adult Life.* New York: Clarendon Press, 1991.
    Long-term studies of cohorts are difficult and, therefore, rare in social science. This book reports on an ongoing study of more than five thousand men and women living throughout Britain, all born in 1946, and interviewed periodically since then.

JACOB LAWRENCE,
THEATRE SERIES, NO. 8:
VAUDEVILLE, 1951

Collection, Hirshhorn Museum and Sculpture Garden,
Smithsonian Institution, Gift of Joseph H. Hirshhorn,
1966. Courtesy of the artist and Francine Seders
Gallery, Seattle.

Social Interaction in Everyday Life

Harold and Sybil are on their way to another couple's home in an unfamiliar section of Clemson, South Carolina. They are now late because, for the last twenty minutes, they have traveled in circles looking for Creek View Drive. Harold, gripping the wheel ever tighter, is doing a slow burn. Sybil, sitting next to him, looks straight ahead, afraid to utter a word. Both realize the evening is off to a bad start (Tannen, 1990:62).

Here we have a simple case of two people unable to locate the home of some friends. But Harold and Sybil are lost in more ways than one, since they fail to grasp why they are growing more and more enraged at their situation and at each other.

Consider the predicament from Harold's point of view. Like most men, Harold cannot tolerate getting lost. The longer he drives around, the more incompetent he feels. Sybil is seething, too, but for a different reason. She does not understand why Harold does not pull over and ask someone where Creek View Drive is. If she were driving, she fumes to herself, they already would have arrived and would now be comfortably settled with drink in hand.

Why don't men ask for directions? Men value their independence and so are uncomfortable asking for help (and also reluctant to accept it). To men, asking for assistance is an admission of inadequacy, an acknowledgement that others know something they don't. If it takes Harold a few more minutes to find Creek View Drive on his own—and secure his self-respect in the process—he thinks the bargain is a good one.

If men pursue self-sufficiency and are sensitive to hierarchy, women are more attuned to others and strive for connectedness. Asking for help seems right to Sybil because, from her point of view, sharing information reinforces social bonds. Requesting directions seems as natural to Sybil as continuing to search on his own appears to Harold. But the two people will not resolve their situation as long as neither one grasps the other's point of view.

Analyzing such examples of everyday life is the focus of this chapter. We begin by presenting many of the building blocks of common experience and then explore the almost magical way in which face-to-face interaction generates reality. Throughout, the discussion highlights the importance of gender to our everyday experiences.

The central concept is **social interaction**, which may be defined as *the process by which people act and react in relation to others*. Social interaction is the key to creating the changing reality we perceive. And in our everyday lives we interact with one another according to particular social guidelines.

Q: "A status, as distinct from the individual who may occupy it, is simply a collection of rights and duties." Ralph Linton (1937:113)

Q: "It is crucial that responsibilities, resources, and rights be assigned to statuses, not to particular individuals. For only by doing so can societies establish general and uniform rules or norms that will apply to many and diverse individuals who are to occupy the statuses . . ." Melvin Tumin (1985:21)

Q: "*Ascribed* statuses are those which are assigned to individuals without reference to their innate differences or abilities. They can be predicted and trained for from the moment of birth. The *achieved* statuses are . . . those requiring special qualities [and] are left open to be filled through competition and individual effort." Ralph Linton (1937:115)

In any rigidly ranked setting, no interaction can proceed until people assess each other's social standing. Thus, military personnel wear clear insignia to designate their level of authority. Don't we size up one another in much the same way in routine interactions, noting a person's rough age, quality of clothing, and manner for clues about social position?

SOCIAL STRUCTURE: A GUIDE TO EVERYDAY LIVING

```
October 21, 1994, Ho Chi Minh City,
Vietnam. This morning we leave the ship
and make our way along the docks toward
the center of Ho Chi Minh City—known to
an earlier generation as Saigon. The
government security officers wave us
through the security gates. Pressed
against the fence are dozens of men who
operate cyclos (bicycles with a small
carriage attached to the front), the
Vietnamese equivalent of taxicabs. We
decline the offers of rides and spend
the next twenty minutes fending off sev-
eral persistent drivers, who cruise
alongside us pleading for our business.
The pressure is uncomfortable. We decide
to cross the street but realize suddenly
that there are no stop signs or signal
lights—and no break at all in the steady
stream of bicycles, cyclos, motorbikes,
```

```
and small trucks. The locals don't bat
an eye—they just walk at a steady pace
across the street, parting waves of
vehicles that close in again immediately
beyond them. Walk right into traffic??
Especially with our small children on
our backs?? Yup, we did it; that's the
way it works in Vietnam.
```

Members of every society rely on social structure to make sense out of everyday situations. As one family's introduction to the streets of Vietnam suggests, the world can be disorienting—even frightening—when cultural norms are unclear. So what, then, are the building blocks of our daily lives?

STATUS

One basic element of social structure is **status,** *a recognized social position that an individual occupies.* Notice that the sociological meaning of the term "status" differs from its everyday meaning of "prestige." In common usage, a bank president has more "status" than a bank teller. Sociologically, however, both "bank president" and "bank teller" are statuses because they represent socially defined positions, even though one does confer more power and prestige than the other.

Every status involves particular duties, rights, and expectations. The statuses people occupy thus guide their behavior in any setting. In the college classroom, for example, professors and students have distinctive, well-defined responsibilities. Similarly, family interaction turns on the interplay of mother, father, daughters, sons, and others. In all these situations, statuses connect us to others, which is why, in the case of families, we commonly call others "relations." In short, a status defines who and what we are *in relation to* others.

Status is also a key component of social identity. Occupational position, for example, is a major part of most people's self-concept throughout life and is quickly offered as part of a social introduction. Even long after retirement, people continue to identify themselves in terms of their life's work.

Status Set

Everyone occupies many statuses simultaneously. The term **status set** refers to *all the statuses a person holds at a given time.* A girl may be a *daughter* to her parents, a *sister* to her siblings, a *friend* to members of her social circle, and a *goalie* to others on her hockey team.

GLOBAL: Typically, members of high-income nations have a larger status set than people in traditional societies for whom kinship represents the core of social organization.
NOTE: In reality, ascribed status and achieved status operate as two endpoints on a continuum.
Q: "Status and role serve to reduce the ideal patterns for social life to individual terms." Ralph Linton (1937:114)

NOTE: Consider introducing the concept of status consistency—the degree of consistency in social ranking—explored in Chapter 10.
NOTE: "Status" has two Latin roots: *Sta* is derived from *stare*, meaning "to stand"; *tus* means "the use of." Thus, status is literally "the use of standing." The term "role" appears to be derived from the French word *rôle*, meaning a roll (of paper) on which is printed an actor's part.

Just as status sets branch out in many directions, they also change over the life course. A child grows into an adult, a student becomes a lawyer, and people marry to become husbands and wives, sometimes becoming single again as a result of divorce or death. Joining an organization or finding a job enlarges our status set; withdrawing from activities diminishes it. Individuals gain and lose dozens of statuses over a lifetime.

Ascribed and Achieved Status

Sociologists classify statuses in terms of how people obtain them. An **ascribed status** is *a social position that someone receives at birth or assumes involuntarily later in life.* Examples of ascribed statuses include being a daughter, a Latino, a teenager, or a widower. Ascribed statuses are matters about which people have little or no choice.

By contrast, an **achieved status** refers to *a social position that someone assumes voluntarily and that reflects personal ability and effort.* Among achieved statuses in the United States are being an honors student, an Olympic athlete, a spouse, a computer programmer, a member of Phi Beta Kappa, or a thief. In each case, the individual has significant choice in the matter.

In practice, of course, most statuses involve some combination of ascription and achievement. That is, people's ascribed statuses influence the statuses they achieve. Adults who achieve the status of lawyer, for example, are likely to share the ascribed trait of being born into relatively privileged families. And any person of a privileged sex, race, ethnicity, or age has far more opportunity to realize desirable achieved statuses than does someone without such advantages. By contrast, many less desirable statuses, such as criminal, drug addict, or being unemployed are more easily "achieved" by people born into poverty.

Master Status

Some statuses matter more than others. A **master status** is *a status that has exceptional importance for social identity, often shaping a person's entire life.* For many people, occupation is often a master status since it conveys a great deal about social background, education, and income. At the extreme, being "a Rockefeller" or "a Kennedy" is enough by itself to push an individual into the limelight.

In a negative sense, serious disease also operates as a master status. Sometimes even lifelong friends shun cancer patients or people with acquired immune deficiency syndrome (AIDS) simply because of their

We learn from what we see. Thus each one of us selects others as role models, people whose behavior we wish to emulate. The National Civil Rights Museum in Memphis, Tennessee, contains this sculpture of Rosa Parks, a woman of color and a seamstress, who boarded a public bus on December 1, 1955, in Montgomery, Alabama. Although she took her place in the section reserved for African Americans, the driver ordered her to give up her seat to a white man. When she courageously refused, police arrested her. The episode led to the Montgomery Bus Boycott, which lasted for a year and finally brought an end to racial segregation on that city's buses.

illness. Most societies of the world also limit the opportunities of women, whatever their abilities, making gender, too, a master status.

Finally, we sometimes dehumanize people with physical disabilities by perceiving them only in terms of their impairments. In the box on page 152, two people with physical disabilities describe this problem.

ROLE

A second major component of social interaction is role, *behavior expected of someone who holds a particular status.* Think of a role as the dynamic expression of a status: Individuals *hold* a status and *perform* a role (Linton, 1937). The obligations and privileges of being a student, for example, require you to fulfill that role by attending classes and completing assignments and, more generally, devoting much of your time to personal enrichment through academic study.

Both statuses and roles vary by culture. In the United States, the status "uncle" refers to a sibling of either one's mother or father; in Vietnam, by contrast, specific terms designate uncles on each side of the

NOTE: Barbara Laslett (1978) points out that role conflict and role strain were probably more pronounced in the Middle Ages than they are today, because parents not only raised children but also produced their food, schooled them, guided their worship, and saw to their health.

NOTE: The Families and Work Institute found that 25% of respondents (employees of Fortune 1000 companies) had refused overtime for family reasons; 24% turned down travel for the same reason; 19% refused to relocate; 10% refused promotions. (*Wall Street Journal*, July 22, 1991:B1)

SOCIAL DIVERSITY

Physical Disability as Master Status

In these research interviews, two women explain how a physical disability can become a master status, defining an individual. The first voice is that of twenty-nine-year-old Donna Finch, who holds a master's degree in social work and lives with her husband and son in Muskogee, Oklahoma. She is also blind.

Most people don't expect handicapped people to grow up, they are always supposed to be children. . . . You aren't supposed to date, you aren't supposed to have a job, somehow you're just supposed to disappear. I'm not saying this is true of anyone else, but in my own case I think I was more intellectually mature than most children, and more emotionally immature. I'd say that not until the last four or five years have I felt really whole.

Rose Helman is an elderly woman living near New York City. She suffers from spinal meningitis and is also blind.

You ask me if people are really different today than in the '20s and

'30s. Not too much. They are still fearful of the handicapped. I don't know if fearful is the right word, but uncomfortable at least. But I can understand it somewhat; it happened to me. I once asked a man to tell me which staircase to use to get from the subway out to the street. He started giving me directions that were confusing, and I said, "Do you mind taking me?" He said, "Not at all." He grabbed me on the side with my dog on it, so I asked him to take my other arm. And he said, "I'm sorry, I have no other arm." And I said, "That's all right, I'll hold onto the jacket." It felt funny hanging onto the sleeve without the arm in it.

Source: Orlansky and Heward (1981).

family, and responsibilities differ accordingly. In every society, too, actual role performance varies according to an individual's unique personality, although some societies permit more personal latitude than others do.

Role Set

Because we occupy many statuses simultaneously—a status set—everyday life is a mix of multiple roles. Robert Merton (1968) introduced the term **role set** to identify *a number of roles attached to a single status.*

Figure 6–1 illustrates the status set and corresponding role sets of one individual. Four statuses are presented, each linked to a different role set. First, this woman occupies the status of "wife," with corresponding roles in relation to her husband ("conjugal roles" such as confidante and sexual partner), with whom she would share a "domestic role" in terms of maintaining the household. Second, she also holds the

status of "mother," with routine responsibilities for her children (the "maternal role") as well as obligations to their school and other organizations (the "civic role"). Third, as a professor, she interacts with students (the "teacher role") as well as with other academics (the "colleague role"). Fourth, her work as a researcher (the "laboratory role") generates the data she uses in her publications (the "author role"). Of course, Figure 6–1 lists only some of this person's status and role sets, since an individual generally occupies several dozen statuses at one time, each linked to a role set. This woman might be, additionally, a daughter caring for aging parents and a member of the city council.

Role Conflict and Role Strain

Members of industrial societies routinely juggle a host of responsibilities demanded by their various statuses and roles. As most mothers can testify, parenting as

Q: "For some types of role exit, society has coined a term to denote exiters: divorcé(e), retiree, recovered alcoholic, widow, alumnus. This is usually the case for exits that are common and have been occurring for a long time . . . In addition to these institutionalized exits, however, there are numerous exits that are simply referred to with the prefix "ex": ex-doctor, ex-executive, ex-nun, ex-convict . . ." Helen Rose Fuchs Ebaugh (1988:1)

RESOURCE: Luigi Pirandello's writing is wonderfully sociological, as the excerpt on this page suggests.
Q: "When I use a word, it means just what I choose it to mean—nothing more nor less." Humpty Dumpty
Q: "Charm is the way of getting the answer yes without asking a clear question." Albert Camus

well as working outside the home taxes both physical and emotional strength. Sociologists thus recognize **role conflict** as *incompatibility among roles corresponding to two or more statuses.*

We experience role conflict when we find ourselves pulled in various directions while trying to respond to the many statuses we hold. Some politicians, for example, decide not to run for national office because the demands of a campaign would impoverish family life; in other cases, ambitious people defer having children or choose to remain childless in order to stay on the "fast track" for career success.

Even the roles linked to a single status may make competing demands on us. The concept of **role strain** refers to *incompatibility among roles corresponding to a single status.* A plant supervisor may enjoy being friendly with other workers. At the same time, however, the supervisor's responsibility for everyone's performance requires maintaining some measure of personal distance from each employee. In short, performing the roles attached to even one status may involve something of a balancing act.

Another strategy for minimizing role conflict is "compartmentalizing" our lives so that we perform roles linked to one status at one time and place, and carry out roles corresponding to another status elsewhere at another time. A familiar example of this scheme is heading home while leaving the job "at work."

Role Exit

After she herself left the life of a Catholic nun to become a university sociologist, Helen Rose Fuchs Ebaugh (1988) began to study *role exit,* the process by which people disengage from important social roles. Studying a range of "exes," including ex-nuns, ex-doctors, ex-husbands, and ex-alcoholics, Ebaugh identified elements common to the process of "becoming an ex."

According to Ebaugh, people initiate the process of role exit by reflecting critically on their existing lives and grappling with doubts about their ability or willingness to persist in a certain role. As they imagine alternative roles, they ultimately reach a point when they decide to pursue a new life.

Even at this point, however, a past role may continue to influence our lives. "Exes" retain a self-image shaped by an earlier role, which may interfere with the drive to build a new sense of self. An ex-nun, for example, may hesitate to wear stylish clothing and makeup.

"Exes" must also rebuild relationships with people who may have known them in their "earlier life" and

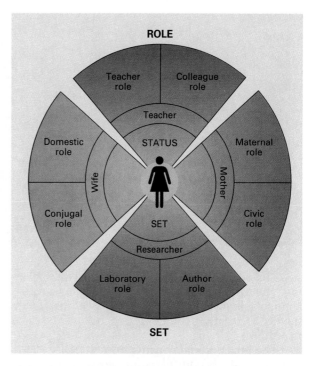

FIGURE 6–1 Status Set and Role Set

who may not realize just how new and unfamiliar their present role may be. And learning new social skills poses another challenge. For example, Ebaugh reports, nuns who begin dating after decades in the church are often startled to learn that sexual norms are now vastly different from those they knew as teenagers.

THE SOCIAL CONSTRUCTION OF REALITY

More than fifty years ago, the Italian playwright Luigi Pirandello skillfully applied the sociological perspective to social interaction. In *The Pleasure of Honesty,* Angelo Baldovino—a brilliant man with a checkered past—enters the fashionable home of the Renni family and introduces himself in a most peculiar way:

> Inevitably we construct ourselves. Let me explain. I enter this house and immediately I become what I have to become, what I can become: I construct myself. That is, I present myself to you in a form suitable to the relationship I wish to achieve with you. And, of course, you do the same with me. (1962:157–58)

GLOBAL: In less economically developed societies, haggling is a common method of establishing value. Often this ritual involves talk and sharing of food and drink, which express good intentions and reaffirm social ties in the midst of pursuing different interests.
NOTE: Illustrating the power of language to define reality: The term *homophobia* (Weinberg, 1973) literally means "fear of sameness." In a political turnaround, this term defines as abnormal not homosexuality but those who condemn it. The term also transforms attitudes toward sexuality from a moral issue (of right and wrong) to a psychological issue of fear (that is, of sickness and health).
DISCUSS: Nowhere is fascination with the use of language more intense than on the college campus, where ideas are our stock in trade. Consider, for example, the ramifications of using two apparently similar phrases "people of color" and "colored people."

Flirting is an everyday experience in reality construction. Each person offers information to the other, and hints at romantic interest. Yet the interaction proceeds with a tentative and often humorous air so that either individual can withdraw at any time without further obligation.

This curious introduction reveals that, while behavior is guided by status and role, each human being has considerable ability to shape what happens moment to moment. "Reality," in other words, is not as fixed as we may think.

The phrase **social construction of reality** identifies *the process by which people creatively shape reality through social interaction.* This idea stands at the foundation of sociology's symbolic-interaction paradigm, as described in earlier chapters. As Angelo Baldovino's remark suggests, especially in an unfamiliar situation, quite a bit of "reality" remains unclear in everyone's mind. So as Baldovino "presents himself" in terms that suit his purposes, and as others do the same, a complex reality emerges, although few people are so "up front" about their deliberate efforts to foster an impression.

Social interaction, then, amounts to negotiating reality. Most everyday situations involve at least some agreement about what's going on, but participants perceive events differently to the extent that they are motivated by disparate interests and intentions.

Steering reality in this way is sometimes referred to as "street smarts." In his biography *Down These Mean Streets*, Piri Thomas recalls moving to a new apartment in New York City's Spanish Harlem, which placed him squarely on the turf of the local street gang. Returning home one evening, young Piri found himself cut off by Waneko, the gang's leader, who was flanked by a dozen of his cohorts.

"Whatta ya say, Mr. Johnny Gringo," drawled Waneko.

Think man, I told myself, *think your way out of a stomping. Make it good.* "I hear you 104th street coolies are supposed to have heart," I said. "I don't know this for sure. You know there's a lot of streets where a whole 'click' is made out of punks who can't fight one guy unless they all jump him for the stomp." I hoped this would push Waneko into giving me a fair one. His expression didn't change.

"Maybe we don't look at it that way."

Crazy, man, I cheer inwardly, *the* cabron *is falling into my setup.* . . . "I wasn't talking to you," I said. "Where I come from, the pres is president 'cause he got heart when it comes to dealing."

Waneko was starting to look uneasy. He had bit on my worm and felt like a sucker fish. His boys were now light on me. They were no longer so much interested in stomping me as seeing the outcome between Waneko and me. "Yeah," was his reply. . . .

I knew I'd won. Sure, I'd have to fight; but one guy, not ten or fifteen. If I lost, I might still get stomped, and if I won I might get stomped. I took care of this with my next sentence. "I don't know you or your boys," I said, "but they look cool to me. They don't feature as punks."

I had left him out purposely when I said "they." Now his boys were in a separate class. I had cut him off. He would have to fight me on his own, to prove his heart to himself, to his boys, and most important, to his turf. He got away from the stoop and asked, "Fair one, Gringo?" (1967:56–57)

This situation reveals the drama—sometimes subtle, sometimes savage—by which human beings creatively build reality. There are limits, of course, to what even the most skillful and persuasive personality can achieve. And, of course, not everyone enters a negotiation with equal standing. Should a police officer have come on the scene of the fight that ensued between Piri and Waneko, both young men might well have ended up in jail.

DISCUSS: Consider other terms that "spin" reality: "unemployed" vs. "between jobs"; "elderly" vs. "elders"; "ladies" vs. "women"; "handicapped children" vs. "exceptional children"; "remedial" vs. "refresher"; "primitive" vs. "nonliterate"; "broken families" vs. "one-parent households"; "sexually active" vs. "promiscuous."

Q: "There is always a rivalry between the spontaneous definitions of the situation made by the member of the organized society and the definitions that society has provided for him." W. I. Thomas (1923:42)

NOTE: Garfinkel's approach runs directly counter to that of Talcott Parsons.

NOTE: Ethnomethodology has roots not only in symbolic interactionism, but also in Alfred Schutz's phenomenology. Moreover, it shares with Berger and Luckmann's work an interest in the everyday round of life, not just a society's grand values or political ideologies.

The Thomas Theorem

By displaying his wits and boxing with Waneko until they both grew tired, Piri Thomas won acceptance that evening and became one of the group. W. I. Thomas (1966:301; orig. 1931) succinctly expressed this insight in what has come to be known as the **Thomas theorem**: *Situations we define as real become real in their consequences.*

Applied to social interaction, Thomas's insight means that although reality is initially "soft" as it is fashioned, it can become "hard" in its effects. In the case of Piri Thomas, having succeeded in defining himself as worthy, this young man *became* worthy in the eyes of his new comrades.

Ethnomethodology

Rather than assuming that reality is something "out there," the symbolic-interaction paradigm posits that reality is created by people in everyday encounters. But how, exactly, do we define reality for ourselves? Answering this question is the objective of *ethnomethodology*, a specialized approach within the symbolic-interaction paradigm.

The term itself has two parts: The Greek *ethno* refers to people and how they understand their surroundings; "methodology" designates a set of methods or principles. Combining them makes **ethnomethodology**, *the study of the way people make sense of their everyday lives.*

Ethnomethodology is largely the creation of Harold Garfinkel (1967), who challenged the then-dominant view of society as a broad, abstract "system" (recall the approach of Emile Durkheim, described in Chapter 4, "Society"). Garfinkel wanted to explore how we make sense of countless familiar situations. On the surface, we engage in intentional speech or action; but these efforts rest on deeper assumptions about the world that we usually take for granted.

Think, for a moment, about what we assume in asking someone the simple question, "How are you?" Do we mean physically? Mentally? Spiritually? Financially? Are we even looking for an answer, or are we "just being polite"?

Ethnomethodology, then, delves into the sense-making process in any social encounter. Because so much of this process is ingrained, Garfinkel argues that the only effective way to expose how we make sense of events is to purposely *break the rules.* Deliberately ignoring conventional rules and observing how people respond, he points out, allows us to tease out how people build a reality. Thus, Garfinkel (1967)

Cultures frame reality in different ways. This man lay on the street in Bombay, India, for several hours and then quietly died. In the United States, such an event would probably have provoked someone to call the rescue squad. In a poor society in which death on the streets is a fact of everyday life, however, many Indians responded not with alarm but with simple decency by stopping to place incense on his body before continuing on their way.

directed his students to refuse to "play the game" in a wide range of situations. Some students living with their parents started acting as if they were boarders rather than children; others entered stores and insisted on bargaining for items; others recruited people into simple games (like tic-tac-toe) only to intentionally flout the rules; still others initiated conversations while slowly moving closer and closer to the other person.

The students first noticed people's reactions. Typically, the "victims" of these rule violations became agitated, indicating that even if reality is taken for granted it is very important to us. Then the students tried to identify exactly *why* people were disturbed, leading to insights about the unspoken agreements that underlie family life, shopping, fair play, and the like.

Because of ethnomethodology's provocative character and its focus on commonplace experiences, some

Seeing Ourselves

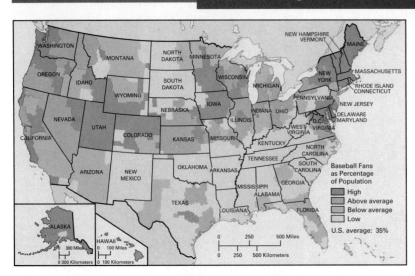

NATIONAL MAP 6–1
Baseball Fans Across the United States

One in three U.S. adults claims to follow baseball. The map shows that fans are concentrated in the northern states from New England to the Pacific Northwest. Why? What categories of people have a world view that celebrates this kind of activity? (Hint: Baseball is more likely to appeal to white males over forty years of age who were born in the United States.)

Source: From Michael J. Weiss, *Latitudes & Attitudes: An Atlas of American Tastes, Trends, Politics, and Passions.* Boston: Little, Brown and Company, 1994.

sociologists view it as less-than-serious research. Even so, ethnomethodology has succeeded in heightening awareness of many unnoticed patterns of everyday life.

Reality Building in Global Perspective

Taking a broader view of reality construction, people do not build everyday experience "out of thin air." In part, how we act or what we see in our surroundings depends on our interests. Scanning the night sky, for example, lovers discover romance, while scientists perceive the same stars as hydrogen atoms fusing into helium. Social background also directs our perceptions, since we build reality out of elements in the surrounding culture. For this reason, residents of, say, Chicago's South Side experience the world differently from those living on the city's affluent Gold Coast.

In truth, there are few common elements to the reality construction that goes on across the United States. Take baseball, the sport long described as our "national pastime." Only about one-third of U.S. adults describe themselves as "fans" and, as National Map 6–1 indicates, they are concentrated in particular regions of the country.

In global perspective, reality construction is even more variable. People waiting for a bus in London typically "queue up" in a straight line; people in New York rarely are so orderly. The law forbids women in Saudi Arabia from driving a car, a constraint unheard of in today's United States. Yet fear of crime in the big cities of this country is considerably greater than it is elsewhere—including London, Paris, Rome, Calcutta, and Hong Kong—and this sense of public danger shapes the daily realities of tens of millions of our citizens.

From these examples, we conclude that people build reality from the surrounding culture. Chapter 3 ("Culture") explained how people the world over derive different meanings from specific gestures, so that sometimes travelers find themselves building a most unexpected reality! Similarly, what we "see" in a book or a film also depends on the assumptions we make about the world. JoEllen Shively (1992) screened "western" films for men of European descent as well as Native-American men. Both categories claimed to enjoy the films but for different reasons. White men interpreted the films as praising rugged people striking out for the West to impose their will on nature. Native-American men, by contrast, saw in the same films a celebration of land and nature apart from any human ambitions.

If people the world over inhabit different realities, are some happier than others? Those living in a high-income society like the United States have reason to feel fortunate. As Figure 6–2 indicates, global survey data reveal that members of our society claim to be happier than most.

Finally, what about the full range of human emotions? Are emotions generically human and, therefore, much the same everywhere? Or is what we feel derived from our culture? Cross-cultural researchers conclude that emotions are rooted in biology—and culture—as the box on pages 158–59 explains.

DRAMATURGICAL ANALYSIS: "THE PRESENTATION OF SELF"

Erving Goffman (1922–1982) enhanced our understanding of everyday life by noting that people interacting behave much like actors performing on a stage. By imagining ourselves as directors scrutinizing what goes on in some situational "theater," we engage in what Goffman called **dramaturgical analysis,** *the investigation of social interaction in terms of theatrical performance.*

Dramaturgical analysis offers a fresh look at two now-familiar concepts. In theatrical terms, a status mirrors a part in a play, and a role serves as a script, supplying dialogue and action for each of the characters. Moreover, in any setting, a person is both actor and audience. Goffman described each individual's "performance" as the **presentation of self,** *an individual's effort to create specific impressions in the minds of others.* Presentation of self, or *impression management,* contains several distinctive elements (Goffman, 1959, 1967).

Performances

As we present ourselves in everyday situations, we convey information—consciously and unconsciously—to others. An individual's performance includes dress (costume), any objects carried along (props), and tone of voice and particular gestures (manner). In addition, people craft their performance according to the setting (stage). We may joke loudly on a sidewalk, for example, but assume a more reverent manner upon entering a church. In addition, individuals design settings, such as a home or office, to enhance a performance by invoking the desired reactions in others.

Consider, for example, how a physician's office conveys information to an audience of patients. Physicians enjoy substantial prestige and power in the United States, a fact immediately grasped by patients upon entering a doctor's office. First, the physician is nowhere to be seen. Instead, in what Goffman describes as the "front region" of the setting, the patient encounters a receptionist who functions as a gatekeeper, deciding if and when the patient can meet the physician. A simple survey of the doctor's waiting

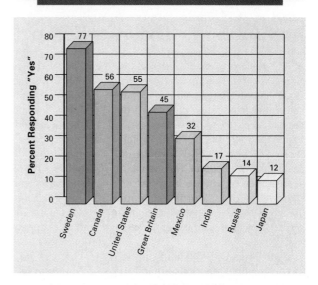

Global Snapshot

FIGURE 6–2 Happiness: A Global Survey
Survey Question: "We are interested in the way people are feeling these days. During the past few weeks, did you ever 'feel on top of the world,' feeling that life is wonderful?"
Source: World Values Survey (1994).

room, with patients (often impatiently) awaiting their call to the inner sanctum, leaves little doubt that the medical team controls events.

The physician's private office and examination room constitute the "back region" of the setting. Here the patient confronts a wide range of props, such as medical books and framed degrees, which together reinforce the impression that the physician has the specialized knowledge necessary to call the shots. In the office, the physician usually remains seated behind a desk—the larger and grander the desk, the greater the statement of power—while the patient is provided with only a chair.

The physician's appearance and manner convey still more information. The usual costume of white lab coat may have the practical function of keeping clothes from becoming soiled, but its social function is to let others know at a glance the physician's status. A stethoscope around the neck or a black medical bag in hand has the same purpose. A doctor's highly technical terminology—frequently

NOTE: When we encounter others, interaction usually proceeds with "small talk," meaning that little is at stake. Only when sufficient information has been exchanged to guide more substantial discussion does "big talk" begin.

Q: "Emotions are shown primarily in the face, not in the body . . . there are facial patterns specific to each emotion." Paul Ekman

NOTE: The words "person" and "mask" are derived from a single root: the Latin word *persona*. Perhaps the ancients well understood Goffman's insights.

GLOBAL SOCIOLOGY

Emotions in Global Perspective: Do We All Feel the Same?

On a New York sidewalk, a woman reacts angrily to the in-line skater who zooms past her. Apart from a few choice words, her facial expression broadcasts a strong emotion that North Americans easily recognize. But would an observer from Nigeria, Nicaragua, or New Guinea be able to interpret her emotion? In other words, do people the world over share similar feelings, and do they express them in the same way?

Paul Ekman (1980) and his colleagues studied emotions around the world, even among members of a small society in New Guinea. They concluded that people throughout the world experience six basic emotions: anger, fear, disgust, happiness, surprise, and sadness. Moreover, people everywhere recognize these feelings in the same distinctive facial gestures. To Ekman, this commonality means that much of our emotional life is universal—rather than culturally variable—and that the display of emotion is biologically programmed in our facial features, muscles, and central nervous system.

But if the reality of emotions is rooted in our biology, Ekman and other researchers note three ways in which emotional life differs significantly in global perspective.

First, *what triggers an emotion varies from one society to another.* Whether people define a particular situation as an insult (causing anger), a loss (calling forth sadness), or a mystical event (provoking surprise and awe) depends on the cultural surroundings of the individual.

Second, *people display emotions according to the norms of their culture.* Every society has rules about when, where, and to whom an individual may exhibit certain emotions. People in the United States typically express emotions more freely in the home among family members than among colleagues in the workplace. Similarly, we expect children to express emotions to parents, although parents are taught to guard their emotions in front of children.

Third, *societies differ in terms of how people cope with emotions.* Some societies encourage the expression of feelings, while others belittle emotions

and demand that their members suppress them. Societies also display significant gender differences in this regard. In the United States, most people consider emotional expression as feminine, expected of women but a sign of weakness in men. In other societies, however, this sex typing of emotions is less pronounced or even reversed.

In sum, emotional life in global perspective has both common and variable elements. People around the world experience the same basic feelings. Witnessing our angry New Yorker who opened this box, an individual from New Guinea quickly would comprehend her expression. But what sparks a particular emotion, to whom someone expresses it, and whether people encourage or discourage the display of emotions are variable products of social learning.

Sources: Ekman (1980a, 1980b), Lutz & White (1986), and Lutz (1988).

mystifying—also emphasizes the hierarchy in the situation. The use of the title "Doctor" by patients who, in turn, are frequently addressed only by their first names also underscores the physician's dominant position. The overall message of a doctor's performance is clear: "I will help you only if you allow me to take charge."

Nonverbal Communication

Novelist William Sansom describes a fictional Mr. Preedy—an English vacationer on a beach in Spain:

He took care to avoid catching anyone's eye. First, he had to make it clear to those potential companions of his holiday that they were of no concern to him whatsoever. He stared through them, round them, over them—eyes lost in space. The beach might have been empty. If by chance a ball was thrown his way, he looked surprised; then let a smile of amusement light his face (Kindly Preedy), looked around dazed to see that there were people on the beach, tossed it back with a smile to himself and not a smile *at* the people. . . .

. . . [He] then gathered together his beach-wrap and bag into a neat sand-resistant pile (Methodical and Sensible Preedy), rose slowly to stretch his huge frame

To most people in the United States, these expressions convey anger, fear, disgust, happiness, surprise, and sadness. But do people elsewhere in the world define them in the same way? Research suggests that all human beings experience the same basic emotions and display them to others in the same basic ways. But culture plays a part by specifying the situations that trigger one emotion or another.

(Big-Cat Preedy), and tossed aside his sandals (Carefree Preedy, after all). (1956; quoted in Goffman, 1959:4–5)

Through his conduct, Mr. Preedy offers a great deal of information about himself to anyone caring to observe him. Notice that he does so without uttering a single word. This illustrates the process of **nonverbal communication,** *communication using body movements, gestures, and facial expressions rather than speech.*

Virtually any part of the body can be used to generate *body language,* that is, to convey information to others. Facial expressions form the most significant element of nonverbal communication. As noted earlier, in the Global Sociology box, smiling and other facial gestures express basic emotions like pleasure, surprise, and anger the world over. Further, people project particular shades of meaning with their faces. We distinguish, for example, between the deliberate smile of Kindly Preedy on the beach, a spontaneous smile of joy at seeing a friend, a pained smile of embarrassment, and a full, unrestrained smile of self-satisfaction that we often associate with the "cat who ate the canary."

GLOBAL: Use of space is another pattern subject to cultural interpretation (or misinterpretation). Across North Africa, from Cairo to Casablanca, people routinely move to within a foot or two when speaking in public. The U.S. traveler may consider such "in your face" behavior to be provocative, which it is not necessarily intended to be.

Q: "If we never tried to seem a little better than we are, how could we improve or 'train ourselves from the outside inward?'" Charles Horton Cooley (1964:352; orig., 1902)
Q: "We are, I fear, getting to know one another. Reticence, secrecy, concealment of self have been transformed into social problems; once they were aspects of civility . . ." Philip Rieff

When we enter the presence of others, we "construct" ourselves and begin a "presentation of self" that has much in common with a dramatic performance. Such a presentation involves clothing (costume), other objects (props), certain typical behavior (script), and it takes place in a particular setting (stage). No wonder the ancient Greeks, who understood the element of acting in everyday life, used the same word for "person" and "mask."

Eye contact is another crucial element of nonverbal communication. Generally, we use eye contact to initiate social interaction. Someone across the room "catches our eye," for example, sparking a conversation. Avoiding the eyes of another, on the other hand, discourages communication. Hands, too, speak for us. Common hand gestures in our culture convey, among other things, an insult, a request for a ride, an invitation for someone to join us, or a demand that others stop in their tracks. Gestures also supplement spoken words. Pointing in a menacing way at someone, for example, intensifies a word of warning, just as shrugging the shoulders adds an air of indifference to the phrase "I don't know," and rapidly waving the arms lends urgency to the single word "Hurry!"

But, as any actor knows, the "perfect performance" is an elusive goal. In everyday performances, some element of body language often contradicts our intended meaning. A teenage boy offers an explanation for getting home late, for example, but his mother doubts his words because he avoids looking her in the eye. The movie star on a television talk show claims that her recent flop at the box office is

"no big deal," but the nervous swing of her leg belies her casual denial. In practical terms, carefully observing nonverbal communication (most of which is not easily controlled) provides clues to deception, in much the same way that a lie detector records telltale changes in breathing, pulse rate, perspiration, and blood pressure.

Yet detecting lies is difficult, because no single bodily gesture directly indicates deceit the way, say, a smile indicates pleasure. Even so, because any performance involves so many expressions, few people can confidently lie without allowing some piece of contradictory information to slip through, arousing the suspicions of a careful observer. Therefore, the key to detecting deceit is to scan the whole performance with an eye for inconsistencies and discrepancies.

Paul Ekman (1985) suggests scrutinizing four elements of a performance—words, voice, body language, and facial expression—for clues to deception.

1. **Words.** Good liars can mentally rehearse their lines and manipulate words with ease. But they may not be able to avoid a simple slip of the tongue—something the performer did not mean to say in quite that way. For example, a young man who is deceiving his parents by claiming that his roommate is a male friend rather than a female lover might inadvertently use the word "she" rather than "he" in a conversation. The more complicated the deception, the more likely a performer is to make a revealing mistake.

2. **Voice.** Tone and patterns of speech are hard to control, so a person trying to hide a powerful emotion, for example, cannot easily prevent the voice from trembling or breaking. Similarly, the individual may speak quickly (a clue to anger) or slowly (indicating sadness). Nervous laughter, inappropriate pauses between words, or nonwords, such as "ah" and "ummm," also hint at discomfort.

3. **Body language.** A "leak" of body language may tip off an observer to deception as well. Subtle body movements, for example, give the impression of nervousness, as does sudden swallowing or rapid breathing. These are especially good clues to deception because few people can control them. Sometimes, *not* using the body in the expected way to enhance words—as when a person tries to fake excitement—also suggests deception.

4. **Facial expressions.** Because facial expressions, too, are hard to control, they give away many

Q: "Male nonverbal communication has certain elements and effects that distinguish it from its female counterpart." Henley, Hamilton, and Thorne (1992:10)

Q: "Both field and laboratory studies have found that people tend to approach females more closely than males, to seat themselves closer to females and otherwise intrude on their territory . . . In the larger aspect of space, women are also less likely to have their own room or other private space in the home." Henley, Hamilton, and Thorne (1992:13)

phony performances, as indicated by Figure 6–3. A sad person feigning happiness, for example, generally "flashes" momentary frowns through a crooked smile. By contrast, raising and drawing together the eyebrows signals genuine fear or worry, since this expression is virtually impossible to make willfully.

In sum, lies are detectable, but training is the key to noticing relevant clues. Another key to spotting deception is knowing the other person well, the reason that parents can usually pick up deceit in their children. Finally, almost anyone can unmask deception when the liar is trying to cover up strong emotions.

Gender and Personal Performances

Because women are socialized to be less assertive than men, they tend to be especially sensitive to nonverbal communication. In fact, gender is a central element in personal performances. Based on the work of Nancy Henley, Mykol Hamilton, and Barrie Thorne (1992), we can extend the present discussion of personal performances to spotlight the importance of gender.

Demeanor

Demeanor—that is, general conduct or deportment—reflects a person's level of social power. Simply put, powerful people enjoy far greater personal discretion in how they act; subordinates act more formally and self-consciously. Off-color remarks, swearing, or casually removing shoes and putting feet up on the desk may be acceptable for the boss, but rarely for employees. Similarly, people in positions of dominance can interrupt the performances of others with impunity, while others are expected to display deference by remaining silent (Smith-Lovin & Brody, 1989; Henley, Hamilton, & Thorne, 1992; Johnson, 1994).

Since women generally occupy positions of lesser power, demeanor is a gender issue as well. As Chapter 13 ("Sex and Gender") explains, about half of all working women in the United States hold clerical or service jobs that place them under the control of supervisors, who are usually men. Women, then, craft their personal performances more carefully than men and display a greater degree of deference in everyday interaction.

Use of Space

How much space does a personal performance require? Here again, power plays a key role, since

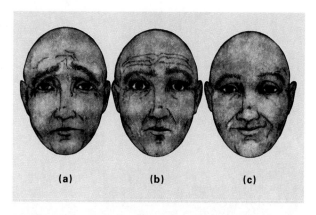

FIGURE 6–3 Which Is An "Honest Face"?
Telling lies is no easy task because most people lack the ability to manipulate all their facial muscles. Looking at the three faces above, the expression of grief in sketch (a) is probably genuine, since few people can deliberately lift the upper eyelids and inner corners of the eyebrows in this way. Likewise, the apprehension displayed in (b) also appears authentic, since intentionally raising the eyebrows and pulling them together is nearly impossible. People who fake emotions usually do a poor job of it, as illustrated by the phony expression of pleasure shown in (c). Genuine delight, for most people, would produce a balanced smile.

using more space conveys a nonverbal message of personal importance. According to Henley, Hamilton, and Thorne (1992), men typically command more space than women do, whether pacing back and forth before an audience or casually lounging on the beach. Why? Our culture traditionally has measured femininity by how *little* space women occupy (the standard of "daintiness"), while gauging masculinity by how *much* territory a man controls (the standard of "turf").

The concept of **personal space** refers to *the surrounding area to which an individual makes some claim to privacy*. In the United States, people typically position themselves several feet apart when speaking; throughout the Middle East, by contrast, individuals interact within a much closer space.

Throughout the world, gender further modifies these patterns. In daily life, men commonly intrude on the personal space of women. A woman's encroachment into a man's personal space, however, is likely to be construed as a sexual overture. Here again, women have less power in everyday interaction than men do.

DISCUSS: Ask members of the class to identify other social situations that are gendered. Can they identify any that are *not* "gendered"?

Q: "A woman's sex is treated as the most salient characteristic of her being; this is not the case for males." Henley, Hamilton, & Thorne

RESOURCE: Deborah Tannen's article on gender and communication is included among the contemporary selections in the companion reader *Seeing Ourselves*.

Notice how this man places his arms around his companion. Does this gesture simply signal affection, or does it imply something about the way our culture defines males and females?

Staring, Smiling, and Touching

Eye contact encourages interaction. Typically, women employ eye contact to sustain conversation more than men do. Men have their own distinctive brand of eye contact: staring. By making women the targets of stares, men are both making a claim of social dominance and defining women as sexual objects.

Although frequently signaling pleasure, *smiling* has a host of meanings. In a male-dominated world, women often smile to indicate appeasement or acceptance of submission. For this reason, Henley, Hamilton, and Thorne maintain, women smile more than men; in extreme cases, smiling may reach the level of nervous habit.

Finally, *touching* constitutes an intriguing social pattern. Mutual touching conveys feelings of intimacy and caring. Apart from close relationships, however, touching is generally something men do to women (although rarely, in our culture, to other men). A male physician touches the shoulder of his female nurse as they examine a report, a young man touches the back of his woman friend as he guides her across the street, or a male skiing instructor looks for opportunities to touch his female students. In these examples—as well as many others—touching may evoke little response, so common is it in everyday life. But it amounts to a subtle ritual by which men express their dominant position in an assumed hierarchy that subordinates women.

Idealization

Complex motives underlie human behavior. Even so, according to Goffman, we construct performances to *idealize* our intentions. That is, we try to convince others (and perhaps ourselves) that what we do reflects ideal cultural standards rather than more selfish motives.

Idealization is easily illustrated by returning to the world of physicians and patients. In a hospital, physicians engage in a performance commonly described as "making rounds." Entering the room of a patient, the physician often stops at the foot of the bed and silently examines the patient's chart. Afterward, physician and patient converse briefly. In ideal terms, this routine involves a physician making a personal visit to inquire about a patient's condition.

In reality, something less exemplary is usually going on. A physician who sees several dozen patients a day may remember little about most of them. Reading the chart gives the physician the opportunity to rediscover the patient's identity and medical problems. Openly revealing the actual impersonality of much medical care would undermine the culturally ideal perception of the physician as deeply concerned about the welfare of others.

Idealization is woven into the fabric of everyday life in countless ways. Physicians, college professors, and other professionals typically idealize their motives for entering their chosen careers. They describe their work as "making a contribution to science," "helping others," "answering a calling from God," or perhaps "serving the community." Rarely do such people concede the less honorable, although common, motives of seeking the income, power, prestige, and leisure these occupations confer.

Taking a broader view, idealization underlies social civility, since we smile and make polite remarks to people we do not like. Such small hypocrisies ease our way through social interactions. Even when we suspect

NOTE: "Embarrass" is derived from words meaning "to block or obstruct." "Tact" is derived from the Latin *tact(us)* meaning "sense of touch."

GLOBAL: There is little comparative data regarding tact. But, logically, one imagines that traditional societies engage in less of it, since reality is better established there.

 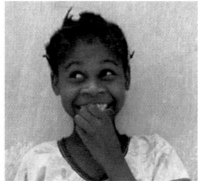 

Hand gestures vary widely from one culture to another. Yet people everywhere define a chuckle, grin, or smirk in response to someone's performance as an indication that one does not take another person seriously. Therefore, the world over, people who cannot restrain their mirth tactfully cover their faces.

that others are putting on an act, rarely do we openly challenge their performance, for reasons we shall explain next.

Embarrassment and Tact

The eminent professor consistently mispronounces the dean's name; the visiting dignitary rises from the table to speak, unaware of the napkin that still hangs from her neck; the president becomes ill at a state dinner. As carefully as individuals may craft their performances, slipups of all kinds frequently occur. The result is *embarrassment*, which, in dramaturgical terms, means the discomfort that follows a spoiled performance. Goffman describes embarrassment simply as "losing face."

Embarrassment looms as an ever-present danger because, first, all performances typically contain some measure of deception. Second, most performances involve a complex array of elements, any one of which, in a thoughtless moment, may shatter the intended impression.

Interestingly, an audience usually overlooks flaws in a performance, thereby allowing an actor to avoid embarrassment. If we do point out a misstep ("Excuse me, but do you know that your fly is open?"), we do it discreetly and only to help someone avoid even greater loss of face. In Hans Christian Andersen's classic fable "The Emperor's New Clothes," the child who blurts out that the emperor is parading around naked is telling the truth, yet is scolded for being rude.

But members of an audience usually do more than ignore flaws in a performance, Goffman explains; typically, they help the performer recover from them. *Tact*, then, amounts to helping another person "save face." After hearing a supposed expert make an embarrassingly inaccurate remark, for example, people may tactfully ignore the comment as if it were never spoken at all. Alternatively, mild laughter may indicate that they wish to dismiss what they have heard as a joke. Or a listener may simply respond, "I'm sure you didn't mean that," acknowledging the statement but not allowing it to destroy the actor's performance.

Why is tact such a common response? Because embarrassment provokes discomfort not simply for one person but for *everyone*. Just as the entire audience feels uneasy when an actor forgets a line, people who observe awkward behavior are reminded of how fragile their own performances often are. Socially constructed reality thus functions like a dam holding back a sea of chaotic possibility. Should one person's performance spring a leak, others tactfully assist in making repairs. Everyone, after all, jointly engages in building culture, and no one wants reality to be suddenly swept away.

In sum, Goffman's research shows that, while behavior is spontaneous in some respects, it is more patterned than we like to think. Almost four hundred years ago, William Shakespeare captured this idea in memorable lines that still ring true:

> All the world's a stage,
> And all the men and women merely players:
> They have their exits and their entrances;
> And one man in his time plays many parts. . . .
> (*As You Like It*, II)

INTERACTION IN EVERYDAY LIFE: TWO ILLUSTRATIONS

We have now examined many elements of social interaction. The final sections of this chapter illustrate key lessons by focusing on two important, yet quite different, elements of everyday life.

Language: The Gender Issue

As Chapter 3 ("Culture") explains, language is the thread that ties members of a society together in the symbolic web we call culture. In everyday life, language conveys meaning on more than one level. Besides the obvious message in what people say, a host of additional meanings are embedded in our language. One such message involves gender. Language defines men and women differently in at least three ways, involving control, value, and attention (Henley, Hamilton, & Thorne, 1992).[1]

Language and Control

A young man astride his new motorcycle rolls proudly into the gas station, and eagerly says to the attendant, "Isn't she a beauty?" On the surface, the question has little to do with gender. Yet, curiously, a common linguistic pattern confers the female "she," and never the male "he," on a man's prized possession.

As we noted at the beginning of this chapter, the language men use often reveals their concern with competence and control. In this case, a man attaches a female pronoun to a motorcycle (car, yacht, or other object) because it reflects *ownership*.

A more obvious control function of language relates to people's names. Traditionally in the United States, and in many other parts of the world, a woman takes the family name of the man she marries. While few people consider this an explicit statement of a man's ownership of a woman, many believe that it reflects male dominance. For this reason, an increasing proportion of married women (currently 10 percent) have retained their own name or merged two family names (Brightman, 1994).

Language and Value

Language usually treats as masculine whatever has greater value, force, or significance. Although we may not think much about it, this pattern is deeply rooted in the English language. For instance, the positive adjective "virtuous," meaning "morally worthy" or "excellent," is derived from the Latin word *vir* meaning "man." By contrast, the derogatory adjective "hysterical" is derived from the Greek word *hyster*, meaning "uterus."

In numerous, more familiar ways, language also confers different value on the two sexes. Traditional masculine terms such as "king" or "lord" have retained their positive meaning, while comparable terms, such as "queen," "madam," or "dame" have acquired negative connotations in contemporary usage. Language thus both mirrors social attitudes and helps to perpetuate them.

Similarly, use of the suffixes "ette" and "ess" to denote femininity generally devalues the words to which they are added. For example, a "major" has higher standing than a "majorette," as does a "host" in relation to a "hostess." And, certainly, men's groups with names such as the Los Angeles Rams carry more stature than women's groups with names like the Radio City Music Hall Rockettes.

Language and Attention

Language also shapes reality by directing greater attention to masculine endeavors. Consider our use of personal pronouns. In the English language, the plural pronoun "they" is neutral as it refers to both sexes. But the corresponding singular pronouns "he" and "she" specify gender. According to traditional grammatical practice, we use "he" along with the possessive "his" and the objective "him" to refer to all people. Thus, we assume that the bit of wisdom "He who hesitates is lost" refers to women as well as to men. But this practice also reflects the traditional cultural pattern of ignoring the lives of women. Some research suggests that people continue to respond to allegedly inclusive male pronouns as if only males were involved (MacKay, 1983).

The English language has no gender-neutral, third-person singular personal pronoun. In recent years, however, the plural pronouns "they" and "them" increasingly have gained currency as singular pronouns ("A person should do as they please"). This usage remains controversial because it violates conventional grammatical rules. Yet, there is no doubt that English is now evolving to accept such gender-neutral constructions.

---

[1] The following sections draw primarily from Henley, Hamilton, & Thorne (1992). Additional material comes from Thorne, Kramarae, & Henley (1983) and others, as noted.

GLOBAL: In Japan, reports Ellen Rudolph (1991), women display subservience to men by speaking more quietly, looking down, and employing more deferential language.
DIVERSITY: "Widower" is the derivative term (from "widow"), indicating that marital standing is more of a master status for women than for men.

Q: "There are very few jokes about sociologists." Peter Berger (1963:1)
NOTE: As an example of humor's origin in incongruity, consider Woody Allen's line: "More than any time in history, mankind faces a crossroads. One path leads to despair and utter hopelessness, the other to total extinction. Let us pray that we have the wisdom to choose correctly."

SOCIOLOGY OF EVERYDAY LIFE

Gender and Language: "You Just Don't Understand!"

In the story that opened this chapter, a couple face a situation that rings all too true to many people: When they are lost, men grumble to themselves, sometimes blaming their partners, but avoid asking others for directions. For their part, women can't understand why not.

Deborah Tannen, who has conducted extensive research on the linguistic differences that separate the sexes, explains why. Men, she claims, see almost every encounter as potentially competitive; thus, getting lost is bad enough without a man asking for help and thereby letting someone else "one up" him. By contrast, because women in the United States hold a generally subordinate position, they are socialized to ask for help. Sometimes, Tannen points out, women will ask for assistance even when they don't need it.

A similar gender-linked problem common to couples involves what men call "nagging." Consider the following exchange (Adler, 1990:74):

Sybil: "What's wrong, honey?"

Harold: "Nothing . . ."

Sybil: "Something is bothering you; I can tell."

Harold: "I told you nothing is bothering me. Leave me alone."

Sybil: "But I can see that something is wrong."

Harold: "OK. Just why do you think something is bothering me?"

Sybil: "Well, for one thing, you're bleeding all over your shirt."

Harold: [now irritated] "It doesn't bother me."

Sybil: [losing her temper] "WELL, IT SURE IS BOTHERING ME!"

Harold: "I'll go change my shirt."

The problem couples face in communicating is that what one partner *intends* by a comment is not always what the other *hears* in the words. To Sybil, her opening question is an effort at cooperative problem solving. She can see that something is wrong with

Harold (who has carelessly cut himself while doing yard work) and she wants to help solve the problem. But Harold interprets her pointing out his problem as belittling, and tries to close off the discussion. Sybil, confident that Harold would take a more positive attitude toward her if he just understood that she only wants to be helpful, repeats herself. This reaction sets in motion a vicious cycle in which Harold, thinking Sybil is trying to manipulate him and make him feel incapable of looking after himself, responds by digging in his heels. His response, in turn, makes Sybil all the more sure that there is a problem that requires attention. And round it goes until somebody loses patience.

In the end, Harold gives in only to the extent that he agrees to change his shirt. But notice that he still refuses to discuss the original problem. Misunderstanding his wife's motives, Harold just wants Sybil to leave him alone. For her part, Sybil fails to understand her husband's view of the situation and walks away thinking that he is unnecessarily grouchy and insensitive.

Sources: Adler (1990) and Tannen (1990).

Even as the English language changes, gender is likely to remain a source of miscommunication between women and men. In the box above, Harold and Sybil—whose misadventures finding a friend's home opened this chapter—return to illustrate how the two sexes often seem to be speaking different languages.

Humor: Playing With Reality

Humor plays a vital part in everyday life. Comedians are among our favorite entertainers, most newspapers carry cartoons, and even professors and members of the clergy include a joke or two in their performances. As with many aspects of social life, however, we largely

NOTE: Another incongruous thought: "My wife and I have no secrets from one another . . . at least none that she knows of . . ."

NOTE: Laughter also accompanies tickling. This is a disruption of what is conventional in a physical sense; tickling is also an ambiguous situation in which one does not know if the other's motives are loving or aggressive.

NOTE: Humor can also be generated by leading an audience to

expect two incongruent realities, one of which fails to materialize. Groucho Marx once quipped: "I worked myself up from nothing to a state of extreme poverty . . ."

NOTE: The link between humor and contrasting realities is inherent in the Monty Python troupe's signature line, "Now for something completely different."

take humor for granted. While everyone laughs at a joke, in other words, few people think about what makes something funny or why humans everywhere like to laugh. Many of the ideas developed in this chapter provide insights into the character of humor, as we shall now see.[2]

The Foundation of Humor

Humor is a product of reality construction; specifically, it stems from the contrast between two, incongruous realities. Generally, one reality is *conventional*, corresponding to what people expect in a specific situation. The other reality is *unconventional*, representing a significant violation of cultural patterns. Humor, therefore, arises from contradiction, ambiguity, and "double meanings" generated by two differing definitions of the same situation. Note how this principle works in one of Woody Allen's lines, "I'm not afraid to die; I just don't want to be there when it happens."

In this example, the first phrase represents a conventional notion; the second half, however, interjects an unconventional—even absurd—meaning that collides with what we are led to expect.

This same simple pattern holds true for virtually all humor. Yogi Berra's quip, "If you come to a fork in the road, take it" sounds like useful advice, but ends up offering nothing at all. Or, notice the twin realities in the statement by frustrated parents, "For their birthday, we're taking the twins to Europe. Next year, maybe we'll go back to get them . . ."

Of course, there are countless ways to mix realities and, thereby, generate humor. In some cases, contrasting realities emerge simply from reordering syllables, as in the case of the (probably fictitious) country song "I'd rather have a bottle in front of me than a frontal lobotomy."

Of course, a joke can be built the other way around, so that the comic leads the audience to *expect* an unconventional answer and gets a very ordinary one. When a reporter asked the famous desperado Willie Sutton why he robbed banks, for example, he replied dryly: "Because that's where the money is." However a joke is constructed, the greater the opposition or incongruity between the two definitions of reality, the greater the potential for humor.

When telling jokes, the comedian can strengthen this opposition in various ways. One technique, favored by Groucho Marx, George Burns, Gracie Allen, and a host of other comics, is to present the first, or conventional, remark in conversation with another actor, then to turn toward the audience (or the camera) when delivering the second, or unconventional, line in a slightly different tone of voice. In one of his films, Groucho swaggers in front of a young woman and brags "This morning I shot a lion in my pajamas." Then, dropping his voice and turning to the camera, he adds, "What the lion was doing in my pajamas *I'll never know . . .*" This "shift of channel" underscores the incongruity of the two parts. Following the same logic, many stand-up comedians also "reset" the audience to conventional expectations by interjecting "But, seriously, folks . . ." after one joke and before the next one.

To construct the strongest contrast in meaning, comedians pay careful attention to their performances—the precise words they use, as well as the timing of each part of the delivery. A joke is "well told" if the comic creates the sharpest possible opposition between the realities, just as humor falls flat in a careless performance. Since the key to humor lies in the opposition of realities, it is not surprising that the climax of a joke is called the *"punch* line."

The Dynamics of Humor: "Getting It"

If people fail to understand both the conventional and unconventional realities embedded in a joke, they usually say, with a puzzled expression, "I don't get it." To "get" humor, members of an audience must understand the two realities underlying the joke well enough to perceive their incongruity.

But getting a joke can be more challenging still, because comics may deliberately omit some of the information listeners must grasp. The audience, therefore, must pay attention to the stated elements of the joke, and then fill in the missing pieces on their own. As a simple case, consider the reflection of movie producer Hal Roach upon reaching his one hundredth birthday:

> If I had known I would live to be one hundred, I would have taken better care of myself!

Here, "getting" the joke depends on realizing that Roach must have taken pretty good care of himself since he lived to be one hundred in the first place. Or take one of W. C. Fields's lines: "Some weasel took the cork out of my lunch." "Some lunch," we think to ourselves to "finish" the joke.

---

[2]The ideas contained in this section are those of the author (1987), except as otherwise noted. The general approach draws on work examined in this chapter, especially the ideas of Erving Goffman.

NOTE: Examples for eliciting the pleasure of "getting jokes": What campus departments or offices would use these call letters for their radio station? WIXL (honors program); WSOS (security office); WURU (counseling service); WYMI (philosophy department); WYYY (religion department); WYRU (sociology department). Barry Glassner and John Western

NOTE: There are almost no jokes about sociologists. So here's one: Q.: How many sociologists does it take to change a light bulb? A.: There's nothing wrong with the light bulb—It's the system!

Q: "Imagination was given to man to compensate him for what he is not; a sense of humor was provided to console him for what he is." Robert Walpole

Of course, some jokes demand more mental effort than others. A more complex example is the following, written on the wall of a college rest room:

Dyslexics of the World, Untie!

To get this one, you must know, first, that dyslexia is a condition in which people routinely reverse letters; second, one must identify the line as an adaptation of Karl Marx's call to the world's workers to unite; third, one must recognize "untie" as an anagram of "unite," as one might imagine a disgruntled dyslexic person would write it.

Why would an audience be required to make this sort of effort in order to understand a joke? Simply because our enjoyment of a joke is heightened by the pleasure of having completed the puzzle necessary to "get it." In addition, once we understand a complex joke, we gain favored status as an "insider" in the larger audience. These insights explain the frustration that accompanies *not* getting a joke: the fear of mental inadequacy coupled with a sense of being socially excluded from a pleasure shared by others. Not surprisingly, "outsiders" in such a situation may fake "getting" the joke; sometimes, too, others may tactfully explain a joke to end another's sense of being left out.

But, as the old saying goes, if a joke has to be explained, it won't be very funny. Besides taking the edge off the language and timing on which the *punch* depends, an explanation completely relieves the audience of any mental involvement, substantially reducing their pleasure.

The Topics of Humor

People throughout the world smile and laugh, signifying humor as a universal human trait. But, living in diverse cultures, the world's people differ in what they find funny. Musicians frequently perform for receptive audiences around the globe; comedians rarely do this, however, demonstrating that humor does not travel well.

October 1, 1994, Kobe, Japan. Can you share a joke with people who live half way around the world? At dinner, I ask two Japanese college women to tell me a joke. "You know 'crayon'?" Asako asks. I nod. "How do you ask for a crayon in Japanese?" I respond that I have no idea. She laughs out loud as she says what sounds like "crayon crayon." Her

Because humor involves challenging established social conventions, comedians typically have been "outsiders," racial and ethnic minorities. Seinfeld is among the latest in a century-old line of Jewish comics who have starred in television and films.

companion Mayumi laughs too. Amy and I sit awkwardly straight-faced. Asako relieves some of our embarrassment by explaining that the Japanese word for "give me" is kureyo, which sounds like "crayon." I force a smile.

What is humorous to the Japanese, then, may be lost on the Chinese, Iraqis, or people in the United States. To some degree, too, the social diversity of our own nation means that even within one country people will find humor in different situations. New Englanders, southerners, and westerners have their own brands of humor, as do Latinos and Anglos, fifteen- and forty-year-olds, Wall Street bankers and hard-hat construction workers.

NOTE: Some topics, in other words, are "off limits," because people expect them to be understood in only one way. The Challenger Space Shuttle disaster was such a case. No jokes were heard for several days after the tragedy; as the shock wore off, a spate of "sick" jokes followed.
NOTE: Laughing at one's own joke is rather rude or odd, because there is no punch at all.

GLOBAL: Illustrating the use of humor to critique society, Soviets used to joke "We pretend to work, and they pretend to pay us . . ."
NOTE: Simple examples to illustrate the elements of humor:
#1: "What do you get when you cross the Atlantic with the *Titanic?*"
#2: "I dunno, what?"
#1: "About halfway . . ."

But, for everyone, humor deals with topics that lend themselves to double meanings or *controversy*. For example, the first jokes many of us learned as children concerned the cultural taboo, sex. The mere mention of "unmentionable acts" or even certain parts of the body can dissolve young faces in laughter. Are there jokes that do break through the culture barrier? Yes, but they must touch upon universal human experiences such as, say, turning on a friend.

```
I try a number of jokes, to little
effect. So many of our jokes are
ethnic, and the two Japanese women, not
grasping much about the U.S. cultural
mix, cannot connect. Inspiration: "Two
fellows are walking in the woods and
come upon a huge bear. One guy leans
over and tightens up the laces on his
running shoes. 'Jake,' says the other,
'what are you doing? You can't outrun
this bear!' 'I don't have to outrun the
bear' responds Jake, 'I just have to
outrun you!'" Smiles all around.
```

The controversy inherent in humor often walks a fine line between what is funny and what is considered "sick." During the Middle Ages, the word *humors* (derived from the Latin *humidus*, meaning "moist") referred to a balance of bodily fluids that regulated a person's health. Today's researchers have come up with scientific justification for the notion that "Laughter is the best medicine": Maintaining a sense of humor is thought to reduce a person's level of unhealthy stress (Robinson, 1983; Haig, 1988). At the extreme, however, people who always take conventional reality lightly go beyond the bounds of a sense of humor and risk being defined as deviant or even mentally ill (a common stereotype depicts insane people laughing uncontrollably, and we have long dubbed mental hospitals "funny farms").

And then there are certain topics that every social group declares as too sensitive for humorous treatment. Of course, one can joke about such things, but doing so courts criticism for telling a "sick" joke (and, therefore, *being* sick). People's religious beliefs, tragic accidents, or appalling crimes are the stuff of "sick" jokes.

The Functions of Humor

If humor is a cultural universal, it must make a significant contribution to social life. Structural-functional analysis points out that humor serves as a social "safety valve," allowing people to release potentially disruptive sentiments safely. By means of humor, we can acceptably discuss a host of cultural taboos, from sex to prejudice to hostility toward parents.

Having strayed into controversy, an individual may also use humor to defuse the situation. Called to account for a remark an audience takes as offensive, a speaker may simply state, "I didn't mean anything by what I said; it was just a joke!" Likewise, an audience may use humor as a form of tact, smiling, as if to say, "We could take offense at what you said, but we'll assume you were only kidding."

Like theater and art, humor allows a society to challenge orthodox ideas and to explore alternatives to the status quo. Sometimes, in fact, humor may actually promote social change by loosening the grip of convention.

Humor and Conflict

If humor holds the potential to liberate those who laugh, it can also be used to oppress others. Men who tell jokes about feminists, for example, typically are voicing some measure of hostility toward them (Powell & Paton, 1988; Benokraitis & Feagin, 1995). Similarly, jokes at the expense of gay people reveal the tensions surrounding sexual orientation in the United States. Generally speaking, humor is a sign of real conflict in situations where one or both parties choose not to bring the conflict out into the open (Primeggia & Varacalli, 1990).

"Put down" jokes, which make one category of people feel good at the expense of another, are common around the globe. After collecting and analyzing jokes from many societies, Christie Davies (1990) concluded that conflict among ethnic groups is one driving force behind humor virtually everywhere. In the typical ethnic joke, the jokester and audience label some disadvantaged category of people as stupid or ridiculous, thereby imputing greater wisdom and skills to people like them. Given the Anglo-Saxon traditions of U.S. society, Poles and other ethnic and racial minorities have long been the "butt" of jokes, as have Newfoundlanders ("Newfies") in eastern Canada, the Irish in Scotland, Sikhs in India, Turks in Germany, Hausas in Nigeria, Tasmanians in Australia, and Kurds in Iraq.

Disadvantaged people, of course, also make fun of the powerful. Women in the United States have long joked about men, just as African Americans portray white people in humorous ways, and poor people poke fun at the rich. Throughout the world, people target

An elderly Jewish woman in a Miami park sees a new face sitting on a bench. "I haven't seen you before," she says by way of an overture. "I just finished forty years in jail," he replies. "What did you do?" "I killed my wife." "So," she concludes hopefully, "you're *single* . . ."

Q: "You can pretend to be serious, but you cannot pretend to be witty." Sacha Guitry

Q: "He who laughs, lasts." Dr. Robert Anthony

NOTE: Recall the example from Chapter 4 that one can cross an international border with valuable information encoded on computer disks and still declare nothing to customs officials.

DISCUSS: Will the twentieth-century shopping center survive in a new century that provides home access to dozens of shopping channels on cable T.V.?

Controversy & Debate

Is New Technology Changing Our Reality?

When Thomas Edison successfully tested the first telephone in 1874, observers were amazed by the feat of talking to others who were "not there." No doubt, people were just as astounded when the first airplane defied gravity and lifted off the ground (1903) or when images appeared out of nowhere on the first television screen (1939).

Is today's new information technology once again reconstructing reality? Absolutely, and the changes are no less amazing. Consider, first, that computers and other information technology have fundamentally altered the U.S. economy: The production of material things (clothing and cars) that defined the industrial age is quickly being replaced by the creation of ideas and images (computer programs and television shows). This trend is changing not only the nature of work, but the skills needed to find employment—working with one's hands is steadily giving way to working with one's head. Moreover, even our legal conception of property is in flux. A million-dollar investment used to mean a factory or a hotel; today, the programming on a single floppy disk can make or break a major corporation.

Second, new information technology is eroding the importance of place in our lives. Edison's telephone greatly extended our "reach";

however, with sound tied to wires, Edison knew exactly where his call was going. Today's cellular technology allows a person to key in a number and reach another person who could be, quite literally, anywhere on the continent—at home, moving in a car, or flying eight miles high. Similarly, the emerging high-technology workplace is now anywhere one can position a computer terminal and fax machine.

Even the centuries-old concepts of national boundaries and citizenship have grown fuzzy, shaken by new technology. Say an employee logs onto a computer terminal in Mexico City and, traveling the "information superhighway," connects to a U.S. bank in Manhattan where she processes transactions throughout the day. Is this "electronic immigrant" part of the labor force of Mexico or the United States?

Third, there is no more basic foundation of our reality than the timeless adage, "Seeing is believing." But digital imagery now allows photographers to combine and manipulate pictures to show anything, computer animation enables movie producers to have humans interact with life-like dinosaurs, and the technology of "virtual reality" means that, connected to computers, we can see, hear, and even feel the "touch" of another person thousands of miles away.

Change is coming to the college scene as well. Historically, students have read textbooks, which augment the "live" performance they observe in the classroom. But books are becoming a smaller and smaller part of publishers' offerings, as we witness a proliferation of images on tape, film, and computer disks. (Not coincidentally, Prentice Hall, publisher of this text, is owned by the entertainment giant Viacom.) In the years to come, textbooks themselves gradually will be replaced by CD-ROMS (this text is already available in this format) or downloaded directly from "Web sites" on the Internet. And, in a world of interactive computer-based instruction, will students need to travel to classrooms to learn? Indeed, will the college classroom itself eventually become obsolete?

Continue the debate . . .

1. *What dangers do you see in new information technology? Might this technology render life more impersonal or threaten our privacy?*

2. *What changes has technology brought to your college: to the library? the classroom?*

3. *In the "electronic decades" to come, what changes would you predict in everyday routines involving recreation, entertainment, paying bills, getting medical checkups, and shopping?*

their leaders with humor, and officials in some countries take such jokes seriously enough to repress them vigorously.

In sum, the significance of humor is no laughing matter. Michael Flaherty (1984, 1990) points out that humor amounts to a means of mental escape from a conventional world that is not entirely to our liking.

With that in mind, it makes sense that a disproportionate number of our nation's comedians come from among the ranks of minorities including Jews and African Americans. As long as we maintain a sense of humor, then, we assert our freedom and are never prisoners of reality. And, in doing so, we change the world and ourselves just a little.

SUMMARY

1. Social structure provides guidelines for behavior, rendering everyday life understandable and predictable.

2. A major component of social structure is status. Within an entire status set, a master status has particular significance.

3. Ascribed statuses are essentially involuntary, while achieved statuses are largely earned. In practice, however, many statuses incorporate elements of both ascription and achievement.

4. Role is the dynamic expression of a status. The incompatibility of roles corresponding to two or more statuses generates role conflict; likewise, incompatible roles linked to a single status produce role strain.

5. The phrase "social construction of reality" conveys the important idea that we all build the social world through our interaction.

6. The Thomas theorem states, "Situations defined as real become real in their consequences."

7. Ethnomethodology seeks to reveal the assumptions and understandings people have of their social world.

8. Dramaturgical analysis studies how people construct personal performances. This approach casts everyday life in terms of theatrical performances, noting the settings of interaction, the use of body language, and how performers often idealize their intentions.

9. Social power affects performances; our society's underlying subordination of women makes them craft their behavior differently than men do.

10. Social behavior carries the ever-present danger of embarrassment. Tact is a common response to a "loss of face" by others.

11. Language is vital to the process of socially constructing reality. In various ways, language defines females and males differently, generally to the advantage of males.

12. Humor stems from the contrast between conventional and unconventional definitions of a situation. Because comedy is framed by a specific culture, people throughout the world find humor in very different situations.

KEY CONCEPTS

achieved status a social position that someone assumes voluntarily and that reflects personal ability and effort

ascribed status a social position that someone receives at birth or assumes involuntarily later in life

dramaturgical analysis Erving Goffman's term for the investigation of social interaction in terms of theatrical performance

ethnomethodology Harold Garfinkel's term for the study of the way people make sense of their everyday lives

master status a status that has exceptional importance for social identity, often shaping a person's entire life

nonverbal communication communication using body movements, gestures, and facial expressions rather than speech

personal space the surrounding area to which an individual makes some claim to privacy

presentation of self an individual's effort to create specific impressions in the minds of others

role behavior expected of someone who holds a particular status

role conflict incompatibility among the roles corresponding to two or more statuses

role set a number of roles attached to a single status

role strain incompatibility among roles corresponding to a single status

social construction of reality the process by which people creatively shape reality through social interaction

social interaction the process by which people act and react in relation to others

status a recognized social position that an individual occupies

status set all the statuses a person holds at a given time

Thomas theorem W. I. Thomas's assertion that situations we define as real become real in their consequences

CRITICAL-THINKING QUESTIONS

1. List a dozen of your own statuses. Do both ascription and achievement play a part in each?

2. Consider ways in which a physical disability can serve as a master status. How do people commonly characterize, say, a person with the physical disability cerebral palsy with regard to mental ability? With regard to sexuality?

3. George Jean Nathan once quipped, "I only drink to make other people interesting." What does this mean in terms of reality construction? Identify the elements of humor within this statement.

4. Paralleling the dramaturgical analysis of a doctor's office found in this chapter, develop a similar analysis of a college classroom. How about a professor's office?

SUGGESTED READINGS

Classic Sources

Erving Goffman. *The Presentation of Self in Everyday Life*. Garden City, N.Y.: Doubleday Anchor Books, 1959.

Erving Goffman's first book is his best-known work.

Peter L. Berger and Thomas Luckmann. *The Social Construction of Reality: A Treatise in the Sociology of Knowledge*. Garden City, N.Y.: Doubleday Anchor Books, 1967.

This book elaborates on the argument that individuals generate meaning through their social interaction.

Contemporary Sources

Adam Phillips. *On Flirtation*. Cambridge: Harvard University Press, 1994.

Flirtation allows us to experiment, and shows that social interaction proceeds in a fluid, unplanned way.

William Rathje and Cullan Murphy. *Rubbish: The Archeology of Garbage*. New York: HarperCollins, 1991.

Researchers at the University of Arizona learned a great deal about people by studying their garbage.

Michele Fine and Adrian Ash. *Women with Disabilities*. Philadelphia: Temple University Press, 1990.

How do people define others with physical disabilities? How do these individuals construct their own identity? This book provides some intriguing insights.

Global Sources

Catherine A. Lutz. *Unnatural Emotions: Everyday Sentiments on a Micronesian Atoll and Their Challenge to Western Theory*. Chicago: University of Chicago Press, 1988.

This report of research on a Pacific island points up how emotions, and the way people think about them, are culturally variable.

Christie Davies. *Ethnic Humor Around the World: A Comparative Analysis*. Bloomington: Indiana University Press, 1990.

Relatively little attention has been paid to the sociological analysis of humor. This book applies a global perspective to the issue.

ED MCGOWIN,
SOCIETY TELEPHONE SOCIETY,
1989

Oil on canvas with carved and painted wood frame, 54"x54".

Groups
and Organizations

Sixty years ago, the opening of a new restaurant in Pasadena, California, attracted little attention from the local community and went unnoticed by the nation as a whole. Yet this seemingly insignificant small business, owned and operated by Mac and Dick McDonald, would eventually spark a revolution in the restaurant industry and provide an organizational model that would be copied by countless other businesses and even schools and churches.

The basic formula the McDonald brothers put into place—which we now call "fast food"—was to serve food quickly and inexpensively to large numbers of people. They trained employees to perform highly specialized jobs, so that one person grilled hamburgers, while others "dressed" them, made french fries, whipped up milkshakes, and presented the food to the customers in assembly-line fashion.

As the years went by, the McDonald brothers prospered, and they moved their single restaurant from Pasadena to San Bernardino. It was there, in 1954, that events took an unexpected turn when Ray Kroc, a traveling blender and mixer merchant, paid a visit to the McDonalds.

Kroc was fascinated by the brothers' efficient system, and, almost immediately, he saw the potential for a greatly expanded system of fast-food restaurants. Initially, Kroc launched his plans in partnership with the McDonald brothers. Soon, however, he bought out their interests and set out on his own to become one of the greatest success stories of all time. Today, fifteen thousand McDonald's restaurants serve people throughout the United States and around the world.

From a sociological point of view, the success of McDonald's reveals much more than the popularity of hamburgers. As this chapter explains presently, the larger importance of this story lies in the extent to which the principles that guide the operation of McDonald's are coming to dominate social life in the United States as well as the rest of the world.

We begin by examining *social groups*, the clusters of people with whom we associate in much of our daily lives. As we shall see, the scope of group life has expanded greatly during this century. From a world built on the family, the local neighborhood, and the small business, the structure of our society now turns on the operation of vast businesses and other bureaucracies that sociologists describe as *formal organizations*. How this expanding scale of life came to dominate our society, and what it means for us as individuals, are the chapter's key objectives.

NOTE: Cooley only came up with the term *primary group*; others introduced the term *secondary group* into sociological terminology, inferring the concept from Cooley's writings. Cooley, who did his first research for the U.S. Census collecting statistics on street railways, became a full-time sociologist at the age of 28.

Q: "By primary groups I mean those characterized by intimate face-to-face association and cooperation. They are primary in several senses, but chiefly in that they are fundamental in forming the social nature and ideals of individuals." Charles Horton Cooley (1962:23; orig. 1909)

NOTE: "Primary" is derived from the Latin word *prime*, meaning "first"; the root of "secondary" is the Latin word *secund(us)*, meaning "following."

Q: "Blood is thicker than water." Old saying

Around the world, families are the most important primary group. In industrial societies, however, numerous friendship groups stand alongside families, joining individuals on the basis of shared interests rather than kinship.

SOCIAL GROUPS

Virtually everyone moves through life with a sense of belonging; this is the experience of group life. A **social group** refers to *two or more people who identify and interact with one another*. Human beings continually come together to form couples, families, circles of friends, neighborhoods, churches, businesses, clubs, and numerous large organizations. Whatever the form, groups encompass people with shared experiences, loyalties, and interests. In short, while maintaining their individuality, the members of social groups also think of themselves as a special "we."

Groups, Categories, and Crowds

People often use the term "group" imprecisely. We now distinguish the group from the similar concepts of category and crowd.

Category

A *category* refers to people who have some status in common. Women, single fathers, military recruits, homeowners, and Roman Catholics are all examples of categories.

Why are categories not considered groups? Simply because, while the individuals involved are aware that they are not the only ones to hold that particular status, the vast majority are strangers to one another.

Crowd

A *crowd* refers to a temporary cluster of individuals who may or may not interact at all. Students sitting together in a lecture hall do engage one another and share some common identity as college classmates; thus, such a crowd might be called a loosely formed group. By contrast, riders hurtling along on a subway train or bathers enjoying a summer day at the beach pay little attention to one another and amount to an anonymous aggregate of people. In general, then, crowds are too transitory and too impersonal to qualify as social groups.

The right circumstances, however, could turn a crowd into a group. People riding in a subway train that crashes under the city streets generally become keenly aware of their common plight and begin to help each other. Sometimes such extraordinary experiences become the basis for lasting relationships.

Primary and Secondary Groups

Acquaintances commonly greet one another with a smile and the simple phrase "Hi! How are you?" The response is usually a well-scripted "Just fine, thanks. How about you?" This answer, of course, is often more formal than truthful. In most cases, providing a detailed account of how you are *really* doing would prompt the other person to beat a hasty and awkward exit.

Sociologists classify social groups by measuring them against two ideal types based on members' level of genuine personal concern. This variation is the key to distinguishing *primary* from *secondary* groups.

According to Charles Horton Cooley (1864–1929), who is introduced in the box, a **primary group** is *a small social group whose members share personal and enduring relationships*. Bound together by *primary relationships*, individuals in primary groups typically spend a great deal of time together, engage in a wide range of common activities, and feel that they know one another well. Although not without periodic conflict, members of primary groups display sincere concern for each other's welfare. The family is every society's most important primary group.

Cooley characterized these personal and tightly integrated groups as *primary* because they are among the first groups we experience in life. In addition, the family and early play groups also hold primary importance in the socialization process, shaping attitudes, behavior, and social identity.

The strength of primary relationships gives people a comforting sense of security. In the familiar social circles of family or friends, people feel they can "be

Q: "In our own life the intimacy of the neighborhood has been broken up by the growth of an intricate mesh of wider contacts which leaves us strangers to people who live in the same house." Charles Horton Cooley (1962:26; orig. 1909)
SOCIAL SURVEY: "How often do you spend an evening with relatives?" (*Student CHIP Social Survey Software*, SOCREL1; GSS 1974–91, N = 14,061) [Note strong correlation with SES.]

Relatives:		
SES	Weekly	Less often
High	26.3%	73.7%
Middle	36.4%	63.6%
Low	42.5%	57.5%

NOTE: Secondary ties may be described as relationships of limited liability.

PROFILE

Charles Horton Cooley: The Primary Group Is Morally Good

Many people fear that life now moves at such a fast pace that individuals are losing touch with one another. This is nothing new: Charles Horton Cooley shared this concern a century ago growing up in a small town and witnessing rapid change all around him.

Home for Cooley was Ann Arbor, Michigan, where he spent his childhood and later returned to teach at the University of Michigan from 1892 until his death. His major contribution to sociology was exploring the character of the primary group.

Cooley noted a disturbing trend: As the United States was becoming more urban and industrialized, people seemed to become ever more individualistic and competitive, displaying less concern for the traditional family and local neighborhood. This transformation made Cooley uneasy because he was convinced of the crucial importance of small, cooperative groups to social life. Primary groups are morally good, he declared, because they engender in people a sense of secure belonging as well as a spirit of fairness and compassion.

Cooley hoped that calling attention to the importance of primary groups might shore up traditional values and sustain social cohesion. Certainly, the United States has continued to change since Cooley's lifetime, and not entirely in ways he would have liked. But even though he died some seventy years ago, many of Cooley's social concerns are with us still.

Sources: Rieff (1962) and Coser (1977).

themselves" without constantly worrying about the impressions they are making.

Members of primary groups generally provide one another with economic and other forms of assistance, as well. But, as important as primary ties are, people generally think of a primary group as an end in itself rather than as a means to other ends. In other words, we prefer to think that kinship or friendship links people who "belong together," rather than people who expect to benefit from each other. For this reason, we readily call on family members or close friends to help us move into a new apartment, without expecting to pay for their services. And we would do the same for them. A friend who never returns a favor, by contrast, is likely to leave us feeling "used" and questioning the depth of the friendship.

Moreover, this personal orientation means that members of a primary group view each other as unique and irreplaceable. We typically do not care who cashes our check at the bank or takes our money at the supermarket checkout. Yet in the primary group—especially the family—we are bound to specific others by emotion and loyalty. So even though brothers and sisters do not always get along, they always remain siblings.

In contrast to the primary group, the **secondary group** is *a large and impersonal social group whose members pursue a specific interest or activity.* In most respects, secondary groups have precisely the opposite characteristics of primary groups. *Secondary relationships* usually involve weak emotional ties and little personal knowledge of one another. Secondary groups vary in duration, but they are frequently short term, beginning and ending without particular significance. Students in a college course, for instance, who may not see one another after the semester ends, exemplify the secondary group.

Weaker social ties permit secondary groups to include many more people than primary groups do. For example, dozens or even hundreds of people may work together in the same office, yet most of them pay only passing attention to one another. Sometimes the passing of time will transform a group from secondary to primary, as with co-workers who share an office for many years. Generally, however, the boundary

TABLE 7–1 Primary Groups and Secondary Groups: A Summary

	Primary ←→ Secondary Group	Group
Quality of relationships	Personal orientation	Goal orientation
Duration of relationships	Usually long term	Variable; often short term
Breadth of relationships	Broad; usually involving many activities	Narrow; usually involving few activities
Subjective perception of relationships	As ends in themselves	As means to an end
Typical examples	Families; circles of friends	Co-workers; political organizations

separating members of a secondary group from non-members is far less clear than it is in primary groups.

Secondary groups lack strong loyalties and emotions because members look to one another only to achieve limited ends. So while members of primary groups display a *personal orientation*, people in secondary groups reveal a *goal orientation*. Secondary ties are not necessarily always aloof or cold, of course. Social interactions among students, co-workers, and business associates are often quite pleasant, even if they are rather impersonal.

In primary groups, members define each other according to *who* they are, that is, in terms of kinship or unique, personal qualities. Members of secondary groups, by contrast, look to one another for *what* they are or what they can do for each other. In secondary groups, in other words, we are always mindful of what we offer others and what we receive in return. This "scorekeeping" comes through most clearly in business relationships. Likewise, the people next door typically expect that a neighborly favor will be reciprocated.

The goal orientation of secondary groups encourages individuals to craft their behavior carefully. In these roles, we remain characteristically impersonal and polite. The secondary relationship, therefore, is one in which the question "How are you?" may be asked without really expecting a truthful answer.

Table 7–1 summarizes the characteristics that distinguish primary and secondary groups. Keep in mind that these traits define two types of social groups in

ideal terms; actual groups in our lives may well contain elements of both. By placing these concepts as ends of a continuum, however, we devise a useful scheme for describing and analyzing group life.

Do some regions of the United States have a more primary orientation than others? A long-standing sociological assertion holds that rural areas and small towns tend toward a greater emphasis on primary relationships while large cities are typically more secondary. While this generalization holds much truth, some urban neighborhoods—especially those populated by people of a single ethnic or religious category—are quite tightly knit. National Map 7–1 offers one indicator of the primary or secondary character of social ties across the United States: a state-by-state survey gauging whether people are likely to resolve interpersonal disputes among themselves or to seek redress formally by turning to the courts.

Finally, what about the world as a whole? In general, primary relationships predominate in low-income, preindustrial societies throughout Latin America, Africa, and Asia in which people's lives revolve around families and local villages. In these countries, especially in rural areas, strangers stand out in the social landscape. By contrast, secondary ties take precedence in high-income, industrial societies, in which people assume highly specialized social roles. Most people in the United States, especially in cities, routinely engage in impersonal, secondary contacts with virtual strangers—people about whom we know very little and whom we may never meet again (Wirth, 1938).

Group Leadership

How do groups operate? One important dimension of group dynamics is leadership. Groups vary in the extent to which members recognize leaders. Large, secondary groups generally place leaders in a formal chain of command; a small circle of friends may have no leader at all. Parents assume leadership roles in families, although husband and wife may disagree about who is really in charge.

Two Leadership Roles

Groups typically benefit from two kinds of leadership (Bales, 1953; Bales & Slater, 1955). **Instrumental leadership** refers to *group direction that emphasizes the completion of tasks*. Members look to instrumental leaders to "get things done." **Expressive leadership**, by contrast, *focuses on collective well-being*. Expressive leaders take less of an interest in the performance

Seeing Ourselves

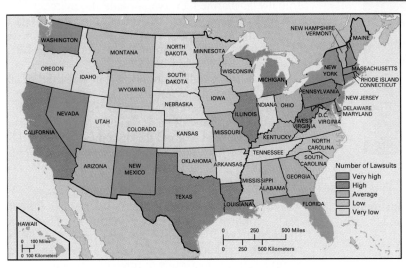

NATIONAL MAP 7–1

The Quality of Relationships: Lawsuits Across the United States

Social conflicts are found everywhere, but whether people tend to resolve them informally or resort to legal action varies from state to state. It stands to reason that, in regions of the country where litigation is least common, people's social ties are typically more primary in character. By contrast, where people are most likely to turn to lawyers, social ties would seem to be more secondary. Looking at the map, what do the states with high levels of litigation have in common? What traits mark the states in which people are reluctant to sue each other?

Source: Prepared by the author using data from Frum & Wolfe (1994).

goals of a group than in group morale and minimizing tension and conflict among members.

Because they concentrate on performance, instrumental leaders usually have formal, secondary relations with other group members. Instrumental leaders give orders and reward or punish people according to their contribution to the group's efforts. Expressive leaders, however, cultivate more personal, primary ties. They offer sympathy to a member having a tough time, work to keep the group united, and lighten serious moments with humor. While successful instrumental leaders enjoy more distant *respect* from members, expressive leaders generally garner more personal *affection*.

In the traditional, North American family, this differentiation of leadership is linked to gender. Conventional cultural norms bestow instrumental leadership on men so that, as fathers and husbands, they assume primary responsibility for earning income, making decisions, and disciplining children. By contrast, expressive leadership is the traditional purview of women. Historically, mothers and wives have encouraged supportive and peaceful relationships among family members. This division of labor partly explains why many children have greater respect for their fathers but closer personal ties with their mothers (Parsons & Bales, 1955; Macionis, 1978).

Of course, increasing equality between men and women has blurred this gender-based distinction between instrumental and expressive leadership. In most group settings, women and men now assume both of these leadership roles.

Three Leadership Styles

Sociologists also characterize group leadership in terms of three orientations to power. *Authoritarian leadership* stresses instrumental concerns, taking personal charge of decision making and demanding strict compliance from subordinates. Although this leadership style may win little affection from group members, a fast-acting authoritarian leader often earns praise in a crisis situation.

Democratic leadership has a more expressive focus, making a point of including everyone in the decision-making process. Although less successful when crises afford little time for discussion, democratic leaders generally draw on the ideas of all members to forge reflective and imaginative responses to the tasks at hand.

Laissez-faire leadership (from the French phrase meaning, roughly, "to leave alone") allows the group to function more or less on its own. This style typically is the least effective in promoting group goals (White & Lippitt, 1953; Ridgeway, 1983).

NOTE: Asch's confederates incorrectly identified lines that varied in length from the standard line by as much as 1 3/4 inches.

Q: "A little doubt came into my mind . . . Even though you know you are right, you wonder why everybody thinks differently. I was doubting myself and was puzzled." One of Solomon Asch's subjects

NOTE: Asch conducted control sessions to test the ability of subjects to make correct comparisons in the absence of group pressure;

overall, 99% of such judgments were correct (compared to 66% in the conformity situation).

DISCUSS: Many studies in social psychology rest on subject deception, a controversial practice covered in Chapter 2's discussion of research ethics. The Milgram experiment is the most troublesome in this regard because it also subjected people to high stress. Is research deception justified?

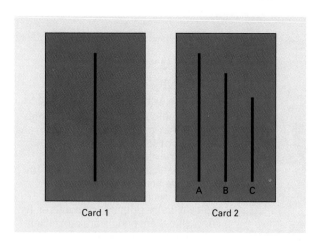

FIGURE 7–1 Cards Used in Asch's Experiment in Group Conformity

Source: Asch (1952).

Group Conformity

Okiki, a thirteen-year-old honors student at a Lorain, Ohio, middle school, sat in class, her arms and legs shaking nervously. In her book bag she concealed a twelve-inch kitchen knife. Her plan was to wait for the bell to ring and then rush to the front of the classroom and, with the help of another student, stab her teacher to death. Why? To settle a grudge against the teacher and to show her classmates (at least a dozen of whom placed bets on whether or not she would "chicken out") that she was worthy of their respect. Hearing about the plot, an assistant principal broke up the plan only minutes before it was to be carried out (Gregory, 1993).

The fact that young teens are anxious about fitting in surprises no one, although many people might be amazed at the lengths some will go to gain acceptance. Social scientists confirm the power of group pressure to shape human behavior and report that it remains strong in adulthood as well as in adolescence.

Asch's Research

Solomon Asch (1952) conducted a classic investigation that revealed the power of group conformity. Asch recruited students for an alleged study of visual perception. Before the actual experiment, however, he revealed to all but one member in each small group that their real purpose was to impose group pressure on the remaining subject. Placing all the students around a table, Asch asked each, in turn, to note the length of a "standard" line, as shown on Card 1 in Figure 7–1, and match it to one of three lines on Card 2.

Anyone with normal vision could easily see that the line marked "A" on Card 2 was the correct choice. Initially, as planned, everyone made the matches correctly. But then Asch's secret accomplices began answering incorrectly, making the naive subject (seated at the table in order to answer next to last) bewildered and uncomfortable.

What happened? Asch found that one-third of all subjects placed in this situation chose to conform to the others by answering incorrectly. His investigation indicates that many of us are willing to compromise our own judgment to avoid the discomfort of being different from others, even from people we do not know.

Milgram's Research

Stanley Milgram—a former student of Solomon Asch—conducted conformity experiments of his own. In Milgram's initial study (1963, 1965; Miller, 1986), a researcher explained to male recruits that they were about to engage in a study of how punishment affects learning. One by one, he assigned them the role of "teacher" and placed another individual—an insider to the study—in a connecting room as the "learner."

The teacher saw the learner sit down in an ominous contraption resembling an electric chair with an electrode attached to one arm. The researcher then had the teacher read aloud pairs of words. In the next step, the teacher repeated the first word of each pair and asked the learner to recall the corresponding second word.

As mistakes occurred, the researcher instructed the teacher to shock the learner using a "shock generator," a bogus but forbidding-looking piece of equipment with a shock switch and a dial marked to regulate electric current from 15 volts (labeled "mild shock") to 300 volts (marked "intense shock") to 450 volts (marked "Danger: Severe Shock" and "XXX").

Beginning at the lowest level, the researcher told the teacher to increase the shock by 15 volts every time the learner made a mistake. The shocks, explained the researcher, would become painful but cause no permanent damage. And so it went. At 75, 90, and 105 volts, the teacher heard audible moans from the learner; at 120 volts, shouts of pain; at 270 volts, screams of agony; and, after 330 volts, deadly silence.

The results show just how readily authority figures can obtain compliance from ordinary people. None of forty subjects assigned in the role of teacher during the initial research even questioned the procedure before 300 volts had been applied, and twenty-six of the subjects—almost two-thirds—went all the way to 450 volts.

NOTE: Milgram found that the physical presence of the experimenter generated the highest level of subject compliance. When commands were issued by telephone, compliance dropped by 20%.

DISCUSS: Pressure to conform comes from many sources other than groups, including media presentations, pronouncements of experts, opinions of significant others, and so on. Ask students to assess the power of such factors to generate conformity.

Q: "Some similarities in status attributes between the individual and the reference group must be perceived or imagined, in order for the comparison to occur at all." Robert K. Merton (1968:296)

NOTE: Regarding reference groups, note Durkheim's contention that failure to have any reference points invites an intolerable lack of constraints that leaves individuals at the mercy of their own passions (which, unlike the case in animals, do not regulate themselves).

Milgram (1964) then modified his research to see if Solomon Asch had documented such a high degree of group conformity only because the task of matching lines seemed trivial. What if groups pressured people to administer electrical shocks?

To investigate, he varied the experiment so that a group of three teachers, two of whom were his accomplices, made decisions jointly. Milgram's rule was that each of the three teachers would suggest a shock level when the learner made an error and they would then administer the lowest of the three suggestions. This arrangement gave the naive subject the power to lessen the shock level regardless of the other two teachers' recommendations.

The accomplices called for increasing the shock level with each error, placing group pressure on the third member to do the same. Responding to this group pressure, subjects applied voltages three to four times higher than in control conditions in which subjects acted alone. Thus Milgram's research suggests that people are surprisingly likely to follow the directions not only of "legitimate authority figures," but also of groups of ordinary individuals.

Janis's Research

Even the experts succumb to group pressure, according to Irving L. Janis (1972, 1989), sometimes making mistakes with far-reaching implications. Janis contends that a number of U.S. foreign policy blunders, including the failure to foresee the Japanese attack on Pearl Harbor that brought the United States into World War II and our ill-fated involvement in the Vietnam War, may have been the result of group conformity among our highest-ranking political leaders.

Common sense tells us that "brainstorming" improves decision making. However, Janis counters that group members often seek quick consensus that closes off discussion, rather than seeking out alternative points of view. Having settled on one "reality," he continues, members may develop an "official" interpretation of events and even come to regard anyone with another opinion as the "opposition." Janis called this process **groupthink**, *the tendency of group members to conform by adopting a narrow view of some issue.*

Illustrating the operation of groupthink, Arthur Schlesinger, Jr. bemoans his role in supporting the Kennedy administration's invasion of Cuba in 1961—an ill-fated plan that provoked international criticism of the United States. The former presidential advisor confesses his guilt "for having kept so quiet during those crucial discussions in the Cabinet Room," adding that the group discouraged anyone from challenging what,

In many traditional societies, children of the same age forge strong loyalties, generally with members of their own sex. Among the Masai in Kenya, for example, boys born during the same four-year period undergo ritual circumcision together and maintain a group bond throughout their lives.

in hindsight, he views as "nonsense" (quoted in Janis, 1972:30, 40).

Reference Groups

How do we assess our own attitudes or behavior? Frequently, we make use of a **reference group,** *a social group that serves as a point of reference in making evaluations or decisions.*

A young man who imagines his family's response to a woman he is dating is using his family as a reference group. Similarly, a banker who assesses her colleagues' reactions to a new loan policy is using her co-workers as a standard of reference. As these examples illustrate, reference groups can be primary or secondary. In either case, the motivation to conform to a group means that the attitudes of others can greatly affect us.

We also use groups that we do *not* belong to for reference. People preparing for job interviews typically notice how those in the company they wish to join dress and act, adjusting their personal performances accordingly. The use of groups by nonmembers illustrates the process of *anticipatory socialization*, described in Chapter 5 ("Socialization"), by which individuals use conformity as a strategy to win acceptance to a particular group.

Stouffer's Research

Samuel A. Stouffer (1949) and his associates conducted a classic study of reference group dynamics

NOTE: Consider the line "It's harder to have made money and lost it than never to have had it at all" in terms of relative deprivation. Or recall the old Cliff Robertson movie "Charly" in which a retarded man is made brilliant by scientists only to face the chilling reality that his condition is temporary.

DISCUSS: Expand the discussion of reference group dynamics by

touching on the concept of relative deprivation (see Chapter 23). A *Times-Mirror* poll found that a growing share of older people in the United States express dissatisfaction with their financial situation, while young people have a more positive view. Actual earning data, however, show the opposite trend, with income among the elderly rising through the 1980s, while that of people in their twenties actually fell.

Throughout the world, the most intense social bonds join two people. Even so, the dyad is also characteristically unstable, since withdrawal of either party causes the group to collapse.

during World War II. In a survey, researchers asked soldiers to evaluate the chances of promotion for a competent soldier in their branch of the service. One might guess that soldiers serving in outfits with a high promotion rate would be optimistic about their future advancement. Yet survey results supported the opposite conclusion: Soldiers in branches of the service with low promotion rates were actually more optimistic about their own chances to move ahead.

The key to this paradox lies in sorting out the groups against which the soldiers measured their progress. Those in branches with low promotion rates looked around them and saw people making no more headway than they were. That is, they had not been promoted, but neither had many others, so they did not feel unjustly deprived.

Soldiers in service branches with high promotion rates, however, could easily think of people who had been promoted sooner or more often than they had. With such people in mind, even soldiers who had been

promoted themselves were likely to feel shortchanged. So these were the soldiers who voiced more negative attitudes in their evaluations.

Stouffer's research demonstrates that we do not make judgments about ourselves in isolation, nor do we compare ourselves with just anyone. Instead, we use specific social groups as standards in developing individual attitudes. Whatever our situation in *absolute* terms, then, we assess our well-being subjectively, *relative* to some specific reference group (Merton, 1968; Mirowsky, 1987).

Ingroups and Outgroups

Everyone favors some groups over others, sometimes based on political outlook, social prestige, or simply manner of dress. On the college campus, for example, left-leaning student activists may look down on fraternity members whom they view as conservative; the Greeks, in turn, may snub the computer "nerds" as well as the "grinds" who study too hard. People in virtually every social setting develop a comparable cluster of positive and negative evaluations.

Such judgments illustrate another key element of group dynamics: the opposition of ingroups and outgroups. An **ingroup** is *a social group commanding a member's esteem and loyalty*. An ingroup exists in relation to an **outgroup**, *a social group toward which one feels competition or opposition*.

Social life is the interplay of both kinds of groups. A campus football team, for example, is both an ingroup to its members and an outgroup for students with no interest in sports. A town's Democrats generally think of themselves as an ingroup in relation to the local Republicans. All ingroups and outgroups work on the principle that "we" have valued characteristics that "they" lack.

Tensions among groups often help to sharpen their boundaries and give people a clearer sense of social identity. However, this form of group dynamics also promotes self-serving distortions of reality. Specifically, research shows, members of ingroups construct overly positive views of themselves and hold unfairly negative views of various outgroups (Tajfel, 1982).

Power also guides intergroup relations. With greater power, members of one ingroup may socially injure people they view as an outgroup. For example, white people have historically viewed people of color in negative terms and subjected them to social, political, and economic disadvantages. Internalizing these negative attitudes, minorities often struggle to overcome negative self-images. In short, ingroups and

Q: "The young always have the same problem—how to rebel and conform at the same time. They have solved this by defying their parents and copying one other." Quentin Crisp
NOTE: Ethnocentrism is one expression of touting one's own ingroup while denigrating those who differ as an outgroup.
NOTE: In the dyad, there can be no "social loafing."

Q: "A dyad . . . depends on each of its two elements alone—in its death, though not in its life: For its life, it needs both, but for its death, only one." Georg Simmel (1950:124)
NOTE: Because of Simmel's focus on the intricate details of situational social life, Everett Hughes dubbed him "the Freud of sociology."

outgroups foster loyalty as well as generating tension and conflict.

Group Size

If you are the first person to arrive at a party, you can observe some fascinating group dynamics. Until about six people enter the room, everyone generally shares a single conversation. But as more people arrive, the group divides into two or more smaller clusters. It is apparent that size plays a crucial role in how group members interact.

To understand why, consider the mathematical connection between the number of people in a social group and the number of relationships among them. As Figure 7–2 shows, two people form a single relationship; adding a third person generates three relationships; adding a fourth person yields six. Increasing the number of people one at a time, then, boosts the number of relationships much more rapidly since every new individual can interact with everyone already there. Thus, five people produce ten relationships and, by the time six people join one conversation, fifteen "channels" connect them. This leaves too many people unable to speak, which is why the group usually divides at this point.

The Dyad

German sociologist Georg Simmel (1858–1918) explored social dynamics in the smallest social groups. Simmel (1950; orig. 1902) used the term **dyad** to designate *a social group with two members*. Throughout the world, most love affairs, marriages, and the closest friendships are dyadic.

What makes the dyad a special relationship? First, explained Simmel, social interaction in a dyad is typically more intense than in larger groups since, in a one-to-one relationship, neither member shares the other's attention with anyone else. Thus dyads have the potential to be the most meaningful social bonds we ever experience.

Second, Simmel explains, like a stool with only two legs, dyads have a characteristic instability. Both members of a dyad must actively sustain the relationship; if either one withdraws, the group collapses. Because of the importance of marriage to society, the marital dyad is supported with legal, economic, and often religious ties. By contrast, a large group such as a volunteer fire company is inherently much more stable, as it can survive the loss of many members.

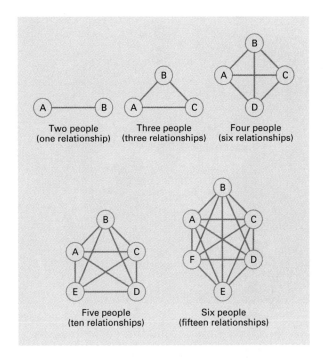

FIGURE 7–2 Group Size and Relationships

Marriage in our society is dyadic; ideally, we expect powerful emotional ties to unite husbands and wives. As we shall see in Chapter 17 ("Family"), however, marriage in other societies may involve more than two people. In that case, the household usually is more stable, although many of the marital relationships are weaker.

The Triad

Simmel also probed the **triad**, *a social group with three members*. A triad encompasses three relationships, each uniting two of the three people. A triad is more stable than a dyad because, should the relationship between any two members become strained, the third can act as a mediator to restore the group's vitality. This bit of group dynamics helps explain why members of a dyad (say, a married couple) often seek out a third person (a counselor) to air tensions between them.

Nonetheless, two of the three can form a coalition to press their views on the third, or two may intensify their relationship, leaving the other feeling like a "third wheel." For example, two members of a triad who develop a romantic interest in each other will understand the old saying "Two's company, three's a crowd."

Q: "Among three elements [of a triad], each one operates as an intermediary between the other two, exhibiting the twofold function of such an organ, which is to unite and to separate." Georg Simmel (1950:135)

SOCIAL SURVEY: "How many of your friends know each other?" (*CHIP1 Social Survey Software*, FRNDKNO1; GSS 1985,

N = 1,423) [Note that low SES people are more likely to have physically localized networks.]

SES	All/most	Few/none
High	55.6%	44.4%
Medium	61.4%	38.6%
Low	64.1%	35.9%

Today's college campuses value social diversity. One of the challenges of this movement is ensuring that all categories of students are fully integrated into campus life. This is not always easy. Following Blau's theory of group dynamics, as the number of minority students increases, these men and women are able to form a group unto themselves, perhaps interacting less with others.

As groups grow beyond three members, they become progressively more stable because the loss of even several members does not threaten the group's existence. At the same time, increases in group size typically reduce the intense personal interaction possible only in the smallest groups. Larger groups are thus based less on personal attachments and more on formal rules and regulations. Such formality helps a large group persist over time, though the group is not immune to change. After all, their numerous members give large groups more contact with the outside world, opening the door to new attitudes and behavior (Carley, 1991).

Does a social group have an ideal size? The answer depends on the group's purpose. A dyad offers unsurpassed emotional intensity, while a group of several dozen members is more stable, capable of accomplishing larger, more complex tasks, and better able to assimilate new members or ideas. People typically find more *personal pleasure* in smaller groups, while deriving greater *task satisfaction* from accomplishments in larger organizations (Slater, 1958; Ridgeway, 1983; Carley, 1991).

Social Diversity

Social diversity affects group dynamics, especially the likelihood that members will interact with someone of another group. Peter Blau (1977, 1982; South & Messner, 1986) points out four ways in which the composition of social groups affects intergroup association.

1. **Large groups turn inward.** Extending Simmel's analysis of group size, Blau explains that the larger a group, the more likely its members are to maintain relationships exclusively among themselves. The smaller the group, by contrast, the more members will reach beyond their immediate social circle.

   To illustrate, consider the efforts of many colleges to enhance social diversity. Increasing the number of, say, international students may add a dimension of difference to a campus, but, as their numbers rise, these students eventually are able to maintain their own distinctive social group. Thus intentional efforts to promote social diversity may well have the unintended effect of promoting separatism.

2. **Heterogeneous groups turn outward.** The more internally heterogeneous a group is, the more likely its members are to interact with members of other groups. We would expect, for example, that campus groups that recruit members of both sexes and people of various ethnic and geographic backgrounds would promote more intergroup contact than those that choose members of only one social type.

3. **Social parity promotes contact.** An environment in which all groups have roughly equal standing encourages people of all social backgrounds to mingle and form social ties. Thus, whether groups insulate their members or not depends on whether the groups themselves form a social hierarchy.

DIVERSITY: Illustrating Blau's analysis, members of small racial and ethnic communities are more likely to marry out of their category than are members of larger categories (cf. Gurak & Fitzpatrick, 1982).

RESOURCE: Elizabeth Bott's classic *Family and Social Network* (The Free Press, 1957 and 1971) relates networks to social class and other aspects of social structure.
NOTE: Networks are a characteristic feature of modern societies in which social connections are not built around localized kinship ties and neighborhood but rather a wide range of individual experiences

SOCIOLOGY OF EVERYDAY LIFE

The Internet: Welcome to Cyberspace!

Its origins seem right out of the 1960s cold war film *Dr. Strangelove*. Three decades ago, government officials and scientists were trying to imagine how to run the country after an atomic attack, which, they assumed, would instantaneously eliminate telephones and television. The brilliant solution was to devise a communication system with no central headquarters, no one in charge, and no main power switch—in short, an electronic web that would link the country in one vast network.

By 1985, the federal government was installing high-speed data lines around the country and the Internet was about to be born. Today, thousands of government offices, as well as colleges and universities across the United States, are joined by the Internet and share in the cost of its operation. Add to this mix millions of other individuals who connect their home computers to this "information superhighway" through a telephone-line modem and a commercial "gateway" such as America Online, Prodigy, and Compuserve.

No one knows precisely how many people make use of the Internet. But a rough 1995 estimate put the total at 50 million individuals in 175 (of 191) countries around the world, making it the largest network in history. And the numbers are doubling each year.

What is available on the Internet? Far more than anyone could ever list in a single directory. Popular activities include electronic mail (start a cyber-romance with a pen pal, write to your textbook author, or even send a message to the president of the United States: president@whitehouse.gov), participating in discussion groups or receiving newsletters on a wide range of topics, or searching libraries across the campus or around the world for books or other information. Because the Internet has no formal rules for its use, its potential defies the imagination.

Ironically, perhaps, it is precisely this chaotic quality that has many people up in arms. Pundits warn that "electronic democracy" may undermine established political practices, parents fear that their technologically sophisticated children may discover sex "on line," and purists bristle at the thought that the Internet may soon be flooded with advertising and other commercial ventures.

In many respects, the "anything goes" character of the Internet mirrors the real world. Not surprisingly, therefore, more and more users are now employing passwords, fees, and other "gates" to build restricted subnetworks limited to people like themselves. From one vast network, then, is emerging a host of smaller social groups.

Sources: Based, in part, on Elmer-DeWitt (1993, 1994) and Hafner (1994).

---

4. **Physical boundaries foster social boundaries.** Blau contends that physical space affects the chances of contacts among groups. To the extent that a social group is physically segregated from others (by having its own dorm or dining area, for example), its members are less apt to engage other people.

Networks

Formally, a **network** is *a web of social ties that links people who identify and interact little with one another.* Think of a network as a "fuzzy" group that brings people into occasional contact without a group's sense of boundaries and belonging. Computer networks, or other high-technology links, now routinely connect people living all over the world. If we consider a group as a "circle of friends," then, we might describe a network as a "social web" expanding outward, often reaching great distances and including large numbers of people.

Some network contacts are regular, as among college friends who years later stay in touch by mail and telephone. More commonly, however, a network includes people we *know of*—or who *know of us*—but with whom we interact infrequently, if at all. As one woman with a widespread reputation as a community organizer explains, "I get calls at home, someone says, 'Are you Roseann Navarro? Somebody told me to call you. I have this problem . . .'" (quoted in Kaminer, 1984:94). For this reason, social networks amount to "clusters of weak ties" (Granovetter, 1973).

NOTE: For more information on cyberspace, see the web site
that supports this textbook.

Q: "No man is an island, entire of itself;
every man is a piece of the continent,
a part of the main . . .

any man's death diminishes me,
because I am involved in mankind.
And therefore never send to know
for whom the bell tolls; it tolls for thee."
John Donne

Window on the World

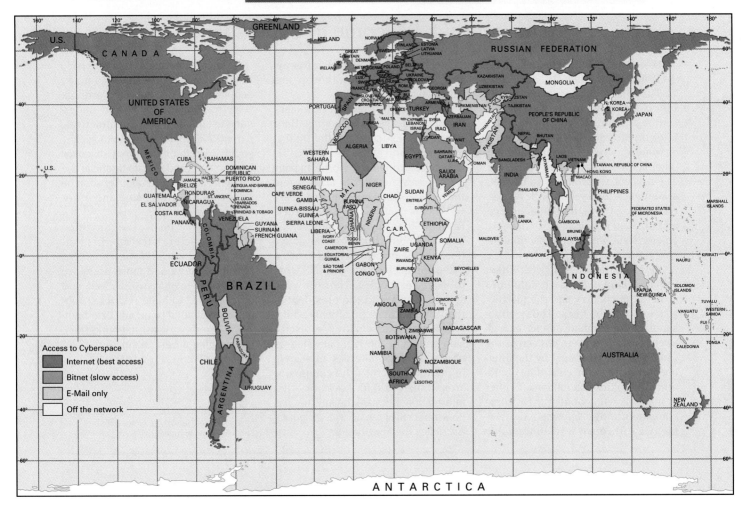

GLOBAL MAP 7–1 Cyberspace: A Global Network

While 175 of 191 world nations are connected to the Internet, a majority of the world's people have
no access to this valuable resource. For one thing, computers are expensive, well out of reach of
ordinary people in low-income countries, especially in Africa. Thus the vast majority of Internet
sites are in the United States, Canada, Western Europe, and Australia. But another barrier to global
communication is language: Born in the U.S., the Internet's available software demands that users
read and write in the Latin alphabet using English. But experts around the world are at work
developing keyboards and interface programs that will link people using various languages.
Perhaps, in the near future, the Internet may be as multicultural as the world it connects.

Source: Copyright © 1993/1995 by The New York Times Co. Reprinted by permission.

Network ties may be weak, but they serve as a
significant resource. For example, many people rely
on their networks to find jobs. Even the scientific

genius Albert Einstein needed a hand in landing his
first job. After a year of unsuccessful interviewing, he
obtained employment only when the father of one

SUPPLEMENTS: Supplementary material on how race, gender, and class affect membership in voluntary associations is included in the *Data File*.
NOTE: The number of voluntary associations in the United States continues to rise; 70 percent of adults belong to at least one (Caplow et al., 1991).

of his classmates put him in touch with an office manager who hired him (Clark, 1971; cited in Fischer, 1977:19). This use of networks to one's advantage suggests that, as the saying goes, *who you know* is often just as important as *what you know.*

Networks are based on peoples' colleges, clubs, neighborhoods, political parties, and informal cliques. Some networks encompass people with considerably more wealth, power, and prestige than others do, which is the essence of describing someone as "well connected." And some people have denser networks than others—that is, they are connected to more people—which is also a valuable social resource. Typically, the most extensive social networks are maintained by people who are young, well educated, and living in urban areas (Marsden, 1987; Markovsky et al., 1993; Kadushin, 1995).

Gender, too, shapes networks. Although the networks of men and women are typically the same size, women include more relatives in their networks, while those of men are filled out with more co-workers. Women's networks, therefore, may not carry quite the same clout as the "old-boy" networks do. Even so, research indicates that, as gender inequality lessens in the United States, this difference is diminishing over time (Moore, 1991, 1992).

Finally, new information technology has generated a global network of unprecedented size in the form of the Internet. The box on page 183 takes a closer look at this twenty-first century form of communication, while Global Map 7–1 shows the extent of the Internet in 1995.

FORMAL ORGANIZATIONS

Throughout human history, most people lived in small groups of family members and neighbors; this pattern was still widespread in the United States a century ago. Today, families and neighborhoods persist, of course, but our lives revolve far more around **formal organizations**, *large, secondary groups that are organized to achieve their goals efficiently.*

Formal organizations, such as corporations or government agencies, differ significantly from families and neighborhoods: Their greater size renders social relationships less personal and fosters a planned, formal atmosphere. In other words, formal organizations operate to accomplish complex jobs rather than to meet personal needs.

When you think about it, organizing a society with some 265 million members is a remarkable feat. Countless tasks are involved, from collecting taxes to

delivering the mail. To meet most of these responsibilities, we rely on large, formal organizations. The United States government, the nation's largest formal organization, employs more than 5 million people in various agencies and the armed forces. Such vast organizations develop lives and cultures of their own, so that as members come and go, the statuses they fill and the roles they perform remain unchanged over the years.

Types of Formal Organizations

Amitai Etzioni (1975) has identified three types of formal organizations, distinguished by why people participate—utilitarian organizations, normative organizations, and coercive organizations.

Utilitarian Organizations

Just about everyone who works for income is a member of a *utilitarian organization,* which provides material rewards for its members. Large business enterprises, for example, generate profits for their owners and income in the form of salaries and wages for their employees. Joining utilitarian organizations is usually a matter of individual choice, although most people must join one or another utilitarian organization to make a living.

Normative Organizations

People join *normative organizations* not for income but to pursue goals they consider morally worthwhile. Sometimes called *voluntary associations,* these include community service groups (such as the PTA, the Lions Club, the League of Women Voters, the Red Cross, and Kiwanis), political parties, religious organizations, and numerous other confederations concerned with specific social issues.

In global perspective, people in the United States are especially likely to be members of voluntary associations (Curtis, Grabb, & Baer, 1992). Figure 7–3 provides a comparative glance at membership in cultural or educational organizations for selected countries.

Coercive Organizations

In Etzioni's typology, *coercive organizations* are distinguished by involuntary membership. That is, people are forced to join the organization as a form of punishment (prisons) or treatment (psychiatric hospitals). Coercive organizations have extraordinary physical

NOTE: The section in Chapter 4, "Max Weber: The Rationalization of Society" provides general background for this discussion of bureaucracy and introduces Weber's thesis of increasing rationalization. Here we focus more narrowly on bureaucracy as a major manifestation of that process.

Q: "Bureaucracy, the rule of no one, has become the modern form of despotism." Mary McCarthy

RESOURCE: An excerpt from Max Weber's analysis of bureaucracy is found in the companion reader, *Seeing Ourselves*.

NOTE: Exemplifying the inefficiency of a prebureaucratic world: Two weeks after the United States and Great Britain signed the Treaty of Ghent ending the War of 1812, 5,000 British troops, unaware of the peace agreement, attacked American forces at New Orleans, resulting in the loss of 2,000 soldiers.

Global Snapshot

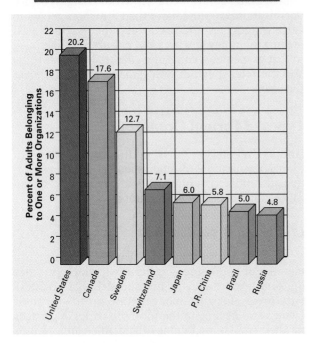

FIGURE 7–3 Membership in Cultural or Educational Organizations
Source: World Values Survey (1994).

features, such as locked doors and barred windows, and are supervised by security personnel (Goffman, 1961). These are settings that segregate people as "inmates" or "patients" for a period of time and sometimes radically alter their attitudes and behavior. Recall from Chapter 5 ("Socialization") the power of *total institutions* to transform a human being's overall sense of self.

From differing vantage points, any particular organization may fall into *all* these categories. A psychiatric hospital, for example, serves as a coercive organization for a patient, a utilitarian organization for a psychiatrist, and a normative organization for a part-time hospital volunteer.

Origins of Bureaucracy

Formal organizations date back thousands of years. Elites who governed early empires relied on government officials to extend their power over millions of people and vast geographical regions. Formal organization allowed these rulers to collect taxes, undertake military campaigns, and construct monumental structures, from the Great Wall of China to the pyramids of Egypt.

The power of these early organizations was limited, however, not because elites lacked grandiose ambition, but by the traditional character of preindustrial societies. Typically, cultural patterns placed greater importance on preserving the past or carrying out "God's will" than on organizational efficiency. Only in the last few centuries did there emerge what Max Weber called a "rational world view," as described in Chapter 4 ("Society"). In the wake of the Industrial Revolution, the organizational structure called *bureaucracy* became commonplace in Europe and North America.

Characteristics of Bureaucracy

Bureaucracy is *an organizational model rationally designed to perform complex tasks efficiently*. In a bureaucratic business or government agency, officials deliberately enact and revise policy to make the organization as efficient as possible. To appreciate the power and scope of bureaucratic organization, consider that any one of 150 million phones in the United States can connect you, within seconds, to any other phone—in homes, businesses, automobiles, even in the middle of a baseball field. Such instant communication is beyond the imagination of those who lived in the ancient world.

Of course, the telephone system depends on technological developments such as electricity, fiber optics, and computers. But neither could the system exist without the organizational capacity to keep track of every telephone call—noting which phone called which other phone, when, and for how long—and presenting all this information to tens of millions of telephone users in the form of monthly bills.

What specific traits promote organizational efficiency? Max Weber (1978; orig. 1921) identified six key elements of the ideal bureaucratic organization.

1. **Specialization.** Through most of human history, everyone pursued the basic goals of securing food and shelter. Bureaucracy, by contrast, assigns to individuals highly specialized duties.

2. **Hierarchy of offices.** Bureaucracies arrange personnel in a vertical hierarchy of offices. Each person is thus supervised by "higher-ups" in the organization while, in turn, supervising others in lower positions.

DISCUSS: Throughout history, people favored "their own kind" (especially kin). A bureaucratic culture erodes ascription in favor of achievement so that favoring kin is transformed into "conflict of interest" and "nepotism." Is nepotism ever justified?

NOTE: Photocopier machines, now essential to bureaucratic organizations, first appeared in the 1950s. Many people were skeptical that they would catch on.

NOTE: Note the rapid growth of the membership of the American Sociological Association: *1910, 256; 1920, 1,021; 1930, 1,530; 1940, 1,034; 1950, 3,241; 1960, 6,875; 1970, 14,156; 1980, 13,304; 1995, 13,000.* In the 1960s, the ASA had 2 employees; today, it has 25. The ASA did not respond to several requests for data about the rising level of dues over time.

Although formal organization is vital to modern, industrial societies, it is far from new. Twenty-five centuries ago, the Chinese philosopher and teacher K'ung Fu-Tzu (known to Westerners as Confucius) endorsed the idea that government offices should be filled by the most talented young men. This led to what was probably the world's first system of civil service examinations. Here, would-be bureaucrats compose essays to demonstrate their knowledge of Confucian texts.

3. **Rules and regulations.** Cultural tradition holds scant sway in bureaucracy. Instead, operations are guided by rationally enacted rules and regulations. These rules control not only the organization's own functioning but, as much as possible, its larger environment. Ideally, a bureaucracy seeks to operate in a completely predictable fashion.

4. **Technical competence.** A bureaucratic organization expects officials to have the technical competence to carry out their official duties. Bureaucracies regularly monitor the performance of staff members. Such impersonal evaluation based on performance contrasts sharply with the custom, followed through most of human history, of favoring relatives—whatever their talents—over strangers.

5. **Impersonality.** In bureaucratic organizations, rules take precedence over personal whim. This impersonality encourages uniform treatment for each client as well as other workers. From this detached approach stems the notion of the "faceless bureaucrat."

6. **Formal, written communications.** An old adage states that the heart of bureaucracy is not people but paperwork. Rather than casual, verbal communication, bureaucracy relies on formal, written memos and reports. Over time, this correspondence accumulates into vast *files*. These files guide the subsequent operation of an organization in roughly the same way that social background shapes the life of an individual.

TABLE 7–2 Small Groups and Formal Organizations: A Comparison

	Small Groups	Formal Organizations
Activities	Members typically engage in many of the same activities	Members typically engage in distinct, highly specialized activities
Hierarchy	Often informal or nonexistent	Clearly defined, corresponding to offices
Norms	Informal application of general norms	Clearly defined rules and regulations
Criteria for membership	Variable, often based on personal affection or kinship	Technical competence to carry out assigned tasks
Relationships	Variable; typically primary	Typically secondary, with selective primary ties
Communications	Typically casual and face to face	Typically formal and in writing
Focus	Person oriented	Task oriented

These traits represent a clear contrast to the more personal character of small groups. Bureaucratic organization promotes efficiency by carefully recruiting personnel and limiting the unpredictable effects of personal tastes and opinions. In smaller, informal groups, members allow one another considerable discretion in their behavior; they respond to each other personally and regard everyone as more or less equal in rank. Table 7–2 summarizes the differences between small social groups and large formal organizations.

The Informal Side of Bureaucracy

Weber's ideal bureaucracy deliberately regulates every activity. In actual organizations, however, human beings have the creativity (or the stubbornness) to resist conforming to bureaucratic blueprints. Sometimes informality helps to meet a legitimate need overlooked by formal regulations. In other situations informality may amount to simply cutting corners in one's job (Scott, 1981).

In principle, power resides in offices, not with the people who occupy them. Nonetheless, the personalities of officials greatly affect patterns of leadership. For example, studies of U.S. corporations document that the qualities and quirks of individuals—including personal charisma and interpersonal skills—have a tremendous impact on organizational outcomes (Halberstam, 1986).

Authoritarian, democratic, and laissez-faire types of leadership—described earlier in this chapter—also reflect individual personality as much as any organizational plan. Then, too, in the "real world" of organizations, leaders and their cronies sometimes seek to benefit personally through abuse of organizational power. And perhaps even more commonly, leaders take credit for the efforts of their subordinates. Many secretaries, for example, have far more authority and responsibility than their official job titles and salaries suggest (Yenerall et al., 1994).

Communication offers another example of how informality creeps into large organizations. Formally, memos and other written communications disseminate information through the hierarchy. Typically, however, individuals cultivate informal networks or "grapevines" that spread information much faster, if not always accurately. Grapevines are particularly important to subordinates because high officials often attempt to conceal important information from them.

Throughout the hierarchy, employees modify or ignore rigid bureaucratic structures for a host of reasons. A classic study of the Western Electric factory in Chicago revealed that few employees reported fellow workers who violated rules, as the company required (Roethlisberger & Dickson, 1939). On the contrary, workers took action against those who *did* blow the whistle on their colleagues, shunning them as "squealers." Although the company formally set productivity standards, workers informally created their own definition of a fair day's work, criticizing those who exceeded it as "rate-busters" and those who fell short as "chiselers."

Such informal social structures suggest that people act to personalize rigidly defined social situations. This leads us to take a closer look at some of the problems of bureaucracy.

Problems of Bureaucracy

Despite our reliance on bureaucracy to manage countless dimensions of everyday life, many members of our society are ambivalent about this organizational form. The following sections review several of the problems associated with bureaucracy, ranging from its tendency

Q: "The impersonal treatment of affairs which are at times of great personal significance to the client gives rise to the charge of 'arrogance' and 'haughtiness' of the bureaucrat." Robert K. Merton (1968:256)

NOTE: Evidence of bureaucracy's pervasiveness: *Federal Tax Regulations 1994* is 6,500 pages. The annual Chrysler Corp. tax return is a paper pile 6 feet tall—the work of 55 accountants.

Q: "The bureaucratic structure exerts a constant pressure upon the official to be methodical, prudent, disciplined . . . This may be exaggerated to the point where primary concern with conformity to the rules interferes with the achievement of the purposes of the organization." Robert K. Merton (1968:252–53)

NOTE: "Pedantry," slavish attention to rules, has the Latin root *ped*, meaning "foot," implying a servile follower.

to dehumanize and alienate individuals to the threats it poses to personal privacy and political democracy.

Bureaucratic Alienation

Max Weber touted bureaucracy as a model of productivity. Nonetheless, Weber was keenly aware of bureaucracy's potential to *dehumanize* those it purports to serve. That is, the same impersonality that fosters efficiency simultaneously denies officials and clients the ability to respond to each other's unique, personal needs. On the contrary, officials must treat each client impersonally as a standard "case."

The impersonal bureaucratic environment, then, gives rise to *alienation*. All too often, Weber contended, formal organizations reduce the human being to "a small cog in a ceaselessly moving mechanism" (1978:988; orig. 1921). The trend toward more and more formal organization, therefore, left him deeply pessimistic about the future of humankind. Although formal organizations are designed to benefit humanity, he feared that humanity might well end up serving formal organizations.

Bureaucratic Inefficiency and Ritualism

Then there is the familiar problem of inefficiency, the failure of a bureaucratic organization to carry out the work it was created to perform. Perhaps the greatest challenge to a large, formal organization is responding to special needs or circumstances. Anyone who has ever tried to replace a lost driver's license, return defective merchandise to a discount store, or change an address on a magazine subscription knows that bureaucracies sometimes can be maddeningly unresponsive.

The problem of inefficiency is captured in the concept of *red tape* (a phrase derived from the red tape used by eighteenth-century English administrators to wrap official parcels and records; Shipley, 1985). Red tape refers to a tedious preoccupation with organizational routines and procedures. Sociologist Robert Merton (1968) points out that red tape amounts to a new twist on the already-familiar concept of group conformity. He coined the term **bureaucratic ritualism** to designate *a preoccupation with rules and regulations to the point of thwarting an organization's goals.*

Ritualism impedes individual and organizational performance as it stifles creativity and imagination. In part, ritualism emerges because organizations, which pay modest, fixed salaries, give officials little or no financial stake in performing efficiently. Then, too, bureaucratic ritualism stands as another expression of

According to Max Weber, bureaucracy is an organizational strategy that promotes efficiency. Impersonality, however, also fosters alienation among employees, who may become indifferent to the formal goals of the organization. The behavior of this municipal employee in Bombay, India, is understandable to members of formal organizations almost anywhere in the world.

the alienation that Weber feared would arise from bureaucratic rigidity (Whyte, 1957; Merton, 1968; Coleman, 1990; Kiser & Schneider, 1994).

Bureaucratic Inertia

If bureaucrats sometimes have little motivation to be efficient, they certainly have every reason to protect their jobs. Thus, officials typically strive to perpetuate their organization even when its purpose has been fulfilled. As Weber put it, "once fully established, bureaucracy is among the social structures which are hardest to destroy" (1978:987; orig. 1921).

Bureaucratic inertia refers to *the tendency of bureaucratic organizations to perpetuate themselves.* Formal organizations, in other words, tend to take on a life of their own beyond their formal objectives. Occasionally, a formal organization that meets its goals will simply disband—as the anti-British Sons of Liberty did after the American Revolution. More commonly, an organization stays in business by redefining its goals so it can continue to provide a livelihood for its members.

NOTE: Evidence of bureaucracy's expansion: In 1950, 10 million farmers were served by 84,373 employees in the Department of Agriculture (ratio of 118:1); by 1990, the numbers were 2.9 million farmers but 129,000 DOA employees (22:1). Based on rates of growth and decline, by 2060 there will be more bureaucrats than farmers. Put otherwise, between 1950 and 1990, the number of farms fell 60 percent, the number of farmers dropped 70 percent, but the number of farm bureaucrats rose 53 percent (Littmann, 1992).

Q: "It is organization which gives birth to the dominion of the elected over the electors, of the mandatories over the mandators, of the delegates over the delegators. Who says organization says oligarchy." Robert Michels

NOTE: "Oligarchy" is derived from the Greek root *oligo*, meaning "few."

George Tooker's painting Government Bureau *is a powerful statement about the human costs of bureaucracy. The artist depicts members of the public in monotonous similitude—reduced from human beings to mere "cases" to be disposed of as quickly as possible. Set apart from others by their positions, officials are "faceless bureaucrats" concerned more with numbers than with providing genuine assistance (notice that the artist places the fingers of the officials on calculators).*

George Tooker, *Government Bureau*, 1956. Egg tempera on gesso panel, 19 5/8 x 29 5/8 inches. The Metropolitan Museum of Art, George A. Hearn Fund, 1956 (56.78).

For example, consider the history of the National Association for Infantile Paralysis, the sponsor of the well-known March of Dimes (Sills, 1969). This organization came into being as part of the drive to find a cure for polio. This goal was accomplished in the early 1950s when Dr. Jonas Salk developed the polio vaccine. Subsequently, however, the March of Dimes did not close up shop; rather, it redirected its efforts toward other medical problems, such as birth defects, and continues to this day.

Oligarchy

Early in this century, Robert Michels (1876–1936) pointed out the link between bureaucracy and political **oligarchy**, *the rule of the many by the few* (1949; orig. 1911). According to what Michels called "the iron law of oligarchy," the pyramidlike structure of bureaucracy places a few leaders in charge of vast and powerful government organizations.

Preindustrial societies did not possess the organizational means for even the most power-hungry ruler to control everyone. But the power of elites increased with the steady expansion of formal organizations and the development of technology over the centuries.

Max Weber credited bureaucracy's strict hierarchy of responsibility with increasing organizational efficiency. By applying Weber's thesis to the organization of government, Michels reveals that this hierarchical structure concentrates power and thus endangers democracy. While the public expects organizational officials to subordinate personal interests to organizational goals, people who occupy powerful positions can—and often do—use their access to information and the media, plus numerous other advantages, to promote their personal interests. Furthermore, bureaucracy also insulates officials from public accountability, whether in the form of a corporate president who is "unavailable for comment" to the local press or a national president seeking to control information by claiming "executive privilege." Oligarchy, then, thrives in the hierarchical structure of bureaucracy and undermines people's control over their elected leaders (Tolson, 1995).

Political competition and checks and balances in this nation's system of government prevent the flagrant oligarchy found in some countries. In 1974, for example, Richard Nixon was forced to resign as president of the United States, and three presidents since then have been defeated in their bids for reelection. Even so, incumbents enjoy a significant advantage in U.S. politics: The 1994 Congressional elections saw only 37 of 408 congressional office holders running for reelection defeated by their challengers.

Parkinson's Law and the Peter Principle

Finally, and on a lighter note, we acknowledge two additional insights concerning the limitations of bureaucratic organizations. The concerns of C. Northcote Parkinson and Laurence J. Peter are

GLOBAL: As an example of successful opposition to entrenched leaders, Brazilian President Fernando Collor de Mello was impeached in 1993 on corruption charges.

THEN AND NOW: In 1956, the cost of a first-class letter was 17 cents (in 1996 dollars); in 1996, it was 32 cents. Postal employees rose from 560,000 to 774,000 over the same period. Ratio of people to postal employees increased only slightly, from 320:1 to 335:1.

DISCUSS: How much validity does the Peter Principle have? What about "Peter's Corollary" that, eventually, all positions in a large organization will be filled with incompetents?

Q: "Specialists without spirit, sensualists without heart; this nullity imagines that it has attained a level of civilization never before achieved." Max Weber (1958:182; orig. 1904–5)

FIGURE 7–4

U.S. Managers by Race, Sex, and Ethnicity, 1995

Source: U.S. Equal Employment Opportunity Commission (1996) and Census Bureau (1996).

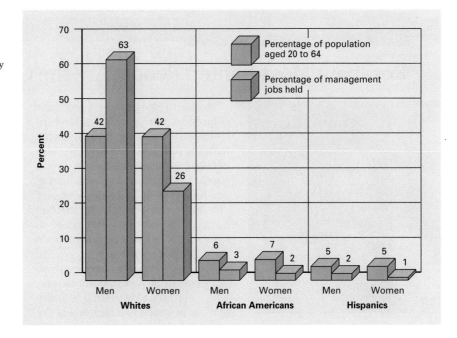

familiar to anyone who has ever been a part of a formal organization.

Parkinson (1957) summed up his understanding of bureaucratic inefficiency with the assertion: *"Work expands to fill the time available for its completion."* Enough truth underlies this tongue-in-cheek assertion that it is known today as Parkinson's Law. To illustrate, assume that a bureaucrat working at the Division of Motor Vehicles processes fifty driver's license applications in an average day. If one day this worker had only twenty-five applications to examine, how much time would the task require? The logical answer is half a day. But Parkinson's Law suggests that if a full day is available to complete the work, a full day is how long it will take.

Because organizational employees have little personal involvement in their jobs, few are likely to seek extra work to fill their spare time. Bureaucrats do strive to *appear* busy, however, and their apparent activity often prompts organizations to take on more employees. The added time and expense required to hire, train, supervise, and evaluate a larger staff make everyone busier still, setting in motion a vicious cycle that results in *bureaucratic bloat*. Ironically, the larger organization may accomplish no more real work than it did before.

In the same light-hearted spirit as Parkinson, Laurence J. Peter (Peter & Hull, 1969) devised the Peter Principle: *"Bureaucrats rise to their level of incompetence."* The logic here is simple: Employees competent at one level of the organizational hierarchy are likely to earn promotion to higher positions. Eventually, however, they will reach a position where they are in over their heads; there, they perform poorly and thus are no longer eligible for promotions.

Reaching their level of incompetence dooms officials to a future of inefficiency. Adding to the problem, after years in the office they have almost certainly learned how to avoid demotion by hiding behind rules and regulations and taking credit for work actually performed by their more competent subordinates.

Gender and Race in Organizations

Rosabeth Moss Kanter, introduced in the box, has analyzed how ascribed statuses such as gender and race figure in the power structure of bureaucratic hierarchies. To the extent that an organization has a dominant social composition, the gender- or race-based ingroup enjoys greater social acceptance, respect, credibility, and access to informal social networks.

As Figure 7–4 shows, white men in the United States represent about 42 percent of the U.S. population between the ages of twenty and sixty-four but hold 63 percent of management jobs. White women, a category of comparable size, trail with about 26 percent of managerial positions (U.S. Equal Employment

RESOURCE: An excerpt from Sally Helgesen's *The Female Advantage* is among the contemporary selections found in the Macionis and Benokraitis reader *Seeing Ourselves*.

DIVERSITY: A growing number of women are trying to resolve role conflicts by leaving organizational jobs ("cashing out") and starting their own small businesses; 400,000 women did so in 1990.

Q: "Bureaucratic organization has usually come into power on the basis of a leveling of economic and social differences." Max Weber

DISCUSS: An interesting question: Do women need to learn about organizations or do organizations need to learn about women?

PROFILE

Rosabeth Moss Kanter: People Are the Greatest Resource

How did a woman who began her career in the 1960s studying communes and other utopian settlements end up shaping the real-world decisions of some of the most successful U.S. corporations? Part of the answer is that many ideas about organizations first raised in the 1960s have now found a receptive audience in corporate boardrooms across the country.

Rosabeth Moss Kanter, a professor of business administration at Harvard University, has helped businesses learn to reorganize for greater success and higher profits. For her work, Kanter has been honored with numerous honorary doctoral degrees, and she has been profiled in various national publications. Her achievements rank her among our nation's most influential women.

Kanter divides her career between academic duties and Goodmeasure, Inc., a corporate consulting firm she and her husband founded. She is the author of several widely read books that apply sociological insights to the task of making corporations more effective.

What lessons does Kanter offer corporate executives that warrant fees as high as $15,000 for a single appearance? She challenges conventional organizational wisdom by demonstrating that *people*—not technology or machinery—are a corporation's most important resource, and by calling on

companies to develop the potential of their employees. Reflecting on her career, Kanter explains:

> I remember when participation was what was being talked about on college campuses by Vietnam war protesters or people looking for student power. Now it's a respectable concept in corporate America, and now very large companies are figuring out how to divide themselves into small units. Many ideas and values of the '60s have been translated into the workplace. Take, for example, the right of workers to free expression, the desirability of participation and teamwork, the idea that authority should not be obeyed unquestioningly, the idea that smaller can be better because it can create ownership and family feeling. All of these are now mainstream ideas.

Sources: Murray (1984) and McHenry (1985).

Opportunity Commission, 1996). The members of various minorities lag further behind, even taking account of their smaller populations.

A smaller representation in the workplace, argues Kanter, may leave women, people of color, and those from economically disadvantaged backgrounds feeling like members of socially isolated outgroups. They are often uncomfortably visible, taken less seriously, and given fewer chances for promotion. Understandably, minorities themselves often end up thinking that they must work twice as hard as those in dominant categories to maintain their present position, let alone advance to a higher position (Kanter, 1977; Kanter & Stein, 1979).

Kanter (1977) finds that providing a structure of unequal opportunities has important consequences for

everyone's on-the-job performance. A company with many "dead-end" jobs, she explains, only encourages workers to become "zombies" with little aspiration, poor self-concept, and little loyalty to the organization. Widespread opportunity, by contrast, motivates employees, turning them into "fast-trackers" with higher aspirations, greater self-esteem, and stronger commitment to the organization.

Finally, Kanter claims that in a corporate environment with wide-open opportunity for advancement, leaders value the input of subordinates and seek to bolster their morale and well-being. It is officials with no real power, she maintains, who jealously guard their own privileges and rigidly ride herd over subordinates.

Organizational research in recent years has also spotlighted differences in management styles linked to gender. Deborah Tannen (1994) claims, for example, that women have a greater "information focus," and more readily ask questions in order to understand an issue. Men, she maintains, share an "image focus" that makes them hesitate in the same situation, wondering what effect asking questions will have on their reputation. In another study of women executives, Sally Helgesen (1990) notes three additional gender-linked patterns. First, women tend to share information more than men do; that is, they "stay involved" and place greater value on communication skills. Second, women are more flexible in their approach to leadership and typically allow subordinates greater autonomy. Third, Helgesen notes, rather than emphasizing a narrow specialization, women are attentive to the interconnectedness of all organizational operations. Because many of today's leading business organizations operate more democratically and seek flexibility in order to contend with complex environments, Helgesen concludes that women bring a "female advantage" to the workplace.

In sum, one key conclusion drawn from recent research is that organizations that become more open and adaptable bring out the best in their employees. The flip side of this trend—in which women are playing a major part—is that, when allowed a more flexible environment, employees best serve the organization.

Humanizing Bureaucracy

Humanizing bureaucracy means *fostering a more democratic organizational atmosphere that recognizes and encourages the contributions of everyone.* Research by Kanter (1977, 1983, 1989; Kanter & Stein, 1980) and others (Peters & Waterman, Jr., 1982) suggests that "humanizing" bureaucracy produces both happier employees and healthier profits. Based on the discussion so far, we can identify three paths to a more humane organizational structure.

1. **Social inclusiveness.** The social composition of the organization should, ideally, make no one feel "out of place" because of gender, race, or ethnicity. The performance of all employees will improve to the extent that no one is subject to social exclusion.
2. **Sharing of responsibilities.** When organizations ease rigid organizational structures, they spread power and responsibility more widely. Managers cannot benefit from the ideas of employees who have no channels for expressing their opinions. Knowing that superiors are open to suggestions

encourages all employees to think creatively, increasing organizational effectiveness.
3. **Expanding opportunities for advancement.** Expanding opportunity reduces the number of employees stuck in routine, dead-end jobs with little motivation to perform well. The organization should give employees at all levels a chance to share ideas and try new approaches, defining everyone's job as the start of an upward career path.

Kanter's work takes a fresh look at the concept of bureaucracy and its application to business organizations. Rigid formality may have made sense in the past, when organizations hired unschooled workers primarily to perform physical labor. But today's educated work force can contribute a wealth of ideas to bolster organizational efficiency—if the organization encourages and rewards innovation.

There is broad support for the idea that loosening up rigid organizations improves performance. Moreover, companies that treat employees as a resource to be developed rather than as a group to be controlled stand out as more profitable. But some critics challenge Kanter's claim that social heterogeneity necessarily yields greater productivity. In controlled comparisons, they maintain, it is homogeneous work groups that typically produce more, while heterogeneous groups are better at generating a diversity of ideas and approaches. Optimal working groups, then, appear to be those that strike a balance: Team members bring to the decision-making process a variety of backgrounds and perspectives yet are similar enough in outlook and goals to effectively coordinate their efforts (Hackman, 1988; Yeatts, 1994).

Self-Managed Work Teams

At mid-century, formal organizations in the United States typically were conventional bureaucracies, run from the top down according to a stern chain of command. Today, especially as U.S. businesses face growing global competition, rigid structures are breaking down. One important element of this trend is the increasing use of the *self-managed work team*. Members of these small groups have the skills necessary to carry out tasks with minimal supervision. By allowing employees to operate within autonomous groups, organizations enhance worker involvement in the job, generate a broader understanding of operations, and raise employee morale. A few U.S. corporations (such as Procter & Gamble) have had autonomous work units since the 1960s. In recent years, many more (including

The recent trend is toward breaking down the rigid structure of conventional bureaucracy. One example of more flexible organizational form is the self-managed work team, whose members have the skills to carry out their tasks creatively and with minimal supervision.

Ford, General Motors, Boeing, Caterpillar, and Digital Equipment) are following suit.

Even though it is difficult to compare the performance of organizations with disparate goals and operations, research indicates that self-managed work teams do boost productivity while heading off some of the problems—including alienation—of the traditional bureaucratic model. In the business world, many companies have found that decentralizing responsibility in this way also raises product quality and lowers rates of employee absenteeism and turnover (Yeatts, 1991, 1995; Maddox, 1995).

Organizational Environment

How any organization performs depends not only on its internal structure but also on the **organizational environment**, *a range of factors external to an organization*

that affects its operation. Such factors include technology, politics, population patterns, the economy, as well as other organizations.

Technology is especially critical in the modern organizational environment. We have already noted that today's organizations could hardly exist without the communications links provided by telephone systems and facsimile (fax) machines and the ability to duplicate, process, and store information afforded by copiers and computers.

Technological changes currently under way are likely to have two somewhat contradictory consequences for organizational structure. On the one hand, the proliferation of personal computers and fax machines affords employees unprecedented access to information; this may produce some leveling in the traditional hierarchy by which top officials kept information and decision making to themselves. On the other hand, computer technology also enables organizational leaders to monitor the activities of workers more closely than ever before (Markoff, 1991).

A second dimension of the organizational environment is *politics*. Changes in law often have dramatic consequences for the operation of an organization, as many industries have learned in the face of new environmental standards imposed by government. In global perspective, a radical change like the reorganization of the Soviet government in 1991 rippled throughout virtually every organization in that country.

Third, *population patterns*—such as the size and composition of the surrounding populace—also affect organizations. The average age, typical education, and social diversity of a local community shape both the available work force and the market for an organization's products or services.

Fourth, the state of the *economy* figures prominently in an organization's well-being. Businesses in the United States expand or contract along with cycles in the overall economy. Even people's ability to get an organization off the ground depends on the availability of funds, which varies according to economic trends and banking policies (Pennings, 1982). Just as important, rising international competition within the global economy has propelled the drive toward more flexible and efficient organizations.

Fifth, *other organizations*, both here and abroad, also form part of the organizational environment. The people who operate a hospital, for example, must be responsive to doctors' and nurses' associations, unions of other hospital workers, as well as the insurance industry. Similarly, to remain competitive, a hospital

NOTE: The McDonaldization of society extends even to McFunerals. Service Corporation International currently operates 662 funeral homes in 39 states and the corporation is aggressively buying operations overseas. SCI now handles about 10 percent of all funerals in the United States. (Myerson, 1993)

NOTE: There are weak countertrends to McDonaldization. For example, the 20s generation is the most likely of all age cohorts to drink micro-brewed beers—perhaps because they are brewed by local companies that pride themselves on creating distinctive tastes as opposed to the standardized blends of the national giants.

NOTE: The United States averages one fast food restaurant per 10,000 people. Which county has the most? It's Socorro County, N.M., with 6 fast food places for 15,400 people.

must be keenly aware of the kinds of equipment and procedures available at other facilities (Fennell, 1980).

In sum, no organization operates in a social vacuum. But, just as formal organizations are shaped by their environment, organizations themselves have an impact on the surrounding society, as we shall now explain.

The McDonaldization of Society

October 9, 1994, Macau. Here we are halfway around the world in the Portuguese colony of Macau—a little nub jutting from the Chinese coast. Few people here speak English, and life on the streets seems a world apart from the urban rhythms of New York, Chicago, or Los Angeles. Then we turn the corner and stand face to face with (who else?) Ronald McDonald! After eating who-knows-what for so long, forgive our failure to resist the lure of the Big Mac! But the most amazing thing is that the food—the burger, fries, and drinks—looks, smells, and tastes exactly the same as it does back home 10,000 miles away!

As noted in the opening to this chapter, McDonald's has enjoyed enormous success.[1] From a single store in the mid-1950s, McDonald's now operates over 15,000 restaurants in the United States and throughout much of the world. There are more than 850 pairs of golden arches in Japan, for example, and the world's largest McDonald's recently opened for business in China's capital city of Beijing.

McDonald's has become a symbol of our way of life; in fact, one poll found that 98 percent of U.S. school children identified Ronald McDonald, making the gleeful clown as much of a celebrity as Santa Claus. Even more important, the organizational principles that underlie McDonald's are steadily coming to dominate our entire society. Our culture is becoming "McDonaldized"—an awkward way of saying that we now model many aspects of life on the famous restaurant chain. Parents buy toys at worldwide chain stores like Toys 'Я' Us; we drive to Jiffy Lube for a ten-minute oil change; face-to-face communication is giving way more and more to voice mail over the telephone, E-mail via computer, and junk mail at the door; more vacations take the form of resort and tour packages; television presents news in the form of ten-second sound bites; college admissions officers size up students they have never met by glancing over their GPA and SAT scores; and professors assign ghostwritten textbooks[2] and evaluate students with tests mass-produced for them by publishing companies. The list goes on and on.

McDonaldization: Four Principles

What do all these developments have in common? According to George Ritzer, the "McDonaldization of society" involves four basic organizational principles.

1. **Efficiency.** Ray Kroc, the marketing genius behind the expansion of McDonald's, set out with the goal of serving a hamburger, french fries, and a milkshake to a customer in fifty seconds. Today, one of the company's most popular items is the Egg McMuffin, an entire breakfast in a single sandwich. In the restaurant, customers bus their own trays or, better still, drive away from the pickup window taking the packaging and whatever mess they make with them.

   Efficiency is now a value virtually without critics in our society. Almost everyone believes that anything that can be done quickly is, for that reason alone, good.

2. **Calculability.** The first McDonald's operating manual declared the weight of a regular raw hamburger to be 1.6 ounces, its size to be 3.875 inches across, and its fat content to be 19 percent. A slice of cheese weighs exactly half an ounce. Fries are cut precisely 9/32 of an inch thick.

   Think about how many objects around the home, the workplace, or the college campus are designed and mass produced uniformly according to a calculated plan. Not just our environment but our life experiences—from traveling the nation's interstates to sitting at home watching television—are now more deliberately planned than ever before.

3. **Uniformity and predictability.** An individual can walk into a McDonald's restaurant anywhere and receive the same sandwiches, drinks, and desserts prepared in precisely the same way. Predictability,

---

[1]This section draws on George Ritzer's (1993) book of the same name.

[2]Half a dozen popular sociology texts were not authored by the person or persons whose names appear on the cover. This book is not one of them.

of course, is the result of a highly rational system that specifies every course of action and leaves nothing to chance.

4. **Control through automation.** The most unreliable element in the McDonald's system is human beings. People, after all, have good and bad days, sometimes let their minds wander, or simply decide to try something a different way. To eliminate, as much as possible, the unpredictable human element, McDonald's has automated its equipment to cook food at fixed temperatures for set lengths of time. Even the cash register at a McDonald's is little more than pictures of the items so as to minimize the responsibility of the human being taking the customer's order.

The scope of McDonaldization is expanding in the United States. Automatic teller machines are replacing banks, highly automated bakeries now produce bread with scarcely any human intervention, and chickens and eggs (or is it eggs and chickens?) emerge from automated hatcheries. In supermarkets, laser scanners are phasing out (less reliable) human checkers. Most of this country's shopping now occurs in malls, in which everything from temperature and humidity to the kinds of stores and products are subject to continuous control and supervision (Idle & Cordell, 1994).

Can Rationality Be Irrational?

No one would challenge the popularity or the efficiency of McDonald's and similar organizations. But there is another side to the story.

Max Weber viewed the increasing rationalization of the world with alarm, fearing that the expanding control of formal organizations would crush the human spirit. As he saw it, rational systems were efficient, but at the terrible cost of dehumanization. Each of the four principles noted above depends on reining in human creativity, discretion, and autonomy. Moreover, as George Ritzer contends, McDonald's food is not particularly good for people nor is the company's extensive use of packaging good for the natural environment. Taking a broader perspective, Ritzer echoes Weber's concern, asserting that "the ultimate irrationality of McDonaldization is that people could lose control over the system and it would come to control us" (1993:145).

Formal Organizations in Japan

We have described efforts to "humanize" U.S. formal organizations. Interestingly, however, organizations in some countries have long been more personal than those in the United States. Organizations in Japan, a small nation that has had remarkable economic success, thrive within a culture of strong collective identity and solidarity. While most members of our society prize rugged individualism, the Japanese maintain traditions of cooperation.

Because of Japan's social cohesiveness, formal organizations in that society approximate very large primary groups. William Ouchi (1981) highlights five distinctions between formal organizations in Japan and their counterparts in industrial societies of the West. In each case, the Japanese organization reflects that society's more collective orientation. The box considers the prospects of applying these five key principles of Japanese organizations in the United States.

1. **Hiring and advancement**. Organizations in the United States hold out promotions and raises in salary as prizes won through individual competition. In Japanese organizations, however, companies hire new graduates together, and all employees of a particular age cohort receive the same salary and responsibilities. Only after several years is anyone likely to be singled out for individual advancement.

2. **Lifetime security**. Employees in the United States expect to move from one company to another to advance their careers. U.S. companies are also quick to lay off employees when economic setbacks strike. By contrast, most Japanese firms hire employees for life, fostering strong, mutual loyalties among members. Japanese companies avoid layoffs by retraining expendable workers for new jobs in the organization.

3. **Holistic involvement**. U.S. workers tend to see the home and the workplace as distinct spheres. Japanese organizations take a different tack, playing a broad role in their employees' lives by providing home mortgages, sponsoring recreational activities, and scheduling social events. Such interaction beyond the workplace strengthens collective identity and offers the respectful Japanese worker an opportunity to voice suggestions and criticisms informally.

4. **Nonspecialized training**. Bureaucratic organization in the United States is based on specialization; many people spend their entire working life at a single task. From the outset, a Japanese organization trains employees in all phases of its operation, again with the idea that employees will remain with the organization for life.

GLOBAL: In William Ouchi's view, the hierarchical structure of U.S. business encourages leaders here to make quick decisions on their own, which are then tough to implement. By contrast, Japanese corporate executives involve many others early on, which slows the decision-making process, but allows subsequent implementation rapidly.

NOTE: As noted in Chapter 4, worker alienation has been linked to rigid bureaucracy (Weber) and rigid class structure (Marx). Japan has a favorable position in both respects. Japanese workers enjoy greater involvement in a more personalized organizational environment. Additionally, the compensation ratio (management/workers) in Japan is roughly half that in the United States.

GLOBAL SOCIOLOGY

The Japanese Model: Will It Work in the United States?

What the company wants is for us to work like the Japanese. Everybody go out and do jumping jacks in the morning and kiss each other when they go home at night. You work as a team, rat on each other, and lose control of your destiny. That's not going to work in this country.

John Brodie
President, United Paperworkers
Local 448
Chester, Pennsylvania

Who can argue with the economic success of the Japanese? Economic competition from Asia (and, increasingly, from Europe) is forcing U.S. companies to reconsider long-time notions about how corporate organizations should operate.

Among the most interesting examples of new organizations are Japanese manufacturing plants built here in the United States. By and large, these "transplant organizations" have been quite successful in terms of productivity, demonstrating the ability of organizations to both adapt to and modify a new environment. Yet some voices in this country—workers, union leaders, and managers—speak as bitterly about transplanting Japanese organizational techniques as they do about importing Japanese cars.

Manufacturing plants operated in the United States by Honda, Nissan, and Toyota employ more than 250,000 people and have achieved the same high level of efficiency and quality that have won these companies praise in Japan. However, this country has been slow to embrace traditional Japanese practices such as worker participation. Our corporate culture still favors rigid hierarchy, praises individualism and personal achievement, and remembers its long history of labor-management conflict. Such factors make proposals to enhance worker participation controversial.

Some employees in the United States disparage worker participation as a thinly veiled strategy to increase their workload. While still responsible for building cars, for instance, workers would also have to worry about quality control, unit costs, and overall efficiency—concerns usually shouldered

To a large extent, organizational life reflects the surrounding culture. But, stirred by the economic power of Japanese corporations, more and more workers in the United States are employing some of Japan's organizational techniques, such as quality control groups. However, few experts think that organizational patterns can be easily transplanted from one society to another.

by management. Moreover, some employees see the broad training favored by the Japanese as a demanding routine of moving from job to job, always having to learn new skills. Many union leaders also are suspicious of new plans formulated by management, fearing that any alliance of workers and managers may undermine union strength. Some managers, too, look cautiously on worker participation programs. Sharing with employees the power to direct production and even schedule vacations does not come easily in light of past practices. Finally, U.S. corporations concentrate on achieving short-term profits, a focus which discourages investing time and money in organizational restructuring.

Primarily due to rising global competition, however, worker participation programs are slowly changing the U.S. workplace. A recent government survey found that 70 percent of large businesses had initiated at least some reforms of this kind. The advantages go right to the bottom line: Productivity and profits are usually higher when workers have a say in decision making. And most employees in worker-participation programs—even those who may not want to sign up for morning jumping jacks—seem happier about their jobs. Workers who have long used only their bodies are now enjoying the opportunity to use their minds as well.

Sources: Hoerr (1989) and Florida & Kenney (1991).

SOCIAL SURVEY: "Should employers be allowed or not allowed to _____" (*Time* poll, 1991)
"listen in on employee telephone conversations" (*Yes*, 6%; *No*, 93%)
"scan the work area with video cameras" (*Yes*, 38%; *No*, 56%)
"require employees to take drug tests" (*Yes*, 76%; *No*, 19%)
Q: "Mind your own business." Phrase appearing on the first coin minted in the United States in 1778.

SOCIAL SURVEY: "How concerned are you about threats to your personal privacy in America today?" (GSS 1982, N = 1,506; *Codebook*, 1994:251)

"Very concerned"   44.6%   "Not concerned at all"   10.9%
"Somewhat concerned"   28.6%   DK/NR   1.5%
"Only a little concerned" 14.4%

Controversy & Debate

Are Large Organizations Threatening Personal Privacy?

Throughout this chapter, we have highlighted the dual character of formal organizations: They enable our society to operate predictably and efficiently while simultaneously invading our lives and manipulating us. So as bureaucracy has expanded in the United States, privacy has declined.

This problem reflects the enormous power of large organizations, their tendency to treat people impersonally, and their practice of collecting information. In recent decades, the threat to privacy has increased as organizations have acquired computers and high-technology surveillance equipment.

Consider the myriad ways in which organizations compile personal information. As they issue driver's licenses, for example, state agencies generate files that they can dispatch to police or other officials at the touch of a button. Similarly, the Internal Revenue Service, the Social Security Administration, regulatory agencies of all kinds, and government programs that benefit veterans, students, the poor, and unemployed people all collect extensive information.

The same kind of data collection is taking place in the private sector. The growth of credit in the U.S. economy has been explosive, with people now carrying 1 billion credit cards (more than five per adult, on average). Such a system is necessary if we are to receive credit from total strangers. But one cost of this convenience is proliferating data banks filled with highly personal information, including our salaries, the cost of our homes, and our debt histories.

We also experience the erosion of privacy in the surveillance cameras that monitor more and more public places, along main street, in shopping malls, and even across college campuses. And then there is the escalating amount of junk mail—now half of all documents the post office delivers. Mailing lists for this material grow exponentially as one company sells our names and addresses to others. Bought a new car recently? If so, you probably have found yourself on the mailing lists of companies that market all kinds of automotive products. Have you ever rented an X-rated video? Many video stores keep records of the movie preferences of customers and pass them along to other businesses whose advertising soon arrives in the mailbox.

Concern about the erosion of privacy in the United States runs high. In response, many states have enacted laws giving citizens the right to examine records about themselves kept by employers, banks, and credit bureaus. The U.S. Privacy Act of 1974 also limits the exchange of personal information among government agencies and permits citizens to examine and correct most government files.

Politics, too, weighs in on this issue. Conservatives denounce the growth of government power, although they treat big business as benign. Liberals take just the opposite approach, condemning big business while favoring expansion of government. Regardless of which political party holds power, citizens' concerns over the erosion of personal privacy will remain strong as new technology continues to alter the character of our lives.

Continue the debate . . .

1. *Look at National Map 7–2. Where are people most concerned about the growing assault on privacy? Can you explain the pattern?*

2. *Have you ever felt your privacy threatened or violated by a large organization? How?*

3. *Do you think government or businesses represent a larger threat to personal privacy? Why?*

Sources: Smith (1979), Dunn (1991), and Miller (1991).

---

5. **Collective decision making.** In the United States, important decisions fall to key executives. Although Japanese leaders also take responsibility for their organization's performance, they involve workers in "quality circles" that seek employee input in any decision that affects them. A closer working relationship is also encouraged by greater economic equality between management and workers. The salary differential between executives and lower-ranking employees is about half that found in the United States.

These characteristics give the Japanese a strong sense of organizational loyalty. The cultural emphasis on *individual* achievement in our society finds its parallel in Japanese *groupism*. By tying their personal interests to those of their company, workers realize their ambitions through the organization.

THE MAP: The more isolated the community, the larger the share of people who fear that big government and big companies are encroaching on our lives. Fears about privacy are greatest among people with moderate incomes who are much more likely to spend a weekend hunting or fishing on their own than taking in a ballgame with friends.

DISCUSS: With regard to social change: Durkheim characterized modernity as a gradual loss of moral bonds (collective conscience) with a concomitant rise of individualism and economic cooperation. But he recognized that modern culture generates limited social cohesion and argued that group membership could enhance social solidarity. But do modern groups exert much moral pull on us?

Seeing Ourselves

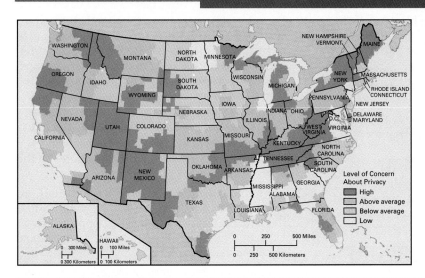

NATIONAL MAP 7–2

Concerns About Privacy Across the United States

At least one in three U.S. adults is concerned about the erosion of privacy. Looking at the map, which details privacy concerns by county, what can you say about people who are most disturbed by this trend? Surprisingly, perhaps, the critics are not big-city residents who avoid eye contact and take refuge in unlisted telephone numbers. Who are they?

Source: *Business Geographics* © 1994 GIS World, Inc., 155 E. Boardwalk Drive, Suite 250, Fort Collins, CO 80525, USA.

GROUPS AND ORGANIZATIONS IN GLOBAL PERSPECTIVE

As this chapter has explained, formal organizations and their surrounding society interact, with each influencing the other. Yet a global perspective reveals that bureaucracy does not take a consistent organizational form; formal organizations in the United States and Japan, for example, differ in significant ways.

Organizations have also changed over time. Several centuries ago, most businesses in Europe and the United States were small, family enterprises. But the Industrial Revolution propelled large, impersonal organizations to the fore. Within this context, officials in Europe and the United States came to define primary relationships at work (such as *nepotism*, favoritism shown to a family member) as an unethical barrier to organizational efficiency.

The development of formal organizations in Japan followed a different route. Historically, that society was even more socially cohesive, organized according to family-based loyalties. As Japan rapidly industrialized, people there did not discard primary relationships as inefficient, as Westerners did. Rather, the Japanese modeled their large businesses on the family, transferring traditional kinship loyalties to corporations.

From our point of view, then, Japan seems to be simultaneously modern and traditional, promoting organizational efficiency by cultivating personal ties. There are indications that Japanese workers are now becoming more individualistic. Yet the Japanese model still demonstrates that organizational life need not be so dehumanizing.

Economically challenged as never before, U.S. businesses are taking a closer look at organizational patterns elsewhere, especially in Japan. In fact, many efforts to humanize bureaucracy in the United States are clear attempts to mimic the Japanese way of doing things.

Beyond the benefits for U.S. business organizations, there is another reason to study the Japanese approach carefully. Our society is less socially cohesive now than the more family-based society Weber knew. A rigidly bureaucratic form of organization only further atomizes the social fabric. Perhaps by following the lead of the Japanese, our own formal organizations can promote—rather than diminish—a sense of collective identity and responsibility.

As some analysts point out, U.S. organizations are still the envy of the world for their productive efficiency; after all, there are few places on earth where the mail arrives as quickly and dependably as in the United States (Wilson, 1991). But the extent of global diversity and change demands that we be cautious about asserting any "absolute truths" about formal organizations and, just as important, that we remain open to new possibilities for reorganizing our future.

SUMMARY

1. Social groups—important building blocks of societies—foster personal development and common identity as well as performing various tasks.

2. Primary groups tend to be small and person oriented; secondary groups are typically large and goal oriented.

3. Instrumental leadership is concerned with realizing a group's goals; expressive leadership focuses on members' collective well-being.

4. The process of group conformity is well documented by researchers. Because members often seek consensus, work groups do not necessarily generate a wider range of ideas than do individuals working alone.

5. Individuals use reference groups—both ingroups and outgroups—to form attitudes and make decisions.

6. Georg Simmel characterized the dyad relationship as intense but unstable; a triad, he noted, can easily dissolve into a dyad by excluding one member.

7. Peter Blau explored how the size, internal homogeneity, relative social parity, and physical segregation of groups all affect members' behavior.

8. Social networks are relational webs that link people who typically have little common identity and limited interaction. The Internet is a vast electronic network linking millions of computers worldwide.

9. Formal organizations are large, secondary groups that seek to perform complex tasks efficiently. According to their members' reasons for joining, formal organizations are classified as utilitarian, normative, or coercive.

10. Bureaucratic organization expands in modern societies to perform many complex tasks efficiently. Bureaucracy is based on specialization, hierarchy, rules and regulations, technical competence, impersonal interaction, and formal, written communications.

11. Ideal bureaucracy may promote efficiency, but bureaucracy also generates alienation and inefficiency, tends to perpetuate itself beyond the achievement of its goals, and contributes to the contemporary erosion of privacy.

12. Formal organizations often mirror oligarchies. Rosabeth Moss Kanter's research has shown that the concentration of power and opportunity in U.S. corporations can compromise organizational effectiveness.

13. Humanizing bureaucracy means recognizing people as an organization's greatest resource. To develop human resources, organizations should spread responsibility and opportunity widely. One way to put this ideal into action is through self-managed work teams.

14. Technology, politics, population patterns, the economy, and other organizations combine to form the environment in which a particular organization must operate.

15. The trend toward "the McDonaldization of society" involves increasing automation and impersonality.

16. Reflecting the collective spirit of Japanese culture, formal organizations in Japan are based on more personal ties than are their counterparts in the United States.

KEY CONCEPTS

bureaucracy an organizational model rationally designed to perform complex tasks efficiently

bureaucratic inertia the tendency of bureaucratic organizations to perpetuate themselves

bureaucratic ritualism a preoccupation with rules and regulations to the point of thwarting an organization's goals

dyad a social group with two members

expressive leadership group leadership that emphasizes collective well-being

formal organization a large secondary group organized to achieve its goals efficiently

groupthink the tendency of group members to conform by adopting a narrow view of some issue

humanizing bureaucracy fostering a more democratic organizational atmosphere that recognizes and encourages the contributions of everyone

ingroup a social group commanding a member's esteem and loyalty

instrumental leadership group leadership that emphasizes the completion of tasks

network a web of social ties that links people who identify and interact little with one another

oligarchy the rule of the many by the few

organizational environment a range of factors external to an organization that affects its operation

outgroup a social group toward which one feels competition or opposition

primary group a small social group in which relationships are both personal and enduring

reference group a social group that serves as a point of reference in making evaluations or decisions

secondary group a large and impersonal social group devoted to some specific interest or activity

social group two or more people who identify and interact with one another

triad a social group with three members

CRITICAL-THINKING QUESTIONS

1. Identify various primary and secondary groups in your own life. What do you like or dislike about each type of setting?

2. What are some of the positive functions of group conformity (for example, fostering team spirit)? Note several dysfunctions.

3. What does the "McDonaldization of society" mean? Cite familiar examples of this trend beyond those discussed in this chapter.

4. How do Japanese organizations differ from those found in the United States? Which organizational type do you prefer? Why?

SUGGESTED READINGS

Classic Sources

George C. Homans. *The Human Group*. New Brunswick, N.J.: Transaction, 1992 (orig. 1950).
This is an early and enduring sociological investigation of the group, the setting for much of our lives.

A. Paul Hare, Edgar F. Borgatta, and Robert F. Bales. *Small Groups: Studies in Social Interaction*. Rev. ed. New York: Alfred A. Knopf, 1965.
This collection of classic contributions to the study of small groups contains important essays by Emile Durkheim, Charles Cooley, Georg Simmel, Solomon Asch, and other notable pioneers in the field.

Contemporary Sources

John P. Walsh. *Supermarkets Transformed: Understanding Organizational and Technological Innovations*. New Brunswick, N.J.: Rutgers University Press, 1993.
Industrial-organizational sociology applies many of this chapter's ideas to the real world of business.

This study illustrates this process by focusing on a familiar setting.

Sally Helgesen. *The Female Advantage: Women's Ways of Leadership*. New York: Doubleday/Currency, 1990.
This intriguing book argues that women typically have a more humanized leadership style that works to the advantage of corporations.

Global Sources

Patricia Caplan. *Class and Gender in India: Women and Their Organizations in a South Indian City*. New York: Tavistock, 1985.
This author analyzes women's associations in the context of national politics in India.

Boye De Mente. *Japanese Etiquette and Ethics in Business*. 5th ed. Lincolnwood, Ill.: NTC Business Books, 1987.
This is one of the best books contrasting formal organizations in the United States with those in Japan.

JOHN NAVA,
2ND OF MAY, 1992, AT LOS ANGELES,
1992

Oil on canvas, 78x108". Collection of Charles Sims,
© John Nava 1997.

Deviance

December 10, 1994,
Casablanca! An
African, European, and
Returning from a stroll
Casablanca, Morocco.
exciting mix of
Middle Eastern cultures.
through the medina, the
medieval section of this coastal, north African city, we confront lines of
police along one of Casablanca's breezy boulevards. Uniformed men stand
between us and the harbor. Their presence has to do with the Islamic conference that has drawn many important leaders to one of the big hotels
nearby. Are the streets closed? No one asks; people seem to halt at an
invisible line some fifty feet from the police officers. I play the brash
urbanite and start across the street to inquire (in broken French) if I
can pass by; but I stop cold as several officers draw a bead on me with
their eyes. Their fingers nervously tap at the grips to their automatic
weapons. This is no time to strike up a conversation.

Every society demands a certain measure of conformity from its members. Sometimes—both in the United States and elsewhere—this process involves the use of armed police. But in the vast majority of cases we conform to cultural patterns for the simple reason that they seem right and natural, part of the reality we inhabit.

This chapter explores many questions dealing with deviance and conformity: Why do societies create cultural norms, including laws, in the first place? Why are some people more likely than others to be accused of violations? To what extent does our country succeed in controlling crime? We begin our investigation by defining several basic concepts.

WHAT IS DEVIANCE?

Deviance is *the recognized violation of cultural norms.* Norms guide virtually all human activities, so the concept of deviance covers a correspondingly broad spectrum. One distinctive category of deviance is **crime**, *the viola-tion of norms a society formally enacts into criminal law.* Even criminal deviance is extensive, ranging from minor traffic violations to serious offenses such as murder. A sub-category of crime, **juvenile delinquency**, refers to *the vio-lation of legal standards by the young.*

Some instances of deviance barely raise eyebrows; other cases command a swift and severe response. Members of our society pay little notice to mild nonconformity like left-handedness or boastfulness; we take a dimmer view of reckless driving or dropping out of school, and we dispatch the police in response to a violent crime like rape.

Not all deviance involves action or even choice. For some categories of individuals, just *existing* may be suffi-cient to provoke condemnation from others. To the young, elderly people sometimes seem hopelessly "out of it"; to whites who are in the majority, the mere presence of people of color may cause discomfort. And affluent people of all ages and races may view the poor as disrep-utable to the extent that they fall short of conventional middle-class standards.

Most examples of nonconformity that come readily to mind are negative instances of rule breaking, such as stealing from a convenience store, neglecting a pet, or driving while intoxicated. But, given our shortcomings, we also define especially righteous people—students who speak up too much in class or people who are enthusias-tic about paying their taxes—as deviant, even if we accord them a measure of respect (Huls, 1987). What deviant actions or attitudes—whether negative or posi-tive—have in common is some evaluation of *difference* that prompts us to regard another person as an "outsider" (Becker, 1966).

Social Control

Because societies have rules, members target each other with efforts at social control. Much of this process is infor-mal, as when we receive praise or criticism from parents, friends, and teachers. Cases of more serious deviance, however, may provoke a response from the **criminal jus-tice system**, *a societal reaction to alleged violations of law utilizing police, courts, and prison officials.*

The kind of deviance people create reflects the moral values they embrace. The Berkeley campus of the University of California has long celebrated its open-minded tolerance of sexual diversity. Thus, in 1992, when Andrew Martinez decided to attend classes wearing virtually nothing, people were reluctant to accuse "The Naked Guy" of immoral conduct. However, in Berkeley's politically correct atmosphere, it was not long before school officials banned Martinez from campus—charging that his nudity constituted a form of sexual harassment.

In sum, deviance is much more than a matter of individual choice or personal failing. *How* a society defines deviance, *whom* individuals brand as deviant, and *what* people decide to do about nonconformity are all issues of social organization. Only gradually, however, have people recognized this essential truth, as we shall now explain.

The Biological Context

Chapter 5 ("Socialization") explained that people a century ago understood—or, more correctly, misunderstood—human behavior as an expression of biological instincts. Understandably, early interest in criminality emphasized biological causes as well. In 1876 Caesare Lombroso (1835–1909), an Italian physician who worked in prisons, declared that criminals have a distinctive physique—low foreheads, prominent jaws and cheekbones, protruding ears, excessive hairiness, and unusually long arms that, taken together, made them resemble the apelike ancestors of human beings.

But Lombroso's work was flawed. Had he looked beyond prison walls, he would have realized that the physical features he attributed exclusively to prisoners actually were found throughout the entire population. We now know that no physical attributes, of the kind described by Lombroso, distinguish criminals from noncriminals (Goring, 1972; orig. 1913).

At midcentury, William Sheldon (1949) took a different tack, positing that body structure might predict criminality. He categorized hundreds of young men in terms of body type and, checking for any criminal history, concluded that delinquency occurred most frequently among boys with muscular, athletic builds. Sheldon Glueck and Eleanor Glueck (1950) confirmed Sheldon's conclusion, but cautioned that a powerful build does not necessarily cause or even predict criminality. The Gluecks postulated that parents treat powerfully built males with greater emotional distance so that they, in turn, grow up to display less sensitivity toward others. Moreover, in a self-fulfilling prophecy, people who expect muscular boys to act like bullies may provoke such aggressive behavior.

Recent genetics research continues to seek possible links between biology and crime. To date, no conclusive evidence connects criminality to any specific genetic flaw. Yet people's overall genetic composition, in combination with social influences, may account for some variation in criminality. In other words, biological factors probably have a real, if modest, effect on whether or not individuals engage in criminal activity (Rowe, 1983; Rowe & Osgood, 1984; Wilson & Herrnstein, 1985; Jencks, 1987).

Critical evaluation. At best, biological theories that trace crime to specific physical traits explain only a small proportion of all crimes. Recent sociobiological research—noting for example, that violent crime is overwhelmingly committed by males or that adults are more likely to abuse foster children than natural children—is promising, but, at this point, we know too little about the links between genes and human behavior to draw any firm conclusions (Daly & Wilson, 1988).

Then, too, because a biological approach spotlights individual behavior, it offers no insight into how

NOTE: Psychology, with its more individualistic orientation, speaks of *personal disorders* rather than *social deviance*.
RESOURCE: Nathaniel Hawthorne's *The Scarlet Letter* is a wonderfully sociological tale of deviance and social control, and of the human spirit courageously emerging from a cloak of conformity.
Q: "When everyone is out to get you, paranoia is quite normal." Johnny Fever

GLOBAL: Although tattoos are widely viewed as deviant in our society, Polynesians regard such skin decoration as a symbol of high social standing. Similarly, even the incest taboo (although universal) has variable kinship application.
GLOBAL: In 17th-century England, not attending church was a crime; in the United States today, attending worship services is free from government mandate.

some kinds of behaviors come to be defined as deviant in the first place. Therefore, although human biology may affect behavior, research currently places far greater emphasis on social influences (Gibbons & Krohn, 1986; Liska, 1991).

Personality Factors

Like biological theories, psychological explanations of deviance focus on cases of individual abnormality, this time involving personality. Some personality traits are hereditary, but most psychologists believe that temperament is shaped primarily by social experiences. Episodes of deviance, then, are viewed as the product of "unsuccessful" socialization.

The work of Walter Reckless and Simon Dinitz (1967) illustrates the psychological approach. These researchers began by asking teachers to categorize twelve-year-old boys as either likely or unlikely to engage in juvenile delinquency. Interviews with both categories of boys and their mothers allowed them to assess each boy's self-concept and how well he related to others. Analyzing their results, they concluded that the "good boys" displayed a strong conscience (or superego, in Sigmund Freud's terminology), coped well with frustration, and identified positively with cultural norms and values. The "bad boys," by contrast, had a weaker conscience, showed little tolerance for frustration, and felt less in tune with conventional culture.

Furthermore, the researchers found that the "good boys" went on to have fewer contacts with the police than the "bad boys." Since all the boys Reckless and Dinitz studied lived in areas where delinquency was widespread, the investigators attributed the tendency to stay out of trouble to a personality that reined in impulses toward deviance. Based on this conclusion, Reckless and Dinitz call their analysis *containment theory.*

Critical evaluation. Psychologists have demonstrated that personality patterns have some connection to delinquency and other types of deviance. Nevertheless, the value of this approach is limited by one key fact: The vast majority of serious crimes are committed by people whose psychological profiles are *normal.*

In sum, both biological and psychological approaches view deviance as an individual attribute without exploring how conceptions of right and wrong initially arise, why people define some rule breakers but not others as deviant, and the role of social power in shaping a society's system of social control. We now

turn to these issues by delving into sociological explanations of deviance.

The Social Foundations of Deviance

Although we tend to think of deviance in terms of the free choice or personal failings of individuals, all behavior—deviance as well as conformity—is shaped by society. There are three social foundations of deviance, identified below.

1. **Deviance varies according to cultural norms.** No thought or action is inherently deviant; it becomes deviant only in relation to particular norms. The life patterns of rural Vermonters, small-town Texans, and urban Californians differ in significant ways; for this reason, what people in each area prize or scorn varies as well. Laws, too, differ from place to place. Texans, for example, can legally consume alcohol in a car, a practice that draws the attention of police in most other states. Casinos entice high rollers in Atlantic City, New Jersey, Las Vegas, Nevada, on Mississippi riverboats, and at several Indian reservations; gambling is illegal everywhere else in the United States. Furthermore, most cities and towns have at least one unique statute: Only in Seattle, for example, is a person suffering from the flu subject to arrest simply for appearing in public.

    In global context, deviance is even more diverse. Albania outlaws any public display of religious faith, such as "crossing" oneself; Cuba can prosecute its citizens for "consorting with foreigners"; police can arrest people in Singapore for selling chewing gum; U.S. citizens risk arrest by their own government for traveling to Libya or Iraq.

2. **People become deviant as others define them that way.** Each of us violates cultural norms regularly, occasionally to the extent of breaking the law. For example, most of us have at some time walked around talking to ourselves or "borrowed" supplies, such as pens and paper, from the workplace. Whether such activities are sufficient to define us as mentally ill or criminal depends on how others perceive, define, and respond to any given situation.

3. **Both rule making and rule breaking involve social power.** The law, Karl Marx asserted, amounts to little more than a strategy by which powerful people protect their interests. For example, the owners of an unprofitable factory have a

DISCUSS: Fashion is a matter of changing conceptions of conformity and deviance. Look ahead to Chapter 23 to the five photos showing changing hair styles in the United States over recent decades. Ask students about the significance they attach to small fashion details: Recall that baseball caps became popular one year then were worn backwards the next.

Q: "I can resist everything except temptation." Oscar Wilde

Q: "Crime is normal because a society exempt from it is utterly impossible." Emile Durkheim (1964:67)

Q: "Crime, then, is necessary; it is bound up with the fundamental conditions of all social life and by that very fact it is useful, because these conditions of which it is a part are themselves indispensable to the normal evolution of morality and law." Emile Durkheim (1964:70)

Artists have an important function in any society: to explore alternatives to conventional notions about how to live. For this reason, while we celebrate artists' creativity, we also accord them a mildly deviant identity. In today's more conservative political climate, some government officials have objected to art that seems to challenge traditional morality. When Cincinnati city officials moved to block the display of photographs by controversial photographer Robert Mapplethorpe, artists publicly displayed their displeasure.

legal right to close their business, even if doing so throws thousands of people out of work. But if workers commit an act of vandalism that closes the same factory for a single day, they are subject to criminal prosecution. Similarly, a homeless person who stands on a street corner denouncing the city government risks arrest for disturbing the peace; a mayoral candidate during an election campaign does exactly the same thing while receiving extensive police protection. In short, norms and their application are linked to social inequality.

STRUCTURAL-FUNCTIONAL ANALYSIS

We now turn to the structural-functional paradigm, which reveals how deviance contributes to a social system and underlies the operation of society.

Emile Durkheim: The Functions of Deviance

In his pioneering study of deviance, Emile Durkheim (1964a, orig. 1895; 1964b, orig. 1893) made the remarkable assertion that there is nothing abnormal about deviance; in fact, it performs four functions essential to society.

1. **Deviance affirms cultural values and norms.** Culture involves moral choices: Unless our lives dissolve into chaos, people prefer some attitudes and behaviors to others. But any conception of virtue rests upon an opposing notion of vice. Just as there can be no good without evil, then, there can be no justice without crime. Deviance, in short, is indispensable to the process of generating and sustaining morality.

2. **Responding to deviance clarifies moral boundaries.** By defining some individuals as deviant, people draw a social boundary between right and wrong. For example, a college marks the line between academic honesty and cheating by disciplining those who commit plagiarism.

3. **Responding to deviance promotes social unity.** People typically react to serious deviance with collective outrage. In doing so, Durkheim explained, they reaffirm the moral ties that bind them. For example, most members of our society joined together in a chorus of condemnation after a terrorist bombed the federal building in Oklahoma City in 1995.

4. **Deviance encourages social change.** Deviant people, Durkheim claimed, push a society's moral boundaries, suggesting alternatives to the status quo and encouraging change. Moreover, he

DISCUSS: Critics blasted rock and roll in the 1950s (Elvis Presley and the Everly Brothers) for undermining morality. Today, of course, rock and roll is mainstream music. Given the increasingly outrageous character of rockers today, ask class members if they find any deviance in contemporary rock music.
RESOURCE: A selection from Durkheim on crime is included in the Macionis and Benokraitis reader, *Seeing Ourselves*.

Q: "I try to avoid temptation, unless I can't resist it." Mae West
DISCUSS: Andres Serrano, who created "Piss Christ," a photograph of a crucifix submerged in the photographer's own urine, maintains that art exerts its greatest power when it is most provocative. Is his work art or obscenity?
Q: "Puritanism is the lurking fear that someone, somewhere, may be happy." H. L. Mencken

declared, today's deviance sometimes becomes tomorrow's morality (1964a:71). In the 1950s, for example, many people denounced rock-and-roll music as a threat to the morals of youth and an affront to traditional musical tastes. Since then, however, rock-and-roll has been swept up in the musical mainstream, becoming a multibillion-dollar industry more "all-American" than apple pie.

An Illustration: The Puritans of Massachusetts Bay

Kai Erikson's (1966) historical investigation of the early Puritans of Massachusetts Bay illustrates Durkheim's analysis. Erikson showed that even the Puritans—a disciplined and highly religious group—created deviance to clarify their moral boundaries. In fact, Durkheim might well have had the Puritans in mind when he wrote:

> Imagine a society of saints, a perfect cloister of exemplary individuals. Crimes, properly so called, will there be unknown; but faults which appear [insignificant] to the layman will create there the same scandal that the ordinary offense does in ordinary consciousness. . . . For the same reason, the perfect and upright man judges his smallest failings with a severity that the majority reserve for acts more truly in the nature of an offense. (1964a:68–69)

Deviance, in short, is not a matter of how good or bad individuals are; it is a necessary product of social living.

But the *kind* of deviance a society condemns depends on the moral issues members of that society seek to clarify. Over time, the Puritans confronted a number of "crime waves." In responding to them, the Puritans sharpened their views on crucial moral quandaries. Thus, they answered questions about how much dissent to allow or what their religious goals should be by celebrating some of their members while branding others as deviants.

And, perhaps most fascinating of all, Erikson discovered that, even though the offenses changed, the Puritans declared a consistent proportion of their number as deviant over time. This stability, concludes Erikson, confirms Durkheim's contention that deviants serve as ethical markers, outlining a society's changing moral boundaries. By constantly defining a small number of people as deviant, in sum, Puritan society ensured that the social functions of deviance were carried out.

No social class stands apart from others as being either criminal or free from criminality. According to various sociologists, however, people with less stake in society and their own future typically exhibit less resistance to some kinds of deviance. Photographer Stephen Shames captured this scene on a Bronx, New York, rooftop in 1983.

Merton's Strain Theory

While deviance is inevitable in all societies, Robert Merton (1938, 1968) argues that excessive violations arise from particular social arrangements. Specifically, the scope and character of deviance depend on how well a society makes cultural *goals* (such as financial success) accessible by providing the institutionalized *means* (such as schooling and job opportunities) to achieve them.

The path to conformity, Merton begins, lies in pursuing conventional goals by approved means. The true "success story," in other words, is someone who gains wealth and prestige through talent and hard work. But not everyone who desires conventional success has the opportunity to attain it. Children raised in poverty, for example, may see little hope of becoming successful if they "play by the rules." As a result, they may seek wealth through one or another kind of crime—say, by dealing cocaine. Merton called this

Q: "Contrary to current ideas, the criminal no longer seems a totally unsociable being, a sort of parasitic element, a strange and inassimilable body, introduced into the midst of society. On the contrary, he plays a definite role in social life." Emile Durkheim (1964:72)

Q: "It is the conflict between culturally accepted values and the socially structured difficulties of living up to these values which exerts pressure toward deviant behavior and disruption of the normative system." Robert K. Merton (1968:245)

Q: ". . . differential pressures for deviant behavior will continue to be exerted upon certain groups and strata as long as the structure of opportunity and the cultural goals remain substantially unchanged." Robert K. Merton (1968:246)

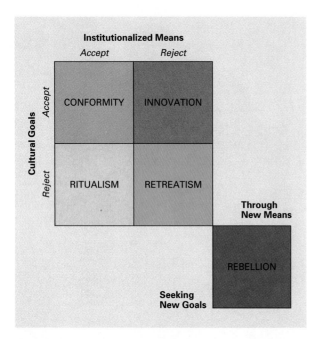

FIGURE 8–1 Merton's Strain Theory of Deviance
Source: Merton (1968).

type of deviance *innovation*—the attempt to achieve a culturally approved goal (wealth) by unconventional means (drug sales). Figure 8–1 characterizes innovation as accepting the goal of success while rejecting the conventional means of becoming rich.

According to Merton, the "strain" between our culture's emphasis on wealth and the limited opportunity to get rich gives rise, especially among the poor, to theft, the selling of illegal drugs, or other forms of street hustling. In some respects, at least, a "notorious gangster" like Al Capone was quite conventional—he pursued the fame and fortune at the heart of the "American dream." But, like many minorities who find the doors to success closed, this bright and enterprising man blazed his own trail to the top. As one analyst of the criminal world put it:

> The typical criminal of the Capone era was a boy who had . . . seen what was rated as success in the society he had been thrust into—the Cadillac, the big bankroll, the elegant apartment. How could he acquire that kind of recognizable status? He was almost always a boy of outstanding initiative, imagination, and ability; he was the kind of boy who, under different conditions, would have been a captain of industry or a key political figure of his time. But he hadn't the opportunity of going to Yale and becoming a banker or broker; there was no passage for him to a law degree from Harvard.

There was, however, a relatively easy way of acquiring these goods that he was incessantly told were available to him as an American citizen, and without which he had begun to feel he could not properly count himself as an American citizen. He could become a gangster. (Allsop, 1961: 236)

The inability to become successful by normative means may also prompt another type of deviance that Merton calls *ritualism* (see Figure 8–1). Ritualists resolve the strain of limited success by abandoning cultural goals in favor of almost compulsive efforts to live "respectably." In essence, they embrace the rules to the point where they lose sight of their larger goals. Lower-level bureaucrats, Merton suggests, often succumb to ritualism as a way of maintaining respectability.

A third response to the inability to succeed is *retreatism*—the rejection of both cultural goals and means so that one, in effect, "drops out." Retreatists include some alcoholics and drug addicts, and some of the street people found in U.S. cities. The deviance of retreatists lies in unconventional living and, perhaps more seriously, in accepting this situation.

The fourth response to failure is *rebellion*. Like retreatists, rebels reject both the cultural definition of success and the normative means of achieving it. Rebels, however, go one step further by advocating radical alternatives to the existing social order. Typically, they call for a political or religious transformation of society, and often join a counterculture.

Deviant Subcultures

Richard Cloward and Lloyd Ohlin (1966) extended Merton's theory in their investigation of delinquent youth. They maintain that criminal deviance results not simply from limited legitimate opportunity but also from available illegitimate opportunity. In short, deviance or conformity grows out of the *relative opportunity structure* that frames young people's lives.

Consider, once again, the life of Al Capone. An ambitious individual denied legitimate opportunity, he organized a criminal empire to take advantage of the country's demand for alcohol during Prohibition (1920–1933). As Capone's life shows, illegal opportunities foster the development of *criminal subcultures* that offer the knowledge, skills, and other resources people need to succeed in unconventional ways. Indeed, gangs may specialize in one or another form of criminality according to available opportunities and resources (Sheley et al., 1995).

But some poor and highly transient neighborhoods may lack almost any form of opportunity—legal

NOTE: Making use of illegitimate means to success explains the gangster's preoccupation with being respected and the desire, eventually, to "go legit." Capone's first employer was a Mafia boss who dubbed himself Mr. Frankie Yale and who ran a speakeasy called the Harvard Inn. Capone often demanded that others address him as "Anthony Brown" and, in time, was delighted to enroll his son at Yale.

NOTE: Another illustration of shifting moral boundaries: It is no coincidence that during the 1980s, a decade when U.S. families tried to come to terms with their growing use of child care, there were numerous child-abuse charges brought against operators of child-care facilities (the McMartin case being the best known). This "crime wave" also reflected the 1979 Mondale Act that increased funding for child-abuse agencies and investigators.

In the Kosovo region of Serbia, as in the United States, young people (especially males) cut off from legitimate opportunity may form deviant subcultures as a strategy to gain the prestige denied them by the larger society.

or illegal. Here, delinquency often surfaces in the form of *conflict subcultures* where violence is ignited by frustration and a desire for fame or respect. Alternatively, those who fail to achieve success, even by criminal means, may sink into *retreatist subcultures,* dropping out through abuse of alcohol or other drugs.

Albert Cohen (1971) asserts that delinquency is most pronounced among lower-class youths because it is they who contend with the least opportunity to achieve success in conventional ways. Sometimes those whom society neglects seek self-respect by building a deviant subculture that "defines as meritorious the characteristics they *do* possess, the kinds of conduct of which they *are* capable" (1971:66). Having a notorious street reputation, for example, may win no points with society as a whole, but it may satisfy a youth's gnawing desire to "be somebody."

Walter Miller (1970) agrees that deviant subcultures typically develop among lower-class youths who contend with the least legitimate opportunity. He spotlights six focal concerns of these deviant subcultures: (1) *trouble*, arising from frequent conflict with teachers and police; (2) *toughness*, the value placed on physical size, strength, and athletic skills, especially among males; (3) *smartness* (or "street smarts"), the ability to outthink or "con" others, and to avoid being similarly taken advantage of; (4) *excitement*, the search for thrills, risk, or danger to escape from a daily routine that is predictable and unsatisfying; (5) a preoccupation with *fate*, derived from the lack of control

these youths feel over their own lives; and (6) *autonomy*, a desire for freedom often expressed as resentment toward figures of authority.

Critical evaluation. Durkheim's pioneering work on the functions of deviance remains central to sociological thinking. Even so, recent critics point out that a community does not always come together in reaction to crime; sometimes, in fact, fear of crime drives people to withdraw from public life altogether (Liska & Warner, 1991).

Derived from Durkheim's analysis, Merton's strain theory has also come under criticism for explaining some kinds of deviance (theft, for example) far better than others (such as crimes of passion or mental illness). In addition, not everyone seeks success in conventional terms of wealth, as strain theory implies. As we noted in Chapter 3 ("Culture"), members of our society embrace many different cultural values and are motivated by various notions of personal success.

The general argument of Cloward and Ohlin, Cohen, and Miller—that deviance reflects the opportunity structure of society—has been confirmed by subsequent research (Allan & Steffensmeier, 1989). However, these theories, too, fall short by assuming that everyone shares the same cultural standards for judging right and wrong. Moreover, we must be careful not to define deviance in ways that unfairly focus attention on poor people. If crime is defined to include stock fraud as well as street theft, offenders are

NOTE: Economically speaking, according to Thomas Szasz (1995), people fall into one of three categories: producers (Merton's conformists); predators (innovators); or parasites (retreatists).

Q: "From this point of view, deviance is not a quality of the act a person commits, but rather a consequence of the application by others of rules and sanctions to an 'offender.' The deviant is one to whom the label has successfully been applied; deviant behavior is behavior that people so label." Howard S. Becker (1966:9)

DISCUSS: People may acquire deviant labels even when they have done nothing at all. What about victims of violent rape—subjected to labeling as deviants based on the misguided assumption that they "led on" the offender? Or individuals with AIDS shunned by employers, friends, and even family members?

The world is full of people who are unusual in one way or another. This Indian man grew the fingernails on one hand for more than thirty years just to do something that no one else had ever done. Should we define such behavior as harmless eccentricity or as evidence of mental illness?

more likely to include affluent individuals. Finally, all structural-functional theories imply that everyone who violates conventional cultural standards will be branded as deviant. Becoming deviant, however, is actually a highly complex process, as the next section explains.

SYMBOLIC-INTERACTION ANALYSIS

The symbolic-interaction paradigm analyzes the creation of deviance as a social process. From this point of view, definitions of deviance and conformity are surprisingly flexible.

Labeling Theory

The central contribution of symbolic-interaction analysis is **labeling theory,** *the assertion that deviance and conformity result, not so much from what people* do, but from how others respond to those actions. Labeling theory stresses the relativity of deviance, meaning that the same behavior may be defined in any number of ways. Howard S. Becker claims that deviance is, therefore, nothing more than "behavior that people so label" (1966:9).

Consider these situations: A woman takes an article of clothing from a roommate; a married man at a convention in a distant city has sex with a prostitute; a member of Congress drives home intoxicated after a party. In each case, "reality" depends on the response of others. Is the first situation a matter of borrowing or is it theft? The consequences of the second case depend largely on whether news of the man's behavior follows him back home. In the third situation, is the official an active socialite or a dangerous drunk? The social construction of reality, then, is a highly variable process of detection, definition, and response.

Because "reality" is relative to time and place, one society's conventions may constitute another's deviance. The box on page 212 describes cockfighting: Is this popular sport a meaningful cultural ritual or simply a vicious abuse of animals?

Primary and Secondary Deviance

Edwin Lemert (1951, 1972) notes that many episodes of norm violation—say, skipping school or underage drinking—provoke little reaction from others and have little effect on a person's self-concept. Lemert calls such passing episodes *primary deviance.*

But what happens if other people take notice of someone's deviance and make something of it? If, for example, people begin to describe a young man as a "boozer," and push him out of their social circle, he may become embittered, drink even more, and seek the company of others who condone his behavior. So the response to initial deviance can set in motion *secondary deviance,* by which an individual engages in repeated norm violations and begins to take on a deviant identity. The development of secondary deviance is one application of the Thomas theorem, which states, "Situations defined as real become real in their consequences."

Stigma

The onset of secondary deviance marks the emergence of what Erving Goffman (1963) called a *deviant career.* As individuals develop a strong commitment to deviant behavior, they typically acquire a **stigma,** *a*

RESOURCE: How important is audience reaction to an episode of deviance in fostering a deviant career? Initial insights into this issue were made by Frank Tannenbaum in *Crime and the Community* (Columbia University Press, 1938).
NOTE: The term "stigma" is derived from a Greek root meaning "tattoo."
Q: "The Greeks, who were apparently strong on visual aids, originated the term *stigma* to refer to bodily signs designed to expose something unusual and bad about the moral status of the signifier." Erving Goffman, *Stigma* (1963)
NOTE: In the late 1950s, Thomas Szasz prepared a short article on the myth of mental illness and submitted it to every major U.S. psychiatric journal—every one rejected it. The article appeared in *The American Psychologist* (1960).

powerfully negative social label that radically changes a person's self-concept and social identity.

Stigma operates as a master status (see Chapter 6, "Social Interaction in Everyday Life"), overpowering other dimensions of social identity so that an individual is diminished and discounted in the minds of others and, consequently, socially isolated. Sometimes an entire community formally stigmatizes individuals through what Harold Garfinkel (1956) calls a *degradation ceremony*. A criminal prosecution is one example, operating much like a high school graduation except that people stand before the community to be labeled in a negative rather than a positive way.

Retrospective Labeling

Once people have stigmatized a person, they may engage in **retrospective labeling**, *the interpretation of someone's past consistent with present deviance* (Scheff, 1984). For example, after discovering that a priest has sexually molested a child, others may rethink his past, perhaps musing, "He always did want to be around young children." Retrospective labeling distorts a person's biography in a highly selective and prejudicial way, guided more by the present stigma than by any attempt to be fair. This process often deepens a person's deviant identity.

Labeling and Mental Illness

Is a woman who believes that Jesus rides the bus to work with her every day seriously deluded or merely expressing her religious faith in a highly graphic way? If a man refuses to bathe, much to the dismay of his family, is he insane or simply unconventional? Is a homeless woman who refuses to allow police to take her to a city shelter on a cold night mentally ill or simply trying to live independently?

Psychiatrist Thomas Szasz—a maverick among mental health professionals—charges that people apply the label of insanity to what is only "difference"; therefore, he concludes, the notion of mental illness should be abandoned (1961, 1970, 1994, 1995). Illness, Szasz argues, is physical and afflicts only the body; mental illness, then, is a myth. The world is full of people whose "differences" in thought or action may irritate us, but difference is no grounds on which to define someone as sick. To do so, Szasz claims, simply enforces conformity to the standards of people powerful enough to impose their will on others.

Many of Szasz's colleagues reject the notion that all mental illness is a fiction. But some have hailed his work for pointing out the danger of abusing medical practice in the interest of promoting conformity. Most of us, after all, experience periods of extreme stress or other mental disability from time to time. Such episodes, although upsetting, are usually of passing importance. If, however, others respond with labeling that forms the basis of a social stigma, the long-term result may be further deviance as a self-fulfilling prophecy (Scheff, 1984).

The Medicalization of Deviance

Labeling theory, particularly the ideas of Szasz and Goffman, helps to explain an important shift in the way our society understands deviance. Over the last fifty years, the growing influence of psychiatry and medicine in the United States has prompted the **medicalization of deviance**, *the transformation of moral and legal issues into medical matters.*

In essence, medicalization amounts to swapping one set of labels for another. In moral terms, we evaluate people or their behavior as "bad" or "good." However, the scientific objectivity of modern medicine passes no moral judgment, utilizing instead clinical diagnoses such as "sick" and "well."

To illustrate, until the middle of this century, people generally viewed alcoholics as weak and morally deficient people, easily tempted by the pleasure of drink. Gradually, however, medical specialists redefined alcoholism so that most people now consider alcoholism a disease, rendering individuals "sick" rather than "bad." Similarly, obesity, drug addiction, child abuse, promiscuity, and other behaviors that used to be moral matters are today widely defined as illnesses for which people need help rather than punishment.

The Significance of Labels

Whether we define deviance as a moral or medical issue has three profound consequences. First, it affects *who responds* to deviance. An offense against common morality typically provokes a reaction by ordinary people or the police. Applying medical labels, however, places the situation under the control of clinical specialists, including counselors, psychiatrists, and physicians.

A second difference is *how people respond* to deviance. A moral approach defines the deviant as an "offender" subject to punishment. Medically, however, "patients" need treatment (for their own good, of course). Therefore, while punishment is designed to fit the crime, treatment programs are tailored to the patient and may involve virtually any therapy that a

Q: "There is so much good in the worst of us, and so much bad in the best of us." Anonymous

NOTE: Colleges have expanded their medical and counseling staffs in recent decades. As a result, what people used to describe as student shortcomings now are cast in terms of various disorders.

NOTE: The medicalization of deviance is one facet of the cultural trend of victimization described in Chapter 3, "Culture."

SOCIAL SURVEY: "Morality is a personal matter and society should not force everyone to follow one standard." (GSS 1988, N = 1,481; *Codebook*, 1994:334)

"Agree strongly"   31.7%   "Disagree strongly"   7.6%
"Agree somewhat"   38.8%   DK/NR   4.4%
"Disagree somewhat"   17.5%

GLOBAL SOCIOLOGY

Cockfighting: Cultural Ritual or Abuse of Animals?

You won't see it on television, but one of the popular sports of the world—from North America to Europe and to Asia—is cockfighting. Legal in parts of Louisiana, Texas, New Mexico, and Arizona, cockfighting is big business in Mexico, and approaches something of a national pastime in the Philippines. There, the local cock pit is as important as the town square in the U.S. midwest: Every settlement has one, and it attracts a crowd on weekends and fiesta days.

On the surface, cockfights are about gambling. An afternoon or evening event might include ten fights. The process begins as the cock owners display their birds to one another, calling out for bets on which is the stronger bird. Members of the audience weigh in with their own cash as a pair of cocks prepares to fight. Taking the money and confirming the bets is the "cristo," by which Filipinos mean that he is expected to be as honest as Christ.

Once the odds of winning have been set and the money is on the table, the actual combat begins. Roosters fight in pairs, each outfitted with a small, sharp blade (each region of the world has its favorite variation as to shape and length) strapped to the rear of the left leg. The cocks need little encouragement to fight, but the owners engage in a bit of strutting of their own, swinging their birds back and forth in front of each other before dropping them on lines drawn in the pit sand. Immediately upon hitting the ground, the hackles rise and the birds fly at one another, merging in a blur of legs and feathers.

Within a few minutes, one bird may collapse from exhaustion; the owner steps in to revive his cock and the process is repeated. Before long, however, a blade finds its mark. The

victor, the bird who will live to fight another day, ends up perching on the vanquished, who will not.

In many parts of the world, cockfighting ranks among the most important male rituals. Many men lavish on their birds the kind of attention they otherwise reserve for their sons. Typically, men raise their roosters for about two years, often at considerable expense, before their fighting careers begin. At that point, cocks take on a crucial cultural function for men. That is, through the ritual of the cockfight, men test their own claims to manhood, establish their own standing in the community pecking order, and pass on to their sons significant lessons about honor, competition, and masculinity.

An outside observer, easily repulsed by the brutality of the cockfight, may readily condemn the practice as unethical. But, sensing the deep importance of the ceremony to insiders, one hangs—looking both ways—on the uneasy edge of uncertainty.

Source: Based on *The Economist* (1994), Harris (1994), and the author's research in the Philippines.

specialist thinks will prevent future deviance (von Hirsh, 1986).

Third, and most important, the two labels differ on the issue of *the personal competence of the deviant person.* Morally speaking, people take responsibility for their behavior whether right or wrong. If we are sick, however, we lose the capacity to control (or even comprehend) our behavior. Defined as incompetent, the deviant person becomes vulnerable to intense,

often involuntary, treatment. For this reason alone, attempts to define deviance in medical terms should be made only with extreme caution.

Sutherland's Differential Association Theory

Learning any social patterns—whether conventional or deviant—is a process that takes place in groups.

Q: "A person becomes delinquent because of an excess of definitions favorable to violation of law over definitions unfavorable to violations of law. This is the principle of differential association." Edwin Sutherland

Q: Summing up his key points, Edwin Sutherland asserts that "Criminal behavior is learned . . . in interaction with other persons . . . [mainly] in intimate personal groups . . . [and] includes techniques of committing the crime . . . [and] motives, drives, rationalizations, and attitudes."

NOTE: Another probable correlate of criminality is intelligence. Travis Hirschi (1995) states that "Research consistently shows that offenders are disadvantaged with regard to intellectual or cognitive skills."

According to Edwin Sutherland (1940), any person's tendency toward conformity or deviance depends on the relative frequency of association with others who encourage conventional behavior or norm violation. This is Sutherland's theory of *differential association.*

Sutherland's theory is illustrated by a study of drug and alcohol use among young adults in the United States (Akers et al., 1979). Analyzing responses to a questionnaire completed by junior and senior high school students, researchers discovered a close link between the extent of alcohol and drug use and the degree to which peer groups encouraged such activity. The investigators concluded that young people embrace delinquent patterns as they receive praise and other rewards for defining deviance rather than conformity in positive terms.

Hirschi's Control Theory

In his *control theory,* Travis Hirschi (1969, 1995) claims that the essence of social control lies in people's anticipation of the consequences of their behavior. Hirschi assumes that everyone finds at least some deviance tempting. Imagining condemnation from family or friends is sufficient to deter most people from temptation; concerns about how transgressions will affect their careers will give others pause. By contrast, individuals who have little to lose from deviance are most likely to become rule-breakers.

Hirschi asserts that conformity arises from four types of social controls.

1. **Attachment.** Strong social attachments encourage conformity; weak relationships in the family, peer group, and school leave people freer to engage in deviance.

2. **Opportunity.** The more one perceives legitimate opportunity, the greater the advantages of conformity. A young person bound for college, one with good career prospects, has a high stake in conformity. By contrast, someone with little confidence in future success drifts more toward deviance.

3. **Involvement.** Extensive involvement in legitimate activities—such as holding a job, going to school and completing homework, or pursuing hobbies—inhibits deviance. People with few such activities—who simply "hang out" waiting for something to happen—have time and energy for deviant activity.

4. **Belief.** Strong beliefs in conventional morality and respect for authority figures restrain tendencies toward deviance. By contrast, people with a weak conscience are more vulnerable to temptation.

Hirschi's analysis draws together a number of ideas presented earlier about the causes of deviant behavior. Note that both relative social privilege and strength of moral character are crucial in generating a stake in conformity to conventional norms (Wiatrowski, Griswold, & Roberts, 1981; Sampson & Laub, 1990; Free, 1992).

Critical evaluation. The various symbolic-interaction theories share a focus on deviance as process. Labeling theory links deviance not to *action* but to the *reaction* of others. Thus some people come to be defined as deviant while others who think or behave in the same way are not. The concepts of stigma, secondary deviance, and deviant career demonstrate how people can incorporate the label of deviance into a lasting self-concept.

Yet labeling theory has several limitations. First, because this theory takes a highly relative view of deviance, it glosses over how some kinds of behavior, such as murder, are condemned virtually everywhere (Wellford, 1980). Labeling theory is thus most usefully applied to less serious deviance, such as sexual promiscuity or mental illness.

Second, the consequences of deviant labeling are unclear. Research is inconclusive as to whether deviant labeling produces subsequent deviance or discourages further violations (Smith & Gartin, 1989; Sherman & Smith, 1992).

Third, not everyone resists the label of deviance; some people may actually relish being defined as deviant (Vold & Bernard, 1986). For example, individuals may engage in civil disobedience leading to arrest to call attention to social injustice.

Both Sutherland's differential association theory and Hirschi's control theory have had considerable influence in sociology. But they provide little insight into why society's norms and laws define certain kinds of activities as deviant in the first place. This important question is addressed by social-conflict analysis, the focus of the next section.

SOCIAL-CONFLICT ANALYSIS

The social-conflict paradigm demonstrates how deviance reflects social inequality. This approach holds that who or what is labeled as deviant depends on the relative power of categories of people.

Deviance and Power

Alexander Liazos (1972) points out that everyday conceptions of deviants—"nuts, sluts, and 'preverts'"—

Artist Frank Romero painted The Closing of Whittier Boulevard *based on a recollection of his youth in East Los Angeles. To many young Latinos, identified here by their distinctive "low-rider" cars, police represent a hostile Anglo culture likely to use heavy-handed tactics to discourage them from venturing out of their neighborhood.*

Frank Romero, *The Closing of Whittier Boulevard*, 1984. Oil on canvas, 6x10 feet.

describe people who share the trait of powerlessness. Bag ladies (not tax evaders) and unemployed men on street corners (not those who profit from wars) carry the stigma of deviance.

Social-conflict theory links deviance to power in three ways. First, the norms—and especially the laws—of any society generally bolster the interests of the rich and powerful. People who threaten the wealthy, either by seizing their property or by advocating a more egalitarian society, come to be tagged as "common thieves" or "political radicals." As noted in Chapter 4 ("Society"), Karl Marx argued that the law (together with all social institutions) tends to support the interests of the rich. Echoing Marx, Richard Quinney makes the point succinctly: "Capitalist justice is by the capitalist class, for the capitalist class, and against the working class" (1977:3).

Second, even if their behavior is called into question, the powerful have the resources to resist deviant labels. Corporate executives who order the dumping of hazardous wastes are rarely held personally accountable for these acts. And, as the O. J. Simpson trial made clear, even when charged with violent crimes, the rich have the resources to vigorously resist being labeled as criminal.

Third, the widespread belief that norms and laws are natural and good masks their political character. For this reason, we may condemn the unequal application of the law but give little thought to whether the *laws themselves* are inherently fair (Quinney, 1977).

Deviance and Capitalism

Also following the Marxist tradition, Steven Spitzer (1980) argues that deviant labels are applied to people who impede the operation of capitalism. First, because capitalism is based on private ownership of wealth, people who threaten the property of others—especially the poor who steal from the rich—are prime candidates for labeling as deviants. Conversely, the rich who exploit the poor rarely are called into question. Landlords, for example, who charge poor tenants high rents and evict those who cannot pay are not considered a threat to society; they are simply "doing business."

Second, because capitalism depends on productive labor, those who cannot or will not work risk deviant labeling. Many members of our society think of people out of work—even if through no fault of their own—as deviant.

Third, capitalism depends on respect for figures of authority, so people who resist authority are labeled as deviant. Examples are children who skip school or talk back to parents and teachers; adults who do not cooperate with employers or police; and anyone who opposes "the system."

Fourth, anyone who directly challenges the capitalist status quo is likely to be defined as deviant. Into this category fall antiwar activists, environmentalists, and labor organizers.

To turn the argument around, society offers positive labels to whomever enhances the operation of capitalism. Winning athletes, for example, have

GLOBAL: Socialist societies also have organized crime; hundreds of criminal organizations now operate in Russia and the number is rising as a market system develops and political freedoms expand.

Q: "It is no longer unthinkable for white-collar criminals to go to prison." Pronouncement by the judge sentencing Ivan Boesky to three years in jail for insider stock trading in 1980s.

NOTE: With regard to corporations shielding individuals from criminal prosecutions, imagine holding a street gang—but not its individual members—responsible for violence.

Q: "The laws are best explained, interpreted, and applied by those whose interest and abilities lie in perverting, confounding, and eluding them. . . . Reward and punishment [are] the two hinges upon which all government turns." Jonathan Swift, *Gulliver's Travels*

celebrity status because they express the values of individual achievement and competition vital to capitalism. Additionally, Spitzer notes, we condemn using drugs of escape (marijuana, psychedelics, heroin, and crack) as deviant, while espousing the use of drugs that promote adjustment to the status quo (such as alcohol and caffeine).

The capitalist system also strives to control threatening categories of people. Those who are a "costly yet relatively harmless burden" on society, says Spitzer, include Robert Merton's retreatists (for example, those addicted to alcohol or other drugs), the elderly, and people with mental and/or physical disabilities. All are subject to control by social welfare agencies. But those who challenge the very underpinnings of the capitalist system, including the inner-city "underclass" and revolutionaries—Merton's innovators and rebels—come under the purview of the criminal justice system and, in times of crisis, military forces such as the National Guard.

Note that both the social welfare and criminal justice systems apply labels that blame individuals and not the system for the control they exert over people's lives. Welfare recipients are deemed unworthy freeloaders; poor people who vent rage at their powerlessness are labeled rioters; anyone who actively challenges the government is branded a radical or a communist; and those who attempt to gain illegally what they cannot otherwise acquire are called common thieves.

White-Collar Crime

As the go-go 1980s came to an end, one Wall Street stockbroker accomplished an astounding feat. In 1987, Michael Milken made headlines by becoming the highest paid U.S. worker in half a century with salary and bonuses totaling $550 million—*about $1.5 million a day*. Such a sum placed Milken right behind Al Capone, whose earnings in 1927 reportedly reached $600 million in current dollars (Swartz, 1989). Milken had something else in common with Capone: The government locked him up—in this case, for business fraud.

Milken's activities exemplify **white-collar crime**, defined by Edwin Sutherland in 1940 as *crimes committed by persons of high social position in the course of their occupations* (Sutherland & Cressey, 1978). As the Milken case illustrates, white-collar crimes do not involve violence and rarely draw uniformed police to a scene with drawn guns. Rather, white-collar crimes are acts by powerful people making use of their occupational positions to enrich themselves or others

From a Marxist point of view, powerful people make the rules to advance their own interests. Thus, no matter what harm they might inflict on the majority, elites are rarely called to account for their actions. U.S. painter Ed McGowin captures this idea in his 1991 painting, Grown Men Playing with Planet Earth.

illegally, often causing significant public harm in the process (Hagan & Parker, 1985; Vold & Bernard, 1986). For this reason, sociologists sometimes call white-collar offenses that occur in government offices and corporate board rooms *crime in the suites* as opposed to *crime in the streets*.

The most common white-collar crimes are bank embezzlement, business fraud, bribery, and antitrust violations. Most cases of white-collar crime, like most street crimes, involve relatively little money and cause limited harm to anyone. But the occasional major crime—like the savings and loan scandal a few years ago—attracts a great deal of attention and causes substantial loss and public harm (Weisburd et al., 1991). The government program to bail out the savings and loan industry ended up costing U.S. taxpayers $600 billion—$2,500 for every person in the country.

Sutherland (1940) argued that most white-collar offenses provoke little reaction from others. When they do, moreover, they typically end up in a civil hearing rather than in a criminal courtroom. *Civil law* regulates business dealings between private parties, while *criminal law* deals with an individual's moral

GLOBAL: A new form of crime, both high-tech and global in character, is pirating copyrighted software. The Internet now allows anyone with a computer and modem to send or receive materials globally. Software piracy is especially pronounced in low-income countries such as Mexico, Brazil, Pakistan, and Malaysia, where perhaps 85% of all software is procured illegally.

Q: "I am as pure as the driven slush." Tallulah Bankhead

DIVERSITY: Edwin Schur argues that sociological analysis has long stressed the positive functions of deviance by women (cf. Kingsley Davis's 1937 analysis of prostitution) with little attention to the structural position of women in relation to men in U.S. society.

Q: ". . . in our society being treated as deviant has been a standard feature of life as a female." Edwin M. Schur

TABLE 8–1 Sociological Explanations of Deviance: A Summary

Theoretical Paradigm	Major Contributions
Structural-functional analysis	While what is deviant may vary, deviance itself is found in all societies; deviance and the social response it provokes sustain the moral foundation of society; deviance may also guide social change.
Symbolic-interaction analysis	Nothing is inherently deviant but may become defined as such through the response of others; the reactions of others are highly variable; the label of deviance may lead to the emergence of secondary deviance and deviant careers.
Social-conflict analysis	Laws and other norms reflect the interests of powerful members of society; those who threaten the status quo generally are defined as deviant; social injury caused by powerful people is less likely to be considered criminal than social injury caused by people who have little social power.

responsibilities to society. In practice, then, a loser in a civil settlement pays for damage or injury, but is not labeled as a criminal. Further, since corporations have the legal standing of persons, white-collar prosecutions commonly target the organization as a whole rather than particular individuals.

And when white-collar criminals are charged and convicted, the odds are they will not go to jail. One accounting shows that fewer than three in ten embezzlers convicted in the U.S. District Court system spent a single day in prison; most were placed on probation (U.S. Bureau of Justice Statistics, 1992).

The main reason for such leniency is that, as Sutherland noted years ago, the public voices less concern about white-collar crime than about street crime. Corporate crime, people seem to feel, victimizes everyone—and no one. White-collar criminals don't stick a gun in anyone's ribs, and the economic costs are usually spread throughout a large population.

Critical evaluation. According to social-conflict theory, inequality in wealth and power guides the creation and application of laws and other norms. This approach asserts that the criminal justice and social

welfare systems act as political agents, controlling categories of people who threaten the capitalist system.

Like other analyses of deviance, however, social-conflict theory has its critics. First, this approach implies that laws and other cultural norms are created directly by and exclusively for the rich and powerful. At the very least, this assumption is an oversimplification, since many segments of our society influence, and benefit from, the political process. Laws also protect workers, consumers, and the environment, sometimes in opposition to the interests of the rich.

Second, social-conflict analysis implies that criminality springs up only to the extent that a society treats its members unequally. However, as Durkheim noted, all societies generate deviance, whatever their economic system.

We have now presented various sociological explanations for crime and other types of deviance. Table 8–1 summarizes the contributions of each approach.

DEVIANCE AND SOCIAL DIVERSITY

The shape of deviance in a society has much to do with the relative power and privilege of different categories of people. The following sections offer two examples: how gender is linked to deviance, and how racial and ethnic hostility motivates hate crimes.

Deviance and Gender

Virtually every society in the world applies more stringent normative controls to women than to men. Historically, our society has restricted the role of women to the home. In the United States even today, women find limited opportunities in the workplace, in politics, and in the military. Elsewhere in the world, the normative constraints placed on women are greater still. In Saudi Arabia, women cannot vote or legally operate motor vehicles; in Iran, women who dare to expose their hair or wear makeup in public can be whipped.

Given the importance of gender to the social construction of deviance, we need to pause a moment to see how gender figures in some of the theories we have already discussed. Robert Merton's strain theory, for example, has a masculine cast in that it defines cultural goals in terms of financial success. Traditionally, at least, this goal has had more to do with the lives of men, while women have been socialized to view success in terms of relationships, particularly marriage and motherhood (Leonard, 1982). A

NOTE: Two people at work are homicide victims each day in the United States; such violence is the leading cause of workplace death for women, the third leading cause of workplace death for men. By occupation, cab drivers lead the risk list.

NOTE: With 16 recorded for 1993, "hate-crime" homicides account for only a tiny fraction of the 21,000 killings annually in the United States.

THE MAP: Because the states that have enacted hate-crime legislation almost exactly mirror those that voted for Democrat Bill Clinton in the 1992 presidential election, the concept of hate crime appears to be a partisan issue. In 1994, one tally put the number of hate crimes at 283, with gays the most common targets (Klanwatch Project of Southern Poverty Law Center).

Seeing Ourselves

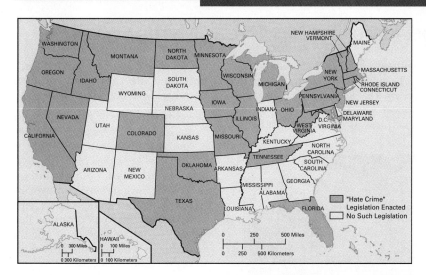

NATIONAL MAP 8–1

Hate-Crime Legislation Across the United States

The states shown in purple have legally mandated harsher penalties for crimes motivated by racial, ethnic, or other bias. Generally, laws of this kind are favored by political liberals. Can you see a pattern in the map? *Hint:* Most of the states that have enacted hate-crime laws supported Democrat Bill Clinton in the 1992 presidential election.

Source: *The New York Times,* June 12, 1993. Copyright © 1993/1995 by *The New York Times* Company. Reprinted by permission.

more woman-focused theory might point up the "strain" caused by the cultural ideals of equality clashing with the reality of gender-based inequality.

Labeling theory, the major approach in symbolic-interaction analysis, offers greater insight into ways in which gender influences how we define deviance. To the extent that we judge the behavior of females and males by different standards, the very process of labeling involves sex-linked biases. Further, because society generally places men in positions of power over women, men often escape direct responsibility for actions that victimize women. In the past, at least, men engaging in sexual harassment or other assaults against women have been tagged with only mildly deviant labels, if they have been punished at all.

By contrast, women who are victimized may have to convince an unsympathetic audience that they are not to blame for what happened. Research confirms an important truth: Whether people define a situation as deviance—and, if so, whose deviance it is—depends on the sex of both the audience and the actors (King & Clayson, 1988). The box on pages 218–19 takes a closer look at date rape, one example of how a double standard has proven harmful to women.

Finally, in a notable irony, social-conflict analysis—despite its focus on social inequality—has long neglected the importance of gender. If, as conflict theory suggests, economic disadvantage is a primary cause of crime, why do women (whose economic position is much worse than that of men) commit far fewer crimes than men do? The section on crime, beginning on page 218, examines crime rates in the United States and addresses this question.

Hate Crimes

More than a decade ago the concept of **hate crime** came into our language to designate *a criminal act against a person or person's property by an offender motivated by racial or other bias.* A hate crime, then, involves both a violation of criminal law and bias on the part of the offender toward the victim on the basis of race, religion, ancestry, sexual orientation, or physical disability.

Although hate crimes are nothing new, the federal government has only tracked them since 1990. While still a small share of all crime, their numbers are rising. A survey conducted in eight U.S. cities by the National Gay and Lesbian Task Force (cited in Berrill, 1992:19–20) found that 20 percent of lesbians and gay men had been physically assaulted because of their sexual orientation; more than 90 percent claimed to have been at least verbally abused for this reason. Research indicates that hate-motivated violence is especially likely to target people who contend with multiple stigmas, such as gay men of color.

National Map 8–1 shows that, as of early 1995, twenty-nine states had enacted hate-crime legislation.

CRITICAL THINKING

Date Rape: Exposing Dangerous Myths

Completing a day of work during a business trip to the courthouse in Tampa, Florida, thirty-two-year-old Sandra Abbott pondered how she would return to her hotel. An attorney with whom she had been working—a pleasant enough man—made the kind offer of a lift. As his car threaded its way through the late afternoon traffic, their conversation was animated. "He was saying all the right things," Abbott recalled, "so I started to trust him."

He asked if she would join him for dinner; she happily accepted. After lingering over an enjoyable meal, they walked together to the door of her hotel room. The new acquaintance angled for an invitation to come in and talk, but Abbott hesitated, sensing that he might have something more on his mind. She explained that she was old-fashioned about relationships but would allow him to come in for a little while with the understanding that talk was *all* they would do.

Sitting on the couch in the room, soon Abbott was overcome with drowsiness. Feeling comfortable in the presence of her new friend, she let

her head fall gently onto his shoulder, and, before she knew it, she fell asleep. That's when the attack began. Abbott was startled back to consciousness as the man thrust himself

Is a person who drinks alcohol to excess capable of making a responsible decision about having sex? What role does alcohol play in date rape on the campus?

upon her sexually. She shouted "No!" but he paid no heed. Abbott describes what happened next:

> I didn't scream or run. All I could think of was my business contacts and what if they saw me run out of my room screaming rape. I thought it was my fault. I felt so filthy, I washed myself over and over in hot water. Did he rape me?, I kept asking myself. I didn't consent. But who's gonna believe me? I had a man in my hotel room after midnight. (Gibbs, 1991a:50)

Abbott knew that she had said "No!" and thus had been raped. She notified the police, who conducted an investigation and turned their findings over to the state attorney's office. But the authorities backed away. In the absence of evidence like bruises, a medical examination, and torn clothes, they noted, there was little point in prosecuting.

The case of Sandra Abbott is all too typical. Even today, in most incidences of sexual attack, a victim makes no report to police, and no offender is arrested. The reason for such inaction

This trend has gratified supporters of hate-crime statutes while strengthening criticism from opponents who characterize such laws as punishing thoughts, not actions. The box on page 220 examines a recent case, which led to a Supreme Court ruling upholding stiffer sentences for crimes motivated by hate.

CRIME

Crime is the violation of statutes enacted into criminal law by a locality, state, or the federal government. Thus, some criminal laws apply everywhere in the

United States; others vary from state to state, and some apply only within a local jurisdiction.

The Components of Crime

Technically, crime is composed of two elements: the *act* itself (or, in some cases, the failure to do what the law requires) and *criminal intent* (in legal terminology, *mens rea*, or "guilty mind"). Intent is a matter of degree, ranging from willful conduct to negligence in which a person does not deliberately set out to hurt anyone but acts (or fails to act) in a manner that may

NOTE: In 1992, the American Medical Association and the Surgeon General declared violent men to be a major threat to women's health. According to the National League of Cities, about one-fourth of visits to emergency rooms by women are for injuries caused by domestic violence.

Q: "The fundamental sociological problem is not crime but the law . . ." Peter Berger (1963:37)

NOTE: Technically, the *corpus delicti* ("body of a crime") is composed of (1) *actus reus* ("guilty act"), which is the physical act (or omission) in violation of criminal law; (2) *mens rea* ("guilty mind") or mental resolve to commit the crime; (3) causal order, by which the criminal intent precedes and is related to the criminal act; and (4) all legal elements, the factors attached to the specific crime in a particular jurisdiction according to the wording of the criminal statute.

is that many people have a misguided understanding of rape. Three false notions about rape are so common in the United States that they might be called "rape myths."

A first myth is that rape involves strangers. A sexual attack brings to mind young men lurking in the shadows who suddenly spring on their unsuspecting victims. But this pattern is the exception rather than the rule: Four out of five rapes are committed by offenders known to their victims. For this reason, people have begun to speak more realistically about *acquaintance rape* or, more simply, *date rape*.

A second myth about rape holds that women provoke their attackers. Surely, many people think, a woman claiming to have been raped must have done *something* to encourage the man, to lead him on, to make him think that she really wanted to have sex.

In the case described above, didn't Sandra Abbott agree to have dinner with the man? Didn't she invite him into her room? Such self-doubt often paralyzes victims. But having dinner with a man—or even inviting him into her hotel room—is hardly a woman's statement of consent to have sex with

him any more than she has agreed to have him beat her with a club.

A third myth is the notion that rape is simply sex. If there is no knife held to a woman's throat, or if she is not bound and gagged, then how can sex be a crime? The answer is simply that *forcing a woman to have sex without her consent is a violent crime*. To accept the idea that rape is sex one would also have to see no difference between brutal combat and playful wrestling. "Having sex" implies intimacy, caring, communication, and, most important of all, consent—none of which is present in cases of rape. Beyond the brutality of being physically violated, date rape also undermines a victim's sense of trust. This psychological burden is especially serious among rape victims under eighteen—half of the total—about one-fourth of whom are attacked by their own fathers (U.S. Department of Justice, 1994).

The more people believe these myths about rape, the more women will fall victim to sexual violence. The ancient Babylonians stoned married women who became victims of rape, convinced that the women had committed adultery. Ideas about rape have

changed little over thousands of years, which helps to explain why, even today, only about one in twenty rapes results in an offender being sent to jail.

Nowhere has the issue of date rape been more widely discussed than on the college campus. The collegiate environment promotes easy friendships and a sense of trust. At the same time, many students have a great deal to learn about relationships and about themselves. So while college life encourages communication, it also invites sexual violence.

To counter this problem, colleges have been facing—and debunking—myths about rape. In addition, attention has centered on the prevalence of alcohol in campus life and the effect of cultural patterns that define sex as a sport. To address the crisis of date rape, everyone needs to understand two simple truths: Forcing sex without a woman's consent is rape, and when a woman says "no," she means just that.

Sources: Gibbs (1991a, 1991b) and Gilbert (1992).

reasonably be expected to cause harm. Juries weigh the degree of intent in determining the seriousness of a crime and may find one person who kills another guilty of first-degree murder, second-degree murder, or negligent manslaughter. Alternatively, they may rule a killing justifiable.

Types of Crime

In the United States, the Federal Bureau of Investigation gathers information on criminal offenses and regularly reports the results in a publication called *Crime*

in the United States. Two major types of offenses make up the FBI "crime index."

Crimes against the person constitute *crimes that direct violence or the threat of violence against others.* Such "violent crimes" include murder and manslaughter (legally defined as "the willful killing of one human being by another"), aggravated assault ("an unlawful attack by one person upon another for the purpose of inflicting severe or aggravated bodily injury"), forcible rape ("the carnal knowledge of a female forcibly and against her will"), and robbery ("taking or attempting to take anything of value from the care, custody, or

NOTE: To understand our changing view of violence, consider how common violence among government officials was two centuries ago. For example, Vice President Aaron Burr shot and killed Alexander Hamilton (the first U.S. Secretary of the Treasury) in a duel in 1804 in Weehawken, New Jersey.

NOTE: Drug abuse is closely linked to serious crime. In 1988, the Justice Department tested men arrested in New York, Washington, D.C., San Diego, and nine other cities and found that 75% tested positive for drug use. "If we're going to do something about the crime rate, we are going to have to confront the drug problem," stated study director James Stewart.

SOCIAL SURVEY: "Do you think the use of marijuana should be made legal or not?" (GSS 1994, N = 2,011; *Codebook*, 1994:109)
"Should" 22.7%   "Should not" 72.1%   DK/NR 5.2%

CRITICAL THINKING

Hate Crimes: Punishing Actions or Attitudes?

On an October evening in 1989, Todd Mitchell, an African-American teenager, and a group of friends were milling around the front of their apartment complex in Kenosha, Wisconsin. They had just watched the film *Mississippi Burning* and were fuming over a scene in which a white man beats a young black boy kneeling in prayer.

"Do you feel hyped up to move on some white people?" asked Mitchell. Minutes later, a young white boy walked toward the group on the other side of the street. Mitchell commanded: "There goes a white boy. Go get him!" The group swarmed around the white boy, knocking him to the ground, beating him up, and leaving him bloody and in a coma. The victors took his tennis shoes as a trophy of their conquest.

The black boys were identified and charged with the beating. At the trial of Todd Mitchell, who acted as the ringleader, the jury took the unusual step of finding the young man guilty of aggravated battery *motivated by racial hatred*. Instead of the typical two-year prison sentence, Mitchell was sentenced to jail for four years.

Three-fifths of the states have now adopted laws enhancing sentences for crimes motivated by bias. Supporters of hate-crime legislation make three arguments in favor of this trend. First, an offender's intentions have always figured in criminal deliberations, so weighing evidence of hatred represents nothing new. Second, crimes motivated by racial or other bias inflame public sentiment more than those carried out for more pedestrian reasons like monetary gain. Third, advocates contend,

Many neighborhoods of U.S. cities seethe with racial hatred. In 1989, a gang of young Italians killed an African-American man who ventured into their Bensonhurst section of Brooklyn in search of a used car. In the weeks that followed, African Americans led marches through the area claiming the right to move freely throughout the city; counter-protestors, too, made their feelings known.

victims of hate crimes typically suffer greater injury than victims of crimes with other motives.

Critics counter that most hate crimes involve, not hard-core racism, but impulsive and situational behavior, often involving juveniles. Even more important, critics maintain, hate-crime law is a direct threat to the First Amendment guarantees of free speech. Under such a law, they explain, courts sentence offenders not just for actions but for underlying attitudes. As Harvard law professor Alan Dershowitz cautions, "As much as I hate bigotry, I fear much more the Court attempting to control the minds of its citizens." In short, according to the critics, hate-crime statutes open the door to punishing beliefs rather than behavior.

In 1993, the Supreme Court upheld the sentence handed down to Todd Mitchell. In a unanimous decision, the justices stated that the government did not intend to punish an individual's beliefs. But, they reasoned, an abstract belief is no longer protected when it becomes the motive for a crime.

Sources: Greenhouse (1993), Jacobs (1993), and Terry (1993).

control of a person or persons by force or threat of force or violence and/or putting the victim in fear").

Crimes against property encompass *crimes that involve theft of property belonging to others.* "Property crimes" range from burglary ("the unlawful entry of a structure to commit a [serious crime] or a theft") to larceny-theft ("the unlawful taking, carrying, leading, or riding away of property from the possession of another"), auto theft ("the theft or attempted theft of a motor vehicle"), and arson ("any willful or malicious burning or attempt to burn the personal property of another").

NOTE: The *State Survey of Prison Inmates, 1991* reported a drop in marijuana use and a rise in cocaine use by prison inmates; half of all inmates claim to have used cocaine in some form (compared to about one-fourth in 1986). About 14% of inmates report committing their offense while under the influence of cocaine or crack.

Q: "I call [juvenile delinquents] drifters . . . Drift is motion gently guided by underlying influences . . . a gradual process [that is] unperceived by the actor, in which the first stage may be accidental . . ." David Matza (1964:29)

Q: "About five times more lowest- than highest-status boys appear in the official records; if records were complete and unselective, we estimate that the ratio would be closer to 1.5:1. . . . As far as we can tell from our data, delinquency among girls is not related to their social status." Martin Gold (1966)

A third category of offenses, not incorporated into major crime indexes, is **victimless crimes**, *violations of law in which there are no readily apparent victims*. So-called crimes without complaint include illegal drug use, prostitution, and gambling. "Victimless crime" is often a misnomer, however. How victimless is a crime when young people abusing drugs may have to steal to support a drug habit? How victimless is a crime if a young pregnant woman smoking crack causes the death or permanent injury of her baby? How victimless is a crime when a young runaway lives a desperate life of prostitution on the streets? And how victimless is a crime when a gambler falls so deeply into debt that he can no longer afford mortgage payments? In truth, the people who commit such crimes are themselves both offenders and victims.

Because public opinion about such activities varies considerably, the laws regulating victimless crimes differ from place to place. In the United States, gambling is legal only in a few locations; prostitution only in one (part of Nevada). Yet both activities are commonplace across the country. Homosexual (and some heterosexual) behavior among consenting adults is legally restricted in about half the states. Where such laws do exist, enforcement is light and selective.

Criminal Statistics

Statistics gathered by the Federal Bureau of Investigation show that crime rates have risen in recent decades, although these rates have remained roughly level since 1980. During the 1990s, police have tallied some 8 million serious crimes annually. Figure 8–2 on page 222 illustrates the trends for various major crimes.

Always read crime statistics with caution, however, since they include only crimes known to the police. The police learn about almost all homicides, but assaults—especially among acquaintances—are far less likely to be reported. The police record an even smaller proportion of property crimes, especially when losses are small. Some victims may not realize that a crime has occurred, or they may assume they have little chance of recovering their property even if they notify the police. And reports of rape, although rising over time, still grossly understate the extent of this crime.

One way to evaluate official crime statistics is through a *victimization survey*, in which a researcher asks a representative sample of people about their experience with crime. People do not always respond fully or truthfully to such surveys, experts acknowledge, but the results of these surveys indicate that actual criminality occurs at a rate two or three times higher than what official reports suggest.

The "Street" Criminal: A Profile

Government statistics paint a broad-brush picture of people arrested for violent and property crimes. We now examine the breakdown of these arrest statistics by age, gender, social class, race, and ethnicity.

Age

Official crime rates rise sharply during adolescence and peak in the late teens, falling thereafter. People between the ages of fifteen and twenty-four represent just 14 percent of the U.S. population, but they accounted for 43.6 percent of all arrests for violent crimes in 1993 and 44.0 percent for property crimes (U.S. Federal Bureau of Investigation, 1994).

In a disturbing trend, most serious crimes are taking place at the hands of younger offenders. Although the murder rate among adults has been falling in recent years, the number of teenagers charged with homicide is up sharply.

Gender

Although each sex constitutes roughly half the population, police collared males in 73.8 percent of all property-crime arrests in 1993. This means that men are arrested three times as often as women for these crimes. In the case of violent crimes, the disparity is even greater: 86.9 percent of arrests involved males and just 13.1 percent were of females (almost a seven-to-one ratio).

Some of this difference reflects the reluctance of law enforcement officials to define women as criminals. Even so, the arrest rate for women has been moving closer to that of men—one indication of increasing sexual equality in our society. Between 1983 and 1992, the increase in arrests of women was greater (37.0 percent) than that for men (14.6 percent) (U.S. Federal Bureau of Investigation, 1994). In global perspective, we see the same pattern, with the greatest sex difference in crime rates marking societies that most limit the social opportunities of women.

Social Class

The FBI does not take note of the social class of arrested persons; thus, no statistical data of the kind just presented are available with regard to the

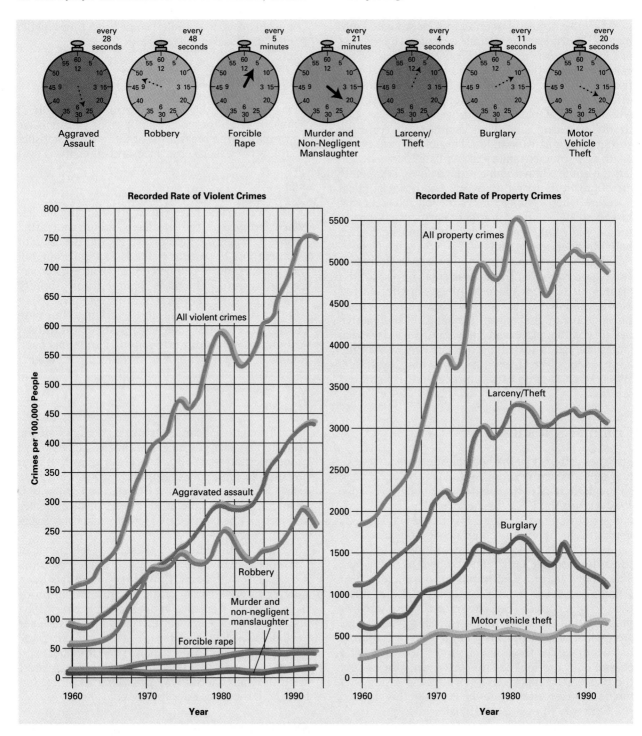

FIGURE 8–2 Crime Rates in the United States, 1960–1993

The graphs represent crime rates for various violent crimes and property crimes during recent decades. "Crime clocks" are another way of describing the frequency of crimes.

Source: U.S. Federal Bureau of Investigation (1995).

socioeconomic status of offenders. Extensive research by social scientists indicates that criminality is more widespread among people of lower social position, yet the connection between class and crime is more complicated than it appears on the surface (Wolfgang, Figlio, & Sellin, 1972; Clinard & Abbott, 1973; Braithwaite, 1981; Thornberry & Farnsworth, 1982; Wolfgang, Thornberry, & Figlio, 1987).

In part, this pattern reflects the historical tendency to view poor people as less worthy than those whose wealth and power confer "respectability" (Tittle & Villemez, 1977; Tittle, Villemez, & Smith, 1978; Elias, 1986). But it is a mistake to equate social disadvantage with criminality. While crime—especially violence—is a serious problem in the poorest inner-city neighborhoods, most people who live in these communities have no criminal records, and most crimes there are committed by relatively few hard-core offenders (Wolfgang, Figlio, & Sellin, 1972; Elliott & Ageton, 1980; Harries, 1990).

Moreover, the connection between social standing and criminality depends on what kind of crime one is talking about (Braithwaite, 1981). If we expand our definition of crime beyond street offenses to include white-collar crime, the "common criminal" suddenly looks much more affluent.

Race and Ethnicity

Both race and ethnicity have a strong correlation to crime rates, although the reasons are many and complex. Official statistics indicate that 66.9 percent of arrests for index crimes in 1993 involved white people. However, arrests of African Americans were higher than for whites in proportion to their numbers: Black people represent 12.5 percent of the population and 33.2 percent of arrests for property crimes (versus 64.4 percent for whites) and 45.7 percent of arrests for violent crimes (52.6 percent for whites) (U.S. Federal Bureau of Investigation, 1994).

What accounts for the disproportionate level of arrests among African Americans? Several factors stand out. To the degree that prejudice related to color or class prompts white police to arrest black people more readily, and leads citizens more willingly to report African Americans to police as suspected offenders, people of color are overly criminalized (Liska & Tausig, 1979; Unnever, Frazier, & Henretta, 1980; Smith & Visher, 1981; Holmes et al., 1993).

Second, race in the United States is closely related to social standing, which, as we have already explained, affects the likelihood of engaging in street crimes. Judith Blau and Peter Blau (1982) contend

The creators of this photograph, part of the United Colors of Benetton advertising campaign, intended to make the statement that people are linked together regardless of color. But so strong are our notions about crime and race that many individuals mistakenly interpreted the photograph as a white police officer escorting a black suspect. What can sociology contribute toward a more accurate understanding of the connection between crime and color?

that criminality is promoted by the sting of being poor in the midst of affluence as poor people come to perceive society as unjust. Because unemployment among African-American adults is double the rate among whites, because two-thirds of black children are born to single mothers (in contrast to one in five white children), and almost half of black children grow up in poverty (as opposed to about one in six white children), no one should be surprised at proportionately higher crime rates for African Americans (Sampson, 1987).

Third, remember that the official crime index excludes arrests for offenses ranging from drunk driving to white-collar violations. Clearly, this omission contributes to the view of the typical criminal as a person of color. If we broaden our definition of crime to include driving while intoxicated, insider stock trading, embezzlement, and cheating on income tax returns, the proportion of white criminals rises dramatically.

Finally, some categories of the population have unusually low rates of arrest. People of Asian descent, who account for about 3 percent of the population, figure in only 1 percent of all arrests. As Chapter 12 ("Race and Ethnicity") documents, Asian Americans enjoy higher than average incomes and have established a highly successful record of educational

There are almost enough guns in the United States to arm every woman, man, and child; about half of all households contain one or more such weapons. The "death clock" in New York City's Times Square tallies both the number of guns and the annual death toll from firearms. Guns are not the only key to our country's high crime rate, since unarmed criminality in the United States is also high by world standards. But the ready availability of guns does contribute to accidental shootings—especially by children—and it also raises the odds that interpersonal violence will become deadly.

achievement, which enhances job opportunities. Moreover, the cultural patterns that characterize Asian-American communities emphasize family solidarity and discipline, both of which inhibit criminality.

Crime in Global Perspective

By world standards, the United States has a lot of crime. The New York metropolitan area recorded 1,182 murders in 1995. Rarely does a day pass with no murder in New York; typically more New Yorkers are hit with stray bullets than are gunned down deliberately in cities elsewhere in the world.

The violent crime rate in the United States stands at about five times that of Europe; the rate of property crime is twice as high. The contrast is even greater between our society and the nations of Asia, including India and Japan, where rates of violent and property crime are among the lowest in the world.

Elliott Currie (1985) suggests that crime stems from our culture's emphasis on individual economic success, frequently at the expense of family and community cohesion. The United States also has extraordinary cultural diversity, the legacy of centuries of immigration. Moreover, economic inequality is higher in this country than in most other industrial societies. Taken together, our society has a relatively weak social fabric, which, combined with considerable frustration among this country's have-nots, generates widespread criminal behavior.

Another contributing factor to violence in the United States is extensive private ownership of guns. Of 23,271 murder victims in the United States in

1993, 69.2 percent died as a result of shootings. By the early 1990s, Texas and several other southern states were reporting that deaths from gunshots exceeded automobile-related fatalities. And, as Figure 8–3 shows, the United States is the runaway leader in handgun deaths among industrial societies.

One recent survey found that just over half of U.S. households have at least one gun, and this percentage seems not to have changed over the last fifty years (Gallup, 1993; Wright, 1995). Put differently, there are at least as many guns in the hands of private individuals as there are adults in the country (roughly one-third of all firearms are handguns). In large part, gun ownership reflects people's fear of crime; yet, the public is also fearful that easy access to guns makes crime more deadly. Concern about gun control led Congress in 1993 to pass the so-called Brady Bill, named for President Ronald Reagan's press secretary who was shot along with the president a decade before. The law requires a seven-day waiting period for the purchase of handguns to discourage impulsive buying and to give police time to perform background checks on purchasers.

But, as critics of gun control point out, waiting periods and background checks at retail gun stores are unlikely to affect criminals, almost all of whom obtain guns illegally (Wright, 1995). Moreover, we should be cautious about viewing gun control as a magic bullet in the war on crime. Elliott Currie notes, for example, that the number of Californians killed each year by knives alone exceeds the number of Canadians killed by weapons of all kinds. Most experts do think, however, that gun control will help lower the level of violence.

Crime rates are soaring in some of the largest cities of the world like Manila, Philippines, and São

SOCIAL SURVEY: "What do you think about U.S. spending on halting the rising crime rate?" (*Student CHIP Social Survey Software*, NATCRIM1; GSS 1973–91, N = 16,140)

	"Too little"	"About right"	"Too much"
Afri Amer	75.7%	18.3%	6.0%
Latino	71.3%	22.7%	6.0%
White Anglo	69.6%	25.0%	5.5%

SOCIAL SURVEY: "Do you happen to have in your home (house or garage) any guns or revolvers?" (GSS 1994, N = 1,977; *Codebook*, 1994:223)

"Yes" 41.0%   "No" 58.7%   DK/NR 0.4%

THEN AND NOW: In 1974, 46% of U.S. adults over 18 owned a gun; in 1995, the figure was 35%.

Paulo, Brazil, which have rapid population growth and millions of desperately poor people. By and large, however, the traditional character of less economically developed societies and their strong family structure allow local communities to control crime informally (Clinard & Abbott, 1973; *Der Spiegel*, 1989).

One exception to this pattern is crimes against women. Rape is surging throughout the world, especially in poor societies. Traditional social patterns that curb the economic opportunities available to women also promote prostitution. Global Map 8–1 on page 226 shows the extent of prostitution in various world regions.

Finally, as noted in earlier chapters, we are experiencing "globalization" on many fronts, including crime. Some types of crime have always been multinational, including terrorism, espionage, and arms dealing (Martin & Romano, 1992).

A more recent case in point is the illegal drug trade. In part, the proliferation of illegal drugs in the United States stems from "demand": There is a very profitable market for cocaine and other drugs in this country, as well as legions of young people willing to risk arrest or even violent death by engaging in the lucrative drug trade. But the "supply" side of the issue also propels drug trafficking. In the South American nation of Colombia, at least 20 percent of the people depend on cocaine production for their livelihood. Furthermore, not only is cocaine Colombia's most profitable export, but it outsells all other exports combined (including coffee). Clearly, then, understanding crimes such as drug dealing requires analyzing social conditions both in this country and around the world.

THE CRIMINAL JUSTICE SYSTEM

The criminal justice system is a society's formal response to crime. In some of the world's countries, military police keep a tight rein on people's behavior; in others, including the United States, officials have more limited powers to respond to specific violations of criminal law. We shall briefly introduce the key elements of this scheme: police, the courts, and the punishment of convicted offenders.

Police

The police serve as the primary point of contact between the population and the criminal justice system. In principle, the police maintain public order

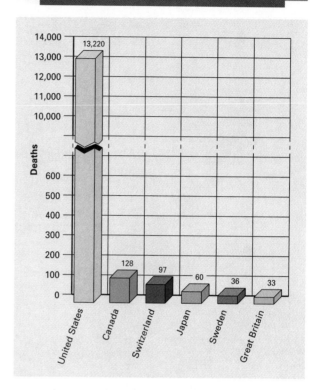

Global Snapshot

FIGURE 8–3 Number of Deaths by Handguns, 1992
Source: Handgun Control, Inc. (1995).

by uniformly enforcing the law. In reality, 550,000 full-time police officers in the United States (in 1992) cannot effectively monitor the activities of 260 million people. As a result, the police exercise considerable discretion about which situations warrant their attention and how to handle them.

How, then, do police carry out their duties? In a study of police behavior in five cities, Douglas Smith and Christy Visher (1981; Smith, 1987) concluded that, because they must respond swiftly, police make several quick assessments that guide their actions. First, how serious is the alleged crime? The more serious police perceive a situation to be, the more likely they are to make an arrest. Second, what is the victim's preference? Generally, if a victim demands that police make an arrest, they are likely to do so. Third, is the suspect

Q: "The entire [criminal justice] system . . . is charged with enforcing the law and maintaining order. What is distinctive about the responsibility of the police is that they are charged with performing these functions where all eyes are upon them and where the going is roughest, on the street." (The President's Commission on Law Enforcement and the Administration of Justice, 1966)

Q: "Don't call a man honest just because he never had a chance to steal." Yiddish proverb

GLOBAL: The People's Republic of China is much more efficient than the United States in disposing of prisoners. In the final days before the Chinese New Year in 1993, courts closed their books on fifty-five people convicted of crimes ranging from fraud to murder; all were quickly sentenced and shot in the back of the head with no delay and little fanfare.

Window on the World

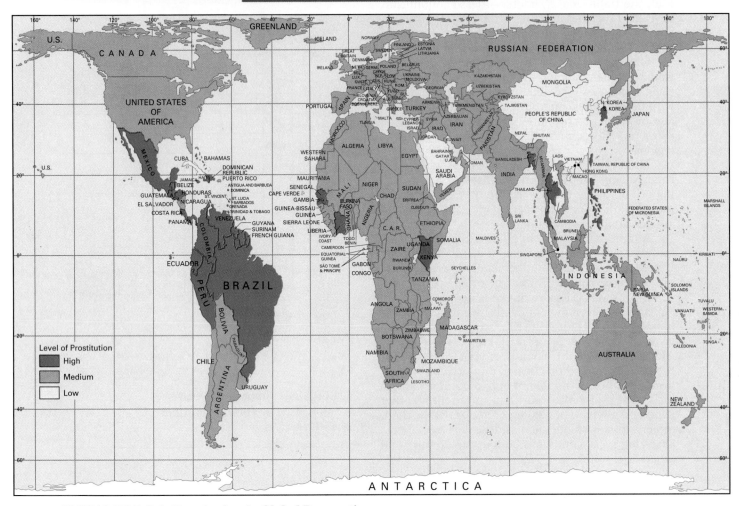

GLOBAL MAP 8–1 Prostitution in Global Perspective

Generally speaking, prostitution is widespread in societies of the world where women have low standing in relation to men. Officially, at least, the now-defunct socialist regimes in Eastern Europe and the former Soviet Union, as well as the People's Republic of China, boast of gender equality, including the elimination of "vice" such as prostitution, which oppresses women. By contrast, in much of Latin America, a region of pronounced patriarchy, prostitution is commonplace. In many Islamic societies patriarchy is also strong, but religious forces act as a counterbalance to restrain this practice. Western, industrial societies display a moderate amount of prostitution.

Source: *Peters Atlas of the World* (1990); updated by the author.

Seeing Ourselves

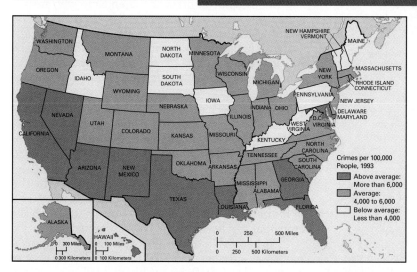

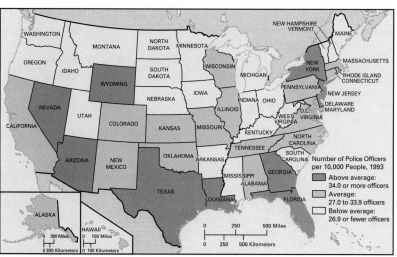

NATIONAL MAP 8–2

The Concentration of Crime and Police Across the United States

The top map reveals the relative crime rates for the various states. The map below shows the range of police strength, from a high of 90.3 police officers for every 10,000 people in Washington, D.C., to a low of 18.9 in South Dakota. Comparing the two maps, what do you conclude about the ability of police—all other things being equal—to curb crime?

Source: Data from U.S. Federal Bureau of Investigation (1995).

cooperative or not? Resisting police efforts increases a suspect's chances of arrest. Fourth, have they arrested the suspect before? Police are more likely to take into custody anyone whom they have arrested before, presumably because this suggests guilt. Fifth, are bystanders present? According to Smith and Visher, the presence of observers prompts police to take stronger control of a situation; arrests also move the encounter from the street (the suspect's turf) to the police department (where law officers have the edge). Sixth, what is the suspect's race? All else being equal,

Smith and Visher contend, police are more likely to arrest people of color than whites, perceiving suspects of African or Hispanic descent as either more dangerous or more likely to be guilty.

Finally, where in the United States is police power the greatest? The ratio of police to citizens is highest in cities with large minority populations and great income disparities between rich and poor. The set of National Maps above shows that states where the hand of law enforcement is heaviest are not always those with the lowest crime rates.

Q: "Of all the institutions in American society, prisons are among the most maligned and vilified." Richard A. Wright

THEN AND NOW: Retribution is part of virtually all ancient codes of law. The Latin concept, *lex talionis*, refers to the "law of exchange" by which an offender's punishment fits the crime.

Q: "Eighty-six percent of incarcerated juveniles owned at least one firearm at some time in their lives; 83% owned a gun at the time

TABLE 8–2 Four Justifications of Punishment: A Summary

Retribution	The oldest justification of punishment that still holds sway today. Punishment is atonement for a moral wrong by an individual; in principle, punishment should be comparable in severity to the deviance itself.
Deterrence	An early modern approach. Deviance is considered social disruption, which society acts to control. People are viewed as rational and self-interested; deterrence works because the pains of punishment outweigh the pleasures of deviance.
Rehabilitation	A modern strategy linked to the development of social sciences. Deviance is viewed as the product of social problems (such as poverty) or personal problems (such as mental illness). Social conditions are improved and offenders subjected to intervention appropriate to their condition.
Societal protection	A modern approach easier to implement than rehabilitation. If society is unable or unwilling to rehabilitate offenders or reform social conditions, people are protected from further deviance by incarceration or execution of the offender.

Courts

After arrest, a court determines a suspect's guilt or innocence. In principle, our courts rely on an adversarial process involving attorneys—one team representing the defendant and another the state—in the presence of a judge who monitors legal procedures.

In practice, however, about 90 percent of criminal cases are resolved prior to court appearance through **plea bargaining**, *a negotiation in which the state reduces the charge against a defendant in exchange for a guilty plea.* For example, the state may offer a defendant charged with burglary a lesser charge of possessing burglary tools in exchange for a guilty plea.

Plea bargaining is widespread because it spares the state the time and expense of trials. In addition, government officials could not possibly bring every case to trial; since the number of cases entering the system more than doubled during the 1980s, this is especially true today. Moreover, a trial is unnecessary if there is little disagreement as to the facts of the case. By selectively trying only a small proportion of the

cases, then, the courts channel their resources into those they deem most important (Reid, 1991).

But this process pressures defendants (who are presumed innocent) to plead guilty. A person can exercise the right to a trial, but only at the risk of receiving a stiffer sentence if found guilty. Plea bargaining may be efficient but, say critics, it circumvents the adversarial process and often undercuts the rights of defendants.

Punishment

In the fall of 1994, Iraqi television offered viewers in Baghdad special coverage of punishment meted out to a man convicted of theft. Viewers cringed at the closeup of a severed human hand, followed by the offender staggering in pain as he clutched the stump of his forearm. Careful observers could also see a black cross that had been branded on his forehead.

Barbaric? No doubt. But this televised punishment was a desperate act by Iraq's leaders to control a rising tide of theft, and it highlights key questions surrounding the act of punishment: Why do governments punish at all? If punishment is necessary, how should it be carried out?

First, the point of purpose: On this score, scholars advance four justifications for punishment.

Retribution

The celebrated justice of the Supreme Court, Oliver Wendell Holmes, stated, "The first requirement of a sound body of law is that it should correspond with the actual feelings and demands of the community." Because people react to crime with a passion for revenge, Holmes continued, "the law has no choice but to satisfy [that] craving" (quoted in Carlson, 1976).

One key reason to punish, then, is to satisfy a society's need for **retribution** or *moral vengeance by which society inflicts suffering on the offender comparable to that caused by the offense.* Retribution rests on a view of society as a moral entity in balance. When criminality upsets this balance, punishment exacted in comparable measure restores the moral order, as suggested by the biblical dictum "An eye for an eye."

Retribution stands as the oldest justification for punishment. During the Middle Ages, most people viewed crime as sin—an offense against God as well as society—that warranted a harsh response. Today, critics charge that retribution does little to reform the offender; even so, this principle retains widespread support.

Deterrence

A second justification for punishment, **deterrence**, amounts to *the attempt to discourage criminality through punishment*. Deterrence reflects the eighteenth-century Enlightenment notion that, as calculating and rational creatures, humans will forgo deviance if they perceive that the pain of punishment outweighs the pleasure of mischief.

Deterrence emerged as reform directed at the harsh punishments based on retribution. Why cut off a hand for stealing, critics asked, if theft can be discouraged with a prison sentence? As the concept of deterrence gained acceptance, execution and physical mutilation of criminals in most industrial societies were replaced by milder forms of punishment such as incarceration.

Punishment may deter crime in two ways. *Specific deterrence* demonstrates to an individual offender that crime does not pay. Through *general deterrence*, the punishment of one person serves as an example to others.

Rehabilitation

The third justification for punishment is **rehabilitation**, *a program for reforming the offender to preclude subsequent offenses*. Rehabilitation paralleled the development of the social sciences in the nineteenth century. According to sociologists of that time (and also since), crime and other deviance spring from an unfavorable environment marked by poverty or a lack of parental supervision. Logically, then, if offenders learn to be deviant, they can also learn to obey the rules; the key is controlling the environment. *Reformatories* or *houses of correction* served as a controlled setting to help people learn proper behavior (recall the description of total institutions in Chapter 5, "Socialization").

Rehabilitation resembles deterrence in that both motivate the offender toward conformity. But rehabilitation emphasizes constructive improvement, while deterrence (like retribution) inflicts suffering on an offender. In addition, while retribution demands that the punishment fit the crime, rehabilitation tailors treatment to the offender. Thus identical crimes would prompt similar acts of retribution but might call for different programs of rehabilitation.

Societal Protection

A final justification for punishment is **societal protection**, *a means by which society renders an offender incapable of further offenses temporarily*

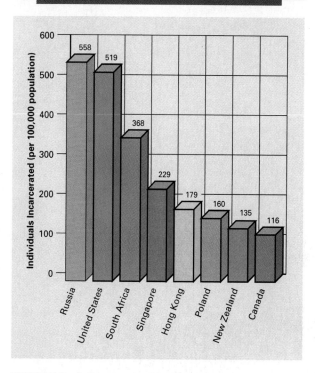

Global Snapshot

FIGURE 8–4 Incarceration Rates, 1993
Source: Mauer (1994).

through incarceration or permanently by execution. Like deterrence, societal protection is a rational approach to punishment and seeks to protect society from crime.

Table 8–2 summarizes these four justifications of punishment. Note, too, Figure 8–4 showing that the United States incarcerates a larger share of its population than most other countries in the world.

Critical evaluation.   We have identified four justifications for punishment. Assessing the actual consequences of punishment, however, is no simple task.

The value of retribution reminds us of Durkheim's contention that punishing the deviant person bolsters people's moral consciousness. To accomplish this objective, punishment was traditionally a public event. Public executions occurred in England until 1868; the last public execution in the United States took place in Kentucky in 1937. Even today, the mass media ensure

DISCUSS: Does the increasing use of lethal injection illustrate the "medicalization of death"? Some oppose this practice because it sugar-coats capital punishment by making suffering less apparent; others hail it as humane; still others, of course, object to any form of capital punishment.

NOTE: Among the 7,000 people executed in the United States during this century, not one was formally declared innocent, although some critics are convinced that several hundred probably were.

NOTE: The minimum age at which an offender can be put to death is now sixteen, based on the Supreme Court's decision in *Thompson v. Oklahoma* (June 1988). The essential issue is how old does a person have to be to be considered consciously evil and to act accordingly?

Q: "Good laws derive from evil habits." Macrobius

Dutch painter Vincent van Gogh (1853–1890) strongly identified with suffering people that he found around him. Perhaps this is why he included his own likeness in this portrait of the dungeon-like prisons of the nineteenth century. Since then, the stark isolation and numbing depersonalization of prison life has changed little. Prisons are still custodial institutions in which officials make few efforts at rehabilitation.

Vincent van Gogh, *Prisoners' Round.* Dutch. Pushkin State Museum, Moscow.

public awareness of executions carried out inside prison walls (Kittrie, 1971).

Nonetheless, it is difficult to prove scientifically that punishment upholds social morality. Often it advances one conception of justice at the expense of another, as when our government imprisons people who refuse to perform military service.

To some degree, punishment serves as a specific deterrent (Wright, 1994). Yet our society also has a high rate of **criminal recidivism,** *subsequent offenses committed by people previously convicted of crimes.* A 1991 study of state prison inmates found that 62 percent had been incarcerated before, and 45 percent had been sentenced three or more times (U.S. Bureau of Justice Statistics, 1991). Put more simply, once released from jail, half of former inmates return to prison within several years. Such a high rate of recidivism raises questions about the extent to which punishment actually deters crime. Then, too, only about one-third of all crimes are known to police, and of these, only about one in five results in an arrest. The old adage that "crime doesn't pay" rings rather hollow when we consider that such a small proportion of offenses ever result in punishment.

General deterrence is even more difficult to investigate scientifically, since we have no way of knowing how people might act if they were unaware of punishments meted out to others. In the debate over capital punishment, permitted in thirty-six states, critics of the practice point to research indicating that the death penalty has limited value as a general deterrent in the United States, which is the only Western, industrial society that routinely executes serious offenders (Sellin, 1980; van den Haag & Conrad, 1983; Archer & Gartner, 1987; Lester, 1987; Bailey & Peterson, 1989; Bailey, 1990; Bohm, 1991).

Prisons accomplish short-term societal protection by keeping offenders off the streets, but they do little to reshape attitudes or behavior in the long term (Carlson, 1976; Wright, 1994). Rehabilitation may be an unrealistic expectation, since, according to Sutherland's theory of differential association, locking someone up among criminals for months or years should simply strengthen criminal attitudes and skills. And because incarceration severs whatever social ties inmates may have in the outside world, individuals may be prone to further crime upon their release, consistent with Hirschi's control theory.

Finally, inmates returning to the surrounding world contend with the stigma of being ex-convicts, often an obstacle to successful integration. One study of young offenders in Philadelphia found that boys who were sentenced to long prison terms—and thus likely to acquire a criminal stigma—later committed both more crimes and more serious ones (Wolfgang, Figlio, & Sellin, 1972).

Ultimately, we should never assume that the criminal justice system—the police, courts, and prisons—can eliminate crime. The point here, made strongly in the final box as it has been throughout this chapter, is simple: Crime and all other deviance are more than simply the acts of "bad people"; they are inextricably bound up in the operation of society itself.

SOCIAL SURVEY: "Do you favor or oppose the death penalty for persons convicted of murder?" (GSS 1994, N = 2,992; *Codebook*, 1994:104)

"Favor" 74.0%   "Oppose" 19.4%   DK/NR 6.6%
(*CHIP1 Social Survey Software*, CAPPUN1,2; GSS 1974–89, N = 18,863)

"Favor"   "Oppose"

	"Favor"	"Oppose"
Men	78.8%	21.2%
Women	70.0%	30.0%
Afri Amer	47.7%	52.3%
Hisp Amer	69.7%	30.3%
Whites	77.5%	22.5%

Q: "In this life one frequently finds greater rewards for vice than for virtue." René Descartes (1641)

Controversy & Debate

What Can Be Done About Crime?

People across the United States are fearful—and fed up—with crime. Dogs for protection, special locks, and security systems have never been more popular. And no wonder: Almost half of U.S. adults claim that they are afraid to walk alone at night in the vicinity of their own homes (NORC, 1994:222). Government spending on crime prevention has risen steadily over the past few decades, but so has the crime rate. What, then, can be done?

Travis Hirschi, sociologist and author of the well-known "control theory," recently offered the radical suggestion that we abandon the criminal justice system as we know it in favor of a new approach. Although his proposals will surely be controversial, they are grounded in decades of research about crime and offenders.

Hirschi begins by pointing out two key characteristics that define the population of criminal offenders. The first is *age*; specifically, crime is a young person's (typically a young *man*'s) game. Crime rates are high in the late teens and early twenties, and they fall quickly thereafter. Second, Hirschi continues, offenders are individuals who take a short-term view of their lives. Most law breakers, claims Hirschi, are individuals "relatively unable to sustain a course of action toward some distant goal, whether that goal be education, friendship, employment, or criminal gain. In fact, the defining characteristic of offenders appears to be *low self-control.*"

These two facts alone, he reasons, mean the criminal justice system, as it currently operates, is not up to the task. For one thing, punishment from the courts is too uncertain (most crimes, after all, go unpunished), and too far removed in time (arrest, trial, and incarceration of criminals often takes a year or more), to deter the typical offender. Thus, Hirschi explains, popular calls for "stiffer sentences" actually have little effect in suppressing crime. And even when offenders are sent off to prison, all but the small percentage of habitual offenders are cared for at taxpayer expense at a time when they are moving beyond the peak "crime years" simply because they are growing older. Statistically speaking, then, offenders aging in prison represent a crime threat already shrinking on its own.

Therefore, rather than trying to incapacitate or rehabilitate adults, society would better protect itself by adopting a whole new approach. Hirschi reasons that we must intervene earlier, directing resources toward young people *before* they commit crimes. One proposal he advances is to restrict the unsupervised activities of teenagers—those at highest risk of criminal behavior. Effective crime control, he explains, depends on regulating the access of teenagers not only to guns and drugs, but also to alcohol, cars, and perhaps even each other.

A second initiative takes effect even earlier in the life course. The most effective way to control crime, Hirschi concludes, is for our society to raise children who learn the key trait of *self-control.* Teaching children to understand the long-term consequences of their behavior is a task ill-suited to government, Hirschi cautions; it is the responsibility of parents. But government can help by targeting seriously dysfunctional families for assistance and by any other means that fosters strong—preferably two-parent—families. Simply "delaying pregnancy among teenage girls," he predicts, "would probably do more to affect long-term crime rates than all the criminal justice programs combined." By increasing the number of caregivers relative to children, Hirschi concludes, society would increase the care and educational resources available to our children and, in the process, protect everyone from crime.

Proposals of this kind will surely provoke criticism. If we reduce support for police and prisons, don't we risk a further outbreak of crime? Without locking up today's offenders, how can we satisfy our society's desire for retribution? Shouldn't we attack the broader conditions that breed crime, such as poverty and racial prejudice? And is it fair to curb the civil rights of *all* teenagers just so *some* would be prevented from committing crimes?

Continue the debate . . .

1. *Do you think limiting teenagers' freedom would reduce crime? What civil rights issues are raised by such a plan?*

2. *Do you think increasing the share of two-parent households would cut the crime rate? Can society realistically shape families in this way?*

3. *Would economic programs directed at reducing poverty diminish the crime problem? What specific programs would you suggest?*

Source: Based on Gottfredson & Hirschi (1995).

SUMMARY

1. Deviance refers to normative violations ranging from mild breaches of etiquette to serious violence.

2. Biological investigation, from Caesare Lombroso's nineteenth-century observations of convicts to recent research in human genetics, has yet to offer much insight into the causes of crime.

3. Psychological study links deviance to abnormal personality stemming from either biological or environmental causes. Psychological theories help to explain some kinds of deviance.

4. Deviance has societal rather than individual roots because it (1) exists in relation to cultural norms, (2) results from a process of social definition, and (3) is shaped by the distribution of social power.

5. Using the structural-functional paradigm, Durkheim asserted that responding to deviance affirms values and norms, clarifies moral boundaries, promotes social unity, and encourages social change.

6. The symbolic-interaction paradigm is the basis of labeling theory, which holds that deviance arises in the reaction of others to a person's behavior. Acquiring a stigma of deviance can lead to secondary deviance and the onset of a deviant career.

7. Following the approach of Karl Marx, social-conflict theory holds that laws and other norms reflect the interests of powerful members of society. Social-conflict theory also spotlights white-collar crimes, which cause extensive social harm even though the offenders are rarely branded as criminals.

8. Official statistics indicate that arrest rates peak in late adolescence, then drop steadily with advancing age. Three-fourths of those arrested for property crimes are males, as are almost nine of ten people charged with violent crimes.

9. People of lower social position commit more street crime than those with greater social privilege. When white-collar crimes are counted among criminal offenses, however, this disparity in overall criminal activity diminishes.

10. More whites than African Americans are arrested for street crimes. However, African Americans are arrested more often than whites in proportion to their respective populations. Asian Americans have lower-than-average rates of arrest.

11. The police exercise considerable discretion in their work. Research reveals that factors such as the seriousness of the offense, the presence of bystanders, and the accused being African American make arrest more likely.

12. Although ideally an adversarial system, U.S. courts resolve most cases through plea bargaining. While efficient, this method nevertheless places less powerful people at a disadvantage.

13. Justifications for punishment include retribution, deterrence, rehabilitation, and societal protection. Because its consequences are difficult to evaluate scientifically, punishment—like deviance itself—sparks controversy among sociologists and the public as a whole.

KEY CONCEPTS

crime the violation of norms a society formally enacts into criminal law

crimes against the person (violent crimes) crimes that direct violence or the threat of violence against others

crimes against property (property crimes) crimes that involve theft of property belonging to others

criminal justice system a societal reaction to alleged violations of the law utilizing police, courts, and prison officials

criminal recidivism subsequent offenses committed by people previously convicted of crimes

deterrence the attempt to discourage criminality through punishment

deviance the recognized violation of cultural norms

hate crime a criminal act against a person or a person's property by an offender motivated by racial or other bias

juvenile delinquency the violation of legal standards by the young

labeling theory the assertion that deviance and conformity result, not so much from what people do, as from how others respond to those actions

medicalization of deviance the transformation of moral and legal issues into medical matters

plea bargaining a legal negotiation in which the state reduces the charge against a defendant in exchange for a guilty plea

rehabilitation a program for reforming the offender to preclude subsequent offenses

retribution moral vengeance by which society inflicts suffering on an offender comparable to that caused by the offense

retrospective labeling the interpretation of someone's past consistent with present deviance

societal protection a means by which society renders an offender incapable of further offenses temporarily through incarceration or permanently by execution

stigma a powerfully negative social label that radically changes a person's self-concept and social identity

victimless crimes violations of law in which there are no readily apparent victims

white-collar crime crimes committed by persons of high social position in the course of their occupations

CRITICAL-THINKING QUESTIONS

1. How does a sociological view of deviance differ from the common-sense notion that bad people do bad things?

2. Identify Durkheim's functions of deviance. From his point of view, could anyone forge a society free from deviance? Why or why not?

3. How does social power affect deviant labeling? How do gender, race, and class figure in this process?

4. Why do you think crime rates have risen in the United States over the last fifty years? Do you agree or disagree with Travis Hirschi's prescription for crime control presented in the chapter's final box? Why?

SUGGESTED READINGS

Classic Sources

Kai Erikson. *Wayward Puritans: A Study in the Sociology of Deviance.* New York: Wiley, 1966.
This historical account of the Puritans of Massachusetts Bay reinforces Durkheim's functional theory of deviance.

Thomas Szasz. *The Myth of Mental Illness: Foundations of a Theory of Personal Conduct.* New York: Harper & Row, 1961.
This influential and controversial treatise condemns the concept of mental illness as a fiction designed to impose conformity on those who are different.

Contemporary Sources

Gregory M. Herek and Kevin T. Berrill. *Hate Crimes: Confronting Violence Against Lesbians and Gay Men.* Newbury Park, Calif.: Sage, 1992.
This collection of essays analyzes the legal, psychological, and social issues surrounding bias crimes against homosexual men and women.

Richard A. Wright. *In Defense of Prisons.* Westport, Conn.: Greenwood Press, 1994.
Noting that prisons are among the most maligned institutions of our society, Wright assesses the strengths and weaknesses of U.S. prisons.

Global Sources

Frances Heidensohn. *Women in Control? The Role of Women in Law Enforcement.* Oxford, U.K.: Clarendon Press, 1992.
This look at the place of women in police work points up differences between the United States and Great Britain.

Ikuyo Sato. *Kamikaze Biker: Parody and Anomy in Affluent Japan.* Chicago: University of Chicago Press, 1991.
In the tradition of Emile Durkheim, this account of juvenile delinquency in Japan highlights the breakdown of traditional social controls that often accompanies material affluence.

ANTONIO RUIZ,
EL CORZO, VERANO,
1937

Social Stratification

On April 10, 1912, slipped away from the docks on its maiden voyage across the proud symbol of the new industrial the ocean liner *Titanic* of Southampton, England, North Atlantic to New York. A age, the towering ship carried twenty-three hundred passengers, some enjoying more luxury than most travelers today could imagine. By contrast, poor immigrants crowded the lower decks, journeying to what they hoped would be a better life in the United States.

Two days out, the crew received radio warnings of icebergs in the area but paid little notice. Then, near midnight, as the ship steamed swiftly and silently westward, a lookout was stunned to see a massive shape rising out of the dark ocean directly ahead. Moments later, the *Titanic* collided with a huge iceberg, almost as tall as the ship itself, which split open its starboard side as if the grand vessel were nothing more than a giant tin can.

Seawater surged into the ship's lower levels, and within twenty-five minutes people were rushing for the lifeboats. By 2:00 in the morning the bow of the *Titanic* was submerged and the stern reared high above the water. Clinging to the deck, quietly observed by those in the lifeboats, hundreds of helpless passengers solemnly passed their final minutes before the ship disappeared into the frigid Atlantic (Lord, 1976).

The tragic loss of more than sixteen hundred lives made news around the world. Looking back dispassionately at this terrible accident with a sociological eye, however, we see that some categories of passengers had much better odds of survival than others. In an age of conventional gallantry, women and children boarded the boats first, so that eighty percent of the casualties were men. Class, too, was at work. Of people holding first-class tickets, more than sixty percent were saved, primarily because they were on the upper decks, where warnings were sounded first and lifeboats were accessible. Only thirty-six percent of the second-class passengers survived, and of the third-class passengers on the lower decks, only twenty-four percent escaped drowning. On board the *Titanic*, class turned out to mean much more than the quality of accommodations: It was truly a matter of life or death.

The fate of the *Titanic* dramatically illustrates the consequences of social inequality for the ways people live—and sometimes whether they live at all. This chapter explores the important concept of social stratification.

Chapter 10 continues the story by highlighting social inequality in the United States, and Chapter 11 examines how our country fits into a global system of wealth and poverty.

Q: "O, when degree is shak'd
    Which is the ladder of all high designs,
    The enterprise is sick! . . .
    Take but degree away, untune that string,
    And hark what discord follows!"
William Shakespeare, *Troilus and Cressida*, on the breakdown
of the "old order," for which he had much sympathy.

Q: "All animals are equal, but some are more equal than others."
George Orwell, *Animal Farm*
DIVERSITY: Regarding Point 4 below, Joan Huber Rytina,
William H. Form, and John Pease found that people of higher social
position saw the United States as a more "open" society. Moreover,
they found that whites perceived more opportunity than blacks did.
[See *American Journal of Sociology* 75, 4 (January 1970):703–16.]

*The personal experience of poverty is captured in
Sebastiao Salgado's haunting photograph, which stands as
a universal portrait of human suffering. The essential
sociological insight is that, however strongly individuals
feel its effects, our social standing is largely a consequence
of the way in which a society (or a world of societies)
structures opportunity and reward. To the core of our
being, then, we are all the products of social stratification.*

WHAT IS SOCIAL STRATIFICATION?

For tens of thousands of years, humans the world over
lived in small hunting and gathering societies.
Although members of these bands might single out
one person as being swifter, stronger, or more skilled in
collecting food, everyone had more or less the same
social standing. As societies became more complex—a
process detailed in Chapter 4 ("Society")—a monumental change came about. The social system elevated
entire categories of people above others, providing one
segment of the population with a disproportionate
amount of money, power, and schooling.

Sociologists use the concept **social stratification**
to refer to *a system by which a society ranks categories of
people in a hierarchy*. Social stratification is a matter of
four basic principles.

1. **Social stratification is a characteristic of society,
   not simply a reflection of individual differences.**
   Members of industrial societies consider social
   standing as a reflection of personal talent and
   effort, although we typically exaggerate the extent
   to which people control their destinies. Did a
   higher percentage of the first-class passengers survive the sinking of the *Titanic* because they were

smarter or better swimmers than the second- and
third-class passengers? Hardly. They fared better
because of their privileged position on the ship.
Similarly, children born into wealthy families are
more likely than those born into poverty to enjoy
health, achieve academically, succeed in their
life's work, and live well into old age. Neither rich
nor poor people are responsible for creating social
stratification, yet this system shapes the lives of
them all.

2. **Social stratification persists over generations.** To
   understand that stratification stems from society
   rather than individual differences, note how
   inequality persists over time. In all societies, parents confer their social positions on their children,
   so that patterns of inequality stay much the same
   from generation to generation.

   Especially in industrial societies, however,
   some individuals do experience **social mobility**,
   change in one's position in a social hierarchy. Social
   mobility may be upward or downward. Our society celebrates the achievements of a Madonna or
   a Bill Cosby, both of whom rose to prominence
   from modest beginnings. But we also acknowledge that people move downward as a result of
   business setbacks, unemployment, or illness.
   More often, people move *horizontally* when they
   exchange one occupation for another that is comparable. For most people, however, social standing
   remains much the same over a lifetime.

3. **Social stratification is universal but variable.**
   Social stratification is found everywhere. At the
   same time, *what* is unequal and *how* unequal it is
   vary from one society to another. Among the
   members of technologically simple societies, social
   differentiation is minimal and based mostly on age
   and sex. With the development of sophisticated
   technology for growing food, societies also forge
   complex and more rigid systems for distributing
   what people produce. As we shall see, industrialization has the effect of increasing social mobility
   and of reducing at least some kinds of social
   inequality.

4. **Social stratification involves not just inequality
   but beliefs.** Any system of inequality not only
   gives some people more resources than others but
   defines certain arrangements as fair. Just as *what* is
   unequal differs from society to society, then, so
   does the explanation of *why* people should be
   unequal. Virtually everywhere, however, people
   with the greatest social privileges express the
   strongest support for their society's system of

NOTE: The Latin root of "caste," *cast(us)*, means "chaste" or "pure;" its later use (for example, the Portuguese word *casta*) means "race" or "blood."

GLOBAL: In the Hindu varna system, *Brahmins* were traditionally priests, *Ksatriyas* were military and political leaders, *Vaishyas* farmers and merchants, *Shudras* the peasants and menial laborers, and *Dasyus* the untouchables outside the varna system. The first

three categories are "twice-born." *Jati* is a more recent development (500 C.E.) including some 3,000 specialized, occupational groups.

GLOBAL: In India, *varna* (a term roughly meaning "color") is a system of ranking; *jati* are groupings of local families. Note also that, despite evident similarities, Hindu *varna* has many differences from the European estate system.

A desire to better one's social position fuels immigration the world over, with the flow of humanity from poorer countries to richer ones. So-called "boat people" from Caribbean nations including Haiti and Cuba have risked their lives in order to find greater opportunity in the United States.

social stratification, while those with fewer social resources are more likely to seek change.

CASTE AND CLASS SYSTEMS

In describing social stratification in particular societies, sociologists often use two opposing standards: "closed" systems that allow little change in social position and "open" systems that permit considerable social mobility (Tumin, 1985).

The Caste System

A **caste system** amounts to *social stratification based on ascription*. A pure caste system, in other words, is "closed" so that birth alone determines one's social destiny with no opportunity for social mobility based on individual efforts. In caste systems, then, categories of people are ranked in a rigid hierarchy.

Two Illustrations: India and South Africa

A number of the world's societies—most of them agrarian—approximate caste systems. One example is India, or at least India's traditional villages in which most people still live. The Indian system of castes (or *varna*, a Sanskrit word that means "color") is composed of four major categories: Brahmin, Kshatriya, Vaishya, and Shudra. On the local level, however, each is composed of hundreds of subcaste (or *jati*) groups.

Caste has also played a key role in the history of South Africa. In this nation's policy of *apartheid*, the 5 million South Africans of European ancestry enjoy a commanding share of wealth and power, dominating some 30 million black South Africans. In a middle position are another 3 million mixed-race people, known as "coloreds," and about 1 million Asians. The box on pages 238–39 describes the current state of South Africa's racial caste system.

In a caste system, birth determines the fundamental shape of people's lives in four crucial respects. First, traditional caste groups are linked to occupation, so that generations of a family perform the same type of work. In rural India, although some occupations (such as farming) are open to all, castes are identified with the work their members do (as priests, barbers, leather workers, street sweepers, and so on). In South Africa, whites still hold almost all the desirable jobs, with most blacks consigned to manual labor and other low-level service work.

No rigid social hierarchy could persist if people married outside their own categories; if they did, what rank would their children hold? To shore up the hierarchy, then, a second trait of caste systems is mandating that people marry others of the same ranking. Sociologists call this pattern *endogamous* marriage (*endo* stems from Greek, meaning "within"). Traditionally, Indian parents select their children's marriage partners, often before the children reach their teens. Until 1985, South Africa banned marriage and even

GLOBAL SOCIOLOGY

Race as Caste: A Report From South Africa

At the southern tip of the African continent lies South Africa, a territory about the size of Alaska, with a 1995 population of some 45 million. The indigenous African people were joined by Dutch traders and farmers who settled the region in the mid-seventeenth century. Early in the nineteenth century, a second wave of colonists—this time British—pushed the descendants of the Dutch settlers inland. By the beginning of this century, the British had gained control of the entire country, naming it the Union of South Africa.

In 1961, formal ties with the United Kingdom ended, making the Republic of South Africa a politically independent nation. But freedom was a reality only for the white minority who dominated the society by imposing the policy of apartheid, or racial separation. A common practice for many years, apartheid was enshrined in a 1948 law denying the black majority South African citizenship, ownership of land, and any formal voice in the government.

Apartheid rendered blacks a subordinate caste, and offered them only the education needed to perform

Nelson Mandela, leader of the African National Congress (ANC), who was imprisoned by the white apartheid government for twenty-seven years, celebrates his election victory as South Africa's first black president.

low-paying jobs deemed inappropriate for whites. So separate were the races that white people earned four times what black people did and even whites of limited means became accustomed to having a black household servant. A final plank in the platform of apartheid was the forcible resettlement of millions of blacks to so-called homelands, poor districts that resemble the desolate reservations that are home to many Indians in the United States.

The prosperous white minority defended apartheid, claiming that blacks threatened their cultural traditions or, more fundamentally, were inferior beings. But resistance to apartheid rose steadily, prompting whites to resort to brutal military repression to maintain their power. Under racially based law, police could arrest and detain any black person for any violation of or opposition to apartheid.

Despite severe repression, violent confrontations became an almost

sex between the races; even now, interracial couples are rare since blacks and whites continue to live in separate areas.

Third, caste guides everyday life so that people remain in the company of "their own kind." Hindus in India enforce this segregation with the belief that a ritually "pure" person of a higher caste will be "polluted" by contact with someone of lower standing. Apartheid in South Africa achieved much the same effect.

Fourth, and finally, caste systems rest on powerful cultural beliefs. Indian culture is built on Hindu traditions that mandate accepting one's life work, whatever it may be, as a moral duty. And, although apartheid is no longer a matter of law, South Africans still cling to notions distinguishing "white jobs" from "black jobs."

Caste and Agrarian Life

Caste systems are typical of agrarian societies, because the lifelong routines of agriculture depend on a rigid sense of duty and discipline. Thus, caste still persists in rural India, half a century after being formally outlawed, even as its grip is easing in the nation's more industrial cities, where most people exercise greater choice about their work and marriage partners (Bahl, 1991). Similarly, the rapid industrialization of South Africa elevated the importance of personal choice and individual rights, making the abolition of apartheid only a matter of time. In the United States, although elements of caste survive, treating people categorically on the basis of their race or sex is now widely denounced as unjust, inviting charges of racism and sexism.

everyday occurrence, sparked primarily by younger blacks impatient for a political voice and economic opportunity. Support for change also swelled outside the country as, during the 1980s, some two hundred U.S. corporations severed economic ties with South Africa. This foreign divestiture staggered the South African economy and effectively pressured the government into making significant reforms.

In 1984, the government granted all South Africans the right to form labor unions, to enter various occupations once restricted to whites, and to own property. Soon afterward, officials abolished a host of "petty apartheid" regulations that segregated the races in public places, including beaches and hospitals.

In 1990, the legalization of the anti-apartheid African National Congress (ANC) and the release from prison of its leader, Nelson Mandela, raised the hope for more basic change. In 1992, a majority of white voters endorsed, in principle, an end to apartheid. Two years later, all South African adults—regardless of race—voted in a national election that swept Nelson Mandela into office as South Africa's new president.

While enraging South African traditionalists, these changes actually have brought about only minimal changes in social stratification. The legal right to own property means little to millions of black people who are dirt poor; opening hospitals to people of every race is an empty gesture for those who cannot afford to pay for medical care; ending racial barriers to the professions offers scant real opportunity to men and women without much schooling. The harsh reality is that more than one-third of all black adults cannot find any work at all, and, by the government's own estimate, half of all black people live in desperate conditions.

The worst off are those called *ukuhleleleka* in the Xhosa language, which means the marginal people. Some 7 million black South Africans fall into this category, living on the edge of society and on the edge of life itself. In Soweto-by-the-Sea, an idyllic-sounding community, thousands of people live crammed into shacks built of packing crates, corrugated metal, cardboard, and other discarded materials. There is no electricity for lights or refrigeration. Without plumbing, people haul sewage in buckets, and a single tap provides water for more than one thousand people. Jobs are hard to come by, partly because Ford and General Motors closed their factories in nearby Port Elizabeth and partly because people keep migrating to the town from regions where life is even worse. Those who can find work are lucky to earn $200 a month.

South Africa has ended white minority rule and, most analysts agree, there is no turning back. Yet undoing centuries of racial caste cannot be accomplished by simple legal mandate. Even when deeply rooted notions about racial inequality are finally overcome, this still-divided society will face the daunting challenge of resolving the underlying problem of intense and persistent poverty among most of its people.

Sources: Fredrickson (1981), Price (1991), Wren (1991), Contreras (1992), and various news reports.

Note, however, that the erosion of caste does not signal the end of social stratification. On the contrary, it simply marks a change in its character, as the next sections explain.

The Class System

Agrarian life relies on the discipline wrought by caste systems; industrial societies, by contrast, depend on developing specialized talents. Industrialization thus erodes caste in favor of a **class system**, *social stratification based on individual achievement.*

A class system is more "open" so that people who gain schooling and skills may experience some social mobility in relation to their parents and siblings. Mobility, in turn, blurs class distinctions. Social boundaries also break down as people immigrate from abroad or move from the countryside to the city, lured by greater opportunity for education and better jobs (Lipset & Bendix, 1967; Cutright, 1968; Treiman, 1970). Typically, newcomers take low-paying jobs, thereby pushing others up the social ladder (Tyree, Semyonov, & Hodge, 1979).

People in industrial societies come to think that everyone is entitled to "rights," rather than just those of particular social standing. The principle of equal standing before the law steadily assumes a central place in the political culture of industrial class systems.

Class systems are no different from caste systems in one basic respect: People remain unequal. But social stratification now rests on personal talent and effort rather than the accident of birth. Careers become not a

NOTE: In the estate system, the terms "gentleman" and "lady" designated people of noble birth. In more democratic North America, the words have come to refer indiscriminately to males and females. Note, too, the link between military officers and nobility, a pattern that persists today with college ROTC graduates entering the military services as officers.
DISCUSS: The moral tone of medieval culture comes through in

the seven deadly sins: covetousness, lust, anger, envy, pride, gluttony, and sloth. Only the last is much of a sin in today's more materialistic world. Ask how our society *demands* envy, pride, gluttony, and so on.
GLOBAL: The U.K.'s richest 1% owned about 66% of the nation's wealth in 1920; this concentration fell to about 18% in 1990 (Wolff, 1995).

matter of moral duty but an issue of individual choice; likewise, class systems allow more individual freedom in the selection of marriage partners.

Status Consistency

Status consistency refers to *the degree of consistency of a person's social standing across various dimensions of social inequality*. In a caste system, limited social mobility generates high status consistency so that the typical person has the same relative ranking with regard to wealth, power, and prestige. By contrast, the greater mobility of class systems allows for lower status consistency. In industrial nations such as the United States, then, a college professor with an advanced degree might enjoy high social prestige while receiving a modest income. Such low status consistency is the key reason that *classes* are less well defined than *castes*.

Caste and Class Together: The United Kingdom

There are no pure caste or class systems; social stratification everywhere involves some combination of these two forms. This mix is particularly striking in the United Kingdom, an industrial nation but one with a long agrarian history.

The Estate System

In the Middle Ages, social stratification in England (which, together with Wales, Scotland, and Northern Ireland constitutes today's United Kingdom of Great Britain and Northern Ireland) took the form of a caste-like system of three estates. A hereditary nobility, or first estate, was composed of 150 families or barely 5 percent of the population (Laslett, 1984). These nobles exercised power and controlled wealth in the form of land. Typically, nobles had no formal occupation at all; to be "engaged in trade" or any other type of work for income was deemed "beneath" the aristocracy. Well tended by servants, many nobles used their leisure time to cultivate refined tastes in art, music, and literature.

The estate system depended on protecting vast landholdings from division by heirs. This was accomplished through the law of *primogeniture* (from Latin meaning "first born"), which mandated that a man's entire property pass to his eldest son or other male relation upon his death. In the process of maintaining a landed aristocracy, however, primogeniture forced younger sons to seek out other sources of support. One

possibility for such men was to enter the clergy—often dubbed the "second estate"—where spiritual power was supplemented by the church's extensive landholdings. Other young men of high birth became military officers, lawyers, or took up work in other "honorable" professions set aside for "gentlemen." And what of women? In an age when no woman could inherit her father's property and few women had the opportunity to earn a living on their own, the daughter of a noble family depended for her security on marrying well.

Below the nobility and the clergy, the vast majority of men and women formed the third estate, or "commoners." With little property, most commoners were serfs working plots of land belonging to nobles. The phrase "one's lot in life" literally describes the daily focus of commoners during the Middle Ages. Unlike the nobility and the clergy, most commoners had little access to schooling and remained illiterate.

As the Industrial Revolution steadily enlarged England's economy, some commoners living in cities gained enough wealth to rival the power of the nobility. The increasing importance of money, along with the extension of schooling and legal rights to more and more people, together blurred social rankings and gave rise to a class system. In a pointed illustration of how far the pendulum has swung, a descendant of nobility, now working for a living as a writer, was asked in an interview if Britain's caste-like estates had finally broken down. Playfully she retorted, "Of course they have, or I wouldn't be here talking to someone like you!" (*New Haven Journal-Courier,* November 27, 1986).

The United Kingdom Today

Social stratification in the United Kingdom today is more of a class system, but one that retains the mark of a long, feudal past. At the top of the hierarchy, a small cluster of British families continues to enjoy inherited wealth, attends expensive schools, and wields political influence. Queen Elizabeth II, who traces her ancestry back through a millennium of aristocracy, reigns as the United Kingdom's head of state, and Parliament's House of Lords is composed of other "peers," most of noble birth. In a sign of the times, however, actual control of government resides in the House of Commons, where the prime minister and other commoners are more likely to have gained their position through achievement than by ascription. Looking beyond the government, most of the leading people in all sectors of British society today are individuals of extraordinary achievement rather than noble birth.

NOTE: Reflecting our more democratic times, an increasing share of English peers (that is, those who sit in the House of Lords) are holders of "life peerages" that are awarded by the Queen for one's lifetime and are not passed on to children as traditional titles are.

NOTE: "Aristocracy" has the Greek root *aristoi*, meaning "the best" (literally, then, "rule of the best"). Elite Greeks took this meaning literally, as did most of the hereditary nobility of medieval Europe.

DISCUSS: Richard Hoggart (1995) argues that aristocracy bolsters standards of excellence (by promoting elitism) so that what is popular is, by definition, mediocre; democracy erodes such standards (through relativism), defining the best as the most popular ("as seen on TV . . ."). Do students believe in "elitism"? Why or why not?

NOTE: Fifty-eight U.S. citizens have been knighted by a British monarch; the last was Ronald Reagan.

Moving down the hierarchy, roughly one-fourth of the population forms the British middle class. Some families are moderately wealthy, with high incomes from professions and business. These richer "commoners," along with the upper class, make up the 10 percent of Britons with significant financial holdings in the form of stocks and bonds (Sherrid, 1986). Most middle-class Britons, however, earn too little to accumulate substantial wealth.

Below the middle class, approximately half of all Britons think of themselves as "working class." As in the United States, members of the working class earn modest incomes, generally by performing manual labor. The decline of British industries such as coal mining and steel production has subjected many working-class families to chronic unemployment. Some have slipped into poverty, joining the remaining one-fourth of Britons who are socially and economically deprived. Lower-class people—or, more simply, the poor—are heavily concentrated in the northern and western regions of the United Kingdom, which are plagued by economic decline.

Today's class system affords the British people some opportunity to move upward or downward. One legacy of the estate system, however, is that social mobility occurs less often in the United Kingdom than in the United States. Compared with members of our society, therefore, Britons are relatively more resigned to remaining in the social position to which they were born (Snowman, 1977; Kerckhoff, Campbell, & Winfield-Laird, 1985).

The greater rigidity of British stratification is exemplified in the importance of accent as a mark of social position. Distinctive patterns of speech develop in any society as people are segregated from one another over time. While people in the United States treat accent as a matter of geography (there is little mistaking a midwestern "twang" or a southern "drawl"), a British accent identifies one as a person of high birth (speaking the "King's English") or someone of common ancestry. So different are these two accents that the British seem to be, as the saying goes, a single people divided by a common language.

Another Example: Japan

Social stratification in Japan also mixes the traditional and the contemporary. Japan is at once the world's oldest, continuously operating monarchy and a modern society in which wealth follows individual achievement.

In 1993, Japan's Crown Prince Naruhito wed Masako Owada, a commoner. The marriage symbolized today's Japan, with one individual representing ancient Japanese traditions and the other the new rise of a highly educated business class. Notice how this official photograph reveals that the princess is actually taller than the prince, perhaps suggesting that Japan is gradually loosening its rigid system by which wives lived in the shadows of their husbands.

Feudal Japan

As early as the fifth century C.E., Japan was an agrarian society with a rigid caste system composed of nobles and commoners and ruled by an "imperial family." Despite the people's belief that the emperor ruled by divine right, limited government organization forced the emperor to delegate much authority to a network of regional nobles or *shoguns*.

Below the nobility stood the *samurai*, or warrior caste. The word *samurai* means "to serve," indicating that this second rank of Japanese society comprised soldiers who cultivated elaborate martial skills and pledged their loyalty to the nobility. To set themselves off from the rest of the commoners, the *samurai* dressed and behaved according to a traditional code of honor.

As in Great Britain, the majority of people in Japan at this time in history were commoners who labored to eke out a bare subsistence. Unlike their European counterparts, however, Japanese commoners were not the lowest in rank. The *burakumin*, or "outcasts," stood further down in that country's hierarchy, shunned by lord and commoner alike. Much like the lowest caste groups in India, "outcasts" lived apart from others, engaged in the most distasteful occupations, and, like everyone else, had no opportunity to change their standing.

Japan Today

Important changes in nineteenth-century Japan—industrialization, the growth of cities, and the opening of Japanese society to outside influences—combined to weaken the traditional caste structure. In 1871, the Japanese legally banned the social category of "outcast," although even today people look down on women and men who trace their lineage to this rank. After Japan's defeat in World War II, the nobility, too, lost legal standing, and, as the years have passed, fewer and fewer Japanese accept the notion that their emperor rules by divine right.

Thus social stratification in contemporary Japan is a far cry from the rigid caste system in force centuries ago. Analysts describe the modern-day Japanese population in terms of social gradations, including "upper," "upper-middle," "lower-middle," and "lower." But since classes have no firm boundaries, they disagree about what proportion of the population falls in each.

Today's Japanese class system also reveals this nation's fascinating ability to weave together tradition and modernity. Because many Japanese people revere the past, family background is never far from the surface in assessing someone's social standing. Therefore, despite legal reforms that assure everyone of equal standing before the law and a modern culture that stresses individual achievement, the Japanese continue to perceive each other through the centuries-old lens of caste.

This dynamic mix echoes from the college campus to the corporate board room. The most prestigious universities—now gateways to success in the industrial world—admit students with outstanding scores on rigorous entrance examinations. Even so, the highest achievers and business leaders in Japan are products of privilege, with noble or *samurai* background. At the other extreme, "outcasts" continue to live in isolated communities cut off from opportunities to better themselves (Hiroshi, 1974; Norbeck, 1983).

Finally, traditional ideas about gender still shape Japanese society. Despite legal reforms that confer formal equality on the sexes, women are clearly subordinate to men in most important respects. Japanese parents are more likely to push sons than daughters toward college, and the nation thus retains a significant "gender gap" in education (Brinton, 1988). As a consequence, women predominate in lower-level support positions in the corporate world, only rarely assuming leadership roles. In this sense, too, individual achievement in Japan's modern class system operates in the shadow of centuries of traditional privileges.

The Former Soviet Union

The former Union of Soviet Socialist Republics (USSR), which rivaled the United States as a military superpower through most of this century, was born out of revolution in 1917. The feudal estate system ruled by a hereditary nobility came to an abrupt end as the Russian revolution transferred most farms, factories, and other productive property from private ownership to state control.

A Classless Society?

This transformation was guided by the ideas of Karl Marx, who asserted that private ownership of productive property was the basis of social classes (see Chapter 4, "Society"). As the state gained control of the economy, Soviet officials boasted that they had engineered a remarkable achievement: humanity's first classless society.

Analysts outside the Soviet Union were always skeptical about this claim of classlessness (Lane, 1984). The occupations of the people in the former Soviet Union, they pointed out, clustered into a four-level hierarchy. At the top were high government officials, or *apparatchiks*. Next came the Soviet intelligentsia, including lower government officials, college professors, scientists, physicians, and engineers. Below them stood the manual workers and, in the lowest stratum, the rural peasantry.

Since people in each of these categories enjoyed very different living standards, the former Soviet Union was never classless in the sense of having no social inequality. But one can say, more modestly, that placing factories, farms, colleges, and hospitals under state control did rein in economic inequality (although not necessarily differences of power) compared to capitalist societies such as the United States.

Q: "Soviet society follows the lead of Lenin towards becoming a classless, communist society." USSR secondary school textbook
NOTE: The Soviet empire in Eastern Europe included the Baltic nations of Estonia, Latvia, and Lithuania, plus Poland, East Germany, Czechoslovakia, Romania, Hungary, and Bulgaria. Between 1989 and 1991 all established their political independence from what is now the Russian Federation.

DIVERSITY: Socialism has done relatively little to incorporate women into positions of power; the ruling elites of both the former Soviet Union and the People's Republic of China, for instance, historically have been almost entirely male.
NOTE: Estimates placed the fortune of the Soviet Communist party, dissolved in August 1991, at roughly $175 billion.

In recent years, the former Soviet Union has moved towards a market economy. Thus economic reforms have made some people quite wealthy, while others have been reduced to selling household goods in order to buy food.

The Second Russian Revolution

<u>November 24, 1994, Odessa, Ukraine.</u> The first snow of our voyage flies about the decks as our ship puts in at Odessa, the former Soviet Union's southernmost port on the Black Sea. A short distance from the dock, we gaze up the Potemkin Steps—the steep stairway leading to the city proper where the first shots of the Russian Revolution rang out. It has been six years since our last visit and much has changed; indeed, the Soviet Union itself has collapsed. Has life improved? Obviously, for some people: There are now chic boutiques in which well-dressed shoppers spend cash for fine wines, designer labels, and imported perfumes. Outside, shiny new Volvos, Mercedes, and even a few Cadillacs stand out against the small Ladas from the "old days." But for most, life seems unmistakably worse. Flea markets line the curbs as families hawk home furnishings. Many are desperate in a town where meat sells for $4 a pound

and the average person earns about $30 a month. Odessa has no lights after about eight o'clock in the evening—the city's strategy to save electricity. The spirits of most people seem as dim as the city streets.

The 1917 Russian revolution radically recast Soviet society as prescribed by Karl Marx (and revolutionary Russian leader Vladimir Lenin). Then in the 1980s, the Soviet Union underwent another sweeping transformation. Economic reforms accelerated when Mikhail Gorbachev came on the scene in 1985. His economic program, popularly known as *perestroika*, meaning "restructuring," sought to solve a dire problem: While the Soviet system had succeeded in minimizing economic inequality, everyone was relatively poor, and living standards lagged far behind those of other industrial nations. Simply put, Gorbachev hoped to stimulate economic expansion by reducing inefficient centralized control of the economy.

Gorbachev's reforms soon escalated into one of the most dramatic social movements in history, as popular uprisings toppled one socialist government after another throughout Eastern Europe and, ultimately, brought down the Soviet system itself. In essence, people blamed their economic plight as well as their lack of basic freedoms on a repressive ruling class of Communist party officials.

GLOBAL: Social hierarchy in the former Soviet Union was based more on power than on wealth. For example, Eduard A. Shevardnadze, Soviet Foreign Minister between 1985 and 1991, claimed an annual salary of $25,000. James Baker, his U.S. counterpart, earned $99,500 and is a millionaire several times over.

NOTE: Even today, Gorbachev is not a rich man; in a personal conversation, his former translator Pavel Palazockenko explained

that Gorbachev is exploring options in light of the gradual withdrawal of various government perks.

NOTE: Fig. 9–1 is consistent with Fig. 9–2, the Kuznets curve. Preindustrial societies typically have greater economic inequality than industrial nations. Note, however, that income inequality also reflects intentional policies, thus ranging from 3:1 or 4:1 in socialist nations and Japan to 10:1 in the U.K. and the U.S.

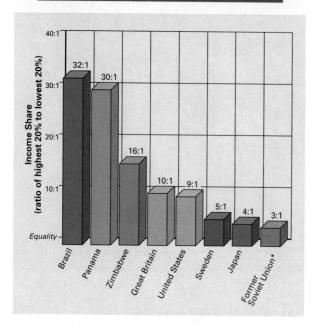

FIGURE 9–1 Economic Inequality in Selected Countries, 1980–1992

*The former Soviet Union did not provide data on economic inequality. Figure is author's estimate based on U.N. data for various nations in the Soviet bloc and other sources.

Source: United Nations Development Programme (1995).

From the Soviet Union's founding in 1917 until its demise in 1991, the Communist party retained a monopoly of power. Near the end, 18 million party members (6 percent of the Soviet people) still made all the decisions about Soviet life while enjoying privileges such as vacation homes, chauffeured automobiles, and access to prized consumer goods and elite education for their children (Zaslavsky, 1982; Shipler, 1984; Theen, 1984). The second Soviet revolution, then, mirrors the first in that it was nothing less than the overthrow of the ruling class.

The rise and fall of the Soviet Union demonstrate that social inequality involves more than economic resources. Figure 9–1 confirms that Soviet society lacked the income disparity typical of Great Britain and the United States. But elite standing in the former Soviet Union was based on power rather than wealth. Thus, even though Mikhail Gorbachev and Boris Yeltsin earned far less than a U.S. president, they wielded awesome power.

And what about social mobility in the Soviet Union? Evidence indicates that during this century there was more upward social mobility in the Soviet Union than in Great Britain, Japan, or even the United States. Why? For one thing, Soviet society lacked the concentrated wealth that families elsewhere pass from one generation to the next. Even more important, industrialization and rapid bureaucratization during this century pushed a large proportion of the working class and rural peasantry upward to occupations in industry and government. In the last few decades, however, the Soviet people experienced decreasing social mobility. Most analysts conclude that the country's earlier high rate of upward movement resulted more from industrial development than from socialism (Dobson, 1977; Lane, 1984; Shipler, 1984).

Oftentimes, as the Soviet experience attests, widespread societal changes affect people's individual social standing in a process sociologists call **structural social mobility,** *a shift in the social position of large numbers of people due more to changes in society itself than to individual efforts.* Half a century ago, industrialization in the Soviet Union created a vast number of new factory jobs that drew rural people to cities. Similarly, the growth of bureaucracy propelled countless Soviet citizens from plowing to paperwork. Now, with new laws sanctioning individual ownership of private property and business, some experts monitoring the changing Soviet scene predict further structural social mobility along with greater economic inequality (Róna-Tas, 1994). But, equal or not, everyone hopes to enjoy a higher standard of living.

Ideology: Stratification's "Staying Power"

Looking around the world at the extent of social inequality, we might wonder how societies persist without distributing their resources more equally. Caste-like systems in Great Britain and Japan lasted for centuries, concentrating land and power in the hands of several hundred families. Even more striking, for two thousand years most people in India accepted the idea that they should be privileged or poor because of the accident of birth.

One key reason for the remarkable persistence of social hierarchies is that they are built on **ideology,** *cultural beliefs that serve to justify social stratification.* Any beliefs—for example, the claim that the rich are smart while the poor are lazy—are ideological to the extent that they bolster the dominance of wealthy elites and suggest that poor people deserve their plight.

Plato and Marx on Ideology

The ancient Greek philosopher Plato (427–347 B.C.E.) defined justice as agreement about who should have what. Every society, Plato explained, teaches its members to view some stratification system as "fair." Karl Marx, too, understood this process, although he was far more critical of inequality than Plato was. Marx took capitalist societies to task for channeling wealth and power into the hands of a few, all the while defining the practice as simply "a law of the marketplace." Capitalist law, Marx continued, defines the right to own property as a bedrock principle. Then, laws of inheritance, which are tied to kinship, funnel money and privileges from one generation to the next. In short, Marx concluded, ideas as well as resources are controlled by a society's elite, which helps to explain why established hierarchies are so difficult to change.

Both Plato and Marx recognized that ideology is rarely a simple matter of privileged people conspiring together to propound self-serving ideas about social inequality. By contrast, ideology usually takes the form of cultural patterns that evolve over a long period of time. As people learn to embrace their society's conception of fairness, they may question the rightness of their own position but are unlikely to challenge the system itself.

Historical Patterns of Ideology

The ideas that shore up social stratification change along with a society's economy and technology. Early agrarian societies depended on slaves to perform burdensome manual labor. Aristotle (384–322 B.C.E.) defended the practice of slavery among the ancient Greeks, noting, for example, that some people with little intelligence deserve nothing better than life under the direction of their natural "betters."

Agrarian societies in Europe during the Middle Ages also required the daily farm labor of most people to support the small aristocracy. In this context, noble and serf learned to view occupation as rightfully determined by birth and any person's work as a matter of moral responsibility. In short, caste systems always rest on the assertion that social ranking is the product of a "natural" order.

The rise of industrial capitalism transformed wealth and power into prizes won by those who display the greatest talent and effort. Class systems celebrate individualism and achievement, so that social standing serves as a measure of personal worthiness. Thus poverty, which called for charity under feudalism, became under industrial capitalism a scorned state of

personal inadequacy. The box on page 246 takes a closer look at the transition from the medieval notion of divinely sanctioned inequality to the modern idea that stratification reflects unequal effort and ability.

Throughout human history, most people have regarded social stratification as unshakable. Especially as traditions weaken, however, people begin to question cultural "truths" and unmask their political foundations and consequences.

For example, historic notions of a "woman's place" today seem far from natural and are losing their power to deprive women of opportunities. For the present, however, the contemporary class system still subjects women to caste-like expectations that they perform traditional tasks out of altruism while men are financially rewarded for their efforts. To illustrate, most chefs are men who work for income while most household cooks are women who perform this role as a household duty.

Yet, while gender differences persist in the United States, there is little doubt that women and men are steadily becoming more equal in important respects. The continuing struggle for racial equality in South Africa also exemplifies widespread rejection of apartheid, which for decades shaped economic, political, and educational life in that nation. Apartheid has never been widely accepted by blacks, and it has lost its support as a "natural" system among whites who reject ideological racism (Friedrich, 1987; Contreras, 1992).

THE FUNCTIONS OF SOCIAL STRATIFICATION

Why are societies stratified at all? One answer, consistent with the structural-functional paradigm, is that social inequality plays a vital part in the operation of society. This influential—and controversial—argument was set forth some fifty years ago by Kingsley Davis and Wilbert Moore (1945).

The Davis-Moore Thesis

The **Davis-Moore thesis** is *the assertion that social stratification has beneficial consequences for the operation of a society.* How else, ask Davis and Moore, can we explain the fact that some form of social stratification has been found everywhere?

Davis and Moore describe our society as a complex system involving hundreds of occupational positions of varying importance. Certain jobs—say, changing spark plugs in a car—are fairly easy and can be performed by almost anyone. Other jobs—such as

CRITICAL THINKING

Ideology: When Is Inequality Unjust?

Inequality is not always injustice; on the contrary, all societies endorse some dimensions of inequality as fair while condemning others as wrong. Justifications for social stratification, then, are culturally variable across history and from place to place.

A millennium ago, a rigid estate system in Europe rested on church teachings that such arrangements reflected the will of God. More specifically, the church endorsed as divinely sanctioned a system by which most people labored as serfs, driving the feudal economy with their muscles. According to the church, nobility was charged with responsibility for defending the realm and maintaining public order. To question this system meant challenging the church and, ultimately, defying God.

The religious justification that supported the medieval estate system for centuries is expressed in the following stanza from "All Things Bright and Beautiful," a hymn sung in parish churches throughout England.

> The rich man in his castle,
> The poor man at his gate,
> He made them high and lowly
> And ordered their estate.

The Industrial Revolution opened the way for newly rich industrialists to topple the feudal nobility. In the process, industrial culture advanced

Medieval Europeans accepted rigid social differences as part of a divine order for the world. This fifteenth-century painting by the Limbourg brothers portrays life as orderly and cyclical. In this example, showing indoor life during January, the Duke of Berry is seated near the fireplace surrounded by attendants. The firescreen behind him appears to give him a halo, surely intended by the artists to suggest the common notion that nobles enjoyed their privileges by grace of God.

Limbourg Brothers, *Le Duc de Berry à table, Tres Riches Heures du Duc de Berry,* January, folio iv, Chantilly, Musée Conde.

a new ideology. Capitalists mocked the centuries-old notion that social hierarchy should depend on the accident of birth. Under God's law, the new thinking went, the most talented and hard-working individuals should dominate society.

John D. Rockefeller (1839–1937), who made a vast fortune in oil, defended the wealth and power of early industrialists as the product of extraordinary effort and initiative. Such a scheme, he contended, was consistent with the laws of nature. The same thinking recast the poor from objects of charity into unworthy people lacking ability and ambition.

The ideological shift from birth to individual achievement as the basis of social inequality was well established by the time early nineteenth-century German writer Johann Wolfgang von Goethe quipped:

> Really to own
> What you inherit,
> You first must earn it
> With your merit.

Clearly, medieval and modern justifications for inequality differ dramatically: What an earlier era viewed as fair, a later one rejected as wrongheaded. Yet both cases illustrate the pivotal role of ideology—cultural beliefs that define a particular kind of hierarchy as fair and natural.

---

transplanting a human organ—are quite difficult and demand the scarce talents of people who have received extensive (and expensive) education. Positions of high day-to-day responsibility that demand special abilities are the most functionally significant.

In general, Davis and Moore explain, the greater the functional importance of a position, the more rewards a society will attach to it. This strategy pays off, since rewarding important work with income, prestige, power, and leisure encourages people to do these

NOTE: From a conservative, meritocratic point of view, social welfare systems penalize activity both on the part of poor people (by providing benefits for idleness) and rich people (by imposing taxes on earnings); they also foster immorality by encouraging the poor to cheat on qualifications for benefits and encouraging the rich to cheat on taxes.

NOTE: In light of the Davis-Moore thesis, seniority is not a

uniformly positive principle. Most brain surgeons, for example, get better with time. Science professors, by contrast, do their best work early in their careers and then slow down. The term-limits debate points up the public perception that legislators are more like the latter than the former. John J. Pitney, Jr. (1995).

Q: "The ruling ideas of each age have ever been the ideas of its ruling class." Karl Marx, *The Communist Manifesto*

things. In effect, by distributing resources unequally, a society motivates each person to aspire to the most significant work possible, and to work better, harder, and longer. The overall effect of a social system of unequal rewards—which is what social stratification amounts to—is a more productive society.

Davis and Moore concede that every society could be egalitarian. But, they caution, rewards could be equal only to the extent that people were willing to let *anyone* perform *any* job. Equality also demands that someone who carries out a job poorly be rewarded on a par with another who performs well. Logic dictates that such a system offers little incentive for people to make their best efforts, and thereby reduces a society's productive efficiency.

The Davis-Moore thesis points out why *some* form of stratification exists everywhere; it does not endorse any *particular* system of inequality. Nor do Davis and Moore specify precisely what reward should be attached to any occupational position. They merely point out that positions a society deems crucial must yield sufficient rewards to draw talent away from less important work.

Meritocracy

The Davis-Moore thesis implies that a productive society is a **meritocracy**, *a system of social stratification based on personal merit.* Such societies hold out rewards to develop the talents and encourage the efforts of everyone. In pursuit of meritocracy, a society promotes equality of opportunity while, at the same time, mandating inequality of rewards. In other words, a pure class system would be a meritocracy, rewarding everyone based on ability and effort. In addition, such a society would have extensive social mobility, blurring social categories as individuals move up or down in the social system depending on their performance.

For their part, caste societies can speak of "merit" (from Latin, meaning "worthy of praise") only in terms of persistence in low-skill labor such as farming. Caste systems, in short, offer honor to those who remain dutifully "in their place."

Although caste systems waste human potential, they are quite orderly. And herein lies a clue to an important question: Why do modern industrial societies resist becoming pure meritocracies by retaining many caste-like qualities? Simply because, left unchecked, meritocracy erodes social structure such as kinship. No one, for example, evaluates family members solely on the basis of performance. Class systems in industrial societies, therefore, retain some caste elements to promote order and social cohesion.

Critical evaluation. By investigating the functions of social stratification, Davis and Moore made a lasting contribution to sociological analysis. Even so, critics point to several flaws in their thesis. Melvin Tumin (1953) wonders, first, if functional importance really explains the high rewards that some people enjoy. Can one even measure functional importance? Perhaps, he suggests, the high rewards our society accords to physicians at least partly results from deliberate efforts by medical schools to limit the supply of physicians and push up the demand for their services.

If so, income and other rewards may have little to do with an individual's functional contribution to society. With an income topping $50 million a year, television personality Oprah Winfrey earns more in two days than the U.S. president earns all year. Would anyone argue that hosting a talk show tops in societal significance the rigors of the presidency? The box takes a critical look at the link between pay and societal importance.

A second charge made by Tumin is that the Davis-Moore thesis exaggerates social stratification's role in developing individual talent. Our society does reward individual achievement, but we also allow families to transfer wealth and power from generation to generation in caste-like fashion. Additionally, for women, people of color, and others with limited opportunities, stratification still raises barriers to personal accomplishment. In practice, Tumin concludes, social stratification functions to develop some people's abilities to the fullest while barring others from ever reaching their potential.

Third, by contending that social stratification benefits all of society, the Davis-Moore thesis ignores how social inequality promotes conflict and, sometimes, even outright revolution. This assertion leads us to the social-conflict paradigm, which provides a very different explanation for the persistence of social hierarchy.

STRATIFICATION AND CONFLICT

Social-conflict analysis argues that, rather than benefiting society as a whole, social stratification provides advantages to some people at the expense of others. This theoretical perspective draws heavily on the ideas of Karl Marx; additional contributions were made by Max Weber.

Karl Marx: Class and Conflict

Karl Marx, whose approach to understanding social inequality is detailed in Chapter 4 ("Society"), identified

CRITICAL THINKING

Big Bucks: Are the Rich Worth What They Earn?

For an hour of work, a Los Angeles priest earns about $5, a bus driver in San Francisco makes about $15, and a Detroit auto worker collects roughly $20. These wages look paltry in comparison to the $25,000 actor Kevin Costner takes home for every hour he spends on a movie set or singer Dolly Parton makes for an hour on a Las Vegas nightclub stage. And what about the $40,000 an hour that Barry Bonds earns for playing baseball with the San Francisco Giants? Or the $100,000 Bill Cosby commands for an hour of entertainment? Or the $200,000 paid to Oprah Winfrey for each hour she chats with guests before the television cameras?

The Davis-Moore thesis states that rewards reflect an occupation's value to society. But are the antics of Bill Cosby worth as much to our society as the work of all one hundred United States senators? In short, do earnings really reflect people's social importance?

Salaries in industrial-capitalist societies like the United States are a product of the market forces of supply and demand. In simple terms, if you can do something better than others, and people value it, you can command greater rewards. According to this view, movie stars, top athletes, skilled professionals, and many business executives have rare talents that are much in demand; thus, they may

earn many times more than the typical worker in the United States.

But critics claim that the market is really a poor evaluator of occupational importance. First, they claim, the U.S. economy is dominated by a small proportion of people who manipulate the system for their own benefit. Corporate executives, for example, pay themselves multimillion dollar salaries and bonuses even in years when their companies flounder. Japanese executives, by contrast, earn far less than their counterparts in this country, yet most Japanese corporations have

Oprah Winfrey is one of the country's highest paid people, earning more than $50 million annually. Are her efforts worth as much as two thousand average workers?

handily outperformed their rivals in the United States.

A second problem with the idea that the market measures people's contributions to society is that many people who make clear and significant contributions receive surprisingly little money for their efforts. Hundreds of thousands of teachers, counselors, and health-care workers contribute daily to the welfare of others for very little salary.

As an example of this gap between societal importance and societal incentives, Wall Street's notorious "junk-bond" king Michael Milken earned $550 million in 1987, benefiting a handful of rich investors. During the same year, health counselor Rachel Stuart helped thirty-five expectant mothers in rural Louisiana deliver healthy babies. Since the cost of neonatal care for a single premature baby runs as high as $200,000, Stuart probably saved the public millions; yet she is paid $4,000 a year for her work (Werman, 1989).

Using social worth to justify income, then, is hazardous. Some defend the market as the most accurate measure of occupational worth; what, they ask, would be better? But others contend that what is lucrative may or may not be socially valuable. From this standpoint, a market system amounts to a closed game in which only a handful of people have the money to play.

---

two major social classes corresponding to the two basic relationships to the means of production: Individuals either (1) own productive property or (2) labor for others. In medieval Europe, the nobility and the church owned the productive land; peasants toiled as farmers. Simi-

larly, in industrial class systems, the capitalists (or the bourgeoisie) own and operate factories, which utilize the labor of workers (the proletariat).

Marx noted great disparities in wealth and power arising from the industrial-capitalist productive system,

NOTE: The term "meritocracy" is associated with Michael Young and his 1957 book, *The Rise of the Meritocracy*. He is also Lord Young of Dartington, member of Parliament. He wrote, "If the soil creates castes, the machine manufactures classes." See a recent article by Young in *Society*, Vol. 31, No. 6 (September/October 1994):84–89.

Q: "There is no more possibility of defeating the operation of [economic] laws than there is of thwarting the laws of nature that determine the humidity of the atmosphere or the revolution of the earth upon its axis." Andrew Carnegie

Q: "God gave me my money." John D. Rockefeller

Q: "The small tradespeople, shopkeepers, and retired tradespeople generally, the handicraftsmen and peasants—all these sink gradually into the proletariat." Karl Marx and Friedrich Engels

John George Brown made a fortune a century ago as a painter who portrayed the world as most people wanted to see it (left). Photographer Jacob Riis, among others, found far less fame during his own lifetime by capturing something closer to the truth. This is Riis's well-known image of New York's "street arabs" (right), who survived as best they could on the mean streets of this growing industrial city.

which, he contended, made class conflict inevitable. In time, he believed, oppression and misery would drive the working majority to organize and, ultimately, to overthrow capitalism.

Marx's analysis was grounded in his observations of capitalism in the nineteenth century, when great industrialists dominated the economic scene. Andrew Carnegie, J. P. Morgan, and John Jacob Astor (one of the few very rich passengers to perish on the *Titanic*) lived in fabulous mansions filled with priceless art and staffed by dozens of servants. Their fortunes were staggering: John Jacob Astor accumulated $25 million; Andrew Carnegie reportedly earned more than $20 million a year as this century began (worth close to $100 million in today's dollars)—all at a time when the wages paid to the average worker totaled roughly $500 a year (Baltzell, 1964; Pessen, 1990).

According to Marx, the capitalist elite draws its strength from more than the operation of the economy. He noted that through the family, opportunity and wealth are passed down from generation to generation. Moreover, the legal system defends this practice through inheritance law. Similarly, exclusive schools bring children of the elite together, encouraging informal social ties that will benefit them throughout their lives. Overall, from Marx's point of view, capitalist society *reproduces the class structure in each new generation.*

Critical evaluation. Exploring how the capitalist economic system generates conflict between classes, Marx's analysis of social stratification has had enormous influence on sociological thinking in recent decades. Because it is revolutionary—calling for the overthrow of capitalist society—Marxism is also highly controversial.

One of the strongest criticisms of the Marxist approach is that it denies one of the central tenets of the Davis-Moore thesis: that motivating people to perform various social roles requires some system of unequal rewards. Marx separated reward from performance, endorsing an egalitarian system based on the principle of "from each according to ability; to each according to need" (1972:388). Critics argue that severing rewards from performance is precisely the flaw that generated the low productivity characteristic of the former Soviet Union and other socialist economies around the world.

Defenders of Marx rebut this line of attack by pointing to considerable evidence supporting Marx's general view of humanity as inherently social rather than unflinchingly selfish (Clark, 1991; Fiske, 1991). They counter that we should not assume that individual rewards (much less monetary compensation alone) are the only way to motivate people to perform their social roles.

In addition, although few doubt that capitalist society does perpetuate poverty and privilege, as Marx asserted, the revolutionary developments he considered inevitable have failed to materialize. The next section explores why the socialist revolution Marx predicted and promoted has not occurred, at least in advanced capitalist societies.

Why No Marxist Revolution?

Despite Marx's prediction, capitalism is still thriving. Why have workers in the United States and other industrial societies not overthrown capitalism? Ralf Dahrendorf (1959) pointed to four reasons.

1. **The fragmentation of the capitalist class.** First, the century since Marx's death has witnessed the fragmentation of the capitalist class in the United States. A century ago, *single families* typically owned large companies; today, *numerous stockholders* fill that position. The diffusion of ownership has also stimulated the emergence of a managerial class, who may or may not be major stockholders (Wright, 1985; Wright, Levine, & Sober, 1992).

2. **White-collar work and a rising standard of living.** A "white-collar revolution" has transformed Marx's industrial proletariat. As Chapter 15 ("The Economy and Work") details, the majority of workers in Marx's time labored either on farms or in factories. They had **blue-collar occupations,** *lower-prestige jobs involving mostly manual labor.* By contrast, most workers today hold **white-collar jobs,** *higher-prestige work involving mostly mental activity.* These occupations include positions in sales, management, and other service work, frequently in large, bureaucratic organizations.

   While many of today's white-collar workers perform repetitive tasks like the industrial workers known to Marx, evidence indicates that most do not think of themselves in those terms. Rather, most white-collar workers now perceive their social positions as higher than those of their blue-collar parents and grandparents. One key reason is that workers' overall standard of living in the United States rose fourfold over the course of the

century in dollars controlled for inflation, even as the work week decreased. As a result of a rising tide of social mobility, our society seems less sharply divided between rich and poor than it did to people during Marx's lifetime (Edwards, 1979; Gagliani, 1981; Wright & Martin, 1987).

3. **More extensive worker organization.** Employees have organizational strengths they lacked a century ago. Workers have won the right to organize into labor unions that can and do make demands of management backed by threats of work slowdowns and strikes. Although union membership is declining, research suggests that well-established unions continue to enhance the economic standing of the workers they represent (Rubin, 1986). Further, today's negotiations between labor and management typically are institutionalized and peaceful, a picture quite different from the often-violent face-offs common before mid-century.

4. **More extensive legal protections.** Since Marx's death, the government has extended laws to protect workers' rights and has given workers greater access to the courts for redressing grievances. Government programs such as unemployment insurance, disability protection, and Social Security also provide workers with substantially greater financial resources than the capitalists of the last century were willing to grant them.

Taken together, these four developments mean that, despite persistent stratification, our society has smoothed out many of capitalism's rough edges. Consequently, social conflict today is less intense than it was a century ago.

A Counterpoint

Many sociologists continue to find value in Marx's analysis, often in modified form (Miliband, 1969; Edwards, 1979; Giddens, 1982; Domhoff, 1983; Stephens, 1986; Boswell & Dixon, 1993; Hout et al., 1993). Advocates of social-conflict theory respond with their own set of four key points, defending Marx's analysis of capitalism.

1. **Wealth remains highly concentrated.** As Marx contended, wealth remains in the hands of the few. In the United States, about half of all privately controlled corporate stock is owned by just 1 percent of individuals, who persist as a capitalist class.

2. **White-collar positions offer little to workers.** As defenders of Marx's thinking see it, the white-collar

In his painting, Work, *U.S. artist Ford Maddox Brown (1821–1893) suggests that the early capitalist era sharply divided U.S. society in the manner that Marx described. Today, more than a century since Brown lived, do you think class differences in the United States have become smaller or greater? Why?*

revolution has delivered little in the way of higher income or better working conditions compared to the factory jobs of a century ago. On the contrary, much white-collar work remains monotonous and routine, especially the low-level clerical jobs commonly held by women.

3. **Progress requires struggle.** Labor organizations may have advanced the interests of the workers over the last half century, but regular negotiation between workers and management hardly signals the end of social conflict. In fact, many of the concessions won by workers came about precisely through the class conflict Marx described. Moreover, workers still strive to gain concessions from capitalists and, in the 1990s, they struggle to hold on to the advances already achieved. As an example, half of all workers in the United States have no company-sponsored pension program.

4. **The law still favors the rich.** Workers have gained some legal protections over the course of this century. Even so, the law still defends the overall distribution of wealth in the United States. Just as important, "average" people cannot use the legal system to the same advantage as the rich do.

In sum, according to social-conflict theory, the fact that no socialist revolution has taken place in the United States hardly invalidates Marx's analysis of capitalism. As we shall see in Chapter 10 ("Social Class in the United States"), pronounced social inequality persists, as does social conflict—albeit less overtly and violently than in the nineteenth century.

Finally, some defenders of capitalism cite the collapse of communist regimes in Eastern Europe and the former Soviet Union as proof of the superiority of capitalism over socialism. Most analysts agree that socialism failed to meet the needs of the people it purported to serve, either in terms of raising living standards or ensuring personal freedoms. But, to be fair, socialism's failings do not excuse flaws in capitalism. Many critics maintain that capitalism in the United States has yet to demonstrate its ability to address problems of public education and desperate poverty, especially among the urban underclass (Uchitelle, 1991). Table 9–1 summarizes the contributions of the two contrasting sociological approaches to understanding social stratification.

Max Weber: Class, Status, and Power

Max Weber, whose approach to social analysis is described in Chapter 4 ("Society"), agreed with Karl Marx that social stratification sparks social conflict, but he differed with Marx in several important respects.

Weber considered Marx's model of two social classes simplistic. Instead, he viewed social stratification as a more complex interplay of three distinct dimensions. First is economic inequality—the issue so

TABLE 9–1 Two Explanations of Social Stratification: A Summary

Structural-Functional Paradigm	Social-Conflict Paradigm
Social stratification keeps society operating. The linkage of greater rewards to more important social positions benefits society as a whole.	Social stratification is the result of social conflict. Differences in social resources serve the interests of some and harm the interests of others.
Social stratification encourages a matching of talents and abilities to appropriate positions.	Social stratification ensures that much talent and ability within society will not be utilized at all.
Social stratification is both useful and inevitable.	Social stratification is useful to only some people; it is not inevitable.
The values and beliefs that legitimize social inequality are widely shared throughout society.	Values and beliefs tend to be ideological; they reflect the interests of the more powerful members of society.
Because systems of social stratification are useful to society as a whole and are supported by cultural values and beliefs, they are usually stable over time.	Because systems of social stratification reflect the interests of only part of society, they are unlikely to remain stable over time.

Source: Adapted in part from Arthur L. Stinchcombe, "Some Empirical Consequences of the Davis-Moore Theory of Stratification," *American Sociological Review*, Vol. 28, No. 5 (October 1963): 808.

vital to Marx—which Weber termed *class* position. Weber's use of "class" refers not to crude categories but to a continuum on which anyone can be ranked from high to low. A second continuum, *status*, measures social prestige. Finally, Weber noted the importance of *power* as a third dimension of social hierarchy.

The Socioeconomic Status Hierarchy

Marx believed that social prestige and power derived from economic position; thus he saw no reason to treat them as distinct dimensions of social inequality. Weber disagreed, recognizing that stratification in industrial societies has characteristically low status consistency. An individual, Weber pointed out, might have high standing on one dimension of inequality but a lower position on another. For example, bureaucratic officials might wield considerable power yet have little wealth or social prestige.

So while Marx viewed inequality in terms of two clearly defined classes, Weber saw something more subtle at work in the stratification of industrial societies. Weber's key contribution in this area, then, lies in identifying the multidimensional nature of social rankings. Sociologists often use the term **socioeconomic status** (SES) to refer to *a composite ranking based on various dimensions of social inequality*.

A population that varies widely in class, status, and power—Weber's three dimensions of inequality—creates a virtually infinite array of social categories, all of which pursue their own interests. Thus, unlike Marx, who focused on conflict between two overarching classes, Weber considered social conflict as highly variable and complex.

Inequality in History

Weber also made a key historical observation, noting that each of his three dimensions of social inequality stands out at different points in the evolution of human societies. Agrarian societies, he maintained, emphasize status or social prestige, typically in the form of honor or symbolic purity. Members of these societies gain such status by conforming to cultural norms corresponding to their rank.

Industrialization and the development of capitalism level traditional rankings based on birth but generate striking material differences in the population. Thus, Weber argued, the crucial difference among people in industrial-capitalist societies lies in the economic dimension of class.

In time, industrial societies witness a surging growth of the bureaucratic state. This expansion of government, coupled with the proliferation of other types of formal organizations, brings power to the fore in the stratification system. Power is also central to the organization of socialist societies, as we see in their extensive government regulation of many aspects of life. The elite members of such societies are mostly high-ranking officials rather than rich people.

This historical analysis underlies a final disagreement between Weber and Marx. Looking to the future, Marx believed that social stratification could be largely eliminated by abolishing private ownership of productive property. Weber doubted that overthrowing capitalism would significantly diminish social stratification in modern societies. While doing so might lessen economic disparity, Weber reasoned, the significance of power based on organizational position would only

NOTE: The Lenskis's analysis of historical changes in human societies—including the types noted here—is found in the first section of Chapter 4, "Society."
Q: "Whether we like to admit it or not, a society which encourages the full flowering of individual liberty is, and can only be, a stratified society." Andrew Hacker

Q: "I have no respect for the passion for equality, which seems to me to be merely idealizing envy." Oliver Wendell Holmes
NOTE: The shrinking stature of the U.S. rich is suggested by this comparison: When William Henry Vanderbilt died in 1885, his obituary covered the entire front page of *The New York Times*. When Sam Walton died in 1992, his death was reported on 1/20th of a page.

increase. In fact, Weber imagined, a socialist revolution might well *increase* social inequality by expanding government and concentrating power in the hands of a political elite. Recent popular uprisings against entrenched bureaucracies in Eastern Europe and the former Soviet Union lend support to Weber's argument.

Critical evaluation. Weber's multidimensional analysis of social stratification retains enormous influence among sociologists, especially in the United States. Some analysts (particularly those influenced by Marx's ideas) argue that while social class boundaries have blurred, striking patterns of social inequality persist in the United States and elsewhere in the industrial world.

As we shall see in Chapter 10 ("Social Class in the United States"), the enormous wealth of the most privileged members of our society contrasts sharply with the grinding poverty of millions who barely meet their day-to-day needs. Moreover, the upward social mobility that historically fueled optimism in this country all but came to a halt in the 1970s, and, during the 1980s, evidence points to an increase in economic inequality. Against this backdrop of economic polarization, the 1990s are marked by a renewed emphasis on "classes" in conflict rather than on the subtle shadings of a "multidimensional hierarchy."

STRATIFICATION AND TECHNOLOGY IN GLOBAL PERSPECTIVE

We can weave together a number of observations made in this chapter by considering the relationship between a society's technology and its type of social stratification. Gerhard Lenski and Jean Lenski's model of sociocultural evolution, detailed in Chapter 4 ("Society"), puts social stratification in historical perspective and also helps us to understand the varying degrees of inequality found around the world today (Lenski, 1966; Lenski, Nolan, & Lenski, 1995).

Hunting and Gathering Societies

Simple technology limits the production of hunting and gathering societies to only what is necessary for day-to-day living. No doubt some individuals are more successful hunters or gatherers than others, but the group's survival depends on all sharing what they have. With little or no surplus, therefore, no categories of people emerge as better off than others. Thus social

stratification among hunters and gatherers, based simply on age and sex, is less complex than among societies with more advanced technology.

Horticultural, Pastoral, and Agrarian Societies

Technological advances generate surplus production, while intensifying social inequality. In horticultural and pastoral societies, a small elite controls most of the surplus. Agrarian technology based on large-scale farming generates even greater abundance; but marked inequality means various categories of people lead strikingly different lives. The social distance between the elite hereditary nobility and the common serfs who work the land looms as large as at any time in human history. In most cases, lords wield godlike power over the masses.

Industrial Societies

Industrialization reverses the historical trend, prompting some decrease in social inequality. The eclipse of tradition and the need to develop individual talents gradually erode caste rankings in favor of greater individual opportunity. Then, too, the increasing productivity of industrial technology steadily raises the living standards of the historically poor majority. Specialized, technical work also demands the expansion of schooling, sharply reducing illiteracy. A literate population, in turn, tends to press for a greater voice in political decision making, further diminishing social inequality. As already noted, continuing technological advances transform much blue-collar labor into higher-prestige white-collar work. All these social shifts help to explain why Marxist revolutions occurred in agrarian societies—such as the former Soviet Union (1917), Cuba (1959), and Nicaragua (1979)—in which social inequality is most pronounced, rather than in industrial societies, as Marx predicted more than a century ago.

Initially, the great wealth generated by industrialization is concentrated in the hands of a few—the pattern so troubling to Marx. In time, however, the share of all property in the hands of the very rich declines somewhat. According to estimates, the proportion of all wealth controlled by the richest 1 percent of U.S. families peaked at about 36 percent just before the stock market crash in 1929; even during the entrepreneurial 1980s, this economic elite owned just one-third of all wealth (Williamson & Lindert, 1980; Beeghley, 1989; *1991 Green Book*).

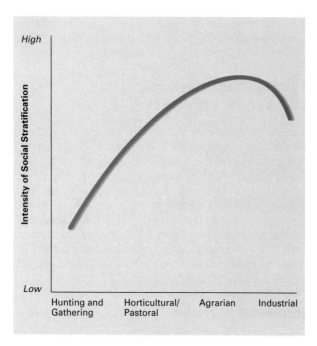

FIGURE 9–2 Social Stratification and Technological Development: The Kuznets Curve

The Kuznets curve reveals that greater technological sophistication is generally accompanied by more pronounced social stratification. The trend reverses itself, however, as industrial societies gradually become more egalitarian. Rigid caste-like distinctions are relaxed in favor of greater opportunity and equality under the law. Political rights are more widely extended, and there is even some leveling of economic differences. The Kuznets curve may also be usefully applied to the relative social standing of the two sexes.

Finally, industrialization diminishes the domination of women by men, a pattern that is strongest in agrarian societies. The movement toward social parity for the sexes derives from the industrial economy's need to cultivate individual talent as well as a growing belief in basic human equality.

The Kuznets Curve

The trend described above can be distilled into the following statement: *In human history, technological progress first sharply increases but then moderates the intensity of social stratification.* So if greater inequality is functional for agrarian societies, then industrial societies benefit from a more egalitarian climate. This historical shift, recognized by Nobel prize–winning economist Simon Kuznets (1955, 1966), is illustrated by the Kuznets curve, shown in Figure 9–2.

Current patterns of social inequality around the world generally square with the Kuznets curve. As shown in Global Map 9–1, industrial societies have somewhat less income inequality—one important measure of social stratification—than nations that remain predominantly agrarian. Specifically, mature industrial societies such as the United States and the nations of Western Europe exhibit less income inequality than the less industrialized countries of Latin America, Africa, and Asia.

Yet income disparity reflects a host of factors beyond technology, especially political and economic priorities. Societies that have had socialist economic systems (including the People's Republic of China, the former Soviet Union, and the nations of Eastern Europe) display relatively little income inequality. Keep in mind, however, that an egalitarian society like the People's Republic of China has an average income level that is quite low by world standards; further, on noneconomic dimensions such as political power, China's society reveals pronounced inequality.

And what of the future? Although the global pattern described by the Kuznets curve appears to be valid, this analysis does not necessarily mean that industrial societies will gradually become less and less stratified. In the abstract, members of our society endorse the principle of equal opportunity for all; even so, this goal has not—and may never—become a reality. The notion of social equality, like all concepts related to social stratification, is controversial, as the final section of this chapter explains.

SOCIAL STRATIFICATION: FACTS AND VALUES

The year was 2081 and everybody was finally equal. They weren't only equal before God and the law. They were equal every which way. Nobody was smarter than anybody else. Nobody was better looking than anybody else. Nobody was stronger or quicker than anybody else. All this equality was due to the 211th, 212th, and 213th Amendments to the Constitution and the unceasing vigilance of agents of the Handicapper General.

With these words, novelist Kurt Vonnegut, Jr. (1961) begins the story of "Harrison Bergeron," an

SOCIAL SURVEY: "Is it government's responsibility to reduce income differences between the rich and the poor?" (*CHIP1 Social Survey Software*, REDISTR; ISSP 1985)

	"Yes"	"No"
U.S.	34.6%	65.4%
Australia	52.6%	47.4%
Germany	66.9%	33.1%
U.K.	71.5%	28.5%
Austria	77.4%	22.6%

NOTE: Figure 11–1 shows the distribution of the world's income by fifths of humanity:
Richest 20%: 70% of income   Fourth 20%: 3% of income
Second 20%: 20% of income   Poorest 20%: 2% of income
Middle 20%: 5% of income

Window on the World

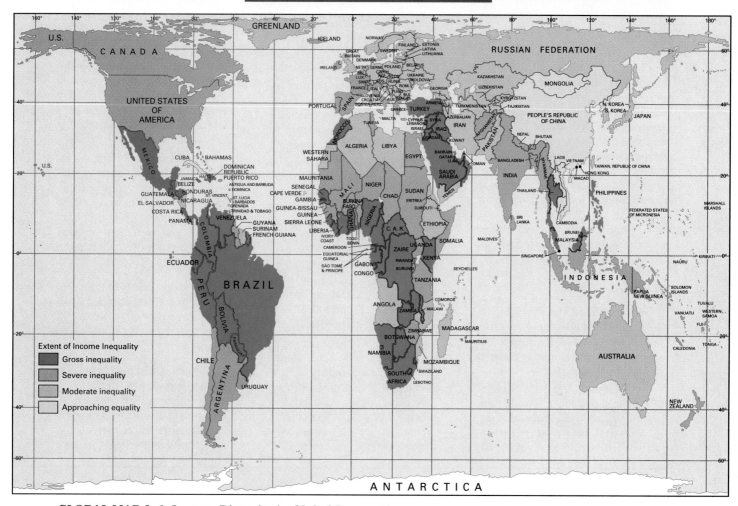

GLOBAL MAP 9–1 Income Disparity in Global Perspective

Societies throughout the world differ in the rigidity and intensity of social stratification as well as in overall standard of living. This map highlights income inequality. Generally speaking, countries that have had centralized, socialist economies (including the People's Republic of China, the former Soviet Union, and Cuba) display the least income inequality, although their standard of living has been relatively low. Industrial societies with predominantly capitalist economies, including the United States and most of Western Europe, have higher overall living standards, accompanied by severe income disparity. The low-income countries of Latin America and Africa (including Mexico, Brazil, and Zaire) exhibit the most pronounced inequality of income.

Source: *Peters Atlas of the World* (1990).

GLOBAL: In 1994, and intriguing in light of the *Bell Curve* debate, the People's Republic of China banned marriages between people deemed likely to produce physically or mentally defective children that would undermine the "quality of the population."

Q: "The more complex a society becomes, the more valuable are the people who are especially good at dealing with complexity." Richard Herrnstein and Charles Murray

Q: "The very same people who scream freedom of expression for Snoop Doggy Dogg or Robert Mapplethorpe . . . would be only too happy to silence—or academically lynch—Charles Murray or his late partner, Richard Herrnstein . . ." Leon R. Kass

Q: "It is the mark of the cultured man that he is aware of the fact that equality is an ethical and not a biological principle." Ashley Montagu

Controversy & Debate

The Bell Curve Debate: Are Rich People Really Smarter?

It is rare when the publication of a new book in the social sciences captures the attention of the public at large. But *The Bell Curve: Intelligence and Class Structure in American Life* by Richard J. Herrnstein and Charles Murray did that and more, igniting a firestorm of controversy over why pronounced social stratification divides our society and, just as important, what to do about it.

The Bell Curve is a long (800-page) book that addresses many critical issues and resists simple summary. But its basic thesis is captured in the following propositions:

1. Something we can describe as "general intelligence" exists; people with more of it tend to be more successful in their careers than those with less.

2. At least half the variation in human intelligence (Herrnstein and Murray use figures of 60 to 70 percent) is transmitted genetically from one generation to another; the remaining variability is due to environmental factors.

3. Over the course of this century—and especially since the "Information Revolution"—intelligence has become more necessary to the performance of our society's top occupational positions.

4. Simultaneously, the best U.S. colleges and universities have shifted their admissions policies away from favoring children of inherited wealth to admitting young people who perform best on standardized tests [such as the Scholastic Aptitude Test (SAT), American College Testing Program (ACT), and Graduate Record Examination (GRE)].

5. As a result of these changes in the workplace and higher education, our society is now coming to be dominated by a "cognitive elite," who are, on average, not only better trained than most people but actually more intelligent.

6. Because more intelligent people are socially segregated on the college campus and in the workplace, it is no surprise that they tend to pair up, marry, and have intelligent children, perpetuating the "cognitive elite."

7. Near the bottom of the social ladder, a similar process is at work: Increasingly, poor people are individuals with lower intelligence, who live segregated from others, and who tend to pass along their modest abilities to their children.

Resting on the validity of the seven assertions presented above, Herrnstein and Murray then offer, as an eighth point, a basic approach to public policy:

8. To the extent that membership in the affluent elite or the impoverished underclass is rooted in intelligence and determined mostly by genetic inheritance, programs to assist underprivileged people

imaginary account of a future United States in which social inequality has been totally abolished. While some people find equality appealing in principle, Vonnegut warns that it can be a dangerous concept in practice. His story describes a nightmare of social engineering in which every individual talent that makes one person different from another has been systematically neutralized by high-handed government agents.

In order to neutralize differences that make one person "better" than another, the state mandates that physically attractive people wear masks that render them average looking, that intelligent people don earphones that generate distracting noise, and that the legs of the best athletes and dancers be precisely fitted with weights to make their movements just as

cumbersome as everyone else's. In short, although we may imagine that social equality would liberate people to make the most of their talents, Vonnegut concludes that an egalitarian society would only succeed in reducing everyone to a lowest common denominator.

This chapter's explanations of social stratification also involve value judgments. The Davis-Moore thesis, which cites universal social stratification, interprets this pattern as evidence that inequality is a necessary element of social organization. Class differences in U.S. society, then, reflect both variation in human abilities and the importance of occupational roles. From this point of view, the specter of equality is a threat to a society of diverse people, since such uniformity (from Head Start to Affirmative Action) will have few practical benefits.

Within weeks of its publication, analysts pro and con were squaring off on television news shows, including *Nightline,* and trading charges across the pages of practically every news magazine in the country. Most social scientists tended to side with *The Bell Curve*'s critics. In response to the book's thesis, critics first questioned exactly what is meant by "intelligence," arguing that anyone's innate abilities can hardly be separated from the effects of socialization. Of course, rich children perform better on intelligence tests, they explained: These people have had all the advantages! Some critics dismiss the concept of "intelligence" outright as phony science. Others take a more moderate view, claiming that we should not think of "intelligence" as the sole cause of achievement since recent research indicates that mental abilities and life experiences are *interactive*, each affecting the other.

In addition, while most researchers who study intelligence agree that genetics does play a part in transmitting intelligence, the consensus is that no more than 25 to 40 percent is inherited—only about half what Herrnstein and Murray claim. Therefore, critics conclude, *The Bell Curve* wrongly misleads readers into thinking that social elitism is both natural and inevitable. In its assumptions and conclusions, moreover, *The Bell Curve* amounts to little more than a rehash of the social Darwinism popular a century ago, which heralded the success of industrial tycoons as merely "the survival of the fittest."

Perhaps, as one commentator noted, the more society seems like a jungle, the more people think of stratification as a matter of blood rather than upbringing. But, despite its flaws and exaggerations, the book's success suggests that *The Bell Curve* raises many issues we cannot easily ignore. Can our democratic system tolerate the "dangerous knowledge" that elites (including not only rich people but also our political leaders) are at least *somewhat* more intelligent than the rest of us? What of *The Bell Curve*'s description—which few challenge—that our society's elites are increasingly insulating themselves from social problems such as crime,

homelessness, and poor schools? As such problems have become worse in recent years, how do we counter the easy explanation that poor people are hobbled by their own limited ability? And, most basically, what should be done to ensure that all people have the opportunity to develop their abilities as fully as possible?

Continue the debate . . .

1. *Do you agree that "general intelligence" exists? Why or why not?*

2. *In general, do you think that people of higher social position are more intelligent than those of low social position? If you think intelligence differs by social standing, which factor is cause and which is effect?*

3. *Do you think sociologists should study controversial issues such as differences in human intelligence? Why or why not?*

Sources: Herrnstein & Murray (1994), Duster (1995), Hauser (1995), Jacoby & Glauberman (1995), and Taylor (1995).

could exist only as the product of the relentless and stifling efforts of officials like Vonnegut's fictitious "Handicapper General."

Social-conflict analysis, advocated by Karl Marx, interpreted universal social inequality in a very different way. Rejecting the notion that inequality is in any sense necessary, Marx condemned social hierarchy as a product of greed. Guided by egalitarian values, he advocated social arrangements that would enable everyone to share all important resources equally. Rather than undermining the quality of life, Marx maintained that equality would enhance human well-being.

Our concluding Controversy and Debate discussion addresses the link between intelligence and social class. This issue—also a mix of facts and values—is among the most troublesome in social science, partly because of the difficulty in defining and measuring "intelligence," but also because the idea that elites are inherently "better" than others challenges our democratic culture.

The next chapter ("Social Class in the United States") takes a close look at inequality in our own society. But, here again, even people who agree on the basic facts often interpret them quite differently. This lesson is repeated in Chapter 11 ("Global Stratification"), which examines inequality among the world's nations and offers two opposing explanations for it. At all levels, then, the study of social stratification involves a complex, ongoing debate that yields no single or simple truth.

SUMMARY

1. Social stratification refers to categories of people ranked in a hierarchy. Stratification is (1) a characteristic of society, not something that merely arises from individual differences; (2) persistent over many generations; (3) universal, yet variable in form; and (4) supported by cultural beliefs.

2. Caste systems, typical of agrarian societies, are based on ascription and permit little or no social mobility. Caste hierarchy, which rests on strong moral beliefs, shapes a person's entire life, including occupation and marriage.

3. Class systems, common to industrial societies, reflect a greater measure of individual achievement. Because the emphasis on achievement opens the way for social mobility, classes are less clearly defined than castes.

4. Historically, socialist societies have claimed to be classless, based on their public ownership of productive property. While such societies may exhibit far less economic inequality than their capitalist counterparts, they are notably stratified with regard to power.

5. Social stratification persists for two reasons—support from various social institutions and the power of ideology to define certain kinds of inequality as both natural and just.

6. The Davis-Moore thesis states that social stratification is universal because it contributes to the operation of society. In class systems, unequal rewards motivate people to aspire to the occupational roles most important to the functioning of society.

7. Critics of the Davis-Moore thesis note that (1) it is difficult to assess objectively the functional importance of any occupational position; (2) stratification prevents many people from developing their abilities; and (3) social stratification often generates social conflict.

8. Karl Marx, a key architect of social-conflict analysis, recognized two major social classes in industrial societies. The capitalists, or bourgeoisie, own the means of production in pursuit of profits; the proletariat, by contrast, offer their labor in exchange for wages.

9. The socialist revolution that Marx predicted has not occurred in industrial societies such as the United States. Some sociologists see this as evidence that Marx's analysis was flawed; others, however, point out that our society is still marked by pronounced social inequality and substantial class conflict.

10. Max Weber identified three distinct dimensions of social inequality: economic class, social status or prestige, and power. Taken together, these three dimensions form a complex hierarchy of socioeconomic standing.

11. Gerhard Lenski and Jean Lenski explained that, historically, technological advances have been associated with more pronounced social stratification. A limited reversal of this trend occurs in advanced, industrial societies, as represented by the Kuznets curve.

12. Social stratification is a complex and controversial area of research because it deals not only with facts but with values that suggest how society should be organized.

KEY CONCEPTS

blue-collar occupations lower-prestige work involving mostly manual labor

caste system a system of social stratification based on ascription

class system a system of social stratification based on individual achievement

Davis-Moore thesis the assertion that social stratification is a universal pattern because it has beneficial consequences for the operation of a society

ideology cultural beliefs that serve to justify social stratification

meritocracy a system of social stratification based on personal merit

social mobility change in people's position in a social hierarchy

social stratification a system by which society ranks categories of people in a hierarchy

socioeconomic status (SES) a composite ranking based on various dimensions of social inequality

status consistency the degree of consistency of a person's social standing across various dimensions of social inequality

structural social mobility a shift in the social position of large numbers of people due more to changes in society itself than to individual efforts

white-collar occupations higher-prestige work involving mostly mental activity

CRITICAL-THINKING QUESTIONS

1. How is social stratification evident on the college campus?

2. Why are agrarian societies typically caste systems? Why does industrialization replace castes with classes?

3. According to the Davis-Moore thesis, why is a college president paid more than a professor? Do you agree with this analysis?

4. In what respects have the predictions of Karl Marx failed to materialize? In what respects does his analysis ring true?

SUGGESTED READINGS

Classic Sources

Lillian Breslow Rubin. *Worlds of Pain: Life in the Working-Class Family*. New York: Basic Books, 1976.
    Based on interviews with fifty working-class families, Rubin skillfully explores the effects of social stratification on everyday life.

C. Wright Mills. *The Power Elite*. New York: Oxford University Press, 1956.
    In this treatise, written in the Marxist tradition, Mills argues that U.S. society is dominated by a small, well-integrated group that controls the economy, the government, and the military.

Contemporary Sources

Mary J. Jackman. *The Velvet Glove: Paternalism and Conflict in Gender, Class, and Race Relations*. Berkeley and Los Angeles: University of California Press, 1994.
    According to this research, relations between elites and subordinates typically are characterized by paternalism, not overt conflict.

Russell Jacoby and Naomi Glauberman, eds. *The Bell Curve Debate: History, Documents, Opinions*. New York: Times Books, 1995.
    Presenting the ideas of dozens of scholars and journalists, this is an excellent collection of commentary and analysis of the *Bell Curve* thesis—the alleged link between intelligence and social class.

Global Sources

Simon Bekker. *Ethnicity in Focus: The South African Case*. Durban: Indicator South Africa, 1993.
    This book traces the recent and complex process by which South Africa seeks to shed the racial foundations of its social inequality.

James Curtis and Lorne Tepperman, eds. *Haves and Have Nots: An International Reader on Social Inequality*. Englewood Cliffs, N.J.: Prentice Hall, 1994.
    This collection of essays presents a global survey of social stratification.

PAUL MARCUS,
PICNIC IN THE BRONX,
1992

Social Class
in the United States

Nigeria Collins died one month and one day after she was born. She now lies in a corner of Evergreen Cemetery in Camden, New Jersey, a small city across the river from Philadelphia. She is not the only infant buried beneath this patch of scrub grass littered with trash and broken glass. Hundreds of other babies lie here in a place that should guard the remains of people who grew up, grew old, and eventually died.

A half-century ago, Camden was one of the busiest industrial cities in the United States. Its shipyard built battleships, its factories turned out record players and other consumer goods, and its processing plants canned soup for a hungry nation.

But today Camden is among the most down-and-out cities in the country. The downward slide started in the 1950s, as people with the initiative and the cash escaped to the leafy green of the surrounding suburbs, leaving behind those with less schooling and fewer skills. Today, two-thirds of Camden's households are poor, and block upon block of housing is falling down, burned out, or boarded up. Camden also bears other familiar marks of cities in crisis: While some two hundred stores sell liquor, there is not a single movie theater; Camden has a flourishing drug trade but no safe park; street violence erupts everywhere, often, and without warning.

This urban tragedy is all the more wrenching because Camden is a city of children: About half of its people (who now number barely 100,000) are under the age of twenty-one. These youngsters cope in a world twisted by poverty, in which drug dealing or prostitution is a way of life; some like Nigeria Collins succumb before they are old enough to know what did them in (Fedarko, 1992).

The story of Camden stands as stark evidence of the pervasive power of social stratification to shape the lives of people throughout the United States. Whether individuals achieve great success or collapse with broken spirits is not a simple matter of individual talents and personal ambitions. Our fate also reflects the distribution of wealth, power, and opportunity in our society.

DIMENSIONS OF SOCIAL INEQUALITY

The United States is distinguished from most countries of the world because we never had a titled aristocracy. With the significant exception of our racial history, this nation has never known a caste system that rigidly ranks categories of people.

Even so, U.S. society is highly stratified. Not only do the rich control most of the money, they also benefit from the most schooling, they enjoy the best health, and they consume the greatest share of almost all goods and services. Such privileges contrast sharply with the poverty of millions of women and men who struggle from day to day simply to secure food and keep a roof over their heads.

People tend to think of the United States as a "middle-class society." Indeed, it is easy to underestimate the extent of stratification in our society for four reasons:

GLOBAL: Additional data for share of income (%) received by top and bottom 20 percent, by country: Lesotho, 60.0/2.9; Botswana, 58.9/3.6; Dominican Republic, 55.6/4.2; Costa Rica, 50.8/4.0; India, 41.3/8.8; Spain, 40/7; Japan, 38/9. (The World Bank, 1995)

GLOBAL: Top ten nations in per capita gross domestic product (using purchasing power parities) for 1993: U.S., $24,740; Switzerland, $23,660; Kuwait, $21,630; Hong Kong, $21,560; United Arab Emirates, $20,940; Japan, $20,850; Canada, $20,230; Norway, $19,780; Belgium, $19,640; Singapore, $19,510. (The World Bank, 1995)

THEN AND NOW: 1970 income data for comparison with Figure 10–1 for each quintile: 40.9%, 23.8%, 17.6%, 12.2%, 5.5%.

THEN AND NOW: Households with income over $100,000 (1993 dollars): 1974, 2.0 million (2.7%); 1993, 5.6 million (5.8%).

TABLE 10–1 U.S. Family Income, 1994

Highest paid . . .	Annually earns at least . . .
0.5%	$1,000,000
1	200,000
5	105,000
10	85,000
20	70,000
30	55,000
40	47,500
50	39,000
60	31,000
70	25,000
80	18,000
90	10,000

Source: U.S. Bureau of the Census (1996) and author calculations.

1. **We support equal standing under the law**. Because our legal system accords equal rights to everyone, we tend to think that all people have basically the same social standing.

2. **Our culture celebrates individual autonomy and achievement**. Our belief that people forge their own destinies through talent and hard work leads us to downplay the significance of birth on social position.

3. **We tend to interact with people like ourselves**. Throughout the United States, primary groups—including family, neighbors, and friends—typically are composed of people with similar social standing (Kelley & Evans, 1995). While we may speak of "how the other half lives," generally we have only brief and impersonal encounters with people very different from ourselves.

4. **The United States is an affluent society**. As noted in Chapter 1 ("The Sociological Perspective"), the overall standard of living in the United States is the highest in the world. Such affluence lulls us into believing that everyone in our society is relatively well off.

When people do acknowledge their differences, they often speak of a "ladder of social class" as if inequality were a matter of a single factor such as money. More accurately, however, social class in the United States has several, more subtle, dimensions. Socioeconomic status (SES), which we examined in Chapter 9 ("Social Stratification"), amounts to a composite measure of social position that encompasses not just money but power, occupational prestige, and schooling.

Income

One important dimension of inequality involves income, *occupational wages or salaries and earnings from investments*. The Bureau of the Census reports that the average (mean) U.S. family income in 1994 was $38,808. The first part of Figure 10–1 illustrates the distribution of income among all families[1] in the country. The richest 20 percent of families (earning at least $70,000 annually, with a mean of about $115,000) received 46.8 percent of all income, while the bottom 20 percent (earning less than $18,000, with a mean of about $10,000) received only about 4.2 percent.

Table 10–1 provides a closer look at income distribution. The highest-paid 5 percent of U.S. families, who earn six-figure incomes (with a mean of $198,336), secured 20.1 percent of all income, surpassing in earnings the lowest-paid 40 percent. At the very top of the pyramid, the richest half of 1 percent earn at least $1 million annually. In short, the bulk of the nation's income is earned by a small proportion of families, while the rest of the population makes do with far less.

As detailed later in this chapter, income disparity in the United States increased during the 1980s as a result of changes in the economy, new tax policies, more two-earner couples, and cuts in social programs that assist low-income people (Levy, 1987; Reich, 1989; Cutler & Katz, 1992). Since 1990, however, income disparity has eased downward, a trend accelerated in 1993 by higher income tax rates on the top-earning 5 percent.

Chapter 9 ("Social Stratification") explained that social inequality declines as industrialization proceeds (according to the Kuznets curve shown in Figure 9–2). Thus, the United States has less income inequality than, say, Venezuela (in South America), Kenya (Africa), or Sri Lanka (Asia). However, as Figure 10–2 on page 264 indicates, U.S. society does permit more income inequality than is found in many other industrial societies.

Wealth

Income is but one component of a person's or family's wealth, *the total value of money and other assets, minus*

---

[1]Some Census Bureau reports use means, others provide median data. For 1994, median family income was $36,782; this figure is lower than the mean because high-income families pull the mean upward. Reported for households rather than families, income statistics are somewhat lower: $32,385 (mean) and $31,241 (median). Most of this difference is due to size: Families averaged 3.20 persons, households 2.67. The Census Bureau defines a household as two or more persons sharing a living unit; they define a family as two or more persons related by blood, marriage, or adoption.

DIVERSITY: Median 1993 household income by age of house-holder: under 25, $19,300; 25–34, $31,300; 35–44, $40,900; 45–54, $46,200; 55–64, $33,500; 65 +, $17,800. (U.S. Bureau of the Census)

DIVERSITY: Median 1993 household wealth by age: under 35, $5,786; 35–44, $29,202; 45–54, $57,755; 55–64, $91,481; 65–69, $92,500; 70–74, $95,748; 75 +, $77,654. (U.S. Bureau of the Census)

GLOBAL: Edward N. Wolff offers wealth inequality coefficients for industrial nations. Zero represents wealth equality; 1.0 reflects all wealth owned by one person. U.S., .34; Italy .31; Canada, .29; Germany, .25; France, .25; Finland .21. (*Top Heavy: A Study of Increasing Inequality of Wealth in America*: Twentieth Century Fund, 1995)

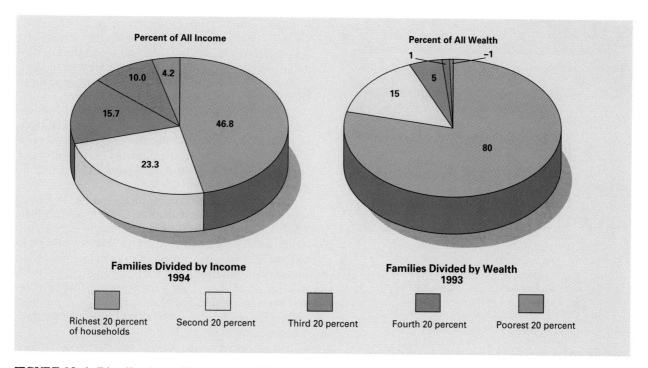

FIGURE 10–1 Distribution of Income and Wealth in the United States

Sources: Income data from U. S. Bureau of the Census (1996); wealth data are author estimates based on the Joint Economic Committee (1986) and Kennickell & Shack-Marquez (1992).

outstanding debts. The second part of Figure 10–1 shows that wealth—in the form of stocks, bonds, real estate, and other privately owned property—is distributed much less equally than income.

In 1993, the richest 20 percent of U.S. families owned approximately 80 percent of the country's entire wealth. High up in this privileged category are the wealthiest 5 percent of families—the "very rich"—who control more than half the nation's property. With wealth into the tens of millions of dollars, the "super rich" comprise the 1 percent of U.S. households that possess one-third of our nation's privately held resources. And capping the wealth pyramid, the one dozen richest U.S. families have a combined net worth approaching $150 billion, which equals the total wealth of 1 million average families, including enough people to fill the cities of Alexandria, Virginia; Akron, Ohio; Anchorage, Alaska; and Albuquerque, New Mexico (Millman et al., 1993; Rogers, 1993; Weicher, 1995).

Recent government calculations place the wealth of the average U.S. household at $37,587, about equal to an average family's annual income. This reflects the value of homes, cars, investments, insurance policies, retirement pensions, furniture, clothing, and all other personal property, minus the home mortgage and other debts (Weicher, 1995). The wealth of average people is not only less than that of the rich, however, it is also different in kind. While "ordinary" wealth usually centers on a home and a car or two—that is, property that generates no income—the greater wealth of the rich is mostly in the form of stocks and other income-producing investments.

When financial liabilities are balanced against assets, the least affluent 40 percent of U.S. families have virtually no wealth at all. The negative percentage shown in Figure 10–1 for the poorest 20 percent of the population means that these people actually live in debt.

Power

In the United States, as elsewhere, wealth stands as an important source of power. Major owners of corporate stock, for example, make decisions that create jobs for ordinary people or scale back operations, throwing men and women out of work.

More broadly, the "super-rich" families who own most of the nation's wealth have a great deal of say about the national political agenda. Thomas Jefferson

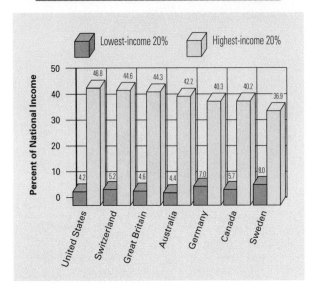

FIGURE 10–2 Income Disparities for Selected Industrial Countries

Source: The World Bank (1995).

(1953; orig. 1785), the third U.S. president and a wealthy man himself, cautioned that the vitality of a democratic system depends on "subdividing property" so that the many, not just the few, have a voice in political affairs.

Chapter 16 ("Politics and Government") delves into the debate surrounding wealth and power. Some analysts concede that the rich have certain advantages but maintain that they hardly dominate the political process. Others counter that, in general, the political agenda reflects the interests of the wealthy.

Occupational Prestige

Occupation, too, is an important element of social standing, since one's job affects all the factors noted thus far: income, wealth, and power. In addition, occupation serves as a key source of social prestige since we commonly evaluate each other according to the kind of work we do, holding some in high esteem while looking down on others.

For more than half a century, sociologists have assessed the social prestige of various occupations

(Counts, 1925; Hodge, Treiman, & Rossi, 1966; NORC, 1994). Table 10–2 presents the results of a recent survey involving a random sample of U.S. adults. In general, people attach high prestige to occupations—such as medicine, law, and engineering—that also generate high income.

Prestige reflects more than just pay, however, since favored occupations typically require considerable ability and demand extensive education and training. By contrast, less prestigious work—as a waitress or janitor, for example—not only pays less but usually requires less ability and schooling.

In global perspective, occupational prestige rankings are much the same in all industrial societies (Ma, 1987; Lin & Xie, 1988). Almost everywhere, white-collar work that involves mental activity free from extensive supervision confers greater prestige than blue-collar occupations that require supervised, manual labor. There are exceptions to this pattern, however. In the United States, for example, a blue-collar police officer enjoys greater social prestige than a white-collar bank teller.

In any society, high-prestige occupations go to privileged categories of people. Reading down from the beginning of Table 10–2, one passes a dozen occupations before reaching "registered nurse," an occupation in which *most* workers are women. Moreover, women are concentrated in so-called pink-collar occupations—service and clerical positions such as secretaries, waitresses, and beauticians—that yield little income and fall near the bottom of the prestige hierarchy. Similarly, reading the table in reverse order shows that many jobs that provide the least amount of prestige and income are commonly performed by people of color. The important point here is that social stratification typically spans various dimensions of inequality (based on income and prestige as well as sex and race) *that are superimposed on each other*, forming a complex, deeply ingrained, and often steep, hierarchy.

Schooling

In industrial societies, schooling is necessary for adults to perform their work; thus, primary, secondary, and some college education is available at public expense. Like other dimensions of inequality, however, more schooling is available to some than to others.

Table 10–3 on page 266 indicates the level of formal education reached by U.S. men and women. According to the table, more than three-fourths of adults have completed high school; just over 20 percent are college graduates.

NOTE: The "Forbes Four Hundred"—a listing of the richest 400 people in the United States—contains interesting facts and patterns about U.S. wealth. This special issue of *Forbes* appears in late October each year. To make the 1995 list, wealth of at least $340 million was needed, with average (mean) wealth more than twice that figure. (In 1980, the list began with individuals worth $230 million.) Fewer than half of the people listed now had appeared there a decade before. Such listings are skewed toward the new-rich corporate elite, whose wealth is mostly in the form of stocks (rather than, say, art) and whose compensation is a matter of public record.

DISCUSS: Consider the extent to which jobs shown in Table 10–2 are gender-linked. What pattern emerges?

Q: "If we command our wealth, we shall be rich and free; if our wealth commands us, we are poor, indeed." Edmund Burke

TABLE 10–2 The Relative Social Prestige of Selected Occupations in the United States

White-collar Occupations	Prestige Score	Blue-collar Occupations	White-collar Occupations	Prestige Score	Blue-collar Occupations
Physician	86		Funeral director	49	
Lawyer	75		Realtor	49	
College/university professor	74		Bookkeeper	47	
Architect	73			47	Machinist
Chemist	73			47	Mail carrier
Physicist/astronomer	73		Musician/composer	47	
Aerospace engineer	72			46	Secretary
Dentist	72		Photographer	45	
Member of the clergy	69		Bank teller	43	
Psychologist	69			42	Tailor
Pharmacist	68			42	Welder
Optometrist	67			40	Farmer
Registered nurse	66			40	Telephone operator
Secondary-school teacher	66			39	Carpenter
Accountant	65			36	Brick/stone mason
Athlete	65			36	Child-care worker
Electrical engineer	64		File clerk	36	
Elementary-school teacher	64			36	Hairdresser
Economist	63			35	Baker
Veterinarian	62			34	Bulldozer operator
Airplane pilot	61			31	Auto body repairperson
Computer programmer	61		Retail apparel salesperson	30	
Sociologist	61			30	Truck driver
Editor/reporter	60		Cashier	29	
	60	Police officer		28	Elevator operator
Actor	58			28	Garbage collector
Radio/TV announcer	55			28	Taxi driver
Librarian	54			28	Waiter/waitress
	53	Aircraft mechanic		27	Bellhop
	53	Firefighter		25	Bartender
Dental hygienist	52			23	Farm laborer
Painter/sculptor	52			23	Household laborer
Social worker	52			22	Door-to-door salesperson
	51	Electrician		22	Janitor
Computer operator	50			09	Shoe shiner

Source: Adapted from *General Social Surveys 1972–1994: Cumulative Codebook* (Chicago: National Opinion Research Center, 1994), pp. 881–89.

Here, again, we see how dimensions of inequality are linked. Schooling affects both occupation and income, since most (but not all) of the better paying, white-collar jobs shown in Table 10–2 require a college degree or other advanced study. On the other hand, most blue-collar occupations that offer lower income and social prestige demand less schooling.

ASCRIPTION AND SOCIAL STRATIFICATION

To a considerable degree, the class system in the United States rewards individual talent and effort. But, our class system also retains distinct elements of caste. Ascription—who we are at birth—greatly influences what we become later in life.

Ancestry

Nothing affects social standing in the United States as much as our birth into a particular family, an event over which we have no control. Ancestry determines our point of entry into the system of social inequality. Some families in the United States, including the duPonts, Rockefellers, Roosevelts, and Kennedys, are renowned around the world. And almost every city and town contain families who have amassed wealth and power on a more modest scale.

Being born to privilege or poverty sets the stage for our future schooling, occupation, and income. Research reveals that at least half of the richest individuals—those with hundreds of millions of dollars in wealth—derived their fortunes primarily from inheritance (Thurow, 1987; Queenan, 1989). By the same token, the

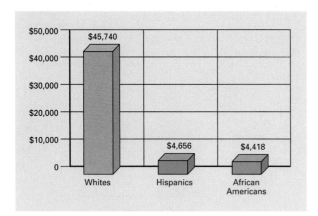

FIGURE 10–3 Average Wealth, by Race and Ethnicity, of the U.S. Population, 1993

Source: U.S. Bureau of the Census (1995).

"inheritance" of poverty and the lack of opportunity that inevitably goes with it just as surely shape the future of those in need. The operation of the family, which serves to transmit property, power, and possibilities from one generation to the next, accounts, more than any other single factor, for the persistence of social stratification.

Race and Ethnicity

Race has a strong connection to social position in the United States. Overall, white people have higher occupational standing than African Americans and also receive more schooling, especially at the college level and beyond. These differences are evident in median income: for African Americans, families earned $21,548 in 1994, which was about 55 percent of the $39,308 earned by white families (U.S. Bureau of the Census, 1995).

Another reason for this disparity involves family patterns: African-American families with children are three times more likely than their white counterparts to have only one parent in the home. Single parenthood, in turn, is a strong predictor of low family income. If we compare only families headed by married couples, the racial disparity shrinks dramatically, with African Americans earning 81 percent of what whites do.

Over time, any income differential builds into a considerable "wealth gap." Figure 10–3 shows that,

while the typical white household has a net worth exceeding $45,000, the comparable figure for Hispanics and African Americans is roughly one-tenth as much. Moreover, the effects of race are significant even among affluent families, as the box on page 267 explains.

Ethnicity, as well as race, shapes social stratification in the United States. Throughout our nation's history, people of English ancestry controlled the most wealth and wielded the greatest power. The rapidly growing Latino population in the United States, by contrast, has long been relatively disadvantaged. In 1993, median family income among all Hispanics was $23,654, 60 percent of the comparable figure for all white families. A detailed examination of how race and ethnicity affect social standing is presented in Chapter 12 ("Race and Ethnicity").

Gender

People of both sexes are born into families at every social level. Yet, on average, women earn lower income, accumulate less wealth, enjoy lower occupational prestige, and rank lower in some aspects of educational achievement than men do.

Perhaps the most dramatic difference, however, is that households headed by women are ten times more likely to be poor than those headed by men. A full picture of the connection between gender and social stratification is found in Chapter 13 ("Sex and Gender").

Religion

Religion, too, has a bearing on social standing in the United States. Among Protestant denominations, with which almost two-thirds of individuals identify,

TABLE 10–3 Schooling of U.S. Adults, 1993 (aged 25 and over)

	Women	Men
Not a high school graduate	**20.0%**	**19.5%**
8 years or less	9.2	9.4
9–11 years	10.8	10.1
High school graduate	**80.0**	**80.5**
High school only	37.4	33.2
1–3 years college	23.4	22.6
College graduate or more	19.2	24.7

Source: U.S. Bureau of the Census (1995).

DIVERSITY: Income is more concentrated among African Americans than among whites. Percent of all income by fifths for 1993: 50.6%; 24.1%; 14.5%; 7.9%; 3.0%.

Q: "No citizen should ever be wealthy enough to buy another, and none poor enough to be forced to sell himself." Jean-Jacques Rousseau, *The Social Contract* (II, 46)

NOTE: As income goes up, the proportion of income spent on necessities declines, while the share allocated to discretionary spending rises. For example, the typical U.S. household spends 12% of income for food; households with incomes above $200,000 spend 2%.

Q: "He who dies rich, dies in disgrace." Andrew Carnegie, industrialist and philanthropist

SOCIAL DIVERSITY

The Color of Money: Being Rich in Black and White

African-American families earn 55 cents to the white family's dollar, a fact that underlies the greater risk of poverty among people of color. But there is another side to black America—an affluent side—that has expanded dramatically in recent decades.

The number of affluent families—those with annual incomes over $50,000—is increasing faster among African Americans than among whites. In 1990, more than 1 million African-American families were financially privileged; adjusted for inflation, this represents a fivefold increase over two decades before. Today, 15 percent of African-American families—more than 2 million adults and their children—are affluent. About 15 percent of Latino families rank as well off, too, while 30 percent of non-Hispanic white families and 35 percent of Asian families have that much income.

The color of money is the same for everyone, but black and white affluence differs in several key respects. First, well-off people of African descent are not *as rich* as their white counterparts. About 45 percent of affluent white families (17 percent of all white families) earn more than $75,000 a year, a standard reached by only 38 percent of affluent African-American families (7 percent of all black families).

Second, African Americans are more likely than white people to achieve affluence through multiple

Rich people come in all colors. But are they all the same?

incomes. Families at this level typically have two employed spouses, perhaps with working children.

Third, affluent African Americans are more likely to derive their income from salaries rather than investments. Three-fourths of affluent white families have investment income, compared to just half of affluent African-American families.

Beyond differences in income, affluent people of color contend with social barriers that do not restrict whites. Even African Americans with the money to purchase a home, for example, may find they are unwelcome as neighbors. This is one reason that a smaller proportion of affluent African-American families (40 percent) live in the suburbs (the richest areas of the country) than do affluent white families (61 percent).

Affluent Americans come in all colors. Yet race has a powerful effect on the lives of affluent people, just as it does on the lives of us all.

Sources: O'Hare (1989), U.S. Bureau of the Census (1995), Weicher (1995).

Episcopalians and Presbyterians have significantly higher social standing, on average, than Lutherans and Baptists. Jews, too, have high social standing, while Roman Catholics hold a more modest position (Roof, 1979; Davidson, Pyle, & Reyes, 1995).

Even John Fitzgerald Kennedy—a member of one of this country's wealthiest and most powerful families—was elected our first Catholic president in 1960 only by overcoming considerable opposition directed against him because of his religion. Understandably, then, throughout our history many upwardly mobile people have converted to a higher-ranking religion (Baltzell, 1979).

SOCIAL CLASSES IN THE UNITED STATES

As Chapter 9 ("Social Stratification") explained, people living in rigid caste systems can tell at a glance anyone's social ranking. Assessing social position in a more fluid class system, however, poses a number of challenges.

Consider the joke about a couple who orders a pizza, asking that it be cut into six slices because they aren't hungry enough to eat eight. While all sociologists acknowledge extensive social inequality in the United States, they have long debated precisely how

NOTE: Erik Olin Wright (1993) argues that classes are discrete categories because (1) they correspond to different mechanisms for generating income, and (2) they are useful for explaining class conflict. An interesting debate on this issue is found in *American Sociological Review*, Vol. 58, No. 1, February 1993.

GLOBAL: The world's richest person is the oil-rich Sultan of Brunei, worth some $35 billion. Not far behind is Taikichiro Mori, worth $15 billion. The fortune of this 90-year-old man—a former professor who left academia to join his father's real estate company in the 1950s—is based on owning 82 buildings in downtown Tokyo. The richest individual in the United States is Microsoft's founder William Henry Gates III (who scored a perfect 800 on his mathematics SAT), worth about $13 billion; close behind is investor Warren Buffett at about $12 billion.

A popular distinction in the United States and elsewhere sets off the "new rich" from people with "old money." Men and women who suddenly begin to earn high incomes tend toward public extravagance because they enjoy the new thrill of high-roller living and they want others to know of their success. Those who grow up surrounded by wealth, by contrast, are more accustomed to their privileges and more quiet about them. In short, the "conspicuous consumption" of the lower-upper class (left) differs from the more private pursuits and characteristic understatement of the upper-upper class (right).

to divide up this social hierarchy. Some follow Karl Marx's thinking and recognize two major classes; others point to as many as six categories (Warner & Lunt, 1941) or even seven (Coleman & Rainwater, 1978). Still others endorse Max Weber's contention that, rather than clear-cut classes, people are ranked in a multidimensional status hierarchy.

Defining classes is difficult because of the relatively low level of status consistency in U.S. society. Especially toward the middle of the hierarchy, standing on one dimension often contradicts one's position on another. A government official, for example, may have the power to administer a multimillion-dollar budget yet earn a modest personal income. Similarly, members of the clergy typically enjoy ample prestige but only moderate power and low pay. Or consider a lucky professional gambler who may win little respect but who accumulates considerable wealth.

Finally, the social mobility typical of class systems—again, most pronounced near the middle—means that social position may well change during one's lifetime. This mobility further blurs the lines between social classes.

Having expressed the necessary reservations, we now proceed to identify four general social classes in the United States: the upper class, the middle class, the working class, and the lower class. To these, moreover, we add a few further distinctions.

The Upper Class

The upper class comprises 5 percent of the U.S. population. The yearly income of upper-class families is at least $100,000 and can exceed ten times that much. As a general rule, the more a family's income is derived from inherited wealth in the form of stocks and bonds, real estate, and other investments, the stronger a family's claim to being upper class.

In 1995, an article in *Forbes* magazine profiled the richest four hundred people in the United States, estimating their combined wealth at $505 billion. Each of these richest individuals had a *minimum* net worth of $340 million, and the group included 128 billionaires. The upper class thus comprises Karl Marx's "capitalists"—those who own much of the nation's productive property.

Besides possessing immense wealth, many members of the upper class work as top corporate executives and as senior government officials, positions which further enhance their power to shape events in the nation and, increasingly, the entire world. Upper-class people also attain extensive education, typically in the most expensive and highly regarded schools and colleges. Historically, though less so today, the upper class has been composed of white Anglo-Saxon Protestants (WASPs) (Baltzell, 1964, 1976, 1988).

DIVERSITY: Typically, suburbs are high-income areas: The suburban area with the highest median income ($59,284 according to the 1990 Census) is Fairfax County, Va.

NOTE: Often members of the "new rich" marry the "old rich" in order to gain the social prestige that cannot be achieved by the mere accumulation of money. For instance, bodybuilder and actor Arnold Schwarzenegger married Maria Shriver, a member of the

Kennedy clan. (*People* magazine described the match as "impeccable pedigree meets impeccable pectorals.")

NOTE: The importance of a college education to middle-class standing is suggested by the practice, common in the United States, of placing college decals on the windows of automobiles.

Q: "The prosperity of the middle and lower classes depends on the good fortune of and light taxes on the rich." Andrew Mellon

Upper-Uppers

Sociologists make a useful distinction between the "upper-upper class" and the "lower-upper class." The *upper-upper class*, often described as "society" or "bluebloods," includes less than 1 percent of the U.S. population (Warner & Lunt, 1941; Coleman & Neugarten, 1971; Baltzell, 1995). Membership is almost always the result of ascription or birth, as suggested by the old quip that the easiest way to become an "upper-upper" is to be born one. These families possess enormous wealth, primarily inherited rather than earned. For this reason, we sometimes say that members of the upper-upper class have *old money*. Noting the favor accorded to this segment of U.S. society, C. Wright Mills commented that "prestige is the shadow of money and power" (1956:83).

Set apart by their wealth, members of the upper-upper class live in a world of exclusive affiliations. They inhabit elite neighborhoods, such as Beacon Hill in Boston, Rittenhouse Square or the Main Line in Philadelphia, the Gold Coast of Chicago, and Nob Hill in San Francisco. Schools and colleges extend this privileged environment. Children typically attend private secondary schools with others of similar background, completing their formal education at high-prestige colleges and universities. In the historical pattern of European aristocrats, they study liberal arts rather than vocationally directed subjects.

Women of the upper-upper class often maintain a full schedule of volunteer work for charitable organizations. Upper-class women, for example, were primarily responsible for establishing the Philadelphia Museum of Art, and that city's old-money families continue to support the organization with donations of time, artworks, and cash. While contributing to the larger community, as Susan Ostrander (1980, 1984) explains, such charitable activities also help families to forge networks that establish them as members of the city's power and prestige elite.

Lower-Uppers

Most upper-class people actually fall into the *lower-upper class*. From the point of view of most of us, such people seem every bit as privileged as the upper-upper class. The major difference, however, is that lower-uppers are the "working rich" who depend on earnings rather than inherited wealth as the primary source of their income.

Especially in the eyes of members of "society," the lower-upper class are merely the "new rich" who can never savor the highest levels of prestige enjoyed by

those with rich and famous grandparents. Thus, while the new rich typically live in the biggest homes, they often find themselves excluded from the clubs and associations of old-money families.

Historically, the American Dream has been to join through exceptional accomplishment not the upper-upper class (difficult except, perhaps, through marriage) but the lower-upper class. The young author whose novel becomes a popular Hollywood movie; the athlete who accepts a million-dollar contract to play in the big leagues; the clever computer whiz who designs a new program that sets a standard for the industry— these are the lucky and talented achievers who reach the level of the lower-upper class. The box on page 270 sharpens the distinction between "society" and high achievers who seem like the rest of us—except that they have made a lot more money.

The Middle Class

Including 40 to 45 percent of the U.S. population, the large middle class exerts a tremendous influence on U.S. culture. Television and other mass media usually depict middle-class people, and most commercial advertising is directed toward these "average" consumers. The middle class encompasses far more racial and ethnic diversity than the upper class. And while many upper-class people (especially upper-uppers) know each other personally, such exclusiveness and familiarity do not characterize the middle class.

Upper-Middles

The top half of this category is often dubbed the *upper-middle class*, based on above-average income in the range of $50,000 to $100,000 a year. Family income may be even greater if both wife and husband work. High income allows upper-middle-class families gradually to accumulate considerable property—a comfortable house in a fairly expensive area, several automobiles, and investments. Two-thirds of upper-middle-class children receive college educations, and postgraduate degrees are common. Many go on to high-prestige occupations (as physicians, engineers, lawyers, accountants, or business executives). Lacking the power of the upper class to influence national or international events, the upper-middle class nonetheless often plays an important role in local political affairs.

Average-Middles

The rest of the middle class falls close to the center of the U.S. class structure. People at the *center*

NOTE: Regional editions of the *Social Register* were published for Newport, Rhode Island (1887; discontinued), New York (beginning in 1888), Philadelphia and Boston (1890), Baltimore (1892), Chicago (1893), Washington, D.C. (1906), and Cleveland-Cincinnati-Dayton (1910). In 1976, these listings were merged into a single, national edition of the book. (Baltzell, 1995)

NOTE: The *Social Register* lists far fewer families (about 40,000) than those whose household wealth exceeds $1 million (about 1.5 million).

Q: "The first and most intense passion that is produced by equality of condition is, I need hardly say, the love of that equality . . . Among democratic nations, men easily attain a certain equality of condition, but they can never attain as much as they desire." Alexis de Tocqueville

CRITICAL THINKING

Caste and Class: The *Social Register* and *Who's Who*

Small and exclusive, the upper-upper class comes closest to being a true social group. There is even a listing of these privileged families: the *Social Register*, first published in 1887 as fortunes grew along with the industrial economy. A century later, some forty thousand conjugal families are included in this inventory of our society's "blue-bloods."

Because membership is typically based on birth, the upper-upper class operates much like a caste: You are either "in" or "out." With tradition as a guide, many upper-upper parents urge their children to seek out partners of their own kind, sustaining the class into another generation. Family is thus crucial to the upper-upper class, as it is to all caste groups. *Social Register* listings are of *families,* not *individuals.*

The listing for David Rockefeller, a member of one of the most socially prominent families in the United States, indicates (1) his family's address and home telephone number; (2) Mrs. Rockefeller's maiden name; (3) the names of the Rockefeller children, noting the boarding schools and colleges they are attending; and (4) exclusive social clubs to which the family belongs. Echoing the practice of idle aristocrats of ages past, entries in the *Social Register* omit any mention of occupation or place of business. Nor do they cite any mark of individual accomplishment.

The lower-upper class, by contrast, is an achievement elite. This larger category of "new-rich" individuals has no clear boundaries, and its members do not engage in formal rituals (like debutante balls) the way old-money families often do.

There is a listing—roughly speaking—of people at this class level: the

Two books: one lists "upper-uppers," the other, "lower-uppers."

national edition of *Who's Who in America.* Here, instead of "established" families, we find individuals distinguished for excellence: outstanding athletes, highly successful business people, college presidents, Nobel prize winners, and famous entertainers.

Who's Who lists a few people, including David Rockefeller, whose families also appear in the *Social Register*, but the information in one has little in common with the writeup in the other. David Rockefeller's entry in *Who's Who* offers a brief biography (date of birth, schooling, and honorary degrees), a list of his accomplishments (military decorations, government service, books authored), and—most important—it specifies his position as board chair of Chase Manhattan Bank. The address provided in *Who's Who* is his place of business.

Comparing the two listings reveals that there are two kinds of elites in the United States. The caste-like *Social Register* lists high-prestige families according to *who they are.* The more class-like *Who's Who* lists individuals on the basis of *what they have done.* But, as the dual writeups on David Rockefeller suggest, social privilege and personal achievement sometimes overlap.

---

of the middle-class typically work in less prestigious white-collar occupations (such as bank tellers, middle managers, or sales clerks) or in highly skilled blue-collar jobs (including electrical work and carpentry). Commonly, household income falls between $35,000 and $50,000 a year, which is close to the mean household income for the United States as a whole ($32,385 in 1994).

Income at this level provides a secure, if modest, standard of living. Middle-class people generally accumulate some wealth over the course of their working lives, most in the form of a house. Middle-class men and women are likely to be high school graduates, but just four in ten young people at this class level attend college, usually enrolling in less expensive state-supported schools.

For more than a century, the Campbell's Soup Company was one of Camden, New Jersey's, major employers. Today, this company is a multinational with production facilities in various locations in the United States and abroad. Recently, the company's owners decided to demolish the antiquated Camden factory, saving only the trademark soup-can water tower, which will be restored as a landmark. For the working people of Camden, the departure of Campbell's is one in a long chain of economic setbacks that has left this city among the poorest in the United States.

The Working Class

Encompassing about one-third of the population, the working class (sometimes called the "lower-middle class") refers to people who have still lower incomes and little or no accumulated wealth. In Marxist terms, the working class forms the core of the industrial proletariat. The blue-collar occupations of the working class generally yield a household income of between $15,000 and $35,000 a year, somewhat below the national average. Working-class families thus find themselves vulnerable to financial problems, especially when confronted by unemployment or illness.

Besides generating less income than the occupations of the middle class, working-class jobs typically yield less personal satisfaction. Tasks tend to be routine, requiring discipline but rarely imagination, and workers are usually subject to continual supervision. Such jobs also provide fewer benefits, like medical insurance and pension programs. About half of working-class families own their homes, usually in lower-cost neighborhoods. College is a goal that only about one-third of working-class children realize.

As these facts suggest, working-class people lack the power to shape events, and many view their lives with a sense of fatalism. Families live in modest neighborhoods because they cannot afford better housing. Many want to send their children to college but do not have the money to cover tuition. They find little satisfaction in their jobs, but they have scant opportunity for upward mobility. Still, many working-class families express a great deal of pride in what they do have, especially in comparison to those who are not working at all.

The Lower Class

The remaining 20 percent of our population make up the lower class. A lack of work and little income render their lives unstable and insecure. In 1993, the federal government classified 39.3 million Americans (15.1 percent of the population) as poor. Millions more—the so-called working poor—are just barely better off. Most lower-class people in the United States are white; however, people of African or Hispanic descent and other minorities are disproportionately represented at the low end of the socioeconomic scale.

About half of the heads of officially poor households do not work at all, in many cases because they are women with children who cannot secure affordable child care. The remainder of the poor and the near poor have low-prestige jobs that provide little intrinsic satisfaction and minimal income. Barely half manage to complete high school, and only one in four enrolls in college. Given limited schooling, many lower-class men and women are functionally illiterate.

Society segregates the lower class—and especially poor minorities—into particular neighborhoods and schools. Although about 40 percent of lower-class families own their own home, they typically are located in the least desirable neighborhoods. Poor districts generally are found in inner cities, but lower-class families also inhabit rural counties, especially in the South.

Wherever they live, lower-class children learn early on the harsh reality that many people consider them only marginal members of society. Observing the struggles of their parents and other lower-class adults, they may see little hope of breaking the cycle of

DIVERSITY: High costs deter the poor from seeking health care. Nonetheless, low-income people have more medical-care contacts (especially emergency-room visits) than more affluent people. The National Health Interview Survey reported 7.9 ER visits per person per year for those in households with under $10,000 in annual income compared to 5.7 for those with $35,000 or more in household income. (U.S. National Center for Health Statisitics)

THEN AND NOW: Changing definition of "necessities" in homes from 1970 to 1990: average square feet, 1710, 2095; garage included, 58%, 82%; 2 1/2 or more bathrooms, 16%, 45%; central air, 34%, 75%; fireplace(s), 35%, 66%. (U.S. Bureau of the Census)
Q: "The more a ruling class is able to assimilate the most prominent men of the dominated classes, the more stable and dangerous its rule." Karl Marx

poverty. Cut off from the resources of an affluent society, lower-class life often generates self-defeating resignation (Jacob, 1986).

Some may simply give up or decide to get by on public assistance. Others, however, work desperately—some at two or three jobs—to make ends meet. In a study conducted in the poor section of a northern city, Carol Stack (1975) noted that, far from lacking initiative and responsibility, residents devised ingenious means to survive. They did so, she concluded, because they simply had no choice.

THE DIFFERENCE CLASS MAKES

September 2, 1995, Mount Vernon, Ohio. My bike leans right, leaving the trail for the rest station that offers a stretch and a drink of water. Here I encounter Linda, a thirty-something woman having trouble with her roller blades. Eye contact and a perplexed look seem a call for help, so I walk over to see if I can assist. Several of her boot buckles require adjustment. Close up, she doesn't look well. "Are you OK?" I ask gently. "Very tired," Linda responds, and goes on to explain why. Now divorced, she cannot pay off her debts with one low-income job, an 11 A.M. to 7 P.M. shift as a computer clerk at a bank in town. Catching four hours of sleep after work, she then drives an hour to Columbus, where she sits at another computer processing catalog orders from 2 A.M. until 10 A.M. That leaves just enough time to drive back to Mount Vernon to start all over again at the bank . . . .

There is little doubt that social stratification affects nearly every dimension of our lives. We will briefly examine some of the ways social standing is linked to our health, values, politics, and family life.

Class and Health

Health is one of the most important correlates of social standing. The lives of those we sometimes describe as the "beautiful people" are enhanced by almost every conceivable advantage. The lives of others (including the woman described above) are frayed by long hours of work and the stress of trying to make ends meet. And for the most forsaken members of our society (such as Nigeria Collins, described in the opening of this chapter), brutal poverty assures that life barely unfolds at all.

Among adults with income above $35,000 annually, half describe their health as "excellent," a claim made by only one-fourth of people earning under $10,000. Conversely, only 4 percent of better-paid people complain of fair or poor health, an assessment made by 23 percent of low-income individuals (U.S. National Center for Health Statistics, 1995).

Plentiful income buys many things that bolster a long life. Nutritious foods, a safe environment, and regular medical care all promote well-being for those who can afford them. Medical costs have risen sharply in recent years to an average $3,300 annually per person in the United States, clearly out of reach for low-income people. Not surprisingly, then, low-income people not only contend with poor health, they do not live as long as others. Poor children are three times more likely than their better-off counterparts to die in the first year of life, and, for those who reach adulthood, they will die some seven years sooner (U.S. Bureau of the Census, 1993).

Men and women in the lower social classes also live and work in more dangerous environments. Factories, mines, and construction sites represent greater threats to health than office buildings, just as poor neighborhoods are all too often plagued by drug use and crime. Over the long term, such conditions cause serious stress; as a result, people with fewer privileges suffer more mental-health problems (Link, Dohrenwend, & Skodol, 1986; Mirowsky & Ross, 1989).

Class and Values

Cultural values, too, vary from class to class. The "old rich" have an unusually strong sense of family history since their social position is based on wealth and social prestige passed down from generation to generation (Baltzell, 1979). With their birthright privileges, upper-uppers also favor understated manners and tastes, as if to say, "I know who I am and I don't have to prove anything to anyone else."

Below the upper class, consumption takes on greater importance to social standing. Thorstein Veblen (1857–1929) coined the term *conspicuous consumption* to refer to the practice of buying expensive clothes, cars, sunglasses, or even bottled water to "make a statement."

RESOURCE: Lillian Rubin's *Worlds of Pain* (Basic, 1976) effectively shows the influence of class on the family life of women. While middle-class women seek personal qualities such as sensitivity and sharing in a spouse, working-class women have greater concern for basic traits such as holding a steady job and refraining from excessive drinking and domestic violence. In short, until their economic standing is secure, women and men have little ability to consider other issues in the relationship.

SOCIAL SURVEY: Unit Five of the Student Social Survey manual allows students to investigate the effects of class on how parents envision the traits of an ideal child.

NOTE: Herrnstein and Murray's controversial book, *The Bell Curve*, states that a 30-point IQ difference separates members of the lower and upper class.

Tolerance is another class-linked value. Due to their greater education and sense of confidence, more well-to-do people express greater tolerance toward controversial behavior such as homosexuality. Less tolerant are working-class people, who grow up in an atmosphere of greater supervision and discipline, and are less likely to attend college (Kohn, 1977; Humphries, 1984; NORC, 1994).

Even the way we think about time varies according to social class. Generations of wealth give upper-class families a keen awareness of the past. Middle-class people, especially those who are upwardly mobile, muse optimistically about the future. The drive for daily survival focuses the attention of lower-class people more on the present, and this present-time orientation reflects the often limited opportunities for advancement available to people in the lower class (Liebow, 1967; Lamar, Jr., 1985; Jacob, 1986).

Class and Politics

Political affiliations tend to follow class lines. By and large, more privileged people in the United States support the Republican party, while those with fewer advantages favor the Democrats.

But, issue by issue, the pattern is more complex. A desire to protect wealth prompts well-off people to take a more conservative approach to economic issues, backing lower taxes and less government regulation of the economy. But on social issues, such as abortion and other feminist concerns, highly educated affluent people are more liberal. People of lower social standing on the other hand, tend to be economic liberals, favoring expanded, government-funded social programs, while at the same time endorsing a more conservative social agenda (Erikson, Luttbeg, & Tedin, 1980; Syzmanski, 1983; Humphries, 1984).

Another clear trend emerges when it comes to political involvement: Individuals with higher incomes, more schooling, and high-prestige, white-collar jobs are more likely to vote and to support various political organizations than are those in the lower class (Hyman & Wright, 1971; Wolfinger & Rosenstone, 1980). This difference stems from the fact that privileged people are better served by the political system.

Class, Family, and Gender

Finally, family life is closely related to social class. Because the typical individual marries someone of comparable social position, distinctive family patterns correspond to each class level. For example, because

Class position influences a host of individual values and attitudes. President John F. Kennedy was born to a family of established power and prestige; his privileged upbringing conferred on him the gentle manner of the upper class. Lyndon Baines Johnson, Kennedy's vice president, was a man of humble origins. Here we see Johnson displaying the spirited style that helped him fight his way to the top; Kennedy responds by trying to restrain what he views as an inappropriate outburst.

Richard Pipes, *Campaign 1960.* © 1997 The Museum of Modern Art, N.Y.

lower-class people marry earlier in life and make less use of birth control, they have more children than middle-class parents do.

Working-class parents encourage children to conform to conventional norms and remain obedient and respectful to authority figures. By contrast, parents of higher social standing transmit different "cultural capital" to their children, motivating them to express their individuality and to use their imagination more freely. This difference reflects parents' expectations about their children's future: The odds are that less privileged children will take jobs demanding close adherence to specified rules, while most advantaged children will enter fields that call for more creativity (Kohn, 1977; McLeod, 1985).

Of course, it stands to reason that the more social resources a family has, the more parents can develop their children's talents and abilities. According to one

Chapter 10 Social Class in the United States **273**

NOTE: Mark Western and Erik Olin Wright (1994) argue that *authority boundaries* (separating managers from nonmanagers) are more permeable than *expertise boundaries* (separating experts from nonexperts); least permeable are *property boundaries* (dividing capitalists from wage laborers).

NOTE: To help students keep the terms straight, note that *intra* is Latin for "within" and *inter* means "between."

NOTE: Our society's belief in opportunity—and even the personal obligation to be upwardly mobile—comes through in admonitions such as "pull yourself up by your own boot straps," which, curiously, is a physical impossibility.

NOTE: Joan Rodgers (1995) estimates that the children of poor parents in the United States have a 16-to-28% chance of becoming poor as adults.

U.S. culture has long embraced the notion that, through talent and hard work, people can set their social position for themselves. How true does this idea ring to you?

Sky's the Limit by Bill Blast, © James Prigoff and Henry Chalfant from Spraycan Art, Thames and Hudson, New York

recent calculation, an affluent family with annual income of $100,000 will spend almost $300,000 raising a child born in 1990 to the age of eighteen. Middle-income people earning in the $40,000-a-year range will spend about $200,000, while families with annual income under $30,000 will spend about $150,000 (Exter, 1991). Such differences underline how privilege tends to beget privilege as family life reproduces the class structure in each generation.

Class also shapes spousal relationships. Elizabeth Bott (1971) documented that working-class couples maintain a rigid division of responsibilities. Middle-class marriages, by contrast, are more egalitarian, sharing more activities and interpersonal intimacy. Keeping this insight in mind, we can understand why divorce is more common among disadvantaged couples, whose limited communication skills may be overwhelmed by the stress of low-income living (Kitson & Raschke, 1981; Fergusson, Horwood, & Shannon, 1984).

SOCIAL MOBILITY

Ours is a dynamic society marked by a significant measure of social mobility as individuals move upward or downward over time. Earning a college degree, securing a higher-paying job, or becoming a member of a two-career household contributes to *upward social mobility*, while dropping out of school, losing a job, or starting to live in a female-headed household may signal *downward social mobility*.

Over the long term, most social mobility is not a matter of individual decisions as much as changes in society itself. During the first half of this century, for example, industrialization expanded the U.S. economy, dramatically raising living standards. Even without being very good swimmers, so to speak, people were able to "ride a rising tide of prosperity." As explained presently, *structural social mobility* in a downward direction has more recently dealt many people economic setbacks.

Sociologists also distinguish between changes within a single generation and shifts between generations of a family. **Intragenerational social mobility** refers to *a change in social position occurring within a person's lifetime.* Sociologists pay even greater attention to **intergenerational social mobility**, *upward or downward social mobility of children in relation to their parents,* because social mobility across generations reflects structural changes in society that affect virtually everyone.

Social Mobility: Myth and Reality

In few societies do people dwell on social mobility as much as in the United States. Historically, moving up has been central to the American Dream. But is there as much social mobility as we like to think?

Studies of intergenerational mobility (that, unfortunately, have focused almost exclusively on men) show that almost 40 percent of the sons of blue-collar workers attain white-collar jobs and almost 30 percent of sons born into white-collar families end up doing blue-collar work. Horizontal mobility—a change of occupation at one class level—is even more common so that about 80 percent of sons show at least some type of social mobility in relation to their fathers (Blau & Duncan, 1967; Featherman & Hauser, 1978).

Available research points to four general conclusions about social mobility in the United States.

1. **Social mobility, at least among men, has been fairly high.** The widespread notion that the United States has considerable social mobility is basically true. We would expect such mobility in an industrial class system.

2. **The long-term trend in social mobility has been upward.** Industrialization, the expansion of the U.S. economy, and the growth of white-collar work over the course of this century have greatly boosted average incomes and living standards.

3. **Within a single generation, social mobility is usually incremental, not dramatic.** Only a very few move "from rags to riches." While sharp rises

NOTE: To some extent, getting ahead economically today depends on limiting or entirely avoiding the expenses of childrearing. YUP-PIES (young, upwardly mobile professionals) are often DINKS (double-income-no-kids).

NOTE: During the recession that opened the 1990s, the process of "scaling back" threatened to transform the "Yuppies" of the 1980s into the "Dumpies" (downwardly mobile professionals) of the 1990s.

DIVERSITY: The number of earners per family has increased in recent decades, meaning people work harder to stay where they are. According to the Department of Labor, in 1950, 66% of families had one earner; by 1993, this figure had dropped to 43%. During this period, two- (or more) earner families increased from 26% to 57%. (U.S. Bureau of Labor Statistics)

or falls in individual fortunes may command public attention, most instances of social mobility involve subtle shadings *within* one class level rather than striking changes *between* classes.

4. **The short-term trend has been stagnation, with some income polarization.** As we shall explain presently, the rise in living standards that carried through most of this century hit a plateau in the early 1970s. Real income (that is, adjusted for inflation) for the U.S. population as a whole also changed little during the 1980s, rising slowly in the early 1990s (Veum, 1992).

Mobility by Income Level

Different categories of people often experience different patterns of mobility, which national figures may mask. Figure 10–4 shows how families in the United States fared between 1980 and 1994 according to their income level. Well-to-do families (the highest 20 percent) saw their average incomes jump from $89,696 in 1980 to $115,608 in 1994, a 29 percent increase. People in the second 20 percent also made gains, albeit a more modest 9.5 percent. While the middle of the population held about even, the lowest-income 20 percent suffered a 6.4 percent loss in earnings.

For families at the very top of the income scale, the last fifteen years have been a windfall. These families, with an average income of $132,451 in 1980, were earning $198,336 in 1994—a 50 percent increase (Edmondson, 1995; U.S. Bureau of the Census, 1996).

Mobility by Race, Ethnicity, and Gender

Patterns of mobility also vary according to race, ethnicity, and gender. White people, generally in a more privileged position to begin with, have been more likely than people of African or Hispanic ancestry to experience upward mobility in recent decades (Featherman & Hauser, 1978; Pomer, 1986). Through the economic expansion of the 1980s, more African Americans entered the ranks of the wealthy, but, overall, the real income of African Americans has not risen in two decades. Placed against a slight up-trend among white people, African-American households earned a smaller percentage of white household income in 1992 (58 percent) than in 1970 (61 percent) (U.S. Bureau of the Census, 1994).

For Latino families, the trend is much the same. Compared to non-Hispanic white households, Latinos' earnings slipped between 1975 (72 percent) and 1993 (69 percent). For both African and Hispanic Americans,

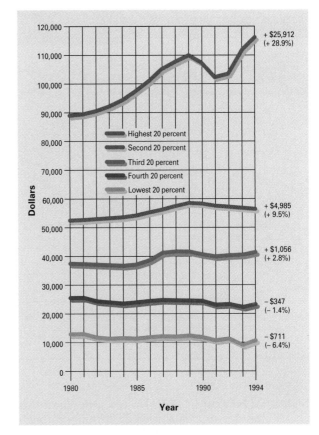

FIGURE 10–4 Mean After-Tax Income, U.S. Families, 1980–1994 (in 1994 dollars, adjusted for inflation)
Source: U.S. Bureau of the Census (1996).

falling wage rates accounted for this structural downward social mobility.

Historically, women have had less opportunity for upward mobility than men. As we shall see in Chapter 13 ("Sex and Gender"), the majority of working women hold clerical jobs (think of secretaries) and service positions (like waitresses). Such work offers little chance for advancement, which effectively limits upward movement. And when marriages end in divorce (as almost half do today), women (but less often men) commonly experience downward social mobility, since they may lose not only income but a host of benefits including health care and insurance coverage.

But scanning the broader picture, we see that, in recent years, the earnings gap between women and men has been closing. Women working full time earned 60 percent as much as men working full time in 1980, with the proportion rising to an all-time

THE MAP: Generally speaking, lower-income counties are those in which pessimism about the future is widespread. One interesting exception is counties containing large college campuses, where many people, although fairly affluent, are doomsayers.

DIVERSITY: During the last decade, some economic polarization occurred in the United States (gini coefficients rose from .366 in 1980 to .447 in 1993). At the middle of the class structure, a "middle-class slide" accounts for about two-thirds of this change. Another one-third improved their economic standing, participating in what could be termed a "middle-class rise."

NOTE: The ubiquitous automatic teller machines (70,000 in the U.S. in 1995; about 130 million people have cards to use them) symbolize the declining demand for lower-skill workers in the service sector.

Seeing Ourselves

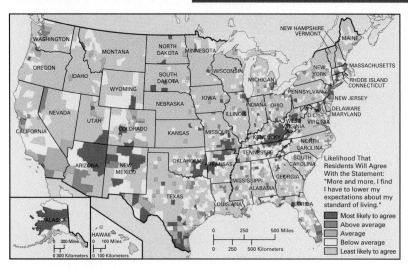

NATIONAL MAP 10–1
"Fear of Falling" Across the United States

This map shows, by county, how likely people are to agree with the statement "More and more, I find I have to lower my expectations about my standard of living." What characterizes regions (including Appalachia in Kentucky and West Virginia) where pessimism is commonplace? But pessimism is pronounced not only in poor rural areas. In rich cities, including New York, Chicago, and Los Angeles, people are also afraid of losing their jobs.

Source: *American Demographics* magazine, February 1994, p. 60. Reprinted with permission. ©1994 *American Demographics* magazine, Ithaca, New York. Data from Yankelovich *Monitor* and Clarita's *Prizm* system.

high of 72 percent in 1993. However, much of this change was due to a *drop* in men's earnings through the 1980s, while the income of women remained about the same (U.S. Bureau of the Census, 1995).

The United States has long been called a "land of opportunity." In truth, this nation has opened the way for many people to realize their dreams, even though some continue to fare far better than others. Looking globally, however, we find that rates of social mobility in the United States during this century roughly match those of other industrial societies. And as the economies of the world become more interrelated, we can expect that structural shifts—both upward and downward—that occur in Europe and Japan will also affect us here in the United States (Lipset & Bendix, 1967; McRoberts & Selbee, 1981; Kaelble, 1986; Erikson & Goldthorpe, 1992).

The "Middle-Class Slide"

The expectation of upward social mobility is deeply rooted in our national culture. Through most of our history, in fact, economic expansion fulfilled the promise of prosperity by raising the overall standard of living. But, as we already noted, beginning in the early 1970s stagnation and—for some categories of

people—actual decline in living standards began to shake our national confidence (Pampel, Land, & Felson, 1977; Blumberg, 1981; Levy, 1987). A number of recent trends points to this reversal in fortunes.

1. **For many workers, earnings have stalled.** The annual income of a fifty-year-old man working full time climbed by 50 percent between 1958 and 1973 (from $21,000 to $32,000 in constant 1990 dollars). Between 1973 and 1994, however, this worker's income remained flat, even as the number of hours he worked rose, and the cost of necessities like housing, education, and medical care soared rapidly upward (DeParle, 1991a; Russell, 1995).

2. **Multiple job-holding is up.** According to the Census Bureau, 4.7 percent of the U.S. labor force worked at two or more jobs in 1975; by 1994, the proportion had risen to 6.0 percent.

3. **More jobs offer little income.** In 1979, the Census Bureau classified 12 percent of full-time workers as "low-income earners" because they brought home less than $6,905; by 1994, this segment had swelled to 16 percent of full-time workers—those earning less than the comparable figure that year of $13,828.

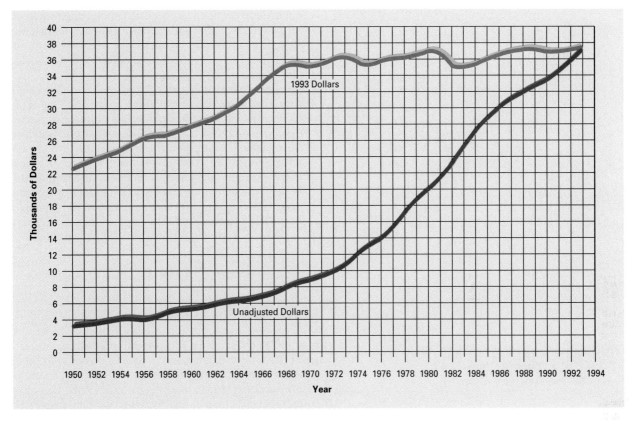

FIGURE 10–5 Median Income, U.S. Families, 1950–1993
Source: U.S. Bureau of the Census (1995).

4. **Young people are remaining at home.** Fully 60 percent of young people, aged twenty to twenty-four, now live with their parents. And the average age at marriage has edged upward three years since 1975 (to 24.5 years for women and 26.5 years for men).

Taken together, these facts paint a disturbing picture. Rather than looking optimistically toward the future, more people in the United States now feel the economic security long associated with middle-class living slipping away. National Map 10–1 reveals where in the United States pessimism about the future is most widespread.

Dubbed the *middle-class slide*, this downward structural mobility is rooted in economic transformation. The brisk pace of economic expansion, long taken for granted, has now slowed for a generation. Figure 10–5 shows median U.S. family income between 1950 and 1993 in constant 1993 dollars. Between 1950 and 1973, median family income

swelled by 65 percent; however, it has moved up only slightly since then (U.S. Bureau of the Census, 1993).

Earlier in this century, the rapid surge in white-collar positions drew millions of workers from blue-collar and farming jobs, encouraging optimistic predictions that the United States was becoming an affluent, middle-class society (Kerckhoff, Campbell, & Winfield-Laird, 1985). Jobs created by the U.S. economy since the 1980s, however, have typically paid *less* than in the past, prompting downward social mobility.

The U.S. Class Structure in Global Perspective

Underlying the middle-class slide is a global economic transformation. Much of the industrial production that offered U.S. workers high-paying jobs a generation ago has been transferred overseas (Rosen, 1987; Thurow, 1987). The United States is now a vast market for industrial goods, such as cars, and popular

RESOURCE: Secretary of Labor Robert Reich's analysis of how the global economy affects inequality in the United States is included in the Macionis and Benokraitis companion reader, *Seeing Ourselves*.

Q: "No man suffers from poverty unless it be more than his fault—unless it be his *sin*." Preacher and social Darwinist Henry Ward Beecher

NOTE: A 1988 news story began by describing Lyndon Johnson standing on Tom Fletcher's porch in Inez, Kentucky, two decades before to launch the War on Poverty (*U.S. News and World Report*, January 11, 1988:18–24). Tom Fletcher was still living in the same house a generation later, and his life was about the same then as it had been two decades before. Perhaps Ronald Reagan was right when he quipped, "We had a war on poverty, and poverty won."

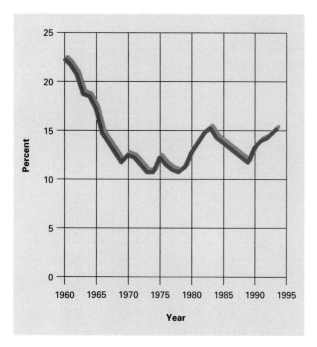

FIGURE 10–6 The Poverty Rate in the United States, 1960–1993

Source: U.S. Bureau of the Census (1995).

items like stereos and cameras, produced in Japan, Korea, and elsewhere.

High-paying jobs in manufacturing, which accounted for 26 percent of the U.S. labor force in 1960, support less than 15 percent of workers today. In their place, the economy now offers jobs in various types of "service work," which typically pay far less. Indicative of this shift, USX (formerly United States Steel) now employs fewer people than McDonald's, which is enjoying a rapid expansion, and fast-food clerks make much less per hour than steel workers do. Not surprisingly, then, one study predicts the fastest-growing jobs throughout the 1990s will be cashiers, nurses, janitors, waiters, and truck drivers (Howe & Strauss, 1991).

The global reorganization of work is not bad news for everyone. On the contrary, this growing global economy is driving the upward social mobility of a highly educated managerial class who specialize in areas such as law, finance, marketing, and computer technology. Moreover, the increasing value of global companies (and a stock market that quintupled between 1980 and 1996) has vastly expanded the wealth of the richest members of our society.

But surging global competition has also unleased a trend toward "downsizing," which has prompted the

largest corporations to eliminate about one-fourth of all jobs since 1980. To make matters worse, many individuals of moderate income have been left without work as their factory jobs have been "exported" overseas (Reich, 1989, 1991).

Just as industrialization spawned prosperity a century ago, today's deindustrialization has hurt the standard of living and shaken the confidence of many people. Compared to a previous generation, far fewer now expect to improve their social position, and a growing number worry about being able to maintain the way of life they knew as children in their parents' home. Women and men are working harder today than ever: Half of today's families have two or more people in the labor force, double the proportion in 1950. Even so, the U.S. standard of living has virtually stalled.

POVERTY IN THE UNITED STATES

Social stratification simultaneously creates "haves" and "have-nots." Poverty is therefore an inevitable product of all systems of social inequality. Sociologists address the concept of poverty in two different ways, however. **Relative poverty** refers to *the deprivation of some people in relation to those who have more*. Relative poverty is universal and unavoidable; even a rich society has some members who live in relative poverty. Much more serious is **absolute poverty**, or *a deprivation of resources that is life threatening*. Defined in this way, poverty is a pressing, but solvable, human problem.

As the next chapter ("Global Stratification") explains, the global dimensions of absolute poverty place the lives of perhaps 800 million people—one in seven of the earth's entire population—at risk. Even in the affluent United States, however, families go hungry, live in inadequate housing, and endure poor health because of the wrenching reality of poverty.

The Extent of U.S. Poverty

As part of President Lyndon Johnson's "war on poverty" in the 1960s, the U.S. government began counting the poor in 1964. Officials established a *poverty threshold*, an annual income level below which a person or family was defined as poor and, therefore, entitled to certain benefits.

By defining poverty in this way, the government intended to approximate the number of people living close to absolute poverty. Mollie Orshansky (1969:38), a government official at the time, described the poverty threshold as the income needed "to purchase a nutritionally adequate diet on the assumption that no

278 Chapter 10 Social Class in the United States

NOTE: In 1904, Robert Hunter (*Poverty*) estimated the U.S. poverty rate at 13% (defining poverty as annual income under $460 in the North and $300 in the South). Living standards rose sharply thereafter; but, in 1963, Michael Harrington (*The Other America*) claimed that at least 20% of the U.S. population was poor. Thus, definitions of poverty are historically specific. (Cf. Gilbert, 1994)

NOTE: Boosting living standards, fertility is down from 18.4 in 1970 to 15.2 in 1995, so household costs are lower for a typical family with children. Real income for a typical male worker has been nearly flat since 1970, but family income is up 20% because more women are working.

NOTE: Since 1959, poverty rates have declined; then, 18 percent of whites and 55 percent of African Americans were poor.

more than a third of the family income is used for food." In simple terms, then, the poverty threshold is three times what the government estimates people must spend to eat. The government keys the exact dollar amount to family size and adjusts it annually to reflect the changing cost of living.

Figure 10–6 shows the official poverty rate as calculated annually since 1960. The long-term trend is downward, although the poverty rate rose early in the 1980s and jumped again after 1989. In 1993, a total of 39.3 million men, women, and children—15.1 percent of the U.S. population—were officially living in poverty. Another 12.5 million people—the *marginally poor*—were supported by incomes no greater than 125 percent of the poverty threshold.

For two adults and two children living in an urban area in 1993, the poverty threshold was $14,763. The income of the typical poor family, however, is about $5,960 *below* the poverty threshold. And, estimates suggest that 40 percent of the poor—those we might term *the poorest of the poor*—struggle to get by on no more than half the income specified as the poverty threshold (U.S. Bureau of the Census, 1995).

Those who have never known poverty cannot easily imagine its consequences. For some children, like Nigeria Collins, whose early death was noted at the beginning of this chapter, poverty means never even having a chance at life. For most, it means a daily life of insecurity, stress, and hunger. Roughly half the officially poor adults and children in the United States endure hunger daily (Schwartz-Nobel, 1981; Physicians' Task Force on Hunger in America, 1987).

Who Are the Poor?

Although no single description covers all poor people, poverty is pronounced among certain categories of our population. Children, people of color, women, and residents of rural areas all are at high risk of being poor. Where these categories overlap, the problem of poverty is especially serious.

Age

A generation ago, the elderly were at greatest risk for poverty. But no longer. From 30 percent in 1967, the poverty rate for seniors over the age of sixty-five plummeted to 12.2 percent in 1993. This translates into just under 4 million elderly poor and means that the elderly now have a poverty rate below the national average. This dramatic decline was due to expanding financial support from government and private employers. Even so, 9.6 percent of the poor are still elderly people.

Today, the burden of poverty falls most heavily on children. In 1993, 22.7 percent of people under age eighteen (15.7 million children) were officially classified as poor. Tallied another way, four in ten of the U.S. poor are children under the age of eighteen. Although there are no comparable data on child poverty available for other countries, selected infant mortality rates suggest that this problem is greater in the United States than in other industrial societies. In fact, despite having the highest overall standard of living in the world, the United States stands twentieth in global child mortality rates. The box offers a closer look at the current problem of child poverty in the United States.

Race and Ethnicity

In absolute numbers, two-thirds of all poor people are white (Latino and non-Latino); about 30 percent are African Americans. But in relation to their overall numbers, African Americans are about three times as likely as white people to be poor. In 1993, 33.1 percent of African Americans (10.9 million people) lived in poverty, compared to about 30.6 percent of Latinos (8.1 million), 15.3 percent of Asians and Pacific Islanders (1.1 million), and 9.9 percent of non-Latino white people (18.9 million). Since 1975, the "poverty gap" between whites and minorities has remained essentially unchanged (U.S. Bureau of the Census, 1995).

Gender and Family Patterns

Of the U.S. poor over age eighteen, 62.3 percent are women and 37.7 percent are men. This disparity reflects the fact that women (but not men) who head households are at high risk of poverty. Of all poor families, 50.9 percent are headed by women with no husband present, while just 5.8 percent of poor families are headed by single men.

Most poor, single women with children do not work. The problem is not just that child care is expensive; most of the jobs for which these women are qualified pay little. In the absence of opportunity for work that will support a household, two-thirds of women in this situation turn to government assistance.

The link between single-parent families and poverty also means that divorce threatens even middle-class women and their children with poverty. Andrew Cherlin (1990) concludes that the income of single-parent families typically plummets by more than one-third within several months of divorce or separation.

SOCIAL DIVERSITY

U.S. Children: Bearing the Burden of Poverty

We cringe at the sight of starving children in countries such as Somalia, the war-torn African nation in which the average person struggles to live on less than $200 a year. But the presence of child poverty in the United States may constitute an even greater tragedy, since ours is such a rich nation with per capita income one hundred times that of Somalia.

More than one in five U.S. children under the age of eighteen is poor— 15.7 million boys and girls. This represents about the same number as when the government's "war on poverty" began thirty years ago. Since then, a national effort to assist the elderly has cut poverty among senior citizens by more than half. Child poverty, however, remains as serious as ever. National Map 10–2 reveals that the concentration of child poverty is greatest across the South.

Like poverty generally, the risk of child poverty varies within our population. In 1993, for the country as a whole, 23 percent of boys and girls under the age of eighteen were poor. But while 18 percent of white children were poor, 41 percent of young Latinos and 46 percent of African-American youngsters were poor.

Reversing our variables, 62 percent of poor children are white, while 33 percent are African American, and 5 percent are Asian; of these, 25 percent are also culturally Hispanic. But while poor children are a diverse lot, they share one key characteristic: They all live in households with low income. In fact, almost half of poor boys and girls are being raised in households with incomes no more than half the poverty threshold (that is, less than $7,382 in 1993).

Researchers have found a strong link between rising rates of child poverty and the increasing share of single-parent households. Today, about eight in ten poor children live in a household with a single mother, and in the same proportion of cases this household contains no full-time worker.

The reasons for poverty, which we shall discuss presently, are complex and controversial, involving both economic trends and changing family patterns. But everyone agrees that no blame lies with the children. Tragically, however, this is precisely where the burden of poverty falls. Practically speaking, social intervention that eliminates the stunting experience of poverty from the lives of children is much cheaper than addressing the problems of unemployment, drug use, crime, and violence that will come later on. So, whether we look at this issue from either a practical or a moral standpoint, should we tolerate this suffering by our society's most vulnerable members?

Seeing Ourselves

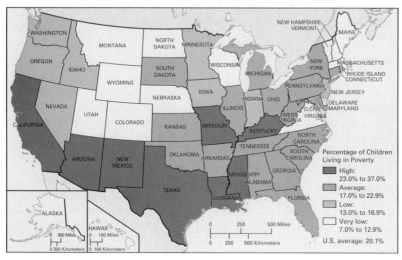

Percentage of Children Living in Poverty

- High: 23.0% to 37.0%
- Average: 17.0% to 22.9%
- Low: 13.0% to 16.9%
- Very low: 7.0% to 12.9%

U.S. average: 20.1%

NATIONAL MAP 10–2 Child Poverty Across the United States
Source: U.S. Bureau of the Census (1996).

Sources: Eggebeen & Lichter (1991), Children's Defense Fund (1995), U.S. Bureau of the Census (1995).

NOTE: The 1993 median income for married-couple families was $43,129; for male heads of household with no wife present, $29,849; for female heads of household with no husband present, $18,545.

DIVERSITY: The rural poverty rate paralleled the trend shown in Figure 10–5, rising from 16.6% in 1973 to 22.9% in 1990.

NOTE: The 1980s also saw a shift in the proportion of federal income tax derived from the richest and poorest taxpayers. Overall, rich people paid more in 1990 than in 1980 but, proportionately, people in the top fifth paid 27.3% of the tax bill in 1980 and only 25.8% in 1990. People in the bottom fifth paid 8.4% in 1980 and 9.7% in 1990.

The term **feminization of poverty** describes *the trend by which women represent an increasing proportion of the poor*. In 1960, 25 percent of all poor households were headed by women; the majority of poor families had both wives and husbands in the home. By 1993, however, the proportion of poor households headed by a single woman had doubled to more than 50 percent.

The feminization of poverty is thus part of a larger change: the rapidly increasing number of households—at all class levels—headed by single women. This trend, coupled with the fact that households headed by women are at high risk of poverty, explains why women (and their children) represent an increasing share of the U.S. poor.

Area of Residence

The greatest concentration of poverty is found in central cities: There, the 1993 poverty rate stood at 21.5 percent. Suburbs, too, have destitute people, but because suburbanites are more affluent, their poverty rate is just 10.3 percent. Thus, the poverty rate for urban areas as a whole is 14.6 percent—lower than the 17.2 percent found in rural areas.

Generally speaking, cities offer higher living standards than the countryside because more jobs and social services are available there. National Map 10–3 on page 282 provides a visual picture of income levels across the United States, indicating the counties in which poverty is most pronounced.

Explaining Poverty

That the richest nation on earth is home to tens of millions of poor people raises serious questions. It is true, as some analysts remind us, that many of the people counted among the officially poor in the United States are better off than the poor in other countries—40 percent of U.S. poor families own their home, for example, and 60 percent own a car (Jenkins, 1992). But it is also the case, as noted earlier, that malnutrition and outright hunger are widespread in this country, along with violence, illness, and a host of other problems that accompany economic deprivation.

Figure 10–7 on page 283 suggests that the public is of two minds about the causes of poverty and how to remedy the problem. One-fourth of respondents to this national survey think the government has the primary responsibility to raise living standards; slightly more counter that people should take responsibility for

A widespread sterotype links poverty to people of color in the inner cities of the United States. Although minorities are more likely to be disadvantaged, most of the U.S. poor are white people. Furthermore, although inner cities have the greatest concentration of poverty, rural residents are at higher risk of poverty than their urban counterparts.

themselves. The greatest number, moreover, choose to straddle the fence, agreeing with both contentions.

We now examine more closely the arguments underlying each of these two approaches to the problem of poverty. Together, they frame a lively and pressing political debate.

One View: Blame the Poor

One side of the issue is based on the following view: *The poor are primarily responsible for their own poverty*. Throughout our history, people in the United States have been a self-reliant lot, embracing the notion that social standing is mostly a matter of talent and individual effort. From this point of view, our society affords considerable opportunity for anyone able and willing to take advantage of it. The poor, then, are those who cannot or will not work, men and women with fewer skills, less schooling, or simply lower motivation. While some people (historically,

THE MAP: The twenty highest-income counties in the United States are in metropolitan areas, seventeen of them along the Eastern seaboard (three of the top five are in New Jersey). Poor counties are likely to be rural, and most are found in the South (eleven of the poorest twenty are in Kentucky and Texas). Low-earning counties also have more single-parent families and more elderly people, while fewer people are in the high-earning age bracket between 45 and 54 years of age.

Q: " . . . it is a vicious cycle: You cannot get a job because you do not have an address, you do not have an address because you do not have any money, and you do not have any money because you do not have a job." Danny Cahill, *Forgotten Voices*, *Unforgettable Dreams*

Seeing Ourselves

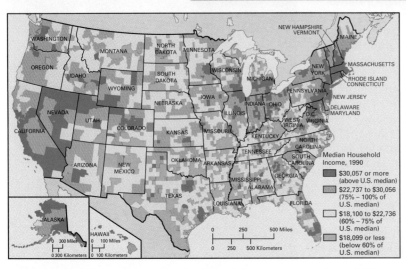

NATIONAL MAP 10–3
Median Household Income Across the United States

This map shows median household income for all 3,014 counties in the United States as recorded by the 1990 census. Surprisingly, just 15 percent of all counties can boast of a median household income greater than the median for the entire country. What do these counties (shown in dark green) have in common? Low-income counties (shown in red) with high rates of poverty also are not randomly spread throughout the nation. What do low-income counties have in common? Do the patterns found here square with our assertion linking affluence to urban areas and poverty to rural places?

Median Household Income, 1990

- $30,057 or more (above U.S. median)
- $22,737 to $30,056 (75% – 100% of U.S. median)
- $18,100 to $22,736 (60% – 75% of U.S. median)
- $18,099 or less (below 60% of U.S. median)

Source: *American Demographics* magazine, Oct. 1992, p. 9. Reprinted with permission. ©1992 *American Demographics* magazine, Ithaca, New York. Data from the 1990 decennial census.

widows and orphans) command our compassion as "worthy poor," this line of reasoning leads us to condemn many people as, in one way or another, undeserving. This view is inherent, to varying degrees, in responses placed on the right side of the continuum in Figure 10–7.

One well-known researcher who held this view was anthropologist Oscar Lewis (1961), who investigated the poor barrios of Latin American cities. Although Lewis doubted that most poor people could do much about their plight, he did not blame them individually for their poverty. Rather, he contended that a *culture of poverty* holds down the poor, fostering resignation to poverty as a matter of fate. Socialized in this environment, children come to believe that there is little point to aspiring to a better life. The result is a self-perpetuating cycle of poverty, as one generation transmits its way of life to the next.

Research in the United States led Edward Banfield (1974) to much the same conclusion. Especially in areas of intense poverty such as the inner cities, claims Banfield, a lower-class subculture has taken hold, eroding personal ambition and achievement. One element of this subculture, as he sees it, is a present-time orientation that encourages living for

the moment. While a future orientation guides most better-off people to study, plan, work hard, and save, Banfield saw poor people as failing to look beyond the moment. In living for the present, he concluded, they perpetuate their own poverty and, therefore, reap more or less what they deserve.

Counterpoint: Blame Society

The other side of the issue can be summed up as follows: *Society is primarily responsible for poverty*. This alternative position, argued by William Ryan (1976), holds that society—not people themselves—distributes the resources and, therefore, is responsible for poverty. Looking at societies around the world from this point of view, we see that those that distribute wealth very unequally (including the United States) face significant relative poverty; societies that strive for more economic equality (such as Sweden and Japan) lack such extremes of social stratification.

Poverty, Ryan insists, is not inevitable; this problem is caused not by personal deficiency but by low income. Ryan interprets any lack of ambition on the part of poor people as a *consequence* rather than a *cause* of

SOCIAL SURVEY: A U.S. Census Bureau survey of poor adults yielded these explanations for not working among those who did not work at all: Ill/disability, 18%; retired, 3%; home or family reasons, 44%; school/other, 23%; could not find work, 13%.

NOTE: About 2.5 million U.S. workers earn the minimum wage. The real value of the minimum wage has dropped about 50 cents since 1991 and currently stands at an all-time low.

DISCUSS: Figure 10–7 indicates that 25% of U.S. adults are liberals on the poverty issue, looking to government for a solution. About 27% are conservatives, who expect individuals to address their own plight. But there is a large (40% +) category who "swing" one way or the other on this issue, indicating that policy in this area is really up for grabs. Ask students to describe their own "policies on poverty."

their lack of opportunity. He therefore dismisses Lewis's and Banfield's analysis as little more than "blaming the victims" for their own suffering.

In Ryan's view, social policies that empower the poor would give them real economic opportunity and yield more economic equality. Support for this view is found on the left side of the continuum in Figure 10–7, where people look to the government to reduce poverty.

Weighing the Evidence

Each of these explanations of poverty has won its share of public support, and each has advocates among government policy makers. As Banfield sees it, society should pursue equality of opportunity, especially for the young, but otherwise people should take responsibility for themselves, and their success will correspond to their talents and interests.

Ryan takes a more activist approach, asserting that government policy should reduce poverty through more equitable redistribution of income. Programs like comprehensive child care, for example, could help poor mothers gain job skills; indeed, the living standard of every poor person could be raised by a tax-funded, guaranteed minimum income for every U.S. family.

Certainly both of these views could be put into practice, and our society periodically leans toward one or the other. Typically, Republican policies are sympathetic toward the first; Democratic strategies are more in tune with the second. But, based on research, what can sociologists contribute to the debate?

There are, of course, numerous data about the poor and all are subject to various interpretations. One fact that advances the position of Lewis and Banfield is that most poor adults in the United States do not hold full-time jobs. Government statistics show that 47.6 percent of the heads of poor families did not work at all during 1993. In fact, only 16.6 percent of the heads of families in poverty worked full time for at least fifty weeks during that year (U.S. Bureau of the Census, 1995). So we can conclude that one major cause of poverty is *not holding a job*.

But the *reasons* that people do not work seem more consistent with Ryan's position. Middle-class women combine working and child rearing, but doing so is much harder for poor women who cannot afford child care. Few U.S. employers provide child-care programs for their employees, and most low-paid workers cannot afford to obtain child care on their own. For their part, low-income men claim that illness or disability has sidelined them, that there are no jobs to

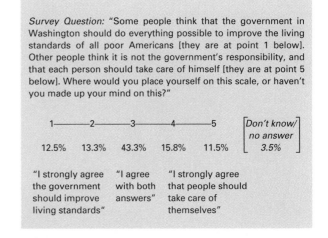

FIGURE 10–7 Government or Individuals: Who Is Responsible for Poverty?

Source: NORC (1994).

be found, or, in the case of the elderly, that they have retired. Realistically or not, most poor adults in the United States feel they have few options or alternatives (Popkin, 1990; Schiller, 1994).

The Working Poor

But not all poor people are jobless, and the *working poor* command the sympathy and support of people on both sides of the poverty debate. In 1993, 16.6 percent of poor heads of households (1.3 million people) labored full time for the entire year and yet could not escape poverty. Another 25.8 percent of these heads of families (2 million people) remained poor despite part-time employment.

From another angle, about 5 percent of full-time workers earn so little that they are classified as poor. This figure represents twice the comparable rate in 1980, revealing, once again, that the 1980s was a difficult decade for low-income people (U.S. Bureau of the Census, 1995).

"Working poverty" places people in a bind. Jobs provide low wages that barely make ends meet but consume the time and energy needed to get training or schooling that might open new doors. Most people are reluctant to risk the job they do have in hopes of finding something better. At the 1994 minimum wage level of $4.25 per hour, a full-time worker could not support a family above the official poverty line (Levitan & Shapiro, 1987; Schwartz & Volgy, 1992).

NOTE: As a case of mixed political attitudes, Jo Phelan et al. (1995) found more educated people to have greater tolerance for the homeless (liberal social attitude) but offer less support for economic assistance to the homeless (conservative economic attitude).

NOTE: According to some estimates, half of homeless women are fleeing abusive partners.

DIVERSITY: The U.S. homeless profile is roughly: 75% unemployed; 35% substance abusers; 25% mentally ill; 25% prison records. The categories overlap somewhat, but estimates of those with drug, alcohol, or mental problems range up to two-thirds of all homeless (though some may be effect rather than cause). In any case, perhaps 400,000 U.S. adults have problems that make it impossible for them to work and live independently—one quarter of one percent of the total U.S. population.

African-American artist Henry O. Tanner (1859–1937) captured the humility and humanity of impoverished people in his painting Thankful Poor. *This insight is important in a society that tends to dismiss poor people as morally unworthy and deserving of their bitter plight.*

Henry O. Tanner, *Thankful Poor,* 1894. Oil on canvas. 35 x 44". William H. and Camille O. Cosby Collection. Philadelphia Museum of Art.

Summing up, individual ability and personal initiative do play a part in shaping everyone's social position. But sociological study highlights how society—not individual character flaws—contribute to poverty. No doubt, some poor people do lack ambition. Overall, however, the poor are *categories* of people—female heads of families, people of color, people isolated from the larger society in inner-city areas—without the same opportunities as others.

Homelessness

Many low-income people in the United States lack the resources to afford even basic housing. In light of the enormous wealth of the United States and its commitment to providing opportunity for everyone, homelessness may be fairly described as a scar on our society that demands an effective response (Schutt, 1989).

Counting the Homeless

There is no precise count of homeless people. Fanning out across the cities of the United States on the night of March 20, 1991, Census Bureau officials tallied 178,828 people at shelters and 49,793 on the streets in neighborhoods where homeless people are known to live. Officials stressed that this count was not intended as an enumeration of homeless people;

it merely helped the Census Bureau to estimate the entire population of the United States more accurately (U.S. Bureau of the Census, 1991).

One problem with this research is that homeless people live not just in cities but also in rural counties, which are the poorest of all. One study estimated that there were 20,000 homeless people in rural Ohio alone (Toomey, First, & Rife, 1990). Therefore, if a complete count of the homeless were done, experts contend, we would find that about 500,000 people are homeless *on any given night* and three times this number—1.5 million people—are homeless *for some time during the course of any year* (Kozol, 1988; Wright, 1989).

Causes of Homelessness

The familiar stereotypes of homeless people— men sleeping in doorways and women carrying all their worldly possessions in a shopping bag—have recently been undermined by the reality of the "new homeless": those thrown out of work because of plant closings, people forced out of apartments by rising rents or the conversion of their buildings into cooperatives, and others unable to meet mortgage or rent payments because they must work for low wages. Today, no stereotype of the homeless paints a complete picture of this varied category of men, women, and children. But virtually all homeless people have one status in common: *poverty*. For that reason, the explanations of poverty already offered also apply to homelessness.

One side of the debate places responsibility on *personal* traits of the homeless themselves. We know, for example, that one-third of homeless people are substance abusers, and one-fourth of homeless adults are mentally ill. More broadly, it should not be surprising that a fraction of 1 percent of our population, for one reason or another, is unable to cope with our complex and highly competitive society (Bassuk, 1984; Whitman, 1989).

On the other side of the debate, advocates assert that homelessness results from *societal* factors, including a small and declining stock of low-income housing in the United States, high unemployment, and the economic transition toward low-paying jobs described earlier (Kozol, 1988; Schutt, 1989; Bohannan, 1991). Supporters of this position claim that one-third of all homeless people are entire families, and children are the fastest-growing category of the homeless. A minister living in a Pennsylvania town that has lost hundreds of industrial jobs due to plant closings describes the real-life effects of economic recession:

> Yes, there are new jobs. There's a new McDonald's and a Burger King. You can take home $450 in a month from jobs like that. That might barely pay the rent. What do you do if someone gets sick? What do you do for food and clothes? These may be good jobs for a teenager. Can you ask a thirty-year-old man who's worked for GM since he was eighteen to keep his wife and kids alive on jobs like that? There are jobs cleaning rooms in the hotel. . . . Can you expect a single mother with three kids to hold her life together with that kind of work? (Kozol, 1988:6)

No one disputes that a large proportion of homeless people are personally impaired, although how much is cause and how much is effect is difficult to assess. But structural changes in the U.S. economy, declining incomes during the 1980s, and government policies that reduced support for lower-income people have all contributed to homelessness.

A comprehensive response to homelessness must consider both personal and societal dimensions of the problem. Increasing the supply of low-income housing (other than shelters) is one important step. But homelessness is more than a housing problem; it is also a *human* problem. People who endure months or years of insecure living come to need various types of social services. Solving the problem of homelessness, therefore, also demands coming to terms with the social damage caused by poverty.

Social scientists debate the causes of poverty, some citing the failings of individuals such as lack of initiative or drug abuse and others pointing to flaws of society including a minimum wage that does not allow a full-time worker to support a family. Whatever side one takes in this controversy, it is impossible to turn away from the drama of children born into poor families. Noted photographer Mary Ellen Marks has followed this family for over a decade. She notes that the children have never known any life but poverty. Whatever their talents may be, are they destined to repeat the ordeal of their parents?

This chapter's closing box examines "welfare," a topic that throws into relief much of our national thinking about social stratification. Just as important, welfare currently is the focus of heated debate in today's political arena.

Finally, the drama of social stratification extends far beyond the borders of the United States. The most striking social disparities are found not by looking inside one country but by comparing living standards in various parts of the world. In Chapter 11, we broaden our investigation of social stratification by focusing on global inequality.

NOTE: Welfare currently involves four federal programs: (1) Aid to Families with Dependent Children (AFDC); (2) AFDC-Unemployed Parent (available in 26 states); (3) Supplemental Security Income (SSI) for qualifying disabled, blind, or over-65 persons; and (4) the Food Stamp Program. All require applicants to qualify according to standards that vary from one place to another.

NOTE: Due to factors including the negative stigma attached to receiving welfare and highly variable eligibility standards, roughly half the women and men eligible for welfare programs never apply for them.

NOTE: The $50 billion home-mortgage tax deduction (85% of which goes to households in the top 20% of income) amounts to five times the $8 billion the government spends annually on low-income housing.

Controversy & *Debate*

The Welfare Dilemma

On a windy, cold day in the winter of 1994, police arrived at the door of a Chicago apartment in a poor neighborhood. After no one responded to their knocks, the officers forced open the door and were aghast at what they found: nineteen children living, without adult supervision, in utter filth. So desperate was the situation that one child tugged on the sleeve of a woman police officer begging "Will you be my mommy? I want to go home with you" (Gibbs:1994:25).

Press accounts such as this one raise troubling questions about our societal health and, especially, the well-being of poor children. And they generate considerable anger in the process. Who is not appalled by the thought of children suffering in this way? To fix the blame, many fingers are quick to point to a government program, one designed to help poor children, but one that has become something of a national scandal—*welfare*.

There is a remarkable consensus regarding "welfare"—no one likes it. Liberals criticize it as an inadequate response to poverty; conservatives charge that it is hurting the people it allegedly helps; and the poor themselves find welfare a complex, confusing, and often degrading program.

It is also important to define our terms: The "welfare state" refers to a host of policies and programs enacted to improve the well-being of the U.S. population. But, by "welfare," most people have in mind one small element of that overall system—Aid to Families with Dependent Children (AFDC), a program by which state governments provide monthly financial support to parents (primarily single women) to care for themselves and their children. In all, some 5 million households received AFDC for some part of the year in 1994.

Conservative critics contend that, rather than alleviating child poverty, AFDC has actually *worsened* the problem for two reasons. First, this form of "welfare" has eroded the traditional family by making living single an attractive alternative to marriage. Especially before reforms in 1990, public assistance regulations provided benefits to poor mothers only if no husband lived in the home. As conservatives see it, AFDC makes it economically beneficial for women to have children outside of marriage and is a key reason for the rapid rise in out-of-wedlock births among poor people. Conservatives highlight the connection between being poor and not being married: Fewer than one in ten married-couple families is poor; more than nine in ten AFDC-supported families is headed by an unmarried woman.

Global Snapshot

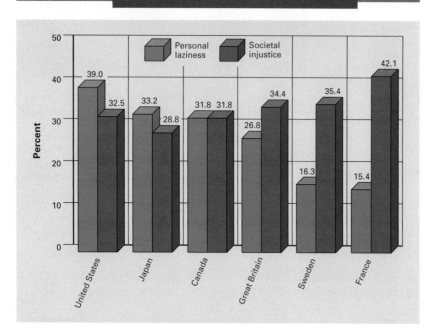

FIGURE 10–8 Assessing the Causes of Poverty

Survey Question: "Why are there people in this country who live in need?" Percentages reflect respondents' identification of either "personal laziness" or "societal injustice" as the primary cause of poverty.

Percentages for each country do not add up to 100 because less frequently identified causes of poverty were omitted from this figure.

Source: World Values Survey (1994).

RESOURCE: The key conservative criticisms of public assistance are found in Charles Murray's *Breaking Ground* (1984). His thesis is that the outlay for welfare must continue to grow because the system fails to alleviate the problems it set out to fix, actually making matters worse.

NOTE: Head Start was funded at $2.8 billion for 1993; it currently serves only about 1% of eligible infants and toddlers.

Q: "I can see the end of public assistance in America." President Franklin Delano Roosevelt (1935)

Q: "Nobody likes welfare. Conservatives worry that it erodes the work ethic, retards productivity, and rewards the lazy. Liberals view the American welfare system as incomplete, inadequate, and punitive. Poor people, who rely on it, find it degrading, demoralizing, and mean." Michael B. Katz (1986:ix)

The second part of the conservative critique holds that government assistance undermines self-reliance among the poor and fosters dependency. Depending on government "handouts," argue critics, is the main reason that 84 percent of poor heads of households do not have steady, full-time jobs. Furthermore, although more than half of nonpoor, single mothers work full time, only 10 percent of single mothers receiving AFDC do. Clearly, conservatives continue, welfare has strayed far from its original purpose of helping nonworking women with children (typically, after the death or divorce of a husband) make the transition to self-sufficiency. On the contrary, "welfare" has become a way of life. Once trapped in dependency, poor women most often raise children who will, themselves, remain poor as adults.

Liberals charge their opponents with using a double standard for assessing government programs. Why, they ask, does our national dander rise at the thought of the government transferring money to poor mothers and children when most "welfare" actually goes to relatively rich people? The AFDC budget runs about $25 billion annually—no small sum, to be sure—but one that pales in comparison to the $50 billion in home-mortgage deductions that homeowners pocket each year, or the $300 billion in annual Social Security benefits Uncle Sam provides to senior citizens, most of whom are quite well off. And what about annual tax write-offs for corporations, which also run into the hundreds of billions? As liberals see it, "wealthfare" is far greater than "welfare," even though public opinion takes the opposite view.

Second, liberals claim that conservatives (and much public opinion) distort the performance of public assistance. The ever-present images of irresponsible "welfare queens" mask the fact that most poor families who turn to public assistance are truly needy. Moreover, the typical family on the AFDC rolls receives just $377 a month, hardly enough to attract people to a "life of welfare dependency." And, in constant dollars, AFDC payments have been declining in recent decades. Overall, liberals fault public assistance as a band-aid approach to the serious social problems of unemployment and poverty in the United States.

As for the charge that public assistance undermines families, liberals concede that the proportion of single-parent families is rising, but they dispute the argument that AFDC is to blame. Rather, they maintain, single parenting is a widespread cultural trend found at all class levels in most industrial societies.

Thus, liberals conclude, programs such as AFDC are not unpopular because they have failed, but because they benefit poor people, a segment of the population long scorned as "undeserving." Our cultural tradition of equating wealth with virtue and poverty with vice allows rich people to display privilege as a "badge of ability" while poverty carries a negative stigma. Richard Sennett and Jonathan Cobb (1973) call this the "hidden injury of class."

Indeed, as shown in Figure 10–8, a greater share of our population attributes poverty to personal laziness. Not surprisingly, then, U.S. society is far less supportive of public assistance for the poor than other industrial nations are. And this attitude translates into an inescapable conclusion: The United States tolerates more economic inequality than our counterparts around the world (look back to Figure 10–2).

Many conservatives believe AFDC and similar programs should be abolished. Many liberals, by contrast, want both to improve and expand them. Are there areas of common ground in this debate? Currently, there is broad support for making income assistance contingent on able-bodied recipients performing useful work ("workfare") and participating in occupational training. Under discussion, too, are proposals to limit the duration of public assistance to a fixed term.

Continue the debate . . .

1. *How does our cultural emphasis on self-reliance explain the criticism surrounding public assistance? Why, then, do people not criticize benefits (like home mortgage deductions) for more well-to-do people?*

2. *Do you think public assistance has become a "way of life" as conservatives charge?*

3. *Do you agree with liberals that an expanded public assistance program would lessen the extent of poverty? Why or why not?*

Sources: Murray (1982), Katz (1986), Mead (1989), Ehrenreich (1991), Weidenbaum (1991), Jensen et al. (1993), and Shapiro (1995).

SUMMARY

1. Social inequality in the United States involves disparities in a host of variables, including income, wealth, and power.

2. White-collar occupations generally confer higher income and more prestige than blue-collar work. The pink-collar occupations typically held by women offer little social prestige or income.

3. Schooling is also a resource that is distributed unequally. More than three-fourths of people over age twenty-five complete high school, but only one-fifth are college graduates.

4. Ascription has a powerful impact on stratification in the United States; ancestry, race and ethnicity, gender, and religion are all related to social position.

5. The upper class, which is small (about 5 percent), includes the richest and most powerful families. Members of the upper-upper class, or the old rich, derive their wealth through inheritance over several generations; those in the lower-upper class, or the new rich, depend on earned income as their primary source of wealth.

6. The middle class includes 40 to 45 percent of the population. The upper-middle class may be distinguished from the rest of the middle class on the basis of higher income, higher-prestige occupations, and more schooling.

7. The working class, sometimes called the lower-middle class, includes about one-third of our population. With below-average income, working-class families have less financial security than those in the middle class. Only one-third of working-class children reach college, and most eventually work in blue-collar or lower-prestige white-collar jobs.

8. About one-fifth of the U.S. population belongs to the lower class, which is defined as those living at or below the official poverty threshold. People of African and Hispanic descent, as well as all women, are disproportionately represented in the lower class.

9. Social class affects nearly all aspects of life, beginning with health and survival in infancy and encompassing a wide range of attitudes and patterns of family living.

10. Social mobility is common in the United States as it is in other industrial societies; typically, however, there are only small changes from one generation to the next.

11. Since the early 1970s, changes in the U.S. economy have reduced the standard of living for low- and moderate-income families. One important contemporary trend is a decline in manufacturing industries in the United States, paralleling growth in low-paying, service-sector jobs.

12. Some 39 million people in the United States are officially classified as poor. About 40 percent of the poor are children under the age of eighteen. Two-thirds of the poor are white, but African Americans and Hispanics are disproportionately represented among low-income people. The "feminization of poverty" refers to the rising share of poor families headed by women.

13. Oscar Lewis and Edward Banfield advanced the *culture of poverty* thesis, which holds that poverty is perpetuated by the social patterns of the poor themselves. Opposing this view, William Ryan argues that poverty is caused by a society's unequal distribution of wealth.

KEY CONCEPTS

absolute poverty a deprivation of resources that is life threatening

feminization of poverty the trend by which women represent an increasing proportion of the poor

income occupational wages or salaries and earnings from investments

intergenerational social mobility upward or downward social mobility of children in relation to their parents

intragenerational social mobility a change in social position occurring during a person's lifetime

relative poverty the deprivation of some people in relation to those who have more

wealth the total value of money and other assets, minus outstanding debts

CRITICAL-THINKING QUESTIONS

1. Assess your own social class. Does your family have consistent standing on various dimensions of social stratification? Why do most people find talking about their own social position awkward?

2. Identify some of the effects of U.S. social stratification on health, values, politics, and family patterns.

3. What categories of people are at high risk of poverty in the United States? What evidence supports the assertion that the poor are responsible for their low social position? That society is primarily responsible for poverty?

4. Why is public assistance for the poor more controversial in the United States than in other industrial nations?

SUGGESTED READINGS

Classic Sources

Robert S. Lynd and Helen Merrell Lynd. *Middletown in Transition: A Study in Cultural Conflicts.* New York: Harcourt, Brace & World, 1937.

In their second sociological study of Muncie, Indiana, a team of researchers led by the Lynds examines life in a Middle American town with a keen eye on the effect of social class.

E. Franklin Frazier. *Black Bourgeoisie: The Rise of a New Middle Class.* New York: The Free Press, 1957.

This mid-century account of the rising affluence of some African Americans examines the interplay of class and race in the experience of upward social mobility.

Contemporary Sources

Charles E. Hurst. *Social Inequality: Forms, Causes, and Consequences.* 2d ed. Boston: Allyn & Bacon, 1995.

This book probes many of the issues raised in this chapter.

Katherine S. Newman. *Declining Fortunes: The Withering of the American Dream.* New York: Basic Books, 1993.

The baby boomers, explains the author, are the first generation that, on average, will not live as well as their parents. But these men and women—a diverse lot—make different sense of this decline.

Elliot Liebow. *Tell Them Who I Am: The Lives of Homeless Women.* New York: The Free Press, 1993.

A renowned ethnographer investigates homelessness among women.

Global Sources

Louise Lamphere, ed. *Structuring Diversity: Ethnographic Perspectives on the New Immigration.* Chicago: University of Chicago Press, 1992.

Based on studies of immigrants in six U.S. cities, various researchers explore how newcomers experience our society's social stratification.

Robert Erikson and John H. Goldthorpe. *The Constant Flux: A Study of Class Mobility in Industrial Societies.* Oxford, U.K.: Clarendon Press, 1992.

This report of a massive research effort explains why rates of social mobility are basically the same in all industrial societies.

CANDIDO PORTINARI,
COFFEE, 1935

Museu Nacional de Belas Artes, Rio de Janeiro.
Photo: Raul Lima.

Global Stratification

October 14, 1994, on the northern Philippines. What clean she was—a girl no years old, hair carefully combed and wearing a freshly laundered dress. Her eyes followed us as we walked past; camera-toting Americans stand out in this, one of the poorest neighborhoods in the entire world.

Smokey Mountain, side of Manila, the caught my eye was how more than seven or eight

Fed by methane from the decomposing garbage, the fires never go out on Smokey Mountain, Manila's vast garbage dump. The smoke envelopes the hills of refuse like a thick fog. But Smokey Mountain is more than a dump, it is a neighborhood that is home to thousands of people. The residents of Smokey Mountain are the poorest of the poor, and one is hard pressed to imagine a setting more hostile to human life. Amidst the smoke and the squalor, men and women walk deliberately about doing what they can to survive, picking plastic bags from the garbage and washing them in the river, stacking flat cardboard boxes up the side of a family's plywood shack. And all over Smokey Mountain are children—children!—kids who must already sense the enormous odds against them. The girls and boys we see are the lucky ones, of course. But what chance do they have, living in families that earn scarcely a few hundred dollars a year? With barely any opportunity for schooling? Year after year, breathing this air?

And, against this backdrop of human tragedy, one lovely little girl has put on a fresh dress and gone out to play . . .

Although they seem worlds away from the comfortable lives of most people in the United States, the residents of Manila's Smokey Mountain are far from unique. Their counterparts live throughout Latin America, Africa, and Asia, indeed in almost every country of the world. There is, of course, poverty in the United States. But, as we shall see, poverty in the poor countries of the world is not only more widespread, it is also far more severe.

GLOBAL ECONOMIC DEVELOPMENT

Chapter 10 ("Social Class in the United States") detailed the income inequality that marks our own society. In global perspective, however, social stratification is even more pronounced. Figure 11–1 on page 292 divides the total global income by fifths of the population. Recall that the richest 20 percent of the U.S. population earns about 47 percent of the national income (see Figure 10–1); the richest 20 percent of the global population, however, receives fully 70 percent of all income. At the other end of the social scale, the poorest 20 percent of the U.S. population earns 4.2 percent of our national income; the

poorest fifth of the world's people, by contrast, struggles to survive on just 2 percent of global income.

Because global income is so concentrated, the average member of a rich society (such as the United States) lives extremely well by world standards. In fact, the living standard of even most people below our government's poverty threshold far surpasses that of the majority of the earth's people.

The Problem of Terminology

After World War II, analysts generated a familiar scheme to describe the unequal distribution of global income. They labeled the rich, industrialized countries the "First World," called the somewhat less industrialized, socialist countries the "Second World," and dubbed the remaining nonindustrialized, poor countries the "Third World."

Although widely used for decades, this "Three Worlds" model has lost validity in recent years. For one thing, it was a product of cold war politics by which the capitalist West (the First World) faced off against the socialist East (the Second World), while the rest of the

Q: "While we may want to keep the term 'Third World' to describe a number of societies that are relatively poor, it would be wrong to see this poverty as being unconnected with the relative wealth of the 'First World.' In short, we need a global perspective if we are to make sense of the pattern of affluence and disadvantage in the world." Andrew Webster (1984:6)

GLOBAL: The share of the world's GNP by fifths of the global population resembles the distribution of wealth in the United States (compare Figures 10–1 and 11–1).

NOTE: The world's total income (value of all goods and services produced annually) is in the range of $20–25 trillion.

GLOBAL: To illustrate the productive power of industrial technology, the GDP of the Netherlands exceeds that of all the countries of sub-Saharan Africa combined.

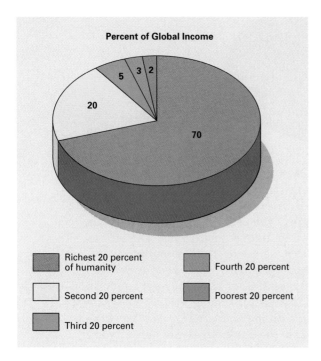

Percent of Global Income

Richest 20 percent of humanity

Second 20 percent

Third 20 percent

Fourth 20 percent

Poorest 20 percent

FIGURE 11–1 Distribution of World Income
Sources: Based on Sivard (1988) and The World Bank (1993).

world (the Third World) remained more or less on the sidelines. But the sweeping transformation of Eastern Europe and the former Soviet Union means that there no longer exists a distinctive Second World; just as important, the superpower opposition that defined the cold war has faded in recent years.

A second problem with the "Three Worlds" model is that it lumped together in the Third World more than one hundred countries at different levels of development. Some relatively better-off nations of the Third World (such as Chile in South America) have ten times the per-person productivity of the poorest countries of the world (including Ethiopia in eastern Africa).

The changes and social differences that mark today's world call for a modestly revised system of classification. Utilizing the terms introduced in Chapter 1 ("The Sociological Perspective"), *high-income countries* are the richest forty nations with the most-developed economies and the highest overall standard of living for their people. Next, the world's ninety *middle-income countries* are somewhat poorer nations whose economic development is more or less typical for the world as a whole. Finally, the remaining sixty *low-income countries* are marked by the lowest productivity and the most severe and extensive poverty.

Compared to the older "Three Worlds" system, this new form of classification has two main advantages. First, it focuses on the key issue of economic development while ignoring the question of whether societies are capitalist or socialist. Second, this revision provides a more precise picture of the relative economic development of the world's countries because it does not lump together all less-industrialized countries into a single Third World.

Nonetheless, classifying the 191 nations on earth into any three categories (or, even more crudely, to divide them into the "rich North" and the "poor South") ignores pronounced differences in their ways of life. The countries at each of the three levels of economic development have rich and varied histories, speak hundreds of languages, and encompass diverse peoples, proud of their cultural distinctiveness.

Keep in mind, too, that just as the world's nations form a social hierarchy that ranges from very rich to very poor, every country on earth is also internally stratified. This means that the extent of global inequality is actually greater than national comparisons suggest, since the most well-off people in rich countries (such as the United States) live worlds apart from the poorest people in low-income countries (like India). With this striking contrast in mind, we can better appreciate the power of visiting Manila's Smokey Mountain dump-dwellers, described at the beginning of this chapter.

High-Income Countries

High-income nations are rich because theirs were the first economies to be transformed by the Industrial Revolution more than two centuries ago, increasing their productive capacity one hundred-fold. To grasp how this development enriched our own region of the world, consider that the typical U.S. household spends more today just caring for pets than the average European household did to meet all its needs during the Middle Ages.

A look back at Global Map 1–1 on page 7 identifies the forty high-income countries of the world. They include most of the nations of Western Europe, including England, where industrialization first took hold about 1750. Canada and the United States are also rich nations; in North America, the Industrial Revolution was well under way by 1850. In Asia, one of the world's leading economic powers is Japan; recent economic growth also places Hong Kong and Singapore in this favored category. Finally, to the south of Asia in the global region known as Oceania,

Japan represents the world's high-income countries, in which industrial technology and economic expansion have produced material prosperity. The presence of market forces is evident in this view of downtown Tokyo (above, left). The Russian Federation represents the middle-income countries of the world. Industrial development has been slower in the former Soviet Union, as socialist economies have performed sluggishly. Residents of Moscow, for example, chafe at having to wait in long lines for their daily needs (above, right). The hope is that the introduction of a market system will raise living standards, although it probably will also increase economic disparity. Bangladesh (right) represents the low-income countries of the world. As the photograph suggests, these nations have limited economic development and rapidly increasing populations. The result is widespread poverty.

Australia and New Zealand also rank as industrial, high-income nations.

Taken together, countries with the most-developed economies cover roughly 25 percent of the earth's land area—including parts of five continents—while lying mostly in the Northern Hemisphere. In mid-1996, the total population of these nations was 870 million, representing about 15 percent of the earth's people. By global standards, rich nations are not densely populated; even so, some countries (such as Japan) are crowded while others (like Canada) are sparsely settled. Inside their borders, however, about three-fourths of the people in high-income countries congregate together in or near cities.

High-income countries reveal significant cultural differences—the nations of Europe, for example, recognize more than thirty official languages. But these countries share an industrial capacity that generates, on average, a rich material life for their people. Per capita income in these societies ranges from about $10,000 annually (in Portugal and Cyprus) to more than $20,000 annually (in the United States and Switzerland).[1] This prosperity is so great that citizens of high-income countries enjoy more than half the world's total income.

Finally, just as people in a single society perform specialized work, so various regions form a global division of labor. Generally speaking, high-income countries dominate the world's scientific efforts and employ the most complex and productive technology. Production in rich societies is capital-intensive, meaning high investments in factories and related machinery. High-income countries also stand at the forefront of new information technology; the majority of the largest

[1]High-income countries have per capita annual income of at least $10,000. For middle- and low-income countries, the comparable figures are $2,500 to $10,000 and below $2,500. All data reflect the United Nations' concept of "purchasing power parities," which avoids distortion caused by exchange rates when converting all currencies to U.S. dollars. Instead, the data represent the local purchasing power of each nation's currency.

When natural disasters strike rich societies, as in the 1993 floods in the midwest region of the United States, property loss is great but the loss of life is low. In poor societies, the converse is true, evident in the aftermath of this cyclone that devastated coastal Bangladesh, killing tens of thousands of poor people who lived on land prone to flooding.

corporations that design and market computers, for instance, are centered in rich societies. With the lion's share of wealth, high-income countries also control the world's financial markets: Upticks and downturns on the financial exchanges of New York, London, and Tokyo affect people throughout the world.

Middle-Income Countries

Middle-income countries are those with per capita income ranging between $2,500 and $10,000, or roughly the median for the world's *nations* (but higher than that of the world's *people* since most people live in low-income countries). These nations have experienced limited industrialization, primarily centered in cities. But about half their people still live in rural areas and engage in agricultural production. Especially in the countryside, schooling, medical care, adequate housing, and even safe water are hard to come by, which represents a standard of living far below what members of high-income societies take for granted.

At the high end of this category, Barbados (Latin America), Greece (Europe), and South Korea (Asia) provide people with about $9,000 in annual income. Ecuador (Latin America), Albania (Europe), and Sri Lanka (Asia) hover at the lower end of this category with roughly $2,500 annually in per capita income. Looking back at Global Map 1–1 (page 7) shows that about ninety of the world's nations fall into this classification, and they are a very diverse lot.

One group of middle-income countries includes the former Soviet Union and the nations of Eastern Europe (in the past, also known as the Second World). The former Soviet Union's military strength rivaled that of the United States, giving it "superpower" status. Its satellite states in Eastern Europe, including Poland, the German Democratic Republic (East Germany), Czechoslovakia, Hungary, Romania, and Bulgaria, had predominantly socialist economies until popular revolts between 1989 and 1991 swept aside their governments. Since then, these nations have begun to introduce market systems. This process, detailed in Chapter 15 ("The Economy and Work"), has yet to solve serious economic woes; on the contrary, in the short term, at least, nations of the former Eastern Bloc are battling high inflation and some people enjoy fewer consumer goods than ever.

In the second category of middle-income countries are most of the oil-producing nations of the Middle East (or, less ethnocentrically, western Asia). These nations, including Saudi Arabia, Oman, and Iran, are very rich, but their wealth is so concentrated that most people receive little benefit and remain poor.

The third, and largest, category of middle-income countries can be found in Latin America and northern and western Africa. These nations (which might be termed the better-off countries of the Third World) include Argentina and Brazil in South America as well as Algeria and Botswana in Africa. Although South Africa's white minority lives as well as people in the

By and large, rich nations such as the United States wrestle with the problem of relative poverty, meaning that poor people get by with less than we think they should have. In poor countries such as Somalia, absolute poverty means that people lack what they need to survive. Here people gather near the Juba River to bury in a common grave family members who died from starvation.

United States, this country, too, must be considered middle income because its majority black population scrapes by with far less income.

Taken together, middle-income countries span roughly 40 percent of the earth's land area, and upwards of 2 billion people, or one-third of humanity, call these nations home. Compared to high-income countries, therefore, these nations are densely populated although, again, some countries in this category (such as El Salvador) are far more crowded than others (like Russia).

Low-Income Countries

Low-income countries of the world, where most people are very poor, are primarily agrarian societies with little industry. These sixty nations, identified in Global Map 1–1 on page 7, are found primarily in central and eastern Africa as well as Asia. Low-income countries (or the poorest nations within the so-called Third World) represent about 35 percent of the planet's land area but are home to half its people. Combining these facts, the population density for poor countries is generally high, although it is much higher in Asian countries (such as Bangladesh and India) than in more sparsely settled central African nations (like Chad or Zaire).

In poor countries, barely 25 percent of the people live in cities; most inhabit villages and farm as their families have done for centuries. In fact, half the world's people are peasants, and most of them live in the low-income countries. By and large, peasants are staunchly traditional, following the folkways of their ancestors. Living without industrial technology, peasants are not very productive, one reason many endure severe poverty. Hunger, minimal housing, and frequent disease all frame the lives of the world's poorest people.

This broad overview of global economic development gives us a foundation for understanding the problem of global inequality. For people living in affluent nations such as the United States, the scope of human want in much of the world is difficult to grasp. From time to time, televised scenes of famine in very poor countries such as Ethiopia and Bangladesh give us a shocking glimpse of the absolute poverty that makes every day a life-and-death struggle. Behind these images lie cultural, historical, and economic forces that we shall explore in the remainder of this chapter.

GLOBAL WEALTH AND POVERTY

October 14, 1994, Manila. With Smokey Mountain behind us, our taxi driver threads his way through heavy traffic as we head for the other side of Manila. The change is amazing: The forbidding smoke and smells of the dump have given way to the polished neighborhoods of Miami or Los Angeles. On the bay in the distance, a cluster of yachts is visible. No more rutted streets; now we glide quietly along wide boulevards lined with trees and filled with expensive Japanese cars. On each side, we pass shopping plazas, upscale hotels, and high-rise office buildings. At every block or so stands the entrance to an exclusive residential enclave set off by gates and protected by security guards. Here, in large, air-conditioned homes, the rich of Manila live and many of the poor work.

To classify a country as "low income" does not mean that only poor people live there. On the contrary, the rich neighborhoods of Manila and Madras (India) testify to the high living standards of some. Indeed, given the low wages paid to most urbanites in these countries, the typical well-to-do household is staffed by several servants and served by a gardener and chauffeur.

But for the majority in the world's poor countries, poverty is the rule. Moreover, with incomes of only several hundred dollars a year, the burden of poverty is greater than it is among the poor of the United States. This does not mean that deprivation here at home constitutes a minor problem. Especially in a rich society, the lack of food, housing, and health care for tens of millions of people—almost half of them children—amounts to a national tragedy. Yet, poverty in poor countries is both *more severe* and *more extensive* than in the United States.

The Severity of Poverty

Poverty in poor countries is more severe than it is in rich nations such as the United States. The data in Table 11–1 suggest why. The first column of figures shows the gross domestic product (GDP) for countries at each level of economic development.[2] Industrial societies have a high economic output primarily because

[2]Gross domestic product refers to all the goods and services on record as produced by a country's economy in a given year. Income earned outside the country by individuals or corporations is excluded from this measure; this is the key difference between GDP and gross national product (GNP), which includes foreign earnings. For countries that invest heavily abroad (Kuwait, for example), GDP is considerably less than GNP; for countries in which other nations invest heavily (Hong Kong), GDP is much higher than GNP. For countries that both invest heavily abroad and have considerable foreign investment at home (like the United States), the two measures are roughly comparable. For the present purpose, simply note the striking differences in productivity of the various world economies.

TABLE 11–1 Wealth and Well-Being in Global Perspective, 1992

Country	Gross Domestic Product ($ billion)	GDP Per Capita (PPP$)*	Quality of Life Index
High-income Countries			
Canada	494	20,520	.950
United States	5,920	23,760	.937
Japan	3,671	20,520	.937
Sweden	221	18,320	.929
Australia	295	18,220	.927
Switzerland	241	22,580	.925
Germany	1,789	21,120	.921
United Kingdom	903	17,160	.916
Middle-income Countries			
Eastern Europe			
Hungary	35	6,580	.856
Poland	84	4,830	.855
Russian Federation	388	6,140	.849
Lithuania	5	3,700	.769
Latin America			
Argentina	229	8,860	.882
Mexico	329	7,300	.842
Brazil	360	5,240	.804
Asia			
South Korea	296	9,250	.882
Thailand	110	5,950	.827
Middle East			
Iran, Islamic Republic of	110	5,420	.770
Saudi Arabia	111	9,880	.762
Africa			
Botswana	4	5,120	.763
Algeria	36	4,870	.732
Low-income Countries			
Latin America			
Honduras	3	2,000	.578
Haiti	...	1,046	.362
Asia			
China, People's Republic of	506	1,950	.594
India	215	1,230	.439
Africa			
Zaire	...	523	.384
Guinea	3	592	.237
Ethiopia	6	330	.227

* These data are the United Nations' new "purchasing power parity" calculations that avoid currency rate distortion by showing the local purchasing power of each domestic currency.

Source: United Nations Development Programme, *Human Development Report, 1995* (New York: Oxford University Press, 1995).

NOTE: Comparatively speaking, the death toll from global poverty (30 fatalities per minute) is ten times that of global war (3 per minute).
SOCIAL SURVEY: "Is it the government's responsibility to reduce income differences between rich and poor?" (*CHIP1 Social Survey Software*, REDISTR; ISSP 1985, N = 3,795)

	"Yes"	"No"
U.S.	34.6%	65.4%
Australia	52.6%	47.4%
Germany	66.9%	33.1%
U.K.	71.5%	28.5%
Austria	77.4%	22.6%

of their industrial technology. A large, industrial nation like the United States had a 1993 GDP of about $6.3 trillion; Japan's GDP stood at about $4.2 trillion. Comparing GDP figures shows that the world's richest nations are thousands of times more productive in terms of goods and services than the poorest countries on earth.

The second column of figures in Table 11–1 indicates per capita GDP in terms of what the United Nations (1995) calls "purchasing power parities," the value of people's income in terms of what it can buy in a local economy. The resulting figures for rich countries like the United States, Switzerland, and Canada are very high—in the range of $20,000. Per capita GDP for middle-income countries, including Brazil, Poland, and Iran, are much lower—in the $5,000 range. And in the world's low-income countries, per capita annual income is no more than just a few hundred dollars. In the African nations of Zaire or Ethiopia, for example, a typical person labors all year long in order to earn what the average worker in the United States reaps in just several days.

The final column of Table 11–1 measures quality of life in the various nations. The quality of life index, calculated by the United Nations (1995), is a composite measure based on a country's life expectancy, income, and education (rates of adult literacy and average number of years of schooling). Index values are decimals that fall between hypothetical extremes of 1 (highest) and zero (lowest). By this calculation, Canadians enjoy the highest quality of life (.950), with residents of the United States and Japan close behind (.937); at the other extreme, people in the African nation of Niger have the world's lowest quality of life (.207).

A key reason for marked disparities in quality of life is that economic productivity is lowest in precisely the regions of the globe where population growth is highest. Figure 11–2 shows the division of global population and global income for countries at each level of economic development. High-income countries are by far the most advantaged with 55 percent of global income supporting just 15 percent of the world's people. Middle-income nations contain about 33 percent of the global population; these people earn about 37 percent of the world's income. This leaves more than half the planet's population with a scant 8 percent of total global income. Factoring together income and population, for every dollar received by individuals in the low-income countries, their counterparts in the high-income nations enjoy twenty-eight dollars.

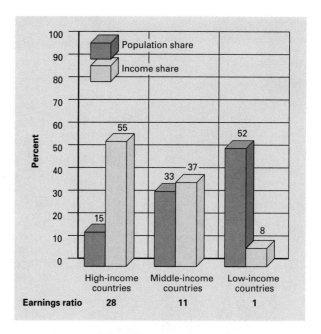

FIGURE 11–2 The Relative Share of Income and Population by Level of Economic Development

Relative Versus Absolute Poverty

A distinction made in the last chapter has an important application to global inequality. The members of rich societies typically focus on the *relative poverty* of some of their members, highlighting how those people lack resources that are taken for granted by others. Relative poverty, by definition, cuts across every society, rich or poor.

But especially important in a global context is the concept of *absolute poverty*, a lack of resources that is life threatening. Human beings in absolute poverty commonly lack the nutrition necessary for health and long-term survival. To be sure, some absolute poverty exists in the United States. Inadequate nutrition that leaves children or elderly people vulnerable to illness and even outright starvation is a reality in this nation. But such immediately life-threatening poverty strikes only a small proportion of the U.S. population; in low-income countries, by contrast, one-third or more of the people are in desperate need.

Since absolute poverty places people at risk of death, we can see the extent of this problem by examining the median age at death around the world. In

THE MAP: The high mortality in low-income societies is all the more striking in light of the fact that infant mortality the world over has actually dropped by half since 1965, from about 125 (per 1,000 live births) to about 65 today.

Q: "In China, we waste nothing but time; in America, you waste everything but time." (Comment made to the author by a student in the People's Republic of China)

GLOBAL: According to calculations by various international agencies, the poorest nation in the world is Ethiopia, with annual per capita consumption below $100. As a result of war and drought, the lives of some 4 million people there are currently at risk.

GLOBAL: Asia has the largest absolute number of poor (some 750 million people; between 20 and 25 percent); Africa has the higher proportion of poor people (35 percent).

Window on the World

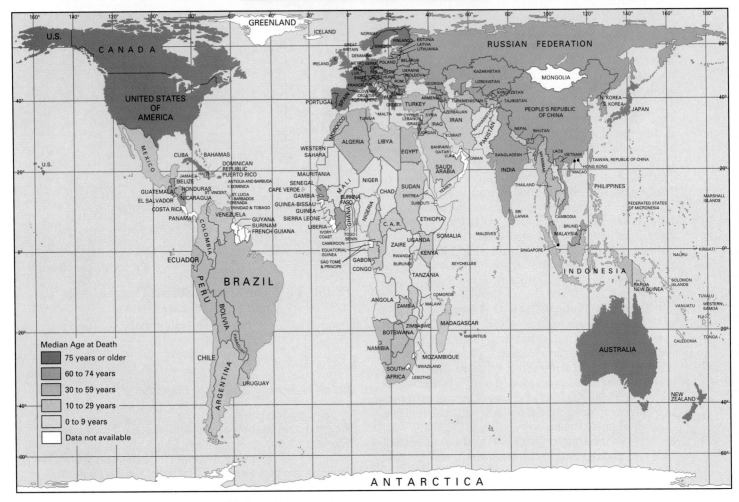

GLOBAL MAP 11–1 Median Age at Death in Global Perspective

This map identifies the age below which half of all deaths occur in any year. In the high-income countries of the world, including the United States, it is the elderly who face death—that is, people age seventy-five or older. In middle-income countries, including most of Latin America, most people die years or even decades earlier. In low-income countries, especially in Africa and parts of Asia, it is children who die, with half of all lives ending before individuals reach ten years of age.

Sources: The World Bank (1993); map projection from *Peters Atlas of the World* (1990).

other words, by what age have half of all people born in a society died? Global Map 11–1 shows that death in high-income countries, on average, occurs among the elderly beyond the age of seventy-five. Death occurs somewhat earlier in middle-income nations, reflecting a lower standard of living. But in many low-income countries of Africa and western Asia, the greater extent of absolute poverty is brought home by the fact that half of all deaths occur among children under the age of ten.

GLOBAL: One indicator of child poverty is the U.N.'s calculation of seriously underweight children below the age of five. In high-income countries, the figure is about 10%. The ten worst rates are for these low-income countries: Afghanistan, 40%; Burkina Faso, 40%; Sri Lanka, 42%; Vietnam, 42%; Pakistan, 42%; Niger, 44%; Mozambique, 47%; Nepal, 51%; India, 63%; Bangladesh, 66%.

GLOBAL: High population growth is associated with a high proportion of children. Share of total population under the age of 14 (1994) for selected countries: Entire world, 31.8%; Japan, 16.6%; U.S., 22%; Brazil, 31.8%; Egypt, 38.8%; Bangladesh, 40.8%; Afghanistan, 42.9%; Iraq, 47.9%; Yemen, 49.3%; Syria, 49.4%. (Among poor societies, Muslim nations have particularly high birth rates.)

The Extent of Poverty

Poverty in poor countries is more extensive than it is in rich nations such as the United States. Chapter 10 ("Social Class in the United States") noted that the U.S. government officially classifies about one in seven people as poor. In low-income countries, however, most people live no better than the poor in our nation, and many people are living close to the edge of survival. As the high death rates among children suggest, the extent of absolute poverty is greatest in Africa, where half the population is malnourished. In the world as a whole, at any given time, 20 percent of the people (about 1 billion) lack the nutrition they need to work regularly. Of these, at least 800 million are at risk for their lives (Sivard, 1988; Helmuth, 1989; United Nations Development Programme, 1993).

Members of rich societies, such as the United States, tend to be overnourished. On average, a member of a high-income society consumes about 3,500 calories daily, an excess that contributes to obesity and related health problems. Most people in low-income countries not only do more physical labor than we do, but they consume only about 2,000 calories daily. In short, they do not consume enough food or, just as important, enough of the right kinds of food.

In simple terms, lack of necessary nutrition makes death a way of life in poor societies. In the ten minutes it takes to read through this section of the chapter, about three hundred people in the world will die of starvation. This amounts to about forty thousand people a day, or 15 million people each year. Even more than in the United States, the burden of poverty in poor countries falls on children. As we have seen, in the poorest nations of central Africa, half of all children die before they reach age ten.

Two further comparisons reveal the human toll of global poverty. First, at the end of World War II, the United States obliterated the Japanese city of Hiroshima with an atomic bomb. The worldwide loss of life from starvation reaches the Hiroshima death toll *every three days.* Second, the annual loss of life stemming from poverty is ten times greater than that resulting from all the world's armed conflicts. Given the magnitude of this problem, easing world hunger is one of the most serious responsibilities facing humanity today.

Poverty and Children

As the last chapter explained, poverty in the United States hits children hardest. The same holds true

Life expectancy is closely related to social-class position. Poor people—especially young males—who struggle to get by in cities around the world, have a strikingly high rate of death and injury from illness, accident, and violence. Some individuals caught up in poverty engage in perilous behavior because they have little reason to think the future will be brighter than the present. The boy shown here, from a poor neighborhood in Rio de Janeiro, died in a "train surfing" accident shortly after this photograph was taken.

worldwide, and the extent and severity of child poverty are greatest in low-income countries. As we have already explained, death often comes early in poor societies, where families lack adequate food, safe water, secure housing, and access to medical care. In many cases, too, children in poor countries leave their families because their chances to survive are better on the streets.

Organizations combating child poverty in the world estimate that poverty forces some 75 million city children in poor countries to beg, steal, sell sex, or serve as couriers for drug gangs in order to provide income for their families. Such a life almost always means dropping out of school and places children at high risk of illness and violence. Many street girls, with little or no access to medical assistance, become pregnant—a case of children who cannot support themselves having still more children.

Another 25 million of the world's children have deserted their families altogether, sleeping and living on the streets as best they can. Roughly half of all street children are found in Latin America. Brazil, where much of the population has flocked to cities in a desperate search for a better life, has millions of street children—many not yet teenagers—living in

NOTE: Illiteracy rates are high in poor societies (about half of all Africans and one-fourth of all Latin Americans can neither read nor write). Throughout the world, illiteracy is considerably more common among women than men. Examples (percent illiterate): Algeria, 43% of men, 68% of women; Bangladesh, 60% of men, 82% of women; Brazil, 21% of men, 24% of women; P.R. China, 21% of men, 49% of women; Saudi Arabia, 29% of men, 70% of women; Tunisia, 40% of men, 60% of women. (United Nations)

DIVERSITY: Of every 100 ministerial-level positions worldwide, four are held by women. By global region: Africa, 2.5; Asia and Pacific Islands, 1.6; Latin America, 4.0; socialist nations, 4.6; industrialized nations, 8.9. (Dr. Nafis Sadik, "Success in Developing Nations Depends on Women," *Popline*, Vol. 13, March–April, 1991, p. 4)

Global Snapshot

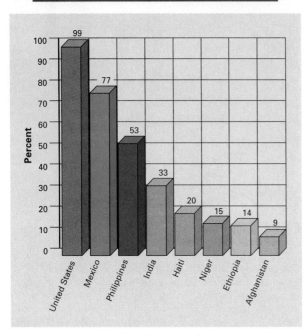

FIGURE 11–3 Percent of Births Attended by Trained Health Personnel
Source: United Nations Development Programme (1995).

makeshift huts, under bridges, or in alleyways. Public response to street children is often anger directed at the children themselves. In Rio de Janeiro, known to many in the United States as Brazil's beautiful seaside resort, police try to keep the numbers of street children in check; when this unrealistic policy fails, however, death squads may sweep through a neighborhood, engaging in a bloody ritual of "urban cleansing." In Rio, several hundred street children are murdered each year (Larmer, 1992; U.S. House of Representatives, 1992).

Poverty and Women

Women in Sikandernagar, one of India's countless rural villages, begin work at 4:00 in the morning, lighting the fires, milking the buffalo, sweeping floors, and walking to the well for water. They care for other family members as they rise. By 8:00, when many people in the United States are just beginning their day, these women move on to their "second shift,"

working under the hot sun in the fields until 5:00 in the afternoon. Returning home, the women gather wood for their fires, all the time searching for whatever plants they can find to enrich the evening meal. The buffalo, too, are ready for a meal, and the women tend to them. It is well past dark before their eighteen-hour day is through (Jacobson, 1993:61).

In rich societies, the work women do is typically unrecognized, undervalued, and underpaid; women receive less income for their efforts than men do. In low-income countries, this pattern is even more pronounced. Women do most of the work in poor societies, and families depend on women's work to provide income. At the same time, just as tradition keeps many women from school, it also accords them primary responsibility for child rearing and maintaining the household. In poor societies, the United Nations estimates, men own 90 percent of the land, representing a far greater gender disparity in wealth than is found in industrial nations. Clearly, multilayered systems of tradition and law subordinate women in poor societies. Caught in a spiral of circumstance that promises little hope for change, women are disproportionately the poorest of the poor. More than 500 million of the world's 800 million people living in absolute poverty are women.

Women in poor countries have limited access to birth control (which, obviously, raises the birth rate), and they typically give birth without the assistance of any trained health personnel. Figure 11–3 draws a stark contrast between high- and low-income countries in this regard.

Overall, gender inequality is strongest in low-income societies, especially in Asia where cultural traditions overwhelmingly favor males. As the box explains, this pattern of denigrating women affects virtually every dimension of life, and has produced a stunning lack of females in some regions of the world (Kishor, 1993).

Correlates of Global Poverty

What accounts for the severe and extensive poverty in low-income countries? The rest of this chapter weaves together explanations from the following facts about poor societies.

1. **Technology.** Almost two-thirds of people in low-income countries farm the land; the productive power of industrial technology is all but absent in these poorest nations. Energy from human muscles or beasts of burden falls far short of the force

RESOURCE: Daphne Topouzis's article "Women's Poverty in Africa" is one of the cross-cultural selections in the Macionis and Benokraitis reader.

GLOBAL: Look ahead to Global Map 20–2, HIV Infection of Adults in Global Perspective, on page 542. Note that while only

10 percent of worldwide HIV infections are found in Southeast Asia, HIV is spreading most rapidly there.

DISCUSS: What effect do you think the empowerment of women (discussed in the box in Chapter 21 with regard to controlling population growth) would have on the sexual slavery trade now booming in Southeast Asia?

GLOBAL SOCIOLOGY

Infanticide and Sexual Slavery: Reports From India and Thailand

Rani, a young woman living in a remote Indian village, returned home from the hospital after delivering a baby girl. There was no joy in the family. On the contrary, upon learning of the birth, the men somberly filed out of the mud house. Rani and her mother-in-law then set about the gruesome task of mashing oleander seeds into several drops of oil to make a poisonous paste, which they forced down the baby's throat. The day came to an end as Rani returned from a nearby field where she had buried the child.

As she walked home, Rani felt not sadness at losing her daughter but bitterness at not bearing a son. Members of her village, like poor people throughout the world (and especially Asia), favor boys while defining girls as an economic liability. Why? Because, in poor societies, most power and wealth falls into the hands of men. Parents recognize that boys are a better investment of their meager resources, since males who survive to adulthood will provide for the family. Then, too, custom dictates that parents of a girl offer a dowry to the family of her prospective husband. In short, given the existing social structure, families are better off with boys and without girls.

One consequence of this double standard is high rates of sex-selective abortion throughout rural India, China, and other Asian nations. Curiously, in India, even villages that lack running water typically have a doctor who performs high-tech amniocentesis or ultrasound to determine the sex of a

fetus. The woman's typical response, upon hearing the results of the test, is either elation at carrying a boy or resolve to terminate the pregnancy quickly so that she may "try again." Although there are no precise counts of abortion and female infanticide, analysts point out that, in some rural regions of Asia, men outnumber women by as many as ten to one.

For girls who manage to survive infancy, gender bias presents overwhelming barriers. Generally speaking, parents provide girls with less food, schooling, and medical care than they give to boys. In times of drought or other crisis, families may leave girls to die while they channel what little resources they have toward the survival of a son.

A global pattern is that poverty forces women into sexual slavery as prostitutes. These four Vietnamese women working in a brothel in Cambodia will never escape their poverty and may well fall victim to AIDS, which is spreading rapidly across Southeast Asia.

Another dimension of gender bias is the exploding growth of sexual slavery involving young women, which has spread rapidly across Southeast Asia. Bangkok, Thailand, is emerging as the sex-tourism capital of the world; prostitution in that country currently claims as many as 800,000 females, half under the age of eighteen. In some cases, parents sell female infants to agents who pay others to raise them, then "harvest their crop" when the girls approach their teenage years and are old enough to work the sex trade. In other cases, girls who see little future in a rural village make their own way to the city, only to fall into the hands of pimps who soon have them working in brothels, soliciting in bars, or performing in sex shows. Pimps provide girls with clothes and housing, but at a price that exceeds the girls' salaries. The result is a system of debt bondage that keeps women virtual prisoners of their unscrupulous employers. Those who run away are pursued by agents and forced to return.

The numbers involved are rapidly mounting: Thailand alone now has 1 to 2 million prostitutes (perhaps 8 percent of the country's female population); about half of these are under age eighteen. The future for these girls and women is bleak. Most suffer from a host of diseases brought on by abuse and neglect, and 40 percent are now infected with the virus that causes AIDS.

Sources: Anderson & Moore (1993) and Santoli (1994).

NOTE: Points 1–3 below are incorporated into modernization theory; points 4–5 are elements of dependency theory. Both theories are discussed later in this chapter.

NOTE: The intensity of the problems of poor societies is most striking in cities. Most of the largest cities of the world are now in poor countries, including Mexico City with some 25 million people.

GLOBAL: On average, people in the United States acquire 13 years of schooling, while those in China average 5 years, Indonesia 4, and Pakistan 2.

NOTE: Modernization theory draws on the ideas of Ferdinand Toennies, Emile Durkheim, and Max Weber. Among the architects of this approach in the United States was Talcott Parsons.

unleashed by steam, oil, gas, or nuclear fuels—the power sources that propel complex machinery. Moreover, poor societies' focus on farming, rather than on specialized production, inhibits development of human skills and abilities.

2. **Population growth.** As Chapter 21 ("Population and Urbanization") explains in detail, countries with the least-developed economies have the world's highest birth rates. Despite the death toll from poverty, the populations of poor countries in Africa, for example, double every twenty-five years. There, more than half the people have yet to enter their childbearing years, so the wave of population growth will roll into the future. Even an expanding economy cannot support vast population surges. During 1993, for example, the population of Kenya swelled by 4 percent; as a result, even with some economic development, living standards actually fell.

3. **Cultural patterns.** Poor societies are typically very traditional. Kinship groups pass folkways and mores from generation to generation. Adhering to long-established ways of life, people resist innovations—even those that promise a richer material life.

   The members of poor societies often accept their fate, although it may be bleak, in order to maintain family vitality and cultural heritage. Such attitudes bolster social bonds, but at the cost of discouraging development. The box explains why traditional people in India respond to their poverty differently than poor people in the United States commonly do.

4. **Social stratification.** Low-income societies distribute their wealth very unequally. Chapter 9 ("Social Stratification") explained that social inequality is more pronounced in agrarian societies than in industrial societies. In the farming regions of Bangladesh, for example, 10 percent of the landowners own more than half the acreage, while almost half of farming families hold title to little or no land of their own (Hartmann & Boyce, 1982). As another example, the richest 10 percent of Central Americans control about three-fourths of that region's land.

5. **Gender inequality.** As we have already explained, poor societies subordinate women even more than industrial societies do. Moreover, women with few opportunities typically have many children, and the needs of a growing population, in turn, restrain economic development. As a result, many analysts conclude that raising living standards in much of the world depends on improving the social standing of women.

6. **Global power relationships.** A final cause of global poverty lies in the relationships among the nations of the world. Historically, wealth flowed from poor societies to rich nations by means of **colonialism,** *the process by which some nations enrich themselves through political and economic control of other countries.* Historical patterns of trade, some analysts claim, spurred certain nations to prosper economically while others simultaneously were made poor. The societies of Western Europe colonized much of Latin America for more than three hundred years and also controlled parts of Asia, notably India, for centuries. Africa, too, endured up to a century of colonization, most of which ended in the 1960s.

   During this century, about 130 former colonies gained their independence, leaving only a small number of countries as colonies today (Strang, 1990). As we shall see, however, a continuing pattern of domination has emerged. **Neocolonialism** (*neo* is a Greek word for "new") amounts to *a new form of global power relationships that involves not direct political control but economic exploitation by multinational corporations.* **Multinational corporations,** in turn, are *large corporations that operate in many different countries.* As Chapter 15 ("The Economy and Work") explains, the power of today's multinational corporations to dominate a poor nation often rivals that of colonial countries in centuries past.

GLOBAL INEQUALITY: THEORETICAL ANALYSIS

There are two major explanations for the unequal distribution of the world's wealth and power—*modernization theory* and *dependency theory.* Each of these approaches advances a thesis to explain why so many of the world's people are poor and why members of rich societies enjoy such relative advantages.

The two explanations overlap to some extent. Both acknowledge the enormous inequality on our planet, and they agree that changes are needed to guarantee the future security of humanity, rich and poor alike. Yet, by emphasizing different causes of global poverty, they reach differing conclusions as to what to do about this pressing problem.

RESOURCE: Robert B. Reich's analysis of the consequences of the emerging global economy for workers in the United States, and David Berreby's article, "The Global Population Crisis," are both included in the Macionis and Benokraitis reader, *Seeing Ourselves: Classic, Contemporary, and Cross-Cultural Readings in Sociology.*

GLOBAL: Assuming that India maintains its current rate of population growth of about 2%, population in that Asian nation will pass the 1 billion mark by 2000 and double again by 2025.
NOTE: India is about ten times as densely populated as the United States.
Q: "In India," observers say, "a child is always in someone's arms."

GLOBAL SOCIOLOGY

A Different Kind of Poverty: A Report From India

Most North Americans know that India is one of the poorest societies of the world: Per capita gross domestic product (GDP) in this low-income Asian nation is only slightly more than $1,000 a year (look back to Table 11–1 on page 296). Deprivation pervades this vast society, home to one-third of all the world's hungry people.

But North Americans do not readily comprehend the reality of poverty in India. Most of the country's 900 million people live in conditions far worse than those our society labels as "poor." A traveler's first experience of Indian life is sobering and sometimes shocking. Arriving in Madras, one of India's largest cities with 7 million inhabitants, a visitor immediately recoils from the smell of human sewage that hangs over the city like a malodorous cloud. Untreated sewage also renders much of the region's water unsafe to drink. The sights and sounds of Madras are strange and intense—streets are choked by motorbikes, trucks, carts pulled by oxen, and waves of people. Along the roads, vendors sit on burlap cloth hawking fruits, vegetables, and cooked food. Seemingly oblivious to the urban chaos all around them, people work, talk, bathe, and even sleep in the streets. Tens of millions of homeless people fill the cities of India.

Madras is also dotted by more than a thousand shanty settlements, containing about half a million people, many of whom have converged on the city from rural villages in search of a better life. Shantytowns are clusters of huts constructed of branches, leaves, and discarded material. These dwellings offer little privacy and lack refrigeration, running water, and bathrooms. The visitor from the United States understandably feels uneasy entering such a community, since the poorest sections of our inner cities seethe with frustration and, oftentimes, explode with violence.

But, here, again, India offers a sharp contrast because its people understand poverty differently than we do. No restless young men hang out at the corner, no drug dealers work the streets, and there is surprisingly little danger. In the United States, poverty often means anger and isolation; in India, even shantytowns are built of strong families—children, parents, and sometimes elderly grandparents—who extend a smile and a welcome.

In traditional societies like India, ways of life change slowly. To most Indians, life is shaped by *dharma*, the Hindu concept of duty and destiny, that encourages them to accept their fate, whatever it may be. Mother Teresa, who has won praise for her work among the poorest of India's people, goes to the heart of the cultural differences: "Americans have angry poverty," she explains. "In India, there is worse poverty, but it is a happy poverty."

Perhaps we should not describe as "happy" anyone who clings to the edge of survival. But the sting of poverty in India is eased by the strength and support of families and communities, a sense that existence has a purpose, and a world view that encourages each person to accept whatever life offers. As a result, the visitor comes away from a first encounter with Indian poverty in confusion: "How can people be so desperately poor, and yet apparently content, vibrant, and so *alive*?"

Low-income societies may be poor, but strong traditions and vital families place most people in a network of social support. Thus people endure poverty with the help of their kin, which contrasts to the often isolating poverty in the United States.

Source: Based on the author's research in Madras, India, November 1988.

Q: "Economic achievement and progress depend largely on human aptitudes and attitudes, on social and political institutions and arrangements which derive from these . . ." P. T. Bauer

RESOURCE: The cultural value placed on achievement is regarded by some sociologists as the crucial factor in advancing or inhibiting development. Cf. Daniel Lerner, *The Passing of Traditional Society: Modernizing the Middle East* (The Free Press, 1958).

GLOBAL: Assuming that (1) about one-sixth of people who have ever lived are living now, (2) virtually all of the people who lived in human history were poor by contemporary standards, and (3) at least one-third of today's global population is poor, then only 5 or 6 percent of humanity has ever known any degree of affluence. According to modernization theory, such affluence (not poverty, which is the norm) is what social scientists must explain.

The value of children in low-income countries includes their ability to earn income. This pattern is especially true in the case of girls. In India, families typically invest in the education of their sons, who may go on to higher earnings. Girls, by contrast, are often kept out of school so they can work full days in factories. This factory offers little pay to girls who produce hand-rolled cigarettes.

Modernization Theory

Modernization theory is *a model of economic and social development that explains global inequality in terms of differing levels of technological development among societies.* Modernization theory emerged in the 1950s, a time when "becoming modern" was a popular idea in the United States and a period of hostility toward the United States in many poor societies. Socialist countries—especially the Soviet Union—were gaining influence among low-income nations by asserting that economic progress was impossible under the sway of rich, capitalist countries. In response, U.S. policy makers framed a broad defense of rich nations' free-market economies that has shaped official foreign policy toward poor nations ever since.[3]

Historical Perspective

Modernization theorists point out that the entire world was poor as recently as several centuries ago. Because poverty has been the norm throughout human history, *affluence*—not deprivation—demands an explanation.

Affluence came within reach of a small segment of humanity in Western Europe during the twilight of the Middle Ages as economic activity expanded. Initially, this economic growth was centered in and around cities. By the beginning of the sixteenth century, exploration of other parts of the world revealed vast commercial potential.

By 1750, Europeans were engaged in trade all over the world. But then an even greater economic force was unleashed as the Industrial Revolution began to transform Western Europe and, soon after, the United States. Industrial technology, coupled with the innovations of countless entrepreneurs, created new wealth on a grand scale. At the outset, modernization theorists concede, this new wealth benefited only a few. Yet industrial technology was so productive that gradually the standard of living of even the poorest people began to rise. Absolute poverty, which had cast a menacing shadow over humanity for its entire history, was finally being routed.

During this century, the standard of living in high-income countries, where the Industrial Revolution began, has jumped at least fourfold. Many middle-income nations in Asia and Latin America are now industrializing, and they, too, are gaining greater wealth. But without industrial technology, low-income countries contend with the same meager productivity they have endured throughout history.

The Importance of Culture

Why didn't the Industrial Revolution sweep away poverty the world over? Modernization theory holds that not every society has been eager to seek out and use new technology. Indeed, depending on culture, some forward-looking societies have eagerly embraced technological innovation while other, more traditional peoples have sternly opposed it.

---

[3]The following discussion of modernization theory draws primarily on Rostow (1960, 1978), Bauer (1981), and Berger (1986).

NOTE: Modernization theory is loosely linked to structural-functional theory; dependency theory has more overt connections to
social-conflict theory.
GLOBAL: Marlise Simons explains how economic development
has undermined the cultural traditions of the Kaiapo in Brazil's
Amazon region. See her article in the Macionis and Benokraitis
reader, or the summary of her work that appears at the opening of
Chapter 24.
NOTE: The subtitle of W. W. Rostow's (1960) work, "A Non-Communist Manifesto," suggests its opposition to Marx's thinking.
Q: "There is widespread agreement today, from Chile to China,
that an economy allowing market forces the fullest feasible sway
will perform better than one in which all decisions are centrally
administered." Peter Berger (1986:130)

Modernization theory identifies *tradition* as the greatest barrier to economic development. In societies that celebrate strong family networks and revere the past, ancient ways offer powerful guides to understanding the present and shaping the future. Predictably, tradition operates as a form of "cultural inertia" that discourages the adoption of technological advances that would improve the standard of living. Even today, a host of peoples from the North American Amish to the Islamic people of Iran and the deeply traditional Semai of Malaysia have battled against technological advances that threaten their strong family relationships, customs, and religious beliefs.

Max Weber (1958; orig. 1904–5) explained that, at the end of the Middle Ages, Western Europe was quite another story: Here was a cultural environment that distinctly favored change. As detailed in Chapter 4 ("Society"), the Protestant Reformation reshaped traditional Catholicism to generate a progress-oriented culture. Material affluence—regarded with suspicion by the Catholic church—became a personal virtue, and individualism steadily undermined the established emphasis on kinship and community. Taken together, these emerging cultural patterns nurtured the Industrial Revolution, which carried one segment of humanity from poverty to prosperity.

Rostow's Stages of Modernization

But, modernization theory holds, the door to affluence remains open to all. Indeed, as technological advances diffuse around the world, all societies are gradually converging on one general form: the industrial model. According to W. W. Rostow (1960, 1978), the process of modernization follows four overarching stages.

1. **Traditional stage.** Any society with longstanding and powerful traditions will resist technological innovation. Socialized to venerate the past, most people in traditional societies cannot even imagine how life could be very different from what they know. Traditionalists, therefore, build their lives around their families and neighborhoods, grant little individual freedom to one another, and in so doing, inhibit change. Life in such communities is often spiritually rich but lacking in material abundance.

   A century ago, much of the world was at this initial stage of economic development. And, because nations such as Bangladesh, Niger, and Somalia are still at the traditional stage, they remain impoverished to this day.

2. **Take-off stage.** As a society begins to shake off the grip of tradition, people start to use their talents and imagination, triggering economic growth. A market emerges as people produce goods not just for their own consumption but to trade with others for profit. The culture is marked by a developing spirit of individualism and a stronger achievement orientation, usually at the expense of family ties and longstanding norms and values.

   Great Britain reached take-off by about 1800, the United States by 1820. Thailand, a middle-income country in eastern Asia, is now at this stage. Such development typically depends on progressive influences from rich nations, including foreign aid, the availability of advanced technology and investment capital, and schooling abroad.

3. **Drive to technological maturity.** By this time, "growth" has become a widely accepted concept, fueling a society's full-scale pursuit of higher living standards. An active, diversified economy drives a population eager to enjoy the benefits of industrial technology. At the same time, however, people begin to realize (and sometimes lament) that industrialization is eroding traditional family and community life. Great Britain reached this point by about 1840, the United States by 1860. Today, Mexico, the U.S. territory of Puerto Rico, and South Korea are among the nations driving to technological maturity.

   By this stage of economic development, absolute poverty has greatly declined. Cities swell with people who stream from the rural hinterland in search of economic opportunity, occupational specialization renders relationships less personal, and heightened individualism sparks movements pressing for expanded political rights. Societies approaching technological maturity also provide basic schooling to all their people, with advanced training for some. Such people discard traditions as "backward," opening the door to further change. The social position of women steadily becomes more equal to that of men. But, in the short term at least, the process of development may subject women to new and unanticipated problems, as the box explains.

4. **High mass consumption.** Economic development driven by industrial technology steadily raises living standards. This rise occurs, Rostow explains, as mass production stimulates mass consumption. Simply put, people soon learn to

GLOBAL SOCIOLOGY

Modernization and Women: A Report From Rural Bangladesh

In global perspective, gender inequality is most pronounced where people are poorest. Economic development, then, gives women opportunities to attend school and to work outside the home, reduces birth rates, and, therefore, weakens traditional male domination.

Along the way, however, the process of modernization often impedes women's progress. Investigating the lives of women in a poor, rural district of Bangladesh, Sultana Alam (1985) observed several hazards of development for women.

First, as economic opportunity draws men from rural areas to cities in search of work, women and children must fend for themselves. Some men sell their land and simply abandon their wives, who are left with nothing but their children.

Second, the waning strength of the family and neighborhood leaves women who are deserted in this way with little assistance. The same holds true for women who become single through divorce or the death of a spouse. In the past, Alam reports, kin or neighbors readily took in a Bangladeshi woman who found herself alone. Today, as Bangladesh struggles to advance economically, the number

One consequence of modernization in developing societies might be termed "the sexualization of women." Rather than being defined in terms of traditional kinship roles, women are increasingly valued for their sexual attractiveness. Do you think it is significant that many of the growing ranks of prostitutes in Asian cities wear Western styles of clothing?

of poor households headed by women is increasing. Rather than enhancing women's autonomy, Alam argues, a new spirit of individualism has actually eroded the social standing of women.

Third, economic development—as well as the growing influence of Western movies and mass media—undermine women's traditional roles as wives, sisters, and mothers in favor of defining women as objects of men's sexual attention. The cultural emphasis on sexuality, familiar to most Westerners, now encourages men in poor countries to abandon aging spouses for younger, more physically attractive partners. The same stress on sex contributes to the world's rising tide of prostitution, noted earlier in this chapter.

Modernization, then, does not affect men and women in the same ways. In the long run, the evidence suggests, modernization does give the sexes more equal standing. In the short run, however, the economic position of many women actually declines, as women are forced to contend with new problems that were virtually unknown in traditional societies.

Sources: Based on Alam (1985) and Mink (1989).

"need" the expanding array of goods that their society produces.

The United States entered the era of high mass consumption around 1900. Other high-income countries were not far behind. Japan, for example, was sufficiently industrialized to become a military power early in this century.

After recovering from the destruction of World War II, the Japanese entered an era of high mass consumption, and Japan's economic output is now second only to that of the United States. Now entering this level of economic development are two of the most prosperous small societies of eastern Asia, Hong Kong and Singapore.

Q: "Capitalism has become one of the most dynamic forces in human history, transforming one society after another, and today it has become established as an international system determining the economic fate of most of mankind and, at least indirectly, its social, political, and cultural fate as well." Peter Berger (1986:115)

GLOBAL: "Divided" countries shed light on the merits of each theory. South Korea (well within the capitalist world economy) has per capita GDP of $7,240 compared to isolated North Korea's figure of $920. For West Germany (1988), the figure was $14,730; East Germany, $8,000.

The Role of Rich Nations

Modernization theory credits high-income countries with a crucial role in global economic development. More specifically, rich societies are the key to alleviating global inequality in the following ways:

1. **Assisting in population control.** We have already noted that population growth is greatest in the poorest societies of the world, where rising population easily overtakes economic advances and lowers the standard of living. As rich nations export birth control technology and promote its use, they help curb population growth, which is crucial to combating poverty. Integral to this process are programs that advance the social standing of women. Once economic development is under way and women are earning more income, their lives are less centered on child rearing, so birth rates begin to decline as they have in industrialized societies.

2. **Increasing food production.** Modernization theory asserts that "high-tech" farming methods, exported from rich to poor nations, raise agricultural yields. Such techniques, collectively referred to as the *Green Revolution*, involve the use of new hybrid seeds, modern irrigation methods, chemical fertilizers, and pesticides.

3. **Introducing industrial technology.** Technological transfers go beyond agricultural innovations. Rich nations accelerate economic growth in poor societies by introducing machinery and information technology. Such cultural diffusion helps to shift the economies of low-income countries from a focus on agriculture to industrial and service work that raises productivity.

4. **Instituting programs of foreign aid.** Investment capital from rich nations boosts the prospects of poor societies striving to reach the take-off stage. Developing countries can use this money to purchase fertilizers and high-technology irrigation projects that raise agricultural productivity as well as building power plants and factories that improve industrial output.

Critical evaluation. Modernization theory, a sweeping analysis of how industrialization transforms social life, has influential supporters among social scientists (Parsons, 1966; W. Moore, 1977, 1979; Bauer, 1981; Berger, 1986; Firebaugh & Beck, 1994). Moreover, this model has guided the foreign policy of the United States and other rich nations for decades. Proponents point to rapid economic development in Asia as proof that the affluence created in Western Europe and North America is within reach of all regions of the world. With the assistance of rich countries, South Korea, Taiwan, the former British colony of Singapore, and Hong Kong, a British colony until 1997, each has a stellar record of economic achievement.

From the outset, however, modernization theory has come under fire from socialist countries (and sympathetic analysts in the West) as a thinly veiled defense of capitalism. Its most serious flaw, according to critics, is that modernization simply has not occurred in many of the world's poor societies. Between 1980 and 1990, in fact, most of the countries of sub-Saharan Africa actually saw their living standards fall.

A second criticism lodged against modernization theory concerns its assessment of the role of rich nations. Modernization theorists contend that the presence of high-income countries ready and willing to offer various kinds of assistance makes economic development easier than ever. But many critics of modernization theory see rich nations more as the cause of global poverty than its solution. Centuries ago, they argue, Europe and North America industrialized from a position of global *strength*; we should not expect low-income countries today to modernize from a position of global *weakness*.

Third, critics charge that modernization theory treats rich and poor nations as worlds unto themselves, failing to see how international relations historically have affected the standing of all nations. It was colonization, they maintain, that boosted the fortunes of Europe to begin with; further, this economic windfall came at the expense of countries in Latin America and Asia that are still reeling from the consequences.

Fourth, critics contend that modernization theory holds up the world's high-income countries as the standard by which the rest of humanity should be judged, betraying an ethnocentric bias. As Chapter 22 ("Environment and Society") explains, our Western conception of "progress" has led us to degrade the physical environment throughout the world. Moreover, not every culture buys into our notions about competitive, materialistic living.

Fifth, and finally, modernization theory draws criticism for locating the causes of global poverty almost entirely in the poor societies themselves. Critics see this analysis as little more than "blaming the victims" for their own plight. Instead, they argue, an analysis of global inequality should focus as much attention on the behavior of *rich* nations as that of poor nations (Wiarda, 1987).

Was the arrival of Europeans in the Western Hemisphere a monument to the bravery of explorers or the greed of conquerors? Bolivian artist Walter Solon Romero sides with the second view in a mural, titled Conquest, *which he painted for San Andras University, La Paz.*

From all these concerns has emerged a second major approach to understanding global inequality. This opposing view is called dependency theory.

Dependency Theory

Dependency theory is *a model of economic and social development that explains global inequality in terms of the historical exploitation of poor societies by rich ones.* Dependency theory offers an analysis of global inequality dramatically different from modernization theory, for it places primary responsibility for global poverty on rich nations. Dependency theory holds that high-income countries have systematically impoverished low-income countries, making poor societies *dependent* on rich ones. According to dependency theorists, this destructive process extends back for centuries and continues today.

Historical Perspective

Everyone agrees that, before the Industrial Revolution, there was little of the affluence present in some parts of the world today. Dependency theory asserts, however, that many poor countries were actually better off economically in the past than they are now. André Gunder Frank (1975), a noted proponent of this approach, argues that the development of rich nations resulted from the same colonial ties that *underdeveloped* poor societies.

Dependency theory hinges on the assertion that the economic positions of the rich and poor nations of the world are linked and cannot be understood correctly in isolation from one another. This analysis maintains that poor nations are not simply lagging behind rich ones on a linear "path of progress." Rather, the increasing prosperity of the high-income countries came largely at the expense of low-income societies. In short, then, some nations became rich *only because other nations became poor*. Both are products of the onset of global commerce that began half a millennium ago.

The Importance of Colonialism

Late in the fifteenth century, Europeans began surveying North America to the west, the massive continent of Africa to the south, and the vast expanse of Asia to the east. Conventional history heralds great explorers such as Christopher Columbus, who sailed westward from Spain in 1492 in search of the Orient. But what Europeans celebrated as "the discovery of the New World" might more correctly be described as the systematic conquest of one region of the world by another (Sale, 1990; Gray, 1991).

Colonization brought vast wealth to European nations. By the nineteenth century, in fact, most of the world had come under the domination of European governments. Spain and Portugal colonized nearly all of Latin America from the sixteenth until the mid-nineteenth centuries. By the beginning of the twentieth century, Great Britain boasted, "The sun never sets on the British Empire." The United States, itself originally thirteen small British colonies on the eastern seaboard, pushed across the continent, purchased Alaska, gained control of Haiti, Puerto Rico, and part of Cuba as well as Guam, the Philippines, and the Hawaiian Islands.

Elsewhere, Europeans in collaboration with Africans initiated a brutal form of human exploitation—the slave trade, which persisted from about 1500 until 1850. But even as the world was rejecting the practice of slavery, Europeans rapidly seized control of Africa itself. As Figure 11–4 shows, Europeans dominated most of the continent, and did so until the early 1960s.

During the last several decades, overt colonialism has largely disappeared from the world. However, according to dependency theory, *political* liberation has not translated into *economic* autonomy. Far from it. Poor societies maintain economic relationships with rich nations that reproduce the pattern of colonial exploitation. This neocolonialism is fueled by a capitalist world economy.

Wallerstein's Capitalist World Economy

Immanuel Wallerstein (1974, 1979, 1983, 1984) explains the origins of contemporary global inequality using a model of the "capitalist world economy."[4] Wallerstein's term *world economy* suggests that the productivity of all nations depends on the operation of a global economic network. He traces the roots of this global system to the economic expansion that began five hundred years ago as rich nations cast their eyes on the wealth of the rest of the world. Centered in the high-income countries, then, the dominant character of the world economy is capitalist.

Wallerstein calls rich nations the *core* of the world economy. Colonialism enriched this core by funneling raw materials from around the globe to Western Europe. Over the longer term, this wealth helped to ignite the Industrial Revolution. Formal colonialism may have ended, but multinational corporations still operate profitably around the world, drawing wealth to North America, Western Europe, and Japan.

Low-income countries represent the *periphery* of the world economy. Originally drawn into this system by colonial exploitation, poor nations continue to support rich ones by providing inexpensive labor, easy access to raw materials, and vast markets for industrial products. A remaining category of countries includes

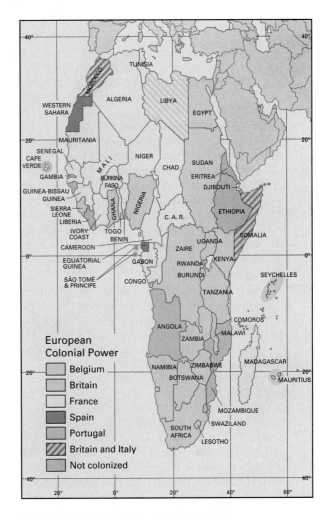

FIGURE 11–4 Africa's Colonial History

those on the *semiperiphery* of the world economy, including middle-income countries like Portugal and South Korea that have closer ties to the global economic core.

According to Wallerstein, the world economy benefits rich societies (by generating profits) and harms the rest of the world (by perpetuating poverty). In short, the world economy imposes a state of dependency on poor nations, which remain under the control of rich ones. This dependency turns on the following three factors:

1. **Narrow, export-oriented economies**. Unlike the diversified economies of core nations, production in poor countries centers on a few raw materials

---

[4]While based on Wallerstein's ideas, this section also reflects the work of Frank (1980, 1981), Delacroix & Ragin (1981), and Bergesen (1983).

GLOBAL: Some poor countries (such as Nicaragua, Mozambique, and Tanzania) have external debt that runs several times higher than annual GNP. Nicaragua's long-term debt of some $9 billion amounts to more than $2,000 per person. With a per capita GNP of $340, people owe many years' income.

Q: On foreign debt in poor countries: "Through this mechanism, the means intended for the development of peoples has turned into

a brake upon development instead, and indeed in some cases has even aggravated underdevelopment." Pope John Paul II, *The Social Concerns of the Church*

NOTE: Arguing that the capitalist world economy is harmful to poor nations, André Gunder Frank maintains that the economies of poor societies have grown mostly during periods of global crisis, such as world wars.

or agricultural products that colonial powers forced laborers to extract or farmers to grow for export. Coffee and fruits from Latin American nations, oil from Nigeria, hardwoods from the Philippines, and palm oil from Malaysia are some of the products central to the economies of these poor societies.

Multinational corporations maintain this pattern today by purchasing raw materials cheaply in poor societies and transporting them to core societies where factories process them for profitable sale. Corporations thus discourage production of food or goods needed by local people in poor nations. These corporations also own a great deal of land and have transformed traditional farmers into low-paid farm laborers. Overall, then, rich nations effectively prevent poor ones from developing industries of their own.

2. **Lack of industrial capacity.** Without an industrial base, poor societies face a double bind. Not only do they count on rich nations to buy their inexpensive raw materials but they also depend on rich nations to sell them whatever expensive manufactured goods they can afford.

In a classic example of this double dependency, British colonialists allowed the people of India to raise cotton, and then shipped Indian cotton back to the English textile mills in Birmingham and Manchester. There, English industrialists wove it into cloth, and traders shipped the finished goods back for profitable sale in India.

Dependency theorists also blast the Green Revolution, widely praised by modernization theorists. To promote agricultural productivity, poor countries end up buying expensive fertilizers, pesticides, and mechanical equipment from core nations. Typically, rich countries profit more from "high-tech" farming in poor societies than do the poor nations themselves.

3. **Foreign debt.** Such unequal trade patterns have plunged poor countries deeper and deeper into debt to industrialized societies. Collectively, the poor nations of the world owe rich countries more than $1 trillion, including hundreds of billions of dollars owed to the United States alone (The World Bank, 1993). This staggering debt is a financial burden few poor societies can bear. Excessive debt, which drains the resources of any society, can destabilize a poor country's economy, making matters worse for nations already reeling from high unemployment and rampant inflation (Walton & Ragin, 1990).

Moreover, the debt crisis requires continuous transfers of wealth from poor to rich societies—roughly $50 billion annually (United Nations Development Programme, 1993)—further impoverishing peripheral societies and increasing their dependency on rich nations. This onerous debt, say dependency theorists, plays into the vicious cycle that makes rich nations richer and poor nations poorer.

Seeing no way out of the "debt trap," some low-income countries have simply stopped making payments. Cuba, for example, refused to make further payments on its $7 billion foreign debt a decade ago. Because failure to repay loans threatens economic growth in rich countries, the United States and other rich nations strongly oppose such actions and have advanced various programs to refinance these debts.

The Role of Rich Nations

Nowhere is the difference between modernization theory and dependency theory sharper than in the role each assigns to rich nations. In investigating the sources of global stratification, modernization theory highlights the *production of wealth*. From this point of view, when rich societies create new wealth through technological innovation, this process does not harm other nations. On the contrary, as rich nations export productive technology and pro-growth attitudes, modernization theorists assert, poor nations will benefit.

By contrast, dependency theory envisions global inequality in terms of the *distribution of wealth*. This approach contends that rich societies have unjustly seized the wealth of the world for their own purposes. That is, the *over*development of some parts of the globe is directly tied to the *under*development of the rest of it.

Dependency theorists dismiss the idea that strategies proposed by rich countries to control population or to boost agricultural and industrial output will help poor countries. They contend that, far from benefiting the vast majority of people in poor societies, such programs provide profits to rich countries (through purchases of high technology), while rewarding not the poor majority but ruling elites who maintain a favorable "business climate" for multinational corporations (Lappé, Collins, & Kinley, 1981).

Hunger activists Frances Moore Lappé and Joseph Collins (1986) claim that the capitalist culture of the United States lulls people into thinking that absolute poverty is somehow inevitable. Following this line of reasoning, poverty results from "natural"

NOTE: Some analysts distinguish between multinational and global corporations. MNCs merely extract raw materials and labor from a poor nation. Global corporations also locate research and development facilities in the local country, which stimulates more economic development. One global corporation is Hewlett Packard, which established a major research and development center in Guadalajara, Mexico.

GLOBAL: Inflation in many poor societies makes it difficult simply to maintain one's standard of living. In Argentina, for example, annual inflation has at times soared to 80,000%.

NOTE: In Lenin's view, Marxist revolutions did not occur in rich societies because international capitalism raised living standards at home by exploiting colonies abroad.

After decades of war and communist rule, Vietnam is now attracting foreign investment, evident in the new high-rise hotels going up in Saigon (Ho Chi Minh City). Will this inflow of capital raise living standards, as modernization theory contends, or block development, as dependency theory maintains?

processes including having too many children and from natural disasters such as droughts. But they challenge this kind of thinking, pointing out that the world produces enough grain so every man, woman, and child could consume 3,600 calories a day, sufficient to make everyone on the planet overweight! Even most of the poorest societies grow enough to feed their people. The problem, therefore, is not production but poverty: Too many people cannot afford to buy available food. This skewed distribution of wealth—including food resources—means that millions in India suffer from malnutrition while this Asian nation *exports* beef, wheat, and rice. Similarly, millions of children go hungry in Africa, a vast continent whose agricultural abundance also makes it a net food exporter.

According to Lappé and Collins, the contradiction of poverty amid plenty stems from the policy of producing food for profits, not people. That is, corporations in rich nations collaborate with elites in poor countries to grow profitable crops for export. Thus, coffee is grown in much of Latin America instead of corn and beans, which are the staples for local consumption. Governments of poor societies often support the practice of growing for export rather than local consumption because food profits help to repay massive foreign debt. The problem is complex, but its core, according to Lappé and Collins, is the global capitalist economic system.

Critical evaluation. The central assertion of dependency theory is that the world's wealth and poverty both result from one interconnected system of global stratification. Citing Latin America and other poor regions of the world, dependency theorists claim that development simply cannot proceed under the constraints presently imposed by rich countries. Addressing global poverty, they conclude, demands more than change within poor societies. Rather, these theorists call for radical reform of the entire world economy so that it operates in the interests of the majority of people.

Critics of the dependency approach identify some important weaknesses in this analysis. First, they charge, dependency theory wrongly contends that the wealth of the high-income nations resulted from stealing resources from poor societies. Farmers, small business owners, and industrialists can and do create new wealth through their imagination and drive. Put another way, wealth is not a zero-sum resource by which some gain only at the expense of others; the entire world's wealth expanded fivefold since 1950, largely due to technological advances and other innovations.

Second, critics reason, if dependency theory were correct in condemning rich nations for creating global poverty, then nations with the strongest ties to rich societies would be among the poorest. However, the low-income countries of the world (like Ethiopia) have had relatively little contact with rich countries. Similarly, critics continue, a long history of trade with rich countries has dramatically improved the economies of nations such as Singapore (a former British colony),

South Korea, Japan, and Hong Kong (since 1842 a British colony that reverts to the People's Republic of China in 1997). In addition, an increasing body of evidence indicates that foreign investment by rich nations fosters economic growth, as modernization theory claims, not economic decline, as dependency theorists assert (Vogel, 1991; Firebaugh, 1992).

Third, critics charge that dependency theory simplistically points the finger at a single factor—world capitalism—as the sole cause of global inequality (Worsley, 1990). By directing attention only to forces outside of poor societies, dependency theory casts poor societies as innocent victims, ignoring factors *inside* these countries that contribute to their economic plight. Sociologists have long recognized the vital role of culture in shaping human behavior. Cultural patterns vary greatly around the world; some societies embrace change readily while others staunchly resist economic development. As we noted earlier, for example, Iran's brand of Islamic fundamentalism has deliberately discouraged economic ties with other countries. Capitalist societies, then, hardly need accept the blame for Iran's economic stagnation.

Nor can rich societies be saddled with responsibility for the reckless behavior of some foreign leaders. Members of poor societies have had to pick up the costs of far-reaching corruption and self-serving military campaigns that have marked the regimes of Ferdinand Marcos in the Philippines, François Duvalier in Haiti, Manuel Noriega in Panama, Mobutu Sese Seko in Zaire, and Saddam Hussein in Iraq. Governments have even withheld food supplies for leverage in internal political struggles as we have seen in the African nations of Ethiopia, Sudan, and Somalia. Other regimes throughout Latin America, Africa, and Asia have failed to support programs to improve the status of women and control population growth.

Fourth, critics chide dependency theorists for downplaying the economic dependency fostered by the former Soviet Union. The Soviet army seized control of most of Eastern Europe during World War II and subsequently dominated the Eastern Bloc nations politically and economically. Many consider the uprisings between 1989 and 1991 against Soviet-installed leaders and the Soviet government itself as popular rejection of a vast Soviet colonial system.

A fifth criticism of dependency theory faults this approach for offering only vague prescriptions for remedying global poverty. Most dependency theorists urge poor societies to sever economic ties to rich countries, and some call for nationalizing foreign-owned industries. Dependency theory implies that the path to ending global poverty begins with the overthrow of international capitalism. At its core, say the critics, dependency theory advocates some sort of world socialism. In light of the failure of government-run socialist societies to meet the needs of their own people, critics ask, should we really expect such a system to lift the entire world toward prosperity?

GLOBAL INEQUALITY: LOOKING AHEAD

Among the most important trends of recent decades is the development of a global economy, which is exacerbating inequality both within our country and around the world. Profitable investments, many of them in poor nations, and lucrative sales by U.S. companies to foreign interests have brought greater affluence to those who already have substantial wealth. At the same time, increasing industrial production abroad has cut factory jobs in this country, exerting downward pressure on wages. The net result: gradual economic polarization in the United States.

Yet looking beyond our own borders, social inequality is far more striking in global context, as this chapter has noted. The concentration of wealth among high-income countries, coupled with the grinding poverty typical of low-income nations, may well constitute the most important dilemma facing humanity in the twenty-first century. To some analysts, rich nations hold the keys to ending world poverty; to others, they are the cause of this tragic problem.

Faced with two radically different approaches to understanding global inequality, we might well wonder which one is "right." As with many controversies in sociology, each view has some merit as well as its own limitations. Table 11–2 summarizes important arguments made by advocates of each approach.

In searching for truth, we must consider empirical evidence. In some regions of the world, such as the "Pacific Rim" of eastern Asia, the market forces endorsed by modernization theory are raising living standards rapidly and substantially. Many Latin American nations (such as Colombia and Chile) also have recorded strong economic growth in recent years. Meanwhile, however, other poor societies, especially in Africa, are experiencing economic turmoil that frustrates hopes for market-based development.

The poor countries that have surged ahead economically have two factors in common. First, they are relatively small. Combined, the Asian nations of South Korea, Taiwan, Hong Kong, Singapore, and Japan

GLOBAL: The United Nations (1994) offers ratios comparing all developing countries to all rich countries (rich baseline = 100) for various social indicators. Life expectancy: 1960, 67; 1992, 84; under-five infant mortality, 80 to 92; daily calorie supply, 72 to 81; access to safe water, 36 to 70; adult literacy, 41 to 71.

NOTE: Many products from rich countries—electricity, technology, communications equipment—are getting cheaper, which helps

raise living standards abroad. The manufactured goods–raw goods exchange rate, in other words, has improved over time.

NOTE: While the *economic* gap between rich and poor countries has remained stable, the divide is narrowing between the two categories of nations on many *social* indicators. This is because rising income in both rich and poor nations produces greater improvement in living standards for lower-income countries.

TABLE 11–2 Modernization Theory and Dependency Theory: A Summary

	Modernization Theory	Dependency Theory
Historical pattern	The entire world was poor just two centuries ago; the Industrial Revolution brought affluence to high-income countries; as industrialization gradually transforms poor societies, all nations are likely to become more equal and alike.	Global parity was disrupted by colonialism, which made some countries rich while simultaneously making other countries poor; barring radical change in the world capitalist system, rich nations will grow richer and poor nations will become poorer.
Primary causes of global poverty	Characteristics of poor societies cause their poverty, including lack of industrial technology, traditional cultural patterns that discourage innovation, and rapid population growth.	Global economic relations—historical colonialism and the operation of multinational corporations—have enriched high-income countries while placing low-income countries in a state of economic dependency.
Role of rich nations	Rich countries can and do assist poor nations through programs of population control, technology transfers that increase food production and stimulate industrial development, and investment capital in the form of foreign aid.	Rich countries have concentrated global resources, conferring advantages on themselves while generating massive foreign debt in low-income countries; rich nations impede the economic development of poor nations.

cover only about one-fifth of the land area and population of India. The economic problems smaller countries face are more manageable; consequently, small societies more effectively administer programs of development. Second, these "best-case" nations have cultural traits in common, especially traditions emphasizing individual achievement and economic success. In other areas of the world, where powerful cultural forces inhibit change and individualism, even smaller nations have failed to turn economic opportunities to their advantage.

The picture now emerging calls into question arguments put forward by both modernization and dependency theories. Theorists for both camps, for instance, are revising their views of the major "paths to development." On the one hand, few societies seeking economic growth now favor a market economy completely free of government control. This view challenges orthodox modernization theory, which endorses a free-market approach to development. On the other hand, recent upheavals in the former Soviet Union and Eastern Europe demonstrate that a global reevaluation of socialism is currently under way. These events, following decades of poor economic performance and political repression, make many poor societies reluctant to consider a government-mandated path to development. Because dependency theory has historically supported socialist economic systems, changes in world socialism will surely generate new thinking here as well.

Hunger is one problem caused by absolute poverty. As the box explains, many analysts wonder if we have the technological means and political will to address it effectively before it overwhelms much of the world.

Although the world's future remains uncertain, we have learned a great deal about global stratification. One key insight, offered by modernization theory, is that poverty is partly a *problem of technology*. A higher standard of living for a surging world population depends on raising agricultural and industrial productivity. A second insight, derived from dependency theory, is that global inequality is also a *political issue*. Even with higher productivity, the human community must address crucial questions concerning how resources are distributed—both within societies and around the globe.

Note, too, that while economic development increases living standards, it also places greater strains on the natural environment. Imagine, for example, if almost 1 billion people in India were suddenly to become "middle class," with automobiles guzzling gasoline and spewing hydrocarbons into the atmosphere.

Finally, the vast gulf that separates the world's richest and poorest people puts everyone at greater risk of war, as those with little act to challenge the social arrangements that threaten their very lives. In the long run, we can achieve peace on this planet only by ensuring that all people enjoy a significant measure of dignity and security.

Q: "For hunger is a curious thing: At first it is with you all the time, waking and sleeping and in your dreams, and your belly cries out incessantly, and there is a gnawing and a pain . . . Then the pain is no longer sharp but dull, and this too is with you always so that you think of food many times a day . . . Then that too is gone, all pain, all desire, only a great emptiness is left, like the sky, like a well in drought, and it is now that the strength drains from your limbs . . ."

Kamala Markandaya, *Nectar in a Sieve*

Q: "One billion more people are being fed today than in the early 1970s, but the number of hungry people continues to increase." John W. Helmuth

NOTE: Crudely speaking, the "optimists" in the world hunger debate lean toward modernization theory; the "pessimists" typically favor dependency theory.

Controversy & Debate

Will the World Starve?

The animals' feet leave their
    prints on the desert's face.
Hunger is so real, so very real,
that it can make you walk around
    a barren tree looking for
    nourishment.
Not once,
Not twice,
Not thrice . . .

These lines, by Indian poet Amit Jayaram, describe the appalling hunger found in Rajasthan, in northwest India. As this chapter has explained, however, hunger casts its menacing shadow not only over regions of Asia, but also over much of Latin America, most of Africa, and even parts of North America. Throughout the world, hundreds of millions of adults do not consume enough food to enable them to work. And, most tragically, some ten million of the world's children die each year because they do not get enough to eat.

At the closing of the last century, humankind took a major step forward by abolishing slavery almost everywhere on the planet. As we near the end of this century, however, what are the prospects for eradicating the wretched misery of human beings enduring daily hunger?

It is easy to be pessimistic. For one thing, the population of poor countries is currently increasing by 90 million people annually—equivalent to adding another Mexico to the world every year. Poor countries can scarcely feed the people they have now; looking ahead a generation to the future, how will they ever feed *double* their current populations?

In addition, as detailed in Chapter 22 ("Environment and Society"), hunger forces poor people to exploit the earth's resources by using short-term strategies for food production that will lead to long-term disaster. For example, to feed the swelling populations of poor, tropical countries, farmers are cutting rain forests in order to increase their farmland. But, without the protective canopy of trees, it is only a matter of time before much of this land turns to desert.

Taken together, rising populations and ecological approaches that borrow against the future raise the specter of hunger and outright starvation escalating well beyond current levels. Regarded pessimistically, the world's future is bleak: unprecedented hunger, human misery, and political calamity.

But there are also some grounds for optimism. Thanks to the Green Revolution, food production the world over is up sharply over the last

SUMMARY

1. In global perspective, social stratification is more pronounced than in the United States. About 15 percent of the world's people live in industrialized, high-income countries and take in 55 percent of the earth's total income. Another one-third of humanity live in middle-income countries with limited industrialization, receiving about 37 percent of all income. Half the world's population live in low-income countries that have yet to industrialize; they earn only 8 percent of global income.

2. While relative poverty is found everywhere, poor societies contend with widespread, absolute poverty. Worldwide, the lives of some 800 million people are at risk. About 15 million people, most of them children, die of starvation every year.

3. Women are more likely than men to be poor nearly everywhere in the world. Gender bias against women is much greater in poor, agrarian societies than it is in industrial societies such as the United States.

4. The poverty found in much of the world is a complex problem reflecting limited industrial technology, rapid population growth, traditional cultural patterns, internal social stratification, male domination, and global power relationships.

5. Modernization theory maintains that successful development hinges on acquiring advanced productive technology. This approach views traditional cultural patterns as the key barrier to modernization.

Q: "Current leftist journals are full of tortured attempts to interpret the developments of the last few years in Europe and elsewhere, most of them attempts to deny the obvious. I have every expectation that sociologists will be whole-hearted participants in this enterprise, bravely led by the old cohorts of dependency theory." Peter Berger (1992)

GLOBAL: Some students think of linguistic pluralism as a mark of underdevelopment. That is, while industrial regions of the world have few languages, less-developed regions have many local tongues. This notion does not hold up well to scrutiny, however. Compare Europe and South Asia: Each covers about 3 million square miles and encompasses just over 30 nations, and in each region the population speaks almost 30 different languages.

fifty years, even outpacing the growth in population. Taking a broader view, the world's economic productivity has risen steadily, so that the average person on the planet has more income now to purchase food and other necessities than ever before.

This growth has increased daily calorie intake as well as life expectancy, access to safe water, and adult literacy, while infant mortality is going down. In fact, looking at these social indicators, we can see the gap between rich and poor countries actually narrowing.

So what are the prospects for eradicating world hunger—especially in low-income nations? Overall, we see less hunger in both rich and poor countries, that is, a smaller *share* of the world's people faces starvation now than, say, in 1960. But as global population increases, with 90 percent of children born in middle- and low-income countries, the *number* of lives at risk is as great today as ever before. Moreover, even though living

standards are rising, there has not been any narrowing of the economic gap between rich and poor countries.

Also bear in mind that aggregate data mask different trends in various world regions. The "best-case" region of the world is eastern Asia, where incomes (controlled for inflation) have tripled over the last generation. It is to Asia that the "optimists" in the global hunger debate typically turn for evidence that poor countries can and do raise living standards and reduce hunger. The "worst-case" region of the world is sub-Saharan Africa, where living standards have actually fallen over the last decade, and more and more people are pushed to the brink of starvation. It is here that high technology is least evident and birth rates are highest. Pessimists typically look to Africa when they argue that poor countries are losing ground in the struggle to keep their people well nourished.

Television brings home the tragedy of hunger every year or so

when news cameras focus on starving people in places like Ethiopia and Somalia. But hunger—and the early death from illness that it brings on—is the plight of millions all year round. The world does have the technical means to feed everyone; the question is do we have the moral determination to do so?

Continue the debate . . .

1. *In your opinion, what are the primary causes of global hunger?*

2. *Do you place responsibility for solving this problem on poor countries or rich ones? Why?*

3. *Do you expect the extent of global hunger to increase or decrease? Why?*

Sources: United Nations Development Programme (1994, 1995).

6. Modernization theorist W. W. Rostow identifies four stages of development: traditional, take-off, drive to technological maturity, and high mass consumption.

7. Arguing that rich societies have the keys to creating wealth, modernization theory cites four ways rich nations can assist poor nations: by bolstering population-control strategies, providing crop-enhancing technologies, encouraging industrial development, and providing investment capital and other foreign aid.

8. Critics of modernization theory maintain that this approach has produced limited economic development in the world, while ethnocentrically assuming that poor societies can follow the path to development taken by rich nations centuries ago.

9. Dependency theory claims that global wealth and poverty are directly linked to the historical operation of the capitalist world economy.

10. The dependency of poor countries on rich ones is rooted in colonialism. Even though most poor countries have won political independence, dependency theorists argue, neocolonialism persists as a form of exploitation carried out by multinational corporations.

11. Immanuel Wallerstein views the high-income countries as the privileged "core" of the capitalist world economy; middle-income nations are the "semiperiphery"; poor societies form the global "periphery."

12. Three factors—export-oriented economies, a lack of industrial capacity, and foreign debt—perpetuate poor countries' dependency on rich nations.

13. Critics of dependency theory argue that this approach overlooks the success of many nations in creating new wealth. Total global wealth, they point out, has increased fivefold since 1950. Furthermore, contrary to the implications of dependency theory, the world's poorest societies are not those with the strongest ties to rich countries.

14. Both modernization and dependency approaches offer useful insights into the development of global inequality. Some evidence supports each view. Less controversial is the urgent need to address the various problems caused by worldwide poverty.

KEY CONCEPTS

colonialism the process by which some nations enrich themselves through political and economic control of other countries

dependency theory a model of economic and social development that explains global inequality in terms of the historical exploitation of poor societies by rich ones

modernization theory a model of economic and social development that explains global inequality in terms of differing levels of technological development among societies

multinational corporation a large corporation that operates in many different countries

neocolonialism a new form of global power relationships that involves not direct political control but economic exploitation by multinational corporations

CRITICAL-THINKING QUESTIONS

1. Do you think advertising (for coffee from Colombia or exotic vacations to Egypt or India) provides an accurate picture of life in low-income countries? Why or why not? Do you think most people in the United States have a realistic understanding of the extent and severity of poverty in the world?

2. Distinguish between relative and absolute poverty. How do the two concepts apply to social stratification in the United States and the world as a whole?

3. Why do many analysts argue that economic development in low-income countries depends on raising the social standing of women?

4. State the basic tenets of modernization theory and dependency theory, and then spell out several criticisms of each approach.

SUGGESTED READINGS

Classic Sources

W. W. Rostow. *The Stages of Economic Growth: A Non-Communist Manifesto.* Cambridge, U.K.: Cambridge University Press, 1960.
  Although this book draws on the thinking of several classic sociologists (including Emile Durkheim and

Max Weber), it represents the first systematic statement of modernization theory.

Frantz Fanon. *The Wretched of the Earth.* New York: Grove Press, 1963.
  This classic analysis highlights the role of colonization, nationalism, and violence in the Algerian struggle for independence.

Contemporary Sources

United Nations Development Programme. *Human Development Report, 1995.* New York: Oxford University Press, 1995.

The World Bank. *World Development Report 1995: Workers in an Integrating World.* New York: Oxford University Press, 1995.

These two annual publications provide a wide range of data on the comparative economic development of the world's nations.

Frances Moore Lappé and Joseph Collins. *World Hunger: Twelve Myths.* New York: Grove Press/Food First Books, 1986.

Peter Berger. *The Capitalist Revolution: Fifty Propositions about Prosperity, Equality, and Liberty.* New York: Basic Books, 1986.

The first of these two books, by two long-time hunger activists, is guided by dependency theory. The second, by a well-known contemporary sociologist, argues the merits of modernization theory.

Global Sources

Nancy Scheper-Hughes. *Death Without Weeping: The Violence of Everyday Life in Brazil.* Berkeley: University of California Press, 1992.

Offering a moving portrait of suffering in the shantytowns of Brazil, this researcher identifies strongly with her subjects and makes an outspoken call for change.

Catherine A. Lutz and Jane L. Collins. *Reading "National Geographic."* Chicago: University of Chicago Press, 1993.

Reviewing more than thirty years of popular *National Geographic* magazines, these researchers argue that this prominent publication presents a sugar-coated vision of life in poor countries.

**HORACE PIPPIN,
MR. PREJUDICE, 1943**

Oil on canvas, 18"x14", Philadelphia Museum of Art:
Gift of Dr. and Mrs. Matthew T. Moore. Photo by
Graydon Wood, 1995.

Race and Ethnicity

On a bright, early years ago, in the city of walked hand-in-hand with his school four blocks from their home. fall day more than forty Topeka, Kansas, a minister daughter to an elementary Linda Brown wanted to enroll in the second grade, but the school refused to admit her. Instead, public-school officials required her to attend another school two miles away, which meant a daily six-block walk to a bus stop where she sometimes waited half an hour for the bus. In bad weather, Linda Brown would be soaking wet by the time the bus came; one day she became so cold at the bus stop that she walked back home. Why, she asked her parents, could she not attend the school only four blocks away?

The answer—difficult for loving parents to give their child—was Linda Brown's introduction to a harsh reality: Skin color made her a second-class citizen in the United States. Her parents began to speak to others in the African-American community about the injustice of preventing black children such as Linda from enrolling in nearby schools attended by white children. Ultimately, a lawsuit went forward on behalf of Linda Brown and several other children and, in 1954, the young girl's question about schooling and skin color was put to the Supreme Court of the United States. In *Brown* v. *the Board of Education of Topeka*, the Supreme Court ruled unanimously that racially segregated schools inevitably provide African Americans with inferior schooling, striking down the historic doctrine of supposedly "separate but equal" education for the two races.

Many people greeted the Supreme Court's *Brown* decision as a great turning point in this country's history, mandating that public education become color blind. Yet, more than four decades later, most U.S. children still attend racially imbalanced schools. Indeed, in a society officially committed to the notion that all people are created equal, race and ethnicity continue to guide the lives of men, women, and children in all sorts of ways.

Globally, the pattern of inequality and conflict based on color and culture is even more pronounced. With the collapse of the former Soviet empire, Ukrainians, Moldavians, Azerbaijanis, and a host of other ethnic peoples in Eastern Europe are struggling to recover their cultural identity after decades of Soviet subjugation. In the Middle East, deep-rooted friction divides Arabs and Jews, while blacks and whites strive to establish a just society in South Africa. In the African nation of Rwanda, the Asian countries of India and Sri Lanka, in the Balkans, and elsewhere in the world, racial and ethnic rifts frequently flare into violent confrontation.

Q: "You cannot become thorough Americans if you think of your-selves in groups. America does not consist of groups. A man who thinks of himself as belonging to a particular national group has not yet become an American." Woodrow Wilson

NOTE: "Race" is derived from Latin meaning "root"; "ethnic" is derived from the Greek, meaning "culture" or "people"; "minority" has a Latin root meaning "smaller" or "lesser."

Q: "The problem of the twentieth century is the problem of the color-line." W. E. B. Du Bois

DIVERSITY: Of the 133,000 interracial births in 1994, black/white couples account for 56,000; Asian/white, 42,000; Native American/white, 22,000; Asian/black, 4,000; Native American/black, 1,500; Native American/Asian, 800; other or unknown, 6,700. (National Center for Health Statistics)

Surely one of the greatest ironies of the human condition is that color and culture—traits that are the roots of our greatest pride—are also those that most often foment hatred and violence and propel us into war. This chapter examines the meaning of race and ethnicity, explains how these social constructs have shaped our history, and suggests why they continue to play such a central part—for better or worse—in the world today.

THE SOCIAL SIGNIFICANCE OF RACE AND ETHNICITY

People in the United States and elsewhere in the world frequently use the terms "race" and "ethnicity" imprecisely and interchangeably. For this reason, we begin with important definitions.

Race

A **race** is *a category composed of people who share biologically transmitted traits that members of a society deem socially significant.* People may classify each other into races based on physical characteristics such as skin color, facial features, hair texture, and body shape.

Racial diversity appeared among our human ancestors as a result of living in different geographical regions of the world. In regions of intense heat, for example, people developed darker skin (from the natural pigment, melanin) that offers protection from the sun; in regions with moderate climates, humans have lighter skin. But such differences are superficial; individuals of all races are members of a single biological species.

People the world over display a bewildering array of racial traits. This variety is the product of migration and intermarriage over the course of human history, so that many genetic characteristics once common to a single place are now evident throughout the world. The most striking racial variation appears in the Middle East (that is, western Asia), that has long served as a "crossroads" of human migration. Striking racial uniformity, by contrast, characterizes more isolated peoples such as the island-dwelling Japanese. But no society lacks genetic mixture, and increasing contact among the world's people will ensure that racial blending will accelerate in the future.

Nineteenth-century biologists responded to the world's racial diversity by developing a three-part scheme of racial classifications. They labeled people with relatively light skin and fine hair as *Caucasian*; they called those with darker skin and coarser, curlier hair *Negroid*; and people with yellow or brown skin and distinctive folds on the eyelids were termed *Mongoloid*.

Sociologists consider such categories misleading, at best, since we now know that no society is composed of biologically pure individuals. In fact, the world traveler notices gradual and subtle racial variations from region to region. The people we might call "Caucasian" (or "Indo-Europeans" or, more commonly, "white people") actually display skin color that ranges from very light (typical in Scandinavia) to very dark (widespread in southern India). We also find the same variation among so-called "Negroids" ("Africans," or more commonly, "black people") and "Mongoloids" (that is, "Asians"). In fact, many "white people" of southern India actually have darker skin than many "black people," including the blond Negroid aborigines of Australia.

Although in the United States we readily distinguish "black" and "white" people, research confirms that our population is genetically mixed. Over many generations, the biological traits of Negroid Africans, Caucasian Europeans, and Mongoloid Native Americans (whose ancestors were Asian) spread widely throughout the Americas. Many "black" people, therefore, have a significant proportion of Caucasian genes, and many "white" people have some Negroid genes. In short, no matter what people may think, race is no black-and-white issue.

Despite the reality of biological mixing, however, people in the United States and around the world are quick to classify each other racially and rank these categories in systems of social inequality. As explained presently, people may also defend racial hierarchy with assertions that one category is inherently "better" or more intelligent than another, although no sound scientific research supports such beliefs. But, because so much is at stake, it is no wonder that societies strive to make racial labeling much more clear than facts permit. Earlier in this century, for example, many southern states legally defined as "colored" anyone who had as little as one thirty-second African ancestry (that is, one African-American great-great-great grandparent). Today, with less of a caste distinction in the United States, the law enables parents to declare the race of a child, if they wish to do so at all.

Indeed, some analysts point out that, in the United States, the concept of race has less and less meaning. For one thing, the number of officially recorded interracial births has doubled in the last fifteen years to 133,000 a year, accounting now for 4 percent of all

GLOBAL: Morocco is a country with a high level of racial mix—southern African, European, and Middle Eastern. Brazil represents another highly varied case with a population descended from all continents.

GLOBAL: Beyond skin color, another racial difference involves height. The Masai of eastern Africa are tall and thin (which helps to dissipate heat in that equatorial climate); the Eskimos and Aleuts of North America, by contrast, are short and stout, which serves to protect them in a far colder habitat.

NOTE: The faces shown below are from Taiwan, Ireland, Botswana, India, Peru, and Egypt.

NOTE: Underlying the trend favoring interracial marriages is the rising affluence of African Americans: 1 of 6 black families earns more than $50,000 annually, compared to 1 in 17 in 1970.

The range of biological variation in human beings is far greater than any system of racial classification allows. This fact is made obvious by trying to place all of the people pictured here into simple racial categories.

births. Moreover, when completing their 1990 census forms, almost 10 million people refused to describe themselves by checking a single racial category. The Census Bureau is likely to respond to the growing racial complexity of our society by adding a new "multiracial" option in the near future (Sandor, 1994; Kalish, 1995).

Ethnicity

Ethnicity is *a shared cultural heritage*. Members of an *ethnic category* have common ancestors, language, or religion that, together, confer a distinctive social identity. The forebears of Polish, Latino, and Chinese Americans, for example, retain cultural patterns rooted in particular areas of the world. More than 30 million people in the United States speak some language other than English in their homes. Moreover, while the United States and Canada are predominantly Protestant societies, most Americans of Spanish, Italian, and Polish ancestry are Roman Catholic, while others of Greek, Ukrainian, and Russian ancestry are members of the Eastern Orthodox church. More than 6 million Jewish Americans (with ancestral ties to various nations) share a distinctive religious history. Similarly, several million women and men in the United States have a Muslim heritage.

Race and ethnicity, then, are quite different, since one is biological and the other is cultural. But the two sometimes go hand in hand. Japanese Americans, for example, have distinctive physical traits and—for those who maintain a traditional way of life—cultural attributes as well. But ethnic distinctiveness should not be viewed as racial. For example, Jews are sometimes described as a race although they are distinctive only in their religious beliefs as well as their history of persecution (Goldsby, 1977).

Finally, ethnicity involves even more variability and mixture than race does, for most people identify with more than one ethnic background, (a person might claim to be, say, German and English). Moreover, people may intentionally modify their ethnicity over time. Some Polish immigrants to the United States gradually shed their cultural background, becoming less

TABLE 12–1 Racial and Ethnic Categories in the United States, 1990

Racial or Ethnic Classification	Approximate U.S. Population	Percent of Total Population
African descent	**29,986,060**	**12.1%**
Hispanic descent	**22,354,059**	**9.0**
Mexican	13,495,938	5.4
Puerto Rican	2,727,754	1.1
Cuban	1,043,932	0.4
Other Hispanic	5,086,435	2.1
Native-American descent	**1,959,234**	**0.8**
American Indian	1,878,285	0.8
Eskimo	57,152	<
Aleut	23,797	<
Asian or Pacific Islander descent	**7,273,662**	**2.9**
Chinese	1,645,472	0.7
Filipino	1,406,770	0.6
Japanese	847,562	0.3
Asian Indian	815,447	0.3
Korean	798,849	0.3
Vietnamese	614,547	0.2
Hawaiian	211,014	<
Samoan	62,964	<
Guamanian	49,345	<
Other Asian or Pacific Islander	821,692	0.3
European descent	**200,000,000**	**80.0**
German	57,947,000	23.3
Irish	38,736,000	15.6
English	32,652,000	13.1
Italian	14,665,000	5.9
French	10,321,000	4.1
Polish	9,366,000	3.8
Dutch	6,227,000	2.5
Scotch-Irish	5,618,000	2.3
Scottish	5,314,000	2.1
Swedish	4,681,000	1.9
Norwegian	3,869,000	1.6
Russian	2,953,000	1.2
Welsh	2,034,000	0.8
Danish	1,635,000	0.6
Hungarian	1,582,000	0.6

People of Hispanic descent can be of any race. Many people also identify with more than one ethnic category. Thus figures total more than 100 percent. White people represent 80 percent of the U.S. population.

< Indicates less than 1/10 of 1 percent.

Source: U.S. Bureau of the Census (1995).

"Polish" and absorbing new ethnic traits from others. In a reversal of this pattern, many people with Native-American ancestry recently have taken a renewed interest in their traditional ethnicity, enhancing this dimension of their identity (Nagel, 1994; Spencer, 1994).

Minorities

A racial or ethnic **minority**[1] is *a category of people, distinguished by physical or cultural traits, who are socially disadvantaged.* Distinct from the dominant "majority," in other words, minorities are set apart and subordinated. The breadth of the term "minority" has expanded in recent years beyond people with particular racial and ethnic traits to include people with physical disabilities; as the next chapter explains, some analysts view all women as minorities as well.

Table 12–1 presents the broad sweep of racial and ethnic diversity in the United States as recorded by the 1990 census. White people of non-Hispanic background continue to predominate numerically; about 80 percent of the national population falls into this broad category. But the absolute numbers and share of population for virtually every minority category grew rapidly during the 1980s. As the box explains, some researchers even project that the historical *minorities*, taken together, will constitute a *majority* of people in the United States sometime during the coming century.

Minorities have two major characteristics. First, they share a *distinctive identity*. Because race is highly visible (and virtually impossible for a person to change), minority men and women typically have a keen awareness of their physical distinctiveness. The significance of ethnicity (which people can change) is more variable. Throughout U.S. history, some people (many Reform Jews among them) have downplayed their historic ethnicity, while others (including many Orthodox Jews) have retained their cultural traditions and lived in distinctive ethnic enclaves.

A second characteristic of minorities is *subordination*. As the remainder of this chapter will demonstrate, U.S. minorities typically have lesser income, lower occupational prestige, and more limited schooling than their counterparts in the majority. With this in mind, we can see that class, race, and ethnicity, as well as gender, are not mutually exclusive issues but are overlapping and reinforcing dimensions of social stratification.

Of course, not all members of any minority category are disadvantaged. Some Latinos, for example, are quite wealthy, certain Chinese Americans are celebrated business leaders, and African Americans are included among our nation's leading scholars. But even

[1]We use the term "minority" rather than "minority group" in the interest of precision; as Chapter 7 ("Groups and Organizations") explains, minorities are categories, not groups.

SOCIAL DIVERSITY

The Coming Minority–Majority?

During the 1980s, Manhattan, the central borough of New York City, gained a *minority-majority*. This means that people of African, Asian, and Latino descent, together with other racial and ethnic minorities, became a majority of the population. As shown in National Map 12–1 on page 324, the same transformation has taken place in 186 counties across the United States (some 6 percent of the total). As early as 2050, according to some projections, minorities will represent a majority of the country.

A look at the 1990 census data confirms the prospect of a minority-majority. Between 1980 and 1990, the "majority" white, non-Hispanic population increased a modest 6 percent. The number of Asians or Pacific Islanders, however, more than doubled, soaring 108 percent. The Hispanic population increased by more than half (53 percent), and the number of Native Americans, Eskimos, or Aleuts jumped by 37 percent. African Americans increased their numbers by 13 percent—twice the white rate. This population growth is highly concentrated, however, with more than half the increase taking place in just three states: California, Florida, and Texas.

Not everyone accepts the conclusion that this country will have a minority-majority in the foreseeable future. Stephan Thernstrom (1990) points out that such a projection rests on two questionable assumptions. First, he explains, the U.S. immigration rate must remain at its current high level despite government projections of a coming downturn. Beyond that, he asks, who can be sure? Second, the high birth rates that characterize many immigrant minorities today must continue. But, Thernstrom points out, as the years pass, immigrants typically begin to behave more or less like everyone else.

But whatever the specific projections, few people doubt that a great change in the racial and ethnic profile of the United States is under way. It seems only a matter of time before people of European ancestry (other than Hispanics) will become minorities as a host of others—those often termed *people of color*—emerge as the majority in the United States.

---

the greatest success rarely allows individuals to transcend their minority standing (Benjamin, 1991). That is, race or ethnicity often serves as a *master status* (described in Chapter 6, "Social Interaction in Everyday Life") that overshadows personal accomplishments.

The term "minority" suggests that these categories of people constitute a small proportion of a society's population. But this is not always the case. For example, black South Africans are a numerical majority in their society, although they are grossly deprived of economic and political power by whites. In the United States, women represent slightly more than half the population but are still struggling to obtain opportunities and privileges enjoyed by men.

PREJUDICE

November 19, 1995, Jerusalem, Israel. Our taxi enters the outskirts of this historic city—a holy place to Jews, Christians, and Muslims. The mere presence of a small group of Ethiopians on the corner provokes a spirited eruption from Razi, our driver. "Those people over there," he begins, "they may be Jews, but they are different. They don't drive cars. They don't want to improve themselves. Even when the government offers them schooling, they don't take it." Shaking his head, he pronounces the Ethiopians "socially incorrigible."

Prejudice is *a rigid and irrational generalization about an entire category of people.* A prejudice is an attitude—a prejudgment—that one applies indiscriminately and inflexibly to some category with little regard for the facts. People commonly hold prejudices about individuals of a particular social class, sex, sexual orientation, age, political affiliation, race, or ethnicity.

Prejudices can be positive or negative. Our positive prejudices tend to exaggerate the virtues of people like ourselves, while our negative prejudices condemn those who differ from us. Negative prejudice runs

THE MAP: Minority-majority counties predominate in the South (where the proportion of African Americans historically has been high) and the Southwest (where immigration from Latin America and Asia has been pronounced).

DISCUSS: Consider how stereotypes figure in the following expressions: "Dutch treat," "French kiss," "Russian roulette," or "gypping" someone (derived from "Gypsy"). What traits make up

stereotypes concerning the Irish? Italians? English?

DIVERSITY: Stereotypes are shaped by cultural values; U.S. stereotypes tend to personally discredit disadvantaged people. Thus, many people stereotype the homeless as mentally ill (although only about one-third are). Likewise, the poor are stereotyped as lazy even though 17% of poor heads of households are full-time "working poor."

Seeing Ourselves

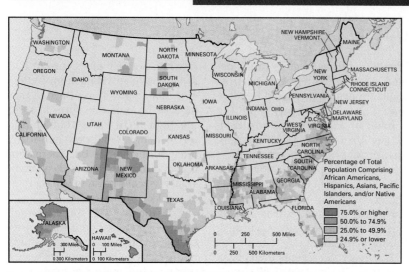

NATIONAL MAP 12–1

Where the Minority-Majority Already Exists

As recorded by the 1990 census, minorities predominate in 186 counties (out of 3,014). That is, the total number of African Americans, Asian Americans, Hispanics, and other minorities exceeds 50 percent of the population. The map also identifies some 40 counties in which minorities together exceed 75 percent of the population and more than 200 counties in which minority population surpasses the 25 percent mark. Why do you think most of these counties are in the South and Southwest?

Source: *Time,* July 12, 1993, p. 15. Copyright © 1993 Time Inc. Reprinted by permisson. Data from the 1990 decennial census.

along a continuum, ranging from mild aversion to outright hostility. Because attitudes are rooted in culture, everyone has at least some measure of prejudice.

Most people recognize that white people commonly hold prejudiced views of minorities. But minorities, too, harbor prejudices, sometimes of whites and often of other minorities. Some Koreans, for example, portray African Americans as being dishonest. African Americans, in turn, sometimes express much the same attitude with regard to Jewish people (Smith, 1996).

Stereotypes

Prejudices combine to form a *stereotype* (*stereo* is derived from Greek meaning "hard" or "solid"), described in Chapter 1 ("The Sociological Perspective") as *a prejudicial, exaggerated description of some category of people.* Because many stereotypes involve emotions like love and loyalty (generally toward members of ingroups) or hate and fear (toward outgroups), they are exaggerated images that are hard to change even in the face of contradictory evidence. For example, some people have a stereotypical understanding of the poor as lazy and irresponsible freeloaders who would rather rely on welfare than support themselves (Waxman, 1983; NORC, 1994). As Chapter 10 ("Social Class in the United States") explained, however, this

stereotype distorts reality since most poor people in the United States are children, working adults, or elderly people.

Stereotypes have been devised for virtually every racial and ethnic minority, and such attitudes may become deeply rooted in a society's culture. In the United States, half of white people stereotype African Americans as lacking motivation to improve their own lives (NORC, 1994:236). Such attitudes assume that social disadvantage is a matter of personal deficiency, which, in most cases, it is not. Moreover, stereotypes of this kind ignore the fact that most poor people in the United States are white and that most African Americans work as hard as anyone else and are *not* poor. In this case the bit of truth in the stereotype is that black people are more likely than white people to be poor (and slightly more likely, if poor, to receive welfare assistance). But by building a rigid attitude out of a few selected facts, stereotypes grossly distort reality.

Racism

A powerful and destructive form of prejudice, **racism** refers to *the belief that one racial category is innately superior or inferior to another.* Racism has pervaded world history. The ancient Greeks, the peoples of India, and the Chinese—despite their many notable achievements—

NOTE: Societies differ in the importance they attach to race. In our society, race has great importance, more than, say, nationality. But to the classical Greeks, color mattered far less than nationality, which determined whether people were free or slaves.

RESOURCES: The role of race in the development of sociology is addressed by James R. Hayes in "Sociology and Racism: An Analysis of the First Era of American Sociology," *Phylon* 37, 4 (1973:330–41)

and Larry Reynolds in "Retrospective on 'Race': The Career of a Concept," *Sociological Focus* 25, 1 (1992:1–14).

NOTE: Keith & Herring (1991) demonstrate that skin tone is strongly correlated with SES among African Americans. It is a better predictor of SES, they conclude, than parental SES.

DIVERSITY: Worth stressing is that race and ethnicity are categories that overlap with class and gender.

were all quick to view "others" as inferior. Racism has also been widespread in our own history, especially as a justification for the enslavement of people of African descent. Today, overt racism in this country has subsided to some degree because of a more egalitarian culture that urges us to evaluate people, in Dr. Martin Luther King's words, "by the content of their character, not the color of their skin." Yet racism persists and, whether blatant or subtle, it continues to cause injury and humiliation to people of color (Feagin, 1991).

Racism and Social Domination

Historically, the assertion that one specific category of people was innately inferior to another has served as a powerful justification for subjecting the targets of these taunts to *social* inferiority. By the end of the last century, European nations and the United States had forged vast empires, often ruthlessly and brutally subjugating foreign peoples with the callous claim that they were somehow less human than the explorers who enslaved them.

In this century, racism was central to the Nazi proclamation that a so-called Aryan super-race of blond-haired, blue-eyed Germans was destined to rule the world. Such racist ideology encouraged the systematic slaughter of anyone deemed inferior, including some 6 million European Jews and millions of Poles, gypsies, homosexuals, and people with physical and mental disabilities.

More recently, racial conflict has intensified in Western Europe with the immigration of people from former colonies as well as from Eastern Europe seeking a higher standard of living. In Germany, France, England, and elsewhere, growing public intolerance of immigrants has fueled a resurgence of Nazi-style rhetoric and tactics. The United States, too, is experiencing increasing racial tensions in cities and on college campuses. Racism—in thought and deed—remains a serious social problem everywhere as people still contend that some racial and ethnic categories are "better" than others. As the box on page 326 explains, however, racial differences in mental abilities are due to environment rather than to biology.

Theories of Prejudice

If prejudice does not represent a rational assessment of facts, what are its origins? Social scientists have come up with various answers to this vexing question, citing the importance of frustration, personality, culture, and social conflict.

In a legal effort to mitigate sharp patterns of social inequality, India reserves half of all government positions for members of castes deemed disadvantaged. Because the government is the largest employer, higher-caste college students fear that this policy will shut them out of the job market after graduation. So intense are these concerns that eleven students killed themselves recently—five by fire—in public protest over this controversial policy.

Scapegoat Theory of Prejudice

Scapegoat theory holds that prejudice springs from frustration. Such attitudes, therefore, are common among people who are themselves disadvantaged (Dollard, 1939). Take the case of a white woman frustrated at the low wages she earns working in a textile factory. Directing hostility at the powerful people who operate the factory carries obvious risks; therefore, she may well attribute her low pay to the presence of minority co-workers. Prejudice of this kind may not go far toward improving the woman's situation, but it serves as a relatively safe way to vent anger, and it may give her the comforting feeling that at least she is superior to someone.

A **scapegoat**, then, is *a person or category of people, typically with little power, whom people unfairly blame for their own troubles.* Because they often are "safe targets," minorities are easily used as scapegoats. The Nazis blamed the Jewish minority for all of Germany's ills fifty years ago. And today some Europeans attribute troubles at home to the presence of Turkish, Pakistani, or other immigrants from abroad.

NOTE: The success of nativists in restricting immigration after 1920 was fueled in part by "evidence" that southern and eastern Europeans had lower intelligence than northern and western Europeans.

Q: "Despite the emotionally charged philosophical and political issues involved, [the connection between race and intelligence] is ultimately an empirical question . . . ." Thomas Sowell

DIVERSITY: While some researchers cite evidence of genetic differences in brain size and intelligence among various racial categories, social scientists have generally condemned such research as inherently racist. A review of some of this evidence and a discussion of research that has unacceptable political consequences is found in Joynson (1994).

Q: "Mentally the Negro is inferior to the white." (Encyclopedia

CRITICAL THINKING

Does Race Affect Intelligence?

Are Asian Americans more intelligent than white people? Is the typical white person smarter than the average African American? Assertions painting one category of people as more intellectually gifted than another have been common throughout the history of the United States. Just as important, such thinking has been used to justify the privileges of the allegedly superior category or even to bar supposedly inferior people from entering this country.

The distribution of human intelligence forms a classic "bell curve," shown in the figure. According to conventional thinking, the average person has an IQ score of 100 (technically, an IQ score is mental age as measured by a test divided by age in years with the result multiplied by one hundred; thus, an eight-year-old who performs like a ten-year-old has an IQ of 10/8=1.2 X 100=120).

In a controversial study of intelligence and social inequality, Richard Herrnstein and Charles Murray (1994) contend that overwhelming research evidence supports the conclusion that race is related to intelligence. More specifically, they place the intelligence quotient (IQ) of people with European ancestry at 100. People of East Asian ancestry exceed that standard slightly, averaging 103; people of African descent fall below that standard, with an average IQ of 90.

Of course, claims of this kind are explosive because they fly in the face of our democratic and egalitarian beliefs by implying that people of one racial type are inherently "better" than another. Indeed, countering such data, some people challenge the validity of intelligence tests and even question whether what we call "intelligence" has much real meaning.

Most social scientists acknowledge the existence of such differences in measured intelligence but reject the notion that some people are "better" than others. Disparities in measured intelligence exist, in other words, but the crucial question is *why*. Is intelligence the work of *nature*, in which case disparities signal that one race is actually superior to another, or does it reflect the forces of *nurture* or environment?

Thomas Sowell, an African-American social scientist, has demonstrated that at least most of the documented racial differences in intelligence are environmental in origin. In a skillful example of sociological detective work, Sowell tracked down IQ scores for various racial and ethnic categories from early in this century. On average, he found, immigrants from European nations such as Poland, Lithuania, Italy, and Greece as well as Asian countries including China and Japan scored ten to fifteen points below the U.S. average (which helped to justify turn-of-the-century laws curbing immigration for fear of "dumbing down" the U.S. population).

Sowell's critical discovery came next: People in these same categories *today* have IQ scores that are average or above average. Among Italian Americans, for example, average IQ jumped almost ten points in fifty years; among Polish and Chinese Americans, the rise was almost twenty points.

Because genetic changes occur over thousands of years and these people largely intermarried among themselves, "nature" simply cannot explain such a dramatic rise in IQ scores. Rather, the evidence points to changing cultural patterns. As immigrants settled in the United States, in other words, their new surroundings affected them in ways that improved their measured intelligence.

Among African Americans, Sowell explains, Northerners have historically outscored Southerners on IQ tests by about ten points. And, among African Americans who migrated from the South to the North after 1940, IQ scores soon rose the same way they did among immigrants from abroad. Thus, controlling for environmental factors, racial IQ differences fade.

What these test-score disparities do tell, Sowell continues, is that *cultural patterns* matter. Asians who score high on tests are no smarter than other people, but they have been raised to value learning and to pursue excellence. For their part, African Americans are no less intelligent than anyone else, but, carrying a legacy of disadvantage, many contend with a cultural environment that discourages self-confidence and achievement.

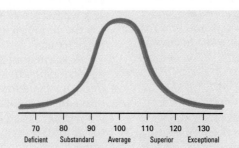

| 70 | 80 | 90 | 100 | 110 | 120 | 130 |
| Deficient | Substandard | Average | | Superior | | Exceptional |

IQ: The Distribution of Intelligence

Sources: Herrnstein & Murray (1994), and Sowell (1994, 1995).

Authoritarian Personality Theory

T. W. Adorno (1950) and his colleagues claimed that extreme prejudice was a personality trait of particular individuals. They based this conclusion on research showing that people who displayed strong prejudice toward one minority were usually intolerant of all minorities. Such people exhibit *authoritarian personalities*, rigidly conforming to conventional cultural values, envisioning moral issues as clear-cut matters of right and wrong, and advocating strongly ethnocentric views. People with authoritarian personalities also look upon society as naturally competitive and hierarchical, with "better" people (like themselves) inevitably dominating those who are weaker.

By contrast, Adorno found, people tolerant toward one minority were likely to be accepting of all. They tend to be more flexible in their moral judgments and believe that, ideally, society should be relatively egalitarian. They feel uncomfortable in any situation in which some people exercise excessive and damaging power over others.

According to these researchers, authoritarian personalities tend to develop in people with little education and harsh and demanding parents. Raised by cold and insistent authority figures, they theorized, children may become angry and anxious people who seek out scapegoats whom they come to define as their social inferiors.

Cultural Theory of Prejudice

A third approach holds that, while extreme prejudice may be characteristic of certain people, some prejudice is common to everyone since such attitudes are embedded in culture. As noted in Chapter 3 ("Culture"), the social superiority of some categories of people is a core value of U.S. culture. Recent multicultural research echoes this idea, and calls for educational programs to help people in the United States move beyond our traditionally Eurocentric attitudes to gain an appreciation of the culture and contributions of those of non-European descent (Asante, 1987, 1988).

For more than forty years, Emory Bogardus (1968) studied the effects of culturally rooted prejudices on interpersonal relationships. He devised the concept of *social distance* to gauge how close or distant people feel in relation to members of various racial and ethnic categories. Interestingly, his research shows that

The efforts of these four women greatly advanced the social standing of African Americans in the United States. Pictured below, from left to right: Sojourner Truth (1797–1883), born a slave, became an influential preacher and outspoken abolitionist who was honored by President Lincoln at the White House. Harriet Tubman (1820–1913), after escaping from slavery herself, masterminded the flight from bondage of hundreds of African-American men and women via the "Underground Railroad." Ida Wells-Barnett (1862–1931), born to slave parents, became a partner in a Memphis newspaper and served as a tireless crusader against the terror of lynching. Marian Anderson (1897–1993), an exceptional singer whose early career was restrained by racial prejudice, broke symbolic "color lines" by singing in the White House (1936) and on the steps of the Lincoln Memorial to a crowd of almost 100,000 people (1939).

NOTE: A century ago, people believed that race (and biology, in general) directly affected human behavior; early anthropology and sociology were central in dispelling this view.
DIVERSITY: The seven leading states in attracting immigrants from abroad (150,000 or more entered between 1985 and 1990) were California, Florida, Texas, New York, New Jersey, Massachusetts, and Illinois.

DIVERSITY: About 8% of U.S. adults report being born outside the United States; 15% claim at least one parent was born abroad. (GSS 1993, N = 1,598; Codebook, 1994:55–56)
Q: "The ordinary English worker hates the Irish worker as a competitor who lowers his standard of life. . . . This antagonism is the secret of the impotence of the English working class . . . it is the secret by which the capitalist class maintains its power." Karl Marx

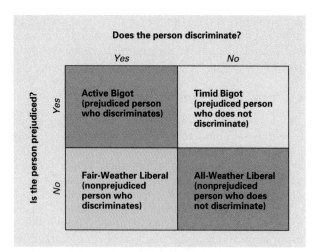

FIGURE 12–1 Patterns of Prejudice and Discrimination

Source: Merton (1976).

people throughout the United States share similar views in this regard, leading Bogardus to conclude that such attitudes are culturally normative.

Bogardus found that members of our society regarded most positively people of English, Canadian, and Scottish background, welcoming close relationships with and even marriage to them. We placed somewhat less of a premium on interactions with people of French, German, Swedish, and Dutch descent. The most negative prejudices, Bogardus discovered, targeted people of African and Asian descent.

If prejudice is widespread, can we dismiss intolerance as merely a trait of a handful of abnormal people, as Adorno asserted? A more all-encompassing approach recognizes some bigotry is within us all as we become well adjusted to a "culture of prejudice."

Conflict Theory of Prejudice

A fourth view, following the social-conflict approach, claims that powerful people utilize prejudice as a strategy to oppress minorities. To the extent that the public looks down on illegal Latino immigrants in the Southwest, for example, rich landowners are able to pay these people low wages for hard work. Similarly, elites benefit from prejudice that divides workers along racial and ethnic lines and discourages them from working together to advance their common interests (Geschwender, 1978; Olzak, 1989).

A different conflict argument, advanced by Shelby Steele (1990), holds that minorities themselves spark conflict by cultivating a climate of *race consciousness*, designed to win them greater power and privileges. Race consciousness, Steele explains, amounts to the assertion that minorities are victims and white people their victimizers. Because of this historical disadvantage, minorities claim they are now entitled to special considerations based on their race. While this strategy may yield short-term gains for minorities, Steele cautions that such policies may precipitate a backlash from white people or others who condemn "special treatment" for anyone on the basis of race or ethnicity.

DISCRIMINATION

Closely related to prejudice is the concept of **discrimination**, *any action that involves treating various categories of people unequally.* While prejudice refers to attitudes, discrimination is a matter of behavior. Like prejudice, discrimination can be either positive (providing special advantages) or negative (placing obstacles in front of particular categories of people). Discrimination also varies in intensity, ranging from subtle to blatant.

Prejudice and discrimination often—but not always—occur together. A personnel manager prejudiced against members of a particular minority may refuse to hire them. Robert Merton (1976) describes such a person as an *active bigot*, as shown in Figure 12–1. Fearing legal action, however, another prejudiced personnel manager may not discriminate, thereby becoming a *timid bigot*. What Merton calls *fair-weather liberals* may be generally tolerant of minorities yet discriminate when it is expedient to do so, such as when a superior demands it. Finally, Merton's *all-weather liberal* is free of both prejudice and discrimination.

Not all kinds of discrimination are wrong. Individuals discriminate all the time, preferring the personalities, favoring the looks, or admiring the talents of particular people. Discriminating in this basic sense of *making distinctions* is necessary to everyday life and rarely causes problems. But discriminating on the basis of race or ethnicity is another matter.

All societies praise some forms of discrimination, in other words, while condemning others. Colleges, for example, systematically favor applicants with greater abilities over those with less aptitude. This kind of discrimination is entirely consistent with our culture-based expectation that the greatest rewards go to people with more ability or those who work harder.

NOTE: Evidence pointing to institutional discrimination: In 1990, the percentages of mortgage applications that were denied, by racial or ethnic category (based on a Federal Reserve Board study of 6,400 loan applications at 9,300 lending institutions), were Asians, 12.9%; whites, 14.4%; Hispanics, 21.4%; African Americans, 33.9%.
NOTE: In Figure 12–1, people who carry out institutional discrimination would fall in the "fair-weather liberal" box.

SOCIAL SURVEY: "How important for getting ahead is being of the right race?" (CHIP1 Social Survey Software, OPRACE1, 2; GSS 1987, N = 1,444)

	"Very important"	"Less important"
Afri Amer	28.8%	71.2%
Hispanics	15.6%	84.4%
Whites	11.9%	88.1%

But what if a college were to favor one category of people (Christians) over another (Jews) regardless of individual talent? Unless the college had a religious mission (making a specific religion directly relevant to performance in school), such a policy would discriminate in a manner both morally wrong and against the law.

In historical terms, principles of fair play change along with economic development. In low-income countries, people routinely favor members of their families, clans, religious groups, and villages. Traditional people typically recognize a moral duty to "look after their own." In high-income, industrial societies, by contrast, cultural norms elevate the individual over the group, so that achievement rather than ascription guides our code of fairness. Many organizations, therefore, seek out the most qualified applicant while forbidding "nepotism" or "conflict of interest" by which employees would favor a relative or reject someone based on race or sex.

Institutional Prejudice and Discrimination

We typically think of prejudice and discrimination as the hateful ideas or actions of specific individuals. But, claimed Stokely Carmichael and Charles Hamilton (1967), far greater harm results from **institutional prejudice or discrimination**, which refers to *bias in attitudes or action inherent in the operation of society's institutions*, including schools, hospitals, the police, and the workplace.

For example, lawyers defending O. J. Simpson during his murder trial contended that racial bias renders the U.S. criminal justice system unfair to African Americans, an allegation shared by a majority of African Americans in the United States (Smolowe, 1994). Even so, note Carmichael and Hamilton, the white majority is slow to condemn or even to recognize institutional prejudice or discrimination since it often involves respected public officials and long-established traditions.

Until the Supreme Court's *Brown* decision in 1954, described in the opening of this chapter, the principle of "separate but equal" legally justified the institutional discrimination by which black and white children attended different schools. In effect, the law before *Brown* upheld institutional racism in the form of an educational caste system. Institutional discrimination remains one of U.S. society's most intractable problems. Despite the *Brown* decision, relatively little has changed since 1954: While no schools remain officially "black" or "white," most U.S. students still attend schools in which one race or the other predominates overwhelmingly. Indeed, in 1991, a court decision recognized that neighborhood schools would never provide equal education as long as our population was divided into racially segregated neighborhoods, with most African Americans living in central cities and most white people (and Asian Americans) living in geographically and politically separate suburbs.

Prejudice and Discrimination: The Vicious Cycle

Prejudice and discrimination frequently reinforce each other. W. I. Thomas offered a simple explanation of this fact, noted in Chapter 6 ("Social Interaction in Everyday Life"). The Thomas theorem states: *If situations are defined as real, they are real in their consequences* (1966:301; orig. 1931). Because people socially construct reality, stereotypes become real to those who believe them and sometimes even to those who are victimized by them. Power also plays a role here, since some categories of people have the ability to enforce their prejudices to the detriment of others.

Prejudice by whites against people of color, for example, does not produce *innate* inferiority but it can produce *social* inferiority, consigning minorities to poverty, low-prestige occupations, and poor housing in racially segregated neighborhoods. If white people interpret social disadvantage as evidence that minorities do not measure up to their standards, they unleash a new round of prejudice and discrimination, giving rise to a *vicious cycle* whereby each perpetuates the other, as illustrated in Figure 12–2, even from generation to generation.

MAJORITY AND MINORITY: PATTERNS OF INTERACTION

Social scientists describe patterns of interaction among racial and ethnic categories in terms of four models: pluralism, assimilation, segregation, and genocide.

Pluralism

Pluralism is *a state in which racial and ethnic minorities are distinct but have social parity*. In a pluralist society, categories of people are socially different, but they share basic social resources more or less equally.

The United States appears to be pluralistic in several respects. Our society provides schooling and other

DIVERSITY: Appearing on all U.S. coins is the Latin phrase *E Pluribus Unum* ("one formed from many"). Whether our society should emphasize the "unum" (which often means, in practice, favoring a dominant cultural tradition) or the "pluribus" (which sometimes causes division) is part of the debate surrounding multiculturalism, as noted in Chapter 3, "Culture." (A multicultural credo might be *E Pluribus Plures*, "many from many.")

Q: "After all, there is but one race—humanity." George Moore
Q: "The future of America can't be sustained if people keep only to their own ways and remain perpetual outsiders. The society has got to turn them into Americans." Allan Bloom
NOTE: We see the effects of assimilation in name changing among U.S. celebrities; see the box, "What's in a Name? How Social Forces Affect Personal Choices," in Chapter 1.

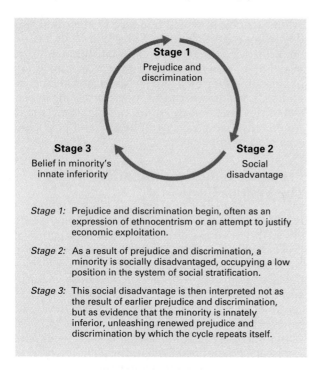

Stage 1
Prejudice and discrimination

Stage 3
Belief in minority's innate inferiority

Stage 2
Social disadvantage

Stage 1: Prejudice and discrimination begin, often as an expression of ethnocentrism or an attempt to justify economic exploitation.

Stage 2: As a result of prejudice and discrimination, a minority is socially disadvantaged, occupying a low position in the system of social stratification.

Stage 3: This social disadvantage is then interpreted not as the result of earlier prejudice and discrimination, but as evidence that the minority is innately inferior, unleashing renewed prejudice and discrimination by which the cycle repeats itself.

FIGURE 12–2 Prejudice and Discrimination: The Vicious Cycle

Prejudice and discrimination can form a vicious cycle, perpetuating themselves, as explained above.

services to all categories of people and promises them equal standing before the law. Moreover, large cities contain dozens of "ethnic villages" where people proudly display the cultural traditions of their immigrant ancestors. In New York these include Spanish Harlem, Little Italy, and Chinatown; in Philadelphia, Italian "South Philly"; in Miami, "Little Havana"; in Chicago, "Little Saigon"; as well as Latino East Los Angeles.

Pluralism is the goal of our society's recent trend toward multiculturalism. As described earlier in Chapter 3 ("Culture"), this scholarly and political initiative seeks to promote respectful tolerance of and social parity for the many cultural traditions that make up our national life.

But, in other respects, the United States remains far from pluralistic. First, while most people appreciate and value their cultural heritage, only a small proportion of minorities want to live and interact only with their "own kind" (NORC, 1994). Second, in many cases, racial and ethnic identity is forced on people by

others who shun them as undesirable. For example, people in many communities in the Appalachian Mountains of the eastern United States remain culturally distinctive because others snub them as "hillbillies." Third, especially in recent years, rising levels of immigration have stretched many people's tolerance for social diversity. One reaction against the new immigrants has been a social movement seeking to establish English as the official language of the United States, hardly a strategy to bolster pluralism.

In global perspective, Switzerland presents a much sharper example of pluralism. In this European nation of almost 7 million people, German, French, and Italian cultural traditions run deep. The Swiss have been relatively successful in maintaining pluralism (albeit involving little difference in color), officially recognizing all three languages. Just as important, the three categories have roughly the same economic standing (Simpson & Yinger, 1972).

Assimilation

Assimilation is *the process by which minorities gradually adopt patterns of the dominant culture.* Assimilation involves changing modes of dress, values, religion, language, or friends.

Many people think of the United States as a "melting pot" in which various nationalities have fused into an entirely new way of life. At the turn of the last century, one immigrant expressed this perception in these words:

> America is God's Crucible, the great melting-pot where all races of Europe are melting and reforming. Here you stand, good folks, think I, when I see them at Ellis Island [historical entry point for many immigrants in New York], here you stand with your fifty groups, with your fifty languages and histories, and your fifty blood-hatreds and rivalries. But you won't be long like that, brothers, for these are the fires of God . . . Germans and Frenchmen, Irishmen and Englishmen, Jews and Russians, into the Crucible with you all! God is making an American! (Zangwill, 1921:33; orig. 1909)

Although the melting-pot image still captures our sense of how this country *ought* to operate, it is misleading as a matter of historical fact. Rather than everyone "melting" into some new cultural pattern, minorities typically adopt the traits (the dress, accent, and sometimes even the names) of the dominant culture established by the earliest settlers.

Not surprisingly, elites tend to favor the assimilation model since it holds them up as the standard to

NOTE: Farley & Frey (1994) found decreasing black-white segregation in young, southern and western metropolitan areas with considerable new construction. Massey & Hajnal (1995) argue that the long-term trend at the state and county level is for less segregation but, at the neighborhood level, toward more segregation.

SOCIAL SURVEY: "If you could find the housing that you would

want and like, would you rather live in a neighborhood that is all black, mostly black, half black, half white, or mostly white?" (GSS 1982, N = 510; African-American respondents; *Codebook*, 1994:152)

"All black"   14.7%   "Mostly white"   5.1%
"Mostly black"   15.8%   DK/NR   10.4%
"Half black, half white"   54.0%

which others should aspire. Many immigrants, too, have been quick to pursue assimilation in the hope that it will free them from the prejudice and discrimination directed against distinctive foreigners and encourage upward social mobility (Newman, 1973). But multiculturalists find fault with the assimilation model because it tends to paint minorities as "the problem" and define them (rather than elites) as the ones who need to do all the changing.

Certainly some assimilation has occurred over the course of our national history (witness the gradual "melting" of neighborhoods previously composed of European immigrants). But some categories of people have "melted" more than others: the Germans and Irish more than the Italians, and the Japanese more than the Chinese or Koreans. Moreover, as fast as some urban "ethnic villages" disappear, new ones emerge, the product of a steady and substantial stream of immigrants. Almost 30 percent of today's New Yorkers are foreign born—the highest percentage in fifty years. No wonder some analysts argue that race and ethnicity endure as basic building blocks of our society (Glazer & Moynihan, 1970; Alba, 1985).

As a cultural process, assimilation involves changes in ethnicity but not in race. For example, many Americans of Japanese descent have discarded their traditional way of life but still maintain their racial identity. However, racial traits do diminish over generations as the result of **miscegenation**, *biological reproduction by partners of different racial categories.* Miscegenation (typically outside of marriage) has occurred throughout U.S. history despite cultural and even legal prohibitions. Norms against miscegenation are now eroding and, while the share of officially recorded interracial births is still just 4 percent, it is rising steadily.

Segregation

Segregation refers to *the physical and social separation of categories of people.* Some minorities, especially religious orders like the Amish, have voluntarily segregated themselves. Mostly, however, majorities segregate minorities involuntarily by excluding them. Various degrees of segregation characterize residential neighborhoods, schools, occupations, hospitals, and even cemeteries. While pluralism fosters distinctiveness without disadvantage, segregation enforces separation to the detriment of a minority.

South Africa's system of apartheid (described in Chapter 9, "Social Stratification") illustrates racial

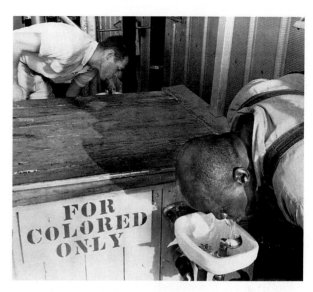

Only a full century after the abolition of slavery did the U.S. government take action to dismantle the "Jim Crow" laws that continued to separate people of European and African ancestry. Until the early 1960s, these laws formally segregated hotels, restaurants, parks, buses, and even drinking fountains. More than three decades later, de facto racial segregation in housing and schooling remains a reality for millions of people of color in the United States.

segregation that has been both rigid and pervasive. Apartheid was created by the European minority it served, and white South Africans historically have enforced this system through the use of brutal power (Fredrickson, 1981). South Africa is now in the process of dismantling apartheid but, as yet, the basic racial structure of South Africa has changed little, and that nation remains essentially two different societies that touch only when blacks provide services for whites.

In the United States, too, racial segregation has a long history. Centuries of slavery gave way to racially separated lodging, schooling, and transportation. Decisions such as the 1954 *Brown* case, described at the beginning of this chapter, have reduced overt and *de jure* (Latin meaning "by law") discrimination in the United States. However, *de facto* ("in fact") segregation continues.

In the 1960s, Karl and Alma Taeuber (1965) assessed the residential segregation of black people and white people in more than two hundred cities in the United States. On a numerical scale ranging from zero (a mixing of races in all neighborhoods) to 100 (racial mixing in no neighborhoods), they calculated an *average* segregation score of 86.2. Subsequent research has shown that segregation has decreased since then, but only slightly; even African Americans with high incomes continue to find that their color closes off opportunities for housing (Hwang et al., 1985; Calmore, 1986; Saltman, 1991; Wilson, 1991; Farley & Frey, 1994; NORC, 1994).

We associate segregation with housing but, as Douglas Massey and Nancy Denton (1989) point out, racial separation involves a host of life experiences beyond neighborhood composition. Many African Americans living in inner cities, these researchers concluded, have little social contact of any kind with the outside world. Such *hypersegregation* affects about one-fifth of all African Americans but only a small fraction of comparably poor whites (Jagarowsky & Bane, 1990).

In short, segregation generally means second-class citizenship for a minority. For this reason, many minority men and women have struggled valiantly against such exclusiveness. Sometimes the action of a single person can make a difference. On December 1, 1955, Rosa Parks boarded a bus in Montgomery, Alabama, and sat in a section designated by law for black people. When a crowd of white passengers boarded the bus, the driver asked Parks and three other African Americans to give up their seats. The three did so, but Rosa Parks refused. The driver left the bus and returned with police, who arrested her for violating the racial segregation laws. A court later convicted Parks and fined her $14. Her stand (or sitting) for justice sparked the African-American community of Montgomery to boycott city buses, ultimately bringing this form of legal segregation to an end (King, 1969).

Genocide

Genocide is *the systematic annihilation of one category of people by another.* This racist and ethnocentric brutality violates nearly every recognized moral standard; nonetheless, it has occurred time and again in the human record.

Genocide figured prominently in centuries of contact between Europeans and the original inhabitants of the Americas. From the sixteenth century on, the Spanish, Portuguese, English, French, and Dutch forcefully colonized vast empires. These efforts decimated the native populations of North and South America, allowing Europeans to gain control of the continents' wealth. Some native people fell victim to calculated killing sprees; most succumbed to diseases carried by Europeans and to which native peoples had no natural defenses (Cottrell, 1979; Butterworth & Chance, 1981; Matthiessen, 1984; Sale, 1990).

Unimaginable horror befell the Jews of Europe during Adolf Hitler's reign of terror in this century. Ultimately, the Nazis exterminated more than 6 million Jewish men, women, and children in what has become known as the Holocaust. In Cambodia between 1975 and 1980, Pol Pot's communist regime slaughtered anyone thought to represent capitalist cultural influences. Condemned to death were men and women able to speak any Western language and even individuals who wore eyeglasses, viewed as a symbol of capitalist culture. In all, some 2 million people (one-fourth of the population) perished in the Cambodian "killing fields" (Shawcross, 1979).

These four patterns of minority-majority interaction have all been played out in the United States. We proudly point to patterns of pluralism and assimilation; only reluctantly do we acknowledge the degree to which our society has been built on segregation (of African Americans) and genocide (of Native Americans). The remainder of this chapter examines how these four patterns have shaped the history and present social standing of major racial and ethnic categories in the United States.

RACE AND ETHNICITY IN THE UNITED STATES

Give me your tired, your poor,
Your huddled masses yearning to breathe free,
The wretched refuse of your teeming shore,
Send these, the homeless, tempest-tossed to me:
I lift my lamp beside the golden door.

These words by Emma Lazarus, inscribed on the Statue of Liberty, express cultural ideals of human dignity, personal freedom, and opportunity. The United States has made way for more immigrants than any country in history, giving these newcomers a chance at the "good life." But our nation's golden door has opened more widely for some than for others. The tension between opportunity and inequality resonates through the entire history of this country's racial and ethnic minorities.

Native Americans

The term "Native Americans" refers to the societies—including Aleuts, Eskimos, Cherokee, Zuni, Sioux,

Mohawk, Aztec, and Inca—who first settled the Western Hemisphere. Some thirty thousand years before Christopher Columbus "discovered" the Americas, these people began migrating from Asia, crossing a land bridge where the Bering Strait off the coast of Alaska is today. Over the centuries they spread throughout the continents of North and South America (Dobyns, 1966).

What some Europeans called "taming the wilderness" actually amounted to the destruction of many ancient civilizations. Exposure to European diseases took a terrible toll among the native peoples, and tens of thousands died at the hands of Europeans seeking land and other wealth. From a population in the millions, the "vanishing Americans" numbered a mere 250,000 by the start of the twentieth century (Tyler, 1973).

It was Columbus who first referred to Native Americans as "Indians"; when he landed in the Bahama Islands in the Caribbean, he thought he had reached India. Columbus described these indigenous Americans as passive and peaceful, in contrast to the more competitive and aggressive ways of the Europeans. Even as Europeans seized the land of Native Americans, the invaders demeaned their victims as thieves and murderers to justify their actions (Unruh, 1979; Josephy, 1982; Matthiessen, 1984; Sale, 1990).

After the Revolutionary War, the new United States government adopted a pluralist approach that recognized Native-American societies but sought to gain more land through treaties. Payment for land was far from fair, however, and when Native Americans refused to surrender their homelands, the U.S. government simply used superior military power to drive them out. In the most tragic incident of its kind, thousands of Cherokees died on a forced march—the Trail of Tears—from their homes in the southeastern United States to reservations in Indian Territory (present-day Oklahoma). By the early 1800s, few Native Americans remained east of the Mississippi River.

In 1871, the United States declared Native Americans wards of the government and set out to resolve "the Indian problem" through forced assimilation. Native Americans continued to lose their land and were well on their way to losing their culture as well. Reservation schools taught English in place of ancestral languages and eroded traditional religion in favor of Christianity. Officials of the Bureau of Indian Affairs took many children from their parents and handed them over to boarding schools, where they were to be resocialized as "Americans." Authorities gave local control of reservation life to the few Native Americans who supported government policies and

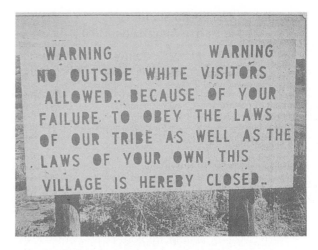

Many outsiders view native peoples of North America more as curious tourist attractions than as cultures that have endured for thousands of years. After visitors repeatedly violated tribal law by photographing sacred dance rituals, the Hopi closed this village as if to say, "If we can't live together in mutual respect, we won't live together at all."

distributed reservation land—traditionally held collectively—as the private property of individual families (Tyler, 1973). Native Americans gradually were taught to be dependent on the government.

Not until 1924 were Native Americans entitled to U.S. citizenship. Since then, the government has acknowledged a host of problems associated with reservation life and encouraged migration and assimilation into the larger society. Some Native Americans have responded by adopting more mainstream cultural patterns and marrying non-Native Americans; many large cities now contain sizable Native-American populations. But Native Americans remain socially deprived: Table 12–2 shows that median family income among this minority population is far below average; moreover, compared to the country as a whole, Native Americans are half as likely to earn a college degree.[2]

Interviewing Native Americans living in a western city, Joan Albon (1971) concluded that this lower social

---

[2]In making comparisons of education and, especially, income, keep in mind that various categories of the U.S. population have different median ages. The 1994 median age for all people in the country was 34.0 years. White people had a median age of 35.0 years; for Native Americans, the figure was 26.7 years. Because people's schooling and income increase over time, such an age difference accounts for some of the disparities shown here.

DIVERSITY: Traditional Native-American cultures tend to be more cooperative than European cultures. The languages of the Navajo and some other Native-American cultures contain no words meaning "free enterprise" or "market system."
NOTE: E. Digby Baltzell, who coined the term WASP, notes that, to many people in the United States, a true WASP is a person whose first name is a last name.

NOTE: WASPs are the only ethnic category found in substantial numbers in virtually every geographic region of the United States.
NOTE: The last nation in the Western Hemisphere to outlaw slavery was Brazil, in 1888. About half the people of color in Brazil are descendants of slaves; blacks have roughly half the income of whites in that middle-income country, and infant mortality is one-third higher.

Table 12–2 The Social Standing of Native Americans, 1990

	Native Americans	Entire United States
Median family income	$21,750	$35,225
Percent in poverty	30.9%	13.1%
Completion of four or more years of college (age 25 and over)	9.3%	20.3%

Source: U.S. Bureau of the Census (1995).

standing partly reflects racial hostility in the United States toward people with dark skin. Some elements of Native-American culture may be at work as well. Few Native Americans have aggressively pursued higher education, and many have limited marketable skills and speak less-than-perfect English. Albon adds that many Native Americans lack the individualism and competitiveness that contribute to success in the United States. This passivity stems from both cooperative traditional values and long dependence on government assistance.

Like other racial and ethnic minorities in the United States, Native Americans have recently reasserted pride in their cultural heritage. As the 1990s began, Native-American organizations reported a surge of new membership applications, and many children are learning to speak native tongues better than their parents (Fost, 1991; Johnson, 1991). In lawsuits against the federal government, some Native Americans have pressed for return of lands, forcibly seized from their ancestors, and sought to gain control of reservation lands. The legal autonomy of reservations has turned out to be an ace-up-the-sleeve for many Native-American tribes, who have built gaming casinos and now control about 20 percent of all gambling in the United States. But such financial windfalls affect relatively few Native peoples; most endure their disadvantages with a profound sense of injustice suffered at the hands of white people (Josephy, 1982; Matthiessen, 1983).

White Anglo-Saxon Protestants

White Anglo-Saxon Protestants (WASPs) were not the first people to inhabit the United States, but they came to dominate this nation once English colonization began. Not until the nineteenth century, in fact, did substantial migration of non-WASPs begin. Most WASPs are still of English ancestry, but the category also includes Scots and Welsh. With more than 50 million people of some English ancestry, one in five members of our society claims WASP background.

Historically, WASP immigrants were highly skilled. Just as important, what we now call the Protestant work ethic motivated them toward hard work and achievement. Also, because their numbers placed them in the majority, WASPs were not subject to the prejudice and discrimination experienced by other immigrants. The historical dominance of WASPs has been so great that, as noted earlier, assimilation into U.S. society has meant that others seek to model themselves after the WASPs.

WASPs were never one single social group; especially in colonial times, there were significant divisions among the WASPs. Vincent Parrillo (1994) points out, for example, that considerable social distance and even hostility set off English Anglicans from Scots-Irish Presbyterians. But, during the nineteenth century, most WASPs joined together to bemoan the presence of new arrivals (Germans in the 1840s, Italians in the 1880s) whom they deemed "undesirable foreigners." Political movements promoted laws to limit the rapidly rising immigration. Those who could afford to pursued a personal solution to the "problem," sheltering themselves in exclusive neighborhoods and restrictive clubs. Thus the 1880s—the decade in which the Statue of Liberty first welcomed immigrants to the United States—also saw the founding of the first country club with all WASP members. Soon afterward, WASPs began publishing the *Social Register* (1887), a listing of members of "society," and established various genealogical organizations such as the Daughters of the American Revolution (1890) and the Society of Mayflower Descendants (1894). Such efforts served to further insulate wealthy WASPs from newly arrived immigrants (Baltzell, 1964).

By about 1930, the growing wealth of other categories of people and more egalitarian values undermined the WASPs' commanding privileges (Baltzell, 1964, 1976, 1988). Exemplifying this shift was the 1960 election of John Fitzgerald Kennedy as the first Irish-Catholic president. Even so, WASPs continue to have great influence; with extensive schooling, they work in high-prestige occupations, enjoy above-average incomes, and still make up most of the upper-upper class (Greeley, 1974; Baltzell, 1979; Roof, 1981; Neidert & Farley, 1985).

Although now under fire by multicultural educational programs, the WASP cultural legacy persists. English remains the dominant language of the United States, and Protestantism is the majority religion. Our

NOTE: John Hope Franklin has pointed out that, historically, racial problems were not limited to the South. In 1776, as the new nation was being formed, slavery was legal in *all* states. By 1850 roughly equal numbers of free blacks (500,000) were found in both the South and the North. Also, segregation and other forms of discrimination were largely Northern in origin, because slavery in the South had spawned other forms of racial control. It was only after abolition that the South adopted Northern forms of discrimination.

DIVERSITY: A 1993 Roper poll of African Americans indicates that 30% preferred that term; 42% favored "black"; 10% preferred "Afro-American"; and 18% favored something else or had no preference. Brad Edmonson (1993)

Q: "There is no Negro problem in the United States; there is only a white problem." Richard Wright

At its foundation, agrarian slavery was an institution built on coercion and violence. As African-American painter Jacob Lawrence shows here, planters utilized the most brutal treatment in an effort to obtain compliance. The wide stance and clenched jaw convey the planter's determination to control the bound man at his feet. But despite the fear that such tactics generated, they also provoked periodic rebellion on the part of slaves.

Jacob Lawrence, *The Planter*, 1937–1938/ tempura on paper/from the Armistad Research Center's Aaron Douglas Collection, New Orleans/11 x 19 inches.

legal system, too, reflects its English origins. But the historical primacy of WASPs is most evident in the widespread use of the terms "race" and "ethnicity" to describe everyone but them.

African Americans

African Americans accompanied Spanish explorers to the New World in the fifteenth century. Most accounts, however, mark the beginning of black history in the United States as 1619, when a Dutch trading ship brought twenty Africans to Jamestown, Virginia. Whether these people arrived as slaves or indentured servants who paid for their passage by performing labor for a specified period, being of African descent on these shores soon became virtually synonymous with being a slave. In 1661, Virginia enacted the first law recognizing slavery (Sowell, 1981).

The southern colonies' plantation system, the region's economic mainstay, depended on slavery. Some white people prospered as plantation owners and, until it was outlawed in 1808, as slave traders. Europeans, in collaboration with Africans, forcibly enslaved and transported to the Americas some 10 million Africans; about 400,000 entered the United States (Sowell, 1981). During the voyage, slaves were chained as human cargo. Filth and disease killed many and drove others to suicide. Overall, perhaps half died en route (Tannenbaum, 1946; Franklin, 1967).

Those who survived the journey faced a life of forced servitude. Although some worked in cities at a variety of trades, most slaves labored in the fields from daybreak until sunset, and for up to twenty hours a day during the harvest (Franklin, 1967). The law empowered slave owners to impose whatever disciplinary measures they deemed necessary to ensure that slaves were productive. Even the killing of a slave by an owner rarely prompted legal action. Owners also divided slave families at public auctions, where human beings were bought and sold as pieces of property. Unschooled and dependent on their owners for all their basic needs, slaves had little control over their destinies (Sowell, 1981).

There were, however, free persons of color in both the North and the South: small-scale farmers, skilled workers, and small-business owners (Murray, 1978). But the lives of most African Americans stood in glaring contradiction to the principles of equality and freedom on which the United States was founded. The Declaration of Independence states:

> We hold these Truths to be self-evident, that all Men are created equal, that they are endowed by their Creator with certain unalienable Rights, that among these are Life, Liberty, and the Pursuit of Happiness.

Most white people, however, did not apply these ideals to black people. In the *Dred Scott* case in 1857, the U.S. Supreme Court addressed the question, "Are blacks citizens?" and answered, "We think they are not, and that they are not included, and were not intended to be included, under the word 'citizens' in the Constitution, and can therefore claim none of the rights

DIVERSITY: In 1965, among African Americans 25–29 years old who had begun college, the percentage of people who went on to complete four years or more was 90% that of whites; by end of 1980s, it had dropped to 60%. (Bunzel, 1991)

RESOURCE: An excerpt from William Julius Wilson's *The Truly Disadvantaged* on the ghetto underclass appears in the Macionis and Benokraitis reader, *Seeing Ourselves*.

DIVERSITY: For a comparison of affluent black people and white people, see the box, "The Color of Money," in Chapter 10.

NOTE: African Americans are now more evident in the mass media, and especially television, where they appear in more favorable roles. In part this is due to advertisers' recognition of the growing African-American audience: Blacks watch about 40% more television, on average, than whites do.

Table 12–3 The Social Standing of African Americans, 1994*

	African Americans	Entire United States
Median family income	$21,548	$36,782
Percent in poverty	33.1%	14.5%
Completion of four or more years of college (age 25 and over)	12.9%	22.2%

*For purposes of comparison with other tables in this chapter, 1990 data are as follows: median family income, $21,423; percent in poverty, 31.9%; completion of four or more years of college, 11.3%.

Source: U.S. Bureau of the Census (1995).

and privileges which that instrument provides for and secures for citizens of the United States" (quoted in Blaustein & Zangrando, 1968:160). Thus arose what Swedish sociologist Gunnar Myrdal (1944) called the *American dilemma*: a democratic society's denial of basic rights and freedoms to an entire category of people. To resolve this dilemma, many white people simply viewed black people as innately inferior.

In 1865, the Thirteenth Amendment to the Constitution ended slavery. Three years later, the Fourteenth Amendment reversed the *Dred Scott* ruling, conferring citizenship on all people born in the United States. The Fifteenth Amendment, ratified in 1870, stated that neither race nor previous condition of servitude should deprive anyone of the right to vote. However, so-called Jim Crow laws—classic cases of institutional discrimination—still divided U.S. society into two racial castes (Woodward, 1974). Especially in the South, white people beat and lynched black people (and some whites) who challenged the racial hierarchy.

The twentieth century has brought dramatic changes to African Americans. After World War I, tens of thousands of men, women, and children deserted the rural South for jobs in northern factories. Most were rewarded with higher incomes, but few escaped racial prejudice and discrimination, which set them apart from white immigrants who had arrived from Europe.

In the 1950s and 1960s, black people and sympathetic white people mobilized for a broad attack on racism. The national civil rights movement led to landmark judicial decisions outlawing racially segregated schools and overt racial discrimination in employment and public accommodations. In addition, the "black power movement" gave African Americans a renewed sense of pride and purpose, which has more recently been reinforced through Afrocentric education, described in Chapter 3 ("Culture").

Gains notwithstanding, people of African descent continue to occupy a subordinate position in the United States, as shown in Table 12–3. The median income of African-American families in 1994 ($21,548) was 55 percent of that earned by white families ($39,308)[3] and substantially below the average for all families across the United States ($36,782). African-American households are also three times as likely as white households to be poor.

The number of African Americans securely in the middle class has risen by half since 1980; three in ten families now earn more than $35,000 a year (18 percent earn above $50,000). But for many African Americans, earnings have slipped during the last fifteen years. This downward slide reflects changes in the U.S. economy by which millions of factory jobs—vital to residents of inner cities—were lost to other countries where labor is cheaper. Thus black unemployment stands at more than twice the level of white joblessness; among African-American teenagers in many cities, the figure exceeds 40 percent (Jacob, 1986; Lichter, 1989; U.S. Bureau of the Census, 1995).

Since 1980, African Americans have made remarkable educational progress, with the share of adults completing high school rising from half to almost three-fourths, almost closing a historical gap between whites and blacks. Between 1980 and 1994, moreover, the share of African-American adults with at least a college degree rose from 8 to 13 percent. But, at the college level, there remains a striking racial disparity: As Table 12–3 shows, African Americans still reach only half the national standard when it comes to completing four years of college (U.S. Bureau of the Census, 1995).

The political clout of African Americans has increased as more and more have registered to vote and elected officials from their own ranks. Black urban migration, along with white movement to the suburbs, has yielded black majorities in many large cities; by 1990 half of this country's ten largest cities had elected black mayors. At the national level, however, just 1 percent of elected leaders are African Americans. After the 1994 Congressional elections, 39 black men and women (of 435) were in the House of Representatives and one black woman (of 100) sat in the Senate.

---

[3]Here again, a median age difference (white people, 35.0; black people, 29.0) accounts for some of the income and educational disparities noted here. This difference also reflects a higher proportion of one-parent families among African Americans. Comparing only married-couple families, African Americans (median income $35,218 in 1993) earned 81 percent as much as white people ($43,675).

Q: "Freedom is not enough. You do not wipe away the scars of centuries by saying: 'Now, you are free to go where you want, do as you desire, and choose the leaders you please.' You do not take a man who for years has been hobbled by chains, liberate him, bring him to the starting line of a race, saying, 'You are free to compete with all others,' and still justly believe that you have been completely fair." Lyndon Johnson (1965)

DIVERSITY: The sense that the Chinese would never assimilate is suggested by historic records such as this population count: "1,200 souls and two Chinamen." (Winnick, 1990)
NOTE: In 1943 the U.S. government extended right of citizenship to Chinese Americans born abroad partly in response to China's status as a military ally in the war against Japan (Japanese Americans born abroad could not become U.S. citizens until 1952).

In sum, for more than 350 years, African Americans have been struggling for social equality in the United States. Our nation can certainly take pride in notable accomplishments: Slavery was ended more than a century ago, and, more recently, this country banned many forms of overt discrimination. Taking a broader view, research reveals that our society is moving along a path of long-term decline in prejudice against African Americans (Firebaugh & Davis, 1988; J. Q. Wilson, 1992). During the 1970s, for example, about 60 percent of adults in the United States supported the right of a white person to refuse to sell a home to a nonwhite buyer; by 1994 that proportion had dropped to 30 percent (NORC, 1994:147).

Assessing the state of African Americans in 1913—fifty years after the abolition of slavery—W. E. B. Du Bois cited the achievements of people of color as grounds for optimism about the future. But Du Bois also cautioned that racial caste remained strong in the United States, and social hierarchy based on race persists to this day.

Asian Americans

Although Asian Americans share racial traits, enormous cultural diversity marks this category of people. The 1990 census placed their number at more than 7 million—approaching 3 percent of the population. As noted earlier (in the "Minority-Majority" box), the Asian and Pacific Islander population more than doubled during the 1980s.

Comprising the largest category of Asian Americans are people of Chinese ancestry (1.6 million), followed by those of Filipino (1.4 million), Japanese (848,000), Asian Indian (815,000), and Korean (800,000) descent. Most Asian Americans live in the western United States; 40 percent live in California (U.S. Bureau of the Census, 1995).

Young Asian Americans command respect as high achievers and are disproportionately represented at our country's best colleges and universities. Many of their elders, too, have made substantial economic and social gains in recent years, with most Asian Americans now living in middle-class suburbs (O'Hare, Frey, & Fost, 1994). Yet Asian Americans often experience aloofness to outright hostility from other people despite (and sometimes because of) this outstanding record of achievement.

Moreover, as we shall see, the "model minority" image of Asian Americans obscures the poverty found within their ranks. We now focus on the history and current standing of Chinese Americans and Japanese

Given the extent of global inequality, it is not surprising that tens of millions of people each year leave their homes in search of more opportunity. This ship, which recently sailed into San Francisco, contained some of the 100,000 Chinese immigrants who annually try to enter this country any way they can.

Americans—the longest-established Asian-American minorities—and conclude with a brief look at the most recent arrivals.

Chinese Americans

Chinese immigration to the United States began with the California Gold Rush of 1849. New towns and businesses sprang up virtually overnight as the new Central Pacific railroad carried eager settlers westward. During this time, some 100,000 Chinese immigrants entered the country eager to offer their labor. Most were hard-working young men willing to take lower-status jobs shunned by whites (Ling, 1971).

But the economy soured in the 1870s, and desperate whites were thrown into a fierce competition with the Chinese for jobs. Suddenly the industriousness of the Chinese and their willingness to work for low wages posed a threat. Illustrating a well-known pattern, economic hard times led to mounting prejudice and discrimination (Boswell, 1986).

Soon, whites acted to legally bar the Chinese from many occupations. Courts also withdrew legal protections, unleashing vicious campaigns against the so-called Yellow Peril. Everyone seemed to line up against the Chinese, and the saying that a person didn't have

TABLE 12–4 The Social Standing of Asian Americans, 1990

	All Asian Americans	Chinese Americans	Japanese Americans	Korean Americans	Filipino Americans	Entire United States
Median family income	$42,240	$41,316	$51,550	$33,909	$46,698	$35,225
Percent in poverty	14.0%	14.0%	7.0%	13.7%	6.4%	13.1%
Completion of four or more years of college (age 25 and over)	37.7%	40.7%	34.5%	34.5%	39.3%	20.3%

Source: U.S. Bureau of the Census (1995).

"a Chinaman's chance" gained currency (Sung, 1967; Sowell, 1981).

In 1882, the U.S. government passed the first of several laws curtailing Chinese immigration. This action created great domestic hardship because, in the United States, Chinese men outnumbered women by almost twenty to one (Hsu, 1971; Lai, 1980). This sex imbalance limiting marriages sent the Chinese population plummeting to about 60,000 by 1920. Chinese women already in the United States, however, were so sought after that they soon became far less submissive to men (Sowell, 1981).

Responding to racial hostility, some Chinese fled eastward; many more sought the relative safety of urban Chinatowns on the West Coast. There Chinese traditions flourished, and kinship networks, called clans, provided financial assistance to individuals and represented the interests of all. At the same time, however, Chinatowns discouraged their residents from learning the English language and from taking jobs outside the local community (Wong, 1971).

A renewed need for labor during World War II prompted President Franklin Roosevelt in 1943 to end the ban on Chinese immigration and to extend the rights of citizenship to Chinese Americans born abroad. Many responded by moving out of Chinatowns and pursuing cultural assimilation. In turn-of-the-century Honolulu, for example, 70 percent of the Chinese people lived in Chinatown; today, the proportion is less than 20 percent.

By 1950, many Chinese Americans had experienced considerable upward social mobility, a trend that continues today. No longer restricted to self-employment in laundries and restaurants, many people of Chinese ancestry now work in a host of high-prestige occupations. Many of these men and women—including several Nobel prize winners—have excelled in science and technology.

As shown in Table 12–4, the median family income of Chinese Americans in 1990 ($41,316) stood above the national average ($35,225)[4]. The higher income of all Asian Americans reflects, on average, a larger number of family members in the labor force.[5] Chinese Americans also have an enviable record of educational achievement: a proportion of college graduates that is twice the national average.

Despite this overall record of success, many Chinese Americans still grapple with subtle (and sometimes overt) prejudice and discrimination. Such hostility is one reason that poverty among Chinese Americans stands above the national average. Poverty is more pronounced among those who remain in the restrictive circle of Chinatowns, where many women and men still work in restaurants or the garment trade. This economic picture has sparked a debate over whether racial and ethnic enclaves assist or exploit their residents (Portes & Jensen, 1989; Zhou & Logan, 1989; Kinkead, 1992; Gilbertson & Gurak, 1993).

Japanese Americans

Japanese immigration to the United States began slowly in the 1860s, reaching only three thousand by 1890. Owners of sugar plantations welcomed Japanese immigrants to the Hawaiian Islands (annexed by the United States in 1898 and made a state in 1959) as a source of cheap labor. Early in this century, however, the number of Japanese entering California rose along with demands for better pay; white people responded by seeking limits to immigration (Daniels, 1971). In 1907 the United States signed an agreement with

---

[4]More recent data, for 1994, place median family income of Chinese Americans at $44,456, above the national figure of $36,782.

[5]Median age for all Asian Americans is 30.4, somewhat below the national median age of 34.0 and the white median of 35.0. But specific categories vary considerably in median age: Japanese, 36.1; Chinese, 32.1; Filipino, 31.1; Korean, 29.1; Asian Indian, 28.9; Cambodian, 19.4; Hmong, 12.5 (U.S. Bureau of the Census, 1995).

NOTE: The suburban area with the largest Asian population is Los Angeles (528,608 in 1990); the only suburban area with an absolute majority of Asian Americans is Honolulu (57%; 270,000).
DIVERSITY: Percentage of Asian Americans who speak a language other than English at home: All Asians, 65%; Hmong, 97%; Chinese, 83%; Koreans, 81%; Filipinos, 66%; Japanese, 43%; Indians, 15%. (U.S. Census Bureau)

DIVERSITY: Social-standing profile of Vietnamese Americans: Median family income (1990): $30,550; percent in poverty: 27.5%; completion of four or more years of college (age 25 and over): 17.4%.
DIVERSITY: Family size varies among Asian Americans from 3.1 persons among Japanese Americans to 6.6 among the Hmong. Typically, income and family size are negatively correlated.

Japan curbing the entry of men, who were deemed the greater economic threat, while allowing Japanese women to immigrate to ease the sex-ratio imbalance. By the 1920s, state laws in California and elsewhere mandated segregation and banned interracial marriage. The net result was that Japanese immigration soon slowed to a trickle. Not until 1952 did the United States extend citizenship to foreign-born Japanese.

Japanese immigrants differed from the Chinese in three ways. First, the number of Japanese immigrants was smaller, so they escaped some of the hostility directed at the more numerous Chinese. Second, the Japanese arrived with greater knowledge about the United States, so they were more skilled in easing racial conflict and assimilating into the larger society (Sowell, 1981). Third, Japanese immigrants favored rural farming to clustering together in cities.

But many white people objected to Japanese ownership of farmland, so California acted in 1913 to bar further purchases. Although principally motivated by economic considerations, such laws also reflected racial hostility, as suggested by this comment from the state's attorney general:

> The fundamental basis of all legislation has been, and is, race undesirability. It seeks to limit [Japanese] presence by curtailing the privileges which they may enjoy here, for they will not come here in large numbers and abide with us if they may not acquire land. (quoted in Kitano, 1980:563)

Foreign-born Japanese (called the *Issei*) responded by placing farmland in the names of their U.S.-born children (*Nisei*), who were constitutionally entitled to citizenship. Others farmed leased land with great success.

Japanese Americans faced their greatest struggle after December 7, 1941, when a Japanese strike force destroyed much of the U.S. naval fleet at Hawaii's Pearl Harbor. Rage toward Japan was directed at the Japanese living in the United States, and some feared Japanese Americans would commit acts of espionage and sabotage. Within a year, President Franklin Roosevelt signed Executive Order 9066, an unprecedented action intended to protect the national security of the United States. This act designated areas of the West Coast as military zones from which anyone considered likely to be disloyal would be relocated inland to remote military reservations. Ninety percent of those with Japanese ancestry—110,000 people in all—found themselves forcibly interned in security camps.

While concern about national security always grows in times of war, this policy has been sharply criticized.

First, it targeted an entire category of people, not one of whom was known to have committed a disloyal act. Second, roughly two-thirds of those imprisoned were *Nisei*, U.S. citizens by birth. Third, although the United States was also at war with Germany and Italy, no such action was taken against people of German or Italian ancestry.

Relocation meant selling homes, furnishings, and businesses on short notice for pennies on the dollar. As a result, almost the entire Japanese-American population was economically devastated. In military prisons—camps surrounded by barbed wire and armed soldiers—families suffered greatly as they were crowded into single rooms, often in buildings that had previously housed livestock (Fujimoto, 1971; Bloom, 1980). The internment ended in 1944, when the Supreme Court declared the policy unconstitutional. In 1988 Congress awarded $20,000 as token compensation to each victim of this policy.

After World War II, Japanese Americans staged a dramatic recovery. Having lost their traditional businesses, they pursued a wide range of new occupations. Because their culture places a high value on education and endorses hard work, Japanese Americans have achieved remarkable success. The 1990 median income of a Japanese-American household was almost 50 percent above the national average. And the rate of poverty among Japanese Americans is half that for the United States as a whole.

Upward social mobility has propelled cultural assimilation and interracial marriage (more than half of married Japanese Americans have a non-Japanese spouse). The third and fourth generations of Japanese Americans (the *Sansei* and *Yonsei*) rarely live in residential enclaves, as many Chinese Americans still do. In the process, many have abandoned their traditions, including the ability to speak Japanese. But the popularity of ethnic associations among Japanese Americans suggests that many seek to maintain some traditional identity (Fugita & O'Brien, 1985).

Overall, Japanese Americans can boast of a clear record of success. Yet many men and women of Japanese descent still feel caught between two worlds, no longer identifying with Japanese cultural traditions yet not winning complete acceptance in the larger world because of racial differences.

Recent Asian Immigrants

More recent immigrants from Asia include Filipinos, Indians, Koreans, Vietnamese, Samoans, and Guamanians. When these newcomers are added to

DIVERSITY: Educational gender gaps: Only among Filipinos are a larger share of women college graduates (42%) than men (36%). Among Koreans, 47% of men but only 26% of women hold a college degree.

Q: "Once America was a microcosm of European nationalities; today, America is a microcosm of the world." Molefi Asante

Q: "A free man carries himself with dignity. He feels respect for others, and for himself. In a free society all are equals, and in a society of free men there exist no prejudices." Olaf Palme

RESOURCE: A resource for the study of racial and ethnic tensions in Europe is *Eurobarometer: Public Opinion in the European Community*, prepared by the Commission of the European Communities (November 1989).

Asian Americans are more likely than any other category of people in the United States to be small-scale entrepreneurs. Although families may earn above-average incomes operating businesses such as this New York grocery store, they typically rely on the labor of many people for long hours.

the existing population of Chinese and Japanese descent, Asian Americans make up this country's fastest-growing minority, accounting for almost half of all immigration to the United States (Winnick, 1990). A brief look at Koreans and Filipinos—both from countries that have had special ties to the United States—reveals the social diversity of newly arriving people from Asia.

Koreans.   The 1990 U.S. Census recorded some 800,000 people of Korean descent; most are recent arrivals. Korean immigration to the United States was insignificant until the 1950s, after this country played a major role in the Korean War. The presence of U.S. troops in South Korea gave our soldiers firsthand experience with Korean culture (contact that, for some, led to marriage) and piqued interest about the United States among many Koreans.

Many Asian immigrants display a strong entrepreneurial spirit. They are slightly more likely than whites, three times more likely than Latinos, and four times more likely than African Americans to own and operate small businesses (U.S. Bureau of the Census, 1995). Among all Asian Americans, moreover, Koreans stand out as the most likely to be entrepreneurs. In New York City, for example, the majority of grocery stores are Korean-owned; similarly, in Los Angeles Koreans operate a large share of local liquor stores.

Many Koreans work long hours; nonetheless, the income of Korean-American families falls slightly below the national average, as shown in Table 12–4. Moreover, Korean Americans have experienced limited social acceptance, even among other categories of Asian Americans. In short, the case of Korean Americans shows that minorities struggle for both economic success and social acceptance.

Filipinos.   With a recorded U.S. population of 1.4 million in 1990, Filipinos are the second largest category of Asian Americans, surpassed only by people of Chinese descent. Many came to this country during the period when the United States controlled the Philippine islands between 1898 (when Spain ceded the country as partial settlement of the Spanish-American War) and 1946 (when the Philippines became an independent republic).

Despite formal control of these Southeast Asian islands, the U.S. government did not grant Filipinos rights of U.S. citizenship. But as laws closed off immigration of other Asian peoples, Filipinos were permitted to come to the United States to take low-paying agricultural jobs, especially in Hawaii and California. The vast majority of Filipino newcomers to the United States were men, which had the predictable effect of keeping the U.S. Filipino population small.

Generally speaking, Filipinos have fared better in this country than most other Asian Americans, as a glance back at Table 12–4 shows. A closer look reveals a mixed pattern by which some Filipinos stand out among successful professionals (especially in medicine), while others struggle in low-skill jobs just trying to get by (Parrillo, 1994).

But the key to the relatively high income of Filipino-American families is gender. Almost three-fourths of Filipino-American women are in the labor force, compared to about half of Korean-American women. Moreover, 42 percent of Filipino-American women have a four-year college degree, an achievement equaled by just 26 percent of Korean-American women. Thus, the typical Filipino-American family has relatively high income because both wives and husbands work, in many cases at high-paying professional occupations.

In sum, the social history of Asians in this country is complex. The Japanese come closest to having achieved social acceptance; for others, especially the Koreans, economic success has not toppled historical prejudice and discrimination. And, while some Asian Americans enjoy considerable prosperity, many

RESOURCE: William O'Hare's "The Rise of Hispanic Affluence" is one of the articles found in the Macionis and Benokraitis reader, *Seeing Ourselves.*
DIVERSITY: Dade County, Fla., remains a national center of Hispanic culture. The composition of its population is 45% Hispanic (mostly Cuban), 37% Anglo, 18% African American, and 1% other categories.

NOTE: Social diversity was much greater in our history than most people realize, and also perhaps greater than it is today. Vincent Parrillo (1994) describes inaccurate comparisons between past and present diversity as the "Dillingham Flaw," named for Vermont's Senator William P. Dillingham who presided over the Congressional Commission on Immigration (1907–1911).

TABLE 12–5 The Social Standing of Hispanic Americans, 1990

	All Hispanics	Mexican Americans	Puerto Ricans	Cuban Americans	Entire United States
Median family income	$23,431	$23,240	$18,008	$31,439	$35,225
Percent in poverty	25.0%	25.0%	37.5%	13.8%	13.1%
Completion of four or more years of college (age 25 and over)	9.2%	6.2%	10.1%	18.5%	20.3%

Source: U.S. Bureau of the Census (1995).

(especially the newcomers) struggle with problems associated with poverty (Lee, 1994).

One thing seems clear: In light of their exceptionally high immigration rate, people of Asian ancestry are certain to play an even more central role in U.S. society in the century to come.

Hispanic Americans

In 1994, there were at least 26 million Hispanics, which is 10.0 percent of the U.S. population. Few people who fall into this category actually call themselves "Hispanics" in everyday conversation. Like Asian Americans, Hispanics are really a cluster of smaller populations, each of which identifies with a particular country. "Hispanic" is thus just a convenient shorthand used by the Census Bureau for collecting and organizing information about diverse peoples who share Spanish heritage perhaps mixed with African and Native-American ancestry (Marín & Marín, 1991). "Latino," an alternative to "Hispanic," finds favor primarily on the West Coast.

About two of three Latinos (at least 15 million) are Mexican Americans, commonly known as "Chicanos." Puerto Ricans are next in population size (2.5 million), followed by Cuban Americans (1.1 million). Other societies of Latin America are represented in smaller numbers, totaling an additional 6 million. Because of a high birth rate and significant immigration, the Hispanic population is currently increasing by almost 1 million a year. According to projections, Hispanics will outnumber African Americans in the United States by 2010 (U.S. Bureau of the Census, 1995).

The U.S. Hispanic population resides primarily in the Southwest and especially in California, where one in four residents is Latino (in greater Los Angeles, the proportion is closer to one in two). National Map 12–2, on page 342, locates counties across the United States with heavy concentrations of Hispanics and contrasts

them with counties containing especially large African-American and Asian-American populations.

The social standing of Hispanics has improved in some respects. One researcher reports that, between 1984 and 1988, the number of Hispanic professionals jumped by half (Schwartz, 1989). Another calculates that the number of affluent Hispanic households (with $50,000 or more in annual income) more than tripled between 1972 and 1993 (U.S. Bureau of the Census, 1995). Nevertheless, the average family income for Hispanics—about $23,912 in 1993—amounts to only a slight increase in real purchasing power compared to 1980. Furthermore, as Table 12–5 indicates, this figure remains well below the national average.[6] As the following sections reveal, however, some categories of Hispanics have fared better than others.

Mexican Americans

Some Mexican-American families have lived for centuries on land ceded by Mexico to the United States at the end of the Mexican-American War (1846–48). Most of today's Mexican Americans, however, are recent immigrants. Between 1970 and 1990, more immigrants entered the United States from Mexico than from any other country. The official Mexican-American population is close to 15 million, but the actual total could be far higher since thousands of people who have passed illegally from Mexico to the United States are not counted by the Census Bureau.

Like other immigrants, many Mexican Americans have worked as low-wage farm laborers or hold other low-paying jobs. Table 12–5 shows that the 1990 median family income for Mexican Americans was

---

[6]The 1994 median age of the U.S. Hispanic population was 26.1 years, well below the national median of 34.0 years. This differential explains some of the disparity in income and education.

THE MAP: Hispanics, African Americans, and Asian Americans cluster in different regions of the United States. Hispanics settle near the "Latin American" side of the country; similarly, most Asian immigrants come to California. Despite a marked northward migration after World War I, the highest concentrations of African Americans remain in the South

SOCIAL SURVEY: "Should immigrants be encouraged to blend into American culture or maintain their own culture more?" (CNN/Gallup Poll, June, 1995)

Blend, 59%   Maintain, 32%   DK/NR, 9%

NOTE: Before the Industrial Revolution, relatively few people moved from one country to another. The word "immigrant" entered the English language only around 1790.

Seeing Ourselves

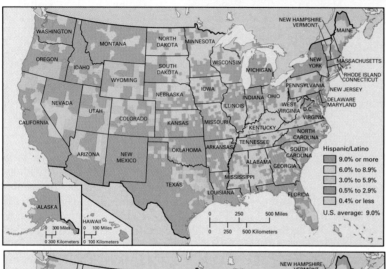

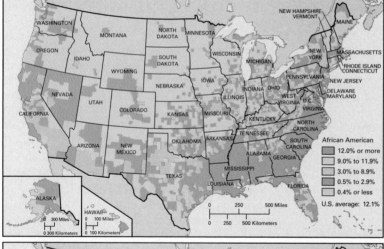

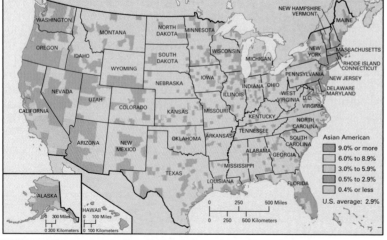

NATIONAL MAP 12–2

The Concentration of Hispanics/Latinos, African Americans, and Asian Americans, by County, 1990

In 1990, Hispanics represented 9 percent of the U.S. population, compared with 12 percent for African Americans and 3 percent for people of Asian descent. These three maps show the geographic distribution of these categories of people. Comparing them, we see that the southern half of the United States is home to far more minorities than the northern half. But are the three concentrated in the same specific areas? What patterns do the maps reveal?

Source: *American Demographics Desk Reference Series,* No. 1, June 1991, pp. 8, 14, 16. Reprinted with permission. © 1991, *American Demographics* magazine, Ithaca, New York. Data from 1990 decennial census.

The strength of family bonds and neighborhood ties is evident in this painting of street life in old San Juan, La Vida en Broma, *by Puerto Rican artist Nick Quijano (1988).*

© Nick Quijano 1997. *La Vida en Broma, 1988: Streetlife in Old San Juan.*

$23,240, about 66 percent of the comparable national figure of $35,225.[7] In 1990, the government classified one-fourth of Chicano families as poor—twice the national average but less than the proportion of African Americans living in poverty. Moreover, despite notable improvement, Mexican Americans receive significantly less education than U.S. adults as a whole and have a higher than average dropout rate.

Puerto Ricans

Puerto Rico (like the Philippines) became a possession of the United States in 1898 at the conclusion of the Spanish-American War. In 1917, Puerto Ricans (but not Filipinos) became American citizens; since then, Puerto Ricans have moved freely to and from the mainland (Fitzpatrick, 1980).

New York City is the center of Puerto Rican life in the continental United States. It was the start of regular airline service between New York City and San Juan, the capital of Puerto Rico, that sparked migration, and, by 1950, New York's Puerto Rican population stood at 187,000 (Glazer & Moynihan, 1970). Today New York is home to about 1 million Puerto Ricans (more than one-third of the total).

Certainly many of these people have found in New York less than they wished. About one-third of that city's Puerto Rican population is severely disadvantaged. Adjusting to culture on the mainland—including, for many, learning English—poses a major challenge; Puerto Ricans with darker skin encounter especially significant prejudice and discrimination. As a result, about as many people return to Puerto Rico each year as arrive from the island.

This "revolving door" pattern has hampered cultural assimilation. Three-fourths of Puerto Rican families in the United States speak Spanish at home, compared with about half of Mexican-American families (Sowell, 1981; Stevens & Swicegood, 1987). Speaking only Spanish may strengthen ethnic identity, but it also limits economic opportunity. In addition, compared to other Hispanics, Puerto Ricans have a higher incidence of female-headed households, which places families at greater risk of poverty.

Table 12–5 shows that 1990 median family income for Puerto Ricans was $18,008, just half the national average. During the 1980s, median Puerto Rican income rose by about 25 percent, but Puerto Ricans remain the most socially disadvantaged Hispanic minority.

Cuban Americans

The U.S. government passed special legislation to allow 400,000 Cuban immigrants to come to this country in the decade following the 1959 Marxist revolution led by Fidel Castro (Perez, 1980). Most settled in Miami, although the Cuban community in New York now numbers over 50,000. Those who fled Castro's Cuba

---

[7]Data for 1993 place median family income at $23,654, 64 percent of the national median of $36,959.

DIVERSITY: About 14% of the U.S. population aged five and older speak a language other than English at home, a total of 31.8 million people in 1990. In 1980, the share was 11% and 23.5 million people. Most of these people (55%) are Spanish-speakers (the 1980 figure was 48%); 14% (4.5 million) are speakers of an Asian language (up from 2.2 million in 1980). More than half of all non-English speakers live in California, New York, and Florida. (U.S. Bureau of the Census, 1993)

DIVERSITY: The coming "minority-majority" is due partly to more rapid population growth among most minorities than among whites. Asians are growing primarily due to immigration, Latinos because of both immigration and natural increase, African Americans mainly due to natural increase. The slower growth among whites is also due primarily to natural increase.

were generally not the "huddled masses" described on the Statue of Liberty but highly educated business and professional people. They wasted little time building much the same success in the United States that they had enjoyed in their homeland (Fallows, 1983).

Table 12–5 shows that the median household income for Cuban Americans in 1990 was $31,439—a relatively high figure that reflects the facts that these people are generally older and more successful than other categories of Hispanics (Krafft, 1993). But note that this income still lags below the national standard, just as poverty among Cuban Americans is higher than average.

Cuban Americans have managed a delicate balancing act—achieving success in the larger society while retaining much of their traditional culture. Of the categories of Hispanics already noted, they are the most likely to speak Spanish in their homes; eight out of ten families do (Sowell, 1981). However, their cultural distinctiveness and their highly visible community enclaves, like Miami's Little Havana district, provoke hostility from some white people.

The 1990 census placed the total number of Cuban Americans at more than 1 million. Substantial population growth during the 1980s followed the so-called Mariel boat lift, the influx of 125,000 refugees from Mariel Harbor in Cuba. Several thousand of these "boat people" had been released from Cuban prisons and mental hospitals, and they became the focus of mass media accounts fueling prejudice against Cuban Americans (Clark, Lasaga, & Regue, 1981; Portes, 1984).

About 90,000 of this second wave of Cuban immigrants settled in the Miami area while others—especially those with darker skin—made their way to cities in the Northeast (Perez, 1980). Typically poorer and less educated than those who had arrived a generation earlier, these recent immigrants clashed with the more conservative and established Cuban community in Miami (Fallows, 1983). But they, too, are quickly putting down roots. Soon after arriving, most applied for resident status so that relatives abroad could also be admitted to the United States.

White Ethnic Americans

The term white ethnics gained currency during the 1960s in recognition of the visible ethnic heritage—and social disadvantages—of many white Americans. This concept conveys the quasi-minority standing of members of the white majority who are not of privileged WASP ancestry. Thus white ethnics have some

non-English European ancestry, perhaps tracing their heritage to Germany, Ireland, Poland, Italy, or other countries. Overall, more than half the women and men in the United States fall into some white ethnic category, and, for many, it forms an important element of personal identity (Alba, 1990).

European immigration was pronounced during the nineteenth century. Initially, the Germans and Irish predominated. Italians, and Jews from many European countries, soon followed. Despite cultural differences, all shared the hope that the United States would offer greater political freedom and economic opportunity than they had known in their homelands. The belief that the streets of their new land were paved with gold contrasted sharply with the reality experienced by the vast majority of immigrants. Jobs were not always easy to find, and most demanded hard labor for low wages.

White ethnics also endured their share of prejudice and discrimination, which rose with the increasing tide of immigration. Nativist organizations opposed the entry of non-WASP Europeans to the United States. Newspaper ads seeking workers in the mid-nineteenth century often carried a warning to new arrivals: "None need apply but Americans" (Handlin, 1941:67).

Some of this prejudice and discrimination was based on class rather than ethnicity, since immigrants with little command of English were typically poor as well. But even distinguished achievers faced hostility. Fiorello La Guardia, the son of immigrants, half Italian and half Jewish, served as mayor of New York between 1933 and 1945 in spite of being rebuked by President Herbert Hoover in words that reveal unambiguous ethnic hatred:

> You should go back where you belong and advise Mussolini how to make good honest citizens in Italy. The Italians are preponderantly our murderers and bootleggers. . . . Like a lot of other foreign spawn, you do not appreciate the country that supports and tolerates you. (Mann, 1959, cited in Baltzell, 1964:30)

Nativists were finally victorious. In 1921 the government enacted legislation that limited immigration by imposing a quota from each foreign country; this quota system remained until 1968. The most severe restrictions were placed on southern and eastern Europeans—people generally with darker skin and with cultural traditions different from those of the dominant WASPs (Fallows, 1983).

In response to widespread bigotry, many white ethnics followed the old pattern of forming supportive

NOTE: Figure 12–3 shows the *number* of immigrants over time; the *proportion* of immigrants was far higher (about 10% of the total population per year) until World War I. In recent years, this proportion has again been rising, although it still is below 3%.

NOTE: The current wave of immigration began in 1965 with liberalization of the old quota system dating from 1924. In essence, "country of origin" ceased to be a key criterion for admission to the United States in favor of special skills and family ties. This sparked a shift from Europe to Latin America and Asia as the source of immigrants, and also allowed many families to join earlier immigrants.

DISCUSS: Ask students to comment on California's Proposition 187 ("Save Our State"), passed in November, 1994, prohibiting illegal immigrants from using state public services. It was never put into practice, however.

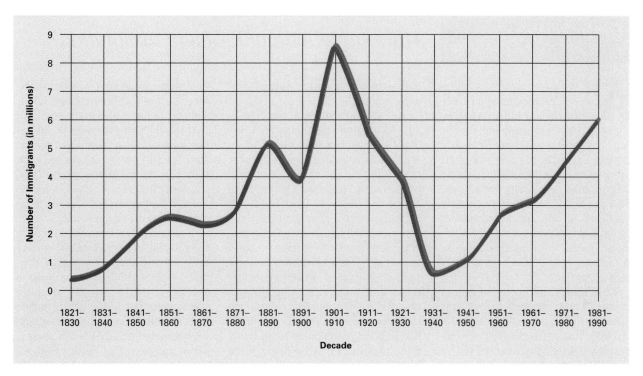

FIGURE 12–3 Immigration to the United States, by Decade
Source: U.S. Immigration and Naturalization Service.

residential enclaves. Some also gained footholds in specialized trades: The Italians entered the construction industry; the Irish worked in various building trades and took civil service jobs; Jews predominated in the garment industry; many Greeks (like the Chinese) worked in the retail food business (Newman, 1973).

White ethnics who prospered were likely to assimilate into the larger society. Many working-class "ethnics," however, still live in traditional neighborhoods. Despite continuing problems, white ethnics have achieved considerable success over the course of this century. Many descendants of immigrants who labored in sweatshops and lived in overcrowded tenements now earn high incomes and enjoy considerable social prestige. As a result, ethnic heritage now serves as a source of pride to many white men and women.

Race and Ethnicity: Looking Ahead

The United States has always been a land of immigrants and will remain so in the foreseeable future. Immigration has generated striking cultural diversity, as well as tales of success, hope, and struggle, told in hundreds of tongues.

For most who came to this country in the great wave of immigration that peaked in 1910, the next two generations brought gradual economic gains and some cultural assimilation. During this period, the United States also extended citizenship to Native Americans (1924), foreign-born Filipinos (1942), Chinese Americans (1943), and Japanese Americans (1952). Although they had gained citizenship in 1868, their continuing disadvantage led African Americans to organize a civil rights movement in the 1950s that sparked further legal reforms.

As Figure 12–3 indicates, a subsequent wave of immigration began after World War II and continued as the government relaxed immigration laws during the 1960s. Since 1990, almost 1 million people have come to the United States each year, a surging flow as large as the "Great Immigration" a century ago (although newcomers now enter a country with five times as many people). Today's immigrants, however, come not from Europe but from Latin America and Asia, with Mexicans, Filipinos, and South Koreans arriving in the largest numbers.

SOCIAL SURVEY: A telephone survey by the National Black Politics Study (1993–94) asked "When will African Americans achieve racial equality?" Responses: "It has been achieved," 5%; "It will be achieved soon," 30%; "Not in my lifetime," 42%; "Never," 23%. (*Time*, 5/2/94:16)

SOCIAL SURVEY: "Have we gone too far in pushing equal rights in this country?" "Yes," 51%; "No," 46%. (White respondents, 54% and 43%; African Americans, 31% and 64%.) (*Newsweek* poll, 2/1–3/95) 1987 responses to same question, "Yes," 42%; "No," 53%.

NOTE: Steele claims that race consciousness is especially effective on the college campus where the claim of black victimization is matched by widespread feelings of guilt among white people.

NOTE: Two-thirds of the U.S. population (including all women and other minorities) are covered by some form of affirmative action.

Controversy & Debate

Affirmative Action: Problem or Solution?

Adarand Constructors, a white-owned Colorado company, submitted the low bid for a federal highway project erecting guard rails. But Adarand never got the job. Despite having to pay a higher price, the government selected Gonzales Construction, a minority-owned firm. Adarand sued, and a bitter company manager, Randy Perch, explained: "What is prejudice? It's when government makes a decision based on something that doesn't matter, like race or gender."

Does race, or ethnicity, or gender matter in how we treat people? This question lies at the heart of the affirmative action debate. To begin, what, exactly, is this controversial policy and how did it originate?

The story started after World War II, when the U.S. government funded higher education for veterans of all races. The so-called G.I. Bill held special promise for African Americans, most of whom needed financial assistance to enroll in college. The program was successful and, by 1960, some 350,000 black men and women had arrived on campus with government funding.

But a problem remained: These individuals were not finding the kinds of jobs for which they qualified. In short, *educational* opportunity was not producing the kind of *economic* opportunity the government had hoped it would.

Thus, in the early 1960s, the Kennedy administration devised a program, soon tagged "affirmative action," to recruit qualified minorities for a range of positions. In simple terms, this policy was designed to throw a broader "net of opportunity" by taking steps to assure the presence of qualified minority candidates when filling jobs. In addition, employers were instructed to carefully monitor hiring, promotion, and admissions policies to eliminate discrimination—even if unintended—against minorities.

Proponents defend affirmative action as a sensible and fair response to our nation's racial and ethnic history. Especially for African Americans, *majority*-preferences were the norm throughout the past, beginning with two centuries of slavery, followed by a century of legal segregation under Jim Crow laws. Supporters point out that the lives of everyone—whether black or white—are affected by the barriers and opportunities faced by their parents and grandparents. Thus, *minority*-preference today is a step toward just compensation for past prejudice and discrimination.

Second, given our racial history, the promise of a "color-blind" society strikes many analysts as empty. Prejudice and discrimination are deep in the fabric of U.S. society; thus we cannot simply endorse the principle of color-blindness and expect everyone to compete fairly. For this reason, some suggest, the notion that we should now strive to take a color-blind approach is merely one element of the recent attack on affirmative action and operates, itself, as a form of prejudice and discrimination.

Third, proponents maintain that affirmative action has worked. Where would minorities be if the U.S. government had not enacted the policy three decades ago? Indeed, they continue,

Many arrivals face much the same prejudice and discrimination experienced by those who came before them. Indeed, recent years have witnessed rising hostility toward foreigners (sometimes called *xenophobia*, with Greek roots meaning "fear of what is strange"). In 1994, California voters passed Proposition 187, which mandates a cut-off in social services (including schooling) to illegal immigrants. And, as the final box explains, the policy of affirmative action seems more controversial than ever.

In today's climate of downsizing and cutbacks, some people scorn newcomers who, they think, come here to take advantage of schooling and other costly social programs (although most analysts conclude that,

as a whole, immigrants contribute much more to the U.S. economy than they draw from it). For some others, of course, simply being racially or ethnically different may be sufficient to spark animosity.

But, whatever the obstacles, many of today's immigrants—like European immigrants of the past—struggle to enter U.S. society without entirely abandoning their traditional culture. Some have also built racial and ethnic enclaves: The Little Havana and Little Saigon of today stand alongside the Little Italy and Germantown of the past. Also like their predecessors, today's immigrants are determined to display race and ethnicity as a source of pride rather than a badge of inferiority.

major employers, such as fire and police departments in large cities, began hiring minorities and women for the first time only because of affirmative action. Moreover, this program has played an important part in the expansion of the African-American middle class.

But affirmative action always drew criticism. Today, Congress is taking aim at all such programs, and public opinion surveys indicate that a majority of adults think we have already done enough to assist minorities.

The first argument made by critics against affirmative action is that what started out as a temporary remedy to ensure fair competition quickly turned into a permanent system of "group preferences" and quotas. In other words, the policy did not remain true to the goal of promoting color-blindness (set out in the 1964 Civil Rights Act). Within a decade, it had become "reverse discrimination," favoring people not because of their performance but because of their race, ethnicity, or sex.

Second, critics contend that affirmative action is polarizing. If racial preferences were wrong in the past, they are wrong now. Moreover, why should whites or men today—many of whom are far from privileged—be penalized for past discrimination for which they were in no way responsible? Our society has undone most of the institutionalized prejudice and discrimination of earlier times, opponents continue, so that minorities can and do enjoy success when they have the talent and make the effort. Giving entire categories of people special treatment inevitably compromises standards, calls into question the real accomplishments of minorities, and provokes a hostile backlash from white people.

The third counterargument is that the benefits of affirmative action go to those who need them least. Favoring minority-owned corporations or allocating places in law school for minorities, in other words, typically helps already privileged people. Affirmative action, however, has done little to remedy the plight of the African-American underclass.

In sum, there are good reasons to argue for and against affirmative action. Indeed, people who believe in the ultimate goal of a society in which no racial or ethnic category dominates others fall on both sides of this debate. The disagreement, then, is not over the idea that people of all colors should have equal opportunity. It lies in whether a single policy—affirmative action—is part of the solution or part of the problem.

Continue the debate . . .

1. *Should all minorities be represented in jobs or universities in proportion to their numbers in the larger population? Why or why not?*

2. *Should affirmative action cover only disadvantaged categories of minorities (say, African Americans and Native Americans) and exclude more affluent categories (such as Japanese Americans)? Why or why not?*

3. *Can sociology play a part in the affirmative action debate? How?*

Sources: NORC (1994), Carr (1995), and Cohen (1995).

SUMMARY

1. Race involves a cluster of biological traits. A century ago scientists identified three broad overarching racial categories: Caucasians, Mongoloids, and Negroids. However, there are no pure races. Ethnicity is a matter not of biology but of shared cultural heritage.

2. Minorities—including those of certain races and ethnicities—are categories of people who are socially distinctive and who have a subordinate social position.

3. A prejudice is an inflexible and distorted generalization about a category of people. Racism, a powerful type of prejudice, is any assertion that one race is innately superior or inferior to another.

4. Discrimination is a pattern of action by which a person treats various categories of people unequally. Institutional discrimination refers to the fact that the law and other social institutions, in contrast to individuals, can treat different categories of people unequally.

5. Pluralism refers to a state in which racial and ethnic categories, although distinct, have equal social standing. Assimilation is a process by which minorities gradually adopt the patterns of the

dominant culture. Segregation means the physical and social separation of categories of people. Genocide involves the extermination of a category of people.

6. Native Americans—the original inhabitants of the Americas—have endured genocide, segregation, and forced assimilation. Today the social standing of Native Americans is well below the national average.

7. WASPs, who predominated among the original European settlers of the United States, continue to enjoy high social position today.

8. African Americans survived two centuries of slavery. Emancipation in 1865 gave way to rigid segregation prescribed by law. Today, despite legal equality, African Americans remain relatively disadvantaged.

9. Chinese and Japanese Americans have suffered both racial and ethnic hostility. Although some prejudice and discrimination continues, both categories now have above-average income and education. More recent immigration—especially of Koreans and Filipinos—has made Asians the fastest-growing racial category of the U.S. population.

10. Hispanics represent many ethnicities rooted in Spanish culture. Mexican Americans, the largest Hispanic minority, are concentrated in the Southwest. Puerto Ricans, one-third of whom live in New York, are poorer. Cubans, concentrated in Miami, are the most affluent category of Hispanics.

11. White ethnics include non-WASPs of European ancestry. While most white ethnics made gains during this century, many still struggle for economic security.

12. Immigration has increased in recent years. No longer primarily from Europe, most newcomers now arrive from Latin America and Asia.

KEY CONCEPTS

assimilation the process by which minorities gradually adopt patterns of the dominant culture

discrimination any action that involves treating various categories of people unequally

ethnicity a shared cultural heritage

genocide the systematic annihilation of one category of people by another

institutional prejudice or discrimination bias in attitudes or action inherent in the operation of society's institutions

minority a category of people, distinguished by physical or cultural traits, who are socially disadvantaged

miscegenation biological reproduction by partners of different racial categories

pluralism a state in which racial and ethnic minorities are distinct but have social parity

prejudice a rigid and irrational generalization about an entire category of people

race a category composed of people who share biologically transmitted traits that members of a society deem socially significant

racism the belief that one racial category is innately superior or inferior to another

scapegoat a person or category of people, typically with little power, whom people unfairly blame for their own troubles

segregation the physical and social separation of categories of people

CRITICAL-THINKING QUESTIONS

1. Clearly differentiate between race and ethnicity. Do you think all nonwhite people should be considered minorities, even if they have above-average income?

2. In what ways do prejudice and discrimination reinforce each other?

3. Are *all* generalizations about minorities wrong? What distinguishes a fair generalization from an unfair stereotype?

4. Do you think U.S. society is color-blind? Should we be? Does affirmative action reduce or exacerbate racial conflict?

SUGGESTED READINGS

Classic Sources

W. E. Burghardt Du Bois. *The Souls of Black Folk.* New York: Penguin Books, 1982; orig. 1903.

This pioneering analysis of racial dynamics in the United States remains a source of insights decades after its publication.

Gunnar Myrdal, with Richard Sterner and Arnold Rose. *An American Dilemma: The Negro Problem and Modern Democracy.* New York: Harper & Brothers, 1944.

This classic investigation of the United States by a noted Swedish social scientist highlights the dilemma posed by a racial caste system in a society aspiring to be democratic.

Contemporary Sources

Vincent N. Parrillo. *Diversity in America.* Thousand Oaks, Calif.: Pine Forge, 1996.

This paperback provides a historical overview of racial and ethnic diversity in the United States and critically assesses the recent emphasis on "multiculturalism."

Gwen Kinkead. *Chinatown: A Portrait of a Closed Society.* New York: HarperCollins, 1992.

This account of New York's Chinatown—the largest of its kind with 150,000 people, most of whom are recent immigrants—is valuable both for its striking analysis of race and ethnicity and its example of challenging fieldwork.

Maria P. P. Root, ed. *Racially Mixed People in America.* Newbury Park, Calif.: Sage, 1992.

This book offers a look at biracial children, whose numbers have risen steadily in the United States.

Global Sources

Eliezer Ben-Raphael and Stephen Sharot. *Ethnicity, Religion, and Class in Israeli Society.* Cambridge, U.K.: Cambridge University Press, 1991.

This investigation of the resurgence of ethnicity in Israel also demonstrates how ethnicity interacts with social class.

Lucy Nguyen-Hong-Nhiem and Joel Martin Halpern, eds. *The Far East Comes Near: Autobiographical Accounts of Southeast Asian Students in America.* Amherst, Mass.: University of Massachusetts Press, 1989.

These personal accounts tell of the challenges faced by people who have moved half a world away from home in search of greater freedom and opportunity.

Sex and Gender

The Duchess of Windsor once quipped, "A woman cannot be too rich or too thin." Perhaps the first half of this observation might apply to men as well, but certainly not the second. Why is it that the $20-billion-a-year cosmetics industry aims almost exclusively at women? Why does the diet industry— which consumes a whopping $40 billion each year—also target women? According to Naomi Wolf (1990), the answer lies in the cultural patterns she calls the "beauty myth." The beauty myth means, first, that society teaches women to measure personal importance, accomplishment, and satisfaction in terms of physical appearance (Backman & Adams, 1991). Curiously, however, this myth also sets up unattainable standards of beauty for most women (such as the Playboy centerfold or the one-hundred-pound New York fashion model), making the quest for beauty ultimately self-defeating. It should not be surprising, argues Wolf, that the beauty myth surfaced in our culture during the 1890s, the 1920s, and the 1980s—all times of anxiety and heightened debate about the social standing of women.

Second, through the beauty myth society teaches women to prize relationships with men, whom, presumably, they attract with their beauty. The relentless pursuit of beauty not only drives women toward being highly disciplined, but it also forces them to be keenly attuned and responsive to men. Beauty-minded women, in short, strive to please men and avoid challenging male power.

A third element of the beauty myth is that society teaches men to possess women who embody beauty. In other words, our concept of beauty both reduces women to objects and motivates men to possess them as if they were dolls rather than human beings.

In short, Wolf asserts, beauty is as much about behavior as appearance. The myth holds that the key to women's personal happiness lies in beauty (or, for men, in possessing a beautiful woman). In fact, however, beauty amounts to an elaborate system—which this chapter explores—through which society teaches both women and men to embrace specific roles and attitudes that place them in a social hierarchy.

SEX AND GENDER

Many people claim that men's and women's differing preoccupations and social patterns—such as a male's concern with getting rich and a female's interest in remaining thin—reflect basic and innate differences between the sexes. But, as we shall see, the different social experiences of women and men are the creation of society far more than biology. To begin, we shall distinguish between the key concepts of sex and gender.

Sex: A Biological Distinction

Sex refers to *the biological distinction between females and males*. Sex is closely related to reproduction, in which both females and males play a part. The female ovum and the male sperm, which join to form a fertilized embryo, each contain twenty-three pairs of chromosomes—biological codes that guide physical development. One of these chromosome pairs determines the child's sex. The mother always contributes an X chromosome;

Primary and Secondary Sex Characteristics

At birth, females and males are distinguished by **primary sex characteristics,** *the genitals, used to reproduce the human species.* Further sex differentiation occurs years later when children reach puberty and their reproductive systems become fully operational. At this point, humans exhibit **secondary sex characteristics,** *bodily development, apart from the genitals, that distinguishes biologically mature females and males.* To accommodate pregnancy, giving birth, and nurturing infants, adolescent females develop wider hips, breasts, and soft fatty tissue, which provides a reserve supply of nutrition for pregnancy and breast-feeding. Usually slightly taller and heavier than females from birth, adolescent males typically develop more muscles in the upper body, more extensive body hair, and voices deeper in tone. These are general differences, however: Some males are smaller, have less body hair, and speak in a higher tone than some females.

Sex is a biological distinction that develops prior to birth. Gender is the meaning that a society attaches to being female or male. Thus, it is culture that divides the range of human behavior, thoughts, and feelings into what people define as feminine or masculine. Moreover, gender differences are also a matter of power, as what is masculine typically has social priority over what is feminine. The importance of gender is not evident among infants, of course, but the ways in which we think of boys and girls set in motion patterns that will continue for a lifetime.

Hermaphrodites

Sex is not always a clear-cut matter. In rare cases, a hormone imbalance before birth produces a **hermaphrodite** (a word derived from Hermaphroditus, the offspring of the mythological Greek gods Hermes and Aphrodite, who embodied both sexes), *a human being with some combination of female and male internal and external genitalia.* Because our culture is uneasy about sexual ambiguity, we often look upon hermaphrodites with confusion and even disgust. By contrast, the Pokot of eastern Africa are indifferent to what they consider a simple biological error, and the Navajo regard hermaphrodites with awe, viewing them as the embodiment of the full potential of both the female and the male (Geertz, 1975).

Transsexuals

Further complicating the story of human sexuality, some people deliberately change their sex. Hermaphrodites may undergo genital surgery to gain the appearance (and occasionally the function) of a sexually normal female or male. Surgery is also commonly considered by **transsexuals,** *people who feel they are one sex though biologically they are the other.* Tens of thousands of transsexuals in the United States have medically altered their genitals to escape the sense of being "trapped in the wrong body" (Restak, 1979, cited in Offir, 1982:146).

the father contributes either an X or a Y. A second X from the father produces a female (XX) embryo; a Y from the father yields a male (XY) embryo. A child's sex, then, is determined at conception.

Within weeks, the sex of an embryo starts to guide its development. If the embryo is male, testicular tissues begin producing testosterone, a hormone that stimulates the development of the male genitals. Without testosterone, the embryo develops female genitals. In the United States, about 105 boys are born for every 100 girls, but a higher death rate among males makes females a slight majority in the population by the time people reach their mid-thirties (U.S. National Center for Health Statistics, 1990).

RESOURCE: J. M. Carrier's comparative look at homosexuality is among the cross-cultural selections in the Macionis and Benokraitis reader, *Seeing Ourselves*.
GLOBAL THEN AND NOW: A 1995 *British Medical Journal* study found that people in Britain lose their virginity at age 17, about three years earlier than in 1950. They found no difference in age of first intercourse among men and women. Use of condoms among teens was about 60%, sharply up since 1950.
NOTE: The gay rights movement maintains that 10% of our society's members are gay, which lends moral urgency to their pursuit of social acceptance and equal standing (Kirk & Madsen, 1989). But a considerable number of recent studies in the U.S. and abroad have challenged this assertion, suggesting that it is simply too high (Crispell, 1992; Cole & Gorman, 1993; Horowitz et al., 1993).

Sexual Orientation

Sexual orientation refers to *an individual's preference in terms of sexual partners: same sex, other sex, either sex, neither sex* (Lips, 1993). For most living things, sexuality is biologically programmed. In humans, however, sexual orientation is bound up in the complex web of cultural attitudes and rules. The norm in all industrial societies is *heterosexuality* (*hetero* is a Greek word meaning "the other of two"), by which a person is sexually attracted to someone of the other sex. However, *homosexuality* (*homo* is the Greek word for "the same"), by which a person is sexually attracted to people of the same sex, is not uncommon. Other sexual orientations are *bisexuality* (attraction to either sex) or *asexuality* (attraction to neither sex).

Although all cultures endorse heterosexuality, many tolerate—and some have even encouraged—homosexuality. Among the ancient Greeks, for instance, elite men celebrated homosexuality as the highest form of relationship, shunning women, whom they considered their intellectual inferiors. In this light, heterosexuality amounted to little more than a reproductive necessity and men who did not engage in homosexuality were defined as deviant. But because homosexual relations do not permit reproduction, no record exists of a society that has favored homosexuality to the exclusion of heterosexuality (Kluckhohn, 1948; Ford & Beach, 1951; Greenberg, 1988).

Homosexuality and the Pursuit of Gay Rights

By the 1960s, homosexuals were becoming more outspoken. By adopting the term *gay*, they were affirming their satisfaction with their sexual orientation. Gays also began to challenge narrow stereotypes—pointing out that the personalities of gay people vary as much as those of "straights"—and to organize in opposition to pervasive discrimination.

In recent years, gay men have faced calamity in the form of acquired immune deficiency syndrome, or AIDS. Since 1980, this deadly disease has not only killed more than 100,000 gay men in the United States (and almost as many nongay people); during the 1980s, it also provoked a renewed outburst of prejudice, discrimination, and outright violence against gays. But the longer-term picture shows a gradual softening of public attitudes. About two-thirds of U.S. adults still define homosexuality as morally wrong (down from three-fourths in the 1970s), but the same majority thinks our society should allow gays and straights equal workplace opportunities (Salholz, 1990; NORC, 1994:212).

Until our society becomes more accepting of homosexuality, some gay people will understandably choose to remain "in the closet," fearfully avoiding public disclosure of their sexual orientation. Heterosexuals can begin to understand what this secrecy means by imagining never speaking about their romances to parents, roommates, or colleagues (Offir, 1982).

For their part, many gay men and gay women (commonly called *lesbians*) have adopted the term *homophobia* (with Greek roots meaning "fear of sameness") to place their opponents on the defensive. This word, first used in the late 1960s, designates an irrational fear of gay people (Weinberg, 1973). Instead of asking "What's wrong with gay people?" this label turns the spotlight on society itself: "What's wrong with people who can't accept this sexual orientation?"

Determining the gay share of the population and the proportion of straight people is a vexing problem for researchers. For one thing, people are not always willing to discuss their sexuality with strangers (or even family members); for another, sexual orientation is not a matter of neat, mutually exclusive categories. Pioneering sex researcher Alfred Kinsey (1948, 1953) described sexual orientation as a continuum, from exclusively homosexual, to equally homosexual and heterosexual, to exclusively heterosexual. Kinsey contended that about 4 percent of males and 2 percent of females have an exclusively same-sex orientation, although he also estimated that at least one-third of men and one-eighth of women had at least one homosexual experience leading to orgasm.

In the wake of the Kinsey studies, most social scientists settled on a figure of 10 percent to describe the proportion of gays in the U.S. population. A comprehensive 1992 survey[1] of sexuality in the United States indicates that precisely how one operationalizes "homosexuality" makes a big difference in the numbers. As Figure 13–1 shows, about 9 percent of U.S. men and 4 percent of U.S. women reported homosexual activity at some time in their lives. The second set of numbers reveals that a significant share of men (less so women) have some childhood homosexual experience that is not repeated after puberty. Finally, 2.8 percent of men and 1.4 percent of women claimed to label themselves as partly or entirely homosexual (Laumann et al., 1994).

---

[1]This national survey involved 3,432 adults, aged eighteen to fifty-nine. Individuals responded to the first two items using a self-administered, anonymous questionnaire, sealed in an envelope before being given to the interviewer; they responded to the third item verbally in an interview.

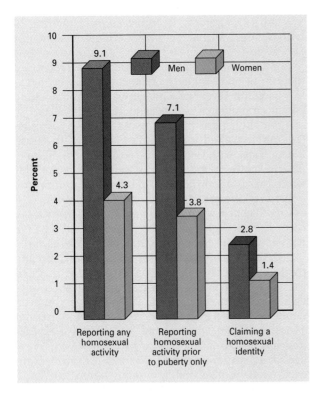

FIGURE 13–1 Measuring Sexual Orientation
Source: Laumann et al. (1994).

Bisexuality

Most people report sexual attraction only to the opposite sex (heterosexuality), while some people are attracted by people of the same sex (a homosexual orientation). Kinsey and his colleagues treated sexual orientation as an "either-or" trait: To be more homosexual is, by definition, to be less heterosexual. But the conventional wisdom is shifting toward a model of sexual orientation by which same-sex and other-sex attractions operate independently. At one extreme, some people experience little sexual attraction to people of either sex, the asexual orientation. At the other, a small share of *bisexual* people feel strong attraction to people of both sexes.

In the recent national sexuality survey noted above, less than 1 percent of adults described themselves as bisexual. But bisexuality is far more popular (at least as a phase) among younger people (especially on college campuses) who reject rigid conceptions of proper relationships (Laumann et al., 1994; Leland, 1995). Many bisexuals, then, do not characterize themselves as either gay or straight. Rather, their behavior may embody elements of both gay and straight living.

The Origins of Sexual Orientation

How does a person develop a particular sexual orientation? There is no definitive answer to this question, but mounting evidence suggests that homosexuality and heterosexuality are rooted in biological factors present at birth and reinforced by our hormone balance as well as social experiences as we grow (Gladue, Green, & Hellman, 1984; Weinrich, 1987; Troiden, 1988; Isay, 1989; Puterbaugh, 1990; Angier, 1992; Gelman, 1992). Noting that most adults who describe themselves as homosexuals have had some heterosexual experience (and many nominal heterosexuals have had at least some homosexual feelings), researchers conclude that sexual orientation is a highly complex human trait affected by both nature and nurture.

Moreover, there is no reason to think that sexual orientation is established in precisely the same way for everyone. At this point, while physical and social scientists have discovered a great deal about sexual orientation, we still have much more to learn.

Gender: A Cultural Distinction

The term *gender*, introduced in Chapter 2 ("Sociological Investigation"), refers to the significance a society attaches to the biological categories of female and male. Gender is evident throughout the social world, shaping how we think about ourselves, guiding our interaction with others, and influencing our work and family life. But gender involves much more than difference; it also involves hierarchy, since men enjoy a disproportionate share of most social resources.

Gender is no simple matter of biological differences between the two sexes. Females and males do differ biologically, of course, but these variations are complex and inconsistent. Beyond the primary and secondary sex characteristics already noted, males around the world average 150 pounds, compared to about 120 pounds for females. In addition, males have more upper-body strength than women do, and men typically outperform women in short-term tests of physical endurance. Yet women outperform men in some tests of long-term endurance because they can draw on the energy derived from greater body fat. Females also outperform males in the ultimate game of life itself: The average life expectancy for men in the United States is now 72.3 years, while women can expect to live 79.0 years (U.S. National Center for Health Statistics, 1995).

Adolescent males exhibit greater mathematical ability, while adolescent females outperform males in verbal skills, differences that researchers attribute to both biology and patterns of socialization (Maccoby & Jacklin, 1974; Baker et al., 1980; Lengermann & Wallace, 1985). Note, however, that research supports the conclusion that there are no overall differences in intelligence between females and males.

Biologically, then, the sexes differ in limited ways, with neither one naturally superior overall. Nevertheless, the deeply rooted *cultural* notion of male superiority may seem so natural that we assume it is the inevitable consequence of sex itself. But society, much more than biology, is at work here, as several kinds of research reveal.

An Unusual Case Study

In 1963 a physician was performing a routine penis circumcision on seven-month-old identical twin boys. While using electrocautery (surgery with a heated needle), the physician accidentally burned off the penis of one boy. Understandably, the parents were horrified. After months of medical consultation, they decided to surgically change the boy's sex and to raise him as a girl.

The parents dressed the child as a girl, let her hair grow long, and treated her according to cultural definitions of femininity. Meanwhile, the brother—born an exact biological copy—was raised as a boy.

Because of their different socialization, each child adopted a distinctive **gender identity**, *traits that females and males, guided by their culture, incorporate into their personalities*. In this extraordinary case, one child learned to think of himself in terms that our culture defines as masculine, while the other child—despite beginning life as a male—soon began to think of herself as feminine. As the twins' mother observed:

> One thing that really amazes me is that [my daughter] is so feminine. I've never seen a little girl so neat and tidy. . . . She is very proud of herself, when she puts on a new dress, or I set her hair. She just loves to have her hair set; she could sit under the dryer all day long to have her hair set. She just loves it. . . . [My daughter] likes for me to wipe her face. She doesn't like to be dirty, and yet my son is quite different. I can't wash his face for anything. . . . She seems to be daintier. (quoted in Money & Ehrhardt, 1972:124)

The girl's development did not proceed smoothly, however, suggesting that some biological forces were coming into play. While feminine in many respects, the researchers reported that she also began to display

In every society, people assume certain jobs, patterns of behavior, and ways of dressing are "naturally" feminine while others are just as obviously masculine. But, in global perspective, we see remarkable variety in such social definitions. These men, Wodaabe pastoral nomads who live in the African nation of Niger, are proud to engage in a display of beauty most people in our society would consider feminine.

some masculine traits, including a desire to gain dominance among her peers. Later, researchers following the case reported that, by the time she was reaching adolescence, she was showing signs of resisting her feminine gender identity (Diamond, 1982). This complex case certainly shows how gender is the product of the social environment, while also revealing that cultural conditioning does not operate free from the influence of biology.

The Israeli Kibbutzim

To investigate the roots of gender, researchers also have focused on collective settlements in Israel, called kibbutzim, where members historically have embraced social equality. Here men and women share in both work and decision making.

Both sexes in the kibbutzim typically perform all kinds of tasks, including child care, building maintenance, cooking, and cleaning. Boys and girls are raised in the same way, with children placed, from the first weeks of life, in dormitories under the care of specially trained personnel. Members of kibbutzim,

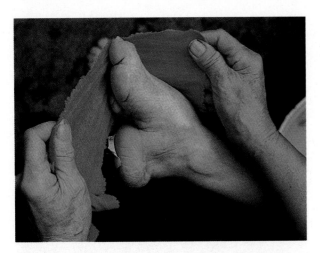

Among the most striking consequences of patriarchy in China is the ancient practice of "foot-binding," by which young girls' feet are tightly wrapped as they grow, with predictable results. Although this practice—now rare—produces what people deem "dainty" proportions, what effect would you imagine this deformity has on the physical mobility of women?

then, regard a person's sex as irrelevant to most of everyday life.

But here, again, we find reason for caution about completely discounting biological forces. Some observers note that women in the kibbutzim have resisted spending much of the day away from their own children. In response to this concern, many of these collectives have returned to more traditional social roles over the years. Such a turnabout, say some researchers, indicates the persistent if subtle influence of biologically rooted differences in the sexes (Tiger & Shepher, 1975). But even if this is so—and this research has its critics—the kibbutzim certainly stand as evidence of the wide cultural latitude people have in defining what is feminine and masculine. They also exemplify how, through conscious efforts, a society can pursue sexual equality just as it can encourage the domination of one sex by the other.

Global Comparisons

To the extent that gender is a dimension of culture, it should vary from society to society; to the degree that it is rooted in biology, the definitions of female and male should be much the same around the world. In a classic, comparative investigation of gender, Margaret Mead studied three societies of New Guinea (1963; orig. 1935). Trekking high into the mountains, Mead observed the Arapesh, whose men and women were remarkably similar in attitudes and behavior. Both sexes, she reported, were cooperative and sensitive to others—what our culture would label "feminine."

Moving south, Mead then studied the Mundugumor, whose culture of head-hunting and cannibalism stood in striking contrast to the gentle ways of the Arapesh. Here, Mead reported, females and males were again alike, although they were startlingly different from the Arapesh. Both Mundugumor females and males were typically selfish and aggressive, traits defined as more "masculine" in the United States.

Finally, traveling west to survey the Tchambuli, Mead discovered a culture that, like our own, defined females and males differently. Yet the Tchambuli reversed many of our notions about gender: Females tended to be dominant and rational, while males were submissive, emotional, and nurturing toward children.

Based on her observations, Mead concluded that what one culture defines as masculine another may consider feminine. Further, she noted that societies can exaggerate or minimize the importance of sex. Mead's research, then, makes a strong case that gender is a variable creation of culture.

In a more wide-ranging study, George Murdock (1937) assessed gender in more than two hundred preindustrial societies. In most societies, he found, hunting and warfare fall to males, while home-centered tasks such as cooking and child care are the purview of females. With only simple technology, preindustrial societies apparently adopt this strategy to benefit from men's greater size and short-term strength; because women bear children, their activities are usually more domestic.

But beyond these general patterns, Murdock found significant variation. About the same number of societies considered agriculture—the core of preindustrial production—to be feminine as to be masculine. In most societies, in fact, farming responsibilities were shouldered by both women and men. When it came to many other tasks—from building shelters to tattooing the body—Murdock documents that societies the world over have been as likely to favor one sex as the other.

In global perspective, then, societies define only a few specific activities consistently as feminine or masculine. And as societies industrialize, with a resulting decrease in the significance of muscle power, even those distinctions are minimized (Lenski, Nolan, & Lenski, 1995). Gender, in sum, is simply too variable

NOTE: Sandra Bem (1993) uses the term "androcentrism" to refer to the belief in male superiority.
NOTE: Patriarchy implies that paternity is the central social relationship. Note the Old Testament emphasis on "begats," one man begetting a son (Rothman, 1995).
NOTE: Research suggests that undergraduate women and men have somewhat different expectations of advisors. One-fourth of women and two-thirds of men had the primary concern that advisors "make concrete and directive suggestions." Three-fourths of women and one-third of men asked advisors to "take the time to know me personally." (The Harvard Assessment Seminars: Explorations with Students and Faculty about Teaching, Learning, and Student Life)
Q: "Conventionality is not morality." Charlotte Brontë

GLOBAL SOCIOLOGY

Patriarchy Breaking Down: A Report From Botswana

As the judge handed down the decision, Unity Dow beamed a smile toward the friends sitting all around her; people in the courtroom joined together in hugs and handshakes. Dow, then a thirty-two-year-old lawyer and citizen of the southern African nation of Botswana, had won the first round in her efforts to overturn the laws by which, she maintains, her country defines women as second-class citizens.

The law that sparked Unity Dow's recent suit against her government specifies the citizenship rights of children. Botswana is traditionally patrilineal, meaning that people trace family membership through males, making children part of their father's—but not their mother's—family line.

Under the law, a child of a Botswanan man and a woman of another nationality is a citizen of Botswana, since in that country legal standing passes through the father. But the child of a Botswanan woman and a man from another nation has no rights of citizenship. Because she married a man from the United States, Unity Dow's children had no citizen's rights in the country where they were born.

The Dow case attracted broad attention because its significance extends far beyond citizenship to the overall legal standing of women and men. In rendering the decision in Dow's favor, High Court Judge Martin Horwitz declared, "The time that women were treated as chattels or were there to obey the whims and wishes of males is long past." In support of his decision, Horwitz pointed to the constitution of Botswana, which guarantees fundamental rights and freedoms to both women and men. Arguing for the government against Dow, Ian Kirby, a deputy attorney

Around the world, patriarchy is most pronounced in less economically developed societies.

general, conceded that the constitution confers equal rights on the two sexes, but he claimed that the law can and should take account of sex where such patterns are deeply rooted in Botswanan male-dominated culture. To challenge such traditions in the name of Western feminism, he continued, amounts to cultural imperialism by which some people seek to subvert an established way of life by advancing foreign notions that are popular elsewhere.

Women from many African nations attended the Dow court case, sensing that a historic change was at hand. And, indeed, this has proven to be the case: As a result of the Dow ruling, the constitution of Botswana was amended to extend citizenship to children such as her own. Symbolically, this transformation greatly enhances the social standing of that nation's women.

To many people in the United States, the Dow case may seem strange, since the notion that men and women are entitled to equal rights and privileges is widely endorsed in our country. But, ironically, it is the United States—not Botswana—that has no constitutional guarantee of equal standing under the law for women and men.

Sources: Author's personal communication with Unity Dow and Shapiro (1991).

---

across cultures to be considered a simple expression of the biological categories of sex. Instead, as with many other elements of culture, what it means to be female and male is mostly a creation of society.

The cultural variability of gender also means that, in any one part of the world, the lives of women and men are subject to transformation over time. The box highlights change in the southern African nation of

Q: "For a guy to walk into a bar and have every woman there be ready to jump into bed with him, he would have to be the world's richest, best looking, and bravest guy. For a woman to get the same response from men, she only has to do her hair." Bill Maher, "Politically Incorrect"

Q: "Why isn't 'man's best friend' woman?" Carol Tavris and Carole Offir

Q: "At the bottom of it all, man's job is to protect woman, and woman's job is to protect her infant; all else is luxury." Steven Goldberg

NOTE: E. Digby Baltzell points out that control of women's sexuality is not simply designed to ensure the domination of women; it is society's means of promoting endogamy, thus defending racial and class hegemony.

TABLE 13–1 Sexism: Echoes of Racial Stereotypes

	Women	African Americans
Link to highly visible biological distinctions	Secondary sex characteristics.	Skin color.
Assertion of innate inferiority	Women are mentally inferior. Women are irresponsible, unreliable, and emotional.	African Americans are mentally inferior. African Americans are irresponsible, unreliable, and pleasure seeking.
Notion of "proper place"	A woman's place is in the home. All women really enjoy being treated "like ladies."	African Americans should remain "in their place." African Americans are content living just as they do.
Notion of the need for protection	Men put women on a pedestal.	White people "take care of" African Americans.
Coping strategies on the part of victims	Behavior flattering to men; letting men think they are better even when they are not. Hiding one's real feelings. Attempting to outwit men.	Deferential behavior toward white people; letting white people think they are better even when they are not. Hiding one's real feelings. Attempting to outwit white people.
Barriers to opportunity	Women don't need an education. Women should be confined to "women's work." Women should stay out of politics.	African Americans don't need an education. African Americans should be confined to "black occupations." African Americans should stay out of politics.
Control strategies on the part of oppressors	Assertive women are "pushy." Ambitious women are trying to be "like men." Violence against women.	Assertive African Americans are "uppity." Ambitious African Americans are trying to be like white people. Violence against African Americans.

Sources: Adapted from Helen Mayer Hacker, "Women as a Minority Group," *Social Forces* 30 (October 1951): 60–69; and "Women as a Minority Group: Twenty Years Later," in Florence Denmark, ed., *Who Discriminates Against Women?* (Beverly Hills, Calif.: Sage, 1974), pp. 124–34.

Botswana, and points up how and why gender is often controversial.

Patriarchy and Sexism

Although conceptions of gender certainly vary, a universal pattern among world societies is some degree of **patriarchy** (literally, "the rule of fathers"), *a form of social organization in which males dominate females.* Despite mythical tales of societies dominated by female "Amazons," the pattern of **matriarchy**, *a form of social organization in which females dominate males,* is not at present part of the human record (Gough, 1971; Harris, 1977; Kipp, 1980; Lengermann & Wallace, 1985).

While some degree of patriarchy may be universal, there is significant variation in the relative power and privilege of females and males around the world. In Saudi Arabia, for example, the power of men over women is as great as anywhere on earth; in the Scandinavian nation of Norway, by contrast, the two sexes approach equality in many respects.

Sexism, *the belief that one sex is innately superior to the other,* stands as an important ideological underpinning of patriarchy. Historically, patriarchy has rested upon a belief in the innate superiority of males who, therefore, legitimately dominate females. As Table 13–1 shows, sexism has much in common with racism: Both are ideologies that support the social domination of one category of people by another.

Also like racism, sexism is more than a matter of individual attitudes. The notion of men's and women's proper "place" is built into various institutions of our society. As we shall see presently, *institutionalized sexism* pervades the operation of the economy, with women highly concentrated in jobs that are less challenging and offer relatively low pay. Similarly, the legal system historically has winked at violence against women, especially violence committed by boyfriends, husbands, and fathers (Landers, 1990).

The Costs of Sexism

Sexism, which is deeply entrenched in our society, has clear costs to women, who are denied opportunities, stand at increased risk of poverty, and endure sexual violence. Taking a broader view, society also loses out to the extent that the full talents and abilities of half the population will never be developed.

RESOURCE: By and large, sociologists accept the view that biology plays no significant role in gender formation. Steven Goldberg's quote is therefore likely to elicit strong disapproval from most sociologists. Goldberg presents his evidence in "Reaffirming the Obvious" and "Utopian Yearning Versus Scientific Curiosity," *Society*, Vol. 23, No. 6 (September/October 1986):4–7 and 29–39.

Q: "Differences between the male and female endocrine/central nervous system are such that—statistically speaking—males have a greater tendency to exhibit whatever behavior is necessary in any environment to attain dominance in hierarchies . . ." Steven Goldberg

DIVERSITY: Without knowing the sex of the person involved, wouldn't people tend to evaluate the traits traditionally linked to females (Table 13–2) as negative?

Even though men benefit in some respects from sexism, their privilege comes at a high price: Masculinity in our culture calls for men to engage in all sorts of high-risk behaviors, including smoking and chewing tobacco, drinking alcohol, participating in physically stressful sports, and even speeding on the road to the point that motor-vehicle accidents are the leading cause of death among young males. Moreover, as Marilyn French (1985) argues, patriarchy compels men to relentlessly seek control—not only of women but of themselves and the entire world. Thus, masculinity is closely linked not only to accidents but also to suicide and violence as well as diseases related to stress. The so-called Type A personality—characterized by chronic impatience, driving ambition, competitiveness, and free-floating hostility—is a recipe for heart disease and almost perfectly matches the behavior that our culture defines as masculine (Ehrenreich, 1983).

Finally, insofar as men seek control over others, they lose the ability to experience intimacy and trust. As one analyst put it, competition is supposed to separate "the men from the boys." In practice, however, it separates men from men—and from everyone else (Raphael, 1988).

Overall, when human feelings, thoughts, and actions are rigidly scripted according to a culture's conceptions of gender, people cannot develop and freely express the full range of their humanity. Society saddles males with the burden of being assertive, competitive, and always in control; simultaneously, society constrains females to be submissive, dependent, and self-effacing, regardless of their individual talents and distinctive personalities.

Is Patriarchy Inevitable?

Technologically simple societies have little control over biological forces. Thus, men's greater physical strength, as well as women's common experience of pregnancy, combine to bolster patriarchy.

Technological advances, however, give members of industrial societies a wider range of choices about gender. Industrial machinery has diminished the primacy of muscle power in everyday life, just as contraception has given women control over pregnancy. Today, then, biological differences provide little justification for patriarchy.

Categorical social inequality—whether based on race, ethnicity, or sex—also comes under attack in the more egalitarian culture of industrial societies. In many industrial nations, law mandates equal employment opportunities for women and men and equal pay for comparable efforts.

**TABLE 13–2 Traditional Notions
of Gender Identity**

Feminine Traits	Masculine Traits
Submissive	Dominant
Dependent	Independent
Unintelligent and incapable	Intelligent and competent
Emotional	Rational
Receptive	Assertive
Intuitive	Analytical
Weak	Strong
Timid	Brave
Content	Ambitious
Passive	Active
Cooperative	Competitive
Sensitive	Insensitive
Sex object	Sexually aggressive
Attractive because of physical appearance	Attractive because of achievement

Nonetheless, in all industrial societies, the two sexes continue to hold different jobs and receive unequal pay, as we will explain presently. So does the persistence of patriarchy mean that it is inevitable? Some sociologists contend that biological factors underlie sex-based differences—especially a greater level of aggressiveness on the part of males. If this is so, of course, the eradication of patriarchy would be difficult and perhaps even impossible (Goldberg, 1974, 1987; Rossi, 1985; Popenoe, 1993). However, most sociologists believe that gender is primarily a social construction, subject to change. Simply because no society has yet eliminated patriarchy, then, does not mean that we must remain prisoners of the past.

To understand why patriarchy has persisted throughout human history, we now examine how gender is rooted and reproduced in society, a process that begins with the way we learn to think of ourselves as children, and continues through the work we perform as adults.

GENDER SOCIALIZATION

From birth until death, human feelings, thoughts, and actions reflect social definitions of the sexes. Children quickly learn that their society defines females and males as different kinds of human beings; by about the age of three, they begin to apply gender standards to themselves (Kohlberg, 1966; Bem, 1981).

Table 13–2 sketches the traits that people in the United States traditionally have used to distinguish "feminine" from "masculine." Note how these

SOCIAL SURVEY: "If the husband in a family wants children, but the wife decides that she does not want any children, is it all right for the wife to refuse to have children?" (GSS 1972–82, N = 12,096; *Codebook*, 1994:233)

"Yes" 59.0%   "No" 30.8%   DK/NR 10.2%

NOTE: Historically, few men were literate; even fewer women were. So that their works would be read, 19th-century women authors

often used male pseudonyms. "George Eliot," for instance, was the pen name of Mary Ann Evans (author of *Silas Marner*). The Brontë sisters all assumed gender-neutral pseudonyms: Charlotte Brontë (*Jane Eyre*) used the name Currer Bell; Anne Brontë (*Agnes Grey*) used Acton Bell; Emily Brontë (*Wuthering Heights*) used Ellis Bell.

NOTE: The phrase "the opposite sex" clearly conveys the idea that gender is a matter of opposition.

PROFILE

Jessie Bernard: Carrying Gender Into Sociology

Now past her ninetieth birthday, Jessie Bernard can look back on a remarkable record of achievement as a sociologist who cast a keen eye on the impact of gender. Bernard notes that past sociologists—even those critical of the status quo—have historically paid little attention to women's lives. Karl Marx, for instance, all but ignored women in his writings.

A key reason for giving short shrift to women, Bernard asserts, is that sociology (like most other disciplines) developed largely under the control of men. One of Bernard's most important contributions lies in revealing how familiar sociological issues and concepts have a built-in male bias.

Consider the topic of social stratification. Sociological research on our class system has focused largely on men to the exclusion of women. We have assumed, in other words, that men *earn* their class position while women simply *derive* their social position from fathers and, subsequently, husbands. Further, in their study of prestige attached to work (look back to Table 10–2), sociologists have long ignored housework, which has been primarily a responsibility of women. By defining occupational prestige so that it almost exclusively relates to men, Bernard reasons, sociologists effectively ignore women in their research.

Bernard's research and writing show us the importance of ensuring that our work addresses the lives of both females and males. Anything less is the study of just half of society.

Sources: Based on Bernard (1981) and author's personal communication with Bernard.

definitions form a pattern of polar opposites setting apart the female and male worlds, even though research indicates that most young people do not develop consistently feminine or masculine personalities (L. Bernard, 1980; Bem, 1993).

Just as gender affects how we *think* of ourselves, so it teaches us to *act* in normative ways. **Gender roles** (or sex roles) are *attitudes and activities that a society links to each sex.* Insofar as our culture defines males as ambitious and competitive, we expect them to engage in team sports and aspire to positions of leadership. To the extent that we define females as deferential and emotional, we expect them to be good listeners and supportive observers.

Gender and the Family

The first question people usually ask about a newborn—"Is it a boy or a girl?"—looms large because the answer involves not just sex but the likely direction of the child's entire life.

In fact, gender is at work even before the birth of a child, since parents generally hope to have a boy rather than a girl. As we noted in Chapter 11 ("Global Stratification"), in China, India, and other strongly patriarchal societies, female embryos are at risk because parents may abort them, hoping later to produce a boy, whose social value is greater (United Nations Development Programme, 1991).

Sociologist Jessie Bernard (1981), introduced in the box, asserts that soon after birth family members usher infants into the "pink world" of girls or the "blue world" of boys. Parents convey gender messages to children by how they, themselves, act and even unconsciously in the way they handle daughters and sons. One researcher at an English university presented an infant dressed as either a boy or a girl to a number of women; her subjects handled the "female" child tenderly, with frequent hugs and caresses, while treating the "male" child more aggressively, often lifting him up high in the air or bouncing him on the knee (Bonner, 1984). The lesson is clear: The female world revolves

GLOBAL: About 85% of U.S. parents express the desire that their children (regardless of sex) attend college. In Japan, 75% of parents want their sons to go to college, but only 30% voice this hope for daughters.

RESOURCE: An excerpt from Deborah Tannen's *You Just Don't Understand* is included in the Macionis and Benokraitis reader, *Seeing Ourselves*.

DIVERSITY: Evidence that the sciences remain largely masculine: Of 2,700 members elected to the National Academy of Sciences since its founding in 1863, only 60 have been women. Vera Rubin (*Science*, July/August 1986:58–65)

Q: "[Men] think themselves superior to women, but they mingle that with the notion of equality between men and women. It's very odd." Jean-Paul Sartre

around passivity and emotion, while the male world places a premium on independence and action.

Gender and the Peer Group

As children reach school age, their lives spill outside the family as they forge ties with others of the same age. Peer groups further socialize their members according to normative conceptions of gender. The box explains how play groups shaped one young boy's sense of himself as masculine.

Janet Lever (1978) spent a year observing fifth graders at play. She concluded that boys engage more in team sports—such as baseball and football—that involve many roles, complex rules, and clear objectives such as scoring a run or a touchdown. These games are nearly always competitive, separating winners from losers. Male peer activities reinforce masculine traits of aggression and control.

By contrast, girls play hopscotch or jump rope, or simply talk, sing, or dance together. Such spontaneous activities have few rules and rarely is "victory" the ultimate goal. Instead of teaching girls to be competitive, Lever explains, female peer groups promote interpersonal skills involving communication and cooperation—presumably the basis for family life.

Carol Gilligan (1982), whose work is highlighted in Chapter 5 ("Socialization"), explains Lever's observations with a gender-based theory of moral reasoning. Boys, Gilligan contends, reason according to abstract principles. For them, "rightness" amounts to "playing by the rules." Girls, by contrast, consider morality more a matter of their responsibilities to others. Thus, the games we play have serious implications for our later lives.

Gender and Schooling

As children near school age, their reading promotes distinctions of gender. A generation ago, children's books typically made males the focus of attention (Weitzman et al., 1972). Males were the main characters, typically mentioned in book titles, and shown in illustrations. Stories portrayed boys as engaged in interesting activities, while girls—more like dolls than living beings—were attractive and compliant observers who concentrated on supporting and pleasing the males at the center of the action.

More recently, a growing awareness among authors, publishers, and teachers of the limiting effects of gender stereotypes on young people has led to changes. Today's books for children portray females and males in a more balanced way.

Through primary and secondary school, however, classroom curricula still encourage children to embrace appropriate gender patterns. For example, schools have long offered young women instruction in typing and home-centered skills such as nutrition and sewing. Classes in woodworking and auto mechanics, conversely, contain mostly young men.

In college, the pattern continues, with men and women tending toward different majors. Men are

---

SOCIOLOGY OF EVERYDAY LIFE

Masculinity as Contest

By the time I was ten, the central fact in my life was the demand that I become a man. By then, the most important relationships by which I was taught to define myself were those I had with other boys. I already knew that I must see every encounter with another boy as a contest in which I must win or at least hold my own. . . . The same lesson continued [in school], after school, even in Sunday School. My parents, relatives, teachers, the books I read, movies I saw, all taught me that my self-worth depended on my manliness, my willingness to stand up to the other boys. This usually didn't mean a physical fight, though the willingness to stand up and "fight like a man" always remained a final test. But the relationships between us usually had the character of an armed truce. Girls weren't part of this social world at all yet, just because they weren't part of this contest. They didn't have to be bluffed, no credit was gained by cowing them, so they were more or less ignored. Sometimes when there were no grownups around we would let each other know that we liked each other, but most of the time we did as we were taught.

Source: Silverstein (1977).

NOTE: Several "firsts" for U.S. women: first woman physician, Elizabeth Blackwell, 1847; ordained minister, Antoinette Blackwell, 1853; surgeon, Mary Thompson, 1863; dentist (DDS), Lucy Hobbs, 1866; lawyer, Arabella Mansfield, 1869; college president, Frances Williard, 1871.

DISCUSS: Is the "rational-emotional" distinction inherently hierarchical? We would tell someone to "control your emotions!" but never "control your intellect!" Rationality tends to be allied with males and dominance.

THEN AND NOW: One indicator of the changing roles of U.S. women: They now represent 40% of business flyers on major airlines, up from 2% in 1970.

NOTE: The trend toward lower male participation in the labor force is due mostly to earlier retirement.

Some recent advertising, typified by this television commercial for Diet Coke, reverses traditional gender definitions by portraying men as the objects of women's sexual attention. Although the reversal is new, the use of gender stereotypes to sell products has long been an element of our way of life.

disproportionately represented in the natural sciences—including physics, chemistry, biology, and mathematics. Women cluster in the humanities (such as English), the fine arts (painting, music, dance, and drama), education courses, and the social sciences (including anthropology and sociology). New areas of study are also likely to be sex linked. Computer science, for example, with its grounding in engineering, logic, and abstract mathematics, predominantly enrolls men, while courses in gender studies, by contrast, are popular among women.

Gender and the Mass Media

Since it first captured the public imagination in the 1950s, television has placed the dominant segment of our population—white males—at center stage. Racial and ethnic minorities were all but absent from television until the early 1970s; only in the last decade have programs featured women in prominent roles.

Even when both sexes appear on camera, men generally play the brilliant detectives, fearless explorers, and skilled surgeons. Women, by contrast, continue to be cast as the less capable characters, often prized primarily for their sexual attractiveness.

Change has come most slowly to advertising, which sells products by conforming to widely established cultural norms. Advertising thus presents the two sexes, more often than not, in stereotypical ways. Historically, ads have shown women in the home, happily using cleaning products, serving foods, modeling clothing, and trying out new appliances. Men, on the other hand, predominate in ads for cars, travel, banking services, industrial companies, and alcoholic beverages. The authoritative "voiceover"—the faceless voice that promotes products on television and radio—is almost always male (Busby, 1975; Courtney & Whipple, 1983).

In a classic study of magazine and newspaper ads, Erving Goffman (1979) found other, more subtle biases. Men, he concluded, are photographed to appear taller than women, implying male superiority. Women were more frequently presented lying down (on sofas and beds) or, like children, seated on the floor. The expressions and gestures of men exude competence and authority, whereas women are more likely to appear in childlike poses. While men focus on the products being advertised, women direct their interest to men, conveying their supportive and submissive role.

Advertising also actively perpetuates Naomi Wolf's "beauty myth," described in the opening of this chapter. The equation runs something like this: By embracing traditional notions of femininity and masculinity, we raise our prospects for personal and professional success. Thus, advertising commands masculine men to drive the "right" car and feminine women to use beauty aids that will help them look younger and more attractive to men.

Gender and Adult Socialization

Reinforced in so many ways by the surrounding culture, gender identity and gender roles come to feel natural long before we reach adulthood. As a result, the attitudes and behavior of adults commonly follow traditional feminine and masculine patterns (Spender, 1980; Kramarae, 1981).

Chapter 6 ("Social Interaction in Everyday Life") reviewed Deborah Tannen's (1990) account of why women and men see many routine situations so differently. Men hate to ask for directions, Tannen notes, because interpersonal exchanges establish a hierarchy, and asking for help amounts to accepting a subordinate place in that hierarchy. But to women, who draw strength from forging and maintaining connections with others, asking for directions is both practical and sensible.

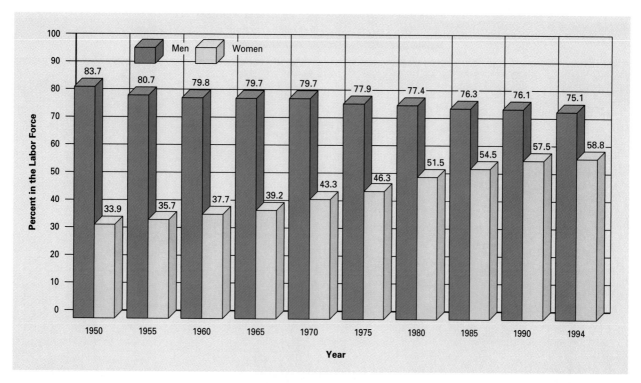

FIGURE 13–2 Men and Women in the U.S. Labor Force
Source: U.S. Bureau of Labor Statistics (1995).

The two sexes, therefore, perceive different meanings in a wide range of everyday experiences. In light of this gender-based disparity, it is not surprising that husbands and wives often have considerable difficulty handling one of the most basic human tasks—simply communicating with each other.

GENDER STRATIFICATION

Gender implies more than how people think and act. The concept of **gender stratification** refers to *a society's unequal distribution of wealth, power, and privilege between the two sexes.* In the United States, as throughout the world, societies allocate fewer valued resources to women than to men. We see gender stratification, first, in the world of work.

Working Men and Women

In 1994, 66.6 percent of people in the United States aged sixteen and over were working for income: 75.1 percent of men and 58.8 percent of women, as shown in Figure 13–2 (U.S. Bureau of Labor Statistics, 1995). This represents a change from 1900, when only about one-fifth of women were in the labor force (typically poor women, who have always worked). Of those in the labor force, 49 percent of all women aged sixteen and over and 62 percent of all comparable men work full time. Thus, the traditional view that working for income is a "man's role" no longer holds true.

Among the factors at work in the changing U.S. labor force are the decline of farming, the growth of cities, shrinking family size, a rising divorce rate, and households that rely on more than one income. Today, 60 percent of married couples depend on two incomes.

In short, the United States and other industrial nations consider women working for income to be the rule rather than the exception. As Global Map 13–1 shows, however, this is not the case in many of the poorer societies of the world.

A common misconception (especially among middle-class people) holds that women in the labor force are childless. But, today, 60 percent of married women with children under six work for income;

Chapter 13 Sex and Gender **363**

Window on the World

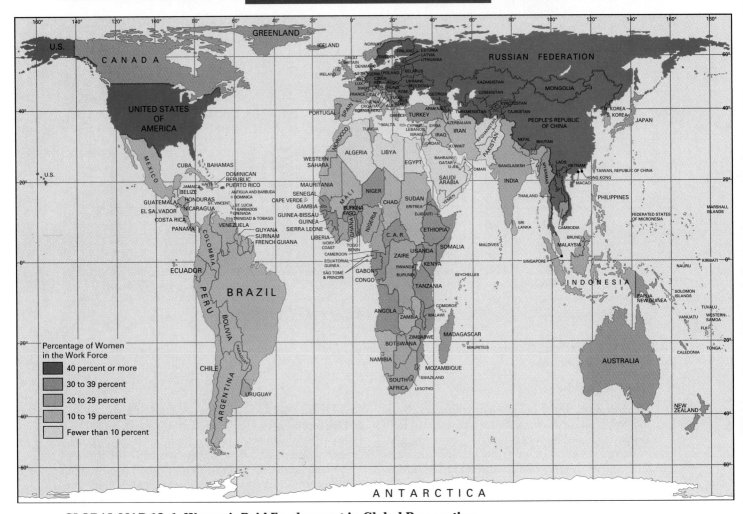

GLOBAL MAP 13–1 Women's Paid Employment in Global Perspective

In 1994, women comprised 46 percent of the labor force in the United States—up almost 10 percent over the last generation. Throughout the industrialized world, at least one-third of the labor force is made up of women. In poor societies, however, women work even harder than they do in this country, but they are less likely to be paid for their efforts. In Latin America, for example, women represent only about 15 percent of the paid labor force; in Islamic societies of northern Africa and the Middle East, the figure is even lower.

Source: *Peters Atlas of the World* (1990).

among married women with children between six and seventeen years of age, 75 percent are employed. For divorced women with children, the comparable figures are 60 percent of women with younger children and 80 percent of women with older children (U.S. Bureau of the Census, 1995). A gradual increase in employer-sponsored child-care programs is giving more women and men the opportunity to combine working and parenting, a trend that is especially important for divorced mothers.

SOCIAL SURVEY: "Do you approve or disapprove of a married woman earning money in business or industry if she has a husband capable of supporting her?" (GSS 1994, N = 1,977; *Codebook*, 1994:200)

"Approve" 79.4%   "Disapprove" 18.4%   DK/NR 2.2%

SOCIAL SURVEY: The same item appears on *STUDENT CHIP Social Survey Software* (GSS 1972–91, N = 17,547).

	"Approve"	"Disapprove"
Women	75.7%	24.3%
Men	74.3%	25.7%
Afri Amer	72.7%	27.3%
Latino	65.5%	34.5%
Whites	75.8%	24.2%

Gender and Occupations

Even though the *proportions* of men and women in the labor force have been converging, the *kind* of work done by the two sexes remains distinct. According to the U.S. Bureau of Labor Statistics (1994), women engage in a narrow range of occupations, with half of working women holding just two types of jobs. Administrative support work, the first category, draws 27 percent of working women, most of whom serve as secretaries, typists, or stenographers. From another angle, 80 percent of all "pink-collar" jobholders are women.

The second category is service work, performed by 18 percent of employed women. These jobs include waitressing and other food-service work as well health-care positions. Both categories of jobs lie at the low end of the pay scale, offer limited opportunities for advancement, and are subject to supervision—most often by men.

Table 13–3 identifies the ten occupations with the highest concentrations of women. The bottom line is that, while increasing numbers of women work for pay, they remain highly segregated in the labor force, suggesting that society continues to view work through the lens of gender (Roos, 1983; Kemp & Coverman, 1989; Charles, 1992; U.S. Bureau of Labor Statistics, 1995).

Men predominate in most other job categories. Men overwhelmingly control the building trades: 98 percent of brickmasons, stonemasons, structural metalworkers, and heavy equipment mechanics are men. Men also hold the lion's share of positions that provide a great deal of income, prestige, and power. For example, 92 percent of engineers, 78 percent of physicians, lawyers, and judges, 70 percent of computer specialists, as well as 55 percent of corporate executives and managers are men. Just 3 percent of top corporate executives in the United States are women (U.S. Bureau of Labor Statistics, 1995).

One recent trend flies in the face of this gender-based male dominance in the work force: Women own an increasing share—currently one-third—of U.S. businesses. The number of women-owned companies jumped by more than 50 percent during the 1980s. Although 80 percent of these businesses are sole proprietorships with a single employee, the success of tens of thousands of women entrepreneurs demonstrates how people with initiative can create opportunities for themselves. Many women find the rewards of self-employment to be far greater than those offered by larger, male-dominated companies (Ando,

TABLE 13–3 Jobs with the Highest Concentrations of Women, 1994

Occupation	Number of Women Employed	Percent in Occupation Who Are Women
1. Dental hygienist	97,000	100%
2. Secretary	3,397,000	98.9%
3. Child-care provider	428,000	98.7%
4. Prekindergarten and kindergarten teachers	496,000	98.1%
5. Child-care worker/ private household	286,000	97.3%
6. Dental assistant	188,000	96.6%
7. Receptionist	931,000	96.4%
8. Early childhood teacher's assistant	416,000	96.4%
9. Cleaner and servant/ private household	500,000	95.8%
10. Dressmaker	82,000	95.8%

Source: U.S. Bureau of Labor Statistics, *Employment and Earnings*, vol. 42, no. 1, January 1995, pp. 174–80.

1990; O'Hare & Larson, 1991; U.S. Bureau of the Census, 1996).

Overall, then, gender stratification permeates the workplace. This hierarchy is easy to spot on the job: Male physicians are assisted by female nurses, male executives have female secretaries, and male airline pilots work with female flight attendants.

Compounding this gender-based inequality, in any field, the greater the income and prestige associated with a job, the more likely it is that the position is held by a man. Among educators, for example, women represent 98 percent of kindergarten teachers, 86 percent of elementary school teachers, 56 percent of secondary school teachers, 43 percent of college and university professors, and 16 percent of college and university presidents (U.S. Bureau of Labor Statistics, 1995; American Council on Education, 1996).

Housework: Women's "Second Shift"

One sound indicator of the global pattern of patriarchy is the extent to which housework—cleaning, cooking, and caring for children—is the province of women. Global Map 13–2 shows that, in general, members of industrial societies divide housework more evenly than people in the poor societies of the world do. But in no nation on earth is housework shared equally.

NOTE: Lennon & Rosenfeld (1994) report that women evaluate their responsibilities for housework according to a social-exchange model: Women without jobs find doing most domestic labor to be fair; those in the labor force do not.

NOTE: South & Spitze (1994) examine household division of labor for various types of households. In married-couple households (versus, say, cohabitants, widowed persons, and divorced persons),

women spend the most time doing housework.

THEN AND NOW: Share of U.S. labor force represented by women: *1893, 17%; 1945, 36%; 1994, 46%.*

THEN AND NOW: In 1950, the U.S. gender earnings ratio was 57%; it is 72% today.

GLOBAL: Gender earnings ratios: Japan, 50%; United States and Great Britain, 70%; France, 80%; Sweden, 85%.

Window on the World

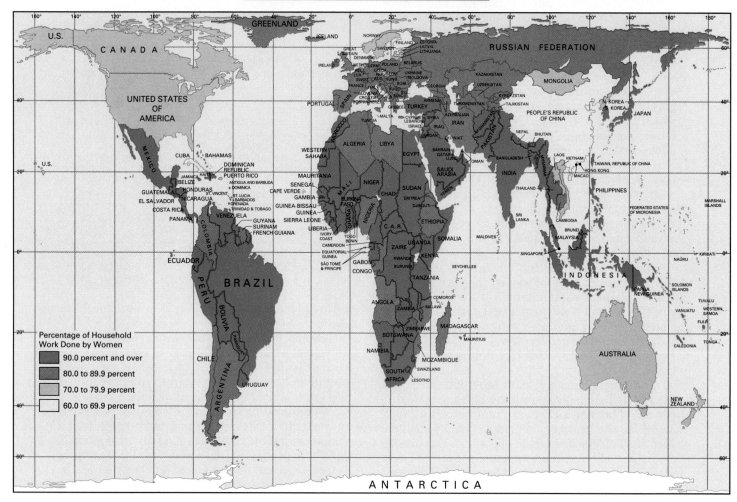

GLOBAL MAP 13–2 Housework in Global Perspective

Throughout the world, a major component of women's routines and identities involves housework. This is especially true in poor societies of Latin America, Africa, and Asia, where women are not generally in the paid labor force. But our society also defines housework and child care as "feminine" activities, even though a majority of U.S. women work outside the home.

Source: *Peters Atlas of the World* (1990); updated by the author.

Surprisingly, despite women's rapid entry into the labor force, the amount of housework performed by women has declined only slightly (and the proportion done by men has not changed at all). Although the typical couple shares in disciplining the children and managing finances, men routinely perform home repairs and yardwork while women see to most daily tasks of shopping, cooking, and cleaning. Consuming, on average, twenty-six hours a week, housework amounts to a "second shift" that women undertake after returning from the workplace each day. In general, then, housework adds stress to many women's lives; those who

DIVERSITY: The gender income gap for year-round, full-time workers varies by race and ethnicity: Among Anglo white people, women earn 72% of men's income; among African Americans, women earn 86% as much; among Hispanics, the figure is 84%.
SOCIAL SURVEY: Gallup poll, 1942: "If women replace men in industry, should they be paid the same wages as men?" Yes, 78%; No, 14%; Undecided, 8%.

Q: "The cost of employing women in management is greater than the cost of employing men. This is a jarring statement, partly because it is true, but mostly because it is something people are reluctant to talk about.... We have become so sensitive to charges of sexism and so afraid of confrontation, even litigation, that we rarely say what we know to be true." Felice Schwartz (1989:65)

have help in maintaining the household suffer less, as do those who choose only the role of full-time home-maker (Schooler et al., 1984; Fuchs, 1986; Hochschild, 1989; Presser, 1993; Keith & Schafer, 1994; Benokraitis & Feagin, 1995).

In sum, men support the idea of women entering the labor force and count on the money women earn. But men nonetheless resist modifying their own behavior to help their partners establish and maintain careers and manageable home lives. Women with high-prestige, high-income jobs certainly have greater power in the household to limit their own housework roles (by hiring outside help). But, typically, men call special attention to any housework they perform, while taking for granted the contributions of women (Komarovsky, 1973; Cowan, 1992; Robinson & Spitze, 1992; Lennon & Rosenfeld, 1994; Heath & Bourne, 1995).

Gender, Income, and Wealth

In 1993, the median earnings for women working full time were $22,469, while men working full time earned $31,077. For every dollar earned by men, then, women earned about 72 cents.

Among full-time workers, 57 percent of women earned less than $25,000 in 1993, compared to 37 percent of comparable men. At the upper end of the income scale, men were five times more likely than women (8.3 percent versus 1.8 percent) to earn more than $75,000 (U.S. Bureau of the Census, 1995).

In global perspective, gender-based income disparity is less pronounced in the United States than in Japan but greater than it is in most other industrial nations, including Australia, Canada, Norway, and Sweden (Rosenfeld & Kalleberg, 1990; United Nations Development Programme, 1995). Over time, however, this disparity has gradually declined in the United States. In 1980, for example, working women earned only 60 percent as much as working men. This trend toward comparable earnings has two sources, however: increasing economic opportunities for women and a recent decline in the earnings of many men (Bernhardt et al., 1995).

Why the income disparity in the first place? The most important reason is the different kinds of work women and men do. As noted earlier, women are concentrated in low-paying clerical and service jobs. In effect, jobs and gender interact: Members of our society tend to perceive jobs with less clout as "women's work," and people also devalue work simply because it is performed by women (Parcel, Mueller,

& Cuvelier 1986; Blum, 1991; England, 1992; Bellas, 1994).

During the 1980s, proponents of gender equality responded to this mindset by proposing a policy of "comparable worth," which means that people should be paid, not according to the historical double standard, but based on the worth of what they actually do. Several nations, including Great Britain and Australia, have adopted such policies, although they have found limited acceptance in the United States. In the absence of such a policy, critics argue, U.S. women lose as much as $1 billion annually.

A second cause of this gender-based income disparity has to do with the family. Both men and women have children, of course, but our culture defines parenting more as a woman's responsibility than a man's. Pregnancy and raising small children keep many younger women out of the labor force altogether at a time when their male peers stand to make significant occupational gains. As a result, women workers have less job seniority than their male counterparts (Fuchs, 1986).

Moreover, women who choose to have children may be reluctant or unable to maintain fast-paced jobs that tie up their evenings and weekends. Career women with children may resolve this classic case of role strain by favoring jobs that offer a shorter commuting distance, more flexible hours, and employer-sponsored child-care services. Women seeking both a career and a family face a serious dilemma, as indicated by the fact that, among executives past the age of forty, 90 percent of men but only 35 percent of women have had a child. Women who do have children, in other words, start to fall behind childless women in terms of earnings.

Felice Schwartz (1989) points out that corporate women risk their careers by having children. Rather than helping to meet the needs of working mothers, the typical corporation interprets a woman's choice to have a child as a sign that she may leave the company, taking with her a substantial investment in time and training. As an alternative, Schwartz calls on corporations to develop "mommy tracks" that allow women to meet family responsibilities while continuing their careers, with less intensity, for specified periods. This proposal has won praise, but it has also provoked strong criticism. Opponents of the "mommy-track" concept fear that it plays into the hands of corporate men who have long stereotyped women as being less attached to careers in the first place. Further, critics add, since companies are unlikely to apply such a plan to men, it can only hurt

TABLE 13–4 Earnings of Full-Time U.S. Workers, by Sex, 1994*

Selected Occupational Categories	Median Income (dollars)		Women's Income as a Percentage of Men's
	Men	Women	
Executives, administrators, and managers	$42,722	$28,876	68%
Professional specialties	$45,136	$31,906	71%
Technical workers	$35,048	$26,324	75%
Sales	$32,327	$18,743	58%
Clerical and other administrative support workers	$26,746	$20,683	77%
Precision production, craft, and repair workers	$27,653	$21,357	77%
Machine operators, assemblers, and inspectors	$23,378	$15,379	66%
Transportation and material movers	$26,532	$19,652	74%
Handlers, equipment cleaners, helpers, and laborers	$17,556	$14,826	84%
Service workers	$20,860	$13,126	63%
Farming, forestry, and fishing workers	$15,655	$10,581	68%
All occupations listed above	$30,407	$21,747	72%

*Workers aged 15 and over.

Source: U.S. Bureau of the Census, *Current Population Reports*, ser. P-60, no. 188 (Washington, D.C.: U.S. Government Printing Office, 1995).

rather than help the career aspirations of corporate women.

The two factors noted so far—type of work and family responsibilities—account for about two-thirds of the earnings disparity between women and men. Researchers conclude that a third factor—discrimina-tion against women—accounts for most of the remain-der (Pear, 1987; Fuller & Schoenberger, 1991).

Because discrimination is illegal, it is often prac-ticed in subtle ways (Benokraitis & Feagin, 1995). Many corporate women encounter a so-called *glass ceiling*, a barrier that is hard to see and formally denied by high company officials, which effectively prevents women from rising above middle management.

For all these reasons, then, women earn less than men within all major occupational categories. As shown in Table 13-4, this disparity varies from job to job, but in only two of these major job classifications do women earn more than 75 percent as much as men do.

Finally, perhaps because women typically outlive men, many people think that women own most of the country's wealth. Government statistics tell a different story: 53 percent of individuals with $1 million or more in assets are men, although widows are highly repre-sented (U.S. Internal Revenue Service, 1993). And just 20 percent of the individuals identified by researchers at *Forbes* and *Fortune* magazines as the richest people in the United States are women.

Gender and Education

Many of our forebears discouraged, and sometimes formally excluded, women from higher education because advanced schooling was considered unneces-sary for homemakers. But times have changed. Around 1980, a majority of all associate's and bache-lor's degrees were earned by women; in 1994, that pro-portion stood at 55 percent (National Center for Education Statistics, 1995).

While the doors of colleges have opened to women, the two sexes still tend to pursue different courses of study, although to a decreasing degree. In 1970, for example, women earned just 17 percent of the bachelor's degrees in natural sciences, computer science, and engineering; by 1992, that proportion had doubled to one-third.

In 1993, women for the first time also received a majority of postgraduate degrees, often a springboard to high-prestige jobs. For all areas of study in 1994, women earned 52 percent of all master's degrees, but only 33 percent of all doctorates (however, 52 percent of all Ph.D.s in sociology went to women). And women now constitute a visible presence in many graduate fields that until recently were virtually all male. For example, in 1970 only a few hundred women received a master's of business administration (M.B.A.) degree; by 1990, the number exceeded twenty-nine thousand (rising from barely 1 percent to 35 percent of all such degrees) (U.S. Bureau of the Census, 1995).

Some professional fields, however, remain pre-dominantly male. In 1992, men received 57 percent of law degrees (LL.B. and J.D.), 64 percent of medical degrees (M.D.), and 68 percent of dental degrees (D.D.S. and D.M.D.) (U.S. Bureau of the Census, 1995). Our society still defines high-paying professions (and the drive and competitiveness needed to succeed in them) as masculine; this fact helps to explain why women begin most preprofessional graduate programs in numbers equal to those of men but are less likely to complete their degrees (Fiorentine, 1987; Fiorentine & Cole, 1992). Nonetheless, the proportion of women in all these professions is rising steadily.

Gender and Politics

A century ago, virtually no women held elected office in the United States. Until the passage of the Nineteenth Amendment to the Constitution in 1920, in fact, women were legally barred from casting a vote in national elections. A few women, however, were candidates for political office even before they could vote. The Equal Rights party nominated Victoria Woodhull for the U.S. presidency in 1872; perhaps it was a sign of the times that she spent election day in a New York City jail. Table 13–5 cites major milestones in women's gradual movement into political life.

Today, thousands of women serve as mayors of cities and towns across the United States, and tens of thousands more hold responsible administrative posts in the federal government. At the state level, women, who in 1970 comprised just 6 percent of state legislators, constituted 21 percent of state legislators in 1995. National Map 13–1 on page 370 shows where in the United States women have made the greatest political gains.

Less change has occurred at the highest levels of politics, although a majority of U.S. adults claim that they would support a qualified woman for any office, including the presidency. After the 1994 national elections, 1 of the 50 state governors was a woman (2 percent); in Congress, women held 49 of 435 seats in the House of Representatives (11 percent), and 8 of 100 seats (8 percent) in the Senate.

Minority Women

Chapter 12 ("Race and Ethnicity") explained that minorities are socially disadvantaged; if so, are minority women doubly handicapped? Generally speaking, the answer is yes.

First, there is the disadvantage associated with race and ethnicity. For example, in 1993, median annual income for African-American women working full time was $20,315, 88 percent as much as the $22,979 earned by white women; Hispanic women earned $17,112, which was 74 percent as much as their white, Anglo counterparts.

Second, there is the obstacle associated with sex. Thus, African-American women earned 86 percent as much as African-American men, while Hispanic women earned 84 percent as much as Hispanic men.

Combining these disadvantages, African-American women earned 64 percent as much as white men, and Hispanic women earned 54 percent as much (U.S. Bureau of the Census, 1995). These disparities reflect minority women's lower positions on the occupational and educational ladders in comparison to white women (Bonilla-Santiago, 1990). Further, whenever the economy sags, minority women

TABLE 13–5 Significant "Firsts" for Women in U.S. Politics

1869	Law allows women to vote in Wyoming territory; Utah follows suit in 1870.
1872	First woman to run for the presidency (Victoria Woodhull) represents the Equal Rights party.
1917	First woman elected to the House of Representatives (Jeannette Rankin of Montana).
1924	First women elected state governors (Nellie Taylor Ross of Wyoming and Miriam ["Ma"] Ferguson of Texas); both followed their husbands into office. First woman to have her name placed in nomination for vice-presidency at the convention of a major political party (Lena Jones Springs).
1931	First woman to serve in the Senate (Hattie Caraway of Arkansas); completed the term of her husband upon his death and won reelection in 1932.
1932	First woman appointed to the presidential cabinet (Frances Perkins, secretary of labor in the cabinet of President F. D. Roosevelt).
1964	First woman to have her name placed in nomination for the presidency at the convention of a major political party (Margaret Chase Smith, a Republican).
1972	First African-American woman to have her name placed in nomination for the presidency at the convention of a major political party (Shirley Chisholm, a Democrat).
1981	First woman appointed to the U.S. Supreme Court (Sandra Day O'Connor).
1984	First woman to be successfully nominated for the vice-presidency (Geraldine Ferraro).
1988	First woman chief executive to be elected to a consecutive third term (Madeleine Kunin, governor of Vermont).
1992	Political "Year of the Woman" yields record number of women in the Senate (six) and the House (forty-eight), as well as (1) first African-American woman to win election to U.S. Senate (Carol Moseley-Braun of Illinois); (2) first state (California) to be served by two women senators (Barbara Boxer and Dianne Feinstein); (3) first woman of Puerto Rican descent elected to the House (Nydia Valasquez of New York).

Sources: Adapted from Sandra Salmans, "Women Ran for Office Before They Could Vote," *New York Times*, July 13, 1984, p. A11, and news reports.

THE MAP: Roughly speaking, women hold the most power in state government in the western states (the region in which women first became state governors). By contrast, the South remains the region in which women are least likely to be in the labor force and where the political clout of women is lowest.

DIVERSITY: Income figures for minority women may seem to indicate that economic disadvantages are due to race and gender alone; however, to draw a complete picture, one would have to factor in differences in education, work histories, age, and so on.

DIVERSITY: Of all families living below poverty level, 51% were headed by women in 1993. Of all poor African-American families, 76.4% were headed by women; for Hispanics, the figure was 47.5%, and for all whites, 43.6%. (U.S. Bureau of the Census, 1994)

Seeing Ourselves

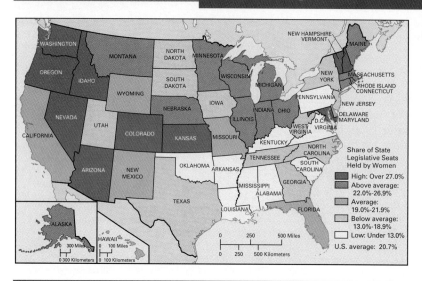

NATIONAL MAP 13–1

Women in State Government Across the United States

Although women represent half of U.S. adults, just 21 percent of seats in state legislatures are held by women. Look at the state-by-state variation in the map. In which regions of the country have women gained the greatest political power? What factors do you think account for this pattern?

Source: From *Time*, August 28, 1995. Copyright © 1995 Time, Inc. Reprinted by permission.

Share of State Legislative Seats Held by Women
- High: Over 27.0%
- Above average: 22.0%-26.9%
- Average: 19.0%-21.9%
- Below average: 13.0%-18.9%
- Low: Under 13.0%

U.S. average: 20.7%

are especially likely to experience declining income and unemployment.

Chapter 10 ("Social Class in the United States") noted that women are disproportionately represented among the nation's poor. Overall, 51 percent of poor families are headed by single women, compared to 6 percent headed by men. But the connection between women and poverty is especially strong among African Americans because of a higher incidence of single parenthood. Thus, three-fourths of poor African-American families are headed by single women, compared to 48 percent of poor Hispanic and 44 percent of poor white families.

In short, gender has a powerful effect on our lives, but never operates alone. A host of other factors, including race, ethnicity, and class, also come into play (Ginsburg & Tsing, 1990).

Are Women a Minority?

Given the clear economic disadvantage of being a woman in our society, it seems reasonable to count all U.S. women as a minority. Subjectively speaking, however, most white women do *not* think of themselves this way (Hacker, 1951; Lengermann & Wallace, 1985). This is partly because, unlike racial and ethnic

minorities, white women are well represented at all levels of the class structure, including the very top.

Bear in mind, however, that women at every class level typically have less income, wealth, education, and power than men do. In fact, patriarchy makes women dependent for much of their social standing on men—first their fathers and later their husbands (J. Bernard, 1981).

Violence Against Women

Perhaps the most wrenching kind of suffering that our society imposes on women is violence. As Chapter 8 ("Deviance") explained, official statistics paint criminal violence as overwhelmingly the actions of men—hardly surprising since aggressiveness is a trait our culture defines as masculine. Furthermore, a great deal of "manly" violence is directed against women, which we also might expect because U.S. society devalues what is culturally defined as feminine.

A 1995 Justice Department report estimated the number of sexual assaults against women at about 500,000 annually, including 310,000 rapes or attempted rapes. To this number can be added perhaps 2 million nonsexual assaults (U.S. Bureau of Justice Statistics, 1995).

DISCUSS: To draw out the link between aggression and masculinity, ask the class what makes a man a "wimp"? A "real man"?
NOTE: In 1993, 5,278 women died as a result of violence; 30% of them were victims of violence perpetrated by a spouse or intimate partner.
Q: "Sexual objectification is the primary process of the subjugation of women . . ." Catharine MacKinnon

NOTE: *Playboy*, which was founded in 1953, had a U.S. circulation of 110,000 in one year, and 1.4 million in ten years. Peak circulation was 6 million in the early 1970s; it has fallen to about half that now, although overseas circulation is up. (Joseph E. Scott and J. Cuvelier, "Violence in *Playboy* Magazine: A Longitudinal Analysis," *Archives of Sexual Behavior*, Vol. 16 (1987): 279–88)

In short, violence is commonplace in our society, and it is closely linked to gender. Violence often erupts where men and women interact most—in the home. Richard Gelles (cited in Roesch, 1984) argues that, with the exception of the police and the military, the family is the most violent organization in the United States. More violent attacks occur in the home, Gelles maintains, than anywhere else. Both sexes suffer from family violence, although, by and large, women sustain more serious injuries than men do (Straus & Gelles, 1986; Schwartz, 1987; Shupe, Stacey, & Hazlewood, 1987; Gelles & Cornell, 1990; Smolowe, 1994). Chapter 17 ("Family") delves more deeply into the problem of family violence.

Violence against women also occurs in casual relationships. As Chapter 8 ("Deviance") explained, the notion that sexual violence involves strangers is a myth; most rapes, for instance, are perpetrated by men known (and sometimes even trusted) by women. A tendency toward sexual violence, in other words, is built into our way of life. Dianne F. Herman (1992) argues that all forms of violence against women—from the wolf whistles that intimidate women on city streets to a pinch in a crowded subway to physical assaults that occur at home—are expressions of a "rape culture." By this, Herman means that men resort to violence as a strategy to dominate women. Sexual violence, then, is fundamentally about *power* rather than sex, and therefore should be understood as a dimension of gender stratification (Griffin, 1982).

Sexual Harassment

Sexual harassment refers to *comments, gestures, or physical contact of a sexual nature that are deliberate, repeated, and unwelcome.* During the 1990s, sexual harassment became an issue of national importance that has already significantly redefined the rules for workplace interaction between the sexes.

Most victims of sexual harassment are women. This is because, first, our culture encourages men to be sexually assertive and to perceive women in sexual terms; social interaction in the workplace, on campus, and elsewhere, then, can readily take on sexual overtones. Second, most individuals in positions of power—including business executives, physicians, bureau chiefs, assembly-line supervisors, professors, and military officers—are men who oversee the work of women. Surveys carried out in widely different work settings confirm that half of women respondents report receiving unwanted sexual attention (Loy & Stewart, 1984; Paul, 1991).

Many public organizations and private companies have adopted policies to discourage forms of behavior, conversation, or images that might create a "hostile or intimidating environment." In essence, such practices seek to remove sexuality from the workplace so that employees can do their jobs while steering clear of traditional notions about female and male relationships. Would a locker room "pinup" like this bother you? Why or why not?

Sexual harassment is sometimes blatant and direct, as when a supervisor solicits sexual favors from a subordinate, coupled with the threat of reprisals if the advances are refused. Behavior of this kind—which not only undermines the dignity of an individual but prevents her from earning a living—is widely condemned. Courts have declared such *quid pro quo* sexual harassment (the Latin phrase means "one thing in return for another") to be an illegal violation of civil rights.

However, the problem of unwelcome sexual attention often involves subtle behavior—sexual teasing, off-color jokes, pinups displayed in the workplace—none of which any individual may *intend* as harassing to another person. But, using the *effect* standard favored by many feminists, such actions add up to creating a *hostile environment* (Cohen, 1991; Paul, 1991). Incidents of this kind are far more complex because they involve very different perceptions of the same behavior. For example, a man may think that showing romantic interest in a co-worker is paying the woman a compliment; she, on the other hand, may deem his behavior offensive and a hindrance to her job performance.

Women's entry into the workplace does not in itself ensure that everyone is treated equally and with

DISCUSS: Ask how the class distinguishes between "erotic" and "pornographic" material. Debate a proper balance among conservative moral concerns, liberal support for freedom of expression, and feminist opposition to the patriarchal dimensions of pornography.

SOCIAL SURVEY: "Being born a man or a woman—how important is that for getting ahead in life?" (GSS 1987, N = 1,285; *Codebook*, 1994:557)

"Essential"	2.7%	"Not very important"	32.8%
"Very important"	11.4%	"Not important at all"	26.5%
"Fairly important"	22.7%	DK/NR	3.9%

NOTE: The legal basis for charges of sexual harassment is Section 703 of Title VII of the 1964 Civil Rights Act that outlaws workplace discrimination based on sex; also Title IX of the Education Amendments of 1972.

respect. Untangling precisely what constitutes a hostile working environment, however, demands clearer standards of conduct than exist at present. Creating such guidelines—and educating the public about them—is likely to take some time (Cohen, 1991; Majka, 1991). In the end, courts (and, ultimately, the court of public opinion) will draw the line between what amounts to "reasonable friendliness" and behavior that is "unwarranted harassment."

Pornography

Pornography, too, underlies sexual violence. Defining pornography has long challenged scholars and lawmakers alike. Unable to set a single, specific standard to distinguish what is, and what is not, pornographic, the Supreme Court allows local cities and counties to decide for themselves what violates "community standards" of decency and lacks any redeeming social value.

But few doubt that pornography (loosely defined) is popular in the United States: X-rated videos, 900 telephone numbers offering sexual conversation, and a host of sexually explicit movies, magazines, and Internet websites together constitute a $7-billion-a-year industry.

Traditionally, society has cast pornography as a moral issue. According to national survey data, 60 percent of U.S. adults endorse the assertion that "sexual materials lead to a breakdown of morals" (NORC, 1994:213).

A more recent view holds that pornography subordinates women. That is, pornography is really a *power* issue because it fosters the notion that men should control both sexuality and women. Catharine MacKinnon (1987) has branded pornography as one foundation of male dominance in the United States because it portrays women in dehumanizing fashion as the subservient playthings of men. Worth noting, in this context, is that the term pornography is derived from the Greek word *porne*, meaning a harlot who acts as a man's sexual slave.

A related charge is that pornography promotes violence against women. Certainly anyone who has viewed more recent "hard-core" videos finds this assertion plausible. Yet demonstrating a scientific cause-and-effect relationship between what people watch and how they act is difficult. Research does support the contention, however, that pornography gives men license to think of women as objects rather than as people. The public as a whole also voices concern about the effects of pornography, with almost half of adults reporting the opinion that pornography encourages men to commit rape (NORC, 1994:213).

Like sexual harassment, pornography gives rise to complex and sometimes conflicting issues. While everyone objects to material deemed offensive, many also endorse the rights of free speech and artistic expression. But pressure to restrict this kind of material is building through the efforts of an unlikely coalition of conservatives (who oppose pornography on moral grounds) and progressives (who condemn it for political reasons).

THEORETICAL ANALYSIS OF GENDER

Although they come to differing conclusions, the structural-functional and social-conflict paradigms each point up the importance of gender to social organization.

Structural-Functional Analysis

The structural-functional paradigm views society as a complex system of many separate but integrated parts. In this approach, every social structure contributes to the overall operation of society.

As Chapter 4 ("Society") explained, members of hunting and gathering societies had little power over the forces of biology. Lacking effective birth control, women experienced frequent pregnancies, and the responsibilities of child care kept them close to home. Likewise, to take advantage of greater male strength, norms guided men toward the pursuit of game and other tasks away from the home. Over many generations, this sexual division of labor became institutionalized and largely taken for granted (Lengermann & Wallace, 1985).

Industrial technology opens up a vastly greater range of cultural possibilities. Human muscle power no longer serves as a vital source of energy, so the physical strength of men loses much of its earlier significance. At the same time, the ability to control reproduction gives women greater choice in shaping their lives. Modern societies come to see that traditional gender roles waste an enormous amount of human talent; yet change comes slowly, because gender is deeply embedded in social mores.

Talcott Parsons: Gender and Complementarity

In addition, as Talcott Parsons (1942, 1951, 1954) explained, gender differences help to integrate society—at least in its traditional form. Gender, Parsons noted, forms a *complementary* set of roles that links men and women together into family units that carry out various functions vital to the operation of society. Women take charge of family life, assuming primary responsibility for managing the household and raising children. Men, by contrast, connect the family to the larger world, primarily by participating in the labor force.

Parsons further argued that distinctive socialization teaches the two sexes their appropriate gender identity and skills needed for adult life. Thus society teaches boys—presumably destined for the labor force—to be rational, self-assured, and competitive. This complex of traits Parsons termed *instrumental*. To prepare girls for child rearing, their socialization stresses what Parsons called *expressive* qualities, such as emotional responsiveness and sensitivity to others.

Society, explains Parsons, promotes gender-linked behavior through various schemes of social control. People incorporate cultural definitions about gender into their own identities, so that failing to be appropriately feminine or masculine produces guilt and fear of rejection by members of the opposite sex. In simple terms, women learn to view nonmasculine men as sexually unattractive, while men learn to avoid unfeminine women.

Critical evaluation. Structural-functionalism advances a theory of complementarity by which gender integrates society both structurally (in terms of what people do) and morally (in terms of what they believe). Although influential at mid-century, this approach is rarely used today by researchers exploring the impact of gender.

For one thing, this analysis assumes a singular vision of society that is not shared by everyone. Poor women, for example, have always worked outside the home as a matter of economic necessity; today, more and more women at all social levels are entering the labor force for various reasons. A second problem, say the critics, is that Parsons's analysis minimizes the personal strains and social costs produced by rigid, traditional gender roles (Giele, 1988). Third and finally, to those whose goals include sexual equality, what Parsons describes as gender complementarity amounts to little more than male domination.

Social-Conflict Analysis

From a social-conflict point of view, gender involves not just differences in behavior but disparities in

Here four of the most successful women in Hollywood—Sharon Stone, Jodie Foster, Demi Moore, and Alicia Silverstone—celebrate their position as film industry tycoons. Yet, given our notions linking gender and power, it is little wonder that popular culture often portrays powerful women in masculine terms.

power. Conventional ideas about gender historically have benefited men while subjecting women to prejudice, discrimination, and sometimes outright violence, in a striking parallel to the treatment of racial and ethnic minorities (Hacker, 1951, 1974; Collins, 1971; Lengermann & Wallace, 1985). Thus, conflict theorists claim, conventional ideas about gender promote not cohesion but tension and conflict, with men seeking to protect their privileges while women challenge the status quo.

As earlier chapters noted, the social-conflict paradigm draws heavily on the ideas of Karl Marx. Yet Marx was a product of his time insofar as his writings focused almost exclusively on men. His friend and collaborator Friedrich Engels, however, did explore the link between gender and social class (1902; orig. 1884).

Friedrich Engels: Gender and Class

Looking back through history, Engels noted that in hunting and gathering societies the activities of

SOCIAL SURVEY: "How important is the women's rights issue to you?" (GSS 1985, N = 804; *Codebook*, 1994:201)
"One of the most important" 9.6% "Not important at all" 11.6%
"Important"   48.4% DK/NR   1.7%
"Not very important"   28.7%
NOTE: An early feminist (and friend of Susan B. Anthony) was Amelia Bloomer, who opposed the hoop skirts of her day. In 1851, she wore a pants outfit designed by a friend, introducing "bloomers" into our language.
Q: "We hold these truths to be self-evident: that all men and women are created equal; that they are endowed by their Creator with certain unalienable rights . . ." Declaration of Sentiments, Seneca Falls, New York (1848)

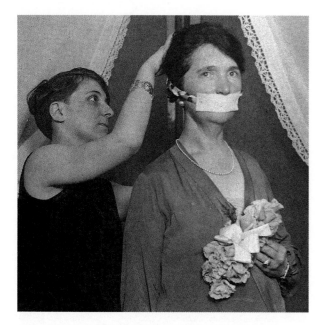

Margaret Higgins Sanger (1883–1966) was a pioneer activist in the crusade for women's reproductive rights, a cause that led her into frequent conflict with the laws of the time. Threatened with arrest if she spoke to a gathering in Boston in 1929, she made a powerful statement by appearing in public with tape over her mouth. Decades later, at the time of her death, some birth control devices (including condoms) still were not freely available in stores everywhere in the United States.

women and men, although different, had comparable importance. A successful hunt may have brought men great prestige, but the vegetation gathered by women constituted most of a society's food supply (Leacock, 1978). As technological advances led to a productive surplus, however, social equality and communal sharing gave way to private property and, ultimately, a class hierarchy. At this point, men gained pronounced power over women. With surplus wealth to pass on to heirs, upper-class men took a keen interest in their children. The desire to control property, then, prompted the creation of monogamous marriage and the family. Ideally, men could be certain of paternity—especially who their sons were—and the law ensured that wealth passed to them. The same logic explains why women were taught to remain virgins until marriage, to remain faithful to their husbands thereafter, and to build their lives around bearing and raising children.

According to Engels, capitalism intensifies this male domination. First, capitalism creates more wealth, which confers greater power on men as wage earners as well as owners and heirs of property. Second, an expanding capitalist economy depends on defining people—especially women—as consumers and convincing them that personal fulfillment derives from owning and using products. Third, to allow men to work, society assigns women the task of maintaining the home. The double exploitation of capitalism, as Engels saw it, lies in paying low wages for male labor and no wages for female work (Eisenstein, 1979; Barry, 1983; Jagger, 1983; Vogel, 1983).

Critical evaluation. Social-conflict analysis highlights how society places the two sexes in unequal positions of wealth, power, and privilege. As a result, the conflict approach is decidedly critical of conventional ideas about gender, claiming that society would be better off if we minimized or even eliminated this dimension of social structure.

But social-conflict analysis, too, has its limitations. One problem, critics suggest, is that this approach casts conventional families—defended by traditionalists as morally positive—as a social evil. Second, from a more practical standpoint, social-conflict analysis minimizes the extent to which women and men live together cooperatively and often quite happily. A third problem with this approach, for some critics, is its assertion that capitalism stands at the root of gender stratification. Agrarian countries, in fact, are typically more patriarchal than industrial-capitalist nations. And socialist societies, too—including the People's Republic of China—remain strongly patriarchal (Moore, 1992).

FEMINISM

Feminism is *the advocacy of social equality for the sexes, in opposition to patriarchy and sexism.* The "first wave" of the feminist movement in the United States began in the 1840s as women opposed to slavery, including Elizabeth Cady Stanton and Lucretia Mott, drew parallels between the oppression of African Americans and the oppression of women (Randall, 1982). The primary objective of the early women's movement was securing the right to vote, which was achieved in 1920. But other disadvantages persisted and a "second wave" of feminism arose in the 1960s and continues today.

Q: "All women are bunnies." Gloria Steinem
SOCIAL SURVEY: "Some people think that the best way for women to improve their position is through women's rights groups (point 1). Other people think that the best way for women to improve their position is for each individual woman to become better trained and more qualified (point 7). Where would you place yourself on this scale?" (GSS 1983, N = 825; *Codebook*, 1994:320)

1 (Women's rights groups), 4.7%   5, 13.7%
2, 2.5%   6, 14.1%
3, 3.6%   7 (Better trained), 43.3%
4, 16.5%   NR, 1.6%

Q: "It is very little for me to have the right to vote, to own property, et cetera, if I may not keep my body, and its uses, in my absolute right." Lucy Stone (1855)

Basic Feminist Ideas

Feminism views the personal experiences of women and men through the lens of gender. How we think of ourselves (gender identity), how we act (gender roles), and our sex's social standing (gender stratification) are all rooted in the operation of our society.

Although people who consider themselves feminists disagree about many things, most support five general principles:

1. **The importance of change.** Feminist thinking is decidedly political; it links ideas to action. Feminism is critical of the status quo, advocating social equality for women and men.

2. **Expanding human choice.** Feminists maintain that cultural conceptions of gender divide the full range of human qualities into two opposing and limited spheres: the female world of emotion and cooperation and the male world of rationality and competition. As an alternative, feminists pursue a "reintegration of humanity" by which each person develops *all* human traits (French, 1985).

3. **Eliminating gender stratification.** Feminism opposes laws and cultural norms that limit the education, income, and job opportunities of women. For this reason, feminists have long advocated passage of the Equal Rights Amendment (ERA) to the U.S. Constitution, which states:

   Equality of rights under the law shall not be denied or abridged by the United States or any State on account of sex.

   The ERA, first proposed in Congress in 1923, has the support of two-thirds of U.S. adults (NORC, 1994:230).

4. **Ending sexual violence.** A major objective of today's women's movement is eliminating sexual violence. Feminists argue that patriarchy distorts the relationships between women and men, and encourages violence against women in the form of rape, domestic abuse, sexual harassment, and pornography (Millet, 1970; J. Bernard, 1973; Dworkin, 1987).

5. **Promoting sexual autonomy.** Finally, feminism advocates women's control of their sexuality and reproduction. Feminists support the free availability of birth control information, which, in some states, was illegal as recently as the 1960s. As Figure 13–3 shows, use of contraception is much less prevalent among married women in most of

Global Snapshot

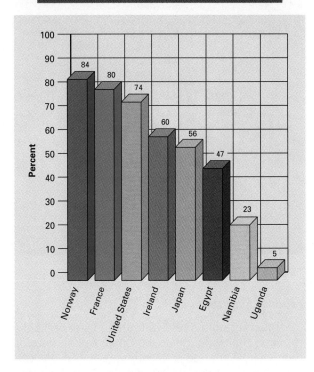

FIGURE 13–3 Use of Contraception by Married Women of Childbearing Age
Source: The World Bank (1995).

the world than it is in the United States. In addition, most feminists support a woman's right to choose whether to bear children or to terminate a pregnancy, rather than allowing men—as husbands, physicians, and legislators—to regulate sexuality. Many feminists also support gay people's efforts to overcome prejudice and discrimination in a predominantly heterosexual culture (Deckard, 1979; Barry, 1983; Jagger, 1983).

Variations Within Feminism

People pursue the goal of sexual equality in different ways, yielding three major divisions within feminism. Although the distinctions among them are far from clear-cut, each describes the problem of patriarchy in somewhat different terms and calls for correspondingly distinctive strategies for social change (Barry, 1983; Jagger, 1983; Stacey, 1983; Vogel, 1983).

Q: "Consider, I address you as a legislator, whether, when men contend for their freedom, and to be allowed to judge for themselves their own happiness, it be not inconsistent and unjust to subjugate women, even though you firmly believe that you are acting in the manner best calculated to promote their happiness? Who made man the exclusive judge, if woman partake with him the gift of reason?" Mary Wollstonecraft, *A Vindication of the Rights of Woman* (1792)

NOTE: Socialist feminists also oppose the family because living in isolated units discourages the solidarity that leads to collective action by women and men.

Q: "Anyone who knows anything about history knows that great social changes are impossible without the feminine ferment." Karl Marx

Violence against women is an important public issue of the 1990s. But, some analysts ask, isn't it men *whose lives are built around the experience of violence? In pursuit of a less violent society, how would you change our culture's definitions of masculinity?*

Liberal Feminism

Liberal feminism is grounded in classic liberal thinking that individuals should be free to develop their own talents and pursue their own interests. Liberal feminists accept the basic organization of our society but seek to expand the rights and opportunities of women. Liberal feminists support the Equal Rights Amendment and oppose prejudice and discrimination that block the aspirations of women.

Liberal feminists also endorse reproductive freedom for all women. They respect the family as a social institution, but call for widely available maternity leave and child care for women who wish to work. They applauded Congressional passage of the Family Leave Act in 1992, which placed the United States in league with more than one hundred nations that guarantee maternity leave for all working women (although unlike that of many European countries, the U.S. policy offers unpaid leave). Moreover, while liberal feminists support the family as a social institution, they contend that families need to change to accommodate the ambitions of both women and men.

With their strong belief in the rights of individuals, liberal feminists do not think that all women need to march in lockstep toward any political goal. Both women and men, working individually, would be able to improve their lives if society simply ended legal and cultural barriers rooted in gender.

Socialist Feminism

Socialist feminism evolved from Marxist conflict theory, in part as a response to how little attention Marx paid to gender, in part as a strategy to challenge both patriarchy and capitalism (Philipson & Hansen, 1992). Engels claimed that patriarchy (like class oppression) has its roots in private property; thus, capitalism intensifies patriarchy by concentrating wealth and power in the hands of a small number of men.

Socialist feminists view the reforms sought by liberal feminism as inadequate. The bourgeois family must be restructured, they argue, to end "domestic slavery" in favor of some collective means of carrying out housework and child care. The key to this goal, in turn, is a socialist revolution that creates a state-centered economy operating to meet the needs of all. Such a basic transformation of society requires that women and men pursue their personal liberation together, rather than individually, as liberal feminists maintain. (Further discussion of socialism appears elsewhere, especially in Chapter 15, "The Economy and Work.")

Radical Feminism

Radical feminism, too, finds the reforms called for by liberal feminism inadequate and superficial. Moreover, radical feminists claim that even a socialist revolution would not end patriarchy. Instead, this variant

NOTE: Radical feminism dovetails with the "children's rights" movement that aspires to free children from dependence on adults.
Q: "The early socialists often argued that problems associated with gender stratification would simply disappear under socialism. The leadership in socialist countries still gives lip service to the ideal of gender equality and includes it among its long-term goals . . ." Charlotte G. O'Kelly and Larry S. Carney

Q: "Differences of age and sex no longer have distinctive social validity for the working class. All are instruments of labor, more or less expensive to use, according to their age and sex." Karl Marx and Friedrich Engels
Q: "No production in philosophy, science, or art, entitled to the first rank, has ever been the work of a woman." John Stuart Mill

of feminism holds that gender equality can be realized only by eliminating the cultural notion of gender itself.

Fundamentally, say radical feminists, gender rests on the biological fact that women bear children. Thus, radical feminists look toward new reproductive technology (see Chapter 17, "Family") to render conventional heterosexual parenting—and thus the historical family—unnecessary. Science already allows conception outside the body, so that there is no necessary link between women's bodies and childbearing. With the demise of motherhood, radical feminists reason, the entire family system (including conventional definitions of motherhood, fatherhood, and childhood) could be left behind, liberating women, men, and children from the tyranny of family, gender, and of sex itself (Dworkin, 1987). Radical feminism clearly envisions a revolution much more far-reaching than that sought by Marx.

Opposition to Feminism

Feminism has provoked criticism and resistance from both men and women who embrace conventional ideas about gender. Some men oppose feminism for the same reasons that many white people have historically opposed social equality for people of color: They want to preserve their own privileges. Other men, including those who are neither rich nor powerful, distrust a social movement (especially its more radical expressions) that advocates socialism or seeks to abolish traditional marriage, family, and parenthood.

Further, for some men, feminism threatens an important basis of their status and self-respect: their masculinity. Men who have been socialized to value strength and dominance understandably feel uneasy about the feminist notion that they can also be gentle and warm (Doyle, 1983).

Some women, as well, shy away from feminism. For example, women who center their lives around their husbands and children may consider feminism a threat to their most cherished values. From this point of view, feminism amounts to an effort to revise the law, the workplace, and the family—in short, to remake all of society—according to the radical political agenda of a few. Feminists, then, would dispose of the traditional values that have guided life and protected individual liberties in the United States for centuries. Additionally, some women worry that, in the process of recasting the conventional "feminine" spheres of life, including the home and the family, women will lose rather than gain power and personal identity (Marshall, 1985).

Resistance to feminism also comes from within academic circles. Some sociologists are decidedly cool toward this approach because, as they see it, feminism ignores a growing body of evidence that men and women innately think and act in different ways. Furthermore, say critics, while feminism has directed considerable attention to enhancing women's presence in the workplace, it has all but ignored the fact that women make a crucial and unique contribution to the development of children—especially in the first years of life (Baydar & Brooks-Gunn, 1991; Popenoe, 1993).

A final area of resistance to feminism involves *how* women's social standing should be improved. Although a large majority of people in the United States believe women should have equal rights, most also believe that women should advance individually, according to their abilities. In a national survey, 70 percent of respondents claimed that women should expect to get ahead on the basis of their own training and qualifications; only 10 percent thought women's rights groups or collective action represent the best approach (NORC, 1994:320). Thus it appears that resistance to feminism is primarily directed at its socialist and radical variants; by contrast, there is widespread support for the principles that underlie liberal feminism.

The embrace of traditional gender patterns is clearly declining in the United States. In 1977, 65 percent of all adults endorsed the statement, "It is much better for everyone involved if the man is the achiever outside the home and the woman takes care of the home and family." By 1994, support for this view had dropped sharply, to 34 percent (NORC, 1994:230).

LOOKING AHEAD: GENDER IN THE TWENTY-FIRST CENTURY

Predictions about the future are, at best, informed speculation. Just as economists disagree about the inflation rate a year from now and political scientists can only guess at the outcome of upcoming elections, sociologists can offer only general observations about the likely future of gender.

Certainly, change has been remarkable. Two centuries ago women in the United States occupied a position that was clearly and strikingly subordinate. Husbands controlled property in marriage, laws barred women from most jobs, from holding political office, and even from voting. Although women today remain socially disadvantaged, the movement toward equality

NOTE: In general, support for feminism is stronger on both coasts than in the Midwest and the South. The states the Democrats carried in the 1992 presidential election look more favorably on feminism than those won by the Republicans.

NOTE: An Iowa study of married women found that 68% preferred the title Mrs.; 6% favored Ms.; 26% were unsure. (*Des Moines Register*)

GLOBAL: In 1990, 10% of the members of the Central Committee of the Communist party in the People's Republic of China were women; none of 19 Politburo members was a woman.

NOTE: Of all people arrested for drunk driving, 95% are men.

Q: "Law may prescribe that the male nipple may be equal to the female one, but they will still not give milk." Allan Bloom

Controversy & Debate

Men's Rights! Are Men Really So Privileged?

"Anti-male discrimination has become far greater in scope, in degree, and in damage than any which may exist against women." Men's rights advocate Richard F. Doyle

Men dominate society, this chapter argues, and benefit from doing so. Men enjoy higher earnings, control more wealth, exercise more power, do less housework, and get more respect than women do. The controversial assertion above, however, sums up an important counterpoint advanced by the "men's rights movement"—that the male world is not nearly as privileged as most people think.

If men are so privileged in our society, why do they turn to crime more often than women do? Moreover, the operation of the criminal justice system emphasizes the *lack* of special privileges accorded to men. Probably most people would not be surprised to learn that police are reluctant to arrest a woman (especially one with children). This fact helps explain why, when police make an arrest for a serious crime, 80 percent of the time the handcuffs go on a male. Moreover, it would seem that men get no break from the courts, since males make up 95 percent of the U.S. prison population. And, despite the fact that women, too, can and do kill, every offender executed during the last several decades has been male.

Culture, too, is not always generous to men. Our way of life praises as "real men" those males who work and live hard, and who typically drink, smoke, and speed on the highways. Given this view of maleness, is it any wonder that men are twice as likely as women to suffer serious assault, three times more likely to fall victim to homicide, and four times more likely to commit suicide? Even more curious, in light of these statistics, is our national preoccupation with violence against *women!* Perhaps, critics suggest, we are in the grip of a cultural double standard that leads us to expect that males will be involved in self-destructiveness, while lamenting the far fewer cases in which brutality harms women. It is this same double standard, the argument continues, that moves women and children out of harm's way while expecting men to "go down with the ship" or to die defending their country on the battlefield.

Child custody is another sore point from the perspective of many men. Despite decades of consciousness-raising in pursuit of gender fairness, and clear evidence that men earn more income than women, courts across the United States routinely settle custody disputes by awarding primary care of children to mothers. And, to make matters worse, men separated from their children by the courts are then stigmatized as "runaway fathers" or "dead-beat dads."

Moreover, the case against male privilege also takes note of the expanding scope of affirmative action laws, which now cover three-fourths of the population (notably excluding white males). In today's affirmative action climate, critics charge, women now have the inside track to college (where they now outnumber men) as well as in the work force (where businesses know they will be called to account for hiring practices).

Nature seems to have plotted against men by giving women, on average, a 10 percent bonus in longevity. But the controversial question is, when society plays favorites, who is favored?

Continue the debate . . .

1. *Do you think that, overall, our culture benefits men or women? Why?*

2. *On the campus, do men's organizations (such as fraternities and athletic teams) enjoy special privileges or not?*

3. *What about the issue of child custody? Should courts routinely favor one parent or another? Why or why not?*

Sources: Based on Doyle (1980) and Scanlon (1992).

has surged ahead. Note, further, that two-thirds of people entering the work force during the 1990s will be women. Truly, today's economy *depends* on the earnings of women (Hewlett, 1990).

Many factors have contributed to this transformation. Most important, industrialization has both broadened the range of human activity and shifted the nature of work from physically demanding tasks that favored male strength to jobs that require more human thought and imagination, which places the talents of women and men on an even footing. Additionally, medical technology has afforded us control over reproduction, so that women's lives today are less constrained by unwanted pregnancies.

Many women and men have also made deliberate efforts in pursuit of social equality. Sexual harassment complaints, for example, now are taken much more seriously in the workplace. And as more women assume positions of power in the corporate and political worlds, social changes in the twenty-first century may turn out to be even greater than those we have already witnessed.

Yet strong opposition to feminism persists. Gender still forms an important foundation of personal identity and family life, and it is deeply woven into the moral fabric of our society. Therefore, attempts to change cultural ideas about the two sexes will continue to provoke opposition. On balance, however, while change is likely to proceed incrementally, the movement toward a society in which women and men enjoy equal rights and opportunities seems certain to gain strength.

SUMMARY

1. Sex is a biological concept; a human fetus is female or male from the moment of conception. Hermaphrodites represent rare cases of people who combine the biological traits of both sexes. Transsexuals are people who feel they are one sex when biologically they are the other.

2. Heterosexuality is the dominant sexual orientation in virtually every society in the world, although people with a bisexual or exclusively homosexual orientation make up a small percentage of the population everywhere.

3. Gender involves how cultures assign human traits and power to each sex. Gender varies historically and across cultures. Some degree of patriarchy, however, exists in every society.

4. Through the socialization process, people link gender with personality (gender identity) and actions (gender roles). The major agents of socialization—the family, peer groups, schools, and the mass media—reinforce cultural definitions of what is feminine and masculine.

5. Gender stratification entails numerous social disadvantages for women. Although most women are now in the paid labor force, a majority of working women hold low-paying clerical or service jobs. Unpaid housework also remains predominantly a task performed by women.

6. On average, U.S. women earn 72 percent as much as men do. This disparity stems from differences in jobs and family responsibilities as well as discrimination.

7. Women now earn a slight majority of all bachelor's and master's degrees. Men still receive a majority of all doctorates and professional degrees.

8. The number of women in politics has increased sharply in recent decades. Still, the vast majority of elected officials nationwide are men.

9. Minority women encounter greater social disadvantages than white women. Overall, minority women earn only half as much as white men, and half the households headed by African-American women are poor.

10. On the basis of their distinctive identity and social disadvantages, all women represent a social minority, although many do not think of themselves in such terms.

11. Violence against women is a widespread problem in the United States. Our society is also grappling with the issues of sexual harassment and pornography.

12. Structural-functional analysis holds that preindustrial societies benefit from distinctive roles for males and females reflecting biological differences between the sexes. In industrial societies, marked gender inequality becomes dysfunctional and slowly decreases. Talcott Parsons claimed that complementary gender roles promote the social integration of families and society as a whole.

13. Social-conflict analysis views gender as a dimension of social inequality and conflict. Friedrich Engels tied gender stratification to the development of

private property. He claimed that capitalism devalues women and housework.

14. Feminism endorses the social equality of the sexes and actively opposes patriarchy and sexism. Feminism also strives to eliminate violence against women, and to give women control over their sexuality.

15. There are three variants of feminist thinking. Liberal feminism seeks equal opportunity for both sexes within current social arrangements; socialist feminism advocates abolishing private property as the means to social equality; radical feminism aims to create a gender-free society.

16. Because gender distinctions stand at the core of our way of life, feminism has encountered strong resistance. Although two-thirds of adults in the United States support the Equal Rights Amendment, this legislation—first proposed in Congress in 1923—has yet to become part of the U.S. Constitution.

KEY CONCEPTS

feminism the advocacy of social equality for the sexes, in opposition to patriarchy and sexism

gender identity traits that females and males, guided by their culture, incorporate into their personalities

gender roles (sex roles) attitudes and activities that a society links to each sex

gender stratification a society's unequal distribution of wealth, power, and privilege between the two sexes

hermaphrodite a human being with some combination of female and male internal and external genitalia

matriarchy a form of social organization in which females dominate males

patriarchy a form of social organization in which males dominate females

primary sex characteristics the genitals, used to reproduce the human species

secondary sex characteristics bodily development, apart from the genitals, that distinguishes biologically mature females and males

sex the biological distinction between females and males

sexism the belief that one sex is innately superior to the other

sexual harassment comments, gestures, or physical contact of a sexual nature that are deliberate, repeated, and unwelcome

sexual orientation an individual's preference in terms of sexual partners: same sex, other sex, either sex, neither sex

transsexuals people who feel they are one sex though biologically they are the other

CRITICAL-THINKING QUESTIONS

1. A recent cover story in a national news magazine characterized bisexuality as "the wild card of erotic life" and a "potent threat to monogamy." Do you agree? Why or why not?

2. What techniques do the mass media use to "sell" women on the value of beauty? How do the media appeal to men?

3. Why is gender a dimension of social stratification? How does gender interact with inequality based on race, ethnicity, and class?

4. What do feminists mean by asserting that "the personal is political"? Explain how liberal, socialist, and radical feminism differ from one another.

SUGGESTED READINGS

Classic Sources

Margaret Mead. *Sex and Temperament in Three Primitive Societies*. New York: William Morrow, 1963; orig. 1935.

This comparative study carried out in New Guinea was an early effort to advance the social equality of the sexes.

Jessie Bernard. *The Female World*. New York: The Free Press, 1981.

This more recent classic explores how females and males live in different, socially constructed worlds.

Contemporary Sources

Judith Lorber. *Paradoxes of Gender*. New Haven, Conn.: Yale University Press, 1994.

This comprehensive survey of the state of gender research argues for classifying gender as a social institution since it shapes all aspects of human behavior.

Pauline Bart, ed. *Violence Against Women: The Bloody Footprints*. Thousand Oaks, Calif.: Sage, 1993.

A number of outspoken analysts charge that violence against women—ranging from pornography to murder—is a routine feature of U.S. society.

Allan Bérubé. *Coming Out Under Fire: The History of Gay Men and Women in World War Two*. New York: The Free Press, 1990.

This interesting book provides the historical context for the recent debate about gays in the military.

Global Sources

Marnia Lazreg. *The Eloquence of Silence: Algerian Women in Question*. New York: Routledge, 1994.

This historical survey of the lives of women in a North African nation suggests that women everywhere—despite profound cultural differences—confront many of the same basic problems.

Cynthia Enloe. *Bananas, Beaches, and Bases: Making Feminist Sense of International Politics*. Berkeley: University of California Press, 1990.

This book pushes the issue of gender into the international arena, arguing that gender (along with race and class) are important dimensions of the geopolitical system.

**ARCHIBALD JOHN MOTLEY, JR.,
MENDING SOCKS, 1924**

Oil on canvas, 111.44x101.60 cm (43 7/8x40 in.).
The Ackland Art Museum, The University of North
Carolina at Chapel Hill, Burton Emmett Collection.

Aging and the Elderly

The book *Final Exit* shot to the top of the bestseller list in 1991. This is a publication about dying—not about the death of a famous person, nor a philosophical treatise on death, but a "how to" manual explaining how to commit suicide. *Final Exit* gives specific instructions for killing yourself in a host of ways, from swallowing sleeping pills, to self-starvation, to suffocation with a plastic bag.

The author of *Final Exit*, Derek Humphry, is a founder and executive director of the Hemlock Society. Since 1980, this organization has offered support and practical assistance to people who wish to die. Humphry argues that the time has come for people in the United States to have straightforward information about how to end their own lives. The immediate and remarkable popularity of *Final Exit*—especially among the elderly—suggests that millions of people agree with him.

Not surprisingly, *Final Exit* sparked controversy. While supporters view the work as a humane effort to assist people who are painfully and terminally ill, critics claim that it encourages suicide by people who are experiencing only temporary depression (Angelo, 1991). A legal battle is also under way as laws are being tested that prohibit doctors—such as Michigan physician Jack Kevorkian—from assisting in the death of a patient.

But the appearance of *Final Exit* also raises broader questions that are no less disturbing and controversial. As this chapter explains, the ranks of the elderly are swelling rapidly as more and more men and women live longer and longer. As a result, younger people are uneasy about their responsibilities toward aging parents. Older people are, on the one hand, fearful of not being able to afford the medical care they may need and, on the other hand, alarmed at the prospect of losing control of their lives to a medical establishment that often seeks to prolong life at any cost. And people of all ages worry whether the health-care system can meet the escalating demands of seniors only by shortchanging the young.

Today, issues relating to aging and the elderly command the attention of policy makers as never before. In some respects, growing old in the United States has never been better: People live longer, have better health care, and experience less poverty than they did a generation ago. But stubborn problems persist. Older people, for example, continue to grapple with prejudice and discrimination. And, as unprecedented numbers of women and men enter old age, new problems loom on the horizon.

THE GRAYING OF THE UNITED STATES

A quiet but powerful revolution is reshaping the United States: The number of elderly people—women and men aged sixty-five and over—is increasing almost three times as fast as the population as a whole. Between 1970 and 1994, while the overall U.S. population rose 28 percent, the number of seniors climbed by 66 percent and the

THEN AND NOW: U.S. population 65 and older: *1974*, 10.3% (22 million); *1994*, 12.7% (33 million).

GLOBAL: In a ranking of the oldest countries (defined in terms of share of population aged 60 and over), the United States ranks 20th (16.9% 60 and older). European nations and Japan are higher on the list. The top five: Sweden (22.8%), Norway (20.9%), Belgium and Italy (20.8%), United Kingdom (20.7%).

THEN AND NOW: Most of the increase in U.S. life expectancy occurred during the first half of this century: *1900*, 47.3 years; *1950*, 68.2; *1960*, 69.7; *1970*, 70.8; *1980*, 73.7; *1990*, 75.4; *1994*, 75.7. (U.S. Census Bureau)

NOTE: The dramatic increase in the number of elderly people in industrial societies means that about half of all people who have ever reached age sixty-five are alive today.

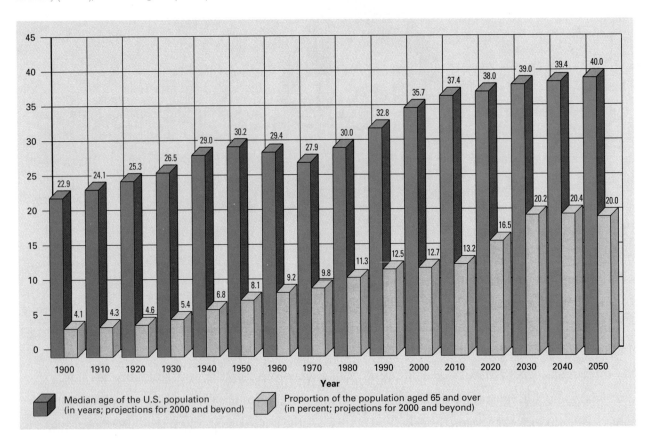

FIGURE 14–1 The Graying of U.S. Society

Source: U.S. Bureau of the Census (1995).

number of people above age eighty-five soared by 150 percent. The effects of this "graying" of the United States promise to be profound.

A few statistical comparisons bring this change into sharp focus. In 1900, half the U.S. population was under twenty-three years of age and only 4 percent had reached sixty-five. By 1990, as Figure 14–1 shows, the median age had climbed to almost thirty-three, with the elderly accounting for more than 12 percent of the population. Looking at absolute numbers, the elderly population jumped tenfold during this century, reaching 35 million in 1995. Looking ahead to the year 2050—within the lifetimes of many readers of this book—the median age will be about forty years and 20 percent of the U.S. population will be over sixty-five. Between now and 2050, the number of elderly people will almost triple to more than 80 million while the number of younger people will increase by barely one-third (U.S. Bureau of the Census, 1995).

As Figure 14–2 suggests, this graying of society characterizes all industrial countries. Typically, rich nations have low birth rates, coupled with increasing longevity. Looking more closely at the United States, we see that, with the end of World War II in 1945, this country experienced a "baby boom" that lasted until about 1965. This large cohort of 75 million "boomers," who are now middle-aged, ensures an "elder boom" early in the next century. But, as it did in other industrial societies, the birth rate in the United States took a sharp turn downward after 1965 (the so-called "baby bust" era), so that in coming decades our population will become increasingly "top heavy."

This century has witnessed a remarkable, thirty-year increase in life expectancy. Females born in 1900 lived, on average, only about forty-eight years; males, forty-six years. By contrast, females born in 1994 can look forward to 79 years of life; men to just over 72 years (U.S. Bureau of the Census, 1995).

NOTE: Examples of the social clout of the baby-boom generation: They defined the 1960s, brought an end to the Vietnam War, got the vote by the time many of them were eighteen, initiated the second wave of feminism, celebrated the first Earth Day, and then raised the drinking age before their own children turned eighteen. (Longino, Jr., 1994)

GLOBAL THEN AND NOW: Japan has the world's greatest life expectancy. In 1947, average life spans were: men, 50.1 years; women, 54.0 years; by 1995, comparable data were 77.0 and 82.6 years.
GLOBAL: In terms of size of the elderly population, the P.R. China leads the world because of its population size—with about 100 million elderly people (roughly 10% of its total population).

Underlying this striking gain in life span are medical advances that have virtually eliminated infectious diseases such as smallpox, diphtheria, and measles, which killed many infants and young people in the past. Just as important, more recent medical strides fend off cancer and heart disease, afflictions common to the elderly. Looking beyond the elderly population, a rising standard of living during this century has promoted the health of people of all ages.

As life becomes longer, the fastest-growing segment of the U.S. population is people over eighty-five, who are already more than twenty times more numerous than they were at the turn of the century. These men and women now number 3.5 million (about 1.4 percent of the total population). Projections place their number at 18 million (about 5 percent of the total) by the year 2050 (Kaufman, 1990; Harbert & Ginsberg, 1991; U.S. Bureau of the Census, 1995).

We can only begin to imagine the consequences of this massive increase in the elderly population. As elderly people steadily retire from the labor force, the proportion of nonworking adults—already about ten times greater than in 1900—will generate ever-greater demands for social resources and programs. And the ratio of elderly people to working-age adults, which analysts call the *old-age dependency ratio*, will almost double in the next fifty years (rising from twenty to thirty-seven elderly people per one hundred people aged eighteen to sixty-four). During this century, the share of federal spending supporting people over sixty-five has already tripled, from 15 percent to almost 50 percent. With more elderly people needing support from fewer workers, can today's baby boomers be assured of security tomorrow (Treas, 1995)?

One key area of concern is the health-care system, because the elderly today account for one-fourth of all medical expenditures. With the skyrocketing costs of medical care, tens of millions of additional elderly men and women will place an unprecedented demand on the health-care system, one that is well beyond current resources.

In terms of everyday experience, interacting with elderly people will become commonplace in coming decades. In recent history, our society has been marked by a considerable degree of age segregation. The young rarely mingle with the old, so that most people know little about aging. In the twenty-first century, as the elderly population of the United States increases, this pattern will change.

But, tomorrow as well as today, how frequently younger people interact with the elderly depends a great deal on where in the country we live. National

Global Snapshot

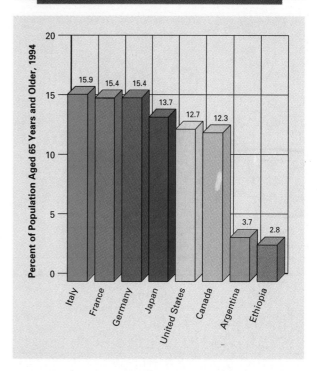

FIGURE 14–2 The Graying of Society
Source: U.S. Bureau of the Census (1995).

Map 14–1, on page 386, takes a look at residential patterns for people aged sixty-five and older.

Finally, the elderly represent an open category in which all of us, if we are lucky, end up. Thus elderly people in the United States are highly diverse, representing all cultures, classes, and races as well as both sexes. Even so, analysts sometimes draw a useful distinction between two cohorts of the elderly. The "younger elderly," who are between sixty-five and seventy-four years of age, are typically autonomous, enjoy good health and financial security, and are likely to be living as couples. The "older elderly" are at least seventy-five years of age and are more likely to be dependent on others because of both health and money problems. Although women outnumber men in the elderly population (due to their greater longevity), this discrepancy increases with advancing age: Among the "older elderly," about two-thirds are women.

NOTE: As the ranks of the elderly swell, our society's share of people under eighteen will drop dramatically. From 36% in 1960, and 26% in 1990, young people will account for just over 20% of the U.S. population by 2030.

NOTE: Looking back to 1820, the median age of the U.S. population was 16.7, similar to that of many poor societies today.

DISCUSS: Does increasing longevity have a serious "downside" in that more people will suffer from illness and disability in old age?

THE MAP: Young people migrate to regions of the country where jobs are plentiful; thus, counties with high proportions of elderly people are those that are contracting economically (especially rural counties in the middle of the country).

NOTE: Looking ahead to Figure 21–2, an age-sex pyramid for the United States, we see the effect of the baby boom and the baby bust.

Seeing Ourselves

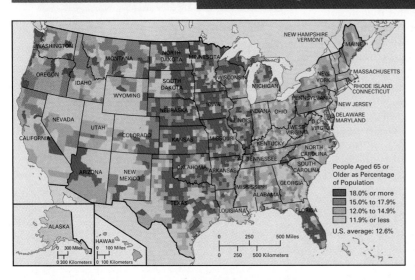

NATIONAL MAP 14–1
The Elderly Population of the United States

Common sense suggests that elderly people live in the Sunbelt, savoring the warmer climate of the South and Southwest. While it is true that Florida has a disproportionate share of people over the age of sixty-five, it turns out that counties with high percentages of older people predominate in the Midwest. What do you think accounts for this pattern? (Hint: Which regions of the United States do *younger* people leave in search of jobs?)

Sources: *American Demographics* magazine, March 1993, p. 34. Reprinted with permission. ©1994, *American Demographics* magazine, Ithaca, New York. Data from the 1990 decennial census.

GROWING OLD: BIOLOGY AND CULTURE

Tracking the graying of the United States is the special focus of **gerontology** (derived from the Greek word *geron*, meaning "an old person"), *the study of aging and the elderly*. Gerontologists explore the biological processes of aging, ask if personalities change as we grow older, and investigate how cultural assumptions about aging vary around the world.

Biological Changes

Aging amounts to a series of gradual, ongoing changes. How we think about life's transitions—whether we cheer our maturity or bemoan our physical decline—depends largely on whether our culture labels such changes as positive or negative. The youth-oriented way of life in the United States hails biological changes that occur early in life. Through childhood and adolescence, we gain responsibility and look forward to expanded legal rights.

But our culture takes a dimmer view of the biological changes that unfold later in life. We commiserate with those entering old age and make jokes about aging to avoid the harsh conclusion that the elderly are on a slippery slope of physical and mental decline. We assume, in short, that by about age forty, people cease growing *up* and begin growing *down*.

Growing old does bring on certain physical problems. Gray hair, wrinkles, loss of height and weight, and an overall decline in strength and vitality all begin in middle age. After the age of fifty, bones become more brittle so that injuries take longer to heal, and the odds of suffering from chronic illnesses (such as arthritis and diabetes) as well as life-threatening conditions (like heart disease and cancer) rise steadily. The sensory abilities—taste, sight, touch, smell, and especially hearing—also become less keen with age (Colloway & Dollevoet, 1977; Treas, 1995).

Without denying that health becomes more fragile with advancing age, the vast majority of older people are neither discouraged nor disabled by their physical condition. Only about one in ten seniors reports trouble walking, and fewer than one in twenty requires intensive care in a hospital or nursing home. No more than 1 percent of the elderly are bedridden. Overall, while 30 percent of people over the age of sixty-five characterize their health as "fair" or "poor" about 70 percent describe their overall condition as "good" or "excellent" (U.S. National Center for Health Statistics, 1994).

Bear in mind, too, that patterns of well-being vary greatly within the elderly population. More health problems beset the "older elderly," those past the age of seventy-five. Moreover, because women typically live longer than men do, women spend more of their lives suffering from chronic disabilities like arthritis. In

Q: "If I had known I was going to live this long, I would have taken better care of myself." Hollywood producer Hal Roach, on his 100th birthday in 1992

RESOURCE: An excerpt from Betty Friedan's new book, *The Fountain of Age*, is included in the third edition of the Macionis and Benokraitis reader, *Seeing Ourselves*.

NOTE: The world's oldest person (as of 1995) is Jeanne Calment of Arles, France, age 120. Although suffering poor hearing and lost vision, her mind is sharp, and she recently released her first vocal album. Asked what kind of future she expects, she responded "A very short one." (Wallis, 1995)

Q: "The older I grow, the more I distrust the common notion that age brings wisdom." H. L. Mencken

The reality of growing old is as much a matter of culture as it is of biology. In the United States, being elderly is often synonymous with being inactive; yet, in Greece and other more traditional countries, old people commonly continue many familiar routines.

addition, well-to-do people are likely to live and work in a healthful and safe environment, which pays benefits well into old age. And, of course, richer people can afford much more preventive medical care. More than 84 percent of elderly people with incomes exceeding $35,000 assess their own health as "excellent" or "very good," while only 58 percent of people with incomes under $10,000 do the same. Income disparity also explains why about three-fourths of elderly white people describe their health in positive terms, in contrast to only half of older African Americans (U.S. National Center for Health Statistics, 1994).

Psychological Changes

Just as we tend to overstate the physical problems of aging, so it is easy to exaggerate the intellectual and psychological changes that accompany growing old. Looking at intelligence over the life course, the conventional wisdom can be summed up in the simple rule: "What goes up must come down" (Baltes & Schaie, 1974).

In recent years, however, gerontologists have cast a critical eye on this assertion. If we operationalize intelligence to spotlight sensorimotor coordination—such as the ability to arrange objects to match a drawing—we indeed find a steady decline after midlife. The facility to learn new material and to think quickly appears to subside as well, although not until much later—typically around the age of seventy. But the ability to apply familiar ideas holds steady with advancing age, and some studies actually show

improvement in verbal and mathematical skills (Baltes & Schaie, 1974; Schaie, 1980).

Most people wonder if they will think differently or have a different outlook when they are older. Gerontologists assure us, for better or worse, that the answer is usually no. Personality changes with advancing age are usually limited to becoming more introspective—that is, more engaged with our own thoughts and emotions—and less materialistic. Generally, therefore, two elderly people who were childhood friends would recognize in each other many of the same personality traits that distinguished them as youngsters (Neugarten, 1971, 1972, 1977; Wolfe, 1994).

Aging and Culture

November 1, 1994, Approaching Kandy, Sri Lanka. Our small van struggles up the steep mountain incline. Breaks in the lush vegetation offer spectacular views, interrupting the conversation, which has turned to growing old. "Then there are no old-age homes in your country?" I ask. "In Colombo and other cities, I am sure," our driver responds, "but not many; we are not like you Americans." "And how is that?" I counter, stiffening a bit. His eyes remain fixed on the road: "We would not leave our fathers and mothers to live alone."

Chapter 14 Aging and the Elderly **387**

NOTE: The sense of "elder" (a term rooted in agrarian societies) is positive; that of "elderly" (in industrial societies) is negative.

GLOBAL: Hoyt Alverson reports that, for the Tswana of southern Africa, the concept of aging is synonymous with the notion of "seeing with one's own eyes." For this traditional society, knowledge is "remembering things past," making the elderly the wisest of all. (*Mind in the Heart of Darkness*, Yale University Press, 1978:171)

Q: "While much of the world thinks Japan is a society where the children look after their elderly parents, that is simply no longer the case." Tsuneo Iida, Nagoya University

RESOURCE: Changes in the traditional care structures in Japan are examined in the film, "Aging in Japan: When Traditional Mechanisms Vanish," available from Films for the Humanities and Sciences, Box 2053, Princeton, NJ 08543.

When do people grow old? How do younger people regard society's oldest members? The variable answers to these questions demonstrate that, while aging is universal, the significance of growing old is a variable element of culture.

At one level, how well—and, more basically, how long—people live is closely linked to a society's technology and overall standard of living. Throughout most of human history, as English philosopher Thomas Hobbes (1588–1679) put it, people's lives were "nasty, brutish, and short" (although Hobbes himself persisted to the ripe old age of ninety-one). In his day, most people married and had children while in their teens, became middle-aged in their twenties, and began to succumb to various illnesses in their thirties and forties. It took several more centuries for a rising standard of living and advancing medical technology to curb deadly infectious diseases. Living to, say, age fifty became commonplace only at the beginning of this century. Since then, a surging standard of living coupled with medical advances have added twenty years to people's longevity in industrial nations.

But living into what we call "old age" is not yet the rule in much of the world. Global Map 14–1 shows that, in the poorest countries, the average life span is still barely fifty years.

Beyond longevity, however, we must examine how societies view their senior members. As Chapter 9 ("Social Stratification") details, all societies display systematic inequality with regard to basic resources. We now turn to how aging figures in this process.

Age Stratification: A Global Assessment

Like race, ethnicity, and gender, age is a basis for socially ranking individuals. **Age stratification**, then, is *the unequal distribution of wealth, power, and privileges among people at different stages in the life course.* As is true of other dimensions of social hierarchy, age stratification varies according to a society's level of technological development.

Hunting and Gathering Societies

As Chapter 4 ("Society") explains, without the technology to produce a surplus of food, hunters and gatherers are nomadic. Their survival depends on physical strength and stamina; thus, as members of these societies become elderly (in this case, reaching about age thirty) they become less active, leading others to consider them an economic burden (Sheehan, 1976).

Pastoral, Horticultural, and Agrarian Societies

With control over raising crops and animals, societies gain the capacity to produce a material surplus; consequently, individuals may accumulate considerable wealth over a lifetime. The most privileged members of these societies are typically the elderly, promoting **gerontocracy**, *a form of social organization in which the elderly have the most wealth, power, and prestige.* Old people, particularly men, are honored (and sometimes feared) by their families and, as the box on page 390 reports in the case of the Abkhasians, they remain active leaders of society until they die. This veneration of the elderly also explains the widespread practice of ancestor worship in agrarian societies.

Industrial Societies

Industrialization pushes living standards upward and advances medical technology, which, in turn, increases life expectancy. But these same forces simultaneously erode the power and prestige of the elderly. In part, this decline reflects a shift in the prime source of wealth from land (typically controlled by the oldest members of society) to factories and other goods (often owned or managed by younger people). The peak earning years among U.S. workers, for instance, occur around age fifty; after that, earnings generally decline.

Urban living also separates the generations physically and encourages children to depend less on their parents and more on their own earning power. Furthermore, because industrial, urban societies change rapidly, the skills, traditions, and life experiences that served the old seem less relevant to the young. Finally, the tremendous productivity of industrial nations means that some members of society do not need to work; as a result, most of the very old and the very young remain in nonproductive roles (Cohn, 1982).

Over the long term, all these factors are transforming *elders* (a term with positive connotations) into the *elderly* (commanding far less prestige). In mature, industrial societies such as the United States and Canada, economic and political leaders are usually middle-aged people who combine seasoned experience with up-to-date skills. In rapidly changing sectors of the economy—especially high-tech fields—many key executives are much younger and sometimes not long out of college. Industrial societies often consign older people to marginal participation in the economy because they lack the knowledge and training demanded by a fast-changing marketplace.

THE MAP: Life expectancy closely parallels level of economic development. Compare this map to Global Map 1–1 on page 7.

NOTE: Life expectancy is affected by changes in infant mortality and tends to exaggerate the change in life span for those who reach old age. In 1900, Americans reaching age 65 typically lived to age 77; by 1990, they could expect to reach 83.

NOTE: The word "elderly" has the root *eld*, from Old English meaning "age," or "old age."

GLOBAL: For the entire world, about 5% of females and 4% of males are over 60 years of age. In poor societies, the figures are lower (3.4% and 3.1%, respectively). For rich nations, they are much higher (9.6% and 6.2%).

Window on the World

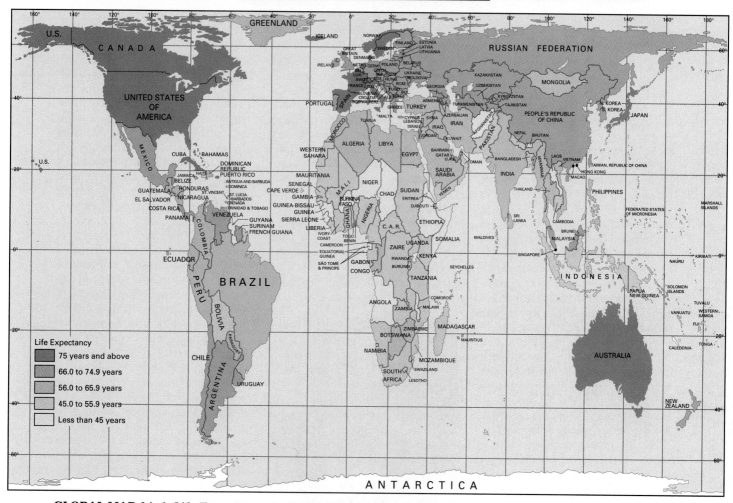

GLOBAL MAP 14–1 Life Expectancy in Global Perspective

Life expectancy has shot upward over the course of this century in industrial countries including Canada, the United States, the nations of Western Europe, Japan, and Australia. A newborn in the United States can expect to live about seventy-five years, and our life expectancy would be greater still were it not for the high risk of death among infants born into poverty. Since poverty is the rule in much of the world, lives are correspondingly shorter, especially in parts of Africa where life expectancy may be as low as forty years.

Source: *Peters Atlas of the World* (1990).

Certainly some elderly men and women remain at the helm of businesses they own but, more commonly, older people predominate in traditional occupations (such as barbers, tailors, and seamstresses) and jobs that involve minimal activity (night security guards, for instance) (Kaufman & Spilerman, 1982).

Japan: An Exceptional Case

Japan stands out as an exception to the rule: With a large proportion of elderly people (about 14 percent and rising rapidly), Japan also maintains a traditional culture that elevates the prestige of older people. Most

DIVERSITY: Currently, about 50,000 people in the U.S. are centenarians; the Census Bureau projects about 75,000 by the year 2000, and 1 million by the year 2040. Of the oldest-of-the-old in 1994, 82% were women, and 84% were white. (African Americans were slightly over-represented among centenarians.)

DIVERSITY: On average, a male in the United States can now look forward to 60 years of health; a female to 63.

NOTE: Academics are aging far faster than the population as a whole. According to the National Center for Education Statistics, by the year 2000, a majority of full-time college faculty members will be aged 60 or older. In every discipline except mathematics, at least one-third of faculty members will be 65 or older by 2002. With increasing college enrollments and many coming retirements, our colleagues should be in rising demand.

GLOBAL SOCIOLOGY

Growing (Very) Old: A Report From Abkhasia

Anthropologist Sula Benet was sharing wine and conversation with a man in Tamish, a small village in the Republic of Abkhasia, once part of the Soviet Union. Judging the man to be about 70, she raised her glass and offered a toast to his long life. "May you live as long as Moses," she exclaimed. The gesture of goodwill fell flat: Moses lived to 120, but Benet's companion was already 119.

An outsider—especially an open-minded anthropologist who studies many of the world's mysteries—should be skeptical of the longevity claims made by some Abkhasians. In one village of twelve hundred visited by Benet, for example, two hundred people declared their age to be more than eighty. But government statistics confirm that, even if some Abkhasians exaggerate their longevity, most outlive the average North American.

What accounts for this remarkable life span? The answer certainly is not the advanced medical technology in which people in the United States place so much faith; many Abkhasians have never seen a physician nor entered a hospital.

The probable explanation is cultural, including diet and physical activity. Abkhasians eat little saturated fat (which is linked to heart disease), use no sugar, and drink no coffee or tea; few smoke or chew tobacco. They consume large amounts of healthful fruits and vegetables and drink lots of buttermilk and low-alcohol wine. Additionally, Abkhasians maintain active lives built around regular physical work for people of all ages.

Moreover, Abkhasians live according to a well-defined and consistent set of traditional values, which confers on all a strong feeling of belonging and

a clear sense of purpose. Here the elderly remain active and valued members of the community, in marked contrast to our own practice of pushing old people to the margins of social life. As Benet explains: "The old [in the United States], when they do not simply vegetate, out of view and out of mind, keep themselves 'busy' with bingo and shuffleboard." For their part, the Abkhasians do not even have a word for old people and have no notion of retiring. Furthermore, younger people accord their senior members great prestige and respect since, in their minds, advanced age confers the greatest wisdom. Elders are indispensable guardians of culture and preside at important ceremonial occasions where they transmit their knowledge to the young. In Abkhasia, in short, people look to the old, rather than the young, for decisions and guidance in everyday life.

Given their positive approach to growing old, Abkhasians expect to lead long and useful lives. They feel needed because, in their own minds and everyone else's, they are. Far from being a burden, elders stand at the center of society.

Source: Based on Benet (1971).

aged people in Japan live with an adult son or daughter and continue to play a significant role in family life. Elderly men in Japan are also more likely than their counterparts in the United States to remain in the labor force, and, in many Japanese corporations, the oldest employees enjoy the greatest respect. But even Japan is steadily becoming more like other industrial societies, in which growing old means giving up a large measure of social importance (Harlan, 1968; Cowgill & Holmes, 1972; Treas, 1979; Palmore, 1982; Yates, 1986).

TRANSITIONS AND PROBLEMS OF AGING

Chapter 5 ("Socialization") explained that we confront change at each stage of life. People must unlearn self-concepts and social patterns that no longer apply to their lives and simultaneously learn to cope with new circumstances. Of all stages of the life course, however, old age presents the greatest personal challenges.

DIVERSITY: By age 75, 52% of women but only 21% of men live alone. At no age do most men live alone.
NOTE: In 1900, there were more men over sixty-five in the United States than there were women. Today the reverse is true. The rate has changed from 100:98 men to women in 1900 to 100:150 in 1990. Higher past death rates for women (especially in childbirth) explain the pattern.

NOTE: Although just 6% of the elderly live in nursing homes, the number of nursing home residents (currently 1.8 million) increased by 25% during the 1980s and may well reach 5 million by 2030.
NOTE: The age distribution among members of the American Sociological Association: 34 and below, 19.9%; 35–39, 12.7%; 40–44, 16.9%; 45–49, 17.9%; 50–54, 11.3%; 55 and older, 21.3%.

Although physical decline in old age is less serious than most younger people think, this change can cause emotional stress. Older people endure more pain, become resigned to limited activities, adjust to greater dependence on others, and see in the death of friends or relatives frequent reminders of their own mortality. Moreover, because our culture places such a premium on youth, aging may spark frustration, fear, and self-doubt (Hamel, 1990). As one retired psychologist recently said of his old age: "Don't let the current hype about the joys of retirement fool you. They are not the best of times. It's just that the alternative is even worse" (Rubenstein, 1991:13).

Erik Erikson (1963, 1980) points out that elderly people must resolve a tension that springs from "integrity versus despair." No matter how much they still may be learning and achieving, older people recognize that their lives are nearing an end. Thus the elderly spend much time reflecting on their past accomplishments and disappointments. To shore up their personal integrity, Erikson explains, older women and men must face up to past mistakes as well as savor their successes. Otherwise, this stage of life may turn into a time of despair—a dead end with little positive meaning.

Research indicates that most people cope fairly well with the challenges of growing old. In a classic study of people in their seventies, Bernice Neugarten (1971) acknowledged that some people develop *disintegrated and disorganized personalities* because they find it nearly impossible to come to terms with old age. Despair is the common thread in these lives, sometimes to the point of making them passive residents of hospitals or nursing homes.

Another segment of Neugarten's subjects, those with *passive-dependent personalities*, were only slightly better off. They have little confidence in their abilities to cope with daily events, sometimes seeking help even if they do not actually need it. Always in danger of social withdrawal, their level of life satisfaction remains relatively low.

A third category of people had *defended personalities*, living independently but fearful of advancing age. Such people try to shield themselves from the reality of old age by valiantly fighting to stay youthful and physically fit. While concerns about health are certainly positive, setting unrealistic standards for oneself can only breed stress and disappointment.

Most of Neugarten's subjects, however, fared far better, displaying what she called *integrated personalities*. As she sees it, the key to successful aging lies in maintaining one's dignity, self-confidence, and optimism while accepting the inevitability of growing old.

TABLE 14–1 Living Arrangements of the Elderly, 1994

	Men	Women
Living alone	16%	40%
Living with spouse	75%	41%
Living with other relatives	6%	17%
Living with nonrelatives	2%	2%
Living in nursing home	1%	1%

Source: U.S. Bureau of the Census (1995).

Given the youth orientation of our society, it is easy for younger people to imagine that the elderly are generally unhappy. But research suggests that, while personal adjustments are inevitable, the experience of growing old in the United States may also provide joy.

Social Isolation

Being alone may provoke anxiety in people of any age; isolation, however, is most common among elderly people. Retirement closes off workplace social interaction, physical problems may limit mobility, and negative stereotypes depicting the elderly as "over the hill" may discourage younger people from close social contact with their elders.

The greatest cause of social isolation, however, is the inevitable death of significant others. Few human experiences affect people as profoundly as the death of a spouse. One study found that almost three-fourths of widows and widowers cited loneliness as their most serious problem (Lund, 1989). Widows and widowers must rebuild their lives in the glaring absence of people with whom, in many instances, they spent most of their adult lives. Some survivors choose not to live at all. One study of elderly men noted a sharp increase in mortality, sometimes by suicide, in the months following the death of their wives (Benjamin & Wallis, 1963).

The problem of social isolation falls most heavily on women, who typically outlive their husbands. Table 14–1 shows that three-fourths of men aged sixty-five and over live with spouses, while only four in ten elderly women do. Forty percent of older women (especially the "older elderly") live alone, compared to 16 percent of older men. More pronounced isolation among elderly women in the United States may account for the research finding that their mental health is not as strong as that of elderly men (Chappell & Havens, 1980). Keep in mind, too, that living alone—which many older people value as a dimension

NOTE: The elderly travel a good deal by car: Projections indicate that elderly people will comprise 20% of the population of North America in 2000, but 28% of drivers on North American roadways.

NOTE: Despite the common image (in the middle class) of retirees heading south to Florida or west to Arizona, only 6% of elderly people report relocating during the past year (compared to 19% of people aged 20 to 64).

NOTE: In 1994, 3.8 million seniors were working or looking for work. Half of elderly workers are employed full time.

SOCIAL SURVEY: "All employees should be required to retire at an age set by law." (GSS 1985; *Codebook*, 1987:379)

"Agree strongly"   5.2%   "Disagree"   42.7%
"Agree"   12.6%   "Disagree strongly" 21.6%
"Neither agree nor disagree" 16.5%   DK/NR   1.4%

of autonomy—presumes the financial means to do so (Mutchler, 1992).

For most older people, families provide the primary source of social support. Ge Lin and Peter Rogerson (1994) found that 60 percent of older people who have no adult children living with them have one living within ten miles. About half of these nearby children visit their parents at least once a week, although much research confirms that daughters are more likely to do so than sons (Stone, Cafferata, & Sangl, 1987).

Retirement

Work provides us not only with earnings; it also figures prominently in our personal identity. Retirement from paid work, therefore, generally entails some reduction in income, diminished social prestige, and loss of purpose in life (Chown, 1977).

Some organizations strive to ease this transition. Colleges and universities, for example, confer the title of "professor emeritus" (from Latin, meaning "fully earned") on retired faculty members, who are permitted to maintain their library, parking, and mail privileges.

For many older people, fresh activities and new interests minimize the personal disruption and loss of prestige brought on by retirement. Volunteer work can be personally rewarding, allowing individuals to apply their career skills to new challenges and opportunities. The American Association of Retired People (AARP), with more than 15 million members over the age of fifty, supports a wide range of volunteer opportunities for experienced seniors. For about one-third of retirees, however, a desire for some combination of social stimulation and greater income draws them back into the labor force, often within a year or two (Mergenbagen, 1994).

Although the idea of retirement is familiar to us, it is actually a recent creation, becoming commonplace only in industrial societies during the last century (Atchley, 1982). Advancing technology reduces the need for everyone to work as well as placing a premium on up-to-date skills. Retirement permits younger workers, who presumably have the most current knowledge and training, to predominate in the labor force. Then, too, the establishment of private and public pension programs provided the economic foundation for retirement. In poor societies that depend on the labor of everyone, and where no pension programs exist, most people work until they become incapacitated.

Around the world, there is little agreement as to when (or even if) a person should retire from paid work. In light of such variability, one might wonder if a society should formally designate any specific age for retirement. Vast differences in the interests and capacities of older people make the notion of a fixed retirement age controversial. As a result, Congress began phasing out mandatory retirement policies in the 1970s and virtually ended the practice by 1987. Statistically, however, the median age at retirement has been dropping, from sixty-eight in 1950 to sixty-three in 1994. By age sixty-five, then, 75 percent of men and 84 percent of women are not in the paid labor force (Mergenbagen, 1994).

In the United States, men more than women have faced the transition of retirement. Elderly women who spend their lives as homemakers do not retire per se, although the departure of the last child from home serves as a rough parallel. As the proportion of women in the labor force continues to rise, of course, both women and men will experience the changes brought on by retirement.

Aging and Poverty

For most people in the United States, retirement leads to a significant decline in income. For many, home mortgages and children's college expenses are paid; yet the costs of medical care, household help, and home utilities typically rise. Many elderly people lack sufficient savings or pension benefits to be self-supporting; while some of the elderly are quite affluent, Social Security is the greatest source of income for those over sixty-five. Thus, poverty rates rise somewhat as people enter old age, as shown in Figure 14–3.

Over time, the rate of poverty among the elderly has gone down. From about 35 percent in 1960, the official poverty rate of elderly people in the United States stood at 12.9 percent in 1994. Early in the 1980s, an important turnaround took place as the poverty rate of the elderly actually fell below that of the nonelderly. Overall, the 1980s were a boom decade for seniors, whose income jumped by more than 20 percent, while income of people under thirty-five actually fell (U.S. Bureau of the Census, 1970, 1995).

Various factors contributed to this financial windfall: Better health now allows people to work more, employer pension programs are more generous, and more couples now enjoy double incomes. Government policy, too, has played a key part, with programs aimed at the elderly (including Social Security) swelling to almost half of all government spending,

DIVERSITY: The earning disparity between men and women rises with age, since older women have less education relative to their male peers than their younger counterparts do. But even among college graduates, different work patterns mean that women aged 25–34 earn 75% of what comparable men do, while women aged 65 and over earn just 38% as much as comparable men.

DIVERSITY: Poverty rates for the elderly by race and ethnicity, 1993: Age 65–74: all, 10.0%, white, 8.2%, African American, 25.5%, Hispanic, 19.0%; Age 75 and over: all, 15.4%, white, 14.0%, African American, 32.0%, Hispanic, 26.1%. (U.S. Bureau of the Census)

SOCIAL SURVEY: The National Aging Center on Elder Abuse reports that in about one-third of cases seniors are abused by adult children at home; spouses come next, with self-abuse through neglect ranking third.

even as spending on children has remained more or less flat.

But, the effects of race and ethnicity are not blunted by growing old. In 1994, the poverty rate among elderly Hispanics (21.4 percent) was twice the rate for their white, non-Hispanic counterparts (10.7 percent); elderly African Americans (28.0 percent) had almost three times the white risk of poverty.

Gender, too, continues to shape the lives of people as they age. Among full-time workers, women over sixty-five had median earnings of $21,548 in 1994; comparable men earned $35,256. A quick calculation shows that this income disparity, by which older full-time working women earn 61 percent as much as all comparable men, is greater than among workers taken as a whole (72 percent). This is because, among workers aged sixty-five and above, women have much less schooling than men and hold lower-paying jobs.

But, of course, the majority of elderly people have retired from the labor force. Thus, a more realistic financial assessment must take account of the entire elderly population—nonworking as well as working. From this point of view, median income is far lower: $8,189 for women and $14,548 for men (a 56 percent gender disparity).

In the United States, then, although the elderly are faring better than ever before, growing old (especially among women and other minorities) still means a growing risk of poverty. One recent study, for example, found that poor elderly households typically spend three-fourths of their income on basic necessities, which amounts to just getting by (Koelln, Rubin, & Picard, 1995).

What is distinctive about the privation of the elderly, however, is that it is often hidden from view. Because of personal pride and a desire to maintain the dignity of independent living, many elderly people conceal financial problems, even from their own families. It is often difficult for people who have supported their children for years to admit that they can no longer provide for themselves, even though it may be through no fault of their own.

Abuse of the Elderly

In the United States, we seem to awaken to social problems in stages: In the case of family violence, child abuse came to light during the 1960s, spouse abuse was first decried in the 1970s, and abuse of the elderly was publicly acknowledged in the 1980s. Abuse of older people takes many forms, from passive neglect

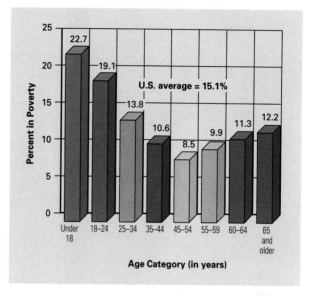

FIGURE 14–3 U.S. Poverty Rates, by Age, 1993
Source: U.S. Bureau of the Census (1995).

to active torment, and includes verbal, emotional, financial, and physical harm. Most elderly people suffer from none of these things, but research reveals that more than 1 million elderly people, out of a total of 35 million (3 percent), suffer serious maltreatment each year, and three times as many sustain abuse at some point. Like family violence against children or women, it is difficult to determine how widespread abuse of the elderly is because victims are understandably reluctant to talk about their plight. But as the proportion of elderly people rises, so does the incidence of abuse (Bruno, 1985; Clark, 1986; Pillemer, 1988; Holmstrom, 1994).

What motivates people to abuse the elderly? Often the cause lies in the stress of caring—financially and emotionally—for aging parents. Today's middle-aged adults represent a "sandwich generation" who may well spend as much time caring for their aging parents as for their own children. This caregiving responsibility is especially pronounced among adult women who not only look after parents and children but hold down jobs as well.

Even in Japan—where tradition demands that adult children care for aging parents at home—more and more people find themselves unable to cope with the caregiving role. Abuse appears to be most common where the stresses are greatest: in families with a very old person suffering from serious health

DIVERSITY: The Age Discrimination in Employment Act of 1967 prohibits age discrimination against workers or job applicants aged 40 to 65. As amended in 1975, it outlaws discrimination in federally funded job programs; in 1986 an additional change banned mandatory retirement in almost all types of jobs.

DIVERSITY: A crucial difference between ageism and racism or sexism is that being old is an *open* category that intersects all others.

SUPPLEMENTS: Making use of the *Student CHIP Social Survey Software*, we note a larger difference in most attitudes between the old and the young than between the sexes.

DISCUSS: Is it age bias? Why are women sometimes named April, May, or June, suggesting a positive attitude toward youth, but women are never called October, November, or December, which implies a negative view of old age? Miriam Corcoran

Various categories of people experience the stages of the life course in distinctive ways. Most men, for example, pass through old age with the support of a partner. Women, who typically outlive men, endure much of their old age alone, a reality poignantly captured in G. G. Kopilak's painting Still Life.

problems. Here, family life may be grossly distorted by demands and tensions that caregivers simply cannot endure, even if their intentions are good (Douglass, 1983; Gelman, 1985; Yates, 1986).

Ageism

In earlier chapters, we explained how ideology—including racism and sexism—seeks to justify the social disadvantages of minorities. Sociologists use the parallel term **ageism** to designate *prejudice and discrimination against the elderly*.

Like racism and sexism, ageism can be blatant (as when individuals deny elderly women or men a job simply because of their age) or subtle (as when people speak to the elderly with a condescending tone, as if they were children) (Kalish, 1979). Also, like racism and sexism, ageism builds physical traits into stereotypes; in the case of the elderly, people consider graying hair, wrinkled skin, and stooped posture as signs of personal incompetence. Negative stereotypes picture the aged as helpless, confused, resistant to change, and generally unhappy (Butler, 1975). Even sentimental notions of sweet little old ladies and charmingly eccentric old gentlemen gloss over older people's individuality, their

distinct personalities, and their long years of experience and accomplishment.

Ageism, like other expressions of prejudice, may have some foundation in reality. Statistically speaking, old people are more likely than young people to be mentally and physically impaired. But we slip into ageism when we make unwarranted generalizations about an entire category of people, most of whom do not conform to the stereotypes.

Recently Betty Friedan, a pioneer of the contemporary feminist movement, asserted that ageism is central to our culture. The box on page 396 takes a closer look at this issue.

The Elderly: A Minority?

As a category of people in this country, the elderly do face social disadvantages. But sociologists disagree as to whether the aged form a minority in the same way as, say, African Americans or women do.

Leonard Breen (1960) was the first to pronounce the elderly a minority, noting that older people have a clear social identity based on their age and, as a category, are subject to prejudice and discrimination. Yet, Gordon Streib (1968) countered, minority status is usually both permanent and exclusive. That is, a person is an African American or woman *for life* and cannot become part of the dominant category of white males. Being elderly, Streib continued, is an *open* status because, first, people are elderly for only part of their lives and, second, everyone who has the good fortune to live long enough eventually grows old.

Streib made a further point. The social disadvantages faced by the elderly are less substantial than those experienced by the minorities described in earlier chapters. For example, old people have never been deprived of the right to own property, to vote, or to hold office, as African Americans and women have. Some elderly people, of course, do suffer economic disadvantages, but these do not stem primarily from old age. Instead, most of the aged poor also happen to fall into categories of people likely to be poor at any age. To Streib, the truth is that "the poor grow old," *not* that "the old grow poor."

In light of this reasoning, and the rising economic fortunes of the elderly, it seems reasonable to conclude that old people are not a minority in the same sense as, say, African Americans and women are. Perhaps the best way to describe the elderly is simply as a distinctive segment of our population with characteristic pleasures and challenges.

DISCUSS: Jenny Hockey and Alison James (1993) claim that, as people transit the life course, they move from the margins to the center and back to the margins. Is this so?
RESOURCE: Robert Butler's statement "The Tragedy of Old Age in America," which challenges various myths about old age, is included among the classics in the Macionis and Benokraitis reader, *Seeing Ourselves*.

DIVERSITY: The elderly are politically active: 70% of seniors claim to have voted in the 1992 national elections, compared to 58% of people 25 to 44 years of age.
NOTE: In another limitation of activity theory, Dale Lund contends that it puts too much emphasis on physical activity.
NOTE: Evidence that tomorrow's elderly will be healthier: Rates of chronic disability among the elderly have been falling steadily.

In sum, growing old involves numerous problems and transitions. Some are brought on by physical decline. But others—including social isolation, adjustment to retirement, risk of poverty, abuse by family members, and ageism—are social problems. In the next section, we will delve into various theoretical perspectives on how society shapes the lives of the elderly.

THEORETICAL ANALYSIS OF AGING

Each of sociology's major theoretical paradigms sheds light on the process of aging in the United States. We examine each in turn.

Structural-Functional Analysis: Aging and Disengagement

Based on the ideas of Talcott Parsons—an architect of the structural-functional paradigm—Elaine Cumming and William Henry (1961) remind us that aging threatens society with disruption as physical decline and death take their toll. Society's response, they claim, is to *disengage* the elderly—to gradually transfer statuses and roles from the old to the young so that tasks are performed with minimal interruption.

Disengagement is thus a strategy to promote the orderly functioning of society by removing aging people from productive roles while they are still able to perform them. Such disengagement has an added benefit in a rapidly changing society, since young workers typically have the most up-to-date skills and training. Formally, then, **disengagement theory** is *the proposition that society enhances its orderly operation by disengaging people from positions of responsibility as they reach old age.*

Disengagement may benefit elderly people as well as society. Aging individuals with diminishing capacities presumably look forward to relinquishing some of the pressures of their jobs in favor of new pursuits of their own choosing (Palmore, 1979b). Society also grants older people greater freedom, so that unusual behavior on their part is construed as harmless eccentricity rather than dangerous deviance.

Critical evaluation. As a strategy for dealing with human decline, disengagement theory explains why rapidly changing, industrial societies typically define their oldest members as socially marginal. But there are also several limitations to this approach.

First, many workers cannot readily disengage from paid work because they do not have sufficient financial security to fall back on. Second, many elderly people—regardless of their financial circumstances—do not wish to disengage from their productive roles. Disengagement, after all, comes at a high price, including loss of social prestige and social isolation. Third, there is no compelling evidence that the benefits of disengagement outweigh its costs to society, which range from the loss of human resources to the increased care of people who might otherwise be able to fend better for themselves. Indeed, as the numbers of elderly people swell, devising ways to help seniors remain independent is a high national priority. Then, too, any useful system of disengagement would have to take account of the widely differing abilities of the elderly themselves.

Symbolic-Interaction Analysis: Aging and Activity

One critical rebuttal to disengagement theory draws heavily on the symbolic-interaction paradigm. **Activity theory** is *the proposition that a high level of activity enhances personal satisfaction in old age.* Because all individuals build their social identities from statuses and roles, this theory maintains, disengagement in old age is bound to undermine the satisfaction and meaning many elderly people find in their lives. What seniors need, in short, are productive and recreational activities that imbue their retirement with meaning and joy.

Activity theory proposes that, to the extent that elderly people do disengage, they substitute new roles and responsibilities for the ones they leave behind. After all, as members of a society that celebrates productivity, the elderly enjoy active lives as much as younger people do. Keep in mind, however, that the elderly are not a monolithic category. Older people have highly varied needs, interests, and physical abilities that guide their choice of activities and their attitudes about aging.

Research supports the general contention of this approach—that elderly people who maintain high activity levels derive the greatest satisfaction from their lives. But advocates of activity theory stress that which activities people pursue, or how vigorously they pursue them, is always an individual matter (Havighurst, Neugarten, & Tobin, 1968; Neugarten, 1977; Palmore, 1979a; Moen, Dempster-McClain, & Williams, 1992).

Chapter 14 Aging and the Elderly **395**

THEN AND NOW: Evidence of the graying of our society includes the rising proportion of college students older than 24: 41% in 1991 versus 33% in 1974. The rise is due to larger older cohorts more than a change in the rate of college attendance. (American Council on Education)

NOTE: In 1993, 57,000 people (.2%) aged 65 or older were enrolled in U.S. colleges and universities.

NOTE: The cultural value of individualism encourages elderly people to fend for themselves. In the name of self-reliance, many poor, elderly men take up residence in single-room occupancy (SRO) hotels. (Cowgill, 1986:49)

NOTE: Looking at a cross-section of the U.S. population, income is highest at about age 50 and wealth is greatest at about age 67 (median wealth of $92,500, up from about $30,000 at age 40).

SOCIAL DIVERSITY

The Fountain of Aging

In 1963, Betty Friedan's book *The Feminine Mystique* asserted that our society defined women only in sexual relation to a man—as wife, mother, or, more commonly, as sex object. Thirty years later, Friedan is issuing another call for change, this time in the way we view the elderly.

Surveying the mass media, Friedan concludes that elderly people are still conspicuous by their absence; only a small percentage of television shows, for example, feature central characters who are over sixty. In addition, when members of our society do think about older people, it is in negative terms: The elderly *lack* jobs, have *lost* their vitality, and *look back* to their youth. In short, the "aging mystique" is that we define being old as little more than a disease, marked by decline and deterioration, for which there is no cure.

This culture-based ageism is as widespread as it is powerful. Why does our society still equate being old with living in a nursing home, when 95 percent of the elderly don't require any such institutionalization? Why do social-service agencies foster dependency in older people rather than encouraging them to live—actively and independently—in society's mainstream?

Responding to this pervasive pessimism, Friedan claims that it is time we started seeking the "fountain of aging" by highlighting the potential and possibilities of this stage of life. All over the United States, there are women and men who are discovering they have far more to contribute than others give them credit for. Playing in orchestras, assisting small business owners, designing housing for the poor, teaching children to read—there are countless ways in which older people can enhance their own lives by engaging people around them. The bottom line, concludes Friedan, is that people do not stop living when they grow old; they grow old when they stop living.

Source: Based on Friedan (1993).

Critical evaluation. Activity theory shifts the focus of analysis from the needs of society (as stated in disengagement theory) to the needs of the elderly themselves. This second approach also highlights social diversity among elderly people, which is an important consideration in formulating any government policy.

However, from a structural-functionalist point of view, this approach tends to exaggerate the well-being and competence of the elderly. Functionalists might ask if we really want elderly people actively serving in crucial roles, say, as physicians or airline pilots. From another perspective, activity theory falls short by overlooking the fact that many of the problems that beset older people have more to do with how society, not any individual, operates. We turn now to that point of view, social-conflict theory.

Social-Conflict Analysis: Aging and Inequality

Social-conflict theory points out that people in different age categories compete for scarce social resources, a fact which contributes to age stratification. By and large, middle-aged people in the United States enjoy the greatest social privileges, while the elderly (as well as children) contend with less power and prestige and face a higher risk of poverty. Employers often shunt elderly workers aside in favor of younger men and women as a means of keeping down wages. As a consequence, conflict theorists note, older people become second-class citizens (Atchley, 1982; Phillipson, 1982).

To conflict theorists, age-based hierarchy is inherent in industrial-capitalist society. Following the ideas

NOTE: Today death is associated with old age; by contrast, a century ago death was common at any age. For instance, none of the Brontë sisters of literary fame lived to the age of 40; Anne (*Agnes Grey*) died at age 29, Emily (*Wuthering Heights*) at 30, and Charlotte (*Jane Eyre*) at 39.

NOTE: A grim demographic fact is that, after age 30, an individual's chance of death doubles every eight years. (Waldrop, 1992)

of Karl Marx, Steven Spitzer (1980) points out that, because our society has an overriding concern with profit, we devalue those categories of people who are economically unproductive. Viewed as mildly deviant because they are less productive than their younger counterparts, Spitzer reasons, the elderly are destined to be marginal members of a society consumed by material gain.

Social-conflict analysis also draws attention to social diversity in the elderly population. Differences of class, race, ethnicity, and gender splinter older people as they do everyone else. Thus the fortunate seniors in higher social classes have far more economic security, greater access to top-flight medical care, and more options for personal satisfaction in old age than others do. Likewise, elderly WASPs typically enjoy a host of advantages denied to older minorities. And women—who represent an increasing majority of the elderly population with advancing age—suffer the social and economic disadvantages of both ageism and sexism.

Critical evaluation. Social-conflict theory adds to our understanding of the aging process by underscoring age-based inequality and explaining how capitalism devalues elderly people who are less productive. The implication of this analysis is that the aged fare better in noncapitalist societies, a view that has some support in research (Treas, 1979).

One shortcoming of this approach goes right to its core contention: Rather than blaming *capitalism* for the lower social standing of elderly people, critics hold that *industrialization* is the true culprit. Thus, they claim, socialism does little to lessen age stratification. Furthermore, the notion that capitalism dooms the elderly to economic distress is challenged by the steady rise in the income of the U.S. elderly population in recent decades.

DEATH AND DYING

> To every thing there is a season,
> And a time for every matter under heaven:
> A time to be born and a time to die . . .

These well-known lines from the Book of Ecclesiastes in the Bible convey two basic truths about human existence: the fact of birth and the inevitability of death. Just as life varies in striking ways across history and around the world, so does death. We conclude this chapter with a brief look at the changing character of death—the final stage in the process of growing old.

Historical Patterns of Death

Throughout most of human history, confronting death was commonplace. No one assumed that a newborn child would live for long, a fact that led parents to delay naming children until they had survived for a year or two. For those fortunate enough to survive infancy, illness prompted by poor nutrition, accidents, and natural catastrophes such as drought or famine combined to make life uncertain, at best.

In times of great need, death was often deliberate, the result of a strategy to protect the majority by sacrificing a group's least productive members. *Infanticide* is the killing of newborn infants; *geronticide*, by contrast, is the killing of the elderly.

If death was routine, it was also readily accepted. Medieval Christianity assured Europeans, for example, that death fit into the divine plan for human existence. To illustrate, historian Philippe Ariès describes how Sir Lancelot, one of King Arthur's fearless Knights of the Round Table, prepared for his own death when he believed himself mortally wounded:

> His gestures were fixed by old customs, ritual gestures which must be carried out when one is about to die. He removed his weapons and lay quietly upon the ground. . . . He spread his arms out, his body forming a cross . . . in such a way that his head faced east toward Jerusalem. (1974:7–8)

As societies gradually gained control over many causes of death, death became less of an everyday occurrence. Fewer children died at birth, and accidents and disease took a smaller toll among adults. Except in times of war or catastrophe, people came to view dying as quite *extra*ordinary, except among the very old. In 1900, about one-third of all deaths in the United States occurred before the age of five, another third occurred before the age of fifty-five, and the remaining one-third of men and women died in what was then defined as old age. By 1995, 85 percent of our population died *after* the age of fifty-five. Thus death and old age have become fused in our culture.

The Modern Separation of Life and Death

Now removed from everyday experience, death seems of us unnatural. If social conditions prepared our ancestors to accept their deaths, modern society, with its youth culture and aggressive medical technology, has fostered a desire for immortality, or eternal youth. In this sense, death has become separated from life.

NOTE: One example of the modern avoidance of death: Few people follow the traditional custom of writing one's own epitaph. Today, even writing a will is considered to be a matter for late in life and is avoided entirely by two-thirds of people in the United States who die without one.

Q: "Death is a subject that is evaded, ignored, and denied by our youth-worshipping, progress-oriented society. It is almost as if we have taken on death as just another disease to be conquered." Joseph L. Braga and Laurie D. Braga, in Kübler-Ross, 1975:x

Q: "God grant me the serenity to accept the things I cannot change,
The courage to change the things I can,
And the wisdom to know the difference."
(The Alcoholics Anonymous Prayer)

Our society has long been concerned with the "good life"; more recently, attention has turned to the idea of a good death. *The hospice movement is an important part of this trend. In some cases, terminally ill patients move to a hospice facility, where a professional staff provides medical support and emotional comfort. In other cases, hospice workers provide care in the familiar surroundings of a person's home.*

Death is also *physically* removed from everyday activities. The clearest evidence of this is that many of us have never seen a person die. While our ancestors typically died at home in the presence of family and friends, most deaths today occur in impersonal settings such as hospitals and nursing homes. Even hospitals commonly relegate dying patients to a special part of the building, and hospital morgues are located well out of sight of patients and visitors alike (Sudnow, 1967; Ariès, 1974).

No doubt, our fear and anxiety about death have propelled the rapid increase in medical research aimed at prolonging life. However, we may be on the verge of forging a new norm relating to death and dying. As the opening of this chapter suggests, many aging people are less terrified of death than they are at the prospect of being kept alive at all costs. In other words, medical technology now threatens personal autonomy by placing doctors rather than dying people in a position to decide when life is to end. The surprising popularity of the book *Final Exit* demonstrates that people want to retain control over their deaths no less than they seek control over their lives.

Consequently, patients and families are now taking the initiative, in many cases choosing not to make use of available medical technology to prolong life. After long deliberation, patients, families, and doctors may decide to forgo any "heroic measures" to resuscitate a person who is dying. Living wills—statements of what medical procedures an individual wants and does not want under specific conditions—are now widespread.

Certainly, this new trend raises problems of its own. Family members may exert subtle pressure on a failing patient to refuse medical care because others wish to be spared emotional stress or a financial burden. Patients and family members will face difficult decisions that are as much moral as they are medical; to assist them, hospitals now offer the services of biomedical ethics committees, composed of physicians, social-service professionals, and members of the clergy. But the emerging consensus is that, while decline and death may be inevitable, people should be able to demand choices about when, where, and perhaps even how they will die.

Bereavement

Chapter 5 ("Socialization") described stages by which people usually confront their own death. Elizabeth Kübler-Ross (1969) claims that individuals initially react with *denial*, then swell with *anger*, try to *negotiate* a divine intervention, gradually fall into *resignation*, and, finally, reach *acceptance*. Those who will grieve the loss of a significant person must also adjust to the approaching death.

According to some researchers, bereavement parallels the stages of dying described by Kübler-Ross. Those close to a dying person, for instance, may initially deny the reality of impending death, reaching the point of acceptance only in time. Other investigators question the validity of any linear "stage theory," arguing that bereavement may not follow a rigid schedule (Lund, Caserta, & Dimond, 1986; Lund, 1989). But all the experts agree that how family and friends view a death influences the attitudes of the person who is dying. Specifically, acceptance by others of the approaching death helps the dying person do the same. Denial of the impending death may isolate the dying person, who is then unable to share feelings and experiences with others.

One recent development intended to provide emotional and medical support to dying people is the *hospice*. Unlike hospitals, which are designed to cure disease, hospices help people have a good death. These care centers work to minimize pain and suffering—either there or at home—and encourage family members to remain close by (Stoddard, 1978).

Even under the most favorable circumstances, bereavement may involve profound grief and social

DISCUSS: People with one year or less to live consume 30% of all Medicare funds; the average person in the United States receives more than one-third of all medical care in the last six months of life. Is this a sensible policy?

Q: "Let us recognize ourselves in this old man or in that old woman." Simone de Beauvoir

Q: "Let us endeavor to live so that when we come to die even the undertaker will be sorry." Mark Twain

Q: Daniel Callahan advocates "an understanding of the process of aging and death that looks to our obligations to the young and to the future, that sees old age as a source of knowledge and insight of value to other age groups, that recognizes the necessity of limits and the acceptance of decline and death, and that values the old for their age and not their continuing youthful vitality." (1987:223)

Controversy & Debate

Setting Limits: Must We "Pull the Plug" on Old Age?

Because death struck at any time, often without warning, our ancestors would have found the question, "Can people live *too long*?" to be absurd. In recent decades, however, a surge in the U.S. elderly population, widespread support for using technology to prolong life, and a dizzying increase in the costs of life-extending medical technology have prompted people to wonder how much old age we can now afford.

Currently, about half of an individual's total lifetime medical costs are incurred during the final years of life, and this share is projected to increase. Against the spiraling costs of prolonging life, then, we may well have to ask if what is technically possible is necessarily socially desirable. As we enter the next century, warns gerontologist Daniel Callahan, a surging elderly population ready and eager to extend their lives will eventually force us either to "pull the plug" on old age or to shortchange everyone else.

To even raise this issue, Callahan concedes, smacks of a lack of caring. But consider that the annual bill for the elderly's health care will top $200 billion by the end of this decade—more than twice the real cost in 1980. This dramatic boost reflects our current policy of directing more and more medical resources toward studying and treating diseases and disabilities common to old age.

So Callahan makes a bold case for limits. He reasons, first, that to spend more on behalf of the elderly we must spend less on others. With a serious problem of poverty among children, he asks, can we continue to direct more money toward the needs of the oldest members of our society at the expense of those just growing up?

Second, Callahan reminds us, a *longer* life does not necessarily make for a *better* life. Costs aside, does stressful heart surgery that may prolong the life of an eighty-four-year-old woman a year or two truly improve the quality of her life? Costs considered, would those resources yield more "quality of life" if used, say, to transplant a kidney into a ten-year-old boy?

Third, Callahan urges us to reconsider our notion of death. Today many people rage against death as an enemy to be conquered at all costs. Yet, he suggests, a sensible health-care program for an aging society must acknowledge death as a natural end to the life course. If we cannot make peace with death for our own well-being, limited financial resources demand that we do so for the benefit of others.

A compelling counterpoint, of course, is that those people who have worked all their lives to make our society what it is should, in their final years, enjoy society's generosity. Moreover, in light of our tradition of personal independence and responsibility, can we ethically deny an aging individual medical care that this person is able and willing to pay for?

What is clear from everyone's point of view is that, in the next century, we will face questions that few would have imagined even fifty years ago: Is optimum longevity good for everyone? Is it even *possible* for everyone?

Continue the debate . . .

1. Should doctors and hospitals devise a double standard, offering more complete care to the youngest people but more limited care to society's oldest members?

2. Do you think our cultural avoidance of death drives us to extend life at all costs?

3. Is the idea of rationing medical care really new? Hasn't our society historically done exactly this by allowing some people to amass more wealth than others?

Source: Callahan (1987).

disorientation that persist for some time. Research reveals that bereavement is less intense among people who accept the death of a loved one and feel that their relationship with the dying person has reached a satisfactory resolution. By taking the opportunity to bring an appropriate closure to their relationship with a dying person, family and friends are better able to comfort and support one another after the death has occurred (Atchley, 1983).

LOOKING AHEAD: AGING IN THE TWENTY-FIRST CENTURY

This chapter has explored a remarkable trend: the "graying" of the United States. We can predict with confidence that the ranks of the elderly will swell dramatically in the decades to come: By 2050, our elderly population alone will exceed the population of the entire country back in 1900. Just as important, one in

GLOBAL: In terms of rates of population growth, middle-income societies (but not low-income countries) stand out, with the Ivory Coast, Indonesia, Costa Rica, Thailand, and Mexico included among the countries with projected increases of elderly people in excess of 200% between 1990 and 2020.

Q: "I'm not afraid to die; I just don't want to be there when it happens." Woody Allen

Q: "Out of life comes death; and out of death, life; Out of the young, the old; and out of the old, the young; Out of waking, sleep; out of sleep, waking; the stream of creation and dissolution never stops." Heraclitus

Q: "Do not go gentle into that good night;
    Rage, rage against the dying of the light."
    Dylan Thomas

five of these seniors will be over the age of eighty-five. Within the next fifty years, in other words, society's oldest members will gain unprecedented visibility and influence in our everyday lives. As this prediction is realized, gerontology, the study of the elderly, will also grow in stature as part of an expansion of research in all fields directed toward aging and the elderly.

The reshaping of the age structure of our society raises many serious concerns. With more people living to an advanced age (and living longer once they reach old age), will the support services they need be available? Remember, too, that as the elderly make unprecedented demands, our society will comprise proportionately fewer younger people to meet their needs. And what about the spiraling medical-care costs of an aging society? As the baby boomers enter old age, some analysts paint a doomsday picture of the United States as a "twenty-first century Calcutta," with desperate and dying elderly people everywhere (Longino, Jr., 1994:13).

But not all the signs are so ominous. For one thing, the health of tomorrow's elderly people (that is, today's young and middle-aged adults) is better than ever: Smoking is way down and the consumption of healthy foods is way up. Such trends probably mean that the elderly of the next century will be more vigorous and independent than their

counterparts are today. Moreover, tomorrow's old people will enjoy the benefits of steadily advancing medical technology although, as the closing box explains, seniors consume a disproportionate share of our national resources, an issue that is already sparking heated debate.

Another positive sign is the surging financial strength of the elderly. Costs of living are certain to rise, but tomorrow's elderly will confront them with unprecedented affluence. Note, too, that the baby boomers will be the first cohort of U.S. seniors in which the vast majority of women have been in the labor force, a fact reflected in their substantial savings and pensions.

On balance, there are reasons for both concern and optimism as we look ahead. But there can be no doubt that younger adults will face a mounting responsibility to care for aging parents. Indeed, as the birth rate drops and the elderly population grows, our society is likely to experience a retargeting of caregiving from the very young to the very old.

Finally, an aging population will almost certainly bring change to the way we view death. In all likelihood, death will become less of a social taboo and become a more natural part of the life course, as it was in centuries past. Should this come to pass, both young and old alike may benefit.

SUMMARY

1. The proportion of elderly people in the United States has risen from 4 percent in 1900 to over 12 percent today; by the middle of the next century 20 percent of our society will be elderly.

2. Gerontology, the study of aging and the elderly, focuses on biological and psychological changes in old age, as well as cultural definitions of aging.

3. Growing old is accompanied by a rising incidence of disease and disability. Younger people, however, commonly exaggerate the extent of disability among the elderly.

4. Psychological research confirms that growing old results in neither overall loss of intelligence nor great change in individual personality.

5. The age at which people are defined as old has varied through history: Until several centuries ago, old age began as early as thirty. In poor societies today, in which life expectancy is substantially lower than in North America, people become old at fifty or even forty.

6. In global perspective, industrialization fosters a decline in the social standing of elderly people.

7. As people age, they commonly experience social isolation brought on by retirement, physical disability, and the death of friends or spouse. Even so, most elderly people look to family members for social support.

8. Since 1960, poverty among the elderly has dropped sharply. The aged poor are categories of people—including single women and people of color—who are likely to be poor regardless of age.

9. Ageism—prejudice and discrimination against old people—serves to justify age stratification.

10. Although many seniors are socially disadvantaged, the elderly encompass people of both sexes and all races, ethnicities, and social classes. Thus older people do not qualify as a minority.

11. Disengagement theory, based on structural-functional analysis, holds that the elderly disengage

from positions of social responsibility before the onset of disability or death. In this way, a society accomplishes the orderly transfer of statuses and roles from an older to a younger generation.

12. Activity theory, based on symbolic-interaction analysis, claims that a high level of activity affords people personal satisfaction in old age.

13. Age stratification is a focus of social-conflict analysis. The emphasis on economic output in capitalist societies leads to a devaluing of those who are less productive, including the elderly.

14. Modern society has set death apart from everyday life, prompting a cultural denial of human mortality. In part, this attitude is related to the fact that most people now die after reaching old age. Recent trends suggest that people are confronting death more directly and seeking control over the process of dying.

KEY CONCEPTS

activity theory the proposition that a high level of activity enhances personal satisfaction in old age

ageism prejudice and discrimination against the elderly

age stratification the unequal distribution of wealth, power, and privileges among people at different stages in the life course

disengagement theory the proposition that society enhances its orderly operation by disengaging people from positions of responsibility as they reach old age

gerontocracy a form of social organization in which the elderly have the most wealth, power, and prestige

gerontology the study of aging and the elderly

CRITICAL-THINKING QUESTIONS

1. Why are the populations of industrial societies getting older? What are some of the likely consequences of this demographic shift?

2. Start with common phrases such as "little old lady" and "dirty old man" and identify ways in which our culture devalues old people.

3. Why does industrialization erode the social standing of the elderly?

4. What important insight about growing old is offered by each of sociology's three major theoretical paradigms?

SUGGESTED READINGS

Classic Source

Robert N. Butler. *Why Survive? Being Old in America.* New York: Harper and Row, 1975.
    This Pulitzer Prize–winning book launched a growing social movement critical of our society's approach to aging.

Contemporary Sources

Judith Treas. "Older Americans in the 1990s and Beyond." *Population Bulletin.* Vol. 50, No. 2 (May 1995). Washington, D.C.: Population Reference Bureau.
    In barely fifty pages, this publication surveys the current state of our society's oldest members and offers predictions about the future.

Robert O. Hansson and Bruce N. Carpenter. *Relationships in Old Age: Coping with the Challenge of Transition.* New York: Guilford Press, 1994.
    This book explores one of the most challenging aspects of growing old: maintaining relationships during a time of transition.

Sara Arber and Jay Ginn. *Gender and Later Life.* Newbury Park, Calif.: Sage, 1992.
    Through the lens of gender, this book explores poverty in later life, ageism, and abuse of the elderly.

Global Source

Margaret Lock. *Encounters with Aging: Mythologies of Menopause in Japan and North America.* Berkeley: University of California Press, 1993.
    This book examines the interaction of gender, aging, biology, and culture in the U.S. and Japan.

DAVID ALFARO SIQUEIROS,
DETAIL OF WORKERS FROM
THE SINDICATO DE ELECTRICITAS, 1937

The Economy and Work

October 20, 1995, Saigon, Vietnam. Sailing slowly up the narrow Saigon River is a riveting experience for anyone who came of age during the 1960s. We need to remember that Vietnam is a <u>country</u> not a <u>war</u>, and that twenty years have passed since the last U.S. helicopter lifted off from the rooftop of the U.S. Embassy, bringing an end to the hostilities.

Saigon (the name Ho Chi Minh City—in honor of the revolutionary leader—is now falling out of use) is on the brink of becoming a boom town. Neon signs cast an eerie hue across the river, bathing the city's waterfront; hotels, bankrolled by Western corporations, now push skyward from a dozen construction sites; taxi meters record fares in U.S. dollars, not Vietnamese dong; Visa and American Express stickers decorate the doors of fashionable shops that cater to shoppers from Japan, France, and (since the U.S. embargo on visiting Vietnam was lifted in 1994) the United States.

There is a heavy irony here: After decades of fighting, the loss of millions of lives on all sides, and the triumphant victory of communist forces, the Vietnamese are making an about-face and turning toward capitalism. What we see today is what might well have happened had the U.S. forces won the war . . .

The tragic clash between Vietnam and the United States was a confrontation between two economic systems—communism and capitalism. What do these economic systems represent that two countries would sacrifice so many lives to defend them? This chapter explores the operation and significance of the economy, widely considered to be the most influential of all social institutions. (The other major social institutions are examined in subsequent chapters: Chapter 16, "Politics and Government"; Chapter 17, "Family"; Chapter 18, "Religion"; Chapter 19, "Education"; and Chapter 20, "Health and Medicine.") We also will investigate the changing character of work in today's world, and note how the economies of the world are now more closely interconnected than ever before.

THE ECONOMY: HISTORICAL OVERVIEW

The **economy** is *the social institution that organizes the production, distribution, and consumption of goods and services.* To call the economy an "institution" implies that it functions in an established manner that is predictable, at least in its general outlines. This is not to say the economy operates to everyone's liking, of course, and sociologists

debate the merits of particular economic arrangements as they critically examine the shape and scope of the other social institutions. *Goods* are commodities ranging from necessities (such as food, clothing, and shelter) to luxury items (such as automobiles, swimming pools, and yachts). *Services* refer to valued activities that benefit others (including the work of religious leaders, physicians, police officers, and telephone operators).

We value goods and services because they ensure survival or because they make life easier, more interesting, or more aesthetically pleasing. The things we produce and consume are also important to our self-image and social identity. How goods and services are distributed, then, shapes the lives of everyone in a number of basic ways.

The complex economies that mark modern industrial societies are themselves the product of centuries of technological innovation. The following sections highlight three technological revolutions that reorganized the means of production and, in the process, brought sweeping changes to many other dimensions of social life.

The Agricultural Revolution

As Chapter 4 ("Society") explained, members of the earliest human societies relied on hunting and gathering to

Q: "The business of the United States is business." President Warren G. Harding
SOCIAL SURVEY: "How much confidence do you have in the people running banks and financial institutions?" (GSS 1994, N = 2,011; *Codebook*, 1994:162)

"A great deal"	17.7%	"Hardly any"	20.0%
"Only some"	60.6%	DK/NR	1.7%

NOTE: The effects of technological advancement are detailed in Chapter 4's opening section, which examines "Society and Technology."
DISCUSS: Chapter 4 defined a social institution as a major sphere of social life organized to meet a basic human need. Engage the class in a discussion about how well the economy and other institutions meet the needs of our society's members.

live off the land. In these technologically simple societies, there was no distinct economy; rather, production, distribution, and consumption of goods were all dimensions of family life.

The development of agriculture about five thousand years ago brought revolutionary change to these societies. Agriculture emerged as people harnessed animals to plows, increasing the productive power of hunting and gathering more than tenfold. The resulting surplus freed some people in society from the demands of food production. Individuals began to adopt specialized economic roles, forging crafts, designing tools, raising animals, and constructing dwellings.

With the development of agriculture under way, towns emerged, soon to be linked by networks of traders dealing in food, animals, and other goods (Jacobs, 1970). These four factors—agricultural technology, productive specialization, permanent settlements, and trade—were the keys to a revolutionary expansion of the economy.

In the process, the world of work became distinct from family life, although production still occurred close to home. In medieval Europe, for instance, most people farmed nearby fields. Both country and city dwellers often labored in their homes—a pattern called *cottage industry*—producing goods sold in frequent outdoor "flea markets" (a term suggesting that not everything was of high quality).

The Industrial Revolution

By the mid-eighteenth century, a second technological revolution was proceeding apace, first in England and soon afterward elsewhere in Europe and North America. The development of industry was to transform social life even more than agriculture had done thousands of years before. Industrialization introduced five notable changes to the economies of Western societies.

1. **New forms of energy**. Throughout history, people derived energy from their own muscles or those of animals. Then, in 1765, English inventor James Watt pioneered the development of the steam engine. Surpassing muscle power a hundred times over, steam engines soon operated large machinery with unprecedented efficiency.

2. **The centralization of work in factories**. Steam-powered machinery soon rendered cottage industries obsolete. Factories—centralized and impersonal workplaces apart from the home—proliferated.

3. **Manufacturing and mass production**. Before the Industrial Revolution, most work involved cultivating and gathering raw materials, such as crops, wood, and wool. The industrial economy shifted most jobs into manufacturing that turned raw materials into a wide range of salable products. For example, factories mass-produced lumber into furniture and transformed wool into clothing.

4. **Specialization**. Typically, a single skilled worker in a cottage industry fashioned a product from beginning to end. Factory work, by contrast, demands specialization so that a laborer repeats a single task over and over, making only a small contribution to the finished product. Thus as factories raised productivity, they also lowered the skill level of the average worker (Warner & Low, 1947).

5. **Wage labor**. Instead of working for themselves or joining together as households, industrial workers entered factories as wage laborers. They sold their labor to strangers who often cared less for them than for the machines they operated. Supervision became routine and intense.

The impact of the Industrial Revolution gradually rippled outward from the factories to transform all of society. Greater productivity steadily raised the standard of living as countless new products and services filled an expanding marketplace. Especially at the outset, however, the benefits of industrial technology were shared very unequally. Some factory owners made vast fortunes, while the majority of industrial workers hovered perilously close to poverty. Children, too, worked in factories or deep in coal mines for pennies a day. Women factory workers, among the lowest paid, endured special hardships, as the box explains.

The Information Revolution and the Postindustrial Society

Industrialization is by nature an ongoing process. In Europe and North America, workers gradually formed labor unions to represent their collective interests in negotiations with factory owners. During this century, governments outlawed child labor, forced wages upward, improved workplace safety, and extended schooling and political rights to a larger segment of the population.

The nature of production itself also has changed. By the middle of this century, the United States was becoming a **postindustrial economy**, *a productive system based on service work and high technology.*

NOTE: The term "spinster," referring to an older, unmarried woman, is derived from those women who spent much of their lives spinning in the early textile mills.

Q: "Women have always worked in factories. Indeed it was women's labor that was initially responsible for the very beginnings of the Industrial Revolution." Ellen Israel Rosen (1987:18)

NOTE: The steam engine was invented in England by Edward Somerset in 1628; the device was not applied to textile machinery for almost 150 years.

NOTE: Because of the low wages and strict control endured by women in early factories, people sometimes called wagons traveling across New England in search of these workers "slavers," a comparison to the slave ships also well known to people of that time.

SOCIAL DIVERSITY

Women in the Mills of Lowell, Massachusetts

Few people paid much attention to Francis Cabot Lowell, ancestor of two prominent Boston families, the Cabots and the Lowells, when he returned from England in 1822. But Lowell carried with him documents that would change the course of the U.S. economy: plans, based on mills operating in England, for this country's first textile factory.

Lowell built his factory astride a waterfall on the Merrimack River in Massachusetts, and soon transformed that farming village into a thriving town. From the outset, 90 percent of the mill workers were women.

The factory owners preferred women because, earning $2 to $3 a week, these workers received only half the wages men did. Many immigrant men were also willing to work for low wages, but prejudice was strong enough to disqualify "foreigners" from any job at all.

Recruiters, driving wagons from one small town to another throughout New England, urged parents to send their daughters to the mill where, they promised, the young women would be properly supervised as they learned skills and discipline. The offer appealed to many families who could

barely provide for their children, and the prospect of getting out on their own surely excited many young women. After all, there were few occupations open to women at that time, and those that were—including teaching and household service—paid even less than factory work.

Once at the Lowell factory, young women settled into dormitory-type housing, paying one-third of their wages for room and board. Employees were subject to a curfew and, as a condition of employment, regularly attended church. Any morally questionable conduct (such as bringing men to their rooms) brought firm disciplinary action.

Factory owners had other motives for their strict rules: They knew that closely supervised women were unable to organize among themselves. Working almost thirteen hours a day, six days a week, the Lowell employees had good reason to seek improvements in their working conditions. Yet any public criticism of the factory, or even having in her possession "radical" literature, could cost a worker her job.

Sources: Based on Eisler (1977) and Wertheimer (1982).

Automated machinery reduced the role of human labor in production, while bureaucracy simultaneously expanded the ranks of clerical workers and managers. Robert Heilbroner (1985) estimates that, a century ago, managers accounted for only 7 percent of employees; now they represent more than one-third of the labor force. More broadly, service industries—such as public relations, health care, advertising, banking, and sales—now employ the bulk of our country's workers. Distinguishing the postindustrial era, then, is a shift from industrial work to service jobs.

Driving this economic change is a third technological transformation: the development of the computer. The *Information Revolution* in the United States and elsewhere is generating new kinds of information, new forms of communication, and changing the character of work just as factories did two centuries ago. The Information Revolution has unleashed three key changes.

1. **From tangible products to ideas.** The industrial era was defined by the production of goods; in the

Q: "[The preindustrial economy] was limited to what could be organized within a family, and within the lifetime of its head." Peter Laslett (1984)

Q: "A fundamental characteristic of the world we have lost was the scene of labor, which was universally supposed to be the home." Peter Laslett (1984)

DISCUSS: As Chapter 4 ("Society") explains, the Industrial Revolution went far beyond mere technological upheaval. What was it for Marx? A capitalist revolution. For Weber? The triumph of rationality. For Durkheim? A process of expanding specialization.

Q: "Among the purposes of a society should be to try to arrange for a continuous supply of work at all times and seasons." Pope Leo XIII

Q: "Banks are more dangerous than standing armies." Thomas Jefferson

Today's high-technology workplace strives for efficiency. Assisted by high-speed computers, a telephone operator can handle hundreds of calls each hour. Several generations ago, by contrast, the local switchboard operator—immortalized by Lily Tomlin in her character role "Ernestine"—had remarkably little to do. Indeed, she had plenty of time to listen in on people's calls and serve as the town's busybody.

postindustrial era, work revolves around creating and manipulating symbols. Computer programmers, writers, financial analysts, advertising executives, architects, and all sorts of consultants represent the workers of the Information Age.

2. **From mechanical skills to literacy skills**. Just as the Industrial Revolution offered opportunities to those who learned a mechanical trade, the Information Revolution demands that workers have literacy skills—the ability to speak, write, and use computer technology. People who can communicate effectively enjoy new opportunities; those who cannot face declining prospects.

3. **The decentralization of work away from factories**. Just as industrial technology (steam power driving massive machines) drew workers together into factories, computer technology now permits many people to work almost anywhere. Indeed, laptop computers and facsimile (fax) machines linked to telephone lines now make the home, a car, or even an airplane a "virtual office." New information technology, in short, is reversing the industrial trend and bringing about a return of home-based "cottage industries."

The need for face-to-face communication as well as the availability of supplies and information still keep most workers in the office. On the other hand, today's more educated and creative labor force no longer requires—and often resists—the close supervision that marked yesterday's factories.

Sectors of the Economy

The three revolutions just described reflect a shifting balance among the three sectors of a society's economy. The **primary sector** is *the part of the economy that generates raw materials directly from the natural environment*. The primary sector, which includes agriculture, animal husbandry, fishing, forestry, and mining, predominates in preindustrial societies. Figure 15–1 indicates that 63 percent of the economic output of low-income countries is produced by the primary sector. The importance of the primary sector declines with economic development. Thus, this sector represents 32 percent of economic activity among middle-income nations and just 4 percent of production among high-income countries like the United States.

The **secondary sector** is *the part of the economy that transforms raw materials into manufactured goods*. This sector grows quickly as societies industrialize, just as manufacturing surged in the United States during the first half of this century. Secondary-sector production includes the refining of petroleum and the use of metals to manufacture tools and automobiles.

The **tertiary sector** is *the part of the economy that generates services rather than goods*. Accounting for just 22 percent of economic output in low-income countries, the tertiary sector grows with industrialization, and dominates the economies of high-income nations as they enter the postindustrial era. Today, about 70 percent of the U.S. labor force is involved in some form of service work, including secretarial and clerical work and positions in food service, sales, law, advertising, and teaching.

The Global Economy

As technology draws people around the world closer together, another important economic transformation is taking place. Recent decades have witnessed the emergence of a **global economy**, *economic activity*

NOTE: Figure 15–1 shows the share of the economy each sector represents by level of income. Even though industrial output constitutes the same 28% relative share in high-income countries and middle-income nations, these two groups are not equally productive in absolute terms. On the contrary, the former greatly outproduce the latter.

NOTE: The shift from an industrial to a service economy can be seen in the falling number of U.S. homes with a workshop and the rising number with a home office equipped with a computer.

NOTE: The *Oxford English Dictionary* explains that the word "capitalism" entered the English language in the late 18th century. Peter Berger claims that Adam Smith never used the term. The etymology of the word reveals a Latin root, *caput*, meaning "of the head."

spanning many nations of the world with little regard for national borders.

The development of a global economy has four main consequences. First, we are seeing a global division of labor by which each region of the world specializes in particular kinds of economic activity. As Global Map 15–1 on page 408 shows, agriculture occupies more than 70 percent of the work force in low-income countries. Global Map 15–2 indicates that industrial production is concentrated in the middle- and high-income nations of the world. The economies of the richest nations, including the United States, now specialize in service-sector activity.

Second, an increasing number of products pass through the economies of more than one nation. Consider, for instance, that workers in Taiwan may manufacture shoes, which a Hong Kong distributor sends to Italy, where they receive the stamp of an Italian designer; another distributor in Rome forwards the shoes to New York, where they are sold in a department store owned by a firm with its headquarters in Tokyo.

A third consequence of the global economy is that national governments no longer control the economic activity that takes place within their borders. In fact, governments cannot even regulate the value of their national currencies, since money is now traded around the clock in the financial centers of Tokyo, London, and New York. Global markets are one consequence of satellite communications that forge information links among the world's major cities.

The fourth consequence of the global economy is that a small number of businesses, operating internationally, now control a vast share of the world's economic activity. One estimate concludes that the six hundred largest multinational companies account for fully half of the earth's entire total economic output (Kidron & Segal, 1991).

The world is still divided into 191 politically distinct nations. But, in light of the proliferation of international economic activity, "nationhood" has lost much of its former significance.

COMPARATIVE ECONOMIC SYSTEMS

Analysts describe the economies of world societies in terms of two models—capitalism and socialism. No society has an economy that is either purely capitalist or purely socialist; these models represent two ends of a spectrum along which all actual economies can be located. Indeed, as the description of Vietnam in the

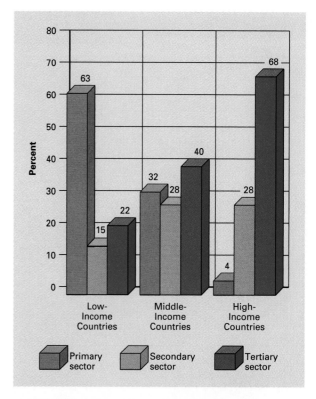

FIGURE 15–1 The Size of Economic Sectors by Income Level of Country
Source: Author estimates based on The World Bank (1995).

chapter opening suggests, many countries move along this continuum in one direction or the other.

Capitalism

Capitalism refers to *an economic system in which natural resources and the means of producing goods and services are privately owned.* Ideally, a capitalist economy has three distinctive features.

1. **Private ownership of property.** A capitalist economy supports the right of individuals to own almost anything. The more capitalist an economy is, the more private ownership there is of wealth-producing property such as factories, real estate, and natural resources.

2. **Pursuit of personal profit.** A capitalist society encourages the accumulation of private property and defines a profit-minded orientation as natural and simply a matter of "doing business." Further, claimed Scottish economist Adam Smith

THE MAP: The two maps show that the economies of low-income nations such as India and the People's Republic of China are dominated by the primary sector. Middle-income countries, like Russia and Greece, have a secondary economic sector that is roughly the same size as their primary sector. The second global map is virtually a negative image of the first.

THEN AND NOW: The decline of farming can be seen in the falling number of farms owned by African Americans: 926,000 in 1920 compared to 19,000 in 1992.

GLOBAL: Worldwide, 2.5 billion (of 5.8 billion) people are employed: 1.4 billion in low-income countries, 660 million in middle-income countries, and 380 million in high-income nations (United Nations, 1995).

Window on the World

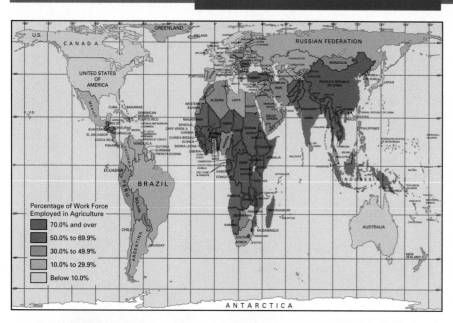

Percentage of Work Force Employed in Agriculture

- 70.0% and over
- 50.0% to 69.9%
- 30.0% to 49.9%
- 10.0% to 29.9%
- Below 10.0%

GLOBAL MAP 15–1
Agricultural Employment in Global Perspective

The primary sector of the economy predominates in societies that are least developed. Thus, in the poor countries of Africa and Asia, half, or even three-fourths, of all workers are farmers. This picture is altogether different among the world's most economically developed countries—including the United States, Canada, Great Britain, and Australia—which have less than 10 percent of their work force in agriculture.

Source: *Peters Atlas of the World* (1990).

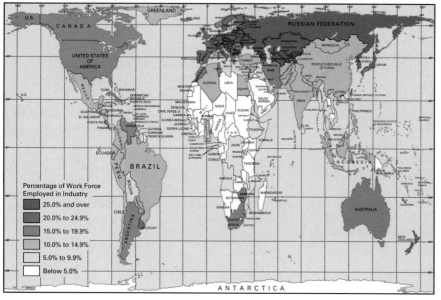

Percentage of Work Force Employed in Industry

- 25.0% and over
- 20.0% to 24.9%
- 15.0% to 19.9%
- 10.0% to 14.9%
- 5.0% to 9.9%
- Below 5.0%

GLOBAL MAP 15–2
Industrial Employment in Global Perspective

The world's poor societies, by and large, have yet to industrialize. For this reason, in the countries of Latin America, Africa, and Asia, a small proportion of the labor force engages in industrial work. The nations of Eastern Europe, along with the Russian Federation, have far more of their workers in industry. In the world's richest societies, we see a reversal of this trend, with more and more workers moving from industrial jobs to service work. Thus, the postindustrial economy of the United States now has about the same share of workers in industrial jobs as the much poorer nation of Argentina.

Source: *Peters Atlas of the World* (1990).

(1723–1790), the individual pursuit of self-interest helps an entire society prosper (1937:508; orig. 1776).

3. **Free competition and consumer sovereignty.** A purely capitalist economy would operate with

no government interference, sometimes called a *laissez-faire* (a French expression meaning "to leave alone") approach. Adam Smith contended that a freely competitive economy regulates itself by the "invisible hand" of the laws of supply and demand.

NOTE: The taxation system of the United States (and, even more so, of European countries) reveals that the government controls much of the "market" economy through taxation. A household earning $60,000 pays 35%–40% in federal, state, and local income taxes, plus another 5%–7% in sales tax on every expenditure, as well as property taxes and other taxes. At a person's death, the government taxes estates worth more than $600,000 at half their value.

The richest one-third of the U.S. population, in short, lose more than half their lifetime earnings to taxes.

GLOBAL: The tax burden in the United States is considerably lower than that of most European nations. U.S. federal tax revenues represent 29% of GDP. Selected data for other nations: Canada, 36%; France, 44%; Denmark, 49%; Sweden, 50%. (U.S. Bureau of the Census)

The productivity of capitalist Hong Kong is evident in the fact that streets are choked with advertising and shoppers. Socialist Beijing, by contrast, is dominated by government buildings rather than a central business district. Here bicyclists glide past the Great Hall of the People.

Smith maintained that the market system is dominated by consumers who select goods and services that offer the greatest value. Producers compete with one another by providing the highest-quality goods and services at the lowest possible price. Thus, while entrepreneurs are motivated by personal gain, everyone benefits from more efficient production and ever-increasing value. In Smith's time-honored phrase, from narrow self-interest comes the "greatest good for the greatest number of people." Government control of an economy would inevitably upset the complex market system, reducing producer motivation, diminishing the quantity and quality of goods produced, and shortchanging consumers.

The United States is the leading capitalist society, yet even here the guiding hand of government plays an extensive role in economic affairs. Through taxation and various regulatory agencies, the government influences what companies produce, the quality and costs of merchandise, the products businesses import and export, and how we consume or conserve natural resources.

The federal government also owns and operates a host of businesses, including the U.S. Postal Service, the Amtrak railroad system, the Tennessee Valley Authority (a large electrical utility company), and the Nuclear Regulatory Commission (which conducts atomic research and produces nuclear materials). The entire U.S. military is also government operated. Federal officials may step in to prevent the collapse of businesses, as in the recent "bailout" of the savings and loan industry. Further, government policies mandate minimum wage levels, enforce workplace safety standards, regulate corporate mergers, provide farm price supports, and funnel income in the form of Social Security, public assistance, student loans, and veterans' benefits to a majority of people in the United States. Not surprisingly, local, state, and federal governments together represent this country's biggest employer, with 14 percent of the labor force on their payrolls (U.S. Bureau of the Census, 1995).

Socialism

Socialism is *an economic system in which natural resources and the means of producing goods and services are collectively owned*. In its ideal form, a socialist economy opposes each of the three characteristics of capitalism just described.

1. **Collective ownership of property**. An economy is socialist to the extent that it limits the right to private property, especially property used in producing goods and services. Laws prohibiting private ownership of property are designed to make housing and other goods available to all, not just to those with the most money.

   Karl Marx asserted that private ownership of productive property spawns social classes as it generates an economic elite. Socialism, then, seeks to lessen economic inequality while forging a classless society.

2. **Pursuit of collective goals**. The individualistic pursuit of profit also stands at odds with the collective orientation of socialism. Socialist values and norms condemn what capitalists celebrate as the entrepreneurial spirit. For this reason, private trading is branded as illegal "black market" activity.

3. **Government control of the economy**. Socialism rejects the idea that a free-market economy regulates itself. Instead of a laissez-faire approach, socialist governments oversee a *centrally controlled* or *command economy*.

   Socialism also rejects the idea that consumers guide capitalist production. From this point of view, consumers lack the information necessary to evaluate products and are manipulated by advertising to buy what is profitable for factory owners rather than what they, as consumers, genuinely need. Commercial advertising thus plays little role in socialist economies.

The People's Republic of China and a number of nations in Asia, Africa, and Latin America—some two dozen in all—model their economies on socialism, placing almost all wealth-generating property under state control (McColm et al., 1991). The extent of world socialism has declined in recent years, however, as societies in Eastern Europe and the former Soviet Union have forged new economic systems increasing the sway of market forces.

Socialism and Communism

Most people equate the terms *socialism* and *communism*. More precisely, as the ideal spirit of socialism, **communism** is *a hypothetical economic and political system in which all members of a society are socially equal*. Karl Marx viewed socialism as a transitory stage on the path toward the ideal of a communist society that had abolished all class divisions. In many socialist societies today, the dominant political party describes itself as communist, but nowhere has the communist goal been achieved.

Why? For one thing, social stratification involves differences of power as well as wealth. Socialist societies have generally succeeded in reducing disparities in wealth only through expanding government bureaucracies and subjecting the population to extensive regulation. In the process, government has not "withered away" as Karl Marx imagined. On the contrary, during this century socialist political elites have gained enormous power and privilege.

Marx would probably have agreed that such a society is a *utopia* (from Greek words meaning "not a place"). Yet Marx considered communism a worthy goal and might well have disparaged reputedly "Marxist" societies such as North Korea, the former Soviet Union, the People's Republic of China, and Cuba for falling far short of his communist ideal.

Democratic Socialism and State Capitalism

A limited measure of socialism, however, does not necessarily stifle democracy. In fact, some of the nations of Western Europe—including Sweden and Italy—have merged socialist economic policies with a democratic political system. Analysts call this "third way" **democratic socialism**, *an economic and political system that combines significant government control of the economy with free elections*.

Under democratic socialism, the government owns some of the largest industries and services, such as transportation, the mass media, and health care. In Sweden and Italy, about 12 percent of economic production is state controlled or "nationalized." That leaves most industry in private hands, but subject to extensive government regulation. High taxation (aimed especially at the rich) funds various social welfare programs, transferring wealth to less-advantaged members of society.

Yet another blend of capitalism and socialism is **state capitalism**, *an economic and political system in which companies are privately owned although they cooperate closely with the government*. Systems of state capitalism are common in the rapidly developing Asian countries along the Pacific Rim. Japan, South Korea, and Singapore, for example, are all capitalist nations, but their governments work closely with large companies, supplying financial assistance or controlling imports of foreign products to help businesses function as competitively as possible in world markets. Countries in East Asia and Western Europe illustrate that there are many ways in which governments and companies can work cooperatively (Gerlach, 1992).

Relative Advantages of Capitalism and Socialism

In practice, how do economic systems differ? Assessing economic models is difficult because all countries mix capitalism and socialism to varying degrees. Moreover, each nation has distinctive cultural attitudes toward work, different natural resources, unequal

NOTE: GDP is the value of goods and services produced within the borders of a country, regardless of who owns or operates them. GNP is the value of goods and services produced by all the facilities owned by citizens of a country, regardless of whether the facilities are located at home or abroad. Therefore, GNP is derived by subtracting from GDP the profits of foreign-owned business in the country and adding to GDP the profits of businesses abroad owned by citizens of that country. Statisticians now use GDP because it allows for more accurate national comparisons as the economy becomes more global.

NOTE: Income data for socialist countries are generally not available, which explains our use of the 1977 data here.

Q: "Under capitalism, man exploits man. Under socialism, the reverse is true." Polish proverb

levels of technological development, and disparate patterns of trade. Some also carry more of the burdens of war than others (Gregory & Stuart, 1985).

Despite these complicating factors, some crude comparisons are revealing. The following sections contrast two categories of countries—those with predominantly capitalist economies and those with mostly socialist economies. The supporting data reflect economic patterns prior to recent changes in the former Soviet Union and Eastern Europe.

Economic Productivity

The most important dimension of economic performance is productivity. A commonly used measure of economic output is gross domestic product (GDP), the total value of all goods and services produced annually by a nation's economy. "Per capita" (or per person) GDP allows us to compare societies of different population size.

Averaging the economic output of the United States, Canada, and the nations of Western Europe at the end of the last decade yields a per capita GDP of about $13,500. The comparable figure for the former Soviet Union and the nations of Eastern Europe was about $5,000. This means that capitalist countries outproduced socialist nations by a ratio of 2.7 to 1 (United Nations Development Programme, 1990).

Economic Equality

How resources are distributed within a society stands as a second crucial issue. A comparative study completed in the mid-1970s calculated income ratios by comparing the earnings of the richest 5 percent of the population and the poorest 5 percent (Wiles, 1977). This research found that societies with predominantly capitalist economies had an income ratio of about 10 to 1; the corresponding figure for socialist countries was 5 to 1.

This comparison of economic performance reveals that *capitalist economies produce a higher overall standard of living but also generate greater income disparity.* Or, put otherwise, *socialist economies create less income disparity but offer a lower overall standard of living.*

Civil Liberties

A society's economic and political systems are closely linked. Capitalism depends on the freedom of producers and consumers to interact without extensive interference from the state. Thus economic capitalism fosters broad civil liberties and political freedom.

Global comparisons indicate that socialist economies generate the greatest economic equality although living standards remain relatively low. Capitalist economies, by contrast, engender more income disparity although living standards are typically higher. As the former Soviet Union has moved towards a market system, however, the majority of people have suffered a decline in living standards, while some people have become quite rich.

For their part, socialist governments strive to maximize economic equality. This goal requires considerable state intervention in the economy, which limits the personal liberty of citizens in ways that the state deems beneficial to the public as a whole. Humanity has yet to devise a social system that ensures political liberty *and* economic equality. In tandem with the drive to improve living standards, many socialist societies are now striving to forge a new balance between these two other worthy objectives as well.

Changes in Socialist Countries

During the last decade, a profound transformation has taken place in many socialist countries of the world.

TABLE 15–1 Participation in the Labor Force by Sex and Race, 1994

	In the Labor Force	
Category of the Population	Number (in millions)	Percentage
Men (aged 16 and over)	**70.8**	**75.1%**
White	60.7	75.9
African-American	7.1	69.1
Women (aged 16 and over)	**60.2**	**58.8**
White	50.4	58.9
African-American	7.4	58.7

Source: U.S. Department of Labor, *Employment and Earnings,* vol. 42, no. 1 (January 1995), pp. 164–66.

Beginning in the shipyards of Poland's port city of Gdansk in 1980, workers began organizing in opposition to their socialist government. Despite struggle and setback, the Solidarity movement eventually succeeded in dislodging Soviet-backed party officials and electing its leader Lech Walesa as national president. Poland is now in the process of introducing market principles into the economy.

Other countries of Eastern Europe, all of which fell under the political control of the former Soviet Union at the end of World War II, also shook off socialist regimes during 1989 and 1990. These nations—including the German Democratic Republic (East Germany), Czechoslovakia, Hungary, Romania, and Bulgaria—have likewise introduced capitalist elements into what had for decades been centrally controlled economies. In 1992, the Soviet Union itself formally dissolved; along the way, the Soviets liberated the Baltic states of Estonia, Latvia, and Lithuania and cast most of the remaining republics, except Georgia and Azerbaijan, into a new Commonwealth of Independent States (now renamed the Russian Federation).

The reasons for these sweeping changes are many and complex. In light of the preceding discussion, however, two factors stand out. First, these predominantly socialist economies grossly underproduced their capitalist counterparts. They were, as we have noted, somewhat successful in achieving economic equality; living standards for everyone, however, were low by Western European standards. Second, the Soviet brand of socialism made for heavy-handed and unresponsive government that rigidly controlled the media as well as the ability of Eastern Europeans to move about, even in their own countries.

In short, socialism did do away with economic elites, as Karl Marx predicted. But, as Max Weber might have foreseen, this system *expanded* the clout of political elites as party bureaucracies grew to gargantuan proportions.

At this stage, the market reforms are proceeding unevenly, with some nations faring better than others. In the short term, the closing of many inefficient, government-run industries has plunged the already struggling economies of Eastern Europe into deeper decline. Within these countries, while some people (including those who have captured lucrative trading agreements with other nations) are thriving, most people are enduring harder times than ever. Although some analysts trumpet their contention that these economies have turned the corner and are now growing, many people remain uncertain about what lies ahead. In the long term, officials contend, the introduction of market forces should raise everyone's standard of living through greater productivity. Even so, to the extent that these countries gradually come to resemble their neighbors to the West, rising prosperity will be accompanied by increasing economic disparity.

WORK IN THE POSTINDUSTRIAL ECONOMY

Change is not restricted to the socialist world; the last century has also transformed the economy of the United States. As of 1994, 131 million people were in the labor force, representing two-thirds of those aged sixteen and over. As shown in Table 15–1, a larger proportion of men (75.1 percent) than women (58.8 percent) hold income-producing jobs, although the gap between them has steadily diminished in recent decades. Among men, the proportion of people of African descent in the labor force (69.1 percent) is somewhat less than the proportion of white people (75.9 percent); among women, roughly the same share of African Americans (58.7 percent) and white people (58.9 percent) are employed.

Age also affects labor force participation. Typically, both women and men join the work force in their teens and early twenties. During their childbearing years, however, women's participation lags behind that of men. After about the age of forty-five, the working profiles of the two sexes again become similar, with a marked withdrawal from the labor force as people approach age sixty-five. After that point in life, only a small proportion of each sex continues to perform, steady, income-producing work.

National Map 15–1 shows labor force participation by county for the United States. Since work and

THE MAP: Counties with low rates of labor force participation not only lack jobs but also are culturally conservative, with high percentages of women who remain at home.

GLOBAL: Fueling the deindustrialization of the United States are the relatively low wage rates typical of poor societies: from about $1.25 an hour in Hong Kong to $.20 an hour in PR China (see Figure 15–4, p. 422).

NOTE: In 1995 *Fortune* added service industries to its Fortune 400—including life insurance companies and banks. Showing the growing significance of information technology, the stock value of Microsoft exceeds that of General Motors.

RESOURCE: Karl Marx's analysis of "alienated labor" is one of the classic selections included in the Macionis and Benokraitis reader, *Seeing Ourselves*.

Seeing Ourselves

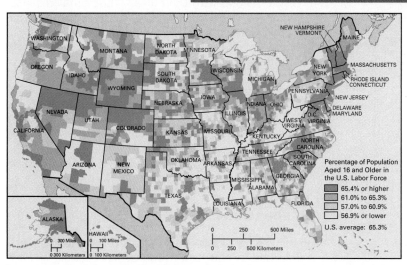

Sources: *American Demographics Desk Reference Series # 4.* Reprinted with permission. ©1992 *American Demographics* magazine, Ithaca, New York. Data from the 1990 decennial census.

NATIONAL MAP 15–1
Labor Force Participation Across the United States

Counties that boast high levels of labor force participation can do so because they have within their borders steady sources of employment, including military bases, recreation areas, and large cities. By contrast, counties with low employment rates generally include a high proportion of elderly people (as well as students). Another important consideration revolves around gender: What do you think is the typical level of employment in regions of the country (stretching from the South up into coal-mining districts of Kentucky and West Virginia) in which traditional cultural norms encourage women to remain in the home?

income go hand in hand, regions of the country with above-average labor force participation tend to be more affluent.

The Decline of Agricultural Work

When this century began, about 40 percent of the U.S. labor force engaged in farming. By the time it ends, this proportion will have fallen to a mere 2 percent. Figure 15–2, on page 414, graphically illustrates this rapid decline, which reflects the diminished role of the primary sector in the U.S. economy.

Even though today's agriculture involves fewer people, farming is more productive than ever. A century ago, a typical farmer grew food for five people; today, one farmer feeds seventy-five. This dramatic rise in productivity also reflects new types of crops, pesticides that increase yields, more efficient machinery, and other advances in farming technology. The average U.S. farm has also doubled in size since 1950, to about 500 acres today.

This process signals the eclipse of "family farms," which are declining in number and produce only a small part of our agricultural yield, in favor of large, *corporate agribusinesses*. But, more productive or not, this transformation has wrought painful adjustments

for farming communities across the country, as a way of life is lost.

From Factory Work to Service Work

Industrialization swelled the ranks of blue-collar workers early in this century. As shown in Figure 15–2, in 1900 more than 40 percent of working people in the United States had industrial jobs—surpassing the share employed in agriculture. By 1950, however, a white-collar revolution had carried a majority of workers into service occupations. By 1994, 90 percent of new jobs were in the service sector, and 70 percent of the entire labor force held white-collar jobs. By contrast, industrial-sector work had slipped to one-fourth of the labor force.

The growth of service occupations is one reason for the widespread description of the United States as a middle-class society. As explained in Chapter 10 ("Social Class in the United States"), however, much service work—including sales positions, secretarial work, and jobs in fast-food restaurants—yields little of the income and prestige of professional white-collar occupations and often provides fewer rewards than factory work. In short, more and more jobs in this postindustrial era provide only a modest standard of living.

DISCUSS: How many of your students work? The University of Michigan's Institute for Social Research estimates that three-fourths of high school seniors worked for income; 40% of all seniors work more than 20 hours a week.

RESOURCE: Work in the secondary labor market is the focus of Mary Romero's article "Maid in the U.S.A." in the *Seeing Ourselves* reader.

THEN AND NOW: U.S. union membership in 1994 was 17.7 million, up 140,000 over the year before—15.5% of all workers are union members, well below the peak of 35.5% in 1945.

SOCIAL SURVEY: "With whom do you most often side in labor disputes—the striking workers or management?" (Yankelovich Partners, Inc., N = 600; June, 1994)
Workers, 50%   *Management*, 24%   *DK/NR*, 26%

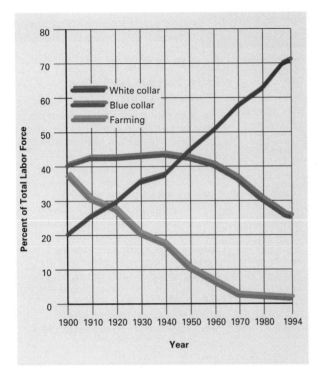

FIGURE 15–2 The Changing Pattern of Work in the United States, 1900–1994

Source: U.S. Department of Labor (1995).

The Dual Labor Market

The change from factory work to service jobs represents a shifting balance between two categories of work (Edwards, 1979). The **primary labor market** includes *occupations that provide extensive benefits to workers*. This favored segment of the labor market contains the traditional white-collar professions and high management positions. These are jobs that people think of as *careers*. Work in the primary labor market provides high income and job security and is also personally challenging and intrinsically satisfying. Such occupations require a broad education rather than specialized training and offer solid opportunity for advancement.

But few of these advantages apply to work in the **secondary labor market**, *jobs providing minimal benefits to workers*. This segment of the labor force is employed in the low-skilled, blue-collar type of work found in routine assembly-line operations, and in low-level service-sector jobs including clerical positions. The secondary labor market offers workers much lower income, demands a longer work week, and affords less job security and opportunity to advance.

Not surprisingly, then, workers in the secondary labor market are most likely to experience alienation and dissatisfaction with their jobs. These problems most commonly beset women and other minorities, who are overly represented in this segment of the labor force (Kohn & Schooler, 1982; Kemp & Coverman, 1989; Hunnicutt, 1990; Greenwald, 1994; Nelson, 1994).

Most new jobs in our postindustrial economy fall within the secondary labor market, and they involve the same kind of unchallenging tasks, low wages, and poor working conditions characteristic of jobs in factories a century ago (Gruenberg, 1980). Moreover, as the box explains, job insecurity is on the rise as the economy shuttles an unprecedented share of workers from one temporary position to another.

Labor Unions

The changing economy has been accompanied by a declining role for **labor unions**, *organizations of workers seeking to improve wages and working conditions through various strategies, including negotiations and strikes*. Membership in labor unions increased rapidly in the United States after 1935, encompassing one-third of the nonfarm labor force by 1950. In absolute numbers, union membership peaked during the 1970s at almost 25 million people. Since then, it has steadily declined to about 16 percent of nonfarm workers, or about 18 million men and women.

The pattern of union decline holds in other high-income countries as well. Yet, unions claim a far smaller portion of workers in the United States than elsewhere. In the Scandinavian countries, at least 80 percent of workers belong to unions; in Europe as a whole, about 40 percent do. In Canada and Japan, the proportion is about one-third (Western, 1993, 1995).

The global decline of unions stems from other trends already noted. First, industrial countries have lost tens of thousands of jobs in the highly unionized factories as industrial jobs are "exported" overseas. Especially in the United States, many plant managers have succeeded in forcing concessions from workers, including, in some cases, the dissolution of labor unions. Moreover, most of the new service-sector jobs being created today are not unionized, and hardly any temporary workers belong to a labor union.

As some analysts see it, however, falling job security may well make union membership a higher priority for workers in the years to come. But to expand their membership, unions will also have to adapt to the new global economy. Instead of seeing foreign workers as a threat to their interests, in short, union

DIVERSITY: The percentage of workers who are actively seeking to change jobs is highest among teens (30%), falls quickly with age to about 8% of men and women aged 35–44, and bottoms out at about 2% among workers over age 65. By age 30, says the Bureau of Labor Statistics, the average U.S. worker has held eight jobs.

NOTE: The *Yellow Pages* periodically updates its listing categories to reflect new consumer trends: recently dropped, for example,

were "go-carts" and "razor sharpening," while "espresso," "karaoke," "foreign exchange brokers," "videoconferencing services," and even "scholarships and financial aid" have been added (Brightman, 1995).

THEN AND NOW: Full-time U.S. employees worked an average of 163 more hours (an extra month of work) in 1987 compared to 1969 (Schor, 1995).

SOCIOLOGY OF EVERYDAY LIFE

The Postindustrial Economy: The "Temping" of the United States

Three hundred years ago, Scottish landlords evicted thousands of tenant farmers so that land could be put to the more profitable use of raising sheep to supply wool to the burgeoning textile factories. Almost overnight, the security of an established way of life vanished. Farmers who were lucky emigrated to North America and started over; the least fortunate starved to death.

Today, as the Information Revolution ushers in the postindustrial economy, economic change is once again undermining job security. A decade ago, workers confidently assumed that hard work and playing by the rules all but guaranteed that their jobs would be there until they were ready to retire. No longer. As one analyst puts it:

The rise of the knowledge economy means a change, in less than twenty years, from an overbuilt system of large, slow-moving economic units to an array of small, widely dispersed economic centers, some as small as an individual boss. In the new economy, geography dissolves, the highways are electronic. Even Wall Street no longer has a reason to be on Wall Street. Companies become concepts . . . and jobs are almost as

susceptible as electrons to vanishing into thin air. (Morrow, 1993:41)

In the short run, at least, the dislocation for U.S. workers is tremendous. Companies scrambling to "remain competitive" in the global economy are "downsizing" and decentralizing to gain "flexibility." These trends mean not only cutting the number of people on the payroll—managers as well as secretaries—but also replacing long-term employees with temporary workers. By hiring "temps," companies no longer have to worry about providing health insurance, paid vacations, or pensions.

And, if next month workers are no longer needed, they can be released without further cost or fear of lawsuits.

"Temping" has become entrenched in the United States: Suppliers of temporary workers—including Manpower and Kelly Services—now dispatch 2 million employees daily. In all, "temps" and other "contingent workers," including part-timers, per-diem workers, and contractors in government and corporate jobs already number 35 million and account for 30 percent of the U.S. labor force—a share that continues to rise.

The easing of the Great Depression more than forty years ago heralded an era of worker-employer relationships based on mutual loyalty. But recent trends are undoing workplace bonds with remarkable speed and at all levels of the labor force. Like workers at the dawn of the industrial era centuries ago, many of today's secretaries, engineers, bank officers, and even corporate executives are finding their job security vanishing before their eyes. For the foreseeable future, most analysts agree, there is probably no going back to the traditional notion of lifetime employment with one company.

Sources: Castro (1993) and Morrow (1993).

leadership will have to forge new international alliances (Mabry, 1992; Church, 1994).

Professions

All kinds of work today are described as professional—we hear of professional tennis players, even

professional exterminators. As distinct from an *amateur* (from Latin meaning "lover," one who acts simply out of love for the activity itself), a professional pursues some task for a living.

More precisely, though, a **profession** is *a prestigious, white-collar occupation that requires extensive formal education.* The term suggests a "profession"—a

SOCIAL SURVEY: Percentage of U.S. adults claiming to trust people in various occupations: pharmacists, 61%; clergy, 54%; public opinion pollsters, 27%; journalists, 20%; lawyers, 17%; advertisers, 12%, car salesmen, 6%. (Fulkerson, 1995)
RESOURCE: Data on small business ownership by women can be found at the Small Business Administration website: www.sbaonline.sba.gov

SOCIAL SURVEY: "The government should provide a decent standard of living for the unemployed." (GSS 1985, N = 1,285; Codebook, 1994:567)
"Strongly agree"   6.2%   "Disagree"   29.2%
"Agree"   29.0%   "Strongly disagree"   5.7%
"Neither agree nor disagree" 25.8%   DK/NR   4.2%

public declaration—of faith or willingness to abide by certain principles. Traditional professions include the ministry, medicine, law, and academia (W. Goode, 1960). Today, workers describe their occupations as professions to the extent that they demonstrate the following four characteristics (Ritzer & Walczak, 1990).

1. **Theoretical knowledge.** Most jobs involve technical skills, but professions demand a theoretical understanding of a field, obtained through extensive schooling and regular interaction with one's peers. Anyone can master first-aid skills, for example, but physicians bring to their work a theoretical understanding of human health and illness.

2. **Self-regulated training and practice.** While most work places people under direct supervision, most professionals are self-employed. Professionals participate in associations that set standards for professional practice, typically including a formal code of ethics.

3. **Authority over clients.** Many jobs—sales work, for example—require people to respond directly to the wishes of customers. Professionals, by contrast, expect their clients to follow their direction and advice. Professionals claim this authority because they possess knowledge that lay people lack.

4. **Orientation to community rather than to self-interest.** The traditional "professing" of faith or duty was a professional's declaration of intention to serve not self-interest but the needs of clients and the broader community. Most business executives readily admit to working in pursuit of profit, but professionals such as priests or college professors rarely admit to financial motives and prefer to think of their work as contributing to the well-being of others. Some professional associations, including the American Medical Association, even forbid their members from advertising their services. This aura of altruism also makes many professionals reluctant to discuss the fees that contribute to their high incomes.

Alongside the traditional professions, a number of other occupations stand as *new professions*. These occupations, which include architecture, counseling, social work, and accountancy, share most of the characteristics just presented.

Many new service occupations in the postindustrial economy have also sought to *professionalize* their work. This claim to professional standing often begins with a new name for the work, one implying that practitioners have acquired special, theoretical knowledge. (These new names have the added benefit of distancing practitioners from their previously less-distinguished reputation.) Government bureaucrats, for example, become "public policy analysts," and dogcatchers are reborn as "animal-control specialists."

Interested parties may also form a professional association that will formally attest to their specialized skills. This organization then begins to license those who perform the work, and develops a code of ethics that emphasizes the occupation's contribution to the community. In its effort to win public acceptance, a professional association may also establish schools or other training facilities and perhaps start a professional journal (Abbott, 1988).

Not every category of workers tries to claim full professional status. Some *paraprofessionals*, including paralegals and medical technicians, possess specialized skills but lack the extensive theoretical education required of full professionals.

Self-Employment

Self-employment—earning a living without working for a large organization—was once commonplace in the United States. C. Wright Mills (1951) estimated that, in the early 1800s, 80 percent of the U.S. labor force was self-employed. Families owned and operated farms, and self-employed, urban workers owned shops and other small businesses or sold their skills on the open market. With the onset of the Industrial Revolution, however, the economy became more centralized so that self-employment diminished, and these workers now account for only 9 percent of the U.S. labor force (10 percent of men and 7 percent of women) (U.S. Bureau of Labor Statistics, 1996).

Lawyers, physicians, and some other professionals have been represented strongly among the ranks of the self-employed. But most self-employed workers are small-business owners, plumbers, carpenters, free-lance writers, editors, artists, house cleaners, child-care providers, and long-distance truck drivers. Overall, the self-employed are more likely to perform blue-collar than white-collar work.

Our society has always painted an appealing picture of working independently: no time clocks to punch, no one looking over your shoulder. For minorities who have long been excluded from particular kinds of work, self-employment has been an effective strategy for broadening economic opportunity (Evans, 1989). Further, self-employment holds the potential—

GLOBAL: Worldwide, some 120 million people are unemployed: one-third in low-income countries, 40% in middle-income nations, and one-fourth in high-income countries (United Nations, 1995).

NOTE: In 1994, the Bureau of Labor Statistics ended its historical practice, when conducting unemployment surveys, of assuming that a woman who answered the door was a housewife uninterested in paid employment. Treating all household members the same has had the effect of boosting the unemployment rate.

GLOBAL: Unemployment rates (1993): Japan, 2.5%; Germany, 5.8%; U.S., 6.8%; Sweden, 8.1%; Netherlands, 8.8%; U.K., 10.4%; Canada, 11.2%; France, 11.8%. (U.S. Census Bureau)

NOTE: The historic trend that linked a high risk of unemployment to blue-collar work shifted in the late 1980s as white-collar executives faced rising joblessness.

During the Great Depression, a time of catastrophic unemployment in the United States, Isaac Soyer painted Employment Agency, *a powerful statement of the personal collapse and private despair that afflict men and women who are out of work.*

Issac Soyer, 1907–1981, *Employment Agency,* 1927. Oil on canvas, 34 1/4 x 15 in. (87 x 114.c cm). Collection of Whitney Museum of American Art, New York. Photo by Geoffrey Clements.

although it is rarely realized—of earning a great deal of money. But for all its advantages, self-employment is vulnerable to fluctuations in the economy, one reason that only one-fifth of small businesses survive for more than ten years. Another common problem is that the self-employed generally lack pension and health-care benefits provided for employees by large organizations.

Finally, in a notable trend, the share of this nation's 15 million small businesses owned by women is up sharply, to almost 40 percent. In fact, small businesses owned by U.S. women now provide more jobs than all the Fortune 500 corporations (Small Business Administration, 1995). Many women find that going into business for themselves affords them greater opportunity, a more enjoyable working environment, and a more flexible schedule than laboring for large organizations.

Unemployment

Every society has some unemployment. Few young people entering the labor force find a job right away; some workers temporarily leave the labor force while seeking a new job, to have children, or because of a labor strike; others suffer from long-term illnesses; still others are illiterate or without the skills to perform useful work.

But the economy itself also generates unemployment. Jobs disappear as occupations become obsolete, as businesses close in the face of foreign competition, and as recessions force layoffs and bankruptcies. Since 1980, for example, the "downsizing" of U.S. businesses has eliminated some 5 million jobs—one-fourth of the total—in this nation's five hundred largest corporations.

Unemployment rates vary over time as they do from country to country. In Japan, for example, 2 percent unemployment is common while, in the United States, the unemployment rate rarely dips below 5 percent of the labor force and no one speaks of an "unemployment problem" until the rate exceeds 7 or 8 percent.

In 1994, 7.9 million people over the age of sixteen were unemployed—about 6 percent of the civilian labor force. As a glance back at National Map 15–1 suggests, some regions of the country, including parts of West Virginia and New Mexico, contend with unemployment at twice the national rate.

Figure 15–3 shows the official unemployment rate for various categories of U.S. workers in 1994 (U.S. Bureau of Labor Statistics, 1995). Unemployment among African Americans stood more than twice as high (11.5 percent) as that among white people (5.3 percent); this disparity is due mostly to the historical concentration of minorities in the secondary labor market. Younger people confront especially high levels of unemployment, and men now have an unemployment rate higher than that for women—a reversal of a historical pattern in the face of an economic contraction in male-dominated blue-collar industrial jobs.

Government unemployment statistics, based on monthly national surveys, generally understate

THEN AND NOW: African-American unemployment, 1930: about 4% vs. 13% today. Richard Vedder and Lowell Gallaway (1993) link this rise to black people's movement out of low-unemployment farming and into urban manufacturing jobs (where layoffs are common) but also to expanding entitlement programs, which have undermined employment.

NOTE: Leslie Dunbar (1988) estimates that a 1% drop in unemployment saves the U.S. government $36 million in assistance payments.
RESOURCE: The lives of gay people in the corporate world are highlighted in the James Woods article, "The Corporate Closet," in the *Seeing Ourselves* reader.

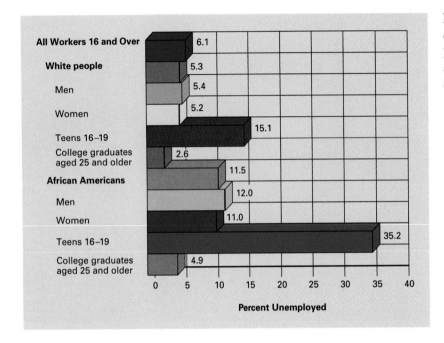

FIGURE 15–3

Official U.S. Unemployment Rate Among Various Categories of Adults, 1994

Source: U.S. Bureau of Labor Statistics (1995).

unemployment for two reasons. First, to be counted among the unemployed, a person must be actively seeking work; "discouraged workers," those who have given up looking for a job, are omitted from the statistics. Second, many people unable to find jobs for which they are qualified settle, at least for a while, for "lesser" employment: A secretary works as a "temp" several days a week or a former college professor drives a taxi while seeking a new teaching position. Such people are counted among the employed, although they might better be described as *under*employed.

On the other hand, statistics also overlook the fact that many people officially out of work receive income "under the table" from odd jobs or even from illegal activity. But, even considering this off-the-books income, the actual level of unemployment is probably several percentage points above the official figure.

The Underground Economy

Although our way of life celebrates individual initiative and free enterprise, the U.S. government requires workers to maintain extensive records and to make regular reports of all economic activity. Any violation of this obligation places transactions within the **underground economy,** *economic activity involving income unreported to the government as required by law.*

On a small scale, most people participate in the underground economy on a regular basis: A family makes extra money by holding a garage sale; another allows its teenage children to babysit for the neighbors without reporting whatever income is received. Nevertheless, most of the underground economy is attributable to criminal activity such as the sale of illegal drugs, prostitution, bribery, extortion, theft, illegal gambling, and loan-sharking.

The single largest segment of the underground economy involves "honest" people who break the law by failing to report some or all of their legally obtained income. Self-employed people such as carpenters, physicians, and owners of small businesses may understate their incomes on tax forms; waiters, waitresses, and other service workers may not report their entire earnings from tips. Even relatively small omissions and misrepresentations, when appearing on millions of individual income tax returns, add up to as much as $170 billion in lost taxes (Speer, 1995).

Social Diversity in the Workplace

The composition of the U.S. labor force has been changing in recent years. Traditionally, white men have been the mainstay of the U.S. paid economy. As explained in Chapter 12 ("Race and Ethnicity"), however, our country's proportion of minorities is rapidly rising. During the 1980s, the increase in African Americans (13 percent) was twice as great as for white people (6 percent); even higher was the jump in the

NOTE: Refer students back to the box on page 323 of Chapter 12, "The Coming Minority-Majority?" for further details on the changing face of minority representation in the United States.
NOTE: National Maps 12–1 and 12–2, on pages 324 and 342, illustrate the areas of the country in which the character of the work force is most affected by racial and ethnic diversity.
Q: "Economics is the study of money and why it is good." Woody Allen

SOCIAL DIVERSITY

The Work Force of the Twenty-First Century

In recent years, the significant rise in the U.S. minority population has been transforming this nation's labor force. As the figure shows, the number of white men in the U.S. labor force is projected to rise by a modest 9 percent during the 1990s. The rate of increase among African-American working men will be twice as great, at 17 percent. Among Hispanic men, the rise will be greater still, 33 percent.

Among women, projected increases will be even larger. But, here again, the gains among minorities will be greatest: A 17 percent rise among white women will be surpassed by a jump of 22 percent among African-American women and 46 percent among Hispanic women.

Thus, non-Hispanic, white men—the traditional backbone of the U.S. labor force—will represent only 9 percent of new workers in the 1990s. By the end of this decade, they will amount to just 45 percent of all workers, a figure that will continue to drop. Companies that begin now to plan for growing social diversity will tap the largest talent pool and enjoy a competitive advantage in the twenty-first century.

Responding effectively to workplace diversity means more than maintaining affirmative-action programs, which are aimed primarily at recruiting. The broader challenge—and greater opportunity—for companies in the next century lies in transforming the workplace environment to develop the potential of all workers. Employees, after all, are a company's most important resource, and utilizing this resource to greatest advantage will require change in several key areas.

First, companies must realize that the needs and concerns of women and other minorities may not be the same as those of white men. For example, corporations will be pressed to provide workplace child care in the future.

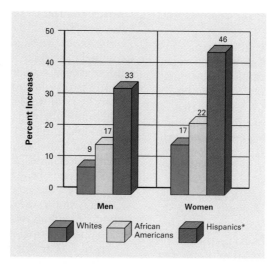

Projected Increase in the Numbers of People in the U.S. Labor Force, 1994–2005
*Hispanics can be of any race.
Source: U.S. Bureau of Labor Statistics (1995).

Second, businesses will have to devise effective strategies for defusing the tensions that arise from social differences. They will have to work harder at treating all workers equally as well as respectfully. If it is to cultivate the full efforts of all workers, the emerging corporate culture cannot tolerate gender- or race-based harassment.

Third, companies will have to rethink current promotion practices. At present, only 2 percent of Fortune 500 top executives are women, and just 1 percent are other minorities. In a broad survey of U.S. companies, the U.S. Equal Employment Opportunity Commission confirmed that white men (42 percent of adults aged twenty to sixty-four) hold 63 percent of management jobs; the comparable figures for white women are 42 and 26 percent; for African Americans, 12 and 5 percent; and, for Hispanics, 10 and 2 percent.

Any informal "glass ceiling" that prevents advancement by skilled workers clearly discourages achievement. In the emerging labor force of the next century, such barriers will deprive companies of their largest source of talent—women and other minorities.

Sources: U.S. Bureau of the Census (1995) and U.S. Equal Opportunity Commission (1995).

Hispanic population (more than 50 percent) and in the numbers of Asian Americans (topping 100 percent). If these trends continue, there will be a "minority-majority" in the United States toward the end of the next century. This change already is having profound consequences in businesses across the country. The box takes a closer look at how the increasing social diversity of our society is affecting the workplace of the 1990s.

SOCIAL SURVEY: "How much confidence do you have in the people running major companies?" (GSS 1994, N = 2,011; *Codebook*, 1994:163)

"A great deal"	25.4%	"Hardly any"	9.9%
"Only some"	61.3%	DK/NR	3.5%

NOTE: More than half of U.S. corporations have total assets valued at less than $100,000. About 80% of U.S. employers have 15 or fewer employees.

NOTE: A significant portion of corporate stock is held by institutional investors (corporations investing in each other). In terms of individuals, about 20% of U.S. residents have such investments (exclusive of pension funds). Most stock is owned by a much smaller proportion of the population, as noted in Chapter 10. Perhaps 10% of Britons are stockholders (again, exclusive of pension funds).

Technology and Work

The central technology of the emerging postindustrial economy is the computer and related devices for processing information. As we noted earlier, the Information Revolution is changing the character of the workplace and even of work itself. Shoshana Zuboff (1982) points to four additional ways in which computers are altering the character of work.

1. **Computers are deskilling labor.** Just as industrial machinery "deskilled" the master crafts workers of an earlier era, so computers now threaten to make the skills of managers obsolete. More and more business decisions are based not on executive decision making but on computer modeling, in which a machine determines whether to buy or sell a product or to approve or reject a loan.

2. **Computers are making work more abstract.** Industrial workers typically have a "hands-on" relationship with their product. Postindustrial workers manipulate words or other symbols in pursuit of more "user-friendly" software or other abstract definition of business success.

3. **Computers limit workplace interaction.** The Information Revolution forces employees to perform most of their work at computer terminals; this system isolates workers from one another.

4. **Computers enhance employers' control of workers.** Computers allow supervisors to monitor each worker's output precisely and continuously, whether employees are working at computer terminals or on an assembly line (Rule & Brantley, 1992).

Making a broader point, Zuboff contends that technology is not socially neutral; rather it shapes the way we work and alters the balance of power between employers and employees. Understandably, then, while workers may hail some dimensions of the Information Revolution, they are likely to oppose others.

CORPORATIONS

At the core of today's capitalist economy lies the **corporation**, *an organization with a legal existence, including rights and liabilities, apart from those of its members.* By incorporating, an organization becomes an entity unto itself, able to enter into contracts and own property. Of some 20 million businesses in the United States, 4 million are incorporated (*Statistics of Income Bulletin*, 1991).

The practice of legally incorporating accelerated with the rise of large businesses a century ago because it offered company owners two advantages. First, incorporation shields them from the legal liabilities of their businesses, protecting personal wealth from lawsuits arising from business debts or harm to consumers. Second, profits earned by corporations receive favorable treatment under the tax laws of the United States.

The largest corporations are owned not by single families but by millions of stockholders, including other corporations. This dispersion of corporate ownership has spread wealth to some extent, making more people small-scale capitalists. Moreover, day-to-day operation of a corporation falls to white-collar executives, who may or may not be major stockholders themselves. Typically, however, a great deal of corporate stock is owned by a small number of the corporation's top executives and directors (Dahrendorf, 1959; Useem, 1980).

Economic Concentration

About half of U.S. corporations are small, with assets worth less than $100,000. The largest corporations, however, dominate our country's economy. Throughout this century, the growth of corporations has resulted in an increasing concentration of national and international economic power. The productive assets of the two hundred largest manufacturing corporations in 1950 were surpassed by those of the biggest one hundred companies in 1970 (Fusfeld, 1982). Corporations on record in 1995 included 445 with assets exceeding $1 billion, representing 72 percent of all corporate assets and 71 percent of total corporate profits (U.S. Bureau of the Census, 1996).

In 1995, the largest U.S. corporation was automaker General Motors, with more than $154 billion in revenue and $199 billion in total assets (*Fortune*, 1995). GM's sales during a single year roughly equaled the tax revenue of 60 percent of the states combined. GM also employed more people (700,000) than did the governments of all the states on the West Coast, including Alaska and Hawaii.

Conglomerates and Corporate Linkages

Economic concentration has spawned **conglomerates**, *giant corporations composed of many smaller corporations.* Conglomerates emerge as corporations enter new markets, spinning off new companies or carrying out takeovers of existing companies. Forging a conglomerate is also a strategy to diversify a company, so that new products can provide a hedge against

Q: "If you have absolutely unrestrained competition in the market-place, pretty soon you'll wind up with no competition at all." Lee Iacocca

Q: "The rare company that is able to retain its share of the market year after year and decade after decade does so by the means of productive efficiency—and deserves praise, not blame." Alan Greenspan.

NOTE: Oligopoly does not preclude successful economic challenges, either in well-established industries like automaking (consider the success of the Japanese in the U.S. auto market) or in new industries like software (note Microsoft's outdistancing of IBM and other rivals to set a world standard).

Q: "The engine that drives enterprise . . . is profit." John Maynard Keynes

declining profits in the original market. Faced with declining sales of tobacco products, for example, R. J. Reynolds merged with Nabisco foods, forming a conglomerate called RJR-Nabisco. Coca-Cola's soft drink market is still growing, but this company now produces fruit drinks, coffee, and bottled water, as well as movies and television programs. Viacom is another giant corporate "umbrella"—1995 revenues reached $11.5 billion—that encompasses many smaller corporations including Paramount (entertainment), Blockbuster (videos and theme parks), MTV, Nickelodeon, and two dozen television and radio stations, as well as Simon & Schuster (publishing), which includes Prentice Hall, publisher of this text (Zoglin, 1996).

Besides conglomerates, corporations are also linked through mutual ownership, since these giant organizations own each other's stock. In today's global economy, many U.S.-based companies have invested heavily in other corporations commonly regarded as their competitors. For instance, Ford owns a significant share of Mazda, General Motors is a major investor in Isuzu, and Chrysler is part owner of Mitsubishi.

One more type of linkage among corporations is the *interlocking directorate*, a social network of people serving simultaneously on the boards of directors of many corporations. These connections give corporations access to valuable information about each other's products and marketing strategies. Antitrust laws forbid linkages of this kind among corporations that compete directly with one another. Yet beneficial linkages persist among noncompeting corporations with common interests—for example, a corporation building tractors may share directors with one that manufactures tires. Indirect linkages also occur when, for example, a member of General Motors' board of directors and a director of Ford both sit on the board of Exxon (Herman, 1981; Scott & Griff, 1985; Weidenbaum, 1995).

Examining the membership of General Motors' board of directors, Beth Mintz and Michael Schwartz (1981) found directors who held comparable positions on the boards of twenty-nine other major corporations. These companies, in turn, shared directors with seven hundred additional corporations, including major banks and insurance companies. Gwen Moore (1979) adds that corporate executives travel in many of the same social circles, allowing them to exchange valuable information informally.

Corporate linkages do not necessarily run counter to the public interest, but they certainly concentrate power and they may encourage illegal activity. Price fixing, for example, is legal in much of the world (the Organization of Petroleum Exporting

McDonald's, which now operates more than fifteen thousand restaurants around the world, illustrates the central role that large corporations play in an expanding global economy. Here, South African children enjoy familiar fare.

Countries—OPEC—meets regularly to try to set oil prices), but not in the United States. By their nature, however, corporate linkages invite price fixing, especially when only a few corporations control an entire market.

Corporations and Competition

The capitalist model assumes that businesses operate independently in a competitive market. But while smaller businesses and self-employed people do represent a competitive sector of the U.S. economy, the corporate core of the economy is largely noncompetitive. Large corporations are not truly competitive because, first, their extensive linkages mean that they do not operate independently. Second, a small number of corporations dominate many large markets.

GLOBAL: Japanese "transplants" utilize nonunion (also younger) workers and produce autos with considerably lower employee costs. While the "big three" pay about $40 per hour, including benefits, Japanese companies pay about $27 hourly.

GLOBAL: U.S. businesses invest about 3% of GNP in new plants, compared to 15% by Japanese businesses. This, in the view of some critics, has reduced U.S. competitiveness.

GLOBAL: Total assets of Japan's biggest companies, as of 1994: Toyota Motors Corp. (9 trillion yen); Matsushita Electrical Industrial Corp. (4.4 trillion yen); Hitachi (3.7 trillion yen); Nissan Motor Co. (3.6 trillion yen); Toshiba Corp. (3.3 trillion yen).

GLOBAL: In recent years, exports have accounted for most of the growth of the U.S. economy; and most of this is the output of multinationals.

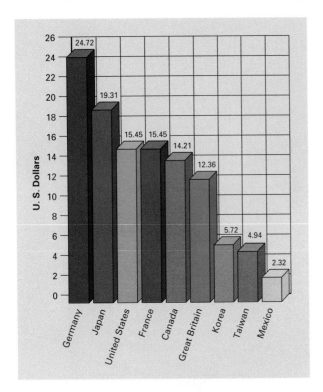

FIGURE 15–4 Average Hourly Wages for Workers in Manufacturing, 1994

Source: Calculations by the author based on Kmitch, Laboy, & Van Damme (1995).

No large company can establish an actual **monopoly,** *domination of a market by a single producer.* The Sherman Antitrust Act, passed in 1890, forbid such dominance because the company could simply dictate prices. But the law does permit lesser economic concentration called **oligopoly,** *domination of a market by a few producers.* Oligopoly results from the vast investment needed to enter a new market such as the auto industry. Certainly the successful entry of foreign-owned corporations into the U.S. automobile market shows that new companies can successfully challenge the biggest corporations. But all large businesses strive to limit competition simply because it places profits at risk.

Although capitalism favors minimal government intervention in the economy, corporate power is now so great—and competition among corporations sometimes so limited—that government regulation may be the only way to protect the public interest. Yet, the government is also the corporate world's single biggest customer, and Washington frequently intervenes to bolster struggling corporations, as in the recent savings and loan bailout. In short, corporations and government

typically work together to make the entire economy more stable and profitable (Madsen, 1980).

Corporations and the Global Economy

Corporations have grown in size and power so fast that they are now responsible for most of the world's economic output. In the process, the largest corporations—centered in the United States, Japan, and Western Europe—have spilled across national borders and now view the entire world as one vast marketplace.

As noted in Chapter 11 ("Global Stratification"), multinationals are large corporations that produce and market products in many different nations. Beatrice Foods, for example, operates factories in thirty countries and sells products in more than one hundred. General Motors, Ford, Exxon, and the other huge multinationals earn much—and in some cases most—of their profits outside the United States.

Corporations become multinational in order to make more money, since most of the planet's resources and three-fourths of the world's people are found in less-developed countries. Worldwide operations, then, offer access to plentiful materials and vast markets. In addition, as indicated in Figure 15–4, labor costs are far lower in poor countries of the world: A manufacturing worker in Taiwan labors all week to earn what a German worker earns in a single day.

The impact of multinationals on poor societies is controversial, as Chapter 11 ("Global Stratification") explains in detail. On one side of the argument, modernization theorists argue that multinationals unleash the great productivity of the capitalist economic system, which will boost economic development (Rostow, 1978; Madsen, 1980; Berger, 1986; Firebaugh & Beck, 1994). Exxon Corporation alone, for example, far outproduces any one of the least-productive nations in the world. Corporations offer poor societies tax revenues, capital investment, new jobs, and advanced technology—taken together, what modernization theorists call a certain recipe for economic growth.

On the other side of the argument, dependency theorists who favor a socialist economy claim that multinationals only intensify global inequality (Vaughan, 1978; Wallerstein, 1979; Delacroix & Ragin, 1981; Bergesen, 1983; Walton & Ragin, 1990). Multinational investment, as they see it, may create a few jobs in poor countries but it also stifles the development of local industries which are a better source of employment. Further, critics charge, multinationals generally push developing countries to produce expensive consumer goods for export to rich nations rather than food

NOTE: Arguments about development on the political right tend to focus on economic productivity; those on the left tend to highlight economic distribution. This mirrors global theories of economic development—modernization theory and dependency (world systems) theory. See discussion of these approaches in Chapter 11, "Global Stratification."

GLOBAL: In 1990, foreign interests invested an estimated $400 billion in the United States; by region, the largest investor is Europe ($250 billion), followed by Asia ($100 billion). The list of individual investor nations is topped by the United Kingdom ($110 billion), Japan ($85 billion), and the Netherlands ($65 billion). (U.S. Census Bureau)

GLOBAL: About half of all consumer items purchased in the United States are made outside the country.

The expansion of Western multinational corporations has altered patterns of consumption throughout the world, creating a homogeneous "corporate culture" that is—for better or worse—undermining countless traditional ways of life.

and other necessities that would bolster the standard of living in local communities. From this standpoint, multinationals establish a system of neocolonialism, making poor societies poorer and increasingly reliant on rich, capitalist societies.

While modernization theory hails the virtues of an unregulated market as the key to a future of progress and affluence for all the world's people, advocates of dependency theory call for replacing market systems with government regulation of economic affairs. The final box takes a closer look at the issue of market versus governmental economies.

LOOKING AHEAD: THE ECONOMY OF THE TWENTY-FIRST CENTURY

Social institutions are organizational strategies by which societies operate to meet the needs of their members. But societies themselves change over time, so that the various institutions always seem somewhat at odds with their missions.

One important transformation highlighted in this chapter revolves around the Information Revolution. New information technology has defined a new era— the postindustrial economy. The share of the U.S. labor force engaged in manufacturing has tumbled to just half of what it was in 1960, while service work has climbed just as quickly. For workers who depend on their industrial skills to earn a living, this major economic shift has brought rising unemployment and declining wages. As we look to the coming century, our society must face up to the fact that millions of men and women lack the language and computer skills needed to participate in the postindustrial economy. Can we afford to consign these workers to the margins of society? How should the government, schools, and families prepare young people to perform the kind of work their society makes available to them?

A second transformation that will define the next century is the emergence of a global economy. Two centuries ago, the ups and downs of a local economy were guided by events or trends that took place within a single town. A century later, local communities throughout the country had become economically interconnected so that prosperity in one place depended on producing goods demanded by people elsewhere. As we approach the next century, economic links are intensifying at the global level. It now makes far less sense to speak of a national economy; what people, say, in a Kansas farm town produce and consume may be affected more by what transpires in the wheat-growing region of Russia than by events in their own state capital. In short, U.S. workers are not only

DISCUSS: How does morality figure in the market system? Some say there is no morality in a market economy, only profit; the political left describes the market as implicitly immoral, since it ignores social good; the political right says that self-seeking is inherently moral, because it represents people freely serving their own chosen ends. Also, a market system offers people freedoms as producers and consumers and bridges national, religious, racial, ethnic, and other historic divides.

DISCUSS: True or false: The political left favors large government and condemns "big business," while the political right favors the market and condemns "big government."

Q: "The general rule is that, while property may be regulated to a certain extent, if regulation goes too far it will be recognized as a taking." Oliver Wendell Holmes

Controversy & Debate

Does "The Market" Serve the Public Interest?

"The Market" or "Government"? Each represents a means of economic decision making, determining what products and services companies produce as well as what people consume. So important is this process that the degree to which the market or government directs the economy represents a key way in which the world's nations define themselves, select their allies, and designate their enemies.

Historically, U.S. society has relied on "the market" for most economic decisions. Generally speaking, we allow the market to set prices as potential buyers and sellers bid for goods and services upward or downward in a changing balance of supply and demand. In doing so, the market coordinates the efforts of countless people, each of whom—to return to

Adam Smith's crucial insight—is motivated only by self-interest.

Defenders also praise the market for discouraging some social bad habits such as racial prejudice. Industrialist J. P. Morgan once commented that, while he would sail only with a gentleman, he would do business with *anyone*—explicit acknowledgement that market transactions focus on value, not the social traits of traders. And, perhaps most important of all, as economists Milton and Rose Friedman remind us, a more-or-less freely operating market system has provided members of our society with an unprecedented economic standard of living.

But others celebrate the role of government in the operation of the U.S. economy. At one level, government steps in to accomplish some tasks that no one would do for profit. Even Adam Smith looked to

government to defend the country against external enemies. Government also has a key role in constructing and maintaining public projects such as roads, utilities, and schools.

Free-marketeers such as the Friedmans counter that virtually any task government undertakes, it performs inefficiently. They point out that the products we enjoy—such as computers, household appliances, and the myriad offerings of supermarkets and shopping centers—are primarily products of the market. By contrast, the least-satisfying goods and services available today—and the Friedmans place public schools, postal service, and railroad passenger service among them—are those operated by the government. Thus, while some government presence in the economy is necessary, supporters of free markets maintain that an economy that

generating new products and services, but we do so in response to factors and forces that are distant and unseen.

Finally, change is causing analysts around the world to rethink conventional economic models. The emerging global economic system revealed socialist economies to be far less productive than their capitalist counterparts, one central cause of the recent collapse of socialist regimes in Eastern Europe and the former Soviet Union. At its peak, socialism organized the productive lives of about one-fourth of humanity; now, the People's Republic of China and Cuba are among the few nations with government-based economies.

Capitalism, too, has seen marked changes and now operates with a significant degree of government regulation. The most significant change in the capitalist system is the emergence of multinational corporations. The global reach of today's giant businesses means that U.S. corporations have expanded into more parts of the world, just as foreign-based corporations are increasing their investment in the United States.

Perhaps we are nearing the end of what some analysts call "the American century." Ours is still the most productive economy in the world. But a turning point occurred in 1990 when, for the first time, foreign corporations owned more of the United States than U.S. corporations owned abroad. Foreign investors now have title to half of the commercial property in downtown Los Angeles, 40 percent in Houston, 35 percent in Minneapolis, and 25 percent in Manhattan (Selimuddin, 1989).

What will be the long-term effects of all these changes? Two conclusions seem inescapable. First, the economic future of the United States and other nations will be played out in a global arena. The emergence of the U.S. postindustrial economy is, after all, inseparable from the increasing industrial production of other nations, especially in Asia's rapidly developing Pacific Rim. Second, everyone confronts the ever-pressing issue of global inequality. Whether the world economy ultimately reduces or deepens the disparity between rich and poor societies will likely be the factor that steers our planet toward peace or belligerence.

Q: Pope John Paul II has charged that both capitalism and socialism have "a tendency toward imperialism" by seeking wealth and power at the expense of low-income nations. (*Sollicitudo Rei Socialis*—"The Social Concerns of the Church")

DISCUSS: Advocates of government regulation argue that such supervision guards against monopoly. Defenders of the market

claim that allowing free international trade forces large companies to be competitive (witness how the Japanese automakers successfully challenged the U.S. Big Three).

NOTE: Microsoft operates as an oligopoly, providing software operating systems for 80% of the world's computers.

operates with minimal state regulation serves the public interest well.

But supporters of government do not concede the argument. Far from it: Many analysts all but dismiss the market as a negative force. For one thing, critics point out, the market has little incentive to produce goods and services that generate little profit, which include just about everything consumed by poor people. Government-directed public housing, for example, stands as a vital resource that no profit-seeking developer would offer independently.

Second, market critics look to government to curb what they see as the market system's self-destructive tendencies. A century ago, for example, the formation of economic monopolies threatened the public interest, prompting the passage of the Sherman Antitrust Act in 1890. Especially since President Roosevelt's "New Deal" of the 1930s, government has performed a host of regulatory functions, intervening in the market to

control inflation, enhance the well-being of workers (by imposing workplace safety standards), and benefit consumers (through product quality controls). Indeed, the power of corporations in U.S. society is so great, conclude the critics, that even the might of the U.S. government cannot effectively defend the public interest.

Third, critics support government's role in curbing what they see as another market flaw: magnifying social stratification. As we have seen, capitalist economies characteristically concentrate income and wealth; a government system of taxation (typically applying higher rates to the rich) counters this tendency in the name of social justice. For a number of reasons, then, the market operating alone does not serve the public interest.

Does the market's "invisible hand" feed us well or pick our pockets? Although many—perhaps most—people in the United States view the market as good, they also support some government role in economic

life to benefit the public. Indeed, government assists not only citizens but business itself by providing investment capital, constructing roads and other infrastructure, and shielding companies from foreign competition. Yet the precise balance struck between market forces and government decision-making continues to underlie much of the political debate in the United States and around the world.

Continue the debate . . .

1. *Why do defenders of the free market assert that "the government that governs best is the government that governs least"?*

2. *In your opinion, does a market system meet the needs of this country's people? Does it serve some better than others?*

3. *What is your impression of the successes and failures of socialist economic systems?*

Sources: Friedman (1980) and Erber (1990).

SUMMARY

1. The economy is the major social institution by which a society produces, distributes, and consumes goods and services.

2. In technologically simple societies, the economy is subsumed within the family. In agrarian societies, most economic activity takes place apart from the home. Industrialization sparks significant economic expansion built around new energy sources, large factories, mass production, and worker specialization.

3. The postindustrial economy is characterized by a productive shift from tangible goods to services. Just as the technology of the Industrial Revolution propelled the industrial economy of the past, the Information Revolution is now advancing the postindustrial economy.

4. The primary sector of the economy generates raw materials; the secondary sector manufactures

various goods; the tertiary sector focuses on providing services. In preindustrial societies, the primary sector predominates; the secondary sector is of greatest importance in industrial societies; the tertiary sector prevails in postindustrial societies.

5. Social scientists describe the economies of today's industrial and postindustrial societies in terms of two models. Capitalism is based on private ownership of productive property and the pursuit of personal profit in a competitive marketplace. Socialism is based on collective ownership of productive property and the pursuit of collective well-being through government control of the economy.

6. Although the U.S. economy is predominantly capitalist, government is broadly involved in economic life. Government plays an even greater role in the "democratic socialist" economies of some

Western European nations and the "state capitalism" of Japan. The former Soviet Union has gradually introduced some market elements into its formerly centralized economy; the nations of Eastern Europe are making similar changes.

7. Capitalism is very productive, yielding a high overall standard of living with extensive civil liberties. Socialism is less productive and restricts civil liberties, but does generate greater economic equality than is found under capitalism.

8. The emergence of a global economy means that nations no longer produce and consume products and services within national boundaries. Moreover, the six hundred largest corporations, operating internationally, now account for most of the earth's economic output.

9. In the United States, agricultural work has declined over the course of this century to just 2 percent of the labor force. The share of blue-collar jobs has also diminished, now accounting for one-fourth of the labor force. The share of white-collar service occupations, however, has been rising rapidly; more than 70 percent of today's labor force perform white-collar work.

10. A profession is a special category of white-collar work based on theoretical knowledge, occupational autonomy, authority over clients, and a claim to serving the community.

11. Work in the primary labor market provides far more rewards than work in the secondary labor market. Most new jobs in the United States are service positions in the secondary labor market, and about one-third of today's workers hold jobs classified as temporary, with no promise of job security.

12. Today, 9 percent of U.S. workers are self-employed. Although many professionals fall into this category, most self-employed workers have blue-collar occupations.

13. Unemployment has many causes, including the operation of the economy itself; in the United States the unemployment rate is generally at least 5 percent.

14. The underground economy, which includes both criminal and legal activity, generates income that goes unreported on income tax forms.

15. Corporations form the core of the U.S. economy. The largest corporations, which are conglomerates, account for most corporate assets and profits. Many large corporations operate as multinationals, producing and distributing products in most nations of the world.

KEY CONCEPTS

capitalism an economic system in which natural resources and the means of producing goods and services are privately owned

communism a hypothetical economic and political system in which all members of a society are socially equal

conglomerates giant corporations composed of many smaller corporations

corporation an organization with a legal existence, including rights and liabilities, apart from those of its members

democratic socialism an economic and political system that combines significant government control of the economy with free elections

economy the social institution that organizes the production, distribution, and consumption of goods and services

global economy economic activity spanning many nations of the world with little regard for national borders

labor unions organizations of workers seeking to improve wages and working conditions through various strategies, including negotiations and strikes

monopoly domination of a market by a single producer

oligopoly domination of a market by a few producers

postindustrial economy a productive system based on service work and high technology

primary labor market occupations that provide extensive benefits to workers

primary sector the part of the economy that generates raw materials directly from the natural environment

profession a prestigious, white-collar occupation that requires extensive formal education

secondary labor market jobs that provide minimal benefits to workers

secondary sector the part of the economy that transforms raw materials into manufactured goods

socialism an economic system in which natural resources and the means of producing goods and services are collectively owned

state capitalism an economic and political system in which companies are privately owned but cooperate closely with the government

tertiary sector the part of the economy that generates services rather than goods

underground economy economic activity generating income that one does not report to the government as required by law

CRITICAL-THINKING QUESTIONS

1. How does the economy operate differently among societies at different stages of technological development?

2. Identify several ways in which the Industrial Revolution reshaped the economy of the United States. How is the Information Revolution transforming the economy once again?

3. What key characteristics distinguish capitalism from socialism? Compare these two systems in terms of productivity, economic inequality, and support for civil liberties.

4. In light of the emerging global economy, some analysts suggest that measurements such as gross domestic product (GDP) are losing their utility. Do you agree?

SUGGESTED READINGS

Classic Sources

Thorstein Veblen. *The Theory of the Leisure Class.* New York: New American Library, 1953; orig. 1899.
    One of the earliest U.S. sociologists explains how patterns of consumption confer social status on people in an increasingly affluent and upwardly mobile society.

Daniel Bell. *The Coming of Post-Industrial Society: A Venture in Social Forecasting.* New York: Harper Colophon, 1976.
    Daniel Bell was among the first sociologists to recognize and analyze the emerging postindustrial society.

Contemporary Sources

Bette Woody. *Black Women in the Workplace: Impacts of Structural Change in the Economy.* Westport, Conn.: Greenwood, 1992.
    Economic changes have different effects on various segments of the labor force. This analysis highlights the consequences of the emerging postindustrial economy for women of color.

J. Clay Smith, Jr. *Emancipation: The Making of the Black Lawyer, 1844–1944.* Philadelphia: University of Pennsylvania Press, 1993.

This historical study of the legal profession demonstrates the significance of race in the world of work.

James A. Yunker. *Socialism Revised and Modernized: The Case for Pragmatic Market Socialism.* New York: Praeger, 1992.
    This author envisions how a fusion of capitalist and socialist models—involving public ownership of larger, profit-seeking corporations—would capitalize on the advantages of both economic systems.

Global Sources

Emilio Zamora. *The World of the Mexican Worker in Texas.* College Station: Texas A&M University Press, 1993.
    By tracing the history of Mexican labor in Texas, this researcher challenges various stereotypes used by employers to subjugate these workers in the labor market.

Suzan Lewis, Dafna N. Izraeli, and Helen Hootsmans. *Dual-Earner Families: International Perspectives.* Newbury Park, Calif.: Sage, 1992.
    This discussion highlights changing economic and family patterns in Hungary, Sweden, Singapore, Japan, India, and elsewhere.

ZHANG HONGTU,
CHAIRMAN MAO,
NUMBER 11, 1989

Politics and Government

On the morning of April 26, 1995, a yellow Ryder truck stood parked in front of the federal building in Oklahoma City. Few among the streams of people passing in and out of the building gave more than a passing glance to the vehicle, and no one imag- ined that it was laden with four thou- sand pounds of high explosives. Then, at 9:02 A.M.—the height of the morning rush hour—the truck was vaporized by a thunderous explosion that people felt thirty miles away. The blast tore into the federal building, collapsing all nine floors of the front facade in a rubble of broken concrete, twisted metal, and shattered lives. At the moment of the blast, some five hundred people were in the building— government workers, citizens conducting routine business, as well as forty children in a day-care center. So extensive was the damage that days passed before authorities set the death toll at one hundred sixty-eight— including nineteen children.

The nation was stunned by the savagery of the attack, and early rumors linked the bombing to Middle Eastern terrorists. But the world soon learned that the driving force behind this unspeakable act was a home-grown phenomenon—several young men, convinced that the federal government represented a great evil, had killed all those innocent people to vent their hatred and, in a distorted way, to make a political statement (Gibbs, 1995; Gleick, 1995).

This chapter investigates the dynamics of power within societies and among nations, explaining the rules of the game and noting why people sometimes break them. **Politics** is *the social institution that distributes power, sets a society's agenda, and makes decisions.* Politics, in short, is about power, a topic about which there is considerable dis-agreement around the world as well as here at home.

POWER AND AUTHORITY

Max Weber (1978; orig. 1921) declared **power** to be *the ability to achieve desired ends despite resistance from others.* History reveals that *force*—physical might or psychologi-cal coercion—is the basic expression of power. But no society exists for long if power derives *only* from force, because people will break rules they do not respect at the first opportunity. Social organization, therefore, depends on generating some consensus about proper goals (cultural values) and the suitable means of attaining them (cultural norms).

The key to social stability is exercising power within some framework of justice. This insight led Weber to focus on the concept of **authority**, *power that people perceive as legitimate rather than coercive.* When parents, professors, or police perform their work in a normative way, their power generally wins respect as authority. The source of authority, Weber continued, differs according to a society's economy.

Traditional Authority

Preindustrial societies, Weber explained, rely on **tradi-tional authority**, *power legitimized through respect for long-established cultural patterns.* Traditional authority is power woven into a society's collective memory, so that it is not only legitimate but almost sacred. The might of Chinese emperors in antiquity was legitimized by tradition, as was the rule of nobles in medieval Europe. In both cases, hereditary family rule within a traditional, agrarian way of life imbued leaders with almost godlike authority.

Traditional authority declines as societies industrialize. Hannah Arendt (1963) explains that traditional authority is compelling only so long as everyone shares the same heritage and world view; this form of authority, then, is undermined by the specialization demanded by industrial

Q: *"Sedis animi est in memoria."* ("The seat of the mind is in memory.") Augustine; the idea is readily applied to traditional authority

Q: "Authority is an institutional phenomenon; it is strongly bound up with faith. It must be believed in . . . . Authority resides not in the person in whom it is conferred by the group or society, but in the recognition and acceptance it elicits in others." Jessie Bernard

NOTE: Ferdinand Toennies, too, described the social roots of authority: He linked authority to (1) advanced age, (2) force, and (3) wisdom or spirit.

GLOBAL: The British have melded traditional and bureaucratic authority by their recent practice of elevating individuals to noble rank based on distinguished accomplishment, but mandating that the rank not pass to any descendants.

production, by modern, scientific thinking, and also by the cultural diversity that accompanies immigration. Thus, no president of today's United States, for example, would claim to rule by the grace of God. Even so, as E. Digby Baltzell (1964) points out, some well-established upper-class families—such as the Roosevelts, the Rockefellers, and the Kennedys—have occupied a privileged position in U.S. society for several generations and enter the political arena with some measure of traditional authority.

If traditional authority plays a smaller part in national politics, it persists in many dimensions of everyday life. Patriarchy, the traditional domination of women by men, is still widespread, although increasingly challenged, in the United States. Less controversial is the traditional authority parents exert over their young children. A common family experience shows that traditional authority is based on a person's status as parent rather than whatever wisdom the particular individual may have acquired. To children who ask *why* they should obey a parental order, parents have long retorted, "Because I said so!" To debate the merits of such a command would, after all, defeat authority by placing parent and child on an equal footing.

Rational-Legal Authority

Weber defined **rational-legal authority** (sometimes called *bureaucratic authority*) as *power legitimized by legally enacted rules and regulations.* Rational-legal authority, then, is legitimized by **government,** *formal organizations that direct the political life of a society.*

As Chapter 7 ("Groups and Organizations") explains, Weber viewed bureaucracy as the organizational backbone of rational, industrial societies. Moreover, according to Weber, just as rationality promotes bureaucracy, so it erodes traditional customs and practices. In their search for justice, in other words, modern people are less likely to venerate the past and more apt to look to formal rules, especially law.

Rationally enacted rules not only guide government in the United States; they also underlie much of our everyday life. The authority of classroom teachers and deans, for example, rests on the offices they hold in bureaucratic colleges and universities. The police, too, are officers within the bureaucracy of local government. Compared to traditional authority, then, rational-legal authority flows not from family background but from organizational position. Thus while a traditional monarch rules for life, a modern president accepts and relinquishes power according to law, with presidential authority remaining in the office.

Charismatic Authority

Max Weber identified charisma as one additional way in which power is transformed into authority. Charisma, a concept detailed in Chapter 18 ("Religion"), designates exceptional personal qualities that people take to be a sign of divine inspiration. In political terms, then, **charismatic authority** is *power legitimized through extraordinary personal abilities that inspire devotion and obedience.* Unlike tradition and rational law, then, charisma has less to do with social organization and is more a trait of individual personality.

Members of societies throughout history have regarded some of their number as especially forceful, creative, and magnetic. Charisma enhances the stature of an established leader, just as it strengthens the appeal of an outside challenger. By turning an audience into followers, charismatics often make their own rules, as if drawing on a higher power. The extraordinary ability of charismatics to challenge the status quo is deeply engrained in global history: Vladimir Lenin guided the overthrow of feudal monarchy in Russia in 1917, Mahatma Gandhi inspired the struggle to free India from British colonialism after World War II, and Martin Luther King, Jr., galvanized the civil rights movement in the United States.

Charisma may arise from personality, but it also reflects a society's expectations about what kind of people emerge as leaders. Patriarchy encourages us to tap men as our national officials, while steering charismatic women toward the arts, the family, and other social contexts traditionally defined as feminine. Yet, in recent years, charismatic women, including Indira Gandhi of India, Benazir Bhutto of Pakistan, Golda Meir of Israel, and Margaret Thatcher of the United Kingdom, have gained international political prominence.

Because charismatic authority emanates from a single individual, any charismatic regime faces a crisis of survival upon the death of its leader. Thus, Weber reasoned, the persistence of a charismatic movement depends on a process he called the **routinization of charisma,** *the transformation of charismatic authority into some combination of traditional and bureaucratic authority.* Christianity, for example, began as a cult driven by the personal charisma of Jesus of Nazareth. After the death of Jesus, followers institutionalized his teachings in a church eventually centered in Rome and built on tradition and bureaucracy. Well routinized, the Roman Catholic church has flourished for two thousand years.

The concept of political liberty burned brightly in the minds of many European thinkers during the eighteenth century as the medieval world drew to a close. In Third of May *(1808), the Spanish painter Francisco Goya (1746–1828) commemorates the death of Madrid citizens at the hands of faceless soldiers. The martyrs shown here are dying not for religious salvation, as is depicted in so much medieval art, but for the modern principle of political freedom.*

Francisco Goya, *Third of May,* Prado, Madrid/Scala/Art Resource.

POLITICS IN GLOBAL PERSPECTIVE

Political systems display marked variety throughout history as well as around the world today. Looking back in time, technologically simple hunting and gathering societies operated like one large family, with few specialized roles. In general, leadership fell to a male with unusual strength, hunting skill, or personal charisma. But leaders of these egalitarian societies exercised little actual power, since they lacked the resources to reward supporters or punish challengers. In the earliest societies, then, leaders were barely discernible from everyone else, and government did not exist as a distinct sphere of life (Lenski, Nolan, & Lenski, 1995).

Agrarian societies, both larger and more complex, benefit from specialized activity and generate a material surplus. These societies become hierarchical, with a small elite gaining control of most wealth and power, and politics moving outside the family realm to become a social institution in its own right. Leaders who manage to pass along their power over several generations may acquire traditional authority, perhaps even claiming divine right to govern. Such leaders also may benefit from Weber's rational-legal authority as they are served by a bureaucratic political administration and system of law.

As politics expands in this way, societal power eventually takes the form of a national government or *political state*. But the political state could develop only according to available technology. Just a few centuries ago, armies moved slowly and communication over even short distances was uncertain. Thus governments could confidently control only very small areas. For this reason, early political empires—such as Mesopotamia in the Middle East about five thousand years ago—actually took the form of many small *city-states* (Stavrianos, 1983).

More complex technology has helped the modern world develop the larger-scale system of *nation-states*. Currently, the world has 191 independent nation-states, each of which operates a political system that is at least somewhat distinctive. Generally speaking, however, the world's political systems fall into four categories: monarchy, democracy, authoritarianism, and totalitarianism.

Monarchy

Monarchy (with Latin and Greek roots meaning "one ruler") is *a type of political system in which a single family rules from generation to generation.* Monarchy is typical of agrarian societies; the Bible, for example, tells of great kings such as David and Solomon.

Today's British monarchy traces its lineage back roughly one thousand years. In Weber's terms, then, monarchy is legitimized by tradition.

During the medieval era, *absolute monarchy*, in which hereditary rulers claimed a virtual monopoly of power based on divine right, flourished from England to China and in parts of the Americas. Monarchs in some nations—including Saudi Arabia—still exercise virtually absolute control over their people.

During this more egalitarian century, however, monarchs have gradually passed from the scene in favor of elected officials. Europe's remaining monarchs—in Great Britain, Spain, Norway, Sweden, Belgium, Denmark, and the Netherlands—now preside over *constitutional monarchies*. They serve as symbolic heads of state, while actual governing is the responsibility of elected politicians, led by a prime minister, according to political principles embodied in a constitution. In these nations, then, the nobility may formally reign, but elected officials actually rule.

Democracy

The historical trend in the modern world has favored **democracy,** *a political system in which power is exercised by the people as a whole.* Members of democratic societies rarely participate directly in decision making; numbers alone make this an impossibility. Instead, a system of *representative democracy* places authority in the hands of elected leaders, who are accountable to the people.

High-income, industrial societies tend to embrace democratic political systems. Economic development and democratic government go together because both depend on a literate populace. Moreover, the traditional legitimization of power in a monarchy gives way in democratic political systems to rational-legal authority. A rational election process places leaders in offices regulated by law. Thus democracy and rational-legal authority are linked just as monarchy and traditional authority are.

But democratic political systems are much more than just leaders and followers; they are built on extensive bureaucracy. Considerable formal organization is necessary to carry out the expanding range of government activities undertaken by democratic societies. As it grows, government gradually takes on a life of its own, revealing an inherent antagonism between democracy and bureaucracy. The federal government of the United States, for example, employs more than 3 million people (excluding the armed forces), making it one of the largest bureaucracies in the world.

Another 15 million people work in some eighty thousand local governments. The great majority of these bureaucrats were never elected and are unknown to the public they purport to serve. To elect them would seem impractical given their numbers and the need for specialized training. But, ironically, while the public focuses attention on a small number of elected leaders, most everyday decision making is carried out by career bureaucrats who are not directly accountable to the people (Scaff, 1981; Edwards, 1985; Etzioni-Halevy, 1985).

Democracy and Freedom: Contrasting Approaches

Despite their distinctive histories and cultural diversity, virtually all industrialized nations in the world claim to be democratic and politically free. This curious fact might make us wonder what societies mean by being politically "free."

The political life of the United States, Canada, and the nations of Europe is shaped by the free-market economic principles of capitalism. Supporters argue that the operation of a market system affords individuals the *personal freedom to pursue whatever they perceive as their self-interest.* Thus, the argument continues, the capitalist approach to political freedom translates into personal liberty—freedom to vote for one's preferred leader or otherwise act with minimal interference from government.

Yet, as the last chapter explained, capitalist societies are marked by a striking inequality of wealth. Such economic disparity, critics counter, gives some people far more choices and opportunities than others. Thus, capitalism looks undemocratic insofar as such a system attends to the needs of only the well-to-do.

Supporters of a socialist economic system, by contrast, point out that socialist politics strive to meet every citizen's basic needs for housing, schooling, a job, and medical care. Thus, the socialist approach to political freedom emphasizes *freedom from basic want.* For example, there is little of the hunger and homelessness we associate with U.S. capitalism in more socialist nations such as Norway and Sweden.

But critics of socialism counter that such systems can be unresponsive to people's needs and aspirations as well as heavy-handed in their suppression of any political opposition. Within the last decade, for example, people living under socialist governments in Eastern Europe overthrew that system in favor of a free market that would, presumably, reduce political repression (and raise living sandards).

NOTE: Generally speaking, the political left (following Rousseau and Marx) seeks to lessen inequality, viewing inequality as equivalent to injustice. The political right (following Plato) maintains that some dimensions of inequality are legitimate or just. Thus, the concept of "authority" has been of more interest to the right, while the left has critiqued legitimizing "ideologies."

Q: "Whether we like to admit it or not, a society which encourages

the full flowering of individual liberty is, and can only be, a stratified society." Andrew Hacker

GLOBAL: Asked which of the two is more important, 72% of a U.S. sample picked freedom (20% equality). Europeans, by contrast, assign roughly equal value to each. (Wattenberg, 1989)

Q: "An oppressive government is more to be feared than a tiger." Confucius

Window on the World

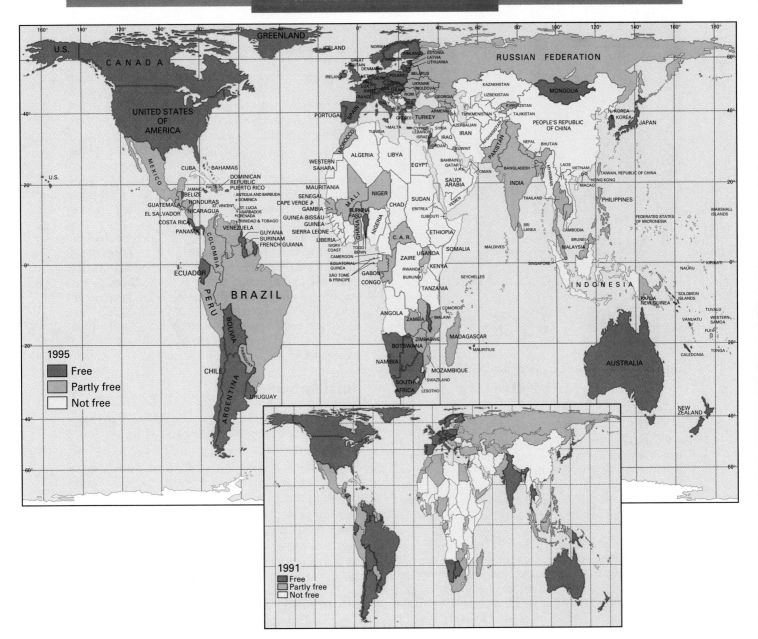

GLOBAL MAP 16–1 Political Freedom in Global Perspective

In 1995, seventy-six of the world's nations, containing 20 percent of all people, were politically "free"—that is, they offered their citizens extensive political rights and civil liberties. Another sixty-one countries that included 40 percent of the world's people were "partly free," with more limited rights and liberties. The remaining fifty-four nations, home to 40 percent of humanity, fall into the category of "not free." In these countries, government sharply restricts individual initiative. Between 1980 and 1991 democracy made significant gains, largely centered in Latin America as well as Eastern Europe. Since 1991, however, the world has witnessed an erosion of political freedom on all continents.

Source: Freedom House (1995).

Chapter 16 Politics and Government   **433**

Q: "Political power grows out of the barrel of a gun." Chinese leader Mao Zedong

NOTE: *Authoritarian* regimes are concerned mostly with overt compliance, while *totalitarian* regimes seek to win "the hearts and minds" of their people.

NOTE: Totalitarianism opposes all pluralism. As an example, anti-Semitism in the former Soviet Union probably was less about religion and more an attempt to quash all loyalties, except those to the state.

Q: "All socialism involves slavery." Herbert Spencer

Q: "Wherever two or three are gathered together, there the party-state desires to be." Timothy Garton Ash (1983:8), on totalitarianism

Q: "Man is born free, and everywhere he is in chains." Jean Jacques Rousseau, *The Social Contract* (1762)

resided in partly free countries, and 40 percent lived in places that were not free (Karatnycky, 1995). Figure 16–1 provides details.

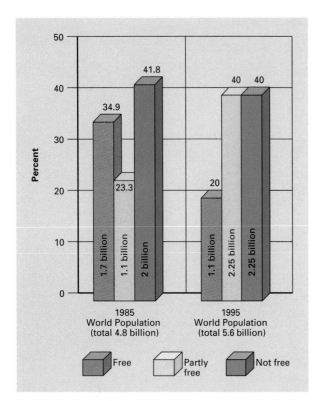

FIGURE 16–1 The Extent of Global Political Freedom, 1985 and 1995

Source: Karatnycky (1995).

These contrasting views of freedom raise an important question: Are economic equality and political liberty compatible? To foster economic equality, socialism tends to infringe on individual initiative. Capitalism, on the other hand, provides broad political liberties, which, in practice, mean little to the poor.

The discussions that follow in this chapter spotlight the varying positons of the world's countries with regard to how much economic inequality they tolerate and the extent of political freedoms they grant to their citizens. Global Map 16–1, on page 433, provides one organization's assessment of political freedom in the world today.

By the beginning of the 1990s, according to Freedom House, a New York–based organization that tracks global political trends, more people in the world were "free" than "not free" for the first time in history. Since then, however, the tide has turned against democracy. In 1995, just 20 percent of the world's people lived in nations that were free; 40 percent

Authoritarianism

As a matter of policy, some nations give their people little voice in politics. **Authoritarianism** refers to *a political system that denies popular participation in government*. An authoritarian government is not only indifferent to people's needs, it lacks the legal means to remove leaders from office, and provides people with little or no way even to express their opinions. Polish sociologist Wlodzimierz Wesolowski (1990:435) sums up authoritarianism this way: "The authoritarian philosophy argues for the supremacy of the state [over other] organized social activity."

The absolute monarchies in Saudi Arabia and Kuwait are highly authoritarian. Other examples of authoritarian regimes are military juntas found today in Congo and Ethiopia, where political dissatisfaction has been widespread. But heavy-handed government does not always breed popular opposition, as we can see in the box on page 435—a look at the "soft authoritarianism" that now thrives in the small Asian nation of Singapore.

Totalitarianism

```
October 22, 1994, near Saigon, Vietnam.
Six students in our group have been
arrested, allegedly for talking to
Vietnamese students and also for taking
pictures at the university. The Viet-
namese Minister of Education has can-
celled the reception tonight, claiming
that our students meeting their stu-
dents represents a threat to this coun-
try's security . . .
```

The most restrictive political form is **totalitarianism**, *a political system that extensively regulates people's lives*. Totalitarian governments emerged only during this century, with the development of the technological means for rigid regulation of a populace. The Vietnamese government closely monitors the activities of its citizens and visitors. Similarly, the government of North Korea utilizes surveillance equipment and sophisticated computers to store vast amounts of information on its citizenry and thereby manipulate an entire population.

Q: In *Democracy in America* (Vol. II, ch. VI), Tocqueville foresaw totalitarian regimes with remarkable accuracy almost a century before they appeared, describing "an innumerable multitude of men, all equal and alike . . . each a stranger to the fate of all the rest . . ." Ruling this mass is "an immense and tutelary power, which takes upon itself alone to secure their gratifications . . . [seeking] to keep them in perpetual childhood . . ."

GLOBAL: Currently, Singapore enjoys economic growth of 9% annually, with unemployment under 2%; just 1% of births are out of wedlock. Note that Freedom House characterizes Singapore as "partly free." Since 1965, this country has had only two leaders (of one party): Lee Kuan Yew and, after 1990, Goh Chok Tong.

NOTE: The growth of government is one dimension of the rise of a service economy.

GLOBAL SOCIOLOGY

"Soft Authoritarianism" or Planned Prosperity?
A Report From Singapore

Singapore, a tiny nation on the tip of the Malay Peninsula with a population of just over 3 million, seems to many to be an Asian paradise. Surrounded by poor societies that grapple with rapidly surging populations, squalid, sprawling cities, and surging crime rates, the affluence, cleanliness, and safety of Singapore make the North American visitor think more of a theme park than a country.

In fact, since its independence from Malaysia in 1965, Singapore has startled the world with its economic development; today, the economy is expanding rapidly and per capita income now rivals that of the United States. But, unlike the United States, Singapore has scarcely any social problems such as crime, slums, unemployment, or children living in poverty. In fact, people in Singapore don't even contend with traffic jams, graffiti on subway cars, or litter in the streets.

The key to Singapore's orderly environment is the ever-present hand of government, which actively promotes traditional morality and regulates just about everything. The state owns and manages most of the country's housing and has a stake in many businesses. It provides tax incentives for family planning and completing additional years of schooling. To keep traffic under control, the government slaps hefty surcharges on cars, pushing the price of a basic sedan up around $40,000.

Singapore made headlines in the United States in 1994 after the government accused U.S. citizen Michael Fay of vandalism and sentenced him to a caning—a penalty illegal in this country. Singapore's laws also permit police to detain a person suspected of a crime without charge or trial and to mandate death by hanging for drug dealing. The government has outlawed some religious groups (including Jehovah's Witnesses) and bans pornography outright. Even smoking in public brings a heavy fine. To ensure that city streets are kept clean, the state forbids eating on the subway, imposes stiff fines for littering, and has even outlawed the sale of chewing gum.

In economic terms, Singapore defies familiar categories. Government control of scores of businesses, including television stations, telephone service, airlines, and taxis seems socialist. Yet, unlike socialist enterprises, these businesses are operated efficiently and very

profitably. Moreover, Singapore's capitalist culture celebrates economic growth (although the government cautions its people about the evils of excessive materialism), and this nation is home to hundreds of multinational corporations.

Singapore's political climate is as unusual as its economy. Members of this society feel the hand of government far more than their counterparts in the United States. Just as important, a single political organization—the People's Action party—has ruled Singapore without opposition since the nation's independence thirty years ago.

Clearly, Singapore is not a politically democratic country. But most people in this prospering nation seem content—even enthusiastic—about their lives. What Singapore's political system offers is a simple bargain: Government demands unflinching loyalty from the populace; in return, it provides a high degree of security and prosperity. Critics charge that this system amounts to a "soft authoritarianism" that stifles dissent and gives government unwarranted control over people's lives. Most of the people of Singapore, however, know the struggles of living elsewhere and, for now at least, consider the tradeoff a good one.

Source: Adapted from Branegan (1993).

Q: "The essential problem of social order is the [legitimation] and not the elimination of social power." E. Digby Baltzell

GLOBAL: After the crackdown, the Chinese government required students at all 67 Beijing universities to take part in a one-month political "refresher" program; also, all college graduates were assigned to work one year in the countryside or in a factory.

THEN AND NOW: "Is big business, big labor, or big government the biggest threat to the nation's future?" Percent answering "big government": *1954*, 16%; *1965*, 35%; *1985*, 50%; *1995*, 67%. (Opinion Research Corp.; Roper Center)

Q: "The number employed in government must forever be very small [because] the indispensable wants of all are not to be obtained without the continual toil of ninety-nine in a hundred of mankind." John Adam (1789)

Although some totalitarian governments claim to represent the will of the people, most seek to bend people to the will of the government. As the term itself implies, such governments represent *total* concentrations of power and prohibit organized opposition of any kind. Denying the populace the right to assemble for political purposes and controlling access to information, these governments thrive in an environment of fear and social atomization. The former Soviet Union, for example, denied most citizens telephone directories, copying equipment, fax machines, and even accurate city maps.

Socialization in totalitarian societies is intensely political, seeking not just outward compliance but inward commitment to the system. In North Korea, pictures of leaders and political messages over loudspeakers are familiar elements of public life that remind citizens that they owe total allegiance to the state. Government-controlled schools and mass media present only official versions of events.

Government indoctrination is especially stringent whenever political opposition surfaces in a totalitarian society. In the aftermath of the 1989 prodemocracy movement in the People's Republic of China, for example, officials demanded that citizens report all "unpatriotic" people—even members of their own families. Further, Chinese leaders subjected all students at Beijing universities to political "refresher" courses.

Totalitarian governments span the political spectrum from the far right (including Nazi Germany) to the far left (North Korea). Many people in the United States view socialist societies as totalitarian by definition because of their extensive government regulation of the economy. Yet socialist economic programs do not necessarily generate a totalitarian political climate. Limited economic socialism—as it exists in Sweden, for example—appears consistent with (and may even enhance) political democracy. Then, too, some societies with capitalist economies (Chile and South Africa, for example) have exercised totalitarian control over the lives of at least most of their citizens (Arendt, 1958; Kornhauser, 1959; Friedrich & Brzezinski, 1965; Nisbet, 1966; Goldfarb, 1989).

A Global Political System?

Chapter 15 ("The Economy and Work") pointed to the emergence of a global economy, meaning that more and more products and services routinely cross national boundaries. In part, the global economy reflects the expanding operations of multinational corporations; it also stems from the Information Revolution that has drawn together the various regions of the world.

Has there been a parallel development of a global political system? On one level, the answer is no. Although most of the world's economic activity now involves more than one nation, the planet remains divided into nation-states, just as it has been for centuries. The United Nations (founded in 1945) might seem like a step toward global government, but it has played a limited role in global politics up to this point.

On another level, however, politics has become a global process. In the minds of some analysts, multinational corporations represent a new political order, since they have enormous power to shape social life throughout the world. From this point of view, politics is dissolving into business as corporations grow larger than governments. As one multinational leader asserted, "We are not without cunning. We shall not make Britain's mistake. Too wise to govern the world, we shall simply own it" (quoted in Vaughan, 1978:20).

Then, too, the Information Revolution has pulled even national politics onto the world stage. Hours before the Chinese government sent troops to Tiananmen Square to crush the 1989 prodemocracy movement, officials "unplugged" the satellite transmitting systems of news agencies in an effort to keep the world from watching as events unfolded that day. Despite their efforts, news of the massacre was flashed around the world minutes after it began via the fax machines in universities and private homes. In short, just as individual nations can no longer control their own economies, so no national government can fully manage the political events that occur within its borders.

POLITICS IN THE UNITED STATES

After winning a war against Great Britain to gain political independence, the United States replaced the British monarchy with a democratic political system. Our nation's commitment to democratic principles has persisted through two centuries, shaped by a distinctive history, economy, and cultural heritage.

U.S. Culture and the Growth of Government

Our cultural emphasis on individualism is written into the Bill of Rights, the first ten amendments to the U.S. Constitution, which guarantees freedom from undue government interference. This cultural heritage

Q: "Just be glad you're not getting all the government you're paying for." Will Rogers
THEN AND NOW: Federal spending: *1960*, $92.2 billion; *1995*, $1.54 trillion (controlled for inflation, a threefold increase). Federal debt: *1960*, $290.5 billion; *1995*, 5.0 trillion (also a threefold increase, controlled for inflation). Federal tax collections from individuals: *1960*, $40.7 billion; *1995*, $588.5 billion (a threefold rise controlled for inflation).
THEN AND NOW: How long during an eight-hour work day one labors to pay taxes: *1929*, :52 (52 minutes); *1940*, 1:29; *1950*, 2:02; *1960*, 2:20; *1970*, 2:32; *1980*, 2:40; *1994*, 2:45. (Tax Foundation, Washington, D.C., 1995.) Tax Freedom Day in 1929 was February 9; in 1994 it was May 5.

is a key reason that many people in the United States support the sentiment of nineteenth-century poet and essayist Ralph Waldo Emerson: "The government that governs best is the government that governs least."

Principles aside, hardly any of us would do away with government entirely because almost everyone thinks it is necessary for some purposes, including securing national defense, operating a system of schools, and maintaining public law and order. Moreover, the government has grown into a vast and complex system of programs and agencies—collectively termed the *welfare state*—that meets some of the needs of those not well served by our capitalist economic system.

In fact, as the United States has become larger, government has expanded even faster, from a federal budget of a mere $4.5 million in 1789 to about $1.5 trillion in 1995. During the first year of our nation's life, the federal government spent just $1.50 for every person in the country; today, per capita federal spending tops $6,000. Government has become so extensive—and expensive—that even our leaders cannot comprehend its scope. The late senator Everett Dirksen is said to have quipped to his colleagues in Congress, "A billion here, a billion there, and pretty soon you're talking about real money."

In terms of bureaucracy, from one government employee serving every eighteen hundred citizens at the nation's founding, today we have one official for every sixteen citizens, counting government at all levels (U.S. Bureau of the Census, 1995). This amounts to almost 20 million workers, a number that now exceeds the total employment in manufacturing. Government workers perform a host of jobs, from managing schools, monitoring civil rights, and setting safety standards for the workplace, to processing student loans and benefits for the elderly, poor people, and veterans. Today, a majority of U.S. adults look to government for at least part of their income (Caplow et al., 1982; Devine, 1985).

As big as U.S. government is, most high-income countries have more expansive welfare states and tax their citizens at higher rates than we do. Figure 16–2 provides a quick comparison.

The Political Spectrum

Political labels—including "conservative," "liberal," and "middle-of-the-roader"—are shorthand for an individual's place on the *political spectrum*. Table 16–1 on page 438 shows how adults in the United States describe themselves in terms of the political spectrum. Slightly more than one-fourth of the respondents fall

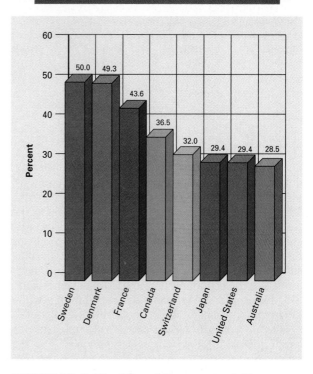

Global Snapshot

FIGURE 16–2 The Size of Government: Tax Revenues as Share of Gross Domestic Product, 1992
Source: U.S. Bureau of the Census (1995).

on the liberal or "left" side, and more than one-third describe themselves as conservative to some degree, placing them on the political "right." A substantial share (35.1 percent) claim to be moderates in the political "middle" (NORC, 1994:82).

One reason for the popularity of the "moderate" label is that many people hold conservative positions on one cluster of issues and liberal views on another (Barone & Ujifusa, 1981; McBroom & Reed, 1990). *Economic issues* focus on economic inequality and the opportunities available for all categories of people. *Social issues* refer to moral concerns about how people live.

Economic Issues

The industrialization of the United States after the Civil War generated enormous wealth, but much of it ended up in the pockets of a small elite. The

SOCIAL SURVEY: "How much confidence do you have in Congress?" (GSS 1994, N = 2,011; *Codebook*, 1994:165)

"A great deal"   7.7%   "Hardly any"   39.2%
"Only some"   50.0%   DK/NR   3.1%

SOCIAL SURVEY: These items show how SES is related to views on economic issues and social issues. (*Student CHIP Social Survey Software*, ABNOMOR1 [GSS 1972–91, N = 20,411] and

EQWLTH1 [GSS 1978–91, N = 10,464]) Undecided Rs omitted.

SES	Pro-choice	Pro-life	Should gov't reduce income differences? "Yes"	"No"
High	58.5%	41.5%	41.4%	58.6%
Middle	44.5%	55.5%	61.3%	38.7%
Low	31.8%	68.2%	75.9%	24.1%

TABLE 16–1 The Political Spectrum: A National Survey, 1994

Survey Question: "We hear a lot of talk these days about liberals and conservatives. I'm going to show you a seven-point scale on which the political views people might hold are arranged from extremely liberal—point 1—to extremely conservative—point 7. Where would you place yourself on this scale?"

1 Extremely liberal	2 Liberal	3 Slightly liberal	4 Middle of the road	5 Slightly conservative	6 Conservative	7 Extremely conservative
2.4 %	11.0 %	12.6 %	35.1 %	15.8 %	16.0 %	3.4 %

[Don't know/no answer 3.8 %]

Source: *General Social Surveys, 1972–1994: Cumulative Codebook* (Chicago: National Opinion Research Center, 1994), p. 82.

Great Depression, which began in 1929, revealed that, despite the undeniable productivity of our capitalist economy, many people had little financial security. The New Deal programs of President Franklin Delano Roosevelt responded to this dilemma by greatly expanding government efforts to promote social welfare. As Roosevelt founded the comtemporary welfare state, he established new programs to regulate many aspects of the economy and provided old-age pensions. Since then, the government has distributed a wider range of financial benefits to more and more people.

Today, both the Democratic and Republican parties—the two major political organizations in the United States—support a large and active federal government, although they disagree about the kinds of activities that government should undertake. Generally speaking, the Democratic party endorses the welfare state, supporting extensive government involvement in the economy; the Republican party, by contrast, seeks to cut back the scope of the welfare state and favors allowing the economy to operate with much less government regulation.

Thus, economic liberals (on the Democratic side of the fence) think that ensuring the health of the economy and an adequate supply of jobs are primary government responsibilities. Economic conservatives (likely to be Republicans) argue that government should interfere as little as possible with the operation of the economy, contending that federal regulations hamper economic productivity.

Social Issues

Social issues are moral matters, ranging from abortion to the death penalty to gay rights and the treatment of minorities. Broadly tolerant of social diversity, social liberals endorse equal rights and opportunities for all categories of people, view abortion as a matter of individual choice, and oppose the death penalty

because, in their view, it does little to discourage crime and has been unfairly applied to minorities.

On the other side of the political spectrum lies the "family values" agenda of social conservatives. Advocates of family values generally support traditional gender roles while opposing public acceptance of gay families and affirmative action and other "special programs" for minorities that, from this point of view, reward people based on group membership rather than individual initiative. Social conservatives condemn abortion and favor the death penalty as a just response to heinous crime.

Overall, the Republican party is more conservative on both economic and social issues while the Democratic party takes a more liberal stand. In practice, then, Republicans celebrate traditional values and individual initiative while Democrats embrace government activism as a means of enhancing social well-being and reducing inequality. Yet each party has conservative and liberal wings so that the difference between a liberal Republican and a conservative Democrat may be insignificant. Further, Republicans as well as Democrats favor big government—as long as it advances their aims. Conservative Republicans (like Ronald Reagan) have sought to expand this country's military strength, for example, while liberal Democrats (like Bill Clinton) have tried to expand the government's "social safety net."

Mixed Positions

Pegging the political views of individuals is difficult because most people do not hold consistent positions on these two kinds of issues. Well-to-do men and women tend to be conservative on economic issues but liberal on social issues (due, in large part, to higher levels of education). Working-class people display the opposite pattern, combining economic liberalism with social conservatism. These women and men, in other words, seek more economic opportunity while taking

NOTE: Generally speaking, Republicans seek to use the power of government to regulate the moral environment, while Democrats enlist government in regulating the economic environment.
NOTE: The policies of the major U.S. parties shift over time. Republicans were the party of civil rights for decades; now Democrats claim that mantle. Democrats supported large deficits; so did Reagan. Democrats endorsed intervention in foreign wars until 1950; now Republicans tend to. Dennis Dedrick
NOTE: Top PAC donations by group: banking and finance, $56 million; energy, $50m; agribusiness, $49m; transportation unions, $46m; insurance, $42m; real estate $41m; media, $38m; government employee unions, $37m; doctors, dentists, nurses, $37m; transportation firms, $30m. (Common Cause, 1995)

pride in conforming to conventional cultural patterns (Nunn, Crocket, & Williams, 1978; Erikson, Luttbeg, & Tedin, 1980; Syzmanski, 1983; Humphries, 1984).

Race and ethnicity modify these patterns slightly. African Americans, with significantly less income overall than white people, are predictably more liberal on economic issues and, since the New Deal era of the 1930s, have overwhelmingly voted Democratic. Yet on many social issues (including reproductive rights for women) disadvantaged African Americans share the views of poor white people and lean in a conservative direction. But when the topic involves race, say, busing school children or increasing government spending to assist minorities, people of African and Hispanic descent are decidedly liberal, even more so than affluent white people (NORC, 1994).

Party Identification

Because so many people hold mixed political attitudes—espousing liberal views on some issues and taking conservative stands on others—party identification is weak in the United States. In this way, our nation differs from European democracies, in which people usually adhere strongly to one political party (Wolfinger, Shapiro, & Greenstein, 1980). Table 16–2 shows the results of a national survey of party identification among U.S. adults (NORC, 1994). Some 47 percent identified themselves—to some degree—as Democrats and about 38 percent favored the Republicans. Twelve percent claimed to be independents, voicing no preference for either major party. Although a large majority have a party preference, most allegiances are weak. Democrat Bill Clinton ousted incumbent Republican George Bush in the 1992 presidential election. Yet in 1994, voters handed Republicans a landslide victory in Congressional elections.

Special-Interest Groups

In 1993, President Clinton proposed reducing the tax deduction for the business lunch. The National Restaurant Association, representing eating and drinking establishments nationwide, mobilized to oppose the idea.

The restaurant industry, as well as associations of elderly people, women's organizations, and environmentalists, each exemplify a **special-interest group,** *a political alliance of people interested in some economic or social issue.* Special-interest groups flourish in societies where political parties are weak, and the United States encompasses a vast array of

TABLE 16–2 Political Party Identification in the United States, 1994

Party Identification	Proportion of Respondents
Democrat	**47.0 %**
Strong Democrat	14.1
Not very strong Democrat	21.5
Independent, close to Democrat	11.4
Republican	**37.5**
Strong Republican	10.7
Not very strong Republican	17.4
Independent, close to Republican	9.4
Independent	**12.3**
Other party, no response	**3.1**

Source: *General Social Surveys, 1972–1994: Cumulative Codebook* (Chicago: National Opinion Research Center, 1994), p. 75.

them. Special-interest groups employ *lobbyists* as their professional advocates in political circles.

One example of a special-interest group concerned with economic issues is the American Federation of Labor–Congress of Industrial Organizations (AFL-CIO), this nation's largest labor union. Special-interest groups that target social issues include the environmentalist Sierra Club, the American Civil Liberties Union, and the National Rifle Association.

Political action committees (PACs) are *organizations formed by special-interest groups, independent of political parties, to pursue political aims by raising and spending money.* Political action committees channel most of their funds directly to candidates likely to support their interests. Since the 1970s, as legal reforms have limited direct contributions to candidates, the number of registered PACs has grown rapidly to more than four thousand (U.S. Federal Election Commission, 1995).

Because of the rising costs of campaigns, most candidates eagerly accept financial contributions from political action committees. In the 1994 congressional election, 24 percent of all funding came from PACs; two-thirds of all Senators seeking reelection received more than $1 million each in PAC contributions. Supporters maintain that PACs represent the interests of a wide spectrum of businesses, unions, and church groups, thereby increasing political participation. Critics counter that organizations supplying cash to politicians expect to be treated favorably in return so that, in effect, PACs seek to buy political influence (Sabato, 1984; Allen & Broyles, 1991; Cook, 1993).

Whether PACs are good or not, they have certainly raised the financial stakes in our political system and

THE MAP: In general, low-turnout regions of the U.S. have a young population. In 1992, another correlate of voter turnout was support for Ross Perot's third-party candidacy. Ironically, then, dissatisfaction with the major parties boosted voter turnout in 1992.

THEN AND NOW: Voter turnouts of 75% to 85% were typical during the 19th century versus about 50% today.

DISCUSS: How do the two major parties court voters? The Republican strategy for winning presidential elections has been to attract affluent people with conservative economic positions (low taxes) while drawing lower-income people with conservative social positions (Willie Horton or Murphy Brown initiatives). Bill Clinton's strength was based on his "New Democrat" image as a moderate on social issues, winning back the so-called "Reagan Democrats."

Seeing Ourselves

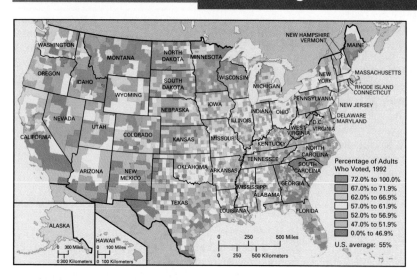

NATIONAL MAP 16–1

Voter Turnout Across the United States

In the 1992 presidential race, just 55 percent of eligible voters went to the polls. The map shows that turnout was high in the North-Central region of the country: In Minnesota, the Dakotas, and Montana, for example, the turnout exceeded 75 percent. By contrast, turnout is low in South Carolina, Georgia, and much of the South. Age is one important correlate of voting, with older people much more likely to vote than young adults. Do you think age plays a part in the regional differences shown here? How?

Source: Lewis, McCracken & Hunt (1994).

---

tipped the scales in favor of incumbents, who have better access to PACs. In the 1994 congressional elections, 60 percent of PAC funds were channeled to incumbents, 91 percent of whom won reelection. Even so, voters turned out scores of incumbents, suggesting that the populace is not held hostage by the greater resources of political incumbents. Moreover, *term limits* is a popular strategy to increase turnover among our elected officials (Theilmann & Wilhite, 1995).

Voter Apathy

In light of the courageous drive of people around the world to gain a greater voice in government—sometimes at the cost of their lives—it is disturbing to note that many people here in the United States seem indifferent to their political rights. The long-term trend is for greater voter *eligibility*—the Fifteenth Amendment, ratified in 1870, enfranchised African-American men; the Nineteenth Amendment extended voting rights to women in 1920; in 1971, the Twenty-Sixth Amendment lowered the voting age to eighteen. However, the share of eligible citizens *who actually vote* has dropped over the course of the last century. The problem of *voter apathy* is also greater in the United States than in most other industrialized democracies (Piven & Cloward, 1988). Even with a slight uptick in turnout, only 55 percent of adults aged eighteen or older claimed to have voted in the 1992

presidential election (U.S. Bureau of the Census, 1993).

Who is and is not likely to vote? Women and men cast ballots in equal numbers. People over sixty-five, however, are twice as likely to vote as young adults. Voting is also more likely among white people (64 percent voted in 1992) than African Americans (59 percent), with Hispanics (32 percent) the least likely of all to vote. Generally speaking, people with the biggest stakes in society are the most likely to go to the polls: homeowners; parents with children at home; people with good jobs, higher incomes, and extensive schooling (Bennett, 1991; Hackey, 1992; Lewis, McCracken, & Hunt, 1994). National Map 16–1 provides a look at the extent of voter apathy across the United States in the 1992 presidential election.

What accounts for nonvoting? First, at any given time, millions of people are sick or disabled; millions more are away from home, having made no arrangement to submit an absentee ballot. Second, many people forget to reregister after moving to a new neighborhood. Third, registration and voting depend on the ability to read and write, which discourages the tens of millions of U.S. adults who have limited literacy skills.

But the heart of voter apathy, as conservatives see it, is *indifference* to politics. Most people who do not vote, they assert, are content with life in the United States. Liberals, and especially political radicals, counter that most nonvoters are so deeply dissatisfied

Q: "No one ever went broke underestimating the intelligence of the American voter." H. L. Mencken
DISCUSS: Does the strength of incumbency run counter to our democratic principles? Indeed, over the last decade or so, members of Congress have been almost as secure in their jobs as members of Britain's House of Lords—a post nobles hold until their death. This inconsistency is surely one reason that the electorates in many

states have now endorsed term limits for their elected officials.
SOCIAL SURVEY: "How much influence do you think people like you have over local government decisions?" (GSS 1987, N = 1,466; Codebook, 1994:313)

"A lot"	14.0%	"None at all"	14.5%
"A moderate amount"	33.8%	DK/NR	2.1%
"A little"	35.7%		

with society that they doubt elections will make any real difference. Thus, from this opposing perspective, voter apathy signifies political *alienation*. Because we know that disadvantaged and powerless people are the least likely to vote, the second explanation is probably closer to the truth.

A final possibility is that apathy stems from our two parties having so much in common. Apathy, in other words, means that people want more of a choice. This insight squares with the fact that many nonvoters were motivated in 1992 to vote for third-party candidate Ross Perot. Perhaps, if parties offered a wider spectrum of political opinion—as they do in European countries—our population would have more reason to vote (Zipp & Smith, 1982; Zipp, 1985; Piven & Cloward, 1988; Lewis, McCracken, & Hunt, 1994).

THEORETICAL ANALYSIS OF POWER IN SOCIETY

Sociologists and political scientists have long debated how power is distributed in the United States. Power is among the most difficult topics of scientific research because decision making is complex and often occurs behind closed doors. Moreover, as Plato recognized more than two thousand years ago, theories about power are difficult to separate from the beliefs and interests of social thinkers themselves. From this mix of facts and values, two competing models of power in the United States have emerged.

The Pluralist Model

Formally, the **pluralist model** is *an analysis of politics that views power as dispersed among many competing interest groups*. This approach is closely tied to structural-functional theory.

Pluralists claim, first, that politics is an arena of negotiation. With limited resources, no organization can expect to realize all its goals. Organizations, therefore, operate as *veto groups*, achieving some success but mostly keeping opponents from reaching all their goals. The political process, then, relies heavily on negotiating alliances and compromises that bridge differences among numerous interest groups and, in the process, produces policies that generate broad-based support. In short, pluralists believe that power is widely dispersed throughout society, and that the political system takes account of all constituencies.

A second pluralist assertion holds that power has many sources—including wealth, political office, social

The power of money has become clear in recent national elections. Steve Forbes, who inherited a publishing empire from his father, ran hard in the 1996 Republican primary, supported by some $25 million of his own money. Despite no experience as an elected official, Forbes managed to win seventy-three convention delegates—at the steep price of $350,000 apiece.

prestige, personal charisma, and organizational clout. Only in exceptional cases do all these sources of power fall into the same hands. Here, again, the conclusion is that power is widely diffused (Dahl, 1961, 1982).

Research Results

Supporting the pluralist model, Nelson Polsby (1959) found that in New Haven, Connecticut, key decisions on various issues—including urban renewal, the nomination of political candidates, and the operation of the schools—were made by different groups. Polsby also noted that few of the upper-class families listed in New Haven's *Social Register* were also economic leaders. Thus, Polsby concluded, no one segment of society rules all the others.

Robert Dahl (1961) investigated New Haven's history and found that, over time, power had become more and more dispersed. Dahl echoed Polsby's judgments, concluding that "no one, and certainly no group of more than a few individuals, is entirely lacking in [power]" (1961:228).

RESOURCE: An excerpt from C. Wright Mills's *The Power Elite* is among the classics included in the Macionis and Benokraitis reader, *Seeing Ourselves*.
NOTE: A more traditionally Marxist view of politics argues that elites need not circulate through the three sectors as Mills claims; the power of the capitalists is sufficient to ensure that politicians serve their interests.

Q: "The executive of the modern state is but a committee for managing the common affairs of the whole bourgeoisie." Marx and Engels
Q: "We can have democracy in this country, or we can have wealth in a few hands, but we can't have both." Justice Louis D. Brandeis
NOTE: The concept of a "military-industrial complex" was used by President Dwight D. Eisenhower in his farewell speech in 1960.

TABLE 16–3 The Pluralist and Power-Elite Models: A Comparison

	Pluralist Model	Power-Elite Model
How is power distributed in the United States?	Dispersed.	Concentrated.
How many centers of power are there?	Many, each with a limited scope.	Few, interconnected, with broad control over society.
How do centers of power relate to one another?	They represent different political interests and thus provide checks on one another.	They represent the same political interests and face little opposition.
What is the relationship between power and the system of social stratification?	Some people have more power than others, but even minorities can organize to gain power. Wealth, social prestige, and political office rarely overlap.	Most people have little power, and the upper class dominates society. Wealth, social prestige, and political office commonly overlap.
What is the importance of voting?	Voting provides the public as a whole with a political voice.	Voting involves choosing between alternatives acceptable to elites.
What, then, is the most accurate description of the U.S. political system?	A pluralist democracy.	An oligarchy—rule by the wealthy few.

The pluralist model implies that the United States is reasonably democratic, granting at least some power to everyone. Pluralists assert that not even the most influential people always get their way, and even the most disadvantaged are able to band together to ensure that some of their political interests are addressed.

The Power-Elite Model

The **power-elite model** is *an analysis of politics that views power as concentrated among the rich.* This second approach is closely allied with the social-conflict paradigm.

The term *power elite* is a lasting contribution of C. Wright Mills (1956), who argued that the upper class holds the bulk of society's wealth, prestige, and power. The power elite constitutes this country's "super-rich" or, in Marxist terms, the capitalists who own and control the lion's share of the economy. These families, broadly linked through business dealings as well as marriage, are able to turn the national agenda toward their own interests.

The power elite, claimed Mills, historically has dominated the three major sectors of U.S. society—the economy, the government, and the military. Elites circulate from one sector to another, consolidating their power as they go. Alexander Haig, for example, has held top positions in private business, served as White House chief of staff under Richard Nixon, was secretary of state under Ronald Reagan, made a bid

for the White House in 1988 as a presidential candidate, and is a retired army general. Haig is far from the exception: A majority of national political leaders enter public life from powerful and highly paid positions—ten of thirteen members of the Clinton cabinet are reputed to be millionaires—and most return to the corporate world later on.

Power-elite theorists challenge claims that the United States is a political democracy; the concentration of wealth and power, they maintain, is simply too great for the average person's voice to be heard. Rejecting pluralist assertions that various centers of power serve as checks and balances on one another, the power-elite model contends that those at the top encounter no real opposition.

Research Results

Over more than fifty years, social scientists have conducted research that helps us evaluate these opposing views of government. Supporting the power-elite position, Robert Lynd and Helen Lynd (1937) studied Muncie, Indiana (which they called "Middletown," to indicate that it was a typical city). They documented the fortune amassed by a single family—the Balls—from their business manufacturing glass canning jars, and showed how the Ball family dominated many dimensions of the city's life. If anyone doubted the Balls' prominence, the Lynds explained, there was no need to look further than the local bank, a university, a

DISCUSS: Is Congress a club for the rich? One in 6 members of Congress (28 of 100 Senators and 50 of 435 members of the House) is a millionaire, compared to 1 out of 200 people in the general population. The richest member in 1994 was Senator Amory Houghton (R - N.Y.) who headed the Corning Glass Works founded by his great-grandfather. The top six Congressional members in wealth include four democrats and two republicans, five men and one woman (Dianne Feinstein, D-Calif.). In the first 3 months of 1994, 45 members of the House spent at least $50,000 of their own money to promote their reelection. The trend is for more rich people to enter Congress because of rising costs of media campaigns.

NOTE: The word "radical" is derived from the Latin meaning "of the root" (a radish is also a root). Thus, radical politics seeks not reform but a change in the system itself.

hospital, and a department store, which all bear the family name. In Muncie, according to the Lynds, the power elite more or less boiled down to a single family.

Floyd Hunter's (1963) study of Atlanta, Georgia, provided further support for the power-elite model. Atlanta, concluded Hunter, had no one dominant family; but there were no more than about forty people who held all the top positions in the city's businesses and controlled the city's politics.

Critical evaluation.   While these two models of power, summarized in Table 16–3, paint quite different pictures of U.S. politics, some evidence validates each interpretation. Yet reviewing all the research on this issue, we find greater support for the power-elite model. Even Robert Dahl (1982)—one of the strongest adherents of the concept of pluralism—concedes that the marked concentration of wealth, as well as the barriers to equal opportunity faced by minorities, constitute basic flaws in our nation's quest for a truly pluralist democracy.

This conclusion squares with survey results. One recent survey asked citizens directly whose interests they think their government serves. As shown in Figure 16–3, people in the United States favor the power-elite position, as their counterparts do in most other countries.

Do these results mean that the pluralist model is entirely wrong? No, but they do suggest that our political system is not as democratic as most people think it is. The universal right to vote is a pluralist achievement, as is the right to form associations to pursue political ends. Even so, major political candidates usually support only those positions acceptable to the most powerful segments of society (Bachrach & Baratz, 1970).

POWER BEYOND THE RULES

Politics is always a matter of disagreement about goals and the means to achieve them. Yet a political system tries to resolve controversy within a system of rules. The foundation of the U.S. political system is the Constitution and its twenty-seven amendments. Countless other regulations guide each political official from the president to the county tax assessor. But political activity sometimes exceeds—or tries to do away with—established practices.

Revolution

Political revolution is *the overthrow of one political system in order to establish another.* In contrast to

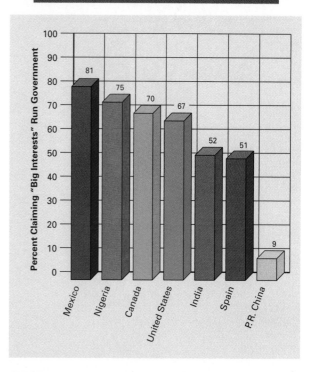

Global Snapshot

FIGURE 16–3 Who Runs the Government?
Survey Question: "Generally speaking, would you say this country is run by a few big interests looking out for themselves, or it is run for the benefit of all the people?"
Source: World Values Survey (1994).

reform, which involves change *within* a system and rarely escalates into violence, revolution implies change *of the system itself*, sometimes sparking violent action. While the revolutions throughout Eastern Europe beginning in 1989 peacefully overthrew communist regimes in numerous countries, fighting in Romania ended thousands of lives.

No type of political system is immune to revolution; nor does revolution invariably produce any one kind of government. The Revolutionary War transformed colonial rule by the British monarchy into democratic government. French revolutionaries in 1789 also overthrew a monarch, only to set the stage for the return of monarchy in the person of Napoleon. In 1917, the Russian Revolution replaced monarchy with a socialist government built on the ideas of Karl Marx. In 1992, the Soviet Union formally came to an

NOTE: Stohl and Lopez (1984) differentiate among three related concepts. *Oppression* is denying some category of people social and economic rights and privileges. *Repression* is more pronounced, coercing one's perceived opponents in order to weaken them. *Terrorism* is more intense still, using violence to force compliance.

Q: "Terrorist? Who says that? George Washington was called a terrorist by the British." Yasir Arafat

GLOBAL: Terrorist acts directed against citizens of the U.S. declined (as did terrorism in general) after 1988.

GLOBAL: There were 177 deaths worldwide from terrorist actions in 1994. Bombs were the most commonly used weapon. Iran, Libya, and Iraq are the countries most often implicated in terrorist incidents, according to the U.S. State Department. (Response to telephone query, 1996)

Because of highly publicized acts of violence against U.S. citizens by Middle Eastern people in recent years, some members of our society tend to link Islam with terrorism. More correctly, however, this religion (like Christianity) seeks harmony and justice. Officials in Egypt have countered a recent wave of terrorism by a few religious extremists by reminding citizens (and outsiders) of their religious responsibility to promote peace.

end, as economic pressures propelled the Russian Federation toward a market system and greater political democracy.

Despite their striking variety, revolutions share a number of traits, according to political analysts (Tocqueville, 1955, orig. 1856; also Davies, 1962; Brinton, 1965; Skocpol, 1979; Lewis, 1984; Tilly, 1986).

1. **Rising expectations.** Although common sense would dictate that revolution is more likely when people are grossly deprived, history shows that revolution generally occurs when people's lives are improving. Rising expectations, rather than bitter resignation, fuel revolutionary fervor.

2. **Unresponsive government.** Revolutionary zeal gains strength to the extent that a government is unwilling or unable to reform, especially when demands for change are made by large numbers of people or powerful segments of society.

3. **Radical leadership by intellectuals.** The English philosopher Thomas Hobbes (1588–1679) observed that political rebellion is often centered in universities. During the 1960s in the United States, students were at the forefront of much of the political unrest that marked that tumultuous decade. Students also played a key role in China's recent prodemocracy movement, as they did in the toppling of socialist governments in Eastern Europe.

4. **Establishing a new legitimacy.** The overthrow of a political system rarely comes easily, but it is more difficult still to ensure a revolution's long-term success. Some revolutionary drives are unified merely by hatred of the past regime and fall victim to internal division once new leaders are installed. Revolutionary movements must also guard against counterrevolutionary drives spearheaded by past leaders; oftentimes, revolutionaries ruthlessly dispose of these former leaders.

Scientific analysis cannot pronounce the effects of revolution as good or bad. The full consequences of such an upheaval depend on one's values and, in any case, take many years to shake out. For example, in the wake of recent revolution, the future of the former Soviet Union remains unsettled.

Terrorism

The recent bombing of the Oklahoma City federal building, described in the opening of this chapter, brought home to the entire nation the deadly nature of **terrorism**, *violence or the threat of violence employed by an individual or a group as a political strategy.* Like revolution, terrorism is a political act beyond the rules of established political systems. Paul Johnson (1981) offers four insights about terrorism.

First, explains Johnson, terrorists try to cast violence as a legitimate political tactic, even though virtually every society condemns such acts. Terrorists also bypass (or are excluded from) established channels of political negotiation. Terror is thus a weak organization's

NOTE: The extreme case of reform is the overthrow of one leader by another—a *coup d'état* (in French, literally "stroke concerning the state"), which involves a basic change in leadership.

NOTE: The U.S. State Department's definition of terrorism: "Premeditated, politically motivated violence perpetrated against noncombatant targets by subnational groups or clandestine state agents, normally intended to influence an audience."

Q: "Since all political systems were created by [people], it follows that [people] can also change them." Peter Berger (1963:128)

Q: "A fanatic is one who can't change his mind and won't change the subject." Winston Churchill

Q:"Politics are almost as exciting as war, and even more dangerous. In war, you can die once; but in politics, many times." Winston Churchill

strategy to harm a stronger foe. For example, the people who held U.S. hostages in the Middle East until 1991 may have been morally wrong to do so, but they succeeded in directing the world's attention to that region of the globe.

Second, Johnson continues, terrorism is a tactic employed not only by groups but also by governments against their own people. **State terrorism** refers to *the use of violence, generally without support of law, against individuals or groups by a government or its agents.* While contrary to democratic political principles, state terrorism figures prominently in authoritarian and totalitarian societies, which survive by inciting fear and intimidation. The left-wing Stalinist regime in the Soviet Union and the right-wing Nazi regime in Germany each routinely employed terror against their own citizens. More recently, Saddam Hussein has ruled Iraq in the same manner.

Third, although democratic societies reject terrorism in principle, democracies are especially vulnerable to terrorists because they afford extensive civil liberties to their people and have minimal police networks. This susceptibility helps to explain the tendency of democratic governments to suspend civil liberties if officials perceive themselves to be under attack. After the Japanese attack on Pearl Harbor at the outset of World War II, the U.S. government feared that Japanese Americans might engage in espionage or terrorism and responded by imprisoning one hundred thousand Japanese-American citizens for the duration of the war.

Generally speaking, citizens of the United States have been the targets of about one in four terrorist incidents worldwide (Jenkins, 1990). Hostage taking and outright killing provoke widespread anger, but devising an effective response to such acts poses several thorny problems. Because most terrorist groups are shadowy organizations with no formal connection to any established state, targeting reprisals may be impossible. Yet, terrorism expert Brian Jenkins warns, the failure to respond "encourages other terrorist groups, who begin to realize that this can be a pretty cheap way to wage war on the United States" (quoted in Whitaker, 1985:29). Then, too, a forcible military reaction to terrorism may broaden the scope of violence, increasing the risk of confrontation with other governments.

Fourth, and finally, terrorism is always a matter of definitions. Governments claim the right to maintain order, even by force, and may brand opponents who use violence as "terrorists." Similarly, political differences may explain why one person's "terrorist" is another's "freedom fighter."

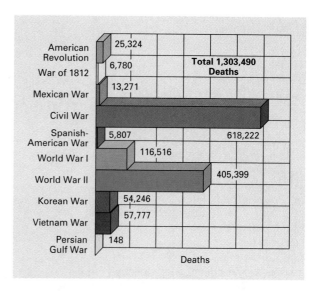

FIGURE 16–4 Deaths of Americans in Ten U.S. Wars

Sources: Compiled from various sources by Maris A. Vinovskis (1989) and the author.

WAR AND PEACE

Perhaps the most critical political issue is **war**, *armed conflict among the people of various societies, directed by their governments.* War is as old as humanity, of course, but the awesome destructiveness of today's nuclear arsenals lends new urgency to understanding international confrontations. Thus, most scholarly investigation of war has the aim of promoting **peace**, *a state of international relations devoid of violence.* Peace implies the absence of war, although not necessarily the lack of all political conflict.

Many people think of war as extraordinary, yet it is peace that is actually rare, existing worldwide only for brief periods during this century. Our nation's short history includes participation in ten large-scale wars, identified in Figure 16–4, which together resulted in the deaths of more than 1.3 million U.S. men and women and caused injury to many times that number. Thousands more died in "undeclared wars" and limited military actions, in countries from the Dominican Republic to Lebanon, Grenada, and Panama.

The Causes of War

The frequency of war in human affairs might imply that there is something natural about armed confrontation. Members of every culture embrace certain

Q: "I am the first to admit that a war is waged in pursuance of political aims." Dwight D. Eisenhower
NOTE: The word "assassin" has the same root in Arabic as the word "hashish." This is because would-be assailants sometimes coaxed one of their numbers to violent action by visions stimulated by the drug.

Q: "I would remind you that extremism in the defense of liberty is no vice . . . and moderation in the pursuit of justice is no virtue." Barry Goldwater
Q: "In the Third World, where one child in ten dies before the age of five, there are six times as many soldiers as there are physicians." Ruth Leger Sivard (1993:6)

GLOBAL SOCIOLOGY

Violence Beyond the Rules:
A Report From the Former Yugoslavia

Former Yugoslavia

War is violent, but it also has rules. Many of the current norms of warfare emerged from the ashes of World War II, when the victorious Allies, including the United States, brought to trial German and Japanese military officials for war crimes. Subsequently, the United Nations has added to the broad principles of fair play in war that have become known as the "Geneva Conventions" (the first of which date back to 1864).

One of the most important principles of the rules of war is that, whatever violence soldiers inflict upon each other, they cannot imprison, torture, rape, or murder civilians; nor can they deliberately destroy civilian property or wantonly bomb or shell cities to foster widespread terror. Even so, a growing body of evidence reveals that all these crimes have occurred as part of the protracted and bloody civil war in the former Yugoslavia. According to U.S. officials, Serbs, Croats, and Muslims have all committed war crimes—tens of thousands of deaths, rapes,

and serious injuries plus an incalculable loss of property. Late in 1993,

Civil wars, such as the conflict in the former Yugoslavia, are among the most tragic forms of bloodshed because a large proportion of casualties are not soldiers but civilians who find themselves in harm's way. Dozens of people died on this street in Sarajevo as mortar rounds fired from the mountains surrounding the city rained down on men, women, and children who were going about their daily lives.

therefore, a United Nations tribunal convened in the Netherlands to assess the evidence and consider possible responses.

After World War II, the Allies successfully prosecuted (and, in several cases, executed) German officers for their crimes against humanity based on evidence culled from extensive Nazi records. This time around, however, the task of punishing offenders will be far more difficult. For one thing, there appear to be no written records of the Balkan conflict; for another, United Nations officials fear that arrests may upset the delicate diplomatic efforts at bringing peace to the region.

Even so, since beginning their investigations in 1993, the United Nations has indicted more than fifty military officers on all sides of the conflict for war crimes. But many observers suspect that—despite a staggering toll in civilian deaths—no one may ever be convicted.

Sources: Adapted from Nelan (1993) and various news reports.

symbols and principles—such as patriotism and freedom—to the point that they are willing to fight to defend (or extend) them. But while many animals are naturally aggressive, research provides no basis for concluding that human beings inevitably wage war under any particular circumstances. Indeed, governments around the world have to use considerable coercion to enlist the support of their people for wars (Lorenz, 1966; Montagu, 1976).

Like all forms of social behavior, warfare is a product of *society* that varies in purpose and intensity from culture to culture. The Semai of Malaysia, among the most peace-loving of the world's people, rarely resort to violence. By contrast, the Yąnomamö, described in Chapter 3 ("Culture"), are quick to wage war with others.

If society holds the key to war or peace, under what circumstances *do* humans engage in warfare?

GLOBAL: From data collected by the U.S. Arms Control and Disarmament Agency, Kuwait has the highest per capita spending on the military at $19,940. Other nations: Saudi Arabia, $2,150; United Arab Emirates, $2,050; United States, $1,110; Israel, $1,100; former Soviet Union, $887; France, $744; Mexico, $13.

Q: "The arms race is not preordained and part of some inevitable course of history. We can make history." Ronald Reagan

GLOBAL: Nations around the world spend an average of 3.5% of GDP on the military; this percentage is about the same for industrial and nonindustrial nations, although the absolute amounts vary, of course.

Q: "The problem with defense spending is to figure out how far you should go without destroying from within what you are trying to defend from without." Dwight D. Eisenhower

In the post–cold war era, tensions between the United States and the former Soviet Union have declined. Even so, the prospects for world peace are hampered by dozens of regional conflicts that persist around the globe. The recent ethnic conflict in the African nation of Rwanda led to tens of thousands of deaths and forced many times this number to become refugees.

Quincy Wright (1987) identifies five factors that promote war.

1. **Perceived threats.** Societies mobilize in response to a perceived threat to their people, territory, or culture. The United States defined Iraq's invasion of Kuwait in 1990 as an immediate threat to national security and subsequently evicted Iraq using military force; by contrast, our government has not defined the ethnic turmoil in the former Yugoslavia in these terms, and the U.S. military presence there has been more limited.

2. **Social problems.** Internal problems that generate widespread frustration may prompt a society's leaders to become aggressive toward others. In this way, societies "construct" enemies as a form of scapegoating. Sluggish economic development in the People's Republic of China, for example, periodically touched off that nation's hostility toward Vietnam, Tibet, and the former Soviet Union.

3. **Political objectives.** Leaders sometimes settle on war as a desirable political strategy. Poor nations, such as Vietnam, have fought wars to end foreign domination. For powerful countries like the United States, a periodic "show of force" (such as the recent deployment of troops in Somalia and Haiti) may enhance global political stature.

4. **Moral objectives.** Rarely do nations claim to fight merely to increase their wealth and power. Leaders infuse military campaigns with moral urgency, rallying people around religious values or secular visions of "freedom." Although few doubted that the 1991 Persian Gulf War was largely about *oil*, U.S. strategists portrayed the mission as a drive to halt a Hitler-like Saddam Hussein.

5. **The absence of alternatives.** A fifth factor promoting war is the absence of alternatives. Article 1 of the United Nations charter defines that organization's task as "maintaining international peace." Despite some notable successes, however, its ability to resolve tensions among self-interested societies has been limited.

In short, war is rooted in social dynamics—on a national and international level. Moreover, even combat has its own system of rules, the violation of which can lead to charges of *war crimes*. The box takes a closer look.

The Costs and Causes of Militarism

The costs of armed conflicts extend far beyond battlefield casualties. Together, the world's nations spend some $5 trillion annually for military purposes. Such expenditures, of course, divert resources from the desperate struggle for survival by millions of poor people throughout the world. Moreover, a large proportion of the world's top scientists concentrate on military research; this resource, too, is siphoned away from other work that might benefit humanity.

In recent years, defense has been the largest single expenditure of the U.S. government, accounting for

SOCIAL SURVEY: "How much confidence do you have in the U.S. military?" (GSS 1994, N = 2,011; *Codebook*, 1994:165)

"A great deal"   36.6%   "Hardly any"   12.2%
"Only some"   48.3%   DK/NR   2.8%

Q: "True individual freedom cannot exist without economic security." Franklin Delano Roosevelt (1944)

RESOURCE: Jack Mendelsohn's article "Arms Control and the New World Order" is included in the Macionis and Benokraitis reader, *Seeing Ourselves*.

Q: "When we discuss national security, we tend too often to give it a military label. It is, in fact, much broader than military power and much more complex. There can be no security without social betterment." Hubert H. Humphrey

Although the two nuclear superpowers—the United States and the Russian Federation—have reduced their arsenals in recent years, global security is threatened by nuclear proliferation. Early in the next century, perhaps fifty nations—many engaged in regional conflicts—will have nuclear weapons.

18 percent of all federal spending, or $272 billion in 1995. This huge expenditure—amounting to about $1,042 for every man, woman, and child in the country—has been prompted by the *arms race*, a mutually reinforcing escalation of military might between the United States and the former Soviet Union.

The United States became a superpower as we emerged victorious from World War II with newly developed nuclear weapons. The atomic bomb was first used in war by U.S. forces to crush Japan in 1945. But the Soviet Union countered by exploding a nuclear bomb of its own in 1949, unleashing the "cold war," by which leaders of each superpower became convinced that their counterparts were committed to military superiority. Ironically, for the next forty years, both sides pursued a policy of escalating military expenditures that neither nation wanted nor could afford.

With the collapse of the Soviet Union in 1992, much of the cold war dissipated. Yet U.S. military expenditures remain high. Some analysts have argued that, all along, the U.S. economy has relied on militarism to generate corporate profits (Marullo, 1987). This approach, closely allied to power-elite theory, maintains that the United States is dominated by a **military-industrial complex,** *the close association among the federal government, the military, and defense industries.* The roots of militarism, then, lie not just in external threats to this nation's security; they also grow from within the institutional structures of our own society.

Another reason for persistent militarism in the post–cold war world is regional conflict. Since the collapse of the Soviet Union, for example, localized wars have broken out in Bosnia, Chechnya, and Rwanda, and tensions still run high in a host of other countries, including Ireland, Iraq, and a divided Korea. Even wars of limited scope have the potential to escalate, involving other countries including the United States. And the danger of regional conflicts is growing as more and more nations gain access to nuclear weapons.

Nuclear Weapons

Despite the easing of superpower tensions, the world still contains almost twenty-five thousand nuclear warheads perched on missiles or ready to be carried by aircraft. This arsenal represents destructive power that one can barely imagine: five tons of TNT for every person on the planet. Should even a small fraction of this stockpile be detonated in war, life as we know it would cease on much of the earth. Albert Einstein, whose genius contributed to the development of nuclear weapons, reflected: "The unleashed power of the atom has changed everything *save our modes of thinking,* and we thus drift toward unparalleled catastrophe." In short, nuclear weapons have rendered unrestrained war unthinkable in a world not yet capable of peace.

At present, although Great Britain, France, and the People's Republic of China have a substantial nuclear capability, the vast majority of nuclear weapons are held by the United States and Russia, which have agreed to reduce their stockpiles of nuclear warheads to about one-fourth their present size by 2003. But

Q: "One of the keys to our thinking in New Zealand is that the nuclear weapons of so-called allies are as dangerous as those of so-called enemies." Helen Clark, member of NZ parliament

NOTE: In 1995, the first class of "infowar" officers graduated from the National Defense University in Washington, D.C. All major branches of the military are setting up information war offices.

NOTE: In the world of information war, computer hackers are the new mercenaries. News reports indicated that several Dutch computer specialists proposed to Saddam Hussein that they would disrupt the U.S. military deployment in the Persian Gulf for $1 million, an offer he declined.

Q: "Democracy presumes a dialogue between people and between nations." Olaf Palme

even as this rivalry winds down, the danger of catastrophic war is increasing along with **nuclear proliferation**, *the acquisition of nuclear-weapons technology by more and more nations.* Most experts agree that Israel, India, Pakistan, North Korea, and South Africa already possess some nuclear weapons, and other nations (including Argentina, Brazil, Iraq, and Libya) are in the process of developing them. By the year 2000, as many as fifty nations could have the ability to fight a nuclear war, a fact that underscores the dangers inherent in any regional conflict (Spector, 1988).

Information Warfare

As earlier chapters have explained, the Information Revolution is changing almost every dimension of social life. In the next century, how will computers reshape warfare?

Currently, military strategists envision future conflict played out not with rumbling tanks and screaming aircraft but with electronic "smart bombs" that would greatly reduce an enemy country's ability to transmit information. In such "virtual wars," soldiers seated at workstation monitors would dispatch computer viruses to shut down an aggressor's communication lines, causing telephones to fall silent, air traffic control and railroad switching systems to fail, computer systems to feed phony orders to field officers, and televisions to broadcast "morphed" news bulletins, prompting people to turn against their leaders.

Like the venom of a poisonous snake, the weapons of "information warfare" can quickly paralyze an adversary, perhaps triggering a conventional military engagement. Another, more hopeful, possibility is that new information technology might not just precede conventional fighting but prevent it entirely. Yet so-called "infowar" also poses new dangers, since, presumably, a few highly skilled operators with sophisticated electronic equipment could also wreak havoc on communications in the United States. As one high-ranking military official noted ominously, "We're more vulnerable than any nation on earth" (Waller, 1995).

The Pursuit of Peace

How can the world reduce the dangers of war? Here are brief sketches of several recent approaches to promoting peace.

1. **Deterrence.** The logic of the arms race linked security to a "balance of terror" between the superpowers. Based on the principle of mutually assured destruction (MAD)—meaning that either side launching a first-strike nuclear attack against the other would sustain massive retaliation—the strategy of deterrence has kept the peace for almost fifty years. But it has three flaws. First, it has fueled an exorbitantly expensive arms race. Second, missiles are now capable of delivering their warheads more quickly than when this strategy was first devised, leaving computers with less time to react to an apparent attack and thereby increasing the risks of unintended war. Third, deterrence cannot curb nuclear proliferation, which poses a growing threat to peace.

2. **High-technology defense.** If technology created the weapons, perhaps it can deliver us from the threat of war. This was the idea behind the *strategic defense initiative* (SDI), proposed by the Reagan administration in 1981. SDI is a complex plan for satellites and ground installations to provide a protective shield or umbrella against enemy missiles. In principle, the system would detect enemy missiles soon after launch and destroy them with lasers and particle beams before they could reenter the atmosphere. If perfected, advocates argue, such a "star wars" defense would render nuclear weapons obsolete.

   But critics charge that even years of research costing trillions of dollars would yield at best a leaky umbrella. The collapse of the Soviet Union also calls into question the need for such an extensive and costly defense scheme.

3. **Diplomacy and disarmament.** Some analysts conclude that the best path to peace involves diplomacy rather than technology (Dedrick & Yinger, 1990). Diplomacy has the appeal of enhancing security through reducing rather than building weapons stockpiles.

   But disarmament, too, has limitations. No nation wishes to become vulnerable to attack by cutting its defenses too deeply. Successful diplomacy, then, depends not on "soft" concession making or "hard" demands, but on all sides sharing responsibility for a common problem (Fisher & Ury, 1988).

   While the United States and the former Soviet Union have succeeded in negotiating arms-reduction agreements, the threat from other nations like Libya, North Korea, and Iraq—all of which desire to build nuclear arsenals—remains large.

4. **Resolving underlying conflict.** In light of the continuing threat of global holocaust, reducing the dangers of nuclear war may depend on resolving

NOTE: As the Republicans see it, the Democrats have been "losing touch" with the people since the 1960s, which, they say, explains the steady erosion of public support for Congress from about 70% approval then to about 20% now. Democrats counter that this slide is due to the rise of big money in U.S. politics.

Q: "What is conservatism? Is it not adherence to the old and tried against the new and untried?" Abraham Lincoln

Q: "Refine and enlarge the public views by passing them through the medium of a chosen body of citizens, whose wisdom may best discern the true interest of their country and whose patriotism and love of justice will be least likely to sacrifice it to temporary or partial considerations." James Madison, *Federalist Papers*

Q: "A man who is not a liberal at sixteen has no heart; a man who is not a conservative at sixty has no head." Benjamin Disraeli

Controversy & Debate

Here Comes "On-line" Democracy!

Today's spectacular advances in communications technology open, for the first time, a mind-boggling array of possibilities for direct citizen participation in political decision-making.

So write sociologists Alvin and Heidi Toffler, suggesting that new information technology is about to reverse the trend of increasing voter apathy and open a new democratic age for the United States. Using computer technology, citizens everywhere might participate in "electronic town meetings," pushing a button on a computer keyboard to record support for or opposition to specific proposals. Citizens could be better informed about the workings of government through an expanding television cable system (similar to C-SPAN that now broadcasts Congressional action). Already, radio talk shows keep us abreast of developing issues as we travel by car; and faxes, electronic mail, and computer-generated messages routinely make their way both to and from Congressional offices. In short, we are entering the age of the "wired Congress," witnessing the birth of "on-line democracy."

But does high technology necessarily make for good politics? Not everyone thinks so. In fact, the trend toward on-line democracy itself has become the subject of intense political debate. The push for high-tech politics began with the Republicans' landslide victory in 1994 that gave the GOP control of both houses of Congress for the first time in more than half a century. Defending their more conservative policies, the Republicans claim people across the country are fed up with the liberal, big-government politics that routinely operate "inside the Beltway" (a reference to the interstate that circles our nation's capital). What better way to defeat the government establishment, they reason, than to open up debate to the "real" voice of the nation—the people in communities from Sarasota to Spokane. Moreover, Republicans continue, by shutting out ordinary people over the years, Congress has adopted and sustained a number of unpopular programs. If the people had been asked in the first place, Republicans contend, this country would not have the high levels of immigration, the rigid affirmative-action programs, and the extensive and expensive bureaucracy that plague us today. As the Republicans see it, all were the creations of liberal, self-righteous politicians who rarely venture outside the Beltway.

The Democrats counter by labeling the current efforts to open the political process "hyperdemocracy." Our system of government, they explain, was erected not as a *direct* democracy but a *representative* democracy. That is, we elect officials to lead rather than merely follow the whims of the voters. The great British statesman Edmund Burke (himself a conservative) charged elected officials to do more than press for their constituents' interests; leaders, he continued, owe the people their judgment. In these days of passion-politics, in which would-be leaders often seek to inflame public opinion, some claim that "on-line" democracy would result in impulsively passing dubious laws. In the early 1960s, Democrats point out, the people of the United States surely were too racially prejudiced to have supported the program of civil rights legislation that Congress enacted. But would we have wanted Congress to do otherwise?

Like it or not, everyone agrees that the new information technology will operate in two directions: affording the people a greater voice to speak to government and also allowing elected leaders greater access to the public when they want to present and defend their own thinking. But the question remains: Is *more* democracy *better* democracy?

Continue the debate . . .

1. *Do you think more direct democracy will be helpful or harmful to the political process?*

2. *Do you tend to see leaders who change their views on the issues as "wafflers" or representatives eager to satisfy voters?*

3. *Do you worry that political leaders might use new information technology to manipulate the public?*

Sources: Toffler & Toffler (1993), McConnell (1995), Roberts (1995), and Wright (1995).

underlying conflicts. Even in the post–cold war era, basic differences between the United States and Russia remain. Moreover, militarism also springs from nationalism, ethnic differences, and class inequality that have sparked regional conflicts in Latin America, Africa, Asia, and the Middle East. If peace is rooted in solving international disputes, why do nations around the world currently spend three thousand times as much money on militarism as they do on addressing the causes of conflict (Sivard, 1988)?

LOOKING AHEAD: POLITICS IN THE TWENTY-FIRST CENTURY

Just as economic systems—the focus of the last chapter—are changing, so are political systems. As we look ahead to the next century, several important dilemmas and trends seem likely to command widespread attention.

One vexing problem in the United States is an inconsistency between our democratic ideals and low public participation in politics. Perhaps, as the power-elite model asserts, this nation's concentration of wealth simply constrains the political agenda to a relatively narrow range of options and policies acceptable to elites. The short-term trend, however, is toward higher turnouts at the polls. This trend—should it continue—may widen the range of issues included in our national political debate.

A second transformation noted in this chapter is the expansion of a global political process. The Information Revolution is changing politics just as it is reformulating the economy (although political change seems to be proceeding somewhat more slowly). Communications technology now allows news and political analysis to move instantly from one point in the world to another. This global flow of information should empower individuals, since governments can no longer seal their borders to new ideas. Today anyone with a television or a short-wave radio (not to mention fax machines and other computer-based devices) has access to various sources of political information. The final box asks whether new information technology is likely to enhance—or undermine—our own version of political democracy.

Third, a global reformulation of political thinking is currently under way. One effect of the cold war between the United States and the Soviet Union was to cast political debate in the form of two rigid political alternatives—the West's democratic capitalism and the East's state-centered socialism. Today, in the post–cold war era, the character of political systems is open to far greater discussion, with various ideas about how to integrate the operation of government and the economy. The system of "state capitalism" found in several Asian nations (notably Japan and South Korea) is but one case in point.

Fourth, and finally, we still face the danger of war in many parts of the world. Even as tensions between the United States and the former Soviet Union have been easing, vast stockpiles of weapons remain, and nuclear technology continues to proliferate. Despite the decline of the Russian Federation as a center of power, new superpowers are likely to arise in the century ahead (the People's Republic of China seems a likely candidate), just as surely as regional conflicts will continue to fester. We can only hope that humanity will enlist forces working for peace—including the United Nations, the expanding global economy, more widespread and rapid communication, and a developing sense of political justice—in the effort to devise a nonviolent solution to the age-old problems that provoke war.

SUMMARY

1. Politics is the major social institution by which a society distributes power and organizes decision making. Max Weber explained that there are three ways to transform coercive power into legitimate authority: through tradition, rationally enacted rules and regulations, and the personal charisma of a leader.

2. Traditional authority is common to preindustrial societies; industrial societies, by contrast, legitimize power through bureaucratic organizations and law. Charismatic authority, which arises in every society, sustains itself through routinization into traditional or rational-legal authority.

3. Monarchy is based on traditional authority and is common in preindustrial societies. Although constitutional monarchies persist in some industrial nations, industrialization favors democracy based on rational-legal authority and extensive bureaucracy.

4. Authoritarian political regimes deny popular participation in government. Totalitarian political systems go even further, tightly regulating people's everyday lives.

5. The world remains divided into 191 politically independent nation-states; one dimension of an emerging global political system, however, is the growing wealth and power of multinational corporations.

Additionally, new technology associated with the Information Revolution means that national governments can no longer control the flow of information across national boundaries.

6. The dramatic growth of the government of the United States during the past two centuries goes far beyond mere population increase; it reflects wider government involvement in the economy and all of society.

7. Liberals and conservatives take different positions on economic and social issues. Liberals call for government regulation of the economy and action to ensure economic equality; conservatives believe the government should not interfere in these arenas. Conservatives, however, do support government regulation of moral issues such as abortion, while liberals argue that government should not interfere in matters of conscience.

8. Special-interest groups advance the political aims of specific segments of the population. These groups employ lobbyists and political action committees to influence the political process.

9. Many people in the United States do not readily describe themselves in political terms, nor do they strongly identify with either the Democratic or the Republican party. Furthermore, only 55 percent of those eligible to vote actually voted in the 1992 national elections.

10. The pluralist model holds that political power is widely dispersed in the United States; the power-elite model takes an opposing view, arguing that power is concentrated in the hands of a small, wealthy segment of the population.

11. Revolution radically transforms a political system. Terrorism, another unconventional political tactic, uses violence in pursuit of political goals. States as well as individuals engage in terrorism.

12. War is armed conflict directed by governments. The development and proliferation of nuclear weapons have increased the threat of global catastrophe. Enhancing world peace ultimately depends on resolving the tensions and conflicts that fuel militarism.

KEY CONCEPTS

authoritarianism a political system that denies popular participation in government

authority power that people perceive as legitimate rather than coercive

charismatic authority power legitimized through extraordinary personal abilities that inspire devotion and obedience

democracy a type of political system in which power is exercised by the people as a whole

government formal organizations that direct the political life of a society

military-industrial complex the close association among the federal government, the military, and defense industries

monarchy a type of political system in which a single family rules from generation to generation

nuclear proliferation the acquisition of nuclear-weapons technology by more and more nations

peace a state of international relations devoid of violence

pluralist model an analysis of politics that views power as dispersed among many competing interest groups

political action committee (PAC) an organization formed by a special-interest group, independent of political parties, to pursue political aims by raising and spending money

political revolution the overthrow of one political system in order to establish another

politics the social institution that distributes power, sets a society's agenda, and makes decisions

power the ability to achieve desired ends despite resistance from others

power-elite model an analysis of politics that views power as concentrated among the rich

rational-legal authority (bureaucratic authority) power legitimized by legally enacted rules and regulations

routinization of charisma the transformation of charismatic authority into some combination of traditional and bureaucratic authority

special-interest group a political alliance of people interested in some economic or social issue

state terrorism the use of violence, generally without support of law, against individuals or groups by a government or its agents

terrorism violence or the threat of violence employed by an individual or group as a political strategy

totalitarianism a political system that extensively regulates people's lives

traditional authority power legitimized through respect for long-established cultural patterns

war armed conflict among the people of various societies, directed by their governments

CRITICAL-THINKING QUESTIONS

1. Distinguish authority from mere power. What forms of authority characterize preindustrial and industrial societies? Why does democracy gradually replace monarchy as societies industrialize?

2. How would you describe the attitudes of the U.S. population on the political spectrum? How is class position linked to political opinions?

3. Contrast the pluralist and power-elite models of societal power. Which do you find more convincing?

4. Do you think that the dangers of war in the world are greater or less than in past generations? Why?

SUGGESTED READINGS

Classic Sources

Alexis de Tocqueville. *Democracy in America.* Garden City, N.Y.: Doubleday-Anchor Books, 1969; orig. 1834, 1840.
    This classic analysis of politics and society was written by a brilliant French aristocrat after a journey through the United States in the early 1830s. Many of Tocqueville's insights about this country's political system remain as fresh and valuable today as when he wrote them.

Hannah Arendt. *The Origins of Totalitarianism.* Cleveland: Meridian Books, 1958.
    This classic description of totalitarianism and its rise in the modern world is written by a woman deeply influenced by her captivity in a Nazi death camp during World War II.

Contemporary Sources

Lyman Tower Sargent, ed. *Extremism in America: A Reader.* New York: New York University Press, 1995.
    This collection of essays probes radical political organizations that advocate violence such as the Oklahoma City bombing.

Mary Ann Glendon. *Rights Talk: The Impoverishment of Political Discourse.* New York: The Free Press, 1991.
    Among the questions posed by this provocative book: Should we claim more and more "rights"? What does this focus on the individual do to our sense of political responsibility for others?

Global Sources

Patrick J. Garrity and Steven A. Maaranen, eds. *Nuclear Weapons in the Changing World: Perspectives from Europe, Asia, and North America.* New York: Plenum, 1992.
    This collection of essays by experts examines nuclear-weapons issues from the points of view of nations in various regions of the world.

Cynthia Enloe. *Bananas, Beaches, and Bases: Making Feminist Sense of International Politics.* Berkeley: University of California Press, 1990.
    This feminist analysis of the world political scene maintains that gender is at the center of global power structures.

FRIDA KAHLO,
MY GRANDPARENTS, MY PARENTS,
AND I (FAMILY TREE), 1936

Oil & tempera on metal panel, 12⅛x13⅝"
(30.7x34.5 cm). The Museum of Modern Art, New
York. Gift of Allan Roos, MD, and B. Mathieu Roos.
Photograph © 1996 The Museum of Modern Art, NY.

Family

The Japanese are in debate on "family values." (relatively rare in Japan) or dren (which is extremely rare). The the midst of a national The problem is not divorce unmarried women having chil- Japanese are simply not having children—not enough, at least, to replace adults of childbearing age. Since 1950, in fact, the average number of children born to a Japanese woman during her lifetime has tumbled from almost five to just over one.

This precipitous decline is no indication that the Japanese have lost their love for children. Quite the contrary. Virtually all young Japanese couples claim to want children, and even screaming babies on a bus or train elicit smiles and sympathy from fellow travelers. The reason for the declining birth rate is that Japanese women display unprecedented reluctance to marry. Back in 1970, only 20 percent of Japanese women reaching the age of thirty had yet to wed; today, that share has doubled to 40 percent.

Why the second thoughts about marriage? For one thing, Japanese culture defines motherhood as a full-time responsibility, which precludes a career. Just as important, the typical Japanese husband works long hours—half are away from home at least twelve hours a day. When he is at home, moreover, the typical Japanese man performs almost no housework and spends little time with his children.

To young women in Japan, therefore, marriage commonly amounts to a daily round of housework, doting on youngsters, and shuttling older children to special "cram" schools where they prepare for all-important college entrance examinations. Faced with such prospects, more women are opting to stay single, live with parents, work, and enjoy plenty of free time and spending money (*The Economist*, 1994).

In the United States, too, the state of the family is a hot topic. Indeed, a rising chorus of voices charges that families in the United States are fast becoming an endangered species. And some hard facts back up their case. The U.S. divorce rate has doubled over the past thirty years so that, if the trend holds, almost half of today's marriages will end in divorce. Marital breakdown, coupled with the fact that almost one in four children is born to an unmarried woman, means that half of U.S. children born today will live with a single parent at some time before reaching age eighteen. Not surprisingly, the proportion of U.S. children living in poverty has been rising steadily in recent years.

Taken together, these facts suggest a basic truth: Families in the United States and in other industrial societies are changing dramatically. Not long ago, the cultural ideal of the family consisted of a working husband, a homemaker wife, and their young children. Today, fewer people embrace such a singular vision of the family, and, at any given time, only about one in four U.S. households fits that description.

This chapter highlights important recent changes in family life, and offers some insights to explain these trends. Yet, as we shall also point out, changing family patterns are nothing new to this country. A century ago, for example, concern over the decline of the family swept the nation as the Industrial Revolution propelled men from farms to factories. Today, of course, many of the same concerns surround the rising share of women whose careers draw them away from home. In short, changes in other social institutions, especially the economy, are leaving their mark—for better or worse—on marriage and family life.

NOTE: Some of the changes in our thinking about family life involve a shift from family *form* to family *function*. In other words, rather than defining the family as a single, traditional form, more people (especially sociologists) seem to be saying "If it works like a family, it *is* a family." The Latin root *familia* means simply "a household."

DIVERSITY: Although the extended family is not favored in the United States partly because of the association of kin and dependency, the poor often establish fictional kin out of need (as in Carol Stack's *All Our Kin*). During economic recessions, families become more extended with, for example, more men and women in their twenties and thirties continuing to live with their parents.

THEN AND NOW: Mean size of U.S. household: *1960*, 3.3; *1970*, 3.1; *1980*, 2.8; *1990*, 2.6; *1994*, 2.6; *2000* (est.), 2.4; *2010* (est.), 2.6.

In modern industrial societies, the members of extended families usually pursue their careers independently while living apart from one another. However, various nuclear families may assemble periodically for rituals such as weddings, funerals, and family reunions.

THE FAMILY: BASIC CONCEPTS

The **family** is *a social institution that unites individuals into cooperative groups that oversee the bearing and raising of children.* These social units are, in turn, built on **kinship**, *a social bond, based on blood, marriage, or adoption, that joins individuals into families.* Although all societies contain families, just who is included under the umbrella of kinship has varied through history, and varies today from one culture to another.

During the twentieth century, most members of our society have regarded a **family unit** as *a social group of two or more people, related by blood, marriage, or adoption, who usually live together.* Initially, individuals are born into a family composed of parents and siblings, which is sometimes called the *family of orientation* because this group is central to socialization. In adulthood, people forge a *family of procreation* in order to have or adopt children of their own.

Throughout the world, families form around **marriage**, *a legally sanctioned relationship, involving economic cooperation as well as normative sexual activity and childbearing, that people expect to be enduring.* Embedded in our language is evidence of a cultural belief that marriage alone is the appropriate context for procreation: Traditionally, people have attached the label of *illegitimacy* to children born out of wedlock; moreover, *matrimony*, in Latin, means "the condition of motherhood." This link between childbearing and marriage has weakened, however, as the proportion of children born to single women (noted earlier to be nearing one in four) has increased.

Some people now object to defining as "families" only married couples and children because that implies that everyone should embrace a single standard of moral conduct. Yet many government programs designate benefits only for members of "families" as conventionally defined, excluding unmarried, committed partners—whether heterosexual or homosexual. As more and more people forge nontraditional family ties, many are now thinking of kinship in terms of *families of affinity*, that is, people with or without legal or blood ties who feel they belong together and wish to define themselves as a family.

What does or does not constitute a family, then, is a moral matter that lies at the heart of the contemporary "family values" debate. The Census Bureau, which uses the conventional definition of family, also plays a role in this discussion: Sociologists who rely on Census Bureau data describing "families" must accept this definition.[1] The trend in public opinion as well as in court decisions, however, favors a wider and more inclusive definition of the "family unit."

THE FAMILY: GLOBAL VARIETY

Typically, members of preindustrial societies take a broad view of family ties, recognizing the **extended family** as *a family unit including parents and children, but also other kin.* Extended families are also called *consanguine families*, meaning that they include everyone with "shared blood." Industrialization, which sparks both geographic and social mobility (see Chapter 15, "The Economy and Work"), gives rise to the **nuclear family**, *a family unit composed of one or two parents and their children.* Because it is based on marriage, the nuclear family is also known as the *conjugal family.* Although many members of our society live in extended families, the nuclear family has become the predominant family form in the United States.

In some nations that have expansive social welfare programs, the government has taken over various family responsibilities. As a result, sociologist David Popenoe explains in the box on pages 458–59, Sweden may have the weakest families in the world.

---

[1]According to the Census Bureau, there were 97.1 million U.S. households in 1994, of which 68.5 million (71 percent) were family households. The remaining living units contained single people or unrelated individuals living together. In 1960, 85 percent of all households were families.

DIVERSITY: Statistically speaking, the typical U.S. family is a married couple, both of whom have graduated from high school and are in the labor force, with one child (mean) or no children (mode), living in a (mortgaged) home that they own. At any given point in time, about 25% of all households have a wife, husband, and one or more children, although more than half take this form during the life course; at any given time, about one in ten households comprises a

working man, homemaker woman, and one or more children although, again, about 25% take this form at some point.

NOTE: Illustrating exogamy is the legal prohibition against homosexual marriages; a case of endogamy is the historical prohibition against interracial marriage.

Q: "Happiness is having a large, loving, caring, close-knit family in another city." George Burns

Window on the World

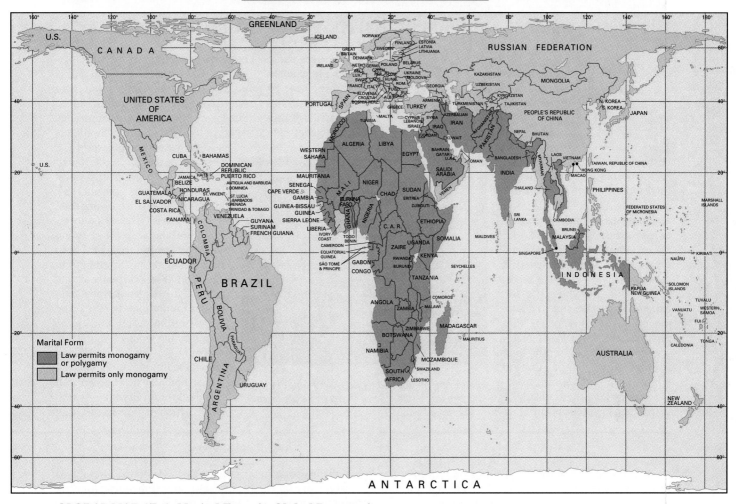

GLOBAL MAP 17–1 Marital Form in Global Perspective

Monogamy is the legally prescribed form of marriage in all industrial societies and throughout the Western Hemisphere. In most African nations, as well as in southern Asia, however, polygamy is permitted by law. In many cases, this practice reflects the historic influence of Islam, a religion that allows a man to have no more than four wives. Even so, most marriages in these traditional societies are monogamous, primarily for financial reasons.

Source: *Peters Atlas of the World* (1990).

Marriage Patterns

Cultural norms, as well as laws, identify people as desirable or unsuitable marriage partners. Some marital norms promote **endogamy**, *marriage between people of the same social category*. Endogamy limits marriage prospects to others of the same age, race, religion, or social class. By contrast, **exogamy** mandates *marriage between people of different social categories*. In rural India, for example, young people are expected to marry someone of the same caste (endogamy), but from a different village (exogamy).

Chapter 17 Family **457**

GLOBAL SOCIOLOGY

The Weakest Families on Earth? A Report From Sweden

Sweden is burdened with few of the social problems that plague the United States. In urban Sweden, there is little of the violent crime, drug abuse, and grinding poverty that has blighted whole regions of our own cities. This Scandinavian nation seems to fulfill the promise of the modern welfare state, with an extensive and professional government bureaucracy that sees to virtually all human needs.

But one drawback of the expanding welfare state, according to David Popenoe, is that Sweden has the weakest families on earth. Because people look to the government—not to spouses—for economic assistance, Swedes are less likely to marry than members of any other

industrialized society. For the same reason, Sweden also has a high share of adults living alone (more than 20 percent, similar to the share in the United States). Moreover, a large proportion of couples live together outside

In Sweden, unmarried women bear half of all children, twice the rate of births by single women in the United States.

of marriage (25 percent versus 6 percent in the United States), and half of all Swedish children (compared to about one in three in the United States) are born to unmarried parents. Average household size in Sweden is also the smallest in the world (2.2 persons versus 2.7 in the United States). Finally, Swedish couples (whether married or not) are more likely to break up than partners in any other country. Popenoe sums up by claiming that the family "has probably become weaker in Sweden than anywhere else—certainly among advanced Western nations. Individual family members are the most autonomous and least bound by the group . . ." (1991:69).

Popenoe contends that a growing culture of individualism and self-fulfillment, coupled with the declining influence of religion, began to erode Swedish

---

Throughout the world, societies pressure people to marry someone of the same social background but of the other sex. The logic of endogamy is simple: People of similar social position pass along their standing to offspring, thereby maintaining traditional social patterns. Exogamy, by contrast, helps to forge useful alliances and promotes cultural diffusion.

In industrial societies today, laws prescribe **monogamy** (from Greek meaning "one union"), *a form of marriage joining two partners*. Our high level of divorce and remarriage, however, suggests that *serial monogamy* is a more accurate description of this nation's marital practice.

Global Map 17–1 , on page 457, shows that while monogamy is the rule throughout the Americas and in Europe, many preindustrial societies—especially in Africa and southern Asia—permit **polygamy** (from Greek meaning "many unions"), *a type of marriage*

uniting three or more people. Polygamy takes two forms. By far the more common is **polygyny** (from the Greek, meaning "many women"), *a type of marriage uniting one male and two or more females*. Islamic societies in Africa and southern Asia, for example, permit men up to four wives. In these societies, however, most families are monogamous all the same because few men have the wealth needed to support several wives and even more children.

Polyandry (from the Greek, meaning "many men" or "many husbands") is *a type of marriage joining one female with two or more males*. This pattern appears only rarely. One example can be seen in Tibet where agriculture is difficult. There, polyandry discourages the division of land into parcels too small to support a family and divides the work of farming among many men. Polyandry has also been linked to female infanticide—the aborting of female fetuses or killing of

NOTE: Of the 68.5 million U.S. families (1994), 41% were married couples without children; 37% were married couples with children; 11% were women heads of households with children; 2% were men heads of household with children; 9% were all other categories. (U.S. Bureau of the Census)

THEN AND NOW: Share of all U.S. adults who are currently married: *1975, 72%; 1994, 62%.*

NOTE: Only 27% of U.S. people aged 15 or older have never been married. Never-married people are typically early in the life course, very rare later on. Among 15-to-24-year-olds, 85% have never married; among those 65 and older, the figure is 4.6%. (U.S. Bureau of the Census)

Q: "They are tremendous aristocrats," cried Henry Adams of the Samoans. "Family is everything!" Quoted in Baltzell (1979:32)

families back in the 1960s. The movement of women into the labor force also plays a part. Sweden has the lowest proportion of women who are homemakers (10 percent versus about 25 percent in the United States) and the highest percentage of women in the labor force (77 percent versus 59 percent in the United States).

But, most important, according to Popenoe, is the expansion of the Swedish welfare state, one of the most far-reaching schemes of its kind. The Swedish government offers citizens a lifetime of services—and high taxes. Swedes can count on the government to give them jobs, sustain their income, deliver and educate their children, provide comprehensive health care, and, when the time comes, pay for their funeral.

Many Swedes supported this welfare program, Popenoe explains, thinking it would *strengthen* families. But with the benefit of hindsight, he concludes, we see that proliferating government programs actually have been *replacing* families. Take the case of child care. The Swedish government operates public child-care centers open to all. As officials see it, this system puts care in the hands of professionals, and makes this service equally accessible regardless of parents' income. At the same time, however, the government offers no subsidy for parents who want to care for children in their own home. In effect, then, government has taken over much of the traditional family function of child rearing.

If this system has solved so many social problems, why should anyone care about the erosion of traditional family life? For two reasons, says Popenoe. First, government can do only at great cost what families used to do for themselves. Recently, Swedes voted to cut back on their burgeoning welfare system because of skyrocketing costs.

Second, can government employees in large child-care centers provide children with the level of love and emotional security they would receive from two parents living as a family? Unlikely, claims Popenoe, noting that small, intimate groups can accomplish some human tasks much better than formal organizations can.

But if the Swedes have gone too far in delegating family responsibilities to government, perhaps we in the United States have not gone far enough. Consider programs allowing new parents time off from work. A Swedish parent may apply for up to eighteen months' leave at 90 percent of his or her salary; in the United States, the 1993 Family and Medical Leave Act allows workers just ninety days—without pay—to care for newborns or sick family members. Should our society try to emulate Sweden? And if we look to government to assist working parents in caring for children, does that strengthen or weaken families?

Sources: Popenoe (1991, 1994); also Herrstrom (1990).

female infants—because a decline in the female population forces men to share women.

Historically, most world societies have permitted more than one marital pattern; even so, most actual marriages have been monogamous (Murdock, 1965). This cultural preference for monogamy reflects two key facts of life: The heavy financial burden of supporting multiple spouses and children as well as the rough numerical parity of the sexes limits the possibility for polygamy.

Residential Patterns

Just as societies regulate mate selection, so they designate where a married couple resides. In preindustrial societies, most newlyweds live with one set of parents, thereby gaining economic assistance and security in the process. Most societies observe a norm of **patrilocality** (Greek for "place of the father"), *a residential pattern by which a married couple lives with or near the husband's family*. But some societies (such as the North American Iroquois) endorse **matrilocality** (meaning "place of the mother"), *a residential pattern by which couples live with or near the wife's family*. Societies that engage in frequent, local warfare tend toward patrilocality since families want their sons close to home to offer protection. Societies that engage in distant warfare present a mixed picture, favoring patrilocality or matrilocality depending on whether sons or daughters have greater economic value (Ember & Ember, 1971, 1991).

Industrial societies show yet another pattern. When finances permit, at least, they favor **neolocality** (Greek meaning "new place"), *a residential pattern by which a married couple lives apart from the parents of both spouses*.

Q: "Despite the profound changes in the nature of the family that have come with the industrialization and urbanization of the past century, today's family remains the basic unit for the protection and rearing of young children, and the center of emotional life. Indeed, its role as the major source of psychological support for its members has, if anything, increased. The family is a 'haven in a heartless world,' an oasis of stable, diffuse and largely unquestioned

love and support." Lenore J. Weitzman (1982:2–3)

NOTE: The incest taboo limits kinship confusion. Rolling Stone Bill Wyman's (age 58) son, Stephen (age 32), announced his intention of marrying the mother (age 45) of his father's ex-wife (age 24). Such a union would make Stephen stepfather to his former stepmother, and Bill step-grandfather to his former wife. Bill would also be his son's son-in-law and the father of his father-in-law!

Patterns of Descent

Descent refers to *the system by which members of a society trace kinship over generations.* Most preindustrial societies trace kinship through only one side of the family—the father or the mother. The more prevalent pattern is **patrilineal descent,** *a system tracing kinship through men.* In a patrilineal system, children are related to others only through their fathers, and fathers typically pass property on to their sons. Patrilineal descent generally characterizes pastoral and agrarian societies, in which men produce the most valued resources. Less common is **matrilineal descent,** *a system tracing kinship through women.* Matrilineal descent, through which mothers pass property to their daughters, is found more frequently in horticultural societies where women are the primary food producers.

Industrial societies with greater gender equality recognize **bilateral descent** ("two-sided descent"), *a system tracing kinship through both men and women.* In this pattern, children recognize as relatives people on both the "father's side" and the "mother's side" of the family.

Patterns of Authority

The predominance of polygyny, patrilocality, and patrilineal descent in the world reflects the universal presence of patriarchy. Without denying that wives and mothers exercise considerable power in every society, as Chapter 13 ("Sex and Gender") explains, no truly matriarchal society has ever existed.

In industrial societies like the United States, more egalitarian family patterns are evolving, especially as increasing numbers of women enter the labor force. However, even here, men are typically heads of households. Parents in the United States also still prefer boys to girls, and typically give children their father's last name.

THEORETICAL ANALYSIS OF THE FAMILY

As in earlier chapters, several theoretical approaches offer a range of insights about the family.

Functions of the Family: Structural-Functional Analysis

The structural-functional paradigm contends that the family performs several vital tasks. From this point of view, the family operates as "the backbone of society."

1. **Socialization.** As explained in Chapter 5 ("Socialization"), the family is the first and most influential setting for socialization. Ideally, parents teach children to be well-integrated and contributing members of society (Parsons & Bales, 1955). Of course, family socialization continues throughout the life cycle. Adults change within marriage, and, as any parent knows, mothers and fathers learn as much from raising their children as their children learn from them.

2. **Regulation of sexual activity.** Every culture regulates sexual activity in the interest of maintaining kinship organization and property rights. One universal regulation is the **incest taboo,** *a cultural norm forbidding sexual relations or marriage between certain kin.* Precisely which kin fall within the incest taboo varies from one culture to another. The matrilineal Navajo, for example, forbid marrying any relative of one's mother. Our bilateral society applies the incest taboo to both sides of the family but limits it to close relatives, including parents, grandparents, siblings, aunts, and uncles. But even brother-sister marriages found approval among the ancient Egyptian, Incan, and Hawaiian nobility (Murdock, 1965).

   Reproduction between close relatives can adversely affect the mental and physical health of offspring. But this biological fact does not explain why, among all species of life, only human beings observe an incest taboo. The key reasons to control incest, then, are social. Why? First, the incest taboo minimizes sexual competition within families by restricting legitimate sexuality to spouses. Second, it forces people to marry outside their immediate families, forging broader alliances. Third, since kinship defines people's rights and obligations toward each other, forbidding reproduction among close relatives protects kinship from collapsing into chaos.

3. **Social placement.** Families are not *biologically* necessary for people to reproduce, but they do provide for the *social* placement of children. Social identity based on race, ethnicity, religion, and social class is ascribed at birth through the family. This fact explains the long-standing preference for so-called legitimate birth. Especially when parents are of similar social position, families clarify inheritance rights and allow for the stable transmission of social standing from parents to children.

4. **Material and emotional security.** People have long viewed the family as a "haven in a heartless world," looking to kin for physical protection, emotional

NOTE: Signaling the personal significance of the family, four of the five most severe "social readjustment experiences" involve kinship: death of a spouse (100), divorce (73), marital separation (65), jail term (63), death of a close family member (63). Holmes & Rahe (1967)
Q: "The bourgeoisie has torn away from the family its sentimental veil, and has reduced the family to a mere money relation." Karl Marx and Friedrich Engels, *The Communist Manifesto*

Q: "Home is the place where, when you have to go there, they have to take you in." Robert Frost
Q: "We do not protest the unequal advantage given . . . by virtue of genetic transmission of qualities of strength and acuity; why, then, should we protest the inheritance of cultural-material qualities . . . which are part of what we think of as family and ancestry?" Robert A. Nisbet (1986:52)

support, and financial assistance. To a greater or lesser extent, most families do provide all these things, although not without periodic conflict. Not surprisingly, then, people living in families tend to be healthier than those living alone.

Critical evaluation. Structural-functional analysis identifies a number of the family's major functions. From this point of view, it is easy to see that society as we know it could not exist without families.

But this approach overlooks the great diversity of U.S. family life. Moreover, it pays little attention to how other social institutions (say, government) could meet at least some of the same human needs. Finally, it minimizes the problems of family life. Established family forms reinforce patriarchy and incorporate a surprising amount of violence, with the dysfunctional effect of undermining individual self-confidence, health, and well-being, especially of women and children.

Inequality and the Family: Social-Conflict Analysis

Like the structural-functional approach, the social-conflict paradigm sees the family as central to the operation of society. But rather than concentrating on ways that kinship benefits society, conflict theorists investigate how the family perpetuates social inequality. The role of families in the social reproduction of inequality takes several forms.

1. **Property and inheritance.** As noted in Chapter 13 ("Sex and Gender"), Friedrich Engels (1902; orig. 1884) traced the origin of the family to the need to identify heirs so that men (especially in the higher classes) could transmit property to their sons. Families thus support the concentration of wealth and reproduce the class structure in each succeeding generation (Mare, 1991).

2. **Patriarchy.** Engels also emphasized how the family promotes patriarchy. The only way men can know who their heirs are is to control the sexuality of women. Thus, Engels continued, families transform women into the sexual and economic property of men. A century ago in the United States, most wives' earnings belonged to their husbands. Although this practice is no longer lawful, men still exert power over women. Despite moving rapidly into the paid work force, women continue to bear major responsibility for child rearing and housework (Fuchs, 1986;

The family is a basic building block of society because it performs important functions such as conferring social position and regulating sexual activity. To most family members, however, the family (at least in ideal terms) is a "haven in a heartless world" in which individuals find a sense of belonging and emotional support, an idea conveyed in Marc Chagall's Scène Paysanne.

Hochschild, 1989; Presser, 1993; Keith & Schafer, 1994; Benokraitis & Feagin, 1995). Patriarchal families offer considerable benefits to men, but they also deprive men of the chance to share in the personal satisfaction and growth derived from close interaction with children.

3. **Race and ethnicity.** Racial and ethnic categories will persist over generations only to the degree that people marry others like themselves. Thus endogamous marriage also shores up the racial and ethnic hierarchy in our own society and elsewhere.

Critical evaluation. Social-conflict analysis reveals another side of family life: its role in maintaining social inequality. During his era, Engels condemned the family as part and parcel of capitalism. Yet noncapitalist societies have families (and family problems) all

Q: "The number of marriages is greater in proportion to the ease and convenience of supporting a family. When families can be easily supported, more persons marry, and earlier in life." Benjamin Franklin (1751)

NOTE: Social-exchange analysis also explains why people who perceive more potential new partners in their surroundings have higher divorce rates. (Cf. South & Lloyd, 1995)

NOTE: Social-exchange analysis represents one kind of rational-choice theory.

Q: "Some kind of family exists in all known human societies, although it is not found in every segment or class of all stratified, state societies. Greek and American slaves, for example, were prevented from forming families." Kathleen Gough (1989:239)

People in every society recognize the reality of physical attraction. But the power of romantic love, captured in Christian Pierre's painting, I Do, *holds surprisingly little importance in traditional societies. In much of the world, it would be less correct to say that* individuals marry individuals *and more true to say that* families marry families. *In other words, parents arrange marriages for their children with an eye to the social position of the kin-groups involved.*

the same. Kinship and social inequality are deeply intertwined, as Engels argued, but the family appears to carry out various societal functions that are not easily accomplished by other means.

Micro-Level Analysis

Both structural-functional and social-conflict analyses take a broad view of the family as a structural system with wide-ranging consequences for our lives. Micro-level approaches, by contrast, explore how individuals shape and experience family life.

Symbolic-Interaction Analysis

Seen from the inside, family life amounts to individuals engaging one another in a changing collage of meanings. People construct family life, building a reality that differs from case to case and from day to day.

In ideal terms, however, family living offers an opportunity for intimacy, a word with Latin roots meaning "sharing fears." That is, as a result of sharing a wide range of activities over a long period of time, members of families forge emotional bonds. Of course, the fact that parents act as authority figures often inhibits their communication with younger children. But, as young people reach adulthood, kinship ties typically "open up" as family members recognize

that they share concern for one another's welfare (Macionis, 1978).

Social-Exchange Analysis

Social-exchange analysis, another micro-level approach, depicts courtship and marriage as forms of negotiation (Blau, 1964). In the case of courtship, dating allows each person the chance to assess the likely advantages and disadvantages of taking the other as a spouse, always keeping in mind the value of what one has to offer in return. In essence, exchange analysts contend, individuals seek to make the best "deal" they can in selecting a partner.

Physical attractiveness is one critical dimension of social exchange. In patriarchal societies around the world, beauty has long been a commodity offered by women on the marriage market. The high value assigned to beauty explains women's traditional concern with physical appearance and their sensitivity about revealing their age. For their part, men have traditionally been assessed according to the financial resources they command. Recently, however, because more and more women are joining the labor force, they are less dependent on men to support them and their children. Thus, the terms of exchange have been converging for men and women.

Critical evaluation. Micro-level analysis offers a useful counterpoint to structural-functional and social-conflict visions of the family as an institutional system. Adopting an interactional or exchange viewpoint, we gain a better sense of the individual's experience of family life and appreciate how people creatively shape this reality for themselves.

Using this approach, however, we run the risk of missing the bigger picture, namely, that family life is similar for people affected by any common set of economic and cultural forces. U.S. families vary in some predictable ways according to social class and ethnicity, and, as the next section explains, they typically evolve through stages linked to the life course.

STAGES OF FAMILY LIFE

The family is dynamic, with marked changes across the life course. Typically, family life begins with courtship, followed by settling into the realities of married life. Next, for most couples at least, is raising children, leading to the later years of marriage after children have left home to form families of their own. We will look briefly at each of these stages.

Courtship

November 2, 1994, Kandy, Sri Lanka. Winding our way through the rain forest of this beautiful island, the van driver Harry is recounting how he met his wife. The two families found each other on the basis of being Buddhist and of a specific caste group. "We got along well, right from the start," recalls Harry. "We had the same background. I suppose she or I could have said 'no.' But 'love marriages' happen in the city, not in the village where I grew up."

People in Sri Lanka, and in preindustrial societies throughout the world, generally consider courtship too important to be left to the young (Stone, 1977). An arranged marriage, representing an alliance forged by two extended families of similar social standing, usually involves a negotiation in terms of wealth, power, and prestige. Romantic love has little to do with it, and parents may make such arrangements when their children are quite young. A century ago in Sri Lanka and India, for example, half of all girls married before reaching the age of fifteen (Mayo, 1927; Mace & Mace, 1960).

Arranged marriages fit into Emile Durkheim's model of *mechanical solidarity* (see Chapter 4, "Society"). Because traditional societies are culturally homogeneous, almost any member of the opposite sex has been suitably socialized to perform the roles of spouse and parent. Thus parents can arrange marriages with little thought to whether or not the two individuals involved are *personally* compatible because they can be confident that virtually any couple will be *culturally* compatible.

Industrialization erodes the importance of extended families, weakens traditions, and enhances personal choice in courtship. Young people now expect to choose their own mates, and they delay doing so until gaining financial security and the experience they need to select a suitable marriage partner. Dating sharpens their skills and may serve as a period of sexual experimentation as well.

Our culture elevates *romantic love*—the experience of affection and sexual passion toward another person—as the basis for marriage. For us, marriage without love is difficult to imagine; popular culture—from remakes of traditional fairy tales like "Cinderella" to today's paperback romance novels—portrays love as the key to a successful marriage. Figure 17–1 provides

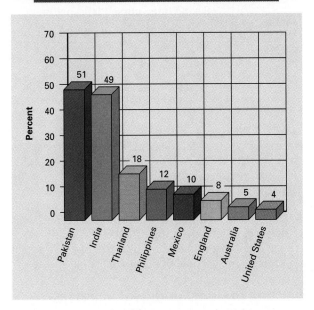

Global Snapshot

FIGURE 17–1 Percentage of College Students Who Express a Willingness to Marry Without Romantic Love

Source: Levine (1993).

a comparative look at the importance of romantic love in several countries. While about half of today's college students in Pakistan and India claim they would marry partners they did not love, only a small percentage of students in industrial nations, including the United States, say they would accept such an arrangement.

Our society's emphasis on romance has some useful consequences. Passionate love motivates individuals to "leave the nest" to form new families of their own, and it may also carry a new couple through difficult adjustments to the realities of living together (Goode, 1959). On the other hand, because feelings wax and wane, romantic love makes for a less stable foundation for marriage than do social and economic considerations—an assertion borne out by this country's high divorce rate compared to societies that afford people less choice in their marriage partners.

But even in this age of choice, sociologists have long recognized that Cupid's arrow is aimed by society more than we like to think. Most people fall in love with others of the same race, comparable age, and

RESOURCE: Among the classics included in the Macionis and Benokraitis reader, *Seeing Ourselves*, is Jessie Bernard's "'His' and 'Her' Marriage."

Q: "What does a woman do for herself and for her children by being fussy about her sexual partners? . . . if she focuses on male traits that are heritable, she sees to it that her kids start with a genetic edge. We aren't all created equal . . . [She also] makes it possible to pick males who will stick around and help raise the kids. A woman is not simply competing for quality sperm; she's competing for the man who goes with it." Heather Trexler Remoff (1984)

NOTE: In a 1986 *Woman's Day* survey, 38% of women claimed that they would not marry the same man again. Although 28% reported feeling "like a lover," about 40% said they were more "like a housekeeper," and 27% said they felt "like a mother."

TABLE 17-1 Frequency of Sexual Activity Among Married Couples

Years Together	Sexual Intercourse (times per month)			
	1 or less	1–4	4–12	12 or more
0–2	6%	11%	38%	45%
2–10	6	21	46	27
10 or more	16	22	45	18

Source: Adapted from Philip Blumstein and Pepper Schwartz, *American Couples* (New York: William Morrow, 1983), p. 196.

similar social class. All societies "arrange" marriages to the extent that they encourage **homogamy** (literally, "like marrying like"), *marriage between people with the same social characteristics.*

In short, "falling in love" may be a strong personal feeling, but it is guided by a host of social forces. Perhaps we exaggerate the importance of romantic love to reassure ourselves that even in the midst of social controls we are capable of making personal choices.

Settling In: Ideal and Real Marriage

Our culture presents marriage to the young in idealized, "happily-ever-after" terms. One consequence of such optimistic thinking is the danger of disappointment, especially for women—who, more than men, are taught to see in marriage the key to future happiness.

Then, too, romantic love involves a good deal of fantasy. We fall in love with others, not necessarily as they are, but as we want them to be (Berscheid & Hatfield, 1983). Only after marriage do many spouses regularly confront each other as they carry out the day-to-day routines of maintaining a household.

Sexuality is one source of disappointment. In the romantic haze of falling in love, people may think of marriage as an endless sexual honeymoon, only to face the sobering realization that sex becomes a less-than-all-consuming passion. While about two in three married people claim to be satisfied with the sexual dimension of their relationship, marital sex does decline over time, as Table 17–1 shows.

Many experts agree that couples with the most fulfilling sexual relationships experience the greatest satisfaction in their marriages. This connection does not mean that sex is the key to marital bliss, but, more often than not, good sex and good relationships go together (Hunt, 1974; Tavris & Sadd, 1977; Blumstein & Schwartz, 1983).

Infidelity—sexual activity outside marriage—is another area in which the reality of marriage does not coincide with our cultural ideal. Traditional marriage vows "to forsake all others" appear to be strong, and in a recent survey, 90 percent of U.S. adults claimed that sex outside of marriage is "always wrong" or "almost always wrong." Even so, 21 percent of men and 13 percent of women indicated on a private, written questionnaire that they had—at least once—been sexually unfaithful to their partners (NORC, 1994:212, 679).

Child Rearing

Adults in the United States overwhelmingly identify raising children as one of life's greatest joys (NORC, 1994:584). This despite the substantial demands children make on the time and energy of parents, sometimes to the point of straining their marriage.

Not surprisingly, then, almost all adults in this society think that a family should contain at least one child. Table 17–2 indicates that most prefer two or three, with few wishing to have four or more children. Smaller families represent a marked change from two centuries ago, when *eight* children was the U.S. average!

Big families pay off in preindustrial societies because children perform needed labor. Indeed, people in these societies generally regard having children as a wife's duty and, without reliable birth-control technology, childbearing is a regular event. Of course, a high death rate in preindustrial societies prevents many children from reaching adulthood; as recently as 1900, one-third of children born in the United States died by age ten (Wall, 1980).

Economically speaking, industrialization transforms children from a vital asset to a burdensome liability. Today the expense of raising a single child exceeds $200,000, including the costs of a college education (U.S. Department of Agriculture, 1993). This expense helps to explain the steady drop in U.S. family size during the twentieth century to one child per family today.[2]

The trend toward smaller families holds true for all other industrial societies as well. But the picture differs sharply in low-income countries in Latin America, Asia, and, especially, Africa, where many women have few alternatives to bearing and raising children. In such societies, four to six children is still the norm.

Not only is parenting expensive, it is a lifetime commitment. As our society has afforded its members more choice about family life, more U.S. adults have

---

[2]According to the U.S. Bureau of the Census (1995), the average number of children under eighteen for all U.S. families was 0.99 in 1994. Among only families with children under eighteen, the medians were 1.84 for whites, 1.35 for African Americans, and 1.57 for Hispanics.

SOCIAL SURVEY: "It is better for all if the man is the achiever outside the home and the woman takes care of the home and the family." (*Student CHIP Social Survey Software*, FEFAM1; GSS 1977, 1985–91, N = 6,752)

	"Agree"	"Disagree"
Men	51.7%	48.3%
Women	44.9%	55.1%

	"Agree"	"Disagree"
High SES	34.7%	65.3%
Middle SES	47.3%	52.7%
Low SES	66.4%	33.6%
Afri Amer	49.2%	50.8%
Latino	48.2%	51.8%
Whites	47.9%	52.1%

opted to delay childbirth or to remain childless. In 1960, almost 90 percent of women between twenty-five and twenty-nine who had ever married had at least one child; by 1992 this proportion had tumbled to 72 percent (U.S. Bureau of the Census, 1995). About two-thirds of parents in the United States claim they would like to devote more of their time to child rearing (Snell, 1990). But unless we are willing to accept some decline in our material standard of living, economic realities demand that most parents pursue careers outside the home. Thus the child-rearing patterns we have described reflect ways of coming to terms with economic change.

As Chapter 13 ("Sex and Gender") explained, most women with young children now work for income. In 1994, 59 percent of women over the age of sixteen were in the work force; among mothers with children under eighteen, 68 percent worked for income (U.S. Bureau of Labor Statistics, 1996). But while women and men share the burden of earning income, women continue to bear the traditional responsibility for raising children and doing housework. Some men in our society are eager parents, yet most resist sharing responsibility for household tasks that our culture historically has defined as "women's work" (Hochschild, 1989; Presser, 1993; Keith & Schafer, 1994).

As more women join men in the labor force, parents have less time for parenting. Children of working parents spend most of the day at school. But perhaps 2 million school-age youngsters (roughly 8 percent of the total) are *latchkey kids* who fend for themselves after school (U.S. Bureau of the Census, 1994). Traditionalists in the "family values" debate caution that increasing numbers of working mothers may be hurting their children, who receive less parenting. Progressives counter that such criticism unfairly faults women for seeking the same opportunities men have long enjoyed.

Congress took a step toward easing the conflict between family and job responsibilities by passing the Family and Medical Leave Act in 1993. This law allows up to ninety days of unpaid leave from work in order to care for a new child or because of a serious family emergency. But, for most U.S. adults, juggling parental and occupational responsibilities still poses a major problem. This dilemma points to the heightened importance of child-care facilities, as the box on page 466 explains.

The Family in Later Life

Increasing life expectancy in the United States means that, barring divorce, couples are likely to remain

TABLE 17–2 The Ideal Number of Children for U.S. Adults, 1994

Number of Children	Proportion of Respondents
0	1.4%
1	2.5
2	52.8
3	22.2
4	9.6
5	1.2
6 or more	0.4
As many as you want	6.1
No response	3.8

Source: *General Social Surveys, 1972–1994: Cumulative Codebook* (Chicago: National Opinion Research Center, 1994), p. 208.

married for a long time. By about age fifty, most have completed the task of raising children. The remaining years of marriage—the "empty nest"—bring a return to living with only one's spouse.

Like the birth of children, their departure requires adjustments, although the marital relationship often becomes closer and more satisfying in midlife. Years of living together may diminish a couple's sexual passion for each other, but mutual understanding and companionship are likely to increase.

Personal contact with children usually continues, since most older adults live a short distance from at least one of their children. Moreover, one-third of all U.S. adults (more than 50 million) are grandparents, and many of these men and women help their daughters and sons with child care and a host of other responsibilities. Among African Americans (who have a high rate of single parenting), many grandmothers assume a central place in family life (Cherlin & Furstenberg, 1986; Crispell, 1993; Jarrett, 1994).

The other side of the coin, explained in Chapter 14 ("Aging and the Elderly"), is that more adults in midlife are facing the challenge of caring for their aging parents. The "empty nest" may not be filled by a parent coming to live in the home, but many adults find that parents living to eighty and beyond require practical, emotional, and financial care that can be more taxing than raising young children. The oldest of the "baby boomers"—now in their fifties—are being touted as the "sandwich generation" because they will spend as many years looking after their aging parents as they did caring for their own offspring.

Retirement also brings further change to family life. If the wife has been a homemaker, the husband's retirement means that spouses will spend much more

THEN AND NOW: Children living with a never-married parent: *1974*, 1.5%; *1994*, 9.6%.

NOTE: The longest marriages in the United States today last about eighty years.

DIVERSITY: Later family life differs by sex: See Table 14–1 on page 391 for the different living arrangements of elderly women and men.

Q: "We think of ourselves as a nation that cherishes its children, but, in fact, America treats its children like excess baggage. Our tax code offers greater incentives for breeding horses than for raising children. We slash school budgets and deny working parents the right to spend even a few weeks with their newborns. We spend 23% of the federal budget on the elderly but less than 5% on children." Sylvia Ann Hewlett

CRITICAL THINKING

Who's Minding the Kids?

Traditionally, the task of providing daily care for young children fell to mothers. But with a majority of mothers and fathers now in the labor force, securing high-quality, affordable child care has become a key priority for parents.

The figure displays the source of care for U.S. children under five years of age whose mothers are working. The most common location of care—utilized in 36 percent of all cases—is the child's own home, where the father or other relative typically provides supervision. An additional 31 percent of children receive care in another person's home, with either relatives or others (often neighbors or friends) looking after them. A small share of children accompany their mothers to work.

A day-care facility or preschool is the setting for the remaining 23 percent of children with working mothers. The proportion in day-care centers has doubled over the last decade because many parents have difficulty finding in-home care for their children.

Some day-care centers handle dozens of children at one time, amounting to "tot lots" in which children, "parked" by their parents for the

day, receive little love and minimal attention. The impersonality of such settings, coupled with rapid turnover in staff, can undermine the warm and consistent nurturing that young children need to develop a sense of trust. Other child-care centers, however, offer a secure and healthful environment. Research suggests that *good* day-care centers are good for children; *bad* facilities are not.

Identifying high-quality child-care facilities is not always easy. Parents

must inspect centers carefully, inquiring about discipline policies, the ratio of children to caregivers, and noting the cleanliness and safety of the surroundings. Such personal investigation is necessary since few states have comprehensive guidelines for operating child-care centers, and some states have none at all.

Source: U.S. Bureau of the Census (1995).

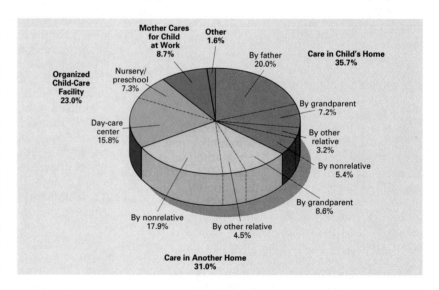

time together. Although the husband's presence is often a source of pleasure to both, it sometimes undermines wives' established routines to the point of intrusion. As one woman bluntly remarked: "I may have married him for better or worse, but not for lunch" (quoted in Kalish, 1982:96).

The final and surely the most difficult transition in married life comes with the death of a spouse. Wives typically outlive their husbands because of

women's longer life expectancy and because wives are usually younger than husbands to begin with. Wives can thus expect to spend a significant period of their lives as widows. The bereavement and loneliness accompanying the death of a spouse are always difficult. This experience may be even harder for widowers, who usually have fewer friends than widows do and may be unskilled at cooking and housework (Berardo, 1970).

THEN AND NOW: Number of teenage mothers: *1970*, 650,000; *1994*, 518,000. Although the numbers are down (fertility generally has decreased), the share of these who are unmarried has risen steadily and rapidly: In *1970*, 200,000 of 650,000 were unmarried; in *1994*, 365,000 of 518,000 were unmarried.

THEN AND NOW: Percent of births to unwed mothers: *1970*: 11% (white, 6%; black, 38%); *1992*, 30% (white, 23%; black, 68%).

RESOURCE: Norval Glenn's article "Are Families *Really* Important?" is one of the contemporary selections in the Macionis and Benokraitis reader, *Seeing Ourselves*.

DIVERSITY: One-parent African-American families represent about half the total, but receive only one-fourth of all black family income.

U.S. FAMILIES: CLASS, RACE, AND GENDER

Dimensions of inequality—social class, ethnicity and race, and gender—are powerful forces that shape marriage and family life. While this section addresses each factor separately, they overlap in all our lives.

Social Class

Social class molds a family's financial security and range of opportunities. Interviewing working-class women, Lillian Rubin (1976) found that wives deemed a good husband to be one who refrained from violence and excessive drinking and held a steady job. Rubin's middle-class informants, by contrast, never mentioned such things; these women simply *assumed* a husband would provide a safe and secure home. Their ideal husband was a man with whom they could communicate easily and share feelings and experiences.

Such differences reflect the fact that people with higher social standing have more schooling, and most have jobs that emphasize verbal skills. In addition, middle-class couples share a wider range of activities, while working-class life is more sharply divided along gender lines. Conventionally masculine ideas of self-control, Rubin explains, can stifle emotional expressiveness on the part of working-class men, prompting women to turn to each other as confidants.

Clearly, what women (and men) conclude that they can hope for in marriage—and what they end up with—is linked to their social class. Much the same holds true for children in families; boys and girls lucky enough to be born into more affluent families enjoy better mental and physical health, develop higher self-confidence, and go on to greater achievement than poor children do (Komarovsky, 1967; Bott, 1971; Rubin, 1976; Fitzpatrick, 1988; McLeod & Shanahan, 1993).

Ethnicity and Race

As Chapter 12 ("Race and Ethnicity") indicates, ethnicity and race are powerful social forces. The effects of both surface in family life.

Latino Families

Latinos in the United States generally bask in the loyalty and support of extended families. Traditionally, Latino parents have exercised greater control over their children's courtship, defining marriage as an alliance of families rather than a union based simply

Historically, Latinos have maintained strong kinship ties. Carmen Lomas Garza's painting Lala's and Tudi's Birthday Party *portrays the extended family that is a foundation of traditional Hispanic culture.*

© 1989 Carmen Lomas Garza. *Cumpleanos de Lala y Tudi,* oil on canvas, 17"x15", Collection of the artist. Photo: Wolfgang Dietze.

on romantic love. A third trait of Latino family life is adherence to conventional gender roles. Machismo—masculine strength, daring, and sexual prowess—is pronounced among some Latinos, while women are both honored and closely supervised.

Assimilation into the larger society is gradually tempering these traditional patterns, however. Many Puerto Ricans who migrate to New York, for example, do not maintain the strong extended families they knew in Puerto Rico. Especially among affluent Hispanic families—whose number has tripled in the last twenty years—the traditional authority of men over women has diminished (Staples & Mirande, 1980; Moore & Pachon, 1985; Nielsen, 1990; O'Hare, 1990).

Some Latinos have become quite prosperous; the overall social standing of this segment of the U.S. population, however, remains below average. The U.S. Census Bureau (1995) reports that, in 1993, the typical Hispanic family had an income of $23,654, about 64 percent of that for all U.S. families. Consequently, many Hispanics contend with the stress of unemployment and other problems that accompany low income.

African-American Families

Analysis of African-American families must begin with the stark reality of economic disadvantage: As noted in earlier chapters, the typical African-American family earned $21,542 in 1993, 58 percent of the

DIVERSITY: Among the poor, female-headed households are predominantly African American; among more affluent people, they are mostly white.

NOTE: The Census Bureau reports that, in 1994, 63% of the 10.1 million African-American children under 18 lived with only one parent (up 97% since 1970). Those families with a woman heading the household (almost all of them) had a median income of $11,093,

31% of the comparable figure for black married-couple families ($35,409).

DIVERSITY THEN AND NOW: U.S. interracial births, 1992: Black/white, 55,890 (1978: 21,438); Asian/white, 42,033 (21,013); Native American/white, 21,819 (12,860); Asian/black, 4,051 (1,669); Native American/black, 1,454 (557); Native American/Asian, 789 (379). Kalish (1995)

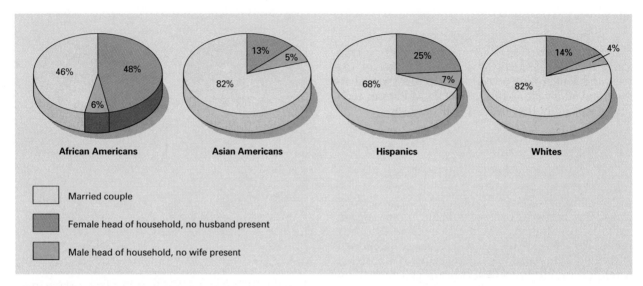

FIGURE 17–2 Family Form in the United States, 1993
Source: U.S. Bureau of the Census (1995).

national average. People of African ancestry are also three times as likely as whites to be poor: Family patterns reflect unemployment, underemployment, and, in many cases, a physical environment replete with crime and drug abuse.

Under these circumstances, maintaining stable family ties is difficult. Note, for example, that 25 percent of African-American women in their forties have never married, compared with about 10 percent of white women of the same age (Bennett, Bloom, & Craig, 1989). This means that African-American women—often with children—are more likely to be single heads of households. As Figure 17–2 shows, women headed 48 percent of all African-American families in 1993, compared with 25 percent of Hispanic families, 13 percent of Asian or Pacific Islander families, and 14 percent of white families (U.S. Bureau of the Census, 1995).

Regardless of race, families headed by single mothers are at high risk of poverty. About one-third of families headed by white women are poor, and the proportion is close to half among women of African or Hispanic ancestry. Note that African-American families with both wife and husband living in the home—which represents half the total—are not as economically vulnerable, earning 81 percent as much as comparable white families. But because 68 percent of African-American children are born to single women, half of all African-American boys and girls grow up in poverty

(Hogan & Kitagawa, 1985; U.S. Bureau of the Census, 1995).

A generation ago, U.S. Senator Daniel Patrick Moynihan (1965) sounded an alarm that the African-American family was in crisis because of a growing number of single mothers and absent fathers. Such families, he argued, could not provide the same level of supervision and care for children and, just as important, were likely to be poor. In Moynihan's view, a cycle of poverty had been unleashed in the African-American community that would pass disadvantage on to future generations.

Critics charged that Moynihan was assuming a narrow conception of family life. As African-American novelist Toni Morrison put it, "I don't think a female running a house is a problem. It is perceived as one because of the notion that a 'head' is a man" (quoted in Angelo, 1989:120).

Others scolded Moynihan for implying that single-parent families were the *cause*—rather than the *consequence*—of poverty. According to William Ryan (1976), saying that people bring poverty on themselves through lifestyle choices amounts to blaming the victims. Underlying both the higher level of poverty and one-parent families among African Americans is societal prejudice, discrimination, and lack of opportunity.

In support of Ryan's position, historical evidence indicates that the proportion of African-American families headed by women, although historically

DIVERSITY: Although the rate of white-black married couples has increased, it remains very low: In *1960*, 126 per 100,000 couples; *1970*, 146 per 100,000; *1980*, 335 per 100,000; *1994*, 546 per 100,000 couples.

DIVERSITY: In 1994, there were 1,283,000 so-called "mixed" marriages (some mix of African American/Asian/Native American/ white), up from 450,000 in 1980. About 4% of U.S. births are

racially mixed children.

DISCUSS: What about interracial adoption? States vary sharply from banning interracial adoption to promoting it. The National Association of Black Social Workers encourages the placement of children first with biological parents, then in "community of origin," then with others (of another race). About 40% of adopted children are African Americans.

higher than among white people, increased after 1940 when African Americans migrated in large numbers to cities. Many of these people left rural areas with few industrial skills, and all were disadvantaged by racial prejudice and discrimination. The predictable result was that African Americans soon were caught up in a world of low-paying jobs that did not provide the financial security necessary to maintain a family (Gutman, 1976; Wilson, 1984).

Although the black middle class has swelled since 1980 to include one in three African-American families, the decline of manufacturing in U.S. cities has hurt blue-collar workers—many blacks among them— whose incomes have slipped. Thus, the black, urban underclass continues to expand. While analysts may disagree about the causes of this problem, Moynihan's prediction thirty years ago has unfortunately come true: A cycle of poverty has expanded among African-American women and their children (Ladner, 1986; Furstenberg, Brooks-Gunn, & Morgan, 1987; U.S. Bureau of the Census, 1995).

At the same time, African Americans have devised distinctive strategies for coping with economic hardship. One source of strength is the extended family, which provides emotional and financial support. Grandparents play a special role: One in eight African-American children lives with a grandparent (twice the Hispanic rate and three times the white rate). Looking beyond the family itself, many black men and women forge networks of people who assume kinlike roles (a substitute "aunt," for instance). Such resourcefulness has allowed people confronting tremendous barriers to care for children and meet their daily needs (Stack, 1975; Cherlin & Furstenberg, 1983; Leslie & Korman, 1989; Ruggles, 1994).

Mixed Marriages

As we have already explained, spouses typically have similar social background with regard to class, race, and ethnicity. Yet the trend among white people, over the course of this century, has been for ethnicity to matter less and less. Thus, a man of German and French ancestry might readily marry a woman of Irish and English background.

Race remains a more formidable consideration, however. Since African, Asian, and Native Americans represent 16 percent of the U.S. population, about that share of marriages would be "mixed" if people paid no attention to race. The actual proportion is not quite 4 percent, attesting to the continuing importance of race in guiding social relations. Even so, the numbers of racially mixed marriages are rising steadily.

Although the proportion of U.S. couples that are racially mixed remains small, their numbers are increasing rapidly. How much importance does race play in your own ideas about courtship?

Black-white marriages are most numerous, as the large African-American population (12 percent of the U.S. total) would lead us to expect. Proportionately, though, whites involved in racially mixed marriages are most likely to choose partners of Asian ancestry (National Center for Health Statistics, 1995).

Gender

Among all races, Jessie Bernard (1982) asserts, every marriage is actually *two* different relationships: a woman's marriage and a man's marriage. Although the extent of patriarchy has diminished with time, even today few marriages are composed of two equal partners. College students of both sexes reported to Mirra Komarovsky (1973, 1976) that their ideal marriage had a dominant husband, evidence that this pattern is deeply embedded in our culture. No doubt, this fact explains why most of us expect men to be older as well as taller than their wives and to have more important careers (McRae, 1986).

What is curious, in light of continuing patriarchy, is the persistent notion that marriage is more beneficial to women than to men (Bernard, 1982). The positive stereotype of the carefree bachelor contrasts sharply with the negative image of the lonely spinster. This idea is rooted in women's historic exclusion from

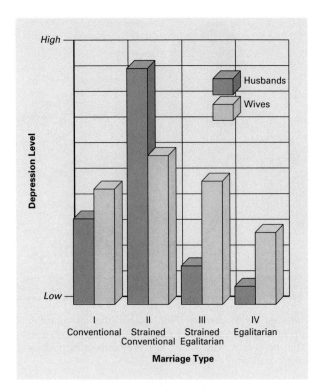

FIGURE 17–3 Depression in Four Types of Marriages
Source: Ross, Mirowsky, & Huber (1983).

the labor force, which made a woman's financial security dependent on marrying well.

But today, Bernard claims, compared to single women, married women have poorer mental health, evince more passive attitudes toward life, and report less personal happiness. Married men, by contrast, live longer than single men, have better mental health, and report being happier. These differences in marriage suggest why, after divorce, men are more eager than women to secure a new partner.

Bernard concludes that there is no better guarantor of long life, health, and happiness for a man than a woman well socialized to perform the "duties of a wife" by devoting her life to caring for him and providing the security of a well-ordered home. She is quick to add that marriage *could* be healthful for women if society would only end the practice of husbands' dominating wives and expecting them to perform all the housework.

A study of psychological depression among spouses in the United States helps to sort out the connections among gender, power, and mental health in marriage (Ross, Mirowsky, & Huber, 1983; Mirowsky & Ross,

1984). In "conventional" marriages (Type I in Figure 17–3), partners agree that only the husband will be employed and the wife will do all housework and child rearing. The researchers found that low to moderate levels of depression characterized spouses in conventional marriages, with men somewhat better off than women. This difference, according to the investigators, is due to husbands' benefiting from income and prestige derived from their jobs, while wives take some satisfaction but no pay for their efforts.

In "strained conventional" marriages (Type II in the figure), the wife joins the husband in the labor force out of necessity, returning home to do all the housework and child rearing as well. This arrangement, as Figure 17–3 shows, is unfavorable for both partners: Depression is high for the wife (with two demanding jobs, one of which she does not want) but higher still for the husband (who thinks he should be able to support his wife but cannot). Note that this is the only marital pattern in which husbands have poorer mental health than wives.

In "strained egalitarian" marriages (Type III), both the husband and wife are happy that they both are working for income; yet, the wife is still responsible for almost all the housework and child care. Here, wives display somewhat lower levels of depression, and husbands benefit even more as they enjoy greater family income.

"Egalitarian" marriages (Type IV) have both husband and wife happily working outside the home but also sharing most family responsibilities. This pattern is linked to the lowest depression levels for both husbands and wives in any of the four types of marriage. The researchers attribute this favorable pattern to the absence of tensions that arise when a working wife must also take full responsibility for housework and child rearing.

These findings support the conclusions by Jessie Bernard (1982) and others that more egalitarian marriages tend to be happier for husbands as well as wives. But such marriages are still relatively rare—probably involving no more than 10 percent of all couples—because conventional ideas about gender are deeply rooted in our way of life.

TRANSITION AND PROBLEMS IN FAMILY LIFE

Ann Landers (1984), a keen observer of the U.S. scene, once remarked that "One marriage out of twenty is wonderful, four are good, ten are tolerable, and five are pure hell." Families can be a source of joy, but the reality of family life sometimes falls far short of this ideal.

THEN AND NOW: U.S. divorce rate: *1955*, 2.2 per 1,000 people; *1994*, 4.6 per 1,000 people.

Q: "It is easier in these United States to walk away from a marriage than from a commitment to purchase a used car. Most contracts cannot be unilaterally abrogated; marriages in contemporary America can be terminated by practically anyone at any time, and without cause." Thomas Morgan

NOTE: Figure 17–4 illustrates the power of social forces in the individual decision to end a marriage: Besides climbing over the course of the century, divorce rates dropped during the depression and rose rapidly at the end of World War II. Note, too, that the recent dip has a demographic component, since the baby boomers are now passing 40, when divorce becomes less likely.

Divorce

Our society strongly supports marriage, and more than nine out of ten people at some point "tie the knot." But many of today's marriages eventually unravel. Figure 17–4 depicts the tenfold increase in the U.S. divorce rate over the last century. By 1994, according to government estimates, four in ten marriages were ending in divorce (for African Americans, the figure was six in ten).

The high U.S. divorce rate can be traced to a number of factors (Huber & Spitze, 1980; Kitson & Raschke, 1981; Thornton, 1985; Waite, Haggstrom, & Kanouse, 1985; Weitzman, 1985; Gerstel, 1987; Furstenberg & Cherlin, 1991; Etzioni, 1993):

1. **Individualism is on the rise.** Today, members of our society spend less time together than in the past. We have become more individualistic, seemingly more concerned with personal happiness and success than with the well-being of families and children.

2. **Romantic love often subsides.** Our culture emphasizes romantic love as a basis for marriage, rendering relationships vulnerable to collapse as sexual passion subsides. There is now widespread support for the notion that one may end a marriage in favor of a new relationship simply to renew excitement and romance.

3. **Women are now less dependent on men.** Their increasing participation in the labor force has reduced wives' financial dependence on husbands. As a practical matter, then, women find it easier to walk away from unhappy marriages.

4. **Many of today's marriages are stressful.** With both partners working outside the home in most cases, jobs consume time and energy that in the past were directed toward family life. Under such circumstances (and given the difficulty of securing good, affordable child care), raising children becomes a particular burden. While children do stabilize some marriages, divorce is most common during the early years of marriage when many couples have young children.

5. **Divorce is more socially acceptable.** Divorce no longer carries the powerful, negative stigma it did a century ago. Couples considering divorce typically do not receive the discouragement from family and friends they once did.

6. **Divorce is legally easier to accomplish.** In the past, courts required divorcing couples to demonstrate that one or both were guilty of behavior

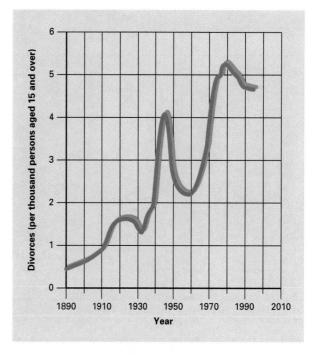

**FIGURE 17–4 The Divorce Rate
for the United States, 1890–1994**
Source: U.S. Bureau of the Census (1995).

such as adultery or physical abuse. Today most states allow divorce simply because a couple decides their marriage has failed. As one law professor notes, "It is easier to walk away from a marriage than from a commitment to purchase a new car" (quoted in Etzioni, 1993). Perhaps this is why nearly half of all U.S. adults now think that a divorce is too easy to obtain (NORC, 1994:210).

The divorce rate has eased downward slightly over the last decade for two reasons. First, the large baby-boomer cohort that was born shortly after World War II is now reaching middle age, when divorce is less common. Second, hard economic times discourage divorce, since living alone typically is more expensive than living in families.

Although the trend of ending marriage may have slowed for the moment, our society still has the highest divorce rate in the world: almost twice as high as Canada, four times as high as Japan, and ten times as high as Italy (U.S. Bureau of the Census, 1995). But Ed Kain (1990) cautions that we commonly exaggerate the stability of marriage in the past when the early death of a spouse ended as many marriages after a few

THE MAP: Correlates of higher divorce on the West Coast include a lower level of religiosity and a higher level of geographical mobility.

NOTE: The divorce rate among remarriages is held down by the fact of advancing age, which discourages marital dissolution.

SOCIAL SURVEY: "Should divorce in this country be easier or more difficult to obtain than it is now?" (*Student CHIP Social Survey Software*, DIVLAW1; GSS 1974–91, N = 14,655)

	"Easier"	"Same"	"Harder"
Afri Amer	51.2%	15.3%	33.5%
Latino	34.0%	19.1%	47.0%
Whites	24.2%	22.3%	53.5%
Women	25.0%	21.8%	53.3%
Men	30.1%	21.1%	48.8%

Seeing Ourselves

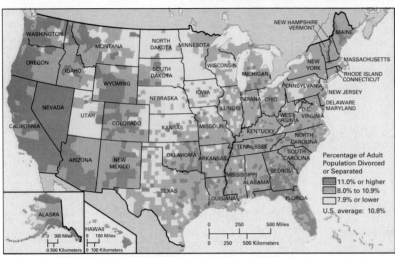

NATIONAL MAP 17–1
Divorced People Across the United States

Overall, about 11 percent of the U.S. population aged fifteen or over are divorced or separated. However, marriages are more vulnerable to breakup in the Pacific region of the country. Nevada has long been the U.S. divorce capital, due to its exceedingly liberal divorce laws. But divorce is also pronounced where religious values are weaker and where people are more likely to move often, thus distancing themselves from family and friends. How would you characterize the West Coast with regard to these factors?

Percentage of Adult Population Divorced or Separated

- 11.0% or higher
- 8.0% to 10.9%
- 7.9% or lower

U.S. average: 10.8%

Source: *American Demographics* magazine, October 1992, p. 5. Reprinted with permission. ©1992, *American Demographics* magazine, Ithaca, New York. Data from the 1990 decennial census.

years as divorce does now. But if marriages used to dissolve due to forces beyond people's control, they are now much more likely to end simply because people want to be single, or married to somebody else.

Who Divorces?

At greatest risk of divorce are young spouses, especially those who marry after a brief courtship, have few financial resources, and have yet to mature emotionally. People of lower social position are also more likely to divorce, usually because of financial strains. At all social levels, the risk of divorce rises if a couple marries in response to an unexpected pregnancy, or when one or both partners have alcohol- or other substance-abuse problems. People who are not religious divorce more readily than those who are.

Divorce also is more common among couples in which women have successful careers, partly due to the strains that arise in two-career marriages and, more important, because financially independent women are less inclined to remain in an unhappy marriage. Finally, men and women who divorce once are more likely to divorce again, presumably because problems follow them from one marriage to another (Booth & White, 1980; Yoder & Nichols, 1980; Glenn & Shelton, 1985).

Divorce is also more likely in some regions of the country than others. National Map 17–1 provides an overview of divorce rates across the United States.

Divorce as Process

Divorce is a form of role exit, as described in Chapter 6 ("Social Interaction in Everyday Life"). Paul Bohannan (1970) and others point to six distinct adjustments divorcing people make:

1. **Emotional divorce.** Distancing oneself from the former spouse usually begins before the formal break occurs. A deteriorating marriage can be fraught with disappointment, indifference, or outright hostility.

2. **Legal divorce.** Since marriage is a legal contract, divorce involves a legal change of status. Often financial settlements are central to a divorce agreement.

3. **Psychic reorganization.** Many divorced people suffer not just from loneliness but a sense that the ending of their marriage represents a personal failure.

4. **Community reorganization.** Ending a marriage requires both partners to reorganize friendships and adjust relations with parents and other family

GLOBAL: Divorce rates for selected countries (1992; per 1,000 married women): U.S., 21; Denmark, 13; U.K., 12; Sweden, 12; Canada, 11; Germany, 7; Italy, 2. (U.S. Bureau of the Census)

Q: "For most [children of divorce], divorce was the most important cause of enduring pain and anomie in their lives." Judith S. Wallerstein and Sandra Blakeslee (1989)

DISCUSS: About $4 billion in court-ordered child support is unpaid in the United States each year. Is this problem caused by courts favoring mothers in custody disputes?

NOTE: "Blended" families are not new; in the past, however, remarriage was more commonly due to death than to divorce.

NOTE: The Census Bureau reports that 7.2 million children live in blended families.

members who are accustomed to seeing each one as part of a couple.

5. **Economic reorganization.** Recent no-fault divorce laws have reduced the amount of alimony and child support paid by men to their former wives. Further, divorce courts often require ex-spouses to sell homes and divide marital assets equally. While divorce raises the living standards of many men (who no longer support wives and children), it can mean financial calamity to women whose earnings are lower than those of their husbands and who may be responsible for supporting children as well (Weitzman, 1985).

6. **Parental reorganization.** More than half of all divorcing couples must resolve the issue of child custody. Our society's conventional practice is still to award custody of children to mothers, based on the notion that women are better parents than men are. A recent trend, however, is toward joint custody, whereby children divide their time between the new homes of their two parents. Joint custody is difficult if divorced parents live far apart or do not get along, but it has the advantage of keeping children in regular contact with both parents (Roman & Haddad, 1978; Cherlin & Furstenberg, 1983).

Because mothers usually gain custody of children but fathers typically earn more income, the well-being of children often depends on fathers making court-ordered child-support payments. As Figure 17–5 indicates, courts award child support in 54 percent of all divorces involving children. Yet, in any given year, nearly half the children legally entitled to support receive only partial payments or no payments at all. The failure of some 2.5 million "dead-beat dads" to support their youngsters prompted federal legislation mandating that employers withhold money from the earnings of parents who fail to pay up. Still, many fathers evade their responsibilities by moving or switching jobs (Weitzman, 1985; Waldman, 1992).

Conventional wisdom holds that divorce is hardest on children. Divorce tears many young people from familiar surroundings, entangles them in bitter family feuds, and frequently distances them from a parent they love. But the greatest tragedy of divorce is that, in their own minds, children often blame themselves for their parents' breakup. For this reason, concludes family counselor Judith Wallerstein, divorce is a disaster for children that can change the trajectory of their entire lives. Perhaps, as others contend, children might

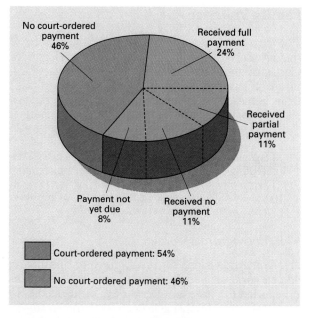

FIGURE 17–5 Payment of Child Support Following Divorce
Source: U.S. Bureau of the Census (1995).

better endure a parental divorce than remain in a family torn by tension or violence. But parents need to be mindful that, in a decision to divorce or not, much more than their own well-being is at stake (Goetting, 1981; Wallerstein & Blakeslee, 1989).

Remarriage

Despite the rising divorce rate, marriage—and remarriage—remain as popular as ever. Four out of five people who divorce remarry, and most do so within five years. Nationwide, almost half of all marriages are now remarriages for at least one partner. Men, who derive greater benefits from wedlock, are more likely to remarry than women are.

Remarriage often creates *blended families*, composed of children and some combination of biological parents and stepparents. Members of blended families thus have to define precisely who is part of the child's nuclear family (Furstenberg, 1984). Blended families also require children to reorient themselves; an only child, for example, may suddenly find she has two older brothers. And, as already noted, the risk of divorce is high for partners in such families. But blended families also offer both young and old the opportunity to relax rigid family roles.

NOTE: In 1993, the FBI recorded 2,697 cases of murder against children. Experts estimate that only half of such cases are recorded. While men are responsible for most child abuse, the younger the child, the more likely women are to be the perpetrators.

DISCUSS: Primary groups are not immune to conflict. Discuss the meaning of the common sayings "You always hurt the ones you love" and "Familiarity breeds contempt."

THEN AND NOW: In 1960, 5% of U.S. children were born to single mothers; the proportion has now risen above 30%. Of these mothers, about 30% are under age 20.

NOTE: Steven Ruggles (1994) reports that the pattern by which African Americans are two to three times more likely than whites to live without one or both biological parents extends back at least to 1880.

Family Violence

The ideal family serves as a haven from the dangers of the outside world. However, from the Biblical story of Cain's killing of his brother Abel to the recent O. J. Simpson case, we see that the disturbing reality of many homes has been **family violence**, *emotional, physical, or sexual abuse of one family member by another.* Sociologist Richard J. Gelles points to a chilling fact:

> The family is the most violent group in society with the exception of the police and the military. You are more likely to get killed, injured, or physically attacked in your home by someone you are related to than in any other social context. (quoted in Roesch, 1984:75)

Violence Against Women

Domestic violence against women occurs among all categories of people. Family brutality often goes unreported to police, but the Bureau of Justice Statistics (1994) estimates that at least 600,000 women are victims of domestic violence each year. Researchers note that men initiate most family violence and that women suffer most of the injuries (Straus & Gelles, 1986; Schwartz, 1987; Shupe, Stacey, and Hazlewood, 1987).

Government statistics show that almost 30 percent of women who are murdered—as opposed to 3 percent of men—are killed by partners or ex-partners. The U.S. death toll from family violence is 1,500 women each year. Overall, women are more likely to be injured by a family member than to be mugged or raped by a stranger or hurt in an automobile accident.

Not long ago, the law declared wives the property of their husbands, so that no man could be charged with raping his wife. By 1995, however, forty states had passed marital rape laws; in some cases, however, such a charge can be made only under specific circumstances such as after a legal separation (Russell, 1982; O'Reilly, 1983; Margolick, 1984; Goetting, 1989).

People who hear about a case of abuse often shake their heads and wonder, "Why didn't she just leave?" The answer is that most physically and emotionally abused women—especially those with children and without much money—have few options. Most wives are also committed to their marriages and believe (however unrealistically) that they can help abusive husbands to change. Some, unable to understand their husbands' violence, blame themselves. Others, raised in violent families, have learned to view assault as part of everyday family life.

In the past, the law regarded domestic violence as a private, family matter. Now, even without separation or divorce, a woman can obtain court protection from an abusive spouse. Today, half the states have added "stalking laws" that prohibit an ex-partner from following or otherwise threatening a woman. Finally, communities across the United States have established shelters that provide counseling as well as temporary housing for women and children driven from their homes by domestic violence.

Violence Against Children

Family violence also victimizes children. Upwards of 3 million children—roughly 4 percent of all youngsters—suffer abuse each year, including several thousand who die as a result. Child abuse entails more than physical injury because abusive adults misuse power and trust to undermine a child's emotional well-being. Child abuse is most common among the youngest and most vulnerable children (Straus & Gelles, 1986; Van Biema, 1994).

Many abused children suffer in silence, believing during their formative years that they are to blame for their own victimization. The initial abuse, compounded by years of guilt, can leave lasting emotional scars that prevent people abused as children from forming healthy relationships as adults.

About 90 percent of child abusers are men, but they conform to no simple stereotype. As one man who entered a therapy group reported, "I kept waiting for all the guys with raincoats and greasy hair to show up. But everyone looked like regular middle-class people" (quoted in Lubenow, 1984). Most abusers, however, share one trait: having been abused themselves as children. Researchers have discovered that violent behavior in close relationships is learned; in families, then, violence begets violence (Gwartney-Gibbs, Stockard, & Bohmer, 1987).

ALTERNATIVE FAMILY FORMS

Most families in the United States are still composed of a married couple who raise children. But, in recent decades, our society has displayed greater diversity in family life.

One-Parent Families

Twenty-six percent of U.S. families with children under eighteen years of age have only one parent in the household—a proportion that more than doubled during the last generation. Put another way, 28 percent of U.S. children now live with only one parent,

NOTE: Edward L. Kain (1990:6) points out that U.S. children were more likely to live in a one-parent family a century ago (due to high mortality) than they are today.

THEN AND NOW: Share of single-parent families: *1970*, 12%; *1994*, 30%. Among African Americans, 35%, 63%; among whites 10%, 24%.

THEN AND NOW: The Census Bureau estimates the number of U.S. cohabiting couples at some 3.7 million, up 60% since 1970.

THEN AND NOW: Share of U.S. population, aged 25–44, that has cohabited: *1987*, 37%; *1994*, 47%. Bumpass & Sweet (1994)

NOTE: Research suggests that cohabitation is inversely correlated with religiosity. Thornton, Axinn, & Hill (1992)

and about half of all children will do so at least some time before reaching the age of eighteen. One-parent families—88 percent of which are headed by a single mother—may result from divorce, death, or the choice of an unmarried woman to have a child. Figure 17–6 compares the share of U.S. births out of wedlock to those for other industrial nations.

Entering the labor force has bolstered women's financial capacity to be single mothers. But single parenthood—especially when the parent is a woman—greatly increases the risks of poverty, as it limits the woman's ability to work and to further her education. At least one-third of women in the United States now become pregnant as unmarried teenagers, and many decide to raise their children on their own. These young women with children—especially if they have the additional disadvantage of being minorities—form the core of the rising problem of child poverty in the United States.

Looking back to Figure 17–2, on page 468, note that 54 percent of African-American families are headed by a single parent. Single parenting is less common among Hispanics (32 percent), among Asian Americans (18 percent), and among non-Hispanic whites (18 percent). Among all categories of people, the trend is toward more single-parent families. Moreover, an increasing number of these one-parent families are multigenerational. In other words, single parents (most of whom are mothers) commonly look to their own parents (again, typically, mothers) for assistance and support. In the United States, then, the rise in single parenting is tied to both a declining role for fathers and the growing importance of grandparenting.

Much contemporary research points to the conclusion that growing up in a one-parent family usually disadvantages children. Some studies indicate that a father and a mother each make a distinctive contribution to a child's social development, so it is unrealistic to expect one parent alone to do as good a job as two working together. But the most serious problem among families with one parent—especially if that parent is a woman—is poverty. On average, children growing up in a single-parent family start out with disadvantages and end up with lesser educational achievement and lower incomes, and face a greater chance of forming one-parent families themselves (Mueller & Cooper, 1984; McLanahan, 1985; Weisner & Eiduson, 1986; Wallerstein & Blakeslee, 1989; Astone & McLanahan, 1991; Li & Wojtkiewicz, 1992; Biblarz & Raftery, 1993; Popenoe, 1993; Shapiro & Schrof, 1995; Webster, Orbuch, & House, 1995).

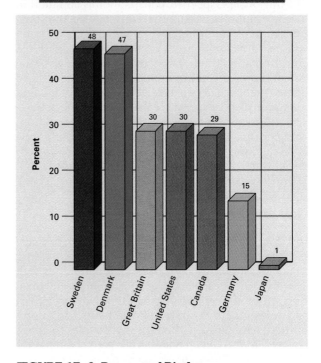

Global Snapshot

FIGURE 17–6 Percent of Births to Unmarried Women, 1991
Source: U.S. Bureau of the Census (1995).

Cohabitation

Cohabitation is *the sharing of a household by an unmarried couple.* A generation ago, widespread use of terms like "shacking up" and "living in sin" indicated disapproval of cohabitation. But, as our society has grown more accepting of premarital sex, the number of cohabiting couples in the United States has increased sharply, from about 500,000 in 1970 to 3.6 million by 1994, a figure that represents 6.3 percent of all couples (U.S. Bureau of the Census, 1995).

Certainly much cohabitation is the product of sexual passion; but, in today's uncertain economic climate, moving in together is also a practical strategy for two people looking to trim expenses. In any case, although most cohabitation occurs among the young, it usually does not lead to marriage. Rather, cohabiting

NOTE: In 1992, *The Star Tribune* in Minneapolis became the first newspaper to list gay "domestic partnerships" on the wedding page.
GLOBAL: Denmark legalized homosexuality in 1930. Half the U.S. states still have laws restricting homosexual behavior. The Danes, Norwegians, and Swedes allow gay and nongay couples equal rights with regard to marriage, inheritance, taxation, and property ownership, but not with regard to adoption of children.

GLOBAL: In Japan, single males are increasing in number. From 1% of men aged 50 in 1920, "never-marrieds" now comprise almost 20% of all 50-year-old men.
NOTE: Economic pressures and marriage later in life are encouraging single men and women to live with parents. In 1990, among single people aged 25–34, 32% of men and 20% of women were living with parents.

is becoming a normative way to test the strength of a serious relationship (Gwartney-Gibbs, 1986).

In global perspective, cohabitation is common in Sweden and other Scandinavian societies as a long-term form of family life, with or without children. By contrast, this family form is rare in more traditional (and Roman Catholic) nations such as Italy. While cohabitation is gaining in popularity in the United States—almost half of people between twenty-five and forty-four years of age have cohabited at some point—such partnerships are still usually of short duration, with perhaps 40 percent of couples marrying after several years, and the remainder splitting up (Blumstein & Schwartz, 1983; Macklin, 1983; Popenoe, 1988, 1991, 1992; Bumpass & Sweet, 1995).

Gay and Lesbian Couples

In 1989, Denmark became the first country to formally recognize homosexual marriages, thereby extending social legitimacy to gay and lesbian couples as well as conferring legal advantages for inheritance, taxation, and joint property ownership. Norway (1993) and Sweden (1995) have followed suit. But none of these nations allows homosexual couples to adopt children. In the United States, while gay people cannot legally marry (but can adopt children), some cities (including San Francisco and New York) allow "registered partnerships" that confer some of the legal benefits of marriage.

Most U.S. gay couples in households including children raise the offspring of previous, heterosexual unions; some couples have adopted children. But many gay parents are quiet about their sexual orientation, not wishing to draw unwelcome attention to their children. In several widely publicized cases in recent years, courts have removed children from homosexual couples, claiming to represent the best interests of the children.

There are at least 1 million gay and lesbian couples in the United States who are now raising one or more children. While this pattern challenges many traditional notions about families in the United States, it also indicates that many gay and lesbian couples perceive the same rewards in child rearing that "straight" couples do (Bell, Weinberg, & Kiefer-Hammersmith, 1981; Gross, 1991; Pressley & Andrews, 1992; Henry, 1993).

Singlehood

Living alone is becoming more common in the United States. In 1950, only one household in ten consisted of a single person. By 1994, this proportion had risen to about one in four: a total of 24 million single adults. Most striking is the surging number of single young women. Elderly widows have always represented a large share of single people; more recently, however, younger women here in the United States are choosing to stay single, just as they are in Japan, as we noted in the chapter opening. In 1960, 28 percent of U.S. women aged twenty to twenty-four were single; by 1994 the proportion had soared to two-thirds. Underlying this trend is women's greater participation in the labor force: Women who are economically secure view a husband as a matter of choice rather than a financial necessity.

By midlife, however, unmarried women encounter a shrinking pool of available men. Because we expect women to "marry up," the older a woman is, the more education she has, and the better her job, the more difficulty she will have in finding a suitable husband (Leslie & Korman, 1989).

NEW REPRODUCTIVE TECHNOLOGY AND THE FAMILY

In 1991, Arlette Schweitzer, a forty-two-year-old librarian living in Aberdeen, South Dakota, became the first woman on record to bear her own grandchildren. Because her daughter was unable to carry a baby to term, Schweitzer agreed to have her daughter's fertilized embryos surgically implanted in her own womb. Nine months later, her efforts yielded healthy twins—a boy and girl (Kolata, 1991).

Such a case illustrates how *new reproductive technology* has created new choices for families and sparked new controversies for society as a whole. The benefits of this rapidly developing technology are exciting; but its use raises daunting ethical questions about the creation and manipulation of life itself.

In Vitro Fertilization

A generation ago, England's Louise Brown became the world's first "test-tube" baby; since then, tens of thousands of people have been conceived in this way. Early in the next century, 2 or 3 percent of the children in industrial societies may be conceived through new birth technologies.

Technically speaking, test-tube babies are the product of *in vitro fertilization*, a procedure whereby the male sperm and the female ovum are united "in glass" rather than in a woman's body. In this complex

Q: "We have Model T laws catching up with space-age technology." Lori Andrews, American Bar Foundation, on legal and ethical issues arising out of new reproductive technologies

Q: "It's ironic that in a world of commerce we have elaborate laws and contracts for insuring some protection and fairness in our financial dealings with one another, but to those we love most, we offer no such guarantees." Marcia Millman

NOTE: Almost 60% of U.S. children live in the Census Bureau's "traditional nuclear family" made up of married biological parents and no one else (by race, 66% white, 28% black, 45% Hispanic). Using a broader definition of family, 77% of children live in two-parent families (not necessarily biological parents nor a married couple). So of kids not in traditional families, half are not at risk, and half may be.

medical procedure, undertaken by some 27,000 U.S. couples each year, doctors use drugs to stimulate the woman's ovaries to produce more than one egg during a reproductive cycle. Then they surgically harvest eggs from her ovaries and combine them with sperm in a laboratory dish. The successful fusion of eggs and sperm produces embryos, which surgeons then either implant in the womb of a woman who is to bear the child or freeze for use at a later time.

The immediate benefit of *in vitro* fertilization is to help couples who cannot conceive normally to have children. Looking further ahead, new birth technologies may eventually reduce the incidence of birth defects. By genetically screening sperm and eggs, medical specialists expect to increase the odds for the birth of a healthy baby (Vines, 1986; Ostling, 1987; Thompson, 1994).

Ethical Issues

Ethical debate over these methods of manipulating life illustrates the concept of *cultural lag* (see Chapter 3, "Culture"), in which society has yet to catch up to the moral implications of a new technology.

The high cost of *in vitro* fertilization (upwards of $100,000) places this procedure within reach of only a small number of people. In addition, as they decide when to employ or withhold this technique, medical experts are in a position to define what constitutes a proper "family." In most cases, doctors and hospitals have restricted *in vitro* fertilization to women under forty years of age who have male partners. Single women, older women, and lesbian couples are only gradually gaining access to this technology.

But all types of new reproductive technology—from laboratory fertilization to *surrogate motherhood*, in which one woman bears a child for another—force us to confront the inadequacy of conventional kinship terms (Is Arlette Schweitzer the mother of the twins she bore? Grandmother? Both?). Then, too, we need to consider that, when it comes to manipulating life, what is technically possible may not always be morally desirable.

LOOKING AHEAD: FAMILY IN THE TWENTY-FIRST CENTURY

In recent decades, transformation in U.S. family life generated controversy, with advocates of "traditional family values" locked in debate with supporters of new family forms and greater personal choice. The closing box focuses on one key dimension of this debate:

For better or worse, the family is certainly changing. But the fact that young people still find marriage so attractive—even amid the most severe adversity—suggests that families will continue to play a central role in society for centuries to come.

Should we work to save the family? Whatever position one takes on the merits of current family trends, change is certain to continue into the coming century. Based on current evidence, we can make five predictions about the future of family life.

First, divorce rates are likely to remain high, even in the face of growing evidence that divorce threatens children. There may be some erosion of support for easy dissolution of marriage, yet several generations of high divorce rates have seriously weakened the idea that marriage is a lifetime commitment. Looking back through history, marital relationships are about as durable today as they were a century ago, when many marriages were cut short by death (Kain, 1990). But more couples now *choose* to end marriages that fail to live up to their expectations. Therefore, although the divorce rate has stabilized recently, it is unlikely that marriage will regain the

Q: "Neither the pessimists who believe that the family is falling apart nor the unbridled optimists who claim that the family has never been in better shape provide an accurate picture of family life in the near future. But . . . what we have come to view as the 'traditional' family will no longer predominate." Andrew Cherlin and Frank F. Furstenberg, Jr.

NOTE: A Census Bureau study of the U.S. poor in 1994 found that

34.6% of people in female-headed households were poor versus 6.1% of people in married-couple households. Of the chronic poor—people poor all year long—only 1.4% lived in married-couple households. Thus, one of the clearest upredictors of whether a child will live in poverty is the marital status of the child's parents.

Q: "Mature adults may be able to do without strong families, but children cannot." David Popenoe

Controversy & Debate   Should We Save the Traditional Family?

Are "traditional families" vital to our way of life? Or are they a barrier to progress? To begin, people typically use the term "traditional family" to mean a married couple who, at some point in their lives, raise children. But the term is more than simply descriptive—it is also a moral statement. That is, support for the traditional family implies that people place a high value on getting and staying married, that parents should place more importance on raising children than to pursuing their own careers, and that society should accord special respect to two-parent families rather than various "alternative lifestyles."

On one side of the debate, David Popenoe notes with alarm the rapid erosion of the traditional family since 1960. Then, married couples with young children accounted for almost half of all households; today, the figure is just 37 percent. Singlehood is up, from 10 percent then to 24 percent of households now. Divorce, too, has become more common, with the rate of marital breakup doubling since

1960 so that half of today's marriages will end in permanent separation. And, because of both divorce and increasing numbers of children born out of wedlock, the share of youngsters living with a single parent at some time before age eighteen has quadrupled since 1960 to half of all children. Combining the last two facts, just one in four of today's children will grow up with two parents and go on to maintain a stable marriage of their own.

In light of such data, Popenoe concludes, the family is not just changing, it is heading toward total collapse. He describes this breakdown as a fundamental shift from a "culture of marriage" to a "culture of divorce." Traditional vows of marital commitment—"till death us do part"—now amount to little more than "as long as I am happy." Drawing on national survey data, Daniel Yankelovich (1994:20) sums up this cultural shift:

The quest for greater individual choice clashed directly with the obligations and social norms that held families and communities together in earlier years. People came to feel that questions of how to live and with whom to live were a matter of individual choice not to be governed by restrictive norms. As a nation, we came to experience the bonds to marriage, family, children, job, community, and country as constraints that were no longer necessary. Commitments have loosened.

The negative consquences of the cultural trend toward weaker families, Popenoe continues, are obvious everywhere: As we pay less and less attention to children, the crime rate goes up along with a host of other problematic behaviors, including smoking, drinking, and premarital sex.

As Popenoe sees it, then, we must work hard and quickly to reverse current trends. Government cannot be the solution (and may even be part of the problem): Since 1960 as government spending on social programs has soared fivefold, the traditional family has grown weaker and weaker.

durability characteristic of the 1950s. One major reason is that increasing numbers of women are able to support themselves, and traditional marriages appeal to fewer of them. Men, as well, are seeking more satisfying relationships. Perhaps we should view the recent trend toward higher divorce rates less as a threat to families than as a sign of change in family form. After all, most divorces still lead to remarriage, casting doubt on the notion that marriage itself is becoming obsolete.

Second, family life in the twenty-first century will be highly variable. We have noted an increasing number of cohabiting couples, one-parent families, gay and lesbian families, and blended families. Most families, of course, still are based on marriage, and

most married couples still have children. But, taken together, the variety of family forms observed today represents a new conception of family life as a matter of choice.

Third, men are likely to continue to play a limited role in child rearing. In the 1950s, a decade many people nostalgically recall as the "golden age" of families, men began to withdraw from active parenting (Snell, 1990; Stacey, 1990). Since then, the share of children growing up in homes without their fathers has passed 25 percent and is continuing to rise. A countertrend is emerging as some fathers—older, on average, and more established in their careers—eagerly jump into parenting. But, on balance, the high U.S. divorce rate and a surge in single motherhood point to

The alternative, Popenoe reasons, is a cultural turnaround by which people will question and ultimately reject the recently popular "me-first" view of our lives in favor of greater commitment to a spouse and children. (We have seen such a turnaround in the case of cigarette smoking.) Yes, concludes Popenoe, we should save the traditional family, and that means we need to affirm publicly the value of marital permanence as well as endorse the two-parent family as best for the well-being of children.

Judith Stacey, who deplores the traditional family, provides a counterpoint. To her, the traditional family is more problem than solution. Striking to the heart of the matter, Stacey writes (1990:269):

The family is not here to stay. Nor should we wish it were. On the contrary, I believe that all democratic people, whatever their kinship preferences, should work to hasten its demise.

The main reason for rejecting the traditional family, Stacey explains, is that it perpetuates and enhances various kinds of social inequality. Families play a key role in maintaining the class hierarchy, transferring wealth as well as "cultural capital" from one generation to another. Moreover, feminists charge that the traditional family is built on patriarchy, which subjects women to their husbands' authority as well as saddling them with most of the responsibility for housework and child care. And from a gay-rights perspective, she adds, a society that values traditional families inevitably denies homosexual men and women equal dignity and participation in social life.

Stacey thus applauds the breakdown of the family as a measure of social progress. Indeed, she views the family not as a basic social institution but as a political construction that serves to elevate one category of people—affluent white males—at the expense of women, homosexuals, and poor people who lack the resources to maintain middle-class respectability.

Moreover, Stacey continues, the concept of "traditional family" is increasingly irrelevant to a diverse society in which people reject singular models of correct behavior and in which both men and women must work for income. What our society needs, Stacey concludes, is not a return to some golden age of the family but political and economic changes (including income parity for women, universal health care, programs to reduce unemployment, and expanded sex education in the schools) that will provide tangible support for our children as well as ensure that people in diverse family forms receive the respect and dignity everyone deserves.

Continue the debate . . .

1. *To strengthen families, Popenoe urges parents to put children ahead of their own careers by limiting their joint working week to sixty hours. Do you agree? Why or why not?*

2. *Judith Stacey asserts that patriarchy cements most stable marriages. Do you agree?*

3. *What policies or programs would you support to enhance the well-being of this country's children?*

Sources: Stacey (1990, 1993), Popenoe (1993), and Council on Families in America (1995).

more children growing up with weaker ties to fathers than ever before. And the evidence is building that the absence of fathers is significantly detrimental to children, at the very least because such families are at high risk of being poor.

Fourth, economic changes will continue to reform marriage and the family. In many families, both household partners must work to ensure the family's financial security. As Arlie Hochschild (1988) points out, the economy is responsible for most of the change in society, but people *feel* these changes in the family. Marriage today is often the interaction of weary men and women: Adults try their best to attend to children, yet worry that popular ideas like "quality time" amount to nothing more than rationalizations for minimal parenting (Dizard & Gadlin, 1990). Two-career couples may advance the goal of gender equality, but the long-term effects on families are likely to be mixed.

Fifth and finally, the importance of new reproductive technologies will increase. While ethical concerns surely will slow these developments, new methods of reproduction will continue to alter the traditional meanings of parenthood.

Despite social changes that have buffeted the family in the United States, most people still report being happy as partners and parents. Marriage and family life today may be more controversial than in the past, but both will likely remain the foundation of our society for some time to come.

SUMMARY

1. All societies are built on kinship, although family forms vary considerably across cultures and over time.

2. In industrial societies such as the United States, marriage is monogamous. Many preindustrial societies, however, permit polygamy, of which there are two types: polygyny and polyandry.

3. In global perspective, patrilocality is most common, while industrial societies favor neolocality and a few societies have matrilocal residence. Industrial societies embrace bilateral descent; preindustrial societies tend to be either patrilineal or matrilineal.

4. Structural-functional analysis identifies major family functions: socializing the young, regulating sexual activity, transmitting social placement, and providing material and emotional support.

5. Social-conflict theories explore how the family perpetuates social inequality by strengthening divisions based on class, ethnicity, race, and gender.

6. Micro-level analysis highlights the variable nature of family life both over time and as experienced by individual family members.

7. Families originate in the process of courtship. Unlike the United States, most societies limit the role of romantic love in the choice of a mate. But even among members of our society, romantic love tends to join people with similar social backgrounds.

8. The vast majority of married couples have children, although family size has decreased over time. The key reason for this decline is industrialization, which transforms children into economic liabilities, encourages women to become educated and to join the labor force, and reduces infant mortality.

9. In later life, marriage changes as children leave home to form families of their own. Many middle-aged couples, however, continue to care for aging parents and are active grandparents. The final stage of married life begins with the death of one spouse, usually the husband.

10. Families differ according to class position, race, and ethnicity. Latino families, for example, tend to maintain extended kinship ties. African-American families are more likely than others to be headed by women. Among all categories of people, well-to-do families enjoy the most options and the greatest financial security.

11. Gender affects family dynamics since husbands play a dominant role in the vast majority of families. Research suggests that marriage provides more benefits to men than to women.

12. Today's divorce rate is ten times higher than a century ago; four in ten current marriages will end in divorce. Most people who divorce—especially men—remarry, often forming blended families that include children from previous marriages.

13. Family violence, victimizing both women and children, is far more common than official records indicate. Adults who abuse family members most often suffered abuse themselves as children.

14. Our society's family life is becoming more varied. One-parent families, cohabitation, gay and lesbian couples, and singlehood have proliferated in recent years. While the law does not recognize homosexual marriages, many gay men and lesbians form long-lasting relationships and, increasingly, are becoming parents.

15. Although ethically controversial, new reproductive technology is altering conventional notions of parenthood.

KEY CONCEPTS

bilateral descent a system tracing kinship through both men and women

cohabitation the sharing of a household by an unmarried couple

descent the system by which members of a society trace kinship over generations

endogamy marriage between people of the same social category

exogamy marriage between people of different social categories

extended family (consanguine family) a family unit including parents and children, but also other kin

family a social institution, found in all societies, that unites individuals into cooperative groups that oversee the bearing and raising of children

family unit a social group of two or more people, related by blood, marriage, or adoption, who usually live together

family violence emotional, physical, or sexual abuse of one family member by another

homogamy marriage between people with the same social characteristics

incest taboo a cultural norm forbidding sexual relations or marriage between certain kin

kinship a social bond, based on blood, marriage, or adoption, that joins individuals into families

marriage a legally sanctioned relationship, involving economic cooperation as well as normative sexual activity and childbearing, that people expect to be enduring

matrilineal descent a system tracing kinship through women

matrilocality a residential pattern in which a married couple lives with or near the wife's family

monogamy a form of marriage joining two partners

neolocality a residential pattern in which a married couple lives apart from the parents of both spouses

nuclear family (conjugal family) a family unit composed of one or two parents and their children

patrilineal descent a system tracing kinship through men

patrilocality a residential pattern in which a married couple lives with or near the husband's family

polyandry a form of marriage joining one female with two or more males

polygamy a form of marriage uniting three or more people

polygyny a form of marriage joining one male with two or more females

CRITICAL-THINKING QUESTIONS

1. How has the emerging postindustrial economy affected family life? What other factors are changing the family?

2. Why do some analysts describe the family as the "backbone of society"? How do families perpetuate social inequality?

3. Do you think that single-parent households do as good a job as two-parent households in raising children? Why?

4. On balance, are families in the United States becoming weaker or not? What evidence supports your contention?

SUGGESTED READINGS

Classic Sources

Herbert G. Gutman. *The Black Family in Slavery and Freedom: 1750–1925*. New York: Pantheon Books, 1976.
   This is one of the most influential studies of the history of the African-American family.

Michael Young and Peter Willmott. *Family and Kinship in East London*. Berkeley: University of California Press, 1992 (orig. 1957).
   One of the best studies of the working-class family, this chronicle reveals the effect of class on family life.

Contemporary Sources

Penelope Leach. *Children First: What Our Society Must Do—And Is Not Doing—For Our Children Today*. New York: Random House, 1995.
   This assessment of the state of U.S. children offers concrete policy proposals that address the highly controversial "family values" debate.

Lillian Rubin. *Families on the Fault Line: America's Working Class Speaks About the Family, the Economy, Race, and Ethnicity*. New York: HarperCollins, 1994.
   Based on four hundred interviews, Rubin conveys working-class families' sense of themselves and their society in hard economic times.

Global Sources

William J. Goode. *World Changes in Divorce Patterns*. New Haven, Conn.: Yale University Press, 1993.
   This global survey explains how divorce is affected by economic patterns such as industrialization; it also explores variation in divorce by class.

Mark Mathabane. *African Women: Three Generations*. New York: HarperCollins, 1994.
   This personal look at three women—a grandmother, a mother, and a sister—by a South African details the struggles common to women under a system of racial oppression.

Religion

About the time most people in the small town of Conyers, Georgia (population 7,380) are waking up, a long line of vehicles already clogs state highway 138. As state troopers wave cars, trucks, and tour buses into fields marked by "Pilgrim Parking" signs, a large crowd—including dozens of men and women in wheelchairs—swells over the thirty-acre farm of Nancy Fowler, a forty-three-year-old former nurse. The commotion began six years ago, when Fowler claims she started seeing visions in the sky of Jesus Christ and the Virgin Mary.

At noon, the crowd begins the Catholic ritual of chanting the Rosary. After almost an hour, Fowler whispers to a select group in her small, one-story home that Mary is descending, barely visible in the brilliant sunlight. The word spreads, and the crowd falls silent, video cameras whirring, as people intently gaze upward at the sun. Suddenly some people shout that they see Mary, and the excitement ripples through the assembled faithful. After some time, an announcer intones, "The Virgin Mary will now bless us," and people thrust their arms upward, holding aloft beads, crosses, and pictures of Christ as their faces radiate a mix of wonder, excitement, and joy.

Although divine sightings of this kind are reported regularly in several locations—the best known are Lourdes in France and Fátima in Portugal—they are most common in the United States. Skeptical people dismiss such extraordinary experiences as little more than self-delusion and the Roman Catholic church officially discourages reports of such miracles, but the prospect of divine revelation draws hundreds of thousands of people each year to Conyers, Georgia, and elsewhere (Smolowe, 1993).

The timeless human fascination with otherworldly truth lies at the heart of religion. This chapter explains what religion is, explores the changing face of religious belief throughout history and around the world, and examines the place of religion in today's modern, scientific culture. As we shall see, religion is a social institution that continues to address questions about the ultimate meaning of life in ways that no other dimension of society can.

RELIGION: BASIC CONCEPTS

French sociologist Emile Durkheim, whose ideas are discussed in detail in Chapter 4 ("Society"), claimed that the focus of religion is "things that surpass the limits of our knowledge" (1965:62; orig. 1915). As human beings, Durkheim explained, we organize our surroundings by defining most objects, events, or experiences as **profane** (from Latin meaning "outside the temple"), *that which is an ordinary element of everyday life*. But we set some things apart, Durkheim continued, by designating them as **sacred**, *that which is defined as extraordinary, inspiring a sense of awe, reverence, and even fear*. Distinguishing the sacred from the profane is the essence of all religious belief. **Religion**, then, is *a social institution involving beliefs and practices based upon a conception of the sacred*.

Around the world, matters of faith vary greatly, with no one thing sacred to everyone on earth. Although people regard most books as profane, Jews view the Torah (the first five books of the Hebrew Bible or Old Testament) as sacred, in the same way that Christians revere the entire Bible and Muslims exalt the Qur'an (Koran).

However a community of believers draws religious lines, Durkheim (1965:62) claimed, people understand profane things in terms of their everyday usefulness: We sit down at a computer or turn the key of a car to accomplish various tasks. What is sacred, however, we set apart from everyday life and regard with reverence. To make clear the

NOTE: Their Latin roots join the words "faith" and "trust."

Q: "Sociologists have a hard time coming to terms with the intensely religious character of the contemporary world. Whether politically on the left or not, they suffer from ideological blinders when it comes to religion, and the tendency is to explain away what cannot be explained. But, ideology apart, parochialism is an important factor here too. Sociologists live in truly secularized milieus—academia and the other institutions of the professional knowledge industry—and it appears that they are no more immune than the sociologically untrained to the common misconception that one can generalize about the world from one's own little corner." Peter Berger (1992:15–16)

NOTE: The Latin root of "religion" is *religare*, "to be tied back," suggesting the link between religion and tradition.

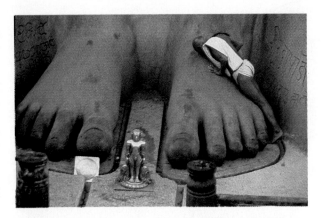

Religion is founded on the idea of the sacred, that which is set apart as extraordinary and which demands our submission. Bowing, kneeling, or prostrating oneself—each a common element of religious devotion—symbolizes this submissiveness.

boundary between the sacred and the profane, Muslims remove their shoes before entering a mosque to avoid defiling a sacred place of worship with soles that have touched the profane ground outside.

The sacred is the focus of **ritual**, which is *formal, ceremonial behavior*. Holy communion is the central ritual of Christianity; the wafer and wine consumed during communion symbolize the body and blood of Jesus Christ, and are never treated as food.

Religion and Sociology

Because religion deals with ideas that transcend everyday experience, neither common sense nor any scientific discipline can verify or disprove religious doctrine. Religion is a matter of **faith**, *belief anchored in conviction rather than scientific evidence*. For instance, the New Testament of the Bible defines faith as "the assurance of things hoped for, the conviction of things not seen" (Heb. 11:1) and exhorts Christians to "walk by faith, not by sight" (2 Cor. 5:7).

Throughout most of human history, human beings living in small societies attributed birth, death, and whatever happened in between to the operation of supernatural forces. Over the course of the last several hundred years, however, science has emerged as an alternative way of understanding the natural world, and scientific sociology offers various explanations of how and why societies operate the way they do.

Some people with strong faith may be disturbed by the thought of sociologists turning a scientific eye to what they hold as sacred. In truth, however, the sociological study of religion is no threat to anyone's faith. Sociologists recognize that religion is central to virtually every culture on earth, and they seek to understand how religious beliefs and practices guide human societies. They offer no comment on the meaning and purpose of human existence, nor can they pass judgment on any religion as right or wrong. Rather, scientific sociology delves into the consequences of religious activity for larger social life.

THEORETICAL ANALYSIS OF RELIGION

Although, as individuals, sociologists may hold any number of religious beliefs—or none at all—they all agree that religion has major importance for the operation of society. Each theoretical paradigm suggests ways in which religion affects social life.

Functions of Religion: Structural-Functional Analysis

Emile Durkheim (1965; orig. 1915) maintained that we confront the power of society every day. Society, he argued, has an existence and power all its own beyond the life of any individual. Thus, society itself is "god-like," surviving the ultimate deaths of its members whose lives it shapes. Durkheim contended that, in religious life, people celebrate the awesome power of their own society.

This insight explains the practice, in every society, of transforming certain everyday objects into sacred symbols of collective life. Members of technologically simple societies, Durkheim explained, do this with the **totem,** *an object in the natural world collectively defined as sacred.* The totem—perhaps an animal or an elaborate work of art—becomes the centerpiece of ritual, symbolizing the power of society to transform individuals into a powerful collectivity. In our society, the flag is a quasi-sacred totem. It is not to be used in a profane manner (say, as clothing) or allowed to touch the ground. In addition, placing the inscription "In God We Trust" on all currency (begun in the 1860s at the time of the Civil War) implies a national bond of religious belief. Local communities across the United States also gain a sense of unity through totemlike symbolism attached to sports teams: from the New England "Patriots," to the Ohio State University "Buckeyes," to the St. Louis "Rams."

Durkheim pointed out three major functions of religion for the operation of society:

SOCIAL SURVEY: Illustrating religious social control, Carol Tavris and Susan Sadd (1977:38) found the following incidence of premarital sex:

"Strongly religious"	61%	"Slightly religious"	86%
"Fairly religious"	78%	"Not religious"	89%

RESOURCE: To the question of creation—"How did *something* come from *nothing?*"—various cultures respond in surprisingly

similar ways. See Raymond Van Over's *Sun Songs: Creation Myths from Around the World* (New York: New American Library, 1980).
Q: "In everyday life it is just as important that some things can be silently taken for granted as that some things are reaffirmed in so many words. Indeed, the most fundamental assumptions about the world . . . are so 'obvious' that there is no need to put them into words." Peter Berger

1. **Social cohesion.** Religion unites people through shared symbols, values, and norms. Religious doctrine and ritual establish rules of "fair play" that make organized social life possible. Religion also speaks eloquently about the vital human dimension of *love*. Thus, religious life underscores both our moral and emotional ties to others (Wright & D'Antonio, 1980).

2. **Social control.** Every society uses religious imagery and rhetoric to promote conformity. Societies infuse many cultural norms—especially mores relating to marriage and reproduction—with religious justification. Looking beyond behavioral norms, religion confers legitimacy on the political system. In medieval Europe, in fact, monarchs claimed to rule by divine right. Few of today's political leaders invoke religion so explicitly, but many publicly ask for God's blessing, implying to audiences that their efforts are right and just.

3. **Providing meaning and purpose.** Religious beliefs offer the comforting sense that the vulnerable human condition serves some greater purpose. Strengthened by such convictions, people are less likely to collapse in despair when confronted by life's calamities. For this reason, major life-course transitions—including birth, marriage, and death—are usually marked by religious observances that enhance our spiritual awareness.

Critical evaluation. Durkheim's structural-functional analysis contends that religion represents the collective life of society. The major weakness of this approach, however, is its tendency to downplay religion's dysfunctions—especially the capacity of strongly held beliefs to generate social conflict. During the early Middle Ages, for example, religious faith was the driving force behind the Crusades, in which European Christians sought to wrest from Muslim control lands that both religions considered to be sacred. Conflict among Muslims, Jews, and Christians continues as a source of political instability in the Middle East today. Social divisions in Northern Ireland are also partly a matter of religious conflict between Protestants and Catholics; Dutch Calvinism historically supported apartheid in South Africa; and religious differences continue to fuel divisions in Algeria, India, Sri Lanka, and elsewhere. In short, nations have long marched to war under the banner of their god, and few analysts dispute the fact that differences in faith have provoked more violence in the world than have differences of social class.

Constructing the Sacred: Symbolic-Interaction Analysis

"Society," asserts Peter Berger (1967:3) "is a human product and nothing but a human product, that yet continuously acts back upon its producer." From a symbolic-interactionist point of view, religion (like all of society) is socially constructed (although perhaps with divine inspiration). Through various rituals, from saying grace before daily meals to annual religious observances such as Easter or Passover, individuals develop the distinction between the sacred and profane. Further, Berger explains, by placing everyday events within a "cosmic frame of reference" people confer on their own fallible, transitory creations "the semblance of ultimate security and permanence" (1967:35–36).

Marriage is a good example. If we look on marriage merely as a contract between two people, we assume that we can end it whenever we want to. But if partners define their relationship as holy matrimony, this bond makes a far stronger claim on them. This fact, no doubt, explains why the divorce rate is lower among people who are more religious.

Especially when humans confront uncertainty and life-threatening situations—such as illness, war, and natural disaster—we bring sacred symbols to the fore. By seeking out sacred meaning in any situation, in other words, we can lift ourselves above life's setbacks and even face the prospect of death with strength and courage.

Critical evaluation. The symbolic-interaction approach views religion as a social construction, placing everyday life under a "sacred canopy" of meaning (Berger, 1967). Of course, Berger adds, the sacred's ability to legitimize and stabilize society depends on its constructed character going unrecognized. After all, we could derive little strength from sacred beliefs if we saw them to be mere devices for coping with tragedy. Then, too, this micro-level view pays scant attention to religion's link with social inequality, to which we now turn.

Inequality and Religion: Social-Conflict Analysis

The social-conflict paradigm highlights religion's support for social hierarchy. Religion, claimed Karl Marx, serves ruling elites by legitimizing the status quo and diverting people's attention from the social inequities of society.

DISCUSS: Do the following two pronouncements of the Roman Catholic church favor Marxism or market capitalism?
Q: "The needs of the poor must take priority over the desires of the rich; and the rights of workers over the maximization of profits." John Paul II

Q: ". . . In today's world . . . the right of economic initiative is often suppressed. Yet it is a right which is important not only for the individual but for the common good. Experience shows that the denial of this right, or its limitation in the name of alleged 'equality' of everyone in society, diminishes, or in practice absolutely destroys the spirit of initiative . . ." John Paul II

Q: "The more of himself man attributes to God, the less he has left in himself." Karl Marx

Q: "Faith is believing when you know it ain't so." Mark Twain

The foundation of all religious life is ritual. Such formal events as baptism, depicted in William H. Johnson's painting I Baptize Thee, *represent life-changing experiences (in Christian terms, "rebirth") that underscore the distinction between the secular and the sacred.*

National Museum of American Art, Washington, D.C./Art Resource, N.Y.

Even today, for example, the British monarch is crowned by the head of the Church of England, illustrating the close alliance between religious and political elites. In practical terms, working for political change may mean opposing the church and, by implication, God. Religion also encourages people to look hopefully to a "better world to come," minimizing the social problems of this world. In one of his best-known statements, Marx offered a stinging criticism of religion as "the sigh of the oppressed creature, the sentiment of a heartless world, and the soul of soulless conditions. It is the opium of the people" (1964:27; orig. 1848).

Gender also figures in religion's tie to social inequality. Virtually all the world's major religions have reflected and encouraged male dominance of social life, as the box on pages 488–89 explains.

During Marx's lifetime, powerful Christian nations of Western Europe justified colonial exploitation of Africa, the Americas, and Asia by claiming that they were merely "converting heathens." In the United States, major churches in the South considered the enslavement of African Americans to be consistent with God's will, and churches throughout the country remain notably segregated to this day. In the words of African-American novelist Maya Angelou, "Sunday at 11:30 a.m., America is more segregated than at any time of the week."

Critical evaluation. Social-conflict analysis reveals the power of religion to legitimize social inequality. Yet critics of religion's conservative face, Marx included, minimize ways in which religion has promoted change as well as equality. Nineteenth-century religious groups in the United States, for example, were at the forefront of the movement to abolish slavery. During the 1950s and 1960s, religious organizations and their leaders (including the Reverend Martin Luther King, Jr.) were at the core of the civil rights movement. During the 1960s and 1970s, many clergy actively opposed the Vietnam War, and, as we explain presently, some have supported revolutionary change in Latin America and elsewhere.

RELIGION AND SOCIAL CHANGE

Religion is not just the conservative force portrayed by Karl Marx. Historically, as Max Weber (1958; orig. 1904–5) pointed out, religion has promoted dramatic social change.

RESOURCE: An excerpt from Max Weber's *The Protestant Ethic and the Spirit of Capitalism* is among the classics included in the Macionis and Benokraitis reader, *Seeing Ourselves.*

Q: "[Rationalization] means that principally there are no mysterious, incalculable forces that come into play, but rather that one can, in principle, master all things by calculation." Max Weber

Q: "A permanent danger of an established church . . . is that a national church might become a nationalistic church." T.S. Eliot

Q: ". . . Established religious institutions have generally had a stake in the status quo and hence have fostered conservatism. . . . On the other hand, as the source of both humanistic values and the strength that can come from believing one is carrying out God's will in political matters, religion has occasionally played a role in movements for radical social change." Gary T. Marx

Max Weber: Protestantism and Capitalism

Max Weber contended that new ideas often operate as engines of change. It was in the wake of Calvinism, he noted, that Western Europe industrialized.

As Chapter 4 ("Society") explains in detail, John Calvin (1509–1564), a leader in the Protestant Reformation, advanced the doctrine of predestination. Calvin held that an all-powerful and all-knowing God predestines some people for salvation while condemning most to eternal damnation. With each individual's fate sealed before birth and known to God alone, the only certainty is what hangs in the balance: eternal peace and glory or hellfire and brimstone.

Driven by anxiety over their fate, Calvinists understandably sought signs of God's favor in *this* world and gradually settled on prosperity as a key symbol of divine favor. This conviction, coupled with their rigid devotion to duty, led Calvinists to become absorbed in the pursuit of success. But riches were never to fuel self-indulgent spending; nor were Calvinists moved to share their wealth with the poor, whose plight they saw as a mark of God's rejection.

As agents of God's work on earth, Calvinists believed that their lifelong "calling" was best fulfilled by reinvesting profits and reaping ever-greater wealth in the process. All the while, they practiced personal thrift and eagerly embraced technological advances that would enhance their efforts. Driven toward worldly success by religious motives, then, they laid the groundwork for the rise of industrial capitalism. In time, the religious fervor that motivated early Calvinists was transformed into a profane Protestant "work ethic," prompting Weber to describe industrial capitalism as a "disenchanted" religion. But his analysis leaves little doubt as to the power of religious thinking to alter the basic shape of society.

Liberation Theology

Christianity has a long-standing concern for the suffering of poor and oppressed people. Historically, the Christian response to poverty has been to strengthen the believer's faith in a better life to come. In recent decades, however, some church leaders and theologians have embraced **liberation theology,** *a fusion of Christian principles with political activism, often Marxist in character.*

This social movement started in the late 1960s in Latin America's Roman Catholic church. In addition to the church's efforts to free humanity from sin, Christian activists are helping people in low-income countries to liberate themselves from abysmal poverty. The message of liberation theology is simple: Social oppression runs counter to Christian morality; it is also preventable. Therefore, as a matter of faith and social justice, Christians must promote greater social equality.

A growing number of Catholic men and women have allied themselves with the poor in the liberation theology movement. The costs of opposing the status quo, however, have been high. Church members—including Oscar Arnulfo Romero, the archbishop of San Salvador (the capital of El Salvador)—have been killed in the violence that engulfs much of that region.

Liberation theology has also polarized the Catholic community by provoking strong criticism. Pope John Paul II condemns this movement for tainting traditional church doctrine with left-wing politics. Despite the pontiff's objections, however, the liberation theology movement has swept through Latin America, fueled by the belief that Christian faith should drive people to improve the condition of the world's poor (Boff, 1984; Neuhouser, 1989).

TYPES OF RELIGIOUS ORGANIZATION

Sociologists have devised a broad scheme to categorize the hundreds of different religious organizations in the United States. The most widely used model takes the form of a continuum, with *churches* at one pole and *sects* at the other. We can describe any actual religious organization, then, in relation to these two ideal types by locating it on the church-sect continuum.

Church and Sect

Drawing on the ideas of his teacher Max Weber, Ernst Troeltsch (1931) defined a **church** as *a type of religious organization well integrated into the larger society.* Churchlike organizations usually persist for centuries and claim as adherents generations of the same family. Churches have well-established rules and regulations and expect their leaders to undergo approved training before being formally ordained.

While concerned with the sacred, a church accepts the ways of the profane world, which gives it broad appeal. Church doctrine conceives of God in highly intellectualized terms (say, as a force for good), and favors abstract moral standards ("Do unto others as you would have them do unto you") over specific mandates for day-to-day living. By teaching morality in safely abstract terms, a church can avoid social

SOCIAL SURVEY: "Where would you place your image of God on the scale [between (1) Mother and (7) Father]?" (GSS 1994, N = 1,977; *Codebook*, 1994:127)

(1) 2.4%	(4) 25.5%	(7) 47.6%
(2) 1.4%	(5) 8.0%	DK/NR 4.7%
(3) 1.7%	(6) 8.8%	

DIVERSITY: The proportion of women serving as clergy in Protestant denominations ranges from 14% for Presbyterians to 35% for Unitarians.

GLOBAL: Some members of a society with an ecclesia see denominations as chaotic: "If Protestantism is a true religion," one Moroccan commented, "why do you Americans have hundreds of denominations?"

SOCIAL DIVERSITY

Religion and Patriarchy: Does God Favor Males?

Two-thirds of U.S. adults envision God primarily or exclusively in male terms (NORC, 1994:127). Because we associate attributes such as wisdom and power with men, it is not surprising that we tend to see God as masculine. By and large, organized religions also favor males, as we can see in passages from the sacred writings of major world religions.

The Qur'an (Koran)—the sacred text of Islam—asserts that men are to have social dominance over women:

Men are in charge of women. . . . Hence good women are obedient . . . As for those whose rebelliousness you fear, admonish them, banish them from your bed, and scourge them. (quoted in Kaufman, 1976:163)

Christianity—the dominant religion of the Western world—has also favored patriarchy. While many Christians revere Mary, the mother of Jesus, the New Testament also includes the following passages, which prescribe a woman's role:

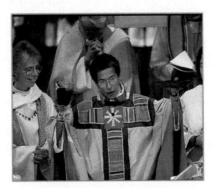

One way that religions support social inequality is by admitting to positions of leadership only certain categories of people. Historically, this has meant the dominance of white men, but this pattern has eroded in recent years. In 1989, for example, Barbara Harris became the first woman of color to be ordained as a bishop in the Episcopal Church.

A man . . . is the image and glory of God; but woman is the glory of man. For man was not made from woman, but woman from man. Neither was man created for woman, but woman for man. (1 Cor. 11:7–9)

As in all the churches of the saints, the women should keep silence in the churches. For they are not permitted to speak, but should be subordinate, as even the law says. If there is anything they desire to know, let them ask their husbands at home. For it is shameful for a woman to speak in church. (1 Cor. 14:33–35)

Wives, be subject to your husbands, as to the Lord. For the husband is the head of the wife as Christ is the head of the church. . . . As the church is subject to Christ, so let wives also be subject in everything to their husbands. (Eph. 5:22–24)

controversy. For example, many churches that, in principle, celebrate the unity of all peoples, have, in practice, all-white memberships. Such duality minimizes conflict between a church and the surrounding political landscape (Troeltsch, 1931).

December 11, 1994, Casablanca, Morocco. The waves of the Atlantic crash along the walls of Casablanca's magnificent coastline mosque, among the largest in the world. From the top of the towering structure, a green laser cuts through the sky pointing to Mecca, the holy city of Islam, toward which the faithful bow in prayer. To pay for this monumental house of worship, King Hassam

II, Morocco's head of state and religious leader, levied a tax on every citizen in his realm, all of whom are officially Muslim. Our notion of the separation of church and state contrasts sharply with this "government religion."

A church generally takes one of two forms. Islam in Morocco represents an **ecclesia,** *a church formally allied with the state.* Ecclesias have been common in history; for centuries Roman Catholicism animated the Roman Empire; Confucianism was the state religion in China until early in this century; the Anglican church remains the official Church of England, as Islam is the official religion of Pakistan and Iran. State churches typically define everyone in the society as a

SOCIAL SURVEY: "Do you favor or oppose women as pastors, ministers, priests, or rabbis in your own faith or denomination?" (GSS 1986, N = 1,334; *Student CHIP Social Survey Software*, FECLERGO)

	"Favor"	"Oppose"
Men	66.4%	33.6%
Women	57.6%	42.4%
13 + years school	69.6%	30.4%
12 years	57.1%	42.9%
0–11 years	54.5%	45.5%
18–34 years of age	69.4%	30.6%
35–64	58.4%	41.6%
65 and up	53.4%	46.6%

Let a woman learn in silence with all submissiveness. I permit no woman to teach or to have authority over men; she is to keep silent. For Adam was formed first, then Eve; and Adam was not deceived, but the woman was deceived and became a transgressor. Yet woman will be saved through bearing children, if she continues in faith and love and holiness, with modesty. (1 Tm. 2:11–15)

Judaism, too, traditionally has bolstered patriarchy. Male Orthodox Jews include the following words in daily prayer:

Blessed art thou, O Lord our
  God, King of the Universe, that
  I was not born a gentile.
Blessed art thou, O Lord our
  God, King of the Universe, that
  I was not born a slave.
Blessed art thou, O Lord our
  God, King of the Universe, that
  I was not born a woman.

In another dimension of religious patriarchy, the major religions have long excluded women from the clergy, although this practice is now being challenged. Islam continues to prohibit women from holding such positions, as does the Roman Catholic church. A growing number of Protestant denominations—including the Church of England—have overturned historical policies and now ordain women. Orthodox Judaism, too, upholds the traditional ban on women serving as rabbis, although Reform Judaism has long elevated women to this role (and is the largest denomination to ordain gay and lesbian people). In 1985, the first woman became a rabbi in the Conservative denomination of Judaism. The proportion of women among students enrolled in seminary schools across the United States has never been higher (now roughly one-third), meaning that further change is only a matter of time.

Challenges to the patriarchal structure of organized religion—from the ordination of women to the introduction of gender-neutral language in hymns and prayers—has sparked heated controversy, delighting progressives while outraging traditionalists. Propelling these developments is a lively feminism within many religious communities today. According to feminist Christians, for example, patriarchy in the church stands in stark contrast to the largely feminine image of Jesus Christ in the Scriptures as 'nonaggressive, noncompetitive, meek and humble of heart, a nurturer of the weak and a friend of the outcast' (Sandra Schneiders, quoted in Woodward, 1989:61).

Feminists argue that unless traditional notions of gender are removed from our understanding of God, women will never have equality with men in the church. Theologian Mary Daly puts the matter bluntly: "If God is male, then male is God" (quoted in Woodward, 1989:58).

member; tolerance of religious difference, therefore, is severely limited.

A **denomination,** by contrast, is *a church, independent of the state, that accepts religious pluralism.* Denominations thrive in societies that formally separate church and state. Ours is such a nation, with dozens of Christian denominations—including Catholics, Baptists, Methodists, and Lutherans—as well as various branches of Judaism and other traditions. While members of a denomination hold to their own beliefs, they recognize the right of others to disagree.

A second general religious form is the **sect,** *a type of religious organization that stands apart from the larger society.* Sect members hold rigidly to their own religious convictions while discounting what others around them claim to be true. In extreme cases, members of a sect may withdraw from society completely in order to practice their religion without interference from outsiders. The Amish, described in Chapter 3 ("Culture"), are an example of a North American sect that has long isolated itself (Kraybill, 1994). Since our culture views religious tolerance as a virtue, members of sects are sometimes accused of being dogmatic in their insistence that they alone follow the true religion (Stark & Bainbridge, 1979).

In organizational terms, sects are less formal than churches. Thus, sect members often engage in highly spontaneous and emotional practices as they worship, while members of churches tend to be passively attentive to their leader. Sects also reject the intellectualized religion of churches, stressing instead the personal experience of divine power. Rodney Stark (1985:314) contrasts a church's vision of a distant God—"Our Father, who art in Heaven"—with a sect's more immediate and accessible God—"Lord, bless this poor sinner kneeling before you now."

NOTE: Churches, with formally ordained (rather than charismatic) leaders, exemplify the routinization of charisma that, as Simmel might have said, favors form over content.

NOTE: The Greek roots of the word "church" refer to "what belongs to God, the greatest power." The word "sect" is derived from Latin, meaning "to cut." The word "cult" is derived from Latin roots meaning "to cultivate, refine, or worship."

GLOBAL: Many Marxist states have been intentionally nonreligious. When Mikhail Gorbachev was sworn in as the U.S.S.R.'s president in 1985, he placed his hand on a copy of that nation's constitution. Albania outlaws any religious gesture; "crossing oneself" can bring a prison sentence.

Q: "In societies under stress, there is a strong tendency for new cults to arise." Felicitas Goodman

In global perspective, the range of human religious activity is truly astonishing. Members of this Christian cult in the Latin American nation of Guatemala observe Good Friday by vaulting over a roaring fire, an expression of their faith that God will protect them.

A further distinction between church and sect turns on patterns of leadership. The more churchlike an organization, the more likely that its leaders are formally trained and ordained. Because more sectlike organizations celebrate the personal presence of God, members expect their leaders to exude divine inspiration in the form of **charisma** (from Greek meaning "divine favor"), *extraordinary personal qualities that can turn an audience into followers*, infusing them with the emotional experience that sects so value.

Sects generally form as breakaway groups from established churches or other religious organizations (Stark & Bainbridge, 1979). Their psychic intensity and informal structure render them less stable than churches, and many sects blossom only to wither and disappear a short time later. The sects that do endure typically become more like churches, losing fervor as they become more bureaucratic and established.

To sustain their membership, many sects rely on active recruitment, or *proselytizing*, of new members. Sects place great value on the experience of *conversion*, a personal transformation or religious rebirth. Members of Jehovah's Witnesses, for example, eagerly share their faith with others in hopes of attracting new members.

Finally, churches and sects differ in their social composition. Because they are more closely tied to the secular world, well-established churches tend to include people of high social standing. Sects, by contrast, attract more disadvantaged people. A sect's openness to new members and promise of salvation and personal fulfillment may be especially appealing to people who perceive themselves as social outsiders. However, as we

shall explain presently, many established churches in the United States have lost membership in recent decades. In the process, a number of sects now find themselves with more affluent members.

Cult

A **cult** is *a religious organization that is substantially outside a society's cultural traditions*. Whereas a sect emerges from within a traditional religious organization, a cult represents something else entirely. Cults typically form around a highly charismatic leader who offers a compelling message of a new way of life.

Because some cult principles or practices may seem unconventional, the popular view of cults pictures them as deviant or even evil. Negative publicity given to a few cults has raised suspicion about any unfamiliar religious group. The Branch Davidians, for example, a cult in Waco, Texas, led by David Koresh, held federal officers at bay for more than fifty days before almost one hundred cult members died in a shootout and subsequent fire in 1993. As a result of such aberrant behavior, some scholars assert that to call a religious community a "cult" amounts to declaring it unworthy (Richardson, 1990).

The connotations of the word "cult" are unfortunate because there is nothing intrinsically wrong with this kind of religious organization. Many longstanding religions—Christianity, Islam, and Judaism included—began as cults. Of course, not all or even most cults flourish for very long. One reason is that cults are even more at odds with the larger society than sects. Many

DISCUSS: Are "Deadheads" a cult? Following the death of Jerry Garcia in 1995, the news media compared the musician to a priest or god and his band to a church.
NOTE: Because animistic peoples perceive the entire world as "enchanted," it may be said that they do not distinguish between the sacred and the secular.
Q: "No man has a body distinct from his soul." William Blake

SOCIAL SURVEY: "The United States Supreme Court has ruled that no state or local government may require the reading of the Lord's Prayer or Bible verses in public schools. What are your views on this?" (GSS 1994, N = 1,977; *Codebook*, 1994:136)
"Approve" 37.3%   "Disapprove" 58.2%   DK/NR 4.6%
Q: "Christianity might be a good thing if anyone ever tried it." George Bernard Shaw

cults demand that members not only accept their doctrine but embrace a radically new lifestyle. As a result, people sometimes accuse cults of brainwashing new members, although research suggests that most people who join cults experience no psychological harm (Barker, 1981; Kilbourne, 1983).

RELIGION IN HISTORY

Religion shapes every society of the world. And, like other social institutions, religion shows considerable variation both historically and cross culturally.

Religion in Preindustrial Societies

Religion predates written history. Archaeological evidence indicates that our human ancestors routinely engaged in religious rituals some forty thousand years ago.

Early hunters and gatherers embraced **animism** (from Latin meaning "the breath of life"), *the belief that elements of the natural world are conscious life forms that affect humanity*. Animistic people view forests, oceans, mountains, even the wind as spiritual forces. Many Native-American societies are animistic, a characteristic that accounts for their historical reverence for the natural environment. Hunters and gatherers conduct their religious life entirely within the family. Members of such societies may look to a *shaman* or religious leader, but there are no full-time, specialized religious leaders.

Belief in a single divine power responsible for creating the world marked the rise of pastoral and horticultural societies. We can trace our society's conception of God as a "shepherd," directly involved in the world's well-being, to the roots of Christianity, Judaism, and Islam, all of whose original followers were pastoral peoples.

As societies develop more productive capacity, religious life expands beyond the family, and priests take their place among other specialized workers. In agrarian societies, the institution of religion gains prominence, as evidenced by the centrality of the church in medieval Europe. Even the physical design of the city casts this dominance in stone, with the cathedral rising above all other structures.

Religion in Industrial Societies

The Industrial Revolution ushered in a growing emphasis on science. Increasingly, people looked to physicians and other practitioners of science for the comfort and certainty they had earlier sought from religious leaders.

Even so, religious thought persists simply because science is powerless to address issues of ultimate meaning in human life. In other words, learning *how* the world works is a matter for scientists, but science is silent on the question of *why* we and the rest of the universe exist at all. Whatever the benefits of science to our material lives, then, religion has a unique capacity to address the spiritual dimension of human existence.

There is little doubt that, because they both offer powerful but distinct ways of viewing the universe, science and religion sometimes fall into an uneasy relationship. Yet, both science and religion play a central role in U.S. culture, with each kind of truth focusing on different facets of human experience.

WORLD RELIGIONS

Religion is found virtually everywhere on our planet, and, remarkably, the diversity of religious expression is almost as wide-ranging as culture itself. Many of the thousands of different religions are highly localized with few followers. *World religions*, by contrast, span large areas and have millions of adherents. We shall briefly describe six world religions, which together claim as adherents some 4 billion people—almost three-fourths of humanity.

Christianity

Christianity is the most widespread religion, with 1.9 billion followers, who constitute roughly one-third of humanity. Most Christians live in Europe or the Americas; more than 85 percent of the people in the United States and Canada identify with Christianity. Moreover, as shown in Global Map 18–1 on page 493, people who are at least nominally Christian represent a significant share of the population in many other world regions, with the notable exceptions of northern Africa and Asia. This diffusion stems from the European colonization of much of the world during the last five hundred years. The dominance of Christianity in the West can be seen in the practice of numbering years on the calendar beginning with the birth of Christ.

Christianity originated as a cult, incorporating elements of its much older predecessor Judaism. Like many cults, Christianity was propelled by the personal charisma of a leader, Jesus of Nazareth, who preached a message of personal salvation. Jesus did not directly challenge the political powers of his day, calling on his followers to "Render therefore to Caesar things that

GLOBAL: Proportion describing the personal significance of religion as very important or quite important: U.S., 78.9%; Italy, 66.8%; Canada, 61.5%; U.K., 44.8%; France, 42.7%; W. Germany, 37.3%; Sweden, 27.2%; Japan, 20.3%. (World Values Survey, 1994)
SOCIAL SURVEY: "Which of these statements comes closest to describing your feelings about the Bible?" (GSS 1994, N = 1,977; Codebook, 1994:137)

"The Bible is the actual word of God and is to be taken literally" 31.1%
"The Bible is the inspired word of God but not everything in it should be taken literally, word for word" 50.7%
"The Bible is an ancient book of fables, legends, history, and moral precepts recorded by men" 14.8%
Other/DK/NR 3.4%

In this outstanding example of folk art, The Lord Will Deliver His People, *African-American artist Amos Finster depicts the central promise of Christianity—salvation from the evils and suffering of the present world.*

National Museum of American Art, Washington, D.C./Art Resource, N.Y.

are Caesar's" (Matt. 22:21). But his message was revolutionary, nonetheless, promising that faith and love would lead to triumph over sin and death.

Christianity is one example of **monotheism**, *belief in a single divine power.* This new religion broke with the Roman Empire's traditional **polytheism**, *belief in many gods.* Yet Christianity has a unique vision of the Supreme Being as a sacred Trinity: God the Creator; Jesus Christ, Son of God and Redeemer; and the Holy Spirit, a Christian's personal experience of God's presence.

The claim that Jesus was divine rests on accounts of his final days on earth. Tried and sentenced to death in Jerusalem on charges that he was a threat to established political leaders, Jesus endured a cruel execution by crucifixion, which transformed the cross into a sacred Christian symbol. According to Christian belief, Jesus was resurrected—that is, he rose from the dead—showing that he was the Son of God.

The apostles of Jesus spread Christianity widely throughout the Mediterranean region. Although the Roman Empire initially persecuted Christians, by the

fourth century Christianity had become an ecclesia—the official religion of what was known as the Holy Roman Empire. What had begun as a cult four centuries before was by then an established church.

Christianity took various forms, including the Roman Catholic church and the Orthodox church, centered in Constantinople (now Istanbul, Turkey). Further division occurred toward the end of the Middle Ages, when the Protestant Reformation in Europe sparked the formation of hundreds of denominations. Dozens of these denominations—the Baptists and Methodists are the two largest—now command sizable followings in the United States (Smart, 1969; Kaufman, 1976; Jacquet & Jones, 1991).

Islam

Islam has some 1.1 billion followers (19 percent of humanity), called Muslims. A majority of people in the Middle East are Muslims, which explains our tendency to associate Islam with Arabs in that region of the world. But most Muslims are *not* Arabs; Global Map 18–2 shows that a majority of people across northern Africa and western Asia are also Muslims. Moreover, significant concentrations of Muslims are found in Pakistan, India, Bangladesh, Indonesia, and the southern republics of the former Soviet Union. Although representing just 1 percent of the population, estimates place the number of North American Muslims at 5 to 10 million (Roudi, 1988; Weeks, 1988; University of Akron Research Center, 1993).

Islam is the word of God as revealed to the prophet Muhammad, who was born in the city of Mecca (now in Saudi Arabia) about the year 570. To Muslims, Muhammad is a prophet, not a divine being as Christians define Jesus. The Qur'an (Koran), sacred to Muslims, is the word of God (in Arabic, "Allah") as transmitted through Muhammad, God's messenger. In Arabic, the word "Islam" means both "submission" and "peace," and the Qur'an urges submission to Allah as the path to inner peace. Muslims express this personal devotion in a daily ritual of five prayers.

Islam spread rapidly after the death of Muhammad, although divisions arose, as they did within Christianity. All Muslims, however, accept the Five Pillars of Islam: (1) recognizing Allah as the one, true God, and Muhammad as God's messenger; (2) ritual prayer; (3) giving alms to the poor; (4) fasting during the month of Ramadan; and (5) making a pilgrimage at least once in a lifetime to the Sacred House of Allah in Mecca (Weeks, 1988; El-Attar, 1991). Like

Q: "All civilizations are based on religion." Arnold Toynbee

GLOBAL: In Japan, the emperor has traditionally been the head priest of the Shinto religion.

GLOBAL: The Church of Sweden (the Lutheran Church) counts all Swedes among its members, unless they officially withdraw from it. The state owns and controls church property and pays clergy as state employees.

DIVERSITY: Muslims hold the Qur'an (Koran) to be the *literal* words of God. For this reason, even translation from Arabic into other languages raises fears of distortion.

NOTE: Literal interpretation of the sacred texts of any religion sharply limits debate among adherents about religious truth, thereby fostering consensus. But literal readings may still reveal inconsistencies; there are, for example, *two* creation stories in Genesis.

Window on the World

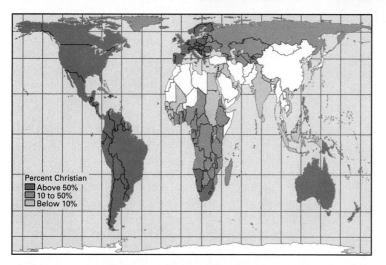

GLOBAL MAP 18–1

Christianity in Global Perspective

Source: *Peters Atlas of the World* (1990).

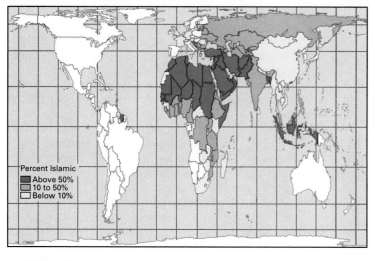

GLOBAL MAP 18–2

Islam in Global Perspective

Source: *Peters Atlas of the World* (1990).

Christianity, Islam holds people accountable to God for their deeds on earth. Those who live obediently will be rewarded in heaven, while evil-doers will suffer unending punishment.

Muslims are also obligated to defend their faith. Sometimes this tenet has justified holy wars against nonbelievers (in roughly the same way that medieval Christians joined the Crusades to recapture the Holy Land from the Muslims). Recently, in Algeria, Egypt, Iran, and elsewhere, some Muslims have sought to rid

their society of Western influences they regard as morally compromising (Martin, 1982; Arjomand, 1988).

Many Westerners view Muslim women as among the most socially oppressed people on earth. Muslim women do lack many of the personal freedoms enjoyed by Muslim men, yet most accept the mandates of their religion. Moreover, patriarchy was well established in the Middle East before the birth of Muhammad. Some defenders of Islam's treatment of women argue that Islam actually improved the social position of women

RESOURCE: The article by Jane I. Smith, "Women and Islam," is among the cross-cultural selections found in the *Seeing Ourselves* reader.
DIVERSITY: More than half of Jewish men and women who have married since 1985 have gentile spouses. What are the consequences of this trend for this religion's future? (Council of Jewish Federations)

GLOBAL: According to the Israeli Central Bureau of Statistics, Israeli Jews represent 27% of world Jewry. About 45% of all Jews live in North America.
NOTE: Jewish assimilation into U.S. society can be seen in the declining concentration of Jews in the Northeast: from 68% in 1930 to 44% in 1990. Another index of religious assimilation: About 55% of U.S. Jews now marry non-Jews.

Followers of Islam reverently remove their shoes—which touch the profane ground—before entering this sacred mosque in the Southeast Asian nation of Brunei.

by demanding that husbands deal justly with their wives. Further, although Islam permits a man to have up to four wives, it admonishes men to have only one wife if having more than one would encourage him to treat women unjustly (Qur'an, "The Women," v. 3).

Judaism

Speaking purely in numerical terms, Judaism, with only 14 million adherents worldwide, is less prominent as a world religion. Only in Israel do Jews represent a national majority. But Judaism has special significance to the United States because the largest concentration of Jews (6 million people) is found in North America.

Jews look to the past as a source of guidance in the present and for the future. And Judaism has deep historical roots that extend back some four thousand years before the birth of Christ to the ancient cultures of Mesopotamia. At this time, Jews were animistic; but this belief was to change after Jacob—grandson of Abraham, the earliest great ancestor—led his people to Egypt.

Under Egyptian rule, Jews endured centuries of slavery. In the thirteenth century B.C.E., a turning point came as Moses, the adopted son of an Egyptian princess, was called by God to lead the Jews from bondage. This exodus (this word's Latin and Greek

roots mean "a marching out") from Egypt is commemorated by Jews today in the annual ritual of Passover. As a result of the Jews' liberation from bondage, Judaism became monotheistic, recognizing a single, all-powerful God.

A distinctive concept of Judaism is the *covenant*, a special relationship with God by which Jews became a "chosen people." The covenant also implies a duty to observe God's law, especially the Ten Commandments as revealed to Moses on Mount Sinai. Jews regard the Bible (or, in Christian terms, the Old Testament) as both a record of their history and a statement of the obligations of Jewish life. Of special importance are the first five books of the Bible (Genesis, Exodus, Leviticus, Numbers, and Deuteronomy), designated as the *Torah* (a word roughly meaning "teaching" and "law"). In contrast to Christianity's central concern with personal salvation, Judaism emphasizes moral behavior in this world.

Judaism is composed of three main denominations. Orthodox Jews (including more than 1 million people in the United States) strictly hold to traditional beliefs and practices, maintaining historical forms of dress, segregating men and women at religious services, and consuming only kosher foods. Such traditional practices set off Orthodox Jews in the United States as the most sectlike. In the mid-nineteenth century, many Jews sought greater accommodation to the larger society, leading to the formation of more churchlike Reform Judaism (now including more than 1.3 million people in this country). More recently, a third segment—Conservative Judaism (with about 2 million adherents)—has established a middle ground between the other two denominations.

All Jews, however, share a keen awareness of their cultural history, which has included battling considerable prejudice and discrimination. A collective memory of centuries of slavery in Egypt, conquest by Rome, and persecution in Europe have shaped Jewish identity. Interestingly, the urban ghetto (derived from the Italian word *borghetto*, meaning settlement outside the city walls) was first home to Jews in Italy, and this form of residential segregation soon spread to other parts of Europe.

Jewish emigration to the United States began in the mid-1600s. Many of these early immigrants prospered, and many were also assimilated into largely Christian communities. But as larger numbers entered the country during the final decades of the nineteenth century, prejudice and discrimination against Jewish people—commonly called *anti-Semitism*—increased. During World War II, anti-Semitism reached a vicious

Window on the World

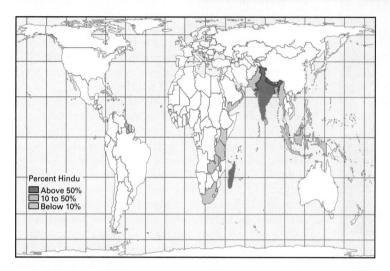

GLOBAL MAP 18-3
Hinduism in Global Perspective
Source: *Peters Atlas of the World* (1990).

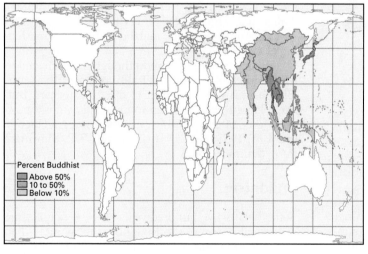

GLOBAL MAP 18-4
Buddhism in Global Perspective
Source: *Peters Atlas of the World* (1990).

peak when Jews experienced the most horrific persecution in modern times as the Nazi regime in Germany systematically annihilated approximately 6 million Jews.

The history of Judaism is a grim reminder of a tragic dimension of the human record—the extent to which religious minorities have been the target of hatred and even slaughter (Bedell, Sandon, & Wellborn, 1975; Holm, 1977; Schmidt, 1980; Seltzer, 1980; B. Wilson, 1982; Eisen, 1983).

Hinduism

Hinduism is the oldest of all the world religions, originating in the Indus River Valley approximately forty-five hundred years ago. Hindus number some 775 million (14 percent of humanity). Global Map 18-3 shows that Hinduism remains an Eastern religion, the predominant creed of India and Pakistan today with a significant presence in a few societies of southern Africa as well as Indonesia.

GLOBAL: One could say that, to the Hindu, nothing is sacred or everything is sacred.
NOTE: The diffusion of religious elements is usually selective. For instance, in the 1960s, many young people in the United States adopted the Hindu concepts of *dharma* (fate) and *karma* (spiritual progression of souls), while scorning the caste system historically associated with Hinduism.

GLOBAL: Eastern religions—Buddhism, Hinduism, Confucianism, Shintoism—are sometimes termed "ethical religions" since they have no gods in the Western sense.
DIVERSITY: By 1990, chaplains in the U.S. armed forces represented 105 religious organizations, including one Buddhist chaplain (some 2,500 military personnel are adherents of this religion).

Buddhists believe that a preoccupation with material things inhibits spiritual development, an idea that is also central to most Western religions. Buddhist monks, therefore, live a simple life devoted to meditation, music, and righteousness in everyday behavior.

Over the centuries, Hinduism and Indian culture have become intertwined, so that now one is not easily described apart from the other. As a result, Hinduism, unlike Christianity, Islam, and Judaism, cannot be diffused widely to other nations. Nevertheless, 1.3 million Hindus living in the United States make this religion a significant part of the cultural diversity of our country.

Hinduism differs from most other religions because it did not spring from the life of any single person. Hinduism also has no sacred writings comparable to the Bible or the Qur'an. Nor does Hinduism even envision God as a specific entity. For this reason, Hinduism—like other Eastern religions, as we shall see—is sometimes thought of as an "ethical religion." Hindu beliefs and practices vary widely, but all Hindus recognize a moral force in the universe that imposes on everyone responsibilities known as *dharma*. One traditional example of dharma is the need to act in concert with the traditional caste system, described in Chapter 9 ("Social Stratification").

A second Hindu principle, *karma*, refers to the belief in the spiritual progress of the human soul. To a Hindu, all actions have spiritual consequences, and proper living contributes to moral development. Karma works through *reincarnation*, a cycle of new birth following death, so that individuals are reborn into a spiritual state corresponding to the moral quality of their previous life. Unlike Christianity and Islam, Hinduism proclaims no ultimate judgment at the hands of a supreme god, although in the cycle of rebirth, each person reaps exactly what that individual has sown. The sublime state of *nirvana* represents spiritual perfection: When a soul reaches this rarefied plateau, it exits the cycle of rebirth.

Looking at Hinduism, we see also that not all religions can be neatly labeled monotheistic or polytheistic. Hinduism may be described as monotheistic because it envisions the universe as a single moral system; yet Hindus perceive this moral order in every element of nature. Rituals, which are central to a Hindu's life, are performed in a variety of ways in countless Indian villages. Most Hindus practice private devotions, including, for example, ritual cleansing following contact with a person of lower caste position. Many also participate in public rituals, such as the *Kumbh Mela*, during which pilgrims flock to the sacred Ganges River to bathe in its purifying waters. This ritual, which occurs every twelve years, attracts 15 to 20 million people, making it the largest gathering of people on earth.

While elements of Hindu thought have characterized some cults in the United States over the years, Hinduism is still unfamiliar to most Westerners. But, like religions better known to us, Hinduism is a powerful force offering both explanation and guidance in life (Pitt, 1955; Sen, 1961; Embree, 1972; Kaufman, 1976; Schmidt, 1980).

Buddhism

Some twenty-five hundred years ago, the rich culture of India also gave rise to Buddhism. Today more than 330 million people (6 percent of humanity) embrace Buddhism, and almost all are Asians. As shown in Global Map 18–4, on page 495, adherents to Buddhism represent more than half the population of Myanmar (Burma), Thailand, Cambodia, and Japan; Buddhism is also widespread in India and the People's Republic of China. Of the world religions considered so far, Buddhism most resembles Hinduism in doctrine, but, like Christianity, its inspiration springs from the life of one individual.

Siddhartha Gautama was born to a high-caste family in Nepal about 563 B.C.E. As a young man, he was preoccupied with spiritual matters. At the age of twenty-nine, he underwent a radical personal transformation, setting off for years of travel and meditation.

His path ended when he achieved what Buddhists describe as *bodhi*, or enlightenment. Understanding the essence of life, Gautama became a Buddha.

Energized by the Buddha's personal charisma, followers spread his teachings—the *dhamma*—across India. During the third century B.C.E., the ruler of India joined the ranks of Buddhists, subsequently sending missionaries throughout Asia and elevating Buddhism to the status of a world religion.

Central to Buddhist belief is the notion that human existence involves suffering. The pleasures of the world are real, of course, but Buddhists see such experiences as transitory. This doctrine is rooted in the Buddha's own travels throughout a society rife with poverty. But the Buddha rejected wealth as a solution to suffering; on the contrary, he warned that materialism inhibits spiritual development. Buddhism's answer to world problems is for individuals to pursue personal, spiritual transformation.

Buddhism closely parallels Hinduism in recognizing no god of judgment; rather, it finds spiritual consequences in each daily action. Another similarity lies in its belief in reincarnation. Here, again, only full enlightenment ends the cycle of death and rebirth, thereby finally liberating a person from the suffering of the world (Schumann, 1974; Thomas, 1975).

When Western people perform religious rituals they typically do so collectively and formally as members of specific congregations. Eastern people, by contrast, visit shrines individually and informally, without joining a specific congregation. For this reason, Asian temples such as this one in Hong Kong, shown above, receive a steady flow of people—families praying, individuals engaged in business, and foreign tourists just watching—that seems somehow inappropriate to the Western visitor.

Confucianism

From about 200 B.C.E. until the beginning of this century, Confucianism was an ecclesia—the official religion of China. Following the 1949 Revolution, religion was suppressed by the communist government of the new People's Republic of China. Although officials provide little in the way of data to establish precise numbers, hundreds of millions of Chinese are still influenced by Confucianism. While almost all adherents to Confucianism live in China, Chinese immigration has introduced this religion to other societies in Southeast Asia. Perhaps one hundred thousand followers of Confucius live in North America.

Confucius or, properly, K'ung-Fu-tzu, lived between 551 and 479 B.C.E. Confucius shared with Buddha a deep concern for the problems and suffering of the world. The Buddha's response was a sectlike spiritual withdrawal from the world; Confucius, by contrast, instructed his followers to engage the world according to a strict code of moral conduct. Thus it was that Confucianism became fused with the traditional culture of China. Here we see a second example of what might be called a "national religion": As Hinduism has remained largely synonymous with Indian culture, Confucianism is enshrined in the Chinese way of life.

A central concept of Confucianism is *jen*, meaning humaneness. In practice, this means that we must always subordinate our self-interest to moral principle. In the family, the individual must display loyalty and consideration for others. Likewise, families must remain mindful of their duties toward the larger community. In this way, layer upon layer of moral obligation integrates society as a whole.

Most of all, Confucianism stands out as lacking a clear sense of the sacred. We could view Confucianism, recalling Durkheim's analysis, as the celebration of society itself as sacred. Alternatively, we might argue that Confucianism is less a religion than a model of disciplined living. Certainly the historical dominance of Confucianism helps to explain why Chinese culture has long taken a skeptical attitude toward the supernatural. If we conclude that Confucianism is best thought of as a disciplined way of life, we must also recognize that it shares with religion a body of beliefs and practices that

	Daily	Weekly	Less often/Never
Women	65.3%	20.2%	14.5%
Men	42.8%	23.6%	33.6%
Afri Amer	72.8%	16.0%	11.2%
Latino	63.4%	21.0%	15.6%

Wh Anglo	52.5%	22.5%	24.9%
High SES	48.6%	25.4%	26.0%
Middle SES	55.4%	21.6%	23.0%
Low SES	63.4%	17.4%	19.2%
65 and older	74.6%	12.0%	13.3%
35–64	56.5%	21.7%	21.8%
18–34	43.8%	26.6%	29.6%

Global Snapshot

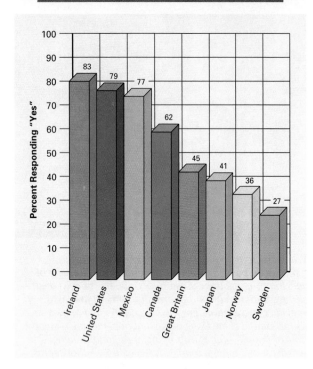

FIGURE 18–1 Religiosity in Global Perspective
Survey Question: "Do you gain comfort and strength from religion?"
Source: World Values Survey (1994).

have as their goal goodness, concern for others, and the promotion of social harmony (Kaufman, 1976; Schmidt, 1980; McGuire, 1987).

Religion: East and West

This overview of world religions points up two general differences between the belief systems that predominate in Eastern and Western societies. First, Western religions (Christianity, Islam, Judaism) are typically deity-based, with a clear focus on God. Eastern religions (Hinduism, Buddhism, Confucianism) tend to be more like ethical codes that make a less clear-cut distinction between the sacred and secular.

Second, the operational unit of Western religious organization is the congregation. That is, people attend a specific place of worship with others, most of

whom are members. Eastern religious organizations, by contrast, are more broadly tied into culture itself. For this reason, for example, a visitor finds a Japanese temple awash with people—tourists and worshipers alike—who come and go on their own schedule, paying little attention to those around them.

These two distinctions do not overshadow the common element of all religions: having a conception of a higher moral force or purpose that transcends the concerns of everyday life. In all these religious beliefs, people of the world find guidance and a sense of purpose for their lives.

RELIGION IN THE UNITED STATES

In global perspective, the United States is a relatively religious nation. As Figure 18–1 illustrates, eight in ten members of our society claim to gain "comfort and strength from religion," a proportion substantially higher than in most other industrial countries.

Although most analysts agree that people in the United States are more religious than most, there is considerable debate about how religious we are. While some scholars contend that religion remains central to our way of life, others wonder if the erosion of the traditional family and the advancing role of science and technology are steadily undermining faith (Collins, 1982; Greeley, 1989; Woodward, 1992; Hadaway, Marler, & Chaves, 1993).

Religious Affiliation

On the surface, at least, most people in the United States claim to be religious. National surveys reveal that 90 percent of U.S. adults voice a religious preference (NORC, 1994:114). According to Table 18–1, six in ten adults call themselves Protestants. Catholicism is the religion of more than one-fourth of respondents, and 2 percent identify with Judaism. Just 9 percent express no religious preference. While growing up, two-thirds of adults attended classes in religious instruction more or less regularly, and 60 percent consider themselves to be a member of some religious organization (NORC, 1994:330–31). Comparisons over time reveal that religious affiliation over the last fifty years has been relatively stable.

National Map 18–1 on page 500 reveals a strong regional pattern in religious affiliation. New England and the Southwest are predominantly Catholic and the South is overwhelmingly Baptist, while Lutherans stand out in the northern Plains states. Members of the Church of Jesus Christ of Latter Day Saints

SOCIAL SURVEY: "How important is following one's conscience even if it means going against what the churches or synagogues say and do?" (GSS 1988, N = 1,481; *Codebook*, 1994:337)
(1) "Very important" 40.9%   (4) 5.9%
(2) 22.5%   (5) "Not very important" 7.4%
(3) 20.5%   DK/NR 2.8%

SOCIAL SURVEY: "How close do you feel to God most of the time?" (GSS 1989, N = 1,006; *Codebook*, 1994:124)
"Extremely close" 28.9%   "Not close at all"   6.4%
"Somewhat close"   52.3%   "Does not believe in God" 2.1%
"Not very close"   8.8%   DK/NR   1.5%
Q: "Religious insanity is very common in the United States." Alexis de Tocqueville

(known as Mormons) are heavily concentrated in and around Utah.

Religiosity

Religiosity designates *the importance of religion in a person's life.* Clearly, identifying with a religion is only one measure of religiosity, and a superficial one at that. How religious the U.S. turns out to be, therefore, depends largely on precisely how we operationalize this concept.

Years ago, Charles Glock (1959, 1962) distinguished five distinct dimensions of religiosity. *Experiential* religiosity refers to the strength of a person's emotional ties to a religion. *Ritualistic* religiosity refers to frequency of ritual activity such as prayer and church attendance. *Ideological* religiosity concerns an individual's degree of belief in religious doctrine. *Consequential* religiosity has to do with how strongly religious beliefs figure in a person's daily behavior. Finally, *intellectual* religiosity refers to a person's knowledge of the history and doctrines of a particular religion. Anyone is likely to be more religious on some dimensions than on others; this inconsistency compounds the difficulty of measuring the concept of religiosity.

How religious, then, are members of our society? When asked directly, almost everyone in the United States (95 percent) claims to believe in a divine power of some kind, although follow-up questions show that only 62 percent agree with the statement: "I know that God exists and have no doubts about it" (NORC, 1994:333). Overall, however, people in the United States certainly seem to have high experiential religiosity.

But on other dimensions of religiosity, the pattern changes. In ideological terms, only about 70 percent, for example, report a belief in life after death. On dimensions of ritualistic religiosity, the numbers drop even lower. For example, only half of adults claim to pray at least once a day, and one-third say they attend religious services on a weekly or almost-weekly basis (NORC, 1994:116, 118, 122).

In short, the question "How religious are we?" yields no easy answers. Keep in mind, too, that being religious is normative in our culture, so that people probably claim to be more religious than they really are. Confirming this suspicion, one team of researchers recently posted observers at every place of worship in Ashtabula County, Ohio; a subsequent survey of county residents indicated that twice as many people claimed that they had attended church on that given Sunday as really did so. A more accurate estimate, in other words, may be that no more than 20 percent of

TABLE 18–1 Religious Identification in the United States, 1994

Religion	Proportion Indicating Preference
Protestant denominations	**59.3%**
Baptist	20.6
Methodist	9.4
Lutheran	6.7
Presbyterian	4.8
Episcopalian	2.2
All others or no denomination	15.6
Catholic	**25.4**
Jewish	**2.0**
Other or no answer	**4.2**
No religious preference	**9.2**

Source: *General Social Surveys, 1972–1994: Cumulative Codebook* (Chicago: National Opinion Research Center, 1994), p. 115.

people attend worship services regularly (Hadaway, Marler, & Chaves, 1993).

Overall, then, most people in the United States claim to be at least somewhat religious. Nonetheless, only about one-third actually are. Moreover, religiosity varies among denominations. Members of sects are the most religious of all, followed by Catholics and then "mainstream" Protestants (Stark & Glock, 1968; Hadaway, Marler, & Chaves, 1993).

Religion and Social Stratification

Sociologists study religion not only to comprehend how people address the sacred but because religious affiliation is related to a host of familiar social patterns.

Social Class

A recent study of *Who's Who in America*—the listing of U.S. high achievers—revealed that Episcopalians, Presbyterians, and United Church of Christ members stood out among those who provided a religious affiliation. Together accounting for less than 10 percent of the population, these categories represented one-third of all high achievers. Jews, too, enjoy high social position, with this 2 percent of the U.S. population accounting for 12 percent of listings.

Research shows that other Protestant denominations—including Congregationalists and Methodists—have a moderate social position, as do Catholics. Lower social standing is typical of Baptists, Lutherans, and members of sects. All these categories, of course,

Seeing Ourselves

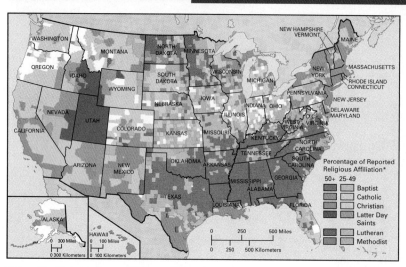

NATIONAL MAP 18-1

Religious Diversity Across the United States

In the vast majority of counties, at least 25 percent of people who report having a religious affiliation are members of the same organization. Thus, although the United States is religiously diverse at the national level, most people live in communities where one denomination predominates. What historical facts might account for this pattern?

*When two or more churches have 25 to 49 percent of the membership in a county, the largest is shown. When no church has 25 percent of the membership that county is left blank. A few exceptions include Palm Beach County in southern Florida, which is primarily Jewish, and Holmes County in central Ohio, which is largely Amish.

Source: The Glenmary Research Center, Atlanta, Georgia (1990).

display some internal variation (Roof, 1979; Davidson, Pyle & Reyes, 1995; Waters, Heath, & Watson, 1995).

By and large, Protestants with high social standing are people of northern European background whose families came to the United States at least a century ago. They encountered little prejudice and discrimination and have had the longest time to establish themselves socially. Roman Catholics, more recent immigrants to the United States, have contended with greater social barriers based on being a minority religion.

Jews command unexpectedly high social standing considering that many are fairly recent immigrants who confronted substantial anti-Semitism from the Christian majority. The reason is mostly cultural, since Jewish traditions place great value on both education and achievement. Although a large proportion of Jews began life in the United States in poverty, many—although certainly not all—improved their social position in subsequent generations.

Ethnicity and Race

Throughout the world, religion is tied to ethnicity. Many religions predominate in a specific geographical region or society. Islam commands the devotion of most (but not all) people within the Arab societies of the Middle East, Hinduism is closely fused with the culture of India, as is Confucianism with the Chinese way of life. Christianity and Judaism, however, diverge

from this pattern: While these religions are predominantly Western, followers are found all over the world.

Religion and national identity come together in the United States as well. Our society, for example, encompasses *Anglo-Saxon* Protestants, *Irish* Catholics, *Russian* Jews, and *Greek* Orthodox. This linking of nation and creed results from the influx of immigrants to the United States from societies with a single major religion. Still, within nearly every ethnic category we find at least some religious diversity. People of English ancestry, for instance, may be Protestants, Roman Catholics, Jews, or followers of other religions.

Historically, the church has been central to the spiritual—and also political—lives of African Americans. Transported to the Western Hemisphere in slave ships, most Africans were forced to embrace Christianity—the dominant religion of European Americans—but they blended Christian belief with elements of African religions. Guided by this eclectic religious mix, many Christian people of color developed rituals that were—by European standards—both spontaneous and emotional. These expressive qualities still characterize many African-American religious organizations today (Frazier, 1965; Roberts, 1980).

As African Americans migrated from the rural South to the industrial cities of the North around 1940, the church played a major role in addressing problems of dislocation, poverty, and prejudice. Moreover, among people often cut off from the

NOTE: The secularization thesis can be linked to Max Weber's account of the "disenchantment" of the world, discussed in Chapter 4.

Q: "In a word, we must discover the rational substitutes for those religious notions that for a long time have served as the vehicle for the most essential moral ideas." Emile Durkheim, *Moral Education* (1961:9)

NOTE: Civil religion is evident in the writing of Jean-Jacques Rousseau, who hated the church but wanted to keep a spirit and discipline in citizenship; curiously, secular conservatives, too, wish to maintain religion's capacity to legitimize public order and maintain the social fabric.

NOTE: "In God We Trust" appeared on U.S. currency in the 1860s; "under God" was added to the Pledge of Allegiance in the 1950s.

larger society, the church provided the opportunity for talented men and women to distinguish themselves as leaders. Ralph Abernathy, Martin Luther King, Jr., and Jesse Jackson each gained international recognition for leadership while serving as ministers in African-American religious organizations.

RELIGION IN A CHANGING SOCIETY

All social institutions evolve over time. Just as the economy, politics, and family life have changed during the course of this century, so has our society's religious life.

Secularization

One of the most important patterns of social change relating to religion is **secularization**, *the historical decline in the importance of the supernatural and the sacred.* For society as a whole, secularization points to the waning influence of religion in everyday life. And as religious organizations become more secular, they direct attention less to otherworldly issues (such as life after death) and more to worldly affairs (such as sheltering the homeless and feeding the hungry). In addition, secularization means that functions once performed mostly by the church (such as charity) are now primarily the responsibility of businesses and government.

Secularization, with Latin roots meaning "the present age," is commonly associated with modern, technologically advanced societies (Cox, 1971; O'Dea & Aviad, 1983). Conventional wisdom holds that secularization is one result of the increasing importance of science in understanding human affairs. Consider that, since mid-century, public schools have taught children little about religion. In broader terms, people perceive birth, illness, and death less as the work of a divine power than as natural stages in the life course. Such events are now more likely to occur in the presence of physicians (scientific specialists) than religious leaders (whose knowledge is based on faith). With the rise of science, religion's sphere of influence has diminished. Theologian Harvey Cox elaborates:

> The world looks less and less to religious rules and rituals for its morality or its meanings. For some, religion provides a hobby, for others a mark of national or ethnic identification, for still others an aesthetic delight. For fewer and fewer does it provide an inclusive and commanding system of personal and cosmic values and explanations. (1971:3)

If Cox is correct, should we expect that religion will disappear completely some day? The consensus among sociologists is "no" (Hammond, 1985; McGuire, 1987). Recall that the vast majority of people in the United States continue to profess a belief in God, and as many people claim to pray each day as vote in national elections. Further, religious affiliation today is actually several times higher than it was in 1850 (Hout & Greeley, 1987).

Secularization does not, then, signal the impending death of religion. Rather, a decline in some dimensions of religiosity (such as belief in life after death) are accompanied by an increase in others (such as religious affiliation). Moreover, in global perspective we see that while religion holds less sway in some regions (the Scandinavian countries, for example), religious fervor is rising in others (such as Algeria) (Cox, 1990).

Our society is also of two minds as to whether secularization is good or bad. Conservative people tend to bemoan the erosion of religion as a mark of moral decline. Progressives, however, herald secularization as liberation from the all-encompassing—and sometimes stifling—beliefs of the past. Further, secularization has brought the practices of many religious organizations (for example, the ordination of both men and women) in line with widespread social attitudes.

Civil Religion

One dimension of secularization is the rise of what Robert Bellah (1975) has called **civil religion**, *a quasi-religious loyalty binding individuals in a basically secular society.* In other words, even if some dimensions of religiosity are weakening, our patriotism and citizenship retain many religious qualities.

Certainly, most people in the United States consider our way of life to be a force for moral good in the world. Many people differ as to what our nation's moral purpose should be, but citizens of all stripes find religious qualities in political movements—liberal and conservative alike (Williams & Demerath, 1991).

Civil religion also involves a range of rituals, from rising to sing the National Anthem at sporting events to sitting down to watch televised public parades several times a year. And, like the Christian cross or the Jewish Star of David, the flag serves as a sacred symbol of our national identity that we expect people to treat with reverence.

Civil religion is not a specific doctrine. It does, however, incorporate many elements of traditional religion into the political system of a secular society.

Chapter 18 Religion **501**

NOTE: "Mainstream" denominations such as Episcopalian and Presbyterian have lost membership in recent years; by contrast, Southern Baptist, Seventh-Day Adventist, and Mormon denominations are gaining in popularity.

Q: "There is no country in the world where the Christian religion retains a greater influence over the souls of men." Alexis de Tocqueville, referring to the United States

GLOBAL: Peter Berger argues that the secularization thesis applies best to European societies, and has less application to the United States.

SOCIAL SURVEY: Characterization of religion respondent was raised in. (GSS 1993, N = 2,992; *Codebook*, 1994:131)

"Fundamentalist" 32.5% "Liberal" 22.1%
"Moderate" 41.8% DK/NR 3.5%

GLOBAL SOCIOLOGY

The Changing Face of Religion: A Report From Great Britain

Great Britain

Although the Church of England enjoys elite status as that nation's official religious organization, Anglicans number only one-fifth of regular worshipers in Great Britain today. As in the United States, membership in Britain's established, "mainstream" churches has been dwindling. The figure demonstrates that support for the Anglican, Roman Catholic, Presbyterian, and Baptist churches is down significantly in recent years.

Overall, however, religiosity in Great Britain is holding steady (although at a level below that of the United States). Why? As the established churches lose members, newer religious organizations are showing surprising

strength. Immigration is behind some of this religious revival: With immigration rising rapidly in Britain, the numbers of Muslims, as well as Sikhs

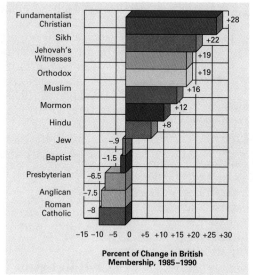

Fundamentalist Christian +28
Sikh +22
Jehovah's Witnesses +19
Orthodox +19
Muslim +16
Mormon +12
Hindu +8
Jew –.9
Baptist –1.5
Presbyterian –6.5
Anglican –7.5
Roman Catholic –8

–15 –10 –5 0 +5 +10 +15 +20 +25 +30

Percent of Change in British Membership, 1985–1990

and Hindus, are steadily increasing. Newly formed cults, too, contribute to religious resurgence. In all, experts believe, as many as six hundred cults exist in Britain at any one time.

But the most significant rise in British religious affiliation can be seen among fundamentalist Christian organizations that embrace highly energetic and musical forms of worship, often under the direction of charismatic leaders. Like their counterparts in the United States, these religious communities typically seek and express the experience of God's presence in a much more spontaneous way than the more staid, "mainstream" churches do.

Sources: Barker (1989) and *The Economist* (1993).

Religious Revival

We have argued that overall religiosity in the United States has been stable in recent decades. But a great deal of change is going on inside the world of organized religion. Membership in established, "mainstream" churches like the Episcopalian and Presbyterian denominations has plummeted by almost 50 percent since 1960. During the same period, affiliation with other religious organizations (including the Mormons, Seventh-Day Adventists, and especially Christian sects) has risen just as dramatically.

Secularization itself may be self-limiting. As churchlike organizations become more worldly, that is, some people within a religious "marketplace" may simply abandon them in favor of more sectlike religious communities that better address their spiritual concerns and whose members exhibit greater religious commitment (Stark & Bainbridge, 1981; Roof &

McKinney, 1987; Jacquet & Jones, 1991; Warner, 1993; Iannaccone, 1994).

Much the same pattern of change can be seen in other industrial societies. The box takes a look at the state of religious affiliation in Great Britain.

Religious Fundamentalism

A key dimension of this change is the growth of **fundamentalism**, *a conservative religious doctrine that opposes intellectualism and worldly accommodation in favor of restoring traditional, otherworldly spirituality*. In the United States, fundamentalism has made the greatest gains among Protestants. Southern Baptists, one such organization, form the largest religious community in the United States. But fundamentalist groups have also proliferated among Roman Catholics and Jews.

In response to what they see as the growing influence of science and the erosion of the conventional

The painting Arts of the South, *by Thomas Hart Benton (1889–1975), suggests that religious fundamentalism is strongly integrated into the community life of rural people in the southern United States.*

Thomas Hart Benton, *Arts of the South*, tempera with oil glaze, 8 x 13 feet, Harriet Russell Stanley, The New Britain Museum of American Art.

family, religious fundamentalists defend their version of traditional values. From this point of view, the liberal churches are simply too tolerant of religious pluralism and too open to change. Religious fundamentalism is distinctive in five ways (Hunter, 1983, 1985, 1987).

1. **Fundamentalists interpret the Scriptures literally.** Fundamentalists insist on a literal interpretation of the Scriptures as a means of countering what they see as excessive intellectualism among more liberal Christian organizations. Fundamentalists hold, for example, that God created the world precisely as described in Genesis.

2. **Fundamentalists do not accept religious pluralism.** Fundamentalists maintain that tolerance and relativism water down personal faith. They maintain, therefore, that their religious beliefs have validity while those of others do not.

3. **Fundamentalists pursue the personal experience of God's presence.** In contrast to the worldliness and intellectualism of other religious organizations, fundamentalism seeks to propagate "good old-time religion" and spiritual revival. To fundamentalist Christians, being "born again" and establishing a personal relationship with Jesus Christ are expected to be clearly evident in a person's everyday life.

4. **Fundamentalism opposes "secular humanism."** Fundamentalists believe that accommodation to the changing world undermines religious conviction. *Secular humanism* is a general term that refers to our society's tendency to look to scientific experts (including sociologists) rather than God for guidance about how to live.

5. **Many fundamentalists endorse conservative political goals.** Although fundamentalism tends to back away from worldly concerns, some fundamentalist leaders have entered the political arena in recent years to oppose what they see as the "liberal agenda" of feminism and gay rights. Fundamentalists oppose abortion as a matter of choice, seek to preserve the traditional two-parent family, urge a return to prayer in the public schools, and scold the mass media for coloring stories with liberal sentiments (Viguerie, 1981; Hunter, 1983; Speer, 1984; Ostling, 1985; Ellison & Sherkat, 1993; Green, 1993).

Taken together, these traits have given fundamentalism a reputation as somewhat rigid and self-righteous. At the same time, this brief sketch also helps us to understand why adherents find in fundamentalism—with its greater religious certainty and emphasis on experiencing God's presence in everyday life—an appealing alternative to the more intellectual, tolerant, and worldly "mainstream" denominations.

Which religions are "fundamentalist"? This term is most correctly applied to conservative Christian organizations in the evangelical tradition, including Pentecostals, Southern Baptists, Seventh-Day Adventists, and Assemblies of God. In national surveys, about 33 percent of U.S. adults describe their religious upbringing as "fundamentalist"; 42 percent claim a

Q: "If a man really wants to make a million dollars, the best way would be to start his own religion." L. Ron Hubbard

Q: "The fact of having been born is a bad augury for immortality." George Santayana

NOTE: In 1991, Arkansas, California, Indiana, Oregon, and West Virginia mandated that children should receive instruction about religions in school, reversing the earlier trend.

NOTE: By the 1950s, the Catholic church claimed that science and religion were not incompatible. In the encyclical *Humani generis*, Pope Pius XII urged both scientists and theologians to study evolution.

Q: "If we do discover a complete theory [of physics] . . . it would be the ultimate triumph of human reason—for then we would truly know the mind of God." Stephen Hawking

Controversy & Debate   *Does Science Threaten Religion?*

At the dawning of the modern age, the Italian physicist and astronomer Galileo (1564–1642) helped initiate the scientific revolution with a series of startling discoveries. Dropping objects from the Leaning Tower of Pisa, he discerned some of the laws of gravity. He also fashioned a telescope and surveyed the heavens, confirming a new proposition that the earth orbited the sun, rather than the other way around.

But his lively scientific imagination got him into trouble: Galileo was denounced by the Roman Catholic church, which had preached for centuries that the earth stood motionless at the center of the universe. Galileo only made matters worse by declaring that religious leaders and Biblical doctrine had no place in the building wave of science. Before long, he found his work banned and himself condemned to house arrest.

From its beginnings, science has maintained an uneasy relationship with religion. Indeed, as the course of Galileo's life makes clear, the claims of one sometimes infringe on the other's truth.

Through this century, too, science and religion have battled over the issue of creation. In the wake of Charles Darwin's masterwork, *On the Origin of Species*, scientists concluded that humanity evolved from lower forms of life over the course of a billion years. Yet the theory of evolution seems to fly in the face of the Biblical account of creation found in Genesis, which states that "God created the heavens and the earth," introducing life on the third day and, on the fifth and sixth days, creating animal life, including human beings, who were fashioned in God's own image.

Galileo would certainly have been intrigued by the famous "Scopes monkey trial" of 1925, in which the state of Tennessee prosecuted a local science teacher, John Thomas Scopes, for instructing his students about evolution in violation of a state law that forbade teaching "any theory that denies the story of the Divine Creation of man as taught in the Bible" and especially any claim that "man descended from a lower order of animals." At the conclusion of the trial, which attracted national attention, the court found Scopes guilty as charged and fined him $100. Because his conviction was reversed on appeal—perhaps to prevent the case from reaching the U.S. Supreme Court—Tennessee law continued to ban the teaching of evolution until 1967. A year later, the U.S. Supreme Court struck down all such laws as unconstitutional—a violation of the Constitution's ban on government-supported religion.

Today—almost four centuries after the silencing of Galileo—many people still ponder the apparently conflicting claims of science and religion. A third of U.S. adults believe the Bible is the literal word of God, and many of these

"moderate" religious tradition; and 22 percent call their religion "liberal" (NORC, 1994:131).

The Electronic Church

In contrast to the small village congregations of years past, some religious organizations—especially fundamentalists—have become electronic churches dominated by "prime-time preachers" (Hadden & Swain, 1981). Electronic religion, a variant found only in the United States, has propelled Oral Roberts, Pat Robertson, Robert Schuller, and others to greater prominence than all but a few clergy have enjoyed in the past. About 5 percent of the national television audience (about 10 million people) regularly tune in to religious television, while perhaps 20 percent (about 40 million) watch some religious programming every week (Martin, 1981; Gallup, 1982; NORC, 1994).

During the 1980s, regular solicitation of contributions brought a financial windfall to some religious organizations. Seen on thirty-two hundred stations in half the countries in the world, for example, Jimmy Swaggart received as much as $180 million annually in donations. But some media-based ministries were corrupted by the power of money. In 1989, Jim Bakker (who began his television career in 1965 hosting a children's puppet show with his wife Tammy Faye) was jailed following a conviction for defrauding contributors. Such cases, although few in number, attracted enormous national attention and undermined public support as people began to wonder whether television preachers were more interested in raising moral standards or cash.

Q: "We have too many men of science, too few of God. We have grasped the mystery of the atom and rejected the Sermon on the Mount. . . . Ours is a world of nuclear giants and ethical infants. We know more about war than about peace, more about killing than about living." General Omar N. Bradley (1948)

Q: "I could be quite a good Catholic if they would only let me pick my own saints and dogmas." Ezra Pound

SOCIAL SURVEY: In a recent *Time*/CNN poll, 55% of U.S. adults thought religion would have a greater role in our society after the year 2000; 37% said a lesser role.

DISCUSS: Do liberal colleges discriminate against religious people? A 1995 Supreme Court ruling (5–4) concluded that the University of Virginia violated free-speech guarantees when it failed to fund a Christian magazine along with other student groups.

people reject scientific findings that seem to run counter to Biblical scripture (NORC, 1994:137).

But there is emerging a middle ground, endorsed by half of U.S. adults (and also many church leaders) who accept that biblical accounts may be inspired by God and represent important philosophical truth without being literally correct in a scientific sense. That is, science and religion represent two different levels of understanding that respond to different kinds of questions. Both Galileo and Darwin devoted their lives to investigating *how* the natural world operates. Yet only religion can address *why* humans and the natural world exist in the first place.

Interestingly, our nation, which is both among the most actively scientific and devoutly religious in the world, embodies the peaceful coexistence of science and religion. Moreover, the more scientists discover about the origins of the universe, the more overwhelming the entire process appears. Indeed, as one scientist recently pointed out, the mathematical odds that some cosmic "Big Bang"

12 billion years ago created the universe and led to the formation of life on earth as we know it today are utterly infinitesimal—surely much smaller than the chance of one person winning a state lottery for twenty weeks in a row. Doesn't such a scientific fact point to the operation of an intelligent and purposeful power in our creation? Can't one be both a religious believer as well as a scientific investigator?

There is another reason to appreciate both scientific and religious thinking: The rapid advances of science continue to present society with vexing ethical dilemmas. Latter-day Galileos have unleashed the power of atomic energy, yet we still struggle to find its rightful use in the world. Similarly, discovering some of the secrets of human genetics has now brought us to the threshold of being able to manipulate life itself, a power that few have the moral confidence to use.

In 1992, a Vatican commission created by Pope John Paul II conceded that the church's silencing of Galileo had been in error. Today, most scientific and religious leaders agree that,

while science and religion represent distinctive truths, their teachings may be complementary. And many believe—in the rush to scientific discovery—that our scientific world has never been more in need of the moral guidance afforded by religion.

Continue the debate . . .

1. *On what grounds do some scientists completely reject religious accounts of human creation? Why do some religious people reject scientific accounts?*

2. *Do you think the sociological study of religion challenges anyone's faith? Why or why not?*

3. *Does it surprise you that about half of U.S. adults think that science is bringing too much change to our way of life? Do you agree or not?*

Sources: Based on Gould (1981) and Hutchingson (1994).

LOOKING AHEAD: RELIGION IN THE TWENTY-FIRST CENTURY

The popularity of media ministries, the rapid growth of religious fundamentalism, and the continuing adherence of millions more people to the "mainstream" churches show that religion will remain a central element of modern society. Moreover, high levels of immigration from many religious countries (in Latin America and elsewhere) will both intensify and diversify the religious character of U.S. society in the decades to come.

In addition, the pace of social change is accelerating. As the world becomes more complex, rapid change often seems to outstrip our capacity to make sense of it all. But rather than undermining religion, this process is firing the religious imagination of

people who seek a sense of religious community and ultimate meaning in life. Tensions between the spiritual world of religion and the secular sphere of science and technology will continue to resonate throughout our way of life; the final box takes a closer look at this dynamic relationship.

Science is simply unable to address the most central human needs and questions. Moreover, technological advances are confronting us with vexing moral dilemmas as never before—from new technologies for creating life to techniques for sustaining the lives of dying people. Against this backdrop of uncertainty, it is little wonder that many people continue to rely on their faith for assurance and hope. No doubt they will continue to do so for some time to come (Cox, 1977; Barker, 1981).

SUMMARY

1. Religion is a major social institution based on distinguishing the sacred from the profane. Religion is a matter of faith, not scientific evidence, which people express through various rituals.

2. Sociology analyzes the social consequences and correlates of religion, but no scientific research can make claims about the ultimate truth or falsity of any religious belief.

3. Emile Durkheim argued that, through religion, individuals experience the power of their society. His structural-functional analysis suggests that religion promotes social cohesion and conformity and confers meaning and purpose on life.

4. Using the symbolic-interaction paradigm, Peter Berger explains that religious beliefs are socially constructed as a means of responding to life's uncertainties and disruptions.

5. Using the social-conflict paradigm, Karl Marx charged that religion promotes social inequality. Historically, however, religious ideals have both supported hierarchy and motivated people to seek greater equality.

6. Max Weber's analysis of Calvinism's contribution to the rise of industrial capitalism demonstrates religion's power to promote social change.

7. Churches, which are religious organizations well integrated into their society, fall into two categories—ecclesias and denominations.

8. Sects, the result of religious division, are marked by suspicion of the larger society as well as charismatic leadership.

9. Cults are religious organizations that embrace new and unconventional beliefs and practices.

10. Technologically simple human societies were generally animistic, with religious life just one facet of family life; in more complex societies, religion emerges as a distinct social institution.

11. Followers of six world religions—Christianity, Islam, Judaism, Hinduism, Buddhism, and Confucianism—represent three-fourths of all humanity.

12. Almost all adults in the United States identify with a religion; about 60 percent claim to have a religious affiliation, with the largest number belonging to various Protestant denominations.

13. How religious we conclude our nation is depends on how we operationalize the concept of religiosity. The vast majority of people say they believe in God, but about only about one-fifth of the U.S. population attends religious services regularly.

14. Secularization refers to the diminishing importance of the supernatural and the sacred. In the United States, while some indicators of religiosity (like membership in "mainstream" churches) have declined, others (such as membership in sects) are on the rise. Such complexity suggests that secularization will not bring on the demise of religion.

15. Civil religion is a quasi-religious belief by which people profess loyalty to their society, often in the form of patriotism.

16. Fundamentalism opposes religious accommodation to the world, favoring a more otherworldly focus. Fundamentalist Christianity also advocates literal interpretation of the Bible, rejects religious diversity, and pursues the personal experience of God's presence. Some fundamentalist Christian organizations actively support conservative political goals.

17. Some of the continuing appeal of religion lies in the inability of science (including sociology) to address timeless questions about the ultimate meaning of human existence.

KEY CONCEPTS

animism the belief that elements of the natural world are conscious life forms that affect humanity

charisma extraordinary personal qualities that can turn an audience into followers

church a type of religious organization well integrated into the larger society

civil religion a quasi-religious loyalty binding individuals in a basically secular society

cult a religious organization that is substantially outside a society's cultural traditions

denomination a church, independent of the state, that accepts religious pluralism

ecclesia a church that is formally allied with the state

faith belief anchored in conviction rather than scientific evidence

fundamentalism a conservative religious doctrine that opposes intellectualism and worldly accommodation in favor of restoring a traditional, otherworldly spirituality

liberation theology a fusion of Christian principles with political activism, often Marxist in character

monotheism belief in a single divine power

polytheism belief in many gods

profane that which is defined as an ordinary element of everyday life

religion a social institution involving beliefs and practices based upon a conception of the sacred

religiosity the importance of religion in a person's life

ritual formal, ceremonial behavior

sacred that which is defined as extraordinary, inspiring a sense of awe, reverence, and even fear

sect a type of religious organization that stands apart from the larger society

secularization the historical decline in the importance of the supernatural and the sacred

totem an object in the natural world collectively defined as sacred

CRITICAL-THINKING QUESTIONS

1. Explain the basic distinction between the sacred and the profane that underlies all religious belief.

2. Explain Karl Marx's contention that religion tends to support the status quo. Develop a counterargument, based on Max Weber's analysis of Calvinism, that religion can serve as a major force for social change.

3. Distinguish between churches, sects, and cults. Is one type of religious organization inherently better than another? Why or why not?

4. What evidence points to a decline in religion in the United States? In what ways does religion seem to be getting stronger?

SUGGESTED READINGS

Classic Sources

Max Weber. *The Protestant Ethic and the Spirit of Capitalism.* New York: Charles Scribner's Sons, 1958 (orig. 1904–5).

This is the classic account of the power of religion to effect sweeping social change.

Edward Franklin Frasier. *The Negro Church in America.* New York: Schocken, 1963.

Frasier offers a historical and comprehensive account of the central place of the church in the African-American community.

Contemporary Sources

Helen Rose Ebaugh. *Women in the Vanishing Cloister: Organizational Decline in Catholic Religious Orders in the United States.* New Brunswick, N.J.: Rutgers University Press, 1993.

This account, written by a nun-turned-sociologist, explores the drop in the number of women in Catholic religious orders since the 1960s.

Wade Clark Roof. *A Generation of Seekers: The Spiritual Journeys of the Baby Boom Generation.* New York: HarperCollins, 1992.

Mounting evidence points to a return to religion for many members of the generation of young people who came of age in the 1960s.

Global Sources

Richard W. Bulliet. *Islam: The View from the Edge.* New York: Columbia University Press, 1994.

Although the heart of Islam lies in the Middle East, Muslims live in North America and around the world. This book examines how Islam differs in its central and peripheral settings.

Christian Smith. *The Emergence of Liberation Theology: Radical Religion and Social Movement Theory.* Chicago: University of Chicago Press, 1991.

This account of liberation theology among politically active Catholics during the 1960s assesses the movement's successes and failures.

Education

Thirteen-year-old Naoko Matsuo has just returned from school to her home in suburban Yokohama, Japan. Instead of dropping off her books and beginning an afternoon of fun, she settles in to do her homework. Several hours later, Naoko's mother reminds her that it is time to leave for the *juku* or "cram school" that she attends for three hours three evenings a week. Mother and daughter travel four stops on the subway to downtown Yokohama and climb to the second floor of an office building where Naoko joins dozens of other girls and boys for intensive training in Japanese, English, math, and science.

Tuition at the *juku* consumes several hundred dollars of the Matsuo family's monthly income. But they recognize the realities of the Japanese educational system, and consider this investment a necessity. The extra hours in the classroom will soon pay off when Naoko takes a national examination to determine her school placement. Three years later, she will face another hurdle with the high school placement exam; this test, once again, will determine the quality of her education. Then will come the final challenge: earning admission to an exclusive national university, a prize won by the one-third of Japanese students who perform best on this examination. Stumbling in the race that is Naoko's next five years will mean learning to settle for less. Like most other Japanese families, the Matsuos are convinced that one cannot work too hard or begin too early to prepare for university admission (Simons, 1989).

Why do the Japanese pay such attention to schooling? In this modern, industrial society, admission to an elite university all but ensures a high-paying, prestigious career. Surveying the world as well as focusing on the United States, this chapter spotlights **education,** *the social institution guiding a society's transmission of knowledge—including basic facts, job skills, and cultural norms and values—to its members.* In industrial societies, as we shall see, much education is a matter of **schooling,** *formal instruction under the direction of specially trained teachers.*

EDUCATION: A GLOBAL SURVEY

Like people in Japan, we in the United States expect children to spend much of their first eighteen years of life in school. As recently as a century ago, however, schooling in our society was a privilege restricted to a small elite. And so it is in poor societies today, where the vast majority of people receive only informal learning within the family.

Schooling and Economic Development

The extent of schooling in any society is closely tied to its level of economic development. Chapter 4 ("Society") explained that our hunting and gathering ancestors lived in societies built around families, without governments, churches, or systems of formal education. Learning amounted to the knowledge and skills adults transmitted to children (Lenski, Nolan, and Lenski, 1995).

In agrarian societies—in which most of the world's people live today—limited schooling imparts practical knowledge needed to perform farming or other traditional tasks. By contrast, the opportunity to study literature, art, history, and science is a privilege generally available only to people freed by wealth from the need to work. The English word "school," in fact, comes down to us from the Greek word for "leisure." In ancient Greece, renowned teachers such as Socrates, Plato, and Aristotle concentrated their efforts on aristocratic men to the exclusion of everyone else. Similarly, in ancient China, the famous philosopher K'ung-Fu-tzu (Confucius) shared his wisdom with only a select few. During the Middle Ages, European

TABLE 19–1 Educational Achievement in the United States, 1910–1993*

Year	High School Graduates	College Graduates	Median Years of Schooling
1910	13.5%	2.7%	8.1
1920	16.4	3.3	8.2
1930	19.1	3.9	8.4
1940	24.1	4.6	8.6
1950	33.4	6.0	9.3
1960	41.1	7.7	10.5
1970	55.2	11.0	12.2
1980	68.7	17.0	12.5
1993	80.2	21.9	12.7

*For persons twenty-five years of age and over. Percentage for high school graduates includes those who go on to college. Percentage of high school dropouts can be calculated by subtracting percentage of high school graduates from 100 percent.

Source: U.S. Bureau of the Census (1995).

education took a step forward as the church established the first colleges and universities. But, here again, the privilege of schooling remained largely restricted to ruling elites.

We find marked diversity in schooling throughout preindustrial societies today, reflecting, in part, the influence of thousands of local cultures. In Iran, for example, education and religion are intertwined, so Islam figures prominently in schooling there. Elsewhere—including Bangladesh (Asia), Zimbabwe (Africa), and Nicaragua (Latin America)—distinctive cultural traditions have molded the process of schooling.

All low-income countries have one trait in common: limited access to schooling. In the poorest nations (including several in central Africa), only half of all elementary-aged children are in school; throughout the world, just half of all children attend secondary school (Najafizadeh & Mennerick, 1992). As a consequence, illiteracy disadvantages one-third of Latin Americans, almost half of Asians, and two-thirds of Africans. Global Map 19–1 displays the extent of illiteracy around the world.

Industrial, high-income societies embrace the principle of schooling for everyone. Industrial production demands that workers gain at least basic skills in the so-called "three Rs"—reading, 'riting, and 'rithmetic. Our society has also looked to schooling as a means of forging a literate citizenry capable of participating in democratic political life.

The United States was among the first countries to pursue the goal of mass education. By 1850 about half the young people between the ages of five and nineteen were enrolled in school. By 1918, every state

had a *mandatory education law* that required children to attend school until at least the age of sixteen or completion of the eighth grade. These laws drew children from farms and factories to classrooms. Table 19–1 shows that a milestone was reached in the mid-1960s when, for the first time, a majority of U.S. adults had earned high school diplomas. Today, four out of five have a high school education, and more than one in five have a four-year college degree. The following sections take a closer look at schooling in several of the world's nations.

Schooling in India

India is a low-income country in which people earn about 5 percent of the income standard in the United States. Consequently, many parents depend on children's earnings. Thus, laws against child labor notwithstanding, many children work in factories—weaving rugs or making handicrafts—up to sixty hours a week, which greatly limits their opportunity for schooling.

In recent decades, the extent of schooling has increased. Most people in India now receive some primary education, typically in crowded school rooms where one teacher attends to upwards of sixty children (more than twice as many as in U.S. classrooms). This is all the schooling most people ever acquire, since less than half pursue secondary education and very few enter college. The overall result is that, across this vast country, only about half the Indian people are literate.

Pronounced patriarchy also shapes Indian education. Indian parents are joyful at the birth of a boy, since he and his future wife both will contribute income to the family. By contrast, families frown on girls as a financial liability, since parents must provide a dowry at the time of her marriage and a daughter's work will then benefit the family of her future husband. Because Indian society offers little incentive to invest in the schooling of girls, 45 percent of boys but only 30 percent of girls attend secondary school. As for the flip side of this cultural denigration of females, a large majority of the children working in Indian factories are girls—a family's way of benefiting from their daughter while they can (United Nations, 1995).

Schooling in Japan

September 30, 1994, Kobe, Japan. Compared to us, the Japanese are, above all, orderly. Young people on the way

THEN AND NOW: Share of Japanese 18-year-olds entering college, *1954*, 10.1%; *1994*, 43.3%. (Japanese Ministry of Education)

GLOBAL: One key to Japanese educational achievement is powerful cultural discipline. Such collective pressure, however, generates collective distinction but produces fewer highly innovative individuals. To illustrate, U.S. men and women have received proportionately more Nobel Prizes than have the Japanese.

Q: "A human being is not, in any proper sense, a human being until he is educated." Horace Mann

NOTE: Since 1970, significant improvements in elementary school enrollment have been reported by most nations in sub-Saharan Africa. Still, many of these societies have a level of schooling that is comparable to that offered in the United States in 1850.

Window on the World

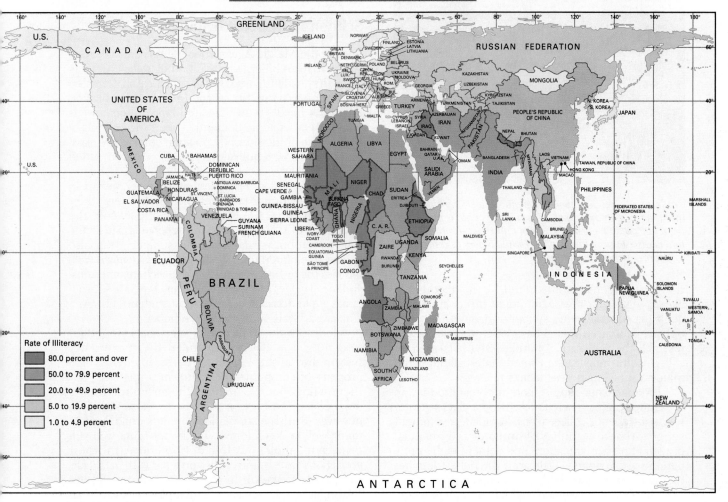

GLOBAL MAP 19–1 Illiteracy in Global Perspective

Reading and writing skills are widespread in every industrial society, with illiteracy rates generally below 5 percent. Throughout Latin America, however, illiteracy is more commonplace—one consequence of limited economic development. In about a dozen nations of the world—many of them in Africa—illiteracy is the rule rather than the exception. In such societies, people rely on what sociologists call "the oral tradition" of face-to-face communication rather than communicating by the written word.

Sources: *Peters Atlas of the World* (1990) and The World Bank (1995).

to school stand out with their uniforms, their armloads of books, and their look of seriousness and purpose.

Schooling has not always been part of the Japanese way of life. Before industrialization brought mandatory education to this country in 1872, only a privileged few enrolled in school. Today, Japan's educational system is widely praised for generating some of the world's highest achievers.

The early grades concentrate on transmitting Japanese traditions, especially obligation to family. By

NOTE: The world's oldest university was founded in Paris early in the 12th century. In England, the oldest is Oxford, also founded early in the 12th century. By the 13th century, historical notes mention "university chests," benefactions for the assistance of poor students—the earliest form of financial aid.

GLOBAL: Women earn about 54% of bachelor's degrees in the United States. In Great Britain, women's share is about 40%.

GLOBAL: British "public" schools number about 1,000 and cost roughly $20,000 a year. Their popularity has dropped in recent years, perhaps due to the high cost and growing opposition by parents to sending off their young children to fend for themselves.

GLOBAL: A U.S. government study determined the following relative proficiency levels for 13-year-olds in mathematics: U.S., 474; Ireland, 504; United Kingdom, 510; Spain, 512; South Korea, 568.

Traditionally, the Japanese have placed a strong emphasis on fitting in with the group. This cultural value is evident in the widespread wearing of school uniforms—a practice that is also gaining favor in the United States as a means to improve school discipline.

their early teens, as illustrated by the account of Naoko Matsuo at the beginning of this chapter, students encounter Japan's system of rigorous and competitive examinations. These written tests, which resemble the Scholastic Aptitude Tests (SATs) used for college admissions in the United States, all but determine a young Japanese student's future.

In Japan, schooling is more meritocratic than in the United States, where family income plays a greater role in a student's college plans. In Japan, government support relieves families of much of the financial burden of higher education. But, without high examination scores, there is little even the richest families can do to place their children in a good university.

More men and women graduate from high school in Japan (90 percent) than in the United States (80 percent). But competitive examinations sharply curb the number of college-bound youths, so that only about 40 percent of high school graduates—compared to 60 percent in the United States—end up entering college. Understandably, then, Japanese students take entrance examinations with the utmost seriousness, and about half attend "cram schools" to prepare for them. Japanese women, most of whom are not in the labor force, often devote themselves to their children's success in school.

Because of the pressure it places on students, Japanese schooling produces impressive results. In a number of fields, notably mathematics and science, young Japanese students outperform students in every other industrial nation, including the United States

(Benedict, 1974; Hayneman & Loxley, 1983; Rohlen, 1983; Brinton, 1988; Simons, 1989).

Schooling in Great Britain

During the Middle Ages, schooling was a privilege of the British nobility, who studied classical subjects since they had little need for the practical skills related to earning a living. But as the Industrial Revolution created a need for an educated labor force, and as working-class people demanded access to schools, a rising share of the British population entered the classroom. Law now requires every British child to attend school until age sixteen.

Traditional social distinctions, however, persist in British education. Many wealthy families send their children to what the British call *public schools*, the equivalent of U.S. private boarding schools. Such elite schools not only teach academic subjects, they also convey to children from wealthy (especially *newly rich*) families the distinctive patterns of speech, mannerisms, and social graces of the British upper class. These academies are far too expensive for most students, however, who attend state-supported day schools.

To lessen the influence of social background on schooling, the British expanded their university system during the 1960s and 1970s, inaugurating a program of competitive entrance examinations. For those who score the highest, the government pays most college costs. Compared with those in Japan, however, British examinations are less crucial, since many well-to-do children who do not score well still manage to enroll in Oxford or Cambridge, the most prestigious British universities on a par with Yale, Harvard, and Princeton in the United States. These "Oxbridge" graduates assume their place at the core of the British power elite: More than two-thirds of the top members of the British government have "Oxbridge" degrees (Sampson, 1982; Gamble, Ludlam, & Baker, 1993).

The overall theme of this brief comparison is that education is shaped by other institutions and social forces. In poor countries, children are more likely to work than go to school, and schooling in countries like India shows the influence of patriarchy. Rich nations adopt mandatory education laws both to forge an industrial work force and to satisfy demands for political democracy. Also woven into the fabric of education are cultural values (note the achievement orientation and intense competition of Japan) and social stratification (pronounced in British schools).

NOTE: In 1779, Thomas Jefferson was among the first proponents of mandatory public education. The public often resisted such laws in the 19th century, so that troops were sometimes called out to escort children to school.

Q: "The actual success of a teacher depends in large measure on the capacity to state the subject matter of instruction in terms of the experience of the [student]." George Herbert Mead

THEN AND NOW: Percentage of U.S. 20–24-year-olds enrolled in school: 1945, 3.9%; 1993, 30.8%.

THEN AND NOW: U.S. adults 25 and over who have completed four years of college: 1960, 7.7%; 1994, 22.2.

THEN AND NOW: U.S. college enrollment in 1890 (156,756) was 3% of 18–21-year-olds; in 1930 (1,100,737), 12%; in 1993 (6,873,000), 52%.

Schooling in the United States

The educational system in the United States, too, has been shaped by both our affluence and democratic principles. Thomas Jefferson thought the new nation could become democratic only if people "read and understand what is going on in the world" (quoted in Honeywell, 1931:13). As Figure 19–1 shows, the United States has an outstanding record of higher education for its people: In no other nation does a larger share of the adult population have a university degree (U.S. Bureau of the Census, 1995).

Schooling in the United States also reflects the value of *equal opportunity*. National surveys show that most people think schooling is crucial to personal success. We like to think that our society offers educational opportunity: Seventy percent endorse the notion that people have the chance to get an education consistent with their abilities and talents (NORC, 1994). But this view better expresses our aspirations than our achievement. Until well into this century, women were all but excluded from higher education and, even today, only among the wealthy do a majority of young people attend college.

Besides trying to make schooling more widely available, our educational system has also stressed the value of *practical* learning, that is, knowledge that has a direct bearing on people's work and interests. The educational philosopher John Dewey (1859–1952) championed *progressive education*, emphasizing practical skills rather than a fixed body of knowledge passed from generation to generation.

Reflecting this pragmatism, today's college students select major areas of study with an eye toward future jobs. The box on page 514 takes a closer look at the changing interests of college students.

THE FUNCTIONS OF SCHOOLING

Structural-functional analysis directs attention to ways in which formal education enhances the operation and stability of society. Central to the socialization process, schooling serves as a cultural lifeline linking the generations.

Socialization

Technologically simple societies transmit their ways of life informally from parents to children. As societies gain complex technology, however, kin can no longer stay abreast of the rapidly expanding range of information and skills, so schooling gradually emerges

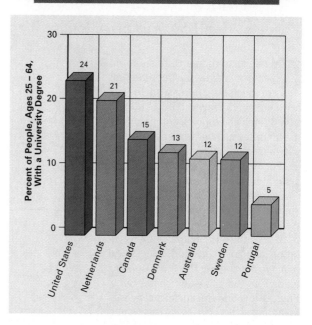

Global Snapshot

FIGURE 19–1 College Degrees in Global Perspective
Source: U.S. Bureau of the Census (1995).

as a distinctive social institution that uses specially trained personnel to convey knowledge needed for adult roles.

At the primary school level, children learn basic language and mathematical proficiency. Secondary school builds on this foundation, and, for many, college allows further specialization. But schools also transmit cultural values and norms. Civics classes, for example, explicitly instruct students in our political way of life. Sometimes important cultural lessons are learned through the operation of the classroom itself. From the earliest grades, spelling bees and classroom drills reveal our keen sense of competitive individualism, enhance respect for authority, and establish norms of fair play. Likewise, rituals such as saluting the flag and singing "The Star-Spangled Banner" foster patriotism.

Cultural Innovation

Educational systems create as well as transmit culture. Schools stimulate intellectual inquiry and critical thinking, sparking the development of new ideas.

THEN AND NOW: One measure of U.S. educational pragmatism is the rapidly growing number of business degrees: *1948*, 38,371 BAs, 2,341 MAs, and 14 doctorates; in *1993*, 249,711 BAs, 89,064 MAs, and 1,339 doctorates.

NOTE: Overall, almost 30% of the U.S. population are attending some school at any given time.

NOTE: The U.S. has 15,025 local school boards.

DISCUSS: Discuss the cultural values implicit in the classroom spelling bee (including competition, individual performance, specific standards of achievement).

DIVERSITY: Dovetailing with the social integration function of schooling is the multiculturalism debate, examined in Chapter 3 ("Culture").

SOCIOLOGY OF EVERYDAY LIFE

Following the Jobs: Trends in Bachelor's Degrees

College attendance in the United States has never been higher, especially among women. For both sexes, however, college education retains an emphasis on practicality: People pursue degrees in fields where they think jobs are plentiful.

Our postindustrial economy has generated the greatest surge in bachelor's degrees in law, as the figure shows. The number of degrees in computer science and communications, both central to the Information Revolution, also rose sharply. Business and management—long the most popular fields for students—also made gains. Engineering and the social sciences—including sociology—are up as well.

By and large, students shy away from majors in areas where the demand for workers is slipping. Library science heads the list of academic fields posting reductions, followed by agriculture, the physical sciences, home economics, education, philosophy and religion.

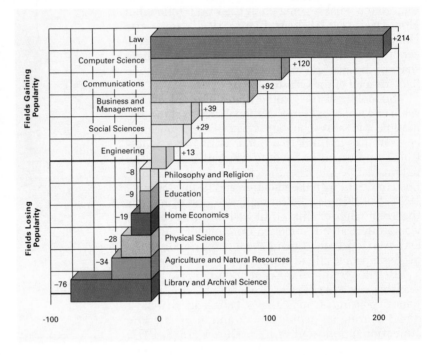

Percentage Changes in Bachelor's Degrees Earned, 1980–1992
Source: U.S. Bureau of the Census (1995).

Today, for example, many college professors engage in research that yields new insights and discoveries. Inquiry in the humanities, the social sciences, and the natural sciences is changing attitudes and behavior throughout the United States and the larger world. Medical research, carried on at major universities, has increased life expectancy, just as research by sociologists and psychologists helps us to take advantage of this longevity.

Social Integration

Schooling works to forge a mass of people into a unified whole. This function is especially important in nations with pronounced social diversity, where various cultures are indifferent or even hostile to one another. In the past, the Soviet Union and Yugoslavia relied on schools to tie their disparate peoples together—without ultimately succeeding—and similar cultural strains mark the United States as well.

Societies in the Americas, Africa, and Asia, encompassing hundreds of ethnic categories, all strive to foster social integration. Schools meet this challenge, first, by establishing a common language that allows for broad communication and forges a national identity. Of course, some ethnic minorities resist state-sponsored schooling for precisely this reason. In the former Soviet Union, for example, Lithuanians, Ukrainians, and Azerbaijanis long chafed at having to learn Russian, which they saw as a threat to their own traditions and emblematic of their domination by outsiders. Similarly, the Amish, a culturally distinctive people in the United States, refuse to send their children to public schools.

A century ago, mandatory education laws in the United States coincided with the arrival of millions of immigrants. Today, too, formal education helps to integrate disparate cultures, as people from Latin America and Asia inject their traditions into the ever-changing cultural mix. In recent years, racial and ethnic minorities have become a numerical majority in many of the largest school districts, igniting a debate over multicultural education (highlighted in Chapter 3, "Culture").

Social Placement

Formal education helps young people assume culturally approved statuses and perform roles that contribute to the ongoing life of society. To accomplish this, schooling operates to identify and develop people's various aptitudes and abilities. Ideally, schools evaluate students' performance in terms of achievement alone while downplaying their social background.

In principle, teachers encourage the "best and the brightest" to pursue the most challenging and advanced studies, while guiding students of more ordinary abilities into educational programs well suited to their talents. Schooling, in short, enhances meritocracy, making personal merit a foundation of future social position and fueling what our society considers desirable social mobility (Hurn, 1978).

Latent Functions of Schooling

Besides these manifest functions of formal education, a number of latent functions are less widely recognized. One is child care. As the number of one-parent families and two-career couples rises, schools have become vital to relieving parents of some child-care responsibilities.

Among teenagers, too, schooling consumes much time and considerable energy, in many cases promoting conformity at a stage of life when the likelihood of unlawful behavior is high. Because many students attend schools well into their twenties, education usefully engages thousands of young people for whom few jobs may be available.

Schools also set the stage for us to establish relationships and networks. In the social circles of the high school, college, and university, many people meet their future spouses. In addition, affiliation with a particular school forms the basis of social ties that provide not only friendship but also valuable career opportunities later on in life.

Critical evaluation. Structural-functional analysis of formal education identifies both manifest and latent contributions of this social institution to an industrial way of life. Yet functionalism skims over one core truth: The quality of schooling is far greater for some than for others. Indeed, critics of the U.S. educational system maintain that schooling actually operates to reproduce the class structure in each generation. In the next section, social-conflict analysis spotlights these issues.

SCHOOLING AND SOCIAL INEQUALITY

Social-conflict analysis takes issue with the functionalist contention that schooling is a meritocratic strategy for developing people's talents and abilities. This view argues that schools routinely tailor education according to students' social background, thereby perpetuating social inequality.

As noted earlier, many of the world's societies have considered schooling more important for males than for females. Although the U.S. education gap between women and men has largely closed in recent decades, many women still study traditionally feminine subjects such as literature, while men pursue mathematics and engineering. And by stressing the experiences of some types of people (say, military generals) while ignoring the lives of others (such as farm women), schools reinforce the values and importance of dominant categories of people. As we shall see, too, affluent people have much more educational opportunity than their poorer counterparts.

Social Control

Social-conflict analysis asserts that schooling acts as a means of social control, reinforcing acceptance of the status quo. In various, sometimes subtle ways, schools operate to reproduce the status hierarchy.

Samuel Bowles and Herbert Gintis (1976) point out that the clamor for public education in the late nineteenth century arose precisely when capitalists were seeking a literate, docile, and disciplined work force. Mandatory education laws ensured that schools would teach immigrants the English language as well as cultural values supportive of capitalism. Compliance, punctuality, and discipline were—and still are—part of what conflict theorists call the **hidden curriculum**, *subtle presentations of political or cultural ideas in the classroom.*

From a functionalist point of view, schooling provides children with the information and skills they will need as adults. A conflict analysis adds that schooling differs according to the resources available to the local community. To the extent that some schools offer children much more than others do, education falls short of its goal of enhancing equality of opportunity.

Standardized Testing

Here is a question of the kind historically used to measure academic ability of school-aged children in the United States:

> Painter is to painting as _____ is to sonnet.
>
> *Answers:*   (a) driver   (c) priest
>   (b) poet   (d) carpenter

The correct answer is (b) *poet*: A painter creates a painting as a poet creates a sonnet. This question purports to measure logical reasoning, but demonstrating this skill depends upon knowing what each term means. Unless students are familiar with sonnets as a Western European form of written verse, they are not likely to answer the question correctly.

Educational specialists claim that bias of this kind has been all but eliminated from standardized tests, since test preparers carefully study response patterns and drop any question that appears to favor one racial or ethnic category over another. Critics, however, maintain that some bias based on class, race, or ethnicity is inherent in any formal testing because questions inevitably reflect our society's dominant culture, thereby placing minorities at a disadvantage (Owen, 1985; Crouse & Trusheim, 1988; Putka, 1990).

School Tracking

Despite continuing controversy over standardized tests, most schools in the United States use them as the basis for **tracking,** *the assignment of students to different types of educational programs.* Tracking is also a common practice in many other industrial societies, including Great Britain, France, and Japan.

The educational justification for tracking is to give students the kind of schooling appropriate to their individual aptitude. For a variety of reasons, including innate ability and level of motivation, some students are capable of more challenging work than others are. Young people also differ in their interests, with some drawn to, say, the study of languages, while others seek training in art or science. Given this diversity of talent and focus, no single program for all students would serve any of them well.

But critics see tracking as a thinly veiled strategy to perpetuate privilege. The basis of this argument is research indicating that social background has as much to do with tracking as personal aptitude does. Students from affluent families generally do well on standardized, "scientific" tests and so are placed in college-bound tracks, while schools assign those from modest backgrounds (including a disproportionate share of the poor) to programs that curb their aspirations and teach technical trades. Tracking, therefore, effectively segregates some students—academically and socially—from others.

Most schools reserve their best teachers for students in favored tracks. Thus high-track boys and girls find that their teachers put more effort into classes, show more respect toward students, and expect more from them. By contrast, teachers of low-track students concentrate on memorization, classroom drill, and other unstimulating techniques. Such classrooms also emphasize regimentation, punctuality, and respect for authority figures.

In light of these criticisms, schools across the United States are now cautious about making tracking assignments and allow greater mobility between tracks. Some have even moved away from the practice entirely. Some tracking seems to be necessary to match instruction with student abilities. But rigid tracking has a powerful impact on students' learning and self-concept. Young people who spend years in higher tracks tend to see themselves as bright and able, whereas those in lower tracks develop lower ambition and self-esteem (Bowles & Gintis, 1976; Persell, 1977; Rosenbaum, 1980; Davis & Haller, 1981; Oakes, 1982, 1985; Hallinan & Williams, 1989; Kilgore, 1991; Gamoran, 1992).

Inequality Among Schools

Just as students are treated differently within schools, schools themselves differ in fundamental ways. One key distinction separates private and public schools.

Public and Private Schools

In 1994, 86 percent of the 65 million U.S. school-aged children attended state-funded public schools. The remainder were in private schools.

A majority of private school students attend one of more than eight thousand *parochial schools* (from the Latin meaning "of the parish") operated by the Roman Catholic church. The Catholic school system grew rapidly a century ago as cities swelled with millions of Catholic immigrants and their children. These schools helped the new arrivals maintain their religious heritage in the midst of a predominantly Protestant society. Today, after decades of flight from the city by white people, many parochial schools enroll non-Catholics, including a growing number of young African Americans whose families eagerly embrace this alternative to the neighborhood public school.

Protestants, especially in fundamentalist denominations, have also founded private schools or Christian academies. Like earlier parochial schools, these Christian schools are favored by parents who want their children to receive religious instruction or seek higher academic and disciplinary standards. For some, however, the Christian school represents a strategy by which parents ensure a racially homogeneous environment for their children in the face of school desegregation mandates (James, 1989).

Additionally, some fifteen hundred nonreligious private schools in the United States enroll students, mostly from well-to-do families. These prestigious and expensive preparatory schools are especially favored by "newly rich" parents eager for their daughters and sons to rub elbows with children with "old money." These institutions—many modeled after boarding schools in Great Britain—are academically outstanding and send a large share of their graduates to equally prestigious and expensive private universities. After learning the mannerisms, attitudes, and social graces of the socially prominent, "preppies" are likely to maintain lifelong school-based networks that confer numerous social advantages.

Are private schools better than public schools? Research indicates that, among children with similar backgrounds, private school students display higher rates of academic achievement than public school students. Private schools seem to generate greater interest in learning than do public schools, probably due to smaller class size and more student-teacher contact. Furthermore, private schools are more academically demanding and enforce stringent disciplinary policies, resulting in a safer, more orderly environment. By and large, all other things being equal, graduates of private schools are more likely than public school graduates to complete college and subsequently enter high-paying occupations (Coleman, Hoffer, & Kilgore, 1981; Coleman & Hoffer, 1987).

Inequality in Public Schooling

A general rule in U.S. education is that the more affluent the community, the better its schools. Winnetka, Illinois—one of the richest areas in the country—spends more than $8,000 annually per student, compared to less than $3,000 in a poor area like Socorro, Texas (Carroll, 1990).

Nationwide, suburban school districts offer better schooling than less-well-funded systems in central cities. This disparity has an important racial dimension, since whites predominate in suburbia, while central cities are home to many African Americans and other minorities. To advance educational equality (often mandated by courts), some communities have initiated *busing*—transporting students to achieve a greater social mix. Although this policy currently affects only 5 percent of U.S. school children, it has generated heated controversy. Busing advocates claim that minority children in poor neighborhoods will have quality schools only if white children from richer neighborhoods attend them. Critics respond that

THE MAP: Relatively affluent regions of the United States have a higher share of young people enrolled in college; in addition, high-enrollment counties are those where people endorse greater opportunities for women (compare to National Map 13–1).
DIVERSITY: Gary Orfield (1994) reports that the percentage of African Americans attending predominantly minority schools was 64% in 1972–73; in 1991–92 it was 66%. Comparable data for

Hispanics, 57% and 73%. Among blacks, 39% attended 90%–100% minority schools in 1972–73; 34% in 1991–92. Comparable data for Hispanics, 23% and 34%.
Q: "Children in one set of schools are trained to be governors; children in the other set are trained to be governed." Jonathan Kozol
Q: "In education, there should be no class distinction." Confucius

Seeing Ourselves

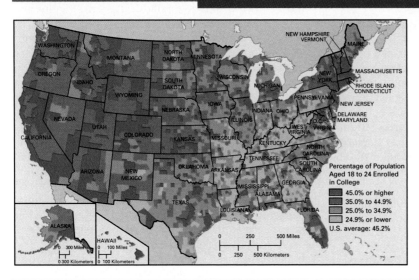

NATIONAL MAP 19–1

College Attendance Across the United States

Generally speaking, college attendance is most common among adults along the Northeast and West coasts. By contrast, adults living in the Midwest and the South (especially the Appalachian region) are the least likely members of our society to attend college. How would you explain this pattern? (Income is one obvious consideration; would people's ideas about gender equality be another?)

Source: *American Demographics* magazine, April 1993, p. 60. Reprinted with permission. ©1993 *American Demographics* magazine, Ithaca, New York.

busing itself is expensive and transporting children undermines the concept of neighborhood schools. But both sides acknowledge that, given the racial imbalance of U.S. urban areas, an effective busing scheme would have to encompass both central cities and the surrounding suburbs—a plan that has almost never been politically feasible.

A classic report by a research team headed by James Coleman (1966) confirmed the handicap of attending predominantly minority schools: larger class size, insufficient libraries, and fewer science labs. But the Coleman report cautioned that money alone does not magically bolster academic quality. Even more important are the cooperative efforts and enthusiasm of teachers, parents, and students themselves. In other words, even if school funding were exactly the same everywhere, the students whose families value and encourage education would still learn more than others (Jencks, 1972). In short, we should not expect schools alone to overcome the effects of marked social inequality.

Yet, schools certainly reflect privilege and disadvantage. As educational critic Jonathan Kozol (1992) concludes, "savage inequalities" in our school system alert young children to the reality that our society has already defined them as winners or losers. And, Kozol continues, all too often the children go on to fulfill this prophecy.

Access to Higher Education

In industrial societies, higher education is a key path to occupational achievement. But while parents typically endorse the idea of sending their children to college, only 61 percent of U.S. high school graduates actually enroll in college the following fall (U.S. Bureau of the Census, 1995). Moreover, among young people eighteen to twenty-four years old, just 45 percent are enrolled in college: National Map 19–1 shows where in the United States college attendance is more or less likely.

The most crucial factor affecting access to U.S. higher education is money. Unlike primary and secondary schooling, which is supported by public funds, people must pay to go to college, which becomes more expensive every year. Even at state-supported institutions, annual tuition averages about $2,500, and the most exclusive private colleges and universities exceed $25,000 a year. Add to these figures the costs of books, supplies, and travel to and from the campus.

Given such expenses, family income is a good predictor of college attendance, as shown in Figure 19–2. Families with incomes of at least $75,000 annually (roughly the richest 20 percent, falling within the upper and upper-middle classes) are more than three times as likely to send a child to college (68 percent do) as families in poverty with less than $10,000 in annual income (19 percent do).

NOTE: Sixty percent of persons 25 years or older who are high school graduates have attained some college education. About 75% of these attended state schools; state funding covers about 80% of their costs. Among college matriculants, only 40% complete a bachelor's degree after six years. The United States has about 1,500 community colleges and 2,100 four-year colleges and universities.
DIVERSITY: In 1993, 42% of white high school graduates went on to college, compared to 36% of Hispanic graduates and 33% of African-American graduates. Moreover, 82% of minorities matriculate in public universities compared to 63% of white students. (American Council on Education)
THEN AND NOW: Number of minority PhDs in the physical sciences: *1975*, 75 of 3,476; *1992*, 261 of 2,731. In the social sciences, *1975*, 256 of 3,500; *1992*, 420 of 5,403.

The financial burden of higher education dissuades many minorities, typically with below-average incomes, from attending college. Figure 19–3 on page 520 shows that whites are more likely than African Americans and Hispanics to complete high school to begin with, and this disparity remains with each step up the educational ladder.

The long-term trend, however, reflects more academic achievement on the part of minorities, and even a closing of the gap with whites. Between 1984 and 1994, the number of African Americans attending college rose by 20 percent; the number of Hispanics on campus shot up by 70 percent. During this same period, the non-Hispanic white increase was a modest 16 percent (U.S. Bureau of the Census, 1995).

But even among those privileged enough to enroll, not everyone gains the same type and quality of education. People of limited financial means typically attend less expensive community colleges and other government-supported schools. Certainly many students receive an excellent education in these public institutions, where the faculty's primary concern is teaching rather than research. But private schools, with high tuition and hefty endowments, offer smaller classes, expose students to renowned researchers, confer higher prestige, and admit students to networks of powerful people (Useem & Karabel, 1986; Monk-Turner, 1990).

Across the board, however, college attendance promises not just intellectual and personal growth but higher income. Over one's working lifetime, in fact, gaining a college degree adds almost $500,000 to personal income (Speer, 1994). Table 19–2 shows why. Women with an eighth-grade education typically earn about $6,500; income rises to almost $11,000 for high

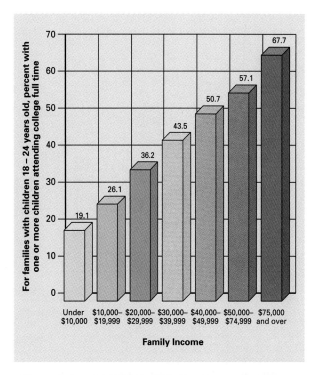

FIGURE 19–2 College Attendance and Family Income, 1993
Source: U.S. Bureau of the Census (1994).

school graduates and averages $22,400 for college graduates. The ratios in parentheses show that a woman with a bachelor's degree earns almost four times as much as her counterpart with four or fewer years of elementary schooling. Considering all levels, men earn on average about 40 percent more than women do; moreover, more schooling boosts men's income at an even greater rate. Finally, bear in mind that some of the earning differential based on education has to do with social background, since the people with the most schooling are likely to come from relatively well-to-do families to begin with.

Credentialism

Sociologist Randall Collins (1979) has dubbed the United States a *credential society,* because people view diplomas and degrees as evidence of ability to perform specialized occupational roles. As modern societies have become more technologically complex, culturally diverse, and socially mobile, a résumé often says more about "who you are" than family background does.

TABLE 19–2 Median Income by Sex and Educational Attainment*

Education	Men	Women
Professional degree	$68,824 (9.2)	$36,645 (6.4)
Doctorate	51,790 (6.9)	39,614 (6.9)
Master's	44,271 (5.9)	30,190 (5.2)
Bachelor's	36,779 (4.9)	22,416 (3.9)
1–3 years of college	26,374 (3.5)	14,408 (2.5)
4 years of high school	21,673 (2.9)	10,909 (1.9)
9–11 years of school	14,220 (1.9)	7,294 (1.3)
5–8 years of school	11,089 (1.5)	6,493 (1.1)
0–4 years of school	7,464 (1.0)	5,759 (1.0)

*Persons aged twenty-five years and over, working full-time, 1993. The earnings ratio, in parentheses, indicates how many times the lowest income level an individual with additional schooling earns.

Source: U.S. Bureau of the Census (1994).

DIVERSITY: College completion (in 1994, aged 25 and over), as in Table 19–1, by sex: 25.1% for men, 19.6% for women; African-American men, 12.8%; African-American women, 13.0%; Asian/Pacific Islander men, 43.2%; Asian/Pacific Islander women, 35.5%; Hispanic men, 9.6%; Hispanic women, 8.6%.

DIVERSITY: By 1994, 72% of African Americans between 18 and 24 had high school diplomas (1980: 70%). Yet black college

matriculation has slipped to about 34% (even as white matriculation has risen to 46%). A gender gap is also evident among African-American students in college: nationally, 59% are women.

THEN AND NOW: Share of adult African-American men and women with a high school diploma: *1980:* 51%, 51%; *1994,* 72%, 74%. Share with college degree: *1980,* 8%, 8%; *1994,* 13%, 13%. (U.S. Census Bureau)

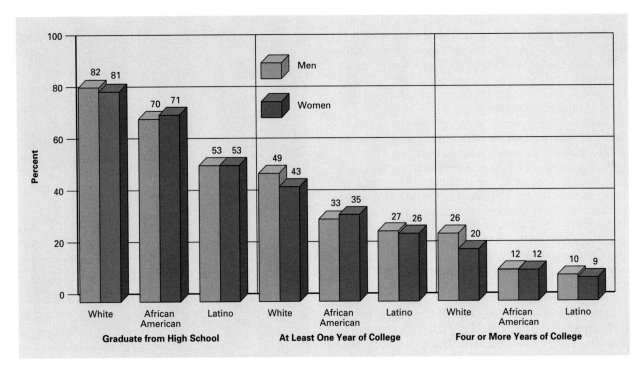

FIGURE 19–3 Educational Achievement for Various Categories of People, Aged 25 Years and Over, 1993

Source: U.S. Bureau of the Census (1994).

Credentialism, then, is *evaluating a person on the basis of educational degrees.* Structural-functional analysis views credentialism as simply the way our modern society goes about ensuring that important jobs are filled by well-trained people. But Collins points out that credentials often bear little relation to the responsibilities of a specific job. In reality, then, advanced degrees serve as a shorthand way to sort out the people with the manners, attitudes, and even color sought by many employers. In short, credentialism operates much like family background as a gate-keeping strategy that restricts prestigious occupations to a small segment of the population.

Finally, this emphasis on credentials in the United States has encouraged *overeducation,* by which many workers have more schooling than they need to perform their jobs. As a result, although we see more and more people with newly minted advanced degrees, our society is creating fewer and fewer jobs calling for highly educated workers; instead, we are witnessing an expansion of low-skill service jobs (described in Chapter 10, "Social Class in the United States").

Privilege and Personal Merit

A key theme of social-conflict analysis deserves to be highlighted: *Schooling transforms social privilege into personal merit.* Attending college, in effect, is a rite of passage for men and women from well-to-do families.

But our cultural emphasis on individualism pushes us to see credentials as "badges of ability," as Richard Sennett and Jonathan Cobb (1973) put it, rather than as symbols of family affluence. When we congratulate the new graduate, we have in mind personal achievement while usually overlooking the social resources that made this accomplishment possible. At the same time, we transform social disadvantage into personal deficiency when we condemn the high school dropout with little thought to the social circumstances that surround that person's life. The box illustrates this process with the words of one bright but disillusioned boy.

Critical evaluation. Social-conflict analysis points up the connection between formal education and social inequality, and shows how schooling transforms privilege into personal worthiness, and social disadvantage

DIVERSITY: In 1992, U.S. universities awarded 40,090 PhDs; African Americans received 1,223 (3%); Latinos 811 (2%) and Native Americans 118 (0.3%). Forty percent of all doctorates earned by African Americans are in education; 11% are in the sciences, and just several dozen are in sociology.

Q: "Discipline is the ultimate tenet of education. Discipline establishes the format, the environment for academic achievement to occur." Joe Clark, controversial principal of Paterson, N.J.'s East-side High School

SOCIAL SURVEY: "Does everyone in this country have an opportunity to obtain an education corresponding to their abilities and talents?" (GSS 1984, N = 1,473; *Codebook*, 1994:97)
"Yes" 69.8%   "No" 27.9%   DK/NR 2.3%

SOCIAL DIVERSITY

"Cooling Out" the Poor:
Transforming Disadvantage Into Deficiency

If schools treat disadvantaged students as "dumb," over time some of them come to believe it. This process of "cooling out" their aspirations for achievement sets into motion a self-fulfilling prophecy by which many poor students end up settling for no more than what society handed them when they were born. Eleven-year-old Ollie Taylor describes his situation in these words:

The only thing that matters in my life is school and there they think I'm dumb and always will be. I'm starting to think they're right. Hell, I know they put all the black kids together in one group if they can,

but that doesn't make any difference either. I'm still dumb. Even if I

look around and know that I'm the smartest in my group, all that means is that I'm the smartest of the dumbest, so I haven't got anywhere at all, have I? I'm right where I always was. Every word those teachers tell me, even the ones I like most, I can hear in their voice that what they're really saying is "All right you dumb kids. I'll make it as easy as I can, and if you don't get it then, you'll never get it. Ever." That's what I hear every day, man. From every one of them. Even the other kids talk that way to me too.

Source: Cottle (1974): 22–24.

into personal deficiency. Critics claim that social-conflict analysis minimizes the extent to which schooling has met the intellectual and personal needs of students, propelling the upward social mobility of many young people in the process. Further, especially in recent years, "politically correct" educational curricula—closely tied to conflict theory—are challenging the status quo on many fronts.

PROBLEMS IN THE SCHOOLS

An intense debate revolves about schooling in the United States. Perhaps because we expect our schools to do so much—equalize opportunity, instill discipline, fire the individual imagination—few people think that public schools are doing an excellent job. Table 19–3 on page 522 shows that about half of all adults give our schools a grade of "C" or below (Roper Center, 1994). The most visible school problems are lack of discipline and outright violence. In addition, many students display little interest in learning, and the record indicates that academic performance is spiraling downward.

School Discipline

Asked to identify the problems of their school, teachers fifty years ago cited talking out of turn, cutting in line, chewing gum, violations of the dress code, and littering. Today's teachers, by contrast, point to drug and alcohol abuse, pregnancy, and violence (Bennett, 1995). It is little wonder that, while almost everyone agrees that schools should teach personal discipline, many think that the job is no longer being done (NORC, 1994:505).

The government estimates that several hundred thousand students and at least one thousand teachers are physically assaulted on school grounds every year. About one-fourth of students attending school in central cities voice fears of being attacked in or around the school. And recent news reports indicate that thousands of young people now routinely arrive at school armed with guns and other deadly weapons (U.S. Bureau of Justice Statistics, 1991).

Disorder spills into schools from the surrounding society. As Chapter 8 ("Deviance") explained, our nation is among the most violent in the world, with

Q: "There has come to be a recognition that many of the issues in education today are not in the domain of educational psychologists, but have to do with the social structure of the school and the world outside the school." James S. Coleman

RESOURCE: The Karp and Yoels article, "Why Don't College Students Participate?" is included in the Macionis and Benokraitis reader, *Seeing Ourselves*.

Q: "Should we produce competent bureaucrats and narrowly trained technicians, or should we develop creative, reflective individuals who will help to transform the world into more democratic forms?" Harvey Holtz (1989:193)

THEN AND NOW: One indicator of dissatisfaction with U.S. schooling is that about 1 million children are now educated at home, up sharply from about 15,000 in 1980.

TABLE 19–3 Grading Public Schools in the United States, 1995

Rating*	Proportion of Respondents
A	8%
B	33
C	37
D	12
FAIL	5
Don't know	5

*These figures reflect the responses of a national sample of U.S. adults to the question: Students are often given the grades A, B, C, D, and FAIL to denote the quality of their work. Suppose the public schools themselves, in this community, were graded in the same way. What grade would you give the public schools here—A, B, C, D, or FAIL?

Source: On-line data from Roper Center for Public Opinion Research, University of Connecticut (1996).

disorder of epidemic proportions in poor communities. Schools do not create the problem of violence, in short, but they do have the power to effect change for the better.

Take the case of Malcolm X Elementary School. The school is located in a poor neighborhood of Washington, D.C., known by residents simply as "the jungle" because, as one local police officer observes, "It's all about survival here." Engulfed by all the urban ills that plague this country, most students at Malcolm X live in poor, single-parent homes, surrounded by prostitution, drugs, and seemingly endless waves of violence.

Yet crossing the threshold of this school brings an unexpected contrast: All the boys are dressed in school uniforms—white shirts and red ties—and all the girls wear plaid jumpers. By and large, the hallways are clean and quiet; classrooms are orderly. The extraordinary achievement of Malcolm X is that students are learning—not out of fear but because they want to.

The key to this remarkable school, as most of the staff sees it, is attitude. Skillful and committed teachers have ignited in students a sense of pride and a hunger to achieve. Principal John Pannell, son of a West Virginia school-bus driver, spells out his simple philosophy this way: "If we don't have high expectations for these children, who will?" For their part, most students do feel that the teachers really care about them. Beaming at her second-grade class, Avis Watts explains, "This is their lifeline really; they know that they'll be fed, loved, and everything else in this school" (Gup, 1992).

While schools like Malcolm X may be the exception, they demonstrate the power of education to bring constructive change to the lives of even the most

disadvantaged students. The key to such success appears to lie in a strong commitment to children, exemplary teaching skills, firm disciplinary policies, and the ability of school officials to garner support from parents and the larger community.

Student Passivity

If some schools are plagued by violence, many more are afflicted by passive, bored students. Some of the responsibility for failing to take advantage of educational opportunity can be placed on television (which now consumes more of young people's time than school does), on parents (who do not foster a desire to learn), and on students themselves. But schools, too, must share the blame, since our educational system has long generated student passivity (Coleman, Hoffer, & Kilgore, 1981).

Bureaucracy

A century ago, formal education in the United States took place in small, personal settings in countless local communities. Today, the one-room schoolhouse has been replaced by huge educational factories. A study of high schools across the United States led Theodore Sizer to identify five ways in which large, bureaucratic schools undermine education (1984:207–9).

1. **Rigid uniformity.** Bureaucratic schools are typically insensitive to the cultural character of local communities. Outside "specialists" (such as state education officials) operate schools with little understanding of the needs of particular students.

2. **Numerical ratings.** School officials define success in terms of numerical attendance records, dropout rates, and achievement test scores. In doing so, they overlook dimensions of schooling difficult to quantify, such as the creativity of students and the energy and enthusiasm of teachers.

3. **Rigid expectations.** Officials expect fifteen-year-olds to be in the tenth grade, and eleventh-graders to score at a certain level on a standardized verbal achievement test. Rarely are exceptionally bright and motivated students permitted to graduate early. Likewise, the system pushes along students who have learned little so they can graduate with their class.

4. **Specialization.** High school students learn Spanish from one person, receive guidance from another, and are coached in sports by still others.

SOCIAL SURVEY: "How important for getting ahead in life is having a good education?" (GSS 1987, N = 1,285; Codebook, 1994:555)

"Essential"	34.7%	"Not very important"	1.3%
"Very important"	48.2%	"Not important at all"	0%
"Fairly important"	14.3%	DK/NR	1.5%

Q: "Instructors who want dialogue to return to the classroom must take it upon themselves to challenge students with a freer, more reflexive form of learning. Professors who rely solely on [lecture-oriented] teaching techniques—but then slouch on their podiums and lament that 'teaching is dead' when these techniques fail—are guilty of murder." Richard A. Wright, "Curing Doonesbury's Disease—A Prescription for Dialogue in the Classroom," Quarterly Journal of Ideology 9, 4 (1985):3–8

Although specialized teachers may have an in-depth grasp of their subjects, no school employee comes to know and appreciate the "complete" student. Students experience this division of labor as a continual shuffling among fifty-minute periods throughout the school day.

5. **Little individual responsibility.** Highly bureaucratic schools do not empower students to learn on their own. Similarly, teachers have little latitude in what and how they teach their classes; they dare not accelerate learning for fear of disrupting "the system."

Of course, some formal organization in schools is inevitable given the immense size of the task. The number of students in the New York City public schools alone now exceeds the student population of the entire country a century ago. But, Sizer maintains, we need to "humanize" schools to make them more responsive to those they claim to serve. He recommends eliminating rigid class schedules, reducing class size, and training teachers more broadly to help them become more involved in the lives of their students. Overall, as James Coleman (1993) recently suggested, schools need to be less "administratively driven" and more "output-driven." Perhaps this transformation could begin by ensuring that graduation from high school depends on what a student has learned rather than simply on the length of time spent in school.

College: The Silent Classroom

Here are the observations of a bright and highly motivated first-year student at a top-flight four-year college. Do they strike a familiar chord?

> I have been disappointed in my first year at college. Too many students do as little work as they can get away with, take courses that are recommended by other students as being "gut" classes, and never challenge themselves past what is absolutely necessary. It's almost like thinking that we don't watch professors but we watch television. (Forrest, 1984:10)

As this student observes, passivity is also common in colleges and universities. Martha E. Gimenez (1989) describes college as the "silent classroom" in which the only voice heard is usually the teacher's. Sociologists tend not to conduct research on the college classroom—a curious fact considering how much time they spend there. A fascinating exception is a study at a coeducational university in which David Karp and William Yoels (1976) found that—even in small classes—

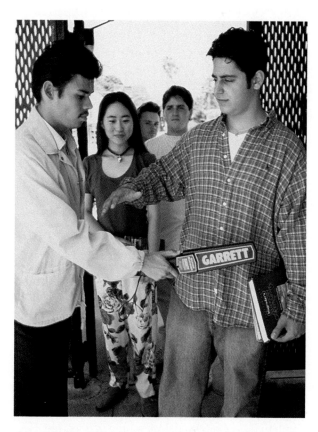

In some cities of the United States, the level of violence has escalated to the point that students are in danger of harm not only while traveling to and from school but also in school itself. Estimates indicate that thousands of young people come to school each day carrying guns and other deadly weapons, forcing administrators to adopt desperate security measures.

just a handful of students said anything at all during the typical class period. In short, Karp and Yoels concluded, passivity is a classroom norm, and they observed that students themselves became irritated with one of their number who was especially talkative.

Gender also affects classroom dynamics. Karp and Yoels note that, in coeducational classes taught by a man, male students dominated most classroom discussion. With women as instructors, however, the two sexes spoke up in roughly the same proportions. Why? Perhaps because women instructors directed questions to women students as frequently as to men, while male teachers favored their male students.

Students offer various explanations for classroom passivity, which are listed in Table 19–4. Note that they see passivity as mostly their own fault, which is,

TABLE 19-4 Student Explanations of Classroom Passivity

	Men		Women	
	Percent	*Rank*	*Percent*	*Rank*
"I had not done the reading assignment."	80.9%	1	76.3%	2
"I didn't know enough about the subject matter."	79.6	2	84.8	1
"The class was too large."	70.4	3	68.9	4
"My ideas were not well enough formulated."	69.8	4	71.1	3
"The course simply isn't meaningful to me."	67.3	5	65.1	5
"I might appear unintelligent in the eyes of the teacher."	43.2	6	41.4	7
"I might appear unintelligent in the eyes of other students."	42.9	7	45.4	6
"The class was too small."	31.0	8	33.6	8
"My comments might negatively affect my grade."	29.6	9	24.3	9
"Other students might not respect my point of view."	16.7	10	12.5	11
"The teacher might not respect my point of view."	12.3	11	12.5	10

Source: David A. Karp and William C. Yoels, "The College Classroom: Some Observations on the Meaning of Student Participation," *Sociology and Social Research,* vol. 60, no. 4 (July 1976):108.

to some degree, a case of the victims of bureaucratic schooling blaming themselves. Long before reaching college, Karp and Yoels explain, students are taught to view instructors as "experts" who serve up "truth." Thus they find little value in classroom discussion, as if the student's proper role were to listen quietly and respectfully take notes. This perception squares with the finding of Karp and Yoels that only 10 percent of class time is devoted to discussion.

Students also realize that instructors generally come to class ready to deliver a prepared lecture. Lecturing allows teachers to present a great deal of material in each class, but only to the extent that they avoid being sidetracked by student questions or comments (Boyer, 1987). Early in each course, the instructor singles out a few students who are willing and able to provide the occasional, limited comments instructors seek. Taken together, these facts form a recipe for passivity on the part of the majority of college students.

Yet faculty can bring students to life in their classrooms by actively involving them in learning. One recent study of classroom dynamics, for example, linked higher levels of student participation to four teaching strategies: (1) calling on students by name when they volunteer, (2) positively reinforcing student participation, (3) asking analytical rather than factual questions and giving students time to answer, and (4) asking for student opinions even when they do not volunteer (Auster & MacRone, 1994).

Dropping Out

If many students are passive in class, others are not there at all. The problem of dropping out—quitting school before earning a high school diploma—leaves young people (many of whom are disadvantaged to begin with) ill equipped for the world of work and at high risk for poverty.

The dropout rate has moved downward in recent decades: Currently about 13 percent of people between the ages of fourteen and twenty-four have dropped out of school, a total of some 3 million young women and men. Dropping out is least pronounced among non-Hispanic whites (12 percent), slightly greater among African Americans (16 percent), and the most serious among Hispanics (33 percent), many of whom have less facility with English than others do (U.S. Bureau of the Census, 1994).

The reasons for dropping out extend beyond problems with English to include lack of active parenting, pregnancy among young women, and the need to work for those whose families are poor. The dropout rate among children growing up in the bottom 20 percent of households ranked by income (27 percent) is ten times higher than that for youngsters whose households fall in the top 20 percent by income (National Center for Education Statistics, 1992). Many dropouts, then, are young people whose parents also have little schooling and provide little incentive for them to complete their studies. Thus low educational achievement often takes the form of a multigenerational cycle of disadvantage.

For young people who drop out of school in a credential society, the risks of unemployment or becoming stuck in a low-paying job are easy to imagine. Faced with this reality, approximately one-third of those who leave school return to the classroom at a later time.

DIVERSITY: Dropping out of college is a growing problem among African Americans. Despite efforts to recruit more minorities, fewer black students finish school. In 1965, of all students beginning college, the proportion of African Americans completing four years was 90% as high as for whites; it has now fallen to about 69%.
NOTE: One study of the mathematical skills of 12th graders concluded that 48.2% knew the basics, 35.6% were below "basics"

level, 13.6% were "proficient," and 2.6% were "advanced." (National Assessment of Educational Progress)
NOTE: A decade after publication of A Nation at Risk, average teacher salaries have climbed, and a number of states have initiated examinations for promotion and graduation, but the dropout rate has changed little, and achievement test scores have risen only slightly.

Academic Standards

Perhaps the most serious educational issue confronting our society involves the quality of schooling. *A Nation at Risk*, a comprehensive report on the quality of U.S. schools prepared in 1983 by the National Commission on Excellence in Education, began with an alarming statement:

> If an unfriendly foreign power had attempted to impose on America the mediocre educational performance that exists today, we might well have viewed it as an act of war. As it stands, we have allowed this to happen to ourselves. (1983:5)

Supporting this conclusion, the report noted that "nearly 40 percent of seventeen-year-olds cannot draw inferences from written material; only one-fifth can write a persuasive essay; and only one-third can solve mathematical problems requiring several steps" (1983:9). Furthermore, scores on the Scholastic Aptitude Test (SAT) have declined since the early 1960s. Then, median scores for students were 500 on the mathematical test and 480 on the verbal test; by 1994, the averages had slipped to 479 and 423. Some of this decline may stem from the increasing share of students taking the standardized test, not all of whom are well prepared (Owen, 1985). But few doubt that schooling has suffered a setback.

A Nation at Risk also noted with alarm the extent of **functional illiteracy**, *reading and writing skills insufficient for everyday living*. Roughly one in eight children in the United States completes secondary school without learning to read or write very well. For young African Americans, the report continued, the proportion is more than one in three. The box on page 526 provides a closer look at this serious national problem.

A Nation at Risk recommends drastic reform. First, it calls for schools to require all students to complete several years of English, mathematics, social studies, general science, and computer science courses. Second, schools should cease pushing along failing students, keeping them in the classroom as long as necessary to teach basic skills. Third, teacher training must improve and teachers' salaries should rise to attract talent into the profession. *A Nation at Risk* concludes that educators must ensure that schools meet public expectations, and we citizens must be prepared to bear the costs of good schools.

Some reforms are already in place: Teachers' salaries have been climbing and more states now require students to pass proficiency examinations before leaving school. But, in comparison to students in other industrial societies, our children still do not perform especially well. U.S. students simply are not as motivated toward academic excellence as their counterparts in Japan, for example, which explains why children here do far less homework—typically less than one hour a night. Moreover, averaging 178 school days per year, U.S. students spend less time in the classroom than their counterparts in virtually every other industrial society: The British require 192 days in school, the Japanese 210 days, the Koreans 222 days, and the Chinese 251 (Walters, 1994). Some educational experts think that we could remedy our schools' poor performance, at least in part, simply by requiring that students spend more time there.

RECENT ISSUES IN U.S. EDUCATION

Our society's schools continuously confront new challenges and technological innovation. This final section—and the final box, on page 528—explore several recent and important educational issues.

School Choice

Some analysts claim that our schools do not teach very well because they have no competition. Thus, giving parents a range of options about where to school their children may force all schools to do a better job. This is the essence of the *school choice* initiative.

Proponents of school choice advocate creating a market for schooling, so that parents and students can shop for the best value. According to one proposal, the government would provide vouchers to all families with school-aged children, allowing them to spend the money at public, private, or parochial schools. Indianapolis, Minneapolis, and Milwaukee recently initiated parental choice plans in hopes that public schools would be forced to perform better in order to win the confidence of families.

But critics (including teachers' unions) charge that school choice amounts to abandoning our nation's commitment to public education. From their point of view, schools that already have bigger budgets will attract the best and brightest children while central city schools will end up as "dumping grounds" for disadvantaged students and those with disciplinary problems. Moreover, research suggests that choice options are utilized by parents who are more educated themselves and who are already more involved in their children's education (Martinez et al., 1995). We are left to

Q: Asked to describe the most miserable state for humanity, Benjamin Franklin responded, "A lonely man on a rainy day who cannot read."

NOTE: Federal literacy programs enroll several million adults each year, a small proportion of those who are functionally illiterate.

SOCIAL SURVEY: "What about U.S. spending on improving the nation's education system?" (*Student CHIP Social Survey Software,*

NATEDUC1; GSS 1973–91, N = 16,374)

	"Too little"	"About right"	"Too much"
Afri Amer	72.1%	26.1%	1.8%
Hispanics	59.9%	36.4%	3.7%
Whites	55.7%	35.1%	9.1%
Total	57.6%	34.2%	8.2%

CRITICAL THINKING

Functional Illiteracy: Must We Rethink Education?

Imagine being unable to read labels on cans of food, instructions for assembling a child's toy, the dosage on a medicine bottle, or even the information on your own paycheck. These are some of the debilitating experiences of *functional illiteracy,* reading and writing skills inadequate for carrying out everyday responsibilities.

As schooling became universal among our population, the U.S. government confidently concluded that illiteracy had been all but eliminated. The truth of the matter—now acknowledged by the government—is that some 25 million adults read and write at no more than a fourth-grade level, and another 25 million have only eighth-grade language skills. This means that one in four adults in the United States is functionally illiterate, and the proportion is higher among the elderly and minorities.

Functional illiteracy is a complex social problem. It is caused partly by an educational system that passes children from one grade to the next whether or not they master the academic skills spelled out in the grade curriculum. Another contributing factor is community indifference to local schools that prevents parents and teachers from working together to improve children's learning. Still another cause is found in the home: Millions of children grow up with illiterate parents who offer little encouragement to learn language skills.

Estimates place the societal cost of functional illiteracy at more than $100 billion a year. This total includes decreased productivity (by workers who perform their jobs improperly) and increased accidents (by people unable to understand written instructions). It also reflects the expense of supporting those unable to read and write well enough to find work who, unable to earn a living, end up either on welfare or in prison.

Correcting this national problem requires one approach for the young and another for adults. To end functional illiteracy, the public must demand that schools not graduate children who have yet to learn basic language abilities. For adults who already suffer from this problem, the answer begins with diagnosis—a difficult issue since many women and men feel deep shame at their plight and avoid disclosing their need for help. Once such people are identified, however, communities must provide adult education programs.

Our society is one of the richest and most powerful nations on earth, yet at least a dozen other countries have a more literate population than we do. For those muddling through life with inadequate communication skills, functional illiteracy is a personal disaster; for all of us, it is an urgent national problem.

Paco learned to read last year. So did Dad.

Literacy Volunteers of America, Inc.

The problem of illiteracy in the United States is most serious among Latinos. In part this is due to a dropout rate among fourteen- to twenty-four-year-olds of almost 30 percent, which is three times the rate among whites or African Americans. The broader issue is that schools fail to teach many Spanish-speaking people to read and write any language very well.

Sources: Based on Kozol (1980, 1985a, 1985b).

Q: "[The magnet school] is a blueprint for school desegregation in the future without relying on mandatory busing, which does not work in a very meaningful way." William Bradford Reynolds

NOTE: The most powerful opponent of school choice programs is the National Education Association (NEA), with more than 2 million members, mostly teachers.

NOTE: The American Federation of Teachers (AFT) put the median U.S. public school teacher's salary at $35,104 in 1993; by state, Connecticut was highest ($48,918 median); lowest was South Dakota ($24,291).

NOTE: Comparing the top ten states in terms of teacher salaries and rates of student graduation from high school, there is only one overlap (New Jersey).

Educators have long debated the proper manner in which to school children with disabilities. On the one hand, such children may benefit from distinctive facilities and specially-trained teachers. On the other hand, they are less likely to be stigmatized as "different" if included in regular classroom settings. What do you consider to be the ramifications of the "special education" versus "inclusive education" debate for the classroom experience of all children, not only those who have disabilities?

wonder whether choice programs could benefit the more disadvantaged of our children.

A more modest form of school choice involves creating *magnet schools*, one thousand of which are now operating across the country. Magnet schools offer special facilities and programs to promote educational excellence in computer science, foreign languages, or science and mathematics. In school districts containing magnet schools, parents can choose the one best suited to a particular student's talents and interests.

Yet another recent development in the school choice movement is *schooling for profit*. According to advocates of this proposal, school systems can be operated by private profit-making companies more efficiently than by local governments. Of course, private schooling is nothing new; more than ten thousand schools are currently operated by private organizations and religious groups. What is new, however, is the assertion that private companies can carry out *mass* education in the United States.

Research confirms that many public school systems suffer from bureaucratic bloat, spending far too much and teaching far too little. Further, it is not surprising that various "choice" proposals are gaining favor in a society that has long looked to competition as a strategy to improve quality. But the results of schooling-for-profit appear mixed. Despite claims that several companies have improved student learning, some cities have cut back on business-run schools. In

1995, for example, Baltimore canceled the contract of the corporation that had taken over nine of its schools in 1992; school boards in Miami and Hartford, Connecticut, have taken similar actions. In short, public school systems perform poorly in many cities; but whether or not private business can improve on this record remains unclear (Toch, 1991; Kanamine, 1995; Putka & Stecklow, 1995).

Schooling People With Disabilities

Mandatory education embodies our society's commitment to provide everyone with a basic education. In 1993, some 5 million children with a wide range of mental and physical disabilities were attending schools in the United States. Nevertheless, many of these boys and girls receive little effective schooling. A highly bureaucratized system of mass education simply does not readily meet the special needs of some children.

Schooling children with disabilities clearly poses a challenge. Many children with physical impairments have difficulty getting to and from school, and those who travel with crutches or wheelchairs cannot negotiate stairs and other obstacles inside school buildings. Children with developmental disabilities like mental retardation require extensive personal attention from specially trained teachers. As a result, many children with mental and physical disabilities have received a public education only because of persistent efforts by parents and other concerned citizens.

NOTE: James Davison Hunter (1991) notes that the American Sociological Association has passed resolutions on a number of political issues, supporting the *Roe v. Wade* decision, gay rights, and calling for an end to aid to El Salvador as well as a boycott of Gallo wines. Moreover, he adds, ASA's policy is to locate its annual meeting with political considerations in mind, for instance, avoiding states that did not pass the ERA.

DISCUSS: Assess Max Weber's contention, detailed in Chapter 2, "Sociological Investigation," that political advocacy necessarily clashes with science.

Q: "An intellectual is a person who uses more words than necessary to tell you more than he knows." Dwight D. Eisenhower

Q: "A university is what a college becomes when the faculty loses interest in students." John Ciardi

Controversy & Debate

Is Political Correctness Undermining Education?

Are you "p.c."? Is your teacher? What about this textbook? The last decade has seen a heightened level of political debate on the college campus. Around 1990, the term *political correctness* entered our language to refer to thinking and acting in accordance with liberal political principles. The term, coined by opponents of "p.c.," implies that truth stems not from scientific evidence but from conformity to approved political orthodoxy. Surveying today's campus scene, James Davison Hunter (1991:211) concludes, "The cultural ethos of the modern university clearly favors a progressivist agenda," including support for feminism, gay rights, and various other movements toward social equality.

Opponents of political correctness argue that left-wing politics threatens the traditional open-mindedness of the university, at its worst transforming professors into political activists and turning teaching into indoctrination. Moreover, some claim political correctness has a "chilling effect" in the classroom, making students wary of expressing opinions about controversial issues (say, homosexuality or racial differences in measured intelligence) for fear of offending others who might, in turn, charge them with "homophobia" or "racism."

Sociology, itself, has fallen victim to political correctness to the extent that the discipline has defined research on politically sensitive issues as taboo. Douglas Massey (1995) asserts that, in recent decades, a number of well-known researchers were ostracized by their peers for publishing the results of solid research that substantiated "unpopular notions" about race and gender.

On the other side of the issue, many people favor political engagement on campus, citing compelling moral considerations. As they see it, there is much injustice in the world that cries out for redress. Richard Rorty (1994) agrees that some academic departments have become "sanctuaries for left-wing political views," but he offers no apology for that fact, noting that his activist colleagues are "doing a great deal of good for people who have gotten a raw deal in our society: women, African Americans, gay men, and lesbians." By keeping the focus on marginalized people, he continues, the politically engaged campus "will, in the long run, help to make our country much more decent, more tolerant and more civilized."

Keep in mind, too, that the extent of "political correctness" is easily exaggerated. While it is probably fair to characterize academia (and sociologists, overall) as politically liberal, virtually any campus includes faculty, administrators, and students who espouse a wide range of political opinions. Furthermore, charges of political correctness in academia are nothing new. Just sixty years ago, for example, a majority of states sought to keep teachers in check by requiring them to sign loyalty oaths before entering the classroom (Hunter, 1991). Perhaps it is true that the more things change . . .

Continue the debate . . .

1. *Overall, do you think that academia has a political bias? What is the bias?*

2. *Should teachers (or textbooks) take explicit political stands on controversial issues?*

3. *Have you or other students remained silent during class discussions for fear of sounding "politically incorrect"?*

About one-fourth of children with disabilities are schooled in special facilities; the rest attend public schools, many participating in regular classes. This reflects the policy of **mainstreaming**, *integrating special students into the overall educational program*. An alternative to segregated "special education" classes, mainstreaming, also known as *inclusive education*, works best for physically impaired students who have no difficulty keeping up with the rest of the class. As an added advantage, children with disabilities learn how to interact with others just as other children benefit from interacting with them.

Mainstreaming is typically less effective for students who have serious mental or emotional impairments. These children may have difficulty matching the performance of other students, and they may simultaneously be deprived of appropriate special education. In any case, mainstreaming may be as expensive as special programs, requiring adaptive facilities and teachers capable of meeting the needs of special children.

NOTE: Higher-education institutions offering the top average salaries for full professor include Harvard, number one at $104,000, to Rutgers, Newark, N.J.; Princeton; and Yale, ranging from $96,500 to $99,300. National averages: full, $63,450 (men, $64,560; women, $57,160); associate, $47,040; assistant, $39,050; instructor, $29,680; lecturer, $32,600; overall average, $49,500. Average at doctorate-granting institutions, $71,290; community colleges, $51,790; private colleges, $84,790; public colleges, $67,560. Forty percent of all faculty are part-timers who earn much less than these figures. Lawyers earn 70% more than professors, on average. (AAUP)

THEN AND NOW: In 1972, about 8% of college students were 35 and older; in 1993, the figure was 18%.

Q: "I am always ready to learn, although I do not always like being taught." Winston Churchill

Adult Education

Most schooling involves young people. However, the share of U.S. students aged twenty-five and older has risen steadily in recent years and now accounts for nearly one in five people in the classroom.

By 1995, more than 25 million U.S. adults were enrolled in some type of educational program. Many are in their mid-twenties; most fall in their late thirties and early forties, but some are well past sixty-five. Adult students—twice as likely to be women as men—are generally a fairly privileged slice of the population with above-average incomes.

What draws adults back to school? The reasons are as varied as the students, but usually the motivation is work related. Most take up part-time study as a way to enhance their careers; this practical emphasis is reflected in high adult enrollments in business, health, and engineering courses. But others, who study everything from astronomy to Zen, return to school simply for the pleasure of learning.

LOOKING AHEAD: SCHOOLING IN THE TWENTY-FIRST CENTURY

Despite the fact that the United States leads the world in higher education, our public school system continues to struggle with serious problems. From what we have learned, it is clear that many of the problems of schools have their roots in the larger society. Thus, as we approach the next century, we cannot expect schools themselves to raise the quality of U.S. education. More realistically, schools will only improve to the extent to which students, teachers, parents, and local communities are committed to excellence and willing to embrace change. Furthermore, as important as issues of excellence are, we must face the parallel problem of educational inequality.

Another important trend now reshaping schools involves technology. Just as the Industrial Revolution had a major impact on schooling in the nineteenth century, computers and the Information Revolution are transforming formal education today. More than 97 percent of schools currently report having computers for instructional use and, across the country, one computer is available, on average, to every eleven students (although, like other dimensions of education, computers are more accessible to affluent children than to poor children) (U.S. Bureau of the Census, 1995).

The promise of new information technology goes beyond helping students learn basic skills to improving the overall quality of learning. Interacting with computers prompts students to be more active learners and has the added benefit of allowing them to progress at their own pace. For students with disabilities who cannot write with a pencil, computers permit easier self-expression. The introduction of computers into schools—in some cases, as early as kindergarten—appears to significantly increase learning speed and retention of information (Fantini, 1986).

The enthusiasm sparked by computers should not blind us to their limitations, however. Computers will never bring to the educational process the personal insight or imagination of a motivated human teacher. Nor can computers tap what one teacher calls the "springs of human identity and creativity" that we discover through exploring literature and language rather than simply manipulating mathematical codes (Golden, 1982:56).

So, despite their proliferation in classrooms, computers have yet to change teaching and learning in any fundamental sense or even to replace the traditional blackboard (Berger, 1991; Elmer-Dewitt, 1991). Thus as our society enters the twenty-first century, we should not look to technology to solve many of the problems—including violence and rigid bureaucracy—that plague our schools. What is needed is a broad plan for social change that refires this country's early ambition to provide high-quality universal schooling—a goal that has so far eluded us.

SUMMARY

1. Education is the major social institution for transmitting knowledge and skills, as well as teaching cultural norms and values. In preindustrial societies, education occurs informally within the family; industrial societies develop formal systems of schooling.

2. The United States was among the first countries to institute compulsory mass education, reflecting both democratic political ideals and the needs of the industrial-capitalist economy.

3. Structural-functional analysis highlights major functions of schooling, including socialization, cultural innovation, social integration, and placing people in the social hierarchy. Among the latent functions of schooling: providing child care and forging social networks.

4. Social-conflict analysis points out how differences in class, race, and gender promote unequal opportunities for schooling. Formal education also serves as a means of generating conformity to produce compliant adult workers.

5. A debate surrounds the use of standardized achievement tests, which some see as a reasonably fair measure of academic aptitude and learning and others claim are culturally biased tools that unfairly define less privileged students as personally deficient.

6. Tracking in school is designed to give students the kind of learning they want and are capable of. Critics maintain that schools track students according to their social background, thereby providing privileged youngsters with a richer and more challenging education.

7. The great majority of young people in the United States attend state-funded public schools. Private schools generally offer a religious education. A small proportion of students—usually well-to-do—attend elite, private preparatory schools.

8. One-fifth of U.S. adults over the age of twenty-five are now college graduates, marking the emergence of a "credential society." People with college degrees enjoy greatly increased lifetime earnings.

9. Most adults in the United States are critical of public schools. Violence permeates many schools, especially those in poor neighborhoods. The bureaucratic character of schools has also fostered high dropout rates and widespread student passivity.

10. Declining academic standards are reflected in today's lower average scores on achievement tests and the functional illiteracy of a significant proportion of high school graduates.

11. The school choice movement seeks to make educational systems more responsive to the public. Innovative options include magnet schools and schools-for-profit, both of which are topics of continuing public-policy debate.

12. Children with mental or physical disabilities historically have been schooled in special classes or not at all. Mainstreaming affords them broader opportunities.

13. Adults represent a growing proportion of students in the United States. Most older learners are women and are engaged in job-related study.

14. The Information Revolution is changing schooling through the increasing use of computers. Although computers permit interactive, self-paced learning, they are not suitable for teaching every subject.

KEY CONCEPTS

credentialism evaluating a person on the basis of educational degrees

education the social institution guiding a society's transmission of knowledge—including basic facts, job skills, and cultural norms and values—to its members

functional illiteracy reading and writing skills insufficient for everyday living

hidden curriculum subtle presentations of political or cultural ideas in the classroom

mainstreaming integrating special students into the overall educational program

schooling formal instruction under the direction of specially trained teachers

tracking the assignment of students to different types of educational programs

CRITICAL-THINKING QUESTIONS

1. Why did widespread schooling develop in the United States only after the Industrial Revolution?

2. Referring to various countries, including the United States, describe ways in which schooling is shaped by economic, political, or cultural factors.

3. From a structural-functional perspective, why is schooling important to the operation of society? From a social-conflict point of view, how does formal education operate to reproduce social inequality?

4. Do you agree with research findings presented in this chapter that, by and large, college students are passive in class? If so, what do you think colleges could do to ensure that classes encourage everyone's active participation?

SUGGESTED READINGS

Classic Sources

John Dewey. *Experience and Education*. New York: Collier, 1963; orig. 1938.
    In this short book—originally presented as a series of lectures—Dewey sketches his vision of progressive education.

James S. Coleman et al. *Equality of Education*. Washington, D.C.: Department of Education, 1966.
    This early assessment of educational inequality in the United States set the agenda for decades of debate over U.S. schooling.

Contemporary Sources

George H. Wood. *Schools That Work: America's Most Innovative Public Education Programs*. New York: Dutton, 1993.
    The good news about education in the United States is that a number of innovative programs are working quite well; this book details some of them.

Nat Hentoff. *Free Speech for Me But Not for Thee: How the American Left and Right Relentlessly Censor Each Other*. New York: HarperCollins, 1992.
    Hentoff reveals how two versions of "political correctness"—the left's demand for "sensitivity" and the right's promotion of "community standards"—are remarkably similar ways of stifling free speech.

Global Sources

Catherine Marshall, ed. *The New Politics of Race and Gender*. Falmer Press, 1993.
    Essays in this collection examine the increasing importance of race and gender in shaping the curriculum, testing, and staffing of schools in the United States, Australia, and Israel.

Nelly P. Stromquist, ed. *Women and Education in Latin America: Knowledge, Power, and Change*. Boulder, Colo.: Lynne Rienner, 1992.
    This book is a collection of thirteen essays that focus on the educational opportunities for women in this important world region.

PHYSICIAN TAKING PATIENT'S
PULSE, CANON OF AVICENNA,
1632

Welcome Institute Library, London.

Health and Medicine

Nineteen-year-old Melody Barrett squirms restlessly on a chair in the waiting room of the medical clinic at her exclusive private college in Minnesota. She feels annoyed and fearful; her roommate pressured her to see the doctor, and she is afraid her parents will be angry if they find out that she is ill. *There isn't anything wrong,* she keeps telling herself. Her parents, both lawyers, live forty miles away in Minneapolis. They expect their daughter home for the weekend, but she is trying to think up an excuse for not going.

This young woman's problem is failing health due to starvation. Far from feeling that she is starving, however, she thinks of herself as fat. She knows that she weighs only eighty-seven pounds, and she expects the doctor to warn her that she weighs far too little for a woman five feet, three inches tall. But for over three years Melody has been preoccupied—her roommate would say obsessed—with being thin.

Melody Barrett's problem, familiar to many college students, is anorexia nervosa, a disorder characterized by what specialists call "severe caloric restriction," or intense, often compulsive dieting. Like most diseases, anorexia nervosa has social as well as biological causes: About 95 percent of its victims are females, most of them white and from affluent families. Many women who contend with eating disorders are pressured by their parents to be high achievers. Although Melody Barrett's case is unusually severe, research suggests that up to half of college-aged women actively try to lose weight, although most of them are not, medically speaking, obese. About one in seven diet to the point that their behavior falls within the clinical description of an eating disorder.

To better appreciate the social foundation of eating disorders,[1] consider a comment once made by the Duchess of Windsor: "A woman," she observed, "cannot be too rich or too thin." Women fall victim to eating disorders because our culture places such stress on women's physical appearance, with slenderness the ideal of femininity (Parrott, 1987). Some researchers assert that our society socializes young women to believe that they are never "too thin to feel fat." Such an attitude pushes women toward a form of "mass starvation" that some critics claim "compares with foot-binding, lip-stretching, and other forms of woman mutilation" found in other cultures (Wooley, Wooley, & Dyrenforth, 1979; Levine, 1987; Robinson, 1987).

Health is obviously the concern of physicians and other medical professionals. But sociologists, too, study health because, as the case of Melody Barrett illustrates and this chapter explains, social forces have a major impact on the well-being of the U.S. population and people throughout the world.

WHAT IS HEALTH?

The World Health Organization (1946:3) defines **health** as *a state of complete physical, mental, and social well-being.* This definition underscores the major theme of this chapter: *Health is as much a social as a biological issue.*

---

[1]This profile of victims of anorexia nervosa is based on Levine (1987). Another eating disorder, *bulimia,* involves binge eating coupled with induced vomiting to inhibit weight gain. The two diseases, which may be two expressions of the same intense concentration on dieting and weight control, have similar victim profiles (cf. Striegel-Moore, Silberstein, & Rodin, 1986).

Medieval medical practice was heavily influenced by astrology, so that physicians and lay people alike attributed disease to astral influence; this is the root of our word "influenza." In this woodcut by Swiss artist Jost Amman (1580), as midwives attend a childbirth astrologers cast a horoscope for the newborn.

Health and Society

The health of any population is shaped by traits of the surrounding society.

1. **People judge their health relative to others.** Standards of health vary from society to society. René Dubos (1980; orig. 1965) points out that early in this century, yaws, a contagious skin disease, was so common in sub-Saharan Africa that people there considered it normal. In truth, then, health is sometimes a matter of having the same diseases as one's neighbors (Quentin Crisp, cited in Kirk & Madsen, 1989).

2. **People pronounce as "healthy" what they hold to be morally good.** Members of our society (especially men) consider a competitive way of life to be "healthy" because it fits in with our cultural mores. (This despite the fact that stress is related to heart disease and many other illnesses.) On the other hand, some people who object to homosexuality on moral grounds label this sexual orientation "sick" even though it is quite natural from a scientific standpoint. In short, ideas about good health constitute a type of social control that encourages conformity to cultural norms.

3. **Cultural standards of health change over time.** Early in this century, some prominent physicians condemned women for enrolling in college, claiming that higher education placed an unhealthy strain on the female brain. Other specialists denounced masturbation as a threat to health. Today, however, such notions elicit little support from the medical community. Conversely, few physicians fifty years ago recognized the dangers of cigarette smoking, a practice that is now widely regarded as a threat to health.

4. **Health relates to a society's technology.** Members of poor societies routinely contend with malnutrition and poor sanitation, which promote high levels of infectious disease. As industrialization raises living standards, our conceptions of health rise as well. But industrial technology also creates new threats to health. As Chapter 22 ("Environment and Society") explains, high-income countries have the capacity to endanger health by overtaxing the world's resources as well as generating various forms of pollution.

5. **Health relates to social inequality.** Every society on earth distributes the resources that promote personal well-being unequally. The physical, mental, and social health of wealthier women and men in the United States is far better than that of poor people, as we shall explain presently. This pattern starts at birth, with infant mortality highest among the poor. Affluent people also live years longer than poor people do.

HEALTH: A GLOBAL SURVEY

Because health is an important dimension of social life, we find pronounced change in human well-being over the long course of history. Similarly, striking differences in health distinguish societies of the world today.

Health in History

Simple technology limited the ability of our ancestors to sustain a healthful environment. Among hunters and gatherers, food shortages sometimes forced mothers to abandon children. Children fortunate enough to

GLOBAL: The leading causes of death in the United States in 1900, as presented in Table 20–1, are leading causes of death in poor societies today.

NOTE: One sign of long-term improvement in nutrition: Lucy, the 3-million-year-old adult fossilized skeleton found in Ethiopia, stood only about 3 feet 6 inches tall; she would have weighed some 65 pounds.

Q: "Hunger may have been the human race's constant companion, and 'the poor may always be with us,' but in the twentieth century, one cannot take this fatalistic view of the destiny of millions of fellow creatures. Their condition is not inevitable but is caused by identifiable forces within the province of rational, human control." Susan George

survive infancy were still vulnerable to a host of injuries and illnesses for which there were few effective treatments, and half died before age twenty. Few lived to forty (Lenski, Nolan, & Lenski, 1995).

The agricultural revolution expanded the supply of food and other resources. Yet due to increasing social inequality, elites enjoyed better health while peasants and slaves faced hunger and endured crowded, unsanitary shelters. Especially in the growing cities of medieval Europe, human waste and other refuse fueled infectious diseases, including plagues that periodically wiped out entire towns (Mumford, 1961).

Health in Low-Income Countries

November 1, 1988, central India. Poverty is not just a matter of what you have; it shapes what you are. Probably most of the people we see in the villages here have never had the benefit of a doctor or a dentist. The detrimental effects on their bodies are all too evident; people look old before their time.

Abject poverty in much of the world cuts life expectancy there far below the seventy or more years typical of rich societies. A look back at Global Map 14–1 on page 389 shows that average life expectancy among Africans barely reaches fifty, and in the world's poorest nations, such as Ethiopia and Somalia, the figure falls to forty.

The World Health Organization reports that 1 billion people around the world—one in five—suffer from serious illness due to poverty. Poor sanitation and malnutrition kill people of all ages, especially children. Health is compromised not just by having too little to eat, but also by consuming only one kind of food, as the box on page 536 explains.

In impoverished countries, sanitary drinking water may be as scarce as the chance for a balanced diet. Contaminated water breeds many of the infectious diseases that imperil both adults and children. The leading causes of death in the United States a century ago, including influenza, pneumonia, and tuberculosis, are still widespread killers in poor societies.

To make matters worse, medical personnel are few and far between, so that the world's poorest people—many of whom live in central Africa—never consult a physician. Global Map 20–1 on page 537 illustrates the availability of doctors throughout the world.

The profession of surgery has existed only for several centuries. Before that, barbers offered their services to the very sick, often cutting the skin to "bleed" a patient. Of course, this "treatment" was rarely effective, but it did produce plenty of bloody bandages, which practitioners hung out to dry. This practice identifies the origin of the red and white barber poles we see today.

Lucas van Leyden, *The Surgeon and the Peasant*, Rijksmuseum, Amsterdam

Against this backdrop of poverty and minimal medical care, it is no wonder that 10 percent of children in poor societies die within their first year. In some countries, half the children never reach adulthood—a pattern that parallels the death rates seen in Europe two centuries ago (George, 1977; Harrison, 1984).

Illness and poverty form a vicious cycle in much of the world. That is, poverty breeds disease, which, in turn, undermines people's ability to earn income. Moreover, when medical technology does curb infectious disease, the populations of poor nations soar.

GLOBAL SOCIOLOGY

Killer Poverty: A Report From Africa

Periodic famine in Africa brings home to people in the affluent United States the horror of starving children. Some of the children portrayed by the mass media appear bloated, while others seem to have shriveled to little more than skin drawn tightly over bones. Both of these deadly conditions, explains Susan George (1977), are direct consequences of poverty.

Children with bloated bodies are suffering from protein deficiency. In West Africa this condition is known as *kwashiorkor*, literally "one-two." The term derives from the common practice among mothers of abruptly weaning a first child upon the birth of a second. Deprived of mother's milk, a baby may receive virtually no protein at all.

Children with shriveled bodies lack both protein and calories. This deficiency is the result of eating little food of any kind.

In either case, children usually do not die of starvation, strictly speaking. Their weakened condition makes them vulnerable to stomach ailments such as gastroenteritis or diseases like measles. The death rate from measles, for example, is a thousand times greater in parts of Africa than in North America.

Depending on a single food also undermines nutrition, causing a deficiency of protein, vitamins, and minerals. Millions of people in low-income countries suffer from goiter, a debilitating, diet-related disease of the thyroid gland. Pellagra, a disease common to people who consume mostly corn, is equally serious, frequently leading to insanity. Those whose diet primarily consists of processed rice are prone to beriberi, which brings on swelling and nerve disorders.

We can understand health as a social issue simply by noting that a host of diseases virtually unknown to members of rich societies are a common experience of life—and death—in poor countries.

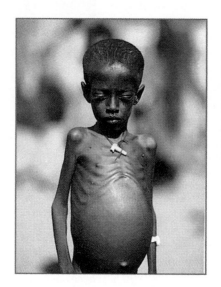

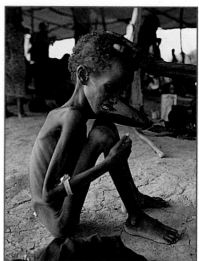

Without resources to ensure the well-being of the people they have now, poor societies can ill afford surging population growth. Thus, efforts to lower death rates in poor countries will ultimately succeed only if they simultaneously reduce birth rates as well.

Health in High-Income Countries

Industrialization dramatically changed patterns of human health in Europe, although, at first, not for the better. By 1800, as the Industrial Revolution was taking hold, factories were choking the cities with people drawn from the countryside in search of economic opportunity. Unprecedented population concentration spawned serious problems of sanitation and overcrowded housing. Moreover, factories continuously fouled the air with smoke, a health threat unrecognized until well into the twentieth century. Accidents in the workplace were also common.

But as the nineteenth century progressed, health in Western Europe and North America improved. This change was mainly due to a rising standard of living that translated into better nutrition and safer housing for the majority of people. After 1850, medical

THEN AND NOW: The U.S. diet is getting healthier. According to the 1990 Census, U.S. annual per capita consumption of red meat fell from 135 pounds in 1970 to 112 pounds in 1990. Gallons of whole milk fell even more, from 27 gallons to about 10. Eggs consumed dropped from 315 to 240. Per capita consumption of broccoli rose from .5 pounds in 1970 to 3.4 pounds in 1992.

NOTE: The Centers for Disease Control reports that more than 9,000 U.S. people die annually from food poisoning; 6.5 million become sick from spoiled food each year.

NOTE: Until the end of the 19th century, Philadelphia drew water from the Delaware River at one point while discharging sewage at another. Such practices were common until the germ theory of disease led to programs to improve environmental quality.

Window on the World

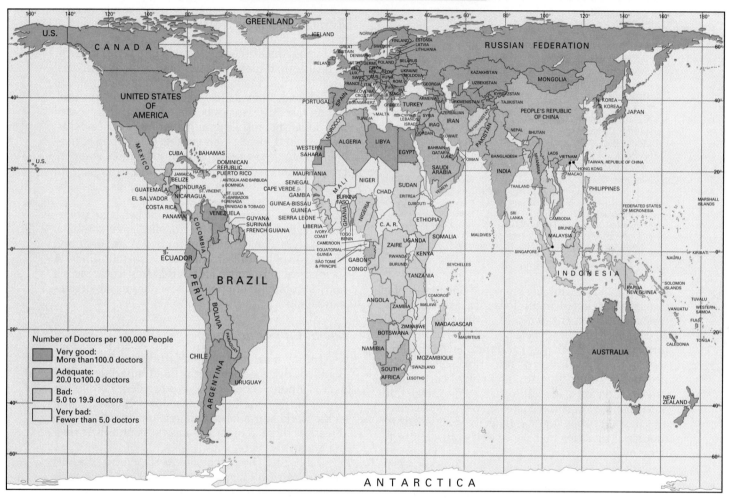

GLOBAL MAP 20–1 The Availability of Physicians in Global Perspective

Medical doctors, widely available to people in rich nations, are perilously scarce in poor societies. While traditional forms of healing do improve health, antibiotics and vaccines—vital for controlling infectious diseases—are often in short supply in poor societies. In these countries, therefore, death rates are high, especially among infants.

Source: *Peters Atlas of the World* (1990).

advances had further promoted health, primarily by controlling infectious diseases. To illustrate, in 1854 John Snow noted the street addresses of London's cholera victims and traced the source of this disease to contaminated drinking water (Rockett, 1994). Soon after, scientists linked cholera to specific bacteria and developed a protective vaccine against the deadly disease. Armed with this knowledge, early environmentalists campaigned against age-old practices such as discharging raw sewage into rivers used for drinking water. As the twentieth century dawned, death rates from infectious diseases had fallen sharply.

Over the long term, industrialization has had a dramatic, beneficial effect on human health. In 1900,

DISCUSS: Do males engage in more risky behavior than females? Percent of high school students, grades 9–12, who report rarely or never using seat belts: national average, 19%; white males, 23%; white females, 12%; African-American males, 35%; African-American females, 26%; Latinos, 22%; Latinas 17%. (Kann et al., 1995)
DIVERSITY: Leading causes of death among 15–24-year-olds by sex and race (1992; Centers for Disease Control):

African-American females: homicide, accidents, cancer, heart disease, AIDS
African-American males: homicide, accidents, suicide, heart disease, AIDS
White females: accidents, cancer, homicide, suicide, heart disease
White males: accidents, suicide, homicide, cancer, heart disease

TABLE 20–1 The Leading Causes of Death in the United States, 1900 and 1994

1900	1994
1. Influenza and pneumonia	1. Heart disease
2. Tuberculosis	2. Cancer
3. Stomach/intestinal diseases	3. Stroke
4. Heart disease	4. Lung disease (noncancerous)
5. Cerebral hemorrhage	5. Accidents
6. Kidney disease	6. Pneumonia and influenza
7. Accidents	7. Diabetes
8. Cancer	8. HIV/AIDS
9. Diseases in early infancy	9. Suicide
10. Diphtheria	10. Chronic liver disease and cirrhosis

Sources: Information for 1900 is from William C. Cockerham, *Medical Sociology,* 2d ed. (Englewood Cliffs, N.J.: Prentice-Hall, 1986), p. 24; information for 1994 is from U.S. Center for Health Statistics, *Monthly Vital Statistics Report* (Hyattsville, Md.: The Center, 1995), vol. 43, no. 13, (Oct. 23, 1995).

influenza and pneumonia prompted one-fourth of all deaths in the United States. Today, these diseases cause fewer than 3 percent of deaths in this country. Table 20–1 shows that other infectious diseases that were once major causes of death now rarely threaten our health.

As the prevalence of infectious diseases has declined, chronic illnesses, including heart disease, cancer, and stroke, are left to claim almost two-thirds of the population of the United States, generally in old age. In short, while nothing alters the reality of death, industrial societies manage to delay our demise for decades.

HEALTH IN THE UNITED STATES

Living in an affluent, industrial society, people in the United States are healthy by world standards. Some categories of people, however, enjoy far better health and well-being than others.

Social Epidemiology: The Distribution of Health

Social epidemiology is *the study of how health and disease are distributed throughout a society's population.* Just as early social epidemiologists examined the origin and spread of epidemic diseases, researchers today find links between health and physical and social environments. Such analysis rests on comparing the health of different categories of people.

Age and Sex

Death is now rare among young people, with two notable exceptions: a rise in mortality resulting from accidents and, more recently, from acquired immune deficiency syndrome (AIDS).

Across the life course, women fare better in terms of health than men. Females have a slight biological advantage that renders them less likely than males to die before or immediately after birth. Then, as socialization takes over, males become more aggressive and individualistic, resulting in higher rates of accidents, violence, and suicide. Our cultural conception of masculinity also pressures adult men to be more competitive, to repress their emotions, and to engage in hazardous behaviors like smoking cigarettes and drinking alcohol to excess.

Doctors describe "coronary-prone behavior" (sometimes tagged the "Type-A personality") as a combination of chronic impatience, uncontrolled ambition, and free-floating hostility toward one's surroundings. A sociological perspective reveals that this syndrome is a fairly accurate description of how our culture defines masculinity.

Social Class and Race

Infant mortality—the death rate among newborns—is twice as high among disadvantaged children as it is among children born to privilege. While the health of the richest children in our nation is the best in the world, our poorest children are as vulnerable to disease as those in many low-income countries, including Sudan and Lebanon.

Table 20–2 shows that almost 80 percent of adults in families with incomes over $35,000 evaluate their health as excellent or very good, while not quite half of those in families earning less than $10,000 make this claim. Conversely, while only about 4 percent of high-income people describe their health as fair or poor, almost one-fourth of low-income people respond this way.

Bear in mind that just as income shapes health, so does health affect income. Members of low-income families miss eight days of school or work each year due to illness, while higher-income people lose only five days a year for this reason (U.S. National Center for Health Statistics, 1994).

Because African Americans are three times as likely as whites to be poor, they are more likely to die in infancy and, as adults, to suffer the effects of violence, drug abuse, and illness. Table 20–3 presents life expectancy for U.S. children born in 1994. Whites can

TABLE 20–2 Assessment of Personal Health by Income, 1993

Family Income	Excellent	Very Good	Good	Fair	Poor
$35,000 and over	47.5%	30.0%	18.2%	3.6%	0.8%
$20,000–$34,999	36.5	29.7	24.7	7.0	2.1
$10,000–$19,999	27.7	25.8	29.6	12.0	4.9
Under $10,000	25.1	23.2	29.1	15.6	7.0

Source: U.S. National Center for Health Statistics, *Current Estimates from the National Health Interview Survey United States, 1993,* series 10, no. 190 (Washington, D.C.: U.S. Government Printing Office, 1994).

expect to live more than seventy-six years; African Americans, about seventy years.

Sex is an even stronger predictor of health than race, since African-American females can expect to outlive males of either race. The table also indicates that 76 percent of white men—but just 58 percent of African-American men—will live to age sixty-five. The comparable chances for women are 86 percent for whites and 78 percent for African Americans.

Poverty condemns people to crowded, unsanitary dwellings that breed infectious diseases. Although tuberculosis is no longer a widespread threat to health in the United States, a higher risk of poverty means that African Americans are four times as likely as whites to die from this disease. Poor people of all races also suffer from nutritional deficiencies. Roughly 20 percent of our population—some 50 million people—can afford neither a healthful diet nor adequate medical care. As a result, wealthy people can expect to die in old age of chronic illnesses such as heart disease and cancer, while poor people generally die younger from infectious diseases brought on by poor nutrition.

Poverty also breeds stress and violence. The leading cause of death among African-American men aged fifteen to twenty-four—who figure prominently in the urban underclass—is homicide. In 1994 about 5,164 African Americans were killed by others of their race—half the number of black soldiers killed in the entire Vietnam War.

Health and Society: Three Examples

Since we all make choices about how to live, we all have some control over our own health. But as the following sections indicate, dangerous behaviors such as cigarette smoking and compulsive dieting are pronounced among certain categories of our population. Sexually transmitted diseases, too, reveal a distinctive social profile.

Cigarette Smoking

Cigarette smoking tops the list of preventable hazards to health. But we can see that smoking has a cultural dimension as well, because it was only after World War I that smoking became popular in the United States. Despite growing evidence of its dangers, smoking remained fashionable even a generation ago. Since then, however, smoking has been redefined as a mild form of social deviance.

As concern about the health effects of smoking has grown, consumption of cigarettes has fallen from its peak in 1960, when almost 45 percent of U.S. adults smoked. By 1994, only 25 percent were smokers (U.S. Bureau of the Census, 1995). Quitting is difficult because cigarette smoke contains nicotine, which is physically addictive. But people also smoke to cope with stress: Divorced and separated people are especially likely to smoke, as are the unemployed and people in the armed forces.

Generally speaking, the less education people have, the greater their chances of smoking. Moreover, a larger share of men (28 percent) than women (24 percent) smoke. But cigarettes—the only form of tobacco use to gain popularity among women—have taken a growing toll on women's health. A decade ago, lung

TABLE 20–3 Life Expectancy for U.S. Children Born in 1994

	Females	Males	Both Sexes
Whites	79.6	73.2	76.5
	(86%)*	(76%)	(81%)
African Americans	74.1	64.9	69.6
	(78%)	(58%)	(67%)
All races	79.0	72.3	75.7
	(85%)	(74%)	(79%)

*Figures in parentheses indicate the chances of living to age sixty-five.

Source: U.S. National Center for Health Statistics (1995).

Evidence of the health hazards of smoking cigarettes first appeared in the 1930s. But cigarettes continued to increase in popularity, helped, in part, by celebrity advertising that was, at best, misleading.

cancer surpassed breast cancer as a leading cause of death among U.S. women.

Some 450,000 men and women die prematurely each year as a direct result of cigarette smoking, which exceeds the combined death toll from alcohol, cocaine, heroin, homicide, suicide, automobile accidents, and AIDS (Mosley & Cowley, 1991). Smokers also endure frequent minor illnesses, such as the flu, and pregnant women who smoke increase the likelihood of spontaneous abortion, prenatal death, and low birth-weight babies. Even nonsmokers exposed to secondhand cigarette smoke have a higher risk of smoking-related diseases.

Tobacco remains a $30 billion business in the United States. The tobacco industry maintains that because the precise link between cigarettes and disease has not been specified, the health effects of smoking remain "an open question." But the tobacco industry is not breathing as easily today as it once did; laws mandating a smoke-free environment are spreading rapidly.

In response to the antismoking trend in the United States, the tobacco industry is selling more products abroad, especially in low-income countries where there is little legal regulation of tobacco sales and advertising. In the United States, however, more and more smokers are trying to break the habit, taking advantage of the fact that someone who has not smoked for ten years has about the same pattern of health as a lifelong nonsmoker.

Eating Disorders

An **eating disorder** is *an intense involvement in dieting or other forms of weight control in order to become very thin.* As the opening of this chapter suggests, eating disorders illustrate how cultural pressures shape human health.

Consider, first, that 95 percent of people who suffer from anorexia nervosa or bulimia are women, mostly from white, relatively affluent families. According to Michael Levine (1987), our culture equates slenderness in women with being successful and attractive to men. On the flip side, Levine adds, overweight people tend to be viewed as "lazy," "ugly," "stupid," and "sloppy."

Studies show that most college-age women (1) widely accept the idea that "guys like thin girls," (2) think being thin is the most crucial dimension of physical attractiveness, and (3) believe that they are not as thin as men would like them to be. In fact, most college women want to be even thinner than college men say women should be. For their part, most men describe their actual body shape as just about what they want it to be; thus, men display little of the dissatisfaction over body shape expressed by women (Fallon & Rozin, 1985).

Chapter 13 ("Sex and Gender") explained that our culture embraces a "beauty myth" that teaches women to exaggerate the importance of physical attractiveness as well as to orient themselves toward pleasing men (Wolf, 1990). Such cultural patterns, Levine continues, encourage women to pursue thinness as a form of perfection. These messages about thinness come from mothers and fathers—especially affluent parents—who pressure a daughter to be "The Best Little Girl in the World." But television and other mass media also play a part in this process, almost exclusively casting actresses and models who are unnaturally thin and unrealistically beautiful.

The common result of our culture's idealized image of women's bodies is low self-image, since few

DISCUSS: How should we combat STDs? Liberals accept that people engage in casual sexual activity and call for widespread availability of birth control devices and sex education; conservatives urge revival of an ethic of abstinence and marital fidelity.
NOTE: Data from the Centers for Disease Control show that, among U.S. high school students, 61% of males and 54% of females have had sexual intercourse.

NOTE: The most common STD, according to the Centers for Disease Control, is now chlamydia, with 450,000 cases reported annually.
NOTE: There are some 50 STDs overall; estimates suggest that one-fifth of the U.S. adult population has one STD other than AIDS. Roughly 7,000 American deaths annually are related to STDs other than AIDS.

women approach our culture's unrealistic standards of beauty. Just as important, those who do are likely to engage compulsively in dieting behavior to the point of risking their health.

Sexually Transmitted Diseasces

Sexual activity, while both pleasurable and vital to the perpetuation of our species, can transmit some fifty illnesses. Sometimes called *venereal diseases* (from Venus, the Roman goddess of love), these ailments are as old as our species. And because our culture has long linked sex to sin, some people regard venereal disease not only as illness but also as a mark of immorality.

Sexually transmitted diseases (STDs) became a national issue during the "sexual revolution" of the 1960s. Before this time, some two out of three men but only about one in ten women had premarital sexual intercourse; today, the figures are closer to three out of four men and two out of three women. With sexual activity typically occurring at an earlier age and with a greater number of partners, STDs have become a serious health problem—a notable exception to the general decline in infectious ailments during this century. In recent years, the growing danger of STDs—and especially AIDS—has prompted something of a sexual counterrevolution that has discouraged casual sex, not necessarily for moral reasons, but out of self-interest (Kain, 1987; Kain & Hart, 1987). The following section provides a brief overview of several common STDs.

Gonorrhea and syphilis.

Among the oldest diseases, gonorrhea and syphilis are caused by a microscopic organism almost always transmitted by sexual contact. Untreated, gonorrhea can cause sterility; syphilis can damage major organs and result in blindness, mental disorders, and death.

Roughly 420,000 cases of gonorrhea and 80,000 cases of syphilis are reported each year, and the actual number may well be several times greater. Both diseases are more common among some populations than others: 81 percent of infections involve African Americans, 13 percent affect whites, 4 percent afflict Latinos, and less than 1 percent are contracted by Asian Americans and Native Americans (Masters, Johnson, & Kolodny, 1988; Moran et al., 1989; U.S. Centers for Disease Control, 1994).

Most cases of gonorrhea and syphilis are easily cured with penicillin, an antibiotic drug developed in the 1940s. Thus, neither disease currently represents a major health problem in the United States.

Genital herpes.

An estimated 20 to 30 million adults in the United States (one in seven) are infected with the genital herpes virus. The infection rate among African Americans, however, is about twice as high as among whites (Moran et al., 1989).

Although far less serious than gonorrhea and syphilis, herpes is incurable. It can be asymptomatic or, periodically, painful blisters may appear on the genitals accompanied by fever and headache. Although not fatal to adults, women with active genital herpes can transmit the disease during a vaginal delivery to an infant, to whom it may be deadly. Such women, therefore, usually give birth by caesarean section.

AIDS.

The most serious of all sexually transmitted diseases is acquired immune deficiency syndrome, or AIDS. Identified in 1981, this disease is incurable and fatal. AIDS is caused by a human immunodeficiency virus (HIV), which attacks white blood cells, the core of the immune system. AIDS thus renders a person vulnerable to a wide range of infectious diseases that eventually bring on death.

AIDS is now the leading killer of young adults aged twenty-five to forty-four in the United States. Some 97,000 new cases of AIDS were reported in the United States during the twelve-month period ending September, 1995, raising the total number of U.S. residents who have contracted this disease to 500,000. Of these, more than 300,000 have already died (U.S.Centers for Disease Control and Prevention, 1995).

In global perspective, some 15 million people are infected with HIV, a figure that could increase threefold or fourfold by the end of this decade. Global Map 20–2, on page 542, shows that the African continent (more specifically, countries south of the Sahara Desert) has the highest HIV infection rate and currently accounts for two-thirds of all world cases. In the cities of central African nations such as Burundi, Rwanda, Uganda, and Kenya, roughly one-fifth of all young adults are infected with HIV (Tofani, 1991). North Americans represent 10 percent of global HIV cases. In the United States, experts estimate the number of infected people at 1 million.

Upon infection, people with HIV display no symptoms whatever; most remain unaware of their condition. Not for a year or longer do any symptoms of AIDS appear. Within five years, one-third of infected people will develop AIDS; half show symptoms of AIDS within ten years, and almost all do within twenty years. With half a million active cases in the United States as of mid-1995, the infection rate is still rising, but at a slower rate than previously. As the

RESOURCE: Loretta Tofani's article, "The AIDS Epidemic in Africa," is included among the cross-cultural selections in the *Seeing Ourselves* reader.

NOTE: 1995 state rates for new AIDS cases range from a high of 274 per 100,000 people in Washington D.C. to 96 in New York, 80 in Florida, 69 in New Jersey, and 60 in California, down to 1.7 in North Dakota.

GLOBAL: Japan is one of the few countries on earth to ban oral contraceptives (the "pill"), which are available only through a doctor's prescription for treatment of irregular menstrual cycles. Japan is among the nations that make greatest use of condoms. The government's logic is that a ban on the pill will maintain the high level of condom use, which should discourage the transmission of HIV.

Window on the World

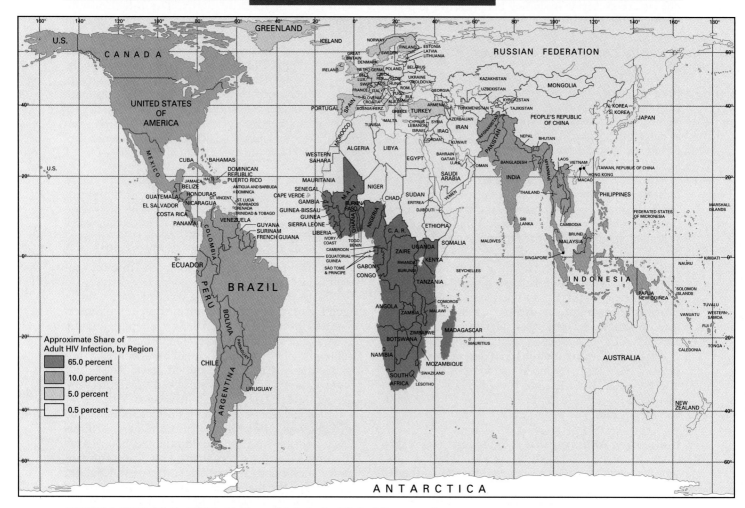

GLOBAL MAP 20–2 HIV Infection of Adults in Global Perspective

Approximately two-thirds of all global HIV cases are recorded in sub-Saharan Africa. This high infection rate reflects the prevalence of other venereal diseases and infrequent use of condoms, factors that promote heterosexual transmission of HIV. South and North America each represent another 10 percent of all cases. The incidence of infection is still low in Europe. Southeast Asia, where HIV is spreading most rapidly, accounts for another 10 percent of infections. Least affected by HIV are countries in North Africa and the Middle East, and the nations of Australia and New Zealand.

Sources: Data from The World Bank (1993); map projection from *Peters Atlas of the World* (1990).

death toll mounts, AIDS has turned out to be nothing less than catastrophic—potentially the most serious epidemic of modern times.

HIV is infectious but not contagious. That is, HIV is transmitted from person to person through blood, semen, or breast milk but *not* through casual contact such as shaking hands, hugging, sharing towels or dishes, swimming together, or even by coughing and sneezing. The risk of acquiring HIV through saliva (as in kissing) is extremely low. Moreover, the risk of contracting HIV through sexual activity is greatly reduced by the use of latex condoms. In the age of AIDS, abstinence or an exclusive relationship with an uninfected person are the only sure ways to avoid contracting HIV.

Specific behaviors place people at high risk for HIV infection. The first is *anal sex,* which can cause rectal bleeding, allowing easy transmission of HIV from one person to another. The practice of anal sex explains why homosexual and bisexual men represent about 55 percent of adolescents and adults with AIDS in the United States.

Sharing needles used to inject drugs is a second high-risk behavior. At present, intravenous drug users account for 24 percent of those with AIDS. Sex with an intravenous drug user is also very risky. Because intravenous drug use is more common among poor people in the United States, AIDS is now becoming a disease of the socially disadvantaged. Although 51 percent of AIDS patients are white people, African Americans (12 percent of the population) account for 31 percent of people with AIDS. Half of all women with the disease and 55 percent of children are African Americans. Similarly, Latinos (7 percent of the population) represent 17 percent of AIDS cases (and 21 percent of women with AIDS). Asian Americans and Native Americans, however, together account for less than 1 percent of people with AIDS (Huber & Schneider, 1992; U.S. Centers for Disease Control and Prevention, 1995).

Using any drug, including alcohol, also increases the risk of being infected with HIV to the extent that it impairs judgment. In other words, even people who understand what places them at risk of infection may act less responsibly once they are under the influence of alcohol, marijuana, or some other drug.

As Figure 20–1 shows, only 7 percent of people with AIDS in the United States became infected through heterosexual contact (although heterosexuals, infected in various ways, account for more than 30 percent of AIDS cases). So the likelihood of a runaway "breakout" of AIDS into the heterosexual population now seems less likely than it did several years ago. But heterosexual activity does transmit HIV, and the danger rises with the number of sexual partners, especially if they fall into high-risk categories. Worldwide, heterosexual relations are the primary means of HIV transmission, accounting for two-thirds of all infections (Eckholm & Tierney, 1990).

AIDS is throwing our health-care system into crisis. The cost of treating a single person with AIDS has already soared to hundreds of thousands of

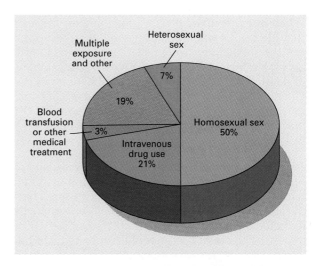

FIGURE 20–1 Types of Transmission for Reported U.S. AIDS Cases, 1995
Source: U.S. Centers for Disease Control and Prevention (1995).

dollars, and this figure may rise as new therapies appear. At present, government health programs, private insurance, and personal savings rarely cover more than a fraction of the cost of treatment. In addition, there is the mounting cost of caring for the children orphaned by this disease, whose numbers, some analysts predict, could reach 80,000 by the end of the 1990s. Overall, there is little doubt that AIDS represents both a medical and a social problem of monumental proportions.

Initially, the government responded slowly to the AIDS crisis, largely because gays and intravenous drug users are widely viewed as deviant. More recently, money allocated for AIDS research has increased rapidly (now totaling more than $4 billion annually), and researchers have identified some drugs, such as AZT, that suppress the symptoms of the disease. But educational programs remain the most effective weapon against AIDS, since prevention is the only way to stop a disease that currently has no cure.

Ethical Issues: Confronting Death

Another connection between health and society involves ethics. Moral questions are more pressing than ever, now that technological advances have given human beings the power to prolong life and, therefore, to draw the line separating life and death. Today, we grapple with how to use these new powers, or whether to use them at all.

When does death occur?

Common sense suggests that life ceases when breathing and heartbeat stop. But the ability to revive or replace a heart and to artificially sustain respiration have rendered such notions of death obsolete. Medical and legal experts in the United States now define death as an *irreversible* state involving no response to stimulation, no movement or breathing, no reflexes, and no indication of brain activity (Ladd, 1979; Wall, 1980).

Do people have a right to die?

The availability of life-extending care means that medical personnel, family members, and patients themselves must face the agonizing burden of deciding when the terminally ill should die.

In 1990, twenty-six-year-old Nancy Cruzan fell into an irreversible coma after an automobile accident. Physicians exhausted their efforts and solemnly assured Cruzan's parents that their daughter would never recover. Certain that their daughter would not wish to live in a permanent vegetative state, the Cruzans sought a legal decision to let Nancy die. The gravity of the case carried it all the way to the U.S. Supreme Court, which supported a patient's right to die by declaring that any competent person can refuse medical treatment or nutrition. Because the Cruzans were able to present "clear and convincing evidence" that this would be Nancy's wish, the court permitted removal of the feeding tube keeping her alive. Nancy Cruzan died twelve days later (Mauro, 1990).

Ten thousand people in the United States are in the same kind of permanent vegetative state as Nancy Cruzan (Howlett, 1990). Thousands more, facing a terminal illness that may cause terrible suffering, consider ending their own lives. Thus courts and government commissions continue to weigh patients' choice against practitioners' obligations to provide all appropriate care. A 1983 presidential commission underlined the primary responsibility of physicians and hospitals: protecting a patient's life. Even so, terminally ill patients (or family members of incompetent patients) may refuse treatment to extend their lives when there is no hope of recovery. But, the commission emphasized, a family decision such as that faced by the Cruzans must be made in the interest of the patient—no one else.

The commission also endorsed an individual's choice to create a *living will*, a statement of personal intention regarding treatment in the event of catastrophic illness. A 1991 federal law requires hospitals, nursing homes, and other medical facilities to honor such documents if patients are unable to speak for themselves due to accident or illness. The law also recognizes people's right to appoint a representative to make their wishes known to doctors or others. The precise legal standing of a living will varies from state to state, as do the policies of particular hospitals. The national trend, however, is toward recognizing the right of people to accept or refuse treatment rather than allowing medical officials alone to act on our behalf.

What about mercy killing?

Mercy killing is the common term for **euthanasia**, *assisting in the death of a person suffering from an incurable disease*. Euthanasia (from the Greek, meaning "a good death") poses an ethical dilemma, being at once an act of kindness and a form of killing.

Support for a patient's right to die (that is, *passive* euthanasia) is growing in the United States. But assisting in the death of another person (*active* euthanasia) still provokes controversy and may violate the law. In 1992, for example, Jack Kevorkian, a physician who has helped people end their lives with his "suicide machine," was arrested in Michigan and charged with murder. No one thinks that Kevorkian's "clients"—people suffering from terminal illnesses—thought of him as their murderer. But our society is uneasy about legally empowering physicians to actively end a life in response to a patient's request.

The debate breaks down roughly as follows. Those who categorically view life—even with suffering—as preferable to death reject both passive and active euthanasia. People who recognize circumstances under which death is preferable to life endorse passive or perhaps active euthanasia, but they face the practical problem of determining just when life should be ended.

Family members also must confront the reality of medical costs, which skyrocket when extraordinary measures are used to prolong life. A single attempt to revive a patient whose heart has stopped may cost $1,500. Monitoring the treatment of 146 critically ill patients over a three-year period, researchers at Duke Medical Center found that just over half could be revived at all, and fewer than ten ever improved enough to leave the hospital. The costs of such heroic medical efforts, however, averaged $150,000 per person (reported in *Time*, March 29, 1993:19). Are such odds good enough to warrant extraordinary medical treatment? Should we consider medical costs at all in making this decision? Our society can no longer duck these questions, since a majority of hospital deaths in the United States now occur through a negotiated

NOTE: Oregon's physician-assisted suicide Proposal 16, the first of its kind in the U.S., passed narrowly in November, 1994. A patient wishing to die must obtain statements from two physicians confirming the terminal illness, and from two other witnesses stating that the patient really wants to die and rationally understands that decision. Then a physician may prescribe a lethal dose of medication, which the patient may decide to take. The proposal is currently undergoing court review.

NOTE: Another problem with the medical establishment has been research that focuses only on males. The famous 1981 study examining whether aspirin reduces heart attacks, for example, utilized 22,000 subjects, all men. In 1990, however, the National Institutes of Health opened an Office of Research on Women's Health.

decision by patients, family members, and physicians (Flynn, 1991; Humphrey, 1991; Markson, 1992).

THE MEDICAL ESTABLISHMENT

Medicine is *a social institution concerned with combating disease and improving health.* Medicine is a vital part of a broader concept of **health care**, which is *any activity intended to improve health.*

Through most of human history, health care was the responsibility of individuals and their families. Medicine emerges only as societies become more productive, assigning their members formal, specialized roles. Such medical practitioners recognize the healing properties of certain plants and offer insights into the emotional and spiritual needs of the ill. From our point of view, traditional healers such as acupuncturists and herbalists may seem like unscientific "witch doctors," but, in truth, they do much to improve human health throughout the world (Ayensu, 1981).

As a society industrializes, health care becomes the responsibility of specially schooled and legally licensed healers, from anesthesiologists to X-ray technicians. Today's medical establishment in the United States took form over the last 150 years.

The Rise of Scientific Medicine

In colonial times, doctors, herbalists, druggists, midwives, and ministers all engaged in various forms of healing arts. But not all did so effectively: Unsanitary instruments, lack of anesthesia, and simple ignorance made surgery a terrible ordeal in which doctors probably killed as many patients as they saved.

Medical specialists gradually learned more about human anatomy, physiology, and biochemistry. By about 1850, doctors had established themselves as self-regulating professionals with medical school degrees. The American Medical Association (AMA), founded in 1847, symbolized the growing acceptance of the new *scientific medicine.* The AMA widely publicized the successes of its members in identifying the cause of life-threatening diseases—bacteria and viruses—and in developing vaccines to combat disease.

Still, other approaches to health care, such as regulating nutrition, also had defenders. The AMA responded boldly—some thought arrogantly—by criticizing these alternative ideas about health. By the early 1900s, state licensing boards agreed to certify only physicians trained in scientific programs approved by the AMA. With control of the certification process,

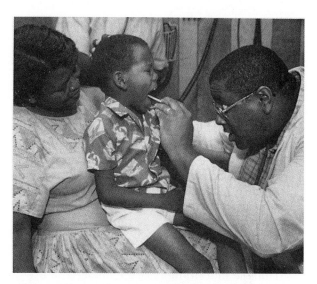

The rise of scientific medicine sparked stunning achievements in our ability to control disease. But it also effectively reduced the number of African Americans in the medical professions and opposed many kinds of healers who traditionally have served rural areas. Michael Cheers, M.D., has tried to turn the tide by transforming an abandoned restaurant into a medical clinic in Tchula, Mississippi. Cheers, who is also an ordained minister and jazz pianist, accepts donations and works overtime in hospital emergency rooms to enable him to treat people who cannot afford to pay for care.

the AMA then began closing down schools teaching other healing skills, limiting the practice of medicine to those with an M.D. degree. In the process, both the prestige and income of physicians rose dramatically. Men and women with M.D. degrees have become among the highest-paid workers in the United States, with annual earnings for private practice that average about $180,000.

Osteopathic physicians (with D.O. degrees) concluded that they had no choice but to fall in line and follow AMA standards. Thus osteopaths, originally concerned with manipulating the skeleton and muscles, today treat illness much as medical doctors (with M.D. degrees) do. Other practitioners—such as chiropractors, herbal healers, and midwives—have held more to their traditional roles, but at the cost of being relegated to the fringe of the medical profession.

Scientific medicine, taught in expensive, urban medical schools, also altered the social profile of doctors. As the AMA closed many rural medical colleges, the number of women, African Americans, and people of modest financial means entering the medical field fell

NOTE: M.D. income varies significantly by specialty and level of experience. Doctors in training earn about $30,000 annually, says the AMA; physicians in general practice average $112,000, and radiologists top the list at $253,000 annually.

DIVERSITY: The American Women's Medical Association reports that, in 1990, there were two women deans in this country's 127 medical schools.

NOTE: About 5% of U.S. adults routinely see a chiropractor.

THEN AND NOW: Share of U.S. physicians who are women: 1960, 7%; 1995, 22%.

NOTE: Ten percent of the U.S. population accounts for 90% of all medical expenditures; 1% accounts for half of all expenditures.

NOTE: By 2005, perhaps half of the U.S. population will be served by an HMO, compared to 17% today.

precipitously. Only in recent decades has medicine seen a turnaround, with women and African Americans now representing 22 percent and 4 percent, respectively, of all physicians (Gordon, 1980; Starr, 1982; Huet-Cox, 1984; U.S. Bureau of Labor Statistics, 1995).

National Map 20–1 shows where the 630,000 U.S. physicians practice. Clearly, people in some parts of the country have far more access to medical specialists than others do.

Holistic Medicine

The scientific model of medicine has recently been tempered by the more traditional notion of **holistic medicine,** *an approach to health care that emphasizes prevention of illness and takes account of a person's entire physical and social environment.*

Holistic practitioners also embrace the use of drugs, surgery, artificial organs, and high technology, but they caution that these developments risk transforming medicine into narrow specialties focusing on symptoms rather than people, disease instead of health. The following are foundations of holistic health care (Duhl, 1980; Ferguson, 1980; Gordon, 1980):

1. **Patients are people.** Holistic practitioners are concerned not only with symptoms but with how each person's environment and lifestyle affect health. For example, the likelihood of illness increases under stress caused by poverty or intense competition at work. Holistic practitioners extend the bounds of conventional medicine, taking an active role in combating environmental pollution and other dangers to public health.

2. **Responsibility, not dependency.** The complexity of contemporary medicine fosters patients' dependence on physicians. Holistic medicine tries to shift some responsibility for health from physicians to patients themselves by enhancing their abilities to engage in health-promoting behavior. Holistic medicine favors a more *active* approach to *health*, rather than a *reactive* approach to *illness*.

3. **Personal treatment.** Conventional medicine locates medical care in impersonal offices and hospitals, which are disease-centered settings. Holistic practitioners favor, as much as possible, a personal and relaxed environment such as the home. Holistic medicine seeks to reestablish the personal social ties that united healers and patients before the era of specialists. The AMA currently recognizes more than fifty specialized areas of medical practice, and a growing proportion of M.D.'s are entering these

high-paying specialties rather than family practice. Thus, there is a need for practitioners who are concerned with the patient in the holistic sense.

Clearly, holistic care does not oppose scientific medicine but shifts its emphasis away from narrowly treating disease toward the goal of achieving the highest possible level of well-being for everyone.

Paying for Health: A Global Survey

As medicine has come to rely on high technology, the costs of health care in industrial societies have skyrocketed. Countries employ various strategies to meet these costs.

Medicine in Socialist Societies

In societies with predominantly socialist economies, the government provides medical care directly to the people. It is an axiom of socialism that all citizens have the right to basic medical care. To translate this ideal of equity into reality, people do not rely on their private financial resources to pay physicians and hospitals; rather, the government funnels public funds to pay medical costs. The state owns and operates medical facilities and pays salaries to practitioners, who are government employees.

People's Republic of China. A poor, agrarian society that is only beginning to industrialize, the People's Republic of China faces the daunting task of attending to the health of more than 1 billion people. Traditional healing arts, including acupuncture and the use of medicinal herbs, are still widely practiced in China. In addition, a holistic concern for the interplay of mind and body marks the Chinese approach to health (Sidel & Sidel, 1982b; Kaptchuk, 1985).

China recently experimented with private medical care, but by 1990 the government had reestablished control over this dimension of life. China's famed barefoot doctors, roughly comparable to U.S. paramedics, have brought some modern methods of medical care to millions of peasants in remote rural villages.

The former Soviet Union. The former Soviet Union is currently struggling to transform a state-dominated economy into more of a market system. For this reason, the scheme for providing medical care is in transition. Nonetheless, the notion that everyone has a right to basic medical care remains strong.

Currently, the government provides medical care funded from taxes. As is the case in the People's

Seeing Ourselves

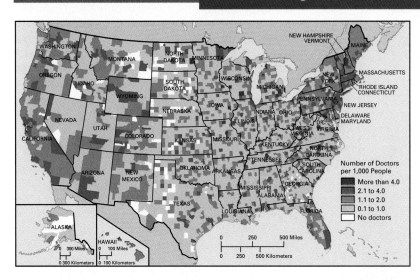

NATIONAL MAP 20–1

The Availability of Physicians Across the United States

There are about 630,000 doctors in the United States, but they are not evenly distributed throughout the population. This map shows the number of doctors for every 1,000 people in counties across the country. In general, people who live along the West Coast and much of the East Coast benefit from the greatest access to doctors. Why do you think doctors cluster in these areas? What consequences do you think this pattern has for public health?

Source: *Time*, June 14, 1993, p. 12. Copyright © 1993 Time Inc. Reprinted by permission.

Republic of China, people do not choose a physician but report to a local government health facility.

Physicians in the former Soviet Union have had lower prestige and income than their counterparts in the United States. Surprisingly, they receive about the same salary as skilled industrial workers (compared to an income six times higher in this country). Worth noting, too, is that about 70 percent of physicians in the Russian Federation are women, compared with about 16 percent in the United States, and, as in our society, occupations dominated by women yield fewer financial rewards.

This system has trained enough physicians to meet the basic needs of a large population. However, rigid bureaucracy makes medical care highly standardized and impersonal. As market reforms are adopted, rigid uniformity will likely diminish, but disparities in the quality of care among various segments of the population may well increase.

Medicine in Capitalist Societies

People living in nations with predominantly capitalist economies are more likely to provide for their own health care in accordance with financial resources and personal preferences. However, the high costs of medical care—beyond the reach of many people—mean that government programs underwrite a considerable proportion of health-related expenses.

Sweden. In 1891 Sweden instituted a compulsory, comprehensive system of government medical care. Citizens of this Scandinavian country pay for health care with their taxes, which are among the highest in the world. In most cases, physicians receive salaries from the government rather than fees from patients, and most hospitals are government managed. Because this medical system resembles that of socialist societies, it is often described as **socialized medicine**, *a health care system in which the government owns and operates most medical facilities and employs most physicians.*

Great Britain. In 1948 Great Britain, too, instituted socialized medicine. The British did not do away with private care, however; today there is a "dual system" of medical services. Thus all British citizens are entitled to medical care provided by the National Health Service, but those who can afford to may purchase more extensive care from doctors and hospitals that operate privately.

Canada. Canada exemplifies the "single-payer" model of health care. Like a vast insurance company, the Canadian government pays doctors and hospitals, which operate privately. But the federal government, in consultation with provincial governments and medical associations, sets a schedule of fees for medical services. Thus Canada has government-funded and regulated medical care but, because practitioners

Global Snapshot

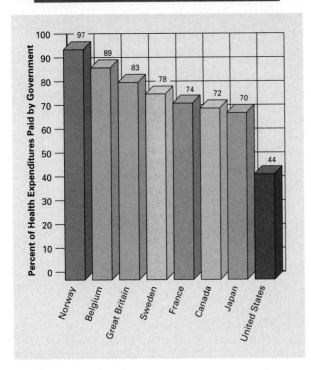

FIGURE 20–2 Extent of "Socialized Medicine" in Selected Countries
Source: U.S. Bureau of the Census (1995).

operate privately, not true socialized medicine. Moreover, some physicians work entirely outside the government-funded system, charging whatever fees they wish.

Canada's system can boast of providing care for everyone at a lower cost than the (nonuniversal) medical system in the United States. At the same time, however, the Canadian system makes less use of state-of-the-art technology and responds slowly to people's needs, often requiring those facing major surgery to wait months or even a year for attention (Grant, 1984; Vayda & Deber, 1984; Rosenthal, 1991).

Japan. Physicians in Japan operate privately, but a combination of government programs and private insurance pays medical costs. As shown in Figure 20-2, the Japanese approach health care much as the Europeans do, with most medical expenses paid through government.

Medicine in the United States

With our primarily private system of medical care, the United States stands alone among industrialized societies in having no government-sponsored medical system that provides care to every citizen. Called a **direct-fee system**, ours is *a medical care system in which patients pay directly for the services of physicians and hospitals.* Thus while Europeans look to government to cover about 80 percent of their medical costs (paid for through taxation), the U.S. government pays less than half this country's medical bills (Lohr, 1988; U.S. Bureau of the Census, 1995).

The mostly private U.S. medical care system allows affluent people to purchase the best medical care in the world. Yet the poor fare worse than their counterparts in Europe. This disparity can be seen in the relatively high death rates among both infants and adults in the United States compared to many European countries (United Nations, 1995).

Why does the United States have no national health care program? First, our society has historically favored limited government in the interest of greater personal liberty. Second, political support for a national medical program has not been strong, even among labor unions, which have concentrated on winning private health care benefits from employers. Third, the AMA and the health insurance industry have strongly and consistently opposed any such program (Starr, 1982).

Figure 20–3 shows that expenditures for medical care increased dramatically between 1950 and 1994, from just $12 billion to more than $880 billion. Medical care absorbed about 5 percent of the gross domestic product in 1950, rising to 14 percent by 1994. This amounted to $3,299 per person, more than any other industrial society spends for medical care, and double the figure in Australia and Japan (U.S. Bureau of the Census, 1995). Who pays the medical bills?

Private insurance programs. In 1992, 180 million people (71 percent) received some medical care benefits from a family member's employer or labor union. Another 35 million people (14 percent) purchased private coverage on their own. Three-fourths of our population thus have private insurance (such as Blue Cross and Blue Shield), although few such programs pay all medical costs (U.S. Bureau of the Census, 1995).

Public insurance programs. In 1965 Congress created Medicare and Medicaid. Medicare pays a portion

DIVERSITY: About 15% of the U.S. population lacks any medical insurance; half of those uninsured are under the age of 25, making people between 18 and 25 the most likely to be without insurance. Among whites, 14% lack insurance; among African Americans, 20%; among Hispanics, 34%. Men are more likely than women to lack coverage, because of the larger numbers of elderly and poor women who participate in Medicaid and Medicare.

NOTE: Health costs are daunting, even to corporations. General Motors, for example, spends some $3 billion per year to provide health care to workers, retirees, and their families, adding hundreds of dollars to the price of the average car.
DIVERSITY: Of U.S. white males in the labor force, 75% are covered by health plans; only 58% of women and other minorities have such protection. (Hersch & White-Means, 1993)

of the medical costs of men and women over sixty-five; in 1993 it covered 35 million women and men, about 14 percent of the population. During the same year, Medicaid, a medical insurance program for the poor, provided benefits to nearly 30 million people, or about 12 percent of the population. An additional 25 million veterans (10 percent of our population) can obtain free care in government-operated hospitals. In all, 35 percent of this country's people enjoy some medical care benefits from the government, but most also participate in a private insurance program.

Health maintenance organizations. An increasing number of people in the United States belong to a **health maintenance organization** (HMO), *an organization that provides comprehensive medical care to subscribers for a fixed fee.* In 1993, some 550 HMOs in the United States enrolled 45 million individuals, about 17 percent of the population. HMOs vary in their costs and benefits, and none provides full coverage. But fixed costs give these organizations a financial interest in keeping their subscribers healthy; therefore, many have adopted a preventive approach to health.

In all, 85 percent of the U.S. population has some medical care coverage, either private or public. Yet most plans pay only part of the cost of treating a serious illness, threatening even middle-class people with financial ruin. And most programs also exclude many medical services, such as dental care and treatment for mental health problems. Most seriously, 40 million people (about 15 percent of the population) have no medical insurance at all. Many more people lose their medical coverage temporarily each year due to layoffs or job changes. While some of these people choose to forgo medical coverage (especially young people who simply take their good health for granted), most work part time or full time for small businesses that provide no health care benefits. In general, then, the people caught in a medical care bind are those (most commonly women and other minorities and their children) with limited incomes who can afford neither to get sick nor to purchase the medical care they need to stay healthy (Altman et al., 1989; Health Insurance Association of America, 1991; Hersch & White-Means, 1993; Smith, 1993).

Recent debate. By 1994, there was strong public support for expanding government-based health care coverage in the United States. Congress considered a number of plans, ranging from a conservative Republican proposal to offer tax credits to people who purchase

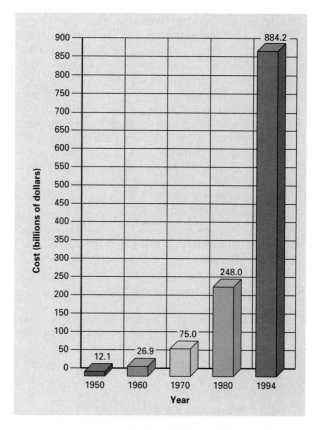

FIGURE 20–3 The Rising Cost of Medical Care in the United States
Source: U.S. Bureau of the Census (1970, 1995).

health insurance to a Canadian-type "single-payer" system sponsored by liberal Democrats.

President Clinton advocated something of a middle ground called "managed competition." The "competition" element of such a program meant that employees would collectively bargain with various medical providers to receive the greatest value. The "managed" dimension referred to government overseeing the entire process to ensure that everyone—regardless of income or present state of health—would have substantial medical coverage.

The essence of the Clinton proposal was to shift medical care away from the traditional, private, fee-for-service system toward various types of health maintenance organizations (HMOs) and government-funded programs. In the process, supporters claimed, costs would fall even as coverage became universal. Critics, however, countered with a "pro-choice" argument that

RESOURCE: A discussion of the sick role by Talcott Parsons is included among the "classics" in the Macionis and Benokraitis reader, *Seeing Ourselves*.
Q: "Physicians have exceedingly high prestige in American society . . . Medicine thus attracts those who value status and income, who seek a challenging and interesting occupation, who enjoy exercising judgment, and who seek to do good." David Mechanic

Q: "We may say that illness is a state of disturbance in the 'normal' functioning of the total human individual, including both the state of the organism as a biological system and of his personal and social adjustments. It is thus partly biological and partly socially defined." Talcott Parsons (1951)
Q: "If you treat a sick child like an adult, and a sick adult like a child, everything usually works out pretty well." Ruth Carlisle

patients should be able to choose their own doctor without government interference. Further, because it would create new government bureaucracies, critics feared, the Clinton plan would raise—not lower—costs, eventually leading to rationing care.

By early 1996, no substantial changes in the U.S. health care system had emerged from Congress. Still, because public concern about health care runs high, this issue will hold center stage for some time to come.

THEORETICAL ANALYSIS OF HEALTH AND MEDICINE

Each of the major theoretical paradigms in sociology provides a means of organizing and interpreting the facts and issues presented in this chapter.

Structural-Functional Analysis

Talcott Parsons (1951) viewed medicine as a social system's way of keeping its members healthy. From this point of view, illness is dysfunctional, undermining the performance of social roles and, thus, impeding the operation of society.

The Sick Role

The normative response to disease, according to Parsons, is for an individual to assume the **sick role**, *patterns of behavior defined as appropriate for people who are ill*. As explained by Parsons, the sick role has four characteristics.

1. **Illness suspends routine responsibilities.** Serious illness relaxes or suspends normal social obligations, such as going to work or attending school. To prevent abuse of this license, however, people do not simply declare themselves ill; they must enlist the support of others—especially a recognized medical expert—before assuming the sick role.

2. **A person's illness is not deliberate.** We assume that sick people are not responsible for their ailments; illness is something that happens to them. Therefore, the failure of ill people to fulfill routine responsibilities should carry no threat of punishment.

3. **A sick person must want to be well.** We also assume that no one wants to be sick. Thus, people suspected of feigning illness to escape responsibility or to receive special attention have no legitimate claim to the sick role.

4. **An ailing person must seek competent help.** People who are ill are obligated to seek competent assistance and to cooperate with health care practitioners. By failing to accept medical help or to follow doctor's orders, a person gives up any claim on the sick role's exemption from routine responsibilities.

The Physician's Role

The physician's role centers on assessing claims of sickness and restoring sick people to normal routines. This responsibility, Parsons explained, rests on specialized knowledge. Physicians expect patients to follow "doctor's orders," and to provide whatever personal information may reasonably assist their efforts.

Although it is inevitably hierarchical, the doctor-patient relationship varies from society to society. In Japan, for example, tradition provides physicians with great authority over patients. One manifestation of this elevated position is that Japanese physicians routinely withhold information about the seriousness of an illness on the grounds that such knowledge might undermine a patient's fighting spirit (Darnton & Hoshia, 1989).

Even three decades ago, physicians in the United States acted in much the same way. But the patient's rights movement embodies the public demand that physicians readily share more and more medical information and offer patients a choice of treatment options. A more egalitarian relationship between doctor and patient is also developing in European societies and, gradually, in Japan as well.

Critical evaluation. Parsons's notion of the sick role illuminates how society accommodates illness, as well as some nonillness situations, such as pregnancy (Myers & Grasmick, 1989). In this scheme, the physician operates as the "gatekeeper," regulating access to the sick role.

One limitation of the sick-role concept is that it applies to acute conditions (like the flu) better than chronic illness (like heart disease), which may not be reversible. Moreover, a sick person's ability to regain health depends on available resources. Many poor people can ill afford either medical care or time off from work.

Critics also question the implication of Parsons's analysis that doctors—rather than people themselves—should bear the primary responsibility for health. Treatment-oriented physicians respond to acute illness, of course; but a more prevention-oriented approach would cast physicians and patients as equal partners in the pursuit of health.

NOTE: There are some 628,000 physicians in the United States, about 78% of whom are men (97% of all nurses are women). Men now receive 64% of medical degrees, so that their representation in the profession is declining.

GLOBAL: Physicians in most poor societies of the world do not share diagnostic information freely with patients.

RESOURCE: A survey article, "The Health of Black America," is included in the Macionis and Benokraitis reader, *Seeing Ourselves*.

DISCUSS: Defining death is a good symbolic-interaction issue. Who participates in the definition of death? When may this definition be a negotiation among parties with various interests? What kinds of power are exercised by patients, family members, clergy, and physicians with scientific training?

Symbolic-Interaction Analysis

Viewed according to the symbolic-interaction paradigm, society is less a grand system than a complex, ever-changing reality. Both health and medical care are thus human constructions that people perceive subjectively.

The Social Construction of Illness

Since we socially construct both health and illness, members of a society where most people go hungry may view malnutrition as quite normal. Similarly, members of our own society defined smoking cigarettes as fashionable for decades, and we are complacent, even today, about the unhealthful effects of a rich diet.

How we respond to illness, too, is based on social definitions that may or may not square with medical knowledge. For instance, people with AIDS contend with fear and sometimes outright bigotry that have no basis in medical fact.

Even the "expert opinions" of medical professionals are influenced by nonmedical factors. U.S. college students, for example, have been known to ignore signs of illness on the eve of a vacation, yet dutifully march into the infirmary before a difficult examination. Health, in short, is not an objective commodity, but a negotiated outcome.

Moreover, how people define a medical situation often affects how they actually feel. Medical experts have long marveled at *psychosomatic* disorders (a fusion of Greek words meaning "mind" and "body"), in which state of mind guides physical sensations (Hamrick, Anspaugh, & Ezell, 1986). As sociologist W. I. Thomas (1931) pointed out, a situation defined as real becomes real in its consequences.

The Social Construction of Treatment

In Chapter 6 ("Social Interaction in Everyday Life"), we used the dramaturgical approach of Erving Goffman to explain how physicians craft their physical surroundings ("the office") and present themselves to others to foster specific impressions of competence and power.

Sociologist Joan Emerson (1970) further illustrates this process of reality construction by analyzing a situation familiar to women, a gynecological examination carried out by a male doctor. After observing seventy-five such examinations, she explains that this setting is especially precarious, because it is so vulnerable to misinterpretation. The man's touching of a woman's genitals—conventionally viewed as a sexual

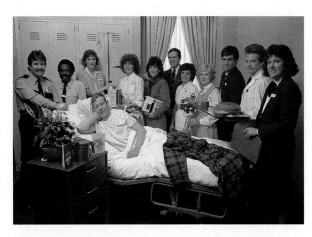

The cost of medical care in the United States has been rising at a dizzying rate. In part, this high rate of increase reflects the fact that hospitals are large, bureaucratic organizations that employ dozens of specialized workers in the treatment of any single patient. Here one man poses for a picture with just the medical staff who directly provide for him.

act and possibly even an assault—must, in this case, be defined as impersonal and professional.

To ensure that people construct reality in this way, doctors and nurses remove sexual connotations as completely as possible. They furnish the examination room with nothing but medical equipment; all personnel wear medical uniforms. Staff members act as if such examinations are simply routine, although, from the patient's point of view, they may be quite unusual.

Further, rapport between physician and patient is established before the examination begins. Once under way, the doctor's performance is strictly professional, suggesting to the patient that inspecting the genitals is no different from surveying any other part of the body. A female nurse is usually present during the examination not only to assist the physician but to dispel any impression that a man and woman are "alone in a room."

The need to manage situational definitions has long been overlooked by medical schools. This omission is unfortunate because, as Emerson's analysis shows, understanding how reality is socially constructed in the examination room is just as crucial as mastering the medical skills required for effective treatment.

Fortunately, medical professionals are gradually recognizing the importance of sociological insights. At the Southwestern Medical School in Dallas, Texas, for

Chapter 20 Health and Medicine **551**

NOTE: Settling the breast implant class-action suit, three companies—Dow Corning, Bristol-Myers Squibb, and Baxter Healthcare—agreed to pay $3.7 billion over 30 years to women claiming injuries. Dow subsequently filed for bankruptcy, raising doubts about eventual payments.

Q: "Since the 1960s, access to medical care for black Americans has improved significantly. In 1963, the proportion of blacks who saw a physician was 18% lower than for whites; by 1982, this gap had been almost eliminated . . . [But given a lower standard of living among blacks,] if there were real parity in access to medical care between the two racial groups, there would be a substantially higher use of health services on the average among black Americans." Robert Blendon, Linda Aiken, Howard Freedman, and Christopher Corey

example, Professor David Hemsell instructs his medical students to actually climb onto an examination table and place their feet in the metal stirrups, with their legs spread apart, to gain an appreciation of the patient's point of view. Hemsell claims, "The only way to understand women's feelings is to be there." He adds, "You can see the impact of being in that position hit them in the face like a two-by-four."

Critical evaluation. One strength of the symbolic-interaction paradigm lies in revealing the relativity of sickness and health. What people view as normal or deviant, healthful or harmful, depends on a host of factors, many of which are not, strictly speaking, medical. This approach also shows that all medical procedures involve a subtle process of reality construction between patient and physician.

But it seems wrong to deny that there are any objective standards of well-being. Certain physical conditions do indeed cause specific negative changes in human capacities, whether we think so or not. People who lack sufficient nutrition and safe water, for example, suffer from their unhealthy environment, however they define their surroundings.

Social-Conflict Analysis

Social-conflict analysis ties health to various dimensions of social inequality. Researchers have focused on three main issues: access to medical care, the effects of the profit motive on treatment, and the politics of medicine.

The Access Issue

Personal health is the foundation of social life. Yet, from a Marxist perspective, capitalist societies make health a commodity, so that health follows wealth. As already noted, this problem is more serious in the United States than in other industrialized societies because our country has no universal health care system.

Most of the 40 million people who lack any health care coverage at present have low incomes. Conflict theorists concede that capitalism does provide excellent health care for the rich; it simply does not provide very well for the rest of the population.

According to radical critics, unequal access to health care in capitalist countries is rooted in class conflict. These critics claim that the concentration of wealth in the United States, in particular, makes the goal of equal medical care impossible to achieve, whatever reforms Congress may enact. Only a wholesale redistribution of economic resources, say the Marxists, would allow medical care to be uniformly available (Bodenheimer, 1977; Navarro, 1977).

The Profit Motive

Beyond the access issue, radical critic John Ehrenreich (1978) argues, the profit motive turns physicians, hospitals, and the pharmaceutical industry into multibillion dollar corporate conglomerates. The quest for ever-increasing profits also encourages questionable medical practices, including ordering needless tests, performing unnecessary surgery, and overly prescribing drugs (Kaplan et al., 1985).

For example, more than 2 million women in the United States have undergone silicone breast-implant surgery, under the assumption that the plastic packets of silicone were safe. Recently, however, it became clear that these implants are not safe enough, a fact apparently known to Dow Corning, their major manufacturer, for decades.

Of the 25 million surgical operations of all kinds performed annually in the United States, three-fourths are "elective," meaning that they are intended to promote a patient's long-term health rather than being prompted by a medical emergency. Critics charge that the decision to perform surgery often reflects the financial interests of surgeons and hospitals as well as the medical needs of patients (Illich, 1976). And, of course, any drugs or medical procedure prescribed for people subjects them to risks, which harm between 5 and 10 percent of patients (Sidel & Sidel, 1982a; Cowley, 1995).

Finally, critics point out, the United States has been all too tolerant of physicians having a direct financial interest in the tests and procedures they order for their patients (Pear & Eckholm, 1991). In short, conflict theorists conclude, health care should be motivated by a concern for people, not profits.

Medicine as Politics

Although medicine declares itself to be politically neutral, scientific medicine frequently takes sides on significant social issues. For example, the medical establishment has long opposed government-operated health care programs. The history of medicine, critics contend, is replete with racial and sexual discrimination, defended by "scientific" facts (Leavitt, 1984). Consider the diagnosis of "hysteria," a term which has its origins in the Greek word *hyster*, meaning "uterus."

NOTE: Several European countries, including the U.K. and France, have enacted laws prohibiting the genital mutilation of women; to date, Minnesota and North Dakota have as well.

DIVERSITY: As late as 1969, some localities in the United States legally required blood products to be labeled with the race of the donor; recipients were able to refuse blood on these grounds.

Q: "Medicine and biology were of crucial importance, providing the basic concepts through which the class and sexual divisions of Victorian society were expressed and ultimately justified." Lesley Doyal (1981:141)

GLOBAL SOCIOLOGY

Female Genital Mutilation: When Medicine Is Politics

In 1993, Meserak Ramsey, a woman born in Ethiopia who now works as a nurse in California, paid a visit to a friend's home. The friend's little girl—eighteen months old—was huddled in the corner of a room in obvious distress. Ramsey was shocked to learn that the girl had recently undergone a clitoridectomy, or female circumcision, whereby the clitoris is surgically removed. This painful procedure is commonly performed by midwives, tribal practitioners, or doctors, typically without anesthesia, on young girls in Nigeria, Togo, Somalia, Egypt, and three dozen other nations in Africa and the Middle East.

According to the patriarchal traditions of these societies, husbands demand that their wives be virgins at marriage and remain sexually faithful thereafter. The point of genital mutilation is to eliminate sexual sensation, thereby making the girl less likely to violate sexual mores. In the process, she becomes more desirable to men. In perhaps one-fifth of all cases, a more severe procedure called infibulation is performed, removing the entire external genital area and stitching the surfaces together leaving only a small hole for urination. At marriage, in such cases, a husband can reopen the wound and ensure himself of his bride's virginity.

Throughout the world, at least 100 million women have endured genital mutilation. There exists no reliable estimate of the number of female genital mutilations in the United States, although probably hundreds if not thousands of such procedures are performed annually. In most cases, immigrant mothers and grandmothers who have themselves been mutilated insist that young girls in their family follow their example. In some cases, immigrant families subject their daughters

to genital mutilation *because* they have come to the United States where sexual mores are lax. "I don't have to worry about her now," one California parent explained to Meserak Ramsey. "She'll be a good girl."

Medically, the consequences of genital mutilation are more than loss of sexual pleasure. Pain is excruciating and may persist, along with the danger of infection, infertility, and even death. Meserak Ramsey herself underwent genital mutilation as a young girl, and since then she has been lucky to have had few medical problems. But she recounts suffering of another kind, brought on by the visit of a young U.S. couple to her home several years ago. Late at night, she heard the woman screaming and burst into the room to investigate, only to realize that the couple was making love and the woman had just had an orgasm. "I didn't understand," Ramsey recalls. "I thought that there must be something wrong with American girls. But now I know that there is something wrong with me." Or with a system that distorts medicine into a brutal form of political and sexual control.

Source: Based on Crossette (1995).

In coining this word, medical professionals apparently suggested that being a woman is synonymous with being sick or crazy. The box takes a look at the gender politics underlying the practice of clitoridectomy, or female genital mutilation.

Surveying the entire medical field, some critics see political mischief in today's scientific medicine. Scientists explain illness in terms of bacteria and viruses, ignoring the effects of social inequality on health. From the scientific perspective, in other words, poor people get sick because of a lack of sanitation and an unhealthy diet, even though poverty may be the underlying cause of these ills. In this way, critics charge, scientific medicine depoliticizes health in the United States by reducing complex political issues to matters of simple biology.

Q: "Humana hospitals do not have the responsibility to provide care for the indigent except in emergencies or in those situations where reimbursement for indigent patients is provided." From Florida certificate-of-need application
Q: "The ways in which the poor die reflect the conditions of their lives." Carol Stack (1975)
Q: "Never accept a drink from a urologist." Erma Bombeck's father

Scientists are learning more and more about the genetic factors that prompt the eventual development of serious diseases. If offered the opportunity, would you want to undergo a genetic screening that would predict the long-term future of your own health?

Critical evaluation. Social-conflict analysis offers another approach to the relationships among health, medicine, and our society. According to this view, social inequality is the reason some people have far better health than others; moreover, conflict theorists denounce the profit motive as inconsistent with the interests of patients.

The most common objection to the conflict approach is that it minimizes the overall improvement in U.S. health through the years and scientific medicine's contribution to our high standard of living today. Even though we could certainly do better, health indicators for our population have risen steadily over the course of this century and compare fairly well with those of other industrial societies.

In sum, sociology's three major theoretical paradigms convincingly argue that health and medicine are social issues. Indeed, as the final box explains, advancing technology is forcing us to confront the social foundations of this institution. The famous French scientist Louis Pasteur (1822–1895) spent much of his life studying how bacteria cause disease. Before his death, he remarked that health depends much less on bacteria than on the social environment in which bacteria operate (Gordon, 1980:7). Explaining Pasteur's insight is sociology's contribution to human health.

LOOKING AHEAD: HEALTH IN THE TWENTY-FIRST CENTURY

At the beginning of this century, deaths from infectious disease were widespread, and scientists had yet to develop basic antibiotics like penicillin. Thus, even common infections represented a deadly threat to health. Today, members of our society take for granted the good health and long life that was the exception, not the rule, a century ago. There is every reason to expect that U.S. health will continue to improve into the next century.

Another encouraging trend is public recognition that, to a significant extent, we can take responsibility for our own health (Caplow et al., 1991). Every one of us can live better and longer if we avoid tobacco, eat sensibly and in moderation, and exercise regularly.

Yet, certain health problems will continue to plague U.S. society in the decades to come. With no cure in sight, it seems likely that the AIDS epidemic will persist for some time. At this point, the only way to steer clear of contracting HIV is to make a personal decision to avoid any of the risky behaviors noted in this chapter.

But the changing social profile of people with AIDS—which increasingly afflicts the poor—reminds us that the United States falls short in addressing the health of marginalized members of our society. Even those among us who do not easily embrace the notion of serving as "our brother's keeper" should recognize the moral obligation that we as a people have to ensure that everyone has the security of medical care.

Finally, repeating a pattern seen in earlier chapters, we find that problems of health are far greater in the poor societies of the world than they are in the United States. The good news is that life expectancy for the world as a whole has been rising—from forty-eight years in 1950 to sixty-five years today—and the biggest gains have been in poor countries (Mosley & Cowley, 1991). But in much of Latin America, Asia, and especially in Africa, hundreds of millions of adults and children lack adequate food, safe water, and needed medical attention. Improving health in the world's poorest societies remains a critical challenge as we enter the next century.

NOTE: We say that most cells contain a nucleus, since red blood cells do not.
DISCUSS: Would you want to know what diseases lie in your future? Half of survey respondents indicate that they would not wish to be tested to learn what diseases they will suffer later in life.
SOCIAL SURVEY: "Would you say your own health, in general, is . . ." (*Student CHIP Social Survey Software*, HEALTH1; GSS

1972–91, N = 18,339)

	"Excellent"	"Good"	"Fair" or "Poor"
Men	34.4%	42.7%	22.9%
Women	31.1%	43.1%	25.8%
Afri Amer	22.3%	42.7%	35.0%
Latino	34.5%	42.6%	23.0%
Whites	33.9%	43.0%	23.1%

Controversy & Debate

The Genetic Crystal Ball: Do We Really Want to Look?

The clear liquid in the laboratory test tube seems ordinary enough, rather like a thick form of water. In one sense it is ordinary but, in another, it represents perhaps the greatest medical breakthrough of all time: *the key to life itself*. The liquid is deoxyribonucleic acid, or DNA, the spiraling molecule found in each cell of the human body—the molecule that contains the blueprints of our being and makes each one of us differerent from every other human.

In medical terms, the human body is composed of some 100 trillion cells, most of which contain a nucleus of twenty-three pairs of chromosomes (one of each pair comes from each parent). Each of these chromosomes is packed with DNA, segments of which are called genes. Genes guide the production of proteins, the building blocks of the human body.

If genetics sounds complex (and it is), the social implications of understanding genetics are no simpler. Scientists have known about DNA since 1952, but now an aggressive program is under way to "map" our genetic landscape. The ambitious goal of the Human Genome Project is nothing less than to understand the operation of each bit of DNA; in essence, to read and understand the computer program that drives our existence. Early results suggest the enormity of the task but are also very promising. And therein lies the greatest question of all: Do we really want to learn the secrets of life itself?

Many scientists offer strong support for the Human Genome Project. They envision for the future a completely new approach to medicine: Rather than treating symptoms, physicians would address the basic causes of illness. Research, they point out, already has identified the genetic abnormalities that cause some forms of cancer, sickle cell anemia, muscular dystrophy, Huntington's disease, cystic fibrosis, and a host of other crippling and deadly afflictions. In the next century, with information from the genetic "crystal ball," screening will allow us to identify people destined to develop serious illnesses, and doctors will be able to manipulate segments of DNA to prevent the onset of diseases before they start.

But many people, both within and outside the scientific community, urge caution in pursuing such research. The problem, they claim, is that no one is sure how genetic information should be used. At its worst, genetic mapping opens the door to Nazi-like efforts at breeding a super-race. Indeed, in 1994, the People's Republic of China initiated a program of marriage regulation and forced abortion to prevent "new births of inferior quality."

It seems inevitable that some parents will seek to use genetic testing to evaluate the future health (or even the eye and hair color) of their unborn child. Should people be permitted to abort a fetus that fails to meet their expectations? Or, further down the road when genetic manipulations become possible, should parents be able to design their own children?

Then there is the issue of "genetic privacy." Should a prospective spouse be able to request a genetic evaluation of her fiancé before agreeing to marry? Should life or health insurance companies be allowed to demand genetic testing before writing policies? Should a corporation be permitted to evaluate job applicants in order to weed out those whose future illnesses might drain their health care funds? Clearly what is scientifically possible is not always morally desirable. Our society is already grappling with questions about how to use the ever-expanding knowledge about human genetics. These ethical dilemmas will only mount as genetic research pinpoints the roots of our makeup in the years to come.

Continue the debate . . .

1. *Through traditional wedding vows, couples pledge to remain together "in sickness and in health." Do you think individuals have a right to know the future health of their potential partner before tying the knot?*

2. *What about the desire of some parents to genetically design their children?*

3. *Where do we turn to devise standards for the proper use of genetic information?*

Sources: Elmer-Dewitt (1994), Thompson (1994), and Nash (1995).

SUMMARY

1. Health is a social as well as a biological issue, and well-being depends on the extent and distribution of a society's resources. Culture shapes both definitions of health and patterns of health care.

2. Through most of human history, health has been poor by today's standards. Health improved dramatically in Western Europe and North America in the nineteenth century, first because industrialization raised living standards and later as medical advances controlled infectious diseases.

3. Infectious diseases were the major killers at the beginning of this century. Today most people in the United States die in old age of heart disease, cancer, or stroke.

4. Health in low-income countries is undermined by inadequate sanitation and hunger. Average life expectancy is about twenty years less than in the United States; in the poorest nations, half the children do not survive to adulthood.

5. In the United States, more than three-fourths of children born today can expect to live to at least age sixty-five. Throughout the life course, however, people of high social position enjoy better health than the poor.

6. Cigarette smoking increased during this century to become the greatest preventable cause of death in the United States. Now that the health hazards of smoking are known, social tolerance for consumption of tobacco products is declining.

7. The incidence of sexually transmitted diseases has risen since 1960, an exception to the general decline in infectious disease.

8. The ability to prolong the lives of terminally ill people is forcing us to confront a number of ethical issues surrounding death and the rights of the dying.

9. Historically a family concern, health care is now the responsibility of trained specialists. The model of scientific medicine underlies the U.S. medical establishment.

10. Holistic healing encourages people to assume greater responsibility for their own health and well-being, and urges professional healers to gain personal knowledge of patients and their environment.

11. Socialist societies define medical care as a right that governments offer equally to everyone. Capitalist societies view medical care as a commodity to be purchased, although most capitalist governments support medical care through socialized medicine or national health insurance.

12. The United States, with a direct-fee system, is the only industrialized society that has no comprehensive medical care program. Most people in this country purchase private health insurance, government insurance, or membership in a health maintenance organization. One in six adults in the United States cannot afford to pay for medical care.

13. Structural-functional analysis links health and medicine to other social structures. A concept central to structural-functional analysis is the sick role, by which the ill person is excused from routine social responsibilities.

14. The symbolic-interaction paradigm investigates how health and medical treatments are largely matters of subjective perception and social definition.

15. Social-conflict analysis focuses on the unequal distribution of health and medical care. It criticizes the U.S. medical establishment for relying too heavily on drugs and surgery, for giving free rein to the profit motive in medicine, and for overemphasizing the biological rather than the social causes of illness.

KEY CONCEPTS

direct-fee system a medical care system in which patients pay directly for the services of physicians and hospitals

eating disorder an intense involvement in dieting or other forms of weight control in order to become very thin

euthanasia (mercy killing) assisting in the death of a person suffering from an incurable disease

health a state of complete physical, mental, and social well-being

health care any activity intended to improve health

health maintenance organization (HMO) an organization that provides comprehensive medical care to subscribers for a fixed fee

holistic medicine an approach to health care that emphasizes prevention of illness and takes account of a person's entire physical and social environment

medicine a social institution concerned with combating disease and improving health

sick role patterns of behavior defined as appropriate for those who are ill

social epidemiology the study of how health and disease are distributed throughout a society's population

socialized medicine a health care system in which the government owns and operates most medical facilities and employs most physicians

CRITICAL-THINKING QUESTIONS

1. Explain why health is as much a social as a biological issue.

2. In global context, which are the "diseases of poverty" that kill people in poor countries? Which are "diseases of affluence," the leading killers in rich nations?

3. Sexually transmitted diseases represent an exception to the historical decline in infectious illness. What social forces are reflected in the rise in STDs since 1960?

4. Do you think the United States should or should not follow the lead of other industrial countries by enacting a government program of health care for everyone? Why?

SUGGESTED READINGS

Classic Sources

Elisabeth Kübler-Ross. *On Death and Dying.* New York: Macmillan, 1969.
  This study of the orderly process of dying illustrates how social research can assist terminally ill patients.

Michel Foucault. *The Birth of the Clinic: An Archaeology of Medical Perception.* New York: Vintage Books, 1975.
  This history of medicine emphasizes not scientific developments but the cultural forces that gradually changed how people thought about illness and health care.

Contemporary Sources

Clyde B. McCoy and James A. Inciardi. *Sex, Drugs, and the Continuing Spread of AIDS.* Los Angeles: Roxbury, 1995.
  The "second wave" of the AIDS epidemic is placing poor people at risk, according to this book.

Susan Sherwin. *No Longer Patient: Feminist Ethics and Health Care.* Philadelphia: Temple University Press, 1992.
  This author argues that ethical issues in medicine should be resolved in a feminist context.

Global Sources

Kaja Finkler. *Women in Pain: Gender and Morbidity in Mexico.* Philadelphia: University of Pennsylvania Press, 1994.
  Women in low-income countries face especially serious threats to health.

Richard Parker and Herbert Daniel. *Sexuality, Politics and AIDS in Brazil: In Another World?* Bristol, Pa.: Taylor & Francis, 1993.
  Based on personal accounts of people with AIDS, the authors contend that the social dynamics linked to this deadly disease are not the same in Brazil as in the United States.

GEORGIA MILLS JESSUP,
RAINY NIGHT DOWNTOWN, 1967

Oil on canvas, 44x48 in. (111.8x121.9 cm). The
National Museum of Women in the Arts. Gift of
Savanna M. Clark.

Population and Urbanization

In 1519 a band of Spanish conquistadors led by Hernando Cortés reached Tenochtitlán, the capital of the Aztec empire. They were stunned by the beautiful, lake-encircled city, teeming with some 300,000 people—more than lived in any European city at that time. Gazing down broad streets, exploring magnificent stone temples, and examining the golden treasures of the royal palace, Cortés and his soldiers wondered if they were dreaming.

Cortés soon set his mind to looting the city's many priceless treasures. At first, he was repelled by the superior military forces of Montezuma and the Aztecs. But Cortés spent the next two years raising a vast army and finally returned to utterly destroy Tenochtitlán. On the rubble of this ancient urban center, he constructed a new city in the European fashion—*Ciudad Imperial de México*, Mexico City.

Today Mexico City is once more fighting for its life. Its soaring population will reach 28 million by the end of this decade—one hundred times the number that astonished Cortés. A triple burden of rising population, urban sprawl, and desperate poverty weighs on Mexico as it does on much of today's world. This chapter examines both population growth and urbanization—two powerful forces that have worked hand in hand to shape and reshape our planet for thousands of years. A steadily increasing population will be one of the most serious challenges facing the world in the coming century, and this compelling drama will be played out in cities of unprecedented size.

DEMOGRAPHY: THE STUDY OF POPULATION

From the point at which the human species emerged about 250,000 B.C.E. until several centuries ago, the population of the entire earth was only some 500 million—less than the number of Europeans today. Life for our ancestors was anything but certain; people were vulnerable to countless diseases, frequent injury, and periodic natural disasters. Powerless in the face of such calamity, one might well be amazed that our species has managed to survive for 10,000 generations.

About 250 years ago, however, world population began to "spike" upward. We now add 90 million people to the planet each year, an increase that pushed the global total to 5.75 billion by early 1996. Ironically, perhaps, human beings have been so successful in reproducing our species that the future well-being of humanity is again in doubt.

The causes and consequences of this human drama form the core of **demography**, *the study of human population.* Demography (from Greek meaning "description of people"), a close cousin of sociology, analyzes the size and composition of a population as well as how people move from place to place. Although much demographic research is a numbers game, the discipline also poses crucial questions about the effects of population growth and its control.

The following sections explain basic demographic concepts.

Fertility

The study of human population begins with how many people are born. **Fertility** is *the incidence of childbearing*

NOTE: Because the United States has a relatively old population—with a median age of 34 years compared to, say, 20 years in Mexico—our crude mortality rate is relatively high compared to Latin America. In Africa, however, where the population is also young, a very high infant mortality rate pushes mortality well above the global average.

THEN AND NOW: U.S. infant mortality rate: *1945, 40; 1995, 7.8.*

NOTE: One dramatic illustration of mortality change: A greater proportion of U.S. babies born today will reach age 65 than survived a single year in 1900.

DIVERSITY: Life expectancy in the U.S. varies by race and sex (1994): for African-American females, 74.1 years; African-American males, 64.9; white females, 79.6; white males, 73.2. Sex has the same effect (6.7 years) that race does (6.9 years).

Global Snapshot

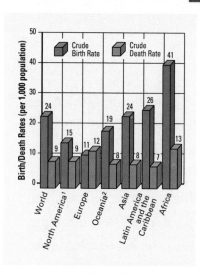
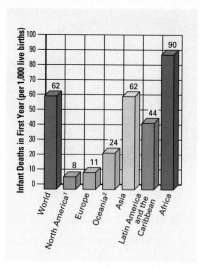
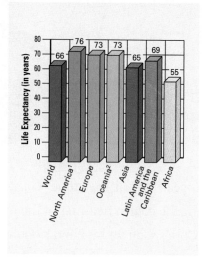

FIGURE 21–1 Crude Birth Rates and Crude Death Rates, Infant Mortality Rates, and Life Expectancy, 1995

[1] United States and Canada

[2] Australia, New Zealand, and South Pacific Islands

Source: Population Reference Bureau (1995).

in a country's population. During their childbearing years, from the onset of menstruation (typically in the early teens) to menopause (usually in the late forties), women are capable of bearing more than twenty children. But *fecundity,* or maximum possible childbearing, is sharply reduced in practice by cultural norms, finances, and personal choice.

Demographers measure fertility using the **crude birth rate,** *the number of live births in a given year for every thousand people in a population.* They calculate the crude birth rate by dividing the number of live births in a year by a society's total population and multiplying the result by 1,000. In the United States in 1995, there were 4.0 million live births in a population of 263 million (National Center for Health Statistics, 1995). According to this formula, then, the crude birth rate was 15.2.

This birth rate is "crude" because it is based on the entire population, not just women in their childbearing years. Comparing the crude birth rates of various countries can be misleading, then, if one society has a larger share of women of childbearing age than another. A crude birth rate also tells us nothing about

how birth rates differ among people of various races, ethnicities, and religions. But this measure is an easy-to-calculate indicator of a society's overall fertility. The first part of Figure 21–1 shows that the crude birth rate of North Americans is low in global perspective.

Mortality

Population size is also affected by **mortality,** *the incidence of death in a country's population.* Corresponding to the crude birth rate, demographers use a **crude death rate,** *the number of deaths in a given year for every thousand people in a population.* This time, we take the number of deaths in a year, divide by the total population, and multiply the result by 1,000. In 1995 there were 2.3 million deaths in the U.S. population of 263 million, yielding a crude death rate of 8.8. As the first part of Figure 21–1 shows, this rate is about the global average.

A third widely used demographic measure is the **infant mortality rate,** *the number of deaths among infants under one year of age for each thousand live births in a given year.* We derive this rate by dividing

THEN AND NOW: The U.S. age-sex pyramid in 1900 resembled that of Mexico today.
DISCUSS: The UN predicts that, between 1995 and 2025, rich societies will grow by 57 million people while poor societies will expand by 1.7 billion people. What are the implications of this pattern?
GLOBAL: One key predictor of fertility is women's income. As wages and salaries rise, fertility falls, and vice versa.

RESOURCE: David Berreby's analysis of "The Global Population Crisis" is included among the cross-cultural selections in the companion reader, *Seeing Ourselves*.
Q: "Although individual women [worldwide] are having fewer children, on average, than their mothers there are simply more women having children, resulting in continuing increases in additions to world population." Population Reference Bureau

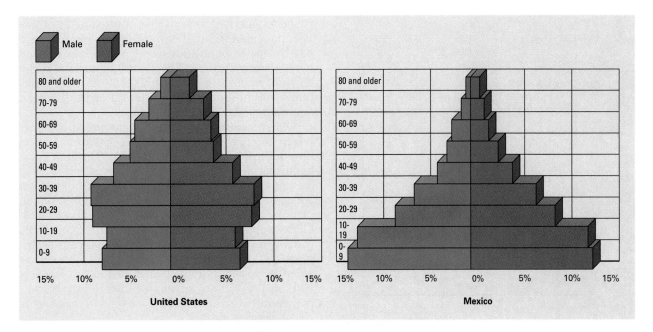

FIGURE 21–2 Age-Sex Population Pyramids for the United States and Mexico
Sources: U.S. Bureau of the Census and Mexican Census data.

natural increase; less economically developed countries (like Mexico) grow almost entirely from natural increase.

To calculate a nation's natural growth rate, demographers subtract the crude death rate from the crude birth rate. The natural growth rate of the U.S. population in 1995 was 6.4 per thousand (the crude birth rate of 15.2 minus the crude death rate of 8.8), or about 0.64 percent annual growth.

Global Map 21–1 shows that population growth in the United States and other industrialized nations is well below the world average of 1.5 percent. The earth's low-growth continents include Europe (currently posting a slight decline: -0.1 percent annual growth), North America (0.7 percent), and Oceania (1.2 percent); Asia (1.7 percent) stands near the global average; Latin America (1.9 percent) and Africa (2.8 percent) constitute the high-growth regions of the world.

A handy rule of thumb is that dividing a society's population growth rate into the number seventy yields the *doubling time* in years. Thus, annual growth of 2 percent (common in Latin America) doubles a population in thirty-five years, and a 3 percent growth rate (found in much of Africa) pares the doubling time to twenty-four years. The rapid population growth of the poorest countries is deeply troubling because they can

barely support the populations they have now (Population Reference Bureau, 1995).

Population Composition

Demographers also study the composition of a society's population at a given point in time. One simple variable is the **sex ratio,** *the number of males for every hundred females in a given population.* In 1995 the sex ratio in the United States was 95.2, or roughly 95 males for every 100 females. Sex ratios are usually below 100 because women typically outlive men. In India, however, the sex ratio is 108. More males than females survive in India because parents value sons more than daughters. Thus women are more likely to abort a female fetus or, after birth, to provide less care to females than to males.

A more complex measure is the **age-sex pyramid,** *a graphic representation of the age and sex of a population.* Figure 21–2 presents two age-sex pyramids, showing the contrasting compositions of the population of the United States and Mexico. The rough pyramid shape of these figures results from higher mortality as people age. Looking at the U.S. pyramid, the bulge corresponding to ages twenty through forty-nine reflects high birth rates from the mid-1940s to the late 1960s, resulting in the *baby boom.* The contraction just

DIVERSITY: Age cohorts play a part in the trend toward the coming "minority-majority." Among people under 35 years of age, one-third are minorities; above 35, one-fifth are minorities.

GLOBAL: Sex-ratio imbalance in Asia is especially high for second and third births. In South Korea, for example, 115 boys are born for every 100 girls as second children; for third children, the figure soars to 190 boys for every 100 girls.

NOTE: Malthus made a personal contribution to population control by having only three children (about half the average for his day); typical for that time, only one of his children lived to adulthood.

GLOBAL: A population comparison of two comparably sized delta lands—Louisiana and Bangladesh—shows that Louisiana has a population of 4.5 million and a growth rate of 1.1%, while Bangladesh has 104 million people and a growth rate of 2.4%.

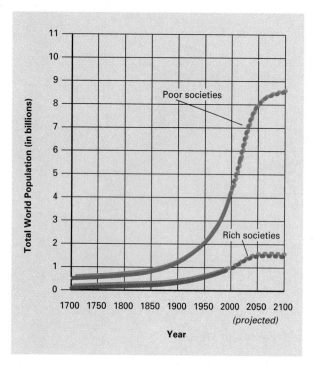

FIGURE 21–3 The Increase in World Population, 1700–2100

below—that is, males and females under twenty—represents the *baby bust* that followed as the birth rate dipped from 25.3 in 1957 to a low of 15.2 in 1995.

Age-sex pyramids not only reflect a society's history, they foretell its future. The age-sex pyramid for Mexico, like that of other lower-income nations, is wide at the bottom (reflecting higher birth rates) and narrows quickly by what we would call middle age (due to higher mortality). Mexico, in short, is a much younger society with a median age of twenty compared to thirty-four in the United States. With a larger share of females still in their childbearing years, we can understand why Mexico's crude birth rate (27) is nearly twice our own (15), and its annual rate of population growth (2.2 percent) is rising almost four times faster than that of the United States (0.6 percent).

HISTORY AND THEORY OF POPULATION GROWTH

Through most of human history, societies favored large families since human labor was the key to productivity. Additionally, until the development of

rubber condoms 150 years ago, controlling birth was uncertain at best. But if birth rates were high, so were death rates, as populations were periodically ravaged by infectious diseases. Thus world population at the dawn of civilization, about 8000 B.C.E., had yet to reach 100 million (the population of the Eastern Seaboard of the United States today).

As shown in Figure 21–3, a demographic shift began about 1800 as the earth's population turned upward, reaching the 1 billion mark. This milestone (requiring all of human history) was repeated by 1930 (barely a century later) when a second billion was added to the planet. In other words, not only did population increase, but the *rate* of growth accelerated. Global population reached 3 billion by 1962 (after just thirty-two years) and 4 billion by 1974 (a scant twelve years later). The rate of world population increase has recently slowed, but our planet passed the 5 billion mark in 1987. In no previous century did the world's population even double. In the twentieth century, it has increased *fourfold*.

Currently, global population is increasing by 90 million people each year, with more than 90 percent of this growth in poor societies. At this rate, experts predict, the earth's people will number 6 billion early in the next century, probably reaching 8 billion by 2025 and passing 10 billion a century from now. Little wonder, then, that global population has become a matter of urgent concern (see also Chapter 22, "Environment and Society").

Malthusian Theory

It was the sudden population growth two centuries ago that sparked the development of demography. Thomas Robert Malthus (1766–1834), an English clergyman and economist, devised a demographic theory that warned of impending social chaos.

To Malthus (1926; orig. 1798), population growth was as certain as the timeless passion between the sexes. Moreover, he predicted a population increase approximating what mathematicians call an *exponential progression*, illustrated by the series of numbers 2, 4, 8, 16, 32, and so on. Noting the accelerating increase in these numbers, Malthus reached the sobering conclusion that world population would soon soar out of control.

Food production would also increase, Malthus reasoned, but only in *arithmetic progression* (as in the series 2, 3, 4, 5, 6) because, even with new agricultural technology, farmland is limited. Malthus's analysis yielded a troubling vision of the future: people reproducing

FIGURE 21–4
Demographic Transition Theory

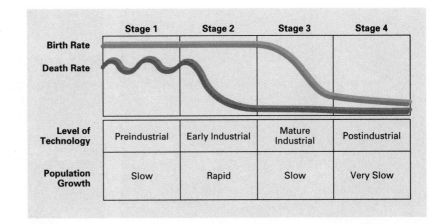

beyond what the planet could feed, leading ultimately to catastrophic starvation.

What of limits to population growth? Malthus foresaw what he called *positive checks*, such as famine, disease, and war, and *preventive checks* like artificial birth control, sexual abstinence, and delayed marriages. He rejected birth control on religious grounds, and his common sense told him people would not abstain from sex or marry very much later. Thus famine stalked humanity's future, Malthus warned, a vision that earned him the moniker of "the dismal parson."

Critical evaluation. Fortunately for us, Malthus's prediction was flawed. First, by 1850 the birth rate in Europe began to drop, partly because children were becoming more of an economic liability than an asset, and partly because people began to use condoms as a means of birth control. Second, Malthus underestimated human ingenuity: Irrigation, fertilizers, and pesticides have increased farm production far more than he imagined, just as factories have generated a bounty of other products.

Critics also chided Malthus for ignoring the role of social inequality in world abundance and famine. For example, Karl Marx (1967; orig. 1867) objected to viewing suffering as a "law of nature" rather than the mischief of capitalism.

Still, we should not entirely dismiss Malthus's distressing prediction. First, habitable land, clean water, and fresh air are certainly finite. And greater industrial productivity has taken a toll on the natural environment. In addition, as medical advances have lowered death rates, world population has risen even faster. Population growth is especially rapid in low-income countries, which are, in fact, experiencing much of the catastrophe Malthus envisioned.

In principle, of course, no level of population growth is sustainable indefinitely. Thus, people everywhere must remain alert to the dangers of population increase.

Demographic Transition Theory

Malthus's rather crude analysis has been superseded by **demographic transition theory,** *a thesis linking demographic changes to a society's level of technological development.* Why did world population soar after 1800? Why is population increase much higher in poor countries than in rich nations?

Demographic transition theory answers these questions by analyzing birth and death rates at four stages of a society's technological development. As shown in Figure 21-4, societies yet to industrialize—those at Stage 1—have high birth rates because of the economic value of children, the absence of effective birth control, and the high risk that children will not survive to adulthood. Death rates, too, are high, due to periodic outbreaks of plague or other infectious disease, low living standards, and a lack of medical technology. But deaths almost offset births, so population increase is modest. This pattern characterized Europe and North America for thousands of years before the Industrial Revolution.

Stage 2—the onset of industrialization—brings a demographic transition as population surges upward. Technology expands food supplies and science combats disease. Death rates fall sharply but birth rates remain high, resulting in rapid population growth. It was in an era like this that Malthus formulated his ideas, and that goes a long way toward explaining his pessimism. Most of the world's least economically developed societies today are still in this high-growth stage.

GLOBAL: Median age in Europe has risen from 30 in 1950 to about 36 today, and will probably reach 40 by 2025. This suggests little overall growth due to natural increase. In Africa, by comparison, during the same period, median age has fallen from about 18 to 17, indicating high population growth.
GLOBAL: In rich societies, women average just under one child during their reproductive lifetimes (counting only those who have children, the median is just under two). In poor societies, virtually all women have children, averaging almost five.
GLOBAL: Europe's population is projected to increase 2% to 743 million by 2025, while the world's population overall jumps by almost 50% to 8 billion.
GLOBAL: Currently, China (25%) and India (16%) together comprise more than 40% of humanity.

The Qampie family, pictured above, lives in Soweto, South Africa. The Pfitzner family, shown on the right, lives in Cologne, Germany. What relationship can you see between a society's level of material affluence and typical family size?

In Stage 3—a mature industrial economy—birth rates drop, finally coming into line with death rates and, once again, curbing population growth. Fertility falls, first, because most children born do survive to adulthood and rising living standards make raising children expensive. Affluence, in other words, transforms offspring from economic assets into economic liabilities. Smaller families, also favored by women working outside the home, are made possible by the widespread availability of birth control devices. As birth rates follow death rates downward, population growth slows further.

The most recent stage corresponds to a postindustrial economy. The birth rate in such societies continues to fall, in part because dual-income couples gradually become the norm and partly because the costs of raising children continue to rise. This trend, coupled with steady death rates, means that, at best, population grows only very slowly. Recent years have witnessed a natural *decrease* in Europe's population, for example.

Critical evaluation. Demographic transition theory suggests that technology holds the key to demographic shifts. Instead of the runaway population increase Malthus feared, this analysis foresees technology reining in population growth.

Demographic transition theory dovetails with modernization theory, one approach to global development examined in Chapter 11 ("Global Stratification"). Modernization theorists are optimistic that industrialization will also solve the population problems that now are placing strains on poor countries. But critics—notably dependency theorists—counter that current economic arrangements only ensure continued poverty in much of the world. Unless there is a significant redistribution of global resources, they maintain, our planet will become increasingly divided into industrialized "haves," enjoying low population growth, and nonindustrialized "have-nots," struggling in vain to feed soaring populations.

Global Population Today: A Brief Survey

What demographic patterns characterize today's world? Drawing on what we have learned so far, we can highlight a number of key trends.

The Low-Growth North

When the Industrial Revolution began, natural increase in Western Europe and North America peaked at 3 percent annually, doubling the population in little more than one generation. But, since then, growth rates have eased downward throughout the Northern Hemisphere and, in 1970, dropped below

NOTE: Population "conservatives" argue that rising populations reflect *success* in combatting death rates; population "liberals" claim that rising population results from *failure* to control births.

GLOBAL: Immunization throughout poor societies has increased dramatically in recent decades. In 1975, 5% of infants were immunized against diseases such as measles, polio, tetanus, and diphtheria. By 1990, about half of all children were immunized against these diseases. One result: In Africa, not just infant mortality rates but the absolute number of infants dying has declined.

GLOBAL: Examples of falling infant mortality rates:

	1975	1995
India	130	74
Vietnam	106	42
Mexico	60	34

1 percent in the United States. As our postindustrial society enters Stage 4, the U.S. birth rate has neared the replacement level of 2.1 children per woman, a point demographers designate as **zero population growth,** *the level of reproduction that maintains population at a steady state.*

Factors holding down population here and in other postindustrial societies include the high proportion of men and women in the labor force, the rising cost of raising children, trends toward later marriage and singlehood, and the use of contraceptives by about two-thirds of women of childbearing age. Voluntary sterilization has increased dramatically to become the most common form of birth control in the United States. Even U.S. Catholics, whose religious doctrine prohibits the use of artificial birth control, no longer differ from others in their contraceptive practices. Finally, abortion has been legal in the United States since 1973, and each year doctors terminate some 1.4 million pregnancies (U.S. Centers for Disease Control, 1995).

Due to immigration as well as natural increase, the U.S. population will continue to grow slowly, approaching 400 million by 2050. Even such a modest increase here and in other industrial countries threatens coming generations, just as it does in poor nations. And, as Chapter 22 ("Environment and Society") explains, an individual in our society uses many times the natural resources that people in poor countries do, placing greater stress on the global environment.

The High-Growth South

Population growth is a serious—and increasing—problem in the poor societies of the Southern Hemisphere. Only a few nations lack industrial technology altogether, placing them at demographic transition theory's Stage 1. Most of Latin America, Africa, and Asia has moved to Stage 2, still primarily agricultural but with some industry. In these nations, advanced medical technology (much supplied by rich societies) has sharply reduced death rates, but birth rates remain high. A look back at Figure 21–3 shows that poor societies now account for two-thirds of the earth's people, a proportion that continues to rise.

In poor countries throughout the world, urban families average four or five children; in rural areas, the number is often six or eight (The World Bank, 1991). No one doubts that world population simply cannot keep increasing at anything like its current rate. At a 1994 global population conference in Cairo,

Dr. Nafiz Sadik is in charge of United Nations efforts to monitor and control the growth of world population. In her view, success in controlling population growth depends directly on our ability to expand the opportunities for education and paid employment for women—especially in poor countries.

delegates from 180 nations agreed not only on the need for vigorous action to contain population growth, but also pointed out the crucial link between population control and the status of women. The box offers a closer look.

In the last decade, the world has made significant progress in lowering fertility. Yet the other half of the demographic equation—death rates—is also crucial. Throughout the world, mortality rates are falling. Although few would oppose medical programs that save lives—mostly of children—this trend exerts upward pressure on population. In fact, population growth in most low-income regions of the world is due *primarily* to declining death rates. After about 1920, when Europe and North America began to export advances in scientific medicine, nutrition, and sanitation around the world, mortality tumbled. Since then, inoculations against infectious diseases and the use of antibiotics and insecticides have pushed down death rates with stunning effectiveness. For example, in Sri Lanka, malaria caused half of all deaths in the 1930s; a decade later, insecticides used to kill malaria-carrying

CRITICAL THINKING

Empowering Women: The Key to Controlling Population Growth

Sohad Ahmad lives in a village fifty miles south of Cairo, Egypt's capital city. Her husband is a farmer and her family is poor. At first glance, one might conclude that this woman's situation fits a stereotype all too typical in low-income countries: desperate poverty pushing families to have more and more children to work the fields and earn more income.

But this is not the case. Sohad Ahmad has had only two children, and she and her husband will have no more. Why does she reject the conventional wisdom that children are an economic asset? One part of the answer is that Egypt's rising population has already created such a demand for land that her family could not afford more even if they could farm it. Another part of the answer is that the Ahmads recognize that a bigger family amounts to more bodies to feed, clothe, and house. In other words, if growing more food requires more hungry workers, how is a family better off? But the third part of the answer is crucial: Sohad Ahmad does not want her life defined only by childbearing. Thus she has made a personal decision to have no more children.

Women like Sohad Ahmad who are taking control of their fertility and seeking greater opportunities are more and more common across Egypt. Indeed, this country has made great progress in reducing its annual population growth from 3.0 percent just ten years ago to 2.3 percent today. This is why the International Conference on Population and Development selected Cairo for its historic 1994 meeting.

The 1994 Cairo conference was not the first of its kind. But it stands out in several respects. First, it had an unprecedented base of participation, with representatives from 180 nations including the United States. In addition, delegates from more than 1,200 nongovernmental organizations also attended the meeting. Second, the Cairo conference reached virtual consensus on a new path toward effective control of global population: elevating the standing of women.

In the past, population control programs have been limited to making birth control technology available to women. This is a crucial objective, since only half the world's married women make use of effective birth control. But it has become clear that more than technology is needed to curb population increase. The larger picture shows that, even with available birth control, population continues to grow in societies that define women's primary responsibility as raising children.

Dr. Nafis Sadik, an Egyptian woman who heads United Nations efforts at population control, sums up the new approach to lowering birth rates: *Give women more choices and they will have fewer children.* In other words, women with access to schooling and jobs, who can decide when and if they wish to marry, and who bear children as a matter of choice will limit their fertility. The door to schooling must be open to older women too, Dr. Sadik adds, since they often exercise great influence in local communities.

The lesson of the Cairo conference—and building evidence from countries around the world—is that controlling population and raising the social standing of women are inseparable objectives.

Sources: Linden (1994) and Ashford (1995).

---

mosquitoes cut the malaria death toll in half. Although we hail such an achievement, this technological advance sent Sri Lanka's population soaring. Similarly, India's infant mortality rate slid from 130 in 1975 to 74 in 1995, a decline that has helped boost that nation's population to 950 million.

In short, in much of the world, fertility is falling. But so is mortality, especially among children. Thus various strategies to control birth are now vital in poor countries where programs to fend off death have worked well in the past.

URBANIZATION: THE GROWTH OF CITIES

October 8, 1994, Hong Kong. The cable train grinds to the top of Victoria Peak where one of the world's spectacular vistas awaits us: gazing down at Hong Kong harbor at night! Tens of thousands of bright, colorful lights ring the water as ships, ferries, and

```
traditional Chinese "junks" churn by.
Although the city seems almost asleep
in the distance below, few settings
match Hong Kong for sheer intensity.
This frantic city is as productive as
the state of Wisconsin or the nation of
Finland. One could sit here for hours
lost in the trance that is Hong Kong.
```

For most of human history, the sights and sounds of great cities such as Hong Kong, New York, or Los Angeles were completely unknown. The world's people lived in small, nomadic groups, moving as they depleted vegetation or searched for migratory game. Not for tens of thousands of years did our human ancestors devise settlements, which now mark the emergence of civilization. First in the Middle East some ten thousand years ago, and eventually on all the continents, cities emerged. But they still held just a small fraction of the earth's people.

Today the largest three or four cities of the world together are home to as many people as the entire planet was then. This fact testifies to the steady march of **urbanization**, *the concentration of humanity into cities.* Urbanization both redistributes the population within a society and transforms many patterns of social life. We will trace these changes in terms of three urban revolutions—the emergence of cities beginning 12,000 years ago, the development of industrial cities after 1750, and the explosive growth of cities in low-income countries today.

The Evolution of Cities

Cities are a relatively new development in human history. Only about 12,000 years ago did our ancestors found the earliest permanent settlements, setting the stage for the *first urban revolution.*

Preconditions of Cities

The founding of cities depended, first, on a *favorable ecology.* As glaciers drew back at the end of the last ice age, people congregated in warm regions with fertile soil. The second prerequisite was *changing technology.* At about the same time, humans discovered how to domesticate animals and cultivate crops. Whereas hunting and gathering demanded continual movement, raising food required people to remain in one place (Lenski, Nolan, & Lenski, 1995). Domesticating animals and plants also yielded a material surplus, which freed some people from concentrating on food production and allowed them to build shelters, make tools, weave clothing, and take part in religious rituals. Thus the founding of cities was truly revolutionary, enhancing productive specialization and raising living standards as never before.

The First Cities

Historians identify Jericho as the first city. This settlement lies to the north of the Dead Sea in disputed land currently occupied by Israel. About 8000 B.C.E., Jericho contained about 600 people. By 4000 B.C.E., numerous cities were flourishing in the Fertile Crescent between the Tigris and Euphrates rivers in present-day Iraq, and urban settlement had begun along the Nile River in Egypt.

Some cities, with populations reaching 50,000, became centers of urban empires. Priest-kings wielded absolute power over lesser nobles, administrators, artisans, soldiers, and farmers. Slaves, captured in frequent military campaigns, labored to build monumental structures like the pyramids of Egypt (Kenyon, 1957; Hamblin, 1973; Stavrianos, 1983; Lenski, Nolan, & Lenski, 1995).

In at least three other areas of the world, cities developed independently. Several large, complex settlements bordered the Indus River in present-day Pakistan starting about 2500 B.C.E. Scholars date Chinese cities from 2000 B.C.E. And in Latin America, urban centers arose around 1500 B.C.E. In North America, however, Native-American societies rarely formed settlements; significant urbanization did not take root here until the arrival of European settlers in the seventeenth century (Lamberg-Karlovsky, 1973; Change, 1977; Coe & Diehl, 1980).

Preindustrial European Cities

Urbanization in Europe began about 1800 B.C.E. on the Mediterranean island of Crete. Cities soon spread throughout Greece, resulting in more than one hundred city-states, of which Athens is the most famous. During its Golden Age, lasting barely a century after 500 B.C.E., Athenians made major contributions to the Western way of life in philosophy, the arts, and politics. Yet Athenian society, numbering some 300,000, rested on the labor of slaves, who comprised one-third of the population. Their democratic principles notwithstanding, Athenian men also denied the rights of citizenship to women and foreigners (Mumford, 1961; Gouldner, 1965; Stavrianos, 1983).

Q: ". . . to be fully functioning human beings both urban and rural medieval people [in Europe] had to be members of the Roman Catholic Church. Religious minorities, notably Jews, were recognized as being mostly outside the mainstream of society . . ." Janet Roebucks (1974:57)

Q: "The bourgeoisie has subjected the country to the rule of the towns. It has created enormous cities, has greatly increased the urban population as compared to the rural, and has thus rescued a considerable part of the population from the idiocy of rural life." Karl Marx and Friedrich Engels

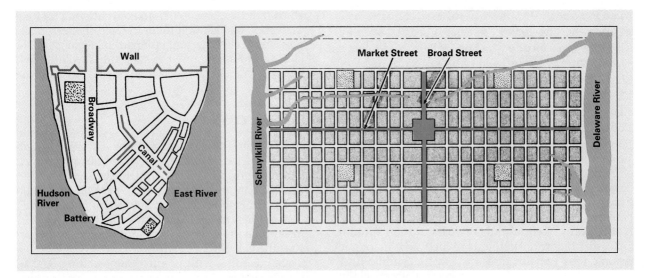

FIGURE 21–5 The Street Plans of Colonial New Amsterdam and Philadelphia
The plan of colonial New Amsterdam, shown at left, exemplifies the preindustrial urban pattern of walls enclosing a city of narrow, irregular streets. Colonial Philadelphia, founded fifty years later, reflects the industrial urban pattern of accessible cities with wide, regularly spaced, parallel and perpendicular streets to facilitate economic activity.

As Greek civilization faded, the city of Rome grew to almost 1 million inhabitants and became the center of a vast empire. By the first century C.E., the militaristic Romans had subdued much of northern Africa, Europe, and the Middle East. In the process, Rome spread its language, arts, and technology. Four centuries later, the Roman Empire fell into disarray, a victim of its gargantuan size, internal corruption, and militaristic appetite. Yet, between them, the Greeks and Romans founded cities across Europe from the Atlantic Ocean all the way to Asia, including Vienna, Paris, London, and Istanbul.

The fall of the Roman Empire initiated an era of urban decline and stagnation lasting six hundred years. Cities became smaller as people drew back within defensive walls and competing warlords battled for territory. About the eleventh century, the "Dark Ages" came to an end as a semblance of peace allowed trade to bring life to cities once again.

Expanding trade prompted medieval cities to tear down their walls. Beneath the towering cathedrals, the narrow and winding streets of London, Brussels, and Florence soon teemed with merchants, artisans, priests, peddlers, jugglers, nobles, and servants. Typically, occupational groups such as bakers, keymakers, and carpenters clustered together in distinct sections or "quarters." Ethnic groups also inhabited their own neighborhoods, often because people kept them out of other districts. The term ghetto (from the Italian word *borghetto*, meaning "outside the city walls") first described the segregation of Jews in medieval Venice.

Industrial European Cities

Throughout the Middle Ages, steadily increasing commerce enriched a new urban middle class or *bourgeoisie* (from the French meaning "of the town"). By the fifteenth century, the power of the bourgeoisie rivaled that of the hereditary nobility.

By about 1750 industrialization was well under way, triggering a *second urban revolution*, first in Europe and then in North America. Factories unleashed productive power as never before, causing cities to grow to unprecedented size. London, the largest European city in 1700, with 550,000 people, swelled to 6.5 million by 1900 (A. Weber, 1963, orig. 1899; Chandler & Fox, 1974). Most of this increase was due to migration from rural areas by people seeking a better standard of living.

Cities not only grew but changed shape as well. The industrial-capitalist city replaced older irregular streets, with broad, straight boulevards, which accommodated the increasing flow of commercial traffic.

Steam and electric trolleys, too, crisscrossed the expanding cities. Lewis Mumford (1961) adds that developers divided cities into regular-sized lots, making land a commodity to be bought and sold. Finally, the cathedrals that had guided the life of medieval cities were soon dwarfed by towering, brightly lit, and frantic central business districts made up of banks, retail stores, and office buildings.

Built for business, cities became increasingly crowded and impersonal. Crime rates rose. Especially at the outset, a small number of industrialists lived in grand style, while for most men, women, and children, factory work proved exhausting and provided bare subsistence.

Organized efforts by workers to improve their plight led to legal regulation of the workplace, better housing, and the right to vote. Public services such as water, sewage, and electricity further enhanced urban living. Today some urbanites still live in poverty, but a rising standard of living has partly fulfilled the city's historical promise of a better life.

The Growth of U.S. Cities

Inhabiting this continent for tens of thousands of years, Native Americans were migratory people, establishing few permanent settlements. Cities first sprang up, then, as a product of European colonization. In 1565, the Spanish made an initial settlement at St. Augustine, Florida, and the English founded Jamestown, Virginia, in 1607. In 1624, the Dutch established New Amsterdam (later called New York), which soon overshadowed these smaller settlements. Today, the United States has two hundred cities with more than 100,000 inhabitants. How ours became an urban society is explained in the brief history that follows.

Colonial Settlement: 1624–1800

Contemporary New York and Boston were, at their founding, tiny villages in a vast wilderness. Dutch New Amsterdam at the southern tip of Manhattan Island (1624) and English Boston (1630) each resembled medieval towns of Europe, with narrow, winding streets that still charm (and frustrate) visitors to lower Manhattan and downtown Boston. New Amsterdam was walled on the north, the site of today's Wall Street. In 1700, Boston was the largest U.S. city, with just 7,000 people.

The rational and expansive culture of capitalism soon transformed these quiet villages into thriving towns built with gridlike streets. Figure 21–5, on page 570, contrasts the medieval shape of early New Amsterdam with the modern grid pattern of Philadelphia, founded half a century later in 1680.

Throughout the colonial era, the United States was still an overwhelmingly rural society. In 1790 the new government's first census tallied barely 4 million people and, as Table 21–1 shows, just 5 percent of them lived in cities.

Urban Expansion: 1800–1860

Early in the nineteenth century, towns began springing up along transportation routes that opened the western frontier. In 1818 the National Road (now Route 40) funneled Easterners from Baltimore through the Appalachian Mountains to the Ohio Valley. A decade later the Baltimore and Ohio Railroad and the Erie Canal (1825) from New York touched off the development of cities along the Great Lakes, including Buffalo, Cleveland, and Detroit. Commerce relied so heavily on water transportation that virtually every one of the largest U.S. cities was founded on a waterway.

By 1860 about one-fifth of the U.S. population lived in cities. Underlying this urban expansion was the Industrial Revolution, centered primarily in the northern states. In 1850, for example, New York City boasted ten times the population of Charleston, South Carolina. In fact, friction between the industrial-urban North and the agrarian-rural South was one key cause of the Civil War (Schlesinger, 1969).

The Great Metropolis: 1860–1950

The Civil War (1861–1865) gave an enormous boost to urbanization, as factories strained to produce

TABLE 21–1 The Urban Population of the United States, 1790–1990

Year	Population (in millions)	Percent Urban
1790	3.9	5.1%
1800	5.3	6.1
1820	9.6	7.3
1840	17.1	10.5
1860	31.4	19.7
1880	50.2	28.1
1900	76.0	39.7
1920	105.7	51.3
1940	131.7	56.5
1960	179.3	69.9
1980	226.5	73.7
1990	253.0	75.2

Source: U.S. Bureau of the Census (1995).

NOTE: Urban growth late in the nineteenth century was nothing less than staggering, contributing to the birth of urban sociology. Chicago, the first city of urban sociology, grew twelve times over between 1870 and 1920.

NOTE: Cities grew upward propelled by advances in building technology. In 1848, five-story iron frame buildings were big news; by 1884, a steel structure in Chicago reached ten stories, and buildings began to utilize elevators (devised in the 1850s). By 1900, skylines reached 30 stories and, on the eve of World War I, New York had 61 buildings more than 20 stories tall. Today, Chicago's Sears Tower is the world tallest (110 stories and 1,454 feet). The technology exists to raise towers to a mile or more, restrained by high cost, the inability to control fire, and people's general reluctance to live that high above the ground.

the tools of battle. Waves of people deserted the countryside for cities in hopes of obtaining better jobs. Following the war, tens of millions of immigrants—most from Europe—settled in the expanding cities to generate a culturally diverse urban mix.

In 1900 New York soared past the 4 million mark, and Chicago—a city of scarcely 100,000 people in 1860—was closing in on 2 million. This growth marked the era of the **metropolis** (from Greek words meaning "mother city"), a *large city that socially and economically dominates an urban area*. Metropolises soon became the manufacturing, commercial, and residential centers of the United States.

Industrial technology not only expanded the population but, once again, changed the physical shape of cities. From the three- or four-story towns in 1850, steel girders and mechanical elevators raised structures over ten stories high in 1880. In 1930, New York's Empire State Building became an urban wonder, a true "skyscraper" stretching 102 stories into the clouds. Pushing upwards as well as outward, cities encompassed a majority of the U.S. population by 1920.

Urban Decentralization: 1950–Present

The industrial metropolis reached its peak about 1950. Since then, something of a turnaround—termed urban decentralization—has occurred as people have deserted the downtowns for outlying suburbs. Thus the large cities of the Northeast and Midwest stopped growing—and some lost considerable population—in the decades after 1950. The 1990 census count tallied half a million fewer New Yorkers, for example, than at mid-century. Instead of densely packed central cities, the urban landscape has evolved into sprawling urban regions, a trend closely tied to the expansion of suburbs.

Suburbs and Central Cities

Just as central cities flourished a century ago, we have recently witnessed the expansion of **suburbs**, *urban areas beyond the political boundaries of a city*. Suburbs began to grow late in the nineteenth century as railroad and trolley lines enabled people to work "downtown" yet leave behind the commotion of the city when they went home (Warner, 1962).

The first suburbanites were well-to-do people, imitating the pattern of the European nobility who shuttled between their town houses and country estates (Baltzell, 1979). But the growth of suburbs was also fueled by racial and ethnic prejudice. Rising immigration was adding to the social diversity of central cities, prompting many to flee to homogeneous, high-prestige enclaves beyond the reach of the masses. In time, of course, less wealthy people also came to view a single-family house on its own piece of leafy suburban ground as part of the American Dream.

The economic boom of the late 1940s, coupled with the mobility offered by increasingly affordable automobiles, placed suburbia within the grasp of the average U.S. household. With World War II over, men and women eagerly returned to family life, igniting the baby boom described earlier in this chapter. Since central cities afforded little space for new housing construction, suburbs blossomed almost overnight. The government weighed in with guaranteed bank loans, and developers offered new, prefabricated homes at unheard-of low prices.

Levittown is the most famous of the low-cost suburbs. Built on potato fields on New York's Long Island in the late 1940s, Abraham Levitt's homes were dismissed by some as lookalike boxes, but snatched up by others as fast as Levitt could build them. By 1970, more of our population lived in the suburbs than in the central cities.

Following the consumers, business, too, began eyeing the suburbs. Soon the suburban mall had largely replaced the downtown stores of the metropolitan era. Manufacturing companies also decentralized into suburban industrial parks far from the high taxes, congested streets, and soaring crime rates of inner cities. The interstate highway system, with its beltways encircling central cities, made moving out to the suburbs almost irresistible for residents and business people alike (Rosenthal, 1974; Tobin, 1976; Geist, 1985).

Decentralization was not good news for everyone, however. Rapid suburban growth soon threw older cities of the Northeast and Midwest into a financial tailspin. Population decline meant falling tax revenues. Further, as affluent people packed for the suburbs, cities were left with the burden of funding expensive social programs for the poor who stayed behind. The overall result was inner-city decay beginning about 1950. Some major cities, such as Cleveland and New York, actually slid to the brink of bankruptcy. Especially to white people, the deteriorating inner cities became synonymous with slum housing, crime, drugs, unemployment, the poor, and minorities. This perception fueled wave after wave of "white flight" and urban decline. Suburbs may have their share of poor housing, congestion, and crime, but they still appeal to many people because they remain largely white, unlike the inner cities whose populations encompass a greater share of people of color (Clark, 1979; Gluck & Meister, 1979; Sternlieb & Hughes, 1983; Logan & Schneider, 1984; Stahura, 1986; Galster, 1991).

The official response to the plight of the central cities was "urban renewal" programs. Federal and local funds have paid for the rebuilding of many inner cities. Yet critics of urban renewal charge that these programs have benefited business communities while doing little to meet the housing needs of low-income residents (Jacobs, 1961; Greer, 1965; Gans, 1982).

Postindustrial Sunbelt Cities

In the new postindustrial economy (see Chapter 15, "The Economy and Work"), people are not only moving beyond the boundaries of central cities; they are also migrating from the Snowbelt to the Sunbelt. The Snowbelt—the traditional industrial heartland of the United States—runs from the Northeast through the Midwest. In 1940, the Snowbelt was home to almost 60 percent of the U.S. population. By 1975, however, the Sunbelt—the South and the West—passed the Snowbelt in overall population and, by 1995, it was home to almost 60 percent of our people.

Table 21–2 shows this demographic shift by comparing the ten largest U.S. cities in 1950 and in 1992. In 1950, eight of the top ten were industrial cities of the Snowbelt, whereas, by 1992, six out of ten were postindustrial cities of the Sunbelt. The box on page 574 provides a snapshot of how our nation's urban profile has changed in recent decades.

Why are Sunbelt cities growing so quickly? Unlike their counterparts in the Snowbelt, the postindustrial cities of the Sunbelt grew *after* urban decentralization began. Since Snowbelt cities have long been enclosed by a ring of politically independent suburbs, outward migration took place at the expense of the central city. Suburbs have played a much smaller role in the history of Sunbelt cities, which have simply expanded outward, annexing land and gaining population in the process. Chicago, for example, covers 228 square miles, whereas Houston now extends over 556.

The great sprawl of the Sunbelt cities does have drawbacks, however. Most Sunbelt cities have limited mass transit systems, so traveling across town is time consuming and automobile ownership is a virtual necessity. Lacking a dense center, Sunbelt cities also generate far less of the excitement and intensity that draw people to New York or Chicago. Critics have long tagged Los Angeles, for example, as a vast cluster of suburbs in search of a center.

TABLE 21–2 The Ten Largest Cities in the United States, 1950 and 1992

1950

Rank	City	Population
1	New York	7,892,000
2	Chicago	3,621,000
3	Philadelphia	2,072,000
4	Los Angeles	1,970,000
5	Detroit	1,850,000
6	Baltimore	950,000
7	Cleveland	915,000
8	St. Louis	857,000
9	Boston	801,000
10	San Francisco	775,000

1992

Rank	City	Population
1	New York	7,312,000
2	Los Angeles	3,490,000
3	Chicago	2,768,000
4	Houston	1,690,000
5	Philadelphia	1,553,000
6	San Diego	1,149,000
7	Dallas	1,022,000
8	Detroit	1,012,000
9	Phoenix	1,012,000
10	San Antonio	966,000

Source: U.S. Bureau of the Census (1995).

Megalopolis: Regional Cities

The decentralization of U.S. cities has produced vast urban areas that encompass numerous municipalities. In 1993 the Bureau of the Census (1995) recognized 253 regional cities, which it calls *metropolitan statistical areas* (MSAs). Each MSA includes at least one city with 50,000 or more people plus densely populated surrounding counties. Almost all of the fifty fastest-growing MSAs are in the Sunbelt.

The biggest MSAs, containing more than 1 million people, are called *consolidated metropolitan statistical areas* (CMSAs). In 1993, there were eighteen CMSAs. Heading the list was New York and adjacent urban areas in Long Island, western Connecticut, and northern New Jersey, with a total population of 20 million. Next in size was the CMSA in southern California that includes Los Angeles, Riverside, and Anaheim, with a population exceeding 15 million (U.S. Bureau of the Census, 1995).

Some regional cities have grown so large that they have collided with one another. Along the East Coast, a four-hundred-mile supercity now extends from New

SOCIOLOGY OF EVERYDAY LIFE

Heading for the Sunbelt

Just as the twentieth century opened with tremendous urban growth in the North and Midwest, the twenty-first century will witness population increase and rapid urbanization across the South and West. The official tally from the 1990 census indicates that, taken as a whole, Snowbelt cities suffered a moderate population decline, while Sunbelt population is soaring.

The figure in the box shows how the largest Snowbelt and Sunbelt cities fared between 1980 and 1992. While two of the six most populous Snowbelt cities posted slight increases in population, four recorded substantial losses. Each of these six Snowbelt

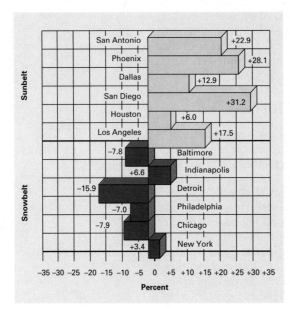

Percent Population Change, 1980–1992
Source: U.S. Bureau of the Census (1995).

cities is now well below its 1950 population peak.

The picture is very different if we turn to the cities of the Sunbelt, where population has grown rapidly since mid-century. All six of the largest Sunbelt cities registeredpopulation gains during the 1980s. The population growth in these Sunbelt cities is dramatic—similar to the explosive increases found in the Snowbelt a century ago.

Which cities—of any size—grew fastest of all during the 1980s? Across the United States, Mesa, Arizona, led the way with a whopping 89 percent gain (to 288,000). Nine other cities had population increases of over 60 percent during that decade—every one of them in the Sunbelt.

England all the way to Virginia. In the early 1960s, French geographer Jean Gottmann (1961) coined the term **megalopolis** to designate *a vast urban region containing a number of cities and their surrounding suburbs.* A megalopolis is composed of hundreds of politically independent cities and suburbs; from an airplane at night, however, one observes what appears to be a single continuous city. Other supercities of this kind sprawl down the eastern coast of Florida and extend from Cleveland west to Chicago. Future megalopolises will undoubtedly emerge, especially in the fast-growing Sunbelt.

URBANISM AS A WAY OF LIFE

Various sociologists in Europe and the United States were among the first to contrast urban and rural life. We will briefly present their accounts of urbanism as a way of life.

Ferdinand Toennies: *Gemeinschaft* and *Gesellschaft*

A century ago, the German sociologist Ferdinand Toennies (1855–1937) set out to chronicle the social characteristics of the new industrial metropolis. He contrasted rural and urban life through two concepts that have become a lasting part of sociology's terminology.

Toennies (1963; orig. 1887) used the German word ***Gemeinschaft*** (meaning roughly "community") to refer to *a type of social organization by which people are bound closely together by kinship and tradition.* Rural villagers, Toennies explained, are joined by kinship, neighborhood, and friendship. *Gemeinschaft,* then, describes any social setting in which people form what amounts to a single primary group.

By and large, argued Toennies, *Gemeinschaft* is not found in the modern city. On the contrary, urbanization fosters ***Gesellschaft*** (a German word meaning roughly "association"), *a type of social organization by*

Q: "Urban life brings physical proximity but social distance among its inhabitants. In rural life, the people are physically far apart but socially together." L. G. Bonald
RESOURCE: The Macionis and Benokraitis reader, *Seeing Ourselves*, includes two urban classics: Georg Simmel's "The Metropolis and Mental Life," and Louis Wirth's "Urbanism As a Way of Life."

Q: "Thus the metropolitan type of man...develops an organ protecting him against the threatening currents and discrepancies of his external environment which would uproot him. He reacts with his head instead of his heart." Georg Simmel
NOTE: Just one-third of U.S. people live in central cities; about 55% live in suburban areas, and the remainder are rural residents.

The painting Peasant Dance *(c.1565), by Pieter Breughel the Elder, conveys the essential unity of rural life forged by generations of kinship and neighborhood. By contrast, Fernand Léger's* The City *(1919) communicates the disparate images and discontinuity of experience that are commonplace in urban areas. Taken together, these paintings capture Toennies's distinction between* Gemeinschaft *and* Gesellschaft.

Pieter Breughel the Elder (c. 1525/30–1569), *Peasant Dance*, c. 1565, Kunsthistorisches Museum, Vienna/Superstock. Fernand Léger, *The City*, 1919, oil on canvas, Philadelphia Museum of Art, A. E. Gallatin Collection.

which people have weak social ties and considerable self-interest. In the *Gesellschaft* scheme, women and men are motivated by their own needs and desires rather than a drive to enhance the well-being of everyone. City dwellers, Toennies suggested, have little sense of community or common identity and look to others mostly as a means of advancing their individual goals. Thus Toennies saw in urbanization the erosion of primary social relations in favor of the temporary, impersonal ties typical of business.

Emile Durkheim: Mechanical and Organic Solidarity

The French sociologist Emile Durkheim, whose ideas are detailed in Chapter 4 ("Society"), agreed with much of Toennies's thinking about cities. Yet Durkheim's analysis highlighted patterns of social solidarity—what binds people together. He conceptualized traditional, rural life as *mechanical solidarity,* social bonds based on shared moral sentiments. With its emphasis on conformity to tradition, this concept bears a striking similarity to Toennies's *Gemeinschaft.*

But if urbanization erodes mechanical solidarity, Durkheim explained, it also generates a new type of bonding, which he termed *organic solidarity*, social bonds based on specialization and interdependence. This concept, which parallels Toennies's *Gesellschaft,*

reveals a key difference between the two thinkers. While each thought the expansion of industry and cities would undermine traditional social patterns, Durkheim took a more optimistic view of this historical transformation. Where societies had been built on *likeness*, Durkheim now observed social organization based on *difference*.

Finally, as noted in Chapter 4, Durkheim did not miss the fact that urban society typically offers more individual choice, moral tolerance, and personal privacy than people find in rural villages. In short, Durkheim concluded, something may be lost in the process of urbanization, but much is gained.

Georg Simmel: The Blasé Urbanite

We previously encountered the ideas of German sociologist Georg Simmel (1858–1918) when we looked at how size affects the social dynamics of small groups (Chapter 7, "Groups and Organizations"). Simmel (1964; orig. 1905) also turned his characteristic micro-level focus to the city, probing how urban life shapes people's attitudes and behavior.

From the point of view of the individual, Simmel explained, the city is a crush of people, objects, and events. Because the urbanite is easily overwhelmed with stimulation, he continued, a *blasé attitude* emerges as a coping strategy. That is, city people learn to respond selectively by tuning out much of what goes on around them. City dwellers are not without sensi-tivity and compassion for others, although they some-times seem "cold and heartless." But urban detachment, as Simmel saw it, is better understood as a technique for social survival by which people stand aloof from most others so they can devote their time and energy to those who really matter.

The Chicago School: Robert Park and Louis Wirth

Sociologists in the United States eagerly joined their European colleagues in exploring the rapidly growing cities. The first major sociology program in the United States took root a century ago at the University of Chicago, then a new metropolis exploding with pop-ulation and cultural diversity. Chicago became the research focus for generations of sociologists, and the work of these men and women yielded a rich understanding of many dimensions of urban life. Although inspired by European theorists like Toen-nies, Durkheim, and Simmel, their unique contribu-tion to U.S. urban sociology was in making the city itself a laboratory for actual research.

Perhaps the greatest urban sociologist of all was Robert Park, who for decades provided the leadership that established sociology in the United States. Park is introduced in the box on page 577.

A second major figure in the Chicago School of urban sociology was Louis Wirth (1897–1952). Wirth's (1938) best-known contribution is a brief essay in which he systematically blended the ideas of Toennies, Durkheim, Simmel, and Park into a comprehensive theory of urban life.

Wirth began by defining the city as a setting with a large, dense, and diverse population. These traits, he argued, combine to form an impersonal, superficial, and transitory way of life. Sharing the teeming streets, urbanites surely come into contact with many more people than rural residents do. But, if city people pay any mind to others, they usually know them only in terms of *what they do*: as bus driver, florist, or grocery store clerk, for instance.

Urban relationships are not only specialized and impersonal, Wirth explained, they are also founded on self-interest. For example, shoppers view grocers as the source of goods, while grocers see shoppers as a source of income. Urban men and women may pleasantly exchange greetings, but friendship is not the reason for their interaction. Finally, limited social involvement coupled with great social diversity also make city

dwellers more tolerant than rural villagers. Rural com-munities often jealously enforce their narrow tradi-tions, but the heterogeneous population of a city rarely shares any single code of moral conduct (T. Wilson, 1985; Wilson, 1995).

Critical evaluation. Both in Europe and in the United States, early sociologists focused on urban life. On balance, this research offers a mixed view of urban living. Toennies and Wirth, especially, worried that the personal ties and traditional morality of rural life are lost in the anonymous rush of the city. On the other hand, Durkheim and Park emphasized urbanism's pos-itive face, including greater personal autonomy and a wider range of life choices.

And what of Wirth's specific claims about urban-ism as a way of life? Decades of research have provided support for only some of his conclusions. Wirth cor-rectly maintained that urban settings do sustain a weaker sense of community than do rural areas. But one can easily forget that conflict is found in the coun-tryside as well as the city. Furthermore, while urban-ites treat most people impersonally, they typically welcome such privacy, and, of course, they do main-tain close personal relationships with a select few (Keller, 1968; Cox, 1971; Macionis, 1978; Wellman, 1979; Lee et al., 1984).

Where the analysis of Wirth and others falls short, too, is in painting urbanism in broad strokes that over-look the effects of class, race, and gender. Herbert Gans (1968) explains that there are many types of urbanites—rich and poor, black and white, Anglo and Latino, women and men—all leading distinctive lives. In fact, cities often intensify these social differences. That is, we see the extent of social diversity most clearly in cities where different categories of people reside in the largest numbers (Spates & Macionis, 1987).

Urban Ecology

Sociologists (especially members of the Chicago School) also developed **urban ecology**, *the study of the link between the physical and social dimensions of cities.* Chapter 22 ("Environment and Society") spotlights cultural ecology, the study of how cultural patterns are related to the physical environment. Urban ecology is one application of this approach, revealing how the physical and social forms of cities influence one another.

Consider, for example, why cities are located where they are. The first cities emerged in fertile regions where the environment favored raising crops and, thus,

	High	Middle	Low
High SES	51.2%	44.7%	4.1%
Middle SES	47.2%	46.1%	6.7%
Low SES	45.9%	45.2%	8.9%
Afri Amer	37.5%	51.2%	11.3%
Latino	41.8%	49.9%	8.3%
Whites	49.4%	44.7%	6.0%

PROFILE

Robert Ezra Park: Walking the City Streets

I suspect that I have actually covered more ground, tramping about in cities in different parts of the world, than any other living man. (1950:viii)

Robert Ezra Park (1864–1944) was a man with a single consuming passion—the city. Walking the streets of the world's great cities, he delighted in observing the full range of human turbulence and triumph. Through his thirty-year career at the University of Chicago, he led a group of dedicated sociologists in direct, systematic observation of urban life.

Park acknowledged his debt to European sociologists including Ferdinand Toennies and Georg Simmel (with whom Park studied in Germany). But Park launched urban sociology in this country by advocating the *direct observation* of the city rather than what amounted to "armchair theorizing" on the part of his European teachers. At Park's urging, generations of sociologists at the University of Chicago rummaged through practically every part of their city.

From this research, Park came to understand the city as a highly ordered mosaic of distinctive regions, including industrial districts, ethnic communities, and vice areas. These so-called "natural areas" all evolved in relation to one another, forming an urban ecology. To Park, the city operates like a living social organism, a true human kaleidoscope. Urban variety, Park maintained, is the key to the timeless attraction of people to cities:

The attraction of the metropolis is due in part to the fact that in the long run every individual finds somewhere among the varied manifestations of city life the sort of environment in which he expands and feels at ease; he finds, in short, the moral climate in which his particular nature obtains the stimulations that bring his innate dispositions to full and free expression. It is, I suspect, motives of this kind . . . which drove many, if not most, of the young men and young women from the security of their homes in the country into the big, booming confusion and excitement of city life. (1967:41; orig. 1925)

Park was well aware that many people saw the city as disorganized and even dangerous. Conceding an element of truth in these assertions, Park still found cities intoxicating. Walking the city streets, he became convinced that urban places offer a better way of life—the promise of greater human freedom and opportunity than we can find elsewhere.

Sources: Based on Park (1967; orig. 1925) and Park (1950).

settlement. Preindustrial societies, concerned with defense, built their cities on mountains (Athens was situated on an outcropping of rock) or surrounded by water (Paris and Mexico City were founded on islands). After the Industrial Revolution, the unparalleled importance of economics led to the founding of cities near rivers and natural harbors that facilitated trade.

Urban ecologists also study the physical design of cities. In 1925 Ernest W. Burgess, a student and colleague of Robert Park, described land use in Chicago in terms of *concentric zones* that look rather like a bull's-eye. City centers, Burgess observed, are business districts bordered by a ring of factories, followed by residential rings with housing that becomes more expensive the farther it stands from the noise and pollution of the city's center.

Homer Hoyt (1939) refined Burgess's observations by noting that distinctive districts sometimes form *wedge-shaped sectors*. For example, one fashionable area may develop next to another, along a major road, or an industrial district may extend outward from a city's center along a railroad line.

Chauncy Harris and Edward Ullman (1945) added yet another insight: As cities decentralize, they lose

Q: This late-medieval poem by Robert Crowley expressed the grow-
ing impersonality of city life:
    "And this is a city,
    In name but in deed
    It is a pack of people
    That seek after meed [profit].
    For officers and all
Do seek their own gain
But for the wealth of the commons
No one taketh pain.
And hell without order
I may it well call
Where every man is for himself
And no man is for all."

The fortunes of cities rise and fall along with economic conditions. By 1975, Atlantic City, long a favorite summer resort for people in New Jersey and neighboring Pennsylvania, had suffered a dramatic decline. Shortly afterward, a new law allowed gambling casinos to open—a strategy that supporters claimed would revitalize the city's economy. A generation later, however, poverty festers in the shadow of glamor. What does this turn of events suggest about the necessary scope of urban renewal programs?

their single-center form in favor of a *multicentered model*. As cities grow, residential areas, industrial parks, and shopping districts typically push away from one another. Few people wish to live close to indus-trial areas, for example, so the city becomes a mosaic of distinct districts.

Social area analysis adds another twist to urban ecology by investigating what people in specific neigh-borhoods have in common. Three factors seem to explain most of the variation—family patterns, social class, and race and ethnicity (Shevky & Bell, 1955; Johnston, 1976). Families with children gravitate to areas offering large apartments or single-family homes and good schools. The rich generally seek high-prestige neighborhoods, often in the central city near many of the city's cultural attractions. People with a common social heritage tend to cluster together in dis-tinctive communities.

Finally, Brian Berry and Philip Rees (1969) have managed to tie together many of these insights. They explain that distinct family types tend to settle in the concentric zones described by Ernest Burgess. Specif-ically, households with few children tend to cluster toward the city's center, while those with more chil-dren live farther away. Social class differences are pri-marily responsible for the sector-shaped districts described by Homer Hoyt as, for instance, the rich occupy one "side of the tracks" and the poor, the other. And racial and ethnic neighborhoods are found

at various points throughout the city, consistent with Harris and Ullman's multicentered model.

Critical evaluation. After almost a century of research, urban ecologists have succeeded in linking the physical and social dimensions of urban life. But, as the researchers themselves concede, their conclu-sions paint an overly simplified picture of urban life. Critics chime in that urban ecology errs to the extent that it implies that cities take shape simply from the choices ordinary people make. Rather, they assert, urban development responds more to powerful elites than to ordinary citizens (Molotch, 1976; Feagin, 1983).

A final criticism holds that urban ecologists have studied only U.S. cities during a single historical period. Little of what we have learned about industrial cities applies to preindustrial towns; similarly, even among industrial cities, socialist settlements differ from their capitalist counterparts. In sum, there is good reason to doubt that any single ecological model will account for the full range of urban diversity.

The Historical Importance of Cities

Cities have stood at the center of human history. Con-sider that the word "civilization" has the Latin root *civis*—meaning "city dweller." Like the ancient Romans, the early Greeks recognized this link; their

RESOURCE: Joe Feagin and Robert Parker take a critical look at the physical and social development of U.S. cities in their article, "The Urban Real Estate Game," included in the Macionis and Benokraitis reader.

GLOBAL: The population density of the United States (1993) is 28 people per square kilometer. The world average is 113. By region:

Africa, 23; Latin America, 28; North America, 13; East Asia, 119; South Central Asia, 123; Europe, 32; Oceania, 3. (United Nations)

GLOBAL: Selected population densities: Macau, 54,286; Hong Kong, 15,671; Taiwan, 1,528; Lebanon, 936; Japan, 861; India, 811; Israel, 705; Haiti, 675; U.K., 628; PRC, 338; Mexico, 127; U.S., 74; Brazil, 48; Canada, 8. (Population Reference Bureau, 1995)

Window on the World

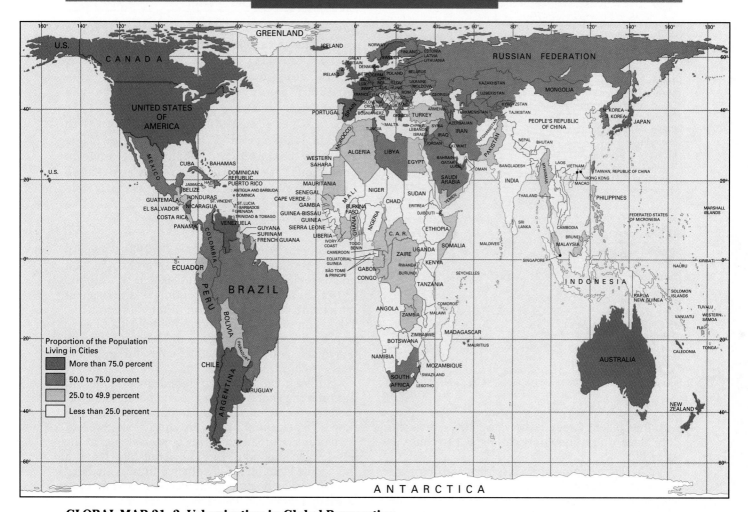

GLOBAL MAP 21–2 Urbanization in Global Perspective

Urbanization is closely linked to economic development. Thus rich nations—including the United States and Canada—have more than three-fourths of their populations in cities, while in the poorest countries of the world—found in Africa and Asia—fewer than one-fourth of the people live in urban centers. Urbanization is now proceeding rapidly in poor countries, however, with emerging "supercities" of unprecedented size.

Source: *Peters Atlas of the World* (1990).

word *polis*—meaning "city"—is the root of politics, the core of Greek life.

But our society has always been ambivalent about urban life. As he assumed the presidency in 1800, Thomas Jefferson repudiated the city as a "pestilence to the morals, the health and the liberties of man"

(quoted in Glaab, 1963:52). Almost a century later, English author and Nobel prize winner Rudyard Kipling echoed those sentiments after a visit to Chicago: "Having seen it, I urgently desire never to see it again. It is inhabited by savages" (quoted in Rokove, 1975:22). Others have disagreed, of course, siding

Chapter 21 Population and Urbanization   **579**

more people; by 2000, projections place 170 cities over this mark.
GLOBAL: One consequence of the extremely rapid growth of Mexican cities is a desire to emigrate to the United States. In response to a recent *Los Angeles Times* survey, 22% of Mexicans in 42 urban centers in Mexico claimed that it was "very likely" or "fairly likely" that they would be living in the United States within one year.

TABLE 21–3 The World's Ten Largest Urban Areas, 1980 and 2000

1980

Urban Area	Population (in millions)
New York, U.S.A.	16.5
Tokyo-Yokohama, Japan	14.4
Mexico City, Mexico	14.0
Los Angeles-Long Beach, U.S.A.	10.6
Shanghai, China	10.0
Buenos Aires, Argentina	9.7
Paris, France	8.5
Moscow, U.S.S.R.	8.0
Beijing, China	8.0
Chicago, U.S.A.	7.7

2000 (projected)

Urban Area	Population (in millions)
Tokyo-Yokohama, Japan	30.0
Mexico City, Mexico	27.9
São Paulo, Brazil	25.4
Seoul, South Korea	22.0
Bombay, India	15.4
New York, U.S.A.	14.7
Osaka-Kobe-Kyoto, Japan	14.3
Tehran, Iran	14.3
Rio de Janeiro, Brazil	14.2
Calcutta, India	14.1

Sources: United Nations (1995) and U.S. Bureau of the Census (1995).

with the ancient Greeks, who viewed the city as the only place where humanity can expect to find the "good life."

Why do cities provoke such spirited and divergent reactions? The answer lies in their ability to encapsulate and intensify human culture. Cities have been the setting for some of the greatest human virtues (the cultural developments of classical Athens) as well as the greatest human failings (the militarism and violence of classical Rome or Nazi Berlin).

For more than 350 years, the United States has steadily urbanized as people have sought a better way of life. Yet, despite the greater economic opportunity that cities afford, many social problems—poverty, crime, racial tensions, environmental pollution—are most serious there.

In short, the city is an intricate weave of noble accomplishments, attractive opportunities, and wretched shortcomings. As we shall see in the concluding sections of this chapter, the greatest test of the city—to raise living standards—is now under way in low-income nations.

URBANIZATION IN POOR SOCIETIES

November 16, 1988, Cairo, Egypt. People call the vast Muslim cemetery in Old Cairo "The City of the Dead." In truth, it is very much alive: Tens of thousands of squatters have moved into the mausoleums, making this place an eerie mix of life and death. Children run across the stone floors, clotheslines stretch between the monuments, and an occasional television antenna protrudes from a tomb roof. In a city gaining one thousand people a day, families live where they can . . .

Twice in human history the world has experienced a revolutionary expansion of cities. The first urban revolution began around 8000 B.C.E. with the first urban settlements, and continued as permanent settlements later appeared on different continents. The second urban revolution took hold about 1750 and lasted for two centuries as the Industrial Revolution touched off rapid growth of cities in Europe and North America.

A third urban revolution started around 1950, but this time the change is taking place not in industrial societies where, as Global Map 21–2 on page 579 shows, 75 percent of people are already city dwellers. Extraordinary urban growth is now occurring in the less-developed nations. In 1950, about 25 percent of the people living in low-income countries inhabited cities; by 1995, the proportion had risen to 42 percent; in another decade, it will exceed 50 percent.

Moreover, in 1950 just seven cities in the world had populations over 5 million, and only two of these were in low-income countries. By 1995, thirty-seven cities had passed this mark, and twenty-five of them were in poor nations.

Table 21–3 looks back to 1980 and ahead to 2000, comparing the size of the world's ten largest urban areas (cities and surrounding suburbs). In 1980, six of the top ten were in industrialized societies, including three in the United States. By the beginning of the next century, however, only four of the ten will be situated in industrialized nations: two in Japan, one in South Korea, and just one in the United States. The majority will be in less economically developed societies.

Not only will these exploding urban areas be the world's largest, they will encompass unprecedented

Every year, some 90 million people are added to the Earth's population. Do you think this rate of growth can be sustained? What are the likely consequences of continuing population increase for the future of our planet?

populations. Relatively rich countries such as Japan may have the resources to provide for cities with upwards of 30 million people, but for poor nations, such as Mexico and Brazil, such supercities will tax resources that are already severely strained.

To understand the third urban revolution, recall that many poor societies are now entering the high-growth stage of demographic transition. Falling death rates continue to fuel population growth in Latin America, Asia, and, especially, Africa. For urban areas, the rate of population increase is *twice* as high because, in addition to natural increase, millions of migrants leave the countryside each year in search of jobs, health care, education, and conveniences like running water and electricity.

Cities do offer more opportunities than rural areas, but they provide no quick fix for the massive problems of escalating population and grinding poverty. Many burgeoning cities in less-developed societies—including Mexico City, described at the beginning of this chapter—are simply unable to meet the basic needs of much of their population. Thousands of rural people stream into Mexico City every day, even though more than 10 percent of the *current* 25 million residents have no running water in their homes, 15 percent lack sewerage facilities, and the city can process only half the trash and garbage produced now. To make matters worse, exhaust from factories and cars chokes everyone, rich and poor alike (Friedrich, 1984; Gorman, 1991).

Like other major cities throughout Latin America, Africa, and Asia, Mexico City is surrounded by wretched shantytowns—settlements of makeshift homes built from discarded materials. As explained in Chapter 11 ("Global Stratification"), even city dumps are home to thousands of poor people, who pick through the waste hoping to find enough to ensure their survival for another day.

LOOKING AHEAD: POPULATION AND URBANIZATION IN THE TWENTY-FIRST CENTURY

The demographic analysis presented in this chapter points to some disturbing trends. We see, first of all, that the earth is gaining unprecedented population because of two parallel shifts: Death rates are dropping even as birth rates remain high in much of the world. The numbers lead us to the sobering conclusion—the focus of the final box—that controlling global population in the next century will be a monumental task.

As we have seen, population growth is currently greatest in the least economically developed countries of the world, those that lack productive capacity to

Q: "Over the last century, population predictions have been renamed population projections out of consideration for the reputations of people making the forecasts." Nicholas Eberstadt (1995)
NOTE: The neo-Malthusians fall within the environmental movement, arguing that growth is a social danger. The anti-Malthusians tend to be economists who follow Adam Smith in viewing growth as good.

Q: "Ten thousand generations to reach 2 billion and then in one human lifetime—ours—we leap from 2 billion toward 10 billion." Vice President Al Gore

Q: "Earth is overpopulated today by a very simple standard: Humanity is able to support itself—often none too well, at that— only by consuming its capital." Paul and Anne Ehrlich

Controversy & Debate

Apocalypse Soon?
Will People Overwhelm the Earth?

Are you worried about the world's increasing population? Think about this: By the time you finish reading this box, the number of people on the planet will rise by more than a thousand. By this time tomorrow, 250,000 more will have been added. As the table below shows, there are about six births for every death on the planet, so that the world's population is marching upward by 90 million annually. Put another way, global population growth amounts to adding another Mexico to the world every year.

fertilizers and plant genetics) could boost the planet's agricultural output. But he maintains that the earth's burgeoning population is rapidly outstripping a host of finite resources. Families in many poor countries can find little firewood; members of rich societies are depleting oil reserves; everyone is draining our reserves of clean water.

Just as important, according to the neo-Malthusians, humanity is steadily poisoning the planet with waste. There is a limit to the earth's capacity to absorb pollution, they warn, and as

spread thinner and thinner as population increases. Rather, the anti-Malthusians counter, people have the capacity to improve their lives. We have yet to determine how many people the earth can support because humans are constantly rewriting the rules, in effect, by deploying new fertilizers, developing new high-yield crops, discovering new forms of energy. Simon points out that today's global economy makes available more resources and products than ever (including energy and a host of consumer goods), and at increasingly low prices. He looks optimistically toward the future, noting that technology, economic investment, and, above all, human ingenuity, have consistently proven the doomsayers wrong. And he is betting they will continue to do so.

Global Population Increase

	Births	Deaths	Net Increase
Year	141,000,000	51,000,000	90,000,000
Month	11,750,000	4,250,000	7,500,000
Day	391,000	141,000	250,000
Hour	16,300	5,875	10,425
Minute	270	98	172
Second	4.5	1.6	2.9

It is no wonder that many population analysts are deeply concerned about the future. The earth has an unprecedented population: Just the 1.6 billion people we have *added* since 1975 exceeds the planet's total in 1900. Might Thomas Robert Malthus—who predicted that population would outstrip the earth's resources and plunge humanity into war and suffering—be right after all?

Lester Brown, a population and environmental activist, represents the *neo-Malthusians* who foresee a coming apocalypse—if we do nothing to change our ways. Brown concedes that Malthus failed to imagine how much technology (especially

the number of people continues to increase, our quality of life inevitably will decline.

But another camp of analysts sharply disagrees. Representing the *anti-Malthusians*, Julian Simon questions "Why the doom and gloom?" Two centuries ago, Simon points out, Malthus predicted global catastrophe. Today, however, there are almost six times as many people on the Earth and, on average, they live longer, healthier lives than ever before. As Simon sees it, the current state of the planet is cause for great celebration.

Simon argues that the neo-Malthusians err in assuming that the world has finite resources that are

Continue the debate . . .

1. *Where do you place your bet? Do you think the earth can support 10 or 12 billion people? Why or why not?*

2. *What are some likely consequences of the fact that almost 90 percent of current population growth is occurring in poor countries?*

3. *Does the world population problem only affect people in low-income countries? What must people in rich societies do to ensure our children's future?*

Sources: Based, in part, on Brown et al. (1993, 1995) and Simon (1994).

GLOBAL: Two-thirds of Mexicans living in cities have at least one child at home; the comparable U.S. figure is 40%.

Q: "In the course of my own lifetime, the earth's population has increased two and a half times, and most of this increase is now to be found in the exploding urban centers, especially in the slums and shantytowns, of Africa, Asia, and Latin America." Isaac Asimov

GLOBAL: Population growth in poor countries has been so rapid in recent decades that roughly 10% of human beings who have ever lived are alive now.

Q: "Children are poor men's riches." Old proverb

Q: "Hell is a city much like London; a populous and smoky city." Percy Bysshe Shelley

Every year, some 90 million people are added to the Earth's population. Do you think this rate of growth can be sustained? What are the likely consequences of continuing population increase for the future of our planet?

populations. Relatively rich countries such as Japan may have the resources to provide for cities with upwards of 30 million people, but for poor nations, such as Mexico and Brazil, such supercities will tax resources that are already severely strained.

To understand the third urban revolution, recall that many poor societies are now entering the high-growth stage of demographic transition. Falling death rates continue to fuel population growth in Latin America, Asia, and, especially, Africa. For urban areas, the rate of population increase is *twice* as high because, in addition to natural increase, millions of migrants leave the countryside each year in search of jobs, health care, education, and conveniences like running water and electricity.

Cities do offer more opportunities than rural areas, but they provide no quick fix for the massive problems of escalating population and grinding poverty. Many burgeoning cities in less-developed societies—including Mexico City, described at the beginning of this chapter—are simply unable to meet the basic needs of much of their population. Thousands of rural people stream into Mexico City every day, even though more than 10 percent of the *current* 25 million residents have no running water in their homes, 15 percent lack sewerage facilities, and the city can process only half the trash and garbage produced now. To make matters worse, exhaust from factories and cars chokes everyone, rich and poor alike (Friedrich, 1984; Gorman, 1991).

Like other major cities throughout Latin America, Africa, and Asia, Mexico City is surrounded by wretched shantytowns—settlements of makeshift homes built from discarded materials. As explained in Chapter 11 ("Global Stratification"), even city dumps are home to thousands of poor people, who pick through the waste hoping to find enough to ensure their survival for another day.

LOOKING AHEAD: POPULATION AND URBANIZATION IN THE TWENTY-FIRST CENTURY

The demographic analysis presented in this chapter points to some disturbing trends. We see, first of all, that the earth is gaining unprecedented population because of two parallel shifts: Death rates are dropping even as birth rates remain high in much of the world. The numbers lead us to the sobering conclusion—the focus of the final box—that controlling global population in the next century will be a monumental task.

As we have seen, population growth is currently greatest in the least economically developed countries of the world, those that lack productive capacity to

Controversy & Debate

Apocalypse Soon? Will People Overwhelm the Earth?

Are you worried about the world's increasing population? Think about this: By the time you finish reading this box, the number of people on the planet will rise by more than a thousand. By this time tomorrow, 250,000 more will have been added. As the table below shows, there are about six births for every death on the planet, so that the world's population is marching upward by 90 million annually. Put another way, global population growth amounts to adding another Mexico to the world every year.

fertilizers and plant genetics) could boost the planet's agricultural output. But he maintains that the earth's burgeoning population is rapidly outstripping a host of finite resources. Families in many poor countries can find little firewood; members of rich societies are depleting oil reserves; everyone is draining our reserves of clean water.

Just as important, according to the neo-Malthusians, humanity is steadily poisoning the planet with waste. There is a limit to the earth's capacity to absorb pollution, they warn, and as

spread thinner and thinner as population increases. Rather, the anti-Malthusians counter, people have the capacity to improve their lives. We have yet to determine how many people the earth can support because humans are constantly rewriting the rules, in effect, by deploying new fertilizers, developing new high-yield crops, discovering new forms of energy. Simon points out that today's global economy makes available more resources and products than ever (including energy and a host of consumer goods), and at increasingly low prices. He looks optimistically toward the future, noting that technology, economic investment, and, above all, human ingenuity, have consistently proven the doomsayers wrong. And he is betting they will continue to do so.

Global Population Increase

	Births	Deaths	Net Increase
Year	141,000,000	51,000,000	90,000,000
Month	11,750,000	4,250,000	7,500,000
Day	391,000	141,000	250,000
Hour	16,300	5,875	10,425
Minute	270	98	172
Second	4.5	1.6	2.9

It is no wonder that many population analysts are deeply concerned about the future. The earth has an unprecedented population: Just the 1.6 billion people we have *added* since 1975 exceeds the planet's total in 1900. Might Thomas Robert Malthus—who predicted that population would outstrip the earth's resources and plunge humanity into war and suffering—be right after all?

Lester Brown, a population and environmental activist, represents the *neo-Malthusians* who foresee a coming apocalypse—if we do nothing to change our ways. Brown concedes that Malthus failed to imagine how much technology (especially

the number of people continues to increase, our quality of life inevitably will decline.

But another camp of analysts sharply disagrees. Representing the *anti-Malthusians*, Julian Simon questions "Why the doom and gloom?" Two centuries ago, Simon points out, Malthus predicted global catastrophe. Today, however, there are almost six times as many people on the Earth and, on average, they live longer, healthier lives than ever before. As Simon sees it, the current state of the planet is cause for great celebration.

Simon argues that the neo-Malthusians err in assuming that the world has finite resources that are

Continue the debate . . .

1. Where do you place your bet? Do you think the earth can support 10 or 12 billion people? Why or why not?

2. What are some likely consequences of the fact that almost 90 percent of current population growth is occurring in poor countries?

3. Does the world population problem only affect people in low-income countries? What must people in rich societies do to ensure our children's future?

Sources: Based, in part, on Brown et al. (1993, 1995) and Simon (1994).

Q: "I'm too dumb for New York City and too ugly for L.A." Waylon Jennings

Q: "A neighborhood is where, when you go out of it, you get beat up." Murray Kempton

Q: "In a genuine community, the antithesis of living for oneself and living for others, selfishness and altruism, is transcended. The self and the others are incorporated in a venture that serves at once as the ground of their self-fulfillment and the focus of their duties . . . all live in a community which is *theirs*." Lawrence Hayworth

Q: "We must restore to the city the maternal, life-nurturing functions, the autonomous activities, the symbiotic associations that have been neglected or suppressed. For the city should be an organ of love . . ." Lewis Mumford (1961:575)

support their present populations, much less their future ones. Most of the privileged inhabitants of high-income nations are spared the trauma of poverty. But supporting about 90 million additional people on our planet each year—80 million of these added to poor societies—will require a global commitment to provide not only food but housing, schools, and employment. The well-being of the entire world may ultimately depend on resolving many of the economic and social problems of poor, overly populated countries and bridging the widening gulf between the "have" and "have-not" societies.

Great concentrations of people have always had the power to intensify the triumphs and tragedies of human existence. Thus the world's demographic, environmental, and social problems are most pronounced in cities, especially in poor nations. In Mexico City, São Paulo (Brazil), Kinshasa (Zaire), Bombay (India), and Manila (the Philippines), urban problems now seem to defy solution, and the end of remarkable urban growth in the world's low-income countries is nowhere in sight.

Earlier chapters point up two different answers to this problem. One view, linked with modernization theory, holds that as poor societies industrialize (as Western Europe and North America did a century ago), greater productivity will simultaneously raise living standards and this, in turn, will reduce population growth. A second view, associated with dependency theory, argues that such progress is unlikely as long as poor societies remain economically dependent on rich ones.

Throughout history, the city has improved people's living standards more than any other type of settlement. The question facing humanity now is whether cities in poor countries will be able to meet the needs of vastly larger populations in the coming century. The answer—which rests on issues of international relations, global economic ties, and simple justice—will affect us all.

SUMMARY

1. Fertility and mortality, measured as crude birth rates and crude death rates, are major components of population growth. In global terms, U.S. population growth is low.

2. Migration, another key demographic concept, has special importance to the historical growth of the United States and to cities everywhere.

3. Demographers use age-sex pyramids to graphically represent the composition of a population and to project population trends. The sex ratio refers to a society's balance of females and males.

4. Historically, world population grew slowly because high birth rates were largely offset by high death rates. About 1750, a demographic transition began as world population rose sharply, mostly due to falling death rates.

5. Thomas Robert Malthus warned that population growth would outpace food production, resulting in social calamity. Others challenge Malthus's ominous predictions, pointing to demographic transition theory's contention that technological advances gradually prompt a drop in birth rates.

6. Research shows that lower birth rates and improved economic productivity in poor societies both result from improving the social position of women.

7. World population is expected to reach 8 billion by the year 2025. Such an increase will likely overwhelm many poor societies, where most of the increase will take place.

8. Closely related to population growth is urbanization. The first urban revolution began with the appearance of cities some 10,000 years ago; by the start of the Common Era, cities had emerged in most regions of the world except for North America.

9. Urbanization parallels a dramatic increase in the division of labor, as people assume a wide range of highly specialized, productive roles in society.

10. Preindustrial cities are characterized by low-rise buildings; narrow, winding streets; and personal social ties.

11. A second urban revolution began about 1750 as the Industrial Revolution propelled rapid urban growth in Europe. This brought about a change in the physical form of cities: Planners created wide, regular streets to facilitate trade. Their emphasis on commercial life and the increasing size of urban areas rendered city life more anonymous.

12. Urbanism came to North America with European settlers. A string of colonial towns dotting the

Atlantic coastline gave way by 1850 to hundreds of new cities from coast to coast.

13. By 1920, a majority of the U.S. population lived in urban settings, and the largest metropolises encompassed millions of inhabitants.

14. Since 1950, U.S. cities have decentralized. The growth of suburbs is one trait of the postindustrial society. Newer, rapidly growing Sunbelt cities are geographically larger than older, Snowbelt cities.

15. Rapid urbanization in Europe during the nineteenth centruy led early sociologists to contrast rural and urban life. Ferdinand Toennies built his analysis around *Gemeinshaft* and *Gesellschaft*. Emile Durkheim's concepts of mechanical solidarity and organic solidarity closely parallel those of Toennies. Georg Simmel claimed that the overstimulation of city life produced a blasé attitude in urbanites.

16. At the University of Chicago, Robert Park hailed cities for permitting greater social freedom. Louis Wirth reasoned that large, dense, heterogeneous populations generated a way of life characterized by impersonality, self-interest, and tolerance of people's differences. Urban ecology studies the interplay of social and physical dimensions of the city.

17. A third urban revolution is now occurring in poor societies of the world, where most of the world's largest cities will soon be found.

KEY CONCEPTS

age-sex pyramid a graphic representation of the age and sex of a population

crude birth rate the number of live births in a given year for every thousand people in a population

crude death rate the number of deaths in a given year for every thousand people in a population

demographic transition theory a thesis linking population patterns to a society's level of technological development

demography the study of human population

fertility the incidence of childbearing in a country's population

Gemeinschaft Toennies's term for a type of social organization by which people are bound closely together by kinship and tradition

Gesellschaft Toennies's designation of a type of social organization by which people have weak social ties and considerable self-interest

infant mortality rate the number of deaths among infants under one year of age for each thousand live births in a given year

life expectancy the average life span of a society's population

megalopolis a vast urban region containing a number of cities and their surrounding suburbs

metropolis a large city that socially and economically dominates an urban area

migration the movement of people into and out of a specified territory

mortality the incidence of death in a country's population

sex ratio the number of males for every hundred females in a given population

suburbs urban areas beyond the political boundaries of a city

urban ecology the study of the link between the physical and social dimensions of cities

urbanization the concentration of humanity into cities

zero population growth the level of reproduction that maintains population at a steady state

CRITICAL-THINKING QUESTIONS

1. Explain the meaning of fertility and mortality rates. Change in which of these two has been of greater importance in increasing global population? Why?

2. How does demographic transition theory link population patterns to technological development?

3. Over the course of history, how have economic and technological changes transformed the physical shape of cities?

4. According to Ferdinand Toennies, Emile Durkheim, Georg Simmel, and Louis Wirth, what characterizes urbanism as a way of life? Note several differences in the ideas of these thinkers.

SUGGESTED READINGS

Classic Sources

Paul R. Ehrlich. *The Population Bomb*. New York: Ballantine Books, 1968.
   This brief book, its reputation tarnished by some predictions that did not come to pass, nevertheless was crucial in igniting the contemporary debate over increasing global population.

Ferdinand Toennies. *Community and Society (Gemeinschaft und Gesellschaft)*. New York: Harper & Row, 1963; orig. 1887.
   This classic comparison of rural and urban social organization—widely cited but rarely read—introduced many of the themes that have shaped urban sociology ever since.

Contemporary Sources

Anthony Downs. *New Visions for Metropolitan America*. Washington, D.C.: Brookings Institute, 1994.
   This analysis examines the core cultural and political values that underlie U.S. cities and urges us to rethink our current ideas about how cities should work.

Stephanie Golden. *The Women Outside: Meaning and Myths of Homelessness*. Berkeley: University of California Press, 1992.
   The author argues that our understanding of the urban problem of homelessness—especially when it involves women—is distorted by a pejorative cultural mythology about the poor.

Global Sources

Belgin Tekçe, Linda Oldham, and Frederic Shorter. *A Place to Live: Families and Health Care in a Cairo Neighborhood*. Cairo, Egypt: American University in Cairo, 1994.
   This study of an "unofficial" settlement of more than 60,000 immigrants to Cairo conveys the challenge of regulating urban growth in a poor country.

David Hakken with Barbara Andrews. *Computing Myths, Class Realities: An Ethnography of Technology and Working People in Sheffield, England*. Boulder, Colo: Westview Press, 1993.
   This community study examines changes within an English manufacturing city during a time of economic decline.

ANATOLY SHDANOW,
WARNING, 1991

Anatoly Shdanow/UNEP.

Environment and Society

The tiny island of Nauru (pronounced NAH-roo) is the world's smallest and most isolated country. Just eight square miles of windswept sand and coral reef, Nauru lies in the South Pacific, roughly 1,700 miles northeast of Australia and hundreds of miles from its nearest neighbor.

Another notable fact is that Nauru's 7,500 people are among the richest on earth. Do they own oil wells? No, their wealth comes from bird droppings. Over hundreds of thousands of years, the excrement from sea birds roosting here has fossilized into a rich phosphate fertilizer. In 1907, German colonists began mining the phosphate, an industry the Australians continued after they took control of the island in 1917. In 1968, Nauru became independent, so that the mining revenues went to the local people, who control a trust fund valued at almost $1 billion.

But all is not well on Nauru. Ninety percent of the island has now been strip-mined. This gives the island yet another distinction—as the most environmentally ravaged place on earth. Its once lush vegetation is all but gone, and in its place lies an eerie moonscape of bare rock canyons. The people, whose easy income from phosphate led them to abandon farming decades ago, now import their food—mostly high-fat canned meats enjoyed with potato chips and beer. As a result, most Nauruans are overweight, suffering from diabetes and high blood pressure. Today, few live past the age of sixty.

Most now realize that their island is no longer habitable. The Nauruans may have money in the bank, but they have lost their way of life and now face the grim reality of abandoning their ancestral home (Shenon, 1995).

Nauru may seem too far removed from our lives to have much meaning. But the tragic course of events that turned this one-time island paradise into an ugly and desolate wasteland is instructive for people everywhere. As one analyst concluded, humanity's remaking of the earth during the last two centuries exceeds changes to our planet from all causes over the last billion years (Milbrath, 1989).

Certainly, many of these changes have benefited humanity. Especially in rich nations, most people enjoy a level of material comfort that our ancestors scarcely could have imagined. However, as the Nauruans have learned, such achievements carry both costs and risks. As this chapter explains, the way of life that has evolved in rich societies places such great strain on the earth's natural environment that it threatens the future of the entire planet. And, at least for the present, this planet is the only home we have.

ECOLOGY: THE STUDY OF THE NATURAL ENVIRONMENT

This chapter draws on **ecology,** *the study of the interaction of living organisms and the natural environment.* Ecology rests on the contributions of researchers in many disciplines, from natural scientists (such as biologists, chemists, and geologists) to social scientists, including sociologists. Here we limit our focus to those aspects of ecology that have a direct connection to concepts and issues already covered in this book.

The concept of the **natural environment** refers to *the earth's surface and atmosphere, including various living organisms as well as the air, water, soil, and other resources necessary to sustain life.* Like every other living species, humans are dependent on the natural environment for everything from basic food, clothing, and shelter to the

DIVERSITY: The concept of "environment" is a cultural construction, varying with ethnicity. Barbara Deutch Lynch

Q: "I am pessimistic about the human race because it is too ingenious for its own good. Our approach to nature is to beat it into submission. We would stand a better chance of survival if we accommodated ourselves to this planet and viewed it appreciatively instead of skeptically and dictatorially." E. B. White

SOCIAL SURVEY: "It is just too difficult for someone like me to do much about the environment." (GSS 1994, N = 1,386; *Codebook*, 1994:645)

"Strongly agree" 4.5%   "Disagree" 45.4%
"Agree" 21.3%   "Strongly disagree" 7.9%
"Neither agree nor disagree" 16.7%   DK/NR 4.2%

materials and advanced sources of energy needed to construct and operate our automobiles, airplanes, and all kinds of electronic devices. Yet humans stand apart from other species of life in our capacity for culture; we alone take deliberate action to remake the world according to our own interests and desires. Thus our species is unique in its capacity to transform the world, for better and worse.

The Role of Sociology

One might wonder what many of the topics found in this chapter—including solid waste, pollution, acid rain, global warming, and biodiversity—are doing in a sociology text. Yet, as Leo Marx (1994) points out, none of these problems is a product of the "natural world" operating on its own. On the contrary, as we shall explain, each results from the specific actions of human beings and are, therefore, *social* issues.

Of course, there are limits to the role sociologists can play in exploring ecological matters. Unless they have technical training in the natural sciences, sociologists will have as much trouble as most other people in assessing the scientific evidence as to whether, say, global warming is actually happening or not or, if it is, whether it will cause rainfall to go up or down. But sociologists can make two vital contributions to ecological debates. First, sociologists can explore what "the environment" means to people of varying social backgrounds. Notions of "wild rivers" or "the frontier" have high emotional significance to people in the western United States, for example, while "gardens" and "the sea" take on special significance to Caribbean Latinos (Lynch, 1993).

Second, sociologists can monitor the public pulse on many environmental issues, reporting people's thoughts and fears (whether grounded or not) about these controversies. Moreover, sociologists analyze why certain categories of people fall on one side of an environmental issue or another (Roberts, 1993).

Third, and perhaps most important, sociologists can demonstrate how human social patterns have caused mounting stress on the natural environment. That is, sociologists can spotlight how environmental problems are linked to particular cultural values, as well as specific political and economic arrangements (Cylke, 1993, 1995).

The Global Dimension

Any comprehensive study of the natural environment must also be global in scope. Regardless of humanity's

political divisions into nation-states, the planet constitutes a single **ecosystem**, defined as *the system composed of the interaction of all living organisms and their natural environment.*

The Greek meaning of *eco* is "house," which reminds us of the simple fact that our planet is our home. Even a brief look at the operation of the global ecosystem confirms that all living things and their natural environment are *interrelated*. Changes to any part of the natural environment ripple through the entire ecosystem, so that what happens in one part of the world inevitably has consequences in another.

To illustrate, consider the effects of our use of chlorofluorocarbons (CFCs, which were marketed under the brand name "Freon") as a propellant in aerosol spray cans and as a gas in refrigerators, freezers, and air conditioners. There is little doubt that CFCs improved our lives in various ways. But as CFCs were released into the air, they accumulated in the upper atmosphere, where, reacting with sunlight, they formed chlorine atoms. These, in turn, destroyed ozone. The ozone layer in the atmosphere serves to limit the amount of harmful ultraviolet radiation reaching the earth from the sun. Thus, recent evidence of a "hole" in the ozone layer (in the atmosphere over Antarctica) may signal a rise in human skin cancers and countless other effects to plants and animals (Clarke, 1984a). In response to the dangers of ozone depletion, the United States and a number of other nations began in the early 1980s to restrict the use of CFCs, and, by 1996, they were all but phased out of use in favor of safer alternatives.

But, given the complexity of the global ecosystem, many threats to the environment go unrecognized. Few Australians who purchased fertilizer for their gardens gave any thought to how they were contributing to the destruction of the island of Nauru, described in the chapter opening. Similarly, as the box explains, the popular, although seemingly innocent, act of eating fast-food hamburgers has significant environmental effects in other parts of the world.

The Historical Dimension

How did humanity gain the power to threaten the natural environment? The most basic part of the answer lies in our capacity for culture, that is, to cultivate the earth. As humans have devised more powerful forms of *technology*—defined in Chapter 3 ("Culture") as knowledge that a society applies to the task of living in its natural surroundings—humans have gained the ability to make and remake the world as we choose.

Q: "The 'control of nature' is a phrase conceived in arrogance, born of the Neanderthal age of biology and philosophy, when it was supposed that nature exists for the convenience of man." Rachel Carson (1962):297

GLOBAL: Even as Costa Rican beef production shot upward after 1960, the per capita consumption of beef in that country fell slightly. This is an example of how making products for export ignores the needs of the local people.

GLOBAL: The global connections that affect ecology are also evident in the case of Nauru (see chapter opening): Australians buying fertilizer, the fertilizer company's investors, and even the Nauruans themselves all participated in the ecological destruction of that island.

GLOBAL SOCIOLOGY

The Global Ecosystem:
The Environmental Consequences of Everyday Choices

People living in high-income nations such as the United States have the greatest power to affect the earth's ecosystem for the simple reason that we consume so much of the planet's resources. Thus, our small, everyday decisions about how we live can add up to large consequences for the planet as a whole.

Consider the commonplace practice of enjoying the all-American hamburger. McDonald's and dozens of other fast-food chains serve billions of hamburgers each year to eager customers across North America, Europe, and Japan. This appetite for beef creates a large market for cattle, which has greatly expanded cattle ranching in Latin America. As our consumption of hamburgers has grown (even as the price of beef has steadily gone up), ranchers in Brazil, Costa Rica, and other Latin American countries are devoting more and more land to cattle grazing.

Latin American cattle graze on grass (rather than being grain fed, as is the practice in this country). This diet produces the lean meat demanded by the fast-food corporations, but it also requires that a great deal of land be dedicated to grazing.

Where is the land to come from? Ranchers in Latin America are solving their land problem by clearing forests at the rate of thousands of square miles each year. These tropical forests, as we shall explain presently, are vital to maintaining the earth's atmosphere. Therefore, forest destruction threatens the well-being of everyone—even the people back in the United States who

enjoy hamburgers without giving a thought to the environment.

Enhancing global consciousness is thus a vital dimension of increasing environmental awareness. Ecologically speaking, our choices and actions ripple throughout the world, even though most of us never realize it. People in the United States are simply looking for a quick hamburger. Fast-food companies are making a profit by serving meals that people want. Ranchers are trying to earn a living by raising beef cattle. No one intends to harm the planet but, taken together, these actions can have serious consequences for everyone.

All people on this planet inhabit a single ecosystem. In a world of countless environmental connections, we need to think critically about the effects of choices we make every day—like what's for lunch!

Source: Based on Myers (1984a).

Members of societies with simple technology—the hunters and gatherers described in Chapter 4 ("Society")—have scarcely any ability to affect the environment, whether they want to or not. On the contrary, the members of such societies are immediately and directly dependent on nature, so that their lives are guided by the migration of game and the rhythm of the seasons. They remain especially vulnerable to natural events, such as fires, floods, droughts, and storms.

Societies at intermediate stages of sociocultural evolution have a somewhat greater capacity to shape the environment. But the environmental impact of horticulture (small-scale farming), pastoralism (the herding of animals), and even agriculture (the use of animal-drawn plows) is limited by the reliance on muscle power for production of food and other goods.

Dramatic change in humans' relationship with the natural environment takes place with the development of industrial technology. Industry replaces muscle power with combustion engines that burn fossil fuels: coal, at first, and then oil. Such machinery affects the environment in two ways—by consuming natural resources and by releasing pollutants into the atmosphere. But, even more important, humans armed with industrial technology become able to bend nature to

DISCUSS: A widespread view is that only "modern" people are concerned about the environment. What do students think? The conventional view that environmental concerns rise along with affluence is challenged by Brechin & Kempton (1994), who argue that "folk societies" are typically environmentally aware.

GLOBAL: More than 90% of nuclear power facilities are in rich nations. The costs and complex technology that have made these

systems controversial there also render them unsuitable for poor societies.

GLOBAL: Poor nations are increasing their consumption of energy rapidly (use has almost tripled since 1970), while in rich nations the use has risen a more modest 20% over the same period.

GLOBAL: The U.S. uses twice the per capita energy that European societies do.

Window on the World

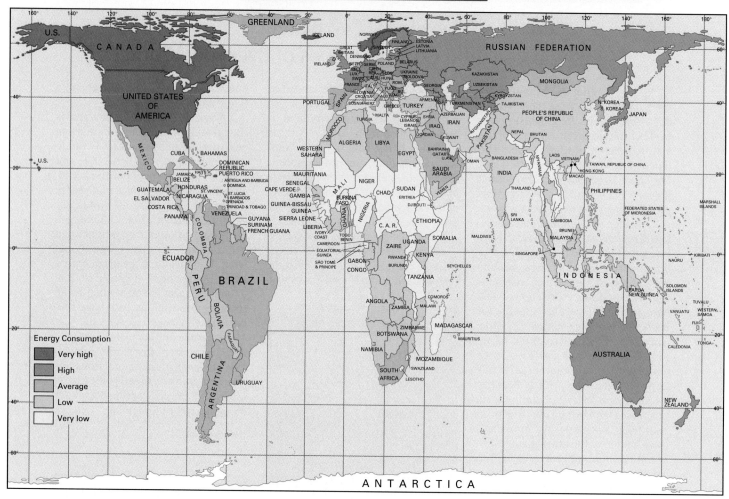

GLOBAL MAP 22–1 Energy Consumption in Global Perspective

The members of industrial societies consume far more energy than others on the planet. The typical U.S. resident uses the same amount of energy in a year as one hundred people in the Central African Republic. This means that the most economically productive societies are also those that place the greatest burden on the natural environment.

Source: *Peters Atlas of the World* (1990).

their will far more than ever before, tunneling through mountains, damming rivers, irrigating deserts, and drilling for oil on the ocean floor.

Global Map 22–1 shows where in the world energy use is highest. The general pattern is clear: It is high-income, industrial societies that place the greatest demands on on the planet's ecosystem. In fact, the

typical adult in the United States consumes one hundred times more energy annually than the average member of the world's poorest societies. Put another way, while the U.S. population accounts for less than 5 percent of the planet's total, we consume roughly one-third of the world's energy. Taking a broader perspective, the members of all high-income societies

NOTE: The increase in productivity of industrial societies is not simply a matter of technology but also of greatly increased energy consumption.

GLOBAL: Net global population increase is 3 per second, 172 per minute, 10,425 per hour, 250,000 per day, 7.5 million per month, and 90 million per year.

GLOBAL: About 80% of world population growth is currently taking place in poor nations.

GLOBAL: The world's ability to feed a growing population depends on greater agricultural efficiency, which, in turn, requires new hybrids as well as curbing topsoil erosion (perhaps 25 billion tons of topsoil are lost annually) and maintaining an adequate supply of water.

represent 20 percent of humanity but utilize 80 percent of all energy (Connett, 1991; Miller, 1992).

But the environmental impact of industrial technology is not limited to energy consumption. Just as important, industrial societies produce one hundred times more goods than agrarian societies do. While these products raise the material standard of living, they greatly escalate the problem of solid waste (because people ultimately throw away most of what they produce) and pollution (because industrial production generates smoke and other toxic substances).

From the outset, people were eager to acquire many of the material benefits of industrial technology. But a century after the dawn of industrial development people began to gauge the long-term consequences of this new technology on the natural environment. Indeed, one defining trait of postindustrial societies is a growing concern for environmental quality.

From today's vantage point, we draw an ironic and sobering conclusion: As we have reached our greatest technological power, we have placed the natural environment—including ourselves and all other living things—at greatest risk (Voight, cited in Bohrmann & Kellert, 1991:ix–x). The evidence is mounting that, in our pursuit of material affluence, humanity is running up an **environmental deficit**, *a situation in which our relationship to the environment, while yielding short-term benefits, will have profound and negative long-term consequences* (Bohrmann, 1990).

The concept of environmental deficit implies three important ideas. First, it reinforces the key assertion that the state of the environment is a *social issue*, reflecting choices people make about how they live. Second, this concept suggests that environmental damage—to the air, land, or water—is often *unintended*. By focusing on the short-term benefits of, say, cutting down forests or using easily disposable packaging, we fail to see (or choose to ignore) their long-term environmental effects. Third, in some but not all respects, the environmental deficit is *reversible*. Inasmuch as societies have created environmental problems, in other words, societies can undo most of them.

Population Increase

Paralleling the development of more powerful technology is a second underlying cause of environmental problems. Ten thousand years ago, at the dawn of civilization, the entire world's population barely reached 100 million, about the population of the Eastern Seaboard of the United States today. Furthermore, population growth was very slow, with gradual increases periodically offset by plague and other catastrophes.

But with the advent of the Industrial Revolution, rising living standards and improving medical technology combined to send death rates in Western Europe plummeting. The predictable result: a sharp upward spike in world population. By 1800, global population had soared to the unprecedented level of 1 billion.

But that was just the beginning. In the decades that followed, global population growth accelerated, reaching the 2 billion point by 1930, 3 billion in 1962, 4 billion in 1974, and 5 billion by 1987. In 1996, the world's population stood at roughly 5.75 billion, with 90 billion people added to the world's total annually (250,000 every day).

The danger of population growth is that it can quickly overwhelm available resources. Consider this old illustration about how runaway growth can wreak havoc on the natural environment (Milbrath, 1989:10):

> A pond has a single water lily growing on it. The lily doubles in size each day. In thirty days, it covers the entire pond. On which day did the lily cover half the pond?

The answer that comes readily to mind—the fifteenth day—is wrong because the lily was not increasing in size by the same amount every day. The correct answer is that the lily covered half the pond on the twenty-ninth day. The lesson of the riddle is that, at an increasing rate of growth, the small lily increases from covering one-eighth of the surface to covering the entire pond in just three days.

To apply the same logic to the earth, most experts now conclude that between 8 and 10 billion people will inhabit our planet by the end of the next century. As Chapters 11 ("Global Stratification") and 21 ("Population and Urbanization") explain, the most rapid population growth now is occurring in the poorest regions of the world. A glance back at Global Map 21–1 on page 562 reveals that the nations of Africa, taken together, are adding to their population at an annual rate approaching 3 percent. If sustained, this high growth rate will almost double that continent's population over the course of the next generation.

Rapid population growth goes hand in hand with poverty. For one thing, a surging population quickly neutralizes any increase in a society's living standards. If a nation's population doubles, doubling its productivity amounts to no gain at all.

And poverty itself strains the environment. Preoccupied with survival, people living on the edge of

NOTE: The book *The Limits to Growth* largely set in motion the later environmental movement; some 3 million copies of the book, published in twenty-seven languages, have been sold.

NOTE: The limits to growth authors called themselves the "club of Rome." Their arguments bring to mind the earlier contentions of Thomas Robert Malthus; thus, they are also known as the "neo-Malthusians."

THEN AND NOW: Patterns of consumption are reflected in the size of homes. In 1970, the average size of a newly constructed home was 1,385 square feet; in 1994, it was 2,100 square feet. Also 80% of today's new homes have central air conditioning, compared to one-third in 1970.

NOTE: Given global connections, argues Lester Milbrath, one principle of environmentalism is that "We can never do just one thing."

Poor countries affect the natural environment primarily by the size of their populations; *rich nations tax the environment because of their* high standard of living. *Today, most people in China use muscle power rather than fossil fuels to move about. But what are the likely environmental consequences of future prosperity in this nation of more than 1 billion people?*

existence are driven to consume whatever resources are at hand, without any thought to the long-term consequences of their actions.

If poor societies suddenly industrialized, what would be the environmental consequences for the billions of people living there? Even at their current population levels, economic development would impose unprecedented stress on the natural environment. To offer just one example, imagine if a poor nation like India were suddenly transformed into a land of prosperity. With its population of 950 million, a "middle-class" India would put almost 1 billion additional cars on its streets. What would that mean for the world's oil reserves or for global air quality?

Cultural Patterns: Growth and Limits

If the world as a whole were suddenly blessed with the material prosperity that people in the United States take for granted, humanity would soon overwhelm the global environment. This conclusion suggests that our planet suffers not just from the problem of economic *under*development in some regions but also from economic *over*development in others.

Let us consider how we construct our cultural notion of "the good life." This is crucial because our cultural outlook, in addition to technology and population growth, is a third factor underlying the environmental deficit.

The Logic of Growth

Why does our society designate specific areas as "parks" or "game reserves"? Doing so seems to imply that, except for these special areas, we may freely use the earth and its resources for productive purposes (Myers, 1991). Such an aggressive approach to the natural environment has long been a central element of our way of life.

Chapter 3 ("Culture") described many of the core values that underlie social life in the United States (Williams, 1970). These included an emphasis on *material comfort*, the belief that money and the things it buys enrich our lives. We also embrace the idea of *progress*, thinking that the future will be better than the present. Moreover, we rely on *science*, looking to experts to apply technology to make our lives better. Taken together, such cultural values form the foundation for *the logic of growth*.

The logic of growth, an optimistic view of the world, holds, first, that people have improved their lives by devising more productive technology and, second, that we shall continue to do so into the future. The logic of growth thus amounts to the assertions that "people are clever," "having things is good (having more is better)," and "life will improve." A powerful force throughout the history of the United States and other Western, industrial societies, the logic of growth has driven individuals to settle the wilderness, clear the land, build towns and roads, and pursue material affluence.

But even optimistic people realize that "progress" generates unanticipated problems, environmental and otherwise. The logic of growth responds by arguing that people (especially scientists and other technology experts) are inventive and will find a way out of any problems that growth places in our path. If, say, present resources should prove inadequate for our future needs, we will come up with new alternative resources that will do the job just as well.

To illustrate, most people in the United States would probably agree that automobiles have greatly improved our lives by providing us with a swift and comfortable means of travel. Automobiles have also made us dependent on oil, but, according to the logic of growth, by the time the growing number of cars in the world threatens to deplete the planet's oil reserves, scientists will have come up with electric, solar, or nuclear engines or some as-yet-unknown technology to free us from oil dependence.

The logic of growth still infuses U.S. culture. But most environmental scientists are critical of this line of reasoning. Lester Milbrath (1989) argues that natural resources such as oil, clean air, fresh water, and the earth's topsoil—all *finite*—simply cannot be replaced by technologically engineered alternatives. He warns that we can and will exhaust them if we continue to pursue growth at any cost.

And what of our faith in human ingenuity and especially the ability of science to resolve problems of scarcity? While conceding that humans are clever at solving problems, Milbrath adds that human resourcefulness, too, has its limits. Do we dare to assume that we will be able to solve every crisis that confronts us, especially those wreaking serious damage on the life-giving environment? Moreover, the more powerful and complex the technology (nuclear reactors, say, compared to gasoline engines), the greater the dangers posed by miscalculation and the more significant the unintended consequences are likely to be. Thus, Milbrath concludes that as we call on the earth to support increasing numbers of people with finite resources, we will almost certainly cause serious injury to the environment, and, ultimately, to ourselves.

The Limits to Growth

If we cannot "invent" our way out of the problems created by the "logic of growth," perhaps we have to come up with an alternative way of thinking about the world. Environmentalists, therefore, propose the counterargument that growth must have limits. The *limits to growth thesis*, stated simply, is that humanity must implement policies to control the growth of pop-

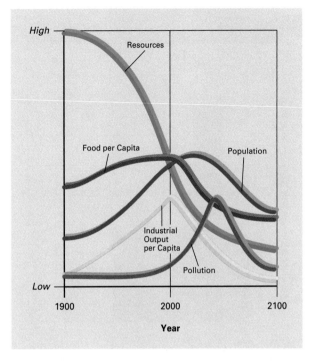

FIGURE 22–1 The Limits to Growth: Projections
Source: Based on Meadows et al. (1972).

ulation, to cut back on production, and to use fewer resources in order to avoid environmental collapse.

The Limits to Growth, a controversial book published in 1972 that had a large hand in launching the environmental movement, uses a computer model to calculate the planet's available resources, rates of population growth, amount of land available for cultivation, levels of industrial and food production, and amount of pollutants released into the atmosphere. The authors contend that the model reflects changes that have occurred since 1900, then projects forward to the end of the next century. Long-range predictions using such a complex model are always speculative and some critics think they are simply wrong (Simon, 1981). But many find the general conclusions of the study, shown in Figure 22–1, convincing.

Following the limits to growth logic, humanity is quickly consuming the earth's finite resources. Supplies of oil, natural gas, and other sources of energy will fall sharply, a little faster or slower depending on policies in rich nations and the speed at which other nations industrialize. While food production per person should continue to rise into the next century, the authors calculate, millions will go hungry because existing food supplies are so unequally distributed

GLOBAL: Heavy reliance on landfills is typical of some industrial nations (U.S., U.K., Australia, Canada) but not others, where incineration is the favored means of disposal (Japan, Sweden, Switzerland, Luxembourg).

GLOBAL: In global perspective, we in the U.S. account for about one-fifth of all the world's trash. In general, the richer the nation, the more materials it consumes and the more it ends up throwing away.

NOTE: In 1993, the space shuttle Endeavor had to change course quickly to avoid a large piece of "space junk" (an old U.S.S.R. rocket). This near-collision raises the specter of future "space pollution." Currently, more than 1,000 pieces of space junk can be seen from earth; the oldest being tracked is the remains of the 1958 Vanguard I satellite.

ENVIRONMENTAL ISSUES

We have reviewed how technological development, population growth, and cultural orientations have placed increasing demands on the natural environment. What, then, is the state of the natural environment today?

Public opinion surveys in the United States and elsewhere reveal serious concern about the natural environment. In general, people in low-income societies who contend with the greatest problems of overpopulation and poverty are most unhappy with their surroundings. Figure 22–2 compares environmental attitudes in selected industrializing and industrial countries (Dunlap, Gallup, & Gallup, 1992).

People in the United States have a more favorable view of their local environments than people in poor countries do. But we, too, are growing more concerned. In one national poll, two-thirds of respondents reported that they thought the natural environment had "gotten worse" over the last twenty years, with 80 percent now claiming to consider themselves "environmentalists" (Gutfeld, 1991a).

In sum, we certainly *perceive* threats to the natural environment. But does our perception accurately mirror reality? In the following survey, we shall briefly examine several key environmental issues, paying particular attention to the United States.

Solid Waste: The "Disposable Society"

As an interesting exercise, carry a trash bag over the course of a single day and collect all the materials you throw away. Most people would be surprised to find that the average person in the United States tosses out close to five pounds of paper, metal, plastic, and other disposable materials daily (about 50 tons over a lifetime). For the country as a whole, this amounts to about 1 billion pounds of solid waste produced *each and every day*. Figure 22–3 shows the composition of a typical household's trash.

It is easy to see why the United States has been dubbed a *disposable society*. Not only are we materially rich, but ours is a culture that values convenience. As a result, we consume more products than virtually any nation on earth, and we purchase much of it with a great deal of packaging. The most commonly cited case is fast food, served with cardboard, plastic, and styrofoam containers that we throw away within minutes. But countless other products—from film to fishhooks—are sold with excessive packaging for the purpose of making the product more attractive to the customer (or harder to shoplift or tamper with).

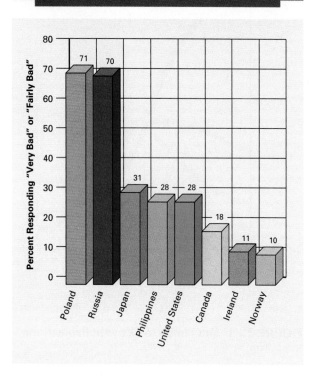

Global Snapshot

FIGURE 22–2 Rating the Local Environment: A Global Survey

Survey Question: "When we say environment, we mean your surroundings—both the natural environment, namely, the air, water, land, plants, and animals—as well as buildings, streets, and the like. Overall, how would you rate the quality of the environment in your local community: very good, fairly good, fairly bad, or very bad?"

Source: Dunlap, Gallup, & Gallup (1992).

throughout the world. By mid-century, the model predicts a hunger crisis serious enough that rising mortality rates will first stabilize population and then send it plunging downward. Depletion of resources will eventually cripple industrial output as well. Only then will pollution rates fall.

The lesson of this study is grim: Current patterns of life are not sustainable for even another century. This leaves us with the fundamental choice of making deliberate changes in how we live, or allowing calamity to force changes upon us.

NOTE: One sign of increasing public concern with solid waste is that, between 1980 and 1990, the weight of discarded grocery packaging dropped by about 10% even as the U.S. population rose 10%. This was accomplished through lighter and more efficient packaging.
DISCUSS: What do people think about junk mail? The U.S. Postal Service delivers about 65 billion pieces annually; 10 billion are thrown out without being opened. The paper in a year's junk mail represents almost 10 million trees (a forest about twice the size of Manhattan island).
DISCUSS: Ask the class to consider depositing in a trash bag that they carry around with them everything they throw away over the course of a day. Discuss and/or examine the results.

Consider, too, that manufacturers market soft drinks, beer, and fruit juices in aluminum cans, glass jars, or plastic containers, which not only consume finite resources but also generate mountains of solid waste. Then there are countless items intentionally designed to be disposable. A walk through any local supermarket reveals shelves filled with pens, razors, flashlights, batteries, and even cameras intended to be used once and dropped in the nearest trash can. Other products—from light bulbs to automobiles—are designed to have a limited useful life, and then become unwanted junk. As Paul H. Connett (1991) points out, even the words we use to describe what we throw away—*waste, litter, trash, refuse, garbage, rubbish*—reveal how little we value what we cannot immediately use and how quickly we push it out of sight and out of mind.

Living in a "disposable society," the average person in the United States consumes 50 times more steel, 170 times more newspaper, 250 times more gasoline, and 300 times more plastic each year than the typical individual in India (Miller, 1992). This high level of consumption means that we in the United States not only use a disproportionate share of the planet's natural resources, but also generate most of the world's refuse.

We like to say that we "throw things away." But the 80 percent of our solid waste that is not burned or recycled never "goes away"; rather, it ends up in landfills. The practice of using landfills, originally intended to improve sanitation, is now associated with several threats to the natural environment.

First, the sheer volume of discarded material is literally filling up landfills all across the country. Especially in large cities like New York, there is simply little room left for disposing of trash. Second, material placed in landfills contributes to water pollution. Although, in most jurisdictions, law now regulates what can be placed in a landfill, the Environmental Protection Agency has identified 30,000 dump sites across the United States containing hazardous materials that are polluting water both above and below the ground. Third, what goes into landfills all too often stays there—sometimes for centuries. Tens of millions of tires, diapers, and other items that we bury in landfills each year do not readily decompose and will become an unwelcome legacy for future generations.

Fifty years ago, it was common practice for manufacturing plants to dispose of all types of hazardous waste simply by dumping them in nearby woods or discharging them into streams. Today, laws in most states impose stiff penalties for such actions, but enforcement has been lax. The problem of solid waste

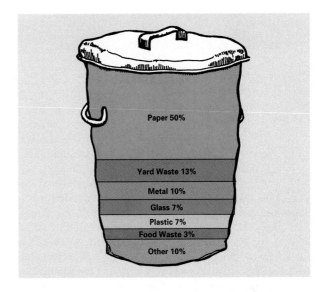

FIGURE 22–3 Composition of Household Trash
Sources: Based on Franklin Associates (1986) and Corley et al. (1993).

includes both the waste products of manufacturing and the solid waste each of us generates daily. To cope with its sheer volume, environmentalists argue that we must turn "waste" into a resource, one that will benefit rather than burden our future.

One way to do this is through *recycling*, reusing resources we would otherwise discard. Recycling is an accepted practice in Japan and many other nations, where at least one-third of waste material is reused. In the United States, by contrast, we recycle just 10 percent of waste materials, mostly thanks to volunteer or government-run programs. But the share is increasing, in part due to laws now enacted in most states that mandate reuse of certain materials such as glass bottles and aluminum cans. Ultimately, recycling will succeed in societies with market-based economies to the extent that it becomes profitable. At present, the demand for most materials that can be recycled is soft. But as recycling processes become more efficient, industry will come to view more and more waste as a useful resource (Corley at al., 1993). The box provides a look at one recycling "success story" in Egypt.

Preserving Clean Water

The oceans, lakes, and streams supply the lifeblood of the global ecosystem. Throughout the history of our species, humans have relied on water for drinking, bathing, cooling, and cooking, for recreation, and a host of other activities.

GLOBAL SOCIOLOGY

Turning the Tide: A Report From Egypt

Egypt

November 14, 1988, Cairo, Egypt. Half an hour from the center of Cairo, Egypt's capital city, the bus bumps along a dirt road and jerks to a stop. It is not quite dawn, and the Mo'edhdhins will soon climb the minarets of Cairo's many mosques to call the Islamic faithful to morning prayers. The driver turns, genuinely bewildered, to the busload of U.S. students and their instructor. "Why," he asks, mixing in a few Arabic words, "do you want to be here? And in the middle of the night?"

Why, indeed? No sooner had we left the bus than smoke and stench, the likes of which we had never before encountered, swirled around us. Eyes squinting, handkerchiefs pressed against noses and mouths, we moved slowly uphill along a path ascending mountains of trash and garbage that extended for miles. We had reached the Cairo dump, where the refuse generated by 15 million people in one of the world's largest cities ends up. We walked hunched over and with great care, guided by only a scattering of light from small fires smoldering around us. Up ahead, through clouds of smoke, we saw blazing piles of trash encircled by people seeking warmth and enjoying companionship.

Human beings actually inhabit this inhuman place, creating a surreal scene, like the aftermath of the next global war. As we approached, the fires cast an eerie light on their faces. We stopped some distance from them, separated by a vast chasm of culture and circumstances. But smiles eased the tension, and soon we were sharing the comfort of their fires. At that moment, the melodious call to prayer sounded across the city.

The people of the Cairo dump, called the Zebaleen, belong to a religious minority—Coptic Christians—in a predominantly Muslim society. Barred by religious discrimination from many jobs, the Zebaleen use donkey carts and small trucks to pick up the city's refuse and haul it here. For decades, the routine has reached a climax at dawn when hundreds of Zebaleen gather at the dump, swarming over the new piles in search of anything of value.

Upon our visit in 1988, we observed men, women, and children picking through Cairo's refuse, filling baskets with anything of value: bits of metal,

---

Yet, the oceans have long served as a vast dumping ground for all kinds of waste. No one can calculate the precise amount of solid waste that has been poured into the world's oceans, but the total certainly exceeds millions of tons. The problems caused by disposing of solid waste in this way are crystal clear: Polluted water kills fish or makes them dangerous to eat, and also spoils a source of great beauty and pleasure.

According to what scientists call the *hydrological cycle*, the earth naturally recycles water and refreshes the land. The process begins as heat from the sun causes the earth's water, 97 percent of which is in the oceans, to evaporate and form clouds. Next, water returns to earth as rain, which drains into streams and rivers and rushes toward the sea. The hydrological cycle not only renews the supply of water but cleans it as well. Because water evaporates at lower temperatures than most pollutants, the water vapor that rises from the seas is relatively pure and free of contaminants, which are left behind. Although the hydrological cycle generates clean water in the form of rain,

however, it does not destroy pollutants that steadily build up in the oceans.

Two key concerns, then, dominate discussions of water and the natural environment. The first is supply; the second is pollution.

Water Supply

Concern over an ample supply of water is hardly new. For thousands of years, since the time of the ancient civilizations of China, Egypt, and Rome, water rights have figured prominently in codes of law. Throughout Europe, aqueducts of brick, built by the ancient Romans, stand as testimony to the historical importance of readily available water.

Today, as Global Map 22–2 on page 598 shows, some regions of the world, especially the tropics, enjoy a plentiful supply of water, although most of the annual rainfall occurs over a relatively brief season. High demand for water, coupled with more modest reserves, make water supply a matter of concern in

strips of ribbon, even scraps of discarded food. Every now and then, someone gleefully displayed a "precious" find that would bring the equivalent of a few dollars in the city. Watching in silence, we became keenly aware of our sturdy shoes and warm clothing and self-conscious that our watches and cameras represented more money than most of the Zebaleen earn in a year.

Today, the Cairo Zebaleen still work the city's streets collecting trash. But much has changed, as they now represent one of the world's environmental success stories. The Zebaleen now have a legal contract to perform this work and, most important, they have established a large recycling center near the dump. There, dozens of workers operate large machines that shred discarded cloth into stuffing to fill furniture, car seats, and pillows. Others separate plastic and metal into large bins for cleaning and sale. In short, the Zebaleen are big business people. Using start-up loans from the World Bank, not only have the Zebaleen constructed an efficient recycling center, they also have built for themselves a modern apartment complex, with electricity and running water.

The Zebaleen are still poor by U.S. standards. But they now own the land on which they live and work, and they are prospering. Certainly, they no longer inhabit the bottom rung of Egyptian society. And many international environmental organizations hope their example will inspire others elsewhere. When the 1992 environmental summit meeting convened in Rio de Janeiro, officials presented the Cairo Zebaleen with the United Nations award for environmental protection.

The Zebaleen people of Cairo have amazed the world with their determination and ingenuity, turning one of the planet's foulest dumps into an efficient recycling center and providing new apartment units for themselves in the process.

Sources: Based on author's visits to Egypt, 1988 and 1994.

much of North America as well as most of Asia; in these areas people look to rivers—rather than rainfall—for their water. Especially in the Middle East, water supply has already reached a critical level. Egypt, for instance, is located in an arid region of the world, where people have long depended on the Nile River for most of their water. But, as the Egyptian population increases, shortages are becoming commonplace. Egyptians today must make do with one-sixth as much water per person from the Nile as they did in 1900, and experts project that the supply will shrink by half again over the next twenty years (Myers, 1984c; Postel, 1993).

Much of the remainder of northern Africa and the Middle East faces an even more critical situation. Within thirty years, according to current predictions, 1 billion people in this region will lack sufficient water. The world has recently witnessed the tragedy of hunger in the African nations of Ethiopia and Somalia. While we recognize the impact of food shortages there, an even more serious problem for these societies is the lack of adequate water for irrigation and drinking.

Surging population and complex technology—especially in manufacturing and power-generating facilities—have greatly increased our appetite for water. The global demand for water (estimated at about 5 billion cubic feet per year) has tripled since 1950 and is expanding faster than the world's population (Postel, 1993).

As a result, even in areas that receive significant rainfall, people are using groundwater faster than it can be naturally replenished. Take the Tamil Nadu region of southern India, for example. There, the rapidly growing population is drawing so much groundwater that the local water table has fallen one hundred feet over the last several decades. In the United States, the pumping of water from the massive Ogallala aquifer, which lies below seven states from South Dakota to Texas, is now so rapid that some experts fear it could be depleted several decades into the next century.

In light of such developments, we must face the reality that water is a valuable, finite resource. Greater conservation of water by individuals (who consume, on

NOTE: A 1993 EPA survey of U.S. drinking water found that systems serving 30 million people had too much lead.

GLOBAL: About 85% of the world's cropland is not artificially irrigated, receiving water only from rainfall. The 15% that is irrigated consumes a greatly disproportionate share of water reserves.

GLOBAL: Irrigation is not only the main source of water use, but a major source of energy consumption. In India, for example, some 8

million irrigation pumps consume one-fourth of that nation's power.

NOTE: Water use by industry in the United States has fallen by one-third since 1950 (as heavy industry has declined overall). This pattern holds true, more or less, for other industrial nations as well.

RESOURCE: Lester Brown's essay "The State of the World's Natural Environment" is one of the contemporary selections in the companion reader, *Seeing Ourselves.*

Window on the World

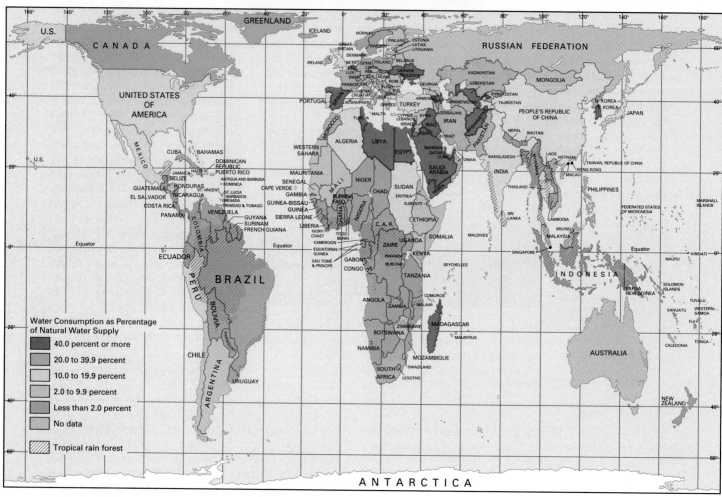

GLOBAL MAP 22–2 Water Consumption in Global Perspective

This map shows each country's water consumption as a percentage of its internal renewable water resources. Nations near the equator consume only a tiny share of their available resources; indeed, as the map shows, much of this region is covered with rain forest. Northern Africa and the Middle East are a different story, however, with dense populations drawing on very limited water resources. As a result, in Libya, Egypt, Saudi Arabia, and other countries, people (especially the poor) do not have as much water as they would like or, often, as they need.

Source: United Nations Development Programme (1995).

average, 10 million gallons over a lifetime) is part of the answer. However, households around the world account for no more than 10 percent of water use. We need to curb water consumption by industry, which currently uses 25 percent of the global total. And, most crucial of all, irrigation channels two-thirds of humanity's water use onto croplands.

New irrigation technology may well reduce this demand in the future. But, here again, we see that population increase, as well as economic growth, are

Q: "We all live downwind." Bumper sticker

THEN AND NOW: Annual U.S. emissions of sulfur dioxide (millions of tons): *1970*, 31; *1995*, 21; carbon dioxide emissions (millions of tons): *1970*, 128; *1995*, 98.

SOCIAL SURVEY: "Modern science will solve our environmental problems with little change to our way of life." (GSS 1994, N =

1,386; *Codebook*, 1994:641)

"Strongly agree"	2.0%
"Agree"	16.7%
"Neither agree nor disagree"	21.5%
"Disagree"	41.6%
"Strongly disagree"	11.5%
DK/NR	6.7%

placing inceasing strains on the ecosystem (Myers, 1984a; Goldfarb, 1991; Falkenmark & Widstrand, 1992; Postel, 1993).

Water Pollution

In large cities—from Mexico City to Cairo to Shanghai—many people have little choice but to drink contaminated water. The poor people of the world suffer most as a result of unsafe water. As Chapter 20 ("Health and Medicine") noted, infectious diseases like typhoid, cholera, and dysentery, all caused by micro-organisms that contaminate water, run rampant in poor nations. Throughout the low-income regions of the world, then, the source of much illness and death can be traced to microbes thriving in polluted water (Clarke, 1984b; Falkenmark & Widstrand, 1992).

Thus, besides ensuring ample *supplies* of water, we must recognize that no society has done an exemplary job of protecting the *quality* of its water. In most areas of the world, tap water is not safe for drinking.

Most people living in the United States take for granted that tap water is free from harmful contaminants, and water quality in the United States is generally good by global standards. However, even here the problem of water pollution is growing steadily. According to the Sierra Club, an environmental activist organization, rivers and streams across the United States absorb some 500 million pounds of toxic waste each year. This pollution results not just from intentional dumping, but also from the runoff of agricultural fertilizers and lawn chemicals. Groundwater supplies are also endangered as hazardous substances leech from thousands of landfills and dump sites across the country.

While even small amounts of pollutants can damage the aquatic ecosystem, only recently have water supplies been protected by law. The federal government's Clean Water Act of 1972 was a first step toward improving this country's water quality. Before its passage, many urban rivers were so polluted that the water was dangerous for drinking or even for bathing, and deadly to fish and other aquatic life. In one of the most egregious examples, Cleveland's Cuyahoga River became so choked with oil and other toxic substances from local manufacturing plants in the late 1960s that it actually caught fire.

Clearing the Air

Most people in the United States are more aware of air pollution than they are of contaminated water, in

The Aral Sea, which straddles Kazakhstan and Uzbekistan in the southwest region of the former Soviet Union, was once a plentiful source of water and fish. Today, due to policies that overly exploited this resource, the sea has all but vanished.

part, because air serves as our constant and immediate environment. Then, too, many U.S. urbanites are familiar with the mix of smoke and fog (the origin of the word "smog") that hangs over our cities.

One of the unanticipated consequences of the development of industrial technology—especially the factory and the motor vehicle—has been a deterioration of air quality. The thick, black smoke belched from factory smokestacks, often twenty-four hours a day, alarmed residents of early industrial cities a century ago. Writing in 1884, for instance, Williard Glazier was stunned by the nighttime view from the hills surrounding the city of Pittsburgh, ablaze with the fires of steel mills and swirling with factory smoke. It was as if someone had lifted the lid on hell itself, Glazier mused, revealing his fellow city dwellers as "tortured spirits writhing in agony" as they fought simply to breathe (cited in Glaab, 1963).

By the end of World War II, such scenes were commonplace in industrial cities of the Northeast and Midwest. By 1950, the rapidly rising number of automobiles were adding to the problem of air pollution, their exhaust fumes shrouding cities like Los Angeles that had escaped the earlier rush of industrial development. On a clear day, Angelenos could see across the city, but there were few clear days.

In London, factory discharge, automobile emissions, and smoke from coal fires used to heat households combined to create what was probably the worst urban air quality of the century. What some British

THE MAP: A few states are home to the sources of most air pollution in the United States. High pollution states contain a large share of this nation's industrial plants and are also home to much of the country's people.

NOTE: Scientists estimate that three-fourths of Europe's remaining forests show damage from acid rain.

SOCIAL SURVEY: "Every time we use coal or oil or gas, we contribute to the greenhouse effect." (GSS 1994, N = 1,386; *Codebook*, 1994:648)

"Definitely true"	13.4%
"Probably true"	45.4%
"Probably not true"	20.6%
"Definitely not true"	4.1%
DK/NR	16.5%

Seeing Ourselves

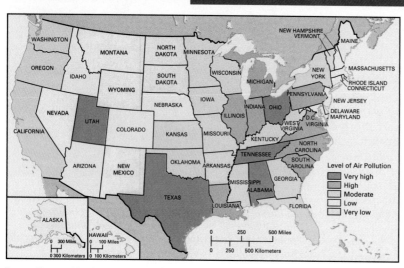

NATIONAL MAP 22–1

Air Pollution Across the United States

The Environmental Protection Agency monitors the emission of 316 compounds into the atmosphere. In 1993, the five states that polluted the air the least were Hawaii, Nevada, Wyoming, North Dakota, and Vermont (although these states each emitted 500,000 pounds of toxics during that year). High-pollution states—including Texas, Alabama, Louisiana, and Indiana—each sent one hundred times as much toxic material into the atmosphere. What traits distinguish high-pollution from low-pollution states?

Source: Prepared by the author using data from the Environmental Protection Agency.

jokingly called "pea soup" was, in reality, a deadly mix of pollution: In the course of just five days in 1952, an especially thick haze that hung over London killed 4,000 people (Clarke, 1984a).

Fortunately, great strides have been made in combating air pollution brought on by our industrial way of life. Laws now mandate the use of low-pollution heating fuels in most cities; the coal fires that choked London a half-century ago, for example, are now forbidden. In addition, scientists have effectively devised new technologies to reduce the noxious output of factory chimneys and, even more important, to lessen the pollution caused by the growing number of automobiles and trucks. The switch to unleaded gasoline initiated in the early 1970s, coupled with changes in engine design and exhaust systems, has reduced the automobile's detrimental environmental impact. Still, with almost 200 million motor vehicles in the United States alone, the challenge of cleaning the air remains daunting. National Map 22–1 identifies the states with the worst air quality.

If the rich societies of the world can breathe a bit more easily than they once did, poor societies contend with an increasing problem of air pollution. For one thing, people in low-income countries still rely on wood, coal, peat, or other "dirty" fuels for cooking fires and to heat their homes. Moreover, many nations are so eager to encourage short-term industrial development that they pay little heed to the longer-term dangers of air pollution. As a result, many cities in Latin America, Eastern Europe, and Asia are plagued by air pollution that rivals the toxic level found in London fifty years ago.

Acid Rain

Acid rain refers to *precipitation that is made acidic by air pollution so that it destroys plant and animal life.* The complex reaction that generates acid rain (or snow) begins as power plants burning fossil fuels (oil and coal) to generate electricity release sulfur and nitrogen oxides into the air. Once the winds sweep these gases into the atmosphere, they react with the air to form sulfuric and nitric acid, which makes atmospheric moisture acidic. Figure 22–4 illustrates the process that creates acid rain.

Taking a closer look at this figure, we also observe that one type of pollution often causes another. In this case, air pollution (from smokestacks) ends up contaminating water (in lakes and streams that collect acid rain). Notice, too, that acid rain is a global phenomenon because the regions that suffer the effects of acid rain may be thousands of miles from the site of the original pollution. For instance, tall chimneys of British power plants have caused the acid rain that has devastated forests and fish in Norway and Sweden up to a thousand miles to the northeast. In the United States, we see a

FIGURE 22–4
The Formation of Acid Rain

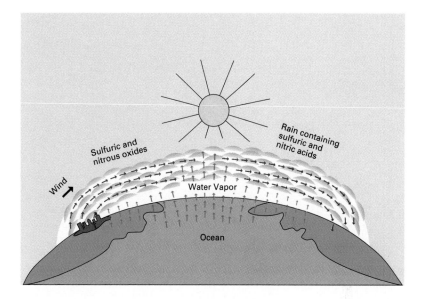

similar pattern as midwestern chimneys poison the nat-ural environment of New England (Clarke, 1984a).

The Rain Forests

Rain forests are *regions of dense forestation, most of which circle the globe close to the equator.* A glance back at Global Map 22–2, on page 598, shows that the largest tropical rain forests are in South America (notably Brazil), but west central Africa and southeast Asia also have sizable rain forests. In all, the world's rain forests cover an area of some 2 billion acres, which accounts for 7 percent of the earth's total land surface.

Like the rest of the world's resources, the rain forests are falling victim to the needs and appetites of the surging human population. As noted earlier in this chapter, the demand for beef has sparked more cattle grazing in Latin America; ranchers typically burn forested areas to increase their supply of grazing land. Just as important is the lucrative hardwood trade. High prices are paid for mahogany and other woods by people in rich societies who have, as environmentalist Norman Myers (1984b:88) puts it, "a penchant for par-quet floors, fine furniture, fancy paneling, weekend yachts, and high-grade coffins." Under such pressure, the world's rain forests are now just half their original size, and they continue to shrink by about 1 percent (65,000 square miles) annually. If this rate of destruc-tion continues unchecked, these forests will vanish before the end of the next century, and, with them, protections for the earth's climate and biodiversity.

Global Warming

Natural scientists explain that rain forests play an important part in removing carbon dioxide (CO_2) from the earth's atmosphere. From the time of the Industrial Revolution, the amount of carbon dioxide humanity has produced (most generated by factories and automo-biles) has risen tenfold. Much of this CO_2 is absorbed by the oceans. But plants, which take in carbon dioxide and expel oxygen, also play a major part in maintaining the chemical balance of the atmosphere.

The problem, then, is that production of carbon dioxide is rising while the amount of plant life on earth is shrinking. To make matters worse, rain forests are being destroyed mostly by burning, which releases even more carbon dioxide into the atmosphere. Experts esti-mate the atmospheric concentration of carbon dioxide is now 10 to 20 percent higher than it was 150 years ago.

In the atmosphere, carbon dioxide behaves much like the glass roof of a greenhouse, letting heat from the sun pass through to the earth while preventing much of it from radiating back away from the planet. Thus ecologists speculate about a possible **green-house effect**, *a rise in the earth's average temperature due to increasing concentration of carbon dioxide in the atmosphere.*

Scientists note a small rise in global temperature (about 1.5 degrees Fahrenheit) over the last century. Some go on to predict that the average temperature of our planet (about 58° F. in recent years) will rise by five to ten degrees during the coming century. This

Chapter 22 Environment and Society **601**

Members of small, simple societies, such as the Tan't Batu, who thrive in the Philippines, live in harmony with nature; such people do not have the technological means to greatly affect the natural world. Although we in complex societies like to think of ourselves as superior to such people, the truth is that there is much we can—and must—learn from them.

warming trend would melt much of the polar ice caps, raise sea levels, and push the oceans up over low-lying land around the world, flooding Bangladesh, for example, and much of the coastal United States, including Washington, D.C., right up to the steps of the White House. On the other hand, the U.S. Midwest—currently one of the most productive agricultural regions in the world—would likely become arid.

Not all scientists share this vision of future global warming. Some point out that global temperature changes have been taking place throughout history, and rain forests have had little or nothing to do with those shifts. Moreover, higher concentrations of carbon dioxide in the atmosphere might actually accelerate plant growth (since plants thrive on this gas), which would serve to correct this imbalance and nudge the earth's temperature downward once again (Silverberg, 1991; Moore, 1995).

Declining Biodiversity

Whatever the effects on this planet's climate, rain forest clearing has another undeniable impact. The disappearance of rain forest is a major factor eroding the earth's *biodiversity*, or, more simply, causing many thousands of species of plant and animal life to disappear forever. While rain forests account for just 7 percent of the earth's surface, they are home to almost half of this planet's living species.

Estimates of the total number of species of animals and plants range from 1.5 million to as high as 30 million. Researchers, in fact, have identified more than one thousand species of ants alone (Wilson, 1991). Several dozen unique species of plants and animals cease to exist each day; but, given the vast number of living species on the earth, why should we be concerned with a loss of biodiversity? Environmentalists point to three reasons. First, our planet's biodiversity provides a vast and varied source of human food. Agricultural technology currently "splices" familiar crops with more exotic plant life to yield crops that are more productive or resistant to insects and disease. In addition, plant geneticists looking into the properties of unfamiliar plant and animal life are working toward generating the quantity and quality of foods necessary to nourish our rapidly increasing population.

Second, the earth's biodiversity is a vital genetic resource. Medical and pharmaceutical industries depend on animal and plant biodiversity in their research to discover compounds that will cure disease and improve our lives. Children in the United States, for example, now have a good chance of surviving leukemia, a disease that was almost a sure killer two generations ago, because of a compound derived from a pretty tropical flower called the rosy periwinkle. The oral birth control pill, used by tens of millions of women in this country, is another product of plant research, this time involving the Mexican forest yam. Scientists have

602 Chapter 22 Environment and Society

NOTE: Increasing global trade itself places great stress on the environment, generating more production, more energy consumption, and more disposal of waste. The energy used annually to power cargo ships roughly equals that consumed by all Brazilians and Turks.

NOTE: Members of our society have always tended to treat "growth" as more or less synonymous with "progress," with both viewed as "better" than the alternatives.

Q: "We don't expect dreamers to explain their dreams; no more would we expect lifestyle participants to explain their lifestyles." Marvin Harris

RESOURCE: Marvin Harris's article "India's Sacred Cow" is included in the Macionis and Benokraitis reader *Seeing Ourselves*, 3/e.

tested tens of thousands of plants for their medical properties, and they have developed hundreds of new medicines each year based on this research.

Third, with the loss of any species of life—whether it is one variety of ant, the spotted owl, the magnificent Asian tiger, or the famed Chinese panda—the beauty and complexity of our natural environment is diminished. And there are clear warning signs: Three-fourths of the world's 9,000 species of birds are currently declining in number.

Finally, keep in mind that, unlike pollution and other environmental problems, the extinction of species is irreversible and final. As a matter of ethics, then, should those who live today make decisions that will impoverish the world for those who live tomorrow? (Myers, 1984b, 1991; Wilson, 1991; Brown, 1993)

SOCIETY AND THE ENVIRONMENT: THEORETICAL ANALYSIS

We have now introduced a number of key concepts and outlined prominent issues facing the natural environment. Sociological theory can help tie this material together to see how environmental concerns reflect the operation of society.

Structural-Functional Analysis

The structural-functional paradigm offers three significant insights about the natural environment. First, as earlier chapters have made clear, this approach highlights the fundamental importance of *values* and *beliefs* to the operation of a social system. Thus, in simple terms, the state of the environment depends largely on our attitude toward the natural world, for values guide human actions.

Members of industrial societies generally see in nature resources to serve our needs; this point of view (examined earlier as the "logic of growth") justifies imposing our human will on the planet. With this orientation, our forebears cleared forests for farmland, dammed rivers for irrigation and water power, covered vast areas with asphalt and concrete, and erected buildings to make cities.

Moreover, Western cultures historically have embraced both materialism and acquisitiveness. That is, we have looked to *things* (sometimes more than, say, kinship or spirituality) as a source of comfort, happiness, and fulfillment. At the same time, we tend to think that if owning *some* things is good, having *more* things is better. Our tendency toward "conspicuous consumption" leads us to purchase and display things

as a way to indicate our social position to others. Such values, not surprisingly, set the stage for the kinds of environmental stress this chapter has described.

Second, structural-functional theory points up the interconnectedness of various dimensions of social life. Our ideas about efficient and private travel, for example, have much to do with the dizzying rate at which industrial societies have produced and consumed motor vehicles. Building and operating hundreds of millions of trucks and automobiles, in turn, has depleted natural resources (like oil) and the quality of the overall environment (especially the air).

Third, structural-functional analysis suggests that, given the many ways in which the operation of society interacts with the natural environment, environmental problems demand far-reaching and multifaceted solutions. We cannot hope to curb the rate at which humanity is consuming the earth's resources, for example, as long as 250,000 people are added to the global population each day. Controlling population growth, in turn, depends on expanding the range of occupational and educational opportunities open to women, so they can opt for alternatives to staying home and having more children.

However difficult the task may be, structural-functionalism provides grounds for optimism that societies can constructively respond to threats to the environment. Consider, once again, the case of air pollution. Air quality plunged with the onset of the Industrial Revolution. But gradually societies in Europe and North America recognized and responded to this problem, enacting new laws and employing new technology to improve air quality. Similarly, just as companies once fouled the natural environment in the process of making money, now new companies are profiting by cleaning up our physical surroundings. In short, because we need a livable natural environment, determined efforts will undoubtedly be brought to bear on whatever environmental problems may arise.

Cultural Ecology

Closely allied with structural-functional theory is **cultural ecology**, *a theoretical paradigm that explores the relationship of human culture and the physical environment.* This paradigm broadens our analysis by exploring not just how culture affects the environment but also how the environment (say, climate or the availability of natural resources) shapes human culture.

First-time travelers to India might well wonder why this nation, that contends with widespread hunger and malnutrition, prohibits the killing of cows.

A challenge of the coming century lies in our moving beyond the notion of discarding "waste" toward the idea of recycling materials in new and creative ways. Perhaps the containers that hold this year's drinks may become the fabric for next year's fashions.

According to Hindu cultural beliefs, cows are sacred animals. To North Americans who enjoy so much beef, this way of thinking is puzzling.

Investigating rural India's ecology, Marvin Harris (1975) concluded that the Hindu veneration of the cow makes sense because cattle's importance extends well beyond their value as a food source. Harris points out that cows cost little to raise, since they consume grasses of no interest to humans. And cows produce two valuable resources: oxen (their neutered offspring) and manure. Unable to afford expensive farm machinery, Indian farmers rely on oxen to power their plows. For Indians, killing cows would be as silly as farmers in the United States destroying factories that build tractors. Furthermore, each year Indians process millions of tons of cow manure into building material and burn "cow pies" as fuel (India has little oil, coal, or wood).

Culture, in short, is shaped by the ecology: Killing cows for food would deprive Indians of homes and a major source of heat.

Critical evaluation. Structural-functional analysis, including the cultural ecology approach, shows that the condition of the natural environment cannot be analyzed apart from the operation of society itself. To its credit, this paradigm reveals the extent to which the environment is a sociological concern.

But critics have pointed out various weaknesses in this paradigm. With regard to cultural ecology, we can see how the natural environment shapes the culture of people with limited technology, but this connection is less obvious in societies with industrial technology.

More broadly, structural-functionalism overlooks issues of social inequality. As we shall note presently, the burdens of environmental pollution are shouldered disproportionately by people with less social power—the poor and minorities. Furthermore, many environmentalists are skeptical of structural-functionalism's optimism about society's capacity to restore the natural world. On the one hand, many people have vested interests in the status quo, even if that threatens the well-being of the general public. Moreover, many of the environmental problems we face—especially rapid population growth—are simply too far out of control at present to justify the optimism voiced by functionalists.

Social-Conflict Analysis

Social-conflict theory highlights the very issues that structural-functionalism tends to overlook: power and inequality. Far from being inevitable, conflict theorists maintain, problems of the natural environment result from social arrangements favored by elites. In other words, social-conflict theory indicts elites for directly or indirectly aggravating environmental problems as they pursue their self-interest. Extending this idea, social-conflict analysis also reminds us that the global disparity of wealth and power has serious environmental consequences.

First, there is the issue of elites. As conflict theorists see it, in the hierarchical organization of U.S. society, a small proportion of our population—what Chapter 16 ("Politics and Government") called the "power elite"—sets the national and global agenda by controlling the world's economy, law, and view of the natural environment.

Early capitalists shepherded the United States into the industrial age, hungrily tapping the earth's resources and frantically turning out manufactured goods in

DIVERSITY: The concept of "environmental racism" partly reflects the movement's concern over its largely white, middle-class membership. (One recent survey found that 43% of readers of the Sierra Club's magazine have postgraduate degrees, ten times the share of the U.S. adult population, with a median income of over $50,000.)

DIVERSITY: The term "environmental racism" was first used in a public speech by Benjamin Chavis, then with the United Church of Christ Commission for Racial Justice (later director of the NAACP) at a 1982 protest in Warren County, North Carolina, over siting of a toxic dump near an African-American community.

NOTE: In 1994, the Clinton administration ordered federal agencies to ensure that their policies and programs do not unfairly inflict environmental harm on poor people or minorities.

pursuit of profits. By and large, it was they who reaped the benefits of the new industrial wealth, while workers toiled in dangerous factories and lived in nearby neighborhoods blighted with smoke, racked with noise, and shaken by the vibrations of the big machines.

Just as important, our society has long winked at the most blatant instances of environmental destruction, even when elite perpetrators run afoul of the law. Corporate pollution, as Chapter 8 ("Deviance") explains, falls under the category of white-collar crime. Such offenses typically escape prosecution; when action is taken, it is usually in the form of fines levied on a company rather than criminal penalties imposed on individuals. Thus, corporate executives who order the burning or burying of toxic waste have been subject to penalties no greater (and sometimes less) than ordinary citizens who throw litter from car windows.

Conflict theorists who embrace a Marxist view of society argue that capitalism itself poses a threat to the environment. The logic of capitalism is the pursuit of profit, and that pursuit demands continuous economic growth. As Marxists see it, what is profitable to capitalists does not necessarily advance the public welfare, nor is it likely to be good for the natural environment. As noted earlier in this chapter, for example, capitalist industries have long ensured ongoing profits by designing products to have a limited useful life (the concept of "planned obsolescence"). Such policies may improve the "bottom line" in the short term, but they raise the long-term risk of depleting natural resources as well as generating overwhelming amounts of solid waste.

A second issue raised by social-conflict theory is inequality. As shown earlier in Global Map 22–1, a small share of the earth's population currently consumes most of its energy. Generally, members of rich societies, including the United States, use most of the earth's resources and, in the process, produce the most pollution. We have achieved our affluent way of life, in short, by exploiting both the earth and the poor of the less-developed countries, and we have poisoned the air and water in the process.

From this point of view, rich nations are actually *over*developed and consume too much. No one should expect that the majority of the earth's people, who live in poor societies, will be able to match the living standard in this country; nor, given the current environmental crisis, would that be desirable. Instead, conflict theorists call for a more equitable distribution of resources among all people of the world as both a matter of social justice and as a strategy to preserve the natural environment (Schnaiberg & Gould, 1994; Szasz, 1994).

Environmental Racism

A specific conflict-theory assertion that has been taking on growing importance is **environmental racism**, *the pattern by which environmental hazards are greatest in proximity to poor people and especially minorities.* Historically, factories that spew pollutants have been built in and near districts inhabited by the poor and people of color, who often work there. As a result of their low incomes, many could afford housing only in undesirable neighborhoods, sometimes in the very shadow of the plants and mills.

In part, however, environmental racism is a deliberate strategy perpetrated by factory owners and powerful officials. No one wants to live in a dangerous environment. But by siting factories and toxic dumps near poor neighborhoods, factory owners ensure that those affected have little power to resist. This means that, historically, the most serious environmental hazards have been found near Newark, New Jersey (not in upscale Bergen County), on Chicago's south side (not wealthy Lake Forest), or on Native-American reservations in the West (not in the affluent suburbs of Denver or Phoenix) (Commission for Racial Justice, United Church of Christ, 1987; Perrolle, 1993; Szasz, 1994; Pollak & Vittas, 1995).

Take the case of Gary, Indiana, where the U.S. Steel (now USX) corporation, founded by industrialist J. P. Morgan in 1901, has its main factory. As the dominant employer in Gary, U.S. Steel had enormous clout in the city's politics. The company offered not only jobs but company housing, which attracted a large work force that swelled the city's population.

If U.S. Steel was Gary's largest employer, it was also the city's biggest polluter. Yet, as Andrew Hurley (1995) explains, some categories of people experienced more harm in terms of poor physical health and high emotional stress than others. Higher-paid employees soon moved to outlying suburbs, clear of the greatest environmental hazards (including smoke, noise, and toxic wastes). Most low-paid workers, by contrast, lived for decades at greater risk, right in the vicinity of the plant. And, grappling with both low wages and racial discrimination in the more desirable neighborhoods, African Americans suffered most of all.

Although workers in many manufacturing industries have organized in opposition to environmental hazards, they have done so with limited success, largely because the people facing the most serious environmental threats have the least social power to begin with.

Critical evaluation. The social-conflict paradigm complements other analyses by raising the important

Although the problem of topsoil erosion in the United States is serious primarily in California, desertification is also widespread in many countries of the world, including Nepal (Asia), Peru (Latin America), Turkey (bridging Europe and Asia), and Sudan and Lesotho (Africa). The causes of desertification are less climatic than human: The cutting of trees, burning of vegetation, and allowing cattle to overgraze land are the major causes of this problem. The overall effect is that, as the world's forests shrink in size, the planet's deserts are expanding.

questions of who sets a society's agenda and who benefits (and suffers) most from decisions that affect us all. Environmental problems, from this point of view, are consequences of a society's class structure and, globally, the world's hierarchy of nations.

Like structural-functionalism, this approach is subject to criticism. While it may be true that elites have always dominated U.S. society, they have not been able to stem a steady tide toward legal protection of the natural environment. These protections, in turn, have yielded significant improvements in our air and water quality.

And what of the charge that capitalism is particularly hostile to the natural world? There is little doubt that capitalism's logic of growth does place stress on the environment. At the same time, however, capitalist societies in North America and, especially, in Europe have made notable strides toward environmental protection. By contrast, the environmental record of socialist societies is far from exemplary. A look back to Figure 22–3 shows that citizens of Poland and Russia—two nations ruled for half a century by socialist governments—are highly critical of environmental quality in their local communities (Dunlap, Gallup, &

Gallup, 1992; Olsen, Lodwick & Dunlap, 1992). This record reflects policies that, for decades, pursued industrialization in utter neglect of environmental concerns, without challenge and with tragic consequences in terms of human health.

Finally, there is little doubt that high-income countries currently place the greatest demands on the natural environment. However, this pattern is already beginning to shift as global population swells in poor countries. And environmental problems are also likely to grow worse to the extent that poor societies develop economically, using more resources and producing more waste and pollutants in the process.

In the long run, all nations of the world share a vital interest in protecting the natural environment. This concern leads us to the final topic of this chapter, the concept of a sustainable environment.

LOOKING AHEAD: TOWARD A SUSTAINABLE SOCIETY AND WORLD

India's great leader Mahatma Gandhi once declared that societies must provide "enough for people's needs, but not for their greed." From an environmental point of view, this means that the earth will be able to sustain future generations only if humanity refrains from rapidly and thoughtlessly consuming finite resources such as oil, hardwoods, and water. Nor can we persist in polluting the air, water, and ground at anything like the current levels. The loss of global forests—through cutting of trees and the destructive effects of acid rain—threatens to undermine the global climate. And we risk the future of the planet by adding people to the world at the rate of 90 million each year.

Today, on every part of the earth inhabited by humanity, the environmental deficit is growing. In effect, our present way of life is borrowing against the well-being of our children and their children. And, taking a global perspective, we see that members of rich societies, who currently consume so much of the earth's resources, are mortgaging the future security of the majority of people who live in the poor countries of the world.

In principle, we could solve the entire range of environmental problems described in this chapter by living in a more *ecocentric* manner, one that makes environmental consequences central to our actions. This is the path to a culture that is sustainable, one that does not increase the environmental deficit. An **ecologically sustainable culture**, then, refers to *a way of life that meets* *the needs of the present generation without threatening the environmental legacy of future generations.*

Sustainable living calls for three basic strategies. The first is the *conservation of finite resources*. We must balance the desire to satisfy our present wants with our responsibility to preserve what will be needed by future generations. Conservation means using resources more efficiently, seeking alternative resources, and, in some cases, learning to live with less.

Technology, no doubt, will provide the key to household devices (from light bulbs to furnaces) that are far more energy efficient than those available at present. Moreover, we should expand development of alternative energy sources, including harnessing the power of the sun, wind, and tides. But while relying on help from new technology, a sustainable way of life will require rethinking the proconsumption attitudes formed during decades of "cheap electricity" and "cheap oil."

The second basic strategy is *reducing waste*. Whenever possible, simply using less is the most effective way to reduce waste. In addition, societies around the world need to expand recycling programs. Success will depend both on dual incentives of educational efforts to enlist widespread support for these initiatives and on legislation requiring the recycling of certain materials. Looking down the road, as recycling programs become commercially profitable, they will be adopted more readily by market-based economies around the world.

The third key element in any plan for a sustainable ecosystem is *bringing world population growth under control*. As we have explained, the current (1996) global population of 5.75 billion is already straining the natural environment. Clearly, the higher world population climbs, the more difficult environmental problems will become. Global population is now increasing by about 1.5 percent each year, a rate that will double the world's people in fewer than fifty years. Few analysts think that the earth can support a population of 10 billion or more; most argue that we must hold the line at about 7 billion. Controlling population growth will require urgent steps in poor regions of the world where growth rates are highest.

But even sweeping environmental strategies—put in place with the best intentions—will fail without some fundamental changes in the ways in which we think about ourselves and our world. By taking an *egocentric* view that sets up our own immediate interests as the standards for how to live, we have obscured several key connections that become clear as we shift to a more *ecocentric* outlook.

First of all, we need to realize that, environmentally speaking, *the present is tied to the future*. Simply put, today's actions shape tomorrow's world. Thus, we must learn to evaluate our short-term choices in terms of their long-range consequences for the natural environment.

Second, rather than viewing humans as "different" from or "better" than other forms of life and assuming that we have the right to dominate the planet, we must acknowledge that *all forms of life are interdependent*. Ignoring this truth not only harms other life forms, it will eventually undermine our own well-being. From the realization that all life figures in the ecological balance must follow specific programs that will protect the earth's biodiversity.

Third, and finally, achieving a sustainable ecosystem will require *global cooperation*. The planet's rich and poor nations are currently separated by a vast chasm of divergent interests, cultures, and living standards. On the one hand, most countries in the northern half of the world are overdeveloped, using more resources than the earth can sustain over time. On the other hand, most nations in the southern half of the world are underdeveloped, unable to meet the basic needs of many of their people. A sustainable ecosystem depends on bold and unprecedented programs of international cooperation. And, while the cost of change will certainly be high, it pales before the eventual cost of not responding to the growing environmental deficit (Humphrey & Buttel, 1982; Burke, 1984; Kellert & Bohrmann, 1991; Brown, 1993).

Along with the ransformations just noted, we will reach the goal of a sustainable society only by critically reevaluating the logic of growth that has dominated our way of life for several centuries. The final box assesses the chances for significant change—even at the cost of economic growth.

In closing, we might well consider that the great dinosaurs dominated this planet for some 160 million years and then perished forever. Humanity is far younger, having existed for a mere quarter of a million years. Compared to the rather dim-witted dinosaurs, our species has the gift of great intelligence. But how wisely will we use this ability? What are the chances that our species will continue to flourish on the earth 160 million years—or even a few thousand years—from now? As Tom Burke (1984) points out, it would be foolish to assume that our present civilization is about to collapse. But it would be equally foolish to ignore the warning signs. One certainty is that the state of tomorrow's world will depend on choices we make today.

Q: "We stand where two roads diverge. But unlike the roads in Robert Frost's poem, they are not equally fair. The road we have long been traveling is deceptively easy, a smooth superhighway on which we progress with great speed, but at its end lies disaster. The other fork in the road, the one 'less traveled by,' offers our last, and only, chance to reach a destination that assures the preservation of our earth." Rachel Carson (1962):277

SOCIAL SURVEY: "Are you willing to accept cuts in your standard of living in order to protect the environment?" (GSS 1994; N = 1,386; *Codebook*, 1994:644)

"Very willing"   4.1%   "Not very willing" 28.1%
"Fairly willing"   26.2%   "Not at all willing" 15.4%
"Neither willing nor unwilling" 22.1%   DK/NR   4.1%

Controversy & Debate

Is the Environmental Movement Radical? Should It Be?

It isn't much, really, in dispute—only the land we live on, the water we drink, the air we breathe, the food we eat, and the energy that supports us. (Aaron Wildavsky)

Judging from many news stories, the environmental movement might seem to be at odds with the main currents of U.S. society. While people in the Pacific Northwest want to continue logging forests to protect their jobs, environmentalists are worried about the spotted owl, endangered by the destruction of his forest habitat. Most people believe that science and technology will improve our lives; environmentalists aren't so sure. What are the facts? How much does the environmental movement challenge the status quo?

The movement itself has changed over time. The "first wave" of environmentalism was little more than a conservation movement that focused on protecting natural wilderness—

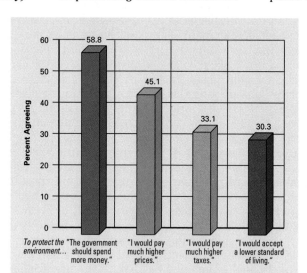

Concern for the Environment: A Survey

especially in the western United States—in the face of rapid development. Conservationists were responsible for setting up scores of national parks as well as founding the U.S. Forest Service. In addition, early activists established the Sierra Club and the National Audubon Society, both of which continue to monitor environmental issues today.

During the 1960s, a "second wave" of environmentalism took root in the United States and became decidedly more critical of our way of life. In 1962, Rachel Carson's book *Silent Spring* explored the dangers of spreading pesticides across the land; agricultural "business as usual," Carson warned, was courting disaster. Before long, environmental concerns had become part of the activist culture

SUMMARY

1. Because the most important factor affecting the state of the natural environment is the way in which human beings organize social life, ecology—the study of how living organisms interact with their environment—is one important focus of sociology.

2. Societies increase the environmental deficit by focusing on short-term benefits and ignoring the long-term consequences brought on by their way of life.

3. Studying the natural environment demands a global perspective. All parts of the ecosystem—including the air, soil, and water—are interconnected. Similarly, actions in one part of the globe have an impact on the natural environment elsewhere.

4. Humanity's enormous influence on the natural environment springs from our capacity for culture. Our manipulation of the environment has expanded over time with the development of complex technology.

5. Through population growth, too, humanity affects the natural environment. The world population has soared upward over the course of the last two centuries and now threatens to overwhelm available natural resources.

6. The "logic of growth" argument defends economic development and asserts that people can

that marked the decade with people chaining themselves to trees to halt logging and blocking ships armed with nuclear weapons.

By 1970, with the celebration of the first "Earth Day," the environmental movement had come of age. Its adherents addressed a wide range of issues—including those covered in this chapter—and, increasingly, they directly challenged many of the practices and priorities that had long marked our way of life. In the early 1980s, the Reagan administration adopted a strong pro-business agenda, and soon the government and the environmental movement were locking horns over population control, land development, and other matters. As Reagan's appointees saw it, environmentalists were a "special interest," far out of the political mainstream.

Some environmentalists, of course, eagerly embrace the label of "radical." To them, basic changes are necessary in our way of life if we are to head off disaster down the road. In particular, they believe, we can no longer place economic growth at the heart of U.S. culture because this core value is causing an increasing environmental deficit.

Other environmentalists take a different tack, arguing that there is nothing at all radical about their movement. From this point of view, we must learn to live in concert with the environment because, politics aside, humanity cannot survive otherwise.

In the end, what environmentalists are saying is that, in light of the risks we face, making basic changes is common sense. And, on the surface at least, the public has come to accept environmentalism. Survey data reveal steady increases in support for this view: About two out of three adults now describe themselves as environmentalists.

But how much change is the U.S. population willing to make? As the figure shows, almost six people in ten think the government should spend more money on environmental issues. Yet a smaller share claims to be willing to pay higher prices or greater taxes in order to protect the environment. And not even one in three respondents is willing to accept a lower standard of living in exchange for greater environmental protection.

Perhaps our society has come to accept the idea that environmentalism is good in principle. But it is far from clear that most people are willing to make the hard choices to achieve a sustainable way of life.

Continue the debate . . .

1. *Do you think limiting economic growth is necessary in order to secure our environmental future? Would you be willing to accept a lower standard of living to protect the natural environment?*

2. *What action have you ever taken (signing a petition, participating in a demonstration, modifying your consumption patterns) in support of the environment?*

3. *Where do you think the major U.S. political parties stand on environmental issues?*

Sources: Based on Dunlap & Mertig (1992); survey data from Dunlap, Gallup, & Gallup (1992), and NORC (1994).

solve environmental problems as they arise. Countering this view, the "limits to growth" thesis states that societies have little choice but to curb development to head off eventual environmental collapse.

7. As a "disposable society," the United States generates 1 billion pounds of solid waste each day. Currently, our society incinerates 10 percent of solid waste, recycles another 10 percent, and disposes of the remaining 80 percent in landfills.

8. Water consumption is rapidly increasing throughout the world. Much of the world—notably northern Africa and the Middle East—is currently approaching a water-supply crisis.

9. The hydrological cycle purifies rainwater, but water pollution from dumping and chemical contamination still poses a serious threat to water quality in the United States. This problem is even more acute in the world's low-income countries.

10. Air quality became steadily worse in Europe and North America after the Industrial Revolution. About 1950, however, a turnaround took place and these societies have made significant progress in curbing air pollution. In low-income countries—especially in cities—air quality remains at unhealthy levels due to burning of "dirty" fuels and little regulation of pollution.

11. Acid rain, the product of pollutants entering the atmosphere, often contaminates land and water thousands of miles away.

12. Rain forests play a vital role in removing carbon dioxide from the atmosphere. Under pressure from commercial interests, the world's rain forests are now half their original size and are shrinking by about 1 percent annually.

13. Global warming refers to predictions that the average temperature of the earth will rise because of increasing levels of carbon dioxide in the atmosphere. Both carbon emissions from factories and automobiles and the shrinking rain forests, which consume carbon dioxide, aggravate this problem.

14. The elimination of rain forests is also reducing the planet's biodiversity, since these tropical regions are home to about half of all living species. Biodiversity, a source of natural beauty, is also critical to agricultural and medical research.

15. Structural-functional theory points out that cultural values have much to do with a society's orientation to the natural environment. Cultural ecology, one application of this approach, explains that a society's climate and natural resources influence culture.

16. Social-conflict analysis highlights the importance of inequality in understanding environmental issues. This perspective blames environmental decay on the self-interest of elites, and notes the pattern of environmental racism whereby the poor—and especially minorities—disproportionately suffer from proximity to environmental hazards. It also places responsibility for the declining state of the world's natural environment primarily on rich societies, which consume the most resources.

17. A sustainable environment is one that does not threaten the well-being of future generations. Achieving this goal will require conservation of finite resources, reducing waste and pollution, and controlling the size of the world's population.

KEY CONCEPTS

acid rain precipitation that is made acidic by air pollution so that it destroys plant and animal life

cultural ecology a theoretical paradigm that explores the relationship of human culture and the physical environment

ecologically sustainable culture a way of life that meets the needs of the present generation without threatening the environmental legacy of future generations

ecology the study of the interaction of living organisms and the natural environment

ecosystem the system composed of the interaction of all living organisms and their natural environment

environmental deficit the situation in which our relationship to the environment, while yielding short-term benefits, will have profound, negative long-term consequences

environmental racism the pattern by which environmental hazards are greatest in proximity to poor people—and especially minorities

greenhouse effect a rise in the earth's average temperature (global warming) due to increasing concentration of carbon dioxide in the atmosphere

natural environment the earth's surface and atmosphere, including various living organisms as well as the air, water, soil, and other resources necessary to sustain life

rain forests regions of dense forestation, most of which circle the globe close to the equator

CRITICAL-THINKING QUESTIONS

1. At one level, chemical spills are technical glitches that we sometimes dismiss as mere "accidents." But what social patterns and cultural values combine to make such occurrences regular events in our lives?

2. What special role can sociology play in understanding the natural environment?

3. What evidence supports the contention that humanity is running up an "environmental deficit"? What evidence suggests that environmental problems are subsiding?

4. In what specific ways would your own life change if we were to establish an environmentally sustainable society?

SUGGESTED READINGS

Classic Sources

Rachel Carson. *Silent Spring.* Boston: Houghton Mifflin, 1962.
  This book about the dangers of chemical pollution helped launch the environmental movement in the United States and elsewhere.

Donella H. Meadows et al. *The Limits to Growth: A Report for the Club of Rome's Project on the Predicament of Mankind.* New York: Universe Books, 1972.
  This study draws on computer modeling to predict future ecological trends. Its conclusions support the "limits to growth" thesis.

Contemporary Sources

Charles L. Harper. *Environment and Society: Social Perspectives on Environmental Issues and Problems.* Englewood Cliffs, N.J.: Prentice Hall, 1995.
  This new text applies various sociological approaches, including major theoretical paradigms, to the study of the environment.

Riley E. Dunlap and Angela G. Mertig, eds. *American Environmentalism: The U.S. Environmental Movement, 1970–1990.* Washington, D.C.: Taylor & Francis, 1992.
  This collection of eight essays surveys environmentalism as a body of knowledge and also as a social movement, domestically and in global perspective.

Global Source

Lester R. Brown et al. *State of the World: A Worldwatch Institute Report on Progress Toward a Sustainable Society.* New York: W. W. Norton, 1996.
  Published annually, this collection of essays focuses on a range of environmental dangers in global perspective.

UMBERTO BOCCIONI,
RIOT IN THE GALLERY, 1909

Umberto Boccioni, *Riot in the Gallery,*
1909/Superstock.

Collective Behavior
and Social Movements

On a bright October 1 million African-American classes, gathered in Washington corners of the United States—many day in 1995, upwards of males, of all ages and all social D.C. Having traveled from all from New York and Chicago, some from as far away as Los Angeles, San Francisco, and even the Hawaiian Islands—they joined together to form a sea of humanity that stretched from the Capitol building all the way to the Lincoln Memorial.

This event was dubbed the "Million Man March." To those assembled, it was a national display of pride, brotherhood, and determination to bring about change. In part, the marchers pledged to rededicate themselves to core cultural values such as self-reliance and making African-American families stronger. In addition, their collective presence in our nation's capital called attention to the fact that U.S. society still withholds full membership from 30 million people based on their skin color.

Such gatherings have been an integral part of the civil rights movement for forty years. As this chapter explains, a **social movement** is *an organized activity that encourages or discourages social change.* Social movements are the most important type of **collective behavior,** *activity involving a large number of people, often spontaneous, and typically in violation of established norms.* Other forms of collective behavior—each giving rise to controversy and some provoking change—are crowds, mobs and riots, rumor and gossip, public opinion, panics and mass hysteria, and fashions and fads.

A half-century ago, sociologists paid little attention to collective behavior, preferring to focus on more established social patterns like the family and social stratification. Because collective behavior deals with actions generally deemed unusual or deviant, in other words, analysts avoided this area of inquiry. The numerous social movements that burst on the scene during the tumultuous 1960s, however, ignited sociological interest in the field of collective behavior (Weller & Quarantelli, 1973; G. Marx & Wood, 1975; Aguirre & Quarantelli, 1983; Turner & Killian, 1987; McAdam, McCarthy, & Zald, 1988).

STUDYING COLLECTIVE BEHAVIOR

Despite its importance, collective behavior is difficult for sociologists to study for the following three reasons.

1. **Collective behavior is wide ranging.** Collective behavior encompasses a sometimes bewildering array of phenomena. The traits common to fads, rumors, and mob behavior, for example, are far from obvious.
2. **Collective behavior is complex.** A rumor seems to come out of nowhere and circulates in countless different settings. For no apparent reason, one new form of dress "catches on" while another does not. And, taking a more sweeping perspective, why would millions of African Americans patiently endure social disadvantages for decades before initiating the modern civil rights movement in the mid-1950s?
3. **Much collective behavior is transitory.** Sociologists can readily study the family because it is an enduring element of social life. Fashions, rumors, and riots, by contrast, tend to arise and dissipate quickly, making them difficult to investigate systematically.

Some researchers counter that these problems apply not just to collective behavior but to *most* forms of human behavior (Aguirre & Quarantelli, 1983). Moreover, collective behavior is not always so elusive; no one is surprised by the crowds that form at sports events and music festivals, and sociologists can study these gatherings firsthand or by reviewing videotapes or audio records. Sometimes researchers can even anticipate natural disasters in order to study the human response they provoke. We know, for

NOTE: Peter Dahlgren characterizes collective behavior as the breakdown of "the smooth rationality upon which the social order rests." Enrico Quarantelli, by contrast, counters that most collective behavior is both continuous and rational.

RESOURCE: The *Student CHIP Social Survey Software* program provides General Social Survey data sets for this chapter.

NOTE: The term "collective behavior" was coined by Robert E. Park; in fact, Park defined sociology as "the science of collective behavior," suggesting a focus on dynamic rather than stable social patterns. (See Ralph Turner's introduction to *Robert E. Park: On Social Control and Collective Behavior*, University of Chicago Press, 1967.)

Q: "The age we are about to enter will in truth be the era of crowds." Gustave Le Bon

example, that forty to eighty major tornadoes occur in particular regions of the United States each year; some sociologists interested in how such disasters affect behavior stand prepared to initiate research on short notice (Miller, 1985). Researchers can also draw on historical documents to reconstruct the details of an unanticipated natural disaster or riot.

While sociologists have learned much about collective behavior, they have not resolved all the problems presented by this area of study. The most serious issue, according to Benigno Aguirre and E. L. Quarantelli (1983), is that sociologists have yet to devise theories that tie together all the diverse actions that fall under the umbrella of "collective behavior."

Questions aside, all collective behavior involves the action of some **collectivity**, *a large number of people whose minimal interaction occurs in the absence of well-defined and conventional norms*. Collectivities are of two kinds. A *localized collectivity* refers to people in physical proximity to one another; this first type is illustrated by crowds and riots. A *dispersed collectivity* or *mass behavior* involves people who influence one another even though they are separated by great distances; examples here include rumors, public opinion, and fashion (Turner & Killian, 1993).

It is important to distinguish collectivities from the already familiar concept of social groups (see Chapter 7, "Groups and Organizations"). Here are three key differences:

1. **Collectivities are based on limited social interaction**. Group members interact directly and frequently. Interaction in localized collectivities such as mobs is limited and temporary. People participating in dispersed collectivities like a fad typically do not interact at all.

2. **Collectivities have no clear social boundaries**. Greater interaction gives group members a sense of common identity usually missing among people engaged in collective behavior. Localized crowds may have a common object of attention (such as a despondent person on a ledge high above the street), but these observers exhibit little sense of unity or coherence. Individuals involved in dispersed collectivities, such as "the public" that turns out to vote for a political candidate, have even less of an awareness of shared membership. People become more aware of "who their friends are" when a social movement gives rise to well-defined factions; even here, however, it is often difficult to discern who falls within the ranks of, say, the pro-life or pro-choice movement.

3. **Collectivities engender weak and unconventional norms**. Conventional cultural norms usually regulate the behavior of group members. Some collectivities, such as people traveling on an airplane, do operate according to social norms, but these rules usually amount to little more than respecting the privacy of people sitting in nearby seats. Other collectivities—such as emotional soccer fans who destroy property as they leave a stadium—spontaneously develop decidedly unconventional norms (Weller & Quarantelli, 1973; Turner & Killian, 1993).

LOCALIZED COLLECTIVITIES: CROWDS

A key form of collective behavior is the **crowd**, *a temporary gathering of people who share a common focus of attention and whose members influence one another*. Historian Peter Laslett (1984) points out that crowds are a modern development; in medieval Europe, large numbers of people assembled in one place only when major armies faced off on the battlefield. Today, however, crowds reaching 25,000 or more are common at sporting events, rock concerts, and even the registration halls of large universities.

But all such crowds are not alike. Herbert Blumer (1969) identified four categories of crowds. A *casual crowd* is a loose collection of people who interact little, if at all. People who gather on the beach or come together at the scene of an automobile accident have only a passing awareness of one another.

A *conventional crowd* results from deliberate planning, as illustrated by a country auction, a college lecture, or a funeral. In each case, interaction typically conforms to norms deemed appropriate for the situation.

An *expressive crowd* forms around an event with emotional appeal, such as a religious revival, a wrestling match featuring Hulk Hogan, or the New Year's Eve celebration in New York's Times Square. Excitement is the main reason people join expressive crowds in the first place, which makes expressive crowds relatively spontaneous and exhilarating for those taking part.

An *acting crowd* is a collectivity fueled by an intense, single-minded purpose, such as an audience rushing the doors of a concert hall or fleeing from a theater that is on fire. Acting crowds are ignited by emotions more powerful than those typical of expressive crowds, often reaching a feverish intensity that sometimes erupts into mob violence.

Q: "Collective behavior is not merely identical with the study of groups. . . . Organizational behavior is the behavior of groups that are governed by established rules or procedures, which have the force of tradition behind them. . . . Collectivities, or the groups within which collective behavior takes place, are not guided in a straightforward fashion by the culture of the society . . ." Ralph H. Turner and Lewis N. Killian (1987:4)

NOTE: The term "mob" is derived from the Latin *mobile vulgus*, meaning the "movable or changeable common people." Note the historical association of mobs with common people.

DIVERSITY: Racial violence has a long history in the United States. Most common were white attacks on black people, Asians, and Native Americans. The pattern of African Americans rioting against whites emerged later, in the 1960s.

Any gathering can change from one type of crowd to another. In 1985, for example, a conventional crowd took form as 60,000 fans assembled in a soccer stadium to watch the European Cup Finals between Italy and Great Britain. Once the game started, however, many British fans, already intoxicated, began taunting the Italians sitting in adjacent stands. At this point, an expressive crowd had formed. The two sides began to throw bottles at each other; then the British surged in a human wave toward the Italians. An estimated 400 million television viewers watched in horror as this acting crowd trampled hundreds of helpless spectators. In minutes, thirty-eight people were dead and another four hundred injured (Lacayo, 1985).

Deliberate action by a crowd is not the product simply of rising emotions. Participants in *protest crowds*—a fifth category we can add to Blumer's list—engage in a variety of actions, including strikes, boycotts, sit-ins, and marches that have political goals (McPhail & Wohlstein, 1983). For example, students on college campuses who gather to demonstrate their opposition to tuition hikes constitute a protest crowd. These crowds vary in emotional energy, ranging from conventional to acting crowds. Sometimes a protest gathering begins peacefully, but individuals become aggressive when confronted with counterdemonstrators, a process illustrated by recent clashes between pro-choice and pro-life activists.

Mobs and Riots

As an acting crowd turns violent, we may witness the birth of a **mob**, *a highly emotional crowd that pursues some violent or destructive goal.* Despite, or perhaps because of, their intense emotion, mobs tend to dissipate rather quickly. The duration of mob action often depends on its precise goals and whether its leadership tries to inflame or stabilize the crowd.

Lynching is the most notorious example of mob behavior in the United States. This term is derived from Charles Lynch, a Virginia colonist who sought to maintain law and order in his own way before formal courts were established. The word soon became synonymous with terrorism and murder outside the legal system.

Lynching has always been colored by race. After the Civil War, whites' efforts to maintain their domination over emancipated African Americans touched off lynch mobs as a highly effective form of social control. African Americans who questioned white superiority or behaved in a nondeferential way risked hanging or being burned alive by vengeful whites.

Much of the exuberance of Beatlemania, which swept up millions of young fans in Europe and North America beginning in the early 1960s, can be traced to the music and personal charisma of the Beatles. But being "part of the crowd" is itself appealing, because collective life generates its own emotional intensity.

Black people and occasionally their white defenders became all-purpose scapegoats.

The activity of lynch mobs—typically composed of low-status whites most threatened by the emancipation of slaves—reached its peak between 1880 and 1930. About 5,000 lynchings were recorded by police in that period; no doubt, many more occurred. Most of these crimes were committed in the Deep South, where the agrarian economy still depended on a cheap and docile labor force, but lynchings took place in virtually every state and victimized every minority. On the western frontier, for example, lynch mobs frequently targeted people of Mexican and Asian descent. In about 25 percent of the cases, whites lynched other whites. The lynching of women, however, was rare; only about a hundred such instances are known, almost all involving women of color (White, 1969, orig. 1929; Grant, 1975).

A frenzied crowd without any particular purpose is a **riot**, *a social eruption that is highly emotional, violent, and undirected.* Unlike the action of a mob, then, a riot usually has no clear goal. Underlying most riots is longstanding anger, set off by some minor incident, that prompts participants to indulge in seemingly

The powers that be have often disparaged popular opposition as a "mob." Such an argument was used to justify police violence against strikers—including ten who died—in a bloody confrontation near Chicago's Republic Steel Mill in 1936. Philip Evergood commemorates the event in his painting American Tragedy.

Philip Evergood, *American Tragedy,* 1936, oil on canvas, 29½ x 39½", Terry Dintenfass Gallery, New York.

random violence against people or property (Smelser, 1962). Whereas a mob action usually ends when a specific violent goal has been achieved (or decisively blocked), a riot tends to disperse only when participants run out of steam or police and community leaders gradually bring them under control.

Throughout our nation's history, riots have erupted as a collective expression of social injustice. Industrial workers, for example, have rioted to vent rage at their working conditions. In 1886, a bitter struggle by Chicago factory workers seeking an eight-hour workday led to the explosive Haymarket Riot, which left eleven dead and scores injured. Rioting born of anger and despair has also been commonplace within this country's penal system.

In addition, race riots have occurred with striking regularity. Early in this century, crowds of whites attacked African Americans in Chicago, Detroit, and other cities. In the 1960s, summers of violent riots rocked numerous inner-city ghettos as seemingly trivial events sparked rage at continuing prejudice and discrimination. In Los Angeles in 1992, an explosive riot was touched off by the acquittal of police officers involved in the beating of Rodney King. The turmoil left more than fifty dead, caused thousands of injuries, and destroyed property worth hundreds of millions of dollars.

Riots are not always fired by hate. They may also burst forth out of positive feelings, such as the high spirits characteristic of young people who flock to resort areas during spring break from college. In March of 1986, for example, the exuberance of vacationing students in Palm Springs, California, erupted into a riot leading to a hundred arrests after crowds of young men began throwing rocks and bottles at passing cars and stripping clothing off terrified women (DeMott, 1986).

Crowds, Mobs, and Social Change

November 2, 1988, Delhi, India. The sidewalk in front of an office building is blocked by a crowd of people staging some kind of protest. The demonstrators chant slogans; anger is in the air. From a window several stories above, a man glances downward—perhaps he is the target of their attention? His expression of disgust leaves little doubt of what he thinks about his accusers.

Ordinary people typically gain power only by acting collectively. Historically, because crowds have been able to effect social change, they have also provoked controversy. Defenders of the established social order have long feared "the mob." In countries around the world, elites know that the masses—organized and focused on a goal—pose a threat to their power. We might bear in mind, however, that collective action condemned by

Q: "Interest in the field [of collective behavior and social movements] has hardly been constant, tending instead to wax and wane partly in response to the level of movement activity in society." Doug McAdam, John D. McCarthy, and Mayer N. Zald

Q: "Usually the judgment that someone has acted irrationally is made in hindsight or by someone who is not in the situation of the actor and thus has a different perspective." Ralph H. Turner and Lewis N. Killian

some people is typically cheered by others as rightful protest. In our own history, the "mob actions" deplored by British officials have come down to us in history books as the valiant efforts of early patriots who risked their lives so our country could be free.

Moreover, crowds share no single political cast: Some call for change and some resist it. Throngs of Romans rallying to the Sermon on the Mount by Jesus of Nazareth, bands of traditional weavers destroying new industrial machinery that was making their skills obsolete, masses of marchers carrying banners and shouting slogans for or against abortion—these and countless other purposeful gatherings across the centuries reveal how crowds enable people to challenge or support their society (Rudé, 1964; Canetti, 1978; Tarrow, 1994).

Explaining Crowd Behavior

What accounts for the behavior of crowds? Over the last century, social scientists have developed several different explanations for collective action.

Contagion Theory

One of the first explanations of collective behavior was formulated by French sociologist Gustave Le Bon (1841–1931) as *contagion theory*. The essence of Le Bon's (1960; orig. 1895) argument is that crowds exert a hypnotic influence over their members. Shielded by the anonymity of a crowd, he claimed, people evade personal responsibility and surrender to a collective mind. As a crowd assumes a life of its own, individual members slip free of social restraints and become irrational creatures driven by contagious emotion. As fear or hate resonates through the crowd, emotions intensify, driving individuals toward a violent outburst.

Critical evaluation. Some of Le Bon's assertions—that crowds foster anonymity and sometimes generate emotion—are surely true. Yet, as Clark McPhail (1991) points out, systematic research reveals that "the madding crowd" does not take on a life of its own, apart from the thoughts and intentions of members. For example, Norris Johnson (1987), investigating panic at a 1979 Who concert in Cincinnati, identified specific factors that sparked the alarm that led to the deaths of eleven people. Causes included an inadequate number of entrance doors, an open-seating policy, and little police supervision. Far from an episode of collective insanity, Johnson concluded, that

crowd was composed of many small groups of people valiantly trying to help each another.

Convergence Theory

Convergence theory holds that motivations for collective action are not born in the crowd but are brought in to the crowd by individual participants. From this point of view, then, crowds amount to a convergence of like-minded individuals. So convergence theory, which asserts that motivation creates the crowd, reverses the causal link implied by contagion theory, which suggests that crowds themselves generate human motivation.

Over the years, for example, whites in various communities have banded together to keep African Americans from moving into their neighborhoods. In such instances, convergence theorists contend, the crowd itself does not generate the racial hatred or the violence; more accurately, hostility among many local people had been simmering for some time. A crowd simply arises from a convergence of people sharing an attachment to a traditionally white neighborhood and opposing the presence of black residents.

Critical evaluation. By linking crowds to broader social forces, convergence theory uncovers the roots of collective action. From this perspective, crowd behavior is not irrational, as Le Bon maintained, but rather stems from social structure and individual decision making (Berk, 1974).

It is probably true, however, that people sometimes do things in a crowd that they would not have the courage to do alone because crowds can diffuse responsibility. In addition, crowds can intensify a sentiment simply by creating a critical mass of like-minded people.

Emergent-Norm Theory

Ralph Turner and Lewis Killian (1993) have developed an *emergent-norm theory* of crowd dynamics. These researchers maintain that social behavior is never entirely predictable; yet, they quickly add, neither are crowds the irrational settings described by Le Bon. And, while similar interests may draw people together, distinctive patterns of behavior do emerge within a crowd itself.

Turner and Killian explain that crowds begin as collectivities in which people have mixed interests and motives. Especially in the case of less stable crowds—expressive, acting, and protest crowds—

Q: "The nearer the people are drawn to the common level of an equal and similar condition, the less prone does each man become to place implicit faith in a certain man or a certain class of men. But his readiness to believe the multitude increases, and opinion is more than ever the mistress of the world." Alexis de Tocqueville

Q: "To regard gossip as 'idle chatter' is to underestimate its usefulness. . . . By making some people 'insiders,' gossip may serve the social needs of other-directed people." Jack Levin and Arnold Arluke (*Gossip: The Inside Scoop*, Plenum, 1987)

norms that guide behavior may surface only in particular settings. Usually leaders start the process of norm construction. For example, one member of a crowd at a rock concert holds up a lit cigarette lighter, to signal praise for the performers, and others follow suit; or a few people in an angry street crowd throw bricks through store windows and others do the same, sparking a riot.

In an infamous incident in New Bedford, Massachusetts, in 1983, a man assaulted a twenty-one-year-old woman, raping her on a barroom floor. Five other men then joined in, repeatedly raping the woman for an hour and a half. Still others in the bar cheered the rapists; apparently, to some people there, this brutal action seemed somehow acceptable, while the rest were too intimidated to assist the woman or even call the police.

Critical evaluation. Emergent-norm theory represents a symbolic-interaction approach to crowd dynamics. Turner and Killian (1972:10) explain that crowd behavior is neither as irrational as contagion theory suggests, nor as purposeful as convergence theory implies. So while crowd behavior responds to participants' motives, it is guided by norms that emerge in a setting as the situation unfolds.

Decision making, then, does play a significant role in crowd behavior, even though it may escape the notice of casual observers. For example, frightened people clogging the exits of a burning theater may appear to be victims of irrational panic but, from their point of view, fleeing a life-threatening situation is certainly a rational alternative to death. Experience and common sense play a part in precisely how people respond to any such event, of course; leaders on the scene also have a hand in guiding crowd response.

Further, emergent-norm theory points out that not every participant embraces emerging norms to the same degree. Some assume leadership roles, others become lieutenants, rank-and-file followers, inactive bystanders, or even opponents (Weller & Quarantelli, 1973; Zurcher & Snow, 1981).

DISPERSED COLLECTIVITIES: MASS BEHAVIOR

It is not just people in physical proximity who participate in collective behavior. Sociologists use the term **mass behavior** to refer to *collective behavior among people dispersed over a wide geographical area.*

Rumor and Gossip

A common example of mass behavior is **rumor**, *unsubstantiated information people spread informally, often by word of mouth*. Although people still pass along rumors through face-to-face communication, modern technology—including telephones, the mass media, and now the Internet—spreads rumors more rapidly and to a greater number of people than ever before.

Rumor has three essential characteristics.

1. **Rumor thrives in a climate of ambiguity**. Rumors arise among people who lack definitive information about a topic of concern. For example, workers fearing a massive layoff, and hearing little official news from management, will usually find themselves awash in rumors. In positive terms, rumor is an effort to define reality in the absence of substantiated facts (Shibutani, 1966; Rosnow & Fine, 1976).

2. **Rumor is unstable**. As people spread a rumor, they alter its content, generally to serve their own interests. Before long, many variations emerge. In a workplace beset by rumors, workers typically play up the shortcomings of management, while executives "spin" information to reflect well on the corporate hierarchy.

3. **Rumor is difficult to stop**. The number of people aware of a rumor increases exponentially as each person relays information to several others. Of course, some rumors dissipate with time, but, in general, only clear, widely dispersed, and convincing information will put a rumor to rest.

Rumor can trigger the formation of crowds or other collective behavior. For this reason, authorities often establish rumor-control centers in times of crisis as a form of information management and social control. Yet some rumors persist for years despite incontrovertible evidence to the contrary; the box on page 619 provides one notable example.

Closely related to rumor is **gossip**, *rumor about the personal affairs of others*. Charles Horton Cooley (1962; orig. 1909) explained that, while rumor involves issues or events of interest to a large segment of the public, gossip concerns a small circle of people who know a particular person. While rumors spread widely, then, gossip is more localized.

Gossip can be an effective strategy for social control as its targets become aware that they are the subject of praise or scorn. People may also gossip about others to elevate their own standing as "insiders" in a

NOTE: Delbert Miller claimed that, in 1945, only a small number of people on his campus learned of the death of President Roosevelt directly from radio reports. Within thirty minutes, however, about 90% of the people had been informed by word of mouth (*American Sociological Review* 10:691–94). Obviously, today's more powerful mass media reduce the significance of word of mouth in spreading national rumor.

NOTE: Levin and Arluke spread a rumor on their campus by widely distributing flyers announcing a fictitious wedding. The flyers were not circulated until a day before the supposed event. Still, the researchers found that, one week later, 52% of a campus sample had heard about the wedding, and 12% claimed to have actually attended it! (1987:14–15)

SOCIOLOGY OF EVERYDAY LIFE

The Rumor Mill: Paul Is Dead!

The 1995 reunion of the remaining Beatles—Paul McCartney, George Harrison, and Ringo Starr—along with the music of their early leader John Lennon reminded the world of the cultural explosion caused by their music in the early 1960s. At the height of their unprecedented fame, the Beatles became the subject of a persistent rumor—the alleged death of Paul McCartney.

The rumor of McCartney's death probably began on October 12, 1969, when a young man telephoned a Detroit disk jockey and made two startling announcements:

1. If you filtered out background noise at the end of the song "Strawberry Fields Forever" on the *Magical Mystery Tour* album, you would hear a voice saying, "I buried Paul!"

2. The phrase "Number 9, Number 9, Number 9" from the song "Revolution 9" on the *White Album*, when played backward, seems to intone, "Turn me on, dead man!"

Two days later, the student newspaper at the University of Michigan carried a story titled "McCartney Is Dead: Further Clues Found." It sent millions of Beatles fans scurrying for their albums to confirm the "evidence."

3. A picture inside the *Magical Mystery Tour* album shows John, George, and Ringo wearing red carnations, while Paul is sporting a black flower.

4. The cover of the *Sergeant Pepper's Lonely Hearts Club Band* album shows a grave with yellow flowers

arranged in the shape of Paul's bass guitar.

5. On the inside of that album, McCartney wears an armpatch with the letters "OPD." Was this the insignia of some police department, or confirmation that Paul had been "Officially Pronounced Dead"?

6. On the back cover of the same album, three Beatles are facing forward while McCartney has his back to the camera.

7. On the album cover of *Abbey Road*, John Lennon is clothed as a clergyman, Ringo Starr wears an undertaker's black tie, and George Harrison is clad in workman's attire as if ready to dig a grave. For his part, McCartney is barefoot—just as Tibetan burial rituals require a corpse ready for interment to be. Further, a Volkswagen nearby displays the license plate "28 IF," correctly indicating that McCartney would have been *28 if* he had not met his demise.

The report in the University of Michigan newspaper provided details of McCartney's alleged "death" in an automobile accident early in November, 1966, and included a photograph that allegedly showed the musician's bloodied head. After the accident, the story continued, music company executives had concocted a scheme to secretly replace Paul with a look-alike imposter.

As his recent television appearance proves, Paul McCartney is very much alive and still jokes about the episode. Few doubt that the Beatles intentionally fabricated some of the "clues" to pique the interest of their fans. But the incident has a serious side, revealing how quickly rumors arise and how long they endure in a climate of distrust. During the late 1960s, many disaffected young people had no trouble believing that the media and other powerful interests would conspire to conceal from the public an event such as McCartney's death.

McCartney himself denied the rumor in a 1969 *Life* magazine interview. But thousands of suspicious readers also noticed that the back of the page containing McCartney's picture had an advertisement for an automobile: Holding this page up to the light, the discerning reader could see that the car lay across McCartney's chest and blocked his head! Another clue!

Sources: Based on Rosnow & Fine (1976) and Kapferer (1992).

Seeing Ourselves

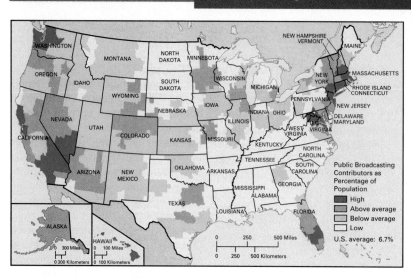

NATIONAL MAP 23-1

Support for Public Broadcasting Across the United States

About 7 percent of people in the United States pledge money to support the Public Broadcasting System (PBS), contributing some $280 million in 1994 to maintain public radio and television (one-seventh of the PBS budget). As the map shows, PBS supporters are concentrated in particular regions of the country. What do you think accounts for this pattern?

Source: *Time* (January 16, 1995). Copyright © 1995 Time, Inc. Reprinted by permission.

---

social group. Those who gossip *too* often, however, may find themselves dismissed as disreputable. The need to control gossip in this way suggests the power of this type of informal communication.

Public Opinion

One form of highly dispersed collective behavior is *public opinion*, which Chapter 5 ("Socialization") defined as widespread attitudes about controversial issues. Although we frequently speak about "the public" in singular terms, there are really many publics forged around a host of issues that attract people's interest. Over the years in the United States, publics have waxed and waned over issues such as water fluoridation, air pollution, the social standing of women, handguns, and health care. As this listing indicates, public issues are important matters about which people disagree (Lang & Lang, 1961; Turner & Killian, 1993). National Map 23-1 provides a sketch of where people do—and do not—support public radio and television.

Note that, on any given issue, anywhere from 2 to 10 percent of people offer no opinion at all, due to ignorance or indifference. Moreover, over time, public interest in some issues rises and falls. For example, concern about the social position of women in the United States ran high during the decades of the women's suffrage movement but declined after 1920 when women won the right to vote. Since the 1960s, a second wave of feminism has again created a public with strong opinions about a host of gender-related issues.

And keep in mind that not everyone's opinion has the same clout on any issue. Some categories of people have more social influence than others because they are better educated, wealthier, or more powerful. As Chapter 16 ("Politics and Government") explained, many special interest groups shape public policy in the United States even though they represent only a small fraction of the population. For example, specialized training and savvy political organizing—not to mention millions in donations to entrenched political figures—give physicians enormous influence over health care policy even though they represent just a tiny fraction of the U.S. population.

Political leaders, special interest groups, and businesses all attempt to influence public tastes and attitudes by using **propaganda**, *information presented with the intention of shaping public opinion.* Although the term has negative connotations, propaganda is not necessarily false. A thin line separates information from propaganda, and this difference is mostly a matter of the presenter's intention. People share information to enlighten others; by contrast, they utilize propaganda to sway an audience toward a particular viewpoint. Political speeches, commercial advertising, and even some college lectures may disseminate propaganda not with the goal of helping people think intelligently for themselves but in an

RESOURCE: Norris Johnson's account of "The Who Concert Panic" is included in the contemporary research found in the companion reader, *Seeing Ourselves*.

Q: "Perhaps there are situations such as a fire in a crowded theater in which people totally ignore others as they try to escape from danger. However, documented cases . . . are surprisingly rare in the literature." Norris Johnson

NOTE: The Greek root of the word "hysteria" is *hystero* meaning "uterus." This etymology reveals the historical association between irrational behavior and women. Moreover, in European and North American history, most witches were women, usually women who did not conform to conventional definitions of femininity.

The most deadly episode of mass hysteria in U.S. history swept up the village of Salem, Massachusetts, in 1692. Fearing witches in their midst, villagers tried and executed twenty people within the year. Such cases of hysteria accompanied the declining strength of religion as the Middle Ages drew to a close.

effort to steer the audience toward thinking or acting in some specific way.

Panic and Mass Hysteria

A **panic** is *a form of localized collective behavior by which people react to a perceived threat or other stimulus with irrational, frantic, and often self-destructive behavior.* The classic illustration of a panic is the scene of people streaming toward exits after someone yells "Fire!" in a crowded theater. As they flee in fear, however, they trample one another, blocking exits so that few actually escape.

Closely related to panic is **mass hysteria**, *a form of dispersed collective behavior by which people respond to a real or imagined event with irrational, frantic, and often self-destructive behavior.* Whether the cause of the mass hysteria is real or not, a large number of people certainly take it very seriously. Parents' unfounded fears that their children may become infected by a schoolmate who has AIDS may cause as much hysteria in a community as the very real danger of an approaching hurricane. Moreover, actions of people in the grip of mass hysteria generally make the situation worse. At the extreme, mass hysteria leads to chaotic flight and sends crowds into panic. People who see others overcome by fear may become more afraid themselves, as hysteria feeds on itself.

During the evening before Halloween in 1938, CBS radio broadcast a dramatization of H. G. Wells's novel *War of the Worlds* (Cantril, Gaudet, & Herzog,

1947; Koch, 1970). From a New York studio, a small group of actors began to perform a program of dance music for a national audience of some 10 million people. Suddenly, they interrupted the performance with a "news report" of explosions on the surface of the planet Mars and, soon after, the crash landing of a mysterious cylinder near a farmhouse in New Jersey. The program then switched to an "on-the-scene reporter" who presented a graphic account of giant monsters equipped with death-ray weapons emerging from the spaceship. An "eminent astronomer," played by Orson Welles, somberly informed the audience that Martians had begun a full-scale invasion. At a time when most people relied on their radios for factual news and many were prepared to believe that intelligent life existed on Mars, this episode was chilling.

Even though three times during the program an announcer identified the broadcast as fiction, more than 1 million people concluded that the events were actually taking place as described. By the time the show was over, thousands were hysterical, gathering in the streets to spread news of the "invasion," while others flooded telephone switchboards with warnings to friends and relatives. Among those who jumped into their cars and fled were a college senior and his roommate:

> My roommate was crying and praying. He was even more excited than I was—or more noisy about it anyway; I guess I took it out in pushing the accelerator to the floor. . . . After it was all over, I started to think about that ride, I was more jittery than when it was

DISCUSS: A rather long-lived fad is Rubik's cube, invented in 1974 by Erno Rubik, a Hungarian architect. Sales exceeded 30 million cubes (and 10 million books on how to solve it) by 1982; subsequently, it fizzled. Another example is the troll doll, devised by a Danish woodcutter as a gift for his daughter in 1959; it became a hit in 1964 and is still around. What other fads can students identify?

NOTE: Contrast transient *fads* with more lasting *trends*, which are rooted in a basic cultural pattern. A recent marketing trend is "value pricing" in fast food, automobiles, and even textbooks, which caught on as the economy sagged in late 1980s. Another example is the McDonaldization trend, discussed in Chapter 7, involving fast food, fast oil changes, and packaged vacations, which responds to our need for quick products on the go. (Letscher, 1994)

Because change in industrial societies is rapid and ongoing, differences in personal appearance—one important kind of fashion—are clearly evident over even a ten-year period. The five photographs (beginning at the top, left) show hair styles commonly worn by men in the 1950s, 1960s, 1970s, 1980s, and 1990s.

happening. The speed was never under 70. I thought I was racing against time. . . . I didn't have any idea exactly what I was fleeing from, and that made me all the more afraid. (Cantril, Gaudet, & Herzog, 1947:52)

Fashions and Fads

Two additional types of collective behavior—fashions and fads—affect people dispersed over a large area. A **fashion** is *a social pattern favored for a time by a large number of people.* In contrast to more established norms, fashion is transitory, sometimes lasting for only months. Fashion characterizes the arts (including painting, music, drama, and literature), the style of buildings, automobiles, and clothes, our use of language, and public opinion. The most widely recognized examples of fashion involve aspects of our personal appearance.

Lyn Lofland (1973) notes that, in preindustrial societies, clothing and personal adornment reflect

traditional *style* that changes little over the years. Categories of people—women and men, and members of various classes and occupations—wear the distinctive clothes and hairstyles of their social and occupational position.

In industrial societies, however, style gives way to fashion for two reasons. First, modern people are less tied to tradition and often eagerly embrace new ways of living. Second, the high social mobility of industrial societies places heightened significance on what people consume. German sociologist Georg Simmel (1971; orig. 1904) explained that people use fashion to craft their presentation of self in pursuit of approval and prestige. According to Simmel, affluent people are typically the trendsetters, since they have the money to spend on luxuries that bespeak privilege. In the lasting phrase of U.S. sociologist Thorstein Veblen (1953; orig. 1899), fashion involves *conspicuous consumption,* meaning that people buy expensive products (whether well made or not) simply to display their wealth to one another.

Less affluent people understandably aspire to own the trappings of wealth, so they snap up less expensive copies of what has become fashionable. In this way, a fashion ripples downward in society. But, as this happens, the fashion eventually loses its prestige, with the wealthy moving on to something new. Fashions, in short, are born at the top of the social hierarchy—on the Fifth Avenues and Rodeo Drives of the rich—rising to mass popularity in bargain stores across the country, and soon are all but forgotten by everyone.

A reversal of this pattern sometimes occurs among rich but egalitarian-minded people who "look downward." In this case, well-off people mimic a fashion that originates among people of lower social position as an expression of identification with the masses. In a classic example of this process, affluent college students favor blue jeans, or dungarees (from a Hindi word for a coarse and inferior fabric). First worn by manual laborers, jeans became the uniform of political activists in the civil rights and antiwar movements in the 1960s and, gradually, of college students across the country. Author Tom Wolfe (1970) coined the phrase "radical chic" to satirize the desire of the rich to look fashionably poor.

A **fad** is *an unconventional social pattern that people embrace briefly but enthusiastically*. Fads, sometimes called *crazes*, are commonplace in affluent industrial societies in which people have the money to spend on amusing, if often frivolous, products. During the 1950s, two young entrepreneurs in California produced a brightly colored plastic version of a popular Australian toy, a hoop three feet in diameter designed to be swung primarily around the waist by gyrating the hips. The "hula hoop" soon rose to the level of a national craze. Within a year, hula hoops disappeared from the scene almost as quickly as they had emerged, but—decades later—they surfaced once again, this time in China.

Streaking—running naked in public—had an even briefer moment in the sun, lasting only a few months in early 1974. Their fleeting duration suggests that fads happen almost at random. But research indicates that the popularity of any fad depends on its acceptance by high-prestige people. In addition, as we see in the case of streaking, fads fade from the scene if subjected to official repression by police or other authority figures (Aguirre, Quarantelli, & Mendoza, 1988).

Fads and fashions both involve dispersed collectivities and last only a short time. But they differ in several respects (Blumer, 1968; Turner & Killian, 1987).

Fads are truly passing fancies—enthusiasms that capture the mass imagination but quickly burn out and disappear. Fashions, by contrast, reflect fundamental cultural values like individuality and sexual attractiveness and tend to evolve over time. In this way, a fashion but rarely a fad becomes incorporated into a society's culture. Streaking, for instance, came out of nowhere and soon vanished, while blue jeans originated in the rough mining camps of Gold Rush California more than a century ago and still influence clothing designs today. Such persistence explains the positive connotation attached to something "fashionable" in contrast to the mildly insulting label "faddish."

SOCIAL MOVEMENTS

Crowds, rumors, fashions, and the other forms of collective behavior we have examined usually have little enduring significance for society as a whole. Social movements, by contrast, are deliberate and consequential forms of collective behavior.

Social movements stand apart from other types of collective behavior in three respects: They have a high degree of internal organization, they last longer, and their purpose is to change or defend some particular social arrangements.

Social movements are far more common today than in the past. Preindustrial societies are tightly integrated by tradition, making social movements extremely rare. Industrial societies, however, foster diversity in the form of subcultures and countercultures so that social movements develop around a wide range of public issues. In recent decades, for example, homosexual men and women—supported by sympathetic heterosexuals—have organized to win economic and legal parity in our society. The gay rights movement has already succeeded in securing legislation in numerous cities and several states forbidding discrimination based on sexual orientation. Like any social movement that challenges conventional practices, this one has sparked a countermovement as traditionalists try to block greater social acceptance of homosexuality. In today's society, almost every significant public issue gives rise to both a social movement favoring change and an opposing countermovement to resist change and reinforce the status quo (Lo, 1982).

Types of Social Movements

Sociologists have classified social movements according to several criteria (Aberle, 1966; Cameron, 1966; Blumer, 1969). One variable asks *who is changed?*,

Q: "All previous historical movements were movements of minorities, or in the interests of minorities. The proletarian movement is the self-conscious, independent movement of the immense majority, in the interest of the immense majority." Karl Marx and Friedrich Engels

NOTE: "Ists" (socialists, fascists, feminists, etc.) are people who subscribe to "isms."

RESOURCE: Jo Freeman's article, "On the Origin of Social Movements," is among the "classics" included in the 3d edition of the Macionis and Benokraitis reader, *Seeing Ourselves.*

NOTE: Joan Fitzgerald and Louise Simmons (1991) point out that to evaluate the success of any social movement, we must look beyond *immediate* effects to assess the movement's contribution to *future* social change.

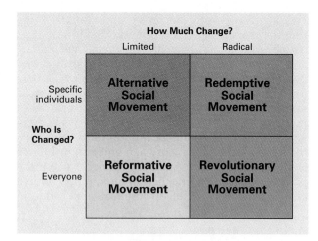

FIGURE 23–1 Four Types of Social Movements
Source: Based onn Aberle (1966).

since some movements target selected people while others try to change everyone. A second variable looks at *how much change?*; some movements attempt to foster only superficial changes in how we live, while others pursue a radical transformation of society. Combining these variables, we can identify four types of social movements, shown in Figure 23–1.

Alternative social movements are the least threatening to the established social order, seeking limited change only in some narrow segment of the population. Planned Parenthood, one example of an alternative social movement, encourages individuals of childbearing age to take the consequences of sexual activity more seriously by practicing birth control.

Redemptive social movements also have a selective focus, but they attempt to induce radical change in those they engage. Examples include fundamentalist Christian organizations that seek to win new members through conversion. The resulting transformation is sometimes so great that converts describe their experience as being "born again."

Reformative social movements aim for only limited social change but target everyone. The multiculturalism movement, described in Chapter 3 ("Culture"), is an educational and political initiative that advocates working toward social parity for all racial and ethnic categories of people. Reformative social movements generally work inside the existing political system. They can be progressive (promoting a new social pattern) or reactionary (countermovements trying to preserve the status quo or to reinstate past social mores). Just as multiculturalists are pushing for greater racial equality, for example, so do various white supremacist

organizations persist in their efforts to maintain the historical dominance of one racial category.

Revolutionary social movements have the most severe and far-reaching consequences of all, striving for basic transformation of a society. Sometimes pursuing specific goals, sometimes spinning utopian dreams, followers of these social movements reject established social institutions as inherently flawed while favoring radically new alternatives. Both the left-wing Communist Party (pushing for government control of the economy) and right-wing militia groups (advocating the destruction of "big government") seek to radically alter our social institutions.

Explaining Social Movements

Because social movements are deliberately organized and often enduring, sociologists find this form of collective behavior somewhat easier to explain than fleeting incidents of mob behavior or mass hysteria. Several theories have come to the fore.

Deprivation Theory

Deprivation theory holds that social movements arise among people who feel deprived. People who feel they lack sufficient income, satisfactory working conditions, important political rights, or basic social dignity may engage in organized collective behavior to bring about a more just state of affairs (Morrison, 1978; Rose, 1982).

The rise of the Ku Klux Klan and the push for so-called Jim Crow laws to enforce segregation throughout the South in the wake of the Civil War exemplify deprivation theory. Emancipation deprived white people, who had formerly owned African Americans as personal property, not only of their economic investment but of their sense of certain superiority. Many whites responded to Emancipation, therefore, by keeping African Americans "in their place"—a strategy designed to perpetuate the whites' relative advantage (Dollard et al., 1939). For their part, African Americans had long experienced much greater deprivation, but the overwhelming power of the white majority gave them relatively little opportunity to organize. Not until well into this century did African Americans forge organizations that successfully pursued racial equality.

As Chapter 7 ("Groups and Organizations") explained, deprivation is a relative concept. Regardless of how much money and power someone accumulates, people feel either well off or deprived compared

Q: "For public interest groups, the best of times *are* the worst of times, since the perception of political crisis can help mobilize political support." Douglas R. Imig and David S. Meyer (1993)

Q: "Psychological attributes of individuals, such as frustration and alienation, have minimal direct impact for explaining the occurrence of rebellion and revolution per se." Carol Mueller

SOCIAL SURVEY: What are your personal feelings about people who organize protests against a government action they strongly oppose?" (GSS 1990, N = 1,217; *Codebook,* 1994:520)

"Extremely favorable"	8.8%	"Unfavorable"	14.2%
"Favorable"	26.5%	"Extremely unfavorable"	5.7%
"Neutral"	33.9%	DK/NR	11.0%

to some category of others—a reference group. **Relative deprivation**, then, is *a perceived disadvantage arising from some specific comparison* (Stouffer et al., 1949; Merton, 1968).

More than a century ago Alexis de Tocqueville (1955; orig. 1856) studied the French Revolution. Why, he asked, did rebellion occur in progressive France rather than in more traditional Germany, where peasants were, by any objective measure, worse off? Tocqueville's answer was that, as bad as their condition was, German peasants had known nothing but feudal servitude and thus had no basis for feeling deprived. French peasants, by contrast, had seen various improvements in their lives that whetted their appetites for more. Thus the French—not the Germans—felt a keen sense of relative deprivation. In analyzing this apparent paradox, Tocqueville pinpointed one of the notable ironies of human history: Increasing prosperity, far from satisfying the population, is likely to promote a spirit of unrest (1955:175; orig. 1856).

Echoing Tocqueville's insight, James C. Davies (1962) suggests that as life gets better, people may take their rising fortunes for granted and come to expect even more. Relative deprivation can set in if the standard of living suddenly stops going up or, worse, begins to drop. As Figure 23–2 illustrates, social movements aimed at changing society coalesce when an extended period of improvement in the standard of living is followed by a shorter period of decline.

Critical evaluation. Deprivation theory reveals the limits of common sense as a predictor of discontent. People do not organize simply because they are suffering in an absolute sense; social movements to promote change are propelled by a perception of relative deprivation. We can discern the underlying truth of this insight by noting that it is found in the work of thinkers as diverse as Marx and Tocqueville.

But since most people experience some discontent all the time, we are left wondering, first, why social movements emerge among certain categories of people and not others. Second, deprivation theory has a tendency toward circular reasoning: We assume that deprivation causes social movements, but often the only evidence of deprivation is the social movement itself (Jenkins & Perrow, 1977). A third limitation of this approach is that while it focuses on the setting in which a social movement develops, it tells us little about movements themselves (McAdam, McCarthy, & Zald, 1988). Fourth, some researchers have claimed that relative deprivation has not turned out to be a very good predictor of social movements (Muller, 1979).

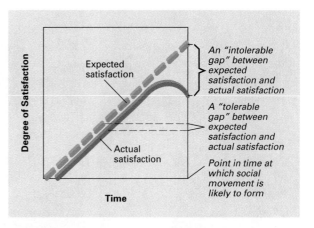

FIGURE 23–2 Relative Deprivation and Social Movements

In this diagram, the solid line represents a rising standard of living over time. The dotted line indicates the expected standard of living, which is typically somewhat higher. James C. Davies describes the difference between the two as "a tolerable gap between what people want and what they get." If the standard of living suddenly drops in the midst of rising expectations, however, this gap grows to an intolerable level. At this point, we can expect social movements to form.
Source: Davies (1962).

Mass-Society Theory

William Kornhauser's *mass-society theory* (1959) argues that social movements attract socially isolated people who feel personally insignificant. From this point of view, social movements characterize large, complex *mass* societies. Further, social movements are more *personal* than *political,* in that they confer a sense of purpose and belonging on people otherwise adrift in society (Melucci, 1989).

This theory holds that categories of people with weak social ties are most readily mobilized into a social movement. People who have a strong sense of social integration, by contrast, are unlikely to join the ranks of a movement for change.

Like Gustave Le Bon, discussed earlier, Kornhauser offers a conservative and critical view of social movements. He regards activists as psychologically vulnerable individuals who eagerly join groups only to have leaders manipulate them, thereby subverting democratic principles. Thus extremist social movements on both ends of the political spectrum typically gain their most ardent support from people who have few other social affiliations.

NOTE: The conservative character of mass-society theory stems from the implication that it is the loss of traditional social ties (and not social inequality) that leads to social movements. Kornhauser follows Tocqueville rather than Marx in focusing on mass movements rather than on class movements. The distinction between mass society and class society is developed further in Chapter 24 ("Social Change: Traditional, Modern, and Postmodern Societies").

NOTE: Mass-society theory has much in common with Hirschi's control theory of deviance (see Chapter 8, "Deviance"): Both suggest that the behavior in question arises among those with few social attachments.

Was the activism of the 1960s a passing phase or is it an ongoing struggle? The evidence is mixed. On the one hand, many members of the generation that came of age in the 1960s have followed the path of Jerry Rubin who, originally one of the "Chicago Seven" responsible for disrupting the 1968 Democratic Party convention, went on to a successful position as a Wall Street stockbroker in the 1980s. On the other hand, however, researchers conclude that many former activists, despite taking on "straight jobs," continue to desire and work for social change in the United States.

Critical evaluation. The strength of Kornhauser's theory lies in its explanation of social movements both in terms of the characteristics of the people who join them and the nature of the larger society. However, from a practical standpoint, if we try to evaluate the notion that mass societies foster social movements, we find it extremely difficult to specify what constitutes a "mass society."

A more political criticism holds that placing the roots of social movements in human psychology tends to minimize the importance of social justice. Put otherwise, this theory suggests that flawed people, rather than a flawed society, underlie the emergence of social movements.

Research support for this theory is mixed. On the down side, some studies conclude that the Nazi movement in Germany did not draw heavily from socially isolated people (Lipset, 1963; Oberschall, 1973). Similarly, urban rioters during the 1960s typically had strong ties to their communities (Sears & McConahay, 1973). In addition, young people who join religious cults generally do not have particularly weak family ties (Wright & Piper, 1986). Finally, researchers who have examined the biographies of 1960s political activists find evidence of deep and continuing commitment to political goals rather than isolation from society or personal aberration (McAdam, 1988, 1989; Whalen & Flacks, 1989).

On the up side, research by Frances Piven and Richard Cloward (1977) shows that a breakdown of routine social patterns does contribute to social movements among poor people. Also, in a study of the New

Mexico State Penitentiary, Bert Useem (1985) found that suspending prison programs that promoted social ties among inmates was followed by an increase in chaotic and violent protest activity.

Structural-Strain Theory

One of the most influential approaches to understanding social movements is *structural-strain theory*, developed by Neil Smelser (1962). This analysis identifies six factors that foster social movements. The more prevalent these conditions are, the greater the likelihood that a social movement will emerge. Smelser's theory also offers insights into which situations spark unorganized mobs or riots and which create highly organized social movements. The prodemocracy movement that transformed Eastern Europe during the late 1980s serves to illustrate how Smelser's six factors operate.

1. **Structural conduciveness.** Social movements arise when significant problems beset a society. The generally low standard of living in Eastern Europe in recent decades, coupled with the political repression of the socialist governments, created widespread dissatisfaction.

2. **Structural strain.** Relative deprivation and other kinds of strain stem from the inability of a society to meet the expectations of its people. The prodemocracy movement in Eastern Europe gained strength because people there could readily see that their quality of life was far lower than

DISCUSS: Use the women's movement to illustrate the stages of Smelser's theory. (1) Historical pattern of patriarchy; women organize in opposition. (2) Strain between U.S. ideal of equality and reality of patriarchy. (3) Early feminist scholarship and organization. (4) First wave of feminism—passage of 13th, 14th, and 15th Amendments extended rights to African-American men but ignored women of both races; second wave of feminism—African-American civil rights movement (predominantly led by men) and the increasing proportion of women in the labor force. (5) Mobilization spearheaded by organizations such as National Organization for Women (NOW); widespread publication of feminist ideas (e.g., *Ms.* magazine, founded in 1972). (6) Passage of the 19th Amendment slowed the women's movement; ERA remains unratified, but legislation has advanced women's social and economic rights.

that of their counterparts in Western Europe or much lower than years of propaganda about the prosperity of socialism had led them to expect.

3. **Growth and spread of an explanation.** Any coherent social movement must formulate a clear statement of a problem, its causes, and likely solutions. To the extent that these are well articulated, people are likely to express their dissatisfaction in an organized, goal-oriented way. If not, frustration may eventually explode in the form of unorganized and unproductive rioting. Intellectuals attributed the plight of Eastern Europe to deep economic and political flaws, while movement leaders proposed constructive strategies to bolster democracy.

4. **Precipitating factors.** Discontent frequently festers for a long time, only to be galvanized into collective action by a specific event. Such an event occurred in 1985 when Mikhail Gorbachev came to power in the Soviet Union and implemented his sweeping program of *perestroika* (restructuring). People in Eastern Europe seized this historic opportunity to reorganize political and economic life as Moscow relaxed its rigid control over their countries.

5. **Mobilization for action.** Widespread concern about a public issue sets the stage for collective action in the form of rallies, leafleting, building alliances with sympathetic organizations, and similar activities. The initial success of the Solidarity movement in Poland—covertly aided by the Reagan administration in the United States and by the Vatican—mobilized people throughout Eastern Europe to press for change. The rate of change accelerated as reform movements gained strength: What had taken a decade in Poland required only months in Hungary and only weeks in other countries.

6. **Lack of social control.** The responses of established authorities, such as political officials, police, and the military, largely determine the outcome of any social movement. Firm repression by the state can weaken or even destroy a social movement, as demonstrated by the crushing of prodemocracy forces in the People's Republic of China. By contrast, Gorbachev adopted a policy of nonintervention in Eastern Europe, thereby increasing the possibility for change there. Ironically, the forces his program unleashed in these neighboring nations soon spread to the Soviet Union itself, ending the historic domination of the Communist party and producing a new political confederation in 1992.

Critical evaluation. Smelser's approach—distinctly social, rather than psychological in focus—recognizes the complexity of social movements and points up how various factors encourage or inhibit their development. Structural-strain theory also explains how social problems may give rise to either organized social movements or more spontaneous mob action or rioting.

Yet Smelser's theory incorporates some of the same circularity of argument found in Kornhauser's analysis. A social movement is caused by strain, he maintains, but frequently the only evidence of this underlying strain appears to be the emerging social movement itself. Finally, this theory overlooks the important role of resources such as the mass media or international alliances in the success or failure of a social movement (Oberschall, 1973; Jenkins & Perrow, 1977; McCarthy & Zald, 1977; Olzak & West, 1991).

Resource-Mobilization Theory

Resource-mobilization theory adds to our understanding of social movements in a critical way. A social movement is unlikely to succeed—or even get off the ground—without substantial resources, including money, human labor, office facilities, communications equipment, access to the mass media, and a positive public image. In short, any social movement rises or falls on its capacity to attract resources, mobilize people, and forge crucial alliances. The collapse of socialism in Eastern Europe was largely the work of dissatisfied people in those countries. But assistance from outside, including fax machines, copiers, telecommunications gear, money, and moral support provided by other nations, was instrumental in efforts first by the Poles and then by people in other nations to topple their leaders.

As this example demonstrates, supplying resources makes outsiders as important as insiders to the outcome of a social movement. Socially disadvantaged people generally lack the money, contacts, leadership skills, and organizational know-how that a successful movement requires, and it is here that sympathetic outsiders often fill the resource gap. In our own country, well-to-do white people, including college students, performed a vital service to the black civil rights movement in the 1960s, and affluent men as well as women have taken a leading role in the current women's movement. Even a small core of powerful resource people can sometimes be enough to link a fledgling social movement to the larger sympathetic audience and practical resources it needs to be successful (McCarthy & Zald, 1977; Snow, Zurcher, & Ekland-Olson, 1980;

Killian, 1984; Snow, Rochford, Jr., Worden, & Benford, 1986; Baron, Mittman, & Newman, 1991; Burstein, 1991; Meyer & Whittier, 1994).

On the other side of the coin, a lack of resources frustrates efforts to bring about intentional change. The history of the AIDS epidemic serves as a case in point. Initially, as the incidence of AIDS was rising in the early 1980s, the government ignored the epidemic. To a large extent, gay communities in cities like San Francisco and New York were left alone to shoulder the responsibility of providing treatment and educational programs. Gradually, as the general public began to grasp the scope of the problem, public pressure prompted local, state, and federal governments to allocate more resources for research, education, and treatment. Galvanizing the public, members of the entertainment industry lent their money, visibility, and prestige to the movement to combat this deadly disease. These extensive resources, together with grassroots organizing by the movement's early leaders, have transformed this fledgling social movement into a well-organized, global coalition of political leaders, educators, and medical specialists.

Critical evaluation. To its credit, resource-mobilization theory recognizes that resources as well as discontent are critical to the success of a social movement. This theory also emphasizes the interplay between social movements and other groups and organizations that are capable of providing or withholding valuable resources. Continuing research in this area suggests that a movement's position in the power structure also affects the strategies it can employ; violence, for example, is a resource that can be used by people seeking entrée into a political system (Grant & Wallace, 1991).

Critics of this approach maintain that even relatively powerless segments of a population can still promote successful social movements if they manage to organize effectively and have strongly committed members. Research by Aldon Morris (1981) shows that people of color drew largely on their own skills and resources to fuel the civil rights movement of the 1950s and 1960s. A second problem with this theory is that it overstates the extent to which powerful people are willing to challenge the status quo. Some rich white people did provide valuable resources to the black civil rights movement, but, more often, elites remain indifferent or opposed to significant change (McAdam, 1982, 1983; Pichardo, 1995).

Overall, the success or failure of a social movement turns on the political struggle between challengers and supporters of intentional change. A strong and united establishment, perhaps aided by a counter-movement, decreases the chances that any social movement will effect meaningful change. If, however, the established powers are divided, the movement's chances of success multiply.

New Social Movements Theory

A final, more recent theoretical approach addresses the changing character of social movements. *New social movements theory* investigates the distinctive features of recent social movements in postindustrial societies of North America and Western Europe (Melucci, 1980; McAdam, McCarthy, & Zald, 1988; Kriesi, 1989; Pakulski, 1993).

Today's most notable social movements are concerned with global ecology, the social standing of women and gay people, reducing the risks of war, and animal rights, among others. One feature of these movements is their national and international scope. As Chapter 16 ("Politics and Government") explains, the power of the state continues to expand in the United States and other postindustrial societies. Not surprisingly, then, the critical response to state policies has also assumed national proportions. As global political connections multiply, moreover, social movements respond by becoming international in scope.

Second, while traditional social movements, such as labor organizations, are concerned primarily with economic issues, new social movements tend to focus on cultural change and the improvement of our social and physical surroundings. The international environmental movement, for example, opposes practices that aggravate global warming and other worldwide threats to the environment.

Third, whereas most social movements of the past were guided by economic interests and elicited strong support from working-class people, new social movements often have noneconomic agendas and usually draw disproportionate support from the middle and upper-middle classes.

Critical evaluation. Because new social movements theory is a recent development, sociologists are still assessing its usefulness. One clear strength of this analysis is its recognition that social movements are increasing in scale in response to the growing power of the state and the development of a global economic and political system. This theory also spotlights the power of the mass media to unite people around the world in pursuit of political goals.

This approach garners criticism, however, for exaggerating the differences between past and present

NOTE: A key contention of new social movements theory is that recruitment into social movements is based more on symbolism (in Weberian terms) than on class interests (in Marxist terms). Indeed, Stanley Aronowitz (1992) suggests that minorities, lesbians, and environmentalists—adherents of the new social movements of the left—may take over the working classes' historic mission to overthrow capitalism.

DIVERSITY: Although some social movements that challenge the status quo have been dominated by men, not all have—the abolition movement, suffrage movement, child-care movements, and anti-drunk driving movements are only a few examples.
RESOURCE: One of the cross-cultural selections in the Macionis and Benokraitis reader, *Seeing Ourselves*, is Brian Russo's "Tiananmen Square: A Personal Chronicle from China."

TABLE 23–1 Theories of Social Movements: A Summary

Deprivation Theory	People forge a movement as a result of experiencing relative deprivation. The social movement is a means of seeking change that brings participants greater benefits. Social movements are especially likely when rising expectations are frustrated.
Mass-Society Theory	People who lack established social ties are mobilized into social movements. Periods of social breakdown are likely to spawn social movements. The social movement gives members a sense of belonging and social participation.
Structural-Strain Theory	People come together because of their shared concern about the inability of society to operate as they believe it should. The growth of a social movement reflects many factors, including a belief in its legitimacy and some precipitating event that provokes action.
Resource-Mobilization Theory	People may join for all the reasons noted above and also because of social ties to existing members. The success or failure of a social movement depends largely on the resources available to it. Also important is the extent of opposition to its goals within the larger society.
New Social Movements Theory	People who become part of social movements are motivated by "quality of life" issues, not necessarily economic concerns. Mobilization is national or international in scope. New social movements arise in response to the expansion of the mass media and the growing power of the state in modern industrial societies to affect people's lives for good or ill.

social movements. The women's movement, for example, focuses on many of the same issues—workplace conditions and pay—that have consumed the energies of labor organizations for decades.

Each of the five theories we have presented offers some explanation for the emergence of social movements; no single theory can stand alone (Kowalewski & Porter, 1992). Table 23–1 summarizes the theories.

Gender and Social Movements

Gender figures prominently in the operation of social movements. In keeping with traditional notions about gender in the United States, men more than women tend to take part in public life—including spearheading social movements.

Investigating "Freedom Summer," a 1964 voter registration project in Mississippi, Doug McAdam (1992) found that movement leaders were more likely to accept an offer of help from men than from women. At that time, most people viewed the potentially dangerous work of registering African-American voters in the midst of considerable opposition and even hostility from whites as "men's work," unsuitable for women. Similarly, he discovered, project leaders were likely to assign women who did join their ranks to clerical and teaching positions, leaving the actual field activities to men. Interestingly, McAdam notes that, by and large, women who participated in Freedom Summer were more qualified than their male counterparts in terms

of years of activism and breadth of organizational affiliations. He concluded that only the most committed women were able to overcome the movement's gender barriers. In short, while women have played leading roles in many social movements (including the abolitionist and feminist movements in the United States), patriarchy has dominated the operation of most social movements—even those that otherwise opposed the status quo.

Stages in Social Movements

Despite the many differences that set one social movement apart from others, all efforts at intentional change unfold in similar stages. Researchers have identified four phases in the life of the typical social movement (Blumer, 1969; Mauss, 1975; Tilly, 1978).

Stage 1: Emergence.   Social movements are built on the perception that all is not well. Some, such as the civil rights and women's movements, are born of widespread dissatisfaction. Others emerge only as a small vanguard group increases public awareness of some issue. Gay activists, for example, have raised public concern about the threat posed by AIDS.

Stage 2: Coalescence.   After emerging, a social movement must define itself and develop a strategy for "going public." Leaders must determine policies, decide on tactics, build morale, and recruit new members. At this stage, the movement may engage in

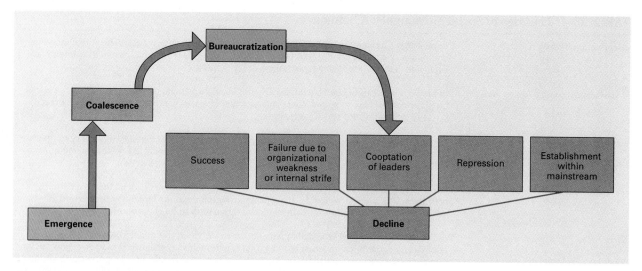

FIGURE 23–3 Stages in the Lives of Social Movements

collective action like rallies or demonstrations to attract media attention in hopes of capturing public notice. Additionally, the movement may form alliances with other organizations to gain necessary resources.

Stage 3: Bureaucratization.   To become an established political force, a social movement must assume bureaucratic traits, as described in Chapter 7 ("Groups and Organizations"). As it becomes "routinized," a social movement depends less on the charisma and talents of a few leaders and relies more on a capable staff. Some social movements do not become established in this way, however. Many activist organizations on college campuses during the late 1960s were galvanized by a single charismatic leader and, consequently, did not endure for long. On the other hand, the well-established National Organization for Women (NOW), despite its changing leadership, offers a steady voice on behalf of feminists.

At the same time, bureaucratization sometimes hinders a social movement. Reviewing social movements in U.S. history, Frances Piven and Richard Cloward (1977) noted that leaders may become so engrossed in building an organization that they neglect the need to sustain sentiments of insurgency among adherents. In such cases, the radical edge of protest is lost.

Stage 4: Decline.   Social movements are inherently dynamic, so a decline need not signal a demise (Wright, 1987). Eventually, however, most social movements do fade. Frederick Miller (1983) spells out four reasons that this may occur.

First, decline may simply signal success as members see nothing more to accomplish. For example, the women's suffrage movement disbanded after it achieved its goal—voting rights for women in the United States. Such clear-cut successes are rare, however, since few social movements have only one specific aim. More commonly, gaining one victory leads to new campaigns. Because issues related to gender extend far beyond voting, the women's movement has recast itself time and again.

Second, a social movement may flag because of organizational factors, such as poor leadership, loss of interest among members, exhaustion of resources, repression by authorities, or excessive bureaucratization. Some people attracted by the verve of a new social movement lose interest when formal routines replace the excitement of early efforts at change. Fragmentation stemming from internal conflicts over goals and tactics is another common problem. Students for a Democratic Society (SDS), a student movement promoting participatory democracy and opposing the war in Vietnam, splintered into several small factions by the end of the 1960s, as members disagreed over strategies for social change.

Third, a social movement may degenerate if the established power structure, through offers of money, prestige, and other rewards, succeeds in diverting leaders from their goals. "Selling out" is one facet of the iron law of oligarchy, noted in Chapter 7 ("Groups and Organizations"), by which organizational leaders may use their positions to enrich themselves. Jerry Rubin, a

Research shows that only a small proportion of people ever demonstrate about important public issues. Why do you think this is the case? Would you take a stand in this way?

political activist of the late 1960s, parlayed his celebrity status as a rebel into a career in the New York financial world. But this transformation can also work the other way: Some people leave lucrative, high-prestige occupations to become activists. Cat Stevens, a rock star of the 1970s, became a Muslim, changed his name to Yusuf Islam, and now promotes the spread of his religion.

Fourth and finally, the demise of a social movement may result from repression. Those in power may crush a movement for change by frightening away participants, discouraging new recruits, and even imprisoning leaders. The intensity of the state's reaction depends on officials' assessment of how revolutionary the social movement is. Until 1990, the government of South Africa, for example, banned the African National Congress (ANC), a political organization that sought to overthrow the state-supported system of apartheid. Even suspected members of the ANC were subject to arrest. In 1990, Pretoria lifted the decades-old ban and released ANC leader Nelson Mandela from prison; in 1994, Mandela became his country's president.

Beyond the reasons noted by Miller, a fifth cause of decline is that a social movement may "go mainstream." Some movements become an accepted part of the system—typically after realizing at least some of their goals—and they no longer challenge the status quo. The U.S. labor movement, for example, is now

well established; its leaders control vast sums of money and, to some critics, at least, now have more in common with the business tycoons they opposed in the past than with the rank-and-file workers.

Figure 23–3 provides a graphic summary of the various stages of social movements.

Social Movements and Social Change

Social movements exist to encourage—or to resist—social change. Whatever the intention, their success varies from case to case. The civil rights movement has certainly pressed this country toward the goal of racial equality, despite opposition from a handful of white supremacist countermovements like the Aryan Nation and the Ku Klux Klan.

Sometimes we overlook the success of past social movements and take for granted the changes that other people struggled so hard to win. Early workers' movements in the United States, for example, battled for decades to end child labor in factories, to limit working hours, to make the workplace safer, and to establish the right to bargain collectively with employers. Legislation protecting the environment is also the product of successful social movements throughout this century. The women's movement in the United States has yet to attain social equality for the sexes, but it has significantly extended the legal rights and economic opportunities of women. In fact, many

THEN AND NOW: Percent of first-year college students who claim to "frequently discuss politics": *1968*, 30%; *1995*, 15%. Percent who view "keeping up with political affairs" as an important life goal: *1966*, 58%; *1995*, 29%. Percent who identify "being well off financially" as an important life goal; *1968*, 38%; *1995*, 74%. (Sax et al., 1995)

SOCIAL SURVEY: In 1973, the following proportion of adults

responded that they had taken part in various kinds of protest actions: (GSS 1973, N = 1,504; *Codebook*, 1994:217)
Picketing for a labor strike 9.5%
A civil rights demonstration 4.3%
An anti-war demonstration 4.9%
A pro-war demonstration 0.4%
A school-related demonstration 5.3%

Controversy & Debate

Are You Willing to Take a Stand?

Are you satisfied with our society as it is? Surely everyone would change some things about our social world. Indeed, based on survey results, a lot of people would change plenty! Research suggests that most people express considerable pessimism about the state of society; in fact, two-thirds of U.S. adults claim that the average person's situation "is getting worse, not better." Just as important, people report little confidence in elected leadership: Three-fourths of respondents conclude that most government officials are "not interested" in the average person's problems (NORC, 1994:186).

Curiously, in light of such concerns, few people are willing to stand up and try to bring about change. Only 10 percent of U.S. adults claim to have ever picketed as part of a labor strike; just 5 percent say they have ever taken part in any other kind of demonstration (NORC, 1994:217).

Many college students probably suspect that age has something to do with such apathy; after all, aren't young people the ones with the interest and the idealism to challenge the status quo? (One of the popular sayings of the activist 1960s was "Never trust anyone over thirty!") But students who entered college in 1995 expressed no more interest in political issues than their parents did.

Asked to select important goals in life from a list, the figure shows that only 28 percent of these first-year students included "keeping up with political affairs," and just 23 percent checked off

"participating in community action programs." Moreover, a small minority of students (15 percent) claim they frequently discuss politics and only a handful (5 percent) expect to engage in a demonstration while in college.

Certainly, many people cite some good reasons to avoid political controversy. Any time we challenge the system—whether on campus or in the national political arena—we risk making enemies, losing a job, or perhaps even sustaining physical injury.

But the most important reason that people in the United States avoid joining social movements may have to do with cultural norms about how change should occur. In our individualistic culture, people favor taking personal responsibility over joining in collective action as a means of addressing social problems. For example, when asked how women or African Americans would best improve their social position, most U.S. adults say that

individuals should become better trained and otherwise sharpen their occupational qualifications. By contrast, only a small minority point to women's groups or civil rights activism as the best way to bring about change (NORC, 1994:319–20). No doubt, this individualistic orientation explains why U.S. adults are half as likely as their European counterparts to join in lawful demonstrations (World Values Survey, 1994).

Sociology, of course, poses a counterpoint to this conventional wisdom. As C. Wright Mills (1959) pointed out decades ago, many of the problems we encounter as individuals are caused by the structure of society. Thus, he maintained, effective solutions to many of life's challenges rest on collective efforts—that is, people willing to join together to take a stand for what they believe.

Continue the debate . . .

1. *Do you think that the reluctance of people in the United States to address problems through collective action shows that they are basically satisfied with their lives? Or that they think individuals acting in concert can't make a difference?*

2. *Have you ever participated in a political demonstration? What were its goals? What did it accomplish?*

3. *Identify ways that life today has been affected by people who got together and took a stand in the past (think about race relations, the state of the environment, the standing of women).*

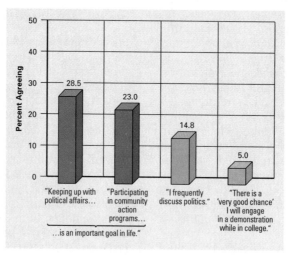

Political Involvement of Students Entering College in 1995: A Survey
Source: Sax et al. (1995).

Q: "I assert that there is no country in Europe in which the public administration has not become, not only more centralized, but more inquisitive and more minute; it everywhere interferes in private concerns more than it did . . ." Alexis de Tocqueville (Book IV, Chapter V)

NOTE: Many social movements fall into one of two categories: *equality movements* seeking social equality for various categories of people (based on class, race, sexual orientation, etc.), and specific *protest movements* targeting gun control, nuclear power, animal experimentation, etc. (Caplow, 1991)

young people are surprised to learn that, earlier in this century, few women worked for income and, in most states, none were permitted to vote.

This broad view leads to one overarching conclusion: We can draw a direct link between social movements and change. In one direction, social transformations such as the Industrial Revolution and the rise of capitalism sparked the emergence of various social movements. Going the other way, the efforts of workers, women, racial and ethnic minorities, and gay people have sent ripples of change throughout our society. Thus social change is both the cause and the consequence of social movements.

LOOKING AHEAD: SOCIAL MOVEMENTS IN THE TWENTY-FIRST CENTURY

Especially since the turbulent decade of the 1960s—marked by widespread social protests and urban rioting—U.S. society has been pushed and pulled by a plethora of social movements and countermovements. Sometimes, tensions explode into violence, as in the case of the 1992 Los Angeles riots following the first trial of police accused of beating Rodney King. In other cases, the struggles are more calm and perhaps more decisive, as with the ongoing tussle between Congressional Democrats supporting social "safety nets" and Republicans decrying "bloated government." Yet people on all sides of controversial issues agree that many of this nation's most profound problems—racial tensions, the size of government, the state of the family—remain unresolved. In addition, of course, new issues—including preserving the environment and gay rights—have recently moved to center stage.

Social movements have always been part of U.S. society, although their focus, tactics, and intensity all change with time. Therefore, we can safely assume that social movements will continue to shape our way of life. However, for two reasons, the scope of social movements is likely to grow. First, the technology of the Information Revolution has drawn the world closer together than ever before. Today anyone with a satellite dish, personal computer, or fax machine can stay abreast of political events, often as they happen. Second, as a consequence of new technology as well as the emerging global economy, social movements are now uniting people throughout the entire world. With the realization that many problems are global in scope has come the understanding that they can be effectively addressed only on an international scale.

SUMMARY

1. A collectivity differs from a social group in its limited social interaction, its vague social boundaries, and its weak and often unconventional norms.

2. Crowds, an important type of collective behavior, take various forms: casual crowds, conventional crowds, expressive crowds, acting crowds, and protest crowds.

3. Crowds that become emotionally intense spawn violence in the form of mobs and riots. Mobs pursue a specific goal; rioting involves undirected destructiveness.

4. Crowds have figured heavily in social change throughout history, although the value of their action depends on one's political outlook.

5. Contagion theory views crowds as anonymous, suggestible, and subject to escalating emotions. Convergence theory links crowd behavior to the traits of participants. Emergent-norm theory suggests that crowds may develop their own behavioral norms.

6. One form of mass behavior is rumor, which thrives in a climate of ambiguity. While rumor involves public issues, gossip deals with personal issues of local interest.

7. Public opinion consists of people's positions on issues, usually controversial, of widespread importance to society. Some people's attitudes carry more weight than others and, on any given issue, a small proportion of the population claims no opinion at all.

8. A panic (in a local area) or mass hysteria (across an entire society) are types of collective behavior by which people respond to a significant event, real or imagined, with irrational, frantic, and often self-destructive behavior.

9. In industrial societies, people adopt fashion as a source of social prestige. A fad is more unconventional than a fashion and is also of shorter duration, although people embrace fads with greater enthusiasm.

10. A social movement entails deliberate activity intended to promote or discourage change. Social movements vary in the range of people they seek to engage and the extent to which they strive to change society.

11. According to deprivation theory, social movements arise in response to relative deprivation more than the lack of well-being in an absolute sense.

12. Mass-society theory holds that people join social movements to gain a sense of belonging and social significance.

13. Structural-strain theory explains the development of a social movement as a cumulative consequence of six factors. Well-formulated grievances and goals encourage the organization of social movements; undirected anger, by contrast, promotes rioting.

14. Resource-mobilization theory ties the success or failure of a social movement to the availability of resources such as money, human labor, and alliances with other organizations.

15. New social movements theory notes that contemporary movements focus on quality-of-life issues that are typically national or international in scope.

16. A typical social movement proceeds through consecutive stages: emergence (defining the public issue), coalescence (entering the public arena), bureaucratization (becoming formally organized), and decline (brought on by failure or, sometimes, success).

17. Past social movements have shaped society in ways that people now take for granted. Just as movements produce change, so change itself sparks social movements.

KEY CONCEPTS

collective behavior activity involving a large number of people, often spontaneous, and typically in violation of established norms

collectivity a large number of people whose minimal interaction occurs in the absence of well-defined and conventional norms

crowd a temporary gathering of people who share a common focus of attention and whose members influence one another

fad an unconventional social pattern that people embrace briefly but enthusiastically

fashion a social pattern favored for a time by a large number of people

gossip rumor about the personal affairs of others

mass behavior collective behavior among people dispersed over a wide geographical area

mass hysteria a form of dispersed collective behavior by which people respond to a real or imagined event with irrational, frantic, and often self-destructive behavior

mob a highly emotional crowd that pursues some violent or destructive goal

panic a form of localized collective behavior by which people react to a perceived threat or other stimulus with irrational, frantic, and often self-destructive behavior

propaganda information presented with the intention of shaping public opinion

relative deprivation a perceived disadvantage arising from a specific comparison

riot a social eruption that is highly emotional, violent, and undirected

rumor unsubstantiated information people spread informally, often by word of mouth

social movement organized activity that encourages or discourages social change

CRITICAL-THINKING QUESTIONS

1. The concept of collective behavior encompasses a broad range of social patterns. What traits do they all have in common?

2. Imagine the aftermath of a football game in which the spirited revelry of a throng of college students turns into a destructive rampage. What unique insights into this event do contagion theory, convergence theory, and emergent-norm theory provide?

3. The 1960s was a decade of unprecedented affluence but also widespread social protest. What sociological insights help to explain this apparent paradox?

4. In what respects do some recent social movements (those concerned with the environment, animal rights, and gun control) differ from older crusades (focusing on, say, civil rights and gender equality)?

SUGGESTED READINGS

Classic Sources

Gustave Le Bon. *The Crowd: A Study of the Popular Mind.* New York: Viking Press, 1960; orig. 1895.
> One of the first studies of crowd behavior, this classic stimulated the investigation of collective behavior and sparked debates on the subject that persist even today.

Jo Freeman, ed. *Social Movements of the Sixties and Seventies.* New York: Longman, 1983.
> This collection of essays, with a useful introductory essay by the editor, investigates social movements in terms of four processes: mobilization, organization, strategy, and decline.

Contemporary Sources

Clark McPhail. *Acting Together: The Social Organization of Crowds.* Hawthorne, N.Y.: Aldine de Gruyter, 1994.
> A review of the research about crowds, this book also critiques various theoretical approaches.

Steven M. Buechler. *Women's Movements in the United States: Woman Suffrage, Equal Rights and Beyond.* New Brunswick, N.J.: Rutgers University Press, 1990.
> This book offers a sociological analysis of the women's movement from the early suffrage campaign to contemporary feminism.

James M. Jasper and Dorothy Nelkin. *The Animal Rights Crusade: The Growth of a Moral Protest.* New York: The Free Press, 1992.
> Here is a survey of the organizations and politics that make up the animal protection crusade, one example of a new social movement.

Global Sources

Hanspeter Kriesi. *Political Mobilization and Social Change: The Dutch Case in Contemporary Perspective.* Brookfield, Vt.: Avebury, 1993.
> Many social movements have swept across Western Europe in recent decades; this book assesses what has changed and what has not.

Gao Yuan. *Born Red: A Chronicle of the Cultural Revolution.* Stanford, Calif.: Stanford University Press, 1987.
> This personal account of one teenager's experiences during the Cultural Revolution in China between 1966 and 1969 explores the causes and consequences of a mass movement that spun out of control.

Social Change:
Traditional, Modern,
and Postmodern Societies

The firelight flickers as Chief Kanhonk sits, as he has done at the end of the day for many years, ready to begin an evening of animated talk and storytelling (Simons, 1995). This is the hour when the Kaiapo, a small society in Brazil's lush Amazon region, celebrate their heritage. Because the Kaiapo are a traditional people with no written language, the elders rely on evenings by the fire to teach their culture and instruct the grandchildren. In the past, evenings like this have been filled with tales of brave Kaiapo warriors fighting off Portuguese traders in pursuit of slaves and gold.

But as the minutes pass, only a few villagers assemble for the evening ritual. "It is the Big Ghost," one man grumbles, explaining the poor turnout. The "Big Ghost" has indeed descended upon them; its bluish glow spilling from windows of homes throughout the village. The Kaiapo children—and many adults as well—are watching television. The consequences of installing a satellite dish in the village several years ago have turned out to be greater than anyone imagined. In the end, what their enemies failed to do to the Kaiapo with guns, they may well do to themselves with prime-time programming.

The Kaiapo are among the 230,000 native peoples who inhabit the country we call Brazil. They stand out because of their striking body paint and ornate ceremonial dress. Recently, they have become rich as profits from gold mining and harvesting mahogany trees have flowed into the settlement. Now they must decide if their newfound fortune is a blessing or a curse.

To some, affluence means the opportunity to learn about the outside world through travel and television. Others, like Chief Kanhonk, are not so sure. Sitting by the fire, he thinks aloud, "I have been saying that people must buy useful things like knives and fishing hooks. Television does not fill the stomach. It only shows our children and grandchildren white people's things." Bebtopup, the oldest priest, nods in agreement: "The night is the time the old people teach the young people. Television has stolen the night" (Simons, 1995:471).

Q: "Man will never fly. Not in a thousand years." Wilbur Wright

Q: "In 1967 two of our most respected futurists, Herman Kahn and Anthony Wiener, published a book entitled *The Year 2000*, now a classic in futurist literature. In that book there is no mention whatever of energy shortage, pollution, ecology, or women's rights—subjects that were to dominate our national debate the very next year after its publication." Richard Farson (1977)

Q: "Every era redefines what of the past remains relevant and what needs to be discarded." Irving Horowitz

Q: "All of us are taking a journey into the future that will last every day of our lives. What will we be seeing and doing? How will we live?" Isaac Asimov

Q: "The major advances in civilization are processes that all but wreck the societies in which they occur." Alfred North Whitehead

The transformation of the Kaiapo raises profound questions about the causes of change and whether change—even in pursuit of a higher material standard of living—is always for the better. Moreover, the drama of the Kaiapo is being played out around the globe as more and more traditional cultures are being lured away from their heritage by the materialism and affluence of rich societies.

This chapter examines social change as a process with both positive and negative consequences. Of particular interest to people in the United States is what sociologists call *modernity*, changes brought about by the Industrial Revolution, and *postmodernity*, more recent transformations sparked by the Information Revolution and the postindustrial economy, which are affecting both the United States and the rest of the world.

WHAT IS SOCIAL CHANGE?

Earlier chapters have examined human societies in terms of both stability and change. Relatively *static* social patterns include status and roles, social stratification, and various social institutions. The *dynamic* forces that have recast humanity's consciousness, behavior, and needs range from innovations in technology to the growth of bureaucracy and the expansion of cities. These are all dimensions of **social change**, *the transformation of culture and social institutions over time*. The process of social change has four key characteristics.

1. **Social change happens everywhere, although the rate of change varies from place to place.** "Nothing is constant except death and taxes," goes the old saying. Yet social patterns related to death have changed dramatically as life expectancy in the United States has doubled since 1850. Taxes, meanwhile, unknown through most of human history, emerged only with complex social organization several thousand years ago. In short, one is hard-pressed to identify anything that is not subject to the twists and turns of change.

   Still, some societies change faster than others. As Chapter 4 ("Society") explained, hunting and gathering societies change quite slowly; members of technologically complex societies, on the other hand, can sense significant change even within a single lifetime.

   Moreover, even in a given society, some cultural elements change more quickly than others. William Ogburn's (1964) theory of *cultural lag* (see Chapter 3) recognizes that material culture (that is, things) usually changes faster than nonmaterial culture (ideas and attitudes). For example, medical techniques that prolong life have developed more rapidly than have ethical standards for deciding when and how to use them.

2. **Social change is sometimes intentional but often unplanned.** Industrial societies actively promote many kinds of change. For example, scientists seek more efficient forms of energy, and advertisers try to convince consumers that life is incomplete without some new gadget. Yet even the experts rarely envision all the consequences of the changes they promote.

   Early automobile manufacturers certainly understood that cars would allow people to travel in a single day distances that had required weeks or months to traverse a century before. But no one foresaw how profoundly the mobility provided by automobiles would reshape U.S. society, scattering family members, threatening the environment, and reshaping cities and suburbs. In addition, automotive pioneers could hardly have predicted the 50,000 deaths each year in car accidents in the United States alone.

3. **Social change often generates controversy.** As the history of the automobile demonstrates, most social change yields both positive and negative consequences. Capitalists welcomed the Industrial Revolution because advancing technology increased productivity and swelled profits. Many workers, however, fearing that machines would make their skills obsolete, strongly resisted "progress."

   In the United States, changing patterns of interaction between black people and white people, between women and men, and between gays and heterosexuals give rise to misunderstandings, tensions, and, sometimes, outright hostility.

4. **Some changes matter more than others.** Some social changes have only passing significance, whereas other transformations resonate for generations. At one extreme, clothing fads among the young burst on the scene and dissipate quickly. At the other, we are still adjusting to powerful technological advances such as television half a century after its introduction. Looking ahead, who can predict with any certainty how computers will transform the entire world during the next century? Will the Information Revolution turn out to be as pivotal as the Industrial Revolution? Like the automobile and television, computers will have both beneficial and deleterious effects, providing new kinds of jobs while eliminating old ones, joining

people together in ever-expanding electronic networks while threatening personal privacy.

CAUSES OF SOCIAL CHANGE

Social change has many causes. And in a world linked by sophisticated communication and transportation technology, change in one place often begets change elsewhere.

Culture and Change

Culture is a dynamic system that continually gains new elements and loses others. Chapter 3 ("Culture") identified three important sources of cultural change. First, *invention* produces new objects, ideas, and social patterns. Through rocket propulsion research, which began in the 1940s, we have engineered high-tech vehicles for space flight. Today we take such technology for granted; during the next century a significant number of people may well travel in space.

Second, *discovery* occurs when people first take note of certain elements of the world or learn to see them in a new way. Medical advances, for example, offer a growing understanding of the human body. Beyond the direct effects for human health, medical discoveries have also stretched life expectancy, setting in motion "the graying of the United States" (see Chapter 14, "Aging and the Elderly").

Third, *diffusion* creates change as trade, migration, and mass communication spread cultural elements throughout the world. Ralph Linton (1937) recognized that many familiar elements of our culture have come to us from other lands. For example, cloth (developed in Asia), clocks (invented in Europe), and coins (devised in Turkey) all originated elsewhere. Generally, material things diffuse more readily than nonmaterial cultural traits. The Kaiapo, described at the beginning of this chapter, have been quick to adopt television but reluctant to embrace the materialism and individualism that sometimes seize those who spend hours watching Western commercial programming.

As a land of immigrants, the United States has steadily changed in response to cultural diffusion. In recent decades, people from Latin America and Asia have been introducing new cultural patterns, clearly evident in the sights, smells, and sounds of cities across the country. Conversely, the global power of the United States ensures that much of our culture—from the taste of hamburgers to the sounds of Harlem rap to the skills of Harvard M.B.A.s—are being diffused to other societies.

Increasing technological sophistication is spreading cultural patterns more widely. In many parts of the world, Western cultural images are now common. Does this portend the emergence of a Western-based McCulture that will supplant thousands of historically distinctive ways of life? What are the advantages and drawbacks of the emergence of a global culture?

Conflict and Change

Tension and conflict within a society also produce change. Karl Marx heralded class conflict as the engine that drives societies from one historical era to another (see Chapter 4, "Society," and Chapter 9, "Social Stratification"). In industrial-capitalist societies, he maintained, struggle between capitalists and workers propels society toward a socialist system of production.

In the century since Marx's death, this model has proven simplistic. Yet, he correctly foresaw that social conflict arising from inequality (involving race and gender as well as social class) would force changes in every society, including our own.

Ideas and Change

Max Weber, too, contributed to our understanding of social change. While Weber acknowledged the importance of conflict based on material production, he traced the roots of social change to the world of ideas. He illustrated his argument by showing how people who display charisma (described in Chapter 16, "Politics and Government," and Chapter 18, "Religion") can convey a message that sometimes changes the world.

DIVERSITY: Percent changing residence between 1993 and 1994, by race and ethnicity: whites, 16%; African Americans, 20%; Hispanics, 22%. Minorities are more likely to move because they are more likely to rent: 60% of Hispanic householders, 57% of blacks, and 33% of whites rent. Renters have almost four times the mobility rate (33% more annually compared to 9% of homeowners). A second factor is age, with minorities being younger, on average.

Median age for whites is 35; for African Americans, 29; for Hispanics, 26. Householders under 30 have high annual mobility rates: 28% (homeowners) and 56% (renters). (Schwartz, 1992; U.S. Bureau of the Census, 1995).

NOTE: One indicator of the increasing pace of social change: While about 10% of all people who have ever lived are breathing today, about 90% of all scientists are now alive.

Weber also highlighted the importance of ideas by revealing how the world view of early Protestants prompted them to embrace industrial capitalism (see Chapter 4, "Society"). By showing that industrial capitalism developed primarily in areas of Western Europe where the Protestant work ethic was strong, Weber (1958; orig. 1904–5) concluded that the disciplined rationality of Calvinist Protestants was instrumental in this change.

Ideas also fuel social movements. Chapter 23 ("Collective Behavior and Social Movements") explained that a social movement may emerge from the determination to modify society in some manner (say, to clean up the environment) or from a sense that existing social arrangements are unjust. The international gay rights movement draws strength from the contention that lesbians and gay men should enjoy rights and opportunities equal to those of the heterosexual majority. Opposition to the gay rights movement, moreover, reveals the power of ideas to inhibit as well as to advance social change.

The Natural Environment and Change

As Chapter 22 ("Environment and Society") detailed, human societies are closely connected to their natural environment. For this reason, change in one tends to produce change in the other.

By and large, our culture casts nature as a force to be tamed and reshaped to human purposes. From the outset, European settlers systematically cut down forests to create fields for farming and to make materials for building; they established towns, extended roads in every direction, and dammed rivers as a source of water and energy. Such human construction not only reflects our cultural determination to master the natural environment; it also points up the centrality of the idea of "growth" in our way of life.

But the consequences of this thinking have placed increasing stress on the natural environment. Our society contends with problems of solid waste and air and water pollution, all the while consuming the lion's share of global resources. A growing awareness that such patterns are not sustainable in the long term is forcing us to confront the need to change our way of life in some basic respects.

Demographic Change

Population growth not only places escalating demands on the natural environment, but it also alters cultural patterns. In cities of the Netherlands, a high-density nation, homes are small and narrow compared to those in the United States, with extremely steep staircases to make efficient use of space. In Tokyo, Japan, commuters routinely endure crowding on subways that would challenge the patience of a lifelong New Yorker.

Throughout our long history, the United States has enjoyed a bounty of physical space, which, no doubt, has affected our notions about personal freedom. Moreover, the fast-paced and anonymous way of life that is typical of populous cities barely resembles that found in the rural villages and small towns common to our past.

Profound change also results from the shifting composition of a population. Our population, collectively speaking, is growing older, as Chapter 14 ("Aging and the Elderly") explained. In 1994, 13 percent of U.S. residents were over age sixty-five, triple the proportion in 1900. By the year 2050, seniors will account for one in five of our residents (U.S. Bureau of the Census, 1995). Medical research and health care services already focus extensively on the elderly, and common stereotypes about old people will be undermined as more men and women enter this stage of life. Our way of life may change in countless additional ways as homes and household products are redesigned to meet the needs of growing ranks of older consumers.

Migration within and among societies is another demographic factor that promotes change. Between 1870 and 1930, tens of millions of immigrants swelled the industrial cities in the United States. Millions of rural people joined them. As a result, farm communities declined, metropolises burgeoned, and the United States became for the first time a predominantly urban society. Similar changes are taking place today as people moving from Snowbelt to Sunbelt states mingle and interact with new immigrants from Latin America and Asia.

Demographic changes have transformed some parts of the United States more than others. National Map 24–1 provides one general indicator of demographic stability, showing where a significant share of residents have lived in their present homes for thirty years or more.

MODERNITY

A central concept in the study of social change is **modernity**, *social patterns linked to industrialization*. In everyday usage, modernity (its Latin root means "lately") designates the present in relation to the past. Sociologists include within this catchall concept the many social patterns set in motion by the Industrial Revolution beginning in Western Europe in the

THE MAP: Signaling the mobility and growth of U.S. society: The average age of housing stock is 26 years—below the median age of the population (34 years). The counties with relatively more long-term residents typically have an older population, and they are also places where economic growth is limited or stagnant. Many of them have lost young people to urban areas offering greater economic prospects. Thus few counties have escaped change of one

kind or another.

DISCUSS: Modernization has not always won people over: Algeria, Ethiopia, and Iran are examples of nations that started on a path toward modernization only to run head on into a strong backlash from powerful segments of the population (largely religious) who insisted on restoring traditional culture.

Q: "Only the wisest and the stupidest do not change." Confucius

Seeing Ourselves

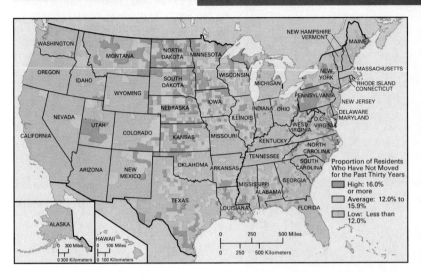

NATIONAL MAP 24–1

Who Stays Put? Residential Stability Across the United States

Overall, only about 14 percent of U.S. residents have not moved during the last thirty years. Counties with a higher proportion of "long-termers" typically have experienced less change over recent decades: Many neighborhoods have been in place since before World War II, and many of the same families live in them. Looking at the map, what can you say about these relatively stable areas? Why are most of these counties rural and away from the coasts?

Source: U.S. Bureau of the Census (1994).

mid-eighteenth century. **Modernization,** then, is *the process of social change initiated by industrialization.* The time line inside the front cover of the text highlights important events that mark the emergence of modernity.

Key Dimensions of Modernization

Peter Berger (1977) notes four major characteristics of modernization:

1. **The decline of small, traditional communities.** Modernity involves "the progressive weakening, if not destruction, of the concrete and relatively cohesive communities in which human beings have found solidarity and meaning throughout most of history" (Berger, 1977:72). For thousands of years, in the camps of hunters and gatherers and in the rural villages of Europe and North America, people lived in small-scale settlements with family and neighbors. Such traditional worlds—based on sentiments and beliefs passed from generation to generation—afford each person a well-defined place. These primary groups limit people's range of experience while conferring a strong sense of identity, belonging, and purpose.

   Small, isolated communities still exist in the United States, of course, but they are now home to only a small percentage of our nation's people.

Even for rural people, rapid transportation and efficient communication, including television, have brought individuals in touch with the pulse of the larger society and even the entire world.

2. **The expansion of personal choice.** To people in traditional, preindustrial societies, life is shaped by forces beyond human control—gods, spirits, or, simply, fate. Steeped in tradition, members of these societies grant one another a narrow range of personal choices.

   As the power of tradition erodes, however, people come to see their lives as an unending series of options, a process Berger calls *individualization.* Recognizing alternatives in everyday life, for example, many people in the United States adopt various "lifestyles" that change over time.

3. **Increasing diversity in beliefs.** In preindustrial societies, strong family ties and powerful religious beliefs enforce conformity while discouraging diversity and change. Modernization promotes a more rational, scientific world view, in which tradition loses its force and morality becomes a matter of individual attitude. The growth of cities, the expansion of impersonal organizations, and social interaction among people from various backgrounds combine to foster a diversity of beliefs and behavior.

4. **Future orientation and growing awareness of time.** People in modern societies think more about the future, while preindustrial people focus

Chapter 24 Social Change: Traditional, Modern, and Postmodern Societies   **641**

Q: "One of the most fundamental traits of modernization is a vast movement from fate to choice in human affairs." Peter Berger
DISCUSS: Are "great people" or "average people" primarily responsible for social change? Historically, conservatives argued the former, since this individualistic position favored traditional hierarchy and elites. Liberals tended toward the more egalitarian, collectivist view.

Q: "Our lives make sense in a thousand ways, most of which we are unaware of, because of traditions that are centuries, if not millennia, old." Robert N. Bellah et al. (1985:282)
NOTE: French artist (Eugène Henri) Paul Gauguin lived from 1848 to 1903; his primitive paintings representing life in Tahiti stood in stark contrast to the tremendous change Western Europe was undergoing during this time of industrialization.

In response to the accelerated pace of change in the late nineteenth century, Paul Gauguin (1848–1903) left his native France for the South Seas where he was captivated by a simpler and seemingly timeless way of life. He romanticized this environment in his 1894 painting The Day of the God (Mahana no Atua).

Paul Gauguin, *The Day of the God (Mahana no Atua)*, 1894, oil on canvas (68.3 x 91.5 cm), Helen Birch Bartlett Memorial Collection, 1926. Photograph © 1994, The Art Institute of Chicago. All rights reserved.

more on the past. Modern people are not only forward looking but optimistic that discoveries and new inventions will enhance their lives.

In addition, modern people organize daily routines according to precise units of time. With the introduction of clocks in the late Middle Ages, sunlight and seasons faded in importance as measures of time's forward march in favor of hours and minutes. Preoccupied with personal gain, modern people calculate time to the moment and generally believe that "Time is money!" Berger points out that one key indicator of a society's degree of modernization is the proportion of people wearing wristwatches.

Finally, recall that modernization touched off the development of sociology itself. As Chapter 1 ("The Sociological Perspective") explained, the discipline originated in the wake of the Industrial Revolution in Western Europe, precisely where social change was proceeding most rapidly. Early European and U.S. sociologists tried to analyze and explain modernization and its consequences—both good and bad—for human beings.

Ferdinand Toennies: The Loss of Community

The German sociologist Ferdinand Toennies, whose brief biography appears in the box, produced the theory of *Gemeinschaft* and *Gesellschaft* (see Chapter 21, "Population and Urbanization"). Like Peter Berger, whose work he influenced, Toennies (1963; orig. 1887) viewed modernization as the progressive loss of *Gemeinschaft*, or human community. As Toennies saw it, the Industrial Revolution undermined the strong social fabric of family and tradition by fostering individualism and a businesslike emphasis on facts and efficiency. European and North American societies gradually became rootless and impersonal as people came to associate mostly on the basis of self-interest—the condition Toennies dubbed *Gesellschaft*.

Early in this century, at least some areas of the United States approximated Toennies's concept of *Gemeinschaft*. Families that had lived for generations in rural towns and villages were tightly integrated into a hard-working, slow-moving way of life. Telephones (invented in 1876) were rare; the first coast-to-coast call was placed only in 1915 (see the time line inside the front cover of this book). Before television (introduced in 1939, widespread after 1950), families entertained themselves, often gathering with friends in the evening—much like Brazil's Kaiapo—to share stories, sorrows, or song. Before the onset of rapid transportation (although Henry Ford's assembly line began in 1908, cars became commonplace only after World War II), many people viewed their hometown as their entire world.

Inevitable tensions and conflicts—sometimes based on race, ethnicity, and religion—characterized

GLOBAL: Most of humanity still lives in powerful, ascriptive communities, thinking of themselves as embedded in kinship, locality, and tradition. From the standpoint of such people throughout the world, we in the United States seem not only affluent but highly individualistic. From our perspective, behavior based on ascriptive solidarities (that is, reflecting categories rather than individual traits) seems wrongheaded and discriminatory.

DISCUSS: What does "success" mean? We have come to use the word "success" in a notably nonspecific manner. Its traditional meaning—to follow or replace another by descent—made sense in a relatively fixed social order with strong social ties. The term's contemporary meaning of achieving individual goals (whatever they may be) suggests a far more fluid social order.

PROFILE

Ferdinand Toennies: Is There Virtue in Modern Society?

Can traditional virtues such as selflessness and honor survive in the rapidly changing modern world? Pioneering sociologist Ferdinand Toennies (1855–1936) spent his life pursuing the answer to this important question. In the process, along with his colleagues Max Weber and Georg Simmel, Toennies helped to establish sociology as an academic discipline in Germany.

Born to a wealthy family in the German countryside, Toennies was raised in comfortable surroundings and received an extensive education. He also learned a great deal from observing the world about him—he was especially fascinated by how the Industrial Revolution was transforming Germany and other European countries.

But, to Toennies, the changes brought on by industrialization did not necessarily contribute to the betterment of humankind. Toennies's work displays a deep distrust of the notion of "progress," which he feared amounted to the steady loss of traditional morality. His influential book *Gemeinschaft und Gesellschaft* (1887) is therefore both a chronicle of modernization and an indictment of an increasingly impersonal world.

Toennies's thesis is that traditional societies, built on kinship and neighborhood, nourish collective sentiments, virtue, and honor.

Modernization washes across traditional society like an acid, eroding human community and unleashing rampant individualism. Toennies stopped short of claiming that modern society was "worse" than societies of the past, and he made a point of praising the spread of rational, scientific thinking. Nevertheless, the growing individualism and selfishness characteristic of modern societies troubled him. Knowing that there could be no return to the past, he looked to the future, hoping that new forms of social organization would develop that would combine modern rationality with traditional collective responsibility.

Source: Based on Cahnman & Heberle (1971).

past communities. According to Toennies, however, the traditional ties of *Gemeinschaft* bound people of a community together, "essentially united in spite of all separating factors" (1963:65; orig. 1887).

Modernity turns societies inside out so that, as Toennies put it, people are "essentially separated in spite of uniting factors" (1963:65; orig. 1887). This is the world of *Gesellschaft* where, especially in large cities, most people live among strangers and ignore those they pass on the street. Trust is hard to come by in a mobile and anonymous society in which, according to researchers, people tend to put their personal needs ahead of group loyalty and a majority of adults claim that "you can't be too careful" in dealing with people (Russell, 1993; NORC, 1994:160). No wonder, as one news report indicated, 15 million men and women attend weekly support groups (also made up of strangers) in which they

establish temporary emotional ties and find someone who is willing simply to *listen* (Leerhsen, 1990).

Critical evaluation. Toennies's theory of *Gemeinschaft* and *Gesellschaft* stands as the most widely cited model for describing modernization. The theory's strength lies in its synthesis of various dimensions of change—growing population, the rise of cities, increasing impersonality in social interaction.

One problem with Toennies's theory is that modern life, while often impersonal, is not completely devoid of *Gemeinschaft*. Even in a world of strangers, friendships are often strong and lasting. Traditions are especially pronounced in many ethnic neighborhoods where residents maintain close community ties.

Another criticism is that Toennies's approach says little about which factors (industrialization,

RESOURCE: Emile Durkheim's "Anomy and Modern Life" is one of the "classics" in the 3d edition of *Seeing Ourselves*.

NOTE: Durkheim's concept of "mechanical solidarity" implies that we can learn the workings of an entire society by examining any one component of it, just as we can understand a physical substance through analysis of a single molecule. This is not true of internally differentiated, organic bodies.

NOTE: The term "lifestyle" emerged only in recent decades as one indication of the growing ability of individuals to shape their own lives (within the limits imposed by their resources, of course).

NOTE: The term "individual," with a Latin root meaning "indivisible," only became widely used in early 19th-century Europe, at a time when traditional social ties were weakening.

George Tooker's 1950 painting The Subway *depicts a common problem of modern life: Weakening social ties and eroding traditions create a generic humanity in which everyone is alike yet each person is an anxious stranger in the midst of others.*

George Tooker, *The Subway,* 1950, egg tempera on composition board, 18⅛ x 36¼", Whitney Museum of American Art, New York. Purchased with funds from the Julianna Force Purchase Award, 50.23.

urbanization, weakening of families) are cause and which are effect. Some analysts have also asserted that Toennies favored—perhaps even romanticized—traditional societies.

Emile Durkheim: The Division of Labor

The French sociologist Emile Durkheim, whose work is examined in Chapter 4 ("Society"), shared Toennies's interest in the profound social changes wrought by the Industrial Revolution. For Durkheim, modernization is marked by an increasing *division of labor,* or specialized economic activity (1964b; orig. 1893). Whereas every member of a traditional society engages in more or less the same daily round of activities, modern societies function by having people perform highly distinctive roles.

Durkheim contended that preindustrial societies are held together by *mechanical solidarity,* social bonds resting on shared moral sentiments. Thus members of preindustrial societies have a sense that everyone is basically alike and belongs together. Mechanical solidarity—or what Toennies called *Gemeinschaft*—depends on a minimal division of labor, so that everyone's life follows much the same path.

With modernization, the division of labor becomes more and more pronounced. Modern societies, then, are held together by *organic solidarity,* bonds of mutual dependency among people who engage in specialized work. Put simply, modern societies are integrated not by likeness but by difference: All of us must depend on others to meet most of our needs. Organic solidarity corresponds to Toennies's concept of *Gesellschaft.*

Despite obvious similarities, Durkheim and Toennies interpreted modernity somewhat differently. To Toennies, modern *Gesellschaft* amounts to the loss of social solidarity—the inevitable result of the gradual erosion of "natural" and "organic" bonds of the rural past, leaving only the "artificial" and "mechanical" ties of the present. Durkheim disagreed and even reversed Toennies's language to bring home the point. He labeled modern society "organic," suggesting that today's world is no less natural than before, and he described traditional societies as "mechanical" because they are so regimented. Thus Durkheim viewed modernization not so much as a loss of community as a change in the basis of community—from bonds of likeness (kinship and neighborhood) to economic interdependence (the division of labor). Durkheim's perspective on modernity is both more complex and more positive than that of Toennies.

Critical evaluation. Durkheim's work stands alongside that of Toennies, which it closely resembles, as a highly influential analysis of modernity. Of the two, Durkheim is clearly the more optimistic; still, he feared that modern societies might become so internally diverse that they would collapse into *anomie,* a condition in which norms and values are so weak and inconsistent that society provides little moral guidance to individuals. In the midst of weak moral claims from society, modern people tend to be egocentric, placing their own needs above those of others.

Evidence supports Durkheim's contention that anomie plagues modern societies. Suicide rates—which Durkheim considered a good index of anomie—have, in fact, risen throughout this century. Moreover, the vast majority of U.S. adults now see moral questions not in clear terms of right and wrong but as "shades of gray," claiming that no single moral standard should be applicable to everyone (NORC, 1994:334).

SOCIAL SURVEY: "Morality is a personal matter and society should not force everyone to follow one standard." (GSS 1988, N = 1,481; *Codebook*, 1994:334)

"Agree strongly"   31.7%   "Disagree strongly"   7.6%
"Agree somewhat"   38.8%   DK/NR   4.4%
"Disagree somewhat" 17.5%

RESOURCE: Max Weber's analysis of "The Disenchantment of

Modern Life" is another of the "classics" in the companion reader, *Seeing Ourselves*.

DISCUSS: Pose to the class the Weberian irony that the more we learn about the natural world, the more uncertainty we feel about ultimate cause and meaning.

NOTE: Two sections of Chapter 4 ("Society") introduced Marx's materialist analysis of change and Weber's idealist analysis.

Max Weber maintained that the distinctive character of modern society was its rational world view. Virtually all of Weber's work on modernity centered on types of people he considered typical of their age: the scientist, the capitalist, and the bureaucrat. Each is rational to the core: The scientist is committed to the orderly discovery of truth, the capitalist to the orderly pursuit of profit, and the bureaucrat to orderly conformity to a rational system of rules.

On the other hand, shared norms and values are still strong enough to give individuals some sense of meaning and purpose. Additionally, whatever the hazards of anomie and atomization, most people seem to value the privacy and personal autonomy that modern society affords.

Max Weber: Rationalization

For Max Weber, whose work is also detailed in Chapter 4 ("Society"), modernity amounts to the progressive replacement of a traditional world view with a rational way of thinking. In preindustrial societies, tradition acts as a constant brake on change. To traditional people, Weber explains, "truth" is roughly synonymous with "what has always been" (1978:36; orig. 1921). In modern societies, by contrast, people see truth as a more personal matter of deliberate calculation. Because efficiency is valued more than reverence for the past, individuals adopt whichever social patterns will allow them to achieve their goals.

Echoing the claim of Toennies and Durkheim that industrialization weakens tradition, Weber declared that modern society had become "disenchanted." What were once unquestioned truths have become subject to matter-of-fact calculations. Embracing rational, scientific thought, in short, modern society turns away from the gods. Throughout his life, Weber explored

various modern "types"—the capitalist, the scientist, the bureaucrat—all of whom share the rational and detached world view Weber believed was coming to dominate humanity.

Critical evaluation.   Compared with Toennies, and especially Durkheim, Weber was a profound critic of modern society. He recognized that science could produce technological and organizational wonders, yet he worried that it was carrying us away from more basic questions about the meaning and purpose of human existence. Weber feared that rationalization, especially in bureaucracies, would erode the human spirit with endless rules and regulations.

However, some of Weber's critics think that the alienation he attributed to bureaucracy is actually a product of social inequality. The contention leads us to the ideas of Karl Marx.

Karl Marx: Capitalism

While other analysts of modernity examined shifting patterns of social order, Marx focused on social conflict. For Marx, modern society was synonymous with capitalism; he saw the Industrial Revolution primarily as a *capitalist revolution*. As Chapter 4 ("Society") explained, Marx contended that the bourgeoisie in medieval Europe emerged as a force to wrest control of society from the feudal nobility. The bourgeoisie were finally

Q: "The bourgeoisie . . . has pitilessly torn asunder the motley feudal ties that bound man to his 'natural superiors,' and has left remaining no other nexus between man and man than naked self-interest, than callous 'cash payment.'" Karl Marx and Friedrich Engels

Q: "The bourgeoisie, during its rule of scarcely one hundred years, has created more massive and more colossal productive forces than have all preceding generations together." Marx and Engels

Q: "A case can be made that the central question of sociology, from its inception in the rather fanciful philosophy of August Comte, has been the question about the nature of modernity." Peter Berger (1986:28)

GLOBAL: Tourism was all but unknown a century ago; today, the entire world copes with hundreds of millions of tourists. This change is one effect of technological advances.

successful when the Industrial Revolution placed a powerful new productive system under their control.

Marx agreed that modernity weakened small-scale communities (as described by Toennies), sharpened the division of labor (as noted by Durkheim), and fostered a rational world view (as asserted by Weber). But he considered these factors simply as conditions necessary for capitalism to flourish. Capitalism, according to Marx, draws population from farms and small towns into an ever-expanding market system centered in the cities; specialization underlies efficient factories; and rationality is exemplified by the capitalists' relentless quest for profits.

Earlier chapters have painted Marx as a spirited critic of capitalist society, but his vision of modernity also incorporates a considerable measure of optimism. Unlike Weber, who viewed modern society as an "iron cage" of bureaucracy, Marx believed that social conflict within capitalist social systems would sow the seeds of revolutionary social change, ultimately producing an egalitarian socialism. Such a society, as he envisioned it, would harness the wonders of industrial technology to enrich people's lives and also rid the world of social classes, the prime source of social conflict and dehumanization. While Marx's evaluation of modern capitalist society was highly negative, then, he imagined a bright future of greater human freedom, blossoming human creativity, and renewed human community.

Critical evaluation. Marx's theory of modernization weaves together many threads in a fabric dominated by capitalism. Yet Marx underestimated the dominance of bureaucracy in modern societies. And in a twist never predicted by Marx, the bloated government apparatus in socialist societies actually stifled the human spirit even more than capitalism does. The recent upheavals in Eastern Europe and the former Soviet Union reveal the depth of popular opposition to rigid state-controlled bureaucracies.

THEORETICAL ANALYSIS OF MODERNITY

The rise of modernity is a complex process involving many dimensions of change, described in previous chapters and summarized in Table 24–1 on page 647. How is one to make sense of so many changes going on all at once? Sociologists have devised two overarching explanations of modern society, one derived from the structural-functional paradigm and one based on the social-conflict approach.

Structural-Functional Theory: Modernity as Mass Society

One broad approach—drawing on the ideas of Ferdinand Toennies, Emile Durkheim, and Max Weber—understands modernization as the emergence of *mass society* (Dahrendorf, 1959; Kornhauser, 1959; Nisbet, 1966, 1969; Baltzell, 1968; Stein, 1972; Berger, Berger, & Kellner, 1974; Pearson, 1993).

A **mass society** is *a society in which industry and expanding bureaucracy have eroded traditional social ties*. A mass society is marked by weak kinship and impersonal neighborhoods so that individuals are socially atomized. In their isolation, members of mass societies typically experience feelings of moral uncertainty and personal powerlessness.

The Mass Scale of Modern Life

Mass-society theory points, first, to the rapidly increasing scale of modern life. Before the Industrial Revolution, Europe and North America constituted an intricate mosaic of countless rural villages and small towns. In these small communities, which inspired Toennies's concept of *Gemeinschaft*, people lived out their lives surrounded by kin and guided by a shared heritage. Gossip was an informal, yet highly effective, means of ensuring rigid conformity to community standards. Limited community size combined with strong moral values to stifle social diversity—the mechanical solidarity described by Durkheim.

For example, in England before 1690, both law and local custom demanded that all people regularly participate in the Christian ritual of Holy Communion (Laslett, 1984). Similarly, only Rhode Island among the New England colonies offered any support for the notion of religious dissent. Because social differences were repressed, subcultures and countercultures rarely flourished and change proceeded slowly. Individuals' social positions were more or less set at birth, with little social mobility.

A surge in population, the growth of cities, and specialized economic activity driven by the Industrial Revolution gradually changed all this. People came to know one another by their functions (for example, as the "doctor" or the "bank clerk") rather than by their kinship group or hometown. The majority of people looked on others simply as a mass of strangers. The face-to-face communication of the village was eventually replaced by the mass media—newspapers, radio, television—as well as computer networks, furthering the process of social atomization. Large organizations steadily assumed more and more

SOCIAL SURVEY: "Right and wrong are not usually a simple matter of black and white; there are many shades of gray." (GSS 1988; N = 1,481; Codebook, 1994:334)

"Agree strongly"   39.8%   "Disagree strongly"   6.9%
"Agree"   42.1%   DK/NR   3.4%
"Disagree somewhat"   7.8%

NOTE: A characteristic of modernity is the rise of tolerance (from the Latin *tolerare*, meaning "to bear"). For most of us, the virtues of tolerance are easy to enumerate, if not always to act on. Contemporary people tend to embrace cultural relativism (especially as their schooling increases); traditional people (and those with less schooling) generally adopt a more ethnocentric, absolutist world view.

TABLE 24–1 Traditional and Modern Societies: The Big Picture

Elements of Society	Traditional Societies	Modern Societies
Cultural Patterns		
Values	Homogeneous; sacred character; few subcultures and countercultures	Heterogeneous; secular character; many subcultures and countercultures
Norms	High moral significance; little tolerance of diversity	Variable moral significance; high tolerance of diversity
Time orientation	Present linked to past	Present linked to future
Technology	Preindustrial; human and animal energy	Industrial; advanced energy sources
Social Structure		
Status and role	Few statuses, most ascribed; few specialized roles	Many statuses, some ascribed and some achieved; many specialized roles
Relationships	Typically primary; little anonymity and privacy	Typically secondary; considerable anonymity and privacy
Communication	Face to face	Face-to-face communication supplemented by mass media
Social control	Informal gossip	Formal police and legal system
Social stratification	Rigid patterns of social inequality; little mobility	Fluid patterns of social inequality; considerable mobility
Gender patterns	Pronounced patriarchy; women's lives centered on the home	Declining patriarchy; increasing number of women in the paid labor force
Economy	Based on agriculture; some manufacturing in the home; little white-collar work	Based on industrial mass production; factories become centers of production; increasing white-collar work
State	Small-scale government; little state intervention in society	Large-scale government; considerable state intervention in society
Family	Extended family as the primary means of socialization and economic production	Nuclear family retains some socialization functions but is more a unit of consumption than of production
Religion	Religion guides world view; little religious pluralism	Religion weakens with the rise of science; extensive religious pluralism
Education	Formal schooling limited to elites	Basic schooling becomes universal, with growing proportion receiving advanced education
Health	High birth and death rates; brief life expectancy because of low standard of living and simple medical technology	Low birth and death rates; longer life expectancy because of higher standard of living and sophisticated medical technology
Settlement patterns	Small scale; population typically small and widely dispersed in rural villages and small towns	Large scale; population typically large and concentrated in cities
Social Change	Slow; change evident over many generations	Rapid; change evident within a single generation

responsibility for daily needs that had once been fulfilled by family, friends, and neighbors; universal public education enlarged the scope of learning; police, lawyers, and formal courts supervised a wide-ranging criminal justice system. Even charity became the work of faceless bureaucrats working for various social welfare agencies.

Geographical mobility, mass communications, and exposure to diverse ways of life erode traditional values. Less certain about what is worth believing, people become more tolerant of social diversity, trumpeting individual rights and freedom of choice. Subcultures and countercultures multiply. Making categorical distinctions among people—that is, treating people differently based on their race, sex, or religion—has come to be defined as backward and unjust. In the process, minorities who have long lived at the margins of society have gained greater power and broader participation in public life. Yet, mass-society theorists fear, transforming people of various backgrounds into a generic mass may end up dehumanizing everyone.

RESOURCE: Georg Simmel's classic about modernity, "The Metropolis and Mental Life," is included in the Macionis and Benokraitis reader, *Seeing Ourselves*.

NOTE: The conservative implication of mass-society theory is that social inequality still persists, but it is not as severe a problem as it was in the 19th century. Instead, the growing state is problematic.

Q: "I assert that there is no country in Europe in which the public administration has not become, not only more centralized, but more inquisitive and more minute; it everywhere interferes in private concerns more than it did . . ." Alexis de Tocqueville (Book IV, Chapter V)

NOTE: Many large charities ceased collecting at home and began soliciting in the workplace several decades ago, recognizing that people were more responsive to co-workers than to neighbors.

Mass-society theory attributes common feelings of isolation in the modern world to rapid social change and the collapse of tradition. Edvard Munch captured this sense of impersonality and anxiety in the modern world in his painting (above) Evening on Karl Johan Street *(1892). Class-society theory, by contrast, ties the experience of powerlessness to the poverty of many amidst the privilege of the few, a situation depicted in Paul Marcus's work,* Dinner Is Served *(1995).*

Top: Edvard Munch, *Evening on Karl Johann Street,* 1892, Scala/Art Resource. *Left:* © Paul Marcus 1995, oil on panel, *Dinner Is Served.*

The Ever-Expanding State

In the small-scale, preindustrial societies of Europe, government amounted to little more than a local noble. A royal family formally reigned over an entire nation but, without efficient transportation or communication, the power of even absolute monarchs fell far short of that wielded by today's political leaders.

As technological innovation allowed government to expand, the centralized state grew in size and importance. At the time the United States gained independence from Great Britain, the federal government was a tiny organization whose prime function was national defense. Since then, government has entered more and more areas of social life—regulating wages and working conditions, establishing standards for products of all sorts, schooling the population, and providing financial assistance to the ill and the unemployed. To pay for such programs, taxes have soared, so that today's average worker labors for four months each year simply to pay for the plethora of government services.

In a mass society, power resides in large bureaucracies, leaving people in local communities little control over their lives. For example, state officials mandate a standardized educational program for local schools, local products must earn government certification, and every citizen must maintain extensive records for purposes of taxation. While such regulations may protect people and enhance uniformity of treatment, they force us to deal more and more with nameless officials in distant and often unresponsive bureaucracies, and they undermine the autonomy of families and neighborhoods.

Critical evaluation. The theory of mass society concedes that the transformation of small-scale communities has positive aspects, but it sees in historical change the loss of an irreplaceable heritage. Modern societies increase individual rights, magnify tolerance of social differences, and raise standards of living. But they seem prone to what Weber feared most—excessive bureaucracy—as well as Toennies's self-centeredness and Durkheim's anomie. Their size, complexity, and tolerance of diversity all but doom traditional values and family patterns, leaving individuals isolated, anxious, and materialistic. As we noted in Chapter 16 ("Politics and Government"), voter apathy has become a serious problem in the United States.

But is it surprising that people in vast, impersonal societies tend to conclude that no one person can make a difference?

Critics of mass-society theory contend that it romanticizes the past. They remind us that many people in small towns were actually eager to set out for the excitement and higher standard of living found in cities. Critics also point out that this approach pays little attention to problems of social inequality. Mass-society analysis, critics conclude, attracts social and economic conservatives who defend conventional morality and often seem indifferent to the historical plight of women and other minorities.

Social-Conflict Theory: Modernity as Class Society

A second interpretation of modernity derives largely from the ideas of Karl Marx. From this point of view, modernity takes the form of a **class society**, *a capitalist society with pronounced social stratification*. This theory holds that inequality underlies widespread feelings of powerlessness. While acknowledging that modern societies have expanded to a mass scale, this approach views the heart of modernization as an expanding capitalist economy with its inevitable inequality (Miliband, 1969; Habermas, 1970; Polenberg, 1980; Blumberg, 1981; Harrington, 1984).

Capitalism

Class-society theory follows Marx in claiming that the growing scale of social life has resulted from the insatiable appetite of capitalism. Because a capitalist economy pursues ever-increasing profits, both production and consumption steadily rise.

According to Marx, capitalism rests on "naked self-interest" (1972:337; orig. 1848). This self-centeredness erodes the social ties that once cemented small-scale communities. Capitalism also fosters impersonality and anonymity by transforming people into commodities, both as a source of labor and a market for capitalist production. The net result is that capitalism reduces human beings to cogs in the machinery of material production.

Capitalism also embraces science, not just as the key to greater productivity but also as an ideology that justifies the status quo. In modern societies, people view their own well-being as a *technical* puzzle to be solved by engineers and other experts rather than through the pursuit of *social* justice (Habermas, 1970). A capitalist culture, for example, seeks to improve health through scientific medicine rather than by eliminating poverty, which undermines many people's health in the first place.

Businesses also raise the banner of scientific logic when they claim that efficiency is achieved only through continual growth. As Chapter 15 ("The Economy and Work") explains, capitalist corporations have reached enormous size and control almost unimaginable wealth. They have done so by "going global," operating as multinationals throughout the world. From the class-society point of view, then, the expanding scale of life is less a function of *Gesellschaft* than it is the inevitable and destructive consequence of capitalism.

Persistent Inequality

Modernity has gradually worn away some of the rigid categorical distinctions that divided nobles and commoners in preindustrial societies. Class-society theory maintains, however, that elites persist, albeit now as capitalist millionaires. In the United States, we may have no hereditary monarchy, but the richest 5 percent of the population nevertheless controls half of all property.

How does the state figure in reducing social inequality? While mass-society theorists believe that government has an expanding role in combating social problems, Marx was skeptical that the state could accomplish more than minor reforms because, as he saw it, the state mostly defends the wealth and privileges of capitalists. Other class-society theorists add that, while working people and minorities enjoy greater political rights and a higher standard of living today, these changes are the fruits of political struggle, often against both capitalists and government officials. Thus, they conclude, despite our pretensions of democracy, power still rests primarily in the hands of those with wealth.

Critical evaluation. Table 24–2 summarizes the interpretations of modernity offered by mass-society theory and class-society theory. While the former focuses on the increasing scale of life and the growth of government, the latter stresses the expansion of capitalism and the persistence of inequality.

Class-society theory also dismisses Durkheim's argument that people in modern societies suffer from anomie, claiming, instead, that they grapple with alienation and powerlessness. Not surprisingly, then, the class-society interpretation of modernity enjoys widespread support among liberals (and radicals) who favor greater equality and call for extensive regulation (or abolition) of the capitalist marketplace.

Q: "Identity is a coherent sense of self. It depends upon the awareness that one's endeavors and one's life make sense, that they are meaningful in the context in which life is lived. It depends also upon stable values, and upon the conviction that one's actions and values are harmoniously related. It is a sense of wholeness, of integration, of knowing what is right and what is wrong and of being able to choose." Alan Wheelis (1958:18)

NOTE: The "lonely crowd" thesis includes the argument that the family had lost its socialization function to schools, various specialists, and the mass media, prompting more other-direction in children.
NOTE: Following Wheelis's argument, we might say that conformity in traditional societies reflects unchanging morality; what we call morality in modern societies is more a matter of conformity to changing public opinion.

TABLE 24–2 Two Interpretations of Modernity: A Summary

	Key Process of Modernization	Key Effects of Modernization
Mass-society theory	Industrialization; growth of bureaucracy	Increasing scale of life; rise of the state and other formal organizations
Class-society theory	Rise of capitalism	Expansion of the capitalist economy; persistence of social inequality

To critics of class-society theory, this analysis overlooks the many ways in which modern societies have grown more egalitarian. After all, while discrimination based on race, ethnicity, and gender still exists, it is now illegal and widely regarded as a form of social deviance. Further, most people in the United States favor unequal rewards, at least insofar as they reflect differences in personal talent and effort.

Moreover, few observers think a centralized economy would cure the ills of modernity in light of socialism's failure to generate a high overall standard of living. Many other social problems found in the United States—from unemployment, homelessness, and industrial pollution, to unresponsive government—have also been commonplace in socialist nations such as the former Soviet Union.

Modernity and the Individual

Both mass- and class-society theories focus on broad patterns of change that have taken place since the Industrial Revolution. From each macro-level approach we can also draw micro-level insights into how modernity shapes individual lives.

Mass Society: Problems of Identity

Modernity liberated individuals from small, tightly knit communities of the past. Most people in modern societies possess unprecedented privacy and freedom to express their individuality. Mass-society theory suggests, however, that extensive social diversity, atomization, and rapid social change make it difficult for many people to establish any coherent identity at all (Wheelis, 1958; Riesman, 1970; Berger, Berger, & Kellner, 1974).

Chapter 5 ("Socialization") explained that people forge distinctive personalities based on their social experience. The small, homogeneous, and slowly changing societies of the past provided a firm (if narrow) foundation for building meaningful identity. Even today, the Amish communities that flourish in the United States and Canada teach young men and women "correct" ways to think and behave. Not everyone born into an Amish community can tolerate these demands for conformity, but most members establish a well-integrated and satisfying personal identity (cf. Hostetler, 1980; Kraybill & Olshan, 1994).

Mass societies, with their characteristic diversity and rapid change, offer only shifting sands on which to build a personal identity. Left to make our own life decisions, many of us—especially those with greater affluence—confront a bewildering array of options. Autonomy has little value without standards for making choices, and in a tolerant mass society, people may find one path no more compelling than the next. Not surprisingly, many people shuttle from one identity to another, changing their lifestyle, relationships, and even religion in search of an elusive "true self." Beset by the widespread "relativism" of modern societies, people without a moral compass have lost the security and certainty once provided by tradition.

To David Riesman (1970; orig. 1950), modernization brings on changes in **social character**, *personality patterns common to members of a particular society*. Preindustrial societies promote what Riesman calls **tradition-directedness**, *rigid conformity to time-honored ways of living*. Members of traditional societies model their lives on what has gone before so that what is "good" is equivalent to "what has always been."

Tradition-directedness, then, carries to the level of individual experience Toennies's *Gemeinschaft* and Durkheim's mechanical solidarity. Culturally conservative, tradition-directed people think and act alike because everyone draws on the same solid cultural foundation. Amish women and men exemplify tradition-direction; in Amish culture, tradition ties everyone to ancestors and descendants in an unbroken chain of righteous living.

Many members of diverse and rapidly changing societies define a tradition-directed personality as deviant because it seems so rigid. Modern people, by and large, prize personal flexibility, the capacity to adapt, and sensitivity to others. Riesman describes this type of social character as **other-directedness**, *a receptiveness to the latest trends and fashions, often expressed in the practice of imitating others*. Because their socialization occurs within societies that are constantly in flux, other-directed people develop fluid identities marked by superficiality, inconsistency, and change. They try on different "selves," almost like so many

Q: "We know that we are in motion but do not know where we are going, and hence cannot predict the values of our children." Alan Wheelis (1958:23)

NOTE: David Reisman used the term "social character" to mean "mode of conformity." Tradition-direction is conformity based on categorical memberships; inner-direction (not addressed in this chapter) is conformity to inwardly held values in the absence of strong

tradition; other-direction is conformity to one's contemporaries.

NOTE: A recent study of other-direction is Woody Allen's *Zelig*, featuring a character whose personality is determined by his surroundings.

NOTE: For mass-society theorists, the essential problem of modernity is *anomie* (as noted by Durkheim); for class-society theorists, it is *alienation* (following Marx).

pieces of new clothing, seek out "role models," and engage in varied "performances" as they move from setting to setting (Goffman, 1959). In a traditional society, such "shiftiness" marks a person as untrustworthy, but in a changing, modern society, the chameleonlike ability to fit in virtually anywhere stands as a valued personal trait.

In societies that value the up-to-date rather than the traditional, people anxiously solicit the approval of others, looking to members of their own generation rather than to elders as significant role models. "Peer pressure" can sometimes be irresistible to people with no enduring standards to guide them. Our society urges individuals to be true to themselves. But when social surroundings change so rapidly, how can people determine to which self they should be true? This problem lies at the root of the identity crisis so widespread in industrial societies today. "Who am I?" is a nagging question that many of us struggle to answer. In truth, this problem is not so much psychological as sociological, reflecting the inherent instability of modern mass society.

Class Society: Problems of Powerlessness

Class-society theory paints a different picture of modernity's effects on individuals. This approach maintains that persistent social inequality undermines modern society's promise of individual freedom. For some, modernity delivers great privilege, but, for many, everyday life means coping with economic uncertainty and a gnawing sense of powerlessness (Newman, 1993).

For minorities, the problem of relative disadvantage looms even larger. Similarly, although women enjoy increasing participation in modern societies, they continue to run up against traditional barriers of sexism. In short, this approach rejects mass-society theory's claim that people suffer from too much freedom. Instead, class-society theory holds, our society still denies a majority of people full participation in social life.

On a global scale, as Chapter 11 ("Global Stratification") explained, the expanding scope of world capitalism has placed more of the earth's population under the influence of multinational corporations. As a result, about two-thirds of the world's income is concentrated in high-income countries, where only 15 percent of its people live. Is it any wonder, class-society theorists ask, that people in poor nations also seek greater power to shape their own lives?

Such problems led Herbert Marcuse (1964) to challenge Max Weber's contention that modern society is rational. Marcuse condemned modern society as irrational because, he maintained, it fails to meet the needs of so many people. While modern capitalist societies produce unparalleled wealth, poverty remains the daily plight of more than a billion people. Moreover, Marcuse argues, technological advances typically reduce people's control over their own lives. The advent of high technology has conferred great power on a core of specialists—not the majority of people—who now control events and dominate the public agenda, whether the issue is energy production or health care. Countering the common view that technology *solves* the world's problems, Marcuse contended that science actually *causes* them. In sum, class-society theory asserts that people suffer because modern societies have concentrated both wealth and power in the hands of a privileged few.

Modernity and Progress

In modern societies, most people expect—and applaud—social change. We link modernity to the idea of *progress* (from Latin, meaning "moving forward"), a state of continual improvement. By contrast, we denigrate stability as stagnation.

This chapter began by describing the Kaiapo of Brazil, for whom affluence has broadened opportunities but weakened traditional heritage. In examining the Kaiapo, we see that social change, with all its beneficial and detrimental consequences, is too complex simply to be equated with progress.

Whether or not we see a given change as progress depends on our underlying values. A rising standard of living among the Kaiapo—or, historically, among the U.S. population—has helped make lives longer and more comfortable. But affluence has also fueled materialism at the expense of spiritual life, rendering any simplistic notions of "progress" suspect. In global context, as Figure 24–1 shows, the U.S. population has considerable confidence in science to improve our lives. Yet, recent surveys show that most adults in the United States also feel that science "makes our way of life change too fast" (NORC, 1994:321).

Social change, then, is inherently complex and controversial. We in the United States are proud of our pursuit of basic human rights, for example. Yet, as Chapter 3 ("Culture") explained, we now have something of a "culture of rights" that emphasizes what others owe us but overlooks our obligations to one another. The box on page 653 sharpens the distinction between rights and obligations by contrasting the modern concept of dignity with the traditional notion of honor.

SOCIAL SURVEY: "One trouble with science is that it makes our way of life change too fast." (GSS 1988, N = 1,481; *Codebook*, 1994:321)
"Agree" 40.2%   "Disagree" 57.7%   DK/NR 2.1%
NOTE: The saying "You can't argue with progress" suggests the inevitable and linear nature of change as our culture sees it.

Q: "'Postmodernism' usually refers to a certain constellation of styles and tones in cultural works; pastiche; blankness; a sense of exhaustion; a mixture of levels, forms, styles; a relish for copies and repetitions; a knowingness that dissolves commitment into irony; acute self-consciousness about the constructed nature of the work; pleasure in the play of surfaces; a rejection of history." Todd Gitlin ("Postmodernism: Roots and Politics," *Dissent*, Winter 1989:100–8.)

Global Snapshot

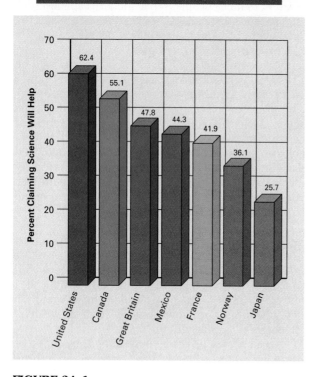

FIGURE 24–1

Support for Science: A Global Survey

Survey Question: "In the long run, do you think the scientific advances we are making will help or harm humankind?"

Source: World Values Survey (1994).

In principle, almost everyone in our society supports the idea that individuals should have considerable autonomy in shaping their own lives. Thus, many people will applaud the demise of traditional conceptions of honor, viewing this trend as a sign of progress. Yet, as people exercise their freedom of choice, they inevitably challenge social patterns cherished by those who maintain a more traditional way of life. For example, people may choose not to marry, to live with someone without marrying, perhaps even to form an intimate partnership with someone of their own sex. To those who endorse individual choice, such changes symbolize progress; to those who value traditional family patterns, however, these developments signal societal decline.

New technology, too, sparks controversy. More rapid transportation and more efficient communication may improve our lives in some respects. However, complex technology has also eroded traditional attachments to hometowns and even to families. Industrial technology has also unleashed an unprecedented threat to the natural environment. In short, we know that social change is accelerating over time, but views may differ sharply as to whether any particular change amounts to progress.

Modernity: Global Variation

October 1, 1994, Kobe, Japan. Riding the computer-controlled monorail high above the streets of Kobe or the two-hundred-mile-per-hour bullet train to Tokyo, we see in Japan the society of the future, in love with high technology. Yet the Japanese remain strikingly traditional in other respects: Few corporate executives and almost no senior politicians are women, young people still accord seniors considerable respect, and public orderliness contrasts to the turmoil and danger of U.S. cities.

Many observers have commented that Japan is a nation at once traditional and modern. This point reminds us that, while it is often useful to contrast traditional and modern social patterns, actual societies often fuse the old and the new in unexpected ways. In the People's Republic of China, to offer another example of this mix, ancient Confucian principles coexist with contemporary socialist thinking. Similarly, in Mexico and much of Latin America, people engage in centuries-old Christian rituals even as they struggle valiantly to pursue economic development.

The description of Brazil's Kaiapo that opened this chapter points up the tensions that typically surround the mixing of traditional and modern social patterns. The broader point is that such combinations are far from unusual—indeed, they are found throughout the world.

POSTMODERNITY

If modernity was the product of the Industrial Revolution, has the Information Revolution propelled us into the postmodern era? A number of scholars answer affirmatively, and use the term **postmodernity** to refer to *social patterns characteristic of postindustrial societies.*

GLOBAL: "Honor" in medieval Europe, "wa" in Japan, and "dharma" in India all express the power of the community to direct the thoughts and behavior of individuals. With modernization, all have tended to erode in favor of "dignity," "choice," and "individual rights."

NOTE: Another implication of the loss of traditional honor in modern societies is the decline of public civility.

DISCUSS: Honor is a matter of specific status; dignity is generically human. One loses honor by violating normative roles; one loses dignity by giving up (or giving away) autonomy. Discuss the differences between "dying with honor" and "dying with dignity."

Q: "What are we calling postmodernity? . . . I must say that I have trouble answering this because I have never clearly understood what was meant . . . by the word 'modernity.'" Michel Foucault

SOCIOLOGY OF EVERYDAY LIFE

What's Happened to Honor?

Honor occupies about the same place in contemporary usage as chastity. An individual asserting it hardly invites admiration, and one who claims to have lost it is an object of amusement rather than sympathy. (1974:83)

Honor is a human virtue that seems distinctly out of place in modern society. This curious concept refers to acting according to traditional cultural norms. Since norms used to be quite different for various categories of people, men claimed honor by acting masculine as women did by being feminine. Honor, in short, is acting like the kind of person you are in a world that rigidly distinguishes between females and males, nobles and serfs, one's own family and outsiders.

Through observing the rules that apply to them, people of any social station can lay claim to honor. During the Middle Ages, European nobles were acting honorably when they performed their feudal obligations toward their social inferiors and displayed

proper respect for their peers. Similarly, commoners acted honorably to the extent that they fulfilled their duties to their superiors and everyone else. Honorable men assumed the cultural ideal of a fatherly, protective role toward women, while never "taking advantage" of them. For their part, women honorably observed proper morals and manners in the presence of men.

With modernization, cultural norms have become weaker and more variable, and categorical distinctions among people have been challenged by drives for social equality. Modern culture, then, holds that all people should treat others as equals. Therefore, although the concept of honor survives among some ethnic communities and traditional occupations like the military, it has less appeal to most members of modern societies.

Modernization enhances a concern for people as *individuals* that is expressed in the concept of *dignity*. Whereas various categories of people have distinctive codes of honor, dignity is a universal human trait, resting

on the inherent value of everyone. We recognize the dignity of others when we acknowledge our common humanity by overlooking social differences.

In the spirit of modern dignity, women may object to men's treating them as women rather than as individuals. The male practices of holding open a door for a woman and paying for a shared meal may be honorable by traditional standards, but now people may view such behavior as an affront to the dignity of women because they underscore gender differences.

As a result, honor is fading from industrial societies. The cultural diversity and rapid social change sweeping across the modern world render as suspect all traditional scripts for living. In contrast to codes of honor that guided people in the past, human beings now value individual self-worth and self-determination, which are the essence of dignity.

Source: Based on Berger, Berger, & Kellner (1974).

Looking more closely, however, we find disagreement about precisely what constitutes postmodernism. This term—long used in literary, philosophical, and even architectural circles—has edged into sociology on a wave of social criticism that has been building since the surge of left-leaning politics in the 1960s. Although there are many variants of postmodern thinking, all share the following five themes (Bernstein, 1992; Borgmann, 1992; Crook, 1992; Hall & Neitz, 1993):

1. **In important respects, modernity has failed.** The promise of modernity was a life free from want. As many postmodernist critics see it, however, the twentieth century was unsuccessful in eradicating

social problems like poverty or even ensuring financial security for many people.

2. **The bright light of "progress" is fading.** Modern people typically look to the future expecting that their lives will improve in significant ways. Members (even leaders) of a postmodern society, however, have less confidence about what the future holds. Furthermore, the buoyant optimism that swept society into the modern era more than a century ago has given way to stark pessimism on the part of most U.S. adults that life is getting worse (NORC, 1994:186).

3. **Science no longer holds the answers.** The defining trait of the modern era was a scientific outlook

NOTE: Postmodernism recognizes that, with the onset of the Information Revolution, ideas are gaining in importance as things decline in significance (New Age thinking as well as fundamentalist religious revival are examples). Such a change prompts us to look critically at the emphasis on material possessions that came with modern, industrial culture.

DISCUSS: Other postmodern changes include: the collapse of culture into various "lifestyles"; the dissolution of social stratification into a mosaic of class and gender and racial categories; weakening political parties; the rise of smaller organizational work groups, suggesting the erosion of traditional bureaucracy; weakening faith in science. (Cf. Stephen Crook, Jan Pakulski, and Malcolm Waters, *Postmodernization: Change in Advanced Societies*, Thousand Oaks, Calif: Sage, 1992)

Sociologist Amitai Etzioni is at the forefront of the communitarian movement, an effort to enlarge our sense of collective responsibility for one another. Etzioni's work drew praise from President Bill Clinton, who invited the sociologist to the White House in 1995.

and a confident belief that technology would make life better. But postmodern critics contend that science has created more problems (such as degrading the environment) than it has solved.

More generally, postmodernist thinkers discredit the foundation of science—the assertion that objective reality and truth exists at all. All reality amounts to so much social construction, they claim; moreover, "deconstructing" science shows that this system of ideas has been widely used for political purposes, especially by powerful segments of society.

4. **Cultural debates are intensifying.** As we have already explained, modernity came wrapped in the bright promise of enhanced individuality and expanding tolerance. Critics claim, however, that the emerging postmodern society falls short of that promise. Feminism asserts that patriarchy continues to shape society today just as multiculturalism seeks to empower minorities long pushed to the margins of social life and left to languish there.

5. **Social institutions are changing.** Industrialization brought sweeping transformation to social institutions; the rise of a postindustrial society is remaking society once again. For example, just as the

Industrial Revolution placed *material things* at the center of productive life, now the Information Revolution has elevated the importance of *ideas*. Similarly, the postmodern family no longer conforms to any singular formula; on the contrary, individuals are devising varied ways of relating to one another.

Critical evaluation. Postmodern critics contend that the United States and other high-income societies have failed in important ways to meet human needs. Yet few would argue that modernity has failed completely; after all, we have seen marked increases in the length and quality of life over the course of this century. Moreover, even if we were to accept postmodernist criticism that science and traditional notions about progress are bankrupt, what are the alternatives?

Then, too, many voices offer strikingly different understandings of recent social trends. The box provides one case in point.

LOOKING AHEAD: MODERNIZATION AND OUR GLOBAL FUTURE

Back in Chapter 1, we imagined the entire world reduced to a village of one thousand people. About 175 residents of this "global village" live in high-income countries, while about half the people receive less than ideal nourishment. Most seriously, 200 people are so poor that they are at risk for their very lives.

The tragic plight of the world's poor shows that some desperately needed change has not occurred at all. Chapter 11 ("Global Stratification") detailed two competing views of why 1 billion people the world over are poor. *Modernization theory* claims that in the past the entire world was poor and that technological change, especially the Industrial Revolution, enhanced human productivity and raised living standards. From this point of view, the solution to global poverty is to promote technological development in poor nations.

For reasons suggested earlier, however, global modernization may be difficult. Recall that David Riesman portrayed preindustrial people as *tradition-directed* and likely to resist change. In response to this cultural brake on development, modernization theorists call for the world's rich societies to offer assistance to poor countries to encourage productive innovation. Industrial nations can speed development by exporting technology to poor regions, welcoming students

NOTE: For a summary of the proliferation of rights, look back at the box about the culture of victimization in Chapter 3, page 72.

Q: Mahatma Gandhi notes seven great dangers to human virtue: wealth without work; pleasure without conscience; knowledge without character; business without ethics; science without humanity; religion without sacrifice; politics without principle.

Q: "Kindness is being nicer to people than they deserve." Anonymous

RESOURCE: William Bennett's article asserting that U.S. culture is in decline appears in the 3d edition of the Macionis and Benokraitis reader, Seeing Ourselves.

Q: "A man cannot get rich if he takes care of his family." Navajo saying

Q: "And, in the end, the love you take is equal to the love you make." The Beatles

CRITICAL THINKING

The United States: A Nation in Decline?

Asked what was his greatest concern about the future of his country, the U.S. novelist Walker Percy responded:

Probably the fear of seeing America, with all its great strength and beauty and freedom . . . gradually subside into decay and be defeated . . . from within by weariness, boredom, cynicism, greed and in the end helplessness before its great problems. . . .

Is the United States, which stood as the world's leading economic and political power during the twentieth century, now a nation in decline? William Bennett, secretary of education in the Reagan administration from 1985 to 1988, points out that, by some measures, the United States is thriving. Between 1960 and 1990, for example, this nation's economic output tripled and median family income (controlled for inflation) climbed by more than one-third. During the same time span, the official poverty rate dropped by half.

Nonetheless, Bennett contends, a number of other indicators of well-being paint a very different—and disturbing—picture of life in the United States as we near the end of this century. Between 1960 and 1990, violent crime shot up fourfold; the number of children born to single mothers as well as the number of children supported by welfare rose more than fivefold; the divorce rate doubled; and teen suicide tripled. Since 1960, television viewing has increased by 35 percent and the average student's College Board scores have fallen by 75 points.

As Bennett sees it, our society cannot fix these problems by throwing money at them. Government expenditures (in constant 1990 dollars) rose fivefold between 1960 and 1990, while our population increased by just 41 percent. Clearly, then, a wide range of serious social problems continues to plague the United States despite (or, perhaps, because of) determined efforts by government to address them. This fact leads Bennett to conclude that our nation's decline is primarily moral—a matter of weakening individual character:

Our society now places less value than before on what we owe to others as a matter of moral obligation; less value on sacrifice as a moral good; less value on social conformity and respectability; and less value on correctness and restraint in matters of physical pleasure and sexuality.

Our current dilemma—that even as we make government bigger and more powerful, many social problems are getting worse—stems from the fact that government can do little to build individual character. Bennett continues:

Our social institutions—families, churches, schools, neighborhoods, and civic associations—have traditionally taken on the responsibility of providing our children with love, order, and discipline—of teaching self-control, compassion, tolerance, civility, honesty, and respect for authority. . . . The social regression of the past thirty years is due in large part to the enfeebled state of our social institutions and their failure to carry out these critical and time-honored tasks.

From Bennett's point of view, the primary values of any society are set not by government but by people living in communities and, especially, by families raising their children. In effect, he concludes, we must not assume that affluence is the best—or even the only—measure of a society's well-being. Moreover, we cannot afford to ignore—nor can we hand over to the government—our basic responsibility to sustain civilization.

Sources: Based, in part, on Bennett (1993).

NOTE: After the Genovese murder, the *New York Times* asked, "Does residence in a great city destroy all sense of personal responsibility for one's neighbors?"

NOTE: In a recent *Time /CNN* poll, more people thought the world would be in better shape (41%) at the end of the next century than feared it would be worse (32%). "About the same" was the reply of 15%.

DISCUSS: Etzioni maintains that U.S. moral revival is possible without the new puritanism of the right or the danger of totalitarianism from the left. While he believes that family is vital, he supports women's equal access to the workplace. He also proposes that schools teach morality, but with no indoctrination.

Q: "Nobody makes a greater mistake than he who does nothing because he could only do a little." Edmund Burke

Controversy & Debate

Personal Freedom and Social Responsibility: Can We Have It Both Ways?

Shortly after midnight on a crisp March evening in 1964, a car pulled into a parking lot alongside a New York apartment complex. Kitty Genovese turned off the headlights, locked the doors of her vehicle, and headed across the blacktop toward the entrance to her building. Moments from safety, she was accosted by a man wielding a knife; as she shrieked in terror, he stabbed her repeatedly. Windows opened above, as curious neighbors searched for the cause of the commotion. But the attack continued—for more than thirty minutes—until Genovese lay dead in the doorway. Subsequent investigation failed to identify the assailant but did confirm a stunning fact: *Not one of dozens of neighbors who witnessed the attack on Kitty Genovese went to the trouble to come to her aid or even to call police.*

More than any other event in recent decades, the Genovese tragedy forced us to confront the question of what we owe others. Members of modern societies prize their individual rights and personal privacy, sometimes withdrawing from public responsibility to the point that society itself seems to collapse. When a cry for help is met by the silence of indifference, have we pushed our modern conception of personal autonomy too far? In a cultural climate of expanding individual rights, can we sustain a sense of human community?

These questions point up the tension between traditional and modern social systems, which is evident in the writings of all the sociologists discussed in this chapter. Toennies, Durkheim, and others concluded that, in a fundamental respect, traditional community and modern individualism are incompatible. That is, society can unite its members in a moral community only the extent that it limits their range of personal choices about how to live. In short, while we value both community and autonomy, we can't have it both ways.

In recent years, sociologist Amitai Etzioni (1993) has tried to strike a middle ground. The "communitarian movement" rests on the simple premise that "strong rights presume strong responsibilities" or, put otherwise, that an individual's pursuit of self-interest must be balanced by a commitment to the larger community.

Etzioni's critique of modernity focuses on the proliferation of individual rights. As he sees it, while people expect the system to provide for them, they are reluctant to support that system. For example, while we believe in the principle of trial by a jury of one's peers, fewer and fewer people today are willing to perform jury duty; similarly, the public is quick to accept government services, but increasingly reluctant to pay taxes.

---

from abroad, and providing foreign aid to stimulate economic growth.

The review of modernization theory in Chapter 11 points to some limited success for these policies in Latin America and, especially, in the small Asian countries of Taiwan, South Korea, Singapore, and Hong Kong. But jump-starting development in the poorest countries of the world poses the greatest challenges. And even where dramatic change has occurred, modernization entails a tradeoff. Traditional people, such as Brazil's Kaiapo, may gain wealth through economic development, but only at the cost of losing their cultural identity and values as they are drawn into the "global village" of McCulture, based on Western materialism, pop music, trendy clothes, and fast food.

One Brazilian anthropologist expressed hope about the future of the Kaiapo: "At least they quickly understood the consequences of watching television.... Now [they] can make a choice" (Simons, 1995:471).

But not everyone thinks that modernization is really an option. According to a second approach to global stratification, *dependency theory*, today's poor societies have little ability to modernize, even if they wanted to. From this point of view, the major barrier to economic development is not traditionalism but the global domination of rich, capitalist societies. Initially, as Chapter 11 explains, this system took the form of colonialism whereby European societies seized much of Latin America, Africa, and Asia. Trading relationships soon enriched England, Spain, and other colonial powers, and their colonies simultaneously became dependent and poor. Almost all societies subjected to this form of domination are now politically independent, but colonial-style ties continue in the form of neocolonialism, with multinational corporations operating throughout the world.

In effect, dependency theory asserts, rich nations achieved their modernization at the expense of poor

Q: "So the journey is over and I am back again where I started, richer by much experience and poorer by many exploded convictions, many perished certainties. . . . Those who like to feel they are always right and to attach a high importance to their own opinions should stay at home. When one is traveling, convictions are mislaid as easily as spectacles; but, unlike spectacles, they are not easily replaced." Aldous Huxley, *Jesting Pilate*

NOTE: A glance back to Figure 11–1, page 292, provides data on the distribution of economic resources around the world.

Richest	20%	70%
2d	20%	20%
Middle	20%	5%
4th	20%	3%
Poorest	20%	2%

Specifically, the communitarians advance four proposals designed to balance individual rights with public responsibilities. First, our society should halt the expanding "culture of rights" by which people have placed their own interests ahead of social responsibility (nothing in the Constitution allows us to do whatever we want to); second, communitarians remind us that all rights involve responsibilities (we cannot simply take from society without giving something back); third, there are certain responsibilities that no one is free to ignore (such as upholding the law and protecting the natural environment); and, fourth, that defending some community interests may require limiting individual rights (protecting public safety, for example, might mean subjecting workers to drug tests).

The communitarian movement appeals to many people who, along with Etzioni, seek to balance personal freedom with social responsibility. But critics have attacked this initiative from both sides of the political spectrum. To those on the left, some vague notion of "social reintegration" falls flat when it comes to addressing problems ranging from voter apathy to street crime. Instead, left-leaning critics contend, what we need are expanded government efforts to enhance equality in U.S. society by curbing the political influence of the rich and actively combating racism and sexism.

Conservatives on the political right also find fault with Etzioni's proposals, but for different reasons (cf. Pearson, 1995). To these critics, the communitarian movement amounts to little more than a rerun of the 1960s leftist agenda. Thus, the communitarian vision of a good society favors some worthy goals (such as protecting the environment) but says little about issues dear to conservatives, such as allowing prayer in the public schools or restoring the strength of traditional families. Moreover, conservatives question whether a free society should engage in the kind of social engineering that Etzioni advocates (such as institutionalizing programs in schools to foster tolerance and requiring young people to perform a year of national service).

Because he draws fire from both the left and the right, some believe that Etzioni has identified a moderate, sensible answer to a vexing problem. On the other hand, it may be that, in a nation as diverse as the United States, people will never readily agree about what they owe themselves—and each other.

Continue the debate . . .

1. *Have you ever failed to come to the aid of someone in need or danger? Why?*

2. *President John F. Kennedy admonished us to "Ask not what your country can do for you, ask what you can do for your country." Do you think people today support this idea? Provide some examples to illustrate your view.*

3. *Do you agree or disagree that our society needs to balance individual rights with more responsibility? Why?*

ones, which provided valuable natural resources and human labor. Even today, the world's poorest countries remain locked in a disadvantageous economic relationship with rich nations, dependent on wealthy countries to buy their raw materials and in return sell them whatever manufactured products they can afford. Overall, dependency theorists conclude, continuing ties with rich societies will only perpetuate current patterns of global inequality.

Whichever approach one finds more convincing, we can no longer isolate the study of the United States from the rest of the world. At the beginning of the twentieth century, a majority of people in today's high-income countries lived in relatively small settlements with limited awareness of the larger world. Now, at the threshold of the twenty-first century, people everywhere participate in a far larger human drama. The world seems smaller, and the lives of all people are increasingly linked. We now discuss the relationships among countries in the same way that people a century ago talked about the expanding ties among cities and towns.

The century now coming to a close has witnessed unprecedented human achievement. Yet solutions to many problems of human existence—including finding meaning in life, resolving conflicts among societies, and eradicating poverty—have eluded us. To this list of pressing matters new concerns have been added in recent years, such as controlling population growth and establishing a sustainable natural environment. As we approach the twenty-first century, we must be prepared to tackle such problems with imagination, compassion, and determination. The challenge is great, but our wide-ranging understanding of human society gives us reason to look to the task ahead with optimism.

SUMMARY

1. Every society changes continuously, intentionally or not, and at varying speeds. Social change often generates controversy.

2. Social change results from invention, discovery, and diffusion as well as social conflict.

3. Modernity refers to the social consequences of industrialization, which, according to Peter Berger, include the erosion of traditional communities, expanding personal choice, increasingly diverse beliefs, and a keen awareness of time, especially the future.

4. Ferdinand Toennies described modernization as the transition from *Gemeinschaft* to *Gesellschaft*, which signifies the progressive loss of community amid growing individualism.

5. To Emile Durkheim, modernization occurred as a function of a society's expanding division of labor. Mechanical solidarity, based on shared activities and beliefs, gradually gives way to organic solidarity, in which specialization makes people interdependent.

6. According to Max Weber, modernity replaces traditional beliefs with a rational world view. He feared the dehumanizing effects of rational organization.

7. Karl Marx saw modernity as the triumph of capitalism over feudalism. Viewing capitalist societies as fraught with social conflict, Marx advocated revolutionary change to achieve a more egalitarian, socialist society.

8. According to mass-society theory, modernity increases the scale of life, enlarging the role of government and other formal organizations in carrying out tasks that previously were performed by family members and neighbors. Cultural diversity and rapid social change make it difficult for people in modern societies to develop stable identities and to find certainty and meaning in their personal lives.

9. Class-society theory states that capitalism is central to Western modernization. This approach charges that, by concentrating wealth, capitalism generates widespread feelings of powerlessness.

10. Social change is too complex and controversial simply to be equated with social progress.

11. Postmodernity refers to cultural traits of postindustrial societies. Postmodern criticism of society centers on the failure of modernity, and specifically science, to fulfill its promise of prosperity and well-being.

12. In a global context, modernization theory links global poverty to the power of tradition. Therefore, some modernization theorists advocate intentional intervention by rich societies to stimulate the development of poor nations.

13. Dependency theory explains global poverty as the product of the world economic system. The operation of multinational corporations ensures that poor societies will remain economically dependent on rich ones.

KEY CONCEPTS

class society a capitalist society with pronounced social stratification

mass society a society in which industry and expanding bureaucracy have eroded traditional social ties

modernity social patterns linked to industrialization

modernization the process of social change initiated by industrialization

other-directedness a receptiveness to the latest trends and fashions, often expressed in the practice of imitating others

postmodernity social patterns characteristic of postindustrial societies

social change the transformation of culture and social institutions over time

social character personality patterns common to members of a particular society

tradition-directedness rigid conformity to time-honored ways of living

CRITICAL-THINKING QUESTIONS

1. Do you think Toennies, Durkheim, Weber, and Marx accurately predicted the character of modern society? How do their visions of society differ?

2. What traits render the United States a "mass society"? Do you consider yourself and most of your friends to be "other-directed"?

3. What is the difference between *anomie* (a trait of mass society) and *alienation* (a characteristic of class society)? Among which categories of the U.S. population would you expect each to be pronounced?

4. What developments lead some analysts to claim that the United States has become a postmodern society?

SUGGESTED READINGS

Classic Sources

Emile Durkheim. *The Division of Labor in Society.* New York: The Free Press, 1964; orig. 1895.
    This is the classic account of social change by one of the founders of sociology.

Derek Sayer. *Capitalism and Modernity: An Excursus on Marx and Weber.* New York: Routledge, 1991.
    This recent book examines the limits of modernity and the prospects for postmodernity through a review of the ideas of two seminal sociologists.

Contemporary Sources

Amitai Etzioni. *The Spirit of Community: Rights, Responsibilities, and the Communitarian Agenda.* New York: Crown Publishers, 1993.
    In what might be called the "handbook of the communitarian movement," Etzioni suggests ways to fuse individual rights with collective responsibility.

Peter Berger, Brigitte Berger, and Hansfried Kellner. *The Homeless Mind: Modernization and Consciousness.* New York: Vintage Books, 1974.

Peter L. Berger. *Facing Up to Modernity: Excursions in Society, Politics, and Religion.* New York: Basic Books, 1977.
    Highly readable, even for undergraduates, these books are filled with interesting insights about the modern world.

Global Sources

Joyce Gelb and Marian Lief Palley, eds. *Women of Japan and Korea: Continuity and Change.* Philadelphia: Temple University Press, 1994.
    This collection of essays surveys the link between women's social standing and society's economic development in two rapidly changing Asian nations.

Wendy Griswold. *Cultures and Societies in a Changing World.* Thousand Oaks, Calif.: Pine Forge Press, 1994.
    Close-up examination of various countries, including Nigeria and China, illustrates this discussion of cultural change.

Glossary

absolute poverty a deprivation of resources that is life threatening

achieved status a social position that someone assumes voluntarily and that reflects personal ability and effort

acid rain precipitation that is made acidic by air pollution and destroys plant and animal life

activity theory the proposition that a high level of activity enhances personal satisfaction in old age

Afrocentrism the dominance of African cultural patterns

ageism prejudice and discrimination against the elderly

age-sex pyramid a graphic representation of the age and sex of a population

age stratification the unequal distribution of wealth, power, and privileges among people at different stages in the life course

agriculture the technology of large-scale farming using plows harnessed to animals or more powerful sources of energy

alienation the experience of isolation resulting from powerlessness

animism the belief that elements of the natural world are conscious life forms that affect humanity

anomie Durkheim's designation of a condition in which society provides little moral guidance to individuals

anticipatory socialization social learning directed toward gaining a desired position

ascribed status a social position that someone receives at birth or assumes involuntarily later in life

assimilation the process by which minorities gradually adopt patterns of the dominant culture

authoritarianism a political system that denies popular participation in government

authority power that people perceive as legitimate rather than coercive

beliefs specific statements that people hold to be true

bilateral descent a system tracing kinship through both men and women

blue-collar occupations lower-prestige work involving mostly manual labor

bureaucracy an organizational model rationally designed to perform complex tasks efficiently

bureaucratic inertia the tendency of bureaucratic organizations to perpetuate themselves

bureaucratic ritualism a preoccupation with rules and regulations to the point of thwarting an organization's goals

capitalism an economic system in which natural resources and the means of producing goods and services are privately owned

capitalists people who own factories and other productive enterprises

caste system a system of social stratification based on ascription

cause and effect a relationship in which change in one variable (the independent variable) causes change in another (the dependent variable)

charisma extraordinary personal qualities that can turn an audience into followers

charismatic authority power legitimized through extraordinary personal abilities that inspire devotion and obedience

church a type of religious organization well integrated into the larger society

civil religion a quasi-religious loyalty binding individuals in a basically secular society

class conflict antagonism between entire classes over the distribution of wealth and power in society

class consciousness Marx's term for the recognition by workers of their unity as a social class in opposition to capitalists and to capitalism itself

class society a capitalist society with pronounced social stratification

class system a system of social stratification based on individual achievement

cohabitation the sharing of a household by an unmarried couple

cohort a category of people with a common characteristic, usually their age

collective behavior activity involving a large number of people, often spontaneous, and typically in violation of established norms

collectivity a large number of people whose minimal interaction occurs in the absence of well-defined and conventional norms

colonialism the process by which some nations enrich themselves through political and economic control of other countries

communism a hypothetical economic and political system in which all members of a society are socially equal

concept a mental construct that represents some part of the world, inevitably in a simplified form

concrete operational stage Piaget's term for the level of human development at which individuals first perceive causal connections in their surroundings

conglomerates giant corporations composed of many smaller corporations

control holding constant all relevant variables except one in order to observe its effect

corporation an organization with a legal existence, including rights and liabilities, apart from those of its members

correlation a relationship by which two (or more) variables change together

counterculture cultural patterns that strongly oppose those widely accepted within a society

credentialism evaluating a person on the basis of educational degrees

crime the violation of norms a society formally enacts into criminal law

crimes against the person (violent crimes) crimes that direct violence or the threat of violence against others

crimes against property (property crimes) crimes that involve theft of property belonging to others

criminal justice system a societal reaction to alleged violations of the law utilizing police, courts, and prison officials

criminal recidivism subsequent offenses committed by people previously convicted of crimes

crowd a temporary gathering of people who share a common focus of attention and whose members influence one another

crude birth rate the number of live births in a given year for every thousand people in a population

crude death rate the number of deaths in a given year for every thousand people in a population

cult a religious organization that is substantially outside a society's cultural traditions

cultural conflict political opposition, often accompanied by social hostility, rooted in different cultural values

cultural ecology a theoretical paradigm that explores the relationship of human culture and the physical environment

cultural integration the close relationship among various elements of a cultural system

cultural lag the fact that cultural elements change at different rates, which may disrupt a cultural system

cultural relativism the practice of judging a culture by its own standards

cultural transmission the process by which one generation passes culture to the next

cultural universals traits that are part of every known culture

culture the beliefs, values, behavior, and material objects that constitute a people's way of life

culture shock personal disorientation that comes from encountering an unfamiliar way of life

Davis-Moore thesis the assertion that social stratification is a universal pattern because it has beneficial consequences for the operation of a society

deductive logical thought reasoning that transforms general ideas into specific hypotheses suitable for scientific testing

democracy a type of political system in which power is exercised by the people as a whole

democratic socialism an economic and political system that combines significant government control of the economy with free elections

demographic transition theory a thesis linking population patterns to a society's level of technological development

demography the study of human population

denomination a church, independent of the state, that accepts religious pluralism

dependency theory a model of economic and social development that explains global inequality in terms of the historical exploitation of poor societies by rich ones

dependent variable a variable that is changed by another (independent) variable

descent the system by which members of a society trace kinship over generations

deterrence the attempt to discourage criminality through punishment

deviance the recognized violation of cultural norms

direct-fee system a medical-care system in which patients pay directly for the services of physicians and hospitals

discrimination an action that involves treating various categories of people unequally

disengagement theory the proposition that society enhances its orderly operation by disengaging people from positions of responsibility as they reach old age

division of labor specialized economic activity

dramaturgical analysis Erving Goffman's term for the investigation of social interaction in terms of theatrical performance

dyad a social group with two members

dysfunction (*See* social dysfunction)

eating disorder an intense involvement in dieting or other forms of weight control in order to become very thin

ecclesia a church that is formally allied with the state

ecologically sustainable culture a way of life that meets the needs of the present generation without threatening the environmental legacy of future generations

ecology the study of the interaction of living organisms and the natural environment

economy the social institution that organizes the production, distribution, and consumption of goods and services

ecosystem the system composed of the interaction of all living organisms and their natural environment

education the social institution guiding a society's transmission of knowledge—including basic facts, job skills, and cultural norms and values—to its members

ego Freud's designation of a person's conscious efforts to balance innate, pleasure-seeking drives and the demands of society

empirical evidence information we can verify with our senses

endogamy marriage between people of the same social category

environmental deficit the situation in which our relationship to the environment, while yielding short-term benefits, will have profound, long-term consequences

environmental racism the pattern by which environmental hazards are greatest in proximity to poor people—and especially minorities

ethnicity a shared cultural heritage

ethnocentrism the practice of judging another culture by the standards of one's own culture

ethnomethodology Harold Garfinkel's term for the study of the way people make sense of their everyday lives

Eurocentrism the dominance of European (especially English) cultural patterns

euthanasia (mercy killing) assisting in the death of a person suffering from an incurable disease

exogamy marriage between people of different social categories

experiment a research method for investigating cause and effect under highly controlled conditions

expressive leadership group leadership that emphasizes collective well-being

extended family (consanguine family) a family unit including parents and children, but also other kin

fad an unconventional social pattern that people embrace briefly but enthusiastically

faith belief anchored in conviction rather than scientific evidence

false consciousness Marx's term for explanations of social problems grounded in the shortcomings of individuals rather than the flaws of society

family a social institution, found in all societies, that unites individuals into cooperative groups that oversee the bearing and raising of children

family unit a social group of two or more people, related by blood, marriage, or adoption, who usually live together

family violence emotional, physical, or sexual abuse of one family member by another

fashion a social pattern favored for a time by a large number of people

feminism the advocacy of social equality for the sexes, in opposition to patriarchy and sexism

feminization of poverty the trend by which women represent an increasing proportion of the poor

fertility the incidence of childbearing in a country's population

folkways a society's customs for routine, casual interaction

formal operational stage Piaget's term for the level of human development at which individuals think abstractly and critically

formal organization a large secondary group organized to achieve its goals efficiently

functional illiteracy reading and writing skills insufficient for everyday living

fundamentalism a conservative religious doctrine that opposes intellectualism and worldly accommodation in favor of restoring a traditional, otherworldly spirituality

Gemeinschaft Toennies's term for a type of social organization by which people are bound closely together by kinship and tradition

gender the significance members of a society attach to being female or male

gender identity traits that females and males, guided by their culture, incorporate into their personalities

gender roles (sex roles) attitudes and activities that a society links to each sex

gender stratification a society's unequal distribution of wealth, power, and privilege between the two sexes

generalized other George Herbert Mead's label for widespread cultural norms and values that we use as references in evaluating ourselves

genocide the systematic annihilation of one category of people by another

gerontocracy a form of social organization in which the elderly have the most wealth, power, and prestige

gerontology the study of aging and the elderly

Gesellschaft Toennies's term for a type of social organization by which people have weak social ties and considerable self-interest

global economy economic activity spanning many nations of the world with little regard for national borders

global perspective the study of the larger world and our society's place in it

gossip rumor about the personal affairs of others

government formal organizations that direct the political life of a society

greenhouse effect a rise in the earth's average temperature (global warming) due to increasing concentration of carbon dioxide in the atmosphere

groupthink the tendency of group members to conform by adopting a narrow view of some issue

hate crime a criminal act against a person or a person's property by an offender motivated by racial or other bias

Hawthorne effect a change in a subject's behavior caused simply by the awareness of being studied

health a state of complete physical, mental, and social well-being

health care any activity intended to improve health

health maintenance organization (HMO) an organization that provides comprehensive medical care to subscribers for a fixed fee

hermaphrodite a human being with some combination of female and male internal and external genitalia

hidden curriculum subtle presentations of political or cultural ideas in the classroom

high culture cultural patterns that distinguish a society's elite

high-income countries industrial nations in which most people enjoy material abundance

holistic medicine an approach to health care that emphasizes prevention of illness and takes account of a person's entire physical and social environment

homogamy marriage between people with the same social characteristics

horticulture technology based on using hand tools to cultivate plants

humanizing bureaucracy fostering a more democratic organizational atmosphere that recognizes and encourages the contributions of everyone

hunting and gathering simple technology for hunting animals and gathering vegetation

hypothesis an unverified statement of a relationship between variables

id Freud's designation of the human being's basic drives

ideal culture (as opposed to real culture) social patterns mandated by cultural values and norms

ideal type Weber's term for an abstract statement of the essential characteristics of any social phenomenon

ideology cultural beliefs that serve to justify social stratification

incest taboo a cultural norm forbidding sexual relations or marriage between certain kin

income occupational wages or salaries and earnings from investments

independent variable a variable that causes change in another (dependent) variable

inductive logical thought reasoning that transforms specific observations into general theory

industrialism technology that powers sophisticated machinery with advanced sources of energy

infant mortality rate the number of deaths among infants under one year of age for each thousand live births in a given year

ingroup a social group commanding a member's esteem and loyalty

institutional prejudice or discrimination bias in attitudes or action inherent in the operation of society's institutions

instrumental leadership group leadership that emphasizes the completion of tasks

intergenerational social mobility upward or downward social mobililty of children in relation to their parents

interview a series of questions a researcher administers personally to respondents

intragenerational social mobility a change in social position occurring during a person's lifetime

juvenile delinquency the violation of legal standards by the young

kinship a social bond, based on blood, marriage, or adoption, that joins individuals into families

labeling theory the assertion that deviance and conformity result, not so much from what people do, as from how others respond to those actions

labor unions organizations of workers seeking to improve wages and working conditions through various strategies, including negotiations and strikes

language a system of symbols that allows members of a society to communicate with one another

latent functions consequences of any social pattern that are unrecognized and unintended

liberation theology a fusion of Christian principles with political activism, often Marxist in character

life expectancy the average life span of a society's population

looking-glass self Cooley's term for the image people have of themselves based on how they believe others perceive them

low-income countries nations with little industrialization in which severe poverty is the rule

macro-level orientation a focus on broad social structures that characterize society as a whole

mainstreaming integrating special students into the overall educational program

manifest functions the recognized and intended consequences of any social pattern

marriage a legally sanctioned relationship, involving economic cooperation as well as normative sexual activity and childbearing, that people expect to be relatively enduring

mass behavior collective behavior among people dispersed over a wide geographical area

mass hysteria a form of dispersed collective behavior by which people respond to a real or imagined event with irrational, frantic, and often self-destructive behavior

mass media impersonal communications directed toward a vast audience

mass society a society in which industry and expanding bureaucracy have eroded traditional social ties

master status a status that has exceptional importance for social identity, often shaping a person's entire life

material culture the tangible things created by members of a society

matriarchy a form of social organization in which females dominate males

matrilineal descent a system tracing kinship through women

matrilocality a residential pattern in which a married couple lives with or near the wife's family

mean the arithmetic average of a series of numbers

measurement the process of determining the value of a variable in a specific case

mechanical solidarity Durkheim's designation of social bonds, based on shared morality, that unite members of preindustrial societies

median the value that occurs midway in a series of numbers arranged in order of magnitude or, simply, the middle case

medicalization of deviance the transformation of moral and legal issues into medical matters

medicine a social institution concerned with combating disease and improving health

megalopolis a vast urban region containing a number of cities and their surrounding suburbs

meritocracy a system of social stratification based on personal merit

metropolis a large city that socially and economically dominates an urban area

micro-level orientation a focus on patterns of social interaction in specific situations

middle-income countries nations characterized by limited industrialization and moderate personal income

migration the movement of people into and out of a specified territory

military-industrial complex the close association among the federal government, the military, and defense industries

minority a category of people, distinguished by physical or cultural traits, who are socially disadvantaged

miscegenation biological reproduction by partners of different racial categories

mob a highly emotional crowd that pursues some violent or destructive goal

mode the value that occurs most often in a series of numbers

modernity social patterns linked to industrialization

modernization the process of social change initiated by industrialization

modernization theory a model of economic and social development that explains global inequality in terms of differing levels of technological development among societies

monarchy a type of political system in which a single family rules from generation to generation

monogamy a form of marriage joining two partners

monopoly domination of a market by a single producer

monotheism belief in a single divine power

mores a society's standards of proper moral conduct

mortality the incidence of death in a country's population

multiculturalism an educational program recognizing past and present cultural diversity in U.S. society and promoting the equality of all cultural traditions

multinational corporation a large corporation that operates in many different countries

natural environment the earth's surface and atmosphere, including various living organisms as well as the air, water, soil, and other resources necessary to sustain life

neocolonialism a new form of global power relationships that involves not direct political control but economic exploitation by multinational corporations

neolocality a residential pattern in which a married couple lives apart from the parents of both spouses

network a web of social ties that links people who identify and interact little with one another

nonmaterial culture the intangible world of ideas created by members of a society

nonverbal communication communication using body movements, gestures, and facial expressions rather than speech

norms rules and expectations by which a society guides the behavior of its members

nuclear family (conjugal family) a family unit composed of one or two parents and their children

nuclear proliferation the acquisition of nuclear weapons technology by more and more nations

objectivity a state of personal neutrality in conducting research

oligarchy the rule of the many by the few

oligopoly domination of a market by a few producers

operationalizing a variable specifying exactly what one intends to measure in assigning a value to a variable

organic solidarity Durkheim's designation of social bonds, based on specialization, that unite members of industrial societies

organizational environment a range of factors external to an organization that affects its operation

other-directedness a receptiveness to the latest trends and fashions, often expressed in the practice of imitating others

outgroup a social group toward which one feels competition or opposition

panic a form of localized collective behavior by which people react to a perceived threat or other stimulus with irrational, frantic, and often self-destructive behavior

paradigm (See theoretical paradigm)

participant observation a research method in which researchers systematically observe people while joining in their routine activities

pastoralism technology based on the domestication of animals

patriarchy a form of social organization in which males dominate females

patrilineal descent a system tracing kinship through men

patrilocality a residential pattern in which a married couple lives with or near the husband's family

peace a state of international relations devoid of violence

peer group a social group whose members have interests, social position, and age in common

personality a person's fairly consistent patterns of thinking, feeling, and acting

personal space the surrounding area to which an individual makes some claim to privacy

plea bargaining a legal negotiation in which the state reduces the charge against a defendant in exchange for a guilty plea

pluralism a state in which racial and ethnic minorities are distinct but have social parity

pluralist model an analysis of politics that views power as dispersed among many competing interest groups

political action committee (PAC) an organization formed by a special-interest group, independent of political parties, to pursue political aims by raising and spending money

political revolution the overthrow of one political system in order to establish another

politics the social institution that distributes power, sets a society's agenda, and makes decisions

polyandry a form of marriage joining one female with two or more males

polygamy a form of marriage uniting three or more people

polygyny a form of marriage joining one male with two or more females

polytheism belief in many gods

popular culture cultural patterns that are widespread among a society's population

population the people who are the focus of research

positivism a means to understand the world based on science

postindustrial economy a productive system based on service work and high technology

postindustrialism technology that supports an information-based economy

postmodernity social patterns characteristic of postindustrial societies

power the ability to achieve desired ends despite resistance from others

power-elite model an analysis of politics that views power as concentrated among the rich

prejudice a rigid and irrational generalization about an entire category of people

preoperational stage Piaget's term for the level of human development at which individuals first use language and other symbols

presentation of self an individual's effort to create specific impressions in the minds of others

primary group a small social group in which relationships are both personal and enduring

primary labor market occupations that provide extensive benefits to workers

primary sector the part of the economy that generates raw materials directly from the natural environment

primary sex characteristics the genitals, used to reproduce the human species

profane that which is defined as an ordinary element of everyday life

profession a prestigious, white-collar occupation that requires extensive formal education

proletariat people who provide labor necessary to operate factories and other productive enterprises

propaganda information presented with the intention of shaping public opinion

qualitative research investigation by which a researcher gathers impressionistic, not numerical, data

quantitative research investigation by which a researcher collects numerical data

questionnaire a series of written questions a researcher supplies to subjects requesting their responses

race a category composed of people who share biologically transmitted traits that members of a society deem socially significant

racism the belief that one racial category is innately superior or inferior to another

rain forests regions of dense forestation, most of which circle the globe close to the equator

rationality deliberate, matter-of-fact calculation of the most efficient means to accomplish a particular goal

rationalization of society Weber's term for the historical change from tradition to rationality as the dominant mode of human thought

rational-legal authority (bureaucratic authority) power legitimized by legally enacted rules and regulations

real culture (as opposed to ideal culture) actual social patterns that only approximate cultural expectations

reference group a social group that serves as a point of reference in making evaluations or decisions

rehabilitation a program for reforming the offender to preclude subsequent offenses

relative deprivation a perceived disadvantage arising from a specific comparison

relative poverty the deprivation of some people in relation to those who have more

reliability the quality of consistent measurement

religion a social institution involving beliefs and practices based upon a conception of the sacred

religiosity the importance of religion in a person's life

replication repetition of research by others

research method a systematic plan for conducting research

resocialization radically altering an inmate's personality through deliberate manipulation of the environment

retribution moral vengeance by which society inflicts suffering on an offender comparable to that caused by the offense

retrospective labeling the interpretation of someone's past consistent with present deviance

riot a social eruption that is highly emotional, violent, and undirected

ritual formal, ceremonial behavior

role behavior expected of someone who holds a particular status

role conflict incompatibility among the roles corresponding to two or more statuses

role set a number of roles attached to a single status

role strain incompatibility among roles corresponding to a single status

routinization of charisma the transformation of charismatic authority into some combination of traditional and bureaucratic authority

rumor unsubstantiated information people spread informally, often by word of mouth

sacred that which is defined as extraordinary, inspiring a sense of awe, reverence, and even fear

sample a part of a population researchers select to represent the whole

Sapir-Whorf hypothesis the hypothesis that people perceive the world through the cultural lens of language

scapegoat a person or category of people, typically with little power, whom people unfairly blame for their own troubles

schooling formal instruction under the direction of specially trained teachers

science a logical system that bases knowledge on direct, systematic observation

secondary analysis a research method in which a researcher utilizes data collected by others

secondary group a large and impersonal social group devoted to some specific interest or activity

secondary labor market jobs that provide minimal benefits to workers

secondary sector the part of the economy that transforms raw materials into manufactured goods

secondary sex characteristics bodily development, apart from the genitals, that distinguishes biologically mature females and males

sect a type of religious organization that stands apart from the larger society

secularization the historical decline in the importance of the supernatural and the sacred

segregation the physical and social separation of categories of people

self George Herbert Mead's term for a dimension of personality composed of an individual's self-awareness and self-image

sensorimotor stage Piaget's designation for the level of human development at which individuals experience the world only through sensory contact

sex the biological distinction between females and males

sexism the belief that one sex is innately superior to the other

sex ratio the number of males for every hundred females in a given population

sexual harassment comments, gestures, or physical contact of a sexual nature that are deliberate, repeated, and unwelcome

sexual orientation an individual's preference in terms of sexual partners: same sex, other sex, either sex, neither sex

sick role patterns of behavior defined as appropriate for those who are ill

social change the transformation of culture and social institutions over time

social character personality patterns common to members of a particular society

social conflict struggle between segments of society over valued resources

social-conflict paradigm a framework for building theory that envisions society as an arena of inequality that generates conflict and change

social construction of reality the process by which people creatively shape reality through social interaction

social control various means by which members of a society encourage conformity to norms

social dysfunction the undesirable consequences of any social pattern for the operation of society

social epidemiology the study of how health and disease are distributed throughout a society's population

social function the consequences of any social pattern for the operation of society

social group two or more people who identify and interact with one another

social institution a major sphere of social life, or societal subsystem, organized to meet a basic human need

social interaction the process by which people act and react in relation to others

socialism an economic system in which natural resources and the means of producing goods and services are collectively owned

socialization the lifelong social experience by which individuals develop their human potential and learn patterns of their culture

socialized medicine a health-care system in which the government owns and operates most medical facilities and employs most physicians

social mobility change in people's position in a social hierarchy

social movement organized activity that encourages or discourages social change

social stratification a system by which society ranks categories of people in a hierarchy

social structure relatively stable patterns of social behavior

societal protection a means by which society renders an offender incapable of further offenses temporarily through incarceration or permanently by execution

society people who interact in a defined territory and share culture

sociobiology a theoretical paradigm that explores ways in which our biology affects how humans create culture

sociocultural evolution the Lenskis' term for the process of change that results from a society's gaining new information, particularly technology

socioeconomic status (SES) a composite ranking based on various dimensions of social inequality

sociology the systematic study of human society

special-interest group a political alliance of people interested in some economic or social issue

spurious correlation an apparent, although false, relationship between two (or more) variables caused by some other variable

state capitalism an economic and political system in which companies are privately owned but cooperate closely with the government

state terrorism the use of violence, generally without support of law, against individuals or groups by a government or its agents

status a recognized social position that an individual occupies

status consistency the degree of consistency of a person's social standing across various dimensions of social inequality

status set all the statuses a person holds at a given time

stereotype an exaggerated description applied to every person in some category

stigma a powerfully negative social label that radically changes a person's self-concept and social identity

structural-functional paradigm a framework for building theory that envisions society as a complex system whose parts work together to promote solidarity and stability

structural social mobility a shift in the social position of large numbers of people due more to changes in society itself than to individual efforts

subculture cultural patterns that set apart some segment of a society's population

suburbs urban areas beyond the political boundaries of a city

superego Freud's designation of the operation of culture within the individual in the form of internalized values and norms

survey a research method in which subjects respond to a series of items in a questionnaire or an interview

symbol anything that carries a particular meaning recognized by people who share culture

symbolic-interaction paradigm a framework for building theory that envisions society as the product of the everyday interactions of individuals

technology knowledge that a society applies to the task of living in a physical environment

terrorism violence or the threat of violence employed by an individual or group as a political strategy

tertiary sector the part of the economy that generates services rather than goods

theoretical paradigm a basic image of society that guides sociological thinking and research

theory a statement of how and why specific facts are related

Thomas theorem W. I. Thomas's assertion that situations we define as real become real in their consequences

total institution a setting in which people are isolated from the rest of society and manipulated by an administrative staff

totalitarianism a political system that extensively regulates people's lives

totem an object in the natural world collectively defined as sacred

tracking the assignment of students to different types of educational programs

tradition sentiments and beliefs passed from generation to generation

traditional authority power legitimized through respect for long-established cultural patterns

tradition-directedness rigid conformity to time-honored ways of living

transsexuals people who feel they are one sex though biologically they are the other

triad a social group with three members

underground economy economic activity generating income that one does not report to the government as required by law

urban ecology the study of the link between the physical and social dimensions of cities

urbanization the concentration of humanity into cities

validity the quality of measuring precisely what one intends to measure

values culturally defined standards by which people assess desirability, goodness, and beauty, and which serve as broad guidelines for social living

variable a concept whose value changes from case to case

victimless crimes violations of law in which there are no readily apparent victims

war armed conflict among the people of various societies, directed by their governments

wealth the total value of money and other assets, minus outstanding debts

white-collar crime crimes committed by persons of high social position in the course of their occupations

white-collar occupations higher-prestige work involving mostly mental activity

zero population growth the level of reproduction that maintains population at a steady state

References

ABBOTT, ANDREW. *The System of Professions: An Essay on the Division of Expert Labor.* Chicago: University of Chicago Press, 1988.

ABERLE, DAVID F. *The Peyote Religion Among the Navaho.* Chicago: Aldine, 1966.

ADLER, JERRY. "When Harry Called Sally . . ." *Newsweek* (October 1, 1990):74.

ADORNO, T. W., ET AL. *The Authoritarian Personality.* New York: Harper & Brothers, 1950.

AGUIRRE, BENIGNO E., and E. L. QUARANTELLI. "Methodological, Ideological, and Conceptual-Theoretical Criticisms of Collective Behavior: A Critical Evaluation and Implications for Future Study." *Sociological Focus.* Vol. 16, No. 3 (August 1983):195–216.

AGUIRRE, BENIGNO E., E. L. QUARANTELLI, and JORGE L. MENDOZA. "The Collective Behavior of Fads: Characteristics, Effects, and Career of Streaking." *American Sociological Review.* Vol. 53, No. 4 (August 1988):569–84.

AKERS, RONALD L., MARVIN D. KROHN, LONN LANZA-KADUCE, and MARCIA RADOSEVICH. "Social Learning and Deviant Behavior." *American Sociological Review.* Vol. 44, No. 4 (August 1979):636–55.

ALAM, SULTANA. "Women and Poverty in Bangladesh." *Women's Studies International Forum.* Vol. 8, No. 4 (1985):361–71.

ALBA, RICHARD D. *Italian Americans: Into the Twilight of Ethnicity.* Englewood Cliffs, N.J.: Prentice Hall, 1985.

———. *Ethnic Identity: The Transformation of White America.* Chicago: University of Chicago Press, 1990.

ALBON, JOAN. "Retention of Cultural Values and Differential Urban Adaptation: Samoans and American Indians in a West Coast City." *Social Forces.* Vol. 49, No. 3 (March 1971):385–93.

ALLAN, EMILIE ANDERSEN, and DARRELL J. STEFFENSMEIER. "Youth, Underemployment, and Property Crime: Differential Effects of Job Availability and Job Quality on Juvenile and Young Adult Arrest Rates." *American Sociological Review.* Vol. 54, No. 1 (February 1989):107–23.

ALLEN, MICHAEL PATRICK, and PHILIP BROYLES. "Campaign Finance Reforms and the Presidential Campaign Contributions of Wealthy Capitalist Families." *Social Science Quarterly.* Vol. 72, No. 4 (December 1991):738–50.

ALLSOP, KENNETH. *The Bootleggers.* London: Hutchinson and Company, 1961.

ALTMAN, DREW, ET AL. "Health Care for the Homeless." *Society.* Vol. 26, No. 4 (May-June 1989):4–5.

AMERICAN COUNCIL ON EDUCATION. "Thirteenth Annual Status Report on Minorities in Higher Education." Washington, D.C.: The Council, 1995.

———. Response to telephone inquiry, 1996.

AMERICAN SOCIOLOGICAL ASSOCIATION. "Code of Ethics." Washington, D.C.: 1984.

ANDERSON, JOHN WARD, and MOLLY MOORE. "World's Poorest Women Suffer in Common." *Columbus Dispatch* (April 11, 1993):4G.

ANDO, FAITH H. "Women in Business." In Sara E. Rix, ed., *The American Woman: A Status Report 1990-91.* New York: Norton, 1990:222–30.

ANG, IEN. *Watching Dallas: Soap Opera and the Melodramatic Imagination.* London: Methuen, 1985.

ANGELO, BONNIE. "The Pain of Being Black" (an interview with Toni Morrison). *Time.* Vol. 133, No. 21 (May 22, 1989):120–22.

———. "Assigning the Blame for a Young Man's Suicide." *Time.* Vol. 138, No. 2 (November 18, 1991):12–14.

ANGIER, NATALIE. "Scientists, Finding Second Idiosyncracy in Homosexuals' Brains, Suggest Orientation is Physiological." *New York Times* (August 1, 1992):A7.

APA. *Violence and Youth: Psychology's Response.* Washington, D.C.: American Psychological Association, 1993.

ARCHER, DANE, and ROSEMARY GARTNER. *Violence and Crime in Cross-National Perspective.* New Haven, Conn.: Yale University Press, 1987.

ARENDT, HANNAH. *The Origins of Totalitarianism.* Cleveland, Ohio: Meridian Books, 1958.

———. *Between Past and Future: Six Exercises in Political Thought.* Cleveland, Ohio: Meridian Books, 1963.

ARIÈS, PHILIPPE. *Centuries of Childhood: A Social History of Family Life.* New York: Vintage Books, 1965.

———. *Western Attitudes Toward Death: From the Middle Ages to the Present.* Baltimore, Md.: Johns Hopkins University Press, 1974.

ARJOMAND, SAID AMIR. *The Turban for the Crown: The Islamic Revolution in Iran.* New York: Oxford University Press, 1988.

ASANTE, MOLEFI KETE. *The Afrocentric Idea.* Philadelphia: Temple University Press, 1987.

———. *Afrocentricity.* Trenton, N.J.: Africa World Press, 1988.

ASCH, SOLOMON. *Social Psychology.* Englewood Cliffs, N.J.: Prentice Hall, 1952.

ASHFORD, LORI S. "New Perspectives on Population: Lessons from Cairo." *Population Bulletin.* Vol. 50, No. 1 (March 1995).

ASTONE, NAN MARIE, and SARA S. MCLANAHAN. "Family Structure, Parental Practices and High School Completion." *American Sociological Review.* Vol. 56, No. 3 (June 1991):309–20.

ATCHLEY, ROBERT C. "Retirement as a Social Institution." *Annual Review of Sociology.* Vol. 8. Palo Alto, Calif.: Annual Reviews, 1982:263–87.

———. *Aging: Continuity and Change.* Belmont, Calif.: Wadsworth, 1983; 2d ed., 1987.

AUSTER, CAROL J. and MIND MacRONE. "The Classroom as a Negotiated Social Setting: An Empirical Study of the Effects of Faculty Members' Behavior on Students' Participation." *Teaching Sociology.* Vol. 22, No. 4 (October 1994):289–300.

AXTELL, ROGER E. *Gestures: The DOs and TABOOs of Body Language Around the World.* New York: Wiley, 1991.

AYENSU, EDWARD S. "A Worldwide Role for the Healing Powers of Plants." *Smithsonian.* Vol. 12, No. 8 (November 1981):87–97.

BABBIE, EARL. *The Practice of Social Research.* 7th ed. Belmont, Calif.: Wadsworth, 1995.

BACHMAN, RONET. *Violence Against Women.* U.S. Bureau of Justice Statistics. Washington, D.C.: U.S. Government Printing Office, 1994.

BACHRACH, PETER, and MORTON S. BARATZ. *Power and Poverty.* New York: Oxford University Press, 1970.

BACKMAN, CARL B., and MURRAY C. ADAMS. "Self-Perceived Physical Attractiveness, Self-Esteem, Race, and Gender." *Sociological Focus.* Vol. 24, No. 4 (October 1991):283–90.

BAHL, VINAY. "Caste and Class in India." Paper presented to the Southern Sociological Society, Atlanta, April, 1991.

BAILEY, WILLIAM C. "Murder, Capital Punishment, and Television: Execution Publicity and Homicide Rates." *American Sociological Review.* Vol. 55, No. 5 (October 1990):628–33.

BAILEY, WILLIAM C., and RUTH D. PETERSON. "Murder and Capital Punishment: A Monthly Time-Series Analysis of Execution Publicity." *American Sociological Review.* Vol. 54, No. 5 (October 1989):722–43.

BAKER, MARY ANNE, CATHERINE WHITE BERHEIDE, FAY ROSS GRECKEL, LINDA CARSTARPHEN GUGIN, MARCIA J. LIPETZ, and MARCIA TEXLER SEGAL. *Women Today: A Multidisciplinary Approach to Women's Studies.* Monterey, Calif.: Brooks/Cole, 1980.

BALES, ROBERT F. "The Equilibrium Problem in Small Groups." In Talcott Parsons et al., eds., *Working Papers in the Theory of Action.* New York: Free Press, 1953:111–15.

BALES, ROBERT F., and PHILIP E. SLATER. "Role Differentiation in Small Decision-Making Groups." In Talcott Parsons and Robert F. Bales, eds.,

666

Family, Socialization and Interaction Process. New York: Free Press, 1955:259–306.

BALTES, PAUL B., and K. WARNER SCHAIE. "The Myth of the Twilight Years." *Psychology Today.* Vol. 7, No. 10 (March 1974):35–39.

BALTZELL, E. DIGBY. *The Protestant Establishment: Aristocracy and Caste in America.* New York: Vintage Books, 1964.

———. "Introduction to the 1967 Edition." In W. E. B. Du Bois, *The Philadelphia Negro: A Social Study.* New York: Schocken, 1967; orig. 1899.

———, ED. *The Search for Community in Modern America.* New York: Harper & Row, 1968.

———. "The Protestant Establishment Revisited." *The American Scholar.* Vol. 45, No. 4 (Autumn 1976):499–518.

———. *Philadelphia Gentlemen: The Making of A National Upper Class.* Philadelphia: University of Pennsylvania Press, 1979; orig. 1958.

———. *Puritan Boston and Quaker Philadelphia.* New York: Free Press, 1979.

———. "The WASP's Last Gasp." *Philadelphia Magazine.* Vol. 79 (September 1988):104–7, 184, 186, 188.

———. *Sporting Gentlemen: From the Age of Honor to the Cult of the Superstar.* New York: Free Press, 1995.

BANFIELD, EDWARD C. *The Unheavenly City Revisited.* Boston: Little, Brown, 1974.

BARASH, DAVID. *The Whispering Within.* New York: Penguin Books, 1981.

BARKER, EILEEN. "Who'd Be a Moonie? A Comparative Study of Those Who Join the Unification Church in Britain." In Bryan Wilson, ed., *The Social Impact of New Religious Movements.* New York: The Rose of Sharon Press, 1981:59–96.

———. *New Religious Movements: A Practical Introduction.* London: Her Majesty's Stationery Office, 1989.

BARON, JAMES N., BRIAN S. MITTMAN, and ANDREW E. NEWMAN. "Targets of Opportunity: Organizational and Environmental Determinants of Gender Integration Within the California Civil Service, 1979–1985." *American Journal of Sociology.* Vol. 96, No. 6 (May 1991): 1362–1401.

BARONE, MICHAEL, and GRANT UJIFUSA. *The Almanac of American Politics.* Washington, D.C.: Barone and Co., 1981.

BARRY, KATHLEEN. "Feminist Theory: The Meaning of Women's Liberation." In Barbara Haber, ed., *The Women's Annual 1982–1983.* Boston: G. K. Hall, 1983:35–78.

BASSUK, ELLEN J. "The Homelessness Problem." *Scientific American.* Vol. 251, No. 1 (July 1984):40–45.

BAUER, P. T. *Equality, the Third World, and Economic Delusion.* Cambridge, Mass.: Harvard University Press, 1981.

BAYDAR, NAZLI, and JEANNE BROOKS-GUNN. "Effect of Maternal Employment and Child-Care Arrangements on Preschoolers' Cognitive and Behavioral Outcomes: Evidence From Children From the National Longitudinal Survey of Youth." *Developmental Psychology.* Vol. 27 (1991):932–35.

BECKER, HOWARD S. *Outside: Studies in the Sociology of Deviance.* New York: Free Press, 1966.

BEDELL, GEORGE C., LEO SANDON, JR., and CHARLES T. WELLBORN. *Religion in America.* New York: Macmillan, 1975.

BEEGHLEY, LEONARD. *The Structure of Social Stratification in the United States.* Needham Heights, Mass.: Allyn & Bacon, 1989.

BELL, ALAN P., MARTIN S. WEINBERG, and SUE KIEFER-HAMMERSMITH. *Sexual Preference: Its Development in Men and Women.* Bloomington: Indiana University Press, 1981.

BELL, DANIEL. *The Coming of Post-Industrial Society: A Venture in Social Forecasting.* New York: Basic Books, 1973.

BELLAH, ROBERT N. *The Broken Covenant.* New York: Seabury Press, 1975.

BELLAH, ROBERT N., RICHARD MADSEN, WILLIAM M. SULLIVAN, ANN SWIDLER, and STEVEN M. TIPTON. *Habits of the Heart: Individualism and Commitment in American Life.* New York: Harper & Row, 1985.

BELLAS, MARCIA L. "Comparable Worth in Academia: The Effects on Faculty Salaries of the Sex Composition and Labor-Market Conditions of Academic Disciplines." *American Sociological Review.* Vol. 59, No. 6 (December 1994):807–21.

BELSKY, JAY, RICHARD M. LERNER, and GRAHAM B. SPANIER. *The Child in the Family.* Reading, Mass.: Addison-Wesley, 1984.

BEM, SANDRA LIPSITZ. "Gender Schema Theory: A Cognitive Account of Sex-Typing." *Psychological Review.* Vol. 88, No. 4 (July 1981):354–64.

———. *The Lenses of Gender: Transforming the Debate on Sexual Inequality.* New Haven, Conn.: Yale University Press, 1993.

BENEDICT, RUTH. "Continuities and Discontinuities in Cultural Conditioning." *Psychiatry.* Vol. 1 (May 1938):161–67.

———. *The Chrysanthemum and the Sword: Patterns of Japanese Culture.* New York: New American Library, 1974; orig. 1946.

BENET, SULA. "Why They Live to Be 100, or Even Older, in Abkhasia." *New York Times Magazine* (December 26, 1971):3, 28–29, 31–34.

BENJAMIN, BERNARD, and CHRIS WALLIS. "The Mortality of Widowers." *The Lancet.* Vol. 2 (August 1963):454–56.

BENJAMIN, LOIS. *The Black Elite: Facing the Color Line in the Twilight of the Twentieth Century.* Chicago: Nelson-Hall, 1991.

BENNETT, NEIL G., DAVID E. BLOOM, and PATRICIA H. CRAIG. "The Divergence of Black and White Marriage Patterns." *American Journal of Sociology.* Vol. 95, No. 3 (November 1989):692–722.

BENNETT, STEPHEN EARL. "Left Behind: Exploring Declining Turnout Among Noncollege Young Whites, 1964–1988." *Social Science Quarterly.* Vol. 72, No. 2 (June 1991):314–33.

BENNETT, WILLIAM J. "Quantifying America's Decline." *Wall Street Journal* (March 15, 1993).

———. "Redeeming Our Time." *Imprimis.* Vol. 24, No. 11 (November 1995). Hillsdale, Mich.: Hillsdale College.

BENOKRAITIS, NIJOLE, and JOE FEAGIN. *Modern Sexism: Blatant, Subtle, and Overt Discrimination.* 2d ed. Englewood Cliffs, N.J.: Prentice Hall, 1995.

BERARDO, F. M. "Survivorship and Social Isolation: The Case of the Aged Widower." *The Family Coordinator.* Vol. 19 (January 1970):11–25.

BERGER, PETER L. *Invitation to Sociology.* New York: Anchor Books, 1963.

———. *The Sacred Canopy: Elements of a Sociological Theory of Religion.* Garden City, N.Y.: Doubleday, 1967.

———. *Facing Up to Modernity: Excursions in Society, Politics, and Religion.* New York: Basic Books, 1977.

———. *The Capitalist Revolution: Fifty Propositions About Prosperity, Equality, and Liberty.* New York: Basic Books, 1986.

BERGER, PETER, BRIGITTE BERGER, and HANSFRIED KELLNER. *The Homeless Mind: Modernization and Consciousness.* New York: Vintage Books, 1974.

BERGER, PETER L., and HANSFRIED KELLNER. *Sociology Reinterpreted: An Essay on Method and Vocation.* Garden City, N.Y.: Anchor Books, 1981.

BERGESEN, ALBERT, ED. *Crises in the World-System.* Beverly Hills, Calif.: Sage, 1983.

BERK, RICHARD A. *Collective Behavior.* Dubuque, Iowa: Wm. C. Brown, 1974.

BERNARD, JESSIE. *The Female World.* New York: Free Press, 1981.

———. *The Future of Marriage.* New Haven, Conn.: Yale University Press, 1982; orig. 1973.

BERNARD, LARRY CRAIG. "Multivariate Analysis of New Sex Role Formulations and Personality." *Journal of Personality and Social Psychology.* Vol. 38, No. 2 (February 1980):323–36.

BERNHARDT, ANNETTE, MARTINA MORRIS, and MARK S. HANDCOCK. "Women's Gains or Men's Losses? A Closer Look at the Shrinking Gender Gap in Earnings." *American Journal of Sociology.* Vol. 101, No. 1 (September 1995):302–28.

BERNSTEIN, RICHARD J. *The New Constellation: The Ethical-Political Horizons of Modernity/Postmodernity.* Cambridge, Mass.: MIT Press, 1992.

BERRILL, KEVIN T. "Anti-Gay Violence and Victimization in the United States: An Overview." In Gregory M. Herek and Kevin T. Berrill, *Hate Crimes: Confronting Violence Against Lesbians and Gay Men.* Newbury Park, Calif.: Sage, 1992:19–45.

BERRY, BRIAN L., and PHILIP H. REES. "The Factorial Ecology of Calcutta." *American Journal of Sociology.* Vol. 74, No. 5 (March 1969):445–91.

BERSCHEID, ELLEN, and ELAINE HATFIELD. *Interpersonal Attraction.* 2d ed. Reading, Mass.: Addison-Wesley, 1983.

BEST, RAPHAELA. *We've All Got Scars: What Boys and Girls Learn in Elementary School.* Bloomington: Indiana University Press, 1983.

BIBLARZ, TIMOTHY J., and ADRIAN E. RAFTERY. "The Effects of Family Disruption on Social Mobility." *American Sociological Review.* Vol. 58, No. 1 (February 1993):97–109.

BILLSON, JANET MANCINI, and BETTINA J. HUBER. *Embarking Upon a Career with an Undergraduate Degree in Sociology.* 2d ed. Washington, D.C.: American Sociological Association, 1993.

BLAU, JUDITH R., and PETER M. BLAU. "The Cost of Inequality: Metropolitan Structure and Violent Crime." *American Sociological Review*. Vol. 47, No. 1 (February 1982):114–29.

BLAU, Peter M. *Exchange and Power in Social Life*. New York: Wiley, 1964.

———. *Inequality and Heterogeneity: A Primitive Theory of Social Structure*. New York: Free Press, 1977.

BLAU, PETER M., TERRY C. BLUM, and JOSEPH E. SCHWARTZ. "Heterogeneity and Intermarriage." *American Sociological Review*. Vol. 47, No. 1 (February 1982):45–62.

BLAU, PETER M., and OTIS DUDLEY DUNCAN. *The American Occupational Structure*. New York: Wiley, 1967.

BLAUSTEIN, ALBERT P., and ROBERT L. ZANGRANDO. *Civil Rights and the Black American*. New York: Washington Square Press, 1968.

BLOOM, LEONARD. "Familial Adjustments of Japanese-Americans to Relocation: First Phase." In Thomas F. Pettigrew, ed., *The Sociology of Race Relations*. New York: Free Press, 1980:163–67.

BLUM, LINDA M. *Between Feminism and Labor: The Significance of the Comparable Worth Movement*. Berkeley: University of California Press, 1991.

BLUMBERG, PAUL. *Inequality in an Age of Decline*. New York: Oxford University Press, 1981.

BLUMER, HERBERT G. "Fashion." In David L. Sills, ed., *International Encyclopedia of the Social Sciences*. Vol. 5. New York: Macmillan and Free Press, 1968:341–45.

———. "Collective Behavior." In Alfred McClung Lee, ed., *Principles of Sociology*. 3d ed. New York: Barnes & Noble Books, 1969:65–121.

BLUMSTEIN, PHILIP, and PEPPER SCHWARTZ. *American Couples*. New York: William Morrow, 1983.

BODENHEIMER, THOMAS S. "Health Care in the United States: Who Pays?" In Vicente Navarro, ed., *Health and Medical Care in the U.S.: A Critical Analysis*. Farmingdale, N.Y.: Baywood Publishing Co., 1977:61–68.

BOFF, LEONARD and CLODOVIS. *Salvation and Liberation: In Search of a Balance Between Faith and Politics*. Maryknoll, N.Y.: Orbis Books, 1984.

BOGARDUS, EMORY S. "Comparing Racial Distance in Ethiopia, South Africa, and the United States." *Sociology and Social Research*. Vol. 52, No. 2 (January 1968):149–56.

BOHANNAN, CECIL. "The Economic Correlates of Homelessness in Sixty Cities." *Social Science Quarterly*. Vol. 72, No. 4 (December 1991):817–25.

BOHANNAN, PAUL. *Divorce and After*. Garden City, N.Y.: Doubleday, 1970.

BOHM, ROBERT M. "American Death Penalty Opinion, 1936–1986: A Critical Examination of the Gallup Polls." In Robert M. Bohm, ed., *The Death Penalty in America: Current Research*. Cincinnati: Anderson Publishing Co., 1991:113–45.

BORMANN, F. HERBERT. "The Global Environmental Deficit." *BioScience*. Vol. 40 (1990):74.

BORMANN, F. HERBERT, and STEPHEN R. KELLERT. "The Global Environmental Deficit." In Bormann, F. Herbert and Stephen R. Kellert, eds., *Ecology, Economics, and Ethics: The Broken Circle*. New Haven, Conn.: Yale University Press, 1991:ix–xviii.

BONILLA-SANTIAGO, GLORIA. "A Portrait of Hispanic Women in the United States." In Sara E. Rix, ed., *The American Woman 1990–91: A Status Report*. New York: Norton, 1990:249–57.

BONNER, JANE. Research presented in "The Two Brains." Public Broadcasting System telecast, 1984.

BOOTH, ALAN, and LYNN WHITE. "Thinking About Divorce." *Journal of Marriage and the Family*. Vol. 42, No. 3 (August 1980):605–16.

BORGMANN, ALBERT. *Crossing the Postmodern Divide*. Chicago: University of Chicago Press, 1992.

BOSWELL, TERRY E. "A Split Labor Market Analysis of Discrimination Against Chinese Immigrants, 1850–1882." *American Sociological Review*. Vol. 51, No. 3 (June 1986):352–71.

BOSWELL, TERRY E., and WILLIAM J. DIXON. "Marx's Theory of Rebellion: A Cross-National Analysis of Class Exploitation, Economic Development, and Violent Revolt." *American Sociological Review*. Vol. 58, No. 5 (October 1993): 681–702.

BOTT, ELIZABETH. *Family and Social Network*. New York: Free Press, 1971; orig. 1957.

BOULDING, ELISE. *The Underside of History*. Boulder, Colo.: Westview Press, 1976.

BOWLES, SAMUEL, and HERBERT GINTIS. *Schooling in Capitalist America: Educational Reform and the Contradictions of Economic Life*. New York: Basic Books, 1976.

BOYER, ERNEST L. *College: The Undergraduate Experience in America*. Prepared by The Carnegie Foundation for the Advancement of Teaching. New York: Harper & Row, 1987.

BRAITHWAITE, JOHN. "The Myth of Social Class and Criminality Reconsidered." *American Sociological Review*. Vol. 46, No. 1 (February 1981):36–57.

BRANEGAN, JAY. "Is Singapore a Model for the West?" *Time*. Vol. 141, No. 3 (January 18, 1993):36–37.

BREEN, LEONARD Z. "The Aging Individual." In Clark Tibbitts, ed., *Handbook of Social Gerontology*. Chicago: University of Chicago Press, 1960:145–62.

BRIGHTMAN, JOAN. "Why Hillary Chooses Rodham Clinton." *American Demographics*. Vol. 16, No. 3 (March 1994):9–11.

BRINTON, CRANE. *The Anatomy of Revolution*. New York: Vintage Books, 1965.

BRINTON, MARY C. "The Social-Institutional Bases of Gender Stratification: Japan as an Illustrative Case." *American Journal of Sociology*. Vol. 94, No. 2 (September 1988):300–34.

BROWN, LESTER R. "Reassessing the Earth's Population." *Society*. Vol. 32, No. 4 (May-June 1995):7–10.

BROWN, LESTER R., ET AL., EDS. *State of the World 1993: A Worldwatch Institute Report on Progress Toward a Sustainable Society*. New York: Norton, 1993.

BROWN, MARY ELLEN, ED. *Television and Women's Culture: The Politics of the Popular*. Newbury Park, Calif.: Sage, 1990.

BRUNO, MARY. "Abusing the Elderly." *Newsweek* (September 23, 1985):75–76.

BUMPASS, LARRY, and JAMES A. SWEET. 1992–1994 National Survey of Families and Households. Reported in "Report from PPA." *Population Today*. Vol. 23, No. 6 (June 1995):3.

BURKE, TOM. "The Future." In Sir Edmund Hillary, ed., *Ecology 2000: The Changing Face of the Earth*. New York: Beaufort Books, 1984:227–41.

BURSTEIN, PAUL. "Legal Mobilization as a Social Movement Tactic: The Struggle for Equal Employment Opportunity." *American Journal of Sociology*. Vol. 96, No. 5 (March 1991):1201–25.

BUSBY, LINDA J. "Sex Role Research on the Mass Media." *Journal of Communications*. Vol. 25 (Autumn 1975):107–13.

BUTLER, ROBERT N. *Why Survive? Being Old in America*. New York: Harper & Row, 1975.

BUTTERWORTH, DOUGLAS, and JOHN K. CHANCE. *Latin American Urbanization*. Cambridge: Cambridge University Press, 1981.

CAHNMAN, WERNER J., and RUDOLF HEBERLE. "Introduction." In *Ferdinand Toennies on Sociology: Pure, Applied, and Empirical*. Chicago: University of Chicago Press, 1971:vii–xxii.

CALLAHAN, DANIEL. *Setting Limits: Medical Goals in an Aging Society*. New York: Simon And Schuster, 1987.

CALMORE, JOHN O. "National Housing Policies and Black America: Trends, Issues, and Implications." In *The State of Black America 1986*. New York: National Urban League, 1986:115–49.

CAMERON, WILLIAM BRUCE. *Modern Social Movements: A Sociological Outline*. New York: Random House, 1966.

CANETTI, ELIAS. *Crowds and Power*. New York: Seabury Press, 1978.

CANTOR, MURIAL G., and SUZANNE PINGREE. *The Soap Opera*. Beverly Hills, Calif.: Sage, 1983.

CANTRIL, HADLEY, HAZEL GAUDET, and HERTA HERZOG. *Invasion from Mars: A Study in the Psychology of Panic*. Princeton, N.J.: Princeton University Press, 1947.

CAPLOW, THEODORE, ET AL. *Middletown Families*. Minneapolis: University of Minnesota Press, 1982.

CAPLOW, THEODORE, HOWARD M. BAHR, JOHN MODELL, and BRUCE A. CHADWICK. *Recent Social Trends in the United States, 1960–1990*. Montreal: McGill-Queen's University Press, 1991.

CARLEY, KATHLEEN. "A Theory of Group Stability." *American Sociological Review*. Vol. 56, No. 3 (June 1991):331–54.

CARLSON, NORMAN A. "Corrections in the United States Today: A Balance Has Been Struck." *The American Criminal Law Review*. Vol. 13, No. 4 (Spring 1976):615–47.

CARMICHAEL, STOKELY, and CHARLES V. HAMILTON. *Black Power: The Politics of Liberation in America*. New York: Vintage Books, 1967.

CARR, LESLIE G. "Colorblindness and the New Racism." Paper presented at the annual meeting, American Sociological Association, Washington, D.C., 1995.

CARROLL, GINNY. "Who Foots the Bill?" *Newsweek*. Special Issue (Fall-Winter 1990):81-85.

CASTRO, JANICE. "Disposable Workers." *Time*. Vol. 131, No. 14 (March 29, 1993):43-47.

CENTER FOR MEDIA AND PUBLIC AFFAIRS. 1991 report by Robert Lichter, Linda Lichter, and Stanley Rothman.

CENTER FOR THE STUDY OF SPORT IN SOCIETY. *1991 Racial Report Card: A Study in the NBA, NFL, and Major League Baseball*. Boston: Northeastern University, 1993.

CHAGNON, NAPOLEON A. *Yąnomamö: The Fierce People*. 4th ed. New York: Holt, Rinehart & Winston, 1992.

CHANDLER, TERTIUS, and GERALD FOX. *3000 Years of Urban History*. New York: Academic Press, 1974.

CHANGE, KWANG-CHIH. *The Archaeology of Ancient China*. New Haven, Conn.: Yale University Press, 1977.

CHAPPELL, NEENA L., and BETTY HAVENS. "Old and Female: Testing the Double Jeopardy Hypothesis." *The Sociological Quarterly*. Vol. 21, No. 2 (Spring 1980):157-71.

CHARLES, MARIA. "Cross-National Variation in Occupational Segregation." *American Sociological Review*. Vol. 57, No. 4 (August 1992):483-502.

CHERLIN, ANDREW. *Marriage, Divorce, Remarriage*. Rev. ed. Cambridge, Mass.: Harvard University Press, 1990.

CHERLIN, ANDREW, and FRANK F. FURSTENBERG, JR. "The American Family in the Year 2000." *The Futurist*. Vol. 17, No. 3 (June 1983):7-14.

———. *The New American Grandparent: A Place in the Family, A Life Apart*. New York: Basic Books, 1986.

CHILDREN'S DEFENSE FUND. *The State of America's Children Yearbook, 1995*. Washington, D.C.: Children's Defense Fund, 1995.

CHOWN, SHEILA M. "Morale, Careers and Personal Potentials." In James E. Birren and K. Warner Schaie, eds., *Handbook of the Psychology of Aging*. New York: Van Nostrand Reinhold, 1977:672-91.

CHURCH, GEORGE J. "Unons Arise—With New Tricks." *Time*. Vol. 143, No. 24 (June 13, 1994):56-58.

CLARK, CURTIS B. "Geriatric Abuse: Out of the Closet." In *The Tragedy of Elder Abuse: The Problem and the Response*. Hearings before the Select Committee on Aging, House of Representatives (July 1, 1986):49-50.

CLARK, JUAN M., JOSE I. LASAGA, and ROSE S. REGUE. *The 1980 Mariel Exodus: An Assessment and Prospect: Special Report*. Washington, D.C.: Council for Inter-American Security, 1981.

CLARK, MARGARET S., ED. *Prosocial Behavior*. Newbury Park, Calif.: Sage, 1991.

CLARK, THOMAS A. *Blacks in Suburbs*. New Brunswick, N.J.: Rutgers University Center for Urban Policy Research, 1979.

CLARKE, ROBIN. "Atmospheric Pollution." In Sir Edmund Hillary, ed., *Ecology 2000: The Changing Face of the Earth*. New York: Beaufort Books, 1984a:130-48.

———. "What's Happening to Our Water?" In Sir Edmund Hillary, ed., *Ecology 2000: The Changing Face of the Earth*. New York: Beaufort Books, 1984b:108-29.

CLINARD, MARSHALL, and DANIEL ABBOTT. *Crime in Developing Countries*. New York: Wiley, 1973.

CLOWARD, RICHARD A., and LLOYD E. OHLIN. *Delinquency and Opportunity: A Theory of Delinquent Gangs*. New York: Free Press, 1966.

COE, MICHAEL D., and RICHARD A. DIEHL. *In the Land of the Olmec*. Austin: University of Texas Press, 1980.

COHEN, ADAM. "A New Push for Blind Justice." *Time*. Vol. 145, No. 7 (February 20, 1995):39-40.

COHEN, ALBERT K. *Delinquent Boys: The Culture of the Gang*. New York: Free Press, 1971; orig. 1955.

COHEN, LLOYD R. "Sexual Harassment and the Law." *Society*. Vol. 28, No. 4 (May-June, 1991):8-13.

COHN, RICHARD M. "Economic Development and Status Change of the Aged." *American Journal of Sociology*. Vol. 87, No. 2 (March 1982):1150-61.

COLEMAN, JAMES S. "Rational Organization." *Rationality and Society*. Vol. 2, (1990):94-105.

———. "The Design of Organizations and the Right to Act." *Sociological Forum*. Vol. 8, No. 4 (December 1993):527-46.

COLEMAN, JAMES S., and THOMAS HOFFER. *Public and Private High Schools: The Impact of Communities*. New York: Basic Books, 1987.

COLEMAN, JAMES, THOMAS HOFFER, and SALLY KILGORE. *Public and Private Schools: An Analysis of Public Schools and Beyond*. Washington, D.C.: National Center for Education Statistics, 1981.

COLEMAN, RICHARD P., and BERNICE L. NEUGARTEN. *Social Status in the City*. San Francisco: Jossey-Bass, 1971.

COLEMAN, RICHARD P., and LEE RAINWATER. *Social Standing in America*. New York: Basic Books, 1978.

COLLINS, RANDALL. "A Conflict Theory of Sexual Stratification." *Social Problems*. Vol. 19, No. 1 (Summer 1971):3-21.

———. *The Credential Society: An Historical Sociology of Education and Stratification*. New York: Academic Press, 1979.

———. *Sociological Insight: An Introduction to Nonobvious Sociology*. New York: Oxford University Press, 1982.

COLLOWAY, N. O., and PAULA L. DOLLEVOET. "Selected Tabular Material on Aging." In Caleb Finch and Leonard Hayflick, eds., *Handbook of the Biology of Aging*. New York: Van Nostrand Reinhold, 1977:666-708.

COMTE, AUGUSTE. *Auguste Comte and Positivism: The Essential Writings*. Gertrud Lenzer, ed. New York: Harper Torchbooks, 1975.

CONNETT, PAUL H. "The Disposable Society." In F. Herbert Bormann and Stephen R. Kellert, eds., *Ecology, Economics, and Ethics: The Broken Circle*. New Haven, Conn.: Yale University Press, 1991:99-122.

CONTRERAS, JOSEPH. "A New Day Dawns." *Newsweek* (March 30, 1992):40-41.

COOK, RHODES. "House Republicans Scored a Quiet Victory in '92." *Congressional Quarterly Weekly Report*. Vol. 51, No. 16 (April 17, 1993):965-68.

COOLEY, CHARLES HORTON. *Social Organization*. New York: Schocken Books, 1962; orig. 1909.

———. *Human Nature and the Social Order*. New York: Schocken Books, 1964; orig. 1902.

CORLEY, ROBERT N., O. LEE REED, PETER J. SHEDD, and JERE W. MOREHEAD. *The Legal and Regulatory Environment of Business*. 9th ed. New York: McGraw-Hill, 1993.

COSER, LEWIS A. *Masters of Sociological Thought: Ideas in Historical and Social Context*. 2d ed. New York: Harcourt Brace Jovanovich, 1977.

COTTLE, THOMAS J. "What Tracking Did to Ollie Taylor." *Social Policy*. Vol. 5, No. 2 (July-August 1974):22-24.

COTTRELL, JOHN, and THE EDITORS OF TIME-LIFE. *The Great Cities: Mexico City*. Amsterdam: 1979.

COUNCIL ON FAMILIES IN AMERICA. *Marriage in America: A Report to the Nation*. New York: Institute for American Values, 1995.

COUNCIL ON INTERNATIONAL EDUCATIONAL EXCHANGE. *Educating for Global Competence: The Report of the Advisory Committee for International Educational Exchange*. New York: The Council, 1988.

COUNTS, G. S. "The Social Status of Occupations: A Problem in Vocational Guidance." *School Review*. Vol. 33 (January 1925):16-27.

COURTNEY, ALICE E., and THOMAS W. WHIPPLE. *Sex Stereotyping in Advertising*. Lexington, Mass.: D.C. Heath, 1983.

COWAN, CAROLYN POPE. *When Partners Become Parents*. New York: Basic Books, 1992.

COWGILL, DONALD, and LOWELL HOLMES. *Aging and Modernization*. New York: Appleton-Century-Crofts, 1972.

COWLEY, GEOFFREY. "The Prescription That Kills." *Newsweek* (July 17, 1995): 54.

COX, HARVEY. *The Secular City*. Rev. ed. New York: Macmillan, 1971; orig. 1965.

———. *Turning East: The Promise and Peril of the New Orientalism*. New York: Simon and Schuster, 1977.

———. "Church and Believers: Always Strangers?" In Thomas Robbins and Dick Anthony, *In Gods We Trust: New Patterns of Religious Pluralism in America*. 2d ed. New Brunswick, N.J.: Transaction, 1990:449-62.

CRISPELL, DIANE. "Grandparents Galore." *American Demographics*. Vol. 15, No. 10 (October 1993):63.

CROOK, STEPHAN, JAN PAKULSKI, and MALCOLM WATERS. *Postmodernity: Change in Advanced Society.* Newbury Park, Calif.: Sage, 1992.

CROSSETTE, BARBARA. "Female Genital Mutilation by Immigrants is Becoming Cause for Concern in the U.S." *New York Times International.* (December 10, 1995):11.

CROUSE, JAMES, and DALE TRUSHEIM. *The Case Against the SAT.* Chicago: University of Chicago Press, 1988.

CUFF, E. C., and G. C. F. PAYNE, EDS. *Perspectives in Sociology.* London: Allen and Unwin, 1979.

CUMMING, ELAINE, and WILLIAM E. HENRY. *Growing Old: The Process of Disengagement.* New York: Basic Books, 1961.

CURRIE, ELLIOTT. *Confronting Crime: An American Challenge.* New York: Pantheon Books, 1985.

CURTIS, JAMES E., EDWARD G. GRABB, and DOUGLAS BAER. "Voluntary Association Membership in Fifteen Countries: A Comparative Analysis." *American Sociological Review.* Vol. 57, No. 2 (April 1992):139–52.

CURTISS, SUSAN. *Genie: A Psycholinguistic Study of a Modern-Day "Wild Child."* New York: Academic Press, 1977.

CUTLER, DAVID M., and LAWRENCE F. KATZ. "Rising Inequality? Changes in the Distribution of Income and Consumption in the 1980s." Working Paper No. 3964. Cambridge, Mass.: National Bureau of Economic Research, 1992.

CUTRIGHT, PHILLIP. "Occupational Inheritance: A Cross-National Analysis." *American Journal of Sociology.* Vol. 73, No. 4 (January 1968):400–16.

CYLKE, F. KURT, JR. *The Environment.* New York: HarperCollins, 1993.

DAHL, ROBERT A. *Who Governs?* New Haven, Conn.: Yale University Press, 1961.

———. *Dilemmas of Pluralist Democracy: Autonomy vs. Control.* New Haven, Conn.: Yale University Press, 1982.

DAHRENDORF, RALF. *Class and Class Conflict in Industrial Society.* Stanford, Calif.: Stanford University Press, 1959.

DALY, MARTIN, and MARGO WILSON. *Homicide.* New York: Aldine, 1988.

DANIELS, ROGER. "The Issei Generation." In Amy Tachiki et al., eds., *Roots: An Asian American Reader.* Los Angeles: UCLA Asian American Studies Center, 1971:138–49.

DANNEFER, DALE. "Adult Development and Social Theory: A Reappraisal." *American Sociological Review.* Vol. 49, No. 1 (February 1984):100–16.

DARNTON, NINA, and YURIKO HOSHIA. "Whose Life Is It, Anyway?" *Newsweek.* Vol. 113, No. 4 (January 13, 1989):61.

DAVIDSON, JAMES D., RALPH E. PYLE, and DAVID V. REYES. "Persistence and Change in the Protestant Establishment, 1930–1992." *Social Forces.* Vol. 74, No. 1 (September 1995):157–75.

DAVIES, CHRISTIE. *Ethnic Humor Around the World: A Comparative Analysis.* Bloomington: Indiana University Press, 1990.

DAVIES, JAMES C. "Toward a Theory of Revolution." *American Sociological Review.* Vol. 27, No. 1 (February 1962):5–19.

DAVIES, MARK, and DENISE B. KANDEL. "Parental and Peer Influences on Adolescents' Educational Plans: Some Further Evidence." *American Journal of Sociology.* Vol. 87, No. 2 (September 1981):363–87.

DAVIS, KINGSLEY. "Extreme Social Isolation of a Child." *American Journal of Sociology.* Vol. 45, No. 4 (January 1940):554–65.

———. "Final Note on a Case of Extreme Isolation." *American Journal of Sociology.* Vol. 52, No. 5 (March 1947):432–37.

DAVIS, KINGSLEY, and WILBERT MOORE. "Some Principles of Stratification." *American Sociological Review.* Vol. 10, No. 2 (April 1945):242–49.

DAVIS, SHARON A., and EMIL J. HALLER. "Tracking, Ability, and SES: Further Evidence on the 'Revisionist-Meritocratic Debate.'" *American Journal of Education.* Vol. 89 (May 1981):283–304.

DECKARD, BARBARA SINCLAIR. *The Women's Movement: Political, Socioeconomic, and Psychological Issues.* 2d ed. New York: Harper & Row, 1979.

DEDRICK, DENNIS K., and RICHARD E. YINGER. "MAD, SDI, and the Nuclear Arms Race." Manuscript in development. Georgetown, Ky.: Georgetown College, 1990.

DELACROIX, JACQUES, and CHARLES C. RAGIN. "Structural Blockage: A Cross-national Study of Economic Dependency, State Efficacy, and Underdevelopment." *American Journal of Sociology.* Vol. 86, No. 6 (May 1981):1311–47.

DEMOTT, JOHN S. "Wreaking Havoc on Spring Break." *Time.* Vol. 127, No. 14 (April 7, 1986):29.

DEPARLE, JASON. "Painted by Numbers, 1980s are Rosy to G.O.P., While Democrats See Red." *New York Times* (September 26, 1991a):B10.

Der Spiegel. "Third World Metropolises Are Becoming Monsters; Rural Poverty Drives Millions to the Slums." In *World Press Review* (October 1989).

DEVINE, JOEL A. "State and State Expenditure: Determinants of Social Investment and Social Consumption Spending in the Postwar United States." *American Sociological Review.* Vol. 50, No. 2 (April 1985):150–65.

DIAMOND, MILTON. "Sexual Identity, Monozygotic Twins Reared in Discordant Sex Roles and a BBC Follow-Up." *Archives of Sexual Behavior.* Vol. 11, No. 2 (April 1982):181–86.

DICKENS, CHARLES. *The Adventures of Oliver Twist.* Boston: Estes and Lauriat, 1886; orig. 1837–39.

DIZARD, JAN E., and HOWARD GADLIN. *The Minimal Family.* Amherst: The University of Massachusetts Press, 1990.

DOBSON, RICHARD B. "Mobility and Stratification in the Soviet Union." *Annual Review of Sociology.* Vol. 3. Palo Alto, Calif.: Annual Reviews, 1977:297–329.

DOBYNS, HENRY F. "An Appraisal of Techniques with a New Hemispheric Estimate." *Current Anthropology.* Vol. 7, No. 4 (October 1966):395–446.

DOLLARD, JOHN, ET AL. *Frustration and Aggression.* New Haven, Conn.: Yale University Press, 1939.

DOMHOFF, G. WILLIAM. *Who Rules America Now? A View of the '80s.* Englewood Cliffs, N.J.: Prentice Hall, 1983.

DONOVAN, VIRGINIA K., and RONNIE LITTENBERG. "Psychology of Women: Feminist Therapy." In Barbara Haber, ed., *The Women's Annual 1981: The Year in Review.* Boston: G. K. Hall, 1982:211–35.

DOUGLASS, RICHARD L. "Domestic Neglect and Abuse of the Elderly: Implications for Research and Service." *Family Relations.* Vol. 32 (July 1983):395–402.

DOYLE, JAMES A. *The Male Experience.* Dubuque, Iowa: Wm. C. Brown, 1983.

DOYLE, RICHARD F. *A Manifesto of Men's Liberation.* 2d ed. Forest Lake, Minn.: Men's Rights Association, 1980.

DU BOIS, W. E. B. *Dusk of Dawn.* New York: Harcourt, Brace & World, 1940.

———. *The Philadelphia Negro: A Social Study.* New York: Schocken Books, 1967; orig. 1899.

DUBOS, RENÉ. *Man Adapting.* New Haven, Conn.: Yale University Press, 1980; orig. 1965.

DUHL, LEONARD J. "The Social Context of Health." In Arthur C. Hastings et al., eds., *Health for the Whole Person: The Complete Guide to Holistic Medicine.* Boulder, Colo.: Westview Press, 1980:39–48.

DUNLAP, RILEY E., GEORGE H. GALLUP, JR., and ALEC M. GALLUP. *The Health of the Planet Survey.* Princeton, N.J.: The George H. Gallup International Institute, 1992.

DUNLAP, RILEY E., and ANGELA G. MERTIG. "The Evolution of the U.S. Environmental Movement from 1970 to 1990: An Overview." In Riley E. Dunlap and Angela G. Mertig, eds., *American Evironmentalism: The U.S. Environmental Movement, 1970–1990.* New York: Taylor & Francis, 1992:1–10.

DUNN, ASHLEY. "Ancient Chinese Craft Shifts Building Designs in the U.S." *The New York Times* (September 22, 1994):1A, B4.

DUNN, WILLIAM. "Peddling Big Brother." *Time.* Vol. 137, No. 25 (June 24, 1991):62.

DURKHEIM, EMILE. *The Division of Labor in Society.* New York: Free Press, 1964a; orig. 1895.

———. *The Rules of Sociological Method.* New York: Free Press, 1964b; orig. 1893.

———. *The Elementary Forms of Religious Life.* New York: Free Press, 1965; orig. 1915.

———. *Suicide.* New York: Free Press, 1966; orig. 1897.

———. *Selected Writings.* Anthony Giddens, ed. Cambridge: Cambridge University Press, 1972.

———. *Sociology and Philosophy.* New York: Free Press, 1974; orig. 1924.

DURNING, ALAN THEIN. "Supporting Indigenous Peoples." In Lester R. Brown et al., eds., *State of the World 1993: A Worldwatch Institute Report on Progress Toward a Sustainable Society.* New York: Norton, 1993:80–100.

DWORKIN, ANDREA. *Intercourse.* New York: Free Press, 1987.

EBAUGH, HELEN ROSE FUCHS. *Becoming an EX: The Process of Role Exit.* Chicago: University of Chicago Press, 1988.

670 References

ECKHOLM, ERIK. "Malnutrition in Elderly: Widespread Health Threat." *New York Times* (August 13, 1985):19–20.

ECKHOLM, ERIK, and JOHN TIERNEY. "AIDS in Africa: A Killer Rages On." *New York Times* (September 16, 1990):A1, 14.

The Economist. "Worship Moves in Mysterious Ways." Vol. 326, No. 7802 (March 13, 1993):65, 70.

———. "Cockfighting: 'Til Death Us Do Part." Vol. 330, No. 7851 (February 19, 1994):30.

———. "Japan's Missing Children." Vol. 333, No. 7889 (November 12, 1994):46.

EDWARDS, DAVID V. *The American Political Experience.* 3d ed. Englewood Cliffs, N.J.: Prentice Hall, 1985.

EDWARDS, RICHARD. *Contested Terrain: The Transformation of the Workplace in the Twentieth Century.* New York: Basic Books, 1979.

EDMONDSON, BRAD. "The Great Money Grab." *American Demographics.* Vol. 17, No. 2 (February 1995):2.

EGGEBEEN, DAVID J., and DANIEL T. LICHTER. "Race, Family Structure and Changing Poverty Among American Children." *American Sociological Review.* Vol. 56, No. 6 (December 1991):801–17.

EHRENREICH, BARBARA. *The Hearts of Men: American Dreams and the Flight from Commitment.* Garden City, N.Y.: Anchor Books, 1983.

EHRENREICH, JOHN. "Introduction." In John Ehrenreich, ed., *The Cultural Crisis of Modern Medicine.* New York: Monthly Review Press, 1978:1–35.

EICHLER, MARGRIT. *Nonsexist Research Methods: A Practical Guide.* Winchester, Mass.: Unwin Hyman, 1988.

EISEN, ARNOLD M. *The Chosen People in America: A Study of Jewish Religious Ideology.* Bloomington: Indiana University Press, 1983.

EISENSTEIN, ZILLAH R., ED. *Capitalist Patriarchy and the Case for Socialist Feminism.* New York: Monthly Review Press, 1979.

EISLER, BENITA. *The Lowell Offering: Writings by New England Mill Women 1840–1845.* Philadelphia and New York: J. B. Lippincott, 1977.

EKMAN, PAUL. "Biological and Cultural Contributions to Body and Facial Movements in the Expression of Emotions." In A. Rorty, ed., *Explaining Emotions.* Berkeley: University of California Press, 1980a:73–101.

———. *Face of Man: Universal Expression in a New Guinea Village.* New York: Garland Press, 1980b.

———. *Telling Lies: Clues to Deceit in the Marketplace, Politics, and Marriage.* New York: Norton, 1985.

EKMAN, PAUL, WALLACE V. FRIESEN, and JOHN BEAR. "The International Language of Gestures." *Psychology Today* (May 1984):64–69.

EL-ATTAR, MOHAMED. Personal communication, 1991.

ELIAS, ROBERT. *The Politics of Victimization: Victims, Victimology and Human Rights.* New York: Oxford University Press, 1986.

ELKIND, DAVID. *The Hurried Child: Growing Up Too Fast Too Soon.* Reading, Mass.: Addison-Wesley, 1981.

ELLIOT, DELBERT S., and SUZANNE S. AGETON. "Reconciling Race and Class Differences in Self-Reported and Official Estimates of Delinquency." *American Sociological Review.* Vol. 45, No. 1 (February 1980):95–110.

ELLISON, CHRISTOPHER G., and DARREN E. SHERKAT. "Conservative Protestantism and Support for Corporal Punishment." *American Sociological Review.* Vol. 58, No. 1 (February 1993):131–44.

ELMER-DEWITT, PHILIP. "The Revolution that Fizzled." *Time.* Vol. 137, No. 20 (May 20, 1991):48–49.

———. "First Nation in Cyberspace." *Time.* Vol. 142, No. 24 (December 6, 1993):62–64.

———. "The Genetic Revolution." *Time.* Vol. 143, No. 3 (January 17, 1994):46–53.

———. "Battle for the Internet." *Time.* Vol. 144, No. 4 (July 25, 1994):50–56.

EMBER, MELVIN, and CAROL R. EMBER. "The Conditions Favoring Matrilocal versus Patrilocal Residence." *American Anthropologist.* Vol. 73, No. 3 (June 1971):571–94.

———. *Anthropology.* 6th ed. Englewood Cliffs, N.J.: Prentice Hall, 1991.

EMBREE, AINSLIE T. *The Hindu Tradition.* New York: Vintage Books, 1972.

EMERSON, JOAN P. "Behavior in Private Places: Sustaining Definitions of Reality in Gynecological Examinations." In H. P. Dreitzel, ed., *Recent Sociology.* Vol. 2. New York: Collier, 1970:74–97.

ENDICOTT, KAREN. "Fathering in an Egalitarian Society." In Barry S. Hewlett, ed., *Father-Child Relations: Cultural and Bio-Social Contexts.* New York: Aldine, 1992:281–96.

ENGELS, FRIEDRICH. *The Origin of the Family.* Chicago: Charles H. Kerr & Company, 1902; orig. 1884.

ENGLAND, PAULA. *Comparable Worth: Theories and Evidence.* Hawthorne, N.Y.: Aldine, 1992.

ERIKSON, ERIK H. *Childhood and Society.* New York: Norton, 1963; orig. 1950.

———. *Identity and the Life Cycle.* New York: Norton, 1980.

ERIKSON, KAI T. *Wayward Puritans: A Study in the Sociology of Deviance.* New York: Wiley, 1966.

ERIKSON, ROBERT, and JOHN H. GOLDTHORPE. *The Constant Flux: A Study of Class Mobility in Industrial Societies.* Oxford: Clarendon Press, 1992.

ERIKSON, ROBERT S., NORMAN R. LUTTBEG, and KENT L. TEDIN. *American Public Opinion: Its Origins, Content, and Impact.* 2d ed. New York: Wiley, 1980.

ETZIONI, AMITAI. *A Comparative Analysis of Complex Organization: On Power, Involvement, and Their Correlates.* Rev. and enlarged ed. New York: Free Press, 1975.

———. "Too Many Rights, Too Few Responsibilities." *Society.* Vol. 28, No. 2 (January-February 1991):41–48.

———. "How to Make Marriage Matter." *Time.* Vol. 142, No. 10 (September 6, 1993):76.

ETZIONI-HALEVY, EVA. *Bureaucracy and Democracy: A Political Dilemma.* Rev. ed. Boston: Routledge & Kegan Paul, 1985.

EVANS, M. D. R. "Immigrant Entrepreneurship: Effects of Ethnic Market Size and Isolated Labor Pool." *American Sociological Review.* Vol. 54, No. 6 (December 1989):950–62.

EXTER, THOMAS G. "The Costs of Growing Up." *American Demographics.* Vol. 13, No. 8 (August 1991):59.

FALK, GERHARD. Personal communication, 1987.

FALKENMARK, MALIN, and CARL WIDSTRAND. "Population and Water Resources: A Delicate Balance." *Population Bulletin.* Vol. 47, No. 3 (November 1992). Washington, D.C.: Population Reference Bureau.

FALLON, A. E., and P. ROZIN. "Sex Differences in Perception of Desirable Body Shape." *Journal of Abnormal Psychology.* Vol. 94, No. 1 (1985):100–5.

FALLOWS, JAMES. "Immigration: How It's Affecting Us." *The Atlantic Monthly.* Vol. 252 (November 1983):45–52, 55–62, 66–68, 85–90, 94, 96, 99–106.

FANTINI, MARIO D. *Regaining Excellence in Education.* Columbus, Ohio: Merrill, 1986.

FARLEY, REYNOLDS, and WILLIAM H. FREY. "Changes in the Segregation of Whites From Blacks During the 1980s: Small Steps Toward a More Integrated Society." *American Sociological Review.* Vol. 59, No. 1 (February 1994):23–45.

FARRELL, MICHAEL P., and STANLEY D. ROSENBERG. *Men at Midlife.* Boston: Auburn House, 1981.

FEAGIN, JOE. *The Urban Real Estate Game.* Englewood Cliffs, N.J.: Prentice Hall, 1983.

FEAGIN, JOE R. "The Continuing Significance of Race: Antiblack Discrimination in Public Places." *American Sociological Review.* Vol. 56, No. 1 (February 1991):101–16.

FEATHERMAN, DAVID L., and ROBERT M. HAUSER. *Opportunity and Change.* New York: Academic Press, 1978.

FEATHERSTONE, MIKE, ED. *Global Culture: Nationalism, Globalization, and Modernity.* London: Sage, 1990.

FEDARKO, KEVIN. "Who Could Live Here?" *Time.* Vol. 139, No. 3 (January 20, 1992):20–23.

FENNELL, MARY C. "The Effects of Environmental Characteristics on the Structure of Hospital Clusters." *Administrative Science Quarterly.* Vol. 29, No. 3 (September 1980):489–510.

FERGUSON, TOM. "Medical Self-Care: Self Responsibility for Health." In Arthur C. Hastings et al., eds., *Health for the Whole Person: The Complete Guide to Holistic Medicine.* Boulder, Colo.: Westview Press, 1980:87–109.

FERGUSSON, D. M., L. J. HORWOOD, and F. T. SHANNON. "A Proportional Hazards Model of Family Breakdown." *Journal of Marriage and the Family.* Vol. 46, No. 3 (August 1984):539–49.

FINKELSTEIN, NEAL W., and RON HASKINS. "Kindergarten Children Prefer Same-Color Peers." *Child Development.* Vol. 54, No. 2 (April 1983):502–8.

FIORENTINE, ROBERT. "Men, Women, and the Premed Persistence Gap: A Normative Alternatives Approach." *American Journal of Sociology*. Vol. 92, No. 5 (March 1987):1118–39.

FIORENTINE, ROBERT, and STEPHEN COLE. "Why Fewer Women Become Physicians: Explaining the Premed Persistance Gap." *Sociological Forum*. Vol. 7, No. 3 (September 1992):469–96.

FIREBAUGH, GLENN. "Growth Effects of Foreign and Domestic Investment." *American Journal of Sociology*. Vol. 98, No. 1 (July 1992):105–30.

FIREBAUGH, GLENN, and FRANK D. BECK. "Does Economic Growth Benefit the Masses? Growth, Dependence, and Welfare in the Third World." *American Sociological Review*. Vol. 59, No. 5 (October 1994):631–53.

FIREBAUGH, GLENN, and KENNETH E. DAVIS. "Trends in Antiblack Prejudice, 1972–1984: Region and Cohort Effects." *American Journal of Sociology*. Vol. 94, No. 2 (September 1988):251–72.

FISCHER, CLAUDE S., ET AL. *Networks and Places: Social Relations in the Urban Setting*. New York: Free Press, 1977.

FISHER, ELIZABETH. *Woman's Creation: Sexual Evolution and the Shaping of Society*. Garden City, N.Y.: Anchor/Doubleday, 1979.

FISHER, ROGER, and WILLIAM URY. "Getting to YES." In William M. Evan and Stephen Hilgartner, eds., *The Arms Race and Nuclear War*. Englewood Cliffs, N.J.: Prentice Hall, 1988:261–68.

FISKE, ALAN PAIGE. "The Cultural Relativity of Selfish Individualism: Anthropological Evidence that Humans Are Inherently Sociable." In Margaret S. Clark, ed., *Prosocial Behavior*. Newbury Park, Calif.: Sage, 1991:176–214.

FITZPATRICK, JOSEPH P. "Puerto Ricans." In *Harvard Encyclopedia of American Ethnic Groups*. Cambridge, Mass.: Harvard University Press, 1980:858–67.

FITZPATRICK, MARY ANNE. *Between Husbands and Wives: Communication in Marriage*. Newbury Park, Calif.: Sage, 1988.

FLAHERTY, MICHAEL G. "A Formal Approach to the Study of Amusement in Social Interaction." *Studies in Symbolic Interaction*. Vol. 5. New York: JAI Press, 1984:71–82.

——. "Two Conceptions of the Social Situation: Some Implications of Humor." *The Sociological Quarterly*. Vol. 31, No. 1 (Spring 1990).

FLORIDA, RICHARD, and MARTIN KENNEY. "Transplanted Organizations: The Transfer of Japanese Industrial Organization to the U.S." *American Sociological Review*. Vol. 56, No. 3 (June 1991):381–98.

FLYNN, PATRICIA. "The Disciplinary Emergence of Bioethics and Bioethics Committees: Moral Ordering and its Legitimation." *Sociological Focus*. Vol. 24, No. 2 (May 1991):145–56.

FORD, CLELLAN S., and FRANK A. BEACH. *Patterns of Sexual Behavior*. New York: Harper & Row, 1951.

FORREST, HUGH. "They Are Completely Inactive . . ." *The Gambier Journal*. Vol. 3, No. 4 (February 1984):10–11.

Fortune. "The Fortune 500." Vol. 131, No. 9 (May 15, 1995): Special issue.

FOST, DAN. "American Indians in the 1990s." *American Demographics*. Vol. 13, No. 12 (December 1991):26–34.

FRANK, ANDRÉ GUNDER. *On Capitalist Underdevelopment*. Bombay: Oxford University Press, 1975.

——. *Crisis: In the World Economy*. New York: Holmes & Meier, 1980.

——. *Reflections on the World Economic Crisis*. New York: Monthly Review Press, 1981.

FRANKLIN, JOHN HOPE. *From Slavery to Freedom: A History of Negro Americans*. 3d ed. New York: Vintage Books, 1967.

FRANKLIN ASSOCIATES. *Characterization of Municipal Solid Waste in the United States, 1960-2000*. Prairie Village, Kans.: Franklin Associates, 1986.

FRAZIER, E. FRANKLIN. *Black Bourgeoisie: The Rise of a New Middle Class*. New York: Free Press, 1965.

FREDRICKSON, GEORGE M. *White Supremacy: A Comparative Study in American and South African History*. New York: Oxford University Press, 1981.

FREE, MARVIN D. "Religious Affiliation, Religiosity, and Impulsive and Intentional Deviance." *Sociological Focus*. Vol. 25, No. 1 (February 1992):77–91.

FREEDOM HOUSE. *Freedom in the World*. New York: Freedom House, 1995.

FRENCH, MARILYN. *Beyond Power: On Women, Men, and Morals*. New York: Summit Books, 1985.

FRIEDAN, BETTY. *The Fountain of Age*. New York: Simon and Schuster, 1993.

FRIEDRICH, CARL J., and ZBIGNIEW BRZEZINSKI. *Totalitarian Dictatorship and Autocracy*. 2d ed. Cambridge, Mass.: Harvard University Press, 1965.

FRIEDRICH, OTTO. "A Proud Capital's Distress." *Time*. Vol. 124, No. 6 (August 6, 1984):26–30, 33–35.

——. "United No More." *Time*. Vol. 129, No. 18 (May 4, 1987):28–37.

FRUM, DAVID, and FRANK WOLFE. "If You Gotta Get Sued, Get Sued in Utah." *Forbes*. Vol. 153, No. 2 (January 1994):70–73.

FUCHS, VICTOR R. "Sex Differences in Economic Well-Being." *Science*. Vol. 232 (April 25, 1986):459–64.

FUGITA, STEPHEN S., and DAVID J. O'BRIEN. "Structural Assimilation, Ethnic Group Membership, and Political Participation Among Japanese Americans: A Research Note." *Social Forces*. Vol. 63, No. 4 (June 1985):986–95.

FUJIMOTO, ISAO. "The Failure of Democracy in a Time of Crisis." In Amy Tachiki et al., eds., *Roots: An Asian American Reader*. Los Angeles: UCLA Asian American Studies Center, 1971:207–14.

FULLER, REX, and RICHARD SCHOENBERGER. "The Gender Salary Gap: Do Academic Achievement, Intern Experience, and College Major Make a Difference?" *Social Science Quarterly*. Vol. 72, No. 4 (December 1991):715–26.

FURSTENBERG, FRANK F., JR. "The New Extended Family: The Experience of Parents and Children After Remarriage." Paper presented to the Changing Family Conference XIII: The Blended Family. University of Iowa, 1984.

FURSTENBERG, FRANK F., JR., J. BROOKS-GUNN, and S. PHILIP MORGAN. *Adolescent Mothers in Later Life*. New York: Cambridge University Press, 1987.

FURSTENBERG, FRANK F., JR., and ANDREW CHERLIN. *Divided Families: What Happens to Children When Parents Part*. Cambridge, Mass.: Harvard University Press, 1991.

FUSFELD, DANIEL R. *Economics: Principles of Political Economy*. Glenview, Ill.: Scott, Foresman, 1982.

GAGLIANI, GIORGIO. "How Many Working Classes?" *American Journal of Sociology*. Vol. 87, No. 2 (September 1981):259–85.

GALLUP, GEORGE, JR. *Religion in America*. Princeton, N.J.: Princeton Religion Research Center, 1982.

GALLUP POLL. *The Gallup Poll Monthly*. December, 1993.

GALSTER, GEORGE. "Black Suburbanization: Has It Changed the Relative Location of Races?" *Urban Affairs Quarterly*. Vol. 26, No. 4 (June 1991):621–28.

GAMBLE, ANDREW, STEVE LUDLAM, and DAVID BAKER. "Britain's Ruling Class." *The Economist*. Vol. 326, No. 7795 (January 23, 1993):10.

GAMORAN, ADAM. "The Variable Effects of High-School Tracking." *American Sociological Review*. Vol. 57, No. 6 (December 1992):812–28.

GANS, HERBERT J. *People and Plans: Essays on Urban Problems and Solutions*. New York: Basic Books, 1968.

——. *Popular Culture and High Culture*. New York: Basic Books, 1974.

——. *Deciding What's News: A Study of CBS Evening News, NBC Nightly News, Newsweek and Time*. New York: Vintage Books, 1980.

——. *The Urban Villagers: Group and Class in the Life of Italian-Americans*. New York: Free Press, 1982; orig. 1962.

GARFINKEL, HAROLD. "Conditions of Successful Degradation Ceremonies." *American Journal of Sociology*. Vol. 61, No. 2 (March 1956):420–24.

——. *Studies in Ethnomethodology*. Cambridge: Polity Press, 1967.

GEERTZ, CLIFFORD. "Common Sense as a Cultural System." *The Antioch Review*. Vol. 33, No. 1 (Spring 1975):5–26.

GEIST, WILLIAM. *Toward a Safe and Sane Halloween and Other Tales of Suburbia*. New York: Times Books, 1985.

GELLES, RICHARD J., and CLAIRE PEDRICK CORNELL. *Intimate Violence in Families*. 2d ed. Newbury Park, Calif.: Sage, 1990.

GELMAN, DAVID. "Who's Taking Care of Our Parents?" *Newsweek* (May 6, 1985):61–64, 67–68.

——. "Born or Bred?" *Newsweek* (February 24, 1992):46–53.

GEORGE, SUSAN. *How the Other Half Dies: The Real Reasons for World Hunger*. Totowa, N.J.: Rowman & Allanheld, 1977.

GERLACH, MICHAEL L. *The Social Organization of Japanese Business*. Berkeley and Los Angeles: University of California Press, 1992.

GERSTEL, NAOMI. "Divorce and Stigma." *Social Problems*. Vol. 43, No. 2 (April 1987):172–86.

GERTH, H. H., and C. WRIGHT MILLS, EDS. *From Max Weber: Essays in Sociology*. New York: Oxford University Press, 1946.

GESCHWENDER, JAMES A. *Racial Stratification in America*. Dubuque, Iowa: Wm. C. Brown, 1978.

GIBBONS, DON C., and MARVIN D. KROHN. *Delinquent Behavior*. 4th ed. Englewood Cliffs, N.J.: Prentice Hall, 1986.

GIBBS, NANCY. "When Is It Rape?" *Time*. Vol. 137, No. 22 (June 3, 1991a):48–54.

———. "The Clamor on Campus." *Time*. Vol. 137, No. 22 (June 3, 1991b):54–55.

———. "How Much Should We Teach Our Children About Sex?" *Time*. Vol. 141, No. 21 (May 24, 1993):60–66.

———. "The Vicious Cycle." *Time*. Vol. 143, No. 25 (June 20, 1994):24–33.

———. "The Blood of Innocents." *Time*. Special Issue. No. 25 (June 1, 1995):57–64.

GIDDENS, ANTHONY. *Sociology: A Brief but Critical Introduction*. New York: Harcourt Brace Jovanovich, 1982.

GIELE, JANET Z. "Gender and Sex Roles." In Neil J. Smelser, ed., *Handbook of Sociology*. Newbury Park, Calif.: Sage, 1988:291–323.

GILBERT, NEIL. "Realities and Mythologies of Rape." *Society*. Vol. 29, No. 4 (May-June 1992):4–10.

GILBERTSON, GRETA A., and DOUGLAS T. GURAK. "Broadening the Enclave Debate: The Dual Labor Market Experiences of Dominican and Colombian Men in New York City." *Sociological Forum*. Vol. 8, No. 2 (June 1993):205–20.

GILLIGAN, CAROL. *In a Different Voice: Psychological Theory and Women's Development*. Cambridge, Mass.: Harvard University Press, 1982.

———. *Making Connections: The Relational Worlds of Adolescent Girls at Emma Willard School*. Cambridge, Mass.: Harvard University Press, 1990.

GIMENEZ, MARTHA E. "Silence in the Classroom: Some Thoughts About Teaching in the 1980s." *Teaching Sociology*. Vol. 17, No. 2 (April 1989):184–91.

GINSBURG, FAYE, and ANNA LOWENHAUPT TSING, EDS. *Uncertain Terms: Negotiating Gender in American Culture*. Boston: Beacon Press, 1990.

GIOVANNINI, MAUREEN. "Female Anthropologist and Male Informant: Gender Conflict in a Sicilian Town." In John J. Macionis and Nijole V. Benokraitis, eds., *Seeing Ourselves: Classic, Contemporary, and Cross-Cultural Readings in Sociology*. 2d ed. Englewood Cliffs, N.J.: Prentice Hall, 1992:27–32.

GLAAB, CHARLES N. *The American City: A Documentary History*. Homewood, Ill.: Dorsey Press, 1963.

GLADUE, BRIAN A., RICHARD GREEN, and RONALD E. HELLMAN. "Neuroendocrine Response to Estrogen and Sexual Orientation." *Science*. Vol. 225, No. 4669 (September 28, 1984):1496–99.

GLAZER, NATHAN, and DANIEL P. MOYNIHAN. *Beyond the Melting Pot*. 2d ed. Cambridge, Mass.: MIT Press, 1970.

GLEICK, SHARON. "Who Are They?" *Time*. Special Issue (June 1, 1995):44–51.

GLENN, NORVAL D., and BETH ANN SHELTON. "Regional Differences in Divorce in the United States." *Journal of Marriage and the Family*. Vol. 47, No. 3 (August 1985):641–52.

GLOCK, CHARLES Y. "The Religious Revival in America." In Jane Zahn, ed., *Religion and the Face of America*. Berkeley: University of California Press, 1959:25–42.

———. "On the Study of Religious Commitment." *Religious Education*. Vol. 62, No. 4 (1962):98–110.

GLUCK, PETER R., and RICHARD J. MEISTER. *Cities in Transition*. New York: New Viewpoints, 1979.

GLUECK, SHELDON, and ELEANOR GLUECK. *Unraveling Juvenile Delinquency*. New York: Commonwealth Fund, 1950.

GOETTING, ANN. "Divorce Outcome Research." *Journal of Family Issues*. Vol. 2, No. 3 (September 1981):350–78.

———. Personal communication, 1989.

GOFFMAN, ERVING. *The Presentation of Self in Everyday Life*. Garden City, N.Y.: Anchor Books, 1959.

———. *Asylums: Essays on the Social Situation of Mental Patients and Other Inmates*. Garden City, N.Y.: Anchor Books, 1961.

———. *Stigma: Notes on the Management of Spoiled Identity*. Englewood Cliffs, N.J.: Prentice Hall, 1963.

———. *Interactional Ritual: Essays on Face to Face Behavior*. Garden City, N.Y.: Anchor Books, 1967.

———. *Gender Advertisements*. New York: Harper Colophon, 1979.

GOLDBERG, STEVEN. *The Inevitability of Patriarchy*. New York: William Morrow, 1974.

———. Personal communication, 1987.

GOLDEN, FREDERIC. "Here Come the Microkids." *Time*. Vol. 119, No. 18 (May 3, 1982):50–56.

GOLDFARB, JEFFREY C. *Beyond Glasnost: The Post-Totalitarian Mind*. Chicago: University of Chicago Press, 1989.

GOLDFARB, WILLIAM. "Groundwater: The Buried Life." In F. Herbert Bormann and Stephen R. Kellert, eds., *Ecology, Economics, and Ethics: The Broken Circle*. New Haven, Conn.: Yale University Press, 1991:123–35.

GOLDSBY, RICHARD A. *Race and Races*. 2d ed. New York: Macmillan, 1977.

GOLDSMITH, H. H. "Genetic Influences on Personality from Infancy." *Child Development*. Vol. 54, No. 2 (April 1983):331–35.

GOODE, WILLIAM J. "The Theoretical Importance of Love." *American Sociological Review*. Vol. 24, No. 1 (February 1959):38–47.

———. "Encroachment, Charlatanism, and the Emerging Profession: Psychology, Sociology and Medicine." *American Sociological Review*. Vol. 25, No. 6 (December 1960):902–14.

GORDON, JAMES S. "The Paradigm of Holistic Medicine." In Arthur C. Hastings et al., eds., *Health for the Whole Person: The Complete Guide to Holistic Medicine*. Boulder, Colo.: Westview Press, 1980:3–27.

GORING, CHARLES BUCKMAN. *The English Convict: A Statistical Study*. Montclair, N.J.: Patterson Smith, 1972; orig. 1913.

GORMAN, CHRISTINE. "Mexico City's Menacing Air." *Time*. Vol. 137, No. 13 (April 1, 1991):61.

GOTTFREDSON, MICHAEL R., and TRAVIS HIRSCHI. "National Crime Control Policies." *Society*. Vol. 32, No. 2 (January-February 1995):30–36.

GOTTMANN, JEAN. *Megalopolis*. New York: Twentieth Century Fund, 1961.

GOUGH, KATHLEEN. "The Origin of the Family." *Journal of Marriage and the Family*. Vol. 33, No. 4 (November 1971):760–71.

GOULD, STEPHEN J. "Evolution as Fact and Theory." *Discover* (May 1981):35–37.

GOULDNER, ALVIN. *Enter Plato*. New York: Free Press, 1965.

———. "The Sociologist as Partisan: Sociology and the Welfare State." In Larry T. Reynolds and Janice M. Reynolds, eds., *The Sociology of Sociology*. New York: David McKay, 1970a:218–55.

———. *The Coming Crisis of Western Sociology*. New York: Avon Books, 1970b.

GRANOVETTER, MARK. "The Strength of Weak Ties." *American Journal of Sociology*. Vol. 78, No. 6 (May 1973):1360–80.

GRANT, DON SHERMAN, II, and MICHAEL WALLACE. "Why Do Strikes Turn Violent?" *American Journal of Sociology*. Vol. 96, No. 5 (March 1991):1117–50.

GRANT, DONALD L. *The Anti-Lynching Movement*. San Francisco: R and E Research Associates, 1975.

GRANT, KAREN R. "The Inverse Care Law in the Context of Universal Free Health Insurance in Canada: Toward Meeting Health Needs Through Public Policy." *Sociological Focus*. Vol. 17, No. 2 (April 1984):137–55.

GRAY, PAUL. "Whose America?" *Time*. Vol. 137, No. 27 (July 8, 1991):12–17.

GREELEY, ANDREW M. *Ethnicity in the United States: A Preliminary Reconnaissance*. New York: Wiley, 1974.

———. *Religious Change in America*. Cambridge, Mass.: Harvard University Press, 1989.

GREEN, JOHN C. "Pat Robertson and the Latest Crusade: Resources and the 1988 Presidential Campaign." *Social Sciences Quarterly*. Vol. 74, No. 1 (March 1993):156–68.

GREENBERG, DAVID F. *The Construction of Homosexuality*. Chicago: University of Chicago Press, 1988.

GREENHOUSE, LINDA. "Justices Uphold Stiffer Sentences for Hate Crimes." *New York Times* (June 12, 1993):1, 8.

GREENWALD, JOHN. "The New Service Class." *Time*. Vol. 144, No. 20 (November 14, 1994):72–74.

GREER, SCOTT. *Urban Renewal and American Cities*. Indianapolis, Ind.: Bobbs-Merrill, 1965.

GREGORY, PAUL R., and ROBERT C. STUART. *Comparative Economic Systems*. 2d ed. Boston: Houghton Mifflin, 1985.

GREGORY, SOPHFRONIA SCOTT. "The Knife in the Book Bag." *Time*. Vol. 141, No. 6 (February 8, 1993):37.

GROSS, JANE. "New Challenge of Youth: Growing Up in a Gay Home." *New York Times* (February 11, 1991):A1, B7.

GRUENBERG, BARRY. "The Happy Worker: An Analysis of Educational and Occupational Differences in Determinants of Job Satisfaction." *American Journal of Sociology.* Vol. 86, No. 2 (September 1980):247–71.

GUP, TED. "What Makes This School Work?" *Time.* Vol. 140, No. 25 (December 21, 1992):63–65.

GUTFELD, ROSE. "Eight of Ten Americans are Environmentalists." *Wall Street Journal* (August 2, 1991):A1.

GUTMAN, HERBERT G. *The Black Family in Slavery and Freedom, 1750–1925.* New York: Pantheon Books, 1976.

GWARTNEY-GIBBS, PATRICIA A. "The Institutionalization of Premarital Cohabitation: Estimates From Marriage License Applications, 1970 and 1980." *Journal of Marriage and the Family.* Vol. 48, No. 2 (May 1986):423–34.

GWARTNEY-GIBBS, PATRICIA A., JEAN STOCKARD, and SUSANNE BOHMER. "Learning Courtship Agression: The Influence of Parents, Peers, and Personal Experiences." *Family Relations.* Vol. 36, No. 3 (July 1987):276–82.

HABERMAS, JÜRGEN. *Toward a Rational Society: Student Protest, Science, and Politics.* Jeremy J. Shapiro, trans. Boston: Beacon Press, 1970.

HACKER, HELEN MAYER. "Women as a Minority Group." *Social Forces.* Vol. 30 (October 1951):60–69.

———. "Women as a Minority Group: 20 Years Later." In Florence Denmark, ed., *Who Discriminates Against Women?* Beverly Hills, Calif.: Sage, 1974:124–34.

HACKEY, ROBERT B. "Competing Explanations of Voter Turnout Among American Blacks." *Social Science Quarterly.* Vol. 73, No. 1 (March 1992):71–89.

HACKMAN, J. R. "The Design of Work Teams." In J. Lorch, ed., *Handbook of Organizational Behavior.* Englewood Cliffs, N.J.: Prentice Hall, 1988:315–42.

HADAWAY, C. KIRK, PENNY LONG MARLER, and MARK CHAVES. "What the Polls Don't Show: A Closer Look at U.S. Church Attendance." *American Sociological Review.* Vol. 58, No. 6 (December 1993):741–52.

HADDEN, JEFFREY K., and CHARLES E. SWAIN. *Prime Time Preachers: The Rising Power of Televangelism.* Reading, Mass.: Addison-Wesley, 1981.

HAFNER, KATIE. "Making Sense of the Internet." *Newsweek* (October 24, 1994):46–48.

HAGAN, JOHN, and PATRICIA PARKER. "White-Collar Crime and Punishment: The Class Structure and Legal Sanctioning of Securities Violations." *American Sociological Review.* Vol. 50, No. 3 (June 1985):302–16.

HAIG, ROBIN ANDREW. *The Anatomy of Humor: Biopsychosocial and Therapeutic Perspectives.* Springfield, Ill.: Charles C. Thomas, 1988.

HALBERSTAM, DAVID. *The Reckoning.* New York: Avon Books, 1986.

HALL, JOHN R., and MARY JO NEITZ. *Culture: Sociological Perspectives.* Englewood Cliffs, N.J.: Prentice Hall, 1993.

HALLINAN, MAUREEN T., and RICHARD A. WILLIAMS. "Interracial Friendship Choices in Secondary Schools." *American Sociological Review.* Vol. 54, No. 1 (February 1989):67–78.

HAMBLIN, DORA JANE. *The First Cities.* New York: Time-Life Books, 1973.

HAMEL, RUTH. "Raging Against Aging." *American Demographics.* Vol. 12, No. 3 (March 1990):42–45.

HAMMOND, PHILIP E. "Introduction." In Philip E. Hammond, ed., *The Sacred in a Secular Age: Toward Revision in the Scientific Study of Religion.* Berkeley: University of California Press, 1985:1–6.

HAMRICK, MICHAEL H., DAVID J. ANSPAUGH, and GENE EZELL. *Health.* Columbus, Ohio: Merrill, 1986.

HANDGUN CONTROL, INC. Data cited in *Time* (December 20, 1993) and various newspaper reports (March 2, 6, 1994).

HANDLIN, OSCAR. *Boston's Immigrants 1790–1865: A Study in Acculturation.* Cambridge, Mass.: Harvard University Press, 1941.

HANEY, CRAIG, CURTIS BANKS, and PHILIP ZIMBARDO. "Interpersonal Dynamics in a Simulated Prison." *International Journal of Criminology and Penology.* Vol. 1 (1973):69–97.

HARBERT, ANITA A., and LEON H. GINSBERG. *Human Services for Older Adults.* Columbia: University of South Carolina Press, 1991.

HAREVEN, TAMARA K. "The Life Course and Aging in Historical Perspective." In Tamara K. Hareven and Kathleen J. Adams, eds., *Aging and Life Course Transitions: An Interdisciplinary Perspective.* New York: Guilford Press, 1982:1–26.

HARLAN, WILLIAM H. "Social Status of the Aged in Three Indian Villages." In Bernice L. Neugarten, ed., *Middle Age and Aging: A Reader in Social Psychology.* Chicago: University of Chicago Press, 1968:469–75.

HARLOW, HARRY F., and MARGARET KUENNE HARLOW. "Social Deprivation in Monkeys." *Scientific American.* Vol. 207 (November 1962):137–46.

HARRIES, KEITH D. *Serious Violence: Patterns of Homicide and Assault in America.* Springfield, Ill.: Charles C. Thomas, 1990.

HARRINGTON, MICHAEL. *The New American Poverty.* New York: Penguin Books, 1984.

HARRIS, CHAUNCEY D., and EDWARD L. ULLMAN. "The Nature of Cities." *The Annals.* Vol. 242 (November 1945):7–17.

HARRIS, JACK DASH. Lecture on cockfighting in the Philippines. *Semester at Sea* (October 27, 1994).

HARRIS, MARVIN. *Cows, Pigs, Wars and Witches: The Riddles of Culture.* New York: Vintage Books, 1975.

———. "Why Men Dominate Women." *New York Times Magazine* (November 13, 1977):46, 115–23.

———. *Cultural Anthropology.* 2d ed. New York: Harper & Row, 1987.

HARRISON, PAUL. *Inside the Third World: The Anatomy of Poverty.* 2d ed. New York: Penguin Books, 1984.

HARTMANN, BETSY, and JAMES BOYCE. *Needless Hunger: Voices From a Bangladesh Village.* San Francisco: Institute for Food and Development Policy, 1982.

HAVIGHURST, ROBERT J., BERNICE L. NEUGARTEN, and SHELDON S. TOBIN. "Disengagement and Patterns of Aging." In Bernice L. Neugarten, ed., *Middle Age and Aging: A Reader in Social Psychology.* Chicago: University of Chicago Press, 1968:161–72.

HAYNEMAN, STEPHEN P., and WILLIAM A. LOXLEY. "The Effect of Primary-School Quality on Academic Achievement Across Twenty-nine High- and Low-Income Countries." *American Journal of Sociology.* Vol. 88, No. 6 (May 1983):1162–94.

HEALTH INSURANCE ASSOCIATION OF AMERICA. *Source Book of Health Insurance Data.* Washington, D.C.: The Association, 1991.

HEATH, JULIA A., and W. DAVID BOURNE. "Husbands and Housework: Parity or Parody?" *Social Science Quarterly.* Vol. 76, No. 1 (March 1995):195–202.

HEILBRONER, ROBERT L. *The Making of Economic Society.* 7th ed. Englewood Cliffs, N.J.: Prentice Hall, 1985.

HELGESEN, SALLY. *The Female Advantage: Women's Ways of Leadership.* New York: Doubleday, 1990.

HELIN, DAVID W. "When Slogans Go Wrong." *American Demographics.* Vol. 14, No. 2 (February 1992):14.

HELMUTH, JOHN W. "World Hunger Amidst Plenty." *USA Today.* Vol. 117, No. 2526 (March 1989):48–50.

HENLEY, NANCY, MYKOL HAMILTON, and BARRIE THORNE. "Womanspeak and Manspeak: Sex Differences in Communication, Verbal and Nonverbal." In John J. Macionis and Nijole V. Benokraitis, eds., *Seeing Ourselves: Classic, Contemporary, and Cross-Cultural Readings in Sociology,* 2d ed. Englewood Cliffs, N.J.: Prentice Hall, 1992:10–15.

HENRY, WILLIAM A., III. "Gay Parents: Under Fire and On the Rise." *Time.* Vol. 142, No. 12 (September 20, 1993):66–71.

HERMAN, DIANNE F. "The Rape Culture." In John J. Macionis and Nijole V. Benokraitis, eds., *Seeing Ourselves: Classic, Contemporary, and Cross-Cultural Readings in Sociology.* 3d ed. Englewood Cliffs, N.J.: Prentice Hall, 1995.

HERMAN, EDWARD S. *Corporate Control, Corporate Power: A Twentieth Century Fund Study.* New York: Cambridge University Press, 1981.

HERRNSTEIN, RICHARD J. *IQ and the Meritocracy.* Boston: Little, Brown, 1973.

HERRNSTEIN, RICHARD J., and CHARLES MURRAY. *The Bell Curve: Intelligence and Class Structure in American Life.* New York: Free Press, 1994.

HERRSTROM, STAFFAN. "Sweden: Pro-Choice on Child Care." *New Perspectives Quarterly.* Vol. 7, No. 1 (Winter 1990):27–28.

HERSCH, JONI, and SHELLY WHITE-MEANS. "Employer-Sponsored Health and Pension Benefits and the Gender/Race Wage Gap." *Social Science Quarterly.* Vol. 74, No. 4 (December 1993):850–66.

HEWLETT, BARRY S. "Husband-Wife Reciprocity and the Father-Infant Relationship Among Aka Pygmies." In Barry S. Hewlett, ed., *Father-Child*

Relations: Cultural and Bio-Social Contexts. New York: Aldine, 1992:153–76.

HEWLETT, SYLVIA ANN. "The Feminization of the Work Force." *New Perspectives Quarterly.* Vol. 7, No. 1 (Winter 1990):13–15.

HIROSHI, MANNARI. *The Japanese Business Leaders.* Tokyo: University of Tokyo Press, 1974.

HIRSCHI, TRAVIS. *Causes of Delinquency.* Berkeley: University of California Press, 1969.

HOCHSCHILD, ARLIE, with ANNE MACHUNG. *The Second Shift: Working Parents and the Revolution at Home.* New York: Viking Books, 1989.

HODGE, ROBERT W., DONALD J. TREIMAN, and PETER H. ROSSI. "A Comparative Study of Occupational Prestige." In Reinhard Bendix and Seymour Martin Lipset, eds., *Class, Status, and Power: Social Stratification in Comparative Perspective.* 2d ed. New York: Free Press, 1966:309–21.

HOERR, JOHN. "The Payoff From Teamwork." *Business Week.* No. 3114 (July 10, 1989):56–62.

HOGAN, DENNIS P., and EVELYN M. KITAGAWA. "The Impact of Social Status and Neighborhood on the Fertility of Black Adolescents." *American Journal of Sociology.* Vol. 90, No. 4 (January 1985):825–55.

HOGGARTH, RICHARD. "The Abuses of Literacy." *Society.* Vol. 55, No. 3 (March-April 1995):55–62.

HOLLANDER, PAUL. "We Are All (Sniffle, Sniffle) Victims Now." *Wall Street Journal* (January 18, 1995):A14.

HOLM, JEAN. *The Study of Religions.* New York: Seabury Press, 1977.

HOLMES, MALCOLM D., HARMON M. HOSCH, HOWARD C. DAUDISTEL, DOLORES PEREZ, and JOSEPH B. GRAVES. "Judges, Ethnicity and Minority Sentencing: Evidence Among Hispanics." *Social Science Quarterly.* Vol. 74, No. 3 (September 1993):496–506.

HOLMSTROM, DAVID. "Abuse of Elderly, Even by Adult Children, Gets More Attention and Official Concern." *Christian Science Monitor* (July 28, 1994):1.

HONEYWELL, ROY J. *The Educational Work of Thomas Jefferson.* Cambridge, Mass.: Harvard University Press, 1931.

HOSTETLER, JOHN A. *Amish Society.* 3d ed. Baltimore: Johns Hopkins University Press, 1980.

HOUT, MICHAEL, and ANDREW M. GREELEY. "The Center Doesn't Hold: Church Attendance in the United States, 1940–1984." *American Sociological Review.* Vol. 52, No. 3 (June 1987):325–45.

HOUT, MIKE, CLEM BROOKS, and JEFF MANZA. "The Persistence of Classes in Post-Industrial Societies." *International Sociology.* Vol. 8, No. 3 (September 1993):259–77.

HOWE, NEIL, and WILLIAM STRAUSS. "America's 13th Generation." *New York Times* (April 16, 1991).

HOWLETT, DEBBIE. "Cruzan's Struggle Left Imprint: 10,000 Others in Similar State." *USA Today* (December 27, 1990):3A.

HOYT, HOMER. *The Structure and Growth of Residential Neighborhoods in American Cities.* Washington, D.C.: Federal Housing Administration, 1939.

HSU, FRANCIS L. K. *The Challenge of the American Dream: The Chinese in the United States.* Belmont, Calif.: Wadsworth, 1971.

HUBER, JOAN, and GLENNA SPITZE. "Considering Divorce: An Expansion of Becker's Theory of Marital Instability." *American Journal of Sociology.* Vol. 86, No. 1 (July 1980):75–89.

HUET-COX, ROCIO. "Medical Education: New Wine in Old Wine Skins." In Victor W. Sidel and Ruth Sidel, eds., *Reforming Medicine: Lessons of the Last Quarter Century.* New York: Pantheon Books, 1984:129–49.

HULS, GLENNA. Personal communication, 1987.

HUMPHREY, CRAIG R., and FREDERICK R. BUTTEL. *Environment, Energy, and Society.* Belmont, Calif.: Wadsworth, 1982.

HUMPHREY, DEREK. *Final Exit: The Practicalities of Self-Deliverance and Assisted Suicide for the Dying.* Eugene, Ore.: The Hemlock Society, 1991.

HUMPHRIES, HARRY LEROY. *The Structure and Politics of Intermediary Class Positions: An Empirical Examination of Recent Theories of Class.* Unpublished Ph.D. dissertation. Eugene: University of Oregon, 1984.

HUNNICUT, BENJAMIN K. "Are We All Working Too Hard? No Time for God or Family." *Wall Street Journal* (January 4, 1990).

HUNT, MORTON. *Sexual Behavior in the 1970s.* Chicago: Playboy Press, 1974.

HUNTER, FLOYD. *Community Power Structure.* Garden City, N.Y.: Doubleday, 1963; orig. 1953.

HUNTER, JAMES DAVISON. *American Evangelicalism: Conservative Religion and the Quandary of Modernity.* New Brunswick, N.J.: Rutgers University Press, 1983.

———. "Conservative Protestantism." In Philip E. Hammond, ed., *The Sacred in a Secular Age.* Berkeley: University of California Press, 1985:50–66.

———. *Evangelicalism: The Coming Generation.* Chicago: University of Chicago Press, 1987.

———. *Culture Wars: The Struggle to Define America.* New York: Basic Books, 1991.

HURLEY, ANDREW. *Environmental Inequalities: Class, Race, and Industrial Pollution in Gary, Indiana, 1945–1980.* Chapel Hill: University of North Carolina Press, 1995.

HURN, CHRISTOPHER. *The Limits and Possibilities of Schooling.* Needham Heights, Mass.: Allyn & Bacon, 1978.

HUTCHINSON, JAMES E. "Science and Religion." *The Herald* (Dade County, Florida). December 25, 1994:1M, 6M.

HWANG, SEAN-SHONG, STEVEN H. MURDOCK, BANOO PARPIA, and RITA R. HAMM. "The Effects of Race and Socioeconomic Status on Residential Segregation in Texas, 1970–1980." *Social Forces.* Vol. 63, No. 3 (March 1985):732–47.

HYMAN, HERBERT H., and CHARLES R. WRIGHT. "Trends in Voluntary Association Memberships of American Adults: Replication Based on Secondary Analysis of National Sample Survey." *American Sociological Review.* Vol. 36, No. 2 (April 1971):191–206.

IANNACCONE, LAURENCE R. "Why Strict Churches Are Strong." *American Journal of Sociology.* Vol. 99, No. 5 (March 1994):1180–1211.

IDE, THOMAS, R., and ARTHUR J. CORDELL. "Automating Work." *Society.* Vol. 31, No. 6 (September-October 1994):65–71.

ILLICH, IVAN. *Medical Nemesis: The Expropriation of Health.* New York: Pantheon Books, 1976.

ISAY, RICHARD A. *Being Homosexual: Gay Men and Their Development.* New York: Farrar, Straus, & Giroux, 1989.

JACOB, JOHN E. "An Overview of Black America in 1985." In James D. Williams, ed., *The State of Black America 1986.* New York: National Urban League, 1986:i-xi.

JACOBS, JAMES B. "Should Hate Be a Crime?" *The Public Interest.* No. 113 (Fall 1993):3–14.

JACOBS, JANE. *The Death and Life of Great American Cities.* New York: Random House, 1961.

———. *The Economy of Cities.* New York: Vintage Books, 1970.

JACOBSON, JODI L. "Closing the Gender Gap in Development." In Lester R. Brown et al., eds., *State of the World 1993: A Worldwatch Institute Report on Progress Toward a Sustainable Society.* New York: Norton, 1993:61–79.

JACOBY, RUSSELL, and NAOMI GLAUBERMAN, EDS. *The Bell Curve Debate.* New York: Random House, 1995.

JACQUET, CONSTANT H., and ALICE M. JONES. *Yearbook of American and Canadian Churches 1991.* Nashville, Tenn.: Abingdon Press, 1991.

JAGAROWSKY, PAUL A., and MARY JO BANE. *Neighborhood Poverty: Basic Questions.* Discussion paper series H-90-3. John F. Kennedy School of Government. Cambridge, Mass.: Harvard University Press, 1990.

JAGGER, ALISON. "Political Philosophies of Women's Liberation." In Laurel Richardson and Verta Taylor, eds., *Feminist Frontiers: Rethinking Sex, Gender, and Society.* Reading, Mass.: Addison-Wesley, 1983.

JAMES, DAVID R. "City Limits on Racial Equality: The Effects of City-Suburb Boundaries on Public-School Desegregation, 1968–1976." *American Sociological Review.* Vol. 54, No. 6 (December 1989):963–85.

JANIS, IRVING. *Victims of Groupthink.* Boston: Houghton Mifflin, 1972.

———. *Crucial Decisions: Leadership in Policymaking and Crisis Management.* New York: Free Press, 1989.

JARRETT, ROBIN L. "Living Poor: Family Life Among Single Parent, African-American Women." *Social Problems.* Vol. 41, No. 1 (February 1994):30–49.

JEFFERSON, THOMAS. Letter to James Madison, October 28, 1785. In Julian P. Boyd, ed., *The Papers of Thomas Jefferson.* Princeton, N.J.: Princeton University Press, 1953:681–83; orig. 1785.

JENCKS, CHRISTOPHER. "Genes and Crime." *The New York Review* (February 12, 1987):33–41.

JENCKS, CHRISTOPHER, ET AL. *Inequality: A Reassessment of the Effect of Family and Schooling in America.* New York: Basic Books, 1972.

JENKINS, BRIAN M. "Terrorism Remains a Threat." Syndicated column, *The Columbus Dispatch* (January 14, 1990):D1.

JENKINS, HOLMAN, JR. "The 'Poverty' Lobby's Inflated Numbers." *Wall Street Journal* (December 14, 1992):A10.

JENKINS, J. CRAIG, and CHARLES PERROW. "Insurgency of the Powerless: Farm Worker Movements (1946–1972)." *American Sociological Review.* Vol. 42, No. 2 (April 1977):249–68.

JENSEN, LIEF, DAVID J. EGGEBEEN, and DANIEL T. LICHTER. "Child Policy and the Ameliorative Effects of Public Assistance." *Social Science Quarterly.* Vol. 74, No. 3 (September 1993):542–59.

JOHNSON, CATHRYN. "Gender, Legitimate Authority, and Leader-Subordinate Conversations." *American Sociological Review.* Vol. 59, No. 1 (February 1994):122–35.

JOHNSON, DIRK. "Census Finds Many Claiming New Identity: Indian." *New York Times* (March 5, 1991):A1, A16.

JOHNSON, NORRIS R. "Panic at 'The Who Concert Stampede': An Empirical Assessment." *Social Problems.* Vol. 34, No. 4 (October 1987):362–73.

JOHNSON, PAUL. "The Seven Deadly Sins of Terrorism." In Benjamin Netanyahu, ed., *International Terrorism.* New Brunswick, N.J.: Transaction Books, 1981:12–22.

JOHNSTON, R. J. "Residential Area Characteristics." In D. T. Herbert and R. J. Johnston, eds., *Social Areas in Cities. Vol. 1: Spatial Processes and Form.* New York: Wiley, 1976:193–235.

JOINT ECONOMIC COMMITTEE. *The Concentration of Wealth in the United States: Trends in the Distribution of Wealth Among American Families.* Washington, D.C.: United States Congress, 1986.

JOSEPHY, ALVIN M., JR. *Now That the Buffalo's Gone: A Study of Today's American Indians.* New York: Alfred A. Knopf, 1982.

KADUSHIN, CHARLES. "Friendship Among the French Financial Elite." *American Sociological Review.* Vol. 60, No. 2 (April 1995):202–21.

KAELBLE, HARTMUT. *Social Mobility in the 19th and 20th Centuries: Europe and America in Comparative Perspective.* New York: St. Martin's Press, 1986.

KAIN, EDWARD L. "A Note on the Integration of AIDS Into the Sociology of Human Sexuality." *Teaching Sociology.* Vol. 15, No. 4 (July 1987):320–23.

———. *The Myth of Family Decline: Understanding Families in a World of Rapid Social Change.* Lexington, Mass.: Lexington Books, 1990.

KAIN, EDWARD L., and SHANNON HART. "AIDS and the Family: A Content Analysis of Media Coverage." Presented to National Council on Family Relations, Atlanta, 1987.

KALISH, RICHARD A. "The New Ageism and the Failure Models: A Polemic." *The Gerontologist.* Vol. 19, No. 4 (August 1979):398–402.

———. *Late Adulthood: Perspectives on Human Development.* 2d ed. Monterey, Calif.: Brooks/Cole, 1982.

KALISH, SUSAN. "Interracial Births Increase as U.S. Ponders Racial Definitions." *Population Today.* Vol. 23, No. 4 (April 1995):1–2.

KAMINER, WENDY. "Volunteers: Who Knows What's in It for Them." *Ms.* (December 1984):93–94, 96, 126–28.

KANAMINE, LINDA. "School Operation Fails For-Profit Test." *USA Today* (November 24, 1995):6A.

KANTER, ROSABETH MOSS. *Men and Women of the Corporation.* New York: Basic Books, 1977.

———. *The Change Masters: Innovation and Entrepreneurship in the American Corporation.* New York: Simon and Schuster, 1983.

———. *When Giants Learn to Dance: Mastering the Challenges of Strategy, Management, and Careers in the 1990s.* New York: Simon and Schuster, 1989.

KANTER, ROSABETH MOSS, and BARRY A. STEIN. "The Gender Pioneers: Women in an Industrial Sales Force." In R. M. Kanter and B. A. Stein, eds., *Life in Organizations.* New York: Basic Books, 1979:134–60.

———. *A Tale of "O": On Being Different in an Organization.* New York: Harper & Row, 1980.

KAPFERER, JEAN-NOEL. "How Rumors Are Born." *Society.* Vol. 29, No. 5 (July-August 1992):53–60.

KAPLAN, ERIC B., ET AL. "The Usefulness of Preoperative Laboratory Screening." *Journal of the American Medical Association.* Vol. 253, No. 24 (June 28, 1985):3576–81.

KAPTCHUK, TED. "The Holistic Logic of Chinese Medicine." In Shepard Bliss et al., eds., *The New Holistic Health Handbook.* Lexington, Mass.: The Steven Greene Press/Penguin Books, 1985:41.

KARATNYCKY, ADRIAN. "Democracies on the Rise, Democracies at Risk." *Freedom Review.* Vol. 26, No. 1 (January-February 1995):5–10.

KARP, DAVID A., and WILLIAM C. YOELS. "The College Classroom: Some Observations on the Meaning of Student Participation." *Sociology and Social Research.* Vol. 60, No. 4 (July 1976):421–39.

KATZ, MICHAEL B. *In the Shadow of the Poorhouse.* New York: Basic Books, 1986.

KAUFMAN, MARC. "Becoming 'Old Old'." *Philadelphia Inquirer* (October 28, 1990):1–A, 10–A.

KAUFMAN, ROBERT L., and SEYMOUR SPILERMAN. "The Age Structures of Occupations and Jobs." *American Journal of Sociology.* Vol. 87, No. 4 (January 1982):827–51.

KAUFMAN, WALTER. *Religions in Four Dimensions: Existential, Aesthetic, Historical and Comparative.* New York: Reader's Digest Press, 1976.

KEITH, PAT M. and ROBERT B. SCHAFER. "They Hate to Cook: Patterns of Distress in an Ordinary Role." *Sociological Focus.* Vol. 27, No. 4 (October 1994):289–301.

KELLER, HELEN. *The Story of My Life.* New York: Doubleday, Page, 1903.

KELLER, SUZANNE. *The Urban Neighborhood.* New York: Random House, 1968.

KELLERT, STEPHEN R., and F. HERBERT BORMANN. "Closing the Circle: Weaving Strands Among Ecology, Economics, and Ethics." In Herbert F. Bohrmann and Stephen R. Kellert, eds., *Ecology, Economics, and Ethics: The Broken Circle.* New Haven, Conn.: Yale University Press, 1991:205–10.

KELLEY, JONATHAN, and M. D. R. EVANS. "Class and Class Conflict in Six Western Nations." *American Sociological Review.* Vol. 60, No. 2 (April 1995):157–78.

KEMP, ALICE ABEL, and SHELLEY COVERMAN. "Marginal Jobs or Marginal Workers: Identifying Sex Differences in Low-Skill Occupations." *Sociological Focus.* Vol. 22, No. 1 (February 1989):19–37.

KENNICKELL, ARTHUR, and JANICE SHACK-MARQUEZ. "Changes in Family Finances from 1983 to 1989: Evidence From the Survey of Consumer Finances." *Federal Reserve Bulletin* (January 1992):1–18.

KENYON, KATHLEEN. *Digging Up Jericho.* London: Ernest Benn, 1957.

KERCKHOFF, ALAN C., RICHARD T. CAMPBELL, and IDEE WINFIELD-LAIRD. "Social Mobility in Great Britain and the United States." *American Journal of Sociology.* Vol. 91, No. 2 (September 1985):281–308.

KIDRON, MICHAEL, and RONALD SEGAL. *The New State of the World Atlas.* New York: Simon and Schuster, 1991.

KILBOURNE, BROCK K. "The Conway and Siegelman Claims Against Religious Cults: An Assessment of Their Data." *Journal for the Scientific Study of Religion.* Vol. 22, No. 4 (December 1983):380–85.

KILGORE, SALLY B. "The Organizational Context of Tracking in Schools." *American Sociological Review.* Vol. 56, No. 2 (April 1991):189–203.

KING, KATHLEEN PIKER, and DENNIS E. CLAYSON. "The Differential Perceptions of Male and Female Deviants." *Sociological Focus.* Vol. 21, No. 2 (April 1988):153–64.

KING, MARTIN LUTHER, JR. "The Montgomery Bus Boycott." In Walt Anderson, ed., *The Age of Protest.* Pacific Palisades, Calif.: Goodyear, 1969:81–91.

KINKEAD, GWEN. *Chinatown: A Portrait of a Closed Society.* New York: HarperCollins, 1992.

KINSEY, ALFRED, ET AL. *Sexual Behavior in the Human Male.* Philadelphia: Saunders, 1948.

———. *Sexual Behavior in the Human Female.* Philadelphia: Saunders, 1953.

KIPP, RITA SMITH. "Have Women Always Been Unequal?" In Beth Reed, ed., *Towards a Feminist Transformation of the Academy: Proceedings of the Fifth Annual Women's Studies Conference.* Ann Arbor, Mich.: Great Lakes Colleges Association, 1980:12–18.

KIRK, MARSHALL, and PETER MADSEN. *After the Ball: How America Will Conquer its Fear and Hatred of Gays in the '90s.* New York: Doubleday, 1989.

KISER, EDGAR, and JOACHIM SCHNEIDER. "Bureaucracy and Efficiency: An Analysis of Taxation in Early Modern Prussia." *American Sociological Review.* Vol. 59, No. 2 (April 1994):187–204.

KISHOR, SUNITA. "'May God Give Sons to All': Gender and Child Mortality in India." *American Sociological Review*. Vol. 58, No. 2 (April 1993):247–65.

KITANO, HARRY H. L. "Japanese." In *Harvard Encyclopedia of American Ethnic Groups*. Cambridge, Mass.: Harvard University Press, 1980:561–71.

KITSON, GAY C., and HELEN J. RASCHKE. "Divorce Research: What We Know, What We Need to Know." *Journal of Divorce*. Vol. 4, No. 3 (Spring 1981):1–37.

KITTRIE, NICHOLAS N. *The Right To Be Different: Deviance and Enforced Therapy*. Baltimore: Johns Hopkins University Press, 1971.

KLUCKHOHN, CLYDE. "As An Anthropologist Views It." In Albert Deuth, ed., *Sex Habits of American Men*. New York: Prentice Hall, 1948.

KMITCH, JANET, PEDRO LABOY, and SARAH VAN DAMME. "International Comparisons of Manufacturing Compensation." *Monthly Labor Review*. Vol. 118, No. 10 (October 1995):3–9.

KOCH, HOWARD. *The Panic Broadcast: Portrait of an Event*. Boston: Little, Brown, 1970.

KOELLN, KENNETH, ROSE M. RUBIN, and MARION SMITH PICARD. "Vulnerable Elderly Households: Expenditures on Necessities by Older Americans." *Social Science Quarterly*. Vol. 76, No. 3 (September 1995):619–33.

KOHLBERG, LAWRENCE. *The Psychology of Moral Development: The Nature and Validity of Moral Stages*. New York: Harper & Row, 1981.

KOHLBERG, LAWRENCE, and CAROL GILLIGAN. "The Adolescent as Philosopher: The Discovery of Self in a Postconventional World." *Daedalus*. Vol. 100 (Fall 1971):1051–86.

KOHN, MELVIN L. *Class and Conformity: A Study in Values*. 2d ed. Homewood, Ill.: Dorsey Press, 1977.

KOHN, MELVIN L., and CARMI SCHOOLER. "Job Conditions and Personality: A Longitudinal Assessment of Their Reciprocal Effects." *American Journal of Sociology*. Vol. 87, No. 6 (May 1982):1257–83.

KOLATA, GINA. "When Grandmother Is the Mother, Until Birth." *New York Times* (August 5, 1991):1, 11.

KOMAROVSKY, MIRRA. *Blue Collar Marriage*. New York: Vintage Books, 1967.

——. "Cultural Contradictions and Sex Roles: The Masculine Case." *American Journal of Sociology*. Vol. 78, No. 4 (January 1973):873–84.

——. *Dilemmas of Masculinity: A Study of College Youth*. New York: Norton, 1976.

KORNHAUSER, WILLIAM. *The Politics of Mass Society*. New York: Free Press, 1959.

KOWALEWSKI, DAVID, and KAREN L. PORTER. "Ecoprotest: Alienation, Deprivation, or Resources?" *Social Sciences Quarterly*. Vol. 73, No. 3 (September 1992):523–34.

KOZOL, JONATHAN. *Prisoners of Silence: Breaking the Bonds of Adult Illiteracy in the United States*. New York: Continuum, 1980.

——. "A Nation's Wealth." *Publisher's Weekly* (May 24, 1985a):28–30.

——. *Illiterate America*. Garden City, N.Y.: Doubleday, 1985b.

——. *Rachel and Her Children: Homeless Families in America*. New York: Crown Publishers, 1988.

——. *Savage Inequalities: Children in America's Schools*. New York: Harper Perennial, 1992.

KRAFFT, SUSAN. "¿Quién es Numero Uno?" *American Demographics*. Vol. 15, No. 7 (July 1993):16–17.

KRAMARAE, CHERIS. *Women and Men Speaking*. Rowley, Mass.: Newbury House, 1981.

KRAYBILL, DONALD B. *The Riddle of Amish Culture*. Baltimore: Johns Hopkins University Press, 1989.

——. "The Amish Encounter With Modernity." In Donald B. Kraybill and Marc A. Olshan, eds., *The Amish Struggle with Modernity*. Hanover, N.H.: University Press of New England, 1994:21–33.

KRAYBILL, DONALD B., and MARC A. OLSHAN, EDS. *The Amish Struggle with Modernity*. Hanover, N.H.: University Press of New England, 1994.

KRIESI, HANSPETER. "New Social Movements and the New Class in the Netherlands." *American Journal of Sociology*. Vol. 94, No. 5 (March 1989):1078–116.

KÜBLER-ROSS, ELISABETH. *On Death and Dying*. New York: Macmillan, 1969.

KUHN, THOMAS. *The Structure of Scientific Revolutions*. 2d ed. Chicago: University of Chicago Press, 1970.

KUZNETS, SIMON. "Economic Growth and Income Inequality." *The American Economic Review*. Vol. XLV, No. 1 (March 1955):1–28.

——. *Modern Economic Growth: Rate, Structure, and Spread*. New Haven, Conn.: Yale University Press, 1966.

LACAYO, RICHARD. "Blood in the Stands." *Time*. Vol. 125, No. 23 (June 10, 1985):38–39, 41.

LADD, JOHN. "The Definition of Death and the Right to Die." In John Ladd, ed., *Ethical Issues Relating to Life and Death*. New York: Oxford University Press, 1979:118–45.

LADNER, JOYCE A. "Teenage Pregnancy: The Implications for Black Americans." In James D. Williams, ed., *The State of Black America 1986*. New York: National Urban League, 1986:65–84.

LAI, H. M. "Chinese." In *Harvard Encyclopedia of American Ethnic Groups*. Cambridge, Mass.: Harvard University Press, 1980:217–33.

LAMAR, JACOB V., JR. "Redefining the American Dilemma." *Time*. Vol. 126, No. 19 (November 11, 1985):33, 36.

LAMBERG-KARLOVSKY, C. C., and MARTHA LAMBERG-KARLOVSKY. "An Early City in Iran." In *Cities: Their Origin, Growth, and Human Impact*. San Francisco: Freeman, 1973:28–37.

LANDERS, ANN. Syndicated column: *Dallas Morning News* (July 8, 1984):4F.

LANDERS, RENE M. "Gender, Race, and the State Courts." *Radcliffe Quarterly*. Vol. 76, No. 4 (December 1990):6–9.

LANE, DAVID. "Social Stratification and Class." In Erik P. Hoffman and Robbin F. Laird, eds., *The Soviet Polity in the Modern Era*. New York: Aldine, 1984:563–605.

LANG, KURT, and GLADYS ENGEL LANG. *Collective Dynamics*. New York: Thomas Y. Crowell, 1961.

LAPPÉ, FRANCES MOORE, and JOSEPH COLLINS. *World Hunger: Twelve Myths*. New York: Grove Press/Food First Books, 1986.

LAPPÉ, FRANCES MOORE, JOSEPH COLLINS, and DAVID KINLEY. *Aid as Obstacle: Twenty Questions about Our Foreign Policy and the Hungry*. San Francisco: Institute for Food and Development Policy, 1981.

LARMER, BROOK. "Dead End Kids." *Newsweek* (May 25, 1992):38–40.

LASLETT, PETER. *The World We Have Lost: England Before the Industrial Age*. 3d ed. New York: Charles Scribner's Sons, 1984.

LAUMANN, EDWARD O., JOHN H. GAGNON, ROBERT T. MICHAEL, and STUART MICHAELS. *The Social Organization of Sexuality: Sexual Practices in the United States*. Chicago: University of Chicago Press, 1994.

LEACOCK, ELEANOR. "Women's Status in Egalitarian Societies: Implications for Social Evolution." *Current Anthropology*. Vol. 19, No. 2 (June 1978):247–75.

LEAVITT, JUDITH WALZER. "Women and Health in America: An Overview." In Judith Walzer Leavitt, ed., *Women and Health in America*. Madison: University of Wisconsin Press, 1984:3–7.

LE BON, GUSTAVE. *The Crowd: A Study of the Popular Mind*. New York: Viking Press, 1960; orig. 1895.

LEE, BARRETT A., R. S. OROPESA, BARBARA J. METCH, and AVERY M. GUEST. "Testing the Decline of Community Thesis: Neighborhood Organization in Seattle, 1929 and 1979." *American Journal of Sociology*. Vol. 89, No. 5 (March 1984):1161–88.

LEE, SHARON M. "Poverty and the U.S. Asian Population." *Social Science Quarterly*. Vol. 75, No. 3 (September 1994):541–59.

LEERHSEN, CHARLES. "Unite and Conquer." *Newsweek* (February 5, 1990):50–55.

LELAND, JOHN. "Bisexuality." *Newsweek* (July 17, 1995):44–49.

LEMERT, EDWIN M. *Social Pathology*. New York: McGraw-Hill, 1951.

——. *Human Deviance, Social Problems, and Social Control*. 2d ed. Englewood Cliffs, N.J.: Prentice Hall, 1972.

LENGERMANN, PATRICIA MADOO, and RUTH A. WALLACE. *Gender in America: Social Control and Social Change*. Englewood Cliffs, N.J.: Prentice Hall, 1985.

LENNON, MARY CLARE, and SARAH ROSENFELD. "Relative Fairness and the Doctrine of Housework: The Importance of Options." *American Journal of Sociology*. Vol. 100, No. 2 (September 1994):506–31.

LENSKI, GERHARD. *Power and Privilege: A Theory of Social Stratification*. New York: McGraw-Hill, 1966.

LENSKI, GERHARD, PATRICK NOLAN, and JEAN LENSKI. *Human Societies: An Introduction to Macrosociology*. 7th ed. New York: McGraw-Hill, 1995.

LEONARD, EILEEN B. *Women, Crime, and Society: A Critique of Theoretical Criminology*. New York: Longman, 1982.

LESLIE, GERALD R., and SHEILA K. KORMAN. *The Family in Social Context.* 7th ed. New York: Oxford University Press, 1989.

LESTER, DAVID. *The Death Penalty: Issues and Answers.* Springfield, Ill.: Charles C. Thomas, 1987.

LEVER, JANET. "Sex Differences in the Complexity of Children's Play and Games." *American Sociological Review.* Vol. 43, No. 4 (August 1978):471–83.

LEVINE, DONALD N. *Georg Simmel: On Individuality and Social Forms.* Chicago: University of Chicago Press, 1971; orig. 1904:294–323.

LEVINE, MICHAEL P. *Student Eating Disorders: Anorexia Nervosa and Bulimia.* Washington, D.C.: National Educational Association, 1987.

LEVINE, ROBERT V. "Is Love a Luxury?" *American Demographics.* Vol. 15, No. 2 (February 1993):27–28.

LEVINSON, DANIEL J., with CHARLOTTE N. DARROW, EDWARD B. KLEIN, MARIA H. LEVINSON, and BRAXTON MCKEE. *The Seasons of a Man's Life.* New York: Alfred A. Knopf, 1978.

LEVITAN, SARA, and ISAAC SHAPIRO. *Working but Poor: America's Contradiction.* Baltimore: Johns Hopkins University Press, 1987.

LEVY, FRANK. *Dollars and Dreams: The Changing American Income Distribution.* New York: Russell Sage Foundation, 1987.

LEWIS, FLORA. "The Roots of Revolution." *New York Times Magazine* (November 11, 1984):70–71, 74, 77–78, 82, 84, 86.

LEWIS, OSCAR. *The Children of Sachez.* New York: Random House, 1961.

LEWIS, PEIRCE, CASEY MCCRACKEN, and ROGER HUNT. "Politics: Who Cares?" *American Demographics.* Vol. 16, No. 10 (October 1994):20–26.

LI, JIANG HONG, and ROGER A. WOJTKIEWICZ. "A New Look at the Effects of Family Structure on Status Attainment." *Social Science Quarterly.* Vol. 73, No. 3 (September 1992):581–95.

LIAZOS, ALEXANDER. "The Poverty of the Sociology of Deviance: Nuts, Sluts and Preverts." *Social Problems.* Vol. 20, No. 1 (Summer 1972):103–20.

LICHTER, DANIEL R. "Race, Employment Hardship, and Inequality in the American Nonmetropolitan South." *American Sociological Review.* Vol. 54, No. 3 (June 1989):436–46.

LICHTER, S. ROBERT, STANLEY ROTHMAN, and LINDA R. ROTHMAN. *The Media Elite: America's New Powerbrokers.* Bethesda, Md.: Adler & Adler, 1986.

LIEBOW, ELLIOT. *Tally's Corner.* Boston: Little, Brown, 1967.

LIN, GE, and PETER ROGERSON. Research reported in Diane Crispell, "Sons and Daughters Who Keep in Touch." *American Demographics.* Vol. 16, No. 8 (August 1994):15–16.

LIN, NAN, and WEN XIE. "Occupational Prestige in Urban China." *American Journal of Sociology.* Vol. 93, No. 4 (January 1988):793–832.

LINDEN, EUGENE. "Can Animals Think?" *Time.* Vol. 141, No. 12 (March 22, 1993):54–61.

———. "More Power to Women, Fewer Mouths to Feed." *Time.* Vol. 144, No. 13 (September 26, 1994):64–65.

LING, PYAU. "Causes of Chinese Emigration." In Amy Tachiki et al., eds., *Roots: An Asian American Reader.* Los Angeles: UCLA Asian American Studies Center, 1971:134–38.

LINK, BRUCE G., BRUCE P. DOHRENWEND, and ANDREW E. SKODOL. "Socio-Economic Status and Schizophrenia: Noisome Occupational Characteristics As a Risk Factor." *American Sociological Review.* Vol. 51, No. 2 (April 1986):242–58.

LINTON, RALPH. "One Hundred Percent American." *The American Mercury.* Vol. 40, No. 160 (April 1937):427–29.

———. *The Study of Man.* New York: D. Appleton-Century, 1937.

LIPSET, SEYMOUR MARTIN. *Political Man: The Social Bases of Politics.* Garden City, N.Y.: Anchor/Doubleday, 1963.

LIPSET, SEYMOUR MARTIN, and REINHARD BENDIX. *Social Mobility in Industrial Society.* Berkeley: University of California Press, 1967.

LISKA, ALLEN E. *Perspectives on Deviance.* 3d ed. Englewood Cliffs, N.J.: Prentice Hall, 1991.

LISKA, ALLEN E., and MARK TAUSIG. "Theoretical Interpretations of Social Class and Racial Differentials in Legal Decision Making for Juveniles." *Sociological Quarterly.* Vol. 20, No. 2 (Spring 1979):197–207.

LISKA, ALLEN E., and BARBARA D. WARNER. "Functions of Crime: A Paradoxical Process." *American Journal of Sociology.* Vol. 96, No. 6 (May 1991):1441–63.

LO, CLARENCE Y. H. "Countermovements and Conservative Movements in the Contemporary U.S." *Annual Review of Sociology.* Vol. 8. Palo Alto, Calif.: Annual Reviews, 1982:107–34.

LOFLAND, LYN. *A World of Strangers.* New York: Basic Books, 1973.

LOGAN, JOHN R., and MARK SCHNEIDER. "Racial Segregation and Racial Change in American Suburbs, 1970–1980." *American Journal of Sociology.* Vol. 89, No. 4 (January 1984):874–88.

LONGINO, JR., CHARLES F. "Myths of An Aging America." *American Demographics.* Vol. 16, No. 8 (August 1994):36–42.

LORD, WALTER. *A Night to Remember.* Rev. ed. New York: Holt, Rinehart & Winston, 1976.

LORENZ, KONRAD. *On Aggression.* New York: Harcourt, Brace & World, 1966.

LOY, PAMELA HEWITT, and LEA P. STEWART. "The Extent and Effects of Sexual Harassment of Working Women." *Sociological Focus.* Vol. 17, No. 1 (January 1984):31–43.

LUBENOW, GERALD C. "A Troubling Family Affair." *Newsweek* (May 14, 1984):34.

LUND, DALE A. "Conclusions about Bereavement in Later Life and Implications for Interventions and Future Research." In Dale A. Lund, ed., *Older Bereaved Spouses: Research With Practical Applications.* London: Taylor-Francis-Hemisphere, 1989:217–31.

LUND, DALE A., MICHAEL S. CASERTA, and MARGARET F. DIMOND. "Gender Differences Through Two Years of Bereavement Among the Elderly." *The Gerontologist.* Vol. 26, No. 3 (1986):314–20.

LUTZ, CATHERINE A. *Unnatural Emotions: Everyday Sentiments on a Micronesia Atoll and Their Challenge to Western Theory.* Chicago: University of Chicago Press, 1988.

LUTZ, CATHERINE A., and GEOFFREY M. WHITE. "The Anthropology of Emotions." In Bernard J. Siegel, Alan R. Beals, and Stephen A. Tyler, eds., *Annual Review of Anthropology.* Palo Alto, Calif.: Annual Reviews, Vol. 15 (1986):405–36.

LYNCH, BARBARA DEUTSCH. "The Garden and the Sea: U.S. Latino Environmenta; Discourses and Mainstream Environmentalism." *Social Problems.* Vol. 40, No. 1 (February 1993):108–24.

LYND, ROBERT S. *Knowledge For What? The Place of Social Science in American Culture.* Princeton, N.J.: Princeton University Press, 1967.

LYND, ROBERT S., and HELEN MERRELL LYND. *Middletown in Transition.* New York: Harcourt, Brace & World, 1937.

LYNOTT, PATRICIA PASSUTH, and BARBARA J. LOGUE. "The 'Hurried Child': The Myth of Lost Childhood on Contemporary American Society." *Sociological Forum.* Vol. 8, No. 3 (September 1993):471–91.

MA, LI-CHEN. Personal communication, 1987.

MABRY, MARCUS. "New Hope for Old Unions?" *Newsweek* (February 24, 1992):39.

MCADAM, DOUG. *Political Process and the Development of Black Insurgency, 1930–1970.* Chicago: University of Chicago Press, 1982.

———. "Tactical Innovation and the Pace of Insurgency." *American Sociological Review.* Vol. 48, No. 6 (December 1983):735–54.

———. *Freedom Summer.* New York: Oxford University Press, 1988.

———. "The Biographical Consequences of Activism." *American Sociological Review.* Vol. 54, No. 5 (October 1989):744–60.

———. "Gender as a Mediator of the Activist Experience: The Case of Freedom Summer." *American Journal of Sociology.* Vol. 97, No. 5 (March 1992):1211–40.

MCADAM, DOUG, JOHN D. MCCARTHY, and MAYER N. ZALD. "Social Movements." In Neil J. Smelser, ed., *Handbook of Sociology.* Newbury Park, Calif.: Sage, 1988:695–737.

MCBROOM, WILLIAM H., and FRED W. REED. "Recent Trends in Conservatism: Evidence of Non-Unitary Patterns." *Sociological Focus.* Vol. 23, No. 4 (October 1990):355–65.

MCCARTHY, JOHN D., and MAYER N. ZALD. "Resource Mobilization and Social Movements: A Partial Theory." *American Journal of Sociology.* Vol. 82, No. 6 (May 1977):1212–41.

MACCOBY, ELEANOR EMMONS, and CAROL NAGY JACKLIN. *The Psychology of Sex Differences.* Palo Alto, Calif.: Stanford University Press, 1974.

MCCOLM, R. BRUCE, JAMES FINN, DOUGLAS W. PAYNE, JOSEPH E. RYAN, LEONARD R. SUSSMAN, and GEORGE ZARYCKY. *Freedom in the World: Political Rights & Civil Liberties, 1990–1991.* New York: Freedom House, 1991.

MCCONNELL, SCOTT. "New Liberal Fear: Hyperdemocracy." *The New York Post* (January 18, 1995):19.

678 References

MacDonald, J. Fred. *Blacks and White TV: African Americans in Television Since 1948.* Chicago: Nelson-Hall, 1992.

Mace, David, and Vera Mace. *Marriage East and West.* Garden City, N.Y.: Doubleday (Dolphin), 1960.

McGuire, Meredith B. *Religion: The Social Context.* 2d ed. Belmont, Calif.: Wadsworth, 1987.

McHenry, Susan. "Rosabeth Moss Kanter." In *Ms.* Vol. 13 (January 1985):62–63, 107–8.

Macionis, John J. "Intimacy: Structure and Process in Interpersonal Relationships." *Alternative Lifestyles.* Vol. 1, No. 1 (February 1978):113–30.

———. "The Search for Community in Modern Society: An Interpretation." *Qualitative Sociology.* Vol. 1, No. 2 (September 1978):130–43.

———. "A Sociological Analysis of Humor." Presentation to the Texas Junior College Teachers Association, Houston, 1987.

———. "Making Society (and, Increasingly, the World) Visible." In Earl Babbie, ed., *The Spirit of Sociology.* Belmont, Calif.: Wadsworth, 1993:221–24.

MacKay, Donald G. "Prescriptive Grammar and the Pronoun Problem." In Barrie Thorne, Cheris Kramarae, and Nancy Henley, eds., *Language, Gender and Society.* Rowley, Mass.: Newbury House, 1983:38–53.

MacKinnon, Catharine A. *Feminism Unmodified: Discourses on Life and Law.* Cambridge, Mass.: Harvard University Press, 1987.

Macklin, Eleanor D. "Nonmarital Heterosexual Cohabitation: An Overview." In Eleanor D. Macklin and Roger H. Rubin, eds., *Contemporary Families and Alternative Lifestyles: Handbook on Research and Theory.* Beverly Hills, Calif.: Sage, 1983:49–74.

McLanahan, Sara. "Family Structure and the Reproduction of Poverty." *American Journal of Sociology.* Vol. 90, No. 4 (January 1985):873–901.

McLeod, Jane D., and Michael J. Shanahan. "Poverty, Parenting, and Children's Mental Health." *American Sociological Review.* Vol. 58, No. 3 (June 1993):351–66.

McLeod, Jay. *Ain't No Makin' It: Aspirations and Attainment in a Low-Income Neighborhood.* Boulder, Colo.: Westview Press, 1995.

McPhail, Clark. *The Myth of the Maddening Crowd.* New York: Aldine, 1991.

McPhail, Clark, and Ronald T. Wohlstein. "Individual and Collective Behaviors Within Gatherings, Demonstrations, and Riots." *Annual Review of Sociology.* Vol. 9. Palo Alto, Calif.: Annual Reviews, 1983:579–600.

McRae, Susan. *Cross-Class Families: A Study of Wives' Occupational Superiority.* New York: Oxford University Press, 1986.

McRoberts, Hugh A., and Kevin Selbee. "Trends in Occupational Mobility in Canada and the United States: A Comparison." *American Sociological Review.* Vol. 46, No. 4 (August 1981):406–21.

Maddox, Setma. "Organizational Culture and Leadership Style: Factors Affecting Self-Managed Work Team Performance." Paper presented at the annual meeting of the Southwest Social Science Association, Dallas, February, 1995.

Madsen, Axel. *Private Power: Multinational Corporations for the Survival of Our Planet.* New York: William Morrow, 1980.

Majka, Linda C. "Sexual Harassment in the Church." *Society.* Vol. 28. No. 4 (May-June 1991):14–21.

Malthus, Thomas Robert. *First Essay on Population 1798.* London: Macmillan, 1926; orig. 1798.

Marcuse, Herbert. *One-Dimensional Man.* Boston: Beacon Press, 1964.

Mare, Robert D. "Five Decades of Educational Assortative Mating." *American Sociological Review.* Vol. 56, No. 1 (February 1991):15–32.

Margolick, David. "Rape in Marriage Is No Longer Within the Law." *New York Times* (December 13, 1984):6E.

Marín, Gerardo, and Barbara Vanoss Marín. *Research With Hispanic Populations.* Newbury Park, Calif.: Sage, 1991.

Markoff, John. "Remember Big Brother? Now He's a Company Man." *New York Times* (March 31, 1991):7.

Markson, Elizabeth W. "Moral Dilemmas." *Society.* Vol. 29, No. 5 (July-August 1992):4–6.

Marriott, Michael. "Fathers Find that Child Support Means Owing More than Money." *New York Times* (July 20, 1992):A1, A13.

Marsden, Peter. "Core Discussion Networks of Americans." *American Sociological Review.* Vol. 52, No. 1 (February 1987):122–31.

Marshall, Susan E. "Ladies Against Women: Mobilization Dilemmas of Antifeminist Movements." *Social Problems.* Vol. 32, No. 4 (April 1985):348–62.

Martin, John M., and Anne T. Romano. *Multinational Crime: Terrorism, Espionage, Drug and Arms Trafficking.* Newbury Park, Calif.: Sage, 1992.

Martin, Richard C. *Islam: A Cultural Perspective.* Englewood Cliffs, N.J.: Prentice Hall, 1982.

Martin, William. "The Birth of a Media Myth." *The Atlantic.* Vol. 247, No. 6 (June 1981):7, 10, 11, 16.

Martinez, Valerie J., R. Kenneth Godwin, Frank R. Kemerer, and Laura Perna. "The Consequences of School Choice: Who Leaves and Who Stays in the Inner City." *Social Science Quarterly.* Vol. 76, No. 1 (September 1995):485–501.

Marullo, Sam. "The Functions and Dysfunctions of Preparations for Fighting Nuclear War." *Sociological Focus.* Vol. 20, No. 2 (April 1987):135–53.

Marx, Gary T., and James L. Wood. "Strands of Theory and Research in Collective Behavior." In Alex Inkeles et al., eds., *Annual Review of Sociology.* Vol. 1. Palo Alto, Calif.: Annual Reviews, 1975:363–428.

Marx, Karl. Excerpt from "A Contribution to the Critique of Political Economy." In Karl Marx and Friedrich Engels, *Marx and Engels: Basic Writings on Politics and Philosophy.* Lewis S. Feurer, ed. Garden City, N.Y.: Anchor Books, 1959:42–46.

———. *Karl Marx: Early Writings.* T. B. Bottomore, ed. New York: McGraw-Hill, 1964a.

———. *Karl Marx: Selected Writings in Sociology and Social Philosophy.* T. B. Bottomore, trans. New York: McGraw-Hill, 1964.

———. *Capital.* Friedrich Engels, ed. New York: International Publishers, 1967; orig. 1867.

———. "Theses on Feuer." In Robert C. Tucker, ed., *The Marx-Engels Reader.* New York: Norton, 1972:107–9; orig. 1845.

Marx, Karl, and Friedrich Engels. "Manifesto of the Communist Party." In Robert C. Tucker, ed., *The Marx-Engels Reader.* New York: Norton, 1972:331–62; orig. 1848.

———. *The Marx-Engels Reader.* Robert C. Tucker, ed. New York: Norton, 1977.

Marx, Leo. "The Environment and the 'Two Cultures' Divide." In James Rodger Fleming and Henry A. Gemery, eds., *Science, Technology, and the Environment: Multidisciplinary Perspectives.* Akron, Ohio: University of Akron Press, 1994:3–21.

Massey, Douglas S. Review of *The Bell Curve: Intelligence and Class Structure in American Life* by Richard J. Herrnstein and Charles Murray. *American Journal of Sociology.* Vol. 101, No. 3 (November 1995):747–53.

Massey, Douglas S., and Nancy A. Denton. "Hypersegregation in U.S. Metropolitan Areas: Black and Hispanic Segregation Along Five Dimensions." *Demography.* Vol. 26, No. 3 (August 1989):373–91.

Masters, William H., Virginia E. Johnson, and Robert C. Kolodny. *Human Sexuality.* 3d ed. Glenview, Ill.: Scott, Foresman/Little, Brown, 1988.

Matthiessen, Peter. *In the Spirit of Crazy Horse.* New York: Viking Press, 1983.

———. *Indian Country.* New York: Viking Press, 1984.

Mauer, Marc. *Americans Behind Bars: The International Use of Incarceration, 1992–1993.* Washington, D.C.: The Sentencing Project, 1994.

Mauro, Tony. "Cruzan's Struggle Left Imprint: Private Case Triggered Public Debate." *USA Today* (December 27, 1990):3A.

Mauss, Armand L. *Social Problems of Social Movements.* Philadelphia: Lippincott, 1975.

Mayo, Katherine. *Mother India.* New York: Harcourt, Brace, 1927.

Mead, George Herbert. *Mind, Self, and Society.* Charles W. Morris, ed. Chicago: University of Chicago Press, 1962; orig. 1934.

Mead, Margaret. *Coming of Age in Samoa.* New York: Dell, 1961; orig. 1928.

———. *Sex and Temperament in Three Primitive Societies.* New York: William Morrow, 1963; orig. 1935.

Meadows, Donella H., Dennis L. Meadows, Jorgan Randers, and William W. Behrens, III. *The Limits to Growth: A Report on the Club of Rome's Project on the Predicament of Mankind.* New York: Universe, 1972.

MELTZER, BERNARD N. "Mead's Social Psychology." In Jerome G. Manis and Bernard N. Meltzer, eds., *Symbolic Interaction: A Reader in Social Psychology*. 3d ed. Needham Heights, Mass.: Allyn & Bacon, 1978.

MELUCCI, ALBERTO. "The New Social Movements: A Theoretical Approach." *Social Science Information*. Vol. 19, No. 2 (May 1980):199–226.

———. *Nomads of the Present: Social Movements and Individual Needs in Contemporary Society*. Philadelphia: Temple University Press, 1989.

MERGENBAGEN, PAULA. "Rethinking Retirement." *American Demographics*. Vol. 16, No. 6 (June 1994):28–34.

MERTON, ROBERT K. "Social Structure and Anomie." *American Sociological Review*. Vol. 3, No. 6 (October 1938):672–82.

———. *Social Theory and Social Structure*. New York: Free Press, 1968.

———. "Discrimination and the American Creed." In *Sociological Ambivalence and Other Essays*. New York: Free Press, 1976:189–216.

MEYER, DAVIS S. and NANCY WHITTIER. "Social Movement Spillover." *Social Problems*. Vol. 41, No. 2 (May 1994):277–98.

MEYROWITZ, JOSHUA, and JOHN MAGUIRE. "Media, Place, and Multiculturalism." *Society*. Vol. 30, No. 5 (July-August 1993):41–48.

MICHELS, ROBERT. *Political Parties*. Glencoe, Ill.: Free Press, 1949; orig. 1911.

MILBRATH, LESTER W. *Envisioning A Sustainable Society: Learning Our Way Out*. Albany: State University of New York Press, 1989.

MILGRAM, STANLEY. "Behavioral Study of Obedience." *Journal of Abnormal and Social Psychology*. Vol. 67, No. 4 (1963):371–78.

———. "Group Pressure and Action Against a Person." *Journal of Abnormal and Social Psychology*. Vol. 69, No. 2 (August 1964):137–43.

———. "Some Conditions of Obedience and Disobedience to Authority." *Human Relations*. Vol. 18 (February 1965):57–76.

MILIBAND, RALPH. *The State in Capitalist Society*. London: Weidenfield and Nicolson, 1969.

MILLER, ARTHUR G. *The Obedience Experiments: A Case of Controversy in Social Science*. New York: Praeger, 1986.

MILLER, DAVID L. *Introduction to Collective Behavior*. Belmont, Calif.: Wadsworth, 1985.

MILLER, FREDERICK D. "The End of SDS and the Emergence of Weatherman: Demise Through Success." In Jo Freeman, ed., *Social Movements of the Sixties and Seventies*. New York: Longman, 1983:279–97.

MILLER, G. TYLER, JR. *Living in the Environment: An Introduction to Environmental Science*. Belmont, Calif.: Wadsworth, 1992.

MILLER, MICHAEL. "Lawmakers Begin to Heed Calls to Protect Privacy." *Wall Street Journal* (April 11, 1991):A16.

MILLER, WALTER B. "Lower Class Culture as a Generating Milieu of Gang Delinquency." In Marvin E. Wolfgang, Leonard Savitz, and Norman Johnston, eds., *The Sociology of Crime and Delinquency*. 2d ed. New York: Wiley, 1970:351–63; orig. 1958.

MILLET, KATE. *Sexual Politics*. Garden City, N.Y.: Doubleday, 1970.

MILLMAN, JOEL, NINA MUNK, MICHAEL SCHUMAN, and NEIL WEINBERG. "The World's Wealthiest People." *Forbes*. Vol. 152, No. 1 (July 5, 1993):66–69.

MILLS, C. WRIGHT. *White Collar: The American Middle Classes*. New York: Oxford University Press, 1951.

———. *The Power Elite*. New York: Oxford University Press, 1956.

———. *The Sociological Imagination*. New York: Oxford University Press, 1959.

MINK, BARBARA. "How Modernization Affects Women." *Cornell Alumni News*. Vol. III, No. 3 (April 1989):10–11.

MINTZ, BETH, and MICHAEL SCHWARTZ. "Interlocking Directorates and Interest Group Formation." *American Sociological Review*. Vol. 46, No. 6 (December 1981):851–69.

MIROWSKY, JOHN. "The Psycho-Economics of Feeling Underpaid: Distributive Justice and the Earnings of Husbands and Wives." *American Journal of Sociology*. Vol. 92, No. 6 (May 1987):1404–34.

MIROWSKY, JOHN, and CATHERINE ROSS. "Working Wives and Mental Health." Presentation to the American Association for the Advancement of Science, New York, 1984.

———. *The Social Causes of Psychological Distress*. Hawthorne, N.Y.: Aldine, 1989.

MOLOTCH, HARVEY. "The City as a Growth Machine." *American Journal of Sociology*. Vol. 82, No. 2 (September 1976):309–33.

MONEY, JOHN, and ANKE A. EHRHARDT. *Man and Woman, Boy and Girl*. New York: New American Library, 1972.

MONK-TURNER, ELIZABETH. "The Occupational Achievement of Community and Four-Year College Graduates." *American Sociological Review*. Vol. 55, No. 5 (October 1990):719–25.

MONTAGU, ASHLEY. *The Nature of Human Aggression*. New York: Oxford University Press, 1976.

MOORE, GWEN. "The Structure of a National Elite Network." *American Sociological Review*. Vol. 44, No. 5 (October 1979):673–92.

———. "Structural Determinants of Men's and Women's Personal Networks." *American Sociological Review*. Vol. 55, No. 5 (October 1991):726–35.

———. "Gender and Informal Networks in State Government." *Social Science Quarterly*. Vol. 73, No. 1 (March 1992):46–61.

MOORE, JOAN, and HARRY PACHON. *Hispanics in the United States*. Englewood Cliffs, N.J.: Prentice Hall, 1985.

MOORE, WILBERT E. "Modernization as Rationalization: Processes and Restraints." In Manning Nash, ed., *Essays on Economic Development and Cultural Change in Honor of Bert F. Hoselitz*. Chicago: University of Chicago Press, 1977:29–42.

———. *World Modernization: The Limits of Convergence*. New York: Elsevier, 1979.

MORAN, JOHN S., S. O. ARAL, W. C. JENKINS, T. A. PETERMAN, and E. R. ALEXANDER. "The Impact of Sexually Transmitted Diseases on Minority Populations." *Public Health Reports*. Vol. 104, No. 6 (November-December 1989):560–65.

MORRIS, ALDON. "Black Southern Sit-in Movement: An Analysis of Internal Organization." *American Sociological Review*. Vol. 46, No. 6 (December 1981):744–67.

MORRISON, DENTON E. "Some Notes Toward Theory on Relative Deprivation, Social Movements, and Social Change." In Louis E. Genevie, ed., *Collective Behavior and Social Movements*. Itasca, Ill.: Peacock, 1978:202–9.

MORROW, LANCE. "The Temping of America." *Time*. Vol. 131, No. 14 (March 29, 1993):40–41.

MORTON, JACKSON. "Census on the Internet." *American Demographics*. Vol. 17, No. 3 (March 1995):52–53.

MOSLEY, W. HENRY, and PETER COWLEY. "The Challenge of World Health." *Population Bulletin*. Vol. 46, No. 4 (December 1991). Washington, D.C.: Population Reference Bureau.

MOYNIHAN, DANIEL PATRICK. *The Negro Family: The Case for National Action*. Washington, D.C.: U.S. Department of Labor, 1965.

———. "Toward a New Intolerance." *The Public Interest*. No. 112 (Summer 1993):119–22.

MUELLER, DANIEL P., and PHILIP W. COOPER. "Children of Single Parent Families: How Do They Fare as Young Adults?" Presentation to the American Sociological Association, San Antonio, Texas, 1984.

MULLER, EDWARD N. *Aggressive Political Participation*. Princeton, N.J.: Princeton University Press, 1979.

MUMFORD, LEWIS. *The City in History: Its Origins, Its Transformations, and Its Prospects*. New York: Harcourt, Brace & World, 1961.

MURDOCK, GEORGE PETER. "Comparative Data on the Division of Labor by Sex." *Social Forces*. Vol. 15, No. 4 (May 1937):551–53.

———. "The Common Denominator of Cultures." In Ralph Linton, ed., *The Science of Man in World Crisis*. New York: Columbia University Press, 1945:123–42.

———. *Social Structure*. New York: Free Press, 1965; orig. 1949.

MURRAY, CHARLES. *Losing Ground: American Social Policy 1950–1980*. New York: Basic Books, 1984.

MURRAY, MEGAN BALDRIDGE. "Innovation Without Geniuses." In *Yale Alumni Magazine and Journal*. Vol. XLVII, No. 6 (April 1984):40–43.

MURRAY, PAULI. *Proud Shoes: The History of an American Family*. New York: Harper & Row, 1978.

MYERS, NORMAN. "Humanity's Growth." In Sir Edmund Hillary, ed., *Ecology 2000: The Changing Face of the Earth*. New York: Beaufort Books, 1984a:16–35.

———. "The Mega-Extinction of Animals and Plants." In Sir Edmund Hillary, ed., *Ecology 2000: The Changing Face of the Earth*. New York: Beaufort Books, 1984b:82–107.

———. "Disappearing Cultures." In Sir Edmund Hillary, ed., *Ecology 2000: The Changing Face of the Earth*. New York: Beaufort Books, 1984c:162–69.

———. "Biological Diversity and Global Security." In F. Herbert Bormann and Stephen R. Kellert, eds., *Ecology, Economics, and Ethics: The Broken Circle*. New Haven, Conn.: Yale University Press, 1991:11–25.

MYERS, SHEILA, and HAROLD G. GRASMICK. "The Social Rights and Responsibilities of Pregnant Women: An Application of Parsons' Sick Role Model." Paper presented to Southwestern Sociological Association, Little Rock, Arkansas, March 1989.

NAGEL, JOANE. "Constructing Ethnicity: Creating and Recreating Ethnic Identity and Culture." *Social Problems*. Vol. 41, No. 1 (February 1994):152–76.

NAJAFIZADEH, MEHRANGIZ, and LEWIS A. MENNERICK. "Sociology of Education or Sociology of Ethnocentrism: The Portrayal of Education in Introductory Sociology Textbooks." *Teaching Sociology*. Vo. 20, No. 3 (July 1992):215–21.

NASH, J. MADELEINE. "To Know Your Own Fate." *Time*. Vol. 145, No. 14 (April 3, 1995):62.

NATIONAL CENTER FOR EDUCATION STATISTICS. *Digest of Education Statistics: 1991*. Washington, D.C.: U.S. Government Printing Office, 1992.

———. *Digest of Education Statistics: 1994*. Washington, D.C.: U.S. Government Printing Office, 1995.

NATIONAL CENTER FOR HEALTH STATISTICS. *Monthly Vital Statistics Report*. Vol. 44, No. 4 (April 1995). Washington, D.C.: U.S. Government Printing Office.

NATIONAL COMMISSION ON EXCELLENCE IN EDUCATION. *A Nation at Risk*. Washington, D.C.: U.S. Government Printing Office, 1983.

NAVARRO, VICENTE. "The Industrialization of Fetishism or the Fetishism of Industrialization: A Critique of Ivan Illich." In Vicente Navarro, ed., *Health and Medical Care in the U.S.: A Critical Analysis*. Farmingdale, N.Y.: Baywood Publishing Co., 1977:38–58.

NEIDERT, LISA J., and REYNOLDS FARLEY. "Assimilation in the United States: An Analysis of Ethnic and Generation Differences in Status and Achievement." *American Sociological Review*. Vol. 50, No. 6 (December 1985):840–50.

NELAN, BRUCE W. "Crimes Without Punishment." *Time*. Vol. 141, No. 2 (January 11, 1993):21.

NELSON, JOEL I. "Work and Benefits: The Multiple Problems of Service Sector Employment." *Social Problems*. Vol. 42, No. 2 (May 1994):240–55.

NEUGARTEN, BERNICE L. "Grow Old with Me. The Best Is Yet to Be." *Psychology Today*. Vol. 5 (December 1971):45–48, 79, 81.

———. "Personality and the Aging Process." *The Gerontologist*. Vol. 12, No. 1 (Spring 1972):9–15.

———. "Personality and Aging." In James E. Birren and K. Warner Schaie, eds., *Handbook of the Psychology of Aging*. New York: Van Nostrand Reinhold, 1977:626–49.

NEUHOUSER, KEVIN. "The Radicalization of the Brazilian Catholic Church in Comparative Perspective." *American Sociological Review*. Vol. 54, No. 2 (April 1989):233–44.

New Haven Journal-Courier. "English Social Structure Changing." November 27, 1986.

NEWMAN, KATHERINE S. *Declining Fortunes: The Withering of the American Dream*. New York: Basic Books, 1993.

NEWMAN, WILLIAM M. *American Pluralism: A Study of Minority Groups and Social Theory*. New York: Harper & Row, 1973.

NIELSEN, JOYCE MCCARL, ED. *Feminist Research Methods: Exemplary Readings in the Social Sciences*. Boulder, Colo.: Westview Press, 1990.

1991 Green Book. U.S. House of Representatives. Washington, D.C.: U.S. Government Printing Office, 1991.

NISBET, ROBERT A. *The Sociological Tradition*. New York: Basic Books, 1966.

———. *The Quest for Community*. New York: Oxford University Press, 1969.

———. "Sociology as an Art Form." In *Tradition and Revolt: Historical and Sociological Essays*. New York: Vintage Books, 1970.

NORBECK, EDWARD. "Class Structure." In *Kodansha Encyclopedia of Japan*. Tokyo: Kodansha, 1983:322–25.

NORC. *General Social Surveys, 1972–1991: Cumulative Codebook*. Chicago: National Opinion Research Center, 1991.

———. *General Social Surveys, 1972–1992: Cumulative Codebook*. Chicago: National Opinion Research Center, 1992.

———. *General Social Surveys, 1972–1994: Cumulative Codebook*. University of Chicago: National Opinion Research Center, 1994.

NUNN, CLYDE Z., HARRY J. CROCKETT, JR., and J. ALLEN WILLIAMS, JR. *Tolerance for Nonconformity*. San Francisco: Jossey-Bass, 1978.

OAKES, JEANNIE. "Classroom Social Relationships: Exploring the Bowles and Gintis Hypothesis." *Sociology of Education*. Vol. 55, No. 4 (October 1982):197–212.

———. *Keeping Track: How High Schools Structure Inequality*. New Haven, Conn.: Yale University Press, 1985.

OBERSCHALL, ANTHONY. *Social Conflict and Social Movements*. Englewood Cliffs, N.J.: Prentice Hall, 1973.

O'DEA, THOMAS F., and JANET O'DEA AVIAD. *The Sociology of Religion*. 2d ed. Englewood Cliffs, N.J.: Prentice Hall, 1983.

OFFIR, CAROLE WADE. *Human Sexuality*. New York: Harcourt Brace Jovanovich, 1982.

OGBURN, WILLIAM F. *On Culture and Social Change*. Chicago: University of Chicago Press, 1964.

O'HARE, WILLIAM P. "In the Black." *American Demographics*. Vol. 11, No. 11 (November 1989):25–29.

———. "The Rise of Hispanic Affluence." *American Demographics*. Vol. 12, No. 8 (August 1990):40–43.

O'HARE, WILLIAM P., WILLIAM H. FREY, and DAN FOST. "Asians in the Suburbs." *American Demographics*. Vol. 16, No. 9 (May 1994):32–38.

OLSEN, MARVIN E., DORA G. LODWICK, and RILEY E. DUNLAP. *Viewing the World Ecologically*. Boulder, Colo.: Westview Press, 1992.

OLZAK, SUSAN. "Labor Unrest, Immigration, and Ethnic Conflict in Urban America, 1880–1914." *American Journal of Sociology*. Vol. 94, No. 6 (May 1989):1303–33.

OLZAK, SUSAN, and ELIZABETH WEST. "Ethnic Conflict and the Rise and Fall of Ethnic Newspapers." *American Sociological Review*. Vol. 56, No. 4 (August 1991):458–74.

O'REILLY, JANE. "Wife Beating: The Silent Crime." *Time*. Vol. 122, No. 10 (September 5, 1983):23–24, 26.

ORLANSKY, MICHAEL D., and WILLIAM L. HEWARD. *Voices: Interviews With Handicapped People*. Columbus, Ohio: Merrill, 1981:85, 92, 133–34, 172.

ORSHANSKY, MOLLIE. "How Poverty is Measured." *Monthly Labor Review*. Vol. 92, No. 2 (February 1969):37–41.

OSTLING, RICHARD N. "Jerry Falwell's Crusade." *Time*. Vol. 126, No. 9 (September 2, 1985):48–52, 55, 57.

———. "Technology and the Womb." *Time*. Vol. 129, No. 12 (March 23, 1987):58–59.

OSTRANDER, SUSAN A. "Upper Class Women: The Feminine Side of Privilege." *Qualitative Sociology*. Vol. 3, No. 1 (Spring 1980):23–44.

———. *Women of the Upper Class*. Philadelphia: Temple University Press, 1984.

OUCHI, WILLIAM. *Theory Z: How American Business Can Meet the Japanese Challenge*. Reading, Mass.: Addison-Wesley, 1981.

OWEN, DAVID. *None of the Above: Behind the Myth of Scholastic Aptitude*. Boston: Houghton Mifflin, 1985.

PAKULSKI, JAN. "Mass Social Movements and Social Class." *International Sociology*. Vol. 8, No. 2 (June 1993):131–58.

PALMORE, ERDMAN. "Predictors of Successful Aging." *The Gerontologist*. Vol. 19, No. 5 (October 1979a):427–31.

———. "Advantages of Aging." *The Gerontologist*. Vol. 19, No. 2 (April 1979b):220–23.

———. "What Can the USA Learn from Japan About Aging?" In Steven H. Zarit, ed., *Readings in Aging and Death: Contemporary Perspectives*. New York: Harper & Row, 1982:166–69.

PAMPEL, FRED C., KENNETH C. LAND, and MARCUS FELSON. "A Social Indicator Model of Changes in the Occupational Structure of the United States: 1947–1974." *American Sociological Review*. Vol. 42, No. 6 (December 1977):951–64.

PARCEL, TOBY L., CHARLES W. MUELLER, and STEVEN CUVELIER. "Comparable Worth and Occupational Labor Market: Explanations of Occupational Earnings Differentials." Paper presented to the American Sociological Association, New York, 1986.

PARENTI, MICHAEL. *Inventing Reality: The Politics of the Mass Media*. New York: St. Martin's Press, 1986.

PARK, ROBERT E. *Race and Culture*. Glencoe, Ill.: Free Press, 1950.

——. "The City: Suggestions for the Investigation of Human Behavior in the Human Environment." In Robert E. Park and Ernest W. Burgess, *The City*. Chicago: University of Chicago Press, 1967; orig. 1925:1–46.

PARKINSON, C. NORTHCOTE. *Parkinson's Law and Other Studies in Administration*. New York: Ballantine Books, 1957.

PARRILLO, VINCENT N. "Diversity in America: A Sociohistorical Analysis." *Sociological Forum*. Vol. 9, No. 4 (December 1994):42–45.

PARROTT, JULIE. "The Effects of Culture on Eating Disorders." Paper presented to Southwestern Social Science Association, Dallas, Texas, March 1987.

PARSONS, TALCOTT. "Age and Sex in the Social Structure of the United States." *American Sociological Review*. Vol. 7, No. 4 (August 1942):604–16.

——. *Essays in Sociological Theory*. New York: Free Press, 1954.

——. *The Social System*. New York: Free Press, 1964; orig. 1951.

——. *Societies: Evolutionary and Comparative Perspectives*. Englewood Cliffs, N.J.: Prentice Hall, 1966.

PARSONS, TALCOTT, and ROBERT F. BALES, EDS. *Family, Socialization and Interaction Process*. New York: Free Press, 1955.

PAUL, ELLEN FRANKEL. "Bared Buttocks and Federal Cases." *Society*. Vol. 28, No. 4 (May-June, 1991):4–7.

PEAR, ROBERT. "Women Reduce Lag in Earnings, But Disparities With Men Remain." *New York Times* (September 4, 1987):1, 7.

PEAR, ROBERT, with ERIK ECKHOLM. "When Healers are Entrepreneurs: A Debate Over Costs and Ethics." *New York Times* (June 2, 1991):1, 17.

PEARSON, DAVID E. "Post-Mass Culture." *Society*. Vol. 30, No. 5 (July-August 1993):17–22.

——. "Community and Sociology." *Society*. Vol. 32, No. 5 (July-August 1995):44–50.

PENNINGS, JOHANNES M. "Organizational Birth Frequencies: An Empirical Investigation." *Administrative Science Quarterly*. Vol. 27, No. 1 (March 1982):120–44.

PEREZ, LISANDRO. "Cubans." In *Harvard Encyclopedia of American Ethnic Groups*. Cambridge, Mass.: Harvard University Press, 1980:256–60.

PERROLLE, JUDITH A. "Comments from the Special Issue Editor: The Emerging Dialogue on Environmental Justice." *Social Problems*. Vol. 40, No. 1 (February 1993):1–4.

PERSELL, CAROLINE HODGES. *Education and Inequality: A Theoretical and Empirical Synthesis*. New York: Free Press, 1977.

PESSEN, EDWARD. *Riches, Class, and Power: America Before the Civil War*. New Brunswick, N.J.: Transaction Books, 1990.

PETER, LAURENCE J., and RAYMOND HULL. *The Peter Principle: Why Things Always Go Wrong*. New York: William Morrow, 1969.

Peters Atlas of the World. New York: Harper & Row, 1990.

PETERS, THOMAS J., and ROBERT H. WATERMAN, JR. *In Search of Excellence: Lessons From America's Best-Run Companies*. New York: Warner Books, 1982.

PHELAN, JO, BRUCE G. LINK, ANN STUEVE, and ROBERT E. MOORE. "Education, Social Liberalism, and Economic Conservatism: Attitudes Toward Homeless People." *American Sociological Review*. Vol. 60, No. 1 (February 1995):126–40.

PHILIPSON, ILENE J., and KAREN V. HANSEN. "Women, Class, and the Feminist Imagination." In Karen V. Hansen and Ilene J. Philipson, eds., *Women, Class, and the Feminist Imagination: A Socialist-Feminist Reader*. Philadelphia: Temple University Press, 1992:3–40.

PHILLIPSON, CHRIS. *Capitalism and the Construction of Old Age*. London: Macmillan, 1982.

PHYSICIANS' TASK FORCE ON HUNGER IN AMERICA. "Hunger Reaches Blue-Collar America." Report issued 1987.

PICHARDO, NELSON A. "The Power Elite and Elite-Driven Countermovements: The Associated Farmers of California During the 1930s." *Sociological Forum*. Vol. 10, No. 1 (March 1995):21–49.

PILLEMER, KARL. "Maltreatment of the Elderly at Home and in Institutions: Extent, Risk Factors, and Policy Recommendations." In U.S. Congress. House. Select Committee on Aging and Senate, Special Committee on Aging. *Legislative Agenda for an Aging Society: 1988 and Beyond*. Washington, D.C.: U.S. Government Printing Office, 1988.

PINES, MAYA. "The Civilization of Genie." *Psychology Today*. Vol. 15 (September 1981):28–34.

PIRANDELLO, LUIGI. "The Pleasure of Honesty." In *To Clothe the Naked and Two Other Plays*. New York: Dutton, 1962:143–98.

PITNEY, JOHN J., JR. "What Scholars Don't Know About Term Limits." *The Chronicle of Higher Education*. Vol. XLI, No. 33 (April 28, 1995):A76.

PITT, MALCOLM. *Introducing Hinduism*. New York: Friendship Press, 1955.

PIVEN, FRANCES FOX, and RICHARD A. CLOWARD. *Poor People's Movements: Why They Succeed, How They Fail*. New York: Pantheon Books, 1977.

——. *Why Americans Don't Vote*. New York: Pantheon Books, 1988.

PLOMIN, ROBERT, and TERRYL T. FOCH. "A Twin Study of Objectively Assessed Personality in Childhood." *Journal of Personality and Social Psychology*. Vol. 39, No. 4 (October 1980):680–88.

POLENBERG, RICHARD. *One Nation Divisible: Class, Race, and Ethnicity in the United States Since 1938*. New York: Pelican Books, 1980.

POLLACK, PHILIP H., III, and M. ELLIOT VITTAS. "Who Bears the Burdens of Environmental Pollution: Race, Ethnicity, and Environmental Equity in Florida." *Social Science Quarterly*. Vol. 76, No. 2 (June 1995):294–310.

POLSBY, NELSON W. "Three Problems in the Analysis of Community Power." *American Sociological Review*. Vol. 24, No. 6 (December 1959):796–803.

POMER, MARSHALL I. "Labor Market Structure, Intragenerational Mobility, and Discrimination: Black Male Advancement Out of Low-Paying Occupations, 1962–1973." *American Sociological Review*. Vol. 51, No. 5 (October 1986):650–59.

POPENOE, DAVID. *Disturbing the Nest: Family Change and Decline in Modern Societies*. New York: Aldine, 1988.

——. "Family Decline in the Swedish Welfare State." *The Public Interest*. No. 102 (Winter 1991):65–77.

——. "The Controversial Truth: Two-Parent Families are Better." *New York Times* (December 26, 1992):21.

——. "American Family Decline, 1960–1990: A Review and Appraisal." *Journal of Marriage and the Family*. Vol. 55, No. 3 (August 1993):527–55.

——. "Parental Androgyny." *Society*. Vol. 30, No. 6 (September-October 1993):5–11.

——. "Scandinavian Welfare." *Society*. Vol. 31, No. 6 (September-October, 1994):78–81.

——. Review of John Snarey's *How Fathers Care for the Next Generation: A Four Decade Study*, in *Contemporary Sociology*. Vol. 23, No. 5 (September 1994):698–700.

POPKIN, SUSAN J. "Welfare: Views From the Bottom." *Social Problems*. Vol. 17, No. 1 (February 1990):64–79.

POPULATION REFERENCE BUREAU. *1995 World Population Data Sheet*. Washington, D.C.: Population Reference Bureau, Inc., 1995.

——. "Past and Future Population Doubling Times, Selected Countries." *Population Today*. Vol. 23, No. 2 (February 1995):6.

Population Today. "Majority of Children in Poverty Live with Parents Who Work." Vol. 23, No 4 (April 1995):6.

PORTES, ALEJANDRO. "The Rise of Ethnicity: Determinants of Ethnic Perceptions Among Cuban Exiles in Miami." *American Sociological Review*. Vol. 49, No. 3 (June 1984):383–97.

PORTES, ALEJANDRO, and LEIF JENSEN. "The Enclave and the Entrants: Patterns of Ethnic Enterprise in Miami Before and After Mariel." *American Sociological Review*. Vol. 54, No. 6 (December 1989):929–49.

POSTEL, SANDRA. "Facing Water Scarcity." In Lester R. Brown et al., eds., *State of the World 1993: A Worldwatch Institute Report on Progress Toward a Sustainable Society*. New York: Norton, 1993:22–41.

POWELL, CHRIS, and GEORGE E. C. PATON, EDS. *Humour in Society: Resistance and Control*. New York: St. Martin's Press, 1988.

PRESSER, HARRIET B. "The Housework Gender Gap." *Population Today*. Vol. 21, No. 7/8 (July-August 1993):5.

PRESSLEY, SUE ANNE, and NANCY ANDREWS. "For Gay Couples, the Nursery Becomes the New Frontier." *Washington Post* (December 20, 1992):A1, A22–23.

PRIMEGGIA, SALVATORE, and JOSEPH A. VARACALLI. "Southern Italian Comedy: Old to New World." In Joseph V. Scelsa, Salvatore J. LaGumina, and Lydio Tomasi, eds., *Italian Americans in Transition*. New York: The American Italian Historical Association, 1990:241–52.

PRINDLE, DAVID F. *Risky Business: The Political Economy of Hollywood.* Boulder, Colo.: Westview Press, 1993.

———. "Take Three on Hollywood Liberalism." *Social Science Quarterly.* Vol. 75, No. 2 (June 1994):458–59.

PRINDLE, DAVID F., and JAMES W. ENDERSBY. "Hollywood Liberalism." *Social Science Quarterly.* Vol. 74, No. 1 (March 1993):136–49.

PUTERBAUGH, GEOFF, ED. *Twins and Homosexuality: A Casebook.* New York: Garland, 1990.

PUTKA, GARY. "SAT To Become A Better Gauge." *Wall Street Journal* (November 1, 1990):B1.

PUTKA, GARY, and STEVE STECKLOW. "Do For-Profit Schools Work? These Seem to for One Entrepreneur." *Wall Street Journal* (June 8, 1994):A1, A4.

QUEENAN, JOE. "The Many Paths to Riches." *Forbes.* Vol. 144, No. 9 (October 23, 1989):149.

QUINNEY, RICHARD. *Class, State and Crime: On the Theory and Practice of Criminal Justice.* New York: David McKay, 1977.

RADEMACHER, ERIC W. "The Effect of Question Wording on College Students." *The Pittsburgh Undergraduate Review.* Vol. 8, No. 1 (Spring 1992):45–81.

RADEMAEKERS, WILLIAM, and RHEA SCHOENTHAL. "Iceman." *Time.* Vol. 140, No. 17 (October 26, 1992):62–66.

RANDALL, VICKI. *Women and Politics.* London: Macmillan, 1982.

RAPHAEL, RAY. *The Men From the Boys: Rites of Passage in Male America.* Lincoln and London: University of Nebraska Press, 1988.

RECKLESS, WALTER C., and SIMON DINITZ. "Pioneering With Self-Concept as a Vulnerability Factor in Delinquency." *Journal of Criminal Law, Criminology, and Police Science.* Vol. 58, No. 4 (December 1967):515–23.

REICH, ROBERT B. "As the World Turns." *The New Republic* (May 1, 1989):23, 26–28.

———. *The Work of Nations: Preparing Ourselves for 21st-Century Capitalism.* New York: Alfred A. Knopf, 1991.

REID, SUE TITUS. *Crime and Criminology.* 6th ed. Fort Worth, Tex.: Holt, Rinehart & Winston, 1991.

REINHARZ, SHULAMIT. *Feminist Methods in Social Research.* New York: Oxford University Press, 1992.

REMOFF, HEATHER TREXLER. *Sexual Choice: A Woman's Decision.* New York: Dutton/Lewis, 1984.

RICHARDSON, JAMES T. "Definitions of Cult: From Sociological-Technical to Popular Negative." Paper presented to the American Psychological Association, Boston, August 1990.

RIDGEWAY, CECILIA L. *The Dynamics of Small Groups.* New York: St. Martin's Press, 1983.

RIEFF, PHILIP. "Introduction." In Charles Horton Cooley, *Social Organization.* New York: Schocken Books, 1962.

RIESMAN, DAVID. *The Lonely Crowd: A Study of the Changing American Character.* New Haven, Conn.: Yale University Press, 1970; orig. 1950.

RILEY, MATILDA WHITE, ANNE FONER, and JOAN WARING. "Sociology of Age." In Neil J. Smelser, ed., *Handbook of Sociology.* Newbury Park, Calif.: Sage, 1988:243–90.

RITZER, GEORGE. *Sociological Theory.* New York: Alfred A. Knopf, 1983:63–66.

———. *The McDonaldization of Society: An Investigation Into the Changing Character of Contemporary Social Life.* Thousand Oaks, Calif.: Pine Forge Press, 1993.

RITZER, GEORGE, and DAVID WALCZAK. *Working: Conflict and Change.* 4th ed. Englewood Cliffs, N.J.: Prentice Hall, 1990.

ROBERTS, J. DEOTIS. *Roots of a Black Future: Family and Church.* Philadelphia: Westminster Press, 1980.

ROBERTS, J. TIMMONS. "Psychosocial Effects of Workplace Hazardous Exposures: Theoretical Synthesis and Preliminary Findings." *Social Problems.* Vol. 40, No. 1 (February 1993):74–89.

ROBERTS, STEVEN V. "Open Arms for Online Democracy." *U.S. News and World Report.* Vol. 118, No. 2 (January 16, 1995):10.

ROBINSON, DAWN. "Toward a Synthesis of Sociological and Psychological Theories of Eating Disorders." Paper presented to Southwestern Social Science Association, Dallas, Texas, March 1987.

ROBINSON, JOYCE, and GLENNA SPITZE. "Whistle While You Work? The Effect of Household Task Performance on Women's and Men's Well-Being." *Social Science Quarterly.* Vol. 73, No. 4 (December 1992):844–61.

ROBINSON, VERA M. "Humor and Health." In Paul E. McGhee and Jeffrey H. Goldstein, eds., *Handbook of Humor Research, Vol. II, Applied Studies.* New York: Springer-Verlag, 1983:109–28.

ROCKETT, IAN R. H. "Population and Health: An Introduction to Epidemiology." *Population Bulletin.* Vol. 49, No. 3 (November 1994). Washington, D.C.: Population Reference Bureau.

RODGERS, JOAN R. "An Empirical Study of Intergenerational Transmission of Poverty in the United States." *Social Science Quarterly.* Vol. 76, No. 1 (March 1995):178–94.

ROESCH, ROBERTA. "Violent Families." *Parents.* Vol. 59, No. 9 (September 1984):74–76, 150–52.

ROETHLISBERGER, F. J., and WILLIAM J. DICKSON. *Management and the Worker.* Cambridge, Mass.: Harvard University Press, 1939.

ROGERS, ALISON. "The World's 101 Richest People." *Fortune.* Vol. 127, No. 13 (June 28, 1993):36–66.

ROHLEN, THOMAS P. *Japan's High Schools.* Berkeley: University of California Press, 1983.

ROKOVE, MILTON L. *Don't Make No Waves, Don't Back No Losers.* Bloomington: Indiana University Press, 1975.

ROMAN, MEL, and WILLIAM HADDAD. *The Disposable Parent: The Case for Joint Custody.* New York: Holt, Rinehart & Winston, 1978.

RÓNA-TAS, ÁKOS. "The First Shall Be Last? Entrepreneurship and Communist Cadres in the Transition From Socialism." *American Journal of Sociology.* Vol. 100, No. 1 (July 1994):40–69.

ROOF, WADE CLARK. "Socioeconomic Differentials Among White Socioreligious Groups in the United States." *Social Forces.* Vol. 58, No. 1 (September 1979):280–89.

———. "Unresolved Issues in the Study of Religion and the National Elite: Response to Greeley." *Social Forces.* Vol. 59, No. 3 (March 1981):831–36.

ROOF, WADE CLARK, and WILLIAM MCKINNEY. *American Mainline Religion: Its Changing Shape and Future.* New Brunswick, N.J.: Rutgers University Press, 1987.

ROOS, PATRICIA. "Marriage and Women's Occupational Attainment in Cross-Cultural Perspective." *American Sociological Review.* Vol. 48, No. 6 (December 1983):852–64.

RORTY, RICHARD. "The Unpatriotic Academy." *New York Times* (February 13, 1994):15.

ROSE, JERRY D. *Outbreaks.* New York: Free Press, 1982.

ROSEN, ELLEN ISRAEL. *Bitter Choices: Blue-Collar Women In and Out of Work.* Chicago: University of Chicago Press, 1987.

ROSENFELD, RACHEL A., and ARNE L. KALLEBERG. "A Cross-National Comparison of the Gender Gap in Income." *American Journal of Sociology.* Vol. 96, No. 1 (July 1990):69–106.

ROSENTHAL, ELIZABETH. "Canada's National Health Plan Gives Care to All, With Limits." *New York Times* (April 30, 1991):A1, A16.

ROSENTHAL, JACK. "The Rapid Growth of Suburban Employment." In Lois H. Masotti and Jeffrey K. Hadden, eds., *Suburbia in Transition.* New York: New York Times Books, 1974:95–100.

ROSNOW, RALPH L., and GARY ALAN FINE. *Rumor and Gossip: The Social Psychology of Hearsay.* New York: Elsevier, 1976.

ROSS, CATHERINE E., JOHN MIROWSKY, and JOAN HUBER. "Dividing Work, Sharing Work, and In-Between: Marriage Patterns and Depression." *American Sociological Review.* Vol. 48, No. 6 (December 1983):809–23.

ROSSI, ALICE S. "Gender and Parenthood." In Alice S. Rossi, ed., *Gender and the Life Course.* New York: Aldine, 1985:161–91.

ROSSI, PETER H. Review of Christopher Jencks, *The Homeless* (Cambridge, Mass.: Harvard University Press). *Society.* Vol. 32, No. 4 (May-June 1995):80–81.

ROSTOW, WALT W. *The Stages of Economic Growth: A Non-Communist Manifesto.* Cambridge: Cambridge University Press, 1960.

———. *The World Economy: History and Prospect.* Austin: University of Texas Press, 1978.

ROTHMAN, STANLEY, STEPHEN POWERS, and DAVID ROTHMAN. "Feminism in Films." *Society.* Vol. 30, No. 3 (March-April 1993):66–72.

ROUDI, NAZY. "The Demography of Islam." *Population Today*. Vol. 16, No. 3 (March 1988):6–9.

ROWE, DAVID C. "Biometrical Genetic Models of Self-Reported Delinquent Behavior: A Twin Study." *Behavior Genetics*. Vol. 13, No. 5 (1983):473–89.

ROWE, DAVID C., and D. WAYNE OSGOOD. "Heredity and Sociological Theories of Delinquency: A Reconsideration." *American Sociological Review*. Vol. 49, No. 4 (August 1984):526–40.

RUBENSTEIN, ELI A. "The Not So Golden Years." *Newsweek* (October 7, 1991):13.

RUBIN, BETH A. "Class Struggle American Style: Unions, Strikes and Wages." *American Sociological Review*. Vol. 51, No. 5 (October 1986):618–31.

RUBIN, LILLIAN BRESLOW. *Worlds of Pain: Life in the Working-Class Family*. New York: Basic Books, 1976.

RUDÉ, GEORGE. *The Crowd in History: A Study of Popular Disturbances in France and England, 1730–1848*. New York: Wiley, 1964.

RUGGLES, STEVEN. "The Origins of African-American Family Structure." *American Sociological Review*. Vol. 59, No. 1 (February 1994):136–51.

RULE, JAMES, and PETER BRANTLEY. "Computerized Surveillance in the Workplace: Forms and Delusions." *Sociological Forum*. Vol. 7, No. 3 (September 1992):405–23.

RUSSELL, CHERYL. "The Master Trend." *American Demographics*. Vol. 15, No. 10 (October 1993):28–37.

———. "Overworked? Overwhelmed?" *American Demographics*. Vol. 17, No. 3 (March 1995):8.

RUSSELL, DIANA E. H. *Rape in Marriage*. New York: Macmillan, 1982.

RYAN, WILLIAM. *Blaming the Victim*. Rev. ed. New York: Vintage Books, 1976.

RYMER, RUSS. *Genie*. New York: HarperPerennial, 1994.

RYTINA, JOAN HUBER, WILLIAM H. FORM, and JOHN PEASE. "Income and Stratification Ideology: Beliefs About the American Opportunity Structure." *American Journal of Sociology*. Vol. 75, No. 4 (January 1970):703–16.

SABATO, LARRY J. *PAC Power: Inside the World of Political Action Committees*. New York: Norton, 1984.

SAGAN, CARL. *The Dragons of Eden*. New York: Ballantine, 1977.

SALE, KIRKPATRICK. *The Conquest of Paradise: Christopher Columbus and the Columbian Legacy*. New York: Alfred A. Knopf, 1990.

SALHOLZ, ELOISE. "The Future of Gay America." *Newsweek* (March 12, 1990):20–25.

SALTMAN, JULIET. "Maintaining Racially Diverse Neighborhoods." *Urban Affairs Quarterly*. Vol. 26, No. 3 (March 1991):416–41.

SAMPSON, ANTHONY. *The Changing Anatomy of Britain*. New York: Random House, 1982.

SAMPSON, ROBERT J. "Urban Black Violence: The Effects of Male Joblessness and Family Disruption." *American Journal of Sociology*. Vol. 93, No. 2 (September 1987):348–82.

SAMPSON, ROBERT J., and JOHN H. LAUB. "Crime and Deviance Over the Life Course: The Salience of Adult Social Bonds." *American Sociological Review*. Vol. 55, No. 5 (October 1990):609–27.

SÀNDOR, GABRIELLE. "The Other Americans." *American Demographics*. Vol. 16, No. 6 (June 1994):36–41.

SANTOLI, AL. "Fighting Child Prostitution." *Freedom Review*. Vol. 25, No. 5 (September-October 1994):5–8.

SAPIR, EDWARD. "The Status of Linguistics as a Science." *Language*. Vol. 5 (1929):207–14.

———. *Selected Writings of Edward Sapir in Language, Culture, and Personality*. David G. Mandelbaum, ed. Berkeley: University of California Press, 1949.

SAX, LINDA J., ALEXANDER W. ASTIN, WILLIAM S. KORN, and KATHRYN M. MAHONEY. *The American Freshman: National Norms for Fall 1995*. Los Angeles: UCLA Higher Education Research Institute, 1995.

SCAFF, LAWRENCE A. "Max Weber and Robert Michels." *American Journal of Sociology*. Vol. 86, No. 6 (May 1981):1269–86.

SCANLON, JAMES P. "The Curious Case of Affirmative Action for Women." *Society*. Vol. 29, No. 2 (January-February 1992):36–42.

SCHAIE, I. WARNER. "Intelligence and Problem Solving." In James E. Birren and R. Bruce Sloane, eds., *Handbook of Mental Health and Aging*. Englewood Cliffs, N.J.: Prentice Hall, 1980:262–84.

SCHEFF, THOMAS J. *Being Mentally Ill: A Sociological Theory*. 2d ed. New York: Aldine, 1984.

SCHELLENBERG, JAMES A. *Masters of Social Psychology*. New York: Oxford University Press, 1978:38–62.

SCHILLER, BRADLEY. "Who Are the Working Poor?" *The Public Interest*. Vol. 155 (Spring 1994):61–71.

SCHLESINGER, ARTHUR. "The City in American Civilization." In A. B. Callow, Jr., ed., *American Urban History*. New York: Oxford University Press, 1969:25–41.

SCHLESINGER, ARTHUR, JR. "The Cult of Ethnicity: Good and Bad." *Time*. Vol. 137, No. 27 (July 8, 1991):21.

SCHMIDT, ROGER. *Exploring Religion*. Belmont, Calif.: Wadsworth, 1980.

SCHOOLER, CARMI, JOANNE MILLER, KAREN A. MILLER, and CAROL N. RICHTAND. "Work for the Household: Its Nature and Consequences for Husbands and Wives." *American Journal of Sociology*. Vol. 90, No. 1 (July 1984):97–124.

SCHUMANN, HANS WOLFGANG. *Buddhism: An Outline of Its Teachings and Schools*. Wheaton, Ill.: The Theosophical Publishing House/Quest Books, 1974.

SCHUTT, RUSSELL K. "Objectivity Versus Outrage." *Society*. Vol. 26, No. 4 (May-June 1989):14–16.

SCHWARTZ, FELICE N. "Management, Women, and the New Facts of Life." *Harvard Business Review*. Vol. 89, No. 1 (January-February 1989):65–76.

SCHWARTZ, JOE. "Rising Status." *American Demographics*. Vol. 11, No. 1 (January 1989):10.

SCHWARTZ, JOHN E., and THOMAS J. VOLGY. *The Forgotten Americans: Thirty Million Working Poor in the Land of Opportunity*. New York: Norton, 1992.

SCHWARTZ, MARTIN D. "Gender and Injury in Spousal Assault." *Sociological Focus*. Vol. 20, No. 1 (January 1987):61–75.

SCHWARTZ-NOBEL, LORETTA. *Starving in the Shadow of Plenty*. New York: McGraw-Hill, 1981.

SCOTT, JOHN, and CATHERINE GRIFF. *Directors of Industry: The British Corporate Network, 1904–1976*. New York: Blackwell, 1985.

SCOTT, W. RICHARD. *Organizations: Rational, Natural, and Open Systems*. Englewood Cliffs, NJ: Prentice Hall, 1981.

SEARS, DAVID O., and JOHN B. MCCONAHAY. *The Politics of Violence: The New Urban Blacks and the Watts Riot*. Boston: Houghton Mifflin, 1973.

SEKULIC, DUSKO, GARTH MASSEY, and RANDY HODSON. "Who Were the Yugoslavs? Failed Sources of Common Identity in the Former Yugoslavia." *American Sociological Review*. Vol. 59, No. 1 (February 1994):83–97.

SELIMUDDIN, ABU K. "The Selling of America." *USA Today*. Vol. 117, No. 2525 (March 1989):12–14.

SELLIN, THORSTEN. *The Penalty of Death*. Beverly Hills, Calif.: Sage, 1980.

SELTZER, ROBERT M. *Jewish People, Jewish Thought: The Jewish Experience in History*. New York: Macmillan, 1980.

SEN, K. M. *Hinduism*. Baltimore: Penguin Books, 1961.

SENNETT, RICHARD, and JONATHAN COBB. *The Hidden Injuries of Class*. New York: Vintage Books, 1973.

SHAPIRO, JOSEPH P. "Welfare: The Myth of Reform." *U.S. News and World Report*. Vol. 188, No. 2 (January 16, 1995):30–40.

SHAPIRO, JOSEPH P., and JOANNIE M. SCHROF. "Honor Thy Children." *U.S. News and World Report*. Vol. 118, No. 8 (February 27, 1995):39–49.

SHAWCROSS, WILLIAM. *Sideshow: Kissinger, Nixon and the Destruction of Cambodia*. New York: Pocket Books, 1979.

SHEEHAN, TOM. "Senior Esteem as a Factor in Socioeconomic Complexity." *The Gerontologist*. Vol. 16, No. 5 (October 1976):433–40.

SHEEHY, GAIL. *Passages: Predictable Crises of Adult Life*. New York: Dutton, 1976.

SHELDON, WILLIAM H., EMIL M. HARTL, and EUGENE MCDERMOTT. *Varieties of Delinquent Youth*. New York: Harper, 1949.

SHELEY, JAMES F., JOSHUA ZHANG, CHARLES J. BRODY, and JAMES D. WRIGHT. "Gang Organization, Gang Criminal Activity, and Individual Gang Members' Criminal Behavior." *Social Science Quarterly*. Vol. 76, No. 1 (March 1995):53–68.

SHENON, PHILIP. "A Pacific Island Nation is Stripped of Everything." *New York Times* (December 10, 1995):3.

SHERMAN, LAWRENCE W., and DOUGLAS A. SMITH. "Crime, Punishment, and Stake in Conformity: Legal and Informal Control of Domestic Violence." *American Sociological Review*. Vol. 57, No. 5 (October 1992):680–90.

SHERRID, PAMELA. "Hot Times in the City of London." *U.S. News & World Report* (October 27, 1986):45–46.

SHEVKY, ESHREF, and WENDELL BELL. *Social Area Analysis*. Stanford, Calif.: Stanford University Press, 1955.

SHIBUTANI, TAMOTSU. *Improvised News: A Sociological Study of Rumor*. Indianapolis, Ind.: Bobbs-Merrill, 1966.

SHIPLER, DAVID K. *Russia: Broken Idols, Solemn Dreams*. New York: Penguin Books, 1984.

SHIPLEY, JOSEPH T. *Dictionary of Word Origins*. Totowa, N.J.: Roman & Allanheld, 1985.

SHIVELY, JOELLEN. "Cowboys and Indians: Perceptions of Western Films Among American Indians and Anglos." *American Sociological Review*. Vol. 57, No. 6 (December 1992):725–34.

SHUPE, ANSON, WILLIAM A. STACEY, and LONNIE R. HAZLEWOOD. *Violent Men, Violent Couples: The Dynamics of Domestic Violence*. Lexington, Mass.: Lexington Books, 1987.

SIDEL, RUTH, and VICTOR W. SIDEL. *A Healthy State: An International Perspective on the Crisis in United States Medical Care*. Rev. ed. New York: Pantheon Books, 1982a.

———. *The Health Care of China*. Boston: Beacon Press, 1982b.

SILLS, DAVID L. "The Succession of Goals." In Amitai Etzioni, ed., *A Sociological Reader on Complex Organizations*. 2d ed. New York: Holt, Rinehart & Winston, 1969:175–87.

SILVERBERG, ROBERT. "The Greenhouse Effect: Apocalypse Now or Chicken Little?" *Omni* (July 1991):50–54.

SILVERSTEIN, MICHAEL. In Jon Snodgrass, ed., *A Book of Readings for Men Against Sexism*. Albion, Calif.: Times Change Press, 1977:178–79.

SIMMEL, GEORG. *The Sociology of Georg Simmel*. Kurt Wolff, ed. New York: Free Press, 1950:118–69.

———. "The Metropolis and Mental Life." In Kurt Wolff, ed., *The Sociology of Georg Simmel*. New York: Free Press, 1964:409–24; orig. 1905.

———. "Fashion." In Donald N. Levine, ed., *Georg Simmel: On Individuality and Social Forms*. Chicago: University of Chicago Press, 1971; orig. 1904.

SIMONS, CAROL. "Japan's *Kyoiku* Mamas." In John J. Macionis and Nijole V. Benokraitis, eds., *Seeing Ourselves: Classic, Contemporary, and Cross-Cultural Readings in Sociology*. Englewood Cliffs, N.J.: Prentice Hall, 1989:281–86.

SIMONS, MARLISE. "The Price of Modernization: The Case of Brazil's Kaiapo Indians." In John J. Macionis and Nijole V. Benokraitis, eds., *Seeing Ourselves: Classic, Contemporary, and Cross-Cultural Readings in Sociology*. 3d ed. Englewood Cliffs, N.J.: Prentice Hall, 1995:470–76.

SIMPSON, GEORGE EATON, and J. MILTON YINGER. *Racial and Cultural Minorities: An Analysis of Prejudice and Discrimination*. 4th ed. New York: Harper & Row, 1972.

SINGER, JEROME L., and DOROTHY G. SINGER. "Psychologists Look at Television: Cognitive, Developmental, Personality, and Social Policy Implications." *American Psychologist*. Vol. 38, No. 7 (July 1983):826–34.

SIVARD, RUTH LEGER. *World Military and Social Expenditures, 1987–88*. 12th ed. Washington, D.C.: World Priorities, 1988.

SIZER, THEODORE R. *Horace's Compromise: The Dilemma of the American High School*. Boston: Houghton Mifflin, 1984.

SKOCPOL, THEDA. *States and Social Revolutions: A Comparative Analysis of France, Russia, and China*. Cambridge: Cambridge University Press, 1979.

SKOLNICK, ARLENE. *The Psychology of Human Development*. New York: Harcourt Brace Jovanovich, 1986.

SLATER, PHILIP E. "Contrasting Correlates of Group Size." *Sociometry*. Vol. 21, No. 2 (June 1958):129–39.

———. *The Pursuit of Loneliness*. Boston: Beacon Press, 1976.

SMALL BUSINESS ADMINISTRATION. News release on census data for women-owned businesses. January 1996.

SMART, NINIAN. *The Religious Experience of Mankind*. New York: Charles Scribner's Sons, 1969.

SMELSER, NEIL J. *Theory of Collective Behavior*. New York: Free Press, 1962.

SMITH, ADAM. *An Inquiry Into the Nature and Causes of the Wealth of Nations*. New York: The Modern Library, 1937; orig. 1776.

SMITH, DOUGLAS A. "Police Response to Interpersonal Violence: Defining the Parameters of Legal Control." *Social Forces*. Vol. 65, No. 3 (March 1987):767–82.

SMITH, DOUGLAS A., and PATRICK R. GARTIN. "Specifying Specific Deterrence: The Influence of Arrest on Future Criminal Activity." *American Sociological Review*. Vol. 54, No. 1 (February 1989):94–105.

SMITH, DOUGLAS A., and CHRISTY A. VISHER. "Street-Level Justice: Situational Determinants of Police Arrest Decisions." *Social Problems*. Vol. 29, No. 2 (December 1981):167–77.

SMITH, ROBERT B. "Health Care Reform Now." *Society*. Vol. 30, No. 3 (March-April 1993):56–65.

SMITH, ROBERT ELLIS. *Privacy: How to Protect What's Left of It*. Garden City, N.Y.: Anchor/Doubleday, 1979.

SMITH, TOM W. Research results reported in "Anti-Semitism Decreases But Persists." *Society*. Vol. 33, No. 3 (March/April 1996):2.

SMITH-LOVIN, LYNN, and CHARLES BRODY. "Interruptions in Group Discussions: The Effects of Gender and Group Composition." *American Journal of Sociology*. Vol. 54, No. 3 (June 1989):424–35.

SMOLOWE, JILL. "A Heavenly Host in Georgia." *Time*. Vol. 141, No. 3 (January 18, 1993):55.

———. "When Violence Hits Home." *Time*. Vol. 144, No. 1 (July 4, 1994):18–25.

SNELL, MARILYN BERLIN. "The Purge of Nurture." *New Perspectives Quarterly*. Vol. 7, No. 1 (Winter 1990):1–2.

SNOW, DAVID A., E. BURKE ROCHFORD, JR., STEVEN K. WORDEN, and ROBERT D. BENFORD. "Frame Alignment Processes, Micromobilization, and Movement Participation." *American Sociological Review*. Vol. 51, No. 4 (August 1986):464–81.

SNOW, DAVID A., LOUIS A. ZURCHER, JR., and SHELDON EKLAND-OLSON. "Social Networks and Social Movements: A Macrostructural Approach to Differential Recruitment." *American Sociological Review*. Vol. 45, No. 5 (October 1980):787–801.

SNOWMAN, DANIEL. *Britain and America: An Interpretation of Their Culture 1945–1975*. New York: Harper Torchbooks, 1977.

SOUTH, SCOTT J., and STEVEN F. MESSNER. "Structural Determinants of Intergroup Association: Interracial Marriage and Crime." *American Journal of Sociology*. Vol. 91, No. 6 (May 1986):1409–30.

SOWELL, THOMAS. *Ethnic America*. New York: Basic Books, 1981.

———. *Race and Culture*. New York: Basic Books, 1994.

———. "Ethnicity and IQ." In Steven Fraser, ed., *The Bell Curve Wars: Race, Intelligence and the Future of America*. New York: Basic Books, 1995:70–79.

SOYINKA, WOLE. "Africa's Culture Producers." *Society*. Vol. 28, No. 2 (January-February 1991):32–40.

SPATES, JAMES L. "Sociological Overview." In Alan Milberg, ed., *Street Games*. New York: McGraw-Hill, 1976a:286–90.

———. "Counterculture and Dominant Culture Values: A Cross-National Analysis of the Underground Press and Dominant Culture Magazines." *American Sociological Review*. Vol. 41, No. 5 (October 1976b):868–83.

———. "The Sociology of Values." In Ralph Turner, ed., *Annual Review of Sociology*. Vol. 9. Palo Alto, Calif.: Annual Reviews, 1983:27–49.

SPATES, JAMES L., and JOHN J. MACIONIS. *The Sociology of Cities*. 2d ed. Belmont, Calif.: Wadsworth, 1987.

SPATES, JAMES L., and H. WESLEY PERKINS. "American and English Student Values." *Comparative Social Research*. Vol. 5. Greenwich, Conn.: JAI Press, 1982:245–68.

SPECTOR, LEONARD S. "Nuclear Proliferation Today." In William M. Evan and Stephen Hilgartner, eds., *The Arms Race and Nuclear War*. Englewood Cliffs, N.J.: Prentice Hall, 1988:25–29.

SPEER, JAMES A. "The New Christian Right and Its Parent Company: A Study in Political Contrasts." In David G. Bromley and Anson Shupe, eds., *New Christian Politics*. Macon, Ga.: Mercer University Press, 1984:19–40.

SPEER, TIBBETT L. "Are College Costs Cutting Enrollment?" *American Demographics*. Vol. 16, No. 11 (November 1994):9–10.

———. "Digging Into the Underground Economy." *American Demographics*. Vol. 17, No. 2 (February 1995):15–16.

SPENCER, MARTIN E. "Multiculturalism, 'Political Correctness,' and the Politics of Identity." *Sociological Forum*. Vol. 9, No. 4 (December 1994):547-67.

SPENDER, DALE. *Man Made Language*. London: Routledge & Kegan Paul, 1980.

SPITZER, STEVEN. "Toward a Marxian Theory of Deviance." In Delos H. Kelly, ed., *Criminal Behavior: Readings in Criminology*. New York: St. Martin's Press, 1980:175-91.

STACEY, JUDITH. *Patriarchy and Socialist Revolution in China*. Berkeley: University of California Press, 1983.

———. *Brave New Families: Stories of Domestic Upheaval in Late Twentieth-Century America*. New York: Basic Books, 1990.

———. "Good Riddance to 'The Family': A Response to David Popenoe." *Journal of Marriage and the Family*. Vol. 55, No. 3 (August 1993):545-47.

STACK, CAROL B. *All Our Kin: Strategies for Survival in a Black Community*. New York: Harper & Row, 1975.

STAHURA, JOHN M. "Suburban Development, Black Suburbanization and the Black Civil Rights Movement Since World War II." *American Sociological Review*. Vol. 51, No. 1 (February 1986):131-44.

STANLEY, LIZ, ED. *Feminist Praxis: Research, Theory, and Epistemology in Feminist Sociology*. London: Routledge & Kegan Paul, 1990.

STANLEY, LIZ, and SUE WISE. *Breaking Out: Feminist Consciousness and Feminist Research*. London: Routledge & Kegan Paul, 1983.

STAPLES, ROBERT, and ALFREDO MIRANDE. "Racial and Cultural Variations Among American Families: A Decennial Review of the Literature on Minority Families." *Journal of Marriage and the Family*. Vol. 42, No. 4 (August 1980):157-72.

STARK, RODNEY. *Sociology*. Belmont, Calif.: Wadsworth, 1985.

STARK, RODNEY, and WILLIAM SIMS BAINBRIDGE. "Of Churches, Sects, and Cults: Preliminary Concepts for a Theory of Religious Movements." *Journal for the Scientific Study of Religion*. Vol. 18, No. 2 (June 1979):117-31.

———. "Secularization and Cult Formation in the Jazz Age." *Journal for the Scientific Study of Religion*. Vol. 20, No. 4 (December 1981):360-73.

STARK, RODNEY, and CHARLES Y. GLOCK. *American Piety: The Nature of Religious Commitment*. Berkeley: University of California Press, 1968.

STARR, PAUL. *The Social Transformation of American Medicine*. New York: Basic Books, 1982.

Statistics of Income Bulletin. Vol. 11, No. 3 (Winter 1991-92).

STAVRIANOS, L. S. *A Global History: The Human Heritage*. 3d ed. Englewood Cliffs, N.J.: Prentice Hall, 1983.

STEELE, SHELBY. *The Content of Our Character: A New Vision of Race in America*. New York: St. Martin's Press, 1990.

STEIN, MAURICE R. *The Eclipse of Community: An Interpretation of American Studies*. Princeton, N.J.: Princeton University Press, 1972.

STEPHENS, JOHN D. *The Transition From Capitalism to Socialism*. Urbana: University of Illinois Press, 1986.

STERNLIEB, GEORGE, and JAMES W. HUGHES. "The Uncertain Future of the Central City." *Urban Affairs Quarterly*. Vol. 18, No. 4 (June 1983):455-72.

STEVENS, GILLIAN, and GRAY SWICEGOOD. "The Linguistic Context of Ethnic Endogamy." *American Sociological Review*. Vol. 52, No. 1 (February 1987):73-82.

STODDARD, SANDOL. *The Hospice Movement: A Better Way to Care for the Dying*. Briarcliff Manor, N.Y.: Stein and Day, 1978.

STONE, LAWRENCE. *The Family, Sex and Marriage in England 1500-1800*. New York: Harper & Row, 1977.

STONE, ROBYN, GAIL LEE CAFFERATA, and JUDITH SANGL. *Caregivers of the Frail Elderly: A National Profile*. Washington, D.C.: U.S. Department of Health and Human Services, 1987.

STOUFFER, SAMUEL A., ET AL. *The American Soldier: Adjustment During Army Life*. Princeton, N.J.: Princeton University Press, 1949.

STRAUS, MURRAY A., and RICHARD J. GELLES. "Societal Change and Change in Family Violence From 1975 to 1985 as Revealed by Two National Surveys." *Journal of Marriage and the Family*. Vol. 48, No. 4 (August 1986):465-79.

STREIB, GORDON F. "Are the Aged a Minority Group?" In Bernice L. Neugarten, ed., *Middle Age and Aging: A Reader in Social Psychology*. Chicago: University of Chicago Press, 1968:35-46.

STRIEGEL-MOORE, RUTH, LISA R. SILBERSTEIN, and JUDITH RODIN. "Toward an Understanding of Risk Factors for Bulimia." *American Psychologist*. Vol. 41, No. 3 (March 1986):246-63.

Student CHIP Social Survey Software. Data sets by Bruner & Macionis. Hanover, N.H.: Zeta Data. © 1992 by James A. Davis.

SUDNOW, DAVID N. *Passing On: The Social Organization of Dying*. Englewood Cliffs, N.J.: Prentice Hall, 1967.

SUMNER, WILLIAM GRAHAM. *Folkways*. New York: Dover, 1959; orig. 1906.

SUNG, BETTY LEE. *Mountains of Gold: The Story of the Chinese in America*. New York: Macmillan, 1967.

SUTHERLAND, EDWIN H. "White Collar Criminality." *American Sociological Review*. Vol. 5, No. 1 (February 1940):1-12.

SUTHERLAND, EDWIN H., and DONALD R. CRESSEY. *Criminology*. 10th ed. Philadelphia: J.B. Lippincott, 1978.

SWARTZ, STEVE. "Why Michael Milken Stands to Qualify for Guinness Book." *Wall Street Journal*. Vol. LXX, No. 117 (March 31, 1989):1, 4.

SYZMANSKI, ALBERT. *Class Structure: A Critical Perspective*. New York: Praeger, 1983.

SZASZ, THOMAS S. *The Manufacturer of Madness: A Comparative Study of the Inquisition and the Mental Health Movement*. New York: Dell, 1961.

———. *The Myth of Mental Illness: Foundations of a Theory of Personal Conduct*. New York: Harper & Row, 1970; orig. 1961.

———. "Mental Illness Is Still a Myth." *Society*. Vol. 31, No. 4 (May-June 1994):34-39.

———. "Idleness and Lawlessness in the Therapeutic State." *Society*. Vol. 32, No. 4 (May/June 1995):30-35.

TAEUBER, KARL, and ALMA TAEUBER. *Negroes in Cities*. Chicago: Aldine, 1965.

TAJFEL, HENRI. "Social Psychology of Intergroup Relations." *Annual Review of Psychology*. Palo Alto, Calif.: Annual Reviews, 1982:1-39.

TANNEN, DEBORAH. *You Just Don't Understand Me: Women and Men in Conversation*. New York: Wm. Morrow, 1990.

———. *Talking from 9 to 5: How Women's and Men's Conversational Styles Affect Who Gets Heard, Who Gets Credit, and What Gets Done at Work*. New York: Wm. Morrow, 1994.

TANNENBAUM, FRANK. *Slave and Citizen: The Negro in the Americas*. New York: Vintage Books, 1946.

TARROW, SIDNEY. *Social Movements, Collective Action and Politics*. New York: Cambridge University Press, 1994.

TAVRIS, CAROL, and SUSAN SADD. *The Redbook Report on Female Sexuality*. New York: Delacorte Press, 1977.

TAYLOR, JOHN. "Don't Blame Me: The New Culture of Victimization." *New York Magazine* (June 3, 1991):26-34.

TERKEL, STUDS. *Working*. New York: Pantheon Books, 1974:1-2, 57-59, 65, 66, 69, 221-22. Copyright © 1974 by Pantheon Books, a division of Random House, Inc.

TERRY, DON. "In Crackdown on Bias, A New Tool." *New York Times* (June 12, 1993):8.

THEEN, ROLF H. W. "Party and Bureaucracy." In Erik P. Hoffmann and Robbin F. Laird, eds., *The Soviet Polity in the Modern Era*. New York: Aldine, 1984:131-65.

THEILMANN, JOHN, and ALLEN WILHITE. "Congressional Turnover: Negating the Incumbent Advantage." *Social Science Quarterly*. Vol. 76, No. 3 (September 1995):594-606.

THOMAS, EDWARD J. *The Life of Buddha as Legend and History*. London: Routledge & Kegan Paul, 1975.

THOMAS, PIRI. *Down These Mean Streets*. New York: Signet, 1967.

THOMAS, W. I. "The Relation of Research to the Social Process." In Morris Janowitz, ed., *W. I. Thomas on Social Organization and Social Personality*. Chicago: University of Chicago Press, 1966:289-305; orig. 1931.

THOMPSON, LARRY. "The Breast Cancer Gene: A Woman's Dilemma." *Time*. Vol. 143, No. 3 (January 17, 1994):52.

———. "Fertility With Less Fuss." *Time*. Vol. 144, No. 20 (November 14, 1994):79.

THORNBERRY, TERRANCE, and MARGARET FARNSWORTH. "Social Correlates of Criminal Involvement: Further Evidence on the Relationship Between Social Status and Criminal Behavior." *American Sociological Review*. Vol 47, No. 4 (August 1982):505-18.

THORNE, BARRIE, CHERIS KRAMARAE, and NANCY HENLEY, EDS. *Language, Gender and Society*. Rowley, Mass.: Newbury House, 1983.

686 References

THORNTON, ARLAND. "Changing Attitudes Toward Separation and Divorce: Causes and Consequences." *American Journal of Sociology*. Vol. 90, No. 4 (January 1985):856–72.

THUROW, LESTER C. "A Surge in Inequality." *Scientific American*. Vol. 256, No. 5 (May 1987):30–37.

TIGER, LIONEL, and JOSEPH SHEPHER. *Women in the Kibbutz*. New York: Harcourt Brace Jovanovich, 1975.

TILLY, CHARLES. *From Mobilization to Revolution*. Reading, Mass.: Addison-Wesley, 1978.

——. "Does Modernization Breed Revolution?" In Jack A. Goldstone, ed., *Revolutions: Theoretical, Comparative, and Historical Studies*. New York: Harcourt Brace Jovanovich, 1986:47–57.

TITTLE, CHARLES R., and WAYNE J. VILLEMEZ. "Social Class and Criminality." *Social Forces*. Vol. 56, No. 22 (December 1977):474–502.

TITTLE, CHARLES R., WAYNE J. VILLEMEZ, and DOUGLAS A. SMITH. "The Myth of Social Class and Criminality: An Empirical Assessment of the Empirical Evidence." *American Sociological Review*. Vol. 43, No. 5 (October 1978):643–56.

TOBIN, GARY. "Suburbanization and the Development of Motor Transportation: Transportation Technology and the Suburbanization Process." In Barry Schwartz, ed., *The Changing Face of the Suburbs*. Chicago: University of Chicago Press, 1976.

TOCH, THOMAS. "The Exodus." *U.S. News & World Report*. Vol. 111, No. 24 (December 9, 1991):68–77.

TOCQUEVILLE, ALEXIS DE. *The Old Regime and the French Revolution*. Stuart Gilbert, trans. Garden City, N.Y.: Anchor/Doubleday Books, 1955; orig. 1856.

TOENNIES, FERDINAND. *Community and Society (Gemeinschaft und Gesellschaft)*. New York: Harper & Row, 1963; orig. 1887.

TOFANI, LORETTA. "AIDS Ravages a Continent, and Sweeps a Family." *Philadelphia Inquirer* (March 24, 1991):1, 15–A.

TOFFLER, ALVIN, and HEIDI TOFFLER. *War and Anti-war: Survival at the Dawn of the 21st Century*. Boston: Little, Brown, 1993.

TOLSON, JAY. "The Trouble With Elites." *The Wilson Quarterly*. Vol. XIX, No. 1 (Winter 1995):6–8.

TOOMEY, BEVERLY, RICHARD FIRST, and JOHN RIFE. Research described in "Number of Rural Homeless Greater Than Expected." Ohio State *Quest* (Autumn 1990):2.

TREAS, JUDITH. "Socialist Organization and Economic Development in China: Latent Consequences for the Aged." *The Gerontologist*. Vol. 19, No. 1 (February 1979):34–43.

——. "Older Americans in the 1990s and Beyond." *Population Bulletin*. Vol. 50, No. 2 (May 1995). Washington, D.C.: Population Reference Bureau.

TREIMAN, DONALD J. "Industrialization and Social Stratification." In Edward O. Laumann, ed., *Social Stratification: Research and Theory for the 1970s*. Indianapolis, Ind.: Bobbs-Merrill, 1970.

TROELTSCH, ERNST. *The Social Teaching of the Christian Churches*. New York: Macmillan, 1931.

TROIDEN, RICHARD R. *Gay and Lesbian Identity: A Sociological Analysis*. Dix Hills, N.Y.: General Hall, 1988.

TUMIN, MELVIN M. "Some Principles of Stratification: A Critical Analysis." *American Sociological Review*. Vol. 18, No. 4 (August 1953):387–94.

——. *Social Stratification: The Forms and Functions of Inequality*. 2d ed. Englewood Cliffs, N.J.: Prentice Hall, 1985.

TURNER, RALPH H., and LEWIS M. KILLIAN. *Collective Behavior*. 2d ed. Englewood Cliffs, N.J.: Prentice Hall, 1972; 3d ed., 1987; 4th ed., 1993.

TYGIEL, JULES. *Baseball's Great Experiment: Jackie Robinson and His Legacy*. New York: Oxford University Press, 1983.

TYLER, S. LYMAN. *A History of Indian Policy*. Washington, D.C.: United States Department of the Interior, Bureau of Indian Affairs, 1973.

TYREE, ANDREA, MOSHE SEMYONOV, and ROBERT W. HODGE. "Gaps and Glissandos: Inequality, Economic Development, and Social Mobility in 24 Countries." *American Sociological Review*. Vol. 44, No. 3 (June 1979):410–24.

UCHITELLE, LOUIS. "But Just Who is That Fairy Godmother?" *New York Times* (September 29, 1991): Section 4, p. 1.

UNITED NATIONS DEVELOPMENT PROGRAMME. *Human Development Report 1990*. New York: Oxford University Press, 1990.

——. *Human Development Report 1991*. New York: Oxford University Press, 1991.

——. *Human Development Report 1993*. New York: Oxford University Press, 1993.

——. *Human Development Report 1994*. New York: Oxford University Press, 1994.

——. *Human Development Report 1995*. New York: Oxford University Press, 1995.

UNIVERSITY OF AKRON RESEARCH CENTER. *National Survey of Religion and Politics 1992*. Akron, Ohio: University of Akron Research Center, 1993.

UNNEVER, JAMES D., CHARLES E. FRAZIER, and JOHN C. HENRETTA. "Race Differences in Criminal Sentencing." *The Sociological Quarterly*. Vol. 21, No. 2 (Spring 1980):197–205.

UNRUH, JOHN D., JR. *The Plains Across*. Urbana: University of Illinois Press, 1979.

U.S. BUREAU OF THE CENSUS. *Statistical Abstract of the United States 1970*. 90th ed. Washington, D.C.: U.S. Government Printing Office, 1970.

——. Press release on homeless count (CB91–117). Washington, D.C.: U.S. Government Printing Office, 1991.

——. *Statistical Abstract of the United States: 1992*. 112th ed. Washington, D.C.: U.S. Government Printing Office, 1992.

——. *Money Income of Households, Families, and Persons in the United States: 1992*. Current Population Reports, Series P-60, No. 184. Washington, D.C.: U.S. Government Printing Office, 1993.

——. *Poverty in the United States: 1992*. Current Population Reports, Series P-60, No. 185. Washington, D.C.: U.S. Government Printing Office, 1993.

——. *Statistical Abstract of the United States: 1993*. 113th ed. Washington, D.C.: U.S. Government Printing Office, 1993.

——. *Educational Attainment in the United States: March 1993 and 1992*. Current Population Reports, Series P-20, No. 476. Washington, D.C.: U.S. Government Printing Office, 1994.

——. *School Enrollment—Social and Economic Characteristics of Students: October 1993*. Current Population Reports, Series P-20, No. 479. Washington, D.C.: U.S. Government Printing Office, 1994.

——. *Statistical Abstract of the United States: 1994*. 114th ed. Washington, D.C.: U.S. Government Printing Office, 1994.

——. *Asset Ownership of Households: 1993*. Current Population Reports, Series P-70, No. 47. Washington, D.C.: U.S. Government Printing Office, 1995.

——. *Current Population Reports*. Series P-60, No. 188. Washington, D.C.: U.S. Government Printing Office, 1995.

——. *Household and Family Characteristics: March 1994*. Current Population Reports, Series P-20, No. 483, Washington, D.C.: U.S. Government Printing Office, 1995.

——. *Income, Poverty, and Valuation of Noncash Benefits: 1993*. Current Population Reports, Series P-60, No. 188. Washington, D.C.: U.S. Government Printing Office, 1995.

——. *Statistical Abstract of the United States: 1995*. 115th ed. Washington, D.C.: U.S. Government Printing Office, 1995.

——. Prepublication data on income and wealth provided by the Census Bureau, 1996.

——. Press release on women-owned businesses, 1996.

——. Response to telephone query, 1996.

U.S. BUREAU OF JUSTICE STATISTICS. *Sourcebook of Criminal Justice Statistics 1990*. Timothy J. Flanagan and Kathleen Maguire, eds. Washington, D.C.: U.S. Government Printing Office, 1991.

——. *Compendium of Federal Justice Statistics, 1989*. Washington D.C.: U.S. Government Printing Office, 1992.

——. *Violence Against Women*. Washington, D.C.: U.S. Government Printing Office, 1994.

——. *National Crime Victimization Survey, 1992–1993*. Washington, D.C.: U.S. Government Printing Office, 1995.

U.S. BUREAU OF LABOR STATISTICS. *Employment and Earnings*. Vol. 41, No. 1 (January). Washington, D.C.: U.S. Government Printing Office, 1994.

——. *Employment and Earnings*. Vol. 42, No. 1 (January). Washington, D.C.: U.S. Government Printing Office, 1995.

——. Unpublished data on U.S. labor force, 1995.

——. *Employment and Earnings.* Vol. 43, No. 1 (January 1996).

——. Response to telephone query, 1996.

U.S. CENTERS FOR DISEASE CONTROL AND PREVENTION. Response to telephone query, 1994.

——. *HIV/AIDS Surveillance Report.* Vol. 7, No. 1. Rockville, Md.: CDC National AIDS Clearinghouse, 1995.

U.S. DEPARTMENT OF AGRICULTURE. Agricultural Research Service. Family Economics Research Group. *Expenditures on a Child by Families, 1992.* Hyattsville, Md.: The Group, 1993.

U.S. DEPARTMENT OF JUSTICE. Press release, June 22, 1994.

USEEM, BERT. "Disorganization and the New Mexico Prison Riot of 1980." *American Sociological Review.* Vol. 50, No. 5 (October 1985):677–88.

USEEM, MICHAEL. "Corporations and the Corporate Elite." In Alex Inkeles et al., eds., *Annual Review of Sociology.* Vol. 6. Palo Alto, Cal.: Annual Reviews, 1980:41–77.

USEEM, MICHAEL, and JEROME KARABEL. "Pathways to Corporate Management." *American Sociological Review.* Vol. 51, No. 2 (April 1986):184–200.

U.S. EQUAL EMPLOYMENT OPPORTUNITY COMMISSION. *Job Patterns for Minorities and Women in Private Industry 1994.* Washington, D.C.: The Commission, 1995.

——. Response to personal query, 1996.

U.S. FEDERAL BUREAU OF INVESTIGATION. *Crime in the United States 1993.* Washington, D.C.: U.S. Government Printing Office, 1994.

——. *Crime in the United States 1994.* Washington, D.C.: U.S. Government Printing Office, 1995.

U.S. FEDERAL ELECTION COMMISSION. *1994 Congressional Funding Sets New Record.* Washington, D.C.: The Commission, 1995.

U.S. HOUSE OF REPRESENTATIVES. "Street Children: A Global Disgrace." Hearing on November 7, 1991. Washington, D.C.: U.S. Government Printing Office, 1992.

U.S. IMMIGRATION AND NATURALIZATION SERVICE. *Statistical Yearbook.* Washington, D.C.: U.S. Government Printing Office, 1995.

U.S. INTERNAL REVENUE SERVICE. *Statistics of Income Bulletin* (Spring 1993).

U.S. NATIONAL CENTER FOR HEALTH STATISTICS. *Vital Statistics of the United States, 1988, Vol. 1, Natality.* Washington, D.C.: U.S. Government Printing Office, 1990.

——. *Current Estimates From the National Health Interview Survey United States, 1993.* Vital and Health Statistics. Series 10, No. 190. Hyattsville, Md.: The Center, 1994.

——. "Annual Summary of Births, Marriages, Divorces, and Deaths: United States, 1994." *Monthly Vital Statistics Report.* Vol. 43, No. 13 (October 23, 1995). Hyattsville, Md.: The Center, 1995.

——. *Current Estimates From the National Health Interview Survey 1994.* Hyattsville, Md.: The Center, 1995.

VAN BIEMA, DAVID. "Parents Who Kill." *Time.* Vol. 144, No. 20 (November 14, 1994):50–51.

VAN DEN HAAG, ERNEST, and JOHN P. CONRAD. *The Death Penalty: A Debate.* New York: Plenum Press, 1983.

VAUGHAN, MARY KAY. "Multinational Corporations: The World as a Company Town." In Ahamed Idris-Soven et al., eds., *The World as a Company Town: Multinational Corporations and Social Change.* The Hague: Mouton Publishers, 1978:15–35.

VAYDA, EUGENE, and RAISA B. DEBER. "The Canadian Health Care System: An Overview." *Social Science and Medicine.* Vol. 18, No. 3 (1984):191–97.

VEBLEN, THORSTEIN. *The Theory of the Leisure Class.* New York: The New American Library, 1953; orig. 1899.

VEUM, JONATHAN R. "Accounting for Income Mobility Changes in the United States." *Social Science Quarterly.* Vol. 73, No. 4 (December 1992):773–85.

VIGUERIE, RICHARD A. *The New Right: We're Ready to Lead.* Falls Church, Va.: The Viguerie Company, 1981.

VINES, GAIL. "Whose Baby Is It Anyway?" *New Scientist.* No. 1515 (July 3, 1986):26–27.

VINOVSKIS, MARIS A. "Have Social Historians Lost the Civil War? Some Preliminary Demographic Speculations." *Journal of American History.* Vol. 76, No. 1 (June 1989):34–58.

VOGEL, EZRA F. *The Four Little Dragons: The Spread of Industrialization in East Asia.* Cambridge, Mass.: Harvard University Press, 1991.

VOGEL, LISE. *Marxism and the Oppression of Women: Toward a Unitary Theory.* New Brunswick, N.J.: Rutgers University Press, 1983.

VOLD, GEORGE B., and THOMAS J. BERNARD. *Theoretical Criminology.* 3d ed. New York: Oxford University Press, 1986.

VON HIRSH, ANDREW. *Past or Future Crimes: Deservedness and Dangerousness in the Sentencing of Criminals.* New Brunswick, N.J.: Rutgers University Press, 1986.

VONNEGUT, KURT, JR. "Harrison Bergeron." In *Welcome to the Monkey House.* New York: Delacorte Press/Seymour Lawrence, 1968:7–13; orig. 1961.

WAITE, LINDA J., GUS W. HAGGSTROM, and DAVID I. KANOUSE. "The Consequences of Parenthood for the Marital Stability of Young Adults." *American Sociological Review.* Vol. 50, No. 6 (December 1985):850–57.

WALDER, ANDREW G. "Career Mobility and the Communist Political Order." *American Sociological Review.* Vol. 60, No. 3 (June 1995):309–28.

WALDMAN, STEVEN. "Deadbeat Dads." *Newsweek* (May 4, 1992):46–52.

WALL, THOMAS F. *Medical Ethics: Basic Moral Issues.* Washington, D.C.: University Press of America, 1980.

WALLER, DOUGLAS. "Onward Cyber Soldiers." *Time.* Vol. 146, No. 8 (August 21, 1995):38–44.

WALLERSTEIN, IMMANUEL. *The Modern World-System: Capitalist Agriculture and the Origins of the European World-Economy in the Sixteenth Century.* New York: Academic Press, 1974.

——. *The Capitalist World-Economy.* New York: Cambridge University Press, 1979.

——. "Crises: The World Economy, the Movements, and the Ideologies." In Albert Bergesen, ed., *Crises in the World-System.* Beverly Hills, Calif.: Sage, 1983:21–36.

——. *The Politics of the World Economy: The States, the Movements, and the Civilizations.* Cambridge: Cambridge University Press, 1984.

WALLERSTEIN, JUDITH S., and SANDRA BLAKESLEE. *Second Chances: Men, Women, and Children a Decade After Divorce.* New York: Ticknor & Fields, 1989.

WALTERS, LAUREL SHAPER. "World Educators Compare Notes." *The Christian Science Monitor: Global Report* (September 7, 1994):8.

WALTON, JOHN, and CHARLES RAGIN. "Global and National Sources of Political Protest: Third World Responses to the Debt Crisis." *American Sociological Review.* Vol. 55, No. 6 (December 1990):876–90.

WARNER, R. STEPHEN. "Work in Progress Toward a New Paradigm for the Sociological Study of Religion in the United States." *American Journal of Sociology.* Vol. 98, No. 5 (March 1993):1044–93.

WARNER, SAM BASS, JR. *Streetcar Suburbs.* Cambridge, Mass.: Harvard University and MIT Presses, 1962.

WARNER, W. LLOYD, and J. O. LOW. *The Social System of the Modern Factory.* Yankee City Series, Vol. 4. New Haven, Conn.: Yale University Press, 1947.

WARNER, W. LLOYD, and PAUL S. LUNT. *The Social Life of a Modern Community.* New Haven, Conn.: Yale University Press, 1941.

WATERS, MELISSA S., WILL CARRINGTON HEATH, and JOHN KEITH WATSON. "A Positive Model of the Determination of Religious Affiliation." *Social Science Quarterly.* Vol. 76, No. 1 (March 1995):105–23.

WATSON, JOHN B. *Behaviorism.* Rev. ed. New York: Norton, 1930.

WAXMAN, CHAIM I. *The Stigma of Poverty: A Critique of Poverty Theories and Policies.* 2d ed. New York: Pergamon Press, 1983.

WEBER, ADNA FERRIN. *The Growth of Cities.* New York: Columbia University Press, 1963; orig. 1899.

WEBER, MAX. *The Protestant Ethic and the Spirit of Capitalism.* New York: Charles Scribner's Sons, 1958; orig. 1904–5.

——. "Science as a Vocation." In H. H. Gerth and C. Wright Mills, *From Max Weber: Essays in Sociology.* New York: Oxford University Press, 1958:129–56; orig. 1918.

——. *Economy and Society.* G. Roth and C. Wittich, eds. Berkeley: University of California Press, 1978.

WEBSTER, PAMELA S., TERRI ORBUCH, and JAMES S. HOUSE. "Effects of Childhood Family Background on Adult Marital Quality and Perceived Stability." *American Journal of Sociology.* Vol. 101, No. 2 (September 1995):404–32.

WEEKS, JOHN R. "The Demography of Islamic Nations." *Population Bulletin.* Vol. 43, No. 4 (December 1988). Washington, D.C.: Population Reference Bureau.

WEICHER, JOHN C. "Getting Richer (At Different Rates)." *Wall Street Journal* (June 14, 1995):A18.

WEIDENBAUM, MURRAY. "The Evolving Corporate Board." *Society*. Vol. 32, No. 3 (March/April 1995):9–20.

WEINBERG, GEORGE. *Society and the Healthy Homosexual*. Garden City, N.Y.: Anchor Books, 1973.

WEINRICH, JAMES D. *Sexual Landscapes: Why We Are What We Are, Why We Love Whom We Love*. New York: Charles Scribner's Sons, 1987.

WEISBURD, DAVID, STANTON WHEELER, ELIN WARING, and NANCY BODE. *Crimes of the Middle Class: White Collar Defenders in the Courts*. New Haven, Conn.: Yale University Press, 1991.

WEISNER, THOMAS S., and BERNICE T. EIDUSON. "The Children of the '60s as Parents." *Psychology Today* (January 1986):60–66.

WEITZMAN, LENORE J. *The Divorce Revolution: The Unexpected Social and Economic Consequences for Women and Children in America*. New York: Free Press, 1985.

WEITZMAN, LENORE J., DEBORAH EIFLER, ELIZABETH HODAKA, and CATHERINE ROSS. "Sex-Role Socialization in Picture Books for Preschool Children." *American Journal of Sociology*. Vol. 77, No. 6 (May 1972):1125–50.

WELLER, JACK M., and E. L. QUARANTELLI. "Neglected Characteristics of Collective Behavior." *American Journal of Sociology*. Vol. 79, No. 3 (November 1973):665–85.

WELLFORD, CHARLES. "Labeling Theory and Criminology: An Assessment." In Delos H. Kelly, ed., *Criminal Behavior: Readings in Criminology*. New York: St. Martin's Press, 1980:234–47.

WELLMAN, BARRY. "The Community Question: Intimate Networks of East Yorkers." *American Journal of Sociology*. Vol. 84, No. 5 (March 1979):1201–31.

WENKE, ROBERT J. *Patterns of Prehistory*. New York: Oxford University Press, 1980.

WERMAN, JILL. "Who Makes What?" *Working Woman* (January 1989):72–76, 80.

WERTHEIMER, BARBARA MAYER. "The Factory Bell." In Linda K. Kerber and Jane De Hart Mathews, eds., *Women's America: Refocusing the Past*. New York: Oxford University Press, 1982:130–40.

WESOLOWSKI, WLODZIMIERZ. "Transition From Authoritarianism to Democracy." *Social Research*. Vol. 57, No. 2 (Summer 1990):435–61.

WESTERN, BRUCE. "Postwar Unionization in Eighteen Advanced Capitalist Countries." *American Sociological Review*. Vol. 58, No. 2 (April 1993):266–82.

———. "A Comparative Study of Working-Class Disorganization: Union Decline in Eighteen Advanced Capitalist Countries." *American Sociological Review*. Vol. 60, No. 2 (April 1995):179–201.

WESTERN, MARK, and ERIK OLIN WRIGHT. "The Permeability of Class Boundaries to Intergenerational Mobility Among Men in the United States, Canada, Norway and Sweden." *American Sociological Review*. Vol. 59, No. 4 (August 1994):606–29.

WHALEN, JACK, and RICHARD FLACKS. *Beyond the Barricades: The Sixties Generation Grows Up*. Philadelphia: Temple University Press, 1989.

WHEELIS, ALLEN. *The Quest for Identity*. New York: Norton, 1958.

WHITAKER, MARK. "Ten Ways to Fight Terrorism." *Newsweek* (July 1, 1985):26–29.

WHITE, RALPH, and RONALD LIPPITT. "Leader Behavior and Member Reaction in Three 'Social Climates.'" In Dorwin Cartwright and Alvin Zander, eds., *Group Dynamics*. Evanston, Ill.: Row, Peterson, 1953:586–611.

WHITE, WALTER. *Rope and Faggot*. New York: Arno Press and *New York Times*, 1969; orig. 1929.

WHITMAN, DAVID. "Shattering Myths About the Homeless." *U.S. News & World Report* (March 20, 1989):26, 28.

WHORF, BENJAMIN LEE. "The Relation of Habitual Thought and Behavior to Language." In *Language, Thought, and Reality*. Cambridge, Mass.: The Technology Press of MIT/New York: Wiley, 1956:134–59; orig. 1941.

WHYTE, WILLIAM FOOTE. *Street Corner Society*. 3d ed. Chicago: University of Chicago Press, 1981; orig. 1943.

WHYTE, WILLIAM H., JR. *The Organization Man*. Garden City, N.Y.: Anchor Books, 1957.

WIARDA, HOWARD J. "Ethnocentrism and Third World Development." *Society*. Vol. 24, No. 6 (September-October 1987):55–64.

WIATROWSKI, MICHAEL A., DAVID B. GRISWOLD, and MARY K. ROBERTS. "Social Control Theory and Delinquency." *American Sociological Review*. Vol. 46, No. 5 (October 1981):525–41.

WILES, P. J. D. *Economic Institutions Compared*. New York: Halsted Press, 1977.

WILLIAMS, RHYS H., and N. J. DEMERATH, III. "Religion and Political Process in an American City." *American Sociological Review*. Vol. 56, No. 4 (August 1991):417–31.

WILLIAMS, ROBIN M., JR. *American Society: A Sociological Interpretation*. 3d ed. New York: Alfred A. Knopf, 1970.

WILLIAMSON, JEFFREY G., and PETER H. LINDERT. *American Inequality: A Macroeconomic History*. New York: Academic Press, 1980.

WILSON, BRYAN. *Religion in Sociological Perspective*. New York: Oxford University Press, 1982.

WILSON, EDWARD O. *Sociobiology: The New Synthesis*. Cambridge, Mass.: Belknap Press of the Harvard University Press, 1975.

———. *On Human Nature*. New York: Bantam Books, 1978.

———. "Biodiversity, Prosperity, and Value." In F. Herbert Bormann and Stephen R. Kellert, eds., *Ecology, Economics, and Ethics: The Broken Circle*. New Haven, Conn.: Yale University Press, 1991:3–10.

WILSON, JAMES Q. *Bureaucracy: What Government Agencies Do and Why They Do It*. New York: Basic Books, 1991.

———. "Crime, Race, and Values." *Society*. Vol. 30, No. 1 (November-December 1992):90–93.

WILSON, JAMES Q., and RICHARD J. HERRNSTEIN. *Crime and Human Nature*. New York: Simon and Schuster, 1985.

WILSON, LOGAN. *American Academics Then and Now*. New York: Oxford University Press, 1979.

WILSON, THOMAS C. "Urbanism and Tolerance: A Test of Some Hypotheses Drawn From Wirth and Stouffer." *American Sociological Review*. Vol. 50, No. 1 (February 1985):117–23.

———. "Urbanism and Unconventionality: The Case of Sexual Behavior." *Social Science Quarterly*. Vol. 76, No. 2 (June 1995):346–63.

WILSON, WILLIAM JULIUS. *The Declining Significance of Race*. Chicago: University of Chicago Press, 1978.

———. "The Black Underclass." *The Wilson Quarterly*. Vol. 8 (Spring 1984):88–99.

———. "Studying Inner-City Social Dislocations: The Challenge of Public Agenda Research." *American Sociological Review*. Vol. 56, No. 1 (February 1991):1–14.

WINKLER, KAREN J. "Scholar Whose Ideas of Female Psychology Stir Debate Modifies Theories, Extends Studies to Young Girls." *Chronicle of Higher Education*. Vol. XXXVI, No. 36 (May 23, 1990):A6–A8.

WINN, MARIE. *Children Without Childhood*. New York: Pantheon Books, 1983.

WINNICK, LOUIS. "America's 'Model Minority'." *Commentary*. Vol. 90, No. 2 (August 1990):22–29.

WIRTH, LOUIS. "Urbanism As a Way of Life." *American Journal of Sociology*. Vol. 44, No. 1 (July 1938):1–24.

WITKIN-LANOIL, GEORGIA. *The Female Stress Syndrome: How to Recognize and Live With It*. New York: Newmarket Press, 1984.

WOLF, NAOMI. *The Beauty Myth: How Images of Beauty Are Used Against Women*. New York: William Morrow, 1990.

WOLFE, DAVID B. "Targeting the Mature Mind." *American Demographics*. Vol. 16, No. 3 (March 1994):32–36.

WOLFE, TOM. *Radical Chic*. New York: Bantam, 1970.

WOLFGANG, MARVIN E., ROBERT M. FIGLIO, and THORSTEN SELLIN. *Delinquency in a Birth Cohort*. Chicago: University of Chicago Press, 1972.

WOLFGANG, MARVIN E., TERRENCE P. THORNBERRY, and ROBERT M. FIGLIO. *From Boy to Man, From Delinquency to Crime*. Chicago: University of Chicago Press, 1987.

WOLFINGER, RAYMOND E., and STEVEN J. ROSENSTONE. *Who Votes?* New Haven, Conn.: Yale University Press, 1980.

WOLFINGER, RAYMOND E., MARTIN SHAPIRO, and FRED J. GREENSTEIN. *Dynamics of American Politics*. 2d ed. Englewood Cliffs, N.J.: Prentice Hall, 1980.

WONG, BUCK. "Need for Awareness: An Essay on Chinatown, San Francisco." In Amy Tachiki et al., eds., *Roots: An Asian American Reader*. Los Angeles: UCLA Asian American Studies Center, 1971:265–73.

WOODWARD, C. VANN. *The Strange Career of Jim Crow*. 3d rev. ed. New York: Oxford University Press, 1974.

WOODWARD, KENNETH L. "Feminism and the Churches." *Newsweek*. Vol. 13, No. 7 (February 13, 1989):58–61.

———. "Talking to God." *Newsweek*. Vol. 119, No. 1 (January 6, 1992):38–44.

———. "The Elite, and How to Avoid It." *Newsweek* (July 20, 1992):55.

WOOLEY, ORLAND W., SUSAN C. WOOLEY, and SUE R. DYRENFORTH. "Obesity and Women—II: A Neglected Feminist Topic." *Women's Studies International Quarterly*. Vol. 2 (1979):81–92.

THE WORLD BANK. *World Development Report 1991: The Challenge of Development*. New York: Oxford University Press, 1991.

———. *World Development Report 1993*. New York: Oxford University Press, 1993.

———. *World Development Report 1995: Workers in an Integrating World*. New York: Oxford University Press, 1995.

WORLD HEALTH ORGANIZATION. *Constitution of the World Health Organization*. New York: World Health Organization Interim Commission, 1946.

World Values Survey, 1990–1993. Ann Arbor, Mich.: Inter-university Consortium for Political and Social Research, 1994.

WORSLEY, PETER. "Models of the World System." In Mike Featherstone, ed., *Global Culture: Nationalism, Globalization, and Modernity*. Newbury Park, Calif.: Sage, 1990:83–95.

WREN, CHRISTOPHER S. "In Soweto-by-the-Sea, Misery Lives On as Apartheid Fades." *New York Times* (June 9, 1991):1, 7.

WRIGHT, ERIK OLIN. *Classes*. London: Verso, 1985.

WRIGHT, ERIK OLIN, ANDREW LEVINE, and ELLIOTT SOBER. *Reconstructing Marxism: Essays on Explanation and the Theory of History*. London: Verso, 1992.

WRIGHT, ERIK OLIN, and BILL MARTIN. "The Transformation of the American Class Structure, 1960–1980." *American Journal of Sociology*. Vol. 93, No. 1 (July 1987):1–29.

WRIGHT, JAMES D. "Address Unknown: Homelessness in Contemporary America." *Society*. Vol. 26, No. 6 (September-October 1989):45–53.

———. "Ten Essential Observations On Guns in America." *Society*. Vol. 32, No. 3 (March-April 1995):63–68.

WRIGHT, QUINCY. "Causes of War in the Atomic Age." In William M. Evan and Stephen Hilgartner, eds., *The Arms Race and Nuclear War*. Englewood Cliffs, N.J.: Prentice Hall, 1987:7–10.

WRIGHT, RICHARD A. *In Defense of Prisons*. Westport, Conn.: Greenwood Press, 1994.

WRIGHT, STUART A. "Social Movement Decline and Transformation: Cults in the 1980s." Paper presented to the Southwestern Social Science Association, Dallas, Texas, March 1987.

WRIGHT, STUART A., and WILLIAM V. D'ANTONIO. "The Substructure of Religion: A Further Study." *Journal for the Scientific Study of Religion*. Vol. 19, No. 3 (September 1980):292–98.

YANKELOVICH, DANIEL. "How Changes in the Economy Are Reshaping American Values." In Henry J. Aaron, Thomas E. Mann, and Timothy Taylor, eds., *Values and Public Policy*. Washington, D.C.: The Brookings Institution, 1994:20.

YATES, RONALD E. "Growing Old in Japan; They Ask Gods for a Way Out." *Philadelphia Inquirer* (August 14, 1986):3A.

YEATTS, DALE E. "Self-Managed Work Teams: Innovation in Progress." *Business and Economic Quarterly* (Fall-Winter 1991):2–6.

———. "Creating the High Performance Self-Managed Work Team: A Review of Theoretical Perspectives." Paper presented at the annual meeting of the Social Science Association, Dallas, February 1995.

YODER, JAN D., and ROBERT C. NICHOLS. "A Life Perspective: Comparison of Married and Divorced Persons." *Journal of Marriage and the Family*. Vol. 42, No. 2 (May 1980):413–19.

YOUNG, MICHAEL. "Meritocracy Revisited." *Society*. Vol. 31, No. 6 (September-October 1994):85–89.

ZANGWILL, ISRAEL. *The Melting Pot*. Macmillan, 1921; orig. 1909.

ZASLAVSKY, VICTOR. *The Neo-Stalinist State: Class, Ethnicity, and Consensus in Soviet Society*. Armonk, N.Y.: M. E. Sharpe, 1982.

ZEITLIN, IRVING M. *The Social Condition of Humanity*. New York: Oxford University Press, 1981.

ZHOU, MIN, and JOHN R. LOGAN. "Returns of Human Capital in Ethnic Enclaves: New York City's Chinatown." *American Sociological Review*. Vol. 54, No. 5 (October 1989):809–20.

ZIMBARDO, PHILIP G. "Pathology of Imprisonment." *Society*. Vol. 9 (April 1972):4–8.

ZIPP, JOHN F. "Perceived Representativeness and Voting: An Assessment of the Impact of 'Choices' vs. 'Echoes.'" *The American Political Science Review*. Vol. 79, No. 1 (March 1985):50–61.

ZIPP, JOHN F., and JOEL SMITH. "A Structural Analysis of Class Voting." *Social Forces*. Vol. 60, No. 3 (March 1982):738–59.

ZUBOFF, SHOSHANA. "New Worlds of Computer-Mediated Work." *Harvard Business Review*. Vol. 60, No. 5 (September-October 1982):142–52.

ZURCHER, LOUIS A., and DAVID A. SNOW. "Collective Behavior and Social Movements." In Morris Rosenberg and Ralph Turner, eds., *Social Psychology: Sociological Perspectives*. New York: Basic Books, 1981:447–82.

Photo Credits

Frontispiece: Paul Liebhardt

CHAPTER 1: Antonio Ruiz (Mexican, b. 1897), *The Bicycle Race*, 1938, 14 1/2" x 16 1/2", oil on canvas, Philadelphia Museum of Art, purchased by Nebinger Fund, xxviii; Robert Burke/Gamma-Liaison, Inc., 1; Paul Liebhardt, 2; Paul Liebhardt, 3; Luc Delahaye/Magnum Photo Inc., 8; Brown Brothers, 11; New York Public Library Picture Collection, 12; Bettmann, 13; © The Pierpont Morgan Library, 1992, NY, m.399, f.5v., 14 (*left*); Archive Photos, 14 (*right*); Bettmann, 15 (*left*); Brown Brothers, 15 (*right*); New York Public Library Picture Collection, 17; Marc Chagall, *I and the Village*, 1911, oil on canvas, 63 5/8 x 59 5/8 inches, The Museum of Modern Art, New York, Mrs. Simon Guggenheim Fund, 18; Marcus, Paul (1953–   ), *The Greatest Show on Earth*, oil on etched wood, H. 76 in. W. 96 in. (183.9 x 243.8cm) The Metropolitan Museum of Art, George A. Hearn Fund, 1988 (1988.53a-c), 19; Brown Brothers, 20; Fateh Al-Moudarres (Syrian), *Les Refugies*, Institute du Monde Arabe, Paris, photo © Phillipe Maillard, 21; Jacob Lawrence, American, b. 1917, *Study for the Munich Olympic Games Poster*, gouache, H. 30 3/8", W. 10 5/8", purchased with funds from P.O.N.C.H.O, courtesy of the artist and Francine Seders Gallery, Seattle, Seattle Art Museum, photo Paul Macapia, 23.

CHAPTER 2: Jonathan Green, 28; Photo by Ruben Burrell, courtesy of Hampton University, 29; Paul Gaugin, France, 1848–1903, *Where Do We Come From? What Are We? Where Are We Going?*, 1897, oil on canvas, 139.1 x 374.6 cm. (54 3/4 x 147 1/2"), Tompkins Collection, courtesy of Museum of Fine Arts, Boston, 31; John Eastcott/Yva Momatiuk/The Image Works, 32; Michael Newman/PhotoEdit, 34; Steve McCurry/Magnum Photo, Inc., 37 (*left*); Argas/Gamma-Liaison, Inc., 37 (*right*); Jeffrey Mark Dunn/Stock Boston, 39; Nubar Alexanian/Woodfin Camp & Associates, 40; Mike Greenbar/The Image Works, 42; Bob Daemmrich/Stock Boston, 44; Lou Jones/The Image Bank, 45; John Sloan (1871–1951), oil on canvas, 30 1/2 x 36 1/8 inches, signed (lower left): John Sloan painted in 1928, The Metropolitan Museum of Art, gift of Friends of John Sloan, 1928 (28.18), 48.

CHAPTER 3: *Memories of the Bitter Past*, Betty LaDuke, 1997, 60; Sylvain Grandadam/Photo Researchers, Inc., 61; Tomas Friedmann/Photo Researchers, Inc., 62; Paul Liebhardt, 63 (*top, left*); Carlos Humberto/TDC/Contact/The Stock Market, 63 (*top, middle*); Paul Liebhardt, 63 (*top, right*); Paul Liebhardt, 63 (*middle, left*); David Austen/Stock Boston, 63 (*middle, middle*); Paul Liebhardt, 63 (*middle, right*); Paul Liebhardt, 63 (*bottom, left*); Jack Fields/Photo Researchers, Inc., 63 (*bottom, right*); G. Humer/Gamma-Liaison, Inc., 64; Jasper Johns, b. 1930, *Three Flags* 1958, encaustic on canvas, 30-7/8 x 45-1/2 x 5"(78.4 x 115.6 x 12.7cm.) 50th anniv. gift Gilman Fnd, Inc, The Lauder Fnd, A. Alfred Taubman, anym. donor, pur. Col. of Whitney Mus of Amer Art NY, lic by VAGA, photo Geoffrey Clements, NY, 65; Jeff Greenberg/Picture Cube, Inc., 66 (*left*); Alex Webb/Magnum Photo, Inc., 66 (*middle*); Pedrick/The Image Works, 66 (*right*); Sabina Dowell, 67 (*left*); CLEO/Jeroboam, Inc., 67 (*middle*); David Young-Wolff/PhotoEdit, 67 (*right*); Penguin Books USA, Inc., 71; Karen Hofer/Actuality, Inc., 72; Reprinted by permission of Margaret Courtney-Clarke; © 1990, 74; Grandma Moses, *Joy Ride*, 1953. Copyright © 1991, Grandma Moses Properties Co., New York, 77; Mark Peters/SIPA Press, 82; Inge Morath/Magnum Photo, Inc., 83; Paul Kuroda/The Orange County Register, 86; Paul Liebhardt, 87; John Moss/Tony Stone Images, 88 (*top, left*); Pete Turner/The Image Bank, 88 (*top, middle*); Brun/Photo Researchers, Inc., 88 (*top, right*); George Holton/Photo Researchers, Inc., 88 (*bottom, left*); Elliot Erwitt/Magnum Photo, Inc., 88 (*bottom, middle*); Bruno Hadjih/Gamma-Liaison, Inc., 88 (*bottom, right*).

CHAPTER 4: Amy Jones, *St. Regis Indian Reservation*, courtesy of Janet Marqusee Fine Arts, New York, 94; Hinterleiner/Gamma-Liaison, Inc., 95; Will Owens/Courtesy of the Lenskis, 96; Patrick Bordes/Photo Researchers, Inc., 97; Victor Englebert/Photo Researchers, Inc., 98; Robert Frerck/Woodfin Camp & Associates, 99; John Coletti/Stock Boston, 104; Brown Brothers, 105; Ron McMillan/Gamma-Liaison, Inc., 107; Sir Luke Fildes (1844–1927), *Awaiting Admission to the Casual Ward*, Royal Holloway and Bedford New College, Surrey (Bridgeman/Art Resource, New York), 108; Gamma-Liaison, Inc., 110; New York Public Library Picture Collection, 111; George Tooker, *Landscape with Figures*, 1963, egg tempera on gesso panel, 26 x 30 inches, private, 114; Bettmann, 115; Elliot Landy/Magnum Photo, Inc., 117 (*left*); Robert Sorbo/AP/Wide World Photos, 117 (*right*); Paul Liebhardt, 118 (*left*); Paul Liebhardt, 118 (*right*).

CHAPTER 5: Hale Woodruff, *Girls Skipping*, 1949, oil on canvas, 24 x 32 inches, courtesy of Michael Rosenfeld Gallery, New York, 122; Blair Seitz/Photo Researchers, Inc., 123; Ted Horowitz/Stock Market, 124 (*left*); Henley & Savage/Stock Market, 124 (*middle*); Tom Pollak/Monkmeyer Press, 124 (*right*); C. 1994 UNICEF, reprinted by permission of Harper Collins Publishers, Inc., 125; UPI/Bettmann, 126; Elizabeth Crews, 128; Keith Carter, 130; Rimma Gervolina & Valeriy Gerlovin, *Manyness*, 1990, courtesy Steinbaum Krauss Gallery, NY, 131; Courtesy of the University of Chicago Archives, 132; Henry Ossawa Tanner, *The Banjo Lesson*, 1893, oil on canvas. Hampton University Museum, Hampton, Virginia, 134; L.S. Stepanowicz/Picture Cube, Inc., 137; Patrick Zachmann/Magnum Photo, Inc., 143; Danny Lyon/Magnum Photo, Inc., 144.

CHAPTER 6: Jacob Lawrence, *Theatre Series, No. 8: Vaudeville, 1951*, tempera on fiberboard with pencil, 29 7/8 x 19 15/16", collection Hirshhorn Museum and Sculpture Garden, Smithsonian Institution, gift of Joseph H. Hirshhorn, 1966, courtesy of the artist and Franc, 148; Macionis, John, 149; Jim Anderson/Woodfin Camp & Associates, 150; John L. Focht, 151; Ian Berry/Magnum Photo, Inc., 152; Dimaggio/Kalish/Stock Market, 154; Paul Liebhardt, 155; David Cooper/Gamma-Liaison, Inc., 159 (*top, left*); Alan Weiner/Gamma-Liaison, Inc., 159 (*top, middle*); Lynn McLaren/Picture Cube, Inc., 159 (*top, right*); Ellis Herwig/Picture Cube, Inc., 159 (*bottom, left*); Richard Pan/The Image Bank, 159 (*bottom, middle*); Erik Leigh Simmone/The Image Bank, 159 (*bottom, right*); Paul Liebhardt, 160; Stephen Lynch/The Image Bank, 162; Paul Liebhardt, 163 (*left*); Paul Liebhardt, 163 (*middle*); Paul Liebhardt, 163 (*right*); Tony Freeman/PhotoEdit, 165; Chris Haston/NBC, Inc., 167.

CHAPTER 7: Ed McGowin, *Society Telephone Society*, 1989, oil on canvas with carved and painted wood frame, 54" x 54", © Ed McGowin 1997, 172; Tony Freeman/PhotoEdit, 173; Frank Siteman/Picture Cube, Inc., 174; Douglas Kirkland/The Image Bank, 179; Paul Liebhardt, 180; Dan Habib/Impact Visuals Photo & Graphics, Inc., 182; Bibliotheque Nationale, Paris, from The Horizon Publishing Co., Inc., 551–5th Avenue, New York, NY 10017 © 1969, 187; Paul Liebhardt, 189; George Tooker, *Government Bureau*, 1956. Egg tempera on gesso panel, 19 5/8 x 29 5/8 inches, The Metropolitan Museum of Art, George A. Hearn Fund, 1956 (56.78), 190; Julie Houck Photography, 192; Gabe Palmer/Stock Market, 194; Karen Kasmauski/Woodfin Camp & Associates, 197.

CHAPTER 8: John Nava, *2nd of May, 1992 at Los Angeles*, 1992, oil on canvas: 78 x 108". Collection of Charles Sims; © John Nava 1997, 202; Benito/Sygma, 203; SIPA Press, 204; Cliff Owen/UPI/Bettmann, 206; Stephen Shames/Matrix International, 207; Paul Liebhardt, 209; Edward Gargan/New York Times Pictures, 210; Jon Levy/Gamma-Liaison, Inc., 212; Frank Romero, *The Closing of Whittier Boulevard*, 1984, oil on canvas, 6 x 10 feet, 214; Ed McGowin, *Grown Men Playing with Planet Earth*, 1991, 215; Mark Peterson/SABA Press Photos, Inc., 218; John Giordano/SABA Press Photos, Inc., 220; Benetton, 223; John Van Hasselt/Sygma, 224; Vincent van Gogh, *Prisoner's Round*, Dutch, Pushkin State Museum, Moscow/Superstock, 230.

CHAPTER 9: Antonio Ruiz, *El Corzo (1964–1985)*, Verano, 1937, Oil on wood 28.5 x 33.5 cm, Collection of Acervo Patrimonial, Secretaria de Hacienda y Credito Publico, Mexico, 234; Ken Marshall/Collection of Joseph M. Ryan, 235; Sebastiao Salgado/Magnum Photo, Inc., 236; Allan Tannenbaum/Sygma, 237; Paula Bronstein/Impact Visuals Photo & Graphics, Inc.,

238; Sygma, 241; Robert Wallis/SABA Press Photos, Inc., 243; Limbourg Brother, *Le Duc de Berry a table*, Tres Riches Heures du Duc de Berry, January, folio iv, Chantilly, Musee Conde, 246; Reuters/Bettmann, 248; Art Resource, 249 (*left*); Jacob Riis/Museum of the City of New York, 249 (*right*); Manchester City Art Gallery/SuperStock, Inc., 251.

CHAPTER 10: © Paul Marcus, 1997. *Picnic in the Bronx*, 1992, oil on wood, 46" x 72", 260; Stephen Shames/Matrix International, 261; Michael Grecco/Stock Boston, 267; Sander/Gamma-Liaison, Inc., 268 (*left*); Burt Glinn/Magnum Photo, Inc., 268 (*right*); Sabina Dowell, 270; AP/Wide World Photos, 271; Richard Pipes (1936–   ), *Campaign 1960* , August 1960, gelatin-silver print, 14x11"(35.6 x 28 cm). The Museum of Modern Art, New York, gift of the photographer, 273; *Sky's the Limit* by Bill Blast, © James Prigoff and Henry Chalfant from Spraycan Art, Thames and Hudson, New York, 274; Tim Carlson/Stock Boston, 281; Henry O. Tanner, *Thankful Poor*, 1894, oil on canvas, 35 x 44 in. William H. and Camille O. Cosby Collection, 284; Mary Ellen Mark Library, 285.

CHAPTER 11: Museu Nacional de Belas Artes, Rio de Janeiro. Photo: Raul Lima, 290; Richard Vogel/Gamma-Liaison, Inc., 291; Tom Wagner/SABA Press Photos, Inc., 293 (*top, left*); Peter Turnley/Black Star, 293 (*top, right*); Thomas Hoepker/Magnum Photo, Inc., 293 (*bottom*); Ron Haviv/SABA Press Photos, Inc., 294 (*left*); Bartholomew/Gamma-Liaison, Inc., 294 (*right*); Christopher Morris/Time/Black Star, 295; Miguel Luis Fairbanks, 299; Patrick Aventurier/Gamma-Liaison, Inc., 301; Steve Maines/Stock Boston, 303; Tom Stodart/Katz/SABA Press Photos, Inc., 304; Paul Liebhardt, 306; James Prigoff, 308; Ben Simmons/Stock Market, 311.

CHAPTER 12: Pippin, Horace. *Mr. Prejudice*, 1943, oil on canvas, 18" x 14", Philadelphia Museum of Art: Gift of Dr. and Mrs. Matthew T. Moore, photo by Graydon Wood, 1995, 318; AP/Wide World Photos, 319; Paul Liebhardt, 321 (*top, left; top, center; bottom, left; bottom, center*); Robert Caputo/Stock Boston, 321 (*top, right*); Lisi Dennis/The Image Bank, 321 (*bottom, right*); Raveendran/Agence France-Presse, 325; Bettman. 327 (left); Culver Pictures, Inc., 327 (*second from left*); Schomburg Center/New York Public Library, 327 (*second from right*); UPI/Bettmann (*right*); Bettmann, 331; Library of Congress, 333; Jacob Lawrence, *The Planter* 1937–1938/Tempera on paper/From the Amistad Research Center's Aaron Douglas Collection, New Orleans/11 x 19 inches, 335; Hardy A. Saffold/SIPA Press, 337; Erich Hartmann/Magnum Photo, Inc., 340; © Nick Quijano 1997. *La Vida en Broma*, 1988: Streetlife in Old San Juan, 343.

CHAPTER 13: © Wendy Seller, 1994. *Magritte & Me*, o/c 34"H x 30"W. Photo courtesy Pepper Gallery, Boston, 350; Mugshots/Stock Market, 351; Barbara Campbell/Gamma-Liaison, Inc., 352; Aspect Picture Library/Stock Market, 355; Explorer/Y. Layma/Photo Researchers, Inc., 356; Joseph B. Bringnolo/The Image Bank, 357; Pennsylvania State University, 360; Jacques M. Chenet/Gamma-Liaison, Inc., 362; Natsuko Utsumi/Gamma-Liaison, Inc., 371; Drew Friedmann, 373; UPI/Bettmann, 374; Jay Silverman/The Image Bank, 376.

CHAPTER 14: Archibald John Motley, Jr. American, 1891–1981. *Mending Socks*, 1924. Oil on canvas, 111.44 x 101.60 cm (43 7/8 x 40 in.) The Ackland Art Museum, The University of North Carolina at Chapel Hill, Burton Emmett Collection, 382; Rob Crandall/Picture Group, 383; Elliot Erwitt/Magnum Photo, Inc., 387 (*left*); Robert Fried/Stock Boston, 387 (*right*); Eve Arnold/Magnum Photo, Inc., 390; SuperStock, Inc., 394; Stephen Castagneto/Gamma-Liaison, Inc., 396; Ira Wyman/Sygma, 398.

CHAPTER 15: Schalkwijk/Art Resource, 402; Paula Bronstein/Impact Visuals Photo & Graphics, Inc., 403; Museum of American Textile History, 405; Archive Photos, 406; Bellavia/REA/SABA Press Photos, Inc., 409 (*left*); John Bryson/Sygma, 409 (*right*); Patrick Ward/Stock Boston, 411; Sabina Dowell, 415; Issac Soyer 1907–1981, *Employment Agency*, 1927. Oil on canvas, 34 1/4 x 45 in. (87 x 114.3 cm), Collection of Whitney Museum of American Art, New York. Photo by Geoffrey Clements, 417; Eric Miller/Impact Visuals Photo & Graphics, Inc., 421; Mayer/Gamma-Liaison, Inc., 423.

CHAPTER 16: Zhang Hongtu, *Chairman Mao #11*, 1989, acrylic, laser photo print and collage, 11 x 8.5", 428; Charles H. Porter, 4th/Sygma, 429; Francisco Goya, *Third of May*/Prado, Madrid/Scala/Art Resource, 431; David Ball/Picture Cube, Inc., 435; Jim Cole/AP/Wide World Photos, 441; Barry Iverson/Time-Life Picture Agency, 444; Peter Northall/Black Star, 446; UPI/Bettmann, 447; Baldeu/Sygma, 448.

CHAPTER 17: Kahlo, Frida. *My Grandparents, My Parents, and I (Family Tree)*, 1936. Oil & tempera on metal panel, 12 1/8 x 13 5/8"(30.7 x 34.5 cm).

The Museum of Modern Art, New York, gift of Allan Roos, MD, and B. Mathieu Roos. Photograph © 1996 The Museum of Modern Art, NY, 454; Richard Kalvar/Magnum Photo, Inc., 455; Stephanie Maze/Woodfin Camp & Associates, 456; Bo Zaunders/Stock Market, 458; Artists Rights Society, 461; SuperStock, Inc., 462; © 1989 Carmen Lomas Garza, *Cumpleanos de Lala y Tudi*, oil on canvas, 17" x 15", collection of the artist, photo:Wolfgang Dietze, 467; Margaret Miller/Photo Researchers, Inc., 469; Stern (Ullal)/Black Star, 477.

CHAPTER 18: © 1994 Dinh Le, *Interconfined*, C-print and linen tape, 55" x 39", 482; Michael A. Schwartz/Gamma-Liaison, Inc., 483; R. Rai/Magnum Photo, Inc., 484; National Museum of American Art, Washington, D.C./Art Resource, NY, 486; Ira Wyman/Sygma, 488; Gilles Peress/Magnum Photo, Inc., 490; National Museum of American Art, Washington, D.C./Art Resource, NY, 492; Hans Hoefer/Woodfin Camp & Associates, 494; Bradshaw/SABA Press Photos, Inc., 496; Hans Kemp/Sygma, 497; Thomas Hart Benton, *Arts of the South*/tempera with oil glaze, 8 x 13 feet/Harriet Russell Stanley/The New Britain Museum of American Art, 503.

CHAPTER 19: Jacob Lawrence, *The Library*, 1960, tempera on fiberboard, 24 x 29 7/8 in.(60.9 x 75.8cm). National Museum of American Art, Washington, D.C., Gift of S.C. Johnson & Son, Inc./Art Resource, NY, 508; Richard Kalvar/Magnum Photo, Inc., 509; Charles Gupton/Stock Boston, 512; John Giordano/SABA Press Photos, Inc., 516 (*left*); Charles Gupton/Stock Boston, 516 (*right*); Leo De Wys, Inc., 521; Michael Newman/PhotoEdit, 523; Literacy Volunteers of America, Inc., 526; Mugshots/Stock Market, 527.

CHAPTER 20: Avicenna, Canon, Isafahan, 1632. Welcome Institute Library, London, 532; Susan Rosenberg/Photo Researchers, Inc., 533; The Granger Collection, 534; 535; W. Campbell/Sygma, 536 (*left*); Steve Lehman/SABA Press Photos, Inc., 536 (*right*); Leyden, *De chirurgijn*, Rijksmuseum, Amsterdam, 535; John Coletti/Picture Cube, Inc., 540; D. Michael Cheers from *Songs of My People*, © New African Visions, Inc., 545; Joseph Nettles/Stock Boston, 551; Catherine Leroy/SIPA Press, 553; Steve Murez/Black Star, 554.

CHAPTER 21: Georgia Mills Jessup (born 1926), *Rainy Night Downtown*, 1967, oil on canvas, 44 x 48 in. (111.8 x 121.9 cm). The National Museum of Women in the Arts, Gift of Savanna M. Clark, 558; John Neubauer/PhotoEdit, 559; Peter Menzel/Material World, 566 (*left*); Peter Ginter/Material World, 566 (*right*); Najlah Feanny/SABA Press Photos, Inc., 567; Pieter Breughel the Elder (c. 1525/30–1569), *Peasant Dance*, c. 1565, Kunsthistorisches Museum, Vienna/Superstock, 575 (*left*); Fernand Leger, *The City*, 1919, oil on canvas, 90 3/4 x 117 1/4, Philadelphia Museum of Art, A.E. Gallatin Collection, 575 (*right*); University of Chicago Library, 577; Bob Krist/Black Star, 578; Jonathan Nourok/PhotoEdit, 581.

CHAPTER 22: © Anatoly Shdanow/UNEP, 586; Michael Friedel/Woodfin Camp & Associates, 587; Peter Martens/Magnum Photo, Inc., 589; A. Ramey/Woodfin Camp & Associates, 592; Thomas Hartwell/Sygma, 597; Utarbekov Nabihan/Press Studio/Lehtikuva/SABA Press Photos, Inc., 599; Eric Pasquier/Sygma, 602; Elizabeth Manglesdorf/S.F. Examiner/SABA Press Photos, Inc., 604; Claus Meyer/Black Star, 606.

CHAPTER 23: Umberto Boccioni, *Riot in the Gallery*, 1909/Superstock, 612; Chien-Chi Chang/Magnum Photo, Inc., 613; Archive Photos, 615; Philip Evergood, *American Tragedy*, 1936, oil on canvas, 29 1/2 x 39 1/2", Terry Dintenfass Gallery, New York, 616; Sabina Dowell, 619; The Granger Collection, 621; Lambert/Archive Photos, 622 (*top, left*); Owen Franken/Stock Boston, 622 (*top, middle*); Charles Harbutt/Actuality Inc., 622 (*top, right*); Terje Rakke/The Image Bank, 622 (*bottom, left*); G & M David de Lossy/The Image Bank, 622 (*bottom, right*); UPI Telephoto/Bettmann, 626 (*left*); Jerry L. Soloway/UPI/Bettmann, 626 (*right*); Donna Binder/Impact Visuals Photo & Graphics, Inc., 631.

CHAPTER 24: Courtesy of The Williams Gallery, Princeton, NJ; © Joan Truckenbrod 1997, 636; Mauri Rautkari/WWF Photo Library, 637; Paul Liebhardt, 639; Paul Gaugin, *The Day of the God (Mahana no Atua)*, 1894, oil on canvas (68.3 x 91.5 cm.), Helen Birch Bartlett Memorial Collection, 1926, 198; Photograph © 1994, The Art Institute of Chicago. All Rights Reserved, 642; Gelehrte Dtld./Bildarchiv Preussischer Kulturbesitz, 643; George Tooker, *The Subway*, 1950, egg tempera on composition board, 18 1/8 x 36 1/8", Whitney Museum of American Art, New York, purchased with funds from the Juliana Force Purchase Award, 50.23, 644; © Paul Marcus 1995, oil on panel *Dinner is Served*, 648 (*left*); Edward Munch, *Evening on Karl Johan Street*, 1892, Scala/Art Resource, 648 (*right*); Dr. Amitai Etzioni/The George Washington University, 654; Rafael Macia/Photo Researchers, Inc., 655.

Index

NAME INDEX

Abbott, Andrew, 416
Abbott, Daniel, 223, 225
Abbott, Sandra, 218, 219
Aberle, David F., 623, 624
Abernathy, Ralph, 501
Adams, Murray C., 351
Addams, Jane, 15
Adler, Jerry, 165
Adorno, T. W., 237
Ageton, Suzanne S., 223
Aguirre, Benigno E., 613, 614, 623
Akers, Ronald L., 213
Alam, Sultana, 306
Alba, Richard D., 331, 344
Albon, Joan, 333
Allan, Emilie Andersen, 209
Allen, Michael Patrick, 439
Allsop, Kenneth, 208
Al-Moudarres, Fateh, 21
Altman, Drew, 549
Alvarez, Marie D., 147
Ambert, Alba N., 147
Amman, Jost, 534
Anderson, John Ward, 301
Anderson, Marian, 327
Ando, Faith, 365
Andrews, Barbara, 585
Andrews, Nancy, 476
Ang, Ien, 138
Angelo, Bonnie, 383, 468
Angelou, Maya, 486
Angier, Natalie, 354
Anspaugh, Gene, 551
Aquinas, St. Thomas, 12
Arber, Sara, 402
Archer, Dane, 230
Arendt, Hannah, 429, 436, 453
Ariès, Philippe, 397, 398
Aristotle, 12, 245, 509
Arjomand, Said Amir, 493
Asante, Molefi Kete, 79, 327
Asch, Solomon, 178
Ashford, 568
Astone, Nan Marie, 475
Astor, John Jacob, 249
Atchley, Robert C., 392, 396, 399
Atkins, Sharon, 109
Aurelius, Marcus, 12
Auster, Carol J., 524
Aviad, Janet O'Dea, 501
Avicenna, 532
Axtell, Roger E., 67
Ayensu, Edward S., 545

Babbie, Earl, 44
Bachrach, Peter, 443
Backman, Carl B., 351
Baer, Douglas, 185
Bahl, Vinay, 238
Bailey, William C., 230
Bainbridge, William Sims, 489,

490, 502
Baker, David, 512
Baker, Mary Anne, 355
Bales, Robert F., 176, 177, 201, 460
Baltes, Paul B., 387
Baltzell, E. Digby, 20, 50–53, 249,
    267–69, 272, 334, 344, 430,
    572, 646
Bane, Mary Jo, 332
Banfield, Edward, 282–83
Banks, Curtis, 42
Barash, David, 89, 91
Baratz, Morton S., 443
Barker, Eileen, 491, 502, 505
Baron, James N., 628
Barone, Michael, 437
Barry, Kathleen, 89, 374, 375
Bart, Pauline, 381
Bassuk, Ellen J., 285
Bauer, P. T., 304, 307
Baydar, Nazli, 376
Beach, Frank A., 353
Beck, Frank D., 307, 422
Becker, Howard S., 203, 210
Bedell, George C., 495
Beeghley, Leonard, 253
Bekker, Simon, 259
Bell, Alan P., 476
Bell, Daniel, 102, 427
Bell, Wendell, 578
Bellah, Robert N., 73, 91, 501
Bellas, Marcia L., 367
Belsky, Jay, 133, 134
Bem, Sandra Lipsitz, 359, 360
Bendix, Reinhard, 239, 276
Benedict, Ruth, 139, 512
Benet, Sula, 390
Benford, Robert D., 628
Benjamin, Bernard, 391
Benjamin, Lois, 29, 30, 36, 43,
    45–47, 323
Bennett, Neil G., 468
Bennett, Stephen Earl, 440
Bennett, William J., 521, 655
Benokraitis, Nijole, 27, 168, 367,
    368, 461
Ben-Raphael, Eliezer, 349
Benton, Thomas Hart, 503
Berardo, F. M., 466
Berger, Brigitte, 646, 650, 653, 659
Berger, Peter L., 2, 27, 39, 145,
    171, 304, 307, 317, 422, 485,
    529, 641, 642, 646, 650,
    653, 659
Bergesen, Albert, 309, 422
Berhardt, Annette, 367
Berk, Richard A., 617
Bernard, Jessie, 360, 370, 375,
    381, 469, 470
Bernard, Larry Craig, 360
Bernard, Thomas J., 213, 215
Bernstein, Richard J., 653

Berrill, Kevin T., 217
Berry, Brian, 578
Berscheid, Ellen, 464
Bérubé, Allan, 381
Best, Raphaela, 134
Bhutto, Benazir, 430
Biblarz, Timothy J., 475
Billson, Janet Mancini, 10, 27
Blakeslee, Sandra, 473, 475
Blast, Bill, 274
Blau, Judith, 223
Blau, Peter M., 22, 223, 274, 462
Blaustein, Albert P., 336
Bloom, David E., 468
Bloom, Leonard, 339
Blum, Linda M., 367
Blumberg, Paul, 276, 649
Blumer, Herbert G., 614, 623, 629
Blumstein, Philip, 464, 476
Bodenheimer, Thomas S., 552
Boff, Leonard, 487
Bohannan, Cecil, 285
Bohannan, Paul, 472
Bohm, Robert M., 230
Bohmer, Jean, 474
Bohrmann, F. Herbert, 591, 607
Bonilla-Santiago, Gloria, 369
Bonner, Jane, 360
Booth, Alan, 472
Borgardus, Emory, 327
Borgatta, Edgar F., 201
Borgmann, Albert, 653
Boswell, Terry E., 250, 337
Bott, Elizabeth, 274, 467
Boulding, Elise, 100
Bourne, David, 367
Bowles, Samuel, 19, 515, 517
Boyce, James, 302
Boyer, Ernest L., 524
Braithwaite, John, 223
Branegan, Jay, 435
Brantley, Peter, 420
Braungart, Margaret M., 81
Braungart, Richard G., 81
Breen, Leonard, 394
Breughel, Pieter the Elder, 575
Brightman, Joan, 164
Brinton, Crane, 444
Brinton, Mary C., 242, 512
Brodie, John, 197
Brody, Charles, 161
Brooks-Gunn, Jeanne, 377, 469
Brown, Ford Maddox, 251
Brown, Lester R., 582, 603,
    607, 611
Brown, Louise, 476
Brown, Mary Ellen, 138, 147
Broyles, Philip, 439
Bruno, Mary, 393
Brzezinski, Zbigniew, 436
Buechler, Steven M., 635
Bulliet, Richard W., 507

Bumpass, Larry, 476
Burgess, Ernest W., 577, 578
Burke, Tom, 607
Burrstein, Paul, 628
Busby, Linda J., 362
Bush, George, 439
Butler, Robert N., 394, 401
Buttel, Frederick R., 607
Butterworth, Douglas, 332

Cafferata, Gail Lee, 392
Cahnman, Werner J., 643
Callahan, Daniel, 399
Calmore, John O., 332
Calvin, John, 113, 487
Cameron, William Bruce, 623
Campbell, Richard T., 241, 277
Canetti, Elias, 617
Cantor, Murial, 138
Cantril, Hadley, 621, 622
Caplan, Patricia, 201
Caplow, Theodore, 437, 554
Capone, Al, 208, 215
Carley, Kathleen A., 182
Carlson, Norman A., 228, 230
Carmichael, Stokely, 329
Carnegie, Andrew, 249
Carpenter, Bruce N., 401
Carr, Leslie G., 347
Carroll, Ginny, 517
Carson, Rachel, 608, 611
Caserta, Michael S., 398
Castro, Fidel, 343
Castro, Janice, 415
Chagall, Marc, 18, 461
Chagnon, Napoleon, 64, 76, 98
Chance, John K., 332
Chandler, Tertius, 570
Change, Kwang Chih, 569
Chappell, Neena L., 391
Charles, Maria, 365
Chaves, Mark, 498, 499
Cherlin, Andrew, 279, 465, 469,
    471, 473
Chown, Sheila M., 392
Church, George, 415
Clark, Curtis B., 393
Clark, Juan M., 344
Clark, Margaret S., 250
Clark, Thomas A., 573
Clarke, Robin, 588, 600, 601
Clayson, Dennis E., 217
Clinard, Marshall, 223, 225
Clinton, Bill, 438, 439, 549, 654
Cloward, Richard A., 208, 209,
    440, 441, 626, 630
Cobb, Jonathan, 287, 520
Cockerham, William C., 538
Coe, Michael D., 569
Cohen, Adam, 347
Cohen, Albert, 209

693

Cohen, Lloyd R., 371, 372
Cohn, Richard M., 388
Cole, Stephen, 369
Coleman, James S., 189, 517, 518, 522, 523, 531
Coleman, Richard P., 268, 269
Collins, Joseph, 310, 311, 317
Collins, Nigeria, 261, 272, 277
Collins, Randall, 373, 498, 519
Colloway, N. O., 386
Columbus, Christopher, 80, 308
Comte, Auguste, 11–17
Confucius, 12, 83, 187, 497, 509
Connett, Paul H., 591, 595
Conrad, John P., 230
Contreras, Joseph, 239, 245
Cook, Rhodes, 439
Cooley, Charles Horton, 131, 174, 175, 618
Cooper, Philip W., 475
Copernicus, 13
Cordell, Arthur J., 196
Corley, Robert N., 595
Cornell, Claire Pedrick, 371
Cortés, Hernando, 559
Coser, Lewis A., 132, 175
Cottle, Thomas J., 521
Cottrell, John, 332
Counts, G. S., 39, 264
Courtney, Alice E., 362
Coverman, Shelley, 365, 414
Cowan, Carolyn Pope, 367
Cowgill, Donald, 390
Cowley, Peter, 540, 552, 554
Cox, Harvey, 501, 505, 576
Craig, Grace, 147
Craig, Patricia H., 468
Cressey, Donald R., 215
Crisp, Quentin, 534
Crispell, Diane, 465
Crocket, Harry J., Jr., 439
Crook, Stephan, 653
Crossette, Barbara, 553
Crouse, James, 516
Cuff, E. C., 106, 110
Cumming, Elaine, 395
Curie, Marie, 82
Currie, Elliott, 224
Curtis, James E., 185, 259
Cutler, 262
Cutright, Phillip, 239
Cuvelier, Steven, 367
Cylke, F. Kurt, Jr., 588

Dahl, Robert, 441, 443
Dahrendorf, Ralf, 250, 420, 646
Daly, Martin, 204
Danefer, Dale, 141
Daniel, Herbert, 557
Daniels, Roger, 338
D'Antonio, William V., 485
Darnton, Nina, 550
Darwin, Charles, 17, 89, 124, 504
Davidson, James D., 267, 500
Davies, Christie, 168, 171
Davies, James C., 444, 625
Davies, Mark, 135
Davis, Kenneth E., 337
Davis, Kingsley, 123, 126, 245–49, 256
Davis, Sharon A., 517
Deber, Raisa B., 548
Deckard, B. Sinclair, 375

Dedrick, Dennis K., 449
Delacroix, Jaques, 309, 422
De Mente, Boye, 201
Demerath, N. J., III, 501
DeMott, John S., 616
Denton, Nancy, 332
Deotis, J., 500
DeParle, Jason, 276
Dershowitz, Alan, 220
Devine, Joel A., 437
Dewey, John, 513, 531
Diamond, Milton, 355
Dickens, Charles, 139
Dickson, William J., 42, 188
Diehl, Richard A., 569
Dimond, Margaret F., 398
Dinitz, Simon, 205
Dirksen, Everett, 437
Disraeli, Benjamin, 54
Dixon, William J., 250
Dizard, Jan E., 479
Dobson, Richard B., 244
Dobyns, Henry F., 333
Dohrenwend, Bruce P., 272
Dollard, John, 325, 624
Dollevoe, Paula L., 386
Domhoff, G. William, 250
Donovan, Virginia K., 127
Douglass, Richard L., 394
Dow, Unity, 357
Doyle, James A., 376, 378
Doyle, Richard F., 378
Du Bois, W. E. B., 20, 30, 47, 59, 337, 349
Dubos, René, 534
Duhl, Leonard J., 546
Duncan, Otis Dudley, 274, 275
Dunlap, Riley E., 594, 606, 609, 611
Dunn, Ashley, 61
Dunn, John, 198
Durkheim, Emile, 4, 5, 12, 15–18, 50, 95, 105, 115–19, 121, 155, 206, 207, 209, 229, 463, 483–85, 576, 644–46, 649, 656, 659
Durning, Alan Thein, 66
Duvalier, François, 312
Dworkin, Andrea, 375, 377
Dyrenforth, Sue R., 533

Ebaugh, Helen Rose, 153, 507
Eckholm, Erik, 543, 552
Edison, Thomas, 168
Edmondson, Brad, 275
Edwards, David V., 432
Edwards, Richard, 250, 414
Eggebeen, David J., 280
Ehrenreich, Barbara, 359
Ehrenreich, John, 552
Ehrhardt, Anke A., 355
Ehrlich, Paul R., 585
Eichler, Margrit, 38
Eiduson, Bernice T., 475
Einstein, Albert, 184
Eisenstein, Zillah R., 374
Eisler, Benita, 405
Ekland-Olson, Sheldon, 627
Ekman, Paul, 67, 158, 160
El-Attar, Mohamed, 492
Elias, Robert, 223
Elkind, David, 139
Elliott, Delbert S., 223
Ellison, Christopher G., 503

Elmer-DeWitt, Philip, 183, 529, 555
Ember, Carol R., 459
Ember, Melvin M., 459
Embree, Ainslie T., 496
Emerson, Joan, 551
Endersby, James W., 138
Endicott, Karen, 97
Engels, Friedrich, 106, 107, 373, 374, 375, 461
Enloe, Cynthia, 381, 453
Erber, 425
Erikson, Kai, 207, 233
Erikson, Robert S., 273, 276, 289, 439
Etzioni, Amitai, 73, 185, 471, 654, 656, 657, 659
Etzioni-Halevy, Eva, 432
Evans, M. D. R., 262, 416
Ezell, David J., 551

Faldenmark, Malin, 599
Falk, Gerhard, 70
Fallon, A. E., 540
Fallows, James, 344
Fanon, Frantz, 316
Fantini, Mario D., 529
Farley, Reynolds, 332, 334
Farnsworth, Margaret, 223
Farrell, Michael P., 141
Fay, Michael, 435
Feagin, Joe R., 168, 325, 367, 368, 461, 578
Featherman, David L., 274
Featherstone, Mike, 27, 86
Fedarko, Kevin, 261
Felson, Marcus, 276
Fennel, Mary C., 195
Ferguson, Tom, 546
Fergusson, D. M., 274
Figlio, Robert M., 223, 230
Fildes, Sir Luke, 108
Fine, Gary Alan, 618, 619
Finkelstein, Neal W., 134
Finster, Amos, 492
Fiorentine, Robert, 369
Firebaugh, Glenn, 307, 312, 337, 422
Fischer, Claude S., 185
Fisher, Elizabeth, 98, 100
Fisher, Roger, 449
Fiske, Alan Paige, 250
Fitzpatrick, Joseph P., 343
Fitzpatrick, Mary Anne, 467
Flacks, Richard, 626
Florida, Richard, 197
Flynn, Patricia, 545
Foch, Terry T., 125
Foner, Anne, 143
Ford, Clellan S., 353
Ford, Henry, 642
Forrest, Hugh, 523
Fost, Dan, 334, 337
Foucalt, Michel, 557
Fox, Gerald, 570
Frank, André Gunder, 307
Franklin, Benjamin, 114
Franklin, John Hope, 335
Frazier, Charles E., 223
Frazier, E. Franklin, 289, 500, 507
Frederickson, George M., 239, 331
Free, Marvin D., 213
Freeman, Jo, 635
French, Marilyn, 359, 375

Freud, Sigmund, 127, 129, 132, 133, 205
Frey, William H., 332, 337
Friedan, Betty, 396
Friedman, Milton, 424, 425
Friedman, Rose, 424
Friedrich, Carl J., 436
Friedrich, Otto, 245, 581
Fuchs, Victor R., 367, 461
Fugita, Stephen S., 339
Fujimoto, Isao, 339
Fuller, Rex, 368
Furstenberg, Frank F., Jr., 465, 469, 471, 473
Fusfeld, Daniel R., 420

Gadlin, Howard, 479
Gagliani, Giorgio, 250
Galileo, 504, 505
Gallup, Alec M., 594, 606, 609
Gallup, George H., Jr., 44, 504, 594, 606, 609
Galster, George, 573
Gamble, Andrew, 512
Gamoran, Adam, 517
Gandhi, Indira, 430
Gandhi, Mahatma, 430, 606
Gans, Herbert J., 78, 138, 573
Garfinkel, Harold, 155, 211
Garrity, Patrick J., 453
Gartin, Patrick R., 213
Gartner, Rosemary, 230
Garza, Carmen Lomas, 467
Gaudet, Hazel, 621, 622
Gauguin, Paul, 31, 642
Gautama, Siddhartha, 496
Geertz, Clifford, 352
Geist, William, 572
Gelb, Joyce, 659
Gelles, Richard J., 371, 474
Gelman, David, 354, 394
Genovese, Kitty, 656
George, Susan, 535, 536
Gerhardt, Uta, 121
Gerlach, Michael L., 410
Gerlovin, Valeriy, 131
Gerlovina, Rimma, 131
Gerstel, Naomi, 471
Gerth, H. H., 113
Geschwender, James A., 328
Gibbons, Dan C., 205
Gibbs, Nancy, 139, 218, 219, 286, 429
Giddens, Anthony, 250
Giele, Janet Z., 373
Gilbert, Neil, 219
Gilbertson, Greta A., 338
Gilligan, Carol, 128–30, 361
Gimenez, Martha E., 523
Ginn, Jay, 402
Ginsberg, Faye, 370
Ginsberg, Leon H., 385
Gintis, Herbert, 19, 515, 517
Giovannini, Maureen, 39
Glaab, Charles N., 579, 599
Gladue, Brian A., 354
Glauberman, Naomi, 257, 259
Glazer, Nathan, 331, 343
Glazier, Williard, 599
Gleick, Sharon, 429
Glendon, Mary Ann, 453
Glenn, Norval D., 472
Glock, Charles Y., 499
Gluck, Peter R., 573

Kitano, Harry H. L., 339
Kitson, Gay C., 274, 471
Kittrie, Nicholas N., 230
Kluckhohn, Clyde, 353
Kmitch, Janet, 422
Koch, Howard, 621
Koelln, Kenneth, 393
Kohlberg, Lawrence, 128–30, 359
Kohn, Melvin L., 59, 134, 273, 414
Kolata, Gina, 476
Kolodny, Robert C., 541
Komarovsky, Mirra, 367, 467, 469
Kopilak, G. G., 394
Koresh, David, 490
Korman, Sheila K., 469, 476
Korn, William S., 81
Kornhauser, William, 436, 646
Kowalewski, David, 629
Kozol, Jonathan, 284, 285, 518, 526
Krafft, Susan, 344
Kramarae, Cheris, 362
Kraybill, Donald B., 77, 89, 489, 650
Kriesi, Hanspeter, 628, 635
Krohn, Marvin D., 205
Kübler-Ross, Elisabeth, 142, 398, 557
Kuhn, Thomas, 16
Kuznets, Simon, 254, 262

Laboy, Pedro, 422
Lacayo, Richard, 615
Ladd, John, 544
Ladner, Joyce A., 469
Laduke, Betty, 60
La Guardia, Fiorello, 344
Lai, H. M., 338
Lamar, Jacob V., Jr., 273
Lamberg-Karlovsky, C. C., 569
Lamphere, Louise, 289
Land, Kenneth C., 276
Landers, Ann, 5, 470
Landers, Rene M., 358
Landon, Alfred E., 44
Lane, David, 242, 244
Lang, Gladys Engel, 620
Lang, Kurt, 620
Lappé, Frances Moore, 310, 311, 317
Larmer, Brook, 300
Larson, Jan, 365
Lasaga, Jose I., 344
Laslett, Peter, 240, 614, 646
Laub, John H., 213
Laumann, Edward O., 75, 353, 354
Lawrence, Jacob, 22, 148
Lazarus, Emma, 332
Lazreg, Marnia, 381
Le, Dinh, 482
Leach, Penelope, 481
Leacock, Eleanor, 97, 374
Leavitt, Judith Walzer, 552
Le Bon, Gustave, 617, 625, 635
Lee, Barrett A., 576
Lee, Sharon M., 340
Leerhsen, Charles, 643
Leland, John, 354
Lemert, Edwin, 210
Lengermann, Patricia Madoo, 355, 356, 370, 372, 373
Lenin, Vladimir, 110, 243, 430

Lennon, Mary Clare, 367
Lenski, Gerhard, 95–102, 106, 117, 118, 121, 253, 356, 431, 509, 535, 569
Lenski, Jean, 95–102, 106, 117, 118, 121, 253, 356, 431, 509, 535, 569
Leonard, Eileen B., 216
Lerner, Richard M., 133, 134
Leslie, Gerald R., 469, 476
Lester, David, 230
Lever, Janet, 134, 361
Levine, Andrew, 250
Levine, Michael P., 533, 540
Levine, Robert V., 463
Levinson, Daniel J., 141
Levitan, Sara, 283
Levitt, Abraham, 572
Levy, Frank, 262, 276
Lewis, Flora, 444
Lewis, Oscar, 282, 283
Lewis, Peirce, 440, 441
Lewis, Suzan, 427
Li, Jiang Hong, 475
Liazos, Alexander, 213
Lichter, Daniel R., 336
Lichter, Daniel T., 138
Lichter, S. Robert, 280
Liebow, Elliot, 273, 289
Limbourg Brothers, 246
Lin, Ge, 392
Lin, Wen, 264
Linden, Eugene, 70, 568
Lindert, Peter H., 253
Ling, Pyau, 337
Link, Bruce G., 272
Linton, Ralph, 82, 151, 639
Lippitt, Ronald, 177
Lips, Hilary, 353
Lipset, Seymour Martin, 239, 276, 626
Liska, Allen E., 205, 209, 223
Littenberg, Ronnie, 127
Lo, Clarence Y. H., 623
Lock, Margaret, 402
Locke, John, 15
Lodwick, Dora G., 606
Lofland, Lyn, 622
Logan, John R., 338, 573
Logue, Barbara J., 139
Lohr, Steve, 548
Lombroso, Caesare, 204
Longfellow, Henry Wadsworth, 50
Longino, Jr., Charles F., 400
Lorber, Judith, 381
Lord, Walter, 235
Lorenz, Konrad, 446
Low, J. O., 404
Lowell, Francis Cabot, 405
Loxley, William A., 512
Loy, Pamela Hewitt, 371
Lubenow, Gerald C., 474
Luckmann, Thomas, 171
Ludlam, Steve, 512
Lund, Dale A., 391, 398
Lunt, Paul S., 268, 269
Luttbeg, Norman R., 273, 439
Lutz, Catherine A., 158, 171, 317
Lynch, Barbara Deutsch, 588
Lynd, Helen Merrell, 289, 442, 443
Lynd, Robert S., 72, 289, 442, 443
Lynott, Patricia Passuth, 139

Ma, Li-Chen, 264
Maaranen, Steven A., 453
Mabry, Marcus, 415
McAdam, Doug, 613, 625, 628, 629
McBroom, William H., 437
McCarthy, John D., 613, 625, 627, 628
McCartney, Paul, 619
McCleod, Jane, 467
Maccoby, Eleanor, 355
McColm, R. Bruce, 410
McConahay, John B., 626
McConnell, Scott, 450
McCoy, Clyde B., 557
McCracken, Casey, 440, 441
McCrae, Susan, 469
Mace, David, 463
Mace, Vera, 463
McGowin, Ed, 172, 215
McGuire, Meredith B., 498, 501
McHenry, Susan, 192
Macionis, John J., 9, 27, 166n, 177, 303, 357, 462, 562, 576
MacKay, Donald G., 164
McKinney, William, 502
MacKinnon, Catharine, 372
Macklin, Eleanor D., 476
McLanahan, Sara S., 475
McLeod, Jay, 273
McPhail, Clark, 615, 617, 635
McRoberts, Hugh A., 276
MacRone, Mind, 524
Maddox, Setma, 194
Madsen, Axel, 422
Madsen, Peter, 534
Maguire, John, 79
Mahoney, Kathryn M., 81
Majka, Linda C., 372
Malthus, Thomas Robert, 564, 565, 582
Mandela, Nelson, 238, 239, 631
Mapplethorpe, Robert, 206
Marcos, Ferdinand, 312
Marcus, Paul, 19, 260, 648
Marcuse, Herbert, 651
Mare, Robert D., 461
Margolick, David, 474
Marín, Barbara VanOss, 40, 41, 59, 340
Marín, Gerardo, 40, 41, 59, 340
Markoff, John, 194
Marks, Mary Ellen, 285
Markson, Elizabeth W., 545
Marler, Penny Long, 498, 499
Marsden, Peter, 185
Marshall, Catherine, 531
Marshall, Susan E., 377
Martin, Bill, 250
Martin, John M., 225
Martin, Richard C., 493
Martin, William, 504
Martineau, Harriet, 15
Martinez, Andrew, 204
Martinez, Valerie J., 525
Marullo, Sam, 448
Marx, Gary T., 613
Marx, Karl, 15, 16, 20, 87, 95, 104–10, 115, 118, 119, 167, 205, 214, 243, 245, 247–53, 257, 268, 360, 373, 376, 397, 409, 410, 412, 443, 485, 486, 565, 625, 639
Marx, Leo, 588

Massey, Douglas, 332, 528
Masters, William H., 541
Mathabane, Mark, 481
Matsuo, Naoko, 509
Matthiessen, Peter, 332, 333, 334
Mauer, Marc, 229
Mauro, Tony, 544
Mauss, Armand L., 629
Mayo, Katherine, 463
Mead, George Herbert, 22, 130–33, 145, 147
Mead, Margaret, 125, 139, 147, 356, 381
Meadows, Donella H., 593, 611
Meir, Golda, 430
Meister, Richard J., 573
Meltzer, Bernard N., 133
Melucci, Alberto, 625, 628
Mendoza, Jorge L., 623
Mennerick, Lewis A., 510
Mergenbagen, Paula, 392
Mertig, Angela G., 609, 611
Merton, Robert K., 18, 152, 180, 189, 207, 208, 215, 328, 625
Messner, Steven F., 182
Meyer, Davis S., 628
Meyrowitz, Joshua, 79
Michels, Robert, 190
Milbrath, Lester W., 587, 591, 592
Milgram, Stanley, 178, 179
Miliband, Ralph, 250, 649
Milken, Michael, 215
Miller, Arthur J., 178
Miller, David L., 59, 614
Miller, Frederick, 630
Miller, G. Tyler, Jr., 591, 595
Miller, Michael, 198
Miller, Walter, 209
Millett, Kate, 375
Millman, Joel, 263
Mills, C. Wright, 9, 11, 27, 113, 259, 269, 416, 442, 632
Mink, Barbara, 306
Mintz, Beth, 421
Mirande, Alfredo, 467
Mirowsky, John, 272, 470
Mirowsky, Robert K., 180
Mitchell, Todd, 220
Mittman, Brian S., 628
Mobutu Sese Seko, 312
Molotch, Harvey, 578
Money, John, 355
Monk-Turner, Elizabeth, 519
Montagu, Ashley, 446
Moore, Gwen, 185, 374, 421
Moore, Joan, 467
Moore, Molly, 301
Moore, Wilbert E., 245–49, 256, 307
Moran, John S., 541
Morgan, J. P., 249
Morgan, S. Philip, 469
Morris, Aldon, 628
Morrison, Denton, 624
Morrison, Toni, 468
Morrow, Lance, 415
Morton, Jackson, 53
Moses, Anna Mary Robertson (Grandma), 77
Mosley, W. Henry, 540, 554
Motley, Archibald, 382
Mott, Lucretia, 374

SUBJECT INDEX

Arms race, 448
Arranged marriage, 463
Artifacts, 75–76
Ascribed status, 151
Asia, 298, 301, 302, 304, 312, 315, 366, 408, 510 (*see also* specific countries)
Asian Americans, 337–41
  and crime, 223–24
  and education, 337, 339, 340
  and family, 468, 475
  geographic distribution of, 342
  and health, 543
  and income, 338, 340
  and intelligence, 326
  population, national map, 342
  population growth, 323, 337
  and poverty, 279
  and workplace, 419
Assimilation, 330–31, 339, 345
Athens, 569
Attention, and language, 96
Australia, 7, 293, 367, 408
Authoritarianism, 434, 435
Authoritarian leadership, 177, 188
Authoritarian personality theory, 327
Authority, 460
  charismatic, 430
  rational-legal, 430, 431
  traditional, 429–30
Azerbaijan, 319, 412, 514

Baby boom, 384, 400, 465, 471, 563, 572
Baby bust, 384, 564
Bangladesh, 295, 302, 305, 306, 492, 510, 602
Barbados, 294
Batek of Malaysia, 97
Beauty myth, 351, 362, 540
Behaviorism, 124, 130
Belgium, 432
Beliefs, 71
Bereavement, 398–99
Bilateral descent, 460
Biodiversity, declining, 602–3
Biology, 125
  and aging, 386–87
  and deviance, 204–5
  and gender, 351–53
  and race, 320–21
Birth control, 374, 375, 564–68
Birth rate, 300, 384, 560, 563–67
Bisexuality, 353, 354
Black Americans (*see* African Americans)
Black power movement, 336
Blasé urban attitude, 575–76
Blended families, 473
Blue-collar occupations, 250, 416
Blue jeans, 623
Body language, 159, 160
Bosnia, 448
Botswana, 294, 357–58
Bourgeosie, 107, 570, 645
Branch Davidians, 490
Brazil, 294, 297, 299–300, 449, 637
Breast implants, 552
Brown v. The Board of Education of Topeka (1954), 319, 329, 331
Buddhism, 496–97
  global map, 495
Bulgaria, 294

Bulimia, 540
Burakumin, 242
Bureaucracy, 430
  characteristics of, 186–88
  and democracy, 432
  and education, 340–41, 522–23
  humanizing, 193
  informality of, 188
  in mass society, 648
  origins of, 186
  privacy and, 198, 199
  problems of, 188–91
  and rationality, 114, 115
  and social movements, 630
Bureaucratic authority, 430, 431
Bureaucratic ritualism, 189
Bushmen, 97
Busing, 517–18

Cable television, 136
Cairo dump, 596–97
Calvinism, 111, 113–14, 118, 485, 487
Cambodia, 332, 496
Camden, New Jersey, 261, 271
Canada, 297, 367, 408, 547–48
Capitalism, 104–6, 119
  and aging, 397
  and alienation, 108–9
  and bureaucracy, 114, 115
  and Calvinism, 113, 487
  characteristics of, 407–8
  and class conflict, 107–8
  and democracy, 432
  and deviance, 214–15
  and gender stratification, 376
  Marxist analysis of, 248–53
  and medicine, 547–48
  and modernity, 645–46, 649
  and natural environment, 606
  and rationality, 111
  versus socialism, 410–11
Capitalist world economy, 309–10
Capital punishment, 229–30, 438
Case studies, 48
Caste system, 237–39
Casual crowds, 614
Category, 174
Catholic Church, 5, 113, 305, 430, 483, 487–89, 492, 498–500, 504, 567
Caucasian, 320
Cause and effect, 34, 35
Chad, 295
Charisma, 490, 492, 639
Charismatic authority, 430
Chechnya, 448
Cherokee Indians, 333
Chicago School, 576
Chicanos, 341
Child abuse, 123, 125, 126, 393, 474
Childbirth, 300
Child care, 419, 466, 515
Child custody, 378, 473
Child labor, 82, 83, 139
  global map, 140
Child rearing, 464–65
Children (*see also* Family)
  and cognitive development, 128–29
  and development of self, 132
  and divorce, 473
  hurried child, 139

  and moral development, 129
  and poverty, 279, 280, 299–300
  and socialization (*see* Socialization)
Chile, 312
China (*see* People's Republic of China)
Chinese Americans, 322, 326, 337–38, 345
Chinese language, 68, 69
Chlorofluorocarbons (CFCs), 588
Christianity, 430, 485–88, 490–92, 500
  global map, 493
Church, defined, 487
Cigarette smoking, 400, 534, 539–40
Cities (*see also* Urbanization)
  evolution of, 14, 569–71
  historical importance of, 578–80
  world's ten largest, 580
City-states, 431, 569
Civil law, 215–16
Civil liberties, 411
Civil religion, 501
Civil Rights Movement, 88, 336, 345, 627, 628, 631
Civil War, 571–72
Class conflict, 107–8, 118
Class consciousness, 107–8
Class (*see* Social class; Social stratification)
Class-society theory, 648–51
Class system, and caste system, 239–42
Clean Water Act of 1972, 599
Clitoridectomy, 553
Closed-ended format, 43
CMSAs (*see* Consolidated metropolitan statistical areas)
Cockfighting, 212
Coercive organizations, 185–86
Cognitive development, 128–29
Cohabitation, 475–76
Cohort, 143
Cold War, 448, 451
Collective behavior, 613–23 (*see also* Social movements)
Collective conscience, 116
Collectivities, 614
College, 264–66
  and African Americans, 336
  attendance, national map, 518
  degrees, 368–69, 513
  majors, and gender, 361–62
  student passivity, 523–24
  trends in bachelor's degrees, 514
Colombia, 312
Colonialism, 302, 308–9, 656
Colonial settlement, 570, 571
Commonwealth of Independent States, 412 (*see also* Soviet Union)
Communications, 8, 52–53, 85, 101, 169
  Internet, 52–53, 183–85
Communism, 106, 410
Communitarian movement, 656–57
Community, loss of, 642–43
Comparable worth policy, 367
Complementarity, theory of, 373

Computers (*see* Information Revolution)
Concentric zone urban model, 577
Concept, 32
Concrete operational stage (Piaget), 128–29
Conflict (*see also* Social conflict)
  role, 152–53
  value, 72–73
Conflict theory of prejudice, 328
Conformity, 178–79
Confucianism, 488, 497–98, 500
Conglomerates, 420–21
Congo, 434
Conjugal family, 456
Consanguine family, 456
Conservative politics, 438–39
Consolidated metropolitan statistical areas (CMSAs), 573
Conspicuous consumption, 268, 272, 603, 622–23
Constitutional monarchy, 432
Contagion theory of crowd behavior, 617
Contraception (*see* Birth control)
Control, scientific, 35
Control theory (Hirschi), 213, 230
Conventional crowds, 614, 615
Conventional level of moral development, 129
Convergence theory of crowd behavior, 617
Conversion, religious, 490
Corporations:
  agribusinesses, 413
  and competition, 421–22
  conglomerates, 420–21
  multinational, 302, 309, 310, 422–23
  women in, 419
Correlation, of variables, 34–35
Cottage industry, 404
Counterculture, 81
Courts, 228
Courtship, 462–64
Creationism, 504–5
Credentialism, 519–20
Credit, 198
Crime, 119, 203 (*see also* Violence)
  components of, 218–19
  and gender, 221
  hate, 217–18, 220
  hate crime legislation, national map, 217
  property, 220, 222, 224
  punishment, 228–31
  and race, 223–24
  and social class, 221, 223
  statistics, 221, 222
  types of, 219–21
  victimless, 221
  white-collar, 215–16
Criminal justice system, 203, 225, 227–31
Criminal law versus civil law, 215–16
Criminal recidivism, 230
Crowds, 174, 614–18
Crude birth rate, 560, 563
Crude death rate, 560, 563
Crusades, 485, 493
Cuba, 205, 253, 255, 309, 310

Cuban Americans, 341, 343–44
Cults, 490–92
Cultural change, 81–82
Cultural conflict, 90
Cultural diversity, 5, 9, 11, 66, 77–86, 182–85 (*see also* Ethnicity; Race)
  counterculture, 81
  and cultural change, 81–82
  cultural relativism, 85
  and deviance, 216–18
  ethnocentrism, 83–84
  multiculturalism, 79–81
  subculture, 78–79
  in workplace, 418–19
Cultural ecology, 603–4
Cultural integration, 82
Cultural lag, 82, 103, 477, 638
Cultural relativism, 85
Cultural theory of prejudice, 327–28
Cultural transmission, 68–69
Cultural universals, 87
Culture, 31, 61–92
  and aging, 387–88
  as constraint, 91
  defined, 62, 65
  diversity (*see* Cultural diversity)
  as freedom, 91
  and gender distinctions, 354–57
  global, 85–86
  and global inequality, 304–5
  high and popular, 77–78
  and human intelligence, 64–65
  ideal and real, 75
  language, 68–70
  norms, 74–75
  of poverty, 282
  and social change, 639
  social-conflict analysis of, 87–88
  and sociobiology, 89, 91
  structural-functional analysis of, 86–87, 89
  symbols, 67–68
  and technology, 75–77
  values and beliefs, 70–74
  of victimization, 72–73
Culture shock, 33, 62, 64, 67–68
Cyprus, 293
Czechoslovakia, 270, 412

Data transmission, global map, 115
Date rape, 218–19
Dating, 462–64
Davis-Moore thesis, 245–49, 256
Day care centers, 466
Death, 142, 397–400
  and bereavement, 398–99
  denial of, 398
  ethics and, 543–45
  historical patterns of, 397
  median age at, global map, 298
  poverty as cause of, 536
  of spouse, 391, 466
Death instinct, 127
Death penalty, 229–30, 438
Death rate, 464, 564, 565, 567
Declaration of Independence, 15, 335
Deductive logical thought, 53
De facto segregation, 331

Degradation ceremony, 211
Dehumanization, 196
Deindustrialization, 278
De jure segregation, 331
Demeanor, 161
Democracy, 72, 432
  political freedom, global map, 433
  as value, 37
Democratic leadership, 177, 188
Democratic socialism, 410
Demographic transition theory, 565–66
Demography, 559–64
  life expectancy, global map, 389
  population growth, global map, 562
  and social change, 640
Denmark, 432, 476
Denomination, religious, 489
Dependency theory of development, 308–13, 422, 566, 656–57
Dependent variable, 34
Depression, 470
Deprivation theory, of social movements, 624–25, 629
Descent, patterns of, 460
Desertification, 606
Deterrence:
  of crime, 228–30
  of war, 449
Development, human, 123–43
Deviance, 31, 116
  and biology, 204–5
  and crime (*see* Crime)
  defined, 203
  functions of, 206–7, 209
  and gender, 216–17
  medicalization of, 211
  and personality, 205
  primary and secondary, 210
  social-conflict analysis of, 213–16
  and social diversity, 216–18
  social foundations, 205–6
  structural-functional analysis, 206–10, 216
  symbolic-interaction analysis of, 210–13, 216
Deviant career, 210
Dharma, 303, 496
Differential association theory, 213–14, 230
Diffusion, of culture, 82, 639
Dignity, versus honor, 651, 653
Diplomacy, 449
Direct-fee medicine, 548
Disabled people, 9, 152, 527–28
Disarmament, 449
Discipline, 521–22
Discovery, 82, 639
Discrimination, 328–30
Disengagement theory of aging, 395
Dispersed collectivities, 614, 618–23
Disposable society, 594–95
Diversity (*see* Cultural diversity)
Division of labor, 116–17, 644–45
Divorce, 119, 279, 471–73, 477–78
DNA (deoxyribonucleic acid), 555
Domestic violence, 371, 375
Double standard, 38–39, 89, 378

Downsizing, 278, 415, 417
Dramaturgical analysis, 22, 157–63, 551
Dred Scott case (1857), 335, 336
Dropping out, 524
Drugs, 213, 221, 225
Dyads, 180, 181

Early adulthood, 141
Earnings (*see* Income)
Eastern Europe, 110, 294, 319, 412, 433, 443, 444, 626–27 (*see also* specific countries)
East Germany, 294, 412
Eating disorders, 533, 540–41
Ecclesia, 488, 492
Ecologically sustainable culture, 606–7
Ecology (*see also* Natural environment)
  defined, 587
Economy, 403–27 (*see also* Work)
  agricultural employment, global map, 408
  and corporations, 420–23
  dependency theory, 308–12
  development, global map, 7, 8
  global, 291–95, 406–7, 422–23, 436
  and government, 409, 422, 424–25
  historical overview of, 403–7
  industrial employment, global map, 408
  modernization theory, 302, 304–8
  organizational environment and, 194
  postindustrial, 404–6, 412–20
  sectors of, 406, 407
  types of systems, 407–12
  underground, 418
Ecosystem, 588
  sustainable, 606–7
Ecuador, 294
Education, 3–4, 18, 19, 264–66, 509–31
  academic standards, 525
  adult, 529
  and African Americans, 4, 80, 266, 336, 517, 519, 520, 524, 525
  and Asian Americans, 337, 339, 340
  changes in student attitudes, 81–82
  and computers, 529
  and disabled, 527–28
  and discipline, 521–22
  dropping out, 524
  and functional illiteracy, 536
  and gender, 368–69
  in global perspective, 509–13
  and Hispanic Americans, 4, 519, 520, 524
  intelligence and, 256–57
  and multiculturalism, 80–81
  and political correctness, 528
  school choice, 525, 527
  social-conflict analysis of, 515–21
  and socialization, 134–35, 361–62, 513
  and stratification, 515–21

structural-functional analysis of, 513–15
  and student passivity, 522–24
  tracking in, 19, 516–17
Efficiency, as value, 71
Ego, 127
Egypt, 493, 580, 596–97
Elderly (*see* Aging)
Electronic church, 504
Electronic mail, 44
Embarrassment, 163
Emergent-norm theory of crowd behavior, 617, 618
Emigration, 561
Emotions, 158–59
Empirical evidence, 31
Empty nest, 465
Enclosure movement, 14
Endogamy, 237, 299, 457–58, 461
Energy consumption, 589–91
  global map, 590
English language, 68, 69, 79–80, 164, 165, 330, 334
Environmental deficit, 591, 606
Environmental movement, 608–9, 631
Environmental racism, 605–6
Environment (*see* Natural environment)
Equality, value of, 262
Equal opportunity, 71, 73
Equal Rights Amendment (ERA), 375, 376
Eros, 127
Eskimos, 323
Espionage, 225
Estate system, 240
Estonia, 412
Ethics:
  and genetic research, 555
  health, 543–45
  and reproductive technology, 477
  research, 39–40
Ethiopia, 295, 297, 311, 312, 315, 434, 597
Ethnicity (*see also* specific categories of people)
  categories, 322
  defined, 321
  minority-majority population, national map, 324
Ethnocentrism, 83–84, 124, 307
Ethnographies, 48
Ethnomethodology, 155–56
Eurocentrism, 79
Euthanasia, 544
Evolution, 504–5
Exogamy, 457–58
Experiment, 41–43, 53
Expressive crowds, 614, 615, 617
Expressive leadership, 176–77
Extended family, 456, 469
Extinction, 603
Eye contact, 160, 162

Facial expressions, 158–61
Facsimile (fax) machines, 112, 406
Factory system, 404, 405
Fads, 613, 622, 623
Fair-weather liberals, 328
Faith, 484
False consciousness, 106
Family, 32, 455–81

Segregation, 319, 329, 331–32
Self, 131–33
  presentation of, 157–63
Self-administered survey, 44
Self-employment, 416–17
Self-managed work teams, 193–94
Semai of Malaysia, 97, 305, 446
Sensorimotor stage (Piaget), 128
Serbia, 209
Serial monogamy, 458
Service work, 365, 367, 413, 414
SES (*see* Socioeconomic status)
Sex, 351–52
Sexism, 358–59
Sex ratio, 563–64
Sexual harassment, 371–72, 375, 379
Sexuality, 139, 464, 465
Sexually transmitted diseases (STDs), 541–43
Sexual orientation, 353–54
Sexual slavery, 301
Shamans, 97, 491
Shoguns, 241
Sick role, 550
Sierra Club, 439, 599
Significant others, 132
Singapore, 205, 292, 306, 307, 311, 410, 434, 435
Singlehood, 476, 478
Slavery, 309, 314, 325, 331, 335, 486
Smiling, 162
Snowball sampling, 46
Social area analysis, 578
Social behaviorism, 130–33
Social change (*see also* Modernity)
  causes of, 639–40
  characteristics of, 638
  and development of sociology, 13–15
  and religion, 486–87
  social movements and, 631–33
Social character, 3, 650
Social class, 3, 31, 261–89 (*see also* Social stratification)
  categories of, 268–72
  and conflict, 107–8
  and crime, 221, 223
  dimensions of inequality, 261–65
  and family and marriage, 273–74, 467
  and gender, 273–74, 373–74
  and health, 272–74, 538–39
  intelligence and, 256–57
  and politics, 273
  and religion, 499–500
  and socialization, 133–34
  and values, 272–73
Social cohesion, 485
Social conflict, 95
Social-conflict paradigm, 19–21, 22 (*see also* individual topics)
Social construction of reality, 153–57 (*see also* Dramaturgical analysis; Symbolic-interaction paradigm)
Social control, 75, 203–4, 485, 515
Social Darwinism, 257
Social distance, 327–28
Social diversity (*see* Cultural diversity)

Social dysfunctions, 18
Social epidemiology, 538
Social-exchange analysis, 22
Social fact, 116
Social functions, 115–17
Social groups, 174–85
  compared to formal organizations, 188
  conformity, 178–79
  diversity of, 182–85
  ingroups and outgroups, 180–81
  leadership, 176–77
  versus other collectivities, 174
  primary and secondary, 174–76
  reference, 179–80
  size, 181–82
  special-interest, 439–40, 620
Social inequality (*see* Social-conflict paradigm; Social stratification)
Social institutions, 105–6, 113
Social integration, 514
Social interaction, 149–71
  dramaturgical analysis, 157–63
  majority and minority, 329–32
  role, 151–53
  social construction of reality, 153–57
  and social structure, 150
  and status, 150–51
Socialism, 109, 110, 251, 313, 432 (*see also* Eastern Europe)
  changes in, 411–12
  characteristics of, 409–10
  and medicine, 546–47
  versus capitalism, 410–11
Social isolation, 125–26, 391–92
Socialist feminism, 376
Socialization, 123–47
  anticipatory, 135, 179
  cognitive development, 128–29
  defined, 123
  and education, 134–35, 361–62, 513
  and family, 133–34, 460
  and freedom, 145
  Freudian model of personality, 127
  and gender, 129–30, 359–63
  and isolation, 125–26
  and life course, 139–43
  and mass media, 135–38
  moral development, 129
  and peer groups, 135
  social behaviorism, 130–33
  and social class, 133–34
  in total institutions, 143–44
  totalitarian, 434, 436
Socialized medicine, 547, 548
Social marginality, 9
Social mobility, 236
  by gender, 275–76
  by income, 275
  middle class slide, 276–77
  by race, 275
  structural, 244, 274
Social movements, 623–33, 640
Social Register, 270, 334
Social responsibility, personal freedom and, 656–57
Social self (*see* Self)
Social solidarity, 95
Social stratification, 3, 235–59

(*see also* Social class; Social-conflict paradigm)
  and ancestry, 265–66
  caste system, 237–39
  defined, 236
  and gender, 266, 363–72
  in global perspective, 253–54, 277–78
  in Great Britain, 240–41
  ideology, 244–46
  income disparity, global map, 255
  in Japan, 241–42
  Marxist analysis, 248–53
  and race, 266
  and religion, 266–67
  social-conflict analysis of, 247–53, 257
  in Soviet Union, 242–44
  structural-functional analysis of, 245–47, 252, 257
  and technology, 254
  Weberian analysis of, 251–53
Social structure, 16–17, 150
Society, 95–121
  defined, 66
  and production, 104–5
  and rationality, 110–15, 118–19
  and social conflict, 104–10, 118–19
  and social function, 115–17, 118–19
  and technology, 96–104, 118–19
Sociobiology, 89, 91, 125
Sociocultural evolution, 96–104
Socioeconomic status (SES), 252
Sociological investigation, 29–59
  basis of, 30–32
  elements of scientific, 32–40
  methods, 40–55
  ten steps in, 55–56
Sociological perspective, 2–15
Sociology:
  defined, 2
  in global perspective, 5–9
  origins of, 11–12
Soft authoritarianism, 434, 435
Solidarity movement, 412, 627
Solid waste, 594–95
Somalia, 295, 305, 312, 315, 447, 597
South Africa, 449
  apartheid in, 237–39, 245, 331, 485
  caste system in, 237–39
South America (*see* specific countries)
South Korea, 101, 294, 305, 307, 309, 312, 410
Soviet Union, 66, 101, 110, 242–44, 253, 255, 293, 294, 312, 313, 412, 436, 443–44, 448, 451, 492, 546–47 (*see also* Commonwealth of Independent States)
Spain, 308, 431, 432
Spanish language, 68, 69, 80, 343
Special-interest groups, 439–40, 620
Specialization, 99, 114, 186, 196, 404, 522–23
Sports:
  baseball fans, national map, 156

theoretical analysis of, 23–25
Spouse abuse, 393
Spurious correlation, 35
Sri Lanka, 294, 319, 463, 485, 567–68
Stalking laws, 474
Standardized testing, 516, 525
Staring, 162
Starvation, 314–15
State capitalism, 410, 451
State terrorism, 445
Statistical manipulation, 54–55
Statistical measures, 33
Status, 150–51
  ascribed and achieved, 151
  master, 151, 152, 211
  socioeconomic, 252
Status consistency, 240, 268
Status set, 150–51
STDs (*see* Sexually transmitted diseases)
Steam engine, 404
Stereotypes, 324, 358, 394
Sterilization, 567
Stigma, 210–11
Strain theory of deviance, 107–8, 216
Strategic defense initiative (SDI), 449
Stratification (*see* Social stratification; individual topics)
Structural-functional paradigm, 16–18, 22 (*see also* individual topics)
Structural social mobility, 244, 274
Structural-strain theory of social movements, 626–27, 629
Student passivity, 516
Students for a Democratic Society (SDS), 630
Subculture, 78–79
  deviant, 208–9
  and poverty, 282
Subjective interpretation, 37–38
Sublimation, 127
Suburbs, 572–73
Success, as value, 71, 74
Sudan, 312, 538
Suicide, 4–5, 115, 116, 383, 391, 644
  in U.S., national map, 16
Sunbelt cities, 573, 574
Superego, 127, 133
Surrogate motherhood, 477
Survey research, 43–47, 53
Survival of the fittest, 17
Sustainable ecosystem, 606–7
Sweden, 367, 410, 432, 436, 458–59, 476
Switzerland, 297
Symbolic-interaction paradigm, 21–22 (*see also* individual topics)
Symbols, cultural, 67–68
Syphilis, 541

Table reading, 47
Tact, 163
Taiwan, 101, 307
Tan't Batu people, 602
Tchambuli of New Guinea, 356
Technology, 404

and culture, 75–76
data transmission, global map, 112
and global poverty, 300, 302
and health, 534
Information Revolution, 101, 102, 104, 169, 404–6, 436, 449, 450, 529, 633, 638–39, 654
limits of, 103–4
and natural environment, 588–91
and organizational environment, 194
and politics, 450
reproductive, 476–77
and research, 52–53
and social stratification, 254
and society, 96–104
and women, 100
and work, 420
Teenage pregnancy, 475
Television, 135–38
viewing, national map, 136
Temporary workers, 415
Tenochtitlán, 559
Terrorism, 225, 444–45
Tertiary economic sector, 406
Thailand, 301, 305, 496
Thanatos, 127
Theological stage, 12
Theory (*see also* individual topics)
defined, 15
paradigm, 15–25
Third estate, 240
Third World (*see* Low-income countries; Middle-income countries)
Thomas Theorem, 155, 329
"Three Worlds" system, 291–92
Tiananmen Square massacre, 436
Tibet, 447, 458
Time, awareness of, 114
Timid bigot, 328
Titanic, 235, 236, 249
Total institutions, 143–44, 186
Totalitarianism, 434, 436
Totem, 484
Touching, 162
Tracking, 19, 516–17
Trade, international, 8–9
Tradition, 110–11, 305
Traditional authority, 429–30
Traditional family, 478–79
Tradition-directedness, 650, 654
Trail of Tears, 333
Transnational corporations (*see* Multinational corporations)
Transportation, 101, 572
Transsexuals, 352
Triads, 181–82
Type A personality, 359, 538

Ukraine, 319, 514
Underground economy, 418

Unemployment, 336, 417–18
United States:
age-sex ratio, 563–64
aging in, 383–85
aging in, national map, 386
air pollution in, national map, 600
college attendance in, national map, 518
culture of, 62, 71–72
divorce rate in, 471
divorce rate in, national map, 472
economy in (*see* Economy)
education in, 19, 513, 514, 516–29
growth of cities in, 571–73
hate crime legislation in, national map, 217
income in (*see* Income)
labor force in, national map, 413
lawsuits in, national map, 177
"McDonaldization" of, 173, 195–96
median household income, national map, 282
medicine in, 538–44
migration in, national map, 561
minority-majority in, 322–23
minority-majority in, national map, 324
occupational prestige in, 264, 265
pessimism about future in, national map, 276
physician availability in, national map, 547
police, concentration of, national map, 227
politics in, 436–41
politics in, national map, 440
poverty in, 278–87
race and ethnicity in, 332–41, 343–45
race and ethnicity in, national maps, 342
religion in, 498–510
social class in, 267–72
suicide in, 16
support for public broadcasting, national map, 620
Upper class, 268–70
Upper-middle class, 269
Upper-upper class, 269, 270
Urban decentralization, 572
Urban ecology, 576–78
Urbanism, 574–80
Urbanization, 568–74, 580–81
global map, 579
in poor societies, 580–81
Urban renewal, 573, 578
USSR (*see* Commonwealth of Independent States; Soviet Union)
Utilitarian organizations, 185

Utopia, 410

Validity, of measurement, 33–34
Values:
cultural, 70–74
inconsistency in, 72–73
language and, 164
and scientific study, 36
and social class, 272–73
Variable, 32, 34–36
VCRs, 136
Venereal disease, 541
Victimization, culture of, 72–73
Victimization survey, 221
Victimless crimes, 221
Vietnam, 403, 407, 434, 447
Vietnamese Americans, 339
Violence:
against children, 123, 125, 126, 393, 474
elderly abuse, 393–94
in schools, 521–23
against women, 217–19, 225, 358, 370–72, 375, 474
Violent crime, defined, 219–20
Voluntary associations, 185
Voter apathy, 440–41

Wage labor, 404
War, 445–49
War crimes, 446
WASPs (*see* White Anglo-Saxon Protestants)
Water consumption, global map, 598
Water pollution, 599
Water supply, 535, 537
Wealth (*see also* Income, Power)
distribution in U.S., 262–63, 266, 267
and gender, 368
Weddings (*see* Marriage)
Welfare, 286–87, 324, 437, 438, 458–59
White Anglo-Saxon Protestants (WASPs), 334–35
White-collar crime, 215–16, 605
White-collar occupations, 250–51, 415–16
White ethnic Americans, 344–45
Wodaabe of Africa, 355
Women (*see also* Family, Feminism, Gender, individual topics, Marriage)
and aging, 141, 391
and beauty myth, 351, 362, 540
and child rearing, 464–65
and eating disorders, 533, 540–41
and gender distinctions, 354–56
and genital mutilation, 553
and housework, 365–67
and housework, global map, 366

and intelligence, 355
Japanese, 241, 242
labor force participation of, 82, 363–65, 412, 413, 419
and life expectancy, 354
in medicine, 545–46
as minority, 369–70
and modernization, 306
Muslim, 493–94
occupations of, 264, 365
paid employment, global map, 364
in politics, 369, 370
and population control, 567, 568
and poverty, 300
and religion, 488–89
technology and changing status of, 100
upper class, 269
violence against, 217–19, 225, 358, 370–72, 375, 474
Women's movement, 88, 627, 629, 631
Women's networks, 185
Work:
agricultural employment, global map, 408
and alienation, 108–9
changing pattern of, 413–14
dual labor market, 414
emergence of postindustrialism and, 102
and gender, 363–65
industrial employment, global map, 408
and introduction of factories, 404, 405
labor force, U.S., 412
labor force, U.S., national map, 413
and occupational prestige, 264–65
professions, 415–16
reorganization of, 277–78
self-employment, 416–17
and technology, 420
temporary, 415
unemployment, 417–18
value of, 71
Work ethic, 334, 487
Working class, 241, 271, 273
Working poor, 271, 283–84
World religions, 491–98
Writing, 68

Xenophobia, 346

Yąnomamö, 62, 64, 76, 446, 987
Yonsei, 339
Yugoslavia, 66, 79, 446, 447

Zaire, 295, 297, 312
Zebaleen of Egypt, 596–97
Zero population growth, 567
Zimbabwe, 510

About the Author

John J. Macionis (pronounced ma-SHOW-nis) grew up in Philadelphia, Pennsylvania. He received his bachelor's degree from Cornell University and his doctorate in sociology from the University of Pennsylvania. His publications are wide-ranging, focusing on community life in the United States, interpersonal intimacy in families, effective teaching, humor, and the importance of global education. He has coedited the companion volume to this text, *Seeing Ourselves: Classic, Contemporary, and Cross-Cultural Readings in Sociology*. Macionis also has written a brief version of this book, *Society: The Basics*, and is coauthor of a forthcoming urban studies text, *Cities and Urban Life*.

John Macionis is professor of sociology at Kenyon College in Gambier, Ohio. He has chaired the Anthropology-Sociology Department, directed Kenyon's multidisciplinary program in humane studies, and presided over the college's faculty.

Professor Macionis has been active in academic programs in other countries, having traveled to some fifty nations. In the fall of 1994, he directed the global education course for the University of Pittsburgh's Semester at Sea program, teaching four hundred students on a floating campus that visited twelve countries as it circled the globe.

Macionis writes, "I am an ambitious traveler, eager to learn—and, through the texts, I try to share much of what I discover with students, many of whom know so little about the rest of the world. For me, traveling and writing are all dimensions of teaching. First and foremost, I am a teacher—a passion for teaching animates everything I do." At Kenyon, Macionis offers a wide range of upper-level courses but his favorite class is Introduction to Sociology, which he schedules every semester. He enjoys extensive contact with students, making an occasional appearance on campus with his guitar and, each term, inviting his students to enjoy a home-cooked meal. Macionis is a frequent visitor to other campuses as well.

The Macionis family—John, Amy, and children McLean and Whitney—live on a farm in rural Ohio. Their home serves as a popular bed and breakfast where they enjoy visiting with old friends and making

new ones. In his free time, Macionis enjoys bicycling through the Ohio countryside, or a warm afternoon might find him out in the barn trying to restore an old tractor to health.

The author welcomes (and responds to) comments and suggestions about this book from faculty and students. Write to Palme House, Kenyon College, Gambier, Ohio 43022. His Internet address is MACIONIS@KENYON.EDU   For more information about all the Macionis textbooks, visit our Web site. Address: http://www.prenhall.com/macionis